HAMMOND
ESSENTIAL
WORLD
ATLAS

HAMMOND World Atlas Corporation

presenting the world

Contents

South America

North America

COUNTRIES OF THE WORLD, STATISTICS, INDEX AND TIME ZONES

The Countries of the World section presents the national flag and important geographic data about each independent country, including area, population, capital, largest city, highest point and monetary unit. The section on World Statistics includes the planets of the solar system, dimensions of the earth, oceans and major seas, major mountain peaks, longest rivers, largest lakes and major islands. A Master Index lists 45,000 places and other features appearing in this atlas, complete with their page numbers and easy-to-use alpha-numeric references. The computer-generated Time Zones of the World reflects the world's most recent time zone changes.

DATE DUE

Essential World Atlas

Using This Atlas

SYMBOLS USED ON MAPS OF THE WORLD

First Order (National) Boundary

Demarcated Land Boundary

Demarcated Water Boundary

Disputed Boundary

Armistice Boundary

De Facto Boundary

Undefined

Second Order (Internal) Boundary

Land/Administrative District Boundary

Water Boundary

Third Order (Internal) Boundary

Land/Administrative District Boundary

Water Boundary

Cities and Towns

Stockholm — First Order (National) Capital

Salt Lake City — Second Order (Internal) Capital

Manchester — Third Order (Internal) Capital

Towns

City District/Neighborhood

City and Urban Area Limits

Transportation

International Airport

Airport

Highways/Roads

Railroads

Ferries

Tunnels (Road, Railroad)

Drainage Features

Shoreline, River

Intermittent River

Canal

Lake, Reservoir

Intermittent Lake

Dry Lake

Salt Pan

Swamp/Marsh

Other Physical Features

▲ Elevation

⊰ Pass

● Falls

✳ Rapids

Desert/Sand Area

Lava Flow

Glacier/Ice Shelf

Cultural Features

Archeological Sites. Ruins

Dam

Park

Wildlife Area

Point of Interest

Well

Air Base

Naval Base

International Date Line

Ancient Walls

Native Reservation/Reserve

Military/Government Reservation

State Park/Recreation Area

National Park/Forest/Recreation/ Wildlife Area

Elevation Legend

Height

| m. ft. |
| 6000 19700 |
| 4000 13000 |
| 2000 6500 |
| 1500 5000 |
| 1000 3300 |
| 500 1600 |
| 200 700 |
| 0 |
| 200 700 |
| 500 1600 |
| 1000 3300 |
| 2000 6500 |
| 3000 9800 |
| 4000 13000 |
| 5000 16400 |
| 6000 19700 |
| m. ft. |

Depth

The color tints in this bar represent both elevation of land areas and depth of the oceans. The changes between colors are labeled in meters and feet. Selective shading for the land areas highlights those regions with significant relief variations. The legend is entered next to each individual map.

ABBREVIATIONS USED IN THE MAPS

Abor. Rsv.	Aboriginal Reserve	Ft.	Fort	NHP	National Historical Park	Pen.	Peninsula
Admin.	Administration	G.	Gulf			Pk.	Peak
AFB	Air Force Base	Govt.	Government	NHS	National Historic Site	Plat.	Plateau
Amm. Dep.	Ammunition Depot	Gd.	Grand			PN	Park National
		Gt.	Great	NL	National Lakeshore	Prom.	Promontory
Arch.	Archipelago	Har.	Harbor			Prsv.	Preserve
Aut.	Autonomous	Hist.	Historic(al)	NM	National Monument	Pt.	Point
B.	Bay	Hts.	Heights			R.	River
Bfld.	Battlefield	I., Is.	Island(s)	NMEM	National Memorial	Rec.	Recreation(al)
Bk.	Brook	Ind. Res.	Indian Reservation			Ref.	Refuge
Br.	Branch	Int'l	International	NMILP	National Military Park	Reg.	Region
C.	Cape	IR	Indian Reservation	No.	Northern	Rep.	Republic
Can.	Canal			NP	National Park	Res.	Reservoir, Reservation
Cap.	Capital	Isth.	Isthmus	NPP	National Park and Preserve	Sa.	Sierra
C.G.	Coast Guard	Jct.	Junction			Sd.	Sound
Chan.	Channel	L.	Lake			So.	Southern
Co.	County	Lag.	Lagoon	NPRSV	National Preserve	SP	State Park
Consv.	Conservation	Mem.	Memorial			Spr., Sprgs.	Spring, Springs
Cord.	Cordillera	Mil.	Military	NRA	National Recreation Area	St.	State
Cr.	Creek	Mon.	Monument			Sta.	Station
Ctr.	Center	Mt.	Mount	NRIV	National River	Stm.	Stream
Dep.	Depot	Mtn.	Mountain	NRSV	National Reserve	Str.	Strait
Depr.	Depression	Mts.	Mountains			Terr.	Territory
Des.	Desert	Nat.	Natural	NS	National Seashore	Tun.	Tunnel
Dist.	District	Nat'l	National			Twp.	Township
DMZ	Demilitarized Zone	Nav.	Naval	NWR	National Wildlife Refuge	UNDOF	United Nations Disengagement Observer Force
		NB	National Battlefield	Obl.	Oblast		
Est.	Estuary			Occ.	Occupied		
Fed.	Federal	NBP	National Battlefield Park	Okr.	Okrug	Val.	Valley
Fk.	Fork			Passg.	Passage	Vill.	Village
For.	Forest	NCA	National Conservation Area				

The Essential World Atlas has been designed to be easy and enjoyable to use. Only a short time is needeed to familiarize yourself with its organization.

MAP SYMBOLS, COLORS AND LABELS

The cartographer selects the natural and cultural features most valuable to the map user. Map legibility requires that small features be represented by symbols that are actually larger than true scale size. Due to the larger symbol sizes and the resulting loss of map space, it is necessary to omit less important features in congested areas.

Most map features are represented by the use of conventional symbols, lines, and patterns printed in appropriate colors. The chart to the left shows the standard symbols used in this atlas. Water features are shown in blue. Lines of various weights, styles, and colors represent the many different linear features in this atlas. Individual point features are represented by a pictorial and/or generic symbol.

Notes may also be added to explain features that cannot be depicted clearly.

MAP SCALES

A map's scale is the relationship of any length on the map to an identical length on the earth's surface. A scale of 1:3M means that one inch on the map represents 3,000,000 inches (47 miles, 76 km.) on the earth's surface. Thus, a 1:1M scale is larger than 1:3M, just as 1/1 is larger than 1/3.

The most densely populated areas in this atlas are shown at a scale of 1:1.14M. Other populous areas are presented at 1:3.4M and 1:6.8M, allowing you to accurately compare areas and distances of similar regions. Remaining regions, including the continent maps, are presented at 1:10.2M and smaller scales.

BOUNDARY POLICIES

This atlas observes the boundary policies of the U.S. Department of State. Disputed, armistice and de facto boundaries are handled with a special symbol treatment. The portrayal of independent nations follows their recognition by the United Nations and/or United States government.

Map Type Styles

Cartographers use a variety of type styles to differentiate between map features. The following styles are used in this Atlas.

Major Political Areas

LUXEMBOURG

Internal Political Divisions

SAXONY-ANHALT

Regions

Polabská Nížina

Cities and Towns

Norfolk Sumter Smyrna

Neighborhoods

BIGGIN HILL

Points of Interest

MISSION SAN BUENAVENTURA

Water Features

L. Elsinore

Capes, Points, Peaks, Passes

Pt. La Jolla   Pacifico Mtn.

Islands, Peninsulas

Cape Breton I.

Mountains, Uplands

Serra do Norte

Deserts, Plains, Valleys

San Fernando Valley

A Word About Names

Our source for all foreign names is the decision lists of the U.S. Board of Geographic Names and/or official foreign government maps and official gazetteers. This atlas also uses accepted conventional names for certain major foreign place names. The U.S. Board of Geographic Names defines a conventional name as "a name approved for use in addition to, or in lieu of, an approved local official name or names."

In order to make the maps more readily understandable to English-speaking readers, many foreign physical features are translated into more recognizable English forms.

The rendering of city, town and village names for the United States follows the forms and spelling of the U.S. Postal Service.

FIGURE 3
Conic Projection

FIGURE 3
Conic Projection
The original idea of a conic projection is to cap the globe with a cone, and then project onto the cone from the planet's center the lines of latitude and longitude (the parallels and meridians). To produce a working map, the cone is simply cut open and laid flat. The conic projection used here is a modification of this idea. A cone can be made tangent to any standard parallel you choose. One popular version of a conic projection, the Lambert Conformal Conic, uses two standard parallels near the top and bottom of the map to further reduce errors of scale.

FIGURE 4
Hammond Optimal Conformal Projection
Like all conformal maps, the Optimal projection preserves angles exactly and minimizes distortion in shapes. This projection is more successful than any previous projection at spreading curvature across the entire map, producing the most distortion-free map possible.

S imply stated, the map-maker's challenge is to project the earth's curved surface onto a flat plane. To achieve this elusive goal, cartographers have developed map projections — equations which govern this conversion of geographic data.

This section explores some of the most widely used projections. It also introduces a new projection, the Hammond Optimal Conformal.

GENERAL PRINCIPLES AND TERMS
The earth rotates around its axis once a day. Its end points are the North and South poles; the line circling the earth midway between the poles is the equator. The arc from the equator to either pole is divided into 90 degrees of latitude. The equator represents 0° latitude. Circles of equal latitude, called parallels, are traditionally shown at every fifth or tenth degree.

The equator is divided into 360 degrees. Lines circling the globe from pole to pole through the degree points on the equator are called meridians, or great circles. All meridians are equal in length, but by international agreement the meridian passing through the Greenwich Observatory near London has been chosen as the prime meridian or 0° longitude. The distance in degrees from the prime meridian to any point east or west is its longitude.

While meridians are all equal in length, parallels become shorter as they approach the poles. Whereas one degree of latitude represents approximately 69 miles (112 km.) anywhere on the globe, a degree of longitude varies from 69 miles (112 km.) at the equator to zero at the poles. Each degree of latitude and longitude is divided into 60 minutes. One minute of latitude equals one nautical mile (1.15 land miles or 1.85 km.).

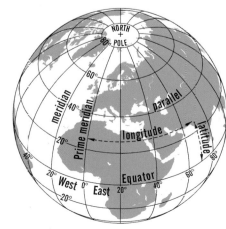

HOW TO FLATTEN A SPHERE: THE ART OF CONTROLLING DISTORTION
There is only one way to represent a sphere with absolute precision: on a globe. All attempts to project our planet's surface onto a plane unevenly stretch or tear the sphere as it flattens, inevitably distorting shapes, distances, area (sizes appear larger or smaller than actual size), angles or direction.

Since representing a sphere on a flat plane always creates distortion, only the parallels or the meridians (or some other set of lines) can maintain the same length as on a globe of corresponding scale. All other lines must be either too long or too short. Accordingly, the scale on a flat map cannot be true everywhere; there will always be different scales in different parts of a map. On world maps or very large areas, variations in scale may be extreme. Most maps seek to preserve either true area relationships (equal area projections) or true angles and shapes (conformal projections); some attempt to achieve overall balance.

PROJECTIONS:
SELECTED EXAMPLES
Mercator (Fig. 1): This projection is especially useful because all compass directions appear as straight lines, making it a valuable navigational tool. Moreover, every small region conforms to its shape on a globe — hence the name conformal. But because its meridians are evenly-spaced vertical lines which never converge (unlike the globe), the horizontal parallels must be drawn farther and farther apart at

FIGURE 1 **Mercator Projection**

FIGURE 2 **Robinson Projection**

higher latitudes to maintain a correct relationship.

Only the equator is true to scale, and the size of areas in the higher latitudes is dramatically distorted.

Robinson (Fig. 2): To create the World-Political and World-Physical maps in this atlas, the Robinson projection was used. It combines elements of both conformal and equal area projections to show the whole earth with relatively true shapes and reasonably equal areas.

Conic (Fig. 3): This projection has been used frequently for air navigation charts and to create most of the national and regional maps in this atlas. (See text in margin at left).

HAMMOND OPTIMAL CONFORMAL
As its name implies, this new conformal projection (Fig. 4) presents the optimal view of an area by reducing shifts in scale over an entire region to the minimum degree possible. While conformal maps generally preserve all small shapes, large shapes can become very distorted because of varying scales, causing considerable inaccuracy in distance measurements. The concept underlying the Optimal Conformal is that for any region on the globe, there is an ideal projection for which scale variation can be made as small as possible. Consequently, unlike other projections, the Optimal Conformal does not use one standard formula to construct a map. Each map is a unique projection — the optimal projection for that particular area.

After a cartographer defines the subject area, a sophisticated computer program evaluates the size and shape of the region, and projects the most distortion-free conformal map possible.

The Solar System

Our Home Star and Its Orbiting Planets

The sun is just one star among billions in our galaxy, the Milky Way. The solar system comprises nine planets (and their named moons): Mercury, Venus, Earth (one moon), Mars (2), Jupiter (48), Saturn (35), Uranus (27), Neptune (9), and the recently "demoted" Pluto (3) (see explanation on bottom of page 7), as well as numerous other smaller objects, such as comets, meteorites, and asteroids. Most asteroids are less than 100 km. in diameter, and nearly all of their paths pass between Mars and Jupiter. Unlike the stars, the planets, their moons, and the small celestial bodies emit no light and are visible to us only because they are illuminated by the sun.

Seen through a telescope, the planets appear as disks of various sizes. Images transmitted from spacecraft provide information about their surface features. The planets move along elliptical orbits on planets which deviate only slightly from that of the earth's orbit. Puzzled by apparent reversals of direction, ancient and medieval observers were unable to explain the motions of the planets as seen from the earth.

Key Data: The Sun	
Diameter:	1,392,000 km
Mass:	333,000 x earth mass
Mean density:	1.409 g/ccm
Distance from earth:	149.6 mill. km
Time of light travel sun—earth:	8 min 20 s

Key Data: The Moon	
Distance earth—moon:	384,403 km
Mass:	0.0123 x earth mass
Mean density:	3.341 g/ccm
Daytime temp.:	214°F
Nighttime temp.:	−240 °F

Planets	Mass (x earth mass)	Density (g/ccm)
Mercury	0.055	5.43
Venus	0.815	5.24
Earth	1.000	5.52
Mars	0.107	3.93
Jupiter	318.0	1.33
Saturn	95.1	0.70
Uranus	14.4	1.30
Neptune	17.2	1.76
Pluto	0.002	1.7

Sizes and Distances

Because the inner, "earthlike" planets Mercury, Venus, Earth, and Mars are composed of metals and rock (rock planets), they are relatively dense. The outer, Jovian planets – Jupiter, Saturn, Uranus, Neptune – and the dwarf planet Pluto consist primarily of gases (including hydrogen, helium, and methane) and frozen water. The asteroid belt lies between the inner and outer planets. The distribution of light and heavy matter took place during the infancy of the solar system, as lighter materials condensed in the colder outer regions of the system. With the exception of Pluto, all of the other planets (known as giant planets) are considerably larger than the earth. The diameter of Jupiter is eleven times greater than that of the earth, that of Saturn almost ten times greater. The sun's diameter is ten times larger than Jupiter's. A comparison of the masses of the objects in the solar system reveals even more marked differences. Added together, the masses of all planets including Pluto amount to only 13% of the sun's mass, and Jupiter alone accounts for 70% of that total. Relative sizes and distances can be illustrated on the basis of the following example: The distance between the sun and Pluto is 5.9 billion kilometers. If the sun had a diameter of one meter, Pluto would measure two millimeters across, and the distance between the two would be four kilometers.

Born of a Cloud of Dust

Some five billion years ago, a cloud of interstellar dust began to condense, a reaction perhaps triggered by a nearby supernova. As gravitational forces increased, the core of the cloud grew increasingly dense, while the concentration of mass in the center accelerated the system's rotation. Gradually, a flat disk formed, from which the planets later emerged. Temperatures at the center of the disk approached eighteen million degrees F, generating nuclear fusion of the hydrogen atoms. The sun began to radiate. At its core, 655 million tons of hydrogen were converted into 650 million tons of helium every second, while five million tons of matter were transformed into energy. Five billion years from now, when its nuclear energy has been consumed, the sun will enter its final phase, at which point it will turn first into a red giant and later into a white dwarf.

The Earth's Reliable Heater

The sun produces temperatures of up to 27 million degrees F at its core. Pressure at that point is 200 billion times that recorded on the earth's surface. The visible surface of the sun is called the photosphere. It is about 400 km thick and has a mean temperature of 9,900 degrees F. Sunspots form where magnetic-field lines break through the surface. Granules (giant bubbles) measuring about 1,500 km in diameter form on the upper surface of the photosphere and bubble upward. Flames of gas (protuberances) shoot forth from the outer layer (the chromosphere), reaching heights up to tens of thousands of kilometers. The outer atmosphere of the sun (the corona) has a very low density and temperatures around 1.8 million degrees F. It extends beyond the photosphere to heights equivalent to several times the radius of the sun.

The Inner Planets

Mercury, the second-smallest planet after to Pluto, is closest to the sun. Humans could not possibly survive its surface temperatures of 780°F during the day and –325°F during the night. The atmosphere (helium, argon) above the moonlike, cratered landscape is extremely thin.

The surface of Venus is not visible from the earth. Thick clouds of carbon dioxide (96%), nitrogen (3%), and trace amounts of water vapor and other gases reflect 65% of the sun's rays, making Venus the third brightest object in the sky, after the sun and the moon. The greenhouse effect caused by its mantle of gases raises the surface temperatures of the planet's craters and lava fields (80%) to temperatures in the range of 850°F. There is no liquid water, and there are no rivers or oceans, only a few dunes.

The distance between the Earth and the sun is favorable to life as we know it, and temperatures are neither too high nor too low.

People long assumed that there could be some form of life on Mars – intelligent or at least primitive life. The pattern of lines on the planet's surface thought to be a network of irrigation canals proved to be an optical illusion however, although valleys marked by meanders do suggest that rivers must have flowed through them at one time. The cold crater landscapes of the "Red Planet" (with lows at the winter polar caps reading -225°F) are marked by rocky deserts. The largest shield volcano on Mars is 700 km wide, 25 km high and presumably several hundred million years old.

The Smallest of the Group

Pluto, the planet in our solar system, was discovered in 1930. Its low surface temperature (−440 °F) cannot support a gaseous atmosphere, and existing gases were presumably frozen out long ago.

Middleweight 1

Little is known about Neptune's internal structure. Its density of 1.76 g/ccm suggests that it has a core of rock, probably surrounded by a mantle of frozen water, methane, ammonia, hydrogen and helium. Neptune's hydrogen atmosphere also contains helium and methane. Only two of its moons had been discovered before 1989.

Predictable Relationships

The planets travel in elliptical orbits on planes which, unlike those of comet orbits, are "tilted" only slightly off the earth's orbital plane. The inner planets, Mercury, Venus, the earth, and Mars, are closest to the sun and receive more warming solar radiation than the distant outer planets, which are accordingly much colder.

Middleweight 2

Seen through a telescope, Uranus appears as a blue-green disk without visible surface features. It was not until 1986 that Voyager 2 provided a more detailed picture, revealing cloud structures, the presence of a magnetic field, and ten previously undiscovered moons. The planet's greater density indicates a composition containing metals heavier than those on Saturn. Its atmosphere consists primarily of hydrogen and helium.

The Solar System

Our Moon

When Astronauts Armstrong and Aldrin took their first steps on the moon on July 21, 1969, they fulfilled an age-old human dream. Since then, plans have been in the making for a manned mission to Mars. Although that goal has yet to be achieved, a number of unmanned spacecraft have explored the depths of space as far away as Neptune.

The Blue Planet

The view from the porthole of a spacecraft shows how lost our planet is in space. Compared with the giant planets or the sun, it seems infinitely small. If mankind is to survive, we must manage our resources wisely. Viewed from outer space, our planet appears predominantly blue.

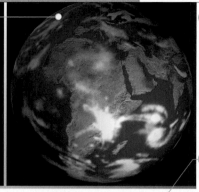

A Glaring Ball of Fire

Only when the sun is just above the horizon can we gaze at it without protecting our eyes. From this position, sunlight travels farther through the atmosphere, and the energy-laden blue rays are largely filtered out. Looking directly at the sun at midday without protection causes irreparable damage to the retina.

Giant Twins

The rings of Saturn and several of Jupiter's moons are clearly visible through even a small telescope. The giant planets Jupiter and Saturn are so large that the earth is dwarfed in comparison. Like other giant planets, Jupiter also has a system of rings, although it is not as prominent as that of Saturn. Both planets have many moons and are encircled by bands of clouds. Their atmospheres consist of hydrogen, helium and minute admixtures of methane and ammonia. Towards the interior, these gases pass through transitions from gaseous to liquid (on the planet's surface) to solid states (at their cores). The two giants have strong magnetic fields.

Io, the innermost planet of Jupiter, became famous through images sent back to earth by Voyager, which provided the first opportunity to observe extraterrestrial volcanic activity. Fountains of lava expelled at speeds of up to 1,000 m/s traveled as high as 300 m above the surrounding areas covered with multi-colored lava and frozen sulfur-dioxide.

It's not easy being Pluto

Originally considered an official planet, in August of 2006 the International Astronomical Union (IAU) downgraded Pluto to a dwarf planet.

According to new rules established by the IAU an offical planet must meet three criteria: 1) it must orbit the sun, 2) be large enough for gravity to have formed it into a sphere, and 3) it must have cleared other objects out of the way in its orbital neighborhood.

Since Pluto orbits among the many other icy objects of the Kuiper Belt – a distinct region beyond the orbit of Neptune – it does not meet the third criterion.

Mars

Venus

Mercury

Earth

Planet Earth

... and it truly does move!

If we could look from a great distance at the supposedly firm and motionless ground on which we normally stand, we would see that it is anything but motionless. Our Earth is a dynamic celestial body which rotates on its own axis and revolves around the sun. The very point at which we stand moves along a complicated orbit through space.

Dancing on a Volcano

An entirely different kind of motion involving shifts in the positions of points on Earth relative to one another ordinarily takes place unnoticed and so slowly that extraordinarily precise instruments are required to prove that it occurs at all. Yet a time-lapse film in which 10 million years are compressed into a single second would provide striking evidence of how much the Earth's appearance has changed since prehistoric times and become the planet we know today. The key terms used to describe this process are "continental drift" and "plate tectonics." The only effects of these changes we perceive directly are the – often disastrous – earthquakes and seaquakes, frequently followed by massive tidal waves, that frequently accompany movements of the large plates in the uppermost layers of the Earth's crust.

Like our perceptions of the positions and movements of objects in the sky, much of what we experience on Earth – the alternation of day and night, the changing seasons – is caused by the motion of the Earth. The alternation of day and night would seem easy enough to explain: The Earth turns completely around its own axis every 24 hours, and thus every place on Earth experiences a sunrise and a sunset. But wait! There are regions on Earth in which the sun doesn't rise for months and doesn't set

again until more months have passed: the polar zones within the Arctic and Antarctic Circles. These periods of time are referred to as polar nights and polar days.

The cause of both – and for the changing seasons everywhere on Earth – is the fact that the Earth's rotational axis is inclined 23.5 degrees to the plane of the Earth's orbit around the sun. Because the angle of the Earth's axis does not change as it revolves around the sun – its northern extension always points towards the North Star – one hemisphere is always closer to the sun: the northern hemisphere during the northern summer and the southern hemisphere during the northern winter. Only at the spring and fall equinoxes, when days and nights are equally long, are the northern and southern hemispheres exposed to the same intensity of solar radiation.

Moon – Calendar – Clock

The Earth has a constant companion on its journey around the sun – the moon. The movements of the Earth and the moon are the basis for our reckoning of time, the rhythm of our clocks, and our calendar system. The corresponding units of time are days, months, and years – the interval between one arrival of the sun at its zenith and the next; the period between full moons, and the length of time it takes the Earth to complete a full revolution around the sun. Precise astronomical observations are required to measure the lengths of these periods. Ancient astronomers discovered that neither a revolution of the Earth around the sun nor of the moon around the Earth equated to a full number of revolutions of the Earth around its own axis. There are approximately 365 ½ days in a year and about 29 ½ days in a (lunar) month. That is what makes designing a precise, reliable calendar such

a difficult matter. Sophisticated correction systems are required to keep the calendar in step with the movements of the celestial bodies. Depending upon the system in use, these systems involve the addition of additional days or months to the calendar at regular intervals (in leap years, for example).

Light and Shadow

During a solar eclipse, the moon passes between the Earth and the sun, whereas a lunar eclipse occurs when the moon moves through the shadow cast by the Earth and thus grows dark. Depending upon their relative positions the sun and the moon may totally or only partially obscured. We can observe a total eclipse of the sun from a place at which the moon's umbra falls. During a total lunar eclipse, the moon is encompassed entirely within the Earth's umbra.

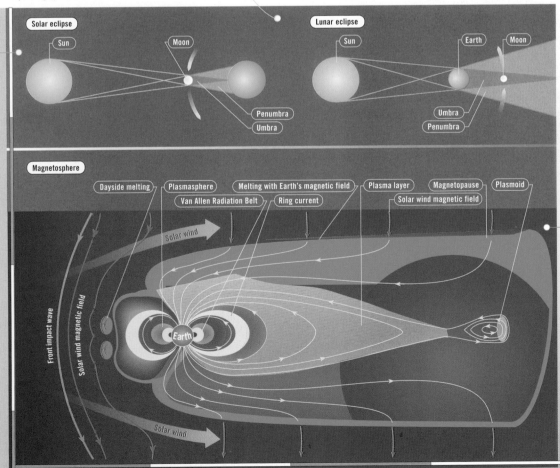

Solar eclipse
Sun
Moon
Penumbra
Umbra

Lunar eclipse
Sun
Earth
Moon
Umbra
Penumbra

Magnetosphere

Dayside melting | Plasmasphere | Melting with Earth's magnetic field | Plasma layer | Magnetopause | Plasmoid
Van Allen Radiation Belt | Ring current | Solar wind magnetic field

Solar wind
Front impact wave
Solar wind magnetic field
Earth
Solar wind

Upper mantle
Lower mantle
Continental cru
Oceanic crust
Outer core
Inner core

An Invisible Cloak

Generated within the Earth's core, the Earth magnetic field is shaped and limited by solar wind, a stream of electrically charged particles emitted by the sun. The space it encloses is known as the magnetosphere. On the side of the Earth facing the sun, the magnetosphere extends to a distance equivalent to between 10 and 20 Earth radii. On the opposite side of the Earth, it pulls a tail measuring some 1,000 Earth radii in length. In the Van Allen radiation belt, electrically charged particles captured from cosmic radiation by the magnetosphere move back and forth between the Earth's magnetic poles. The term "plasma" denotes a gas consisting of positively and negatively charged particles, whose charges offset one another. Plasmoids are lumps of plasma that are cut off and catapulted from the tail of the magnetosphere.

Occasional corrections to clock time are required, usually in late June and/or late December, for a different reason: the irregular rotation of the Earth. This irregularity was not discovered until the 1930s, following the invention of quarz clocks that were more exact than the Earth's own rotation. These smaller corrections involve the addition of leap seconds.

The Earth Seen from Space

Although mankind has long been aware that the Earth is an object in space, like the sun and the moon, people did not truly appreciate that fact until the age of space exploration began in the early sixties. The image shows an early docking maneuver during the Gemini 8 mission in 1966.

A Glowing Hot Core inside a Cool Shell

In terms of its static structure, the Earth can be divided roughly into a crust, a mantle, and a core. We distinguish between the upper and the lower mantle, while the core consists of an outer and an inner core. The crust and the mantle are composed of rock, while the core consists primarily of iron and nickel. The outer core (iron and iron oxide) is molten liquid. The inner core (iron and nickel) is solid. The continental crust is considerably thicker than the oceanic crust.

Like a Tilted Top

Seasonal temperature differences are attributable to the fact that the Earth's rotational axis is not precisely perpendicular to the plane of its orbit around the sun. As a result, the Earth tips its northern polar region toward the sun during the northern summer, while the southern polar region is inclined toward the sun during the northern winter. In the first case, the northern hemisphere is exposed to stronger solar radiation; in the second, it is the southern hemisphere that is bathed in warmer sunlight. At the spring and autumn equinoxes, when days and nights are of equal length, the northern and southern hemispheres are exposed to the same amount of solar radiation.

The larger figures representing the Earth illustrate the distribution of sunlight at the summer solstice (around June 21st, on the left) and at the winter solstice (around December 21st, on the right).

The amount of warmth received by the various regions of the globe, and thus the temperature characteristics of the four seasons, depend largely upon the angle at which solar radiation reaches the Earth, which is in turn a function of the time of day, geographic latitude, and the time of year.

The elliptical shape of the Earth's orbit also exerts a small influence on temperatures. At the most distant (aphelion) and the nearest points (perihelion) to the sun, the distance between the Earth and the sun is 1.7 per cent greater or smaller than its mean distance. Thus at these points, solar radiation is also nearly 3.5 per cent stronger or weaker, respectively.

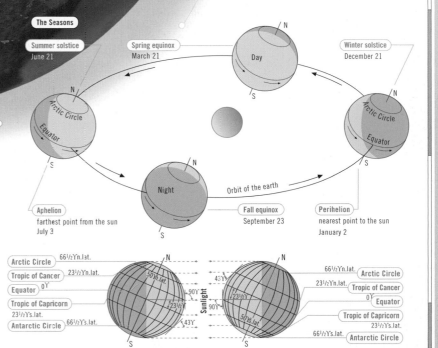

The Seasons

Summer solstice
June 21

Spring equinox
March 21

Day

Winter solstice
December 21

Arctic Circle

Equator

Arctic Circle

Equator

Night

Orbit of the earth

Aphelion
farthest point from the sun
July 3

Fall equinox
September 23

Perihelion
nearest point to the sun
January 2

Arctic Circle	66½Yn.lat.
Tropic of Cancer	23½Yn.lat.
Equator	0Y
Tropic of Capricorn	23½Ys.lat.
Antarctic Circle	66½Ys.lat.

66½Yn.lat.	Arctic Circle
23½Yn.lat.	Tropic of Cancer
0Y	Equator
23½Ys.lat.	Tropic of Capricorn
66½Ys.lat.	Antarctic Circle

Earthquakes - Danger from the Depths

When the ground begins to shake beneath our feet

Well into the Middle Ages, earthquakes were regarded as the work of mythical, supernatural beings or signs of the wrath of God. The quake that destroyed Lisbon in cataclysmic waves of fire and flooding on November 1, 1775 caused many people to wonder about the validity of prevailing philosophical systems. Could anyone still look upon our world as the "best of all possible worlds," as a planet governed by reliable natural laws?
And why had Lisbon, of all places, a city of churches and monasteries devoted to piety, been singled out by God for such terrible punishment? That earthquake marked the beginning of the science of seismology. The Portuguese minister Pombal had reports compiled by observers all over the country. The British engineer John Michell computed the speed of the shock waves. Questions were raised about the origin and the causes of the quake.

The Restless Earth

Although we rarely notice it, the Earth's crust is constantly moving. The oceans and atmosphere are subject to patterns of natural motion, and so are the seemingly fixed landmasses of the continents, though their movements are so slow that we do not perceive them. Much more obvious – and dangerous – are the brief (lasting less than a minute), abrupt, and rapid shifts of larger segments of crust caused by tensions inside the Earth. The amplitude of these movements of ground may amount to as much as several decimeters. The energy released in the process spreads in the form of elastic waves through the Earth's interior: longitudinal and transverse waves. Longitudinal waves (also known as P or primary waves) move faster and arrive at a given distant point sooner than transverse waves (S or secondary waves). The slowest but most highly energized waves are surface waves (L and Rayleigh waves).

The source of an earthquake, known as the focus or hypocenter, may be near the surface or deep within the Earth's crust. Based upon its distance from the epicenter, the point of greatest surface movement, seismologists distinguish between shallow, intermediate, and deep-focus earthquakes. At depths below 720 km, rock is so soft and malleable that no abrupt shifts occur.

On average, 10,000 earthquakes classified as grade 4 or higher on the Richter Scale are recorded annually. Between 10 and 15 of these cause significant damage. In 1999, more than 22,000 people died as a result of earthquakes, while the average death toll for the preceding years is about 10,000. Some 15 percent of the Earth's land area is subject to severe earthquake activity. Another 40 percent is classified as virtually risk-free.

Measuring Earthquake Energy and Effects

Earthquakes are registered and recorded in seismograms using highly sensitive measuring instruments known as seismographs. The direction, distance, and energy of an earthquake can be derived from the data in the seismogram, i.e. the amplitude of the waves generated by an earthquake. Energy is expressed as magnitude, which is computed on the basis of ground amplitude, wave duration, and a calibration function. Earthquakes are classified on the Richter Scale of Earthquake Magnitude according to the maximum amplitude measured at a distance of 100 km from the epicenter. Magnitude values range from zero to between 7.7 and 8.6, but the scale has no upper limit.

California Awaits "The Big One"

The United States Geological Survey (USGS) estimates the probability of a major earthquake in northern California by the year 2020 at 70 per cent. USGS experts anticipate a seismic event comparable to the San Francisco earthquake of 1906, which measured 8.3 on the Richter Scale and laid much of the city to waste, causing numerous fires and killing some 2,000 people. The quake in Northridge near Los Angeles in 1994 took 60 human lives, and total damage was valued at $ 30–40 billion (a U.S. record). The American West Coast is one of the most severely endangered regions in the world. The Pacific Plate thrusts against the North American Plate along several fault lines, the best known of which is the San Andreas fault. These movements are not gradual and consistent but abrupt and violent, and they are responsible for a seemingly endless series of earthquakes. Some 7,800 earthquakes are registered in California each year, although most of them can only be detected by sensitive seismographic instruments.

Seismic Waves Explore the Earth's Interior

Physical bores are mere pinpricks in the Earth's crust (at about 13 km, the deepest bore ever made reached a depth equivalent to only about 0.2 per cent of the Earth's radius). We learn a great deal more about the structure of the Earth's interior from seismic waves that penetrate to the core and beyond. This method is the basis for the shell model of the Earth, with a crust (50–70 km thick beneath the continents, 5–10 km thick below the oceans), a mantle (2,900 km thick, divided in two by a transition zone), and a core (outer core to a depth of 5,200 km, inner core to a depth of 6,371 km). Correlations between wave speeds and experimental findings generate conclusions about the density, the temperature, and the chemical and mineral composition of the different zones.

Are Earthquakes Predictable?

People in ancient China observed unusual behavior in animals immediately preceding earthquake events, although they realized this only later. Today, even seismologists disagree about whether the location, time, and magnitude of an earthquake can be predicted. Researchers have been trying to identify reliable signs for decades. Using automatic recording devices, they systematically measure changes in specific characteristics – temperature, chemical composition, gas concentration (radon) and electrical groundwater resistance, groundwater levels and spring behavior, movements at fault lines, and deformations of the Earth's surface. All of these phenomena can – but do not necessarily – indicate impending earthquake activity.

Crisis Management – Emergency Disaster Aid

In industrialized countries threatened by earthquakes, such as Japan, the U. S. (especially California), and Italy, plans have been made for responses to natural disasters. Kindergarten and school children in Japan and California learn rules for behavior when danger threatens. Public emergency disaster exercises are conducted on a broad basis in Japan. Plans are modified in response to experience gained in such emergencies. California has established a network of decentralized emergency aid stations staffed and equipped to meet specific local needs. The central Japanese authority failed to respond adequately during the Kobe earthquake.

Earthquake-Proof Construction – Only an Illusion?

The first building designed to resist earthquake shock was erected by American architect Frank Lloyd Wright in Tokyo between 1916 and 1922. It survived the earthquake of 1923 virtually undamaged. In the years since, architects have employed special methods of stable or flexible construction at locations in Japan, California,

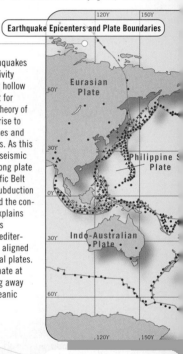

Earthquake Epicenters and Plate Boundaries

Zones of Critical Seismic Activity

Ninety per cent of all earthquakes are caused by seismic activity (volcanism and collapsing hollow areas in the Earth account for the remainder). Thus the theory of plate tectonics has given rise to new insights into the causes and distribution of earthquakes. As this map of epicenters shows, seismic activity is most intense along plate margins. The Circum-Pacific Belt coincides primarily with subduction zones (these incline toward the continental interiors, which explains the locations of deep-focus earthquakes), while the Mediterranean-Transasian Belt is aligned with converging continental plates. Weaker earthquakes originate at the edges of plates moving away from another near mid-oceanic ridges.

Where the Ball Rolls – the First Seismograph

The first device used to register earthquake activity was invented in China in the first century AD. The pot-bellied vessel is adorned with eight dragon figures, each facing a crouching toad positioned on the base below. When a tremor occurs, the pendulum inside begins to swing. The mouth of the dragon on the side opposite the direction of the shock wave opens and drops a ball into the mouth of the toad beneath it. This was believed to indicate the direction of the earthquake.

An Earthquake Exposes Weaknesses in Japanese Society

The quake that shook the Japanese industrial and port city of Kobe in the early morning of January 17, 1995 lasted no more than a few seconds. More than 20,000 buildings were heavily damaged or destroyed; 6,432 people were killed, and 350,000 lost their homes. The supports beneath 500 m of the Hanshin Highway collapsed, and the supposedly earthquake-proof elevated road crashed to the ground. The multi-story buildings nearby remained undamaged. The seemingly well-organized disaster aid and rescue system was largely ineffective.

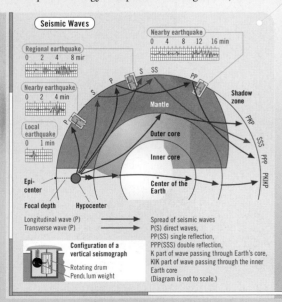

Seismic Waves

Nearby earthquake
0   4   8   12   16 min

Regional earthquake
0   2   4   8 mir

Nearby earthquake
0   2   4 min

Local earthquake
0   1 min

Epicenter

Focal depth   Hypocenter

Mantle

Shadow zone

Outer core

Inner core

Center of the Earth

Longitudinal wave (P)
Transverse wave (P)

Configuration of a vertical seismograph
Rotating drum
Pendulum weight

Spread of seismic waves
P(S) direct waves,
PP(SS) single reflection,
PPP(SSS) double reflection,
K part of wave passing through Earth's core,
KIK part of wave passing through the inner Earth core
(Diagram is not to scale.)

Earthquakes - Danger from the Depths

and other parts of the world. A number of countries have enacted corresponding building regulations in the past few years. Cellular construction techniques and "sandwich structures" comprised of steel and rubber plates built into the foundations of high-rise buildings absorb earthquake shocks. Steel structures are generally safer than stone or brick buildings. Wood-frame buildings may also offer satisfactory earthquake resistance if certain safety requirements are met. Schools, hospitals and other public buildings are subject to particularly stringent regulations. Recent experience has shown that many bridges, highway ramps, and similar structures need upgrading to meet safety requirements. Loose substrata, especially made-made fills or embankments, are very susceptible to earthquake damage. Much depends on the quality of construction – an issue of concern in developing countries. It is important to consider that the greatest damage incurred during major earthquakes (e.g. San Francisco, 1906 and Kobe, 1995) resulted from fire (broken gas lines). Although earthquakes cannot be prevented, precautionary measures reduce damage significantly.

A "Bend" in the Landscape

Only rarely are movements of the Earth's crust as obvious as in this photo: a bend of 3 to 5 meters in the railway line near Izmit, Turkey in August 1999.

Building Structure and Building Damage

With shops and underground parking areas, the basement level is the weakest part of many otherwise robust reinforced concrete structures. When it collapses, the entire building may fall. (Wufeng, Taiwan, 9/21/1999).

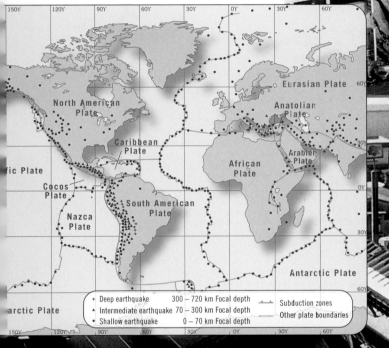

HOTEL 10F

Volcanism – Unbridled Forces from the Earth's Interior

Fertile Soil – Ever-Present Danger

In the early morning hours of August 27, 1883, the small volcanic island of Krakatoa in the Sundra Strait was shaken by violent explosions which virtually blew the island paradise apart. The enormous bang was heard more than 5,000 km away, and atmospheric pressure rose by 1.45 millibars in Tokyo. Massive tremors that triggered tsunamis traveling at the speed of an airliner battered the coastlines of Java and Sumatra. Roughly 36,000 people lost their lives as a direct result of the eruptions. And this was by no means the worst volcanic disaster in history. Eruptions on the Indonesian island of Sumbawa in 1815 ejected more than 180 cubic km of lava and ash (compared to only 20 cubic km on Krakatoa). The volcano, the tidal waves, and the famine that followed were responsible for some 90,000 deaths. Dust in the atmosphere darkened the sky for weeks.

A Bubbling Inferno Beneath Us

The solid crust that floats on the hot molten rock of the upper mantle is actually very thin. Continental crust attains a maximum thickness of 70 km, while oceanic crust is ordinarily between 5 and 10 km thick. (Imagine

An Eruption in Hawaii

An eruption of Kilauea in Hawaii begins with a fountain of lava lasting several hours. Escaping gas catapults the red-hot molten mass hundreds of meters into the air.

"Rushing Stream"

This is the literal translation of the Islandic word for geyser (geysir). Rainwater seeping into the hot volcanic underground is heated and ejected – often at regular intervals – through fissures in the rock. (photo: geysers in the Rotorua region of New Zealand). The process is a part of the waning phase of volcanic activity.

Volcanic Breakthrough in a Glacier

In 1996, the volcano beneath the Vatnajökull Glacier in Iceland melted a hole in the ice cap, sending clouds of ash as high as 4,000 m into the air. The lava eruptions that followed were accompanied by severe earth-quakes.

Aa and Pahoehoe Lava

A skin forms on the surface of the thin, red-hot pahoehoe lava as it flows. Once it has cooled and solidified, the lava may look much like lengths of intertwining twisted ropes or strings.

A Volcanic Blessing

Geothermal energy is a readily available alternative energy source in volcanically active regions like Italy, Iceland, and New Zealand.

Volcanism - Unbridled Forces from the Earth's Interior

an orange measuring 12 cm in diameter with a peel only 0.3 mm thick!). And thus it is no wonder that the Earth's thin crust is extremely fragile. Molten rock accumulates in large magma chambers beneath the surface and rises where faults or openings develop. Magma that emerges at the surface is called lava.

Harmless and Dangerous Volcanoes

The flow characteristics of lava depend on its chemical composition and gas content. Thin, basaltic lava (50% SiO2) of the kind that erupts from Kilauea (Hawaii) is often ejected in towering fountains which then flow smoothly from the crater. Andesitic magma rich in silicic acid (60 % SiO2) is catapulted from volcanic Mount Saint Helens to heights of several kilometers. Gases escape easily from thin magma, whereas thick, highly gaseous magma builds up high pressures that are released suddenly and explosively near the surface, where outside pressure decreases rapidly. At these points, lava shoots from the volcano like champagne from a shaken bottle. Basaltic lava forms relatively flat (12 degrees) shield volcanoes like those in Hawaii, or basalt floors (Dekkan, India).

Acidic lava tends to erupt violently, although it may also flow quietly down volcanic slopes. Alternating deposits of lava and tuff form cone-shaped stratovolcanoes with slopes as steep as 30 degrees. The most famous volcano of this type is Fujiama in Japan. When underground pressure has no means of escape, domes of lava form, raising the overlying layers and the Earth's surface above. The destructive power of explosive eruptions makes living in these areas extremely dangerous. The worst outbreak of this kind occurred at the Montagne Pelée on the island of Martinique in 1902. Extremely hot air (1,440° F) loaded with ash enveloped the nearby city of Saint-Pierre in a red-hot cloud, killing 29,000 people. The only survivor was found at the island prison.

Volcanoes – Gigantic Dirt Canons

Volcanic eruptions also hurl huge blocks of rock (bombs) far into the surrounding countryside. Fine particles are shot up to 10 km into the atmosphere, where they may circulate around the Earth for years. Bombs, lapilli (fragments measuring from two to 64 mm), and fine ash fall to the ground, forming volcanic tuff. Fragments that have not cooled sufficiently fuse into clinkers. Rock baked from larger masses becomes volcanic breccia. Storms among the high clouds above the volcano bring heavy rains, often causing massive mudflows that obliterate everything in their paths to the valleys below.

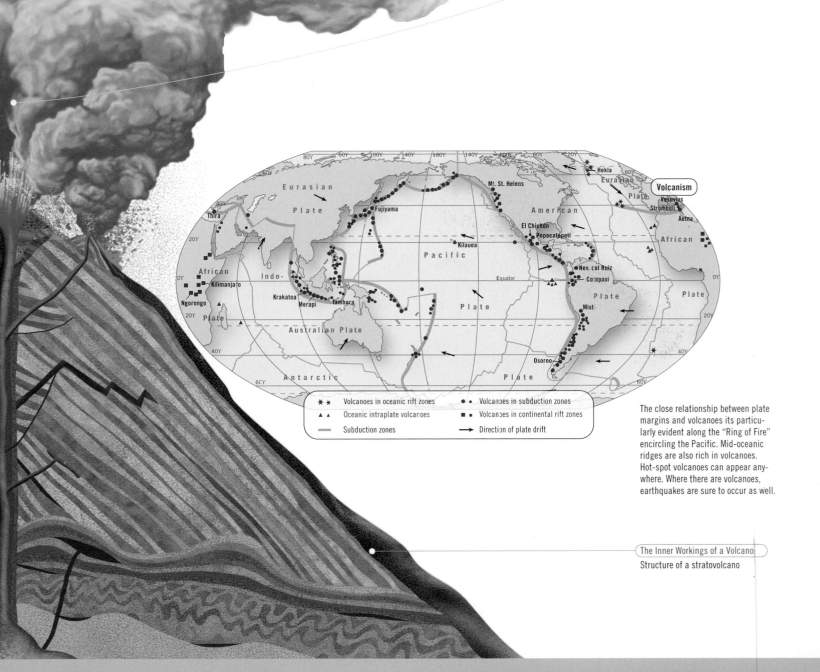

Volcanoes in oceanic rift zones
Oceanic intraplate volcanoes
Subduction zones
Volcanoes in subduction zones
Volcanoes in continental rift zones
Direction of plate drift

The close relationship between plate margins and volcanoes its particularly evident along the "Ring of Fire" encircling the Pacific. Mid-oceanic ridges are also rich in volcanoes. Hot-spot volcanoes can appear anywhere. Where there are volcanoes, earthquakes are sure to occur as well.

The Inner Workings of a Volcano:
Structure of a stratovolcano

Natural Disasters - Human Catastrophes

Does Mankind Pose a Challenge to Nature?

The media provide news about a terrible natural disaster somewhere in the world virtually every day. Our television screens show us images of devastation and often of the dramatic events themselves as they unfold. Sober assessments of underlying causes are often overshadowed in the public mind by such sensational reports.

Yet there are several questions we cannot ignore: "To what extent are we humans at fault?" Is mankind inevitably doomed to destruction, or can we find a way to avert it?

A Devastating Christmas Present

On Christmas Day of 1974, Tropical Storm Tracy battered the city of Darwin in northern Australia. With average wind speeds of 140 kilometers per hour and gusts peaking at 260 kilometers per hour, the storm completely destroyed more than 5,000 of the 8,000 lightweight houses built on stilts. Forty-nine people died, and property damage amounted to 3 billion Australian dollars. Of Darwin's 45,000 inhabitants, 25,000 were evacuated by air, while 10,000 people fled the city by car toward the south. This was the greatest natural disaster in Australia's history.

Flight from the Inferno

In early April 1991, Pinatubo, a volcano on the Philippine island of Luzon, erupted again for the first time in human memory. In June, the mountain collapsed and lost 300 meters of elevation. Red-hot clouds spread like avalanches, covering distances of as much as 20 km. Ten cubic km of ash, gas, and other erupted matter were catapulted into the stratosphere to heights of up to 40 km. Torrential rains generated by a tropical storm turned the accumulated ash into massive streams of mud. More than 200,000 people fled the looming catastrophe; 400 lives were lost. The expulsion of ash and particles containing sulphuric acid caused average temperatures in the atmosphere near ground level to sink by as much as 0.9° F — worldwide.

Tornadoes – Dangerous Twisters

The narrow funnel of a tornado dips threateningly earthward. The air rising inside the funnel rotates at speeds that accelerate to a maximum of 200 kilometers per hour toward the inside. The suction force generated inside the funnel rips buildings apart and bursts lungs and blood vessels in human victims. Objects carried away become dangerous projectiles; dust and water are hurled high into the atmosphere. The path of the funnel, which moves at speeds between 50 and 60 kilometers per hour, is narrow and clearly delineated, and so is its wake of destruction — and destruction is almost always total. The extensive damage is attributable in part to the prevalence of lightweight, wood-frame buildings in the United States.

Disasters Mark the Course of the Earth's History

The history of the Earth teaches us that catastrophic events have always played a role in global and regional developments and have even impacted on the evolution of living organisms. Yet from our somewhat short-sighted present-day perspective, we tend to overlook the length of time involved in these processes. Experts continue to debate the question of whether the mass extinction of life forms some 65 million years ago was caused by a collision with an extraterrestrial body, a severe outbreak of volcanic activity, or other geological, perhaps tectonic events. Most agree, however, that the extinction of the dinosaurs (along with many other forms of animal life) paved the way for the development of mammals and thus ultimately for the origin of Homo sapiens. But when we speak of natural disasters, we are usually thinking of events that affect human beings directly.

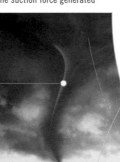

Cyclones

Natural Disasters - Human Catastrophes

The Earth's Vast Destructive Potential

The "restless Earth" poses many dangers. Earthquakes and volcanic eruptions are concentrated in certain regions. While it is impossible to prevent such events from occurring, precautions can be taken against their consequences. The number of severe earthquakes (measuring 7.0 or above on the Richter Scale) did not increase worldwide during the twentieth century. Yet the toll in human lives and property damage has risen steadily, due to increasing population and building density, to the spread of settlements into endangered areas people once avoided, to the increasing value of property and goods (concentrated primarily in metropolitan areas) that has accompanied the rise in living standards, and to the increased susceptibility of modern societies and technologies to damage. Explosive population growth is another significant factor. The Kobe earthquake (1995) clearly showed seismic activity affects not only devel-

oping countries but often industrialized nations as well. And much the same applies to volcanism. We find ourselves in the midst of a heated debate about the dangers posed by the Earth's atmosphere and waters. Is the number of incidents rising? Are they growing in severity? And what or who is to blame – nature or mankind? A closely related issue is the question of mankind's impact on climate. Hurricanes are not the only destructive climatic phenomenon. Extended periods of heavy rain or snow storms; hail, ice, droughts; heat waves and periods of extreme cold; forest, bush, and prairie fires caused by lightning; avalanches, fog and smog all leave destruction in their wake. Excessive precipitation causes floods, landslips, and mudslides.

Stormy Times

The most dangerous storms originate in the Tropics: hurricanes along the coasts of Central and North America, typhoons over the waters off East and Southeast Asia, and cyclones in the Bay of Bengal (Bangladesh). They often wander for days over the sea in a westerly direction, only to turn suddenly north or south just before landfall. Their low pressure areas measure between 300 and 1,000 km in diameter. The center (known as the eye) of such storms is virtually cloudless and calm. It is encircled by a spiral of clouds that rotates at speeds up to 400 kilometers per hour. Torrential rain falls from massive cloud formations towering to heights of more than 15,000 meters. Storms that reach land wreak tremendous destruction, to which tidal waves also contribute, but then quickly lose intensity and dissipate. Hurricane Andrew caused $30 billion in damage. Katrina, ultimately is expected to cost about $200 billion. In Bangladesh, more than 300,000 people lost their lives in flooding caused by cyclones in 1970. The energy bundled in such storms is equivalent to that of several atomic bombs.

The tornadoes that occur frequently in the Midwestern United States are born when warm, moist air from the Gulf of Mexico is overlayered by dry, cool air from the Rocky Mountains or the Arctic. The temperature differential (between 36° and 54°F) generates incredibly high wind speeds. An average of 750 tornadoes are registered in the U.S. every year. They have costs the lives of hundreds of people – despite the well-organized warning system.

Tropical storms (cyclones)
- highly destructive
- severe to very severe
- weak to moderate
- Tornadoes

Major paths of movement
→ Tropical storms
→ Non-tropical storms

Dangerous Tropical Storms

Tropical storms originate over waters with surface temperatures of at least 48°F in northern and southern latitudes between 5° and 30° during the late summer and early fall. A mass of moist, warm air with towering formations of cumulonimbus clouds gathers above the water. Condensation of the water vapor releases huge amounts of heat energy which accelerate the movement of rising air and the speed of the whirling mass of clouds. Tropical storms are generated by wavelike disruptions along the edge of the subtropical high-pressure belt or by the intrusion of low-pressure centers from the west-wind zone into the tropical circulation belt. Due to deflection caused by the Earth's rotation (Coriolis effect), storms spin clockwise in the southern hemisphere and counter-clockwise in the northern hemisphere. Cyclonic storms do not occur near the equator, as the Coriolis effect is too weak to accelerate the rotating masses of air.

When the Earth Slides Away

Saturation of debris or "soft," porous rock on mountain slopes or hillsides by heavy, sustained rainfall or melting snow can cause extensive landslips or mudslides. When these huge masses of mud and debris are carried into the valleys and rivers, the descending wave cuts a broad path of destruction through the landscape. Mudslides of this kind occur often in the Apennines (photo taken near Sarno, east of Mt. Vesuvius), especially in areas where slopes have been stripped of vegetation through deforestation or overgrazing.

Those Who Look for Trouble ...

The map divides the eastern and southeastern coasts of the United States into 58 numbered sections (each 80 km wide). Based on long-term observation, it is possible to estimate the probability of hurricane activity in a given year as a percentage value. The number of "normal" hurricanes (wind speeds higher than 33 meters per second) is entered in the inner row of boxes; "major" hurricanes (56 meters per second and higher) are listed in the outer row, which has several large gaps. Hurricane activity is most frequent in August and September.

Year in, Year out ...

Floods caused by high water on the Rhine (photo: Cologne) and its tributaries are practically a regular occurrence. Data gathered at water-level measuring stations enable authorities to issue advance warnings and initiate evacuation procedures. Dykes and ad hoc precautionary measures (such as mobile protective walls) can help prevent some but by no means all flood damage. Flooding in 1993 and 1995 caused total property damage estimated at five billion dollars.

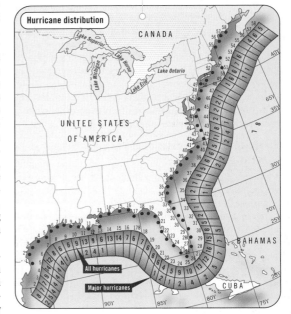

Hurricane distribution

The Great Flood Yet to Come?

High water is ordinarily caused by unusually long periods of heavy precipitation or by rapid melting of winter snows. Repeated reports of catastrophic flooding evoke the impression that these disastrous events are becoming more frequent. Are they a by-product of global climatic changes that are reflected in increasingly heavy precipitation in Central Europe and the American Midwest? Catastrophic floods have occurred often in the past, as high-water marks show, but they had less far-reaching consequences, as agriculture and housing development were much less extensive than they are today. Various human interventions in the balance of nature have accelerated runoff activity and increased the danger of flooding. Prime examples are deforestation, ground-surface sealing (roads, housing developments, etc.), soil compaction (resulting from machine plowing and the conversion of meadowlands to fields), riverbed constriction with dams and dykes, river straightening, and the draining of wetlands (along the Mississippi, Missouri, and Red Rivers, for example), in combination with ground settlement and rising riverbed levels caused by accumulating silt deposits. Awakened from their lethargy by the increasing frequency and impact of floods, experts and regulatory authorities have instituted renaturation programs for river areas. Efforts to restore natural flood plains (retention areas) often encounter stiff opposition from local farmers, however.

Vegetation - The Earth's Botanical Cloak

Plant and Human Life — A Reassessment

According to the Book of Genesis, God created plants on the third day, calling upon the Earth to "bring forth grass, the herb yielding seed … and the tree yielding fruit … and God saw that it was good." (Genesis 1:11). Mankind arrived on the scene soon afterward. By current reckoning, human beings have since destroyed about 30% of the original 62 million square kilometers of forest on Earth, transformed much of our planet's vast grasslands into arid wastelands (desertification) through overcultivation, and altered the character of natural vegetation in many regions of the world. We have intervened in natural patterns of growth and distribution, manipulated genetic makeup through breeding experiments, and replaced local flora with secondary growth over wide areas. Yet despite this massive human intervention in the plant kingdom, more than 99% of the Earth's biomass — about 1.8 trillion tons of organic material (300 tons for every living human being) — is vegetable matter.

The Foundation of Human and Animal Life

In his famous "Canticle of the Sun," Saint Francis of Assisi spoke of "… Earth, our Mother, who feeds us in her sovereignty and produces various fruits and colored flowers and herbs." The words of Saint Francis reflect an uncomplicated view of nature and an implicit recognition of the close and vital cosmic relationship between all living organisms (the biosphere) and the Earth's inorganic crust (the lithosphere), a mystery that was not solved by modern biological science until many years later. Biologists, ecologists and biochemists agree that animal, and thus of course human life could not exist in its present form without the Earth's botanical cloak.

Plants as Chemical Factories and Nutrient Pumps

The leaves of plants contain chlorophyll (the pigment that makes them green), which they use to convert water taken up by their roots and carbon dioxide (CO_2) absorbed from the air into glucose (sugar) with the aid of light (solar energy) captured on their surfaces in a complicated process known as photosynthesis. Through their roots, which in some plants (wheat, for example) form networks of microscopically fine fibrous tendrils with combined lengths of up to several hundred kilometers, they absorb a wide variety of elements essential to all life on Earth from the soil. These they process along with the glucose into organic matter, referred to collectively as biomass (the dry weight of organic matter).

Through this process, a number of elements essential to many physiological processes, such as iron, phosphorus, calcium, magnesium, nitrogen, and sulfur, are incorporated into biomass and passed along through the food chain to herbivorous animal organisms and ultimately to carnivores (including humans as well, regardless of whether they actually eat meat or not, since the consumption of animal protein is virtually unavoidable for modern consumers).

In this way, the massive global nutrient pump of natural vegetation extracts more than two cubic kilometers per year – roughly six billion tons – of minerals and substances of all kinds from the Earth's crust and makes them available as sustenance to animals and human beings (approximately one ton for every living human being on Earth).

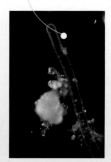

A root hair launches a biochemical attack on a calcite mineral: the first stage in the transition from mineral to chemical substance.

Soil-Building Vegetation

Vegetable biomass consumed by animal organisms is returned to the eternal mineral cycle as feces or in the bodies of dead organisms themselves. Unconsumed biomass is also remineralized when humus is formed through the decomposition of fallen leaves and dead plants. Mineral replacement resulting from biochemical and physical root activity, on the one hand, and the accumulation of biomass, on the other, are important soil-building processes which work within an ecological network in collaboration with such non-biological factors as the warmth and moisture of vegetation in a specific region.

Trees — Unsung "Environmental Helpers"

Trees are the largest forms of plant life. A deciduous tree between 15 and 20 meters high generates three million liters of oxygen annually (four times as much as a single human being needs in a year) through the process of photosynthesis. In one year, the same tree also filters as much as 7,000 kg of dust from the air with its foliage and extracts up to 7,000 liters of water from the soil through its root system, thus contributing significantly to the prevention of soil erosion – a problem that can assume catastrophic proportions in deforested areas. For every human being on Earth today, there are about 500 trees at work providing these important environmental services.

How Do the Little Flowers Grow, and How Do Plants Give Us Food?

The preceding description shows how very important the plant kingdom is. In light of the crucial role plants play in our lives, it is shocking to realize how little we know about them. Most people in the industrialized countries of the world can name at least 20 different makes of car but not nearly as many kinds of plants! Yet botanists have now identified more than 360,000 varieties, of which about 180,000 are blossoming plants.

It is not the species of so-called "higher plants" classified into families of trees, shrubs, flowers, and grasses that are so difficult to identify with certainty. The real difficulty and suspense begins with the attempt to establish clear scientific distinctions among the varieties of "lower plant organisms" or microflora: fungi, the various species of algae, lichens as symbiotic communities of fungi and algae, and even the types of bacteria that are classified as forms of plant life – the "little beasties" discovered and described by Antonie van Leewenhoek (1632–1723) with the aid of his home-made microscope.

Although between 10,000 and 50,000 edible varieties of plants are available for human consumption, only about 150 to 200 species (between 0.3 and 2 %) are actually used for nutritional purposes. Over 75 % of all energy consumed by human beings in the form of vegetable matter comes from only about ten crop plants (between 0.002 and 0.1 % of all edible species of plants).

The Earth's Coat of Brightly Colored Stripes

Plants have no means of locomotion, and thus the characteristics they exhibit as indicator plants at the present stage of evolutionary development are always evidence of their adaptation to prevailing conditions in their local environments (known as habitat conditions). These include such features as water-retention organs (in cactuses or agaves in arid regions), shallow, broad root systems (like those of the birch tree) in permafrost regions where soil thaws only for a few months during the summer, or a thick coat of hair as protection against evaporation in alpine regions (edelweiss is an example). Thus we understand why belts of vegetation corresponding generally to the Earth's climatic zones, communities of plants known by botanists as vegetation zones, cover the Earth like a brightly-colored striped coat. And the same explanation applies to the typical vegetation patterns in mountainous regions that reflect the increasing lack of heat at progressively higher elevations, a phenomenon described with specific reference to South America by Alexander von Humboldt as early as the late eighteenth century.

(2) Tundra Vegetation

With average annual temperatures normally below 5°F, permafrost soil thaws only briefly to a depth of a few centimeters in the summer. With a growth period of 30–90 days, this type of vegetation, which forms a continuous belt only in the northern hemisphere, is characterized by an extraordinary abundance of lichens (in the Arctic north) and treeless, summer-green, flower-covered meadows (in the subpolar south).

(11) Alpine Vegetation

The most impressive alpine vegetation is found in the Andes (see photographs). Here the hierarchy of vegetation levels, from the tropical rain forest to the Paramo to the high tropical grasslands (moist puna) and the frost-prone, high, cold puna at elevations of about 5,000 m, where grass is sparse but lichens are plentiful, reflect the effects of diminishing warmth at progressively higher elevations.

The upper layer of permafrost soil thaws in the early summer.

Tundra meadows blossom in mid-summer.

Soil erosion following deforestation in Peru

Vegetation - The Earth's Botanical Cloak

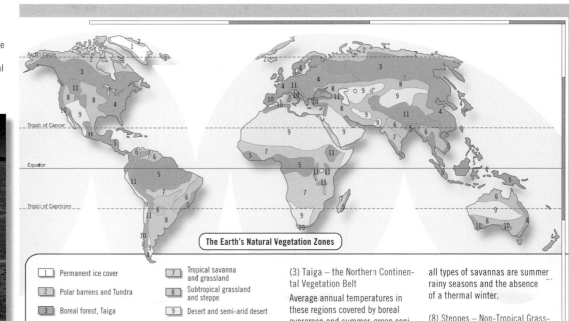

(5) Tropical deciduous forest

Despite annual precipitation often exceeding 1,000 mm, these forests of long-trunked trees that turn fully green only near their tops during the summer rainy season have a relatively short growth period, as water is scarce during the rest of the year (photo: Caprivi, Namibia). The monsoon forests of southern and Southeast Asia represent a special form of this class of vegetation.

The Earth's Natural Vegetation Zones

1	Permanent ice cover
2	Polar barrens and Tundra
3	Boreal forest, Taiga
4	Temperate forest and cultivated land
5	Tropical rain forest
6	Tropical deciduous forest
7	Tropical savanna and grassland
8	Subtropical grassland and steppe
9	Desert and semi-arid desert
10	Mediterranean vegetation, sclerophyllous plants
11	Alpine vegetation

Sparse cold puna with cushion grass and lichens

Moist puna of the Altiplano with grazing llamas

Transition from tropical mountain to mist forest

(4) Forests of the Temperate Zone

The summer-green deciduous and mixed forests that once prevailed throughout this climate zone, which with average annual temperatures of between 43 and 54°F and growth periods of 200 days or longer offers ideal conditions for agriculture, have fallen victim to large-scale deforestation and have been replaced in isolated areas by second-growth forests used primarily for wood production.

(3) Taiga – the Northern Continental Vegetation Belt

Average annual temperatures in these regions covered by boreal evergreen and summer-green coniferous forests comprising only a few species, which span the globe only in the permafrost regions of the northern hemisphere, range near 32°F. Covering some 20 million square km (about 13 % of the Earth's dry land), they represent the world's largest forest formation.

(5) Tropical Rain Forest

In the tropics, where rain falls the year round and annual precipitation often exceeds 2,000 mm, temperatures determine the character of forests. Multi-tiered, evergreen equatorial rain forest – a habitat for a wide range of species – is predominant in low-lying areas with mean annual temperatures of 72–82°F. Mountain forests with fewer species are prevalent at elevations over 1,000 m and average temperatures of 57–72°F. Mist forests characterized by beard lichens, epiphytes, and tree ferns predominate only at elevations of over 2,000 m and at average temperatures of only 40–57°F. Together, these three forest types occupy a total area of about 12.5 million square km (approximately 8 % of the dry land on Earth). They are seriously endangered, particularly at lower elevations, by logging operations and large-scale deforestation. The most common natural form of vegetation along the tropical coasts are mangrove forests, although they have now been almost totally destroyed.

(7) Savannas – Maximum Landscape Diversity

Savannas are generally thought of as expansive tropical grasslands (like the Serengeti). Actually, they display a number of different faces. Although grass is the dominant ground cover in all savanna landscapes, the spectrum of plant formations encompasses dry, thorny shrub vegetation, flourishing bush growth, densely wooded areas, and even true forests (such as the gallery forests along riverbanks or the Mopane and Miombo woodlands of southern Africa). Common to all types of savannas are summer rainy seasons and the absence of a thermal winter.

(8) Steppes – Non-Tropical Grasslands Under the Plow

Where grasslands once stretched to the horizon in climates with dry summers and often extremely cold winters (on the North American prairies or the black-earth regions of southern Russia), human beings have replaced the natural vegetation of the dry, short-grass and moister, long-grass steppes with vast grain fields. In many places, such industrial-scale farming operations have contributed to soil deterioration by clearing the way for wind and water erosion.

(9) Desert Vegetation

Vegetation in deserts and semi-arid regions (where climates are only slightly more favorable), is ideally adapted to the extreme conditions of their environments (scarcity of water, heat, nocturnal or winter frost, sand storms, etc.). Higher forms of plant life have developed appropriate survival tools: water-retaining organs, leaf coverings that inhibit evaporation, suspension of metabolic activity during extremely dry periods ("latent life") or disproportionately large (relative to above-ground biomass) underground plant organs (primarily roots). Microflora – ordinarily overlooked by human beings – is represented in abundance on the surface in the form of algae, fungi, and blankets of lichens that can even be seen in satellite images.

(10) Mediterranean Vegetation

The original natural vegetation of the Mediterranean regions, which are classified as subtropical climate zones with wet winters, was evergreen sclerophyllous forest (holm oak forests in the actual Mediterranean region). Extreme overuse by humans has caused much of this original vegetation to be replaced by meager second-growth formations such as broad-leaved shrubs and small trees (matorral, chaparral or maquis) and even poorer scrubland vegetation (garrigue).

The Changing Global Climate

... and Mankind's Role in the Process

The history of the Earth's climate is one of changes, some gradual, others rapid and dramatic. Periods of relative stability and calm like the Holocene, which began some 10,000 years ago, are the exception rather than the rule. Yet it was precisely this climatic stability that allowed human civilization to develop. Today, the extent of human intervention in climatic processes is increasing. Are we merely a minor disruptive factor in the interplay of these powerful forces of nature, or does mankind pose a serious threat to the global climatic balance?

Variations in the Earth's Orbit

Some 20,000 years ago, at the peak of the last ice age, substantial portions of North America and northern Europe were covered by sheets of ice several thousand meters thick. This ice extended deep into the North American continent to the region now covered by the Great Lakes. The land south of the ice was arctic steppe, much like today's tundra regions. On basis of bore samples taken from deposits thousands and even millions of years old, from layers of sediment on the ocean floor or from continental ice in Antarctica and Greenland, for example, it has been possible to reconstruct temperature patterns and many other characteristics of past climate. For at least two million years, the Earth's climate has been governed by relatively regular cycles. Ice ages lasting roughly 100,000 years have alternated with warm periods usually about 10,000 years long. These cycles are caused by subtle shifts in the Earth's orbit around the sun and in the inclination of the Earth's axis. These changes, known as Milankovitch variations, affect the seasonal and geographic distribution of solar radiation – although the total amount of radiation that reaches the Earth remains constant. It is not entirely clear why the Earth's climate reacts so dramatically to these changing radiation patterns. One crucial factor is apparently the intensity of summer sunlight over the continents of the northern hemisphere, for when the snows of the past winter do not melt completely, large sheets of ice begin to form. They reflect solar radiation and thus lead to further cooling. Our understanding of Milankovitch variations suggests that the Holocene is an unusually long warm phase, which would mean that a new ice age is not to be expected for several tens of thousands of years.

Abrupt Climatic Shifts

Scientists have learned only fairly recently that the last ice age was marked by a series of very abrupt and drastic changes in climate. In the course of these so-called Dansgaard-Oeschger Events (of which more than 20 are known to have occurred during the last ice age), average temperatures in the North Atlantic region rose rapidly – within only a few years – by between 11 and 14°F. These unusually warm periods lasted several hundreds or thousands of years. Their effects were felt around the globe – even in the Antarctic. Evidently, sudden shifts in the course of marine currents played a significant role in these sudden climatic changes.

Even the Holocene, the current, relatively stable warm period, has not been free of climatic changes. Some 5,500 years ago, the Sahara was transformed from a landscape of swamps, lakes and areas of vegetation inhabited by many large animals and human beings into the desert we know today. In all likelihood, this process was set in motion by a shift in the Earth's orbit which triggered a fatal chain of events: a gradual decrease in rainfall resulting in diminished plant growth which led in turn to further reduction in precipitation.

The Radiation Budget

The Earth's temperature is regulated by a simple radiation budget. On average, the energy received from the sun is equal to the energy radiated by the Earth into space. If too much energy is received, temperatures rise and the Earth radiates more heat until balance is

Frozen Lake, 1830
From the fifteenth to the eighteenth century, temperatures in Europe were 1.8 to 3.6° F cooler than today. This cool period is known as the "Little Ice Age." Lake Constance froze over completely about every 20 years during that period but only once during the twentieth century (1963). Inhabitants of the alpine regions often experienced failed harvests and famine during the "Little Ice Age." This View of Frozen Lake Constance was painted by the local artist Nicolaus Hug in 1830.

The Changing Global Climate

restored. If the Earth had no atmosphere, its average temperature would be somewhere near 0° F. The atmosphere inhibits thermal radiation from the Earth's surface, primarily due to the insulating effect of water vapor and carbon dioxide, the so-called greenhouse gases. Consequently, the Earth's surface warms until the radiation balance is restored at today's average temperature of about 59° F. It is this natural greenhouse effect that makes our planet inhabitable. Changes in the composition of the atmosphere or in the surface area of reflective ice and cloud masses can affect the radiation budget and thus raise or lower temperatures.

The Human Factor

Human impact on the global climate dates back to the Middle Ages, when people began clearing forests to make room for farmland, thereby increasing carbon dioxide levels in the atmosphere and creating lighter areas of surface that reflect more sunlight. But it was not until the Industrial Revolution in the first half of the nineteenth century that mankind developed the means to disrupt the delicate radiation balance significantly. The leading cause of these man-made changes is the use of fossil fuels – coal, petroleum, and natural gas. The fossil fuel we burn in a single year took roughly a million years to accumulate. The carbon contained in these materials oxidizes during combustion and is released into the air as carbon dioxide (CO_2). About half of it remains in the atmosphere, while the remainder is absorbed by the oceans and the biosphere. Since the beginning of the Industrial Age, the carbon-dioxide concentration in the atmosphere has risen from 280 parts per million (ppm) to 360 ppm, and the greenhouse effect has grown stronger accordingly. Other gases released in the course of human activities intensify the greenhouse effect even further. Examples are methane and fluorocarbons, which are also responsible for the ozone hole.

Concentrations of greenhouse gases in the atmosphere have risen in recent years, raising average global temperatures by about 1.25° F – over both land and sea. Mountain glaciers are melting all over the world (total glacier volume in the Alps has already decreased by half). Artic Ice has become almost 40 per cent thinner over the past 30 years.

Using sophisticated pattern-recognition techniques, climatologists have attempted to determine the extent to which these trends are actually attributable to anthropogenic emissions and to identify other possible causes (such as fluctuations in the sun). Their findings indicate that, at the very least, the accelerated warming trend observed since 1970 is largely a man-made phenomenon.

Scientists warned as early as the late nineteenth century on the basis of simple computations that increasing concentrations of carbon dioxide in the atmosphere would lead to global warming. Today, the world's climate can be simulated with the aid of powerful computers, which make it possible both to reconstruct past climate patterns and to project scenarios for the future. If concentrations of greenhouse gases in the atmosphere continue to rise at the current pace, we can expect global temperatures to rise by between 2.7 and 9.9 degrees F over the next hundred years. Should this happen, the earth will be warmer than it has been at any time during the past 100,000 years. One consequence would be a rise in sea level of between 20 and 90 centimeters, which would persist for centuries even if the warming trend were halted. Warming would also lead to changes in precipitation patterns and thus possibly to drought and flooding, endangering many existing ecosystems in the process. Low-lying coastal regions would be threatened by flooding caused by storms, and several island nations in the Pacific would disappear beneath the sea.

In an effort to slow the process of global warming, most of the nations participating in the international conference in Kyōto, Japan in 1997 signed a Climate Treaty that obliges industrial nations to reduce emissions of greenhouse gases to five per cent below 1990 levels by the year 2012. The treaty is not yet in force, as only a few nations have ratified it, and it represents, at best, only a first small step toward effective climate protection.

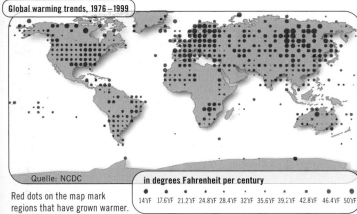

Global warming trends, 1976 – 1999

Quelle: NCDC

in degrees Fahrenheit per century

14°F   17.6°F   21.2°F   24.8°F   28.4°F   32°F   35.6°F   39.2°F   42.8°F   46.4°F   50°F

Red dots on the map mark regions that have grown warmer. Blue dots show those that have cooled. Insufficient data is available for the remaining areas.

Saharan Rock Painting

Until about 6,000 years ago, the Sahara was much greener than it is today. A large number of rock drawings offer evidence of a much moister climate. The buffalo Homoioceras antiquus (Oued Djerat, Tassili n'Ajjer, Algeria) became extinct during the early Holocene.

The Radiation Budget and the Greenhouse Effect

Assuming a value of 100 % for the amount of solar radiation that actually effects the global radiation budget (342.5 Watts per square meter), only 45 % (on long-term, global average) actually reaches the Earth's surface. The remainder is absorbed or scattered. The total reflective capacity of the earth (including the atmosphere and clouds) is referred to as the Earth's albedo, and amounts to 30 % on a yearly average.
The effective heat radiated by the Earth's surface is 18 %. This equates to the difference between 114 % – the value which would be expected if the Earth had no atmosphere – and 96 % – for radiation reflected back by the atmosphere (the greenhouse effect). The difference between incoming solar radiation and outgoing terrestrial radiation (27 %) at the surface is offset by heat currents.

Threatening Hole

In 1985, British researchers discovered a hole in the ozone layer of the upper atmosphere – our shield against dangerous cosmic radiation. One of the causes identified was the release of industrially produced fluorocarbons, such as those used in spray cans, into the atmosphere. The Montreal Protocol of 1987 called for a global ban on these gases, to be achieved in a step-by-step process. They are hardly used at all today, and scientists now predict that the ozone hole will gradually close over the next several decades. It will probably take more than 100 years to restore the ozone layer completely, however.

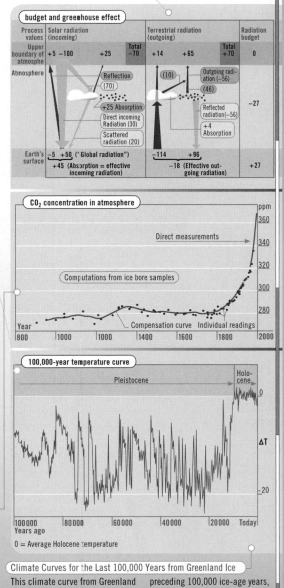

budget and greenhouse effect

Process values	Solar radiation (incoming)				Terrestrial radiation (outgoing)				Radiation budget
Upper boundary of atmosphe	+5 −100	+25		Total −70	+14	+65		Total +70	0
Atmosphere		Reflection (70)			(10)	Outgoing radiation (−56)			
	+25 Absorption					(46)			−27
	Direct incoming Radiation (30)					Reflected radiation (−56)			
	Scattered radiation (20)					+4 Absorption			
Earth's surface	−5 +50 ("Global radiation")				−114	+96			+27
	+45 (Absorption = effective incoming radiation)				−18 (Effective outgoing radiation)				

CO_2 concentration in atmosphere

Direct measurements

Computations from ice bore samples

Year   Compensation curve   Individual readings

800   1000   1000   1400   1600   1800   2000

ppm
360
340
320
300
280

100,000-year temperature curve

Pleistocene   Holocene

0

ΔT

−20

100 000   80 000   60 000   40 000   20 000   Today
Years ago

0 = Average Holocene temperature

Alarming Rise

Analyses of air bubbles in Antarctic ice and measurements taken at Mauna Loa (Hawaii) since 1957 tell us a great deal about carbon-dioxide concentration in the atmosphere: about 280 ppm during warm periods like the Holocene, 200 ppm during the ice ages, and more

Climate Curves for the Last 100,000 Years from Greenland Ice

This climate curve from Greenland shows the consistently warm climate of the past 10,000 years, the Holocene period. During the preceding 100,000 ice-age years, the climate was not only much colder but also subject to sudden fluctuations.

Religions of the World

One Divine Power? Many Concepts of Divinity

Religion is an expression of human responses to the experience of divinity in ritual and doctrine. It appears n different forms in different cultures and at different times, and though distinct from other manifestations of culture, it both reflects and shapes them at the same time. Religion is always community-oriented and always involves standards of ethics, although these may differ significantly from one set of beliefs and principles to another. Religion takes public form in rituals and pilgrimages, at specific places, and in the teachings of religious leaders. Religious faith informs and molds the lives of those who share it.

A Ubiquitous Phenomenon

All human societies since prehistoric times have embraced religious beliefs of some kind. We distinguish between two basic types of religion. The first is known as "primary religion." The origin and basis for all religions, it is still clearly evident today in "tribal religions" (frequently, though imprecisely and even inaccurately referred to as "natural" or "animistic" religions). These systems of belief have primarily local or regional relevance and generally govern communal life in small societies. They provide guidance and support at critical points in life – birth, puberty, marriage, death and mourning – through "rites of passage." Events marking seasonal transitions, such as planting and harvest or the winter and summer solstices, are also celebrated in rituals and serve as fixed points of reference for communal life, much like Christmas and Easter in western societies.

The second group, "secondary religions," comprises systems of belief and ritual which can be traced to the teachings or activities of founders, reformers, and charismatic leaders. They include the five major religions of the world: Judaism, Christianity, Islam, Buddhism, and Hinduism. They all pose the question of truth, which plays no role at all in primary religions, whose "natural" legitimacy is grounded in the specific societies that embrace them. Many secondary religions have sacred scriptures, which contain the basic tenets of ethics, faith, and behavior to which their adherents subscribe. Because they claim possession of universal truth, they tend to assume a missionary character, and their founders are the central focus of teaching and devotion. Buddhism, Christianity, and Islam are prime examples of this tendency. As they spread throughout the world, these secondary religions have had to come to grips with

Christian Africa

The majority of people in most of the countries of central and southern Africa are Christians. More than one-third of African Christians are members of the Catholic Church, which actively promotes the education and development of native clerics. The "Independent Churches" embody a form of Christianity that deliberately makes room for traditional aspects of African tribal cultures.

Religion by the Book

An Ethiopian monk demonstrates the art of manuscript illumination while writing a page of the Bible in Amharic, which becomes established as the liturgical language of the Ethiopian Church.

Sacred Waters

A bath in the sacred Ganges River is believed to purify the soul of a Hindu. The ghats (bathing steps) at the pilgrimage center in Varanasi provide easy access to the Ganges.

Traditional Healer

In many African religions, misfortune, disease, and death are attributed to evil spells cast by witches. Only the healer (photo: Susa Madela, Sorcerer of Lightning, 1902–1988) can provide protection.

Islamic Pilgrimage

The Ka'bah, an empty, windowless building inside the Great Mosque in Mecca was a sacred shrine in the city even during pre-Islamic times. All Muslims are obliged to make at least one pilgrimage to Mecca in their lifetime. Pilgrims walk around the shrine seven times.

Religions of the World

Tropic of Cancer

Guadalupe

Salt Lake City

Great Lakes

ATLANTIC

PACIFIC

Equator

OCEAN

Tropic of Capricorn

Christianity			Islam	
Protestantism		Judaism		Sunni
Roman Catholicism		Significant		Shi'a
Eastern Orthodox Churches		◆ Jewish communities		
Other Christian sects				Hinduism

Religions of the World

primary religions. In the process, they have adopted and adapted existing sacred rituals, places and times, reinterpreting them and casting out whatever elements could not be reconciled with their teachings. Buddhism developed into Mahayana Buddhism in China, for example, in response to regional influences. Christianity split into an eastern (Orthodox) branch under the influence of the religions of Greece and Asia Minor and a western (Roman) form of Catholicism oriented toward the more dogmatic Roman religions. Islam adopted pre-Islamic and existing Judaic and Christian elements, as the life of Mohammed clearly shows.

When the great religions face a loss of vitality and begin to abandon their original doctrines under the influence of progressive enlightenment, modern patterns of thought, and the pressure of political systems, reformers appear, new sects are founded, and fundamentalist revival movements take shape, as we witness all over the world today. This tendency is reflected in new religious movements and sects in Japan (Tenrykyo and others), the United States (Mormons, Children of God, etc.), Latin America (Umbanda, voodoo cults), India (neo-Hinduism), and Africa (Kimbanguism, Aladura churches, etc.) as well as the emphatically pious New-Age religions.

Religion – a Source of Conflict?

All religions strive to control the lives of their members, and thus they play an important role in public life. Radical, often fundamentalist religious movements also seek to exert political influence, although they often expose themselves to manipulation by political forces as well. In view of the dangers all societies face in today's world, religions would do well to remember their humanitarian function and support the growth of a system of ethics that will enable human beings to live together in peace.

Religions of the World				
Religions	Date of origin	Sacred scriptures	Number of adherents	% of world population
Christianity	30 AD	Bible	2 bn	33 % – increasing in the Third World
Islam	622 AD	Koran	1.3 bn	20 % – increasing
Hinduism and neo-Hinduism	c. 1,500 BC	Vedas, Upanishads	900 mil.	15 % – stagnant
Atheists and agnostics	–	–	900 mil.	15 % – decreasing
Buddhism	c. 530 BC	Tipitaka	360 mil.	6 % – stagnant
Chinese Religious Complex (ancestor and nature worship, Taoism, Confucianism*)	c. 1,500 BC	–	230 mil.	5 %
Tribal religions	prehistoric	Oral tradition	91 mil.	2 %
Yoruba religions: voodoo cults, Umbanda, etc.	?	–	30 mil.	< 1 %
New religious movements (Caodaism, Soka-Gakkai, Ananda Marge, etc.)	19th/20th c.	–	30 mil.	< 1 %
Sikhism	1500 AD	Adi Granth	18 mil.	< 1 %
Judaism	Babylonian exile (587–538 BC)	Torah, Talmud	15 mil.	< 1 %
Shamanism	prehistoric	Oral tradition	12 mil.	< 1 %
Spiritism*	after 1800	–	10 mil.	< 1 %
Baha'i	1863 AD	The Most Holy Book	4 mil.	< 1 %
Shintō	6th c. AD	Kojiki, Nihonzi, Fudoki	4 mil.	< 1 %
Jainism	6th/5th c. BC	Extensive canon in Prakrit literature	3 mil.	< 1 %
Parsiism	500 – 250 BC	Avesta	150,000	< 1 %

* not a religion in the strict sense

Jewish Marriage Rites

Bride and groom cover their heads with a tallit (prayer cloak) during the marriage ceremony.

The Desert – Origin of all Great Religions

The Israelites were nomads, like these shepherds on the Sinai Peninsula. They are believed to have worshiped protector gods and local divinities originally. Every tribe had its own god, to whom access was gained through the tribal elders ("fathers").

Harmony and Peace

Meditation is an important religious exercise for Buddhists, as it relieves the heart of suffering and the mind of ignorance. The simple saffron-colored robe symbolizes simplicity and self-denial; the fig tree recalls the bodhi tree beneath which Buddha achieved enlightenment.

Northern and southern Buddhism
Lamaistic Buddhism
Chinese Religious Complex (Confucianism, Taoism)
Shinto
Tribal religions, Shamanism
New religious movements
Religious shrines and sites
Unpopulated areas

Global Linguistic Diversity

One World – Thousands of Languages

Depending upon the criteria applied in distinguishing them, between 2,500 and 6,500 languages are spoken on Earth. These widely diverging figures reflect both the difficulty involved in differentiating with certainty between a dialect and a language and our lack of knowledge about many languages spoken by very small groups in regions such as the Amazon Basin, New Guinea, and the African interior.

European languages account for only a small portion of the total. Somewhere between 70 and 165 different tongues are spoken on the continent. More languages (nearly 750!) are spoken in Papua New Guinea than in any other single country in the world. Only very few countries are completely unilingual (Iceland is one). Most countries are home to speakers of several or many different tongues and their variants. A number of languages die out every year, and discoveries of new languages are rare even today.

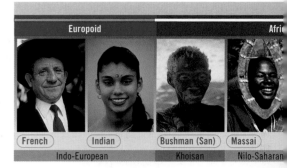

Europoid — Afri[...]
French | Indian | Bushman (San) | Massai
Indo-European | Khoisan | Nilo-Saharan

Dead Languages – Living Legacies

Some languages die out with their last speakers, while others are preserved as funds of knowledge, taught in schools (classical Arabic), used only in religious contexts (Old Hebrew), or studied as fixed points of historical reference in linguistics (Sanskrit). Still others serve as a source of new scientific terminology (Greek, Latin) or retain their vitality as literary languages (classical Chinese).

English – A Dominant World Language

Languages are affected by globalization as well. English has become the dominant language worldwide, although it ranks far behind Chinese in terms of numbers of native speakers. In sports and culture, in the high-tech world of computers and telecommunication, in the realm of travel and leisure activities, in scientific discourse and business correspondence, English has attained a degree of appeal, prestige, and influence that is unrivalled by any other language at the global level. International organizations exert considerable influence on language policy in support of other tongues. At the UN, for example, Arabic, Chinese, French, Russian, and Spanish join English as official languages. The European Union has even awarded official status to the national languages of all its member states.

Ethnic Revival – Grass Roots Resistance

The emancipation movements of the sixties and seventies led to a reassessment of the importance of language within the context of ethnic revival. Emphasis suddenly shifted from "utility" and "suitability" in a global sense to concern for linguistic diversity. "Minority" languages and tongues spoken in now independent former colonies were recognized as worthy of equal status and treatment. Languages which for centuries had been preserved and passed from one generation to the next only in oral form were systematically analyzed and described, transposed into a standardized written form, and documented in learning and reference materials such as textbooks, teachers' guides, dictionaries, and grammars (examples include Faeroese, a Germanic island language, and Swahili, the lingua franca in Africa). Bilingual or trilingual traffic and street signs, multilingual billboards, and enhanced media presence now offer striking visible and audible evidence of the new status of many once-neglected languages.

Writing Systems – Keys to Language

Human beings have employed a wide range of different writing systems to present natural, spoken language in visual form for more than three millennia. People of the ancient Egyptian, Inuit, and Maya cultures developed various forms of hieroglyphics, the Sumerians created a cuneiform system, while people of other civilizations established systems comprised of signs for words or syllables. Most forms of writing employed today make use of letters or symbols representing specific sounds. The writing systems now used in Europe and North America derive from the Phoenician alphabet developed in the 10th century BC, which also provided the basis for both the Arabic and Hebrew writing systems. Linguists have identified four major groups of alphabets: Greek (Latin, Coptic, Cyrillic, Armenian, Georgian), Semitic (Arabic, Hebrew, Ethiopian), Indian (Devanagari, Bengali, Tibetan, Burman, Thai, Khmer), and East Asian (Chinese, Japanese, Korean).

Every human has a language, but not everyone has command of its written form. Illiteracy is actually quite widespread and is particularly prevalent in the Third World. In Haiti, for example, 55% of the population cannot read or write. Illiterates account for 40% of the population of the Central African Republic, and 62% of all Yemenese are unable to read a newspaper or write even a short note. Even the rich industrialized countries of the world face the problem of illiteracy, with up to 5% of their inhabitants unable to read or express themselves in written form and thus virtually excluded from the mainstream of cultural and economic life.

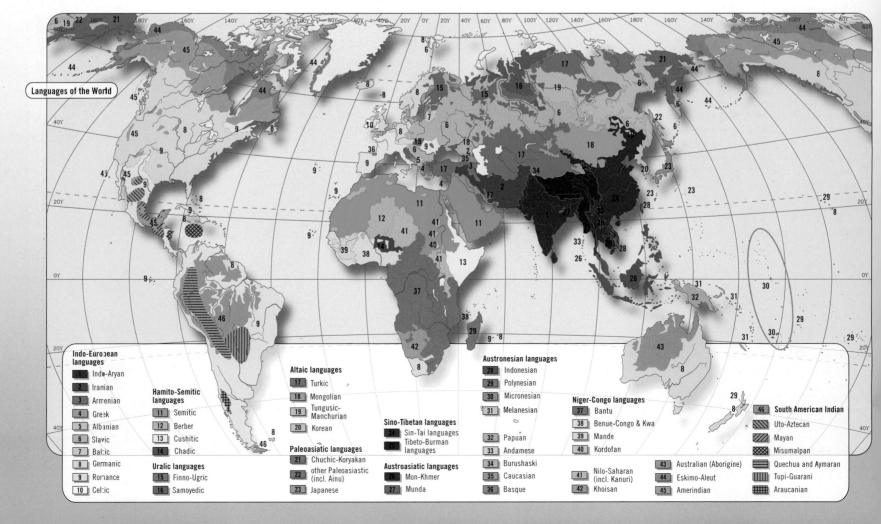

Languages of the World

Indo-European languages
1 Indo-Aryan
2 Iranian
3 Armenian
4 Greek
5 Albanian
6 Slavic
7 Baltic
8 Germanic
9 Romance
10 Celtic

Hamito-Semitic languages
11 Semitic
12 Berber
13 Cushitic
14 Chadic

Uralic languages
15 Finno-Ugric
16 Samoyedic

Altaic languages
17 Turkic
18 Mongolian
19 Tungusic-Manchurian
20 Korean

Paleoasiatic languages
21 Chuchic-Koryakan
22 other Paleoasiastic (incl. Ainu)
23 Japanese

Sino-Tibetan languages
24 Sin-Tai languages
25 Tibeto-Burman languages

Austroasiatic languages
26 Mon-Khmer
27 Munda

Austronesian languages
28 Indonesian
29 Polynesian
30 Micronesian
31 Melanesian
32 Papuan
33 Andamese
34 Burushaski
35 Caucasian
36 Basque

Niger-Congo languages
37 Bantu
38 Benue-Congo & Kwa
39 Mande
40 Kordofan

41 Nilo-Saharan (incl. Kanuri)
42 Khoisan

43 Australian (Aborigine)
44 Eskimo-Aleut
45 Amerindian

46 South American Indian
Uto-Aztecan
Mayan
Misumalpan
Quechua and Aymaran
Tupi-Guarani
Araucanian

Global Linguistic Diversity

East Asian		Arctic	Amerindian		Oceanian		Australian
Pygmy	Chinese	Tibetan	Inuit	Maya	Yanomami	Polynesian	Melanesian	Australian
Niger-Kordofan	Sino-Tibetan		Eskimo-Aleut	Amerindian		Austronesian		Australian

Linguistic Diversity – a Curse?
Did all humans originally speak a single language? The idea (no longer accepted) is expressed in the biblical story of the Tower of Babylon (painting by Pieter Bruegel the Elder, 1563), in which linguistic diversity is described as God's punishment for human pride and greed for power.

Linguistic Exchange – The Foreign Element

All languages have changed over the course of centuries. Apart from natural, organic evolution, languages are influenced significantly by contact among speakers of different linguistic communities – conquerors and conquered peoples, neighboring linguistic groups, etc. In this way, languages enrich one another with "foreign material" (adopted and adapted words and forms). These phenomena are referred to by historical linguistics as strata: Substrates are traces of the language of a conquered or exterminated people left behind in the language of the victors (e.g. remnants of Celtic in the Romance languages). Superstrata are elements introduced by a conquering group into the language of a subjugated people but which do not displace the original language (e.g. Franconian influences on French). Adstrata are linguistic influences which do not reflect hierarchical relationships (e.g. contacts between speakers of Germanic and Romance languages along linguistic boundaries).

The Birth of New Languages: Pidgin and Creole Forms

Pidgin and Creole languages are the products of a special form of linguistic interaction which takes place primarily when speakers of different native tongues communicate with each other. Such languages have developed through trading activity and in economies significantly influenced by slavery in the New World, Africa, Southeast Asia, and Oceania. Pidgin languages are characterized by markedly simplified structures that facilitate communication but are found in neither of the original native languages involved. Pidgin languages that become established and are passed on to succeeding generations are known as Creoles. Many Creole languages have been standardized and adopted as official national languages (in Haiti, Mauritius, and the Seychelles, for example) and thus contribute to local or national identity.

The Future of Languages

Though many have predicted the eventual demise of linguistic diversity, languages have proven astonishingly resilient. Even today, there are those who hope and believe that globalization will result in the establishment of English as the worldwide medium for communication. Yet efforts have also been undertaken to have the right to speak one's native language firmly anchored in international human rights conventions. Slowly but surely, people are beginning to realize that linguistic diversity has the capacity to enrich humanity and is not, as the Bible suggests, God's punishment for human pride, vanity, and greed. In the age of technology, languages that remain open to progress and capable of integrating it into their dynamic systems will survive and ensure the preservation of linguistic diversity in the 21st century.

A Monument to Language
A prime example of a literary language developed through deliberate effort is Afrikaans, which is spoken in South Africa. The unique monument to language erected in Paarl near Cape Town commemorates the linguistic movement founded by the Boers in 1875.

The Physiognomy of Diversity
Portraits of people from selected ethnic groups and their language families (lower print bar).

Geographic distribution of languages on Earth

- 32% Asia
- 3% Europe
- 15% America
- 19.5% Australia & Oceania
- 30.5% Africa

Most widely spoken languages by number of speakers as native and second language

millions	
940	Chinese
475	English
395	Hindi
375	Spanish
300	Russian
215	Arabic
200	Bengali
185	Portuguese
155	Malayan-Indonesian
125	Japanese
122	French
118	German
100	Urdu

Overcoming Social Ostracism
Of the 880 million illiterates in the world, two thirds are women. 120 million children do not attend proper schools – due primarily to a lack of money. The photo shows a Massai "bush school" in East Africa.

Bilingual Street Sign
Increasing attention is now being given to linguistic minorities in many countries (photo: sign in French and Occitan in Agde). Distinctions are expressed in different print sizes.

Rue
Hôtel du cheval blanc
PORTA DE LA FONT

The Earth from Space

Topographic Image

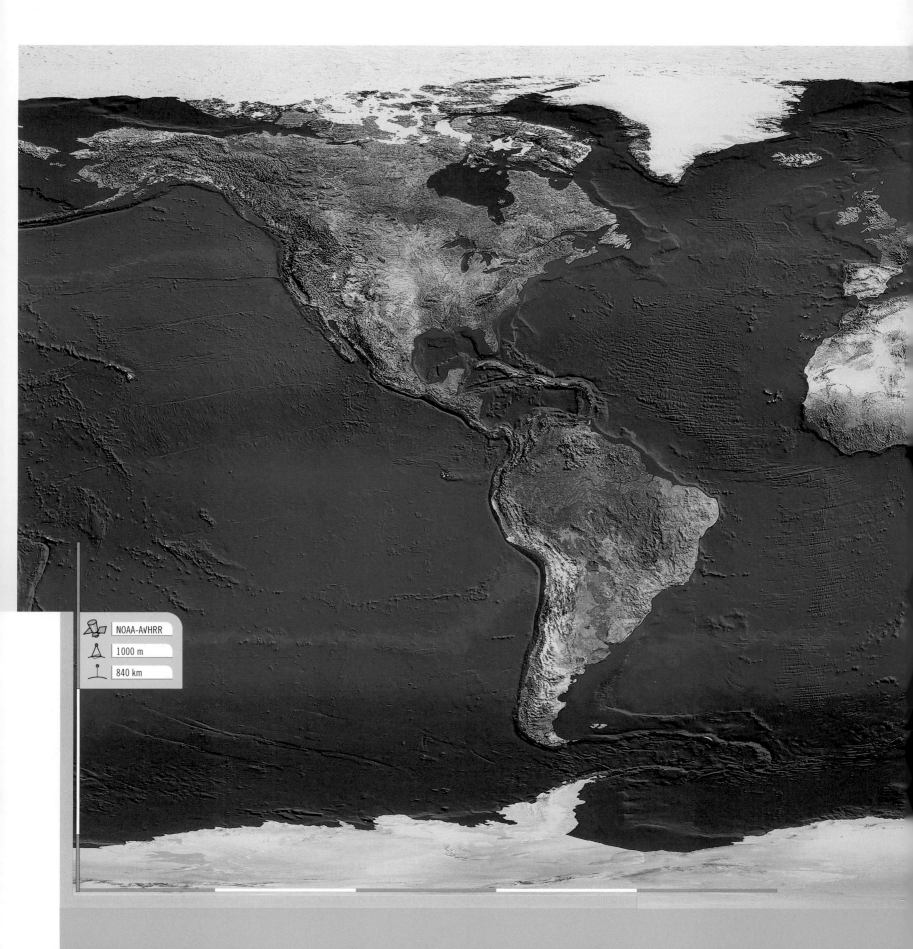

NOAA-AVHRR

1000 m

840 km

View of the Earth from Space

Several thousand images from the U.S. NOAA Satellite Series were required to compile this completely cloudless picture of the Earth.

In the projection selected for this satellite imagery map, the polar regions extend along the full length of the Equator. The continents are true to form to north and south latitudes of about 35 degrees, but distortion grows more extreme toward the poles.

This composite satellite image gives a good overview of major landscapes of the continents and their vegetation patterns. A particularly striking feature is the belt of deserts that encircles the globe.

(Copyright: GEOSPACE / World Sat International Corp. 2000)

Bodies of Water   Rivers – Blood Vessels of a Country

	Landsat ETM
	15 m
	705 km
	Nov. 3, 1999

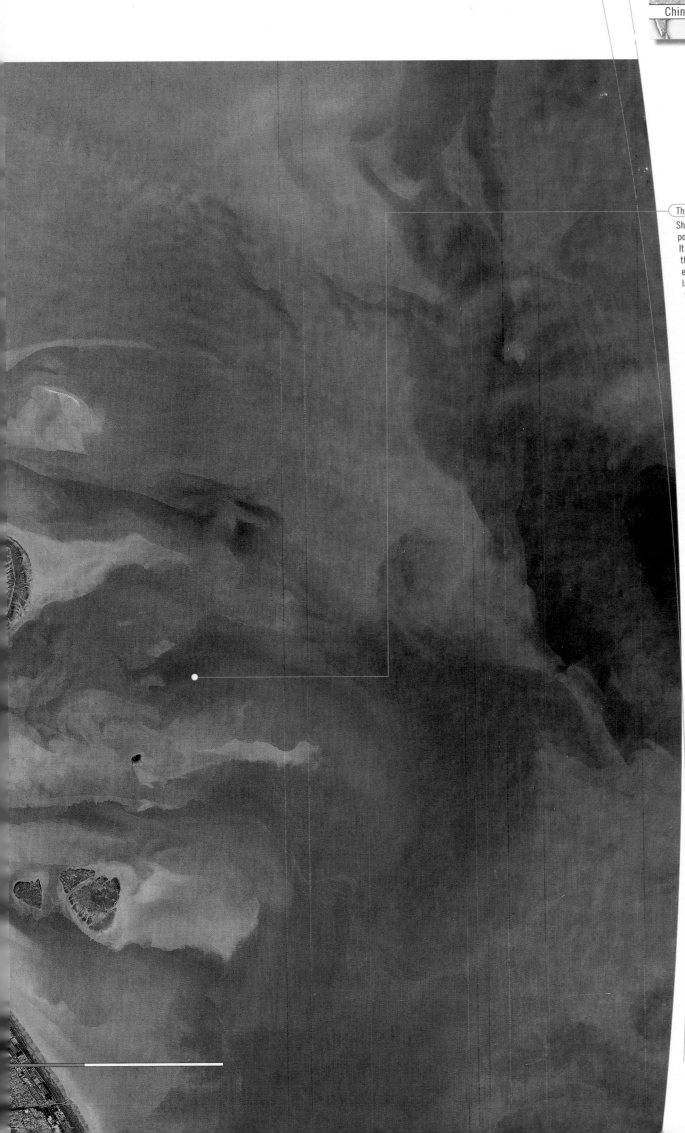

The Mouth of the Yangtze (Chang)

Shanghai is China's most important port and its largest metropolis. It radiates from the confluence of the Huang River and the Yangtze east of Tai Lake. At the turn of the last century, the city was home to some 12 million people, and nearly 20 million people live in greater metropolitan Shanghai. The opening of China to international trade has spurred rapid growth in the city in recent years, to which an expansive system of urban freeways and a number of new high-rise complexes bear witness. The amount of developed land nearly doubled between 1980 and 2000. In the process, the belt of vegetation that once encircled the city (visible in places as spots of light-green coloration in the satellite image) was obliterated. Development has been especially intensive in the Pudong district on the right bank the Huang, where large areas the old city were demolished and replaced by new business and industrial centers.

Coastal Formations   The Largest Reef on Earth

Landsat TM

30 m

705 km

July 13, 2000

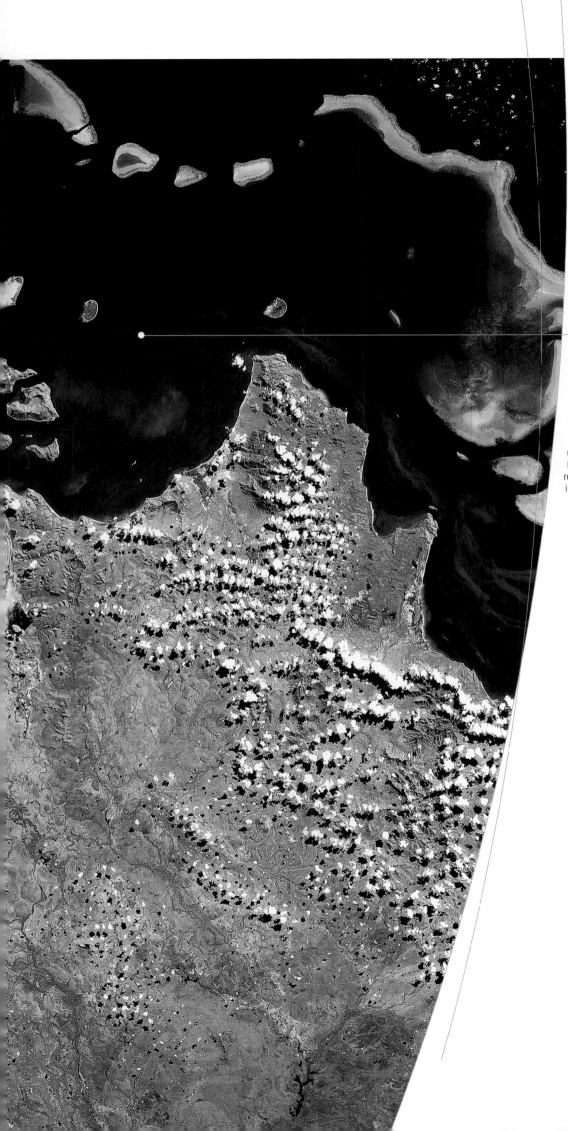

The Great Barrier Reef

The world's largest coral reef runs parallel to the coast of Australia off the shores of Queensland. This satellite image shows Princess Charlotte Bay on the southern coast of the Cape York Peninsula.

The chain of elongated, oval or circular coral reefs is discernable only from the air. Covered only by shallow waters, they appear as turquoise and light blue areas that stand out clearly against the deep blue of the open sea.

The view from the air tells us something else as well. The Great Barrier Reef is not a continuous, linear reef system but instead comprises a large number of individual reefs of different sizes distributed in a picturesque pattern in the lagoon.

Deserts

Shifting Seas of Sand

The Sahara near Amguid in Algeria

The Sahara presents a very different face in many places. Landscapes can be distinguished on the basis of differences in surface material — exposed rock, gravel, sand, or salt clay. A large portion of the image is occupied by the debris-covered surfaces of the Hamada de Tinrhert (light gray and reddish brown areas). This bolder-strewn desert is known as Serir in Algeria. The second type of desert in the Sahara is characterized by sand sheets and dunes. A prominent feature of the landscape in this satellite image is the tongue of sand in the upper portion of the picture, with its regular pattern of star-shaped figures. Salt clay plains (bluish-turquoise coloration) are found in the broad depressions where the wadis — dry valleys through which water flows only after heavy rains — grow wider. The dark brown areas are the northern fingers of the Tassili-n-Ajjer range, with peaks as high as 1,800 m.

Landsat ETM

30 m

705 km

Winter 1987

Vegetation and Land Use

Carving New Settlements from the Desert

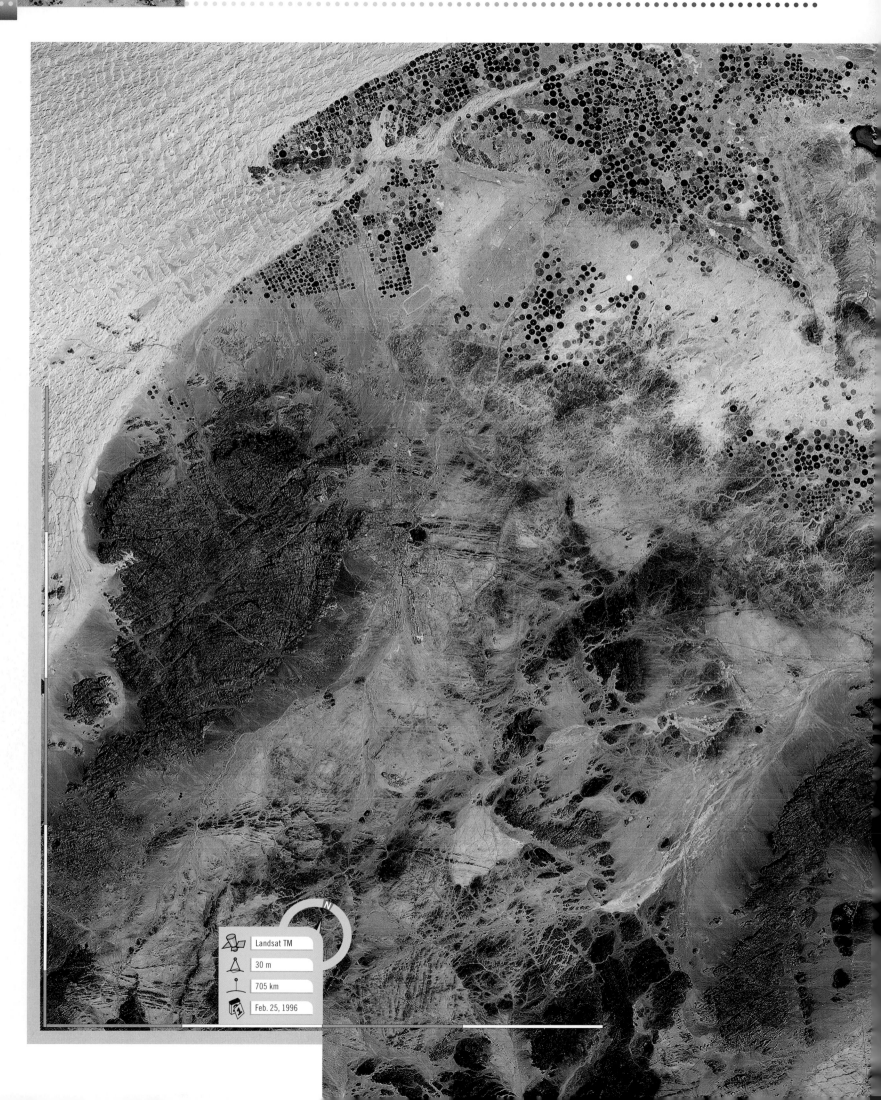

Landsat TM

30 m

705 km

Feb. 25, 1996

(Saudi Arabia – Hā'il)

Expansive plateaus irregularly interspersed with ranges of mountains and inselbergs characterize the topography of the Central Arabian Highlands. In the north, the crystalline highlands extend to the edge of the sand desert of An Nafūd. Circular patches are distributed like confetti over the yellow sand of the Wadi Ha'il – small areas of cultivation in the midst of the arid desert, irrigated with rotating sprinkler systems fed to a certain extent with fossil water. Conveyed by pumps and pipelines, the water is distributed for specified periods of time in fine veils of rain. This process enables farmers to fertilize their fields efficiently by adding plant nutrients to the water. Excessive irrigation creates swampy soil conditions, which make the fields difficult to tend. Evaporation rates are extremely high in the hot, arid regions of Saudi Arabia, and changing wind patterns can lead to unequal distribution of water vapor.

Settlement Patterns   City and Country

Landsat TM + Spot PAN

30 m

705 km

Aug. 14, 1993
July 7, 1993

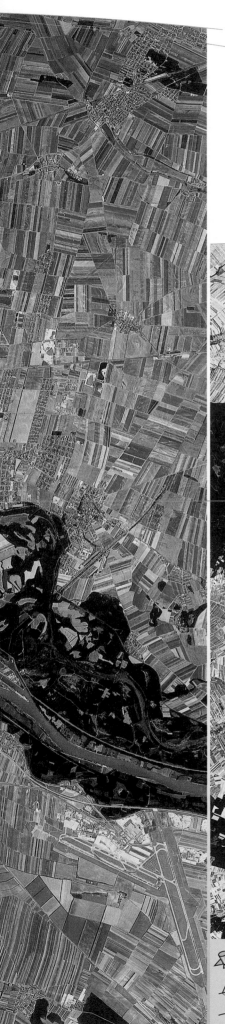

Vienna

Positioned favorably where the Alps descend to the Great
Hungarian Plain at a major crossroads of traditional
European trading routes from north to south, the Danube
metropolis developed from a village into a world city
within only few centuries.

The Danube, whose course has been artificially altered
twice during the past several centuries, forms the region's
natural axis. The former meanders of the Old Danube
in the northern part of the satellite image serve as important urban recreation areas today.

The New Danube, which runs parallel to the river, was
created in 1970 to prevent flooding. A by-product of this
water-regulation measure is the Danube Island, a
popular park and recreation area for the people of Vienna.

Neusiedler Lake

Despite its size – approximately 296 sq. km, including
120 sq. km of encircling reed growth, Neusiedler
Lake is neither fed nor drained by a river of significant
size. Its cloudy greenish-gray coloration is not
caused by pollution but is a sign of the presence of
billions of suspended particles that never sink
entirely to the bottom of the shallow, windswept lake.
The border between Austria and Hungary is vividly
documented in this satellite image. The landscape
in the Austrian state of Burgenland is covered by an
intricate quilt of small strip parcels indicating intensive cultivation. These stand in stark contrast to
the large block fields on the other side of the border
– remnants of the collective farms of a bygone era.

Landsat TM +
Spot PAN

30 m

705 km

Aug. 14, 1993
Aug. 10, 1992

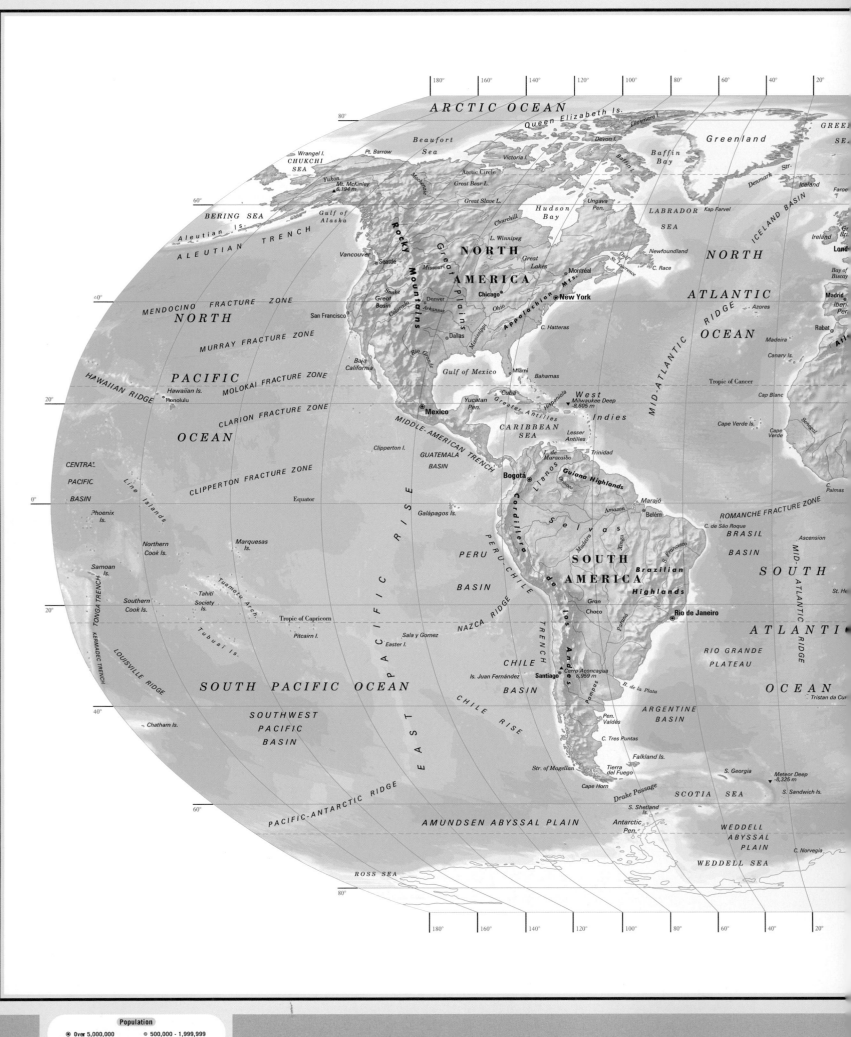

Population

◉ Over 5,000,000   ⊙ 500,000 - 1,999,999

⊕ 2,000,000 - 4,999,999   ○ Under 500,000

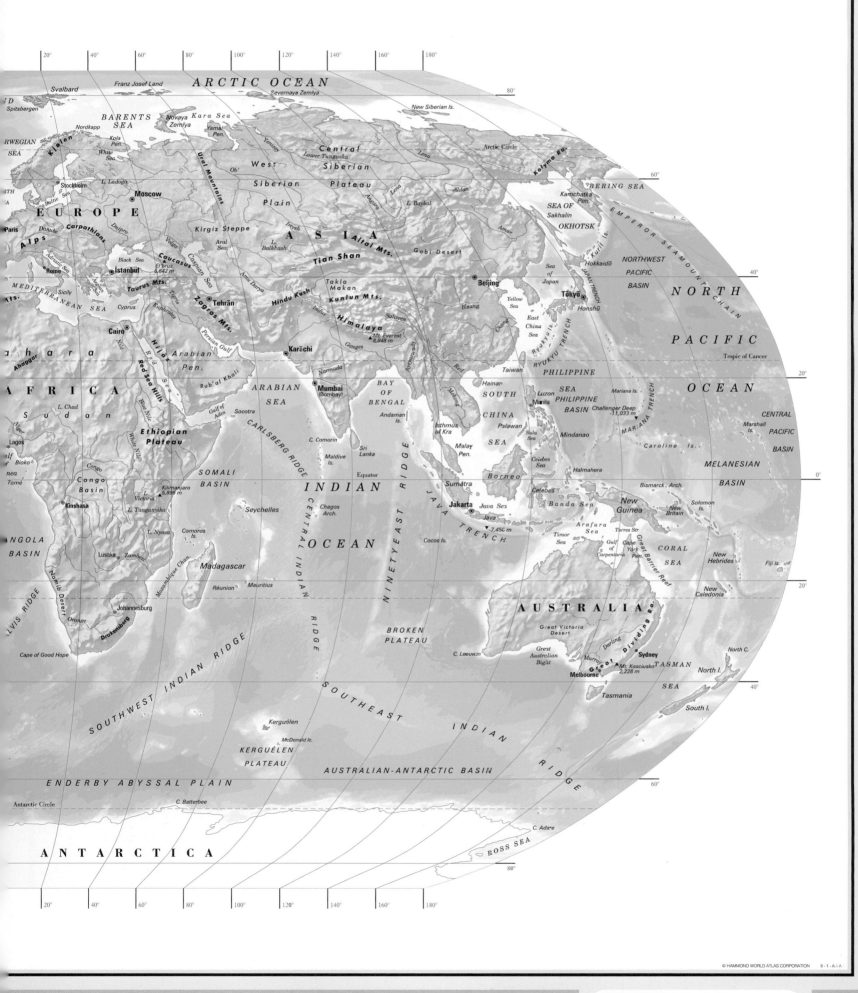

ARCTIC OCEAN

Svalbard
Franz Josef Land
Spitsbergen
Severnaya Zemlya
New Siberian Is.
80°
BARENTS
SEA
Kara Sea
Nordkapp
Novaya
Zemlya
Yamal
Pen.
Kjølen
Kola
Pen.
White
Sea
Yenisey
Central
Lower Tunguska
Siberian
Lena
Arctic Circle
Kolyma Ra.
BERING SEA
NORWEGIAN
SEA
West
Siberian
Plateau
Kamchatka
Pen.
NORTHWEST
PACIFIC
BASIN
Stockholm
L. Ladoga
Ob'
Plain
Angara
L. Baykal
Aldan
SEA OF
OKHOTSK
Sakhalin
Hokkaidō
EUROPE
Moscow
Kirgiz Steppe
Irtysh
A S I A
Altai Mts.
Gobi Desert
Amur
Kuril Is.
Honshū
NORTH
Paris
Danube
Carpathians
Dnipro
Volga
Aral
Sea
Tian Shan
Sea
of
Japan
JAPAN TRENCH
Alps
Adriatic Sea
Black Sea
Caucasus
El'brus
5,642 m
Caspian Sea
L.
Balkhash
Beijing
Huang
Yellow
Sea
Tōkyō
PACIFIC
Rome
Istanbul
Takla
Makan
East
China
Sea
Sicily
Taurus Mts.
Cyprus
Zagros Mts.
Tehrān
Hindu Kush
Kunlun Mts.
Ryukyu Is.
MEDITERRANEAN SEA
Aegean Sea
Euphrates
Tigris
Indus
Himalaya
Saluen
Mekong
Taiwan
RYUKYU TRENCH
Tropic of Cancer
Cairo
Hila
Arabian
Persian Gulf
Mt. Everest
8,848 m
Ganges
Hainan
PHILIPPINE
Sahara
Nile
Red Sea Hills
Pen.
Karāchi
Normada
Red
SOUTH
SEA
Ahaggar
Rub'al Khali
ARABIAN
Mumbai
(Bombay)
BAY
OF
BENGAL
CHINA
Luzon
Mariana Is.
OCEAN
20°
AFRICA
Sudan
White Nile
Blue Nile
SEA
Gulf of
Aden
Socotra
Andaman
Is.
SEA
Palawan
Manila
PHILIPPINE
BASIN
Challenger Deep
-11,033 m
MARIANA TRENCH
CENTRAL
PACIFIC
BASIN
L. Chad
Niger
Ethiopian
Plateau
CARLSBERG RIDGE
C. Comorin
Isthmus
of Kra
Malay
Pen.
Sulu
Sea
Mindanao
Marshall
Is.
Lagos
Bioko
Congo
Maldive
Is.
Sri Lanka
Andaman
Is.
Celebes
Sea
Halmahera
Caroline Is.
MELANESIAN
Tomé
Congo
Basin
SOMALI
BASIN
Equator
Sumatra
Borneo
Bismarck Arch.
BASIN
nea
Kinshasa
L.
Victoria
Kilimanjaro
5,895 m
INDIAN
Seychelles
Chagos
Arch.
Java Sea
Celebes
Banda Sea
New
Guinea
New
Britain
Solomon
Is.
NGOLA
BASIN
L. Tanganyika
Jakarta
Java
-7,450 m
New
Hebrides
Lusaka
Zambezi
OCEAN
Comoros
Is.
L. Nyasa
JAVA TRENCH
Arafura
Sea
Timor
Sea
Torres Str
Gulf
of
Carpentaria
Cape
York
Pen.
Great Barrier Reef
CORAL
SEA
Fiji Is.
NINETYEAST RIDGE
Madagascar
Réunion
Mauritius
CENTRAL INDIAN RIDGE
Mozambique Chan.
Cocos Is.
AUSTRALIA
New
Caledonia
20°
Namib Desert
Johannesburg
Orange
Drakensberg
BROKEN
PLATEAU
Great Victoria
Desert
C. Leeuwin
Great
Australian
Bight
Darling
Great Dividing Ra.
Sydney
North C.
ALVIS RIDGE
Cape of Good Hope
Murray
Melbourne
Mt. Kosciusko
2,228 m
TASMAN
SEA
North I.
40°
SOUTHWEST INDIAN RIDGE
SOUTHEAST
Tasmania
South I.
Kerguélen
INDIAN
McDonald Is.
KERGUÉLEN
PLATEAU
AUSTRALIAN-ANTARCTIC BASIN
RIDGE
60°
ENDERBY ABYSSAL PLAIN
Antarctic Circle
C. Batterbee
C. Adare
ANTARCTICA
ROSS SEA
80°

20° 40° 60° 80° 100° 120° 140° 160° 180°

© HAMMOND WORLD ATLAS CORPORATION

Europe - Physical

Height

| m. ft. |
| 6000 / 19700 |
| 4000 / 13000 |
| 2000 / 6500 |
| 1500 / 5000 |
| 1000 / 3300 |
| 500 / 1600 |
| 200 / 700 |
| 0 |
| 200 / 700 |
| 500 / 1600 |
| 1000 / 3300 |
| 2000 / 6500 |
| 3000 / 9800 |
| 4000 / 13000 |
| 5000 / 16400 |
| 6000 / 19700 |

Depth

Scale 1:20,500,000 Hammond Optimal Conformal

MI   200   400   600
KM 200 400 600 800

Asia - Physical

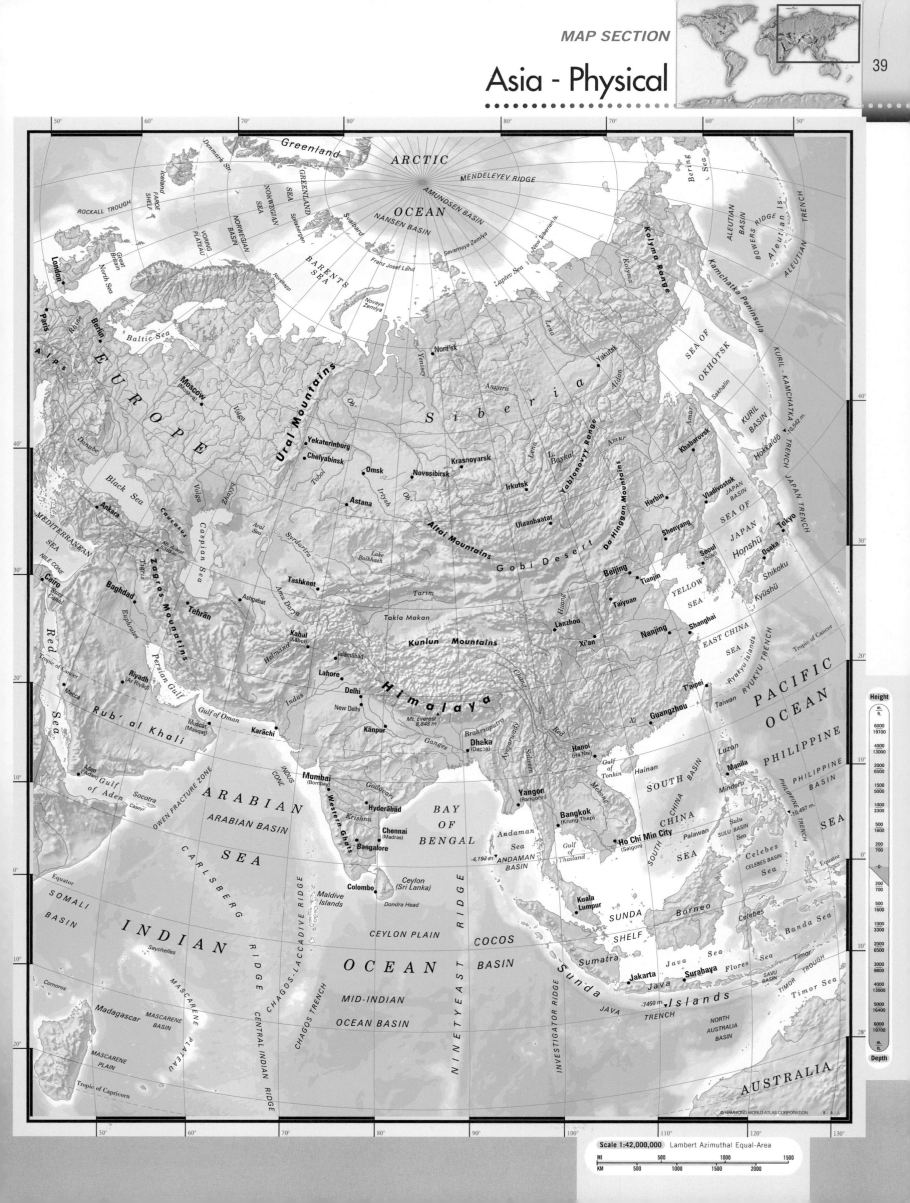

Scale 1:42,000,000   Lambert Azimuthal Equal-Area

| MI | 500 | 1000 | 1500 |
| KM | 500 | 1000 | 1500 | 2000 |

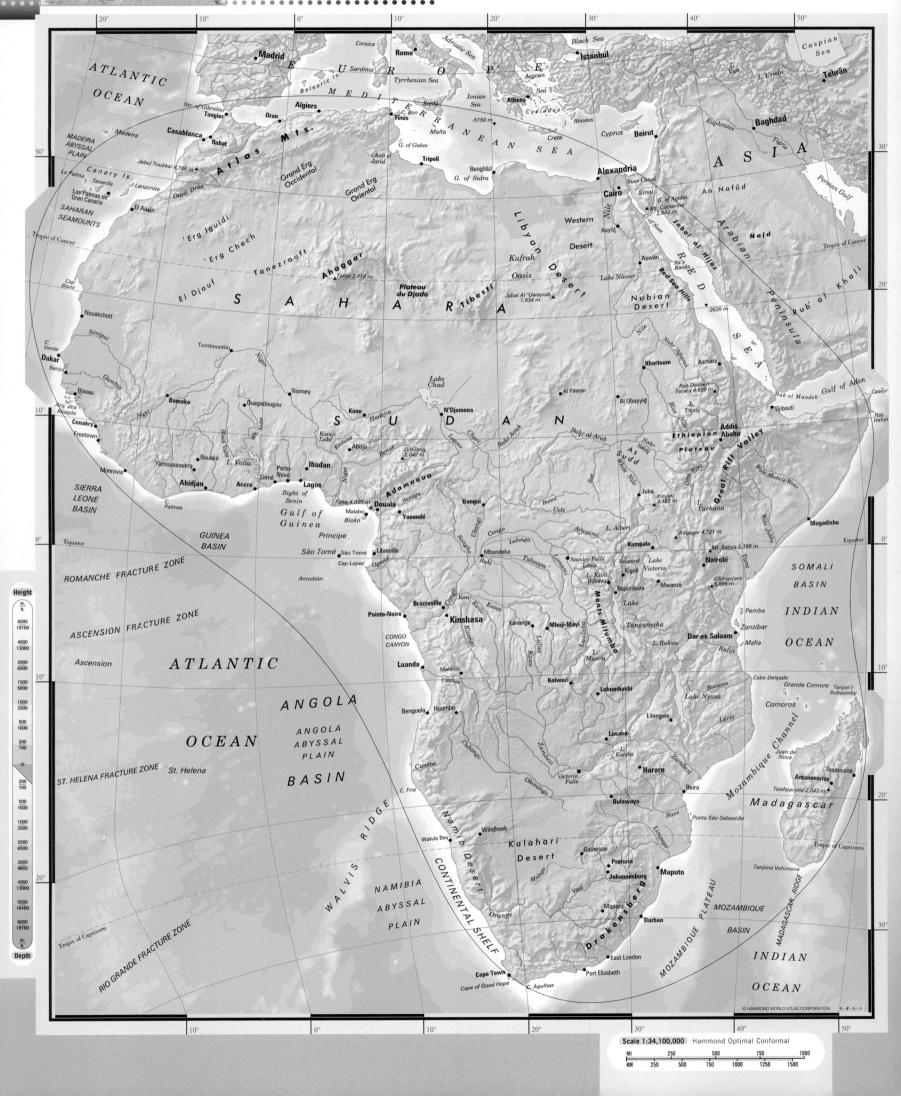

Scale 1:34,100,000   Hammond Optimal Conformal

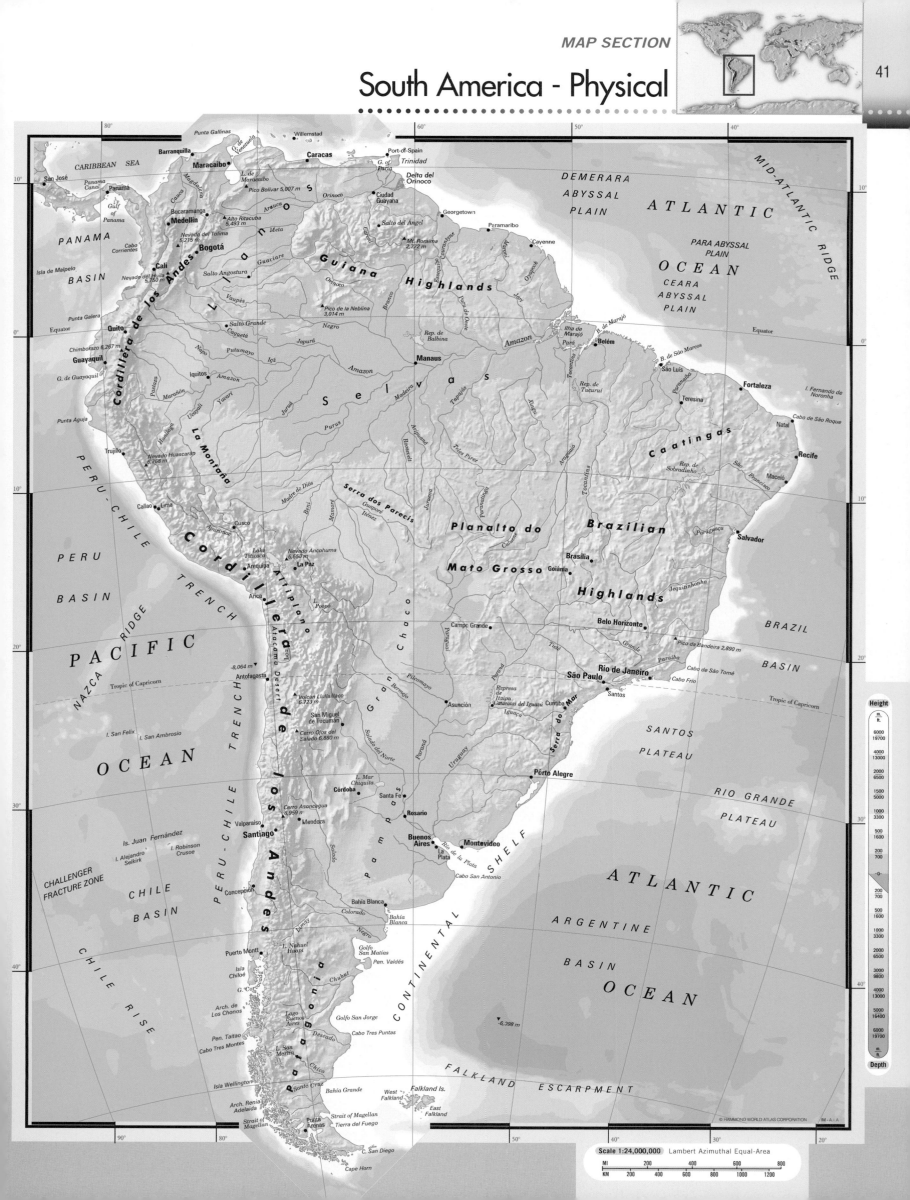

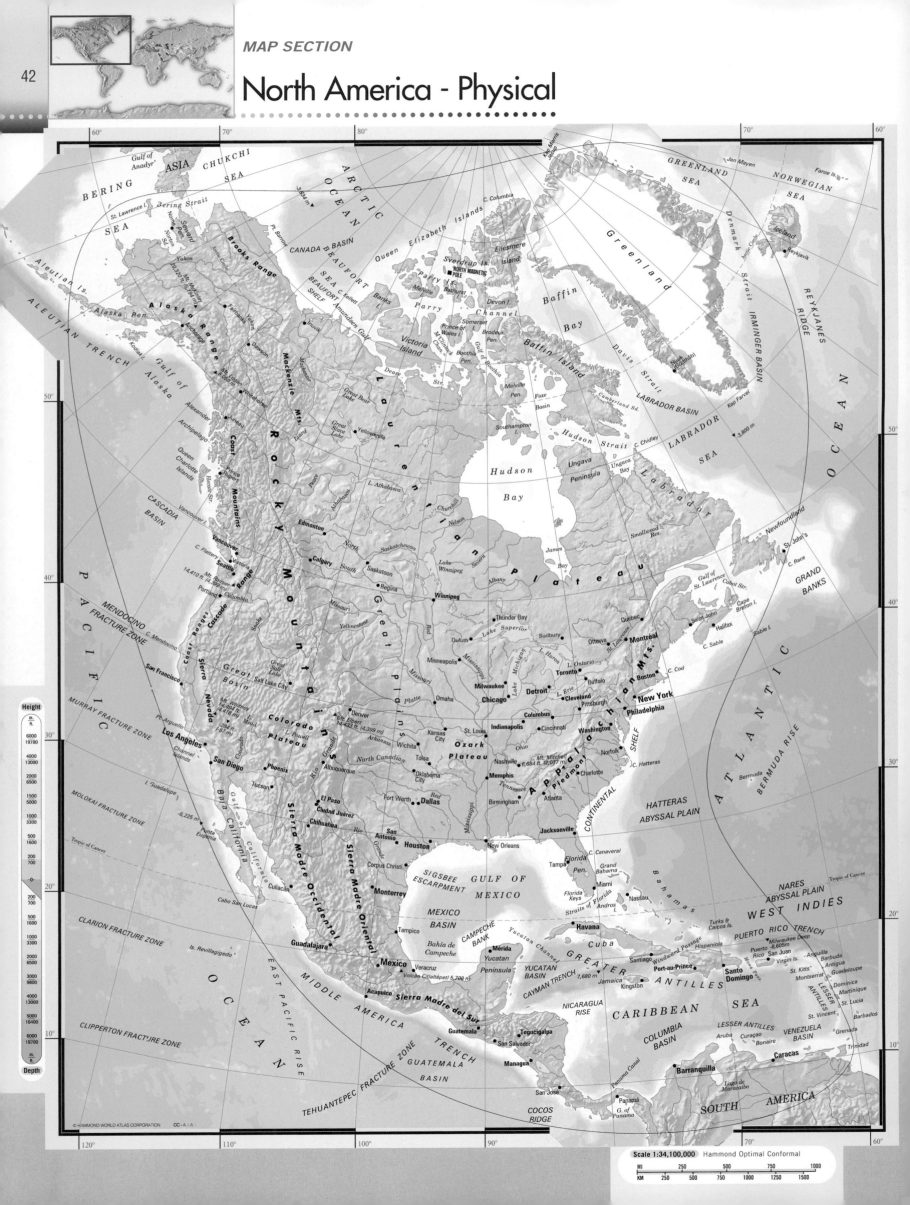

North America - Physical

Scale 1:34,100,000 Hammond Optimal Conformal

World Map Section

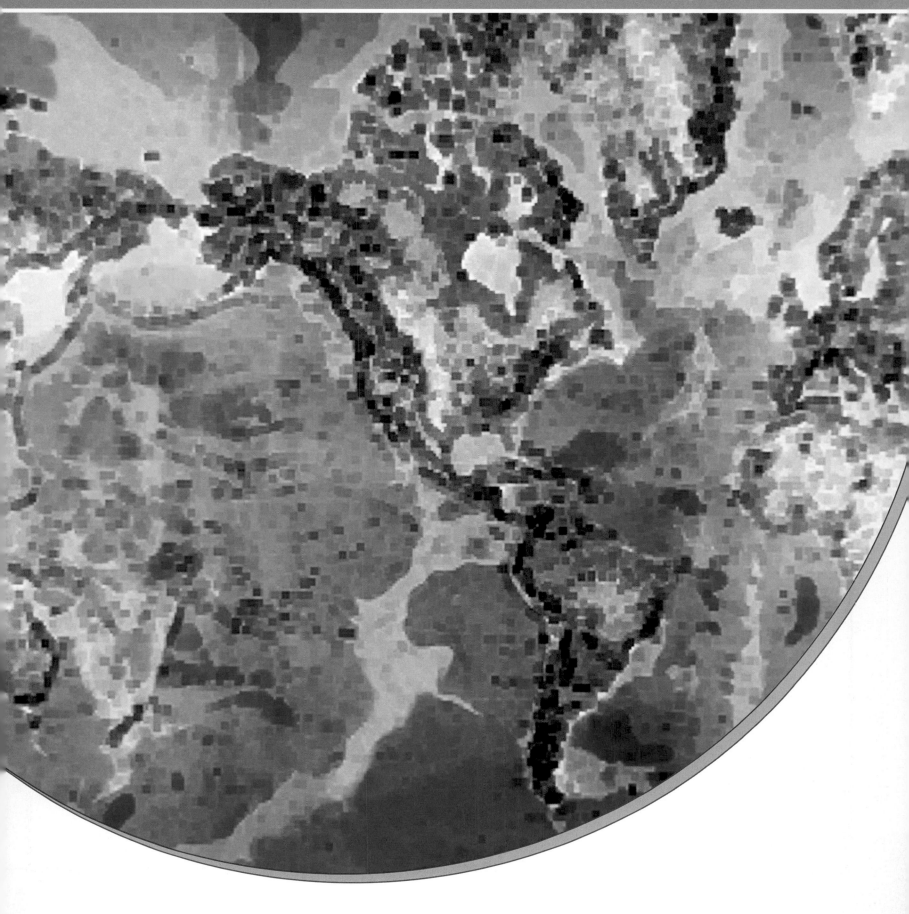

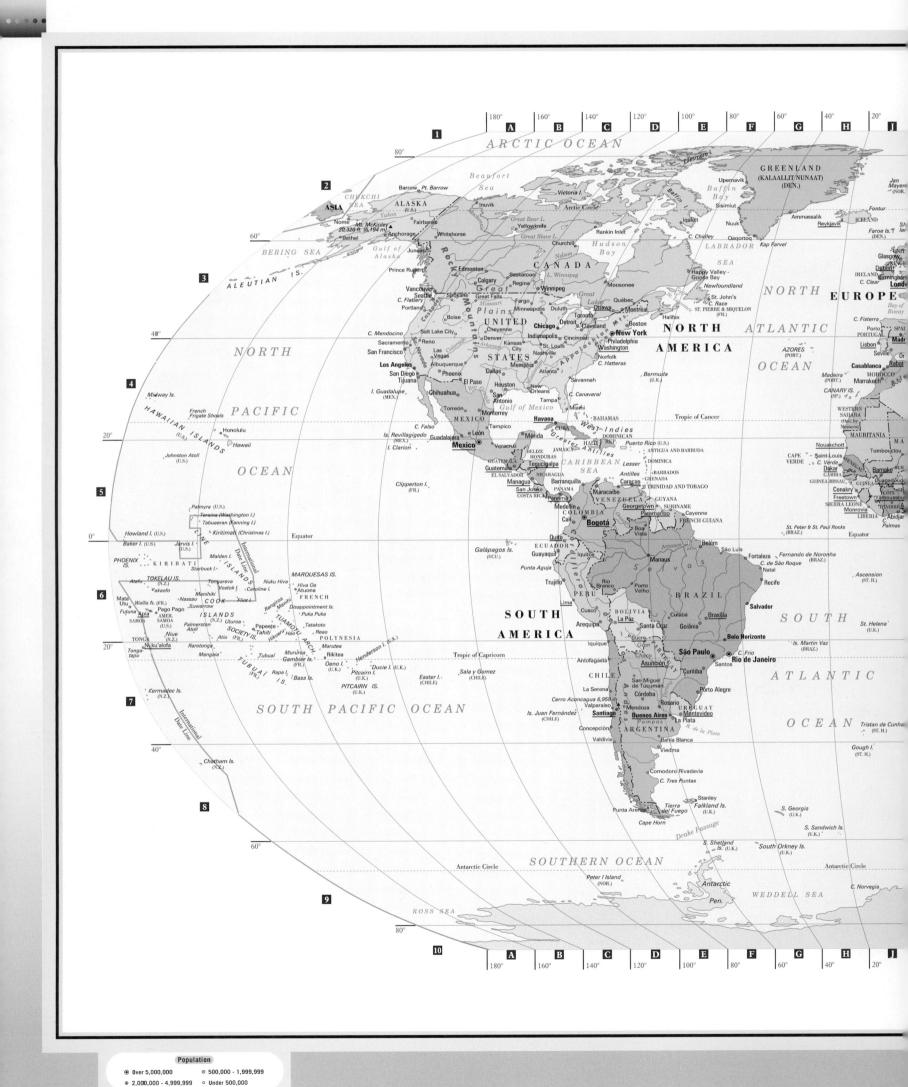

Population

- ⊙ Over 5,000,000
- ⊛ 2,000,000 - 4,999,999
- ⊙ 500,000 - 1,999,999
- ⊙ Under 500,000

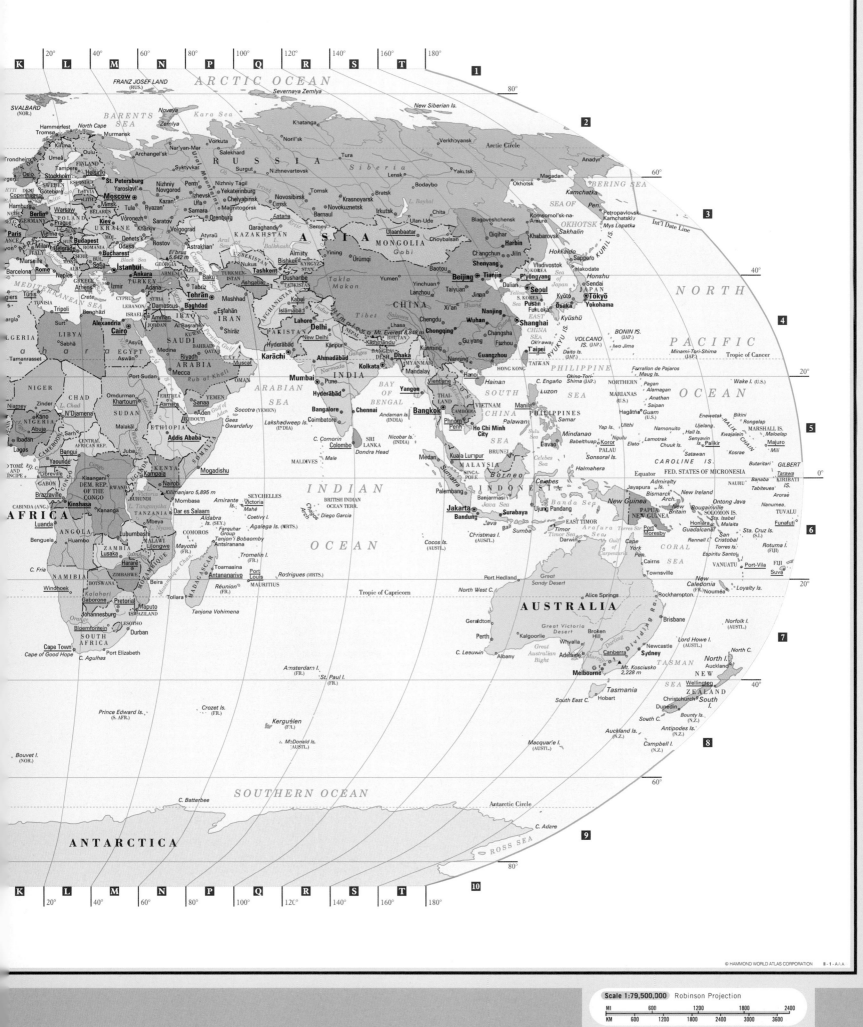

Scale 1:79,500,000 Robinson Projection

Europe - Geographical Comparisons

TOPOGRAPHY

SQ. MI.	SQ. KM.	SQ. MI.	SQ. KM.	SQ. MI.	SQ. KM.
UNDER 656	UNDER 200	1640-3281	500-1000	6562-16404	2000-5000
656-1640	200-500	3281-6562	1000-2000	OVER 16404	OVER 5000

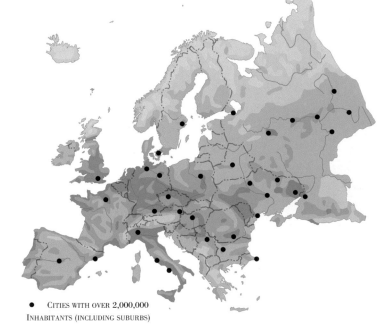

● CITIES WITH OVER 2,000,000
INHABITANTS (INCLUDING SUBURBS)

POPULATION DISTRIBUTION

DENSITY PER		SQ. MI.	SQ. KM.	SQ. MI.	SQ. KM.
SQ. MI.	SQ. KM.	130 TO 260	50 TO 100	3 TO 25	1 TO 10
OVER 260	OVER 100	25 TO 130	10 TO 50	UNDER 3	UNDER 1

LAND USE

- CEREALS, LIVESTOCK
- DAIRY, LIVESTOCK
- LIVESTOCK HERDING
- SPECIAL CROPS
- FRUIT AND TRUCK FARMING
- PASTURE LIVESTOCK
- DAIRY, CEREALS
- GENERAL FARMING, LIVESTOCK
- FORESTS
- NONPRODUCTIVE

MINERAL RESOURCES

ENERGY & FUELS
- ◆ COAL
- ⬟ LIGNITE
- ▲ NATURAL GAS
- ● PETROLEUM
- ■ URANIUM

IRON & FERROALLOYS
1. CHROMIUM
2. COBALT
3. IRON ORE
4. MANGANESE
5. MOLYBDENUM
6. NICKEL
7. TUNGSTEN
8. VANADIUM

OTHER MAJOR RESOURCES
1. ANTIMONY
2. ASBESTOS
3. BAUXITE
4. COPPER
5. FLORSPAR
6. GRAPHITE
7. LEAD
8. MAGNESITE
9. MERCURY
10. PHOSPHATES
11. PLATINUM
12. POTASH
13. SILVER
14. SULFER
15. TITANIUM
16. ZINC

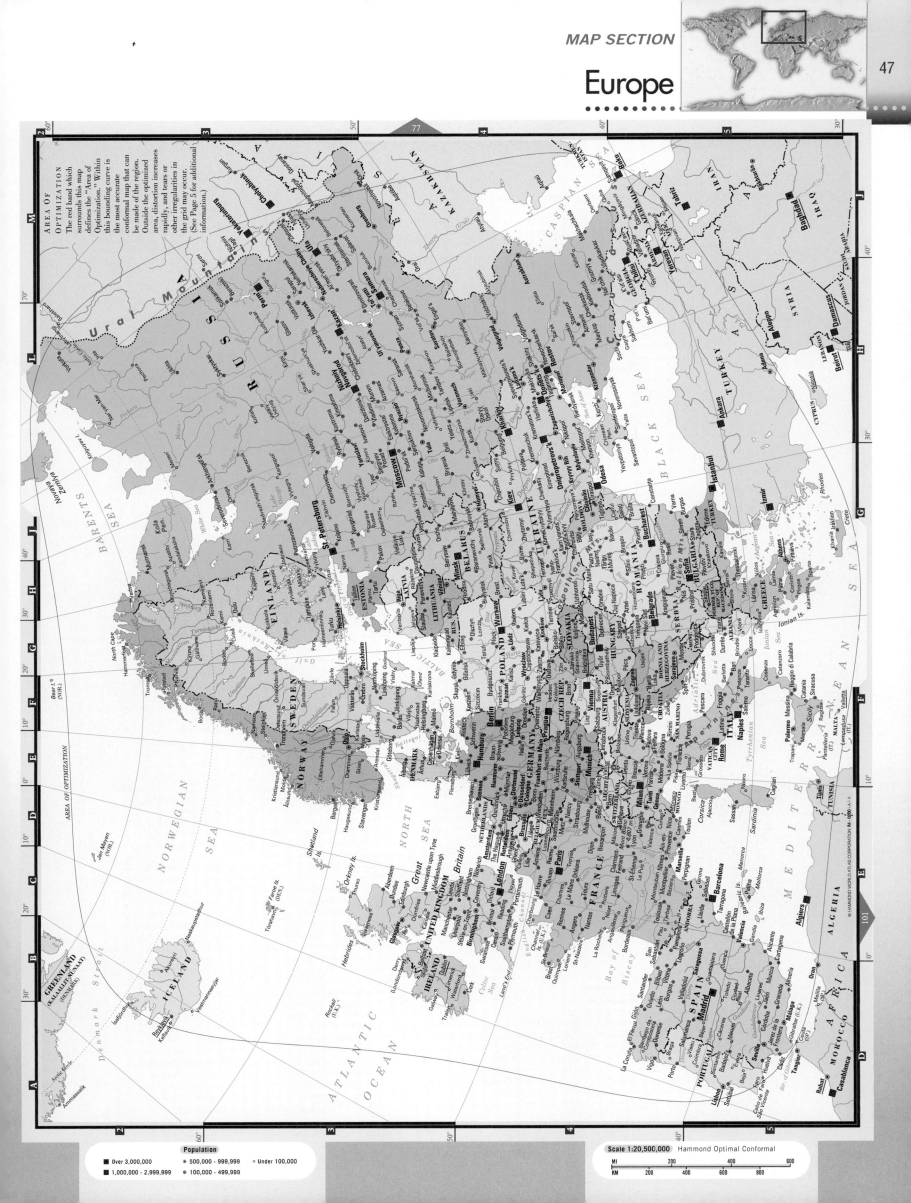

Europe

AREA OF OPTIMIZATION
The red band which surrounds this map defines the "Area of Optimization." Within this bounding curve is the most accurate conformal map that can be made of the region. Outside the optimized area, distortion increases rapidly, and tears or other irregularities in the grid may occur. (See Page 5 for additional information.)

AREA OF OPTIMIZATION

Population

■ Over 3,000,000	● 500,000 - 999,999	○ Under 100,000
■ 1,000,000 - 2,999,999	• 100,000 - 499,999	

Scale 1:20,500,000 Hammond Optimal Conformal

MI 200 400 600
KM 200 400 600 800

© HAMMOND WORLD ATLAS CORPORATION IM-0200-A-1-A

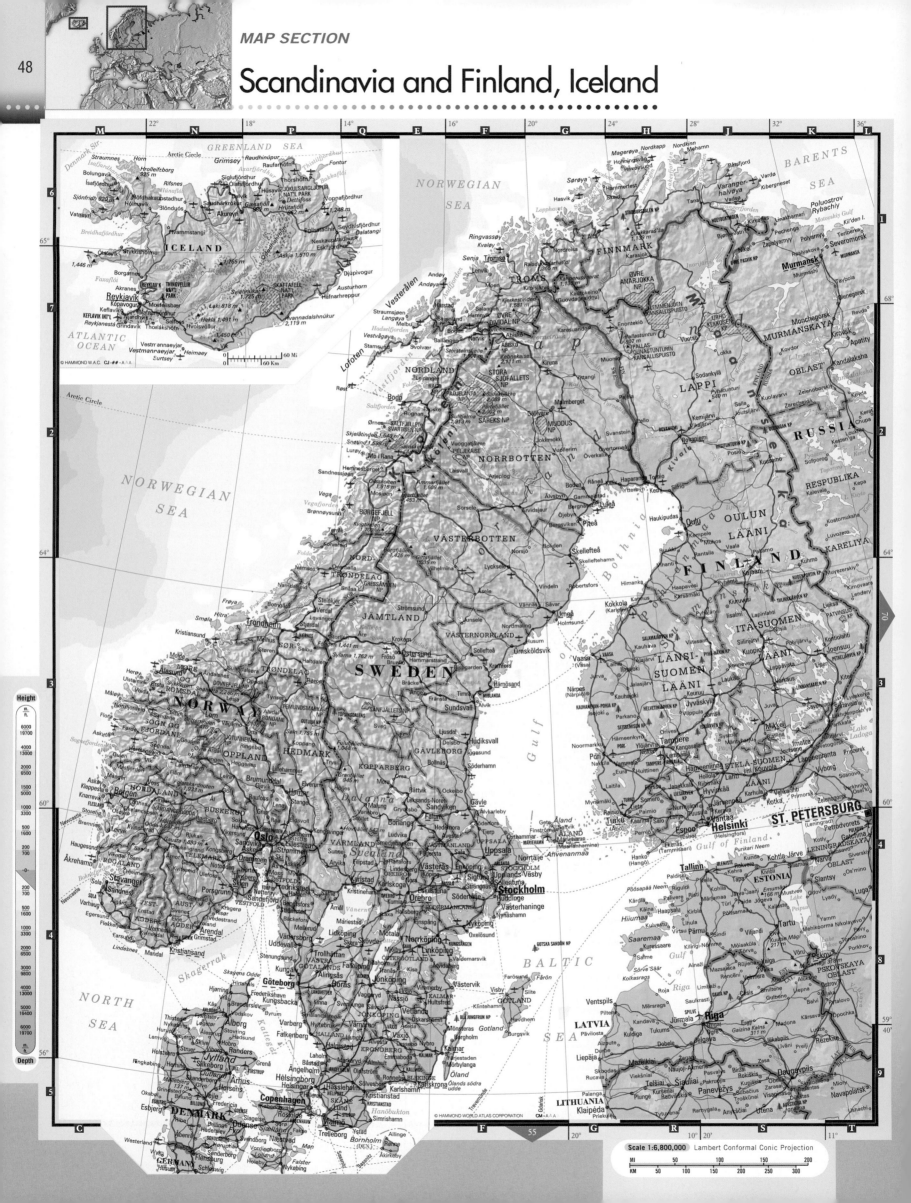

Scandinavia and Finland, Iceland

Scale 1:6,800,000 Lambert Conformal Conic Projection

© HAMMOND W.A.C.

© HAMMOND WORLD ATLAS CORPORATION

© Hammond World Atlas Corporation

Scale 1:3,400,000   Lambert Conformal Conic Projection

Population

■ Over 2,000,000 ● 500,000 - 999,999 ● 100,000 - 249,999 ○ 10,000 - 29,999
■ 1,000,000 - 1,999,999 ● 250,000 - 499,999 ○ 30,000 - 99,999 ○ Under 10,000

Scale 1:1,140,000 Lambert Conformal Conic Projection

© Hammond World Atlas Corporation

Scale 1:1,140,000 Lambert Conformal Conic Projection

Population

■ Over 2,000,000	◉ 500,000 - 999,999	◎ 100,000 - 249,999	○ 10,000 - 29,999
■ 1,000,000 - 1,999,999	◉ 250,000 - 499,999	◎ 30,000 - 99,999	○ Under 10,000

Scale 1:3,400,000 Lambert Conformal Conic Projection

Netherlands, Northwestern Germany

Population

■ Over 2,000,000	◉ 500,000 - 999,999
■ 1,000,000 - 1,999,999	◉ 250,000 - 499,999

Scale 1:1,140,000   Lambert Conformal Conic Projection

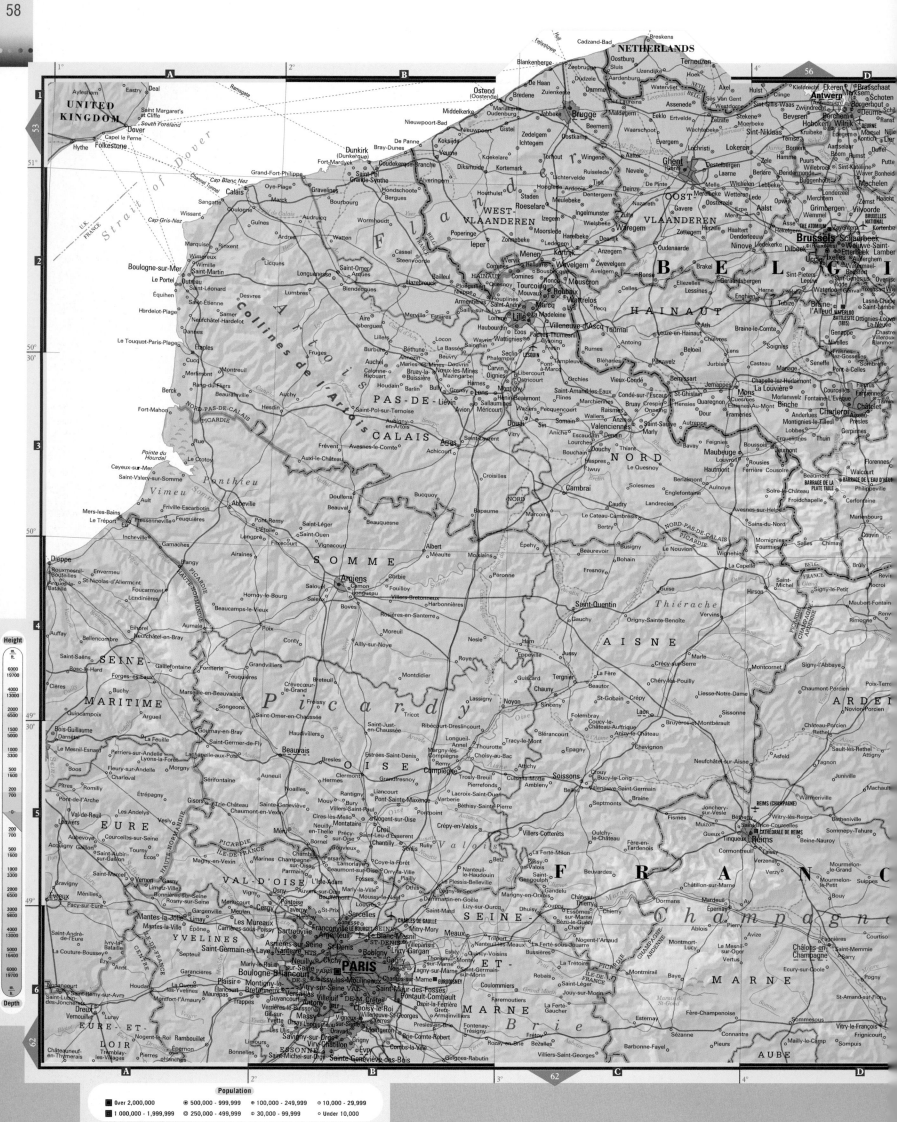

Scale 1:1,140,000   Lambert Conformal Conic Projection

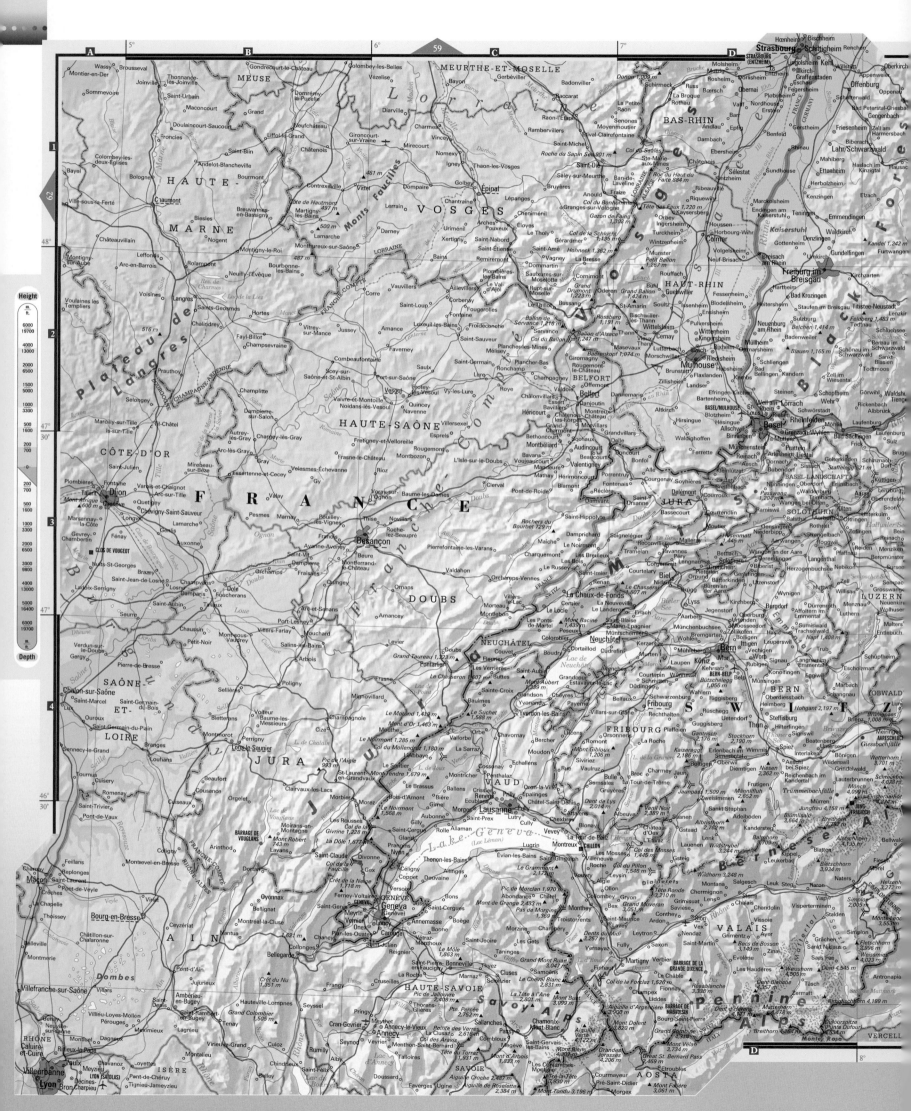

Central Alps Region

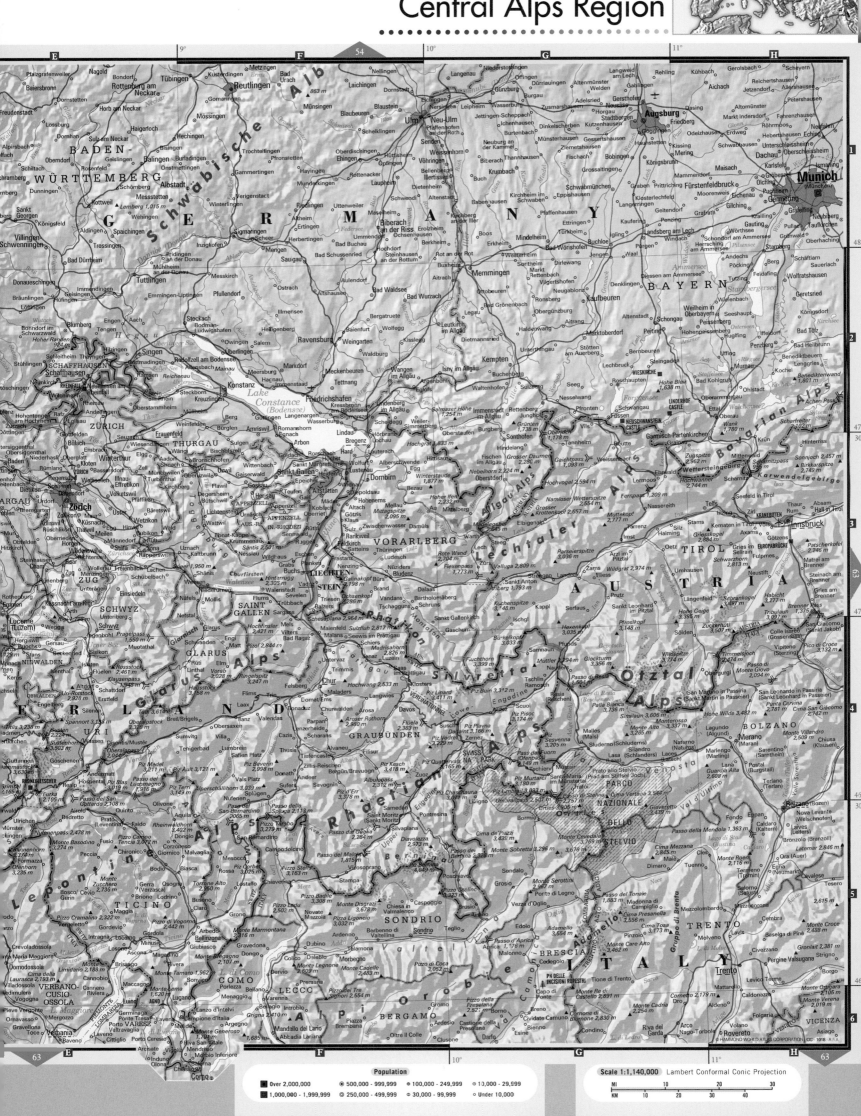

Population
- Over 2,000,000
- 1,000,000 - 1,999,999
- 500,000 - 999,999
- 250,000 - 499,999
- 100,000 - 249,999
- 30,000 - 99,999
- 10,000 - 29,999
- Under 10,000

Scale 1:1,140,000 Lambert Conformal Conic Projection

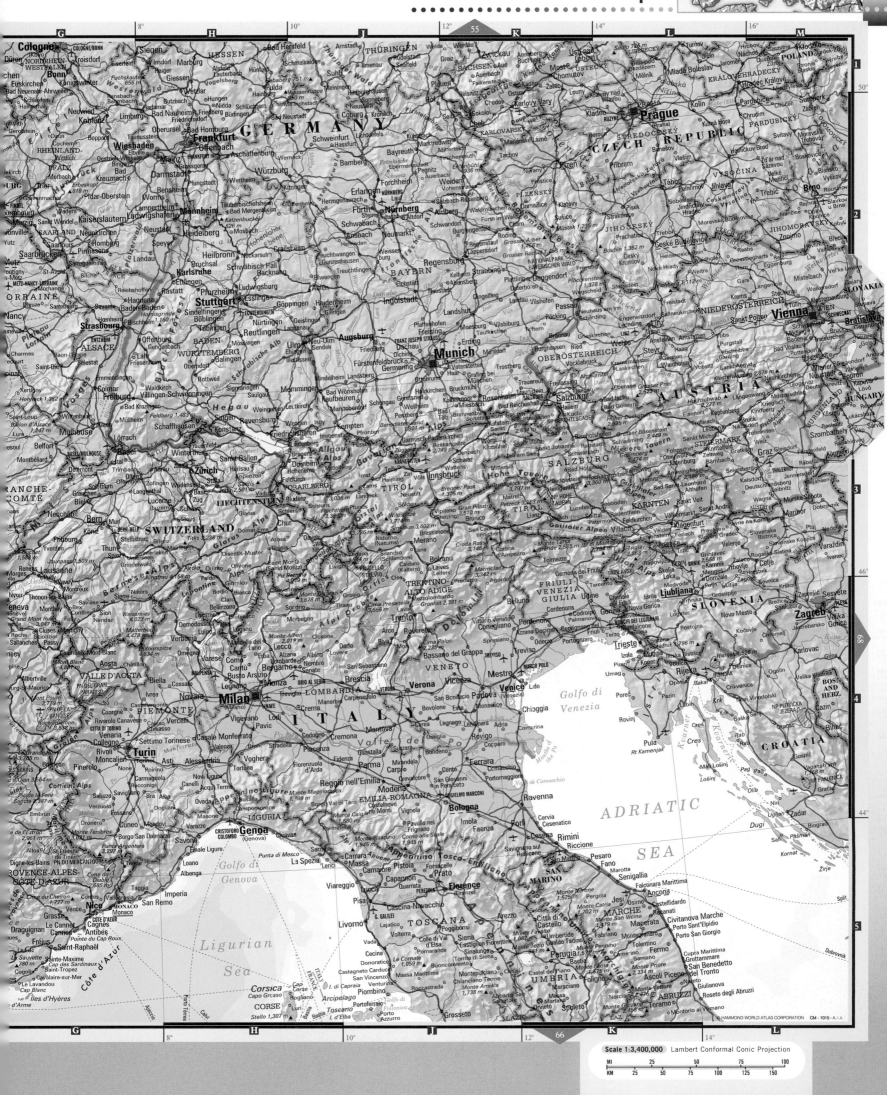

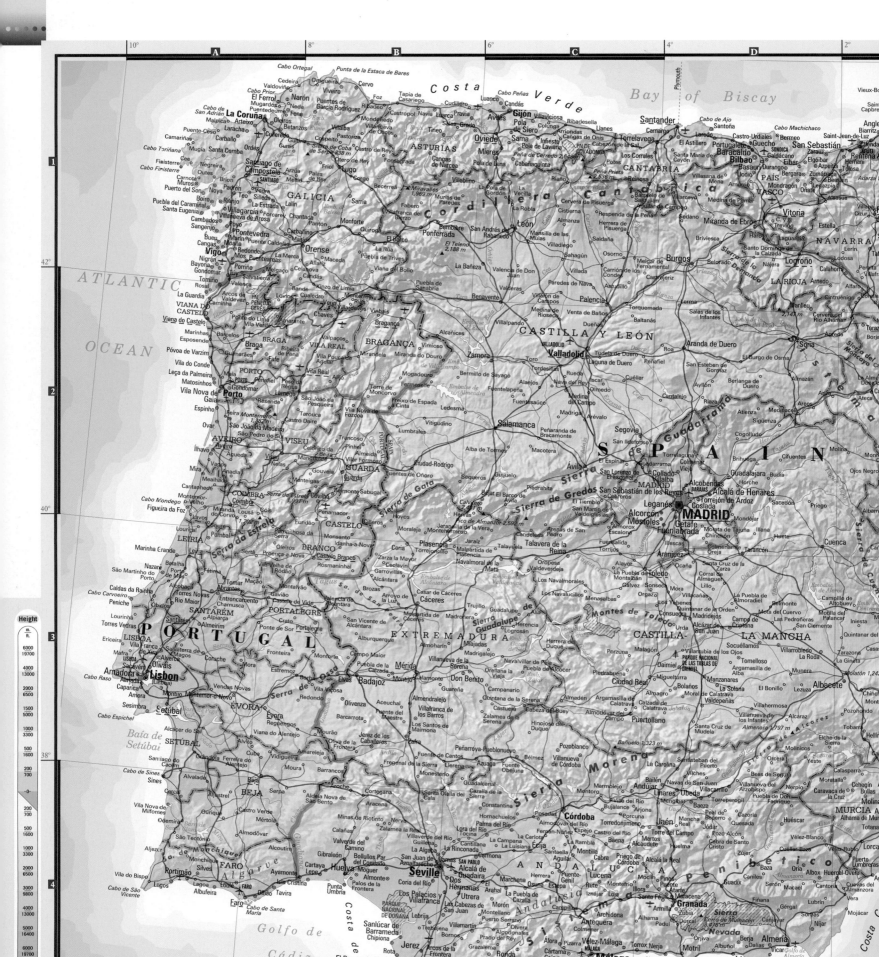

Spain and Portugal map showing the Iberian Peninsula.

Population

■ Over 2,000,000	⊙ 500,000 – 999,999	⊙ 100,000 – 249,999	⊙ 10,000 – 29,999
■ 1,000,000 – 1,999,999	⊙ 250,000 – 499,999	⊙ 30,000 – 99,999	○ Under 10,000

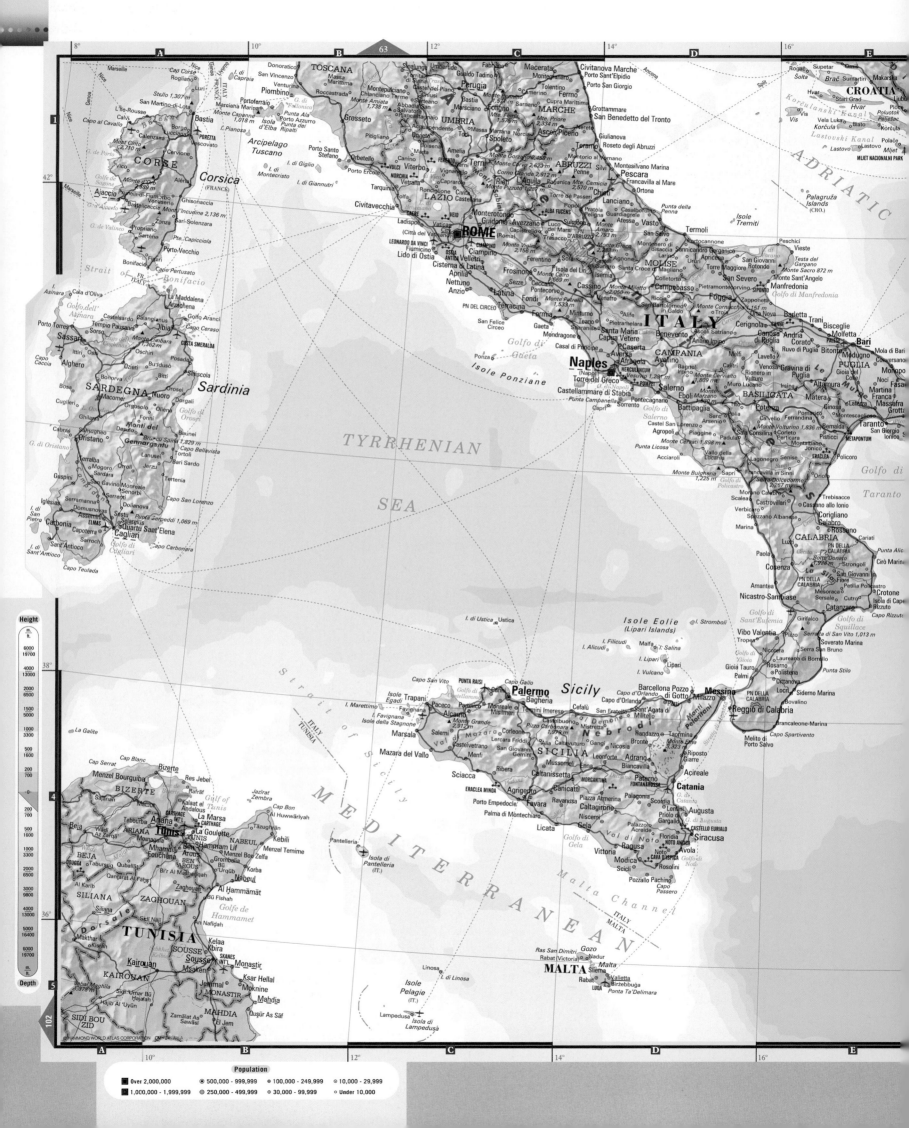

Southern Italy, Albania, Greece

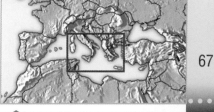

Population

■ Over 2,000,000
■ 1,000,000 - 1,999,999
● 500,000 - 999,999
◉ 250,000 - 499,999
● 100,000 - 249,999
◉ 30,000 - 99,999
● 10,000 - 29,999
○ Under 10,000

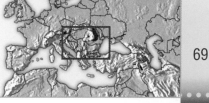

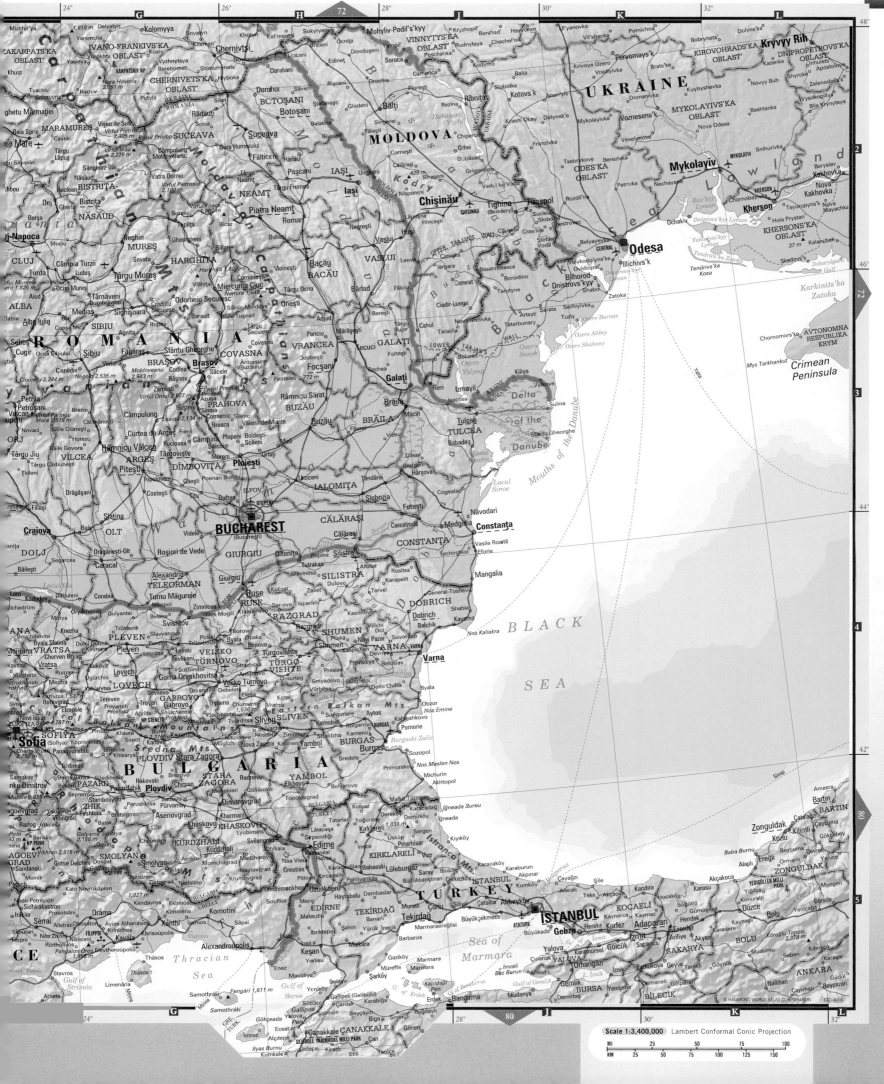

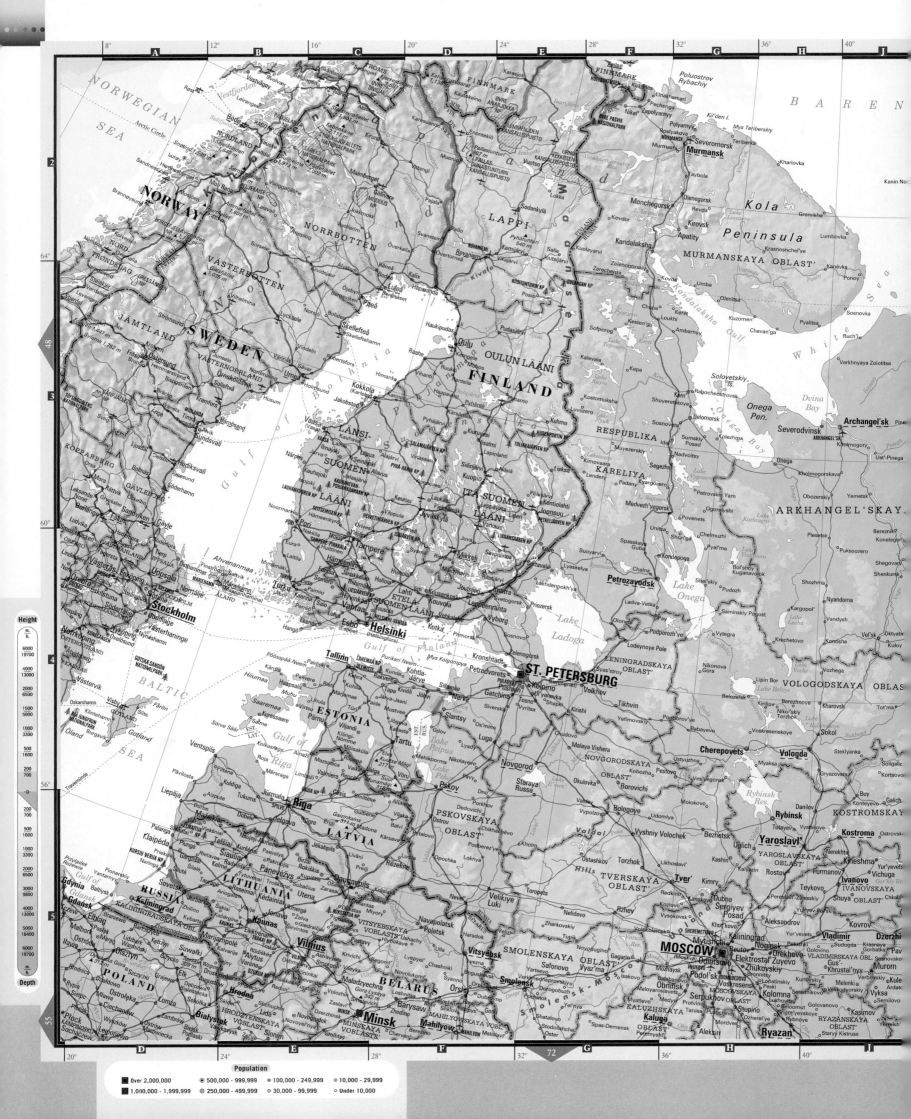

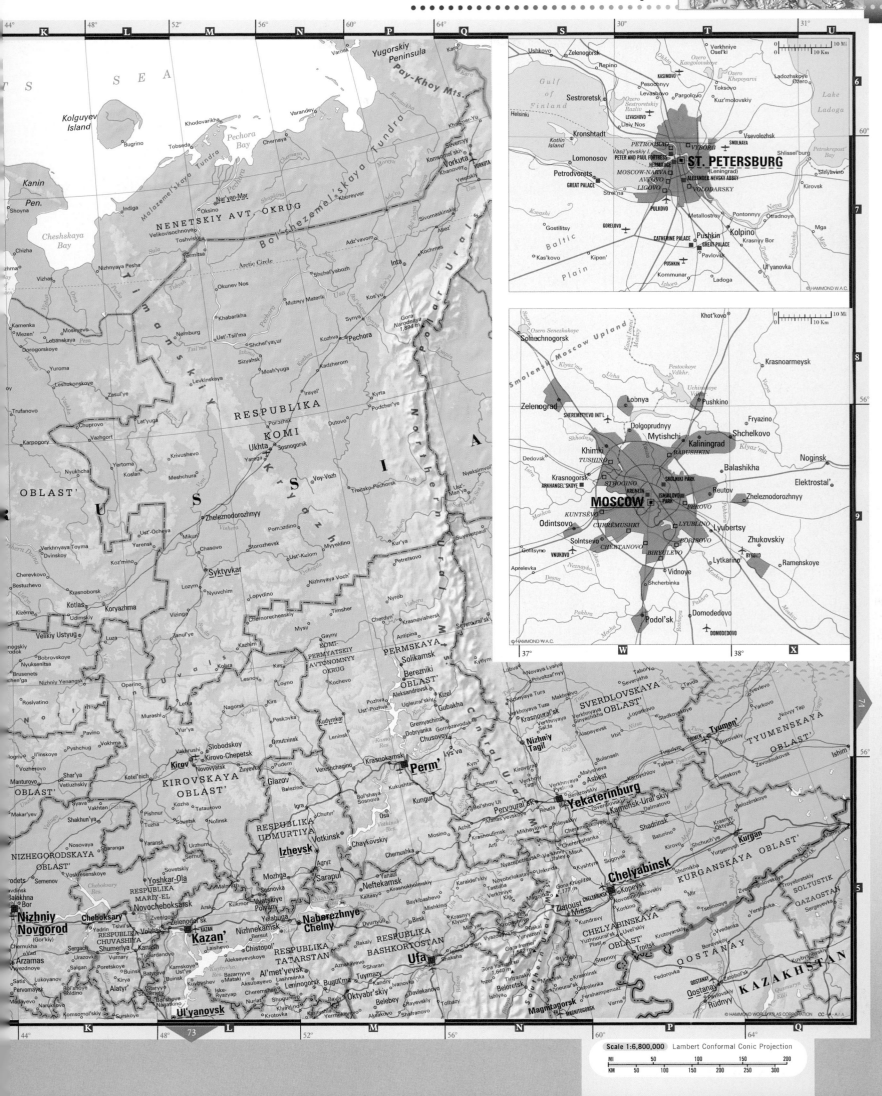

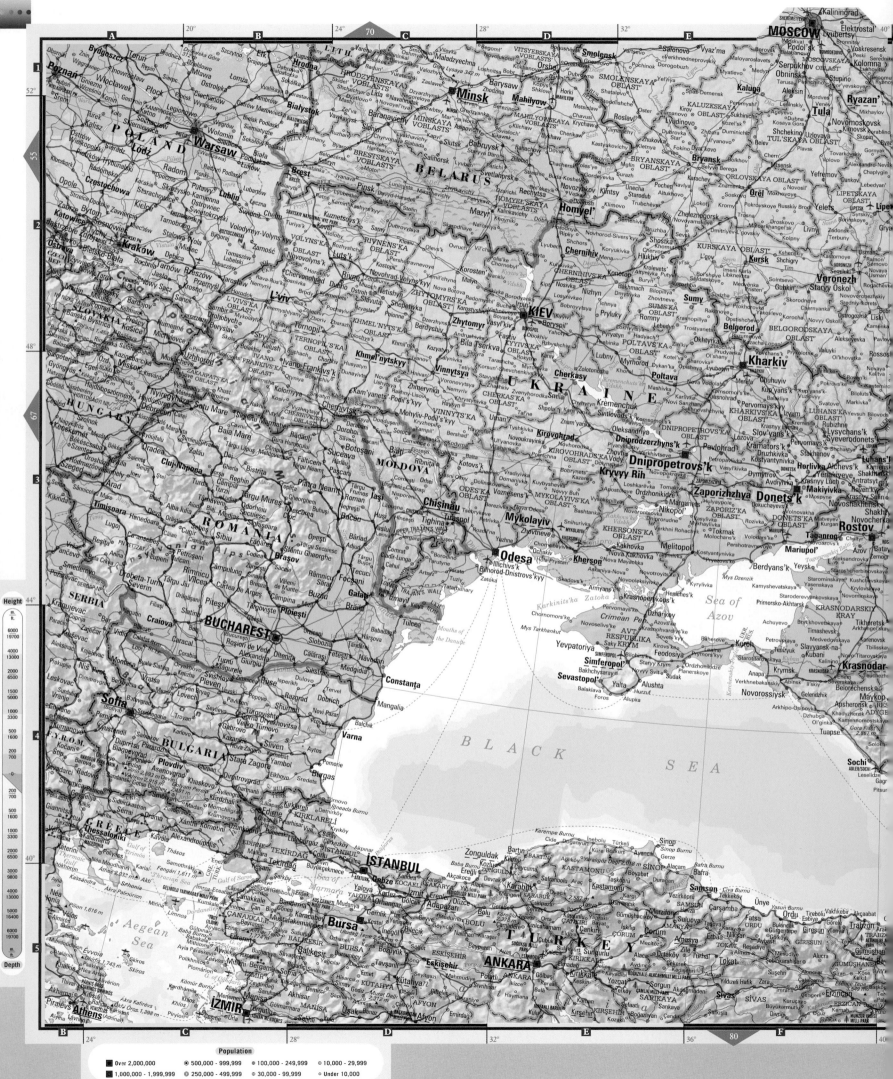

Scale 1:6,800,000   Lambert Conformal Conic Projection

MI   50   100   150   200

KM   50   100   150   200   250   300

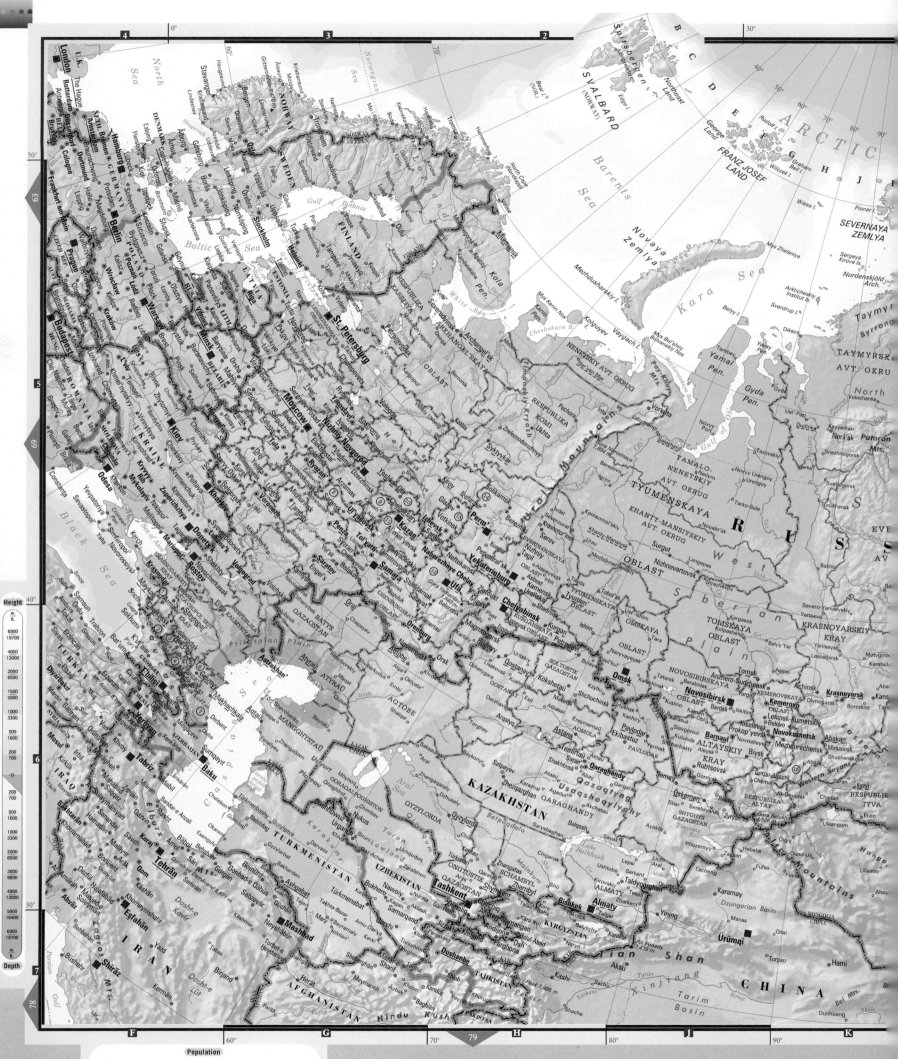

Russia and Neighboring Countries

RUSSIA
(Administrative divisions are named only when they differ from their respective capitals.)

1. RESPUBLIKA ADYGEYA
2. RESPUBLIKA KARACHAYEVO-CHERKESIYA
3. RESPUBLIKA KABARDINO-BALKARIYA
4. RESPUBLIKA SEVERNAYA OSETIYA-ALANIYA
5. RESPUBLIKA INGUSHETIYA
6. RESPUBLIKA CHECHNYA
7. RESPUBLIKA DAGESTAN
8. RESPUBLIKA MORDOVIYA
9. RESPUBLIKA CHUVASHIYA
10. RESPUBLIKA MARIY-EL
11. RESPUBLIKA TATARSTAN
12. RESPUBLIKA BASHKORTOSTAN
13. RESPUBLIKA UDMURTIYA
14. KOMI-PERMYATSKIY AVTONOMNYY OKRUG
15. RESPUBLIKA KHAKASIYA
16. UST'-ORDYNSKIY BURYATSKIY AVT. OKRUG
17. AGINSKIY BURYATSKIY AVT. OKRUG

© HAMMOND WORLD ATLAS CORPORATION   CM-29-A-A

Scale 1:20,500,000   Lambert Conformal Conic Projection

MI   200   400   600
KM   200   400   800

Asia - Geographical Comparisons

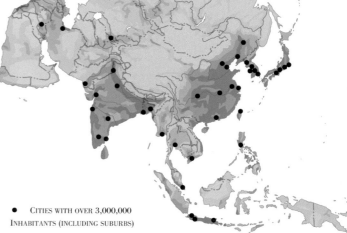

● CITIES WITH OVER 3,000,000
INHABITANTS (INCLUDING SUBURBS)

TOPOGRAPHY

SQ. MI.	SQ. KM.	SQ. MI.	SQ. KM.	SQ. MI.	SQ. KM.
UNDER 656	UNDER 200	1640-3281	500-1000	6562-16404	2000-5000
656-1640	200-500	3281-6562	1000-2000	OVER 16404	OVER 5000

POPULATION DISTRIBUTION

DENSITY PER		SQ. MI.	SQ. KM.	SQ. MI.	SQ. KM.
SQ. MI.	SQ. KM.	130 TO 260	50 TO 100	3 TO 25	1 TO 10
OVER 260	OVER 100	25 TO 130	10 TO 50	UNDER 3	UNDER 1

LAND USE

CEREALS, LIVESTOCK	DIVERSIFIED TROPICAL & SUBTROPICAL CROPS	SPECIAL CROPS	
CASH CROPS, MIXED FARMING	LIVESTOCK RANCHING & HERDING	FORESTS	
DAIRY, LIVESTOCK		NONPRODUCTIVE	

MINERAL RESOURCES

ENERGY & FUELS
◆ COAL
⬟ LIGNITE
▲ NATURAL GAS
● PETROLEUM
■ URANIUM

IRON & FERROALLOYS
1 CHROMIUM
2 COBALT
3 IRON ORE
4 MANGANESE
5 MOLYBDENUM
6 NICKEL
7 TUNGSTEN

OTHER PRINCIPAL RESOURCES
1 ANTIMONY
2 ASBESTOS
3 BAUXITE
4 BORAX
5 COPPER
6 DIAMONDS
7 GOLD
8 GRAPHITE
9 LEAD
10 MAGNESITE
11 MERCURY
12 MICA
13 PHOSPHATES
14 PLATINUM
15 POTASH
16 SILVER
17 SULFUR
18 TIN
19 TITANIUM
20 ZINC

AREA OF
OPTIMIZATION

The red band which
surrounds this map
defines the "Area of
Optimization." Within
this bounding curve is
the most accurate
conformal map that can
be made of the region.
Outside the optimized
area, distortion increases
rapidly, and tears or
other irregularities in
the grid may occur.
(See Page 5 for additional
information.)

Population
■ Over 3,000,000   ★ 500,000-999,999   ○ Under 100,000
■ 1,000,000-2,999,999   ● 100,000-499,999

Scale 1:47,700,000   Hammond Optimal Conformal

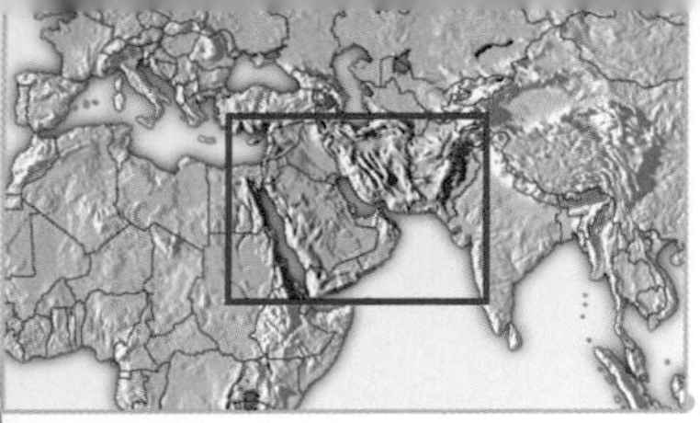

Southwestern Asia

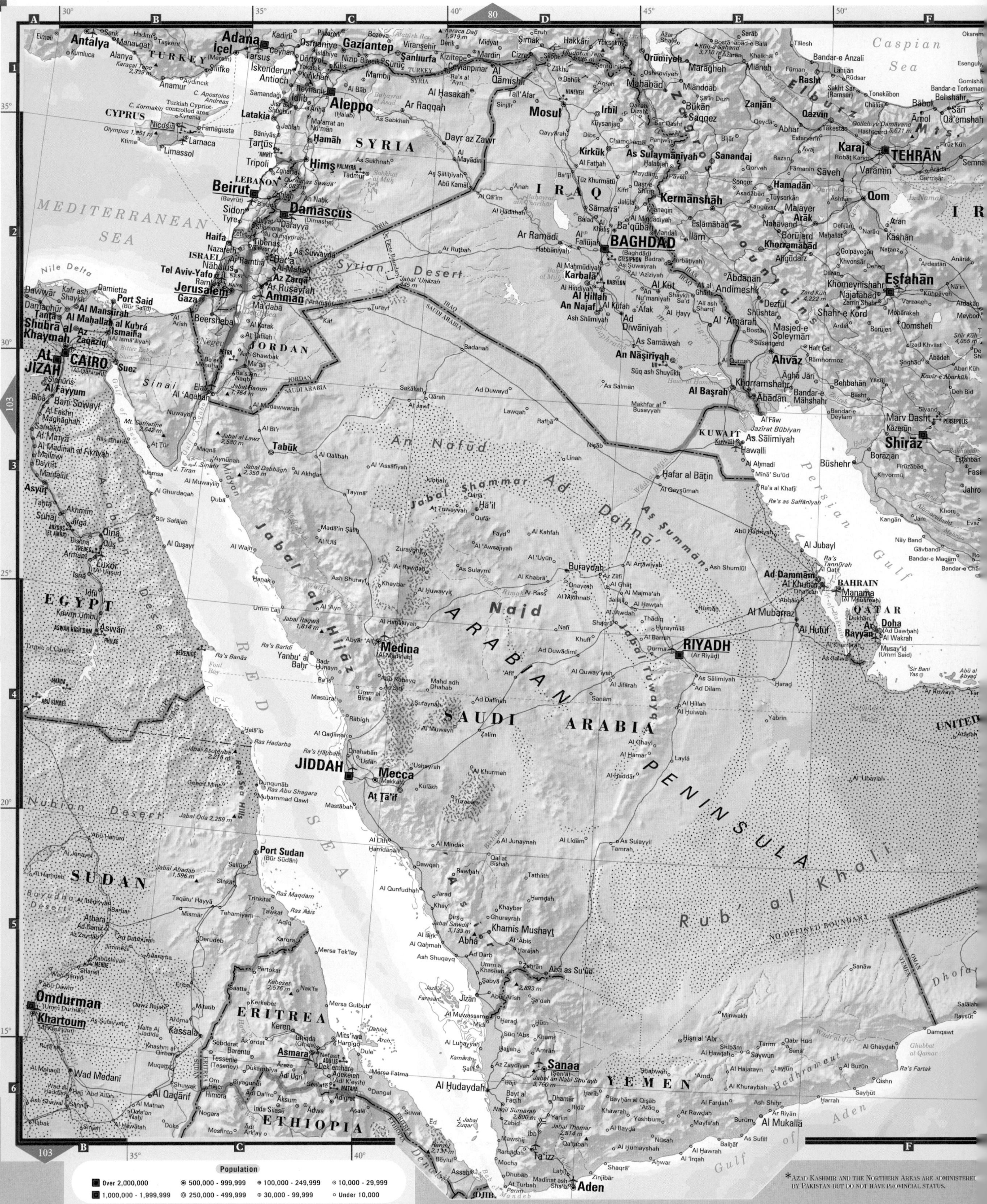

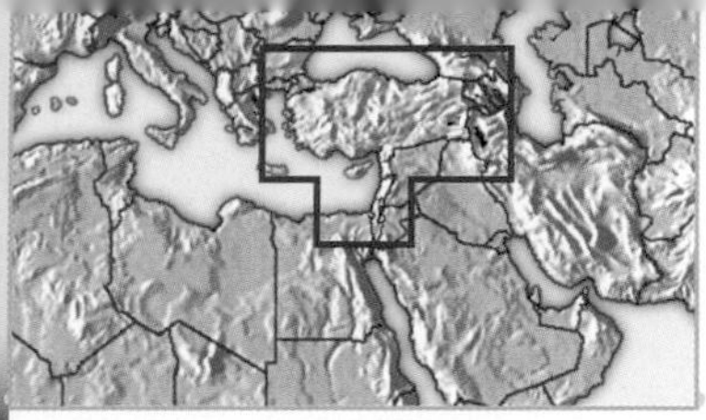

MAP SECTION

Eastern Mediterranean Region

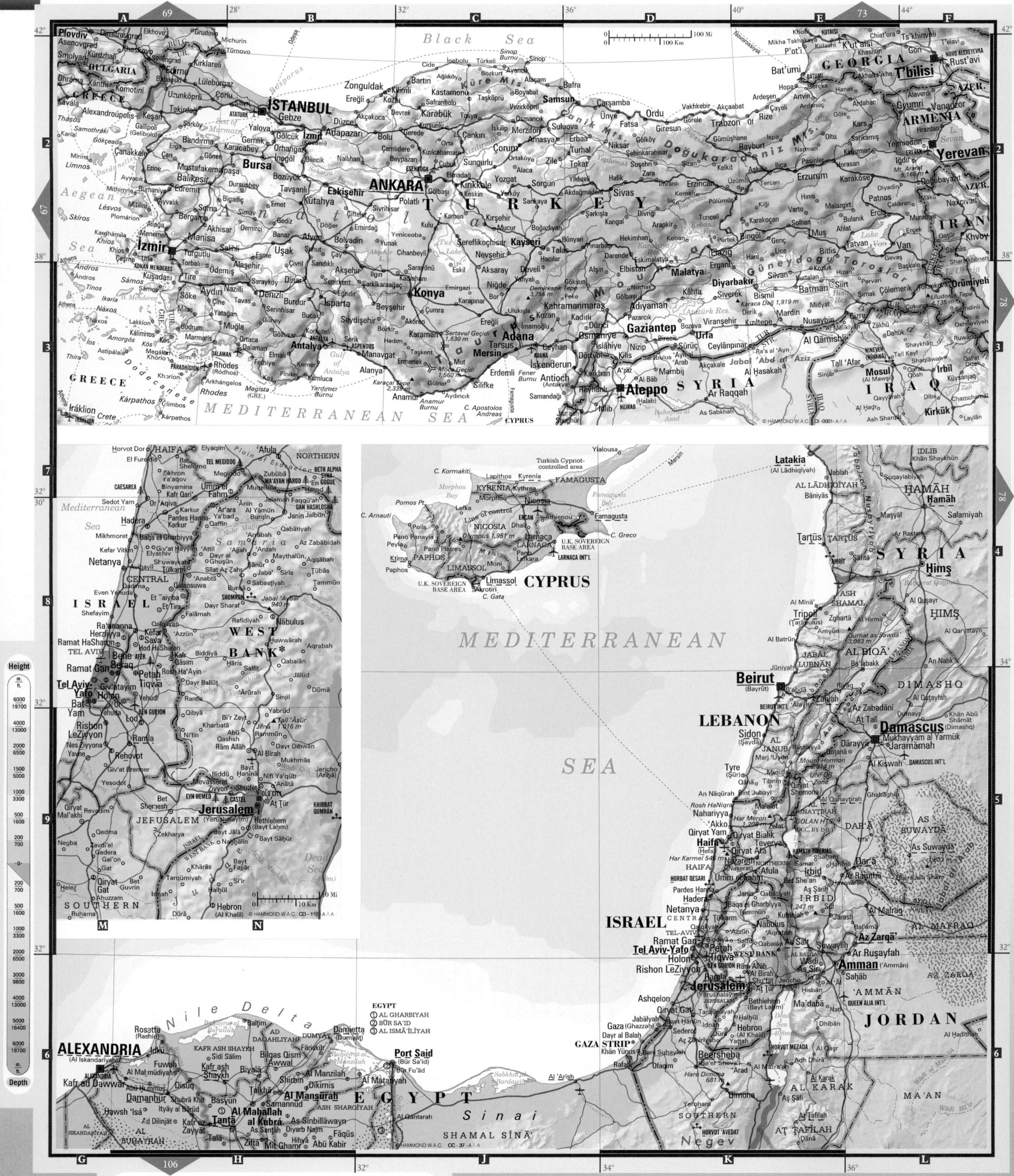

Population

- Over 2,000,000
- 1,000,000 - 1,999,999
- 500,000 - 999,999
- 250,000 - 499,999
- 100,000 - 249,999
- 30,000 - 99,999
- 10,000 - 29,999
- Under 10,000

Population

- ■ Over 2,000,000
- ■ 1,000,000 - 1,999,999
- ⊙ 500,000 - 999,999
- ⊙ 250,000 - 499,999
- ◉ 100,000 - 249 999
- ◎ 30,000 - 99,999
- ◦ 10,000 - 29,999
- ◦ Under 10,000

*AZAD KASHMIR AND THE NORTHERN AREAS ARE ADMINISTERED BY PAKISTAN BUT DO NOT HAVE PROVINCIAL STATUS.

Scale 1:9,000,000 Lambert Conformal Conic Projection

MI   100   200   300
KM   100   200   300   400

Height
m. ft.
6000 19700
4000 13000
2000 6500
1500 5000
1000 3300
500 1600
200 700
-0-
200 700
500 1600
1000 3300
2000 6500
3000 9800
4000 13000
5000 16450
6000 19700
m. ft.
Depth

Scale 1:9,000,000   Lambert Conformal Conic Projection

SEA OF JAPAN

PACIFIC

OCEAN

EAST

CHINA

SEA

KOREA STRAIT

SOUTH KOREA

Population

■ Over 2,000,000	◉ 500,000 - 999,999	◎ 100,000 - 249,999	◦ 10,000 - 29,999
■ 1,000,000 - 1,999,999	◉ 250,000 - 499,999	◦ 30,000 - 99,999	◦ Under 10,000

Honshū

Tōkyō

Sagami Sea

FUJI-HAKONE-IZU NATIONAL PARK

Tamba Uplands

KYŌTO

Kyōto

Ōtsu

SHIGA

HYŌGO

Kōbe

Amagasaki

ŌSAKA

Higashi-Ōsaka

Sakai

NARA

MIE

Tsu

NAGOYA

AICHI

Toyota

Okazaki

Yokkaichi

Ise Bay

Gifu

Scale 1:3,400,000   Lambert Conformal Conic Projection

Population
- ■ Over 2,000,000
- ■ 1,000,000 - 1,999,999
- ● 500,000 - 999,999
- ● 250,000 - 499,999
- ● 100,000 - 249,999
- ● 30,000 - 99,999
- ● 10,000 - 29,999
- ○ Under 10,000

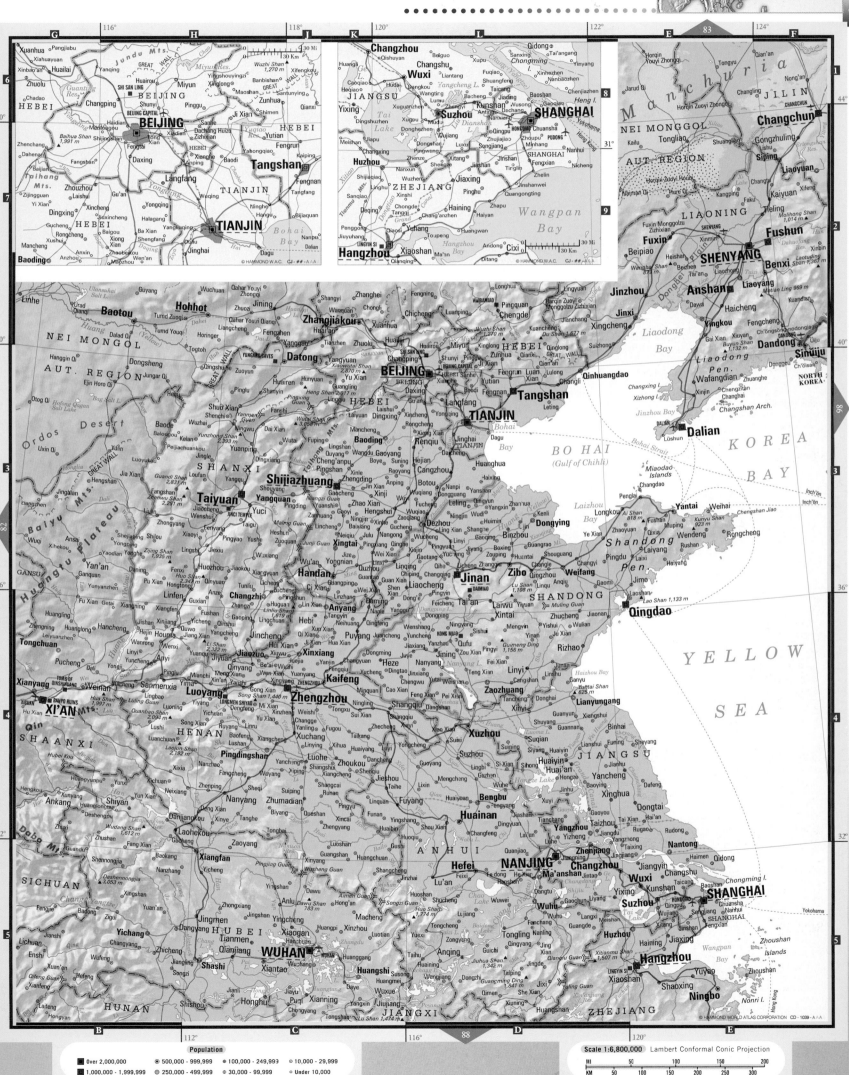

Population

■ Over 2,000,000	● 500,000 - 999,999
■ 1,000,000 - 1,999,999	● 250,000 - 499,999

● 100,000 - 249,993   ○ 10,000 - 29,999
● 30,000 - 99,999   ○ Under 10,000

Scale 1:6,800,000   Lambert Conformal Conic Projection

MI   50   100   150   200
KM   50   100   150   200   250   300

Southeastern China, Taiwan, Philippines

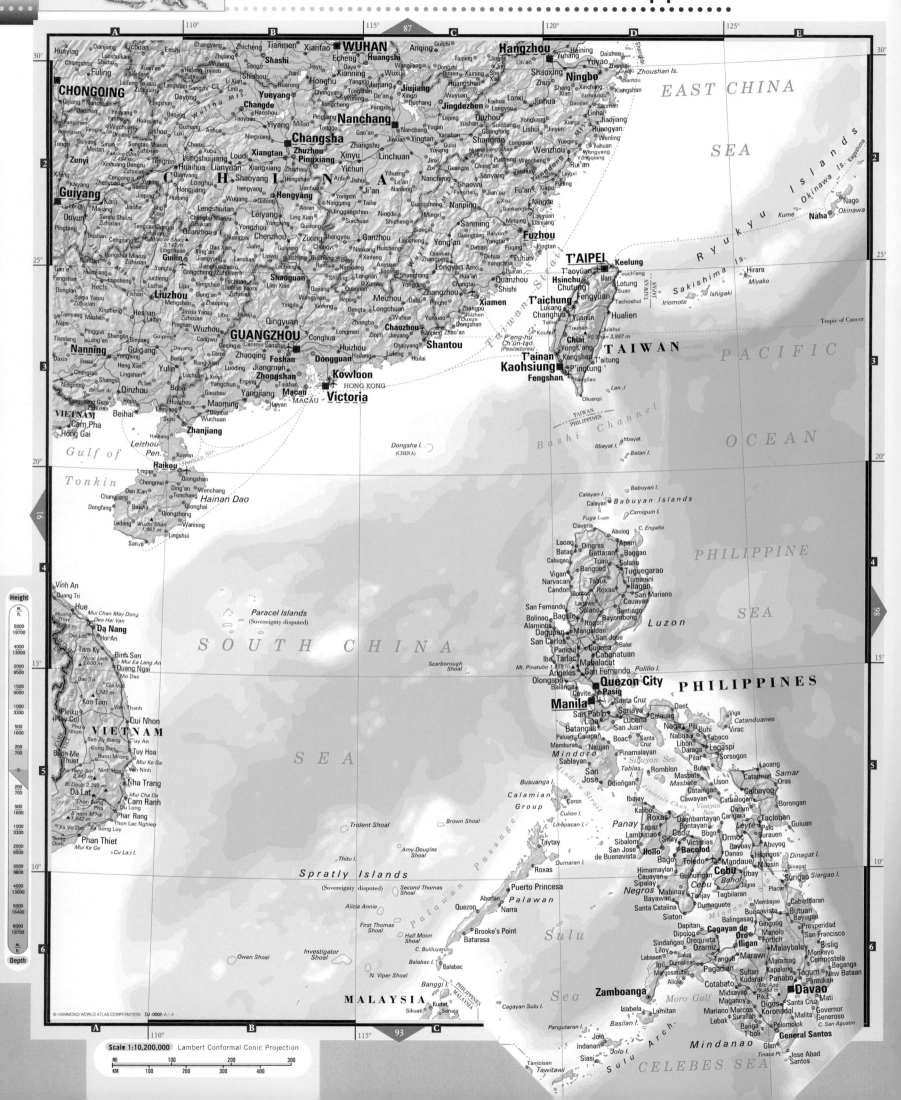

Scale 1:10,200,000   Lambert Conformal Conic Projection

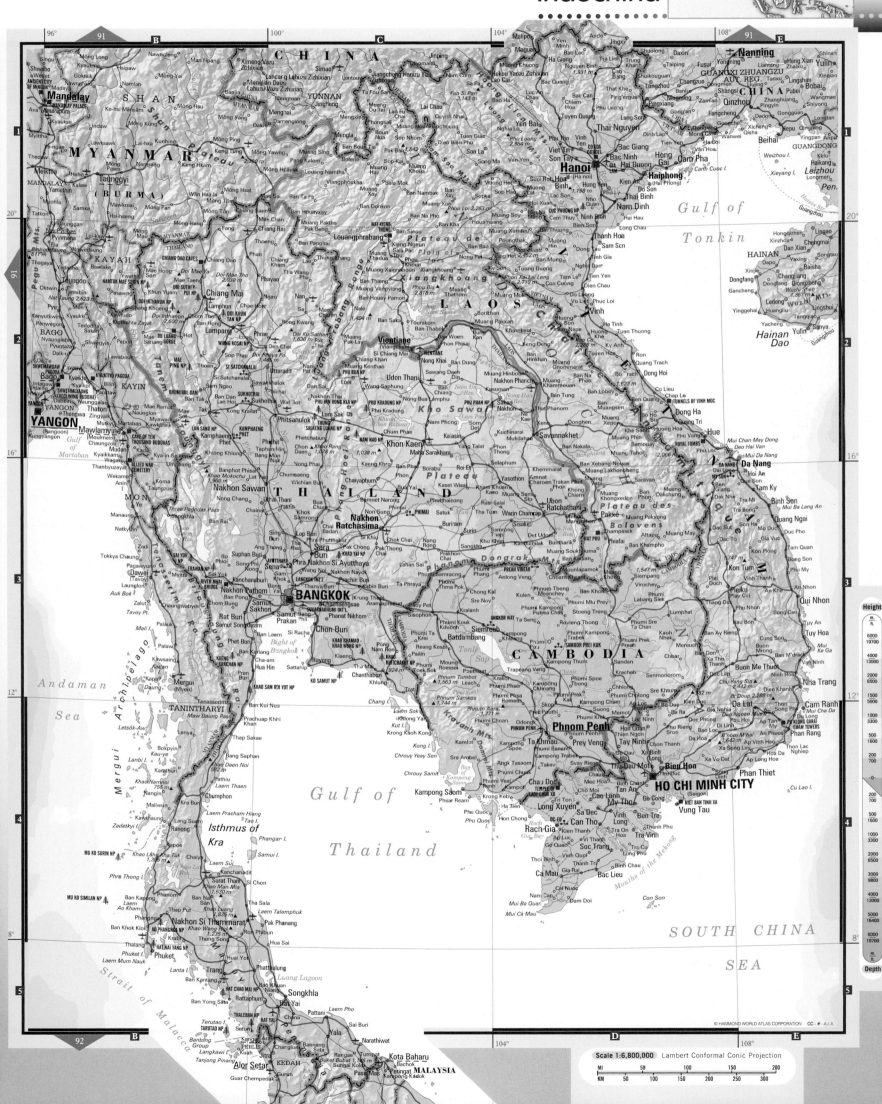

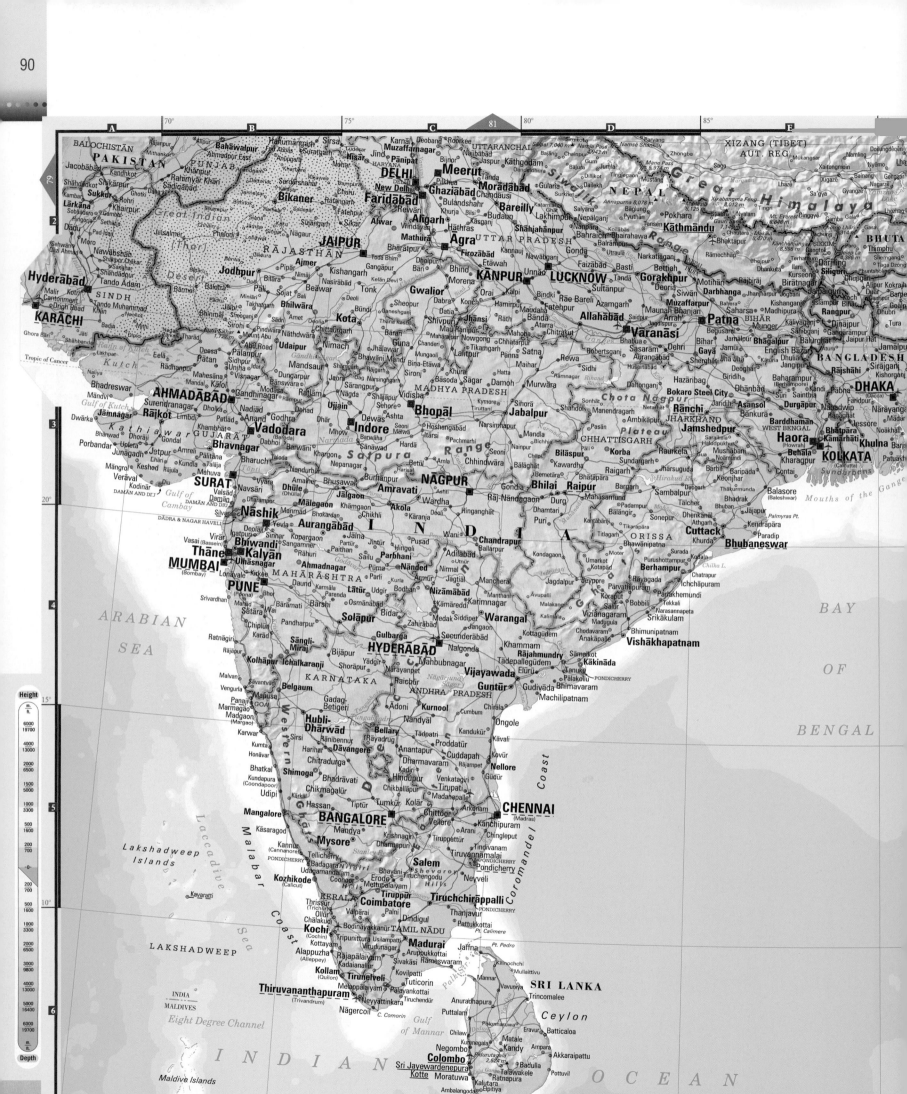

Population

■ Over 2,000,000   ● 500,000 - 999,999   ● 100,000 - 249,999   ● 10,000 - 29,999
■ 1,000,000 - 1,999,999   ● 250,000 - 499,999   ● 30,000 - 99,999   ● Under 10,000

Scale 1:10,200,000 Lambert Conformal Conic Projection

- ● CITIES WITH OVER 500,000
  INHABITANTS (INCLUDING SUBURBS)

TOPOGRAPHY

SQ. MI.	SQ. KM.	SQ. MI.	SQ. KM.	SQ. MI.	SQ. KM.
UNDER 656	UNDER 200	1640-3281	500-1000	6562-16404	2000-5000
656-1640	200-500	3281-6562	1000-2000	OVER 16404	OVER 5000

POPULATION DISTRIBUTION

DENSITY PER		SQ. MI.	SQ. KM.	SQ. MI.	SQ. KM.
SQ. MI.	SQ. KM.	25 TO 130	10 TO 50	UNDER 3	UNDER 1
OVER 130	OVER 50	3 TO 25	1 TO 10		

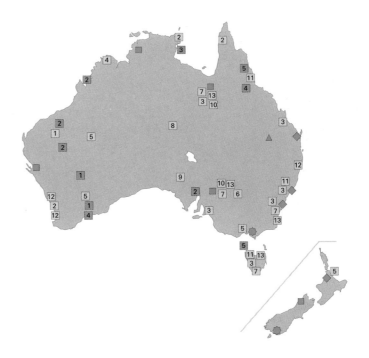

LAND USE

- CEREALS, LIVESTOCK
- LIVESTOCK RANCHING & HERDING
- DAIRY, LIVESTOCK
- PASTURE LIVESTOCK
- CASH CROPS, MIXED FARMING
- FORESTS
- UNPRODUCTIVE

MINERAL RESOURCES

ENERGY & FUELS
- ◆ COAL
- ⬟ LIGNITE
- ▲ NATURAL GAS
- ■ URANIUM

IRON & FERROALLOYS
- 1 COBALT
- 2 IRON ORE
- 3 MANGANESE
- 4 NICKEL
- 5 TUNGSTEN

OTHER MAJOR RESOURCES
- 1 ASBESTOS
- 2 BAUXITE
- 3 COPPER
- 4 DIAMONDS
- 5 GOLD
- 6 GYPSUM
- 7 LEAD
- 8 MICA
- 9 OPALS
- 10 SILVER
- 11 TIN
- 12 TITANIUM
- 13 ZINC

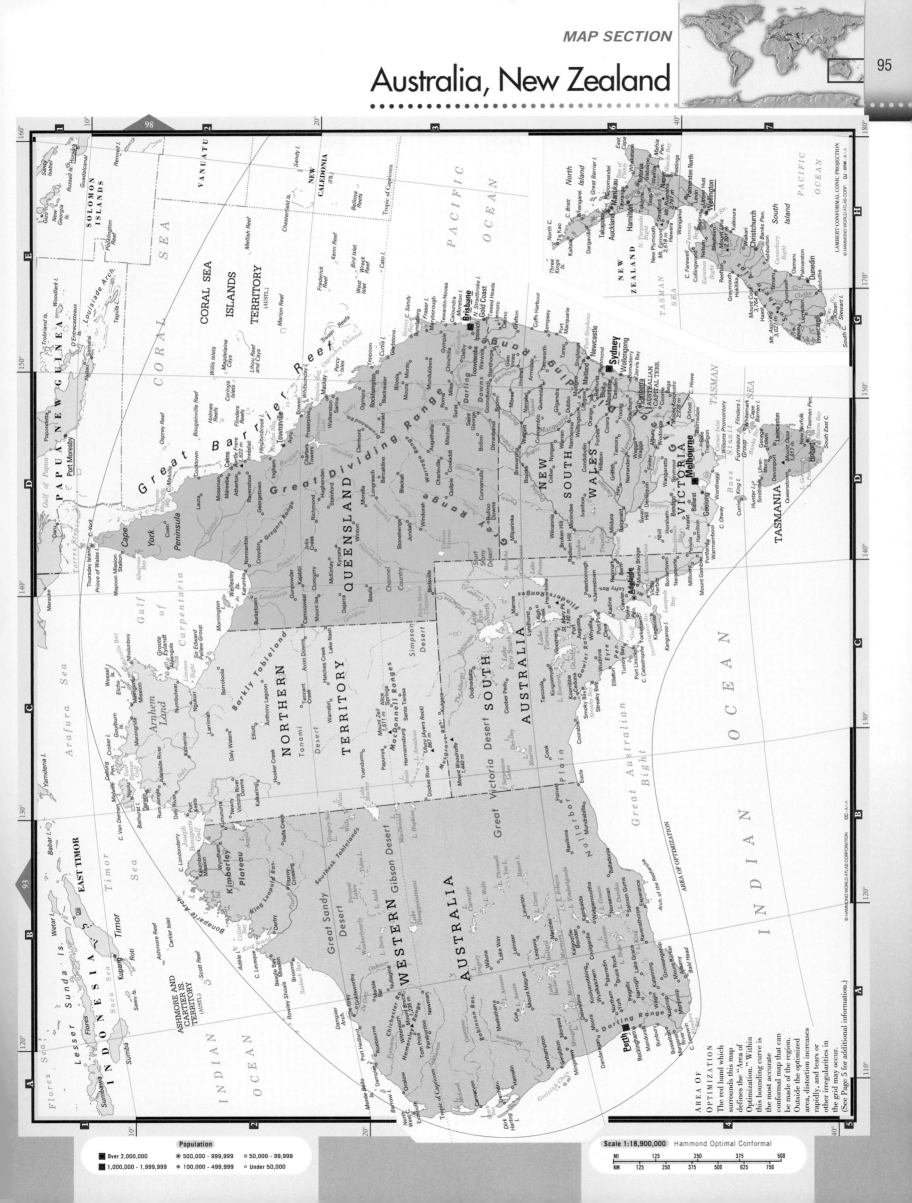

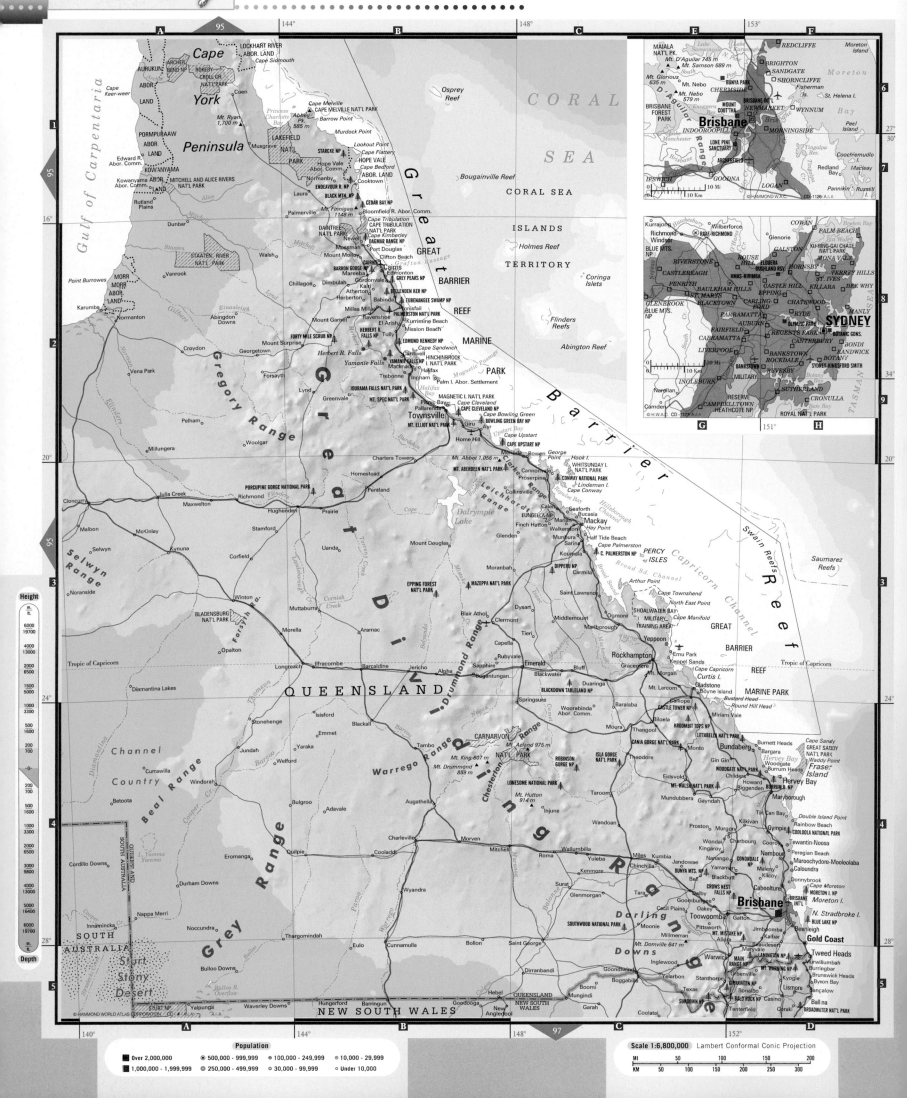

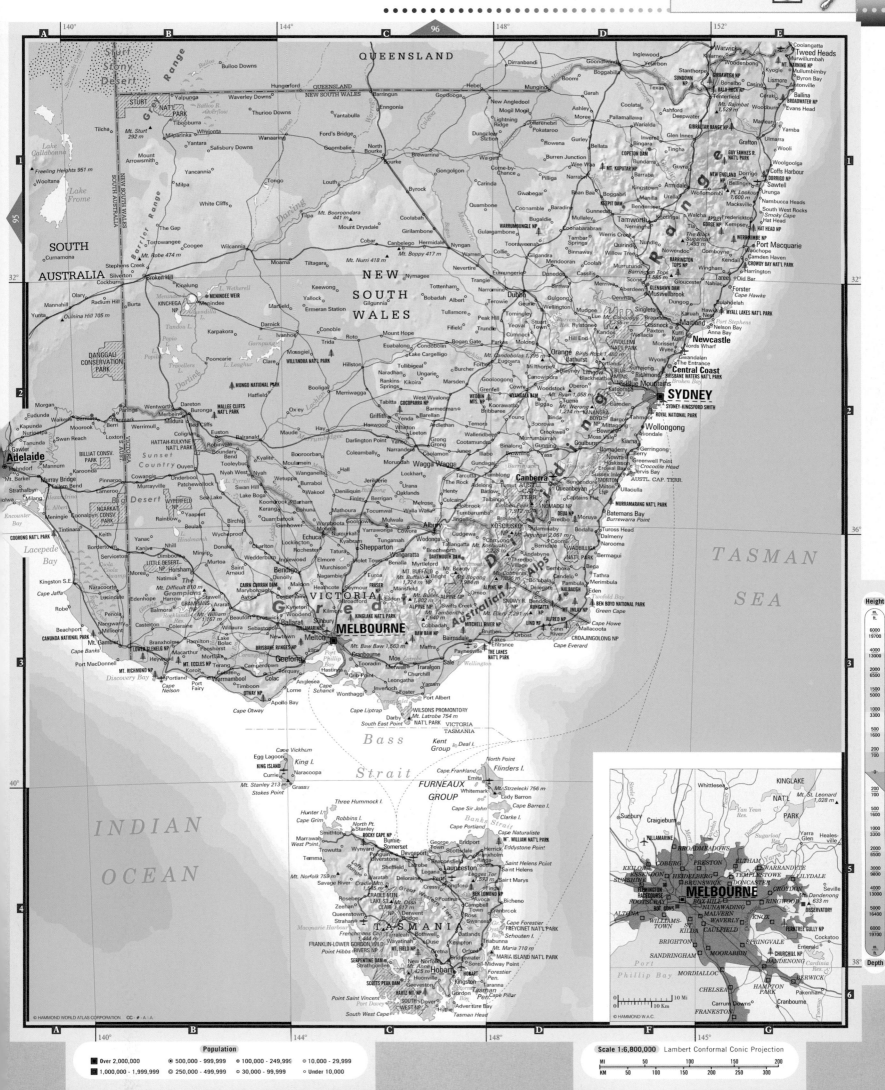

Population

■ Over 2,000,000	● 500,000 - 999,999	● 100,000 - 249,999	○ 10,000 - 29,999
■ 1,000,000 - 1,999,999	● 250,000 - 499,999	○ 30,000 - 99,999	○ Under 10,000

Height

Depth

Scale 1:6,800,000   Lambert Conformal Conic Projection

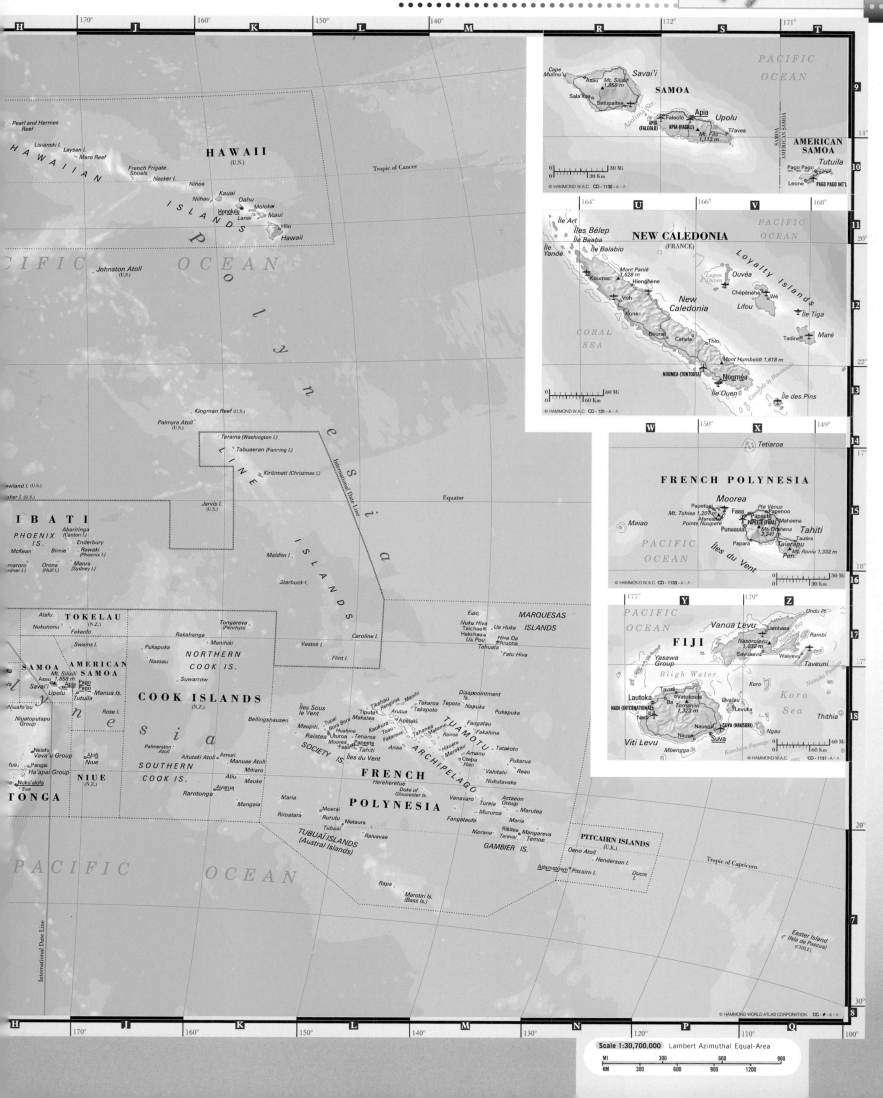

Africa - Geographical Comparisons

TOPOGRAPHY

SQ. MI.	SQ. KM.	SQ. MI.	SQ. KM.	SQ. MI.	SQ. KM.
UNDER 656	UNDER 200	1640-3281	500-1000	6562-16404	2000-5000
656-1640	200-500	3281-6562	1000-2000	OVER 16404	OVER 5000

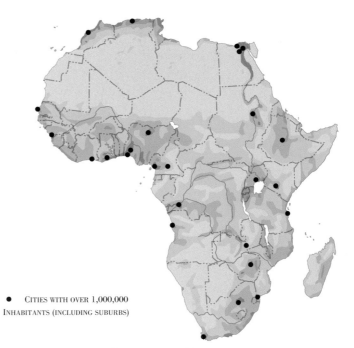

● CITIES WITH OVER 1,000,000
INHABITANTS (INCLUDING SUBURBS)

POPULATION DISTRIBUTION

DENSITY PER		SQ. MI.	SQ. KM.	SQ. MI.	SQ. KM.
SQ. MI.	SQ. KM.	130 TO 260	50 TO 100	3 TO 25	1 TO 10
OVER 260	OVER 100	25 TO 130	10 TO 50	UNDER 3	UNDER 1

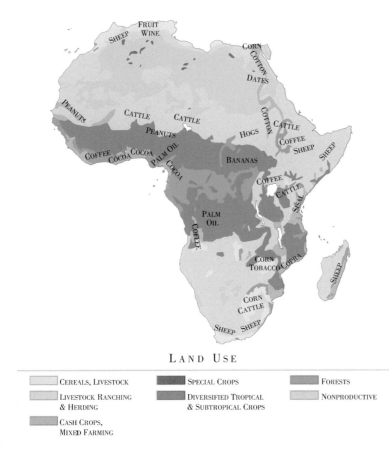

LAND USE

▨ CEREALS, LIVESTOCK	▨ SPECIAL CROPS	▨ FORESTS	
▨ LIVESTOCK RANCHING & HERDING	▨ DIVERSIFIED TROPICAL & SUBTROPICAL CROPS	▨ NONPRODUCTIVE	
▨ CASH CROPS, MIXED FARMING			

MINERAL RESOURCES

ENERGY & FUELS	IRON & FERROALLOYS	OTHER MAJOR RESOURCES	
◆ COAL	1 CHROMIUM	1 ANTIMONY	7 LEAD
▲ NATURAL GAS	2 COBALT	2 ASBESTOS	8 MICA
● PETROLEUM	3 IRON ORE	3 BAUXITE	9 PHOSPHATES
■ URANIUM	4 MANGANESE	4 COPPER	10 PLATINUM
	5 NICKEL	5 DIAMONDS	11 TIN
	6 VANADIUM	6 GOLD	12 ZINC

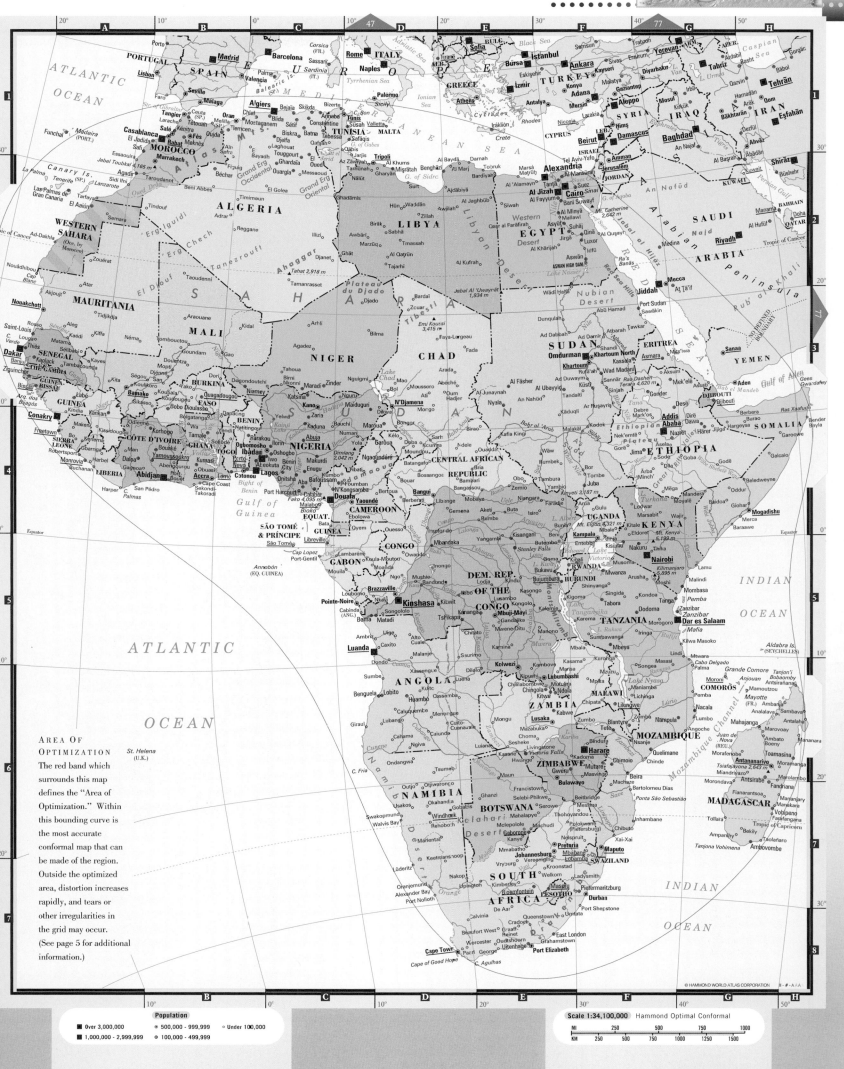

AREA OF OPTIMIZATION
The red band which surrounds this map defines the "Area of Optimization." Within this bounding curve is the most accurate conformal map that can be made of the region. Outside the optimized area, distortion increases rapidly, and tears or other irregularities in the grid may occur.
(See page 5 for additional information.)

Population

■ Over 3,000,000	● 500,000 - 999,999	○ Under 100,000
■ 1,000,000 - 2,999,999	⊛ 100,000 - 499,999	

Scale 1:34,100,000   Hammond Optimal Conformal

| MI | 250 | 500 | 750 | 1000 |
| KM | 250 | 500 | 750 | 1000 | 1250 | 1500 |

© Hammond World Atlas Corporation

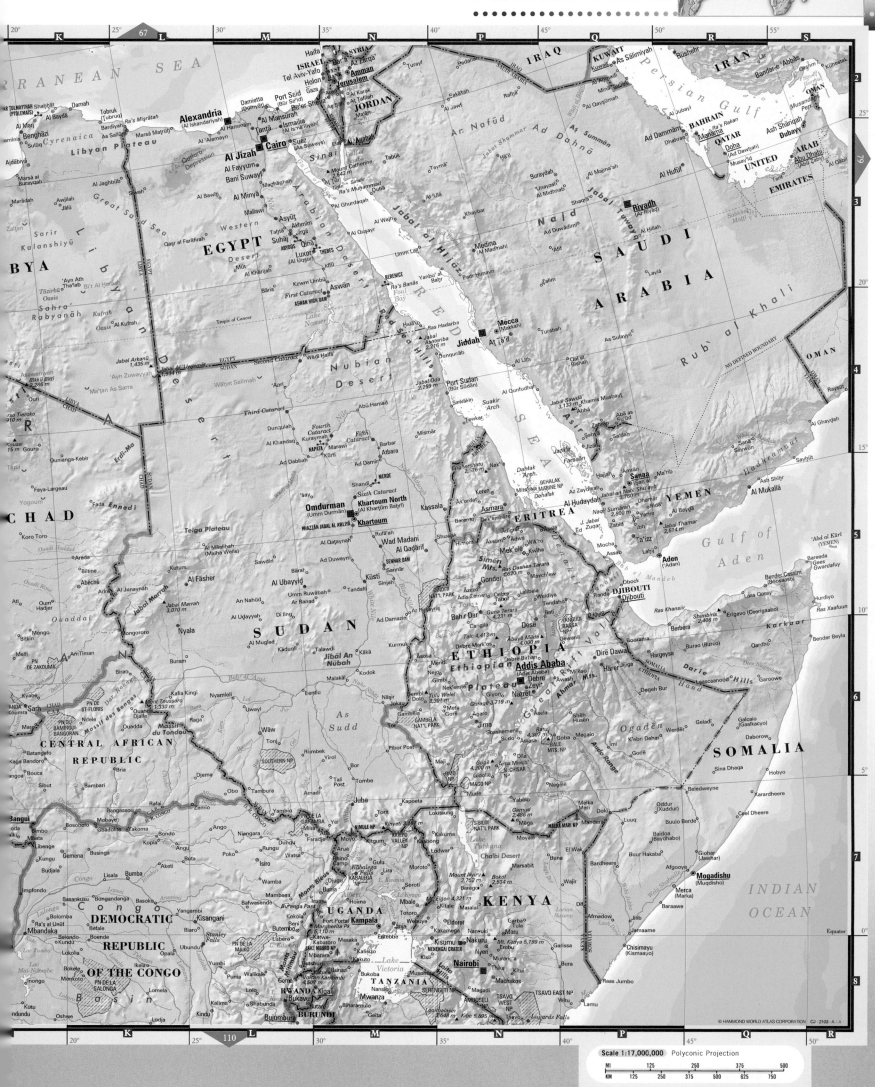

Scale 1:17,000,000   Polyconic Projection

MI   125   250   375   500

KM   125   250   375   500   625   750

Height
m.
ft.
6000 19700
4000 13000
2000 6500
1500 5000
1000 3300
500 1600
200 700
0
200 700
500 1600
1000 3300
2000 6500
3000 9800
4000 13000
5000 16400
6000 19700
Depth

© HAMMOND WORLD ATLAS CORPORATION   CC · # · A · A

Population

Symbol	Range
■	Over 2,000,000
●	500,000 - 999,999
●	100,000 - 249,999
●	10,000 - 29,999
■	1,000,000 - 1,999,999
●	250,000 - 499,999
○	30,000 - 99,999
○	Under 10,000

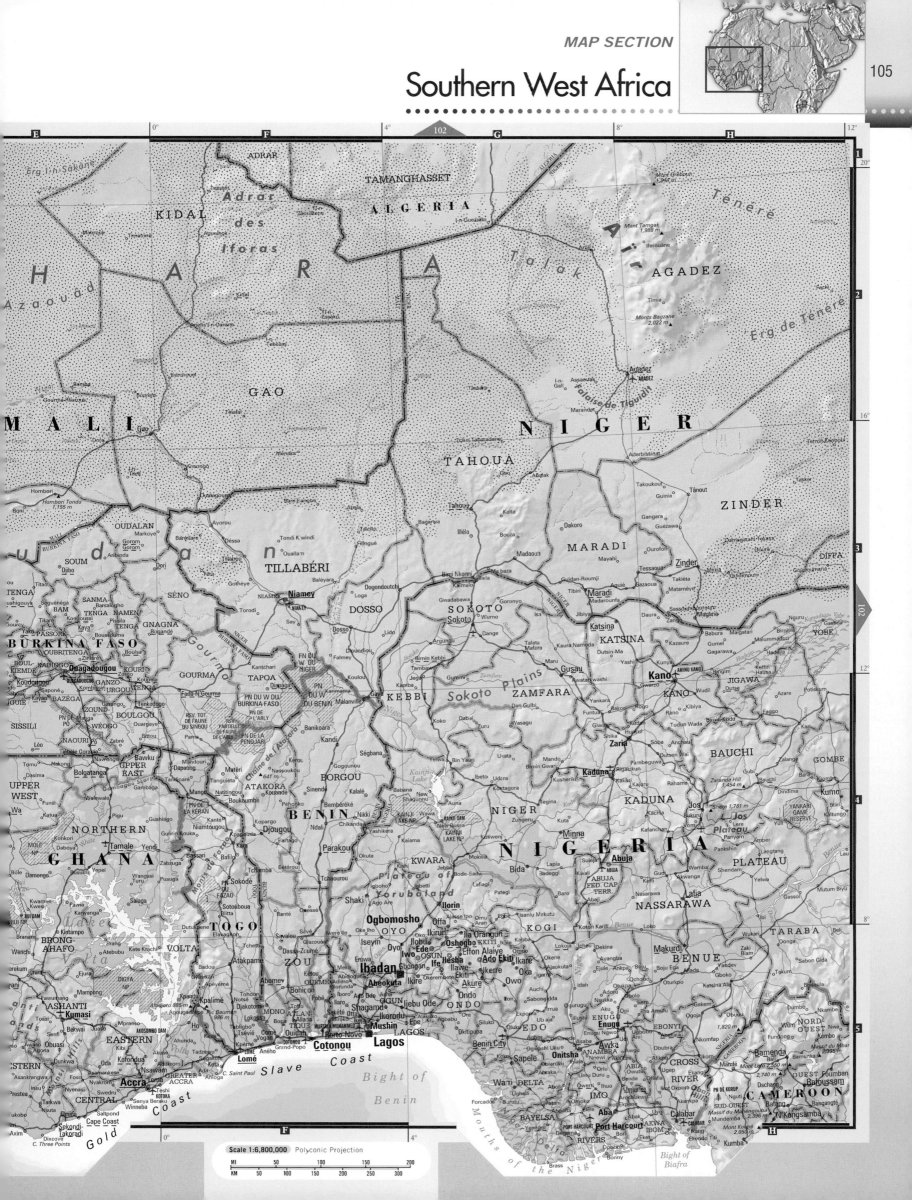

Scale 1:6,800,000 · Polyconic Projection

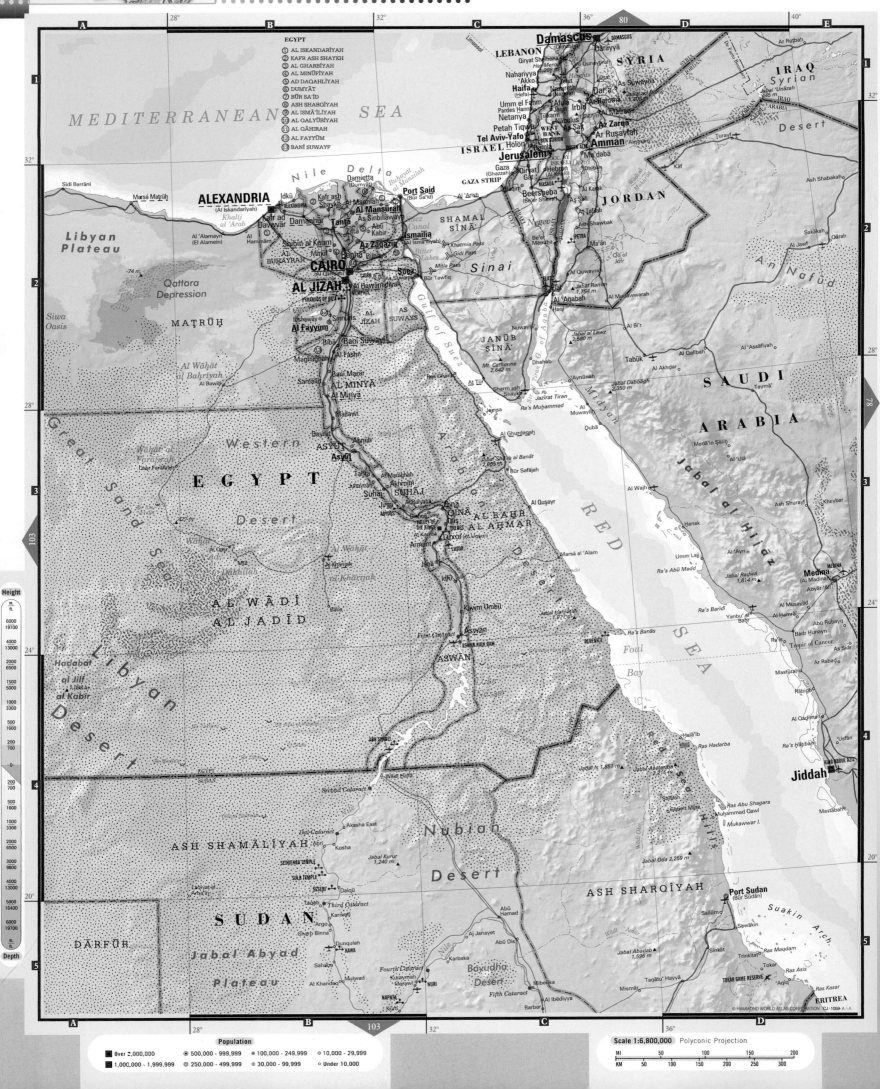

EGYPT
① AL ISKANDARĪYAH
② KAFR ASH SHAYKH
③ AL GHARBĪYAH
④ AL MINŪFĪYAH
⑤ AD DAQAHLĪYAH
⑥ DUMYĀT
⑦ BŪR SAʿĪD
⑧ ASH SHARQĪYAH
⑨ AL ISMĀʿĪLĪYAH
⑩ AL QALYŪBĪYAH
⑪ AL QĀHIRAH
⑫ AL FAYYŪM
⑬ BANĪ SUWAYF

MEDITERRANEAN SEA

Libyan Plateau

Qattara Depression

Siwa Oasis

MAṬRŪḤ

EGYPT

Great Sand Sea

Western

Desert

AL WĀDĪ AL JADĪD

Libyan Desert

Hadabat al Jilf al Kabīr

DĀRFŪR

ASH SHAMĀLĪYAH

SUDAN

Jabal Abyad Plateau

Nubian Desert

ASH SHARQĪYAH

Bayuda Desert

ALEXANDRIA (Al Iskandarīyah)

CAIRO (Al Qāhirah)

AL JĪZAH

Al Fayyūm

AL MINYĀ

ASYŪṬ

SUHĀJ

QINĀ

AL BAHR AL AHMAR

ASWĀN

ASWAN HIGH DAM

ABU SIMBEL

Nile Delta

Port Said (Būr Saʿīd)

Suez Canal

Ismailia

SHAMAL SĪNĀ

Sinai

Gulf of Suez

JANŪB SĪNĀ

Mt. Catherine 2,642 m

Gulf of Aqaba

RED SEA

Foul Bay

Tropic of Cancer

Suakin Arch.

Port Sudan (Būr Sūdān)

LEBANON

SYRIA

Damascus

ISRAEL

Jerusalem

Tel Aviv-Yafo

Haifa

WEST BANK

GAZA STRIP

JORDAN

Amman

Az Zarqā

IRAQ

Syrian Desert

An Nafūd

SAUDI ARABIA

Jabal al Hijāz

Medina (Al Madīnah)

Jiddah

ERITREA

Height
m. / ft.
6000 / 19700
4000 / 13000
2000 / 6500
1500 / 5000
1000 / 3300
500 / 1600
200 / 700
0
200 / 700
500 / 1600
1000 / 3300
2000 / 6500
3000 / 9800
4000 / 13000
5000 / 16400
6000 / 19700
Depth

Population

■ Over 2,000,000
■ 1,000,000 - 1,999,999
● 500,000 - 999,999
● 250,000 - 499,999
● 100,000 - 249,999
● 30,000 - 99,999
● 10,000 - 29,999
○ Under 10,000

Scale 1:6,800,000   Polyconic Projection

MI   50   100   150   200
KM   50   100   150   200   250   300

© HAMMOND WORLD ATLAS CORPORATION   CJ-1059-A-A

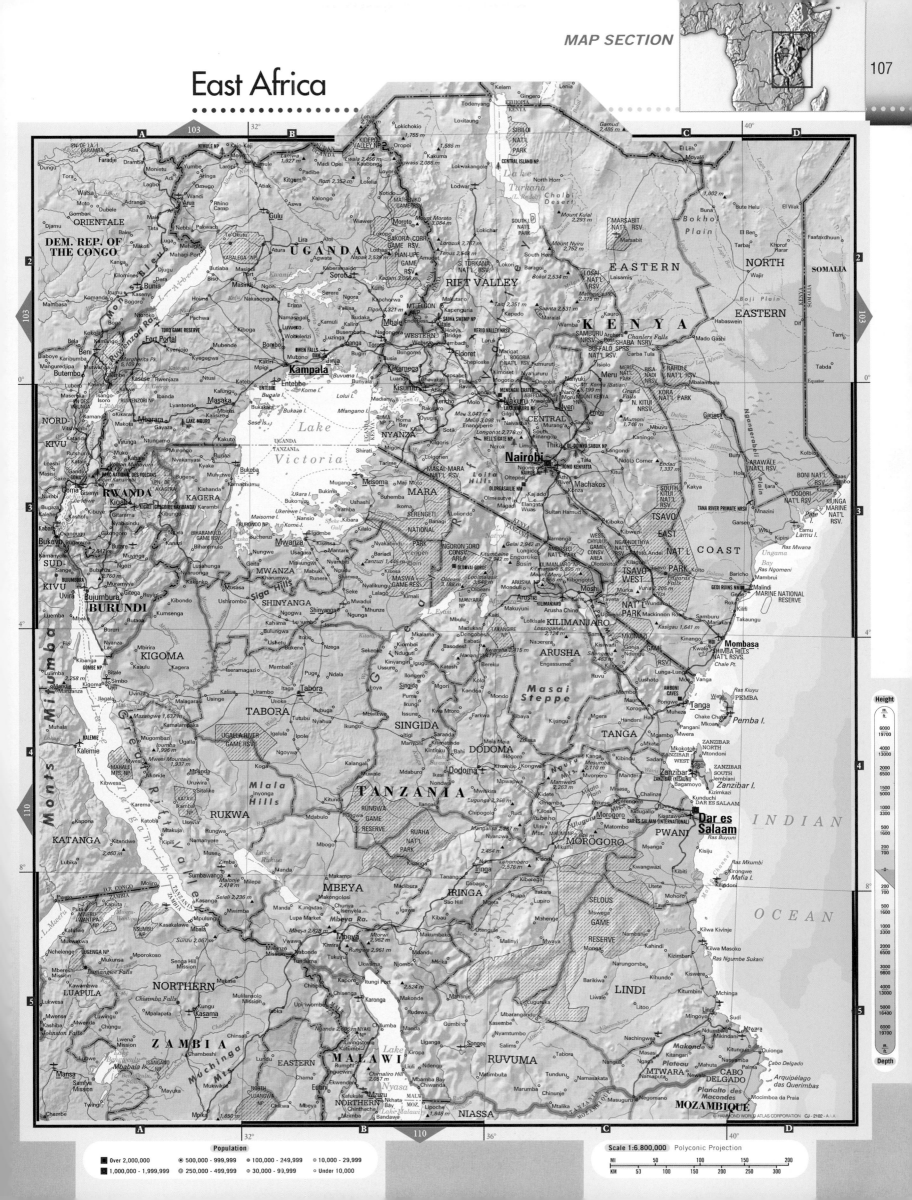

East Africa

Scale 1:6,800,000   Polyconic Projection

Population

■ Over 2,000,000
■ 1,000,000 - 1,999,999
● 500,000 - 999,999
● 250,000 - 499,999
● 100,000 - 249,999
● 30,000 - 93,999
○ 10,000 - 29,999
○ Under 10,000

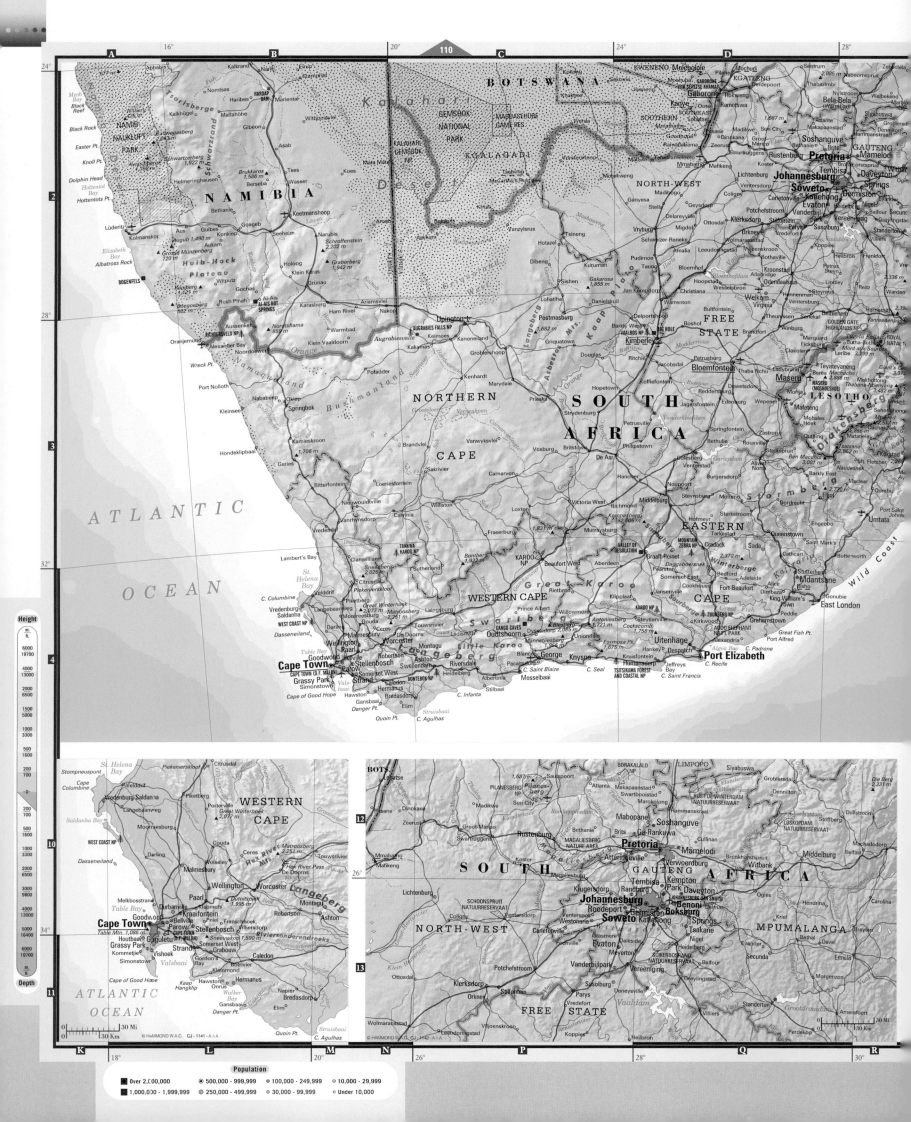

Scale 1:6,800,000   Polyconic Projection

Southern Africa

Population

■ Over 2,000,000	● 500,000 - 999,999	○ 50,000 - 99,999
■ 1,000,000 - 1,999,999	● 100,000 - 499,999	○ Under 50,000

Scale 1:17,000,000 Polyconic Projection

MI 125   250   375   500

KM 125   250   375   500   625   750

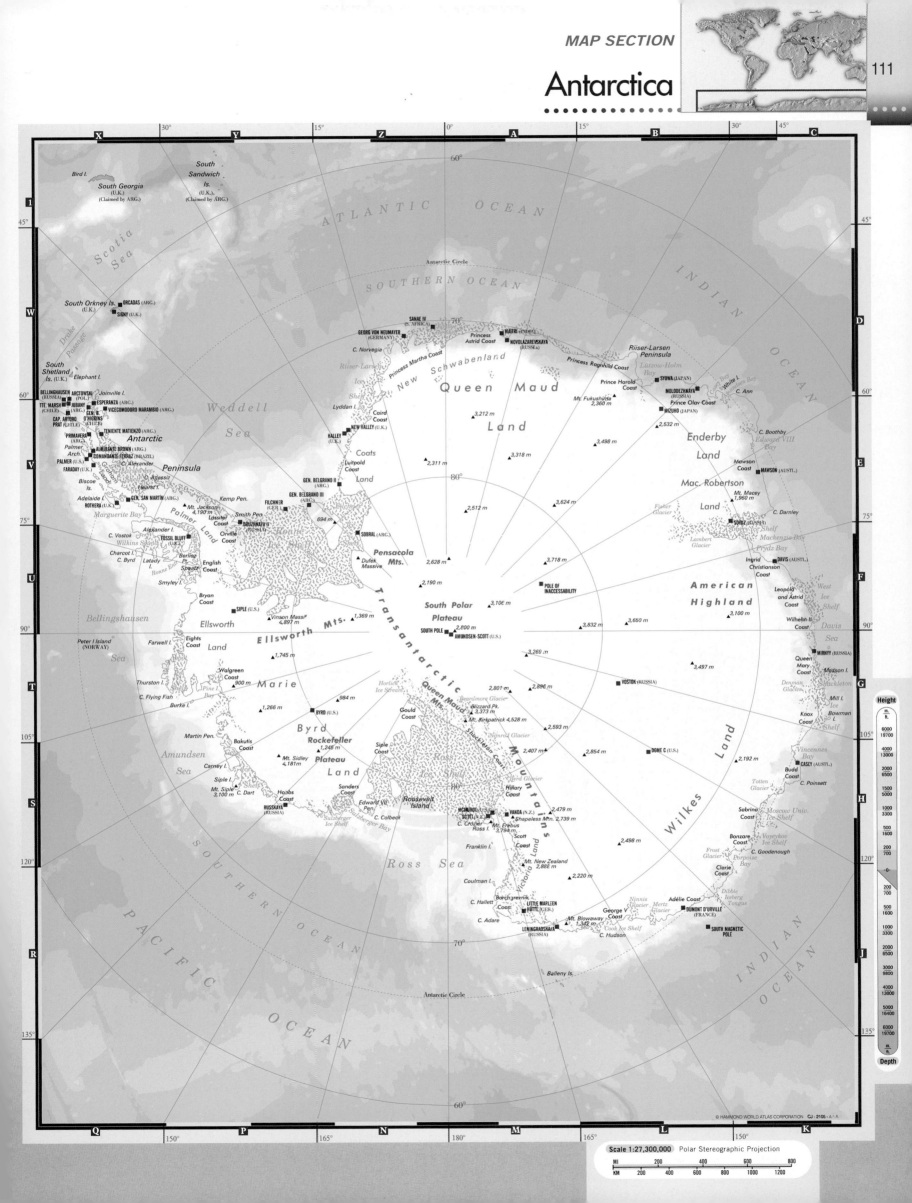

South America - Geographical Comparisons

TOPOGRAPHY

SQ. MI.	SQ. KM.	SQ. MI.	SQ. KM.	SQ. MI.	SQ. KM.
UNDER 656	UNDER 200	1640-3281	500-1000	6562-16404	2000-5000
656-1640	200-500	3281-6562	1000-2000	OVER 16404	OVER 5000

POPULATION DISTRIBUTION

● CITIES WITH OVER 1,000,000 INHABITANTS (INCLUDING SUBURBS)

DENSITY PER

SQ. MI.	SQ. KM.	SQ. MI.	SQ. KM.	SQ. MI.	SQ. KM.
OVER 260	OVER 100	130 TO 260	50 TO 100	3 TO 25	1 TO 10
		25 TO 130	10 TO 50	UNDER 3	UNDER 1

LAND USE

CEREALS, LIVESTOCK	DIVERSIFIED TROPICAL CROPS
LIVESTOCK & MIXED FARMING	LIVESTOCK GRAZING & RANCHING
TRUCK FARMING, SPECIAL CROPS	
FORESTS	NONPRODUCTIVE

MINERAL RESOURCES

ENERGY & FUELS
- ◆ COAL
- ▲ NATURAL GAS
- ● PETROLEUM
- ■ URANIUM

IRON & FERROALLOYS
- 1 CHROMIUM
- 2 IRON ORE
- 3 MANGANESE
- 4 MOLYBDENUM
- 5 NICKEL
- 6 TUNGSTEN

OTHER MAJOR RESOURCES
- 1 ANTIMONY
- 2 ASBESTOS
- 3 BAUXITE
- 4 COPPER
- 5 DIAMONDS
- 6 GOLD
- 7 IODINE
- 8 LEAD
- 9 MICA
- 10 NITRATES
- 11 PHOSPHATES
- 12 SILVER
- 13 TIN
- 14 TITANIUM
- 15 ZINC

South America

ATLANTIC

OCEAN

ATLANTIC

OCEAN

SURINAME

FRENCH GUIANA

Tumuc-Humac Mts.

St. Peter and St. Paul Rocks (BRAZIL)

Fernando de Noronha (BRAZIL)

Equator

Macapá

Belém

Santarém

B R Z I L

Planalto do Mato Grosso

Planalto Central

Brasília

Goiânia

Campo Grande

Belo Horizonte

Rio de Janeiro

São Paulo

Teresina

Fortaleza

Natal

Recife

Maceió

Salvador

Vitória da Conquista

Ilhéus

Tropic of Capricorn

Ilha da Trindade (BRAZIL)

Ilhas Martin Vaz (BRAZIL)

© HAMMOND WORLD ATLAS CORPORATION CJ 2107 - A A

Scale 1:14,800,000 Lambert Conformal Conic Projection

MI 100 200 300 400
KM 100 200 300 400 500 600

Southeastern Brazil

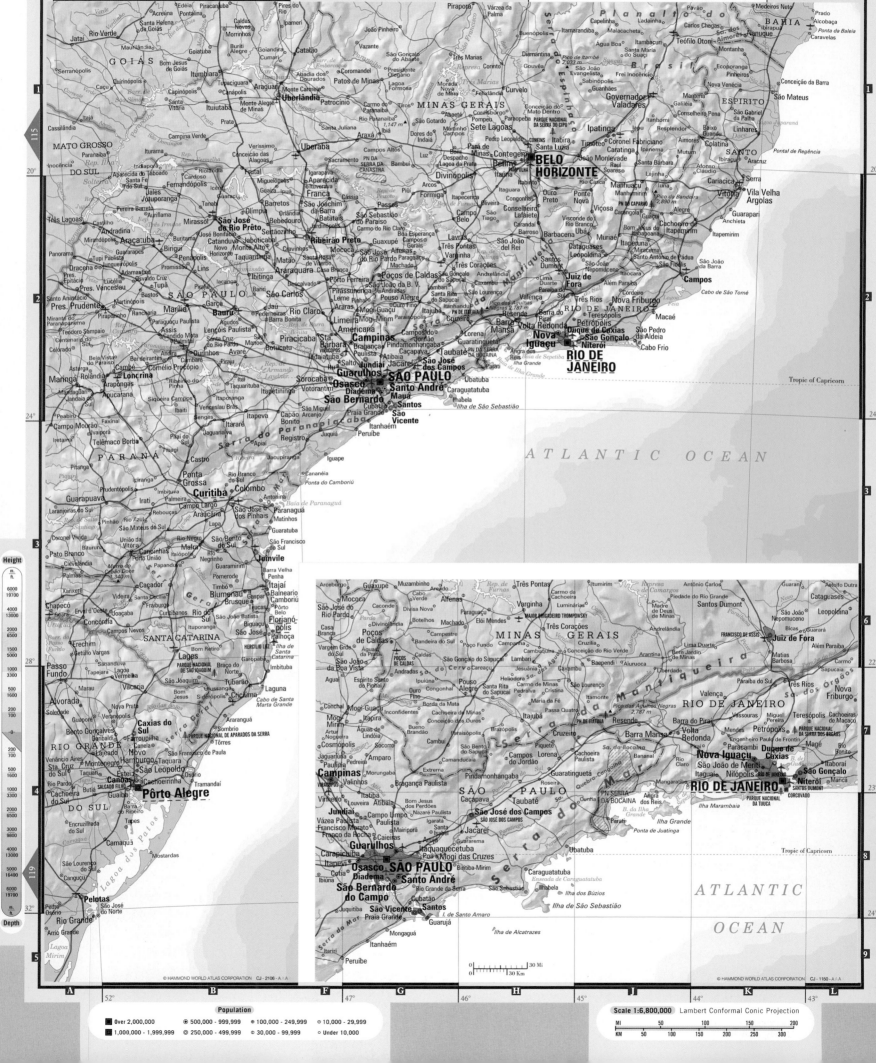

Population

- ■ Over 2,000,000
- ⊚ 500,000 - 999,999
- ⦿ 100,000 - 249,999
- ⊙ 10,000 - 29,999
- ■ 1,000,000 - 1,999,999
- ⊚ 250,000 - 499,999
- ● 30,000 - 99,999
- ○ Under 10,000

Scale 1:6,800,000 Lambert Conformal Conic Projection

MI   50   100   150   200

KM   50   100   150   200   250   300

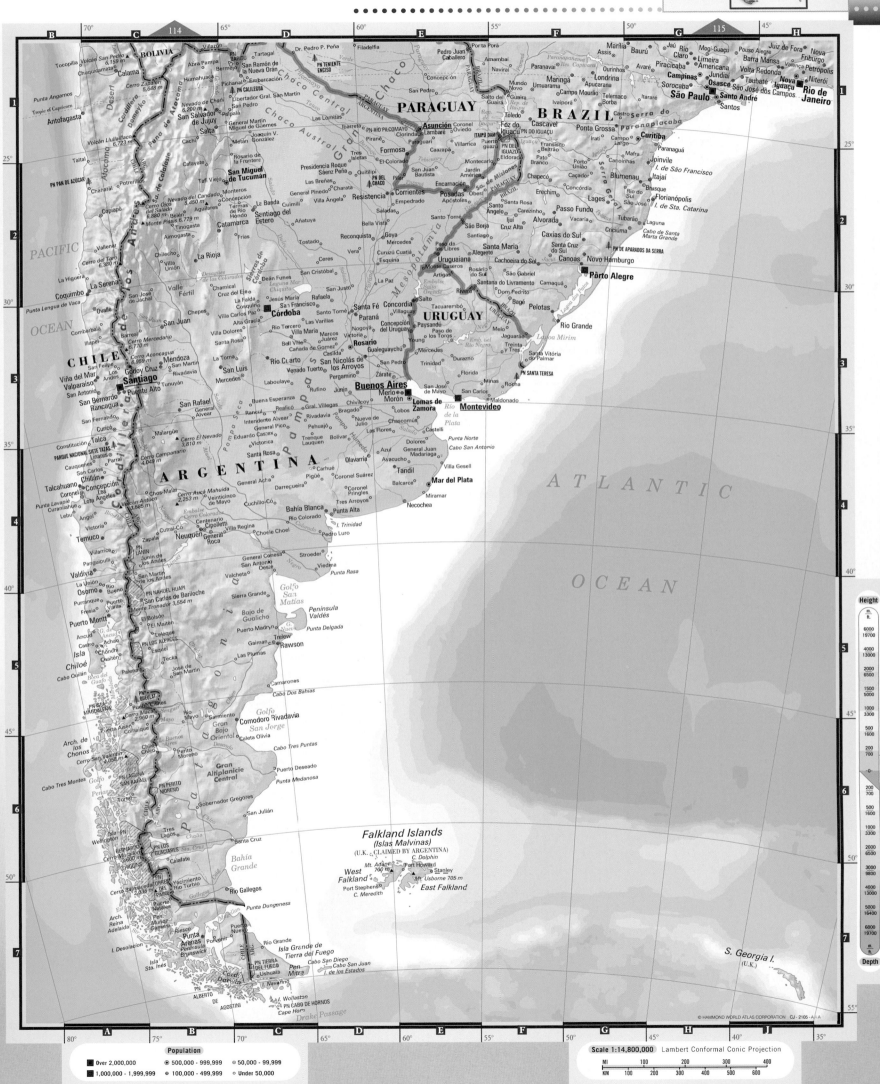

Falkland Islands
(Islas Malvinas)
(U.K., CLAIMED BY ARGENTINA)

West Falkland   East Falkland

A T L A N T I C

O C E A N

PACIFIC

OCEAN

BOLIVIA

PARAGUAY

BRAZIL

CHILE

ARGENTINA

URUGUAY

Buenos Aires

Santiago

Montevideo

São Paulo

Rio de Janeiro

Asunción

Curitiba

Pôrto Alegre

Córdoba

Rosario

Mar del Plata

S. Georgia I.
(U.K.)

© HAMMOND WORLD ATLAS CORPORATION   CJ - 2106 · A A A

Population	
■ Over 2,000,000	● 500,000 - 999,999
■ 1,000,000 - 1,999,999	● 100,000 - 499,999
● 50,000 - 99,999	○ Under 50,000

Height

Depth

Scale 1:14,800,000   Lambert Conformal Conic Projection

MI   100   200   300   400
KM   100   200   300   400   500   600

Southern Chile and Argentina

Scale 1:6,800,000 Lambert Conformal Conic Projection

North America - Geographical Comparisons

TOPOGRAPHY

SQ. MI.	SQ. KM.	SQ. MI.	SQ. KM.	SQ. MI.	SQ. KM.
UNDER 656	UNDER 200	1640-3281	500-1000	6562-16404	2000-5000
656-1640	200-500	3281-6562	1000-2000	OVER 16404	OVER 5000

● CITIES WITH OVER 2,000,000
INHABITANTS (INCLUDING SUBURBS)

POPULATION DISTRIBUTION

DENSITY PER		SQ. MI.	SQ. KM.	SQ. MI.	SQ. KM.
SQ. MI.	SQ. KM.	130 TO 260	50 TO 100	3 TO 25	1 TO 10
OVER 260	OVER 100	25 TO 130	10 TO 50	UNDER 3	UNDER 1

LAND USE

	CEREALS, LIVESTOCK		COTTON & SPECIAL CROPS		DAIRY
	LIVESTOCK RANCHING & LIMITED AGRICULTURE		DIVERSIFIED TROPICAL CROPS		FORESTS
	FRUIT, TRUCK & MIXED FARMING		GENERAL FARMING		UNPRODUCTIVE

MINERAL RESOURCES

ENERGY & FUELS	IRON & FERROALLOYS	OTHER MAJOR RESOURCES		
◆ COAL	1 COBALT	1 ANTIMONY	7 GOLD	13 PLATINUM
▲ NATURAL GAS	2 IRON ORE	2 ASBESTOS	8 GRAPHITE	14 POTASH
● PETROLEUM	3 MANGANESE	3 BAUXITE	9 LEAD	15 SILVER
■ URANIUM	4 MOLYBDENUM	4 BORAX	10 MERCURY	16 SULFUR
	5 NICKEL	5 COPPER	11 MICA	17 TITANIUM
	6 TUNGSTEN	6 FLUORSPAR	12 PHOSPHATES	18 ZINC
	7 VANADIUM			

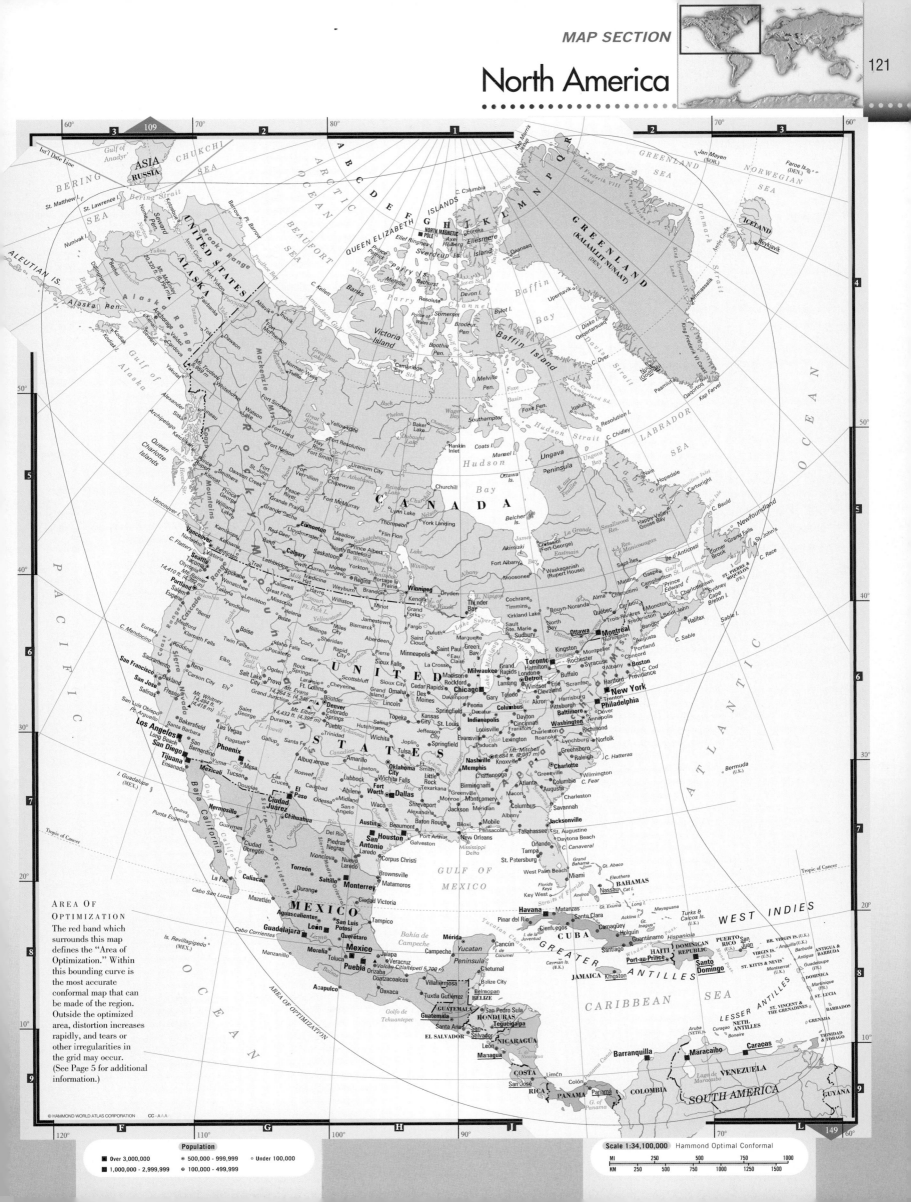

AREA OF OPTIMIZATION

The red band which surrounds this map defines the "Area of Optimization." Within this bounding curve is the most accurate conformal map that can be made of the region. Outside the optimized area, distortion increases rapidly, and tears or other irregularities in the grid may occur. (See Page 5 for additional information.)

© HAMMOND WORLD ATLAS CORPORATION   CC - A A A

Population

■ Over 3,000,000	⊛ 500,000 - 999,999	○ Under 100,000
■ 1,000,000 - 2,999,999	⊛ 100,000 - 499,999	

Scale 1:34,100,000 Hammond Optimal Conformal

MI   250   500   750   1000
KM 250 500 750 1000 1250 1500

Middle America and Caribbean

ATLANTIC OCEAN

PACIFIC OCEAN

CARIBBEAN SEA

Scale 1:10,200,000 Lambert Conformal Conic Projection

Map continued at right

Map continued at left

© HAMMOND W.A.C. CJ-156-AAA

© HAMMOND WORLD ATLAS CORPORATION

Scale 1:13,600,000   Lambert Conformal Conic Projection

Scale 1:13,600,000 Lambert Conformal Conic Projection

MI 100 200 300 400

KM 100 200 300 400 500 600

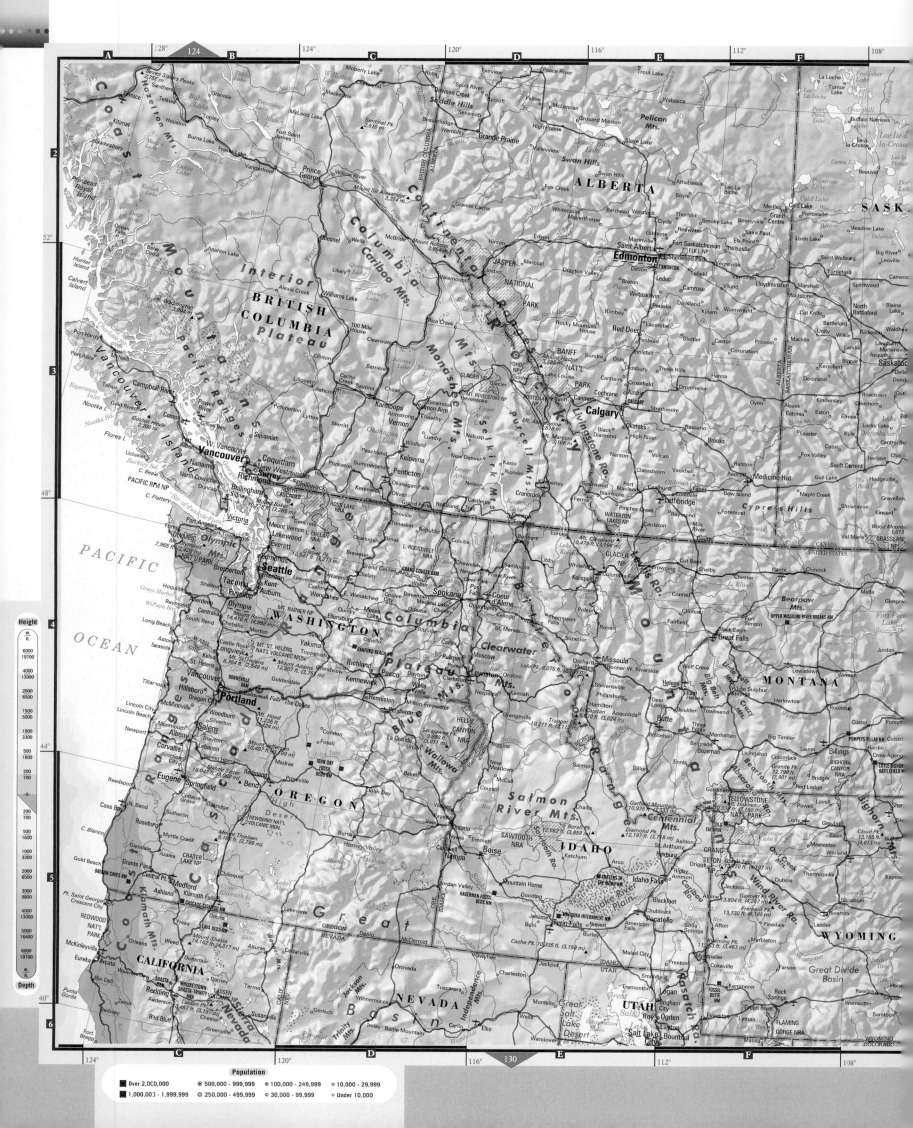

Population

■ Over 2,000,000 ● 500,000 - 999,999 ● 100,000 - 249,999 ● 10,000 - 29,999
■ 1,000,000 - 1,999,999 ● 250,000 - 499,999 ● 30,000 - 99,999 ○ Under 10,000

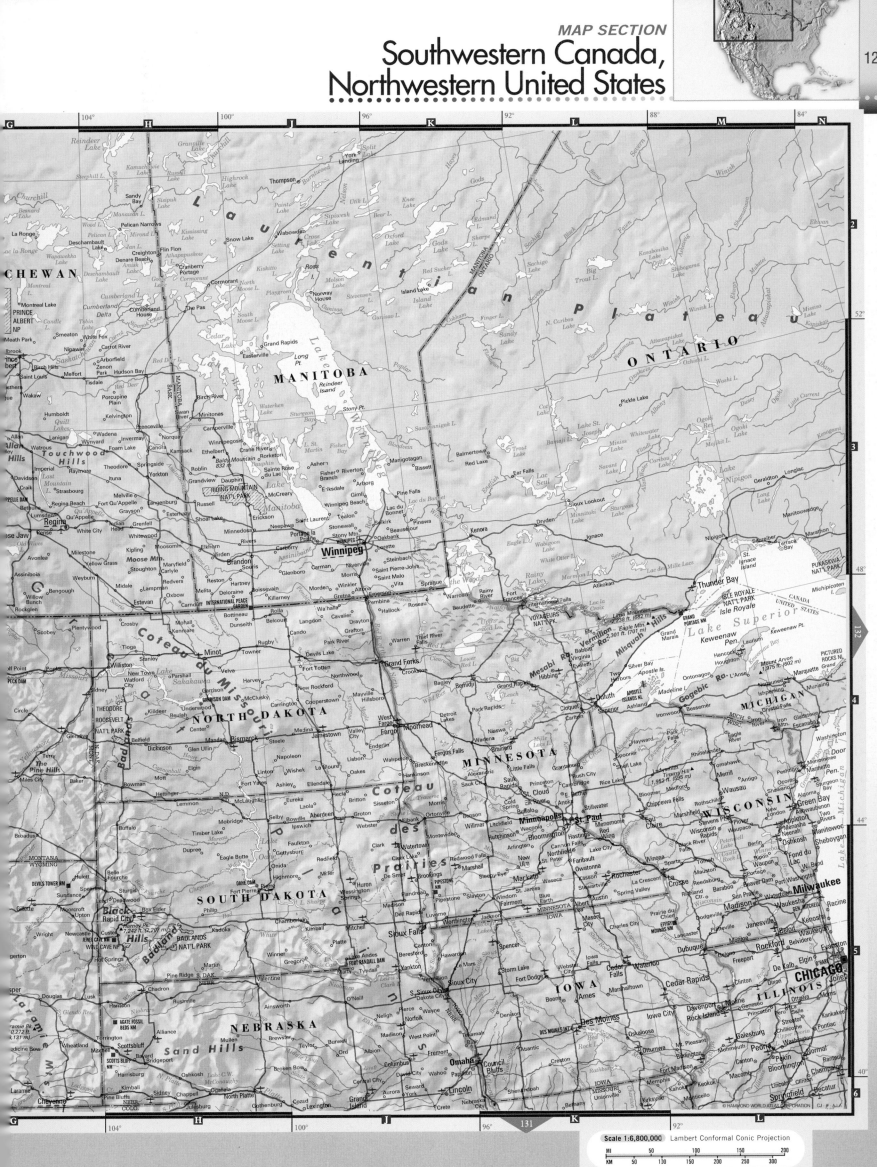

Scale 1:6,800,000   Lambert Conformal Conic Projection

MI   50   100   150   200

KM   50   130   150   250   300

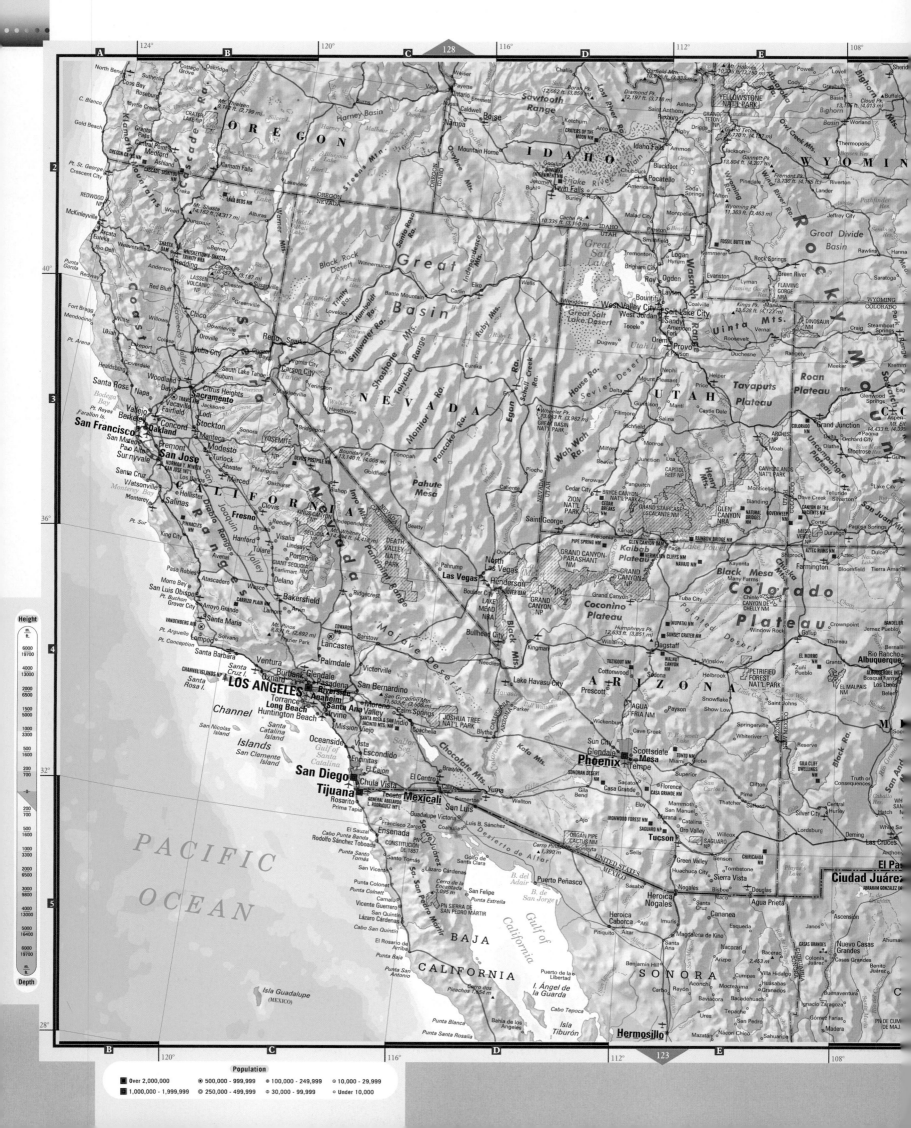

Population

■ Over 2,000,000
■ 1,000,000 - 1,999,999
● 500,000 - 999,999
● 250,000 - 499,999
● 100,000 - 249,999
◉ 30,000 - 99,999
◎ 10,000 - 29,999
○ Under 10,000

Southwestern United States

Scale 1:6,800,000   Lambert Conformal Conic Projection

MI | 50 | 100 | 150 | 200

KM 50 | 100 | 150 | 200 | 250 | 300

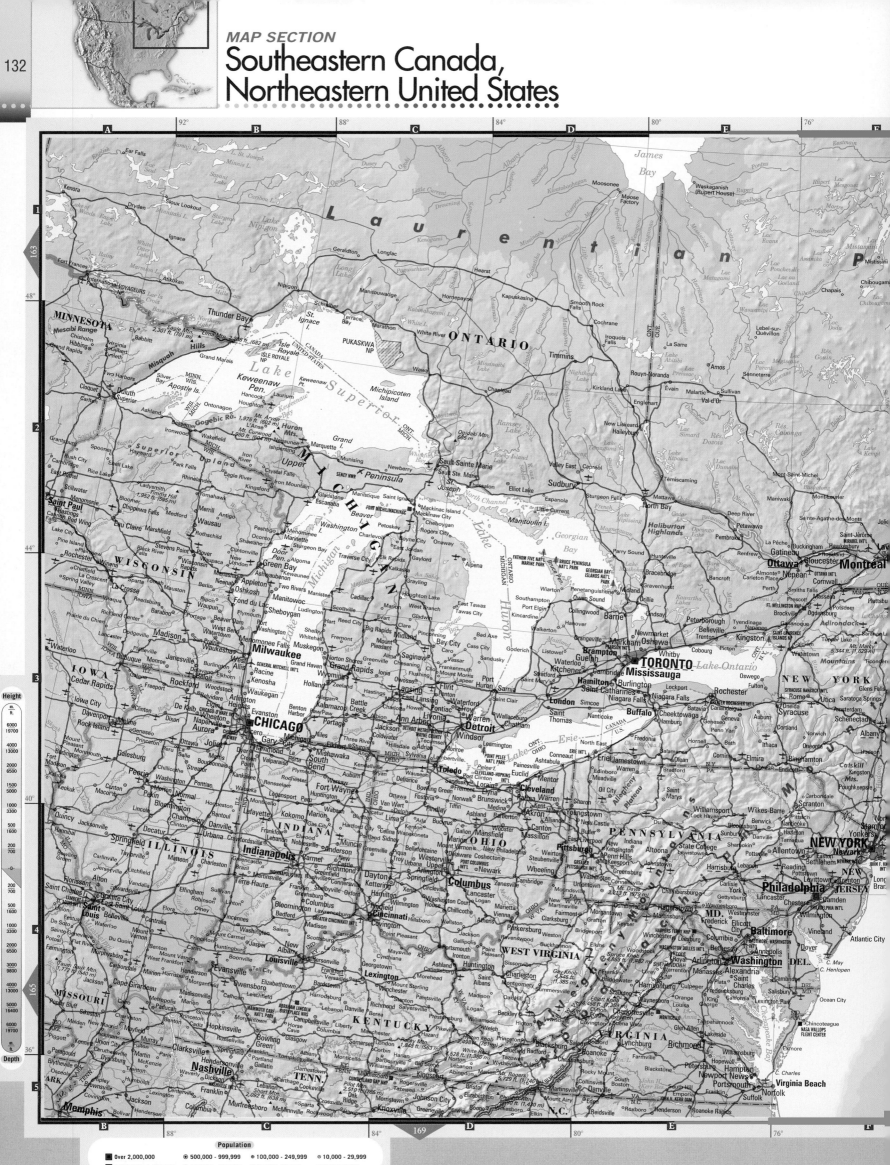

Population
- ■ Over 2,000,000
- ◉ 500,000 - 999,999
- ● 100,000 - 249,999
- ○ 10,000 - 29,999
- ■ 1,000,000 - 1,999,999
- ◉ 250,000 - 499,999
- ● 30,000 - 99,999
- ○ Under 10,000

72° 159 G 68° H 64° J 60° K 52°

QUÉBEC

Gulf of
St. Lawrence

Île d'Anticosti

NEWFOUNDLAND
AND LABRADOR

Newfoundland

Gaspé Peninsula

NEW
BRUNSWICK

PRINCE
EDWARD
ISLAND

CAPE BRETON
HIGHLANDS NP

Cabot Strait

Cape Breton

ST. PIERRE & MIQUELON
(FRANCE)

NOVA
SCOTIA

MAINE

ATLANTIC

OCEAN

Sable I.
(CAN.)

NEW
HAMPSHIRE

Gulf
of
Maine

Boston

C. Cod
CAPE COD
NAT'L
SEASHORE

MASS.

Long Island

Nantucket I.
Martha's
Vineyard
Block
Island

PEEL

King City

YORK

Greenwood
Brougham
Green River

DURHAM

Bowmanville
Newcastle

Oshawa

Richmond Hill
Markham
Pickering

Whitby

Ajax

ONTARIO

SCARBOROUGH

NORTH YORK

Brampton

PEARSON

YORK
EAST
YORK

TORONTO

Lake

TORONTO

Mississauga

CANADA
UNITED STATES

Ontario

HALTON

Oakville

Burlington

ROYAL BOTANICAL
GARDEN

Hamilton

HAMILTON-
WENTWORTH

NIAGARA

OLD FORT
NIAGARA

NEW
YORK

Saint
Catharines

Niagara
Falls

NIAGARA

ERIE

Buffalo

Lake Erie

West Seneca

MONTCALM

LES PAYS-
D'EN-HAUT

LA RIVIÈRE-
DU-NORD

St-Jérôme

L'ASSOMPTION

L'Assomption

LES MOULINS

LAJEMMERAIS

Terrebonne

Repentigny

MIRABEL

BLAINVILLE

LAVAL

Laval

VILLE
DE
MONTRÉAL

Longueuil

Montréal

MONTRÉAL-TRUDEAU

LA VALLÉE
DU
RICHELIEU

LES JARDINS-DE-
NAPIERVILLE

BEAUHARNOIS-
SALABERRY

LE HAUT-
RICHELIEU

72° G M 74° N 73° 30' P Q 79° 30' R S 79°

Scale 1:6,800,000 Lambert Conformal Conic Projection

MI   50   100   150   200
KM   50   100   150   200   250   300

© HAMMOND WORLD ATLAS CORPORATION CJ-2111-AAA

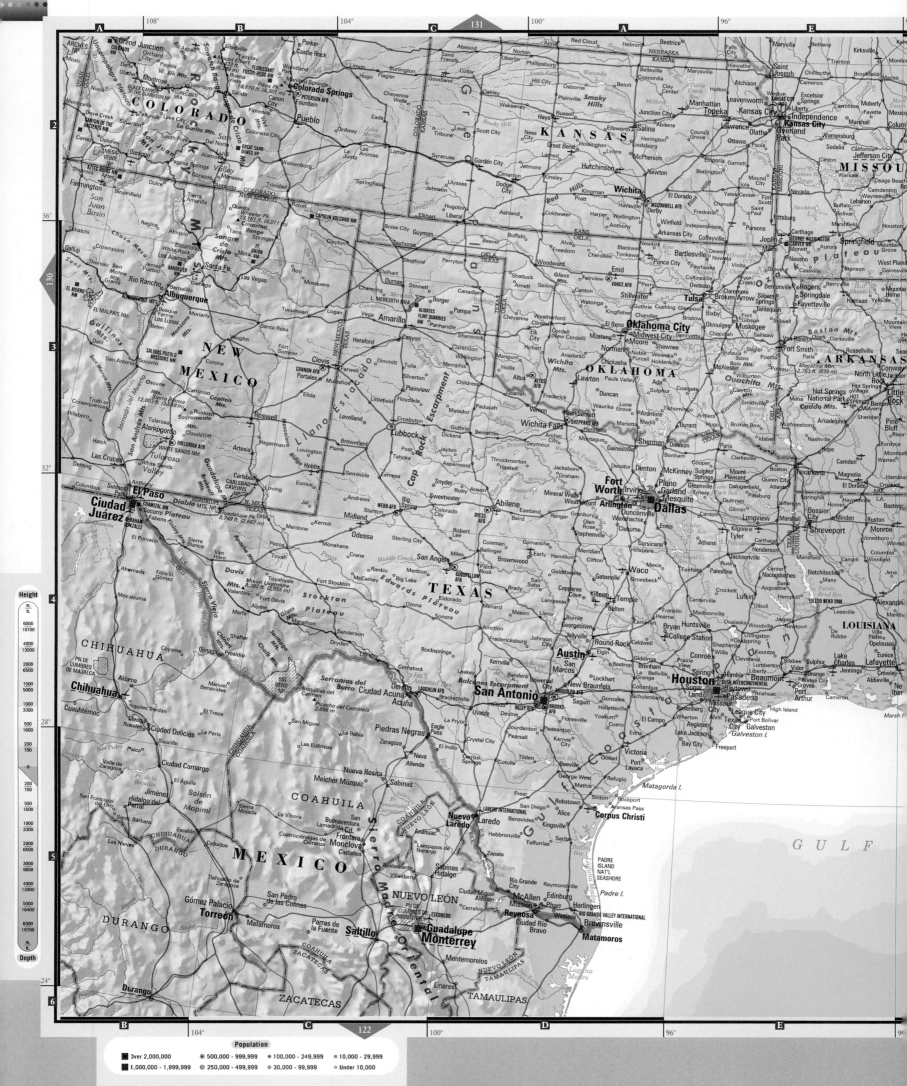

Population

■ Over 2,000,000	● 500,000 - 999,999	● 100,000 - 249,999	○ 10,000 - 29,999
■ 1,000,000 - 1,999,999	● 250,000 - 499,999	○ 30,000 - 99,999	○ Under 10,000

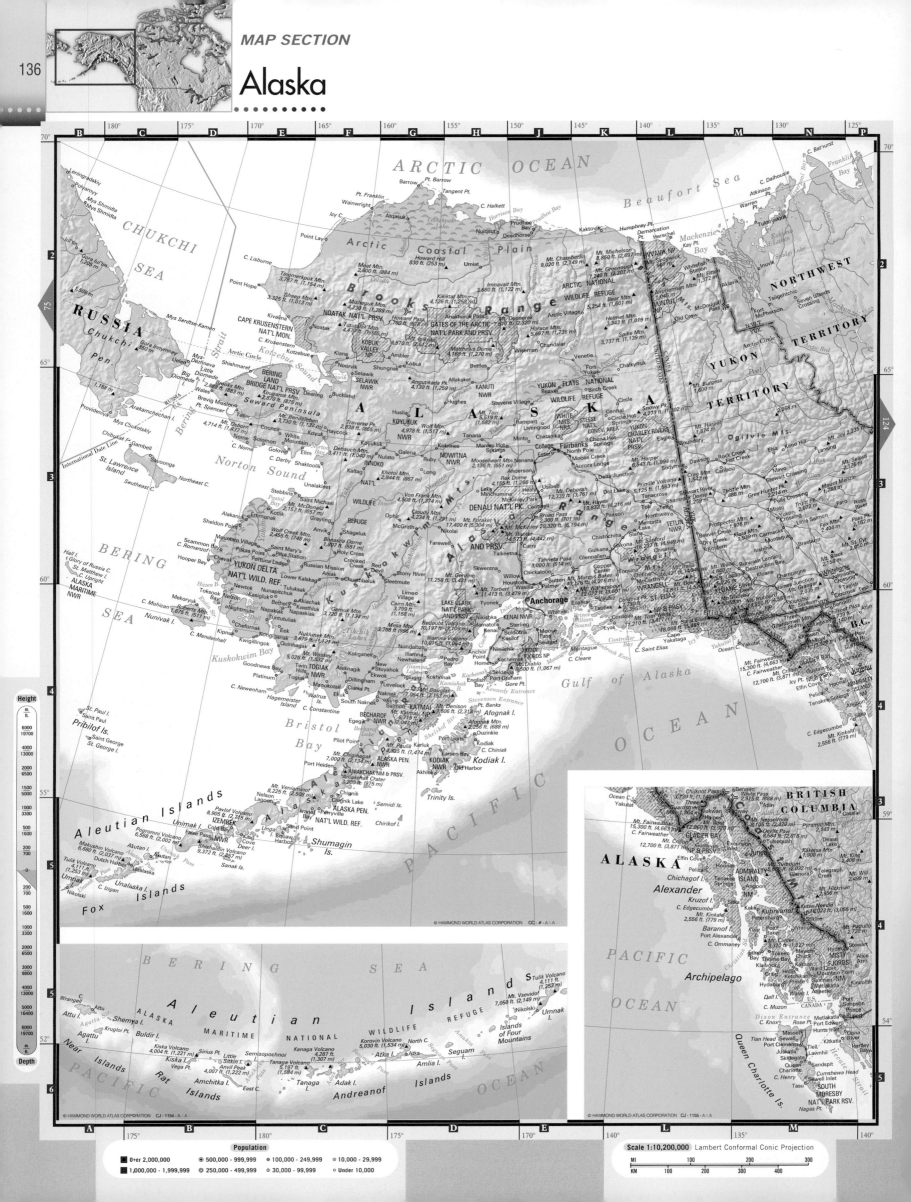

Population

■ Over 2,000,000
■ 1,000,000 - 1,999,999
● 500,000 - 999,999
● 250,000 - 499,999
● 100,000 - 249,999
● 30,000 - 99,999
○ 10,000 - 29,999
○ Under 10,000

Scale 1:10,200,000 Lambert Conformal Conic Projection

Height

m. ft.
6000 19700
4000 13000
2000 6500
1500 5000
500 1600
200 700
0
200 700
500 1600
1000 3300
2000 6500
3000 9800
4000 13000
5000 16400
6000 19700

Depth

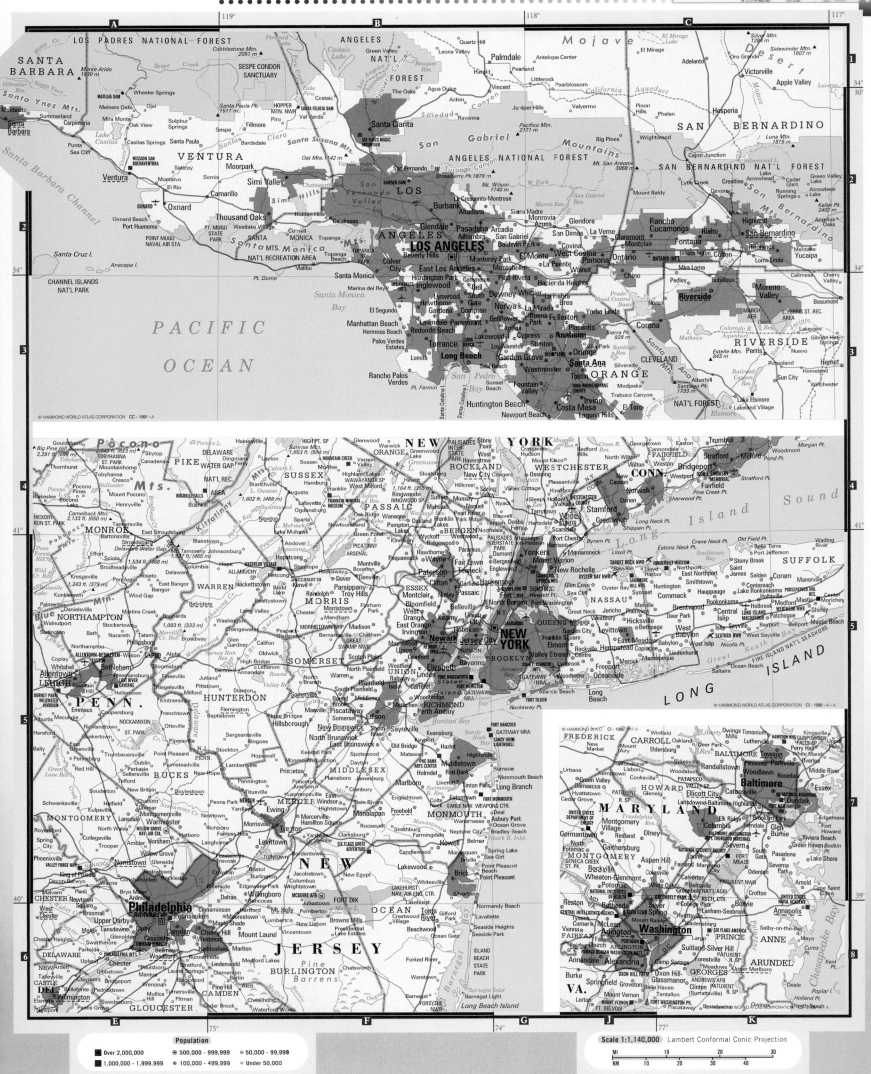

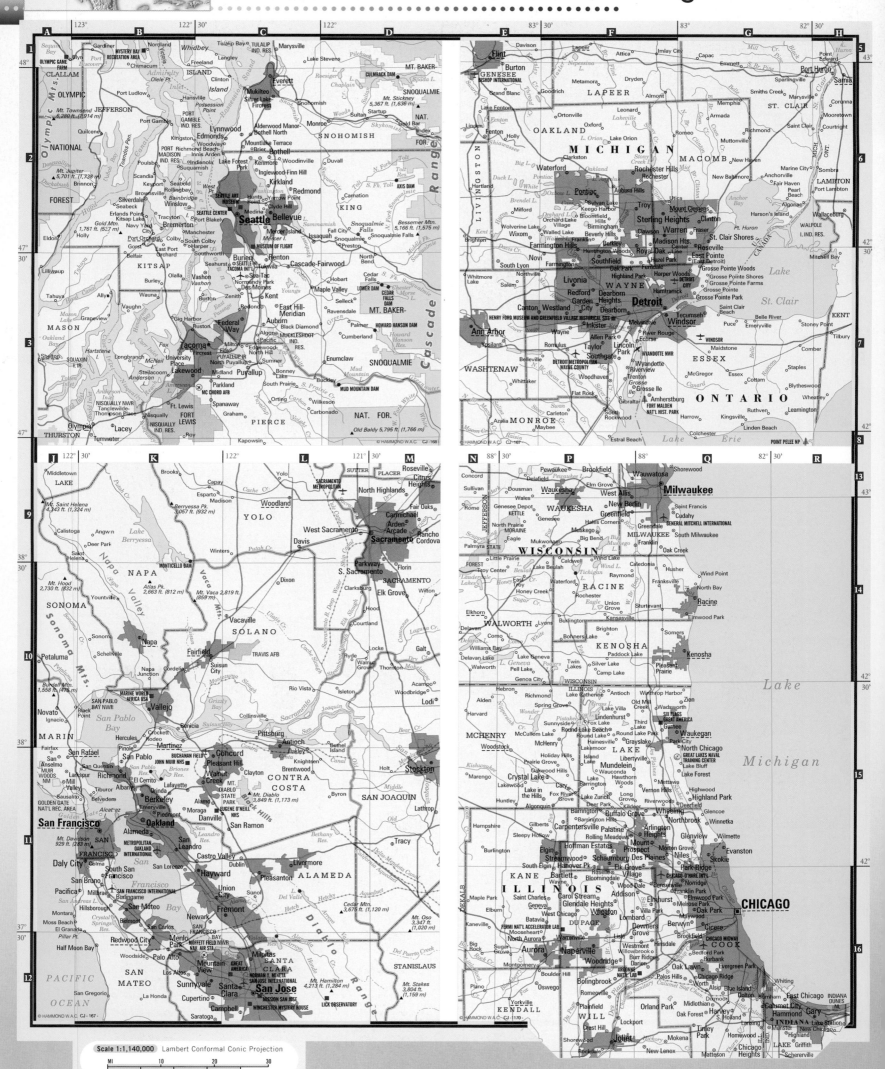

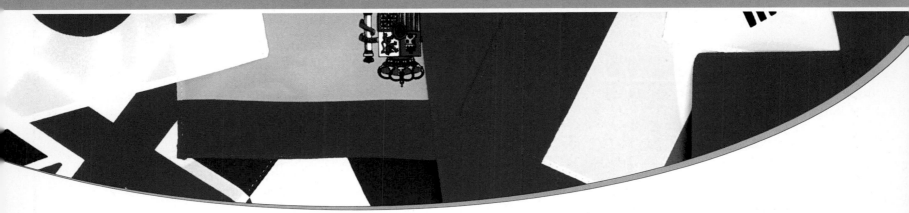

World Flags and Reference Guide

Countries of the World

Afghanistan
Page/Location: 79/H2
Area: 250,775 sq. mi.
   649,507 sq. km.
Population: 29,547,078
Capital: Kabul
Largest City: Kabul
Highest Point: Noshaq
Monetary Unit: Afghani

Albania
Page/Location: 67/F2
Area: 11,110 sq. mi.
   28,749 sq. km.
Population: 3,544,808
Capital: Tiranë
Largest City: Tiranë
Highest Point: Korab
Monetary Unit: lek

Algeria
Page/Location: 102/F2
Area: 919,519 sq. mi.
   2,381,740 sq. km.
Population: 33,357,089
Capital: Algiers
Largest City: Algiers
Highest Point: Tahat
Monetary Unit: Algerian dinar

Andorra
Page/Location: 65/F1
Area: 174 sq. mi.
   450 sq. km.
Population: 69,865
Capital: Andorra la Vella
Largest City: Andorra la Vella
Highest Point: Coma Pedrosa
Monetary Unit: euro

Angola
Page/Location: 110/C3
Area: 481,351 sq. mi.
   1,246,700 sq. km.
Population: 10,978,552
Capital: Luanda
Largest City: Luanda
Highest Point: Morro de Môco
Monetary Unit: kwanza

Antigua and Barbuda
Page/Location: 123/J4
Area: 171 sq. mi.
   443 sq. km.
Population: 68,320
Capital: St. John's
Largest City: St. John's
Highest Point: Boggy Peak
Monetary Unit: East Caribbean dollar

Argentina
Page/Location: 117/C4
Area: 1,068,296 sq. mi.
   2,766,890 sq. km.
Population: 39,144,753
Capital: Buenos Aires
Largest City: Buenos Aires
Highest Point: Cerro Aconcagua
Monetary Unit: peso argentino

Armenia
Page/Location: 73/H5
Area: 11,506 sq. mi.
   29,800 sq. km.
Population: 3,325,307
Capital: Yerevan
Largest City: Yerevan
Highest Point: Aragats
Monetary Unit: dram

Australia
Page/Location: 95
Area: 2,966,136 sq. mi.
   7,682,300 sq. km.
Population: 19,913,144
Capital: Canberra
Largest City: Sydney
Highest Point: Mt. Kosciusko
Monetary Unit: Australian dollar

Austria*
Page/Location: 63/L3
Area: 32,375 sq. mi.
   83,851 sq. km.
Population: 8,174,762
Capital: Vienna
Largest City: Vienna
Highest Point: Grossglockner
Monetary Unit: euro

Azerbaijan
Page/Location: 73/H4
Area: 33,436 sq. mi.
   86,600 sq. km.
Population: 7,868,385
Capital: Baku
Largest City: Baku
Highest Point: Bazardüzü
Monetary Unit: manat

Bahamas,The
Page/Location: 123/F2
Area: 5,382 sq. mi.
   13,939 sq. km.
Population: 299,697
Capital: Nassau
Largest City: Nassau
Highest Point: Mt. Alvernia
Monetary Unit: Bahamian dollar

Bahrain
Page/Location: 78/F3
Area: 240 sq. mi.
   622 sq. km.
Population: 677,886
Capital: Manama
Largest City: Manama
Highest Point: Jabal Dukhān
Monetary Unit: Bahraini dinar

Bangladesh
Page/Location: 90/E3
Area: 55,598 sq. mi.
   144,000 sq. km.
Population: 141,340,476
Capital: Dhākā
Largest City: Dhākā
Highest Point: Keokradong
Monetary Unit: taka

Barbados
Page/Location: 123/J5
Area: 186 sq. mi.
   430 sq. km.
Population: 278,289
Capital: Bridgetown
Largest City: Bridgetown
Highest Point: Mt. Hillaby
Monetary Unit: Barbadian dollar

Belarus
Page/Location: 47/G3
Area: 80,154 sq. mi.
   207,600 sq. km.
Population: 10,310,520
Capital: Minsk
Largest City: Minsk
Highest Point: Dzyarzhynskaya
Monetary Unit: Belarusian ruble

Belgium*
Page/Location: 54/C3
Area: 11,781 sq. mi.
   30,513 sq. km.
Population: 10,348,276
Capital: Brussels
Largest City: Brussels
Highest Point: Botrange
Monetary Unit: euro

Belize
Page/Location: 122/D4
Area: 8,867 sq. mi.
   22,966 sq. km.
Population: 272,945
Capital: Belmopan
Largest City: Belize City
Highest Point: Victoria Peak
Monetary Unit: Belize dollar

Benin
Page/Location: 105/F4
Area: 43,483 sq. mi.
   112,620 sq. km.
Population: 7,250,033
Capital: Porto-Novo
Largest City: Cotonou
Highest Point: Sokbaro
Monetary Unit: CFA franc

Bhutan
Page/Location: 90/E2
Area: 18,147 sq. mi.
   47,000 sq. km.
Population: 2,185,569
Capital: Thimphu
Largest City: Thimphu
Highest Point: Kula Kangri
Monetary Unit: ngultrum

Bolivia
Page/Location: 114/F7
Area: 424,163 sq. mi.
   1,098,582 sq. km.
Population: 8,724,156
Capital: La Paz; Sucre
Largest City: La Paz
Highest Point: Nevado Sajama
Monetary Unit: boliviano

Bosnia and Herzegovina
Page/Location: 68/C3
Area: 19,940 sq. mi.
   51,645 sq. km.
Population: 4,007,608
Capital: Sarajevo
Largest City: Sarajevo
Highest Point: Maglič
Monetary Unit: marka

Botswana
Page/Location: 110/D5
Area: 231,803 sq. mi.
   600,370 sq. km.
Population: 1,561,973
Capital: Gaborone
Largest City: Gaborone
Highest Point: Tsodilo Hills
Monetary Unit: pula

Brazil
Page/Location: 113/D3
Area: 3,286,470 sq. mi.
   8,511,965 sq. km.
Population: 184,101,109
Capital: Brasilia
Largest City: São Paulo
Highest Point: Pico da Neblina
Monetary Unit: real

Brunei
Page/Location: 92/D2
Area: 2,226 sq. mi.
   5,765 sq. km.
Population: 365,251
Capital: Bandar Seri Begawan
Largest City: Bandar Seri Begawan
Highest Point: Bukit Pagon
Monetary Unit: Brunei dollar

Bulgaria*
Page/Location: 69/G4
Area: 42,823 sq. mi.
   110,912 sq. km
Population: 7,517,973
Capital: Sofia
Largest City: Sofia
Highest Point: Musala
Monetary Unit: lev

Burkina Faso
Page/Location: 105/E3
Area: 105,869 sq. mi.
   274,200 sq. km.
Population: 13,574,820
Capital: Ouagadougou
Largest City: Ouagadougou
Highest Point: Tena kourou
Monetary Unit: CFA franc

Burundi
Page/Location: 107/A3
Area: 10,747 sq. mi.
   27,835 sq. km.
Population: 6,231,221
Capital: Bujumbura
Largest City: Bujumbura
Highest Point: Heha
Monetary Unit: Burundi franc

Cambodia
Page/Location: 89/D3
Area: 69,898 sq. mi.
   181,036 sq. km.
Population: 13,363,421
Capital: Phnom Penh
Largest City: Phnom Penh
Highest Point: Phnum Aoral
Monetary Unit: riel

Cameroon
Page/Location: 102/H7
Area: 183,568 sq. mi.
   475,441 sq. km.
Population: 16,063,678
Capital: Yaoundé
Largest City: Douala
Highest Point: Mt. Fako
Monetary Unit: CFA franc

*Member of the European Union

Canada
Page/Location: 124
Area: 3,851,787 sq. mi.
9,976,139 sq. km.
Population: 32,507,874
Capital: Ottawa
Largest City: Toronto
Highest Point: Mt. Trudeau
Monetary Unit: Canadian dollar

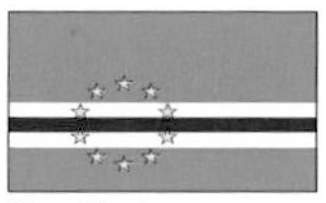

Cape Verde
Page/Location: 44/H5
Area: 1,557 sq. mi.
4,033 sq. km.
Population: 415,294
Capital: Praia
Largest City: Praia
Highest Point: Mt. Fogo
Monetary Unit: Cape Verde escudo

Central African Republic
Page/Location: 103/J6
Area: 240,533 sq. mi.
622,980 sq. km.
Population: 3,742,482
Capital: Bangui
Largest City: Bangui
Highest Point: Mt. Ngaoui
Monetary Unit: CFA franc

Chad
Page/Location: 103/J4
Area: 495,752 sq. mi.
1,283,998 sq. km.
Population: 9,538,544
Capital: N'Djamena
Largest City: N'Djamena
Highest Point: Emi Koussi
Monetary Unit: CFA franc

Chile
Page/Location: 113/B6
Area: 292,257 sq. mi.
756,946 sq. km.
Population: 15,827,180
Capital: Santiago
Largest City: Santiago
Highest Point: Nevado Ojos del Salado
Monetary Unit: Chilean peso

China
Page/Location: 77/J6
Area: 3,705,386 sq. mi.
9,596,960 sq. km.
Population: 1,294,629,555
Capital: Beijing
Largest City: Shanghai
Highest Point: Mt. Everest
Monetary Unit: yuan

Colombia
Page/Location: 114/D3
Area: 439,513 sq. mi.
1,138,339 sq. km.
Population: 42,310,775
Capital: Bogotá
Largest City: Bogotá
Highest Point: Pico Cristóbal Colón
Monetary Unit: Colombian peso

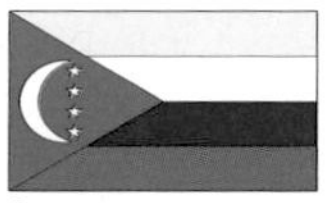

Comoros
Page/Location: 109/G5
Area: 838 sq. mi.
2,170 sq. km.
Population: 651,901
Capital: Moroni
Largest City: Moroni
Highest Point: Karthala
Monetary Unit: Comorian franc

Congo, Dem. Rep. of the
Page/Location: 101/E5
Area: 905,563 sq. mi.
2,345,410 sq. km.
Population: 58,317,930
Capital: Kinshasa
Largest City: Kinshasa
Highest Point: Margherita Peak
Monetary Unit: Congolese franc

Congo, Rep. of the
Page/Location: 101/D4
Area: 132,046 sq. mi.
342,000 sq. km.
Population: 2,998,040
Capital: Brazzaville
Largest City: Brazzaville
Highest Point: Mt. Berongou
Monetary Unit: CFA franc

Costa Rica
Page/Location: 122/E5
Area: 19,730 sq. mi.
51,100 sq. km.
Population: 3,956,507
Capital: San José
Largest City: San José
Highest Point: Cerro Chirripó Grande
Monetary Unit: Costa Rican Colón

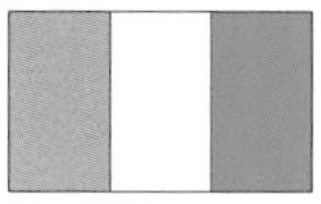

Côte d'Ivoire
Page/Location: 104/D5
Area: 124,504 sq. mi.
322,465 sq. km.
Population: 17,327,724
Capital: Yamoussoukro
Largest City: Abidjan
Highest Point: Mt. Nimba
Monetary Unit: CFA franc

Croatia
Page/Location: 68/B3
Area: 22,050 sq. mi.
57,110 sq. km.
Population 4,435,960
Capital: Zagreb
Largest City: Zagreb
Highest Point: Dinara
Monetary Unit: Croatian kuna

Cuba
Page/Location: 123/F3
Area: 42,803 sq. mi.
110,860 sq. km.
Population: 11,308,764
Capital: Havana
Largest City: Havana
Highest Point: Pico Turquino
Monetary Unit: Cuban peso

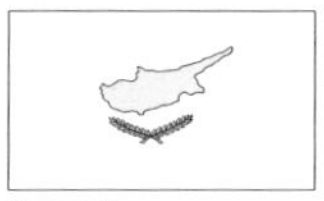

Cyprus*
Page/Location: 80/J4
Area: 3,571 sq. mi.
9,250 sq. km.
Population: 775,927
Capital: Nicosia
Largest City: Nicosia
Highest Point: Olympus
Monetary Unit: euro

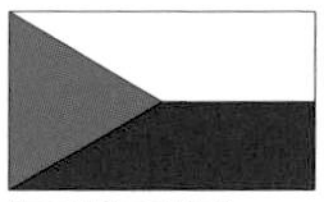

Czech Republic*
Page/Location: 55/H4
Area: 30,387 sq. mi.
78,703 sq. km.
Population: 10,246,178
Capital: Prague
Largest City: Prague
Highest Point: Sněžka
Monetary Unit: Czech koruna

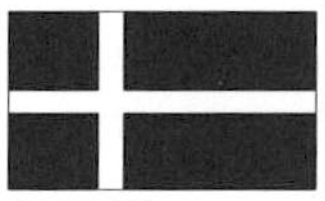

Denmark*
Page/Location: 48/C5
Area: 16,629 sq. mi.
43,069 sq. km.
Population: 5,413,392
Capital: Copenhagen
Largest City: Copenhagen
Highest Point: Yding Skovhøj
Monetary Unit: Danish krone

Djibouti
Page/Location: 103/P5
Area: 8,494 sq. mi.
22,000 sq. km.
Population: 466,900
Capital: Djibouti
Largest City: Djibouti
Highest Point: Moussa Ali
Monetary Unit: Djibouti franc

Dominica
Page/Location: 123/J4
Area: 290 sq. mi.
751 sq. km.
Population: 69,278
Capital: Roseau
Largest City Roseau
Highest Point: Morne Diablotins
Monetary Unit: East Caribbean dollar

Dominican Republic
Page/Location: 123/H4
Area: 18,815 sq. mi.
48,730 sq. km.
Population: 8,833,634
Capital: Santo Domingo
Largest City: Santo Domingo
Highest Point: Pico Duarte
Monetary Unit: Dominican peso

East Timor
Page/Location: 93/G5
Area: 5,743 sq. mi.
14,874 sq. km.
Population: 1,019,252
Capital: Dili
Largest City: Dili
Highest Point: Teta Mailau
Monetary Unit: U. S. dollar

Ecuador
Page/Location: 114/C4
Area: 109,483 sq. mi.
283,561 sq. km.
Population: 13,971,798
Capital: Quito
Largest City: Guayaquil
Highest Point: Chimborazo
Monetary Unit: U.S. dollar

Egypt
Page/Location: 106/B3
Area: 386,659 sq. mi.
1,001,447 sq. km.
Population: 76,117,421
Capital: Cairo
Largest City: Cairo
Highest Point: Mt. Catherine
Monetary Unit: Egyptian pound

El Salvador
Page/Location: 122/D5
Area: 8,124 sq. mi.
21,040 sq. km.
Population: 6,587,541
Capital: San Salvador
Largest City: San Salvador
Highest Point: El Pital
Monetary Unit: Salvadoran colón

Equatorial Guinea
Page/Location: 102/G7
Area: 10,831 sq. mi.
28,052 sq. km.
Population: 523,051
Capital: Malabo
Largest City: Malabo
Highest Point: Basile
Monetary Unit: CFA franc

Eritrea
Page/Location: 103/N5
Area: 46,842 sq. mi.
121,320 sq. km.
Population: 4,447,307
Capital: Asmara
Largest City: Asmara
Highest Point: Soira
Monetary Unit: nafka

Estonia*
Page/Location: 70/E4
Area: 17,413 sq. mi.
45,100 sq. km.
Population: 1,401,945
Capital: Tallinn
Largest City: Tallinn
Highest Point: Munamägi
Monetary Unit: kroon

Ethiopia
Page/Location: 103/N5
Area: 435,184 sq. mi.
1,127,127 sq. km.
Population: 67,851,281
Capital: Addis Ababa
Largest City: Addis Ababa
Highest Point: Ras Dejen
Monetary Unit: birr

Fiji
Page/Location: 98/G6
Area: 7,055 sq. mi.
18,272 sq. km.
Population: 880,874
Capital: Suva
Largest City: Suva
Highest Point: Tomaniivi
Monetary Unit: Fijian dollar

Finland*
Page/Location: 48/H2
Area: 130,128 sq. mi.
337,032 sq. km.
Population: 5,214,512
Capital: Helsinki
Largest City: Helsinki
Highest Point: Haltia
Monetary Unit: euro

France*
Page/Location: 62/D3
Area: 211,208 sq. mi.
547,030 sq. km.
Population: 60,424,213
Capital: Paris
Largest City: Paris
Highest Point: Mont Blanc
Monetary Unit: euro

Gabon
Page/Location: 102/H7
Area: 103.346 sq. mi.
267,666 sq. km.
Population: 1,355,246
Capital: Libreville
Largest City: Libreville
Highest Point: Mt. Iboundji
Monetary Unit: CFA franc

Gambia, The
Page/Location: 104/B3
Area: 4,363 sq. mi.
11,300 sq. km.
Population: 1,546,848
Capital: Banjul
Largest City: Banjul
Highest Point: 174 ft. (53 m)
Monetary Unit: dalasi

Georgia
Page/Location: 73/G4
Area: 26,911 sq. mi.
69,700 sq. km.
Population: 4,909,633
Capital: T'bilisi
Largest City: T'bilisi
Highest Point: Mt'a Shkhara
Monetary Unit: lari

Germany*
Page/Location: 54/E3
Area: 137,803 sq. mi.
356,910 sq. km.
Population: 82,424,609
Capital: Berlin
Largest City: Berlin
Highest Point: Zugspitze
Monetary Unit: euro

Ghana
Page/Location: 105/E4
Area: 92,099 sq. mi.
238,536 sq. km.
Population: 20,757,032
Capital: Accra
Largest City: Accra
Highest Point: Afadjato
Monetary Unit: cedi

*Member of the European Union

Greece*
Page/Location: 67/G3
Area: 50,944 sq. mi.
131,945 sq. km.
Population: 10,647,529
Capital: Athens
Largest City: Athens
Highest Point: Mt. Olympus
Monetary Unit: euro

Grenada
Page/Location: 123/J5
Area: 133 sq. mi.
344 sc. km.
Population: 39,357
Capital: St. George's
Largest City: St. George's
Highest Point: Mt. St. Catherine
Monetary Unit: East Caribbean dollar

Guatemala
Page/Location: 122/C4
Area: 42,042 sq. mi.
108,899 sq. km.
Population: 14,280,596
Capital: Guatemala
Largest City: Guatemala
Highest Point: Tajumulco
Monetary Unit: quetzal

Guinea
Page/Location: 104/C4
Area: 94,925 sq. mi.
245,856 sq. km.
Population: 9,246,462
Capital: Conakry
Largest City: Conakry
Highest Point: Mt. Nimba
Monetary Unit: Guinea franc

Guinea-Bissau
Page/Location: 104/B3
Area: 13,948 sq. mi.
36,125 sq. km.
Population: 1,388,363
Capital: Bissau
Largest City: Bissau
Highest Point: 984 ft. (300 m)
Monetary Unit: CFA franc

Guyana
Page/Location: 114/G3
Area: 83,000 sq. mi.
214,970 sq. km.
Population: 705,803
Capital: Georgetown
Largest City: Georgetown
Highest Point: Mt. Roraima
Monetary Unit: Guyana dollar

Haiti
Page/Location: 123/G4
Area: 10,694 sq. mi.
27,697 sq. km.
Population: 7,656,166
Capital: Port-au-Prince
Largest City: Port-au-Prince
Highest Point: Pic la Selle
Monetary Unit: gourde

Honduras
Page/Location: 122/D4
Area: 43,277 sq. mi.
112,087 sq. km.
Population: 6,823,568
Capital: Tegucigalpa
Largest City: Tegucigalpa
Highest Point: Cerro de las Minas
Monetary Unit: lempira

Hungary*
Page/Location: 68/D2
Area: 35,919 sq. mi.
93,030 sq. km.
Population: 10,032,375
Capital: Budapest
Largest City: Budapest
Highest Point: Kékes
Monetary Unit: forint

Iceland
Page/Location: 48/N7
Area: 39,768 sq. mi.
103,000 sq. km.
Population: 282,151
Capital: Reykjavik
Largest City: Reykjavik
Highest Point: Hvannadalshnukúr
Monetary Unit: króna

India
Page/Location: 77/G7
Area: 1,269,339 sq. mi.
3,287,588 sq. km.
Population: 1,065,070,607
Capital: New Delhi
Largest City: Mumbai
Highest Point: Kanchenjunga
Monetary Unit: Indian rupee

Indonesia
Page/Location: 93/E4
Area: 741,096 sq. mi.
1,919,440 sq. km.
Population: 238,452,952
Capital: Jakarta
Largest City: Jakarta
Highest Point: Puncak Jaya
Monetary Unit: rupiah

Iran
Page/Location: 78/F2
Area: 636,293 sq. mi.
1,648,000 sq. km.
Population: 69,018,924
Capital: Tehrān
Largest City: Tehrān
Highest Point: Qolleh-ye Damāvand
Monetary Unit: Iranian rial

Iraq
Page/Location: 78/D2
Area: 168,753 sq. mi.
437,072 sq. km.
Population: 25,374,691
Capital: Baghdad
Largest City: Baghdad
Highest Point: Haji Ibrahim
Monetary Unit: Iraqi dinar

Ireland*
Page/Location: 49/A4
Area: 27,136 sq. mi.
70,282 sq. km.
Population: 3,969,558
Capital: Dublin
Largest City: Dublin
Highest Point: Carrauntoohil
Monetary Unit: euro

Israel
Page/Location: 80/J5
Area: 8,019 sq. mi.
20,770 sq. km.
Population: 6,199,008
Capital: Jerusalem
Largest City: Jerusalem
Highest Point: Har Meron
Monetary Unit: new Israeli shekel

Italy*
Page/Location: 47/F4
Area: 116,303 sq. mi.
301,225 sq. km.
Population: 58,057,477
Capital: Rome
Largest City: Rome
Highest Point: Mont Bianco
Monetary Unit: euro

Jamaica
Page/Location: 123/F4
Area: 4,243 sq. mi.
10,990 sq. km.
Population: 2,713,130
Capital: Kingston
Largest City: Kingston
Highest Point: Blue Mountain Pk.
Monetary Unit: Jamaican dollar

Japan
Page/Location: 83/M4
Area: 145,882 sq. mi.
377,835 sq. km.
Population: 127,333,002
Capital: Tokyo
Largest City: Tokyo
Highest Point: Fujiyama
Monetary Unit: yen

Jordan
Page/Location: 78/C2
Area: 34,445 sq. mi.
89,213 sq. km.
Population: 5,611,202
Capital: Ammān
Largest City: Ammān
Highest Point: Jabal Ramm
Monetary Unit: Jordanian dinar

Kazakhstan
Page/Location: 74/G5
Area: 1,049,150 sq. mi.
2,717,300 sq. km.
Population: 16,798,552
Capital: Astana
Largest City: Almaty
Highest Point: Khan-Tengri
Monetary Unit: Kazakhstani tenge

Kenya
Page/Location: 107/C2
Area: 224,960 sq. mi.
582,646 sq. km.
Population: 32,021,856
Capital: Nairobi
Largest City: Nairobi
Highest Point: Mt. Kenya
Monetary Unit: Kenya shilling

Kiribati
Page/Location: 98/H5
Area: 277 sq. mi.
717 sq. km.
Population: 100,798
Capital: Tarawa
Largest City: —
Highest Point: Banaba Island
Monetary Unit: Australian dollar

Korea, North
Page/Location: 86/D3
Area: 46,540 sq. mi.
120,539 sq. km.
Population: 22,697,553
Capital: P'yŏngyang
Largest City: P'yŏngyang
Highest Point: Paektu-san
Monetary Unit: North Korean won

Korea, South
Page/Location: 86/D4
Area: 38,023 sq. mi.
98,480 sq. km.
Population: 48,598,175
Capital: Seoul
Largest City: Seoul
Highest Point: Halla-san
Monetary Unit: South Korean won

Kuwait
Page/Location: 78/E3
Area: 6,880 sq. mi.
17,820 sq. km.
Population: 2,257,549
Capital: Kuwait
Largest City: As Sālimiyah
Highest Point: 1,003 ft. (306 m)
Monetary Unit: Kuwaiti dinar

Kyrgyzstan
Page/Location: 81/B3
Area: 76,641 sq. mi.
198,500 sq. km.
Population: 4,965,081
Capital: Bishkek
Largest City: Bishkek
Highest Point: Pik Pobedy
Monetary Unit: som

Laos
Page/Location: 89/C2
Area: 91,428 sq. mi.
236,800 sq. km.
Population: 6,068,117
Capital: Vientiane
Largest City: Vientiane
Highest Point: Phou Bia
Monetary Unit: kip

Latvia*
Page/Location: 70/E4
Area: 24,749 sq. mi.
64,100 sq. km.
Population: 2,332,078
Capital: Riga
Largest City: Riga
Highest Point: Gaizina Kalns
Monetary Unit: Latvian lat

Lebanon
Page/Location: 80/K5
Area: 4,015 sq. mi.
10,399 sq. km.
Population: 3,777,218
Capital: Beirut
Largest City: Beirut
Highest Point: Qurnat as Sawdā'
Monetary Unit: Lebanese pound

*Member of the European Union

Lesotho
Page/Location: 109/D3
Area: 11,720 sq. mi.
30,355 sq. km.
Population: 1,865,040
Capital: Maseru
Largest City: Maseru
Highest Point: Thabana-Ntlenyana
Monetary Unit: loti

Liberia
Page/Location: 104/C5
Area: 43,000 sq. mi.
111,370 sq. km.
Population: 3,390,635
Capital: Monrovia
Largest City: Monrovia
Highest Point: Mt. Wuteve
Monetary Unit: Liberian dollar

Libya
Page/Location: 103/J2
Area: 679,358 sq. mi.
1,759,537 sq. km.
Population: 5,631,585
Capital: Tripoli
Largest City: Tripoli
Highest Point: Bīkkū Bīttī
Monetary Unit: Libyan dinar

Liechtenstein
Page/Location: 61/F3
Area: 61 sq. mi.
158 sq. km.
Population: 33,436
Capital: Vaduz
Largest City: Vaduz
Highest Point: Grauspitz
Monetary Unit: Swiss franc

Lithuania*
Page/Location: 70/D5
Area: 25,174 sq. mi.
65,200 sq. km.
Population: 3,584,836
Capital: Vilnius
Largest City: Vilnius
Highest Point: Juozapines
Monetary Unit: litas

Luxembourg*
Page/Location: 59/E4
Area: 999 sq. mi.
2,587 sq. km.
Population: 462,690
Capital: Luxembourg
Largest City: Luxembourg
Highest Point: Buurgplaatz
Monetary Unit: euro

Macedonia (F.Y.R.O.M.)
Page/Location: 67/G2
Area: 9,781 sq. mi.
25,333 sq. km.
Population: 2,071,210
Capital: Skopje
Largest City: Skopje
Highest Point: Korab
Monetary Unit: denar

Madagascar
Page/Location: 109/H8
Area: 226,657 sq. mi.
587,041 sq. km.
Population: 17,501,871
Capital: Antananarivo
Largest City: Antananarivo
Highest Point: Maromokotro
Monetary Unit: Malagasy franc

Malawi
Page/Location: 110/F3
Area: 45,747 sq. mi.
118,485 sq. km.
Population: 11,906,855
Capital: Lilongwe
Largest City: Blantyre
Highest Point: Sapitwa
Monetary Unit: Malawi kwacha

Malaysia
Page/Location: 92/C2
Area: 127,316 sq. mi.
329,750 sq. km.
Population: 23,522,482
Capital: Kuala Lumpur
Largest City: Kuala Lumpur
Highest Point: Gunung Kinabalu
Monetary Unit: ringgit

Maldives
Page/Location: 77/G9
Area: 115 sq. mi.
298 sq. km.
Population: 339,330
Capital: Male
Largest City: Male
Highest Point: 8 ft. (2.4 m)
Monetary Unit: rufiyaa

Mali
Page/Location: 102/E4
Area: 478,764 sq. mi.
1,240,000 sq. km.
Population: 11,956,788
Capital: Bamako
Largest City: Bamako
Highest Point: Hombori Tondo
Monetary Unit: CFA franc

Malta*
Page/Location: 66/D5
Area: 122 sq. mi.
316 sq. km.
Population: 403,342
Capital: Valletta
Largest City: Valletta
Highest Point: Ta'Dmejrek
Monetary Unit: euro

Marshall Islands
Page/Location: 98/G3
Area: 70 sq. mi.
181 sq. km.
Population: 57,738
Capital: Majuro
Largest City: —
Highest Point: 33 ft. (10 m)
Monetary Unit: U.S. dollar

Mauritania
Page/Location: 104/B2
Area: 397,953 sq. mi.
1,030,700 sq. km.
Population: 2,998,563
Capital: Nouakchott
Largest City: Nouakchott
Highest Point: Kediet Ijill
Monetary Unit: Ouguiya

Mauritius
Page/Location: 109/T15
Area: 718 sq. mi.
1,860 sq. km.
Population: 1,220,481
Capital: Port Louis
Largest City: Port Louis
Highest Point: Mont Piton
Monetary Unit: Mauritian rupee

Mexico
Page/Location: 122/A3
Area: 761,601 sq. mi.
1,972,546 sq. km.
Population: 104,959,594
Capital: Mexico
Largest City: Mexico
Highest Point: Citlaltépetl
Monetary Unit: Mexican peso

Micronesia
Page/Location: 98/D4
Area: 271 sq. mi.
702 sq. km.
Population: 108,155
Capital: Palikir
Largest City: Kolonia
Highest Point: Totolom
Monetary Unit: U.S. dollar

Moldova
Page/Location: 72/C3
Area: 13,012 sq. mi.
33,700 sq. km.
Population: 4,446,455
Capital: Chişinău
Largest City: Chişinău
Highest Point: Dealul Balanesti
Monetary Unit: leu

Monaco
Page/Location: 63/G5
Area: 0.7 sq. mi.
1.9 sq. km.
Population: 32,270
Capital: Monaco
Largest City: —
Highest Point: Mont Agel
Monetary Unit: euro

Mongolia
Page/Location: 82/D2
Area: 606,163 sq. mi.
1,569,962 sq. km.
Population: 2,751,314
Capital: Ulaanbaatar
Largest City: Ulaanbaatar
Highest Point: Nayramadlīn Orgil
Monetary Unit: tughrik

Montenegro
Page/Location: 68/D4
Area: 5,333 sq. mi.
13,812 sq. km.
Population: 620,150
Capital: Podgorica
Largest City: Podgorica
Highest Point: Bobotov Kuk
Monetary Unit: euro

Morocco
Page/Location: 102/C1
Area: 172,414 sq. mi.
446,550 sq. km.
Population: 32,209,101
Capital: Rabat
Largest City: Casablanca
Highest Point: Jebal Toubkal
Monetary Unit: Moroccan dirham

Mozambique
Page/Location: 110/G4
Area: 309,494 sq. mi.
801,590 sq. km.
Population: 18,811,731
Capital: Maputo
Largest City: Maputo
Highest Point: Monte Binga
Monetary Unit: metical

Myanmar (Burma)
Page/Location: 91/G3
Area: 261,969 sq. mi.
678,500 sq. km.
Population: 42,720,196
Capital: Yangon (Rangoon)
Largest City: Yangon (Rangoon)
Highest Point: Hkakabo Razi
Monetary Unit: kyat

Namibia
Page/Location: 110/C5
Area: 318,694 sq. mi.
825,418 sq. km.
Population: 1,954,033
Capital: Windhoek
Largest City: Windhoek
Highest Point: Königstein
Monetary Unit: Namibian dollar

Nauru
Page/Location: 98/F5
Area: 7.7 sq. mi.
20 sq. km.
Population: 12,809
Capital: Yaren (district)
Largest City: —
Highest Point: 200 ft. (61 m)
Monetary Unit: Australian dollar

Nepal
Page/Location: 77/H7
Area: 54,663 sq. mi.
141,577 sq. km.
Population: 27,070,666
Capital: Kāthmāndu
Largest City: Kāthmāndu
Highest Point: Mt. Everest
Monetary Unit: Nepalese rupee

Netherlands*
Page/Location: 56/B5
Area: 14,413 sq. mi.
37,330 sq. km.
Population: 16,318,199
Capital: The Hague; Amsterdam
Largest City: Amsterdam
Highest Point: Vaalserberg
Monetary Unit: euro

New Zealand
Page/Location: 95/H6
Area: 103,736 sq. mi.
268,676 sq. km.
Population: 3,993,817
Capital: Wellington
Largest City: Auckland
Highest Point: Mt. Cook
Monetary Unit: New Zealand dollar

Nicaragua
Page/Location: 122/D5
Area: 49,998 sq. mi.
129,494 sq. km.
Population: 5,232,216
Capital: Managua
Largest City: Managua
Highest Point: Pico Mogotón
Monetary Unit: gold cordoba

Niger
Page/Location: 102/G4
Area: 489,189 sq. mi.
1,267,000 sq. km.
Population: 11,360,538
Capital: Niamey
Largest City: Niamey
Highest Point: Bagzane
Monetary Unit: CFA franc

Nigeria
Page/Location: 102/G6
Area: 356,668 sq. mi.
923,770 sq. km.
Population: 137,253,133
Capital: Abuja
Largest City: Lagos
Highest Point: Chappal Waddi
Monetary Unit: naira

Norway
Page/Location: 48/C3
Area: 125,053 sq. mi.
323,887 sq. km.
Population: 4,574,560
Capital: Oslo
Largest City: Oslo
Highest Point: Galdhøppigen
Monetary Unit: Norwegian krone

Oman
Page/Location: 79/G4
Area: 82,031 sq. mi.
212,460 sq. km.
Population: 2,903,165
Capital: Muscat
Largest City: Muscat
Highest Point: Jabal ash Shams
Monetary Unit: Omani rial

Pakistan
Page/Location: 79/H3
Area: 310,403 sq. mi.
803,944 sq. km.
Population: 153,705,278
Capital: Islāmābād
Largest City: Karāchi
Highest Point: K2 (Godwin-Austen)
Monetary Unit: Pakistani rupee

*Member of the European Union

Palau
Page/Location: 98/C4
Area: 177 sq. mi.
        458 sq. km.
Population: 20,016
Capital: Koror
Largest City: Koror
Highest Point: Mt. Ngerchelchauus
Monetary Unit: U.S. dollar

Panama
Page/Location: 123/E6
Area: 30,193 sq. mi.
        78,200 sq. km.
Population: 3,000,463
Capital: Panamá
Largest City: Panamá
Highest Point: Barú
Monetary Unit: balboa

Papua New Guinea
Page/Location: 98/D5
Area: 178,259 sq. mi.
        461,690 sq. km.
Population: 5,420,280
Capital: Port Moresby
Largest City: Port Moresby
Highest Point: Mt. Wilhelm
Monetary Unit: kina

Paraguay
Page/Location: 113/D5
Area: 157,047 sq. mi.
        406,752 sq. km.
Population: 6,191,368
Capital: Asunción
Largest City: Asunción
Highest Point: Cerro Pero
Monetary Unit: guaraní

Peru
Page/Location: 114/C5
Area: 496,222 sq. mi.
        1,285,215 sq. km.
Population: 28,863,494
Capital: Lima
Largest City: Lima
Highest Point: Nevado Huascarán
Monetary Unit: nuevo sol

Philippines
Page/Location: 88/D5
Area: 115,830 sq. mi.
        300,000 sq. km.
Population: 86,241,697
Capital: Manila
Largest City: Manila
Highest Point: Mt. Apo
Monetary Unit: Philippine peso

Poland*
Page/Location: 55/K2
Area: 120,725 sq. mi.
        312,678 sq. km.
Population: 38,626,349
Capital: Warsaw
Largest City: Warsaw
Highest Point: Rysy
Monetary Unit: zloty

Portugal*
Page/Location: 64/A3
Area: 35,549 sq. mi.
        92,072 sq. km.
Population: 10,119,250
Capital: Lisbon
Largest City: Lisbon
Highest Point: Serra da Estrela
Monetary Unit: euro

Qatar
Page/Location: 78/F3
Area: 4,247 sq. mi.
        11,000 sq. km.
Population: 840,290
Capital: Doha
Largest City: Doha
Highest Point: Tuwayyir al Hamir
Monetary Unit: Qatari riyal

Romania*
Page/Location: 69/F3
Area: 91,699 sq. mi.
        237,500 sq. km.
Population: 22,355,551
Capital: Bucharest
Largest City: Bucharest
Highest Point: Moldoveanu
Monetary Unit: lei

Russia
Page/Location: 74/H3
Area: 6,592,812 sq. mi.
        17,075,400 sq. km.
Population: 144,112,353
Capital: Moscow
Largest City: Moscow
Highest Point: El'brus
Monetary Unit: Russian ruble

Rwanda
Page/Location: 107/A3
Area: 10,169 sq. mi
        26,337 sq. km.
Population: 7,954,013
Capital: Kigali
Largest City: Kigali
Highest Point: Karisimbi
Monetary Unit: Rwanda franc

Saint Kitts and Nevis
Page/Location: 123/J4
Area: 104 sq. mi.
        269 sq. km.
Population: 38,836
Capital: Basseterre
Largest City: Basseterre
Highest Point: Mt. Liamuiga
Monetary Unit: East Caribbean dollar

Saint Lucia
Page/Location: 123/J5
Area: 238 sq. mi.
        616 sq. km.
Population: 164,213
Capital: Castries
Largest City: Castries
Highest Point: Mt. Gimie
Monetary Unit: East Caribbean dollar

Saint Vincent and the Grenadines
Page/Location: 123/J5
Area: 131 sq. mi.
        340 sq. km.
Population: 117,193
Capital: Kingstown
Largest City: Kingstown
Highest Point: Soufière
Monetary Unit: East Caribbean dollar

Samoa
Page/Location: 99/H6
Area: 1,104 sq. mi.
        2,860 sq. km.
Population: 177,714
Capital: Apia
Largest City: Apia
Highest Point: Mt. Silisili
Monetary Unit: tala

San Marino
Page/Location: 63/K5
Area: 23.4 sq. mi.
        60.6 sq. km.
Population: 28,503
Capital: San Marino
Largest City: San Marino
Highest Point: Monte Titano
Monetary Unit: euro

São Tomé and Príncipe
Page/Location: 102/F7
Area: 371 sq. mi.
        960 sq. km.
Population: 181,565
Capital: São Tomé
Largest City: São Tomé
Highest Point: Pico de São Tomé
Monetary Unit: dobra

Saudi Arabia
Page/Location: 78/D4
Area: 756,981 sq. mi.
        1,960,582 sq. km.
Population: 25,100,425
Capital: Riyadh
Largest City: Riyadh
Highest Point: Jabal Sawdā'
Monetary Unit: Saudi riyal

Senegal
Page/Location: 104/B3
Area: 75,954 sq. mi.
        196,720 sq. km.
Population: 10,852,147
Capital: Dakar
Largest City: Dakar
Highest Point: 1,906 ft. (581 m)
Monetary Unit: CFA franc

Serbia
Page/Location: 68/D3
Area: 34,185 sq. mi.
        88,538 sq. km.
Population: 10,212,395
Capital: Belgrade
Largest City: Belgrade
Highest Point: Daravica
Monetary Unit: Yugoslav new dinar

Seychelles
Page/Location: 45/M6
Area: 176 sq. mi.
        455 sq. km.
Population: 80,832
Capital: Victoria
Largest City: Victoria
Highest Point: Morne Seychellois
Monetary Unit: Seychelles rupee

Sierra Leone
Page/Location: 104/B4
Area: 27,699 sq. mi.
        71,740 sq. km.
Population: 5,883,889
Capital: Freetown
Largest City: Freetown
Highest Point: Loma Mansa
Monetary Unit: leone

Singapore
Page/Location: 92/B3
Area: 244 sq. mi.
        632.6 sq. km.
Population: 4,767,974
Capital: Singapore
Largest City: Singapore
Highest Point: Bukit Timah
Monetary Unit: Singapore dollar

Slovakia*
Page/Location: 55/K4
Area: 18,924 sq. mi.
        49,013 sq. km.
Population: 5,423,567
Capital: Bratislava
Largest City: Bratislava
Highest Point: Gerlachovský Štit
Monetary Unit: Slovak koruna

Slovenia*
Page/Location: 68/B3
Area: 7,898 sq. mi.
        20,456 sq. km.
Population: 1,938,282
Capital: Ljubljana
Largest City: Ljubljana
Highest Point: Triglav
Monetary Unit: euro

Solomon Islands
Page/Location: 98/E6
Area: 11,500 sq. mi.
        29,785 sq. km.
Population: 523,617
Capital: Honiara
Largest City: Honiara
Highest Point: Mt. Makarakomburu
Monetary Unit: Solomon Islands dollar

Somalia
Page/Location: 103/Q6
Area: 246,200 sq. mi.
        637,658 sq. km.
Population: 8,304,601
Capital: Mogadishu
Largest City: Mogadishu
Highest Point: Shimbiris
Monetary Unit: Somali shilling

South Africa
Page/Location: 110/D6
Area: 471,008 sq. mi.
        1,219,912 sq. km.
Population: 42,718,530
Capital: Cape Town; Pretoria
Largest City: Johannesburg
Highest Point: Njesuti
Monetary Unit: rand

Spain*
Page/Location: 64/C2
Area: 194,881 sq. mi.
        504,742 sq. km.
Population: 40,280,780
Capital: Madrid
Largest City: Madrid
Highest Point: Pico de Teide
Monetary Unit: euro

*Member of the European Union

Countries of the World

Sri Lanka
Page/Location: 90/D6
Area: 25,332 sq. mi.
65,610 sq. km.
Population: 19,905,165
Capital: Colombo
Largest City: Colombo
Highest Point: Pidurutalagala
Monetary Unit: Sri Lanka rupee

Sudan
Page/Location: 103/L5
Area: 967,494 sq. mi.
2,505,809 sq. km.
Population: 39,148,162
Capital: Khartoum
Largest City: Omdurman
Highest Point: Kinyeti
Monetary Unit: Sudanese dinar

Suriname
Page/Location: 115/G3
Area: 63,039 sq. mi.
163,270 sq. km.
Population: 436,935
Capital: Paramaribo
Largest City: Paramaribo
Highest Point: Juliana Top
Monetary Unit: Suriname guilder

Swaziland
Page/Location: 109/E2
Area: 6,705 sq. mi.
17,366 sq. km.
Population: 1,169,241
Capital: Mbabane; Lobamba
Largest City: Mbabane
Highest Point: Emlembe
Monetary Unit: lilangeni

Sweden*
Page/Location: 48/E3
Area: 173,665 sq. mi.
449,792 sq. km.
Population: 8,986,400
Capital: Stockholm
Largest City: Stockholm
Highest Point: Kebnekaise
Monetary Unit: krona

Switzerland
Page/Location: 60/D4
Area: 15,943 sq. mi.
41,292 sq. km.
Population: 7,450,867
Capital: Bern
Largest City: Zürich
Highest Point: Dufourspitze
Monetary Unit: Swiss franc

Syria
Page/Location: 78/C1
Area: 71,498 sq. mi.
185,180 sq. km.
Population: 18,016,874
Capital: Damascus
Largest City: Damascus
Highest Point: Jabal ash Shaykh
Monetary Unit: Syrian pound

Taiwan
Page/Location: 88/D3
Area: 13,971 sq. mi.
26,185 sq. km.
Population: 22,749,838
Capital: T'aipei
Largest City: T'aipei
Highest Point: Yü Shan
Monetary Unit: new Taiwan dollar

Tajikistan
Page/Location: 74/H6
Area: 55,251 sq. mi.
143,100 sq. km.
Population: 7,011,556
Capital: Dushanbe
Largest City: Dushanbe
Highest Point: Pik Imeni Ismail Samani
Monetary Unit: somoni

Tanzania
Page/Location: 107/B4
Area: 364,699 sq. mi.
945,090 sq. km.
Population: 36,588,225
Capital: Dar es Salaam
Largest City: Dar es Salaam
Highest Point: Kilimanjaro
Monetary Unit: Tanzanian shilling

Thailand
Page/Location: 89/C3
Area: 198,455 sq. mi.
513,998 sq. km.
Population: 64,865,523
Capital: Bangkok
Largest City: Bangkok
Highest Point: Doi Inthanon
Monetary Unit: baht

Togo
Page/Location: 105/F4
Area: 21,927 sq. mi.
56,790 sq. km.
Population: 5,556,812
Capital: Lomé
Largest City: Lomé
Highest Point: Mt. Agou
Monetary Unit: CFA franc

Tonga
Page/Location: 99/H7
Area: 289 sq. mi.
748 sq. km.
Population: 110,237
Capital: Nuku'alofa
Largest City: Nuku'alofa
Highest Point: Kao Island
Monetary Unit: pa'anga

Trinidad and Tobago
Page/Location: 123/J5
Area: 1,980 sq. mi.
5,128 sq. km.
Population: 1,096,585
Capital: Port-of-Spain
Largest City: Port-of-Spain
Highest Point: El Cerro del Aripo
Monetary Unit: Trin. and Tob. dollar

Tunisia
Page/Location: 102/G1
Area: 63,170 sq. mi.
163,610 sq. km.
Population: 10,032,050
Capital: Tūnis
Largest City: Tūnis
Highest Point: Jebel ech Chambi
Monetary Unit: Tunisian dinar

Turkey
Page/Location: 80/C2
Area: 301,382 sq. mi.
780,580 sq. km.
Population: 68,893,918
Capital: Ankara
Largest City: İstanbul
Highest Point: Mt. Ararat
Monetary Unit: Turkish lira

Turkmenistan
Page/Location: 74/F6
Area: 188,455 sq. mi.
488,100 sq. km.
Population: 4,863,169
Capital: Ashgabat
Largest City: Ashgabat
Highest Point: Ayrybaba
Monetary Unit: manat

Tuvalu
Page/Location: 98/G5
Area: 9.78 sq. mi.
25.33 sq. km.
Population: 11,468
Capital: Funafuti
Largest City: —
Highest Point: 16 ft. (5 m)
Monetary Unit: Australian dollar

Uganda
Page/Location: 107/B2
Area: 91,076 sq. mi.
235,887 sq. km.
Population: 26,404,543
Capital: Kampala
Largest City: Kampala
Highest Point: Margherita Peak
Monetary Unit: Ugandan shilling

Ukraine
Page/Location: 72/D2
Area: 233,089 sq. mi.
603,700 sq. km.
Population: 47,732,079
Capital: Kiev
Largest City: Kiev
Highest Point: Hoverla
Monetary Unit: hryvnia

United Arab Emirates
Page/Location: 78/F4
Area: 29,182 sq. mi.
75,581 sq. km.
Population: 2,523,915
Capital: Abu Dhabi
Largest City: Dubayy
Highest Point: Jabal Yibir
Monetary Unit: Emirian dirham

United Kingdom*
Page/Location: 49/C3
Area: 94,399 sq. mi.
244,493 sq. km.
Population: 60,270,708
Capital: London
Largest City: London
Highest Point: Ben Nevis
Monetary Unit: pound sterling

United States
Page/Location: 126
Area: 3,618,765 sq. mi.
9,372,610 sq. km.
Population: 301,139,947
Capital: Washington, D.C.
Largest City: New York
Highest Point: Mt. McKinley
Monetary Unit: U.S. dollar

Uruguay
Page/Location: 117/E3
Area: 68,039 sq. mi.
176,220 sq. km.
Population: 3,440,205
Capital: Montevideo
Largest City: Montevideo
Highest Point: Cerro Catedral
Monetary Unit: Uruguayan peso

Uzbekistan
Page/Location: 74/G5
Area: 172,741 sq. mi.
447,400 sq. km.
Population: 26,410,416
Capital: Tashkent
Largest City: Tashkent
Highest Point: Adelunga Toghi
Monetary Unit: sum

Vanuatu
Page/Location: 98/F6
Area: 5,700 sq. mi.
14,763 sq. km.
Population: 202,609
Capital: Port-Vila
Largest City: Port-Vila
Highest Point: Tabwemasana
Monetary Unit: vatu

Vatican City
Page/Location: 66/C2
Area: 0.17 sq. mi.
0.44 sq. km.
Population: 911
Capital: —
Largest City: —
Highest Point: 246 ft. (75 m)
Monetary Unit: euro

Venezuela
Page/Location: 114/E2
Area: 352,143 sq. mi.
912,050 sq. km.
Population: 25,017,387
Capital: Caracas
Largest City: Caracas
Highest Point: Pico Bolívar
Monetary Unit: bolívar

Vietnam
Page/Location: 89/D2
Area: 127,243 sq. mi.
329,560 sq. km.
Population: 82,689,518
Capital: Hanoi
Largest City: Ho Chi Minh City
Highest Point: Fan Si Pan
Monetary Unit: dong

Yemen
Page/Location: 78/E5
Area: 203,849 sq. mi.
527,970 sq. km.
Population: 20,024,867
Capital: Sanaa
Largest City: Aden
Highest Point: Nabī Shu'ayb
Monetary Unit: Yemeni rial

Zambia
Page/Location: 110/E3
Area: 290,568 sq. mi.
752,618 sq. km.
Population: 10,462,436
Capital: Lusaka
Largest City: Lusaka
Highest Point: Mafinga Hills
Monetary Unit: Zambian kwacha

Zimbabwe
Page/Location: 110/E4
Area: 150,803 sq. mi.
390,580 sq. km.
Population: 12,671,860
Capital: Harare
Largest City: Harare
Highest Point: Inyangani
Monetary Unit: Zimbabwe dollar

*Member of the European Union

World Statistics, Index, and Time Zones

ELEMENTS OF THE SOLAR SYSTEM

	Mean Distance from Sun: in Miles	in Kilometers	Period of Revolution around Sun	Period of Rotation on Axis	Equatorial Diameter in Miles	in Kilometers	Surface Gravity (Earth = 1)	Mass (Earth = 1)	Mean Density (Water = 1)	Number of Satellites
Mercury	35,990,000	57,900,000	87.97 days	58.7 days	3,032	4,880	0.38	0.055	5.4	0
Venus	67,240,000	108,200,000	224.70 days	243.7 days†	7,521	12,104	0.91	0.815	5.2	0
Earth	93,000,000	149,700,000	365.26 days	23h 56m	7,926	12,755	1.00	1.00	5.5	1
Mars	141,610,000	227,900,000	686.98 days	24h 37m	4,221	6,794	0.38	0.107	3.9	2
Jupiter	483,675,000	778,400,000	11.86 years	9h 55m	88,846	142,984	2.36	317.8	1.3	62‡
Saturn	886,572,000	1,426,800,000	29.46 years	10h 30m	74,898	120,536	0.92	95.2	0.7	59‡
Uranus	1,783,957,000	2,871,000,000	84.01 years	17h 14m†	31,763	51,118	0.89	14.5	1.3	27
Neptune	2,795,114,000	4,498,300,000	164.79 years	16h 6m	30,778	49,532	1.13	17.1	1.6	13‡
Pluto*	3,670,000,000	5,906,400,000	247.70 years	6.4 days†	1,413	2,274	0.07	0.002	2.1	3‡

† Retrograde motion   ‡ Includes provisionally named satellites   * Pluto is no longer considered a planet by the International Astronomical Union.

Source: NASA, National Space Science Center

DIMENSIONS OF THE EARTH

	Area in: Sq. Miles	Sq. Kilometers
Superficial area	196,939,000	510,072,000
Land surface	57,506,000	148,940,000
Water surface	139,433,000	361,132,000

	Distance in: Miles	Kilometers
Equatorial circumference	24,902	40,075
Polar circumference	24,860	40,007
Equatorial diameter	7,926.4	12,756.4
Polar diameter	7,899.8	12,713.6
Equatorial radius	3,963.2	6,378.2
Polar radius	3,949.9	6,356.8
Volume of the Earth	2.6×10^{11} cubic miles	10.84×10^{11} cubic kilometers
Mass or weight	6.6×10^{21} short tons	6.0×10^{21} metric tons
Maximum distance from Sun	94,600,000 miles	152,000,000 kilometers
Minimum distance from Sun	91,300,000 miles	147,000,000 kilometers

OCEANS AND MAJOR SEAS

	Area in: Sq. Miles	Sq. Kms.	Greatest Depth in: Feet	Meters
Pacific Ocean	63,855,000	165,384,000	36,198	11,033
Atlantic Ocean	31,744,000	82,217,000	28,374	8,648
Indian Ocean	28,417,000	73,600,000	25,344	7,725
Arctic Ocean	5,427,000	14,056,000	17,880	5,450
Caribbean Sea	970,000	2,512,300	24,720	7,535
Mediterranean Sea	969,000	2,509,700	16.896	5,150
South China Sea	895,000	2,318,000	15.000	4,600
Bering Sea	875,000	2,266,250	15,800	4,800
Gulf of Mexico	600,000	1,554,000	12,300	3,750
Sea of Okhotsk	590,000	1,528,100	11,070	3,370
East China Sea	482,000	1,248,400	9,500	2,900
Yellow Sea	480,000	1,243,200	350	107
Sea of Japan	389,000	1,007,500	12,280	3,740
Hudson Bay	317,500	822,300	846	258
North Sea	222,000	575,000	2,200	670
Black Sea	185,000	479,150	7,365	2,245
Red Sea	169,000	437,700	7,200	2,195
Baltic Sea	163,000	422,170	1,506	459

THE CONTINENTS

	Population	Total Area in: Sq. Miles	Total Area in: Sq. Kms.	Percent of World's Land
Asia	4,004,788,000	17,128,500	44,362,815	29.5
Africa	935,813,000	11,707,000	30,321,130	20.2
North America	523,686,000	9,363,000	24,250,170	16.2
South America	380,017,000	6,879,725	17,818,505	11.9
Antarctica	— — —	5,405,000	14,000,000	9.4
Europe	727,228,000	4,057,000	10,507,630	7.0
Australia	20,434,000	2,967,893	7,686,850	5.1

MAJOR SHIP CANALS

	Length in: Miles	Kms.	Minimum Depth in: Feet	Meters
Volga-Baltic, Russia	225	362	–	–
Baltic-White Sea, Russia	140	225	16	5
Suez, Egypt	100.76	162	42	13
Albert, Belgium	80	129	16.5	5
Moscow-Volga, Russia	80	129	18	6
Volga-Don, Russia	62	100	–	–
Göta, Sweden	54	87	10	3
Kiel (Nord-Ostsee), Germany	53.2	86	38	12
Panama Canal, Panama	50.72	82	41.6	13
Houston Ship, U.S.A.	50	81	36	11

LARGEST ISLANDS

	Area in: Sq. Miles	Sq. Kms.
Greenland	840,000	2,175,600
New Guinea	305,000	789,950
Borneo	286,000	740,740
Madagascar	226,656	587,040
Baffin, Canada	195,928	507,454
Sumatra, Indonesia	164,000	424,760
Honshu, Japan	88,000	227,920
Great Britain	84,400	218,896
Victoria, Canada	83,896	217,290
Ellesmere, Canada	75,767	196,236
Celebes, Indonesia	72,986	189,034
South I., New Zealand	58,393	151,238
Java, Indonesia	48,842	126,501
North I., New Zealand	44,187	114,444
Cuba	42,803	110,860
Newfoundland, Canada	42,031	108,860
Luzon, Philippines	40,420	104,688
Iceland	39,768	103,000
Mindanao, Philippines	36,537	94,631
Hokkaidō, Japan	30,436	78,829
Sakhalin, Russia	29,500	76,405
Hispaniola, Haiti & Dom. Rep.	29,399	76,143

	Area in: Sq. Miles	Sq. Kms.
Ireland	27,136	70,282
Banks, Canada	27,038	70,028
Tasmania, Australia	26,410	68,402
Ceylon, Sri Lanka	25,332	65,610
Svalbard, Norway	23,957	62,049
Devon, Canada	21,331	55,247
Novaya Zemlya (north isl.), Russia	18,600	48,200
Tierra del Fuego, Chile & Argentina	18,301	47,400
Marajó, Brazil	17,991	46,597
Alexander, Antarctica	16,700	43,250
Axel Heiberg, Canada	16,671	43,178
Melville, Canada	16,274	42,150
Southampton, Canada	15,913	41,215
New Britain, Papua New Guinea	14,100	36,519
Taiwan	13,836	35,835
Kyushu, Japan	13,770	35,664
Hainan, China	13,127	33,999
Prince of Wales, Canada	12,872	33,338
Spitsbergen, Norway	12,355	31,999
Vancouver, Canada	12,079	31,285
Timor, Indonesia	11,527	29,855
Sicily, Italy	9,926	25,708

	Area in: Sq. Miles	Sq. Kms.
Somerset, Canada	9,570	24,786
Sardinia, Italy	9,301	24,090
Shikoku, Japan	6,860	17,767
New Caledonia, France	6,530	16,913
Nordaustlandet, Norway	6,409	16,599
Samar, Philippines	5,050	13,080
Negros, Philippines	4,906	12,707
Palawan, Philippines	4,550	11,785
Panay, Philippines	4,446	11,515
Jamaica	4,232	10,961
Hawaii, United States	4,038	10,458
Viti Levu, Fiji	4,010	10,386
Cape Breton, Canada	3,981	10,311
Mindoro, Philippines	3,759	9,736
Kodiak, Alaska, U.S.A.	3,670	9,505
Cyprus	3,572	9,251
Puerto Rico, U.S.A.	3,435	8,897
Corsica, France	3,352	8,682
New Ireland, Papua New Guinea	3,340	8,651
Crete, Greece	3,218	8,335
Anticosti, Canada	3,066	7,941
Wrangel, Russia	2,819	7,301

PRINCIPAL MOUNTAINS

	Height in : Feet	Meters		Height in : Feet	Meters		Height in : Feet	Meters
Everest, Nepal-China	29,028	8,848	Pissis, Argentina	22,241	6,779	Margherita (Ruwenzori), Africa	16,795	5,119
K2 (Godwin Austen), Pakistan-China	28,250	8,611	Mercedario, Argentina	22,211	6,770	Kazbek, Georgia-Russia	16,558	5,047
Känchenjunga, Nepal-India	28,208	8,598	Huascarán, Peru	22,205	6,768	Puncak Jaya, Indonesia	16,503	5,030
Lhotse, Nepal-China	27,923	8,511	Llullaillaco, Chile-Argentina	22,057	6,723	Blanc, France	15,771	4,807
Makalu, Nepal-China	27,789	8,470	Nevada Ancohuma, Bolivia	21,489	6,550	Klyuchevskaya Sopka, Russia	15,584	4,750
Dhaulagiri, Nepal	26,810	8,172	Chimborazo, Ecuador	20,561	6,267	Fairweather, Br. Col., Canada	15,300	4,663
Nanga Parbat, Pakistan	26,660	8,126	McKinley, Alaska	20,320	6,194	Dufourspitze (Mte. Rosa), Italy-Switzerland	15,203	4,634
Annapurna, Nepal	26,504	8,078	Trudeau, Yukon, Canada	19,524	5,951	Ras Dashen, Ethiopia	15,157	4,620
Nanda Devi, India	25,645	7,817	Cotopaxi, Ecuador	19,347	5,897	Matterhorn, Switzerland	14,691	4,478
Rakaposhi, Pakistan	25,550	7,788	Kilimanjaro, Tanzania	19,340	5,895	Whitney, California, U.S.A.	14,494	4,418
Kongur Shan, China	25,325	7,719	El Misti, Peru	19,101	5,822	Elbert, Colorado, U.S.A.	14,433	4,399
Tirich Mir, Pakistan	25,230	7,690	Pico Cristóbal Colón, Colombia	18,947	5,775	Rainier, Washington, U.S.A.	14,410	4,392
Gongga Shan, China	24,790	7,556	Huila, Colombia	18,865	5,750	Shasta, California, U.S.A.	14,162	4,317
Ismail Samani Peak, Tajikistan	24,590	7,495	Citlaltépetl (Orizaba), Mexico	18,700	5,700	Pikes Peak, Colorado, U.S.A.	14,110	4,301
Pobedy Peak, Kyrgyzstan	24,406	7,439	Damavand, Iran	18,605	5,671	Finsteraarhorn, Switzerland	14,022	4,274
Chomo Lhari, Bhutan-China	23,997	7,314	El'brus, Russia	18,510	5,642	Mauna Kea, Hawaii, U.S.A.	13,796	4,205
Muztag, China	23,891	7,282	St. Elias, Alaska, U.S.A.-Yukon, Canada	18,008	5,489	Mauna Loa, Hawaii, U.S.A.	13,677	4,169
Cerro Aconcagua, Argentina	22,831	6,959	Dykh-tau, Russia	17,070	5,203	Jungfrau, Switzerland	13,642	4,158
Ojos del Salado, Chile-Argentina	22,572	6,880	Batian (Kenya), Kenya	17,058	5,199	Grossglockner, Austria	12,457	3,797
Bonete, Chile-Argentina	22,546	6,872	Ararat, Turkey	16,946	5,165	Fujiyama, Japan	12,389	3,776
Tupungato, Chile-Argentina	22,310	6,800	Vinson Massif, Antarctica	16,864	5,140	Cook, New Zealand	12,349	3,764

LONGEST RIVERS

	Length in: Miles	Kms.		Length in: Miles	Kms.		Length in: Miles	Kms.
Nile, Africa	4,145	6,671	Rio Grande, Mexico-U.S.A.	1,885	3,034	Kama, Russia	1,252	2,031
Amazon, S. America	4,007	6,448	Syrdariya-Naryn, Asia	1,859	2,992	Don, Russia	1,222	1,967
Mississippi-Missouri-Red Rock, U.S.A.	3,710	5,971	Indus, Asia	1,800	2,897	Red, U.S.A.	1,222	1,966
Chang Jiang (Yangtze), China	3,500	5,633	Danube, Europe	1,775	2,857	Columbia, U.S.A.-Canada	1,214	1,953
Ob'-Irtysh, Russia-Kazakhstan	3,362	5,411	Brahmaputra, Asia	1,700	2,736	Tigris, Asia	1,181	1,901
Yenisey-Angara, Russia	3,100	4,989	Tocantins, Brazil	1,677	2,699	Darling, Australia	1,160	1,867
Huang He (Yellow), China	2,950	4,747	Salween, Asia	1,675	2,696	Angara, Russia	1,135	1,827
Congo, Africa	2,780	4,474	Euphrates, Asia	1,650	2,655	Sungari, Asia	1,130	1,819
Amur-Shilka-Onon, Asia	2,744	4,416	Xi (Si), China	1,650	2,655	Pechora, Russia	1,124	1,809
Lena, Russia	2,734	4,400	Amu Darya, Asia	1,616	2,601	Snake, U.S.A.	1,038	1,670
Mackenzie-Peace-Finlay, Canada	2,635	4,241	Nelson-Saskatchewan, Canada	1,600	2,575	Churchill, Canada	1,000	1,609
Paraná-La Plata, S. America	2,630	4,232	Orinoco, S. America	1,600	2,575	Pilcomayo, S. America	1,000	1,609
Mekong, Asia	2,610	4,200	Paraguay, S. America	1,584	2,549	Uruguay, S. America	994	1,600
Niger, Africa	2,580	4,152	Kolyma, Russia	1,562	2,514	Platte-N. Platte, U.S.A.	990	1,593
Missouri-Red Rock, U.S.A.	2,564	4,125	Ganges, Asia	1,550	2,494	Ohio, U.S.A.	981	1,578
Yenisey, Russia	2,500	4,028	Zhayyq (Ural), Kazakhstan-Russia	1,509	2,428	Magdalena, Colombia	956	1,538
Mississippi, U.S.A.	2,348	3,778	Japurá, S. America	1,500	2,414	Pecos, U.S.A.	926	1,490
Murray-Darling, Australia	2,310	3,718	Arkansas, U.S.A.	1,450	2,334	Oka, Russia	918	1,477
Volga, Russia	2,290	3,685	Colorado, U.S.A.-Mexico	1,450	2,334	Canadian, U.S.A.	906	1,458
Madeira, S. America	2,013	3,240	Negro, S. America	1,400	2,253	Colorado, Texas, U.S.A.	894	1,439
Purus, S. America	1,995	3,211	Dnepr (Dnyapro, Dnipro), Russia-Belarus-Ukraine	1,368	2,202	Dnister (Nistru), Ukraine-Moldova	876	1,410
Yukon, Alaska-Canada	1,979	3,185	Orange, Africa	1,350	2,173	Fraser, Canada	850	1,369
Zambezi, Africa	1,950	3,138	Ayeyarwady, Myanmar	1,325	2,132	Rhine, Europe	820	1,319
São Francisco, Brazil	1,930	3,106	Brazos, U.S.A.	1,309	2,107	Northern Dvina, Russia	809	1,302
St. Lawrence, Canada-U.S.A.	1,900	3,058	Ohio-Allegheny, U.S.A.	1,306	2,102	Ottawa, Canada	790	1,271

PRINCIPAL NATURAL LAKES

	Area in: Sq. Miles	Sq. Kms.	Max. Depth in: Feet	Meters		Area in: Sq. Miles	Sq. Kms.	Max. Depth in: Feet	Meters
Caspian Sea, Asia	143,243	370,999	3,264	995	Lake Eyre, Australia*	3,500-0	9,065-0	–	–
Lake Superior, U.S.A.-Canada	31,820	82,414	1,329	405	Lake Titicaca, Peru-Bolivia	3,200	8,288	1,000	305
Lake Victoria, Africa	26,628	69,215	270	82	Lake Nicaragua, Nicaragua	3,100	8,029	230	70
Lake Huron, U.S.A.-Canada	23,010	59,596	748	228	Lake Athabasca, Canada	3,064	7,936	400	122
Lake Michigan, U.S.A.	22,400	58,016	923	281	Reindeer Lake, Canada*	2,568	6,651	–	–
Aral Sea, Kazakhstan-Uzbekistan	15,830	41,000	213	65	Lake Turkana (Rudolf), Africa	2,463	6,379	240	73
Lake Tanganyika, Africa	12,650	32,764	4,700	1,433	Ysyk-Köl, Kyrgyzstan	2,425	6,281	2,303	702
Lake Baykal, Russia	12,162	31,500	5,316	1,620	Lake Torrens, Australia*	2,230	5,776	–	–
Great Bear Lake, Canada	12,096	31,328	1,356	413	Vänern, Sweden	2,156	5,584	328	100
Lake Nyasa (Malawi), Africa	11,555	29,928	2,320	707	Nettilling Lake, Canada*	2,140	5,543	–	–
Great Slave Lake, Canada	11,031	28,570	2,015	614	Lake Winnipegosis, Canada	2,075	5,374	38	12
Lake Erie, U.S.A.-Canada	9,940	25,745	210	64	Lake Albert, Africa	2,075	5,374	160	49
Lake Winnipeg, Canada	9,417	24,390	60	18	Kariba Lake, Zambia-Zimbabwe	2,050	5,310	295	90
Lake Ontario, U.S.A.-Canada	7,540	19,529	775	244	Lake Nipigon, Canada	1,872	4,848	540	165
Lake Balkhash, Kazakhstan	7,081	18,340	87	27	Lake Mweru, Africa	1,800	4,662	60	18
Lake Chad, Africa*	7,000	18,130	25	8	Lake Manitoba, Canada	1,799	4,659	12	4
Lake Ladoga, Russia	6,900	17,871	738	225	Lake Khanka, China-Russia	1,700	4,403	33	10
Lake Maracaibo, Venezuela	5,120	13,261	100	31	Lake Kioga, Uganda	1,700	4,403	25	8
Tonle Sap, Cambodia*	3,860-965	10,000-2,500	–	–	Lake of the Woods, U.S.A.-Canada	1,679	4,349	70	21
Lake Onega, Russia	3,761	9,741	377	115					

* Figures subject to great seasonal variations.

Index of the World

This index is a comprehensive listing of the places and geographic features found in the atlas. Names are arranged in strict alphabetical order, without regard to hyphens or spaces. Every name is followed by the country or area to which it belongs. Except for cities, towns, countries and cultural areas, all entries include a reference to feature type, such as province, river, island, peak, and so on. The page number and alpha-numeric code appear in blue to the left of each listing. The page number directs you to the largest scale map on which the name can be found. The code refers to the grid squares formed by the horizontal and vertical lines of latitude and longitude on each map. Following the letters from left to right and the numbers from top to bottom helps you to quickly locate the square containing the place or feature. Inset maps have their own alpha-numeric codes. Names that are accompanied by a point symbol are indexed to the symbol's location on the map. Other names are indexed to the initial letter of the name. When a map name contains a subordinate or alternate name, both names are listed in the index. To conserve space and provide room for more entries, many abbreviations are used in this index. The primary abbreviations are listed below.

Index Abbreviations

A
Ab,Can	Alberta
Abor.	Aboriginal
Acad.	Academy
ACT	Australian Capital Territory
A.F.B.	Air Force Base
Afld.	Airfield
Afg.	Afghanistan
Afr.	Africa
Ak,US	Alaska
Al,US	Alabama
Alb.	Albania
Alg.	Algeria
Amm. Dep.	Ammunition Depot
And.	Andorra
Ang.	Angola
Angu.	Anguilla
Ant.	Antarctica
Anti.	Antigua and Barbuda
Ar,US	Arkansas
Arch.	Archipelago
Arg.	Argentina
Arm.	Armenia
Arpt.	Airport
Aru.	Aruba
ASam.	American Samoa
Ash.	Ashmore and Cartier Islands
Aus.	Austria
Austl.	Australia
Aut.	Autonomous
Az,US	Arizona
Azer.	Azerbaijan
Azor.	Azores

B
Bahm.	Bahamas, The
Bahr.	Bahrain
Bang.	Bangladesh
Bar.	Barbados
BC,Can	British Columbia
Bela.	Belarus
Belg.	Belgium
Belz.	Belize
Ben.	Benin
Berm.	Bermuda
Bfld.	Battlefield
Bhu.	Bhutan
Bol.	Bolivia
Bor.	Borough
Bosn.	Bosnia and Herzegovina
Bots.	Botswana
Braz.	Brazil
Brln.	British Indian Ocean Territory
Bru.	Brunei
Bul.	Bulgaria
Burk.	Burkina Faso
Buru.	Burundi
BVI	British Virgin Islands

C
Ca,US	California
CAfr.	Central African Republic
Camb.	Cambodia
Camr.	Cameroon
Can.	Canada
Can.	Canal
Canl.	Canary Islands

(continued)
Cap.	Capital
Cap. Dist.	Capital District
Cap. Terr.	Capital Territory
Cay.	Cayman Islands
C.d'Iv.	Côte d'Ivoire
C.G.	Coast Guard
Chan.	Channel
Chl.	Channel Islands
Co.	County
Co,US	Colorado
Col.	Colombia
Com.	Comoros
Cont.	Continent
CpV.	Cape Verde Islands
CR	Costa Rica
Cr.	Creek
Cro.	Croatia
CSea.	Coral Sea Islands Territory
Ct,US	Connecticut
Ctr.	Center
Ctry.	Country
Cyp.	Cyprus
Czh.	Czech Republic

D
DC,US	District of Columbia
De,US	Delaware
Den.	Denmark
Depr.	Depression
Dept.	Department
Des.	Desert
DF	Distrito Federal
Dist.	District
Djib.	Djibouti
Dom.	Dominica
Dpcy.	Dependency
D.R.Congo	Democratic Republic of the Congo
DRep.	Dominican Republic

E
Ecu.	Ecuador
Emb.	Embankment
Eng.	Engineering
Eng,UK	England
EqG.	Equatorial Guinea
Erit.	Eritrea
ESal.	El Salvador
Est.	Estonia
Eth.	Ethiopia
ETim.	East Timor
Eur.	Europe

F
Falk.	Falkland Islands
Far.	Faroe Islands
Fed. Dist.	Federal District
Fin.	Finland
Fl,US	Florida
For.	Forest
Fr.	France
FrAnt.	French Southern and Antarctic Lands
FrG.	French Guiana
FrPol.	French Polynesia
FYROM	Former Yugoslav Rep. of Macedonia

G
Ga,US	Georgia
Galp.	Galapagos Islands

Gam.	Gambia, The
Gaza	Gaza Strip
GBis.	Guinea-Bissau
Geo.	Georgia
Ger.	Germany
Gha.	Ghana
Gib.	Gibraltar
Glac.	Glacier
Gov.	Governorate
Govt.	Government
Gre.	Greece
Grld.	Greenland
Gren.	Grenada
Grsld.	Grassland
Guad.	Guadeloupe
Guat.	Guatemala
Gui.	Guinea
Guy.	Guyana

H
Har.	Harbor
Hi,US	Hawaii
Hist.	Historic(al)
Hon.	Honduras
Hts.	Heights
Hun.	Hungary

I
Ia,US	Iowa
Ice.	Iceland
Id,US	Idaho
Il,US	Illinois
IM	Isle of Man
In,US	Indiana
Ind. Res.	Indian Reservation
Indo.	Indonesia
Int'l	International
Ire.	Ireland
Isl., Isls.	Island, Islands
Isr.	Israel
Isth.	Isthmus
It.	Italy

J
Jam.	Jamaica
Jor.	Jordan

K
Kaz.	Kazakhstan
Kiri.	Kiribati
Ks,US	Kansas
Kuw.	Kuwait
Ky,US	Kentucky
Kyr.	Kyrgyzstan

L
La,US	Louisiana
Lab.	Laboratory
Lag.	Lagoon
Lakesh.	Lakeshore
Lat.	Latvia
Lcht.	Liechtenstein
Ldg.	Landing
Leb.	Lebanon
Les.	Lesotho
Libr.	Liberia
Lith.	Lithuania
Lux.	Luxembourg

M
Ma,US	Massachusetts
Madg.	Madagascar
Madr.	Madeira
Malay.	Malaysia
Mald.	Maldives
Malw.	Malawi
Mart.	Martinique
May.	Mayotte

Mb,Can	Manitoba
Md,US	Maryland
Me,US	Maine
Mem.	Memorial
Mex.	Mexico
Mi,US	Michigan
Micr.	Micronesia, Federated States of
Mil.	Military
Mn,US	Minnesota
Mo,US	Missouri
Mol.	Moldova
Mon.	Monument
Mona.	Monaco
Mong.	Mongolia
Mont.	Montenegro
Monts.	Montserrat
Mor.	Morocco
Moz.	Mozambique
Mrsh.	Marshall Islands
Mrta.	Mauritania
Mrts.	Mauritius
Ms,US	Mississippi
Mt.	Mount
Mt,US	Montana
Mtn., Mts.	Mountain, Mountains
Mun. Arpt.	Municipal Airport
Myan.	Myanmar

N
NAm.	North America
Namb.	Namibia
NAnt.	Netherlands Antilles
Nat'l	National
Nav.	Naval
NB,Can	New Brunswick
Nbrhd.	Neighborhood
NC,US	North Carolina
NCal.	New Caledonia
ND,US	North Dakota
Ne,US	Nebraska
Neth.	Netherlands
Nf,Can	Newfoundland
Nga.	Nigeria
NH,US	New Hampshire
NI,UK	Northern Ireland
Nic.	Nicaragua
NJ,US	New Jersey
NKor.	North Korea
NM,US	New Mexico
NMar.	Northern Mariana Islands
Nor.	Norway
NS,Can	Nova Scotia
Nv,US	Nevada
Nun.,Can	Nunavut
NW,Can	Northwest Territories
NY,US	New York
NZ	New Zealand

O
Obl.	Oblast
Oh,US	Ohio
Ok,US	Oklahoma
On,Can	Ontario
Or,US	Oregon

P
Pa,US	Pennsylvania
PacUS	Pacific Islands, U.S.
Pak.	Pakistan

Pan.	Panama
Par.	Paraguay
Par.	Parish
PE,Can	Prince Edward Island
Pen.	Peninsula
Phil.	Philippines
Phys. Reg.	Physical Region
Pitc.	Pitcairn Islands
Plat.	Plateau
PNG	Papua New Guinea
Pol.	Poland
Port.	Portugal
Poss.	Possession
Pkwy.	Parkway
PR	Puerto Rico
Pref.	Prefecture
Prov.	Province
Prsv.	Preserve
Pt.	Point

Q
Qu,Can	Quebec

R
Rec.	Recreation(al)
Ref.	Refuge
Reg.	Region
Rep.	Republic
Res.	Reservoir, Reservation
Reun.	Réunion
RI,US	Rhode Island
Riv.	River
Rom.	Romania
Rsv.	Reserve
Rus.	Russia
Rvwy.	Riverway
Rwa.	Rwanda

S
SAfr.	South Africa
Sam.	Samoa
SAm.	South America
SaoT.	São Tomé and Príncipe
SAr.	Saudi Arabia
Sc,UK	Scotland
SC,US	South Carolina
SD,US	South Dakota
Seash.	Seashore
Sen.	Senegal
Serb.	Serbia
Sey.	Seychelles
SGeo.	South Georgia and Sandwich Islands
Sing.	Singapore
Sk,Can	Saskatchewan
SKor.	South Korea
SLeo.	Sierra Leone
Slov.	Slovenia
Slvk.	Slovakia
SMar.	San Marino
Sol.	Solomon Islands
Som.	Somalia
Sp.	Spain
Spr., Sprs.	Spring, Springs
SrL.	Sri Lanka
Sta.	Station
StH.	Saint Helena
Str.	Strait
StK.	Saint Kitts and Nevis
StL.	Saint Lucia

StP.	Saint Pierre and Miquelon
StV.	Saint Vincent and the Grenadines
Sur.	Suriname
Sval.	Svalbard
Swaz.	Swaziland
Swe.	Sweden
Swi.	Switzerland

T
Tah.	Tahiti
Tai.	Taiwan
Taj.	Tajikistan
Tanz.	Tanzania
Ter.	Terrace
Terr.	Territory
Thai.	Thailand
Tn,US	Tennessee
Tok.	Tokelau
Trg.	Training
Trin.	Trinidad and Tobago
Trkm.	Turkmenistan
Trks.	Turks and Caicos Islands
Tun.	Tunisia
Tun.	Tunnel
Turk.	Turkey
Tuv.	Tuvalu
Twp.	Township
Tx,US	Texas

U
UAE	United Arab Emirates
Ugan.	Uganda
UK	United Kingdom
Ukr.	Ukraine
Uru.	Uruguay
US	United States
USVI	U.S. Virgin Islands
Ut,US	Utah
Uzb.	Uzbekistan

V
Va,US	Virginia
Val.	Valley
Van.	Vanuatu
VatC.	Vatican City
Ven.	Venezuela
Viet.	Vietnam
Vill.	Village
Vol.	Volcano
Vt,US	Vermont

W
Wa,US	Washington
Wal,UK	Wales
Wall.	Wallis and Futuna
WBnk.	West Bank
Wi,US	Wisconsin
Wild.	Wildlife, Wilderness
WSah.	Western Sahara
WV,US	West Virginia
Wy,US	Wyoming

Y
Yem.	Yemen
Yk,Can	Yukon Territory

Z
Zam.	Zambia
Zim.	Zimbabwe

149
A – Alofi

A

58/B2 Aa (riv.), Fr.
56/D5 Aa (riv.), Ger.
57/G5 Aa (riv.), Ger.
59/F2 Aachen, Ger.
56/C5 Aalburg, Neth.
63/J2 Aalen, Ger.
56/B4 Aalsmeer, Neth.
58/D2 Aalst, Belg.
56/D5 Aalten, Neth.
58/C1 Aalter, Belg.
60/E3 Aarau, Swi.
60/D3 Aare (riv.), Swi.
60/E3 Aargau (canton), Swi.
59/D2 Aarschot, Belg.
58/D1 Aartselaar, Belg.
82/E5 Aba, China
105/G5 Aba, Nga.
107/A2 Aba, D.R. Congo
78/D5 Abā as Su'ūd, SAr.
114/G5 Abacaxis (riv.), Braz.
106/C5 Abadab, Jabal (peak), Sudan
78/E2 Ābādān, Iran
78/F2 Ābādeh, Iran
116/C1 Abaeté, Braz.
115/J4 Abaetetuba, Braz.
98/G4 Abaiang (atoll), Kiri.
126/D4 Abajo (mts.), Ut,US
74/K4 Abakan, Rus.
114/D6 Abancay, Peru
82/G3 Abaq Qi, China
64/E3 Abarán, Sp.
99/H5 Abariringa (Canton) (atoll), Kiri.
78/F2 Abar Kūh, Iran
83/N3 Abashiri, Japan
74/H5 Abay, Kaz.
103/N6 Ābaya Hayk' (lake), Eth.
81/F1 Abaza, Rus.
66/B1 Abbadia San Salvatore, It.
58/A3 Abbeville, Fr.
134/E4 Abbeville, La,US
135/H3 Abbeville, SC,US
96/B3 Abbot (mt.), Austl.
111/T Abbot Ice Shelf, Ant.
51/G6 Abbots Bromley, Eng,UK
52/D5 Abbotsbury, Eng,UK
79/K2 Abbottābād, Pak.
56/B4 Abcoude, Neth.
80/E3 'Abd al 'Azīz, Jabal (mts.), Syria
73/K1 Abdulino, Rus.
103/K5 Abéché, Chad
109/E2 Abel Erasmuspas (pass), SAfr.
98/G4 Abemama (atoll), Kiri.
104/E5 Abengourou, C.d'Iv.
54/E1 Åbenrå, Den.
63/J2 Abens (riv.), Ger.
105/F5 Abeokuta, Nga.
50/D5 Aber, Wal,UK
52/B2 Aberaeron, Wal,UK
52/C1 Aberangell, Wal,UK
52/B2 Aberath, Wal,UK
52/C3 Abercarn, Wal,UK
52/C3 Aberdare, Wal,UK
50/D6 Aberdaron, Wal,UK
124/G2 Aberdeen (lake), Nun,Can.
49/D2 Aberdeen, Sc,UK
135/F3 Aberdeen, Ms,US
129/J4 Aberdeen, SD,US
128/C4 Aberdeen, Wa,US
52/B1 Aberdyfi, Wal,UK
49/D2 Aberfeldy, Sc,UK
49/C2 Aberfoyle, Sc,UK
52/C3 Abergavenny, Wal,UK
50/E5 Abergele, Wal,UK
52/B2 Aberporth, Wal,UK
50/D6 Abersoch, Wal,UK
52/C3 Abersychan, Wal,UK
130/B2 Abert (lake), Or,US
52/C3 Abertillery, Wal,UK
52/B2 Aberystwyth, Wal,UK
78/D5 Abhā, SAr.
78/E1 Abhar, Iran
103/P5 Abhe Bad (lake), Djib., Eth.
104/D5 Abidjan, C.d'Iv.
85/J7 Abiko, Japan
131/H3 Abilene, Ks,US
134/D3 Abilene, Tx,US
53/E3 Abingdon, Eng,UK
132/D4 Abingdon, Va,US
133/R10 Abino (pt.), On,Can.
131/F3 Abiquiu, NM,US
132/E1 Abitibi (lake), On,Can.
132/D1 Abitibi (riv.), On,Can.
73/G4 Abkhaz Aut. Rep., Geo.
106/B3 Abnūb, Egypt
104/E5 Aboisso, C.d'Iv.
105/F5 Abomey, Ben.
68/E2 Abony, Hun.
88/C6 Aborlan, Phil.
48/G3 Åbo (Turku), Fin.
49/D2 Aboyne, Sc,UK
88/D4 Abra (riv.), Phil.
123/G3 Abraham's Bay, Bahm.
64/A3 Abrantes, Port.
117/C1 Abra Pampa, Arg.
106/B4 'Abrī, Sudan
68/F2 Abrud, Rom.
66/C1 Abruzzi (reg.), It.
66/C2 Abruzzo Nat'l Park, It.
128/F4 Absaroka (range), Mt, Wy,US
78/F4 Abū al Abyaḑ (isl.), UAE
79/F4 Abu Dhabi (Abū Ẓaby) (cap.), UAE
106/C5 Abū Dīs, Sudan
106/B4 Abu el-Husein, Bîr (well), Egypt
106/C5 Abū Hamad, Sudan
106/C4 Abu Hashim, Bi'r (well), Egypt
80/H6 Abū Ḩummuş, Egypt
105/G4 Abuja (cap.), Nga.
105/G4 Abuja Cap. Terr., Nga.
80/H6 Abū Kabīr, Egypt
78/D2 Abū Kamāl, Syria
85/G2 Abukuma (hills), Japan
85/G2 Abukuma (riv.), Japan
88/D4 Abulog, Phil.
106/A3 Abu Minqâr, Bîr (well), Egypt
114/E6 Abuná (riv.), Bol.
114/E5 Abunã (riv.), Braz.
90/B3 Abu Road, India
106/D4 Abu Shagara, Ras (cape), Sudan
106/B4 Abu Simbel (ruins), Egypt
103/N5 Ābuyē Mēda (peak), Eth.
88/E5 Abuyog, Phil.
79/F4 Abū Ẓaby (Abu Dhabi) (cap.), UAE
66/A4 Abyaḑ, Ar Ra's al (cape), Tun.
106/B3 Abydos (ruins), Egypt
133/G2 Acadia Nat'l Park, Me,US
123/N9 Acaponeta, Mex.
122/B4 Acapulco, Mex.
114/G5 Acari (riv.), Braz.
123/H6 Acarigua, Ven.
122/B4 Acatlán, Mex.
105/E5 Accra (cap.), Gha.
51/F4 Accrington, Eng,UK
118/B4 Achao, Chile
105/H2 Achegour (well), Niger
83/K2 Acheng, China
58/B3 Achicourt, Fr.
58/B3 Achiel-le-Grand, Fr.
133/N6 Achigan (riv.), Qu,Can.
74/K4 Achinsk, Rus.
104/D2 Achmîm (well), Mrta.
49/C2 Achnasheen, Sc,UK
59/G3 Acht, Hohe (peak), Ger.
66/D4 Acireale, It.
123/G3 Acklins (isl.), Bahm.
51/G4 Ackworth Moor Top, Eng,UK
96/C4 Acland (peak), Austl.
53/H1 Acle, Eng,UK
118/C2 Aconcagua, Cerro (peak), Arg.
115/L5 Acopiara, Braz.
63/H4 Acqui Terme, It.
114/E6 Acre (riv.), Braz., Peru
116/B1 Acreúna, Braz.
67/L7 Acropolis, Gre.
99/M7 Actaeon Group (isls.), FrPol.
137/B2 Acton, Ca,US
115/L5 Açu, Braz.
118/Q9 Aculeo (lake), Chile
132/D3 Ada, Oh,US
131/H4 Ada, Ok,US
68/E3 Ada, Serb.
125/J1 Adair (cape), Nun,Can.
64/C2 Adaja (riv.), Sp.
136/C6 Adak (isl.), Ak,US
136/C6 Adak (str.), Ak,US
119/M7 Adam (peak), Falk.
116/B2 Adamantina, Braz.
105/H5 Adamawa (plat.), Camr., Nga.
128/D3 Adams (lake), BC,Can.
128/C4 Adams (peak), Wa,US
80/C3 Adana, Turk.
69/K5 Adapazarı, Turk.
111/M Adare (cape), Ant.
64/E1 Adarza (mtn.), Fr.
63/H4 Adda (riv.), It.
103/M4 Ad Dabbah, Sudan
78/D3 Ad Dahnā' (des.), SAr.
103/M5 Ad Damazin, Sudan
103/M4 Ad Damīr, Sudan
78/F3 Ad Dammām, SAr.
80/H6 Ad Daqahlīyah (gov.), Egypt
78/F3 Ad Dawḩah (Doha) (cap.), Qatar
80/H6 Ad Dilinjāt, Egypt
103/N6 Addis Ababa (cap.), Eth.
138/Q16 Addison, Il,US
78/D2 Ad Dīwānīyah, Iraq
108/D4 Addo Elephant Nat'l Park, SAfr.
103/M5 Ad Duwaym, Sudan
111/V Adelaide (isl.), Ant.
97/A2 Adelaide, Austl.
124/G2 Adelaide (pen.), Nun,Can.
108/D4 Adelaide, SAfr.
137/C1 Adelanto, Ca,US
57/G5 Adelebsen, Ger.
111/K Adélie (coast), Ant.
103/Q5 Aden (gulf), Afr., Asia
78/D6 Aden, Yem.
57/H2 Adendorf, Ger.
93/H4 Adi (isl.), Indo.
63/J4 Adige (Etsch) (riv.), It.
103/N5 Ādīgrat, Eth.
90/C4 Adilābād, India
105/E2 Adiora (well), Mali
132/F2 Adirondack (mts.), NY,US
103/N6 Ādīs Ābeba (Addis Ababa) (cap.), Eth.
103/N5 Ādīs Zemen, Eth.
78/C6 Ādī Ugri, Erit.
80/D3 Adıyaman, Turk.
69/H2 Adjud, Rom.
122/B3 Adjuntas (res.), Mex.
51/F4 Adlington, Eng,UK
125/H1 Admiralty (inlet), Nun,Can.
98/D5 Admiralty (isls.), PNG
138/B2 Admiralty (inlet), Wa,US
136/M4 Admiralty I. Nat'l Mon., Ak,US
85/L9 Ado (riv.), Japan
105/F5 Ado, Nga.
85/M9 Adogawa, Japan
90/C4 Ādoni, India
62/C5 Adour (riv.), Fr.
64/D4 Adra, Sp.
66/D4 Adrano, It.
102/E2 Adrar, Alg.
104/B1 Adrar (reg.), Mrta.
102/E1 Adrar bou Nasser (peak), Mor.
105/F1 Adrar des Iforas (mts.), Mali
103/K5 Adré, Chad
63/K4 Adria, It.
132/C3 Adrian, Mi,US
53/F5 Adur (riv.), Eng,UK
103/N5 Ādwa, Eth.
51/G4 Adwick le Street, Eng,UK
75/P3 Adycha (riv.), Rus.
72/F3 Adygeya, Resp., Rus.
73/G4 Adzhar Aut. Rep., Geo.
71/N2 Adz'va (riv.), Rus.
67/J3 Aegean (sea), Gre., Turk.
54/F1 Ærø (isl.), Den.
52/B2 Aeron (riv.), Wal,UK
57/G4 Aerzen, Ger.
50/E1 Ae, Water of (riv.), Sc,UK
105/F5 Afadjoto (peak), Gha.
99/X15 Afareaitu, FrPol.
80/M8 Afek Nat'l Park, Isr.
62/B3 Aff (riv.), Fr.
79/H2 Afghanistan (ctry.)
103/Q7 Afgooye, Som.
136/H3 Afognak (isl.), Ak,US
136/H4 Afognak (mtn.), Ak,US
104/C2 Afollé (reg.), Mrta.
116/D2 Afonso Cláudio, Braz.
66/D2 Afragola, It.
101/* Africa (cont.)
80/D2 Afşin, Turk.
56/C2 Afsluitdijk (IJsselmeer) (dam), Neth.
57/F5 Afte (riv.), Ger.
128/F5 Afton, Wy,US
80/K5 'Afula, Isr.
80/B2 Afyon, Turk.
102/H4 Agadem, Niger
105/G2 Agadez, Niger
105/H2 Agadez (dept.), Niger
102/D1 Agadir, Mor.
45/M6 Agalega (isls.), Mrts.
105/F2 Agamor (well), Mali
85/F2 Agano (riv.), Japan
103/N6 Āgaro, Eth.
91/F3 Agartala, India
111/V Agassiz (cape), Ant.
125/T6 Agassiz (ice field), Nun,Can.
131/G2 Agate Fossil Beds Nat'l Mon., Ne,US
136/A5 Agattu (isl.), Ak,US
136/A5 Agattu (str.), Ak,US
105/G5 Agbor, Nga.
104/D5 Agboville, C.d'Iv.
73/H5 Agdam, Azer.
62/E5 Agde, Fr.
62/E5 Agde, Cap d' (cape), Fr.
62/D4 Agen, Fr.
85/H7 Ageo, Japan
54/E1 Agerbæk, Den.
57/E6 Agger (riv.), Ger.
68/E1 Aggteleki Nat'l Park, Hun.
50/B3 Aghagallon, NI,UK
78/E2 Āghā Jārī, Iran
123/N8 Agiabampo, Estero de (bay), Mex.
75/M4 Aginskiy Buryatskiy Aut. Okrug, Rus.
82/G1 Aginskoye, Rus.
50/B1 Agivey, NI,UK
62/E5 Agly (riv.), Fr.
69/G3 Agnita, Rom.
85/M10 Ago, Japan
63/H4 Agogna (riv.), It.
137/B2 Agoura Hills, Ca,US
62/D5 Agout (riv.), Fr.
90/C2 Āgra, India
66/E2 Agri (riv.), It.
73/H5 Ağrı (Ararat) (peak), Turk.
66/C4 Agrigento, It.
98/D3 Agrihan (isl.), NMar.
67/G3 Agrinion, Gre.
118/C3 Agrio (riv.), Arg.
66/D2 Agropoli, It.
71/M4 Agryz, Rus.
123/G6 Aguachica, Col.
123/H4 Aguadilla, PR
122/C4 Agua Dulce, Mex.
123/E6 Aguadulce, Pan.
130/E4 Agua Fria Nat'l Mon., Az,US
116/F7 Aguaí, Braz.
65/P10 Agualva-Cacém, Port.
122/D4 Aguan (riv.), Hon.
116/B2 Aguapeí (riv.), Braz.
123/N7 Agua Prieta, Mex.
123/H6 Aguaro-Guariquito Nat'l Park, Ven.
116/H6 Águas (hills), Braz.
122/A3 Aguascalientes, Mex.
122/A3 Aguascalientes (state), Mex.
116/G6 Águas da Prata, Braz.
116/G7 Águas de Lindóia, Braz.
116/B1 Aguavermelha (res.), Braz.
116/B2 Agudos, Braz.
64/A2 Águeda, Port.
64/B2 Agueda (riv.), Sp.
102/C3 Agüenit, WSah.
85/M10 Agui, Japan
98/D3 Aguijan (isl.), NMar.
64/C4 Aguilar, Sp.
64/C1 Aguilar de Campóo, Sp.
117/C2 Aguilares, Arg.
64/E4 Aguilas, Sp.
123/P10 Aguililla de Iturbide, Mex.
65/X17 Agüimes, Canl.,Sp.
123/G5 Aguja (cape), Col.
108/M11 Agulhas (cape), SAfr.
116/C2 Agulhas Negras (peak), Braz.
93/E5 Agung (vol.), Indo.
88/E6 Agusan (riv.), Phil.
123/G5 Agustín Codazzi, Col.
102/G3 Ahaggar (plat.), Alg.
56/E4 Ahaus, Ger.
80/E2 Ahlat, Turk.
57/E5 Ahlen, Ger.
90/B3 Ahmadābād, India
90/B4 Ahmadnagar, India
79/K3 Ahmadpur East, Pak.
103/P6 Ahmar (mts.), Eth.
50/B2 Ahoghill, NI,UK
59/F3 Ahr (riv.), Ger.
57/H1 Ahrensburg, Ger.
57/F5 Ahse (riv.), Ger.
123/P9 Ahuacatlán, Mex.
126/W13 Ahuimanu, Hi,US
123/N7 Ahumada, Mex.
78/E2 Ahvāz, Iran
48/F4 Ahvenanmaa (prov.), Fin.
108/B2 Ai-Ais Hot Springs, Namb.
85/E3 Aichi (pref.), Japan
126/W13 Aiea, Hi,US
62/E4 Aigoual (mtn.), Fr.
62/F4 Aigues (riv.), Fr.
65/F1 Aigues Tortes y Lago de San Mauricio Nat'l Park, Sp.
85/F1 Aikawa, Japan
135/H3 Aiken, SC,US
123/F6 Ailigandí, Pan.
98/F4 Ailinglapalap (atoll), Mrsh.
50/C1 Ailsa Craig (isl.), Sc,UK
98/G3 Ailuk (atoll), Mrsh.
87/C5 Aimen Guan (pass), China
116/D1 Aimorés, Braz.
60/B5 Ain (dept.), Fr.
62/F4 Ain (riv.), Fr.
102/G1 'Aïn Beïda, Alg.
102/D2 Aïn Ben Tili, Mrta.
67/G3 Aínos (peak), Gre.
67/G3 Aínos Nat'l Park, Gre.
51/F4 Ainsdale, Eng,UK
102/E1 'Aïn Sefra, Alg.
131/H2 Ainsworth, Ne,US
105/G2 Aïr (plat.), Niger
128/E3 Airdrie, Ab,Can.
49/D3 Airdrie, Sc,UK
59/D5 Aire (riv.), Fr.
51/G4 Aire (riv.), Eng,UK
58/B2 Aire, Canal de (can.), Fr.
51/E5 Aire, Point of (pt.), Wal,UK
58/B2 Aire-sur-la-Lys, Fr.
125/J2 Air Force (isl.), Nun,Can.
51/F3 Airton, Eng,UK
63/J2 Aisch (riv.), Ger.
58/D3 Aiseau-Presles, Belg.
118/B5 Aisén del General Carlos Ibáñez del Campo (reg.), Chile
87/E3 Ai Shan (mtn.), China
136/L3 Aishihik, Yk,Can.
59/E3 Aisne (riv.), Belg.
58/C4 Aisne (dept.), Fr.
58/C5 Aisne (riv.), Fr.
102/E1 Aïssa (peak), Alg.
85/M9 Aitō, Japan
99/J6 Aitutaki (atoll), Cookls.
69/F2 Aiud, Rom.
116/J7 Aiuruoca (riv.), Braz.
62/F5 Aix-en-Provence, Fr.
62/F4 Aix-les-Bains, Fr.
67/H4 Aíyina, Gre.
67/H3 Aíyion, Gre.
85/F2 Aizu-Wakamatsu, Japan
91/F3 Āīzwal, India
66/A2 Ajaccio, Fr.
66/A2 Ajaccio (gulf), Fr.
133/R8 Ajax, On,Can.
82/D3 Aj Bogd (peak), Mong.
102/K1 Ajdābiyā, Libya
106/C5 Aj Janayet, Sudan
68/C2 Ajka, Hun.
90/B2 Ajmer, India
130/D4 Ajo, Az,US
64/D1 Ajo, Cabo de (cape), Sp.
122/A4 Ajuchitlán, Mex.
85/F1 Aka (riv.), Japan
85/N10 Akabane, Japan
81/F1 Akademik Obruchev (mts.), Rus.
85/F3 Akaishi-dake (mtn.), Japan
106/B4 Akasha East, Sudan
84/D3 Akashi, Japan
85/K10 Akashi (str.), Japan
81/B4 Akbaytal (pass), Taj.
80/D2 Akçaabat, Turk.
80/D3 Akçakale, Turk.
69/K5 Akçakoca, Turk.
104/B2 Akchâr (reg.), Mrta.
80/C2 Akdağmadeni, Turk.
78/G4 Akdar, Al Jabal (mts.), Oman
85/N9 Akechi, Japan
48/D3 Akershus (co.), Nor.
103/K7 Aketi, D.R. Congo
73/G4 Akhaltsikhe, Geo.
67/H3 Akharnaí, Gre.
67/G3 Akhelóos (riv.), Gre.
80/A2 Akhisar, Turk.
106/B3 Akhmīm, Egypt
73/H3 Akhtuba (riv.), Rus.
73/H2 Akhtubinsk, Rus.
72/E2 Akhtyrka, Ukr.
84/C4 Aki, Japan
85/H7 Aki (riv.), Japan
85/H7 Akigawa, Japan
125/H3 Akimiski (isl.), NW,Can.
85/H7 Akishima, Japan
83/N4 Akita, Japan
104/B2 Akjoujt, Mrta.
90/D6 Akkaraipattu, SrL.
80/K5 'Akko, Isr.
104/D2 'Aklé 'Aouâna (dune), Mali, Mrta.
84/D3 Akō, Japan
102/H7 Akoga, Gabon
90/C3 Akola, India
103/N4 Āk'ordat, Erit.
105/F5 Akosombo (dam), Gha.
125/K2 Akpatok (isl.), Nun,Can.
81/C3 Akqi, China
67/J2 Ákrathos, Ákra (cape), Gre.
48/C4 Åkrehamn, Nor.
67/G4 Akrítas, Ákra (cape), Gre.
131/G2 Akron, Co,US
132/D3 Akron, Oh,US
81/C4 Aksai Chin (reg.), China, India
80/C2 Aksaray, Turk.
82/C4 Aksay, China
80/B2 Akşehir, Turk.
80/B2 Akşehir (lake), Turk.
81/C2 Aksoran (peak), Kaz.
81/D3 Aksu, China
81/C3 Aksu (riv.), China
103/N5 Āksum, Eth.
67/J2 Aktí (pen.), Gre.
84/B4 Akune, Japan
48/N6 Akureyri, Ice.
136/E5 Akutan (isl.), Ak,US
136/E5 Akutan (passg.), Ak,US
105/G5 Akwa Ibom (state), Nga.
91/F3 Akyab (Sittwe), Myan.
73/L2 Ak'yar, Rus.
69/K5 Akyazı, Turk.
82/B3 Ala (riv.), China
135/G3 Alabama (state), US
135/G4 Alabama (riv.), Al,US
135/G3 Alabaster, Al,US
80/C2 Alaca, Turk.
80/C2 Alaçam, Turk.
135/H4 Alachua, Fl,US
73/H4 Alagir, Rus.
62/E4 Alagnon (riv.), Fr.
115/L6 Alagoinhas, Braz.
64/B2 Alagón (riv.), Sp.
48/G3 Alajärvi, Fin.
122/E5 Alajuela, CR
81/D2 Alaköl (lake), Kaz.
106/B2 Al 'Alamayn (El Alamein), Egypt
98/D3 Alamagan (isl.), NMar.
78/E2 Al 'Amārah, Iraq
78/F3 'Alāmarvdasht (riv.), Iran
138/K11 Alameda, Ca,US
122/E5 Alamikamba, Nic.
122/B3 Alamo, Mex.
130/D4 Alamo (lake), Az,US
138/K11 Alamo, Ca,US
130/D3 Alamo, Nv,US
131/F4 Alamogordo, NM,US
123/N8 Alamos, Mex.
131/F3 Alamosa, Co,US
48/G3 Åland (isls.), Fin.
54/F2 Aland (riv.), Ger.
80/C3 Alanya, Turk.
109/J7 Alaotra (lake), Madg.
135/H4 Alapaha (riv.), Ga,US
69/K5 Alaplı, Turk.
64/D3 Alarcón (res.), Sp.
80/B2 Alaşehir, Turk.
80/L6 Al 'Āşimah (gov.), Jor.
136/* Alaska (state), US
136/J4 Alaska (gulf), Ak,US
136/F4 Alaska (pen.), Ak,US
136/H3 Alaska (range), Ak,US
136/B5 Alaska Maritime Nat'l Wild. Ref., Ak,US
136/G4 Alaska Pen. Nat'l Wild. Ref., Ak,US
63/H5 Alassio, It.
71/K5 Alatyr', Rus.
73/H4 Alaverdi, Arm.
48/G3 Alavus, Fin.
50/D5 Alaw (riv.), Wal,UK
50/D5 Alaw, Llyn (lake), Wal,UK
81/B4 Alayskiy (mts.), Kyr.
75/R3 Alazeya (riv.), Rus.
78/E2 Al 'Azīzīyah, Iraq
102/H1 Al 'Azīzīyah, Libya
63/H4 Alba, It.
69/F2 Alba (co.), Rom.
80/D3 Al Bāb, Syria
64/E3 Albacete, Sp.
106/C3 Al Baḩr al Aḩmar (gov.), Egypt
63/F2 Alba Iulia, Rom.
80/K5 Al Balqā' (gov.), Jor.
106/C3 Al Balyanā, Egypt
133/F1 Albanel (lake), Qu,Can.
67/F2 Albania (ctry.)
95/A4 Albany, Austl.
125/H3 Albany (riv.), On,Can.
138/K11 Albany, Ca,US
135/G4 Albany, Ga,US
132/C4 Albany, Ky,US
132/F3 Albany (cap.), NY,US
128/C4 Albany, Or,US
78/E2 Al Başrah, Iraq
108/A2 Albatross (pt.), Namb.
106/B2 Al Bawīţī, Egypt
103/K1 Al Bayḑā, Libya
135/H3 Albemarle, NC,US
135/J2 Albemarle (sound), NC,US
63/H4 Albenga, It.
64/C2 Alberche (riv.), Sp.
97/A2 Albert (inlet), Austl.
59/E2 Albert (can.), Belg.
58/B4 Albert, Fr.
107/A2 Albert (lake), D.R. Congo, Ugan.
124/E3 Alberta (prov.), Can.
113/E2 Alberti, Arg.
68/D2 Albertirsa, Hun.
123/K5 Albert Lea, Mn,US
107/A2 Albert Nile (riv.), Ugan.
119/J8 Alberto de Agostini Nat'l Park, Chile
108/Q13 Alberton, SAfr.
63/G4 Albertville, Fr.
135/G3 Albertville, Al,US
62/E5 Albi, Fr.
63/H4 Albino, It.
132/C3 Albion, Mi,US
131/H2 Albion, Ne,US
80/L4 Al Biqā' (gov.), Leb.
80/K5 Al Biqā' (Bekaa) (val.), Leb.
80/K6 Al Bīrah, WBnk.
56/B5 Alblasserdam, Neth.
48/D4 Ålborg, Den.
64/D4 Albox, Sp.
52/D1 Albrighton, Eng,UK
64/A4 Albufeira, Port.
80/H6 Al Buḩayrah (gov.), Egypt
61/F4 Albula (riv.), Swi.
130/F4 Albuquerque, NM,US
64/B3 Alburquerque, Sp.
69/C3 Albury, Austl.
65/P10 Alcabideche, Port.
64/A3 Alcácer do Sal, Port.
64/C4 Alcalá de Guadaira, Sp.
64/D2 Alcalá de Henares, Sp.
64/D4 Alcalá la Real, Sp.
66/C4 Alcamo, It.
65/E2 Alcanadre (riv.), Sp.
65/E2 Alcanar, Sp.
65/E2 Alcañiz, Sp.
64/B3 Alcantara (res.), Sp.
64/E4 Alcantarilla, Sp.
64/D3 Alcarez (range), Sp.
138/K11 Alcatraz (isl.), Ca,US
64/C4 Alcaudete, Sp.
64/D3 Alcázar de San Juan, Sp.
53/E2 Alcester, Eng,UK
65/E3 Alcira, Sp.
135/H3 Alcoa, Tn,US
64/D2 Alcobendas, Sp.
65/Q10 Alcochete, Port.
65/E2 Alcora, Sp.
64/D2 Alcorcón, Sp.
135/H3 Alcovy (riv.), Ga,US
65/E3 Alcoy, Sp.
101/G5 Aldabra (isls.), Sey.
134/B4 Aldama, Mex.
75/N4 Aldan, Rus.
75/N4 Aldan (plat.), Rus.
75/P3 Aldan (riv.), Rus.
81/G2 Aldarhaan, Mong.
53/E4 Aldbourne, Eng,UK
51/H4 Aldbrough, Eng,UK
53/H2 Alde (riv.), Eng,UK
53/H2 Aldeburgh, Eng,UK
110/B2 Aldeia Viçosa, Ang.
59/F2 Aldenhoven, Ger.
50/B2 Aldergrove, NI,UK
51/F5 Alderley Edge, Eng,UK
53/E4 Aldermaston, Eng,UK
53/F4 Aldershot, Eng,UK
138/C2 Alderwood Manor-Bothell North, Wa,US
134/E4 Aldine, Tx,US
53/E1 Aldridge, Eng,UK
104/B2 Aleg, Mrta.
116/D2 Alegre, Braz.
117/E2 Alegrete, Braz.
113/A6 Alejandro Selkirk (isl.), Chile
72/E2 Aleksandriya, Ukr.
70/H4 Aleksandrov, Rus.
71/N4 Aleksandrovsk, Rus.
83/N1 Aleksandrovsk-Sakhalinskiy, Rus.
55/K2 Aleksandrów Kujawski, Pol.
55/K3 Aleksandrów Łódzki, Pol.
81/B1 Alekseyevka, Kaz.
72/F2 Alekseyevka, Rus.
70/H5 Aleksin, Rus.
68/E4 Aleksinac, Serb.
116/L6 Além Paraíba, Braz.
62/D2 Alençon, Fr.
115/H4 Alenquer, Braz.
126/T10 Alenuihaha (chan.), Hi,US
80/D3 Aleppo (Ḩalab), Syria
118/B4 Alerce Andino Nat'l Park, Chile
125/S6 Alert (pt.), Nun,Can.
68/F2 Aleşd, Rom.
63/H4 Alessandria, It.
48/C3 Ålesund, Nor.
136/E5 Aleutian (isls.), Ak,US
136/G4 Aleutian (range), Ak,US
111/V Alexander (cape), Ant.
111/V Alexander (isl.), Ant.
136/L4 Alexander (arch.), Ak,US
135/G3 Alexander City, Al,US
67/H2 Alexándria, Gre.
69/G4 Alexandria, Rom.
134/E4 Alexandria, La,US
129/K4 Alexandria, Mn,US
137/J8 Alexandria, Va,US
106/B2 Alexandria (Al Iskandarīyah), Egypt
97/A2 Alexandrina (lake), Austl.
67/J2 Alexandroúpolis, Gre.
128/C2 Alexis Creek, BC,Can.
81/D1 Aley (riv.), Rus.
81/D1 Aleysk, Rus.
65/E3 Alfafar, Sp.
78/D2 Al Fallūjah, Iraq
65/P10 Alfama, Port.
65/P11 Alfarim, Port.
64/E1 Alfaro, Sp.
103/L5 Al Fāsher, Sudan
106/B2 Al Fashn, Egypt
78/D1 Al Fatḩah, Iraq
78/E3 Al Fāw, Iraq
106/B2 Al Fayyum, Egypt
106/B2 Al Fayyum (gov.), Egypt
59/F3 Alfbach (riv.), Ger.
57/G5 Alfeld, Ger.
116/H6 Alfenas, Braz.
67/G4 Alfiós (riv.), Gre.
51/J5 Alford, Eng,UK
97/D3 Alfred Nat'l Park, Austl.
51/G5 Alfreton, Eng,UK
53/G5 Alfriston, Eng,UK
59/G2 Alfter, Ger.
73/L2 Alga, Kaz.
48/C4 Ålgård, Nor.
64/C4 Algeciras, Sp.
65/E3 Algemesí, Sp.
102/F2 Algeria (ctry.)
57/G4 Algermissen, Ger.
65/N8 Algete, Sp.
106/B2 Al Gharbīyah (gov.), Egypt
66/A2 Alghero, It.
106/C3 Al Ghurdaqah, Egypt
102/F1 Algiers (cap.), Alg.
65/E3 Alginet, Sp.
108/D4 Algoa (bay), SAfr.
114/D4 Algodón (riv.), Peru
138/P15 Algonquin, Il,US
65/P10 Algueirão, Port.
78/D2 Al Ḩadīthah, Iraq
80/E3 Al Ḩaḑr, Iraq
79/G4 Al Ḩajar ash Sharqī (mts.), Oman
79/G5 Al Ḩallānīyah (isl.), Oman
64/D4 Alhama de Granada, Sp.
64/E4 Alhama de Murcia, Sp.
137/B2 Alhambra, Ca,US
106/B2 Al Ḩammām, Egypt
65/Q10 Alhandra, Port.
80/E3 Al Ḩasakah, Syria
64/C4 Alhaurín el Grande, Sp.
106/B2 Al Ḩawāmidīyah, Egypt
78/E2 Al Ḩayy, Iraq
78/D2 Al Ḩillah, Iraq
78/D2 Al Hindīyah, Iraq
102/E1 Al Hoceima, Mor.
78/E3 Al Hufūf, SAr.
80/A2 Aliağa, Turk.
67/G2 Aliákmon (riv.), Gre.
67/G2 Aliákmonos (lake), Gre.
78/E2 'Alī al Gharbī, Iraq
78/E2 'Alī ash Sharqī, Iraq
134/C3 Alibates Flint Quarries Nat'l Mon., Tx,US
73/J5 Āli-Bayramlı, Azer.
106/C5 Al Ibēdiyya, Sudan
69/J5 Alibeyköy, Turk.
65/E3 Alicante, Sp.
96/A1 Alice (riv.), Austl.
66/E3 Alice (pt.), It.
134/D5 Alice, Tx,US
95/C3 Alice Springs, Austl.
135/F3 Aliceville, Al,US
88/D6 Alicia, Phil.
66/D3 Alicudi (isl.), It.
90/C2 Alīgarh, India
78/E2 Alīgudarz, Iran
102/J8 Alima (riv.), Congo
48/E4 Alingsås, Swe.
90/B2 Alīpur, Pak.
90/E2 Alīpur Duār, India
106/B2 Al Iskandarīyah (gov.), Egypt
106/B2 Al Iskandarīyah (Alexandria), Egypt
106/C2 Al Ismā'īlīyah (gov.), Egypt
106/C2 Al Ismā'īlīyah (Ismailia), Egypt
108/D3 Aliwal North, SAfr.
103/K2 Al Jaghbūb, Libya
66/B5 Al Jamm, Tun.
80/K5 Al Janūb (gov.), Leb.
106/B2 Al Jīzah, Egypt
106/B2 Al Jīzah (gov.), Egypt
103/K5 Al Junaynah, Sudan
64/A4 Aljustrel, Port.
80/K6 Al Karak, Jor.
80/L6 Al Karak (gov.), Jor.
106/C3 Al Karnak, Egypt
59/E2 Alken, Belg.
79/G4 Al Khābūrah, Oman
80/K6 Al Khalīl (Hebron), WBnk.
78/D2 Al Khāliş, Iraq
106/B5 Al Khandaq, Sudan
106/B3 Al Khārijah, Egypt
103/M4 Al Kharţūm Baḩrī (Khartoum North), Sudan
78/F3 Al Khobar, SAr.
102/H1 Al Khums, Libya
56/B3 Alkmaar, Neth.
102/H3 Alkoum (well), Alg.
78/D2 Al Kūfah, Iraq
103/K3 Al Kufrah, Libya
78/E2 Al Kūt, Iraq
80/K4 Al Lādhiqīyah (Latakia), Syria
90/D2 Allahābād, India
129/G3 Allan, Sk,Can.
129/G3 Allan (hills), Sk,Can.
133/R9 Allanburg, On,Can.
91/G4 Allanmyo, Myan.
129/L3 Allan Water (riv.), On,Can.
102/H1 'Allāq (well), Libya
106/C4 'Allāqī, Wādī al (dry riv.), Egypt
132/C3 Allegan, Mi,US
132/D4 Allegheny (mts.), US
132/E3 Allegheny (plat.), Pa,US
132/E3 Allegheny (riv.), Pa,US
118/D3 Allen, Arg.
51/F2 Allen (riv.), Eng,UK
50/B5 Allen, Bog of (swamp), Ire.
51/F2 Allendale, Eng,UK
135/H3 Allendale, SC,US
122/A2 Allende, Mex.
138/F7 Allen Park, Mi,US
137/E5 Allentown, Pa,US
90/C6 Alleppey, India
57/G3 Aller (riv.), Ger.
57/H4 Allerkanal (can.), Ger.
61/G3 Allgäu (mts.), Aus., Ger.
131/G2 Alliance, Ne,US
132/D3 Alliance, Oh,US
62/E3 Allier (riv.), Fr.
62/D3 Allones, Fr.
133/G1 Alma, Qu,Can.
132/C3 Alma, Mi,US
131/H2 Alma, Ne,US
64/A3 Almada, Port.
64/C3 Almadén, Sp.
78/B3 Al Madīnah al Fikrīyah, Egypt
80/L5 Al Mafraq, Jor.
118/D2 Almafuerte, Arg.
102/E1 Al Maghrib (reg.), Alg., Mor.
64/D3 Almagro, Sp.
80/H6 Al Maḩallah al Kubrá, Egypt
80/H6 Al Maḩmūdīyah, Egypt
78/D2 Al Maḩmūdīyah, Iraq
80/E3 Al Mālikīyah, Syria
81/A3 Almalyk, Uzb.
78/F3 Al Manāmah (Manama) (cap.), Bahr.
130/B2 Almanor (lake), Ca,US
65/E3 Almansa, Sp.
80/H6 Al Manşūrah, Egypt
80/H6 Al Manzilah, Egypt
64/D4 Almanzora (riv.), Sp.
64/C2 Almanzor, Pico de (peak), Sp.
106/B3 Al Marāghah, Egypt
102/K1 Al Marj, Libya
115/J6 Almas (riv.), Braz.
106/B2 Al Maţarīyah, Egypt
81/C3 Almaty, Kaz.
80/E3 Al Mawşil (Mosul), Iraq
78/D1 Al Mayādin, Syria
65/E3 Almazora, Sp.
57/F5 Alme (riv.), Ger.
64/A3 Almeirim, Port.
56/D4 Almelo, Neth.
115/K7 Almenara, Braz.
64/D3 Almenara (mtn.), Sp.
64/B2 Almendra (res.), Sp.
64/B3 Almendralejo, Sp.
56/C4 Almere, Neth.
64/D4 Almería, Sp.
65/D4 Almeria (gulf), Sp.
71/M5 Al'met'yevsk, Rus.
48/E4 Älmhult, Swe.
64/C5 Almina (pt.), Sp.
106/B2 Al Minūfīyah (gov.), Egypt
106/B2 Al Minyā, Egypt
106/B3 Al Minyā (gov.), Egypt
78/D2 Al Miqdādiyah, Iraq
119/J7 Almirante Montt (gulf), Chile
67/H3 Almirós, Gre.
67/J5 Almiroú (gulf), Gre.
64/C3 Almodóvar del Campo, Sp.
64/C4 Almodóvar del Río, Sp.
49/D2 Almond (riv.), Sc,UK
132/E2 Almonte, On,Can.
64/B4 Almonte, Sp.
65/E3 Almoradí, Sp.
116/D1 Almores (range), Braz.
78/E3 Al Mubarraz, SAr.
103/L5 Al Muglad, Sudan
64/D4 Almuñécar, Sp.
49/C2 Alness, Sc,UK
99/J6 Alofi (cap.), Niue

98/H6 Alofi (isl.), Wall.
91/G2 Along, India
67/H3 Alónnisos (isl.), Gre.
93/F5 Alor (isls.), Indo.
64/C4 Álora, Sp.
92/B2 Alor Setar, Malay.
98/E6 Alotau, PNG
56/D5 Alpen, Ger.
132/D2 Alpena, Mi,US
115/J5 Alpercatas (mts.), Braz.
56/B4 Alphen aan de Rijn, Neth.
64/A3 Alpiarça, Port.
134/C4 Alpine, Tx,US
128/F5 Alpine, Wy,US
64/B4 Alportel, Port.
47/E4 Alps (mts.), Eur.
85/F3 Alps-Minami Nat'l Park, Japan
79/G4 Al Qābil, Oman
103/N5 Al Qaḍīrif, Sudan
106/B2 Al Qāhirah (Cairo) (cap.), Egypt
106/B2 Al Qāhirah (gov.), Egypt
106/B2 Al Qalyūbīyah (gov.), Egypt
80/E3 Al Qāmishlī, Syria
106/B3 Al Qaṣr, Egypt
103/M5 Al Qaṭaynah, Sudan
102/H3 Al Qaṭrūn, Libya
80/K5 Al Qunayṭirah (prov.), Syria
106/C3 Al Quṣayr, Egypt
80/L4 Al Quṣayr, Syria
80/L5 Al Quṭayfah, Syria
53/E1 Alrewas, Eng,UK
54/F1 Als (isl.), Den.
60/D2 Alsace (reg.), Fr.
60/C2 Alsace, Ballon d' (mtn.), Fr.
51/F5 Alsager, Eng,UK
128/F3 Alsask, Sk,Can.
64/D1 Alsasua, Sp.
59/F2 Alsdorf, Ger.
54/E3 Alsfeld, Ger.
138/Q16 Alsip, Il,US
57/H1 Alster (riv.), Ger.
51/F2 Alston, Eng,UK
51/F4 Alt (riv.), Eng,UK
48/G1 Alta, Nor.
137/B2 Altadena, Ca,US
115/G5 Alta Floresta, Braz.
118/D1 Alta Gracia, Arg.
122/D5 Alta Gracia, Nic.
81/D1 Altai (mts.), Asia
135/H4 Altamaha (riv.), Ga,US
115/H4 Altamira, Braz.
122/B3 Altamira, Mex.
135/H4 Altamonte Springs, Fl,US
66/E2 Altamura, It.
122/C4 Altar de los Sacrificios (ruins), Guat.
82/B2 Altay, China
74/J4 Altay, Resp., Rus.
74/J4 Altayskiy Kray, Rus.
61/E4 Altdorf, Swi.
63/J2 Altdorf bei Nürnberg, Ger.
65/E3 Altea, Sp.
57/E6 Altena, Ger.
57/F5 Altenau (riv.), Ger.
57/F5 Altenbeken, Ger.
54/G3 Altenburg, Ger.
55/G2 Altentreptow, Ger.
123/P8 Alteres, Mex.
56/D5 Alter Rhein (riv.), Ger.
57/G1 Altes Land (reg.), Ger.
51/H4 Althorpe, Eng,UK
114/E7 Altiplano (plat.), Bo., Peru
54/F2 Altmark (reg.), Ger.
63/J2 Altmühl (riv.), Ger.
63/K3 Altmünster, Aus.
115/J6 Alto (peak), Braz.
115/H7 Alto Araguaia, Braz.
110/C2 Alto Cuale, Ang.
53/F4 Alton, Eng,UK
132/B4 Alton, Il,US
97/F5 Altona, Austl.
129/J3 Altona, Mb,Can.
132/E3 Altoona, Pa,US
114/D6 Alto Purús (riv.), Peru
115/K5 Altos, Braz.
51/F5 Altrincham, Eng,UK
82/C4 Altun (mts.), China
122/D4 Altun Ha (ruins), Belz.
130/B2 Alturas, Ca,US
131/H4 Altus, Ok,US
131/H4 Altus (res.), Ok,US
131/H4 Altus A.F.B., Ok,US
103/M5 Al Ubayyiḍ, Sudan
103/L5 Al Uḍayyah, Sudan
106/C3 Al Uqṣur (Luxor), Egypt
72/E3 Alushta, Ukr.
103/L3 Al 'Uwaynāt (peak), Sudan
131/H3 Alva, Ok,US
53/E2 Alvechurch, Eng,UK
64/A3 Alverca, Port.
65/P10 Alverca do Ribatejo, Port.
48/E4 Alvesta, Swe.
52/D4 Alveston, Eng,UK
134/E4 Alvin, Tx,US
48/F3 Älvkarleby, Swe.
48/E4 Älvsborg (co.), Swe.
48/G2 Älvsbyn, Swe.
106/B3 Al Wādī al Jadīd (gov.), Egypt
90/C2 Alwar, India
50/E5 Alwen (riv.), Wal,UK
82/E4 Alxa Youqi, China
82/F4 Alxa Zuoqi, China
55/N1 Alytus, Lith.
63/K2 Alz (riv.), Ger.
63/H4 Alzano Lombardo, It.
59/F4 Alzette (riv.), Lux.
106/C2 Al `Aqabah, Jor.
114/D4 Amacayacú Nat'l Park, Col.
78/B4 Amada (ruins), Egypt
103/M6 Amadi, Sudan
125/J2 Amadjuak (lake), Nun,Can.
64/A3 Amadora, Port.
85/L10 Amagasaki, Japan
84/B4 Amagi, Japan
85/F3 Amagi-san (mtn.), Japan
93/G4 Amahai, Indo.
84/A4 Amakusa (sea), Japan
48/E4 Åmål, Swe.
82/G1 Amalat (riv.), Rus.
67/G4 Amaliás, Gre.
90/C3 Amalner, India
117/E1 Amambaí, Braz.
115/H8 Amambaí (riv.), Braz.
98/B2 Amami (isls.), Japan
66/E3 Amantea, It.
99/L6 Amanu (atoll), FrPol.
64/A2 Amarante, Port.
89/B1 Amarapura, Myan.
130/C3 Amargosa (dry riv.), Ca, Nv,US
134/C3 Amarillo, Tx,US
66/D1 Amaro (peak), It.
80/C2 Amasya, Turk.
85/J7 Amatsukominato, Japan
59/E2 Amay, Belg.
115/H4 Amazon (riv.), SAm.
115/G4 Amazônia (Tapajós) Nat'l Park, Braz.
90/C4 Ambajogai, India
79/L2 Ambāla, India
90/D6 Ambalangoda, SrL.
109/H8 Ambalavao, Madg.
109/J6 Ambanja, Madg.
109/H6 Ambaro (bay), Madg.
114/C4 Ambato, Ecu.
109/H7 Ambato Boeny, Madg.
109/H8 Ambatofinandrahana, Madg.
109/H7 Ambatolampy, Madg.
109/J7 Ambatondrazaka, Madg.
67/H4 Ámbelos, Ákra (cape), Gre.
63/J2 Amberg, Ger.
51/G5 Ambergate, Eng,UK
90/D3 Ambikāpur, India
109/J6 Ambilobe, Madg.
109/J7 Ambinaninony, Madg.
51/G1 Amble, Eng,UK
137/E5 Ambler, Pa,US
51/F3 Ambleside, Eng,UK
58/A2 Ambleteuse, Fr.
59/F3 Amblève (riv.), Belg.
109/H9 Amboasary, Madg.
109/J6 Ambohitra, Tampon (peak), Madg.
93/G4 Ambon, Indo.
93/G4 Ambon (isl.), Indo.
109/H8 Ambositra, Madg.
109/H9 Ambovombe, Madg.
110/B2 Ambriz, Ang.
98/F6 Ambrym (isl.), Van.
136/B6 Amchitka (isl.), Ak,US
136/B6 Amchitka (passg.), Ak,US
123/P9 Ameca, Mex.
59/F3 Amel, Belg.
56/C2 Ameland (isl.), Neth.
56/B5 Amer (chan.), Neth.
111/F American (highland), Ant.
138/M9 American (riv.), Ca,US
138/B3 American (lake), Wa,US
116/C2 Americana, Braz.
128/E5 American Falls, Id,US
130/D2 American Falls (res.), Id,US
130/E2 American Fork, Ut,US
99/J6 American Samoa (terr.), US
135/G3 Americus, Ga,US
63/L3 Ameringkogel (peak), Aus.
56/C4 Amersfoort, Neth.
53/F3 Amersham, Eng,UK
111/E Amery Ice Shelf, Ant.
129/K5 Ames, Ia,US
53/E4 Amesbury, Eng,UK
67/H3 Ámfissa, Gre.
75/N3 Amga (riv.), Rus.
75/T3 Amguema (riv.), Rus.
83/M1 Amgun' (riv.), Rus.
133/H2 Amherst, NS,Can.
138/F7 Amherstburg, On,Can.
66/B1 Amiata (peak), It.
58/B4 Amiens, Fr.
75/U4 Amila (isl.), Ak,US
45/M6 Amirante (isls.), Sey.
129/H2 Amisk (lake), Sk,Can.
134/C4 Amistad (res.), Mex., US
131/G5 Amistad Nat'l Rec. Area, Tx,US
131/K5 Amite (riv.), La,US
90/C3 Amla, India
136/D6 Amlia (isl.), Ak,US
50/D5 Amlwch, Wal,UK
80/K6 Ammān (cap.), Jor.
52/C3 Amman (riv.), Wal,UK
52/C3 Ammanford, Wal,UK
48/E2 Ammarfjället (peak), Swe.
136/K2 Ammerman (mtn.), Yk,Can.
61/H2 Ammersee (lake), Ger.
128/F5 Ammon, Id,US
89/D3 Amnat Charoen, Thai.
59/F5 Amnéville, Fr.
78/F1 Āmol, Iran
65/P10 Amora, Port.
67/J4 Amorgós (isl.), Gre.
135/F3 Amory, Ms,US
132/E1 Amos, Qu,Can.
109/J8 Ampangalana (can.), Madg.
109/H9 Ampanihy, Madg.
90/D6 Amparai, SrL.
116/G7 Amparo, Braz.
109/J6 Ampasindava (bay), Madg.
65/F2 Amposta, Sp.
53/F2 Ampthill, Eng,UK
133/H1 Amqui, Qu,Can.
90/C3 Amravati, India
90/B3 Amreli, India
78/C2 'Amrīt (ruins), Syria
79/K2 Amritsar, India
54/E1 Amrum (isl.), Ger.
56/B4 Amstel (riv.), Neth.
56/B4 Amstelveen, Neth.
45/N7 Amsterdam (isl.), FrAnt.
56/B4 Amsterdam (cap.), Neth.
132/F3 Amsterdam, NY,US
56/C5 Amsterdam-Rijnkanaal (can.), Neth.
63/L2 Amstetten, Aus.
103/K5 Am Timan, Chad
77/F5 Amudar'ya (riv.), Asia
136/D5 Amukta (passg.), Ak,US
125/S7 Amund Rignes (isl.), Nun,Can.
111/D Amundsen (bay), Ant.
111/S Amundsen (sea), Ant.
124/D1 Amundsen (gulf), NW,Can.
111/A Amundsen-Scott, Ant.
83/M1 Amur (riv.), China, Rus.
99/K6 Amuri, Cookls.
75/N4 Amur Obl., Rus.
64/D1 Amurrio, Sp.
83/M1 Amursk, Rus.
75/N4 Amurskaya Oblast, Rus.
106/C5 'Amur, Wādī (dry riv.), Sudan
80/K4 Amyūn, Leb.
99/L6 Anaa (atoll), FrPol.
75/L3 Anabar (riv.), Rus.
137/A2 Anacapa (isl.), Ca,US
123/J6 Anaco, Ven.
128/E4 Anaconda, Mt,US
131/H4 Anadarko, Ok,US
75/T3 Anadyr', Rus.
75/U3 Anadyr' (gulf), Rus.
75/T3 Anadyr' (range), Rus.
75/T3 Anadyr' (riv.), Rus.
67/J4 Anáfi (isl.), Gre.
78/D2 'Ānah, Iraq
137/C3 Anaheim, Ca,US
128/B2 Anahim Lake, BC,Can.
122/A2 Anáhuac, Mex.
134/E4 Anahuac, Tx,US
90/D4 Anakāpalle, India
109/H6 Analalava, Madg.
109/J7 Analamaitso (plat.), Madg.
123/F3 Ana María (gulf), Cuba
92/C3 Anambas (isls.), Indo.
105/G5 Anambra (state), Nga.
80/C3 Anamur, Turk.
80/C3 Anamur (pt.), Turk.
84/D4 Anan, Japan
90/B3 Anand, India
90/C5 Anantapur, India
79/L2 Anantnag, India
81/C3 Anan'yevo, Kyr.
72/F3 Anapa, Rus.
119/K7 Añapi (peak), Arg.
115/J7 Anápolis, Braz.
115/H4 Anapu (riv.), Braz.
115/G8 Anastácio, Braz.
98/D3 Anathan (isl.), NMar.
80/B2 Anatolia (reg.), Turk.
117/D2 Añatuya, Arg.
114/F3 Anauá (riv.), Braz.
133/Q9 Ancaster, On,Can.
88/A2 Anchangzhen, China
138/G6 Anchor (bay), Mi,US
136/J3 Anchorage, Ak,US
133/G2 Ancienne-Lorette, Qu,Can.
114/E7 Ancohuma (peak), Bol.
63/K5 Ancona, It.
118/B4 Ancud, Chile
118/B4 Ancud (gulf), Chile
83/K2 Anda, China
114/D6 Andahuaylas, Peru
109/J7 Andaingo Gara, Madg.
48/C3 Åndalsnes, Nor.
64/C4 Andalusia (aut. comm.), Sp.
135/G4 Andalusia, Al,US
91/F5 Andaman (sea), Asia
91/F5 Andaman (isls.), India
91/F5 Andaman & Nicobar Is. (terr.), India
109/J6 Andapa, Madg.
58/A4 Andelle (riv.), Fr.
48/F1 Andenes, Nor.
59/E3 Andenne, Belg.
48/F1 Anderdalen Nat'l Park, Nor.
58/D3 Anderlues, Belg.
59/G3 Andernach, Ger.
136/N2 Anderson (riv.), NW,Can.
130/B2 Anderson, Ca,US
132/C3 Anderson, In,US
135/H3 Anderson, SC,US
134/E4 Anderson, Tx,US
138/B3 Anderson (isl.), Wa,US
113/C4 Andes (mts.), SAm.
48/F1 Andfjorden (fjord), Nor.
90/C4 Andhra Pradesh (state), India
67/H5 Andikíthira (isl.), Gre.
109/J7 Andilamena, Madg.
78/E2 Andīmeshk, Iran
67/J4 Andíparos (isl.), Gre.
116/B2 Andira, Braz.
81/B3 Andizhan, Uzb.
64/D1 Andoain, Sp.
86/E4 Andong, SKor.
86/E4 Andong (lake), SKor.
65/F1 Andorra (ctry.)
65/E2 Andorra, Sp.
65/F1 Andorra la Vella (cap.), And.
53/E4 Andover, Eng,UK
137/F5 Andover, NJ,US
48/E1 Andøya (isl.), Nor.
116/G7 Andradas, Braz.
116/B2 Andradina, Braz.
65/G3 Andraitx, Sp.
109/H7 Andranomavo (riv.), Madg.
136/C6 Andreanof (isls.), Ak,US
116/J6 Andrelândia, Braz.
134/C3 Andrews, Tx,US
66/E2 Andria, It.
109/H8 Andringitra (mts.), Madg.
109/J6 Androntany (cape), Madg.
123/F3 Andros (isl.), Bahm.
67/J4 Ándros (isl.), Gre.
132/G2 Androscoggin (riv.), Me, NH,US
64/C3 Andújar, Sp.
118/C4 Anecón Grande (peak), Arg.
118/E4 Anegada (bay), Arg.
123/J4 Anegada (isl.), BVi.
123/J4 Anegada (passage), NAm.
75/N6 Aného, Togo
98/G7 Aneityum (isl.), Van.
65/F1 Aneto, Pico de (peak), Sp.
88/B2 Anfu, China
117/B1 Angamos (pt.), Chile
82/E1 Angara (riv.), Rus.
82/E1 Angarsk, Rus.
48/E3 Ånge, Swe.
57/E5 Angel (riv.), Ger.
123/M8 Ángel de la Guarda (isl.), Mex.
88/D4 Angeles, Phil.
137/B2 Angeles Nat'l Forest, Ca,US
134/E4 Angelina (riv.), Tx,US
54/E1 Angeln (reg.), Ger.
114/F2 Angel, Salto (falls), Ven.
138/F6 Angelus (lake), Mi,US
48/E2 Ångermanälven (riv.), Swe.
55/H2 Angermünde, Ger.
62/C3 Angers, Fr.
89/C3 Angkor (ruins), Camb.
89/D4 Angk Tasaom, Camb.
50/D5 Anglesey (isl.), Wal,UK
62/C5 Anglet, Fr.
134/E4 Angleton, Tx,US
62/D3 Anglin (riv.), Fr.
89/C2 Ang Nam Ngum (lake), Laos
103/L7 Ango, D.R. Congo
118/B3 Angol, Chile
110/C3 Angola (ctry.)
132/C3 Angola, In,US
122/C4 Angostura (res.), Mex.
62/D4 Angoulême, Fr.
65/S12 Angra do Heroísmo, Azor.,Port.
116/J8 Angra dos Reis, Braz.
81/B3 Angren, Uzb.
89/C3 Ang Thong, Thai.
103/K7 Angu, D.R. Congo
123/J4 Anguilla (isl.), UK
136/G2 Angutikada (peak), Ak,US
115/H8 Anhanduí (riv.), Braz.
59/D3 Anhée, Belg.
91/K2 Anhua, China
87/D4 Anhui (prov.), China
136/G4 Aniakchak (crater), Ak,US
136/G4 Aniakchak Nat'l Mon. & Prsv., Ak,US
58/C3 Aniche, Fr.
130/F3 Animas (riv.), Co, NM,US
68/E3 Anina, Rom.
83/N2 Aniva (bay), Rus.
48/H3 Anjalamkoski, Fin.
90/B3 Anjār, India
85/N10 Anjō, Japan
62/C3 Anjou (hist. reg.), Fr.
109/H6 Anjouan (isl.), Com.
80/C2 Ankara (cap.), Turk.
109/J7 Ankaratra, Massif (plat.), Madg.
134/C2 Ankaree (riv.), Co,US
109/H8 Ankazoabo, Madg.
89/E3 An Khe, Viet.
55/G2 Anklam, Ger.
89/D3 Anlong Veng, Camb.
56/D2 Anloo, Neth.
87/C5 Anlu, China
111/D Ann (cape), Ant.
133/G3 Ann (cape), Ma,US
132/E4 Anna (lake), Va,US
102/G1 Annaba, Alg.
63/K1 Annaberg-Buchholz, Ger.
80/L4 An Nabk, Syria
50/B3 Annaclone, NI,UK
78/C3 An Nafūd (des.), SAr.
103/L5 An Nahūd, Sudan
78/D2 An Najaf, Iraq
49/B3 Annalee (riv.), Ire.
50/C3 Annalong, NI,UK
89/D2 Annamitique, Chaine (mts.), Laos, Viet.
51/E2 Annan, Sc,UK
49/D3 Annan (riv.), Sc,UK
137/J8 Annandale, Va,US
56/B3 Anna Pavlowna, Neth.
118/B5 Anna Pink (bay), Chile
137/K8 Annapolis (cap.), Md,US
90/D2 Annapurna (mtn.), Nepal
78/C3 An Naqb, Ra's, Jor.
138/E7 Ann Arbor, Mi,US
78/E2 An Nāṣirīyah, Iraq
97/C4 Anne (peak), Austl.
63/G4 Annecy, Fr.
89/E3 An Nhon, Viet.
135/G3 Anniston, Al,US
102/F8 Annobón (isl.), EqG.
62/F4 Annonay, Fr.
78/E2 An Nu'manīyah, Iraq
85/M10 Anō, Japan
65/K7 Anoia (riv.), Sp.
129/K4 Anoka, Mn,US
109/J7 Anosibe an' Ala, Madg.
105/G2 Anou-Zeggarene (wadi), Niger
89/E4 An Phuoc, Viet.
87/D5 Anqing, China
57/F5 Anröchte, Ger.
59/E2 Ans, Belg.
63/J2 Ansbach, Ger.
123/G4 Anse-d'Hainault, Haiti
63/L2 Ansfelden, Aus.
86/B2 Anshan, China
91/J2 Anshun, China
134/D3 Anson, Tx,US
86/D4 Ansŏng, SKor.
98/E4 Ant (atoll), Micr.
53/H1 Ant (riv.), Eng,UK
80/D3 Antakya (Antioch), Turk.
109/J6 Antalaha, Madg.
80/B3 Antalya, Turk.
80/B3 Antalya (gulf), Turk.
109/H7 Antananarivo (cap.), Madg.
109/H7 Antananarivo (prov.), Madg.
111/W Antarctic (pen.), Ant.
111/* Antarctica (cont.)
116/B4 Antas (riv.), Braz.
58/D5 Ante (riv.), Fr.
64/C4 Antequera, Sp.
131/H3 Anthony, Ks,US
130/F4 Anthony, NM,US
102/D2 Anti-Atlas (mts.), Mor.
63/G5 Antibes, Fr.
133/J1 Anticosti (isl.), Qu,Can.
62/D2 Antifer, Cap d' (cape), Fr.
132/B2 Antigo, Wi,US
133/J2 Antigonish, NS,Can.
123/J4 Antigua (isl.), Ant. & Barb.
123/J4 Antigua and Barbuda (ctry.)
80/K5 Anti-Lebanon (mts.), Leb.
138/L10 Antioch, Ca,US
138/P15 Antioch, Il,US
80/D3 Antioch (Antakya), Turk.
45/T8 Antipodes (isls.), NZ
131/J4 Antlers, Ok,US
117/B1 Antofagasta, Chile
58/C2 Antoing, Belg.
109/J6 Antongil (bay), Madg.
108/C4 Antoniesberg (peak), SAfr.
116/B3 Antonina, Braz.
131/F3 Antonito, Co,US
122/B4 Anton Lizardo (pt.), Mex.
58/B6 Antony, Fr.
50/B2 Antrim, NI,UK
50/B2 Antrim (dist.), NI,UK
50/B1 Antrim (mts.), NI,UK
109/H7 Antsalova, Madg.
109/H7 Antsirabe, Madg.
109/J6 Antsiranana, Madg.
109/J6 Antsiranana (prov.), Madg.
109/H6 Antsohihy, Madg.
118/C3 Antuco (vol.), Chile
59/E1 Antwerp (prov.), Belg.
58/D1 Antwerp (Antwerpen), Belg.
90/D6 Anuradhapura, SrL.
136/B6 Anvil (vol.), Ak,US
88/C2 Anxi, China
87/C3 Anyang, China
82/D4 A'nyêmaqên (mts.), China
87/B4 Anyi, China
83/M2 Anyuy (riv.), Rus.
58/C2 Anzegem, Belg.
74/J4 Anzhero-Sudzhensk, Rus.
58/C3 Anzin, Fr.
66/C2 Anzio, It.
85/L9 Aogaki, Japan
89/B4 Ao Kham (pt.), Thai.
83/N3 Aomori, Japan
67/G2 Aóos (riv.), Gre.
89/B4 Ao Phangnga Nat'l Park, Thai.
89/C4 Aoral (peak), Camb.
63/G4 Aosta, It.
104/C2 Aoudaghost (ruins), Mrta.
103/K5 Aouk (riv.), CAfr., Chad
104/C2 Aoukar (reg.), Mrta.
102/F2 Aoulef, Alg.
85/M10 Aoyama, Japan
102/J3 Aozou, Chad
134/B4 Apache (mts.), Tx,US
135/G4 Apalachicola, Fl,US
116/B4 Aparados da Serra Nat'l Park, Braz.
116/C2 Aparecida, Braz.
116/B2 Aparecida do Taboado, Braz.
88/D4 Aparri, Phil.
123/F6 Apartadó, Col.
99/L6 Apataki, FrPol.
68/D3 Apatin, Serb.
70/G2 Apatity, Rus.
123/P10 Apatzingán, Mex.
122/B4 Apaxtla, Mex.
89/D4 Ap Binh Chau, Viet.
56/C4 Apeldoorn, Neth.
56/D4 Apeldoornsch (can.), Neth.
57/E2 Apen, Ger.
47/F4 Apennines (mts.), It.
92/C3 Api (cape), Indo.
93/E5 Api (peak), Indo.
81/D5 Api (mtn.), Nepal
99/S9 Apia (cap.), Samoa
115/G6 Apiacás (mts.), Braz.
116/B3 Apiaí, Braz.
89/D4 Ap Loc Thanh, Viet.
89/E4 Ap Long Hoa, Viet.
89/D4 Ap Luc, Viet.
88/E6 Apo (mt.), Phil.
99/R9 Apolima (str.), Samoa
116/B1 Aporé (riv.), Braz.
132/B2 Apostle (isls.), Wi,US
117/E2 Apóstoles, Arg.
80/C3 Apostolos Andreas (cape), Cyp.
127/K4 Appalachian (mts.), US
61/F3 Appenzell Ausser Rhoden (canton), Swi.
61/F3 Appenzell Inner Rhoden (canton), Swi.
56/D2 Appingedam, Neth.
51/F2 Appleby, Eng,UK
53/E1 Appleby Magna, Eng,UK
133/S9 Appleton, NY,US
132/B2 Appleton, Wi,US
137/C1 Apple Valley, Ca,US
66/D2 Apricena, It.
66/C2 Aprilia, It.
72/F3 Apsheronsk, Rus.
97/E1 Apsley Gorge Nat'l Park, Austl.
89/E4 Ap Tan My, Viet.
126/U11 Apua (pt.), Hi,US
63/J4 Apuane (mts.), It.
116/B2 Apucarana, Braz.
123/H6 Apure (riv.), Ven.
114/D6 Apurímac (riv.), Peru
89/E4 Ap Vinh Hao, Viet.
106/C2 Aqaba (gulf), Asia
78/B3 Aqaba (gulf), Egypt, SAr.
106/D5 'Aqīq, Sudan
81/E4 Aqqikkol (lake), China
78/D1 'Aqrah, Iraq
73/K2 Aqsay, Kaz.
81/C2 Aqsū (riv.), Kaz.
73/J4 Aqtaū, Kaz.
73/L2 Aqtöbe, Kaz.
73/L3 Aqtöbe Obl., Kaz.
115/G8 Aquidauana, Braz.
115/G8 Aquidauana (riv.), Braz.
62/C4 Aquitaine (reg.), Fr.
82/D4 Ar (riv.), China
85/F2 Ara (riv.), Japan
103/L5 'Arab (riv.), Sudan
135/G3 Arab, Al,US
106/C2 'Arabah, Wādī (dry riv.), Egypt
78/D3 Arabian (pen.), Asia
79/H5 Arabian (sea), Asia
106/C3 Arabian (des.), Egypt
80/L5 'Arab, Jabal al (mts.), Syria
106/B2 'Arab, Kalīj al (gulf), Egypt
72/E4 Araç (riv.), Turk.
115/L6 Aracaju, Braz.
115/L4 Aracati, Braz.
116/B2 Araçatuba, Braz.
64/B4 Aracena, Sp.
116/D1 Aracruz, Braz.
115/K7 Araçuaí, Braz.
68/E2 Arad, Rom.
68/E2 Arad (co.), Rom.
103/K4 Arada, Chad
78/F1 Arādān, Iran
78/D4 'Arafāt, Jabal (mtn.), SAr.
98/C5 Arafura (sea), Austl., Indo.
115/H7 Aragarças, Braz.
73/H4 Aragats, Gora (peak), Arm.
65/E2 Aragon (aut. comm.), Sp.
64/E1 Aragón (riv.), Sp.
115/J5 Araguaia (riv.), Braz.
115/H5 Araguaia Nat'l Park, Braz.
115/J5 Araguaína, Braz.
116/B1 Araguari, Braz.
115/H3 Araguari (riv.), Braz.
115/J7 Araguari (riv.), Braz.
116/C1 Araguari (Valhas) (riv.), Braz.
115/J5 Araguatins, Braz.
85/F2 Arai, Japan
78/E2 Arāk, Iran
136/D3 Arakamchechan (isl.), Rus.
91/F3 Arakan (mts.), Myan.
67/G3 Árakhthos (riv.), Gre.
73/H5 Araks (Aras) (riv.), Eur., Asia
74/G5 Aral, Kaz.
74/G5 Aral (sea), Uzb., Kaz.
73/J2 Aralsor (lake), Kaz.
78/F2 Ārān, Iran
49/H7 Aran (isl.), Ire.
49/A4 Aran (isls.), Ire.
64/D2 Aranda de Duero, Sp.
68/E3 Arandelovac, Serb.
64/D2 Aranjuez, Sp.
50/E6 Aran Mawddwy (mtn.), Wal,UK
134/D5 Aransas Pass, Tx,US
98/G4 Aranuka (atoll), Kiri.
115/L5 Arapiraca, Braz.
80/D2 Arapkir, Turk.
116/B2 Arapongas, Braz.
116/B4 Araranguá, Braz.
116/B2 Araraquara, Braz.
116/C2 Araras, Braz.
97/B3 Ararat, Austl.
73/H5 Ararat (peak), Turk.
115/K5 Araripina, Braz.
73/H5 Aras (riv.), Asia
104/C2 Aratane (well), Mrta.
114/F4 Arauá (riv.), Braz.
114/D2 Arauca, Col.
116/B3 Araucária, Braz.
98/E5 Arawa, PNG
116/C1 Araxá, Braz.
103/N6 Ārba Minch', Eth.
129/H2 Arborfield, Sk,Can.
129/J3 Arborg, Mb,Can.
49/D2 Arbroath, Sc,UK
62/F5 Arc (riv.), Fr.
63/G4 Arc (riv.), Fr.
62/C4 Arcachon, Fr.
62/C4 Arcachon (lag.), Fr.
62/C4 Arcachon, Pointe d' (pt.), Fr.
137/B2 Arcadia, Ca,US
135/H5 Arcadia, Fl,US
130/A2 Arcata, Ca,US
70/J2 Archangel'sk, Rus.
64/E3 Archena, Sp.
96/A1 Archer (riv.), Austl.
96/A1 Archer Bend Nat'l Park, Austl.
134/D3 Archer City, Tx,US
130/E3 Arches Nat'l Park, Ut,US
64/C4 Archidona, Sp.
118/C3 Arco (pass), Arg.
63/J4 Arco, It.
128/E5 Arco, Id,US
116/C2 Arcos, Braz.
64/C4 Arcos de la Frontera, Sp.
115/L5 Arcoverde, Braz.
44/A1 Arctic (ocean)
136/F2 Arctic (coast. pl.), Ak,US
136/J2 Arctic Nat'l Wild. Ref., Ak,US
136/M2 Arctic Red River, NW,Can.
69/G5 Arda (riv.), Bul.
80/E2 Ardahan, Turk.
78/F2 Ardakān, Iran
48/C3 Årdalstangen, Nor.
80/E2 Ardanuç, Turk.
51/E6 Arddleen, Wal,UK
62/F4 Ardèche (riv.), Fr.
138/M9 Arden-Arcade, Ca,US
59/E4 Ardennes (for.), Eur.
58/D4 Ardennes (dept.), Fr.
59/D4 Ardennes, Canal des (can.), Fr.
80/E2 Ardeşen, Turk.
50/C3 Ardglass, NI,UK
64/B3 Ardila (riv.), Sp.
131/H4 Ardmore, Ok,US
137/E5 Ardmore, Pa,US
58/C2 Ardooie, Belg.
50/C2 Ards (dist.), NI,UK
50/C3 Ards (pen.), NI,UK
48/E3 Åre, Swe.
116/G6 Areado, Braz.
115/L4 Areia Branca, Braz.
123/N9 Arena (pt.), Mex.
130/B3 Arena (pt.), Ca,US
115/G6 Arenápolis, Braz.
64/C2 Arenas de San Pedro, Sp.
119/K8 Arenas, Punta de (pt.), Arg.
48/D4 Arendal, Nor.
56/C6 Arendonk, Belg.
50/E6 Arenig Fawr (mtn.), Wal,UK
65/L6 Arenys de Mar, Sp.
65/L6 Arenys de Munt, Sp.
114/D7 Arequipa, Peru
64/C2 Arévalo, Sp.
63/J5 Arezzo, It.
62/C5 Arga (riv.), Sp.
64/D3 Argamasilla de Alba, Sp.
64/C3 Argamasilla de Calatrava, Sp.
65/N9 Arganda, Sp.
63/G5 Argens (riv.), Fr.
62/C2 Argentan, Fr.
63/G4 Argentera (peak), It.
58/B6 Argenteuil, Fr.
117/C4 Argentina (ctry.)
119/J7 Argentino (lake), Arg.
65/L6 Argentona, Sp.
69/G3 Argeş (co.), Rom.
69/G3 Argeş (riv.), Rom.
79/J2 Arghandab (riv.), Afg.
106/B5 Argo, Sudan
67/H4 Argolis (gulf), Gre.
59/E5 Argonne (for.), Fr.
67/H4 Árgos, Gre.
67/G3 Argostólion, Gre.
58/A4 Argueil, Fr.
130/B4 Arguello (pt.), Ca,US
104/A1 Arguin (bay), Mrta.
83/H1 Argun (riv.), China, Rus.
81/E2 Argut (riv.), Rus.
102/C3 Arhreijît (well), Mrta.
48/D4 Århus, Den.
66/A4 Ariana, Tun.
66/A4 Ariana (gov.), Tun.
66/D2 Ariano Irpino, It.
64/C1 Arianza (riv.), Sp.
114/D7 Arica, Chile
84/D3 Arida, Japan
137/A1 Arido (mt.), Ca,US
62/D5 Ariège (riv.), Fr.
69/K5 Arifiye, Turk.
80/K6 Arīḥā (Jericho), WBnk.
131/G3 Arikaree (riv.), Co,US
123/J5 Arima, Trin.
115/G6 Arinos (riv.), Braz.
114/F5 Aripuanã (riv.), Braz.
114/F5 Ariquemes, Braz.
106/C2 'Arīsh, Wādī al (dry riv.), Egypt
109/H7 Arivonimamo, Madg.
65/F1 Arize (riv.), Fr.
130/D4 Arizona (state), US
123/F5 Arjona, Col.
64/C4 Arjona, Sp.
134/E3 Arkadelphia, Ar,US
49/C2 Arkaig, Loch (lake), Sc,UK
131/K4 Arkansas (riv.), US
134/E3 Arkansas (state), US
135/F3 Arkansas City, Ar,US
131/H3 Arkansas City, Ks,US
103/K3 Arkanū (peak), Libya
70/H3 Arkhangel'skaya Obl., Rus.
50/B6 Arklow, Ire.
55/G1 Arkona, Kap (cape), Ger.
90/C5 Arkonam, India
51/G4 Arksey, Eng,UK
74/H2 Arkticheskiy Institut (isls.), Rus.
64/C1 Arlanza (riv.), Sp.
64/C1 Arlanzón (riv.), Sp.
62/F5 Arles, Fr.
58/C3 Arleux, Fr.
135/G4 Arlington, Ga,US
129/K4 Arlington, Mn,US
134/D3 Arlington, Tx,US
137/J8 Arlington, Va,US
138/Q15 Arlington Heights, Il,US
59/E4 Arlon, Belg.
105/F4 Arly Nat'l Park, Burk.
138/G6 Armada, Mi,US
50/B3 Armagh, NI,UK
50/B3 Armagh (dist.), NI,UK
62/F3 Armançon (riv.), Fr.
116/B2 Armando Laydner (res.), Braz.
106/C3 Armant, Egypt
73/G3 Armavir, Rus.
63/G5 Arme, Cap d' (cape), Fr.
73/H4 Armenia (ctry.)
114/C3 Armenia, Col.
58/B2 Armentières, Fr.
123/P10 Armeria, Mex.
97/D1 Armidale, Austl.
64/D4 Armilla, Sp.
50/B1 Armoy, NI,UK
118/E2 Armstrong, Arg.
128/D3 Armstrong, BC,Can.
51/G4 Armthorpe, Eng,UK
90/C4 Ārmūr, India
125/J3 Arnaud (riv.), Qu,Can.
80/J4 Arnauti (cape), Cyp.
53/E3 Arncott, Eng,UK
64/D1 Arnedo, Sp.
58/B2 Arnèke, Fr.
131/H3 Arnett, Ok,US
56/C5 Arnhem, Neth.
90/C5 Arni, India
63/J5 Arno (riv.), It.
98/G4 Arno (atoll), Mrsh.
51/G5 Arnold, Eng,UK
63/K3 Arnoldstein, Aus.
62/E3 Arnon (riv.), Fr.
132/E2 Arnprior, On,Can.
57/F6 Arnsberg, Ger.
51/F3 Arnside, Eng,UK
54/F3 Arnstadt, Ger.
62/E3 Aron (riv.), Fr.
65/X16 Arona, Canl.
58/B4 Aronde (riv.), Fr.
98/G5 Arorae (atoll), Kiri.
93/H5 Aro Usu (cape), Indo.
81/A1 Arqalyq, Kaz.
58/B2 Arques, Fr.
90/D2 Arrah, India
103/M5 Ar Rahad, Sudan
115/H6 Arraias (riv.), Braz.
51/H4 Arram, Eng,UK
78/D2 Ar Ramādī, Iraq
80/L5 Ar Ramthā, Jor.
49/C3 Arran (isl.), Sc,UK
80/D3 Ar Raqqah, Syria
58/B3 Arras, Fr.
80/L4 Ar Rastan, Syria
65/F1 Arrats (riv.), Fr.
65/Y16 Arrecife, Canl.
118/E2 Arrecifes, Arg.
62/B2 Arrée (mts.), Fr.
122/C4 Arriaga, Mex.
116/A5 Arrio Grande, Braz.
78/E4 Ar Riyāḍ (Riyadh) (cap.), SAr.
62/F3 Arroux (riv.), Fr.
64/B3 Arroyo de la Luz, Sp.
130/B4 Arroyo Grande, Ca,US
80/L5 Ar Ruṣayfah, Jor.
103/M5 Ar Ruṣayriṣ, Sudan
78/F4 Ar Ruways, SAr.

151
Arsen – Bamin

83/L3 **Arsen'yev**, Rus.
99/T11 **Art** (isl.), NCal.
67/G3 **Árta**, Gre.
67/G3 **Arta** (gulf), Gre.
64/A1 **Arteijo**, Sp.
83/L3 **Artem**, Rus.
122/E3 **Artemisa**, Cuba
137/B3 **Artesia**, Ca,US
131/F4 **Artesia**, NM,US
96/C3 **Arthur** (pt.), Austl.
117/E3 **Artigas**, Uru.
58/A2 **Artois** (reg.), Fr.
58/B2 **Artois, Collines de l'** (hills), Fr.
116/F7 **Artur Nogueira**, Braz.
81/C4 **Artux**, China
80/E2 **Artvin**, Turk.
93/H5 **Aru** (isls.), Indo.
107/A2 **Arua**, Ugan.
123/H5 **Aruba** (isl.), Neth.
116/G8 **Arujá**, Braz.
53/F5 **Arun** (riv.), Eng,UK
91/F2 **Arunāchal Pradesh** (state), India
53/F5 **Arundel**, Eng,UK
90/C6 **Aruppukkottai**, India
93/F3 **Arus** (cape), Indo.
107/C3 **Arusha**, Tanz.
107/C4 **Arusha** (prov.), Tanz.
99/L6 **Arutua** (atoll), FrPol.
103/L7 **Aruwimi** (riv.), D.R. Congo
82/E2 **Arvayheer**, Mong.
48/F2 **Arvidsjaur**, Swe.
48/E4 **Arvika**, Swe.
130/C4 **Arvin**, Ca,US
132/B2 **Arvon** (peak), Mi,US
81/A3 **Arys'**, Kaz.
62/B3 **Arz** (riv.), Fr.
71/J5 **Arzamas**, Rus.
64/A1 **Arzúa**, Sp.
59/E1 **As**, Belg.
54/G3 **Aš**, Czh.
48/D4 **Ås**, Nor.
78/E2 **Asadābād**, Iran
104/D5 **Asagny Nat'l Park**, C.d'Iv.
92/A3 **Asahan** (riv.), Indo.
84/C3 **Asahi** (riv.), Japan
85/G2 **Asahi-Bandai Nat'l Park**, Japan
83/N3 **Asahi-dake** (mtn.), Japan
83/N3 **Asahikawa**, Japan
85/H7 **Asaka**, Japan
85/M9 **Asake** (riv.), Japan
103/P5 **Āsalē**, Erit.
85/F2 **Asama-yama** (mtn.), Japan
90/E3 **Asansol**, India
103/J3 **Asawanwah** (well), Libya
71/P4 **Asbest**, Rus.
108/C3 **Asbestos** (mts.), SAfr.
137/F5 **Asbury Park**, NJ,US
122/D4 **Ascención** (bay), Mex.
44/J6 **Ascension** (isl.), StH.
57/E5 **Ascheberg**, Ger.
54/F3 **Aschersleben**, Ger.
66/A1 **Asco** (riv.), Fr.
66/C1 **Ascoli Piceno**, It.
66/D2 **Ascoli Satriano**, It.
53/F4 **Ascot**, Eng,UK
103/P5 **Āseb**, Erit.
103/N6 **Āsela**, Eth.
69/G4 **Asenovgrad**, Bul.
82/G2 **Asgat**, Mong.
53/G4 **Ash**, Eng,UK
53/E4 **Ashampstead**, Eng,UK
105/E5 **Ashanti** (reg.), Gha.
105/E5 **Ashanti** (uplands), Gha.
51/G5 **Ashbourne**, Eng,UK
95/H7 **Ashburton**, NZ
52/C5 **Ashburton**, Eng,UK
53/E1 **Ashby** (can.), Eng,UK
51/G6 **Ashby-de-la-Zouch**, Eng,UK
52/D3 **Ashchurch**, Eng,UK
123/D3 **Ashcroft**, BC,Can.
135/J3 **Asheboro**, NC,US
129/J3 **Ashern**, Mb,Can.
135/H3 **Asheville**, NC,US
129/M2 **Asheweig** (riv.), On,Can.
53/F1 **Ashfordby**, Eng,UK
79/G1 **Ashgabat** (cap.), Trkm.
133/Q8 **Ashgrove**, On,Can.
51/G1 **Ashington**, Eng,UK
85/L10 **Ashiya**, Japan
84/C4 **Ashizuri-misaki** (cape), Japan
131/H3 **Ashland**, Ks,US
132/D4 **Ashland**, Ky,US
132/D3 **Ashland**, Oh,US
128/C5 **Ashland**, Or,US
132/B2 **Ashland**, Wi,US
129/J4 **Ashley**, ND,US
95/B2 **Ashmore and Cartier Is.** (terr.), Austl.
80/L4 **Ash Shamāl** (gov.), Leb.
78/D2 **Ash Shāmīyah**, Iraq
79/G3 **Ash Shāriqah**, UAE
80/E3 **Ash Sharqāt**, Iraq
80/H6 **Ash Sharqīyah** (gov.), Egypt
90/C3 **Ashta**, India
132/D3 **Ashtabula**, Oh,US
128/F4 **Ashton**, Id,US
51/F5 **Ashton-in-Makerfield**, Eng,UK
51/F5 **Ashton-under-Lyne**, Eng,UK
132/B2 **Ashwaubenon**, Wi,US
53/F2 **Ashwell**, Eng,UK
77/* **Asia** (cont.)
66/A2 **Asinara** (gulf), It.
66/A2 **Asinara** (isl.), It.
74/J4 **Asino**, Rus.
78/D5 **'Asīr** (mts.), SAr., Yemen
106/D5 **Asis, Ras** (cape), Sudan
80/E2 **Aşkale**, Turk.
51/E3 **Askam in Furness**, Eng,UK
48/D4 **Asker**, Nor.
51/G4 **Askern**, Eng,UK
48/D4 **Askim**, Nor.
67/G2 **Áskion** (peak), Gre.
48/P6 **Askja** (crater), Ice.
48/C3 **Askøy**, Nor.
103/N4 **Asmara** (cap.), Erit.
58/B6 **Asnières-sur-Seine**, Fr.
84/B4 **Aso Nat'l Park**, Japan
103/M5 **Āsosa**, Eth.
84/B4 **Aso-san** (mtn.), Japan
106/D4 **Asoteriba, Jabal** (peak), Sudan
51/E2 **Aspatria**, Eng,UK
65/E3 **Aspe**, Sp.
130/F3 **Aspen**, Co,US
137/J7 **Aspen Hill**, Md,US
134/C3 **Aspermont**, Tx,US
65/F1 **Aspin, Col d'** (pass), Fr.
67/H3 **Asprópirgos**, Gre.
128/G2 **Asquith**, Sk,Can.
104/C2 **'Assâba, Massif de l'** (reg.), Mrta.
80/D3 **As Sabkhah**, Syria
80/K6 **Aş Şāfī**, Jor.
78/E3 **As Sālimīyah**, Kuw.
78/E4 **As Sālimīyah**, SAr.
103/L1 **As Sallūm**, Egypt
80/K5 **As Salţ**, Jor.
91/F2 **Assam** (state), India
78/E2 **As Samāwah**, Iraq
80/H6 **As Sanţah**, Egypt
80/K5 **Aş Şarīḩ**, Jor.
58/D2 **Asse**, Belg.
66/A3 **Assemini**, It.
56/D2 **Assen**, Neth.
58/C1 **Assenede**, Belg.
102/J1 **As Sidr**, Libya
80/H6 **As Sinbillāwayn**, Egypt
129/G3 **Assiniboia**, Sk,Can.
128/E3 **Assiniboine** (peak), BC,Can.
129/J3 **Assiniboine** (riv.), Mb,Can.
132/F1 **Assinika** (lake), Qu,Can.
116/B2 **Assis**, Braz.
65/G1 **Assou** (riv.), Fr.
103/M6 **As Sudd** (reg.), Sudan
78/E1 **As Sulaymānīyah**, Iraq
78/E3 **Aş Şummān** (mts.), SAr.
80/L5 **As Suwaydā'**, Syria
80/L5 **As Suwaydā'** (dist.), Syria
78/D2 **Aş Şuwayrah**, Iraq
106/C2 **As Suways** (gov.), Egypt
106/C2 **As Suways** (Suez), Egypt
81/B1 **Astana** (cap.), Kaz.
56/C6 **Asten**, Neth.
63/H4 **Asti**, It.
116/L6 **Astolfo Dutra**, Braz.
53/E2 **Aston**, Eng,UK
52/D2 **Aston on Clun**, Eng,UK
116/B2 **Astorga**, Braz.
128/C4 **Astoria**, Or,US
73/J3 **Astrakhan'**, Rus.
73/H3 **Astrakhanskaya Obl.**, Rus.
64/B1 **Asturias** (aut. comm.), Sp.
53/E2 **Astwood Bank**, Eng,UK
85/L10 **Asuka**, Japan
85/N9 **Asuke**, Japan
98/D3 **Asuncion** (isl.), NMar.
117/E2 **Asunción** (cap.), Par.
122/B4 **Asunción Ixtaltepec**, Mex.
107/B2 **Aswa** (riv.), Ugan.
106/C3 **Aswān**, Egypt
106/C4 **Aswān** (gov.), Egypt
106/C4 **Aswan High** (dam), Egypt
106/B3 **Asyūţ**, Egypt
106/B3 **Asyūţ** (gov.), Egypt
106/C2 **Asyūţī, Wādī al** (dry riv.), Egypt
117/C2 **Atacama** (des.), Chile
117/C1 **Atacama, Puna de** (plat.), Arg.
105/F4 **Atacora** (range), Ben.
99/H5 **Atafu** (atoll), Tok.
105/F5 **Atakpamé**, Togo
85/F3 **Atami**, Japan
104/B1 **Atar**, Mrta.
64/D4 **Atarfe**, Sp.
90/D2 **Atarra**, India
82/D3 **Atas Bogd** (peak), Mong.
130/B4 **Atascadero**, Ca,US
80/D3 **Atatürk** (res.), Turk.
103/M4 **Atbara**, Sudan
103/M4 **Atbara (Atbarah)** (riv.), Eth., Sudan
81/A1 **Atbasar**, Kaz.
131/K5 **Atchafalaya** (bay), La,US
135/F4 **Atchafalaya** (riv.), La,US
131/J3 **Atchison**, Ks,US
105/E5 **Atebubu**, Gha.
48/G1 **Ateelva** (riv.), Nor.
123/P9 **Atengo** (riv.), Mex.
66/C1 **Aterno** (riv.), It.
58/C2 **Ath**, Belg.
128/E2 **Athabasca**, Ab,Can.
124/E3 **Athabasca** (riv.), Ab,Can.
124/F3 **Athabasca** (lake), Ab, Sk,Can.
129/H2 **Athapuskow** (lake), Mb,Can.
102/K1 **Āthār Ţulmaythah** (Ptolemaïs) (ruins), Libya
135/G3 **Athens**, Al,US
135/H3 **Athens**, Ga,US
132/D4 **Athens**, Oh,US
135/G3 **Athens**, Tn,US
134/E3 **Athens**, Tx,US
67/L7 **Athens (Athínai)** (cap.), Gre.
53/E1 **Atherstone**, Eng,UK
51/F4 **Atherton**, Eng,UK
49/B4 **Athlone**, Ire
67/J2 **Áthos** (peak), Gre.
103/J5 **Ati**, Chad
116/G8 **Atibaia**, Braz.
116/G7 **Atibaia** (riv.), Braz.
132/B1 **Atikokan**, On,Can.
99/K7 **Atiu** (isl.), Cooks.
136/C5 **Atka** (isl.), Ak,US
73/H2 **Atkarsk**, Rus.
136/M2 **Atkinson** (pt.), NW,Can.
135/G3 **Atlanta** (cap.), Ga,US
134/E3 **Atlanta**, Tx,US
44/G3 **Atlantic** (ocean)
129/K5 **Atlantic**, Ia,US
137/G5 **Atlantic Beach**, NY,US
105/F5 **Atlantique** (prov.), Ben.
102/E2 **Atlas** (mts.), Afr.
138/K10 **Atlas** (peak), Ca,US
102/E1 **Atlas Saharien** (mts.), Alg., Mor.
136/M4 **Atlin** (lake), BC,Can.
122/B4 **Atlixco**, Mex.
135/G4 **Atmore**, Al,US
102/B3 **Atoui** (dry riv.), Mrta.
79/G1 **Atrak** (riv.), Iran
114/C2 **Atrato** (riv.), Col.
85/H7 **Atsugi**, Japan
85/N10 **Atsumi**, Japan
85/N10 **Atsumi** (pen.), Japan
80/K6 **Aţ Ţafīlah**, Jor.
78/D4 **Aţ Ţā'if**, SAr.
80/L5 **At Tall**, Syria
135/G3 **Attalla**, Al,US
125/H3 **Attawapiskat** (riv.), On,Can.
57/E6 **Attendorn**, Ger.
63/K3 **Attersee** (lake), Aus.
58/C5 **Attichy**, Fr.
53/E2 **Attleborough**, Eng,UK
53/H2 **Attleborough**, Eng,UK
136/A5 **Attu** (isl.), Ak,US
106/C2 **Aţ Ţūr**, Egypt
80/K6 **Aţ Ţūr**, WBnk.
78/D6 **At Turbah**, Yem.
118/D2 **Atuel** (riv.), Arg.
48/F4 **Åtvidaberg**, Swe.
130/B3 **Atwater**, Ca,US
131/G3 **Atwood**, Ks,US
73/J3 **Atyraū**, Kaz.
73/J3 **Atyraū Obl.**, Kaz.
122/E4 **Auas**, Hon.
59/E4 **Aubange**, Belg.
58/D6 **Aube** (dept.), Fr.
62/F2 **Aube** (riv.), Fr.
62/F4 **Aubenas**, Fr.
58/C6 **Aubetin** (riv.), Fr.
58/A5 **Aubette** (riv.), Fr.
62/E4 **Aubin**, Fr.
135/G3 **Auburn**, Al,US
130/B3 **Auburn**, Ca,US
132/C3 **Auburn**, In,US
133/G2 **Auburn**, Me,US
131/J2 **Auburn**, Ne,US
132/E3 **Auburn**, NY,US
138/C3 **Auburn**, Wa,US
138/F6 **Auburn Hills**, Mi,US
118/C3 **Aucá Mahuida** (peak), Arg.
62/D5 **Auch**, Fr.
58/B3 **Auchel**, Fr.
49/D2 **Auchenblae**, Sc,UK
50/E2 **Auchencairn**, Sc,UK
49/C3 **Auchinleck**, Sc,UK
95/H6 **Auckland**, NZ
45/S8 **Auckland** (isls.), NZ
62/E5 **Aude** (riv.), Fr.
58/D2 **Auderghem**, Belg.
62/A3 **Audierne** (bay), Fr.
51/F6 **Audlem**, Eng,UK
51/F5 **Audley**, Eng,UK
103/P6 **Audo** (range), Eth.
59/E5 **Audun-le-Tiche**, Fr.
63/K1 **Aue**, Ger.
63/K1 **Auerbach**, Ger.
63/J2 **Auerbach in der Oberpfalz**, Ger.
50/A3 **Augher**, NI,UK
50/B3 **Aughnacloy**, NI,UK
108/C3 **Augrabies Falls Nat'l Park**, SAfr.
108/C3 **Augrabiesvalle** (falls), SAfr
61/G1 **Augsburg**, Ger.
108/A2 **Augub** (peak), Namb.
66/D4 **Augusta**, It.
66/D4 **Augusta** (gulf), It.
135/H3 **Augusta**, Ga,US
133/G2 **Augusta** (cap.), Me,US
57/F5 **Augustdorf**, Ger.
55/M2 **Augustów**, Pol.
89/B3 **Auk Bok** (isl.), Myan.
65/M9 **Aulencia** (riv.), Sp.
62/B2 **Aulne** (riv.), Fr.
58/C3 **Aulnoye-Aymeries**, Fr.
58/B5 **Aunette** (riv.), Fr.
108/B2 **Auob** (dry riv.), Namb.
108/C2 **Auobrivier** (dry riv.), SAfr.
98/G4 **Aur** (atoll), Mrsh.
90/C4 **Aurangābād**, India
90/D3 **Aurangābād**, India
62/B3 **Auray**, Fr.
62/D5 **Aureilhan**, Fr.
57/E2 **Aurich**, Ger.
116/B2 **Auriflama**, Braz.
62/E4 **Aurillac**, Fr.
131/F3 **Aurora**, Co,US
138/P16 **Aurora**, Il,US
131/J3 **Aurora**, Mo,US
131/H2 **Aurora**, Ne,US
96/A1 **Aurukun Abor. Land**, Austl.
132/C2 **Au Sable** (riv.), Mi,US
55/K3 **Auschwitz** (Oświęcim), Pol.
62/E5 **Aussillon**, Fr.
48/C4 **Aust-Agder** (co.), Nor.
124/G2 **Austin** (isl.), Nun,Can.
129/K5 **Austin**, Mn,US
130/C3 **Austin**, Nv,US
134/D4 **Austin** (cap.), Tx,US
95/* **Australia** (cont.) (ctry.)
97/C3 **Australian Alps** (mts.), Austl.
97/D3 **Australian Cap. Terr.**, Austl.
63/L3 **Austria** (ctry.)
48/P7 **Austurhorn** (pt.), Ice.
58/B3 **Authie** (riv.), Fr.
123/P10 **Autlán de Navarro**, Mex.
58/B5 **Automne** (riv.), Fr.
62/F3 **Autun**, Fr.
62/E4 **Auvergne** (reg.), Fr.
58/B5 **Auvers-sur-Oise**, Fr.
62/D4 **Auvézère** (riv.), Fr.
62/E3 **Auxerre**, Fr.
60/B3 **Auxonne**, Fr.
132/D2 **Aux Sables** (riv.), On,Can.
125/K2 **Auyuittuq Nat'l Park**, Nun,Can.
114/D6 **Auzangate** (peak), Peru
62/E3 **Avallon**, Fr.
133/K2 **Avalon** (pen.), Nf,Can.
116/B2 **Avaré**, Braz.
53/E4 **Avebury**, Eng,UK
64/A2 **Aveiro**, Port.
64/A2 **Aveiro** (dist.), Port.
58/C2 **Avelgem**, Belg.
118/F2 **Avellaneda**, Arg.
66/D2 **Avellino**, It.
58/A4 **Avelon** (riv.), Fr.
130/B3 **Avenal**, Ca,US
58/A58 **Aver** (riv.), Fr.
66/D2 **Aversa**, It.
123/J4 **Aves** (isl.), Ven.
48/F3 **Avesta**, Swe.
62/D4 **Aveyron** (riv.), Fr.
66/C1 **Avezzano**, It.
49/D2 **Aviemore**, Sc,UK
62/F5 **Avignon**, Fr.
64/C2 **Ávila de los Caballeros**, Sp.
64/C1 **Avilés**, Sp.
58/B3 **Avion**, Fr.
64/B3 **Avis**, Port.
50/B6 **Avoca**, Ire.
50/B6 **Avoca** (riv.), Ire.
66/D4 **Avola**, It.
62/E2 **Avon**, Fr.
52/C6 **Avon** (riv.), Eng,UK
52/D4 **Avon** (riv.), Eng,UK
53/E2 **Avon** (riv.), Eng,UK
53/E5 **Avon** (riv.), Eng,UK
50/B6 **Avonbeg** (riv.), Ire.
129/G3 **Avonlea**, Sk,Can.
50/B6 **Avonmore** (riv.), Ire.
52/D4 **Avonmouth**, Eng,UK
62/C2 **Avranches**, Fr.
58/B4 **Avre** (riv.), Fr.
62/C3 **Avrillé**, Fr.
85/L10 **Awaji**, Japan
84/D3 **Awaji** (isl.), Japan
80/L5 **A'waj, Nahr al** (riv.), Syria
59/E2 **Awans**, Belg.
103/N6 **Āwasa**, Eth.
103/P5 **Āwash Wenz** (riv.), Eth.
108/A2 **Awasibberge** (peak), Namb.
102/H2 **Awbārī**, Libya
49/C2 **Awe, Loch** (lake), Sc,UK
103/K2 **Awjilah**, Libya
48/P6 **Axarfjördhur** (bay), Ice.
52/D4 **Axbridge**, Eng,UK
52/D4 **Axe** (riv.), Eng,UK
52/D5 **Axe** (riv.), Eng,UK
56/A6 **Axel**, Neth.
125/S7 **Axel Heiberg** (isl.), Nun,Can.
105/E5 **Axim**, Gha.
67/H2 **Axios** (riv.), Gre.
52/D5 **Axminster**, Eng,UK
71/N5 **Ay** (riv.), Rus.
84/D3 **Ayabe**, Japan
118/F3 **Ayacucho**, Arg.
114/D6 **Ayacucho**, Peru
81/E4 **Ayakkum** (lake), China
81/D2 **Ayaköz**, Kaz.
81/D2 **Ayaköz** (riv.), Kaz.
85/M10 **Ayama**, Japan
104/E5 **Ayamé, Barrage d'** (dam), C.d'Iv.
64/B4 **Ayamonte**, Sp.
80/C2 **Ayancık**, Turk.
123/F6 **Ayapel**, Col.
85/H7 **Ayase**, Japan
114/D6 **Ayaviri**, Peru
79/J1 **Āybak**, Afg.
80/N8 **'Aybāl, Jabal** (Har Eval) (mtn.), WBnk.
80/A3 **Aydın**, Turk.
80/C3 **Aydıncık**, Turk.
95/C3 **Ayers Rock** (Uluru) (peak), Austl.
91/G4 **Ayeyarwady** (riv.), Myan.
67/J3 **Áyios Evstrátios** (isl.), Gre.
67/J5 **Áyios Ioánnis, Ákra** (cape), Gre.
67/J5 **Áyios Nikólaos**, Gre.
53/F3 **Aylesbury**, Eng,UK
53/G4 **Aylesford**, Eng,UK
53/H4 **Aylesham**, Eng,UK
124/F2 **Aylmer** (lake), NW,Can.
53/H1 **Aylsham**, Eng,UK
80/D3 **'Ayn al 'Arab**, Syria
103/K2 **'Ayn Ath Tha'lab**, Libya
78/D1 **'Ayn, Ra's al**, Syria
103/K3 **'Ayn Zuwayyah** (well), Libya
75/S3 **Ayon** (isl.), Rus.
65/E3 **Ayora**, Sp.
102/D3 **'Ayoûn 'Abd el Mâlek** (well), Mrta.
96/B2 **Ayr**, Austl.
49/C3 **Ayr**, Sc,UK
49/C3 **Ayr** (riv.), Sc,UK
50/D3 **Ayre, Point of** (pt.), Eng,UK
51/H3 **Ayton**, Eng,UK
69/H4 **Aytos**, Bul.
62/C3 **Aytré**, Fr.
122/B4 **Ayutla**, Mex.
89/C3 **Ayutthaya** (ruins), Thai.
80/A2 **Ayvacık**, Turk.
80/A2 **Ayvalık**, Turk.
59/E3 **Aywaille**, Belg.
65/F3 **Azahar** (coast), Sp.
85/M9 **Azai**, Japan
128/C5 **Azalea**, Or,US
90/D2 **Azamgarh**, India
114/D6 **Azángaro**, Peru
102/G2 **Azao** (peak), Alg.
105/E2 **Azaouâd** (reg.), Mali
105/G2 **Azaouak, Vallée de l'** (wadi), Mali, Niger
80/D3 **A'zāz**, Syria
73/H4 **Azerbaijan** (ctry.)
103/N5 **Āzezo**, Eth.
81/E1 **Azhu-Tayga, Gora** (peak), Rus.
114/C4 **Azogues**, Ecu.
65/R12 **Azores** (aut. reg.), Port.
65/R12 **Azores** (isls.), Port.
72/F3 **Azov**, Rus.
72/E3 **Azov** (sea), Rus., Ukr.
64/D1 **Azpeitia**, Sp.
130/F3 **Aztec**, NM,US
130/E3 **Aztec Ruins Nat'l Mon.**, NM,US
123/G4 **Azua**, DRep.
64/C3 **Azuaga**, Sp.
85/M9 **Azuchi**, Japan
123/F6 **Azuero** (pen.), Pan.
118/F3 **Azul**, Arg.
85/G2 **Azuma-san** (mtn.), Japan
85/F2 **Azumaya-san** (mtn.), Japan
63/G5 **Azur, Côte d'** (coast), Fr.
137/C2 **Azusa**, Ca,US
80/L5 **Az Zabadānī**, Syria
106/B2 **Az Zagāzīg**, Egypt
63/K4 **Azzano Decimo**, It.
80/L5 **Az Zarqā'**, Jor.
102/H1 **Az Zāwiyah**, Libya

B

99/Y18 **Ba**, Fiji
89/E3 **Ba** (riv.), Viet.
99/U11 **Baaba** (isl.), NCal.
80/N9 **Ba'al Ḩazor** (Tall 'Āşūr) (mtn.), WBnk.
61/E3 **Baar**, Swi.
56/C4 **Baarn**, Neth.
82/D2 **Baatsagaan**, Mong.
79/J2 **Baba** (mts.), Afg.
69/F4 **Baba** (peak), Bul.
72/D4 **Baba Burnu** (pt.), Turk.
69/J3 **Babadag**, Rom.
69/H5 **Babaeski**, Turk.
114/C4 **Babahoyo**, Ecu.
93/G5 **Babar** (isl.), Indo.
107/B4 **Babati**, Tanz.
52/C5 **Babbacombe** (bay), Eng,UK
129/L4 **Babbitt**, Mn,US
130/C3 **Babbitt**, Nv,US
103/P5 **Bab el Mandeb** (str.), Afr., Asia
98/C4 **Babelthuap** (isl.), Palau
72/A2 **Babia Gora** (peak), Pol.
91/H3 **Babian** (riv.), China
128/B2 **Babine** (lake), BC,Can.
124/D3 **Babine** (riv.), BC,Can
78/F1 **Bābol**, Iran
72/D1 **Babruysk**, Bela.
88/D4 **Babuyan** (isls.), Phil.
76/D2 **Babylon** (ruins), Iraq
137/G5 **Babylon**, NY,US
115/J4 **Bacabal**, Braz.
115/H4 **Bacajá** (riv.), Braz.
93/G4 **Bacan** (isl.), Indo.
69/H2 **Bacău**, Rom.
69/H2 **Bacău** (co.), Rom.
89/D1 **Bac Can**, Viet.
89/D1 **Bac Giang**, Viet.
124/G2 **Back** (riv.), Nun,Can.
132/E2 **Back** (lake), On,Can.
137/K7 **Back** (riv.), Md,US
68/D3 **Bačka** (reg.), Serb.
68/D3 **Bačka Palanka**, Serb.
68/D3 **Bačka Topola**, Serb.
63/H2 **Backnang**, Ger.
52/D4 **Backwell**, Eng,UK
89/D4 **Bac Lieu**, Viet.
89/D1 **Bac Ninh**, Viet.
88/D5 **Bacolod**, Phil.
89/D1 **Bac Quang**, Viet.
68/D2 **Bácsalmás**, Hun.
68/D2 **Bács-Kiskun** (co.), Hun.
53/H1 **Bacton**, Eng,UK
51/F4 **Bacup**, Eng,UK
129/H4 **Bad** (riv.), SD,US
90/C5 **Badagara**, India
82/E3 **Badain Jaran** (des.), China
64/B3 **Badajoz**, Sp.
65/L7 **Badalona**, Sp.
57/G6 **Bad Arolsen**, Ger.
132/D3 **Bad Axe**, Mi,US
57/F6 **Bad Berleburg**, Ger.
57/H2 **Bad Bevensen**, Ger.
59/G2 **Bad Breisig**, Ger.
54/F1 **Bad Doberan**, Ger.
57/G5 **Bad Driburg**, Ger.
63/M2 **Baden**, Aus.
63/H2 **Baden-Baden**, Ger.
54/E4 **Baden-Württemberg** (state), Ger.
57/F4 **Bad Essen**, Ger.
55/H2 **Bad Freienwalde**, Ger.
57/H5 **Bad Gandersheim**, Ger.
63/K3 **Bad Goisern**, Aus.
57/H5 **Bad Harzburg**, Ger.
54/E3 **Bad Hersfeld**, Ger.
63/H1 **Bad Homburg vor der Höhe**, Ger.
59/G2 **Bad Honnef**, Ger.
79/J4 **Badīn**, Pak.
63/K3 **Bad Ischl**, Aus.
63/G2 **Bad Kreuznach**, Ger.
60/D2 **Bad Krozingen**, Ger.
129/H4 **Badlands** (uplands), ND,US
129/H5 **Badlands** (hills), SD,US
129/H5 **Badlands Nat'l Park**, SD,US
57/H6 **Bad Langensalza**, Ger.
57/H5 **Bad Lauterberg**, Ger.
57/F5 **Bad Lippspringe**, Ger.
63/H2 **Bad Mergentheim**, Ger.
57/G4 **Bad Munder am Deister**, Ger.
59/F2 **Bad Münstereifel**, Ger.
63/H1 **Bad Nauheim**, Ger.
57/G4 **Bad Nenndorf**, Ger.
59/G2 **Bad Neuenahr-Ahrweiler**, Ger.
63/J1 **Bad Neustadt an der Saale**, Ger.
57/F4 **Bad Oeynhausen**, Ger.
54/F2 **Bad Oldesloe**, Ger.
57/G5 **Bad Pyrmont**, Ger.
79/J3 **Badrāh**, Pak.
54/G5 **Bad Reichenhall**, Ger.
57/H5 **Bad Sachsa**, Ger.
57/H4 **Bad Salzdetfurth**, Ger.
57/F4 **Bad Salzuflen**, Ger.
54/F3 **Bad Salzungen**, Ger.
57/F5 **Bad Sassendorf**, Ger.
54/F2 **Bad Schwartau**, Ger.
54/F2 **Bad Segeberg**, Ger.
57/G6 **Bad Sooden-Allendorf**, Ger.
61/H2 **Bad Tölz**, Ger.
90/D6 **Badulla**, SrL.
63/M3 **Bad Vöslau**, Aus.
57/G6 **Bad Wildungen**, Ger.
57/E2 **Bad Zwischenahn**, Ger.
64/C4 **Baena**, Sp.
116/J6 **Baependi**, Braz.
59/F2 **Baesweiler**, Ger.
64/D4 **Baeza**, Sp.
105/H5 **Bafang**, Camr.
125/H1 **Baffin** (isl.), Nun,Can.
125/K1 **Baffin** (bay), Can.,Grld.
134/D5 **Baffin** (bay), Tx,US
102/H7 **Bafia**, Camr.
104/D4 **Bafing** (riv.), C.d'Iv., Gui.
104/C3 **Bafing** (riv.), Gui., Mali
105/H5 **Bafoussam**, Camr.
80/C2 **Bafra**, Turk.
104/B2 **Bafrechié** (well), Mrta.
103/L7 **Bafwasende**, D.R. Congo
87/B3 **Bag** (salt lake), China
102/H5 **Baga**, Nga.
88/E6 **Baganga**, Phil.
105/G3 **Bagaroua**, Niger
81/E3 **Bagda** (mts.), China
119/G1 **Bagé**, Braz.
88/D4 **Baggao**, Phil.
52/B4 **Baggy** (pt.), Eng,UK
78/D2 **Baghdad** (Baghdād) (cap.), Iraq
66/C3 **Bagheria**, It.
79/J1 **Baghlān**, Afg.
52/C3 **Baglan**, Wal,UK
129/K4 **Bagley**, Mn,US
62/D5 **Bagnères-de-Bigorre**, Fr.
62/F4 **Bagnols-sur-Cèze**, Fr.
88/D5 **Bago**, Phil.
104/D3 **Bagoe** (riv.), C.d'Iv., Mali
89/B2 **Bago (Pegu)** (div.), Myan.
88/D4 **Baguio**, Phil.
102/J5 **Baguirmi** (reg.), Chad
103/H2 **Bagzane** (peak), Niger
123/F2 **Bahamas** (ctry.)
90/E3 **Baharampur**, India
81/B6 **Bahāwalnagar**, Pak.
79/K3 **Bahāwalpur**, Pak.
107/B4 **Bahi**, Tanz.
122/D4 **Bahía** (isls.), Hon.
123/M8 **Bahia Asunción**, Mex.
118/E3 **Bahía Blanca**, Arg.
123/M8 **Bahía de los Angeles**, Mex.
90/D3 **Bahía Honda**, Cuba
123/M8 **Bahía Kino**, Mex.
123/M8 **Bahía Tortugas**, Mex.
103/N5 **Bahir Dar**, Eth.
79/G4 **Bahlah**, Oman
90/D2 **Bahraich**, India
78/F3 **Bahrain** (ctry.)
78/F3 **Bahrain** (gulf), Bahr., SAr.
78/D2 **Baḩr al Milḩ** (lake), Iraq
103/K6 **Bahr Aouk** (riv.), CAfr., Chad
106/B2 **Baḩrīyah, Al Wāḩāt al** (oasis), Egypt
87/C2 **Bai** (riv.), China
87/C4 **Bai** (riv.), China
69/F2 **Baia Mare**, Rom.
69/F2 **Baia Sprie**, Rom.
102/J6 **Baïbokoum**, Chad
83/J2 **Baicheng**, China
81/D3 **Baicheng**, China
69/G3 **Băicoi**, Rom.
103/P7 **Baidoa**, Som.
87/D5 **Baidong** (lake), China
133/G1 **Baie-Comeau**, Qu,Can.
125/J3 **Baie-du-Poste**, Qu,Can.
133/G2 **Baie-Saint-Paul**, Qu,Can.
133/K1 **Baie Verte**, Nf,Can.
87/G7 **Baigou** (riv.), China
78/D2 **Ba'īji**, Iraq
75/L4 **Baikal (Baykal)** (lake), Rus.
51/G4 **Baildon**, Eng,UK
64/D3 **Bailén**, Sp.
69/F3 **Băileşti**, Rom.
58/B2 **Bailleul**, Fr.
82/E5 **Bailong** (riv.), China
87/C4 **Bailu** (riv.), China
51/H5 **Bain** (riv.), Eng,UK
135/G4 **Bainbridge**, Ga,US
138/B2 **Bainbridge** (isl.), Wa,US
81/D4 **Bairab** (lake), China
136/F3 **Baird** (inlet), Ak,US
134/D3 **Baird**, Tx,US
97/C3 **Bairnsdale**, Austl.
80/L6 **Bā'ir, Wādī** (riv.), Jor.
62/D5 **Baïse** (riv.), Fr.
90/D2 **Baitadi**, Nepal
89/D2 **Bai Thuong**, Viet.
65/P10 **Baixa de Banheira**, Port.
116/D1 **Baixo Guandu**, Braz.
82/E4 **Baiyin**, China
87/B3 **Baiyu** (mts.), China
88/C2 **Baiyun**, China
119/J7 **Baja** (pt.), Chile
68/D2 **Baja**, Hun.
123/L8 **Baja California** (pen.), Mex.
123/L7 **Baja California** (state), Mex.
123/M8 **Baja California Sur** (state), Mex.
93/F5 **Bajawa**, Indo.
68/D4 **Bajina Bašta**, Serb.
97/E1 **Bajmba** (peak), Austl.
68/D3 **Bajmok**, Serb.
123/F4 **Bajo Nuevo** (isl.), Col.
93/E3 **Bakayan** (peak), Indo.
104/B3 **Bakel**, Sen.
124/G2 **Baker** (lake), Nun,Can.
119/J6 **Baker** (riv.), Chile
99/H4 **Baker** (isl.), PacUS
130/C4 **Baker**, Ca,US
129/G4 **Baker**, Mt,US
130/D3 **Baker**, Nv,US
128/D4 **Baker**, Or,US
128/C3 **Baker** (peak), Wa,US
130/C4 **Bakersfield**, Ca,US
51/G5 **Bakewell**, Eng,UK
72/E3 **Bakhchisaray**, Ukr.
72/E2 **Bakhmach**, Ukr.
78/E2 **Bākhtarān**, Iran
78/F3 **Bakhtegān** (lake), Iran
48/P6 **Bakkaflói** (bay), Ice.
102/H8 **Bakoumba**, Gabon
104/C4 **Bakoye** (riv.), Gui., Mali
73/J4 **Baku** (cap.), Azer.
111/S **Bakutis** (coast), Ant.
114/E6 **Bala** (mts.), Bol.
50/E6 **Bala**, Wal,UK
93/E2 **Balabac** (str.), Malay., Phil.
88/C6 **Balabac**, Phil.
88/C6 **Balabac** (isl.), Phil.
80/L5 **Ba'labakk**, Leb.
99/U12 **Balabio** (isl.), NCal.
78/D2 **Balad**, Iraq
90/D3 **Bālāghāt**, India
66/A1 **Balagne** (range), Fr.
65/F2 **Balaguer**, Sp.
62/C5 **Balaïtous** (mtn.), Fr.
110/F3 **Balaka**, Malw.
71/J4 **Balakhna**, Rus.
73/H1 **Balakovo**, Rus.
79/H1 **Bālā Morghab**, Afg.
69/G2 **Bălan**, Rom.
122/C4 **Balancán**, Mex.
88/D5 **Balanga**, Phil.
89/E3 **Ba Lang An** (cape), Viet.
90/D3 **Bālāngir**, India
73/J2 **Balaözen** (riv.), Kaz.
71/W9 **Balashikha**, Rus.
73/G2 **Balashov**, Rus.
68/D1 **Balassagyarmat**, Hun.
68/C2 **Balaton** (lake), Hun.
68/C2 **Balatonfüred**, Hun.
118/F3 **Balcarce**, Arg.
50/E2 **Balcary** (pt.), Sc,UK
69/J4 **Balchik**, Bul.
95/G7 **Balclutha**, NZ
53/F4 **Balcombe**, Eng,UK
134/D4 **Balcones Escarpment** (plat.), Tx,US
135/H2 **Bald** (peak), Va,US
53/F3 **Baldock**, Eng,UK
97/E1 **Bald Rock Nat'l Park**, Austl.
137/C2 **Baldwin Park**, Ca,US
129/H3 **Baldy** (peak), Mb,Can.
65/F3 **Balearic (Baleares)** (isls.), Sp.
116/E1 **Baleia, Ponta da** (pt.), Braz.
125/K3 **Baleine** (riv.), Qu,Can.
125/J3 **Baleine, Grande Rivière de la** (riv.), Qu,Can.
125/J3 **Baleine, Petite Rivière de la** (riv.), Qu,Can.
103/N6 **Bale Mountains Nat'l Park**, Eth.
59/F1 **Balen**, Belg.
88/D4 **Baler**, Phil.
90/E3 **Baleshwar**, India
82/H1 **Baley**, Rus.
90/B2 **Bali**, India
92/D5 **Bali** (isl.), Indo.
92/D5 **Bali** (sea), Indo.
80/A2 **Balıkesir**, Turk.
93/E4 **Balikpapan**, Indo.
88/D6 **Balingasag**, Phil.
61/E1 **Balingen**, Ger.
69/F4 **Balkan** (mts.), Eur.
73/K4 **Balkhan Obl.**, Trkm.
81/B2 **Balkhash** (lake), Kaz.
80/B4 **Ballagan** (pt.), Ire.
50/C1 **Ballantrae**, Sc,UK
97/B3 **Ballarat**, Austl.
90/C4 **Ballarpur**, India
50/D3 **Ballaugh**, IM,UK
111/L **Balleny** (isls.), Ant.
97/E1 **Ballina**, Austl.
49/A3 **Ballina**, Ire.
49/A4 **Ballinasloe**, Ire.
50/B2 **Ballinderry** (riv.), NI,UK
134/D4 **Ballinger**, Tx,US
50/B1 **Ballintoy**, NI,UK
50/C2 **Ballycarry**, NI,UK
50/B1 **Ballycastle**, NI,UK
50/B2 **Ballyclare**, NI,UK
50/C2 **Ballyeaston**, NI,UK
50/A3 **Ballygawley**, NI,UK
50/C3 **Ballygowan**, NI,UK
50/C3 **Ballyhalbert**, NI,UK
50/A1 **Ballykelly**, NI,UK
50/B2 **Ballymena**, NI,UK
50/B2 **Ballymena** (dist.), NI,UK
50/B1 **Ballymoney**, NI,UK
50/B1 **Ballymoney** (dist.), NI,UK
50/C3 **Ballynahinch**, NI,UK
50/C2 **Ballynure**, NI,UK
50/C3 **Ballyquintin** (pt.), NI,UK
50/C2 **Ballywalter**, NI,UK
119/J7 **Balmaceda** (peak), Chile
68/E2 **Balmazújváros**, Hun.
129/K3 **Balmertown**, On,Can.
116/B3 **Balneario Camboriú**, Braz.
119/T12 **Balneario Carras**, Uru.
96/C4 **Balonne** (riv.), Austl.
90/B2 **Bālotra**, India
87/B3 **Balougou**, China
81/B2 **Balqash**, Kaz.
90/D2 **Balrāmpur**, India
69/G3 **Balş**, Rom.
53/E2 **Balsall Common**, Eng,UK
115/J5 **Balsas**, Braz.
115/J5 **Balsas** (riv.), Braz.
122/A4 **Balsas** (riv.), Mex.
48/F4 **Baltic** (sea), Eur.
55/K1 **Baltic** (spit), Pol., Rus.
80/H6 **Balţīm**, Egypt
137/K7 **Baltimore**, Md,US
137/K7 **Baltimore Highlands-Lansdown**, Md,US
55/K1 **Baltiysk**, Rus.
57/E1 **Baltrum** (isl.), Ger.
79/H3 **Baluchistan** (reg.), Iran, Pak.
90/E2 **Bālurghāt**, India
57/E6 **Balve**, Ger.
73/J3 **Balykshi**, Kaz.
105/E3 **Bam** (prov.), Burk.
81/F5 **Bam** (lake), China
79/G3 **Bam**, Iran
102/H5 **Bama**, Nga.
132/A1 **Bamaji** (lake), On,Can.
104/D3 **Bamako** (cap.), Mali
104/D3 **Bamako** (reg.), Mali
114/C5 **Bambamarca**, Peru
103/K6 **Bambari**, CAfr.
63/J2 **Bamberg**, Ger.
135/H3 **Bamberg**, SC,US
51/F4 **Bamber Ridge**, Eng,UK
48/D4 **Bamble**, Nor.
116/C2 **Bambuí**, Braz.
105/H5 **Bamenda**, Camr.
79/J2 **Bāmīān**, Afg.
103/K6 **Bamingui-Bangoran Nat'l Park**, CAfr.

152
Bamoa – Bento

123/N8 Bamoa, Mex.
52/C5 Bampton, Eng,UK
79/H3 Bampūr (riv.), Iran
98/F5 Banaba (isl.), Kiri.
104/D3 Banamba, Mali
104/B4 Banana (isls.), SLeo.
110/B2 Banana, D.R. Congo
90/B2 Banās (riv.), India
106/C4 Banās, Ra's (pt.), Egypt
68/E3 Banatsko Novo Selo, Serb.
80/B2 Banaz, Turk.
50/B3 Banbridge, NI,UK
50/B3 Banbridge (dist.), NI,UK
53/E2 Banbury, Eng,UK
102/B3 Banc d'Arguin Nat'l Park, Mrta.
89/C2 Ban Chiang (ruins), Thai.
49/D2 Banchory, Sc,UK
122/D4 Banco Chinchorro (isls.), Mex.
132/E2 Bancroft, On,Can.
93/H4 Banda (isls.), Indo.
93/G5 Banda (sea), Indo.
92/A2 Banda Aceh, Indo.
85/G2 Bandai-Asahi Nat'l Park, Japan
85/G2 Bandai-san (mtn.), Japan
104/D5 Bandama (riv.), C.d'Iv.
104/D4 Bandama Blanc (riv.), C.d'Iv.
104/D4 Bandama Rouge (riv.), C.d'Iv.
79/H3 Bandar Beheshtī (Chāh Behār), Iran
79/G3 Bandar-e 'Abbās, Iran
78/E1 Bandar-e Anzalī, Iran
78/F3 Bandar-e Būshehr, Iran
78/E2 Bandar-e Māhshahr, Iran
78/F1 Bandar-e Torkeman, Iran
92/D3 Bandar Seri Begawan (cap.), Bru.
116/D2 Bandeira (peak), Braz.
130/F4 Bandelier Nat'l Mon., NM,US
134/D4 Bandera, Tx,US
123/N9 Banderas (bay), Mex.
104/E3 Bandiagara, Mali
81/B5 Bandipura, India
69/H5 Bandırma, Turk.
69/J5 Bandırma (gulf), Turk.
91/J5 Ban Don, Viet.
110/C1 Bandundu, D.R. Congo
92/C5 Bandung, Indo.
65/E3 Bañeres, Sp.
49/D2 Banff, Sc,UK
128/E3 Banff Nat'l Park, Ab, BC,Can.
104/D4 Banfora, Burk.
88/D6 Bañga, Phil.
90/C5 Bangalore, India
105/H5 Bangangté, Camr.
103/K7 Bangassou, CAfr.
93/E2 Bangau, Tanjong (cape), Malay.
93/F4 Banggai (isls.), Indo.
81/C5 Banggong (lake), China
89/D2 Banghiang (riv.), Laos
92/C4 Bangka (isl.), Indo.
92/B4 Bangka (str.), Indo.
89/C3 Bangkok (bight), Thai.
89/C3 Bangkok (Krung Thep) (cap.), Thai.
90/E3 Bangladesh (ctry.)
89/C5 Bang Lang (res.), Thai.
50/C2 Bangor, NI,UK
50/D5 Bangor, Wal,UK
133/G2 Bangor, Me,US
51/F6 Bangor-is-y-Coed, Wal,UK
110/D2 Bangu, D.R. Congo
88/D4 Bangued, Phil.
103/J7 Bangui (cap.), CAfr.
106/B2 Banhā, Egypt
110/F5 Banhine Nat'l Park, Moz.
123/G4 Baní, DRep.
104/D3 Bani (riv.), Mali
104/D3 Banifing (riv.), Burk., Mali
79/L2 Banihāl (pass), India
106/B2 Banī Mazār, Egypt
135/J2 Banister (riv.), Va,US
80/K6 Banī Suhaylah, Gaza
106/B2 Banī Suwayf, Egypt
106/B2 Banī Suwayf (gov.), Egypt
80/K4 Bāniyās, Syria
68/C3 Banja Luka, Bosn.
92/D4 Banjarmasin, Indo.
104/A3 Banjul (cap.), Gam.
89/B5 Ban Kantang, Thai.
91/J4 Ban Kengkok, Laos
88/C2 Bankengting, China
89/D3 Ban Khampho, Laos
89/C5 Ban Khuan Niang, Thai.
97/B3 Banks (cape), Austl.
97/C4 Banks (str.), Austl.
124/C3 Banks (isl.), BC,Can.
124/D1 Banks (isl.), NW,Can.
136/H4 Banks (pt.), Ak,US
128/D4 Banks (lake), Wa,US
98/F6 Banks (isls.), Van.
96/H8 Bankstown, Austl.
90/E3 Bānkurā, India
67/H1 Bankya, Bul.
89/D2 Ban Loboy, Laos
89/E3 Ban Mdrack, Viet.
89/D2 Ban Mong, Viet.
89/D2 Ban Muangsen, Laos
49/B4 Bann (riv.), Ire.
50/B2 Bann (riv.), NI,UK
89/D2 Ban Nape, Laos
79/K2 Bannu, Pak.
68/D3 Banovići, Bosn.
89/C4 Ban Pak Phanang, Thai.
89/D3 Ban Phon, Laos
87/B4 Banpo (ruins), China
89/C2 Ban Sieou, Laos
55/K4 Banská Bystrica, Slvk.
69/F5 Bansko, Bul.
55/K4 Banskobystrický (reg.), Slvk.
53/F4 Banstead, Eng,UK
90/B3 Bānswāra, India
88/D5 Bantayan, Phil.
92/D5 Bantenan (cape), Indo.
89/C2 Ban Thabok, Laos
89/B5 Bantong Group (isls.), Thai.
64/C3 Bañuelo (mtn.), Sp.
89/D3 Ban Xebang-Nouan, Laos
92/A3 Banyak (isls.), Indo.
65/G1 Banyoles, Sp.
92/D5 Banyuwangi, Indo.
111/J Banzare (coast), Ant.
87/B3 Baode, China
87/D3 Baodi, China
87/C3 Baoding, China
89/D1 Bao Ha, Viet.
82/F5 Baoji, China
91/J2 Baojing, China
89/D1 Bao Lac, Viet.
89/D4 Bao Loc, Viet.
87/E5 Baoshan, China
91/G2 Baoshan, China
87/B2 Baotou, China
104/D4 Baoulé (riv.), C.d'Iv., Mali
104/C3 Baoulé (riv.), Mali
90/D4 Bāpatla, India
80/K5 Bāqa el Gharbiyya, Isr.
89/D4 Ba Quan (cape), Viet.
81/C2 Baqanas (riv.), Kaz.
78/D2 Ba'qūbah, Iraq
58/D5 Bar (riv.), Fr.
68/D4 Bar, Mont.
89/D4 Ba Ra, Viet.
103/P7 Baraawe, Som.
92/E4 Barabai, Indo.
74/H4 Barabinsk, Rus.
132/B3 Baraboo, Wi,US
64/D1 Baracaldo, Sp.
80/L5 Baradá (riv.), Syria
118/F2 Baradero, Arg.
103/M5 Bārah, Sudan
123/G4 Barahona, DRep.
81/C5 Bārā Lācha La (pass), India
92/D3 Baram (cape), Malay.
92/D3 Baram (riv.), Malay.
114/G2 Barama (riv.), Guy.
90/B4 Bārāmati, India
79/K2 Baramula, India
90/C2 Bāran, India
72/C1 Baranavichy, Bela.
136/L4 Baranof (isl.), Ak,US
68/C3 Baranya (co.), Hun.
116/D1 Barão de Cocais, Braz.
69/G2 Baraolt, Rom.
59/E3 Baraque de Fraiture (hill), Belg.
93/G5 Barat Daya (isls.), Indo.
116/D2 Barbacena, Braz.
123/J5 Barbados (ctry.)
106/C5 Barbar, Sudan
65/F1 Barbastro, Sp.
64/C4 Barbate de Franco, Sp.
125/T6 Barbeau (peak), Nun,Can.
65/L6 Barbera del Vallès, Sp.
126/V13 Barbers (pt.), Hi,US
109/E2 Barberton, SAfr.
132/D3 Barberton, Oh,US
62/C4 Barbezieux-Saint-Hilaire, Fr.
90/E3 Barbil, India
51/F3 Barbon, Eng,UK
132/D4 Barbourville, Ky,US
123/J4 Barbuda (isl.), Ant. & Barb.
68/F2 Barcău (riv.), Rom.
66/D3 Barcellona Pozzo di Gotto, It.
65/L7 Barcelona, Sp.
123/J5 Barcelona, Ven.
64/A2 Barcelos, Port.
55/J2 Barcin, Pol.
96/A4 Barcoo (riv.), Austl.
68/C3 Barcs, Hun.
55/L2 Barczewo, Pol.
102/J3 Bardaï, Chad
80/J6 Bardawīl, Sabkhat al (lag.), Egypt
55/L4 Bardejov, Slvk.
103/P7 Bardheere, Som.
51/H5 Bardney, Eng,UK
90/B3 Bārdoli, India
50/D6 Bardsey (isl.), Wal,UK
132/C4 Bardstown, Ky,US
103/R5 Bareeda, Som.
90/C2 Bareilly, India
56/B5 Barendrecht, Neth.
62/D2 Barentin, Fr.
45/L2 Barents (sea)
103/N4 Barentu, Erit.
62/C2 Barfleur, Pointe de (pt.), Fr.
90/D3 Bargarh, India
52/C3 Bargoed, Wal,UK
57/H1 Bargteheide, Ger.
82/F1 Barguzin (riv.), Rus.
90/D2 Barhaj, India
133/G2 Bar Harbor, Me,US
53/G2 Bar Hill, Eng,UK
90/C2 Bāri, India
66/E2 Bari, It.
102/F1 Barika, Alg.
122/C4 Barillas, Guat.
123/G6 Barinas, Ven.
110/C2 Baringa-Twana, D.R. Congo
90/E3 Baripāda, India
116/B2 Bariri, Braz.
106/B3 Bārīs, Egypt
90/F3 Barisāl, Bang.
92/B4 Barisan (mts.), Indo.
92/D4 Barito (riv.), Indo.
117/C1 Baritu Nat'l Park, Arg.
133/S9 Barker, NY,US
128/B3 Barkley (sound), BC,Can.
132/C4 Barkley (lake), Ky,US
51/F6 Barlaston, Eng,UK
51/G4 Barlby, Eng,UK
59/E6 Bar-le-Duc, Fr.
66/E2 Barletta, It.
58/B3 Barlin, Fr.
55/H2 Barlinek, Pol.
117/E2 Barmejo (riv.), Arg.
90/B2 Barmer, India
52/B1 Barmouth, Wal,UK
57/G1 Barmstedt, Ger.
79/L2 Barnāla, India
51/G2 Barnard Castle, Eng,UK
81/D1 Barnaul, Rus.
137/F6 Barnegat (bay), NJ,US
56/C4 Barneveld, Neth.
55/G2 Barnim (reg.), Ger.
51/F4 Barnoldswick, Eng,UK
51/G4 Barnsley, Eng,UK
51/G4 Barnsley (co.), Eng,UK
52/B4 Barnstaple, Eng,UK
52/B4 Barnstaple (Bideford) (bay), Eng,UK
57/G5 Barntrup, Ger.
135/H3 Barnwell, SC,US
90/B3 Baroda, India
79/K1 Barowghīl (Khyber) (pass), Afg.
90/F2 Barpeta, India
123/H5 Barquisimeto, Ven.
50/D1 Barr, Sc,UK
115/K6 Barra, Braz.
116/B2 Barra Bonita, Braz.
116/B2 Barra Bonita (res.), Braz.
122/E5 Barra del Colorado Nat'l Park, CR
115/G7 Barra do Bugres, Braz.
115/J5 Barra do Corda, Braz.
115/H7 Barra do Garças, Braz.
116/K7 Barra do Piraí, Braz.
116/B4 Barra do Ribeiro, Braz.
116/J7 Barra Mansa, Braz.
114/C4 Barranca, Peru
114/C6 Barranca, Peru
114/D2 Barrancabermeja, Col.
123/N8 Barranca del Cobre Nat'l Park, Mex.
118/C2 Barrancas, Chile
123/G5 Barranquilla, Col.
116/B3 Barra Velha, Braz.
115/J6 Barreiras, Braz.
64/A3 Barreiro, Port.
109/G7 Barren, Nosy (isls.), Madg.
116/B2 Barretos, Braz.
128/E2 Barrhead, Ab,Can.
50/D1 Barrhill, Sc,UK
132/E2 Barrie, On,Can.
97/B1 Barrier (range), Austl.
128/C3 Barrière, BC,Can.
138/P15 Barrington, Il,US
138/P15 Barrington Hills, Il,US
97/D1 Barrington Tops (peak), Austl.
97/D1 Barrington Tops Nat'l Park, Austl.
96/B2 Barron Gorge Nat'l Park, Austl.
116/D2 Barroso, Braz.
96/B1 Barrow (pt.), Austl.
124/G1 Barrow (str.), Nun,Can.
49/B4 Barrow (riv.), Ire.
136/G1 Barrow (pt.), Ak,US
51/H6 Barrowby, Eng,UK
51/F4 Barrowford, Eng,UK
51/E3 Barrow-in-Furness, Eng,UK
52/C4 Barry, Wal,UK
73/L4 Barsakel'mes (salt pan), Uzb.
79/L5 Bārshi, India
57/G4 Barsinghausen, Ger.
57/E2 Barssel, Ger.
130/C4 Barstow, Ca,US
62/F2 Bar-sur-Aube, Fr.
81/B4 Bartang (riv.), Taj.
54/G1 Barth, Ger.
69/L5 Bartın, Turk.
131/J3 Bartlesville, Ok,US
138/P16 Bartlett, Il,US
123/F3 Bartolomé Masó, Cuba
110/G5 Bartolomeu Dias, Moz.
53/F3 Barton in the Clay, Eng,UK
53/E5 Barton on Sea, Eng,UK
53/E1 Barton under Needwood, Eng,UK
51/H4 Barton-upon-Humber, Eng,UK
55/L1 Bartoszyce, Pol.
135/H5 Bartow, Fl,US
122/E6 Barú (vol.), Pan.
92/B3 Barumun (riv.), Indo.
92/A3 Barus, Indo.
82/C2 Baruun Huuray (reg.), Mong.
82/G2 Baruun-Urt, Mong.
90/C3 Barwāha, India
90/B3 Barwāni, India
97/D1 Barwon (riv.), Austl.
55/J3 Barycz (riv.), Pol.
70/F5 Barysaw, Bela.
73/H1 Barysh, Rus.
103/J7 Basankusu, D.R. Congo
64/D1 Basauri, Sp.
118/F2 Basavilbaso, Arg.
52/D1 Baschurch, Eng,UK
60/D2 Basel, Swi.
60/D3 Baselland (canton), Swi.
66/E2 Basento (riv.), It.
108/E3 Bashee (riv.), SAfr.
88/D3 Bashi (chan.), Phil., Tai.
81/E1 Bashkaus (riv.), Rus.
71/M5 Bashkortostan, Resp., Rus.
88/D6 Basilan (isl.), Phil.
93/F2 Basilan (peak), Phil.
53/G3 Basildon, Eng,UK
66/D2 Basilicata (reg.), It.
90/C3 Bāsim, India
128/F4 Basin, Wy,US
53/E4 Basingstoke, Eng,UK
80/F2 Başkale, Turk.
132/F2 Baskatong (res.), Qu,Can.
90/C3 Bāsoda, India
103/K7 Basoko, D.R. Congo
64/D1 Basque Provinces (aut. comm.), Sp.
60/D1 Bas-Rhin (dept.), Fr.
97/C3 Bass (str.), Austl.
99/L7 Bass (isls.), FrPol.
67/G4 Bassae (ruins), Gre.
128/E3 Bassano, Ab,Can.
63/J4 Bassano del Grappa, It.
110/G5 Bassas da India (isl.), Reun., Fr.
91/F4 Bassein, Myan.
91/F4 Bassein (riv.), Myan.
90/B4 Bassein, India
59/E2 Bassenge, Belg.
62/C2 Basse-Normandie (reg.), Fr.
51/E2 Bassenthwaite (lake), Eng,UK
123/J4 Basse-Terre (cap.), Guad.
123/J4 Basse-Terre (isl.), Guad.
123/J4 Basseterre (cap.), StK.
57/F3 Bassum, Ger.
132/B1 Basswood (lake), On,Can., Mn,US
48/E4 Båstad, Swe.
90/D2 Bastī, India
66/A1 Bastia, Fr.
66/C1 Bastia, It.
59/E3 Bastogne, Belg.
116/B2 Bastos, Braz.
134/F3 Bastrop, La,US
134/D4 Bastrop, Tx,US
80/H6 Basyūn, Egypt
102/G7 Bata, EqG.
122/E3 Batabanó (gulf), Cuba
88/D4 Batac, Phil.
75/P3 Batagay, Rus.
79/L2 Batāla, India
64/A3 Batalha, Port.
88/D3 Batan (isl.), Phil.
103/J6 Batangafo, CAfr.
88/D5 Batangas, Phil.
116/C2 Batatais, Braz.
138/P16 Batavia, Il,US
132/E3 Batavia, NY,US
72/F3 Bataysk, Rus.
91/H5 Batdambang, Camb.
96/H9 Bate (bay), Austl.
102/H8 Batéké (plat.), Congo
97/D2 Batemans Bay, Austl.
135/H3 Batesburg, SC,US
135/F3 Batesville, Ar,US
135/F3 Batesville, Ms,US
52/D4 Bath, Eng,UK
52/D4 Bath and Northeast Somerset (co.), Eng,UK
133/G3 Bath, Me,US
132/E3 Bath, NY,US
97/D2 Bathurst, Austl.
133/H2 Bathurst, NB,Can.
136/N1 Bathurst (cape), NW,Can.
124/F2 Bathurst (inlet), Nun,Can.
125/R7 Bathurst (isl.), Nun,Can.
103/P5 Batī, Eth.
81/F2 Batik (mts.), China
78/E3 Bāṭin, Wādī al (dry riv.), SAr.
51/G4 Batley, Eng,UK
80/E3 Batman, Turk.
102/G1 Batna, Alg.
135/F4 Baton Rouge (cap.), La,US
102/H7 Batouri, Camr.
133/F2 Batsican (riv.), Qu,Can.
137/F6 Batsto (riv.), NJ,US
82/F2 Batsümber, Mong.
45/M9 Batterbee (cape), Ant.
51/G3 Battersby, Eng,UK
90/D6 Batticaloa, SrL.
128/F2 Battle (riv.), Ab, Sk,Can.
53/G5 Battle, Eng,UK
128/F3 Battle (cr.), Mt,US
132/C3 Battle Creek, Mi,US
128/F2 Battleford, Sk,Can.
130/C2 Battle Mountain, Nv,US
68/E2 Battonya, Hun.
82/E2 Battsengel, Mong.
103/N6 Batu (peak), Eth.
93/E3 Batu (cape), Indo.
92/A4 Batu (isls.), Indo.
92/D3 Batu (bay), Malay.
92/D3 Batu (peak), Malay.
93/F4 Batudaka (isl.), Indo.
92/D3 Batuensambang (peak), Indo.
92/B3 Batu Gajah, Malay.
73/G4 Bat'umi, Geo.
92/B3 Batu Pahat, Malay.
92/B3 Batu Puteh (peak), Malay.
92/B4 Baturaja, Indo.
115/L4 Baturité, Braz.
80/M8 Bat Yam, Isr.
73/J2 Batys Qazaqstan (obl.), Kaz.
105/H4 Bauchi (state), Nga.
129/K3 Baudette, Mn,US
125/L1 Bauld (cape), Nf,Can.
105/F5 Bauman (peak), Togo
57/G6 Baunatal, Ger.
116/B2 Bauru, Braz.
55/H3 Bautzen, Ger.
61/G3 Bavarian Alps (mts.), Aus., Ger.
92/C4 Bawang (cape), Indo.
97/C3 Baw Baw (peak), Austl.
97/C3 Baw Baw Nat'l Park, Austl.
92/D5 Bawean (isl.), Indo.
105/E4 Bawku, Gha.
123/F3 Bayamo, Cuba
123/H4 Bayamón, PR
82/D5 Bayan Har (mts.), China
82/E2 Bayanhongor, Mong.
82/E3 Bayanleg, Mong.
81/F2 Bayannur, Mong.
82/E2 Bayan-Ovoo, Mong.
82/D2 Bayan-Uul, Mong.
131/G2 Bayard, Ne,US
88/D6 Bayawan, Phil.
59/G3 Baybach (riv.), Ger.
88/D5 Baybay, Phil.
80/E2 Bayburt, Turk.
132/D3 Bay City, Mi,US
134/E4 Bay City, Tx,US
74/G2 Baydaratskaya (bay), Rus.
82/D2 Baydrag (riv.), Mong.
105/G5 Bayelsa (state), Nga.
63/K2 Bayerischer Wald Nat'l Park, Ger.
54/F4 Bayern (state), Ger.
115/M5 Bayeux, Braz.
62/C2 Bayeux, Fr.
119/T11 Baygorria, Artificial de (res.), Uru.
78/E6 Bayḥān al Qiṣāb, Yem.
75/L4 Baykal (mts.), Rus.
82/F1 Baykal (Baikal) (lake), Rus.
135/G4 Bay Minette, Al,US
88/D5 Bayombong, Phil.
64/A1 Bayona, Sp.
135/H4 Bayonet Point, Fl,US
62/C5 Bayonne, Fr.
137/F5 Bayonne, NJ,US
137/G5 Bayport, NY,US
79/H1 Bayram-Ali, Trkm.
69/H5 Bayramıç, Turk.
63/J2 Bayreuth, Ger.
80/K5 Bayrūt (Beirut) (cap.), Leb.
132/E2 Bays (lake), On,Can.
135/F4 Bay Saint Louis, Ms,US
65/E1 Bayse (riv.), Fr.
52/D1 Bayston Hill, Eng,UK
80/K6 Bayt Laḥm (Bethlehem), WBnk.
134/E4 Baytown, Tx,US
106/C5 Bayūda (des.), Sudan
88/E6 Bayugan, Phil.
137/G5 Bayville, NY,US
64/D4 Baza, Sp.
73/H4 Bazardyuzyu, Gora (peak), Rus.
110/G5 Bazaruto (isl.), Moz.
105/E4 Bazèga (prov.), Burk.
132/F2 Bazin (riv.), Qu,Can.
137/F6 Beachwood, NJ,US
53/G5 Beachy Head (pt.), Eng,UK
52/C2 Beacon (hill), Wal,UK
53/F3 Beaconsfield, Eng,UK
52/B5 Beaford, Eng,UK
96/A4 Beal (mts.), Austl.
109/J6 Bealanana, Madg.
128/B3 Beale (cape), BC,Can.
131/G4 Beals (cr.), Tx,US
52/D5 Beaminster, Eng,UK
109/H9 Beampingaratra (ridge), Madg.
133/R9 Beamsville, On,Can.
129/K2 Bear (lake), Mb,Can.
74/C2 Bear (isl.), Nor.
136/K2 Bear (mtn.), Ak,US
136/K3 Bear (mtn.), Ak,US
128/F5 Bear (lake), Id, Ut,US
128/F5 Bear (riv.), Id, Ut,US
111/M Beardmore (glac.), Ant.
128/F3 Bearpaw (mts.), Mt,US
49/C3 Bearsden, Sc,UK
128/F4 Beartooth (mts.), Mt, Wy,US
135/F4 Bear Town, Ms,US
64/D1 Beasain, Sp.
64/D3 Beas de Segura, Sp.
123/G4 Beata (cape), DRep.
131/H2 Beatrice, Ne,US
50/E1 Beattock, Sc,UK
130/C3 Beatty, Nv,US
62/F5 Beaucaire, Fr.
121/C2 Beaufort (sea), Can., US
135/H3 Beaufort, SC,US
108/C4 Beaufort West, SAfr.
62/D3 Beaugency, Fr.
133/N7 Beauharnois, Qu,Can.
62/F4 Beaujolais (mts.), Fr.
53/E5 Beaulieu, Eng,UK
50/D5 Beaumaris, Wal,UK
58/B3 Beaumetz-les-Loges, Fr.
137/C3 Beaumont, Ca,US
134/E4 Beaumont, Tx,US
58/B5 Beaumont-sur-Oise, Fr.
62/F3 Beaune, Fr.
62/D3 Beaupréau, Fr.
59/D3 Beauraing, Belg.
129/J3 Beauséjour, Mb,Can.
58/B5 Beauvais, Fr.
128/G2 Beauval, Sk,Can.
128/F2 Beaver (riv.), Ab, Sk,Can.
124/D2 Beaver (riv.), Yk,Can.
131/G3 Beaver (riv.), Co,US
131/G3 Beaver (riv.), Ks, Ne,US
132/C2 Beaver (isl.), Mi,US
131/G3 Beaver (riv.), NM, Ok,US
131/G3 Beaver, Ok,US
130/D3 Beaver, Ut,US
136/K3 Beaver Creek, Yk,Can.
132/B3 Beaver Dam, Wi,US
128/E4 Beaverhead (riv.), Mt,US
128/D2 Beaverlodge, Ab,Can.
129/L2 Beaver Stone (riv.), On,Can.
90/B2 Beāwar, India
116/B2 Bebedouro, Braz.
51/E5 Bebington, Eng,UK
57/G7 Bebra, Ger.
53/H2 Beccles, Eng,UK
68/E3 Bečej, Serb.
102/E1 Bechar, Alg.
136/G4 Becharof (lake), Ak,US
136/G4 Becharof Nat'l Wild. Ref., Ak,US
59/F5 Beckingen, Ger.
51/H5 Beckingham, Eng,UK
132/D4 Beckley, WV,US
57/F5 Beckum, Ger.
69/G2 Beclean, Rom.
51/G3 Bedale, Eng,UK
56/D7 Bedburg, Ger.
56/D5 Bedburg-Hau, Ger.
52/C3 Beddau, Wal,UK
50/D5 Beddgelert, Wal,UK
96/B1 Bedford (cape), Austl.
133/F2 Bedford, Qu,Can.
53/F2 Bedford, Eng,UK
132/C4 Bedford, In,US
132/E4 Bedford, Va,US
53/G2 Bedford Level (reg.), Eng,UK
53/F2 Bedfordshire (co.), Eng,UK
51/G1 Bedlington, Eng,UK
102/H4 Bedouaram (well), Niger
56/D2 Bedum, Neth.
52/C3 Bedwas, Wal,UK
53/E2 Bedworth, Eng,UK
96/D4 Beenleigh, Austl.
52/C5 Beer, Eng,UK
52/C5 Beer Head (pt.), Eng,UK
58/C1 Beernem, Belg.
80/K6 Beersheba (Be'er Sheva'), Isr.
59/D1 Beerzel, Belg.
56/D6 Beesel, Neth.
51/G6 Beeston, Eng,UK
134/D4 Beeville, Tx,US
103/K7 Befale, D.R. Congo
57/F5 Bega (riv.), Ger.
90/C3 Begamganj, India
73/K4 Begarslan (peak), Trkm.
68/E3 Bega Veche (riv.), Rom.
75/M2 Begichev (isl.), Rus.
50/B2 Beg, Lough (lake), NI,UK
48/D3 Begna (riv.), Nor.
90/E2 Begusarai, India
115/H3 Béhague (pt.), FrG.
92/B4 Behala (str.), Indo.
78/F2 Behbahān, Iran
59/F5 Behren-lès-Forbach, Fr.
78/F1 Behshahr, Iran
81/F3 Bei (mts.), China
88/A2 Bei (riv.), China
83/K2 Bei'an, China
82/D4 Beida (riv.), China
89/E1 Beihai, China
87/H7 Beijing (cap.), China
87/H6 Beijing (prov.), China
56/D3 Beilen, Neth.
82/C5 Beilu (riv.), China
89/D1 Beilun (pass), China
87/E2 Beipiao, China
110/F4 Beira, Moz.
87/C4 Beiru (riv.), China
80/K5 Beirut (Bayrūt) (cap.), Leb.
110/E5 Beitbridge, Zim.
68/F2 Beiuş, Rom.
64/B3 Beja, Port.
64/A4 Beja (dist.), Port.
66/A4 Beja, Tun.
66/A4 Beja (gov.), Tun.
102/F1 Bejaïa, Alg.
64/C2 Béjar, Sp.
79/J3 Bejhi (riv.), Pak.
80/K5 Bekaa (Al Biqā') (val.), Leb.
92/C5 Bekasi, Indo.
68/E2 Békés, Hun.
68/E2 Békés (co.), Hun.
68/E2 Békéscsaba, Hun.
109/H8 Bekily, Madg.
105/E5 Bekwai, Gha.
90/B3 Bela, India
79/J3 Bela, Pak.
68/E3 Bela Crkva, Serb.
68/F4 Bela Palanka, Serb.
47/G3 Belarus (ctry.)
65/P10 Belas, Port.
115/G8 Bela Vista, Braz.
116/B2 Bela Vista do Paraíso, Braz.
71/M5 Belaya (riv.), Rus.
73/G2 Belaya Kalitva, Rus.
72/D2 Belaya Tserkov', Ukr.
55/K3 Bełchatów, Pol.
125/S7 Belcher (chan.), Nun,Can.
125/H3 Belcher (isls.), Nun,Can.
129/J3 Belcourt, ND,US
71/M5 Belebey, Rus.
103/Q7 Beled Weyne, Som.
117/C2 Belén, Arg.
130/F4 Belen, NM,US
119/S12 Belén de Escobar, Arg.
69/G4 Belene, Bul.
64/B1 Belesar (res.), Sp.
103/N5 Beles Wenz (riv.), Eth.
72/F1 Belev, Rus.
50/C2 Belfast (cap.), NI,UK
50/C2 Belfast (dist.), NI,UK
133/G2 Belfast, Me,US
50/C2 Belfast Lough (inlet), NI,UK
129/H4 Belfield, ND,US
60/C2 Belfort, Fr.
60/C2 Belfort (dept.), Fr.
90/B4 Belgaum, India
54/C3 Belgium (ctry.)
72/F2 Belgorod, Rus.
72/D3 Belgorod-Dnestrovskiy, Ukr.
72/F2 Belgorodskaya Obl., Rus.
128/F4 Belgrade, Mt,US
68/E3 Belgrade (Beograd) (cap.), Serb.
68/E4 Beli Drim (riv.), Serb.
68/D3 Beli Manastir, Cro.
68/F4 Beli Timok (riv.), Serb.
92/C4 Belitung (isl.), Indo.
122/D4 Belize (ctry.)
122/D4 Belize City, Belz.
68/E3 Beljanica (peak), Serb.
75/P2 Bel'kovskiy (isl.), Rus.
125/H2 Bell (pen.), Nun,Can.
132/E1 Bell (riv.), Qu,Can.
137/B3 Bell, Ca,US
128/B2 Bella Coola, BC,Can.
50/B2 Bellaghy, NI,UK
90/C4 Bellary, India
117/E2 Bella Vista, Arg.
66/A3 Bellavista (cape), It.
138/G7 Belle (riv.), On,Can.
138/G6 Belle (riv.), Mi,US
58/C5 Belleau, Fr.
50/B3 Belleek, NI,UK
132/D3 Bellefontaine, Oh,US
129/G4 Belle Fourche (riv.), SD, Wy,US
60/B5 Bellegarde-sur-Valserine, Fr.
135/H5 Belle Glade, Fl,US
137/J8 Belle Haven, Va,US
62/B3 Belle-Ile (isl.), Fr.
133/K1 Belle Isle (str.), Nf, Qu,Can.
96/B2 Bellenden Ker Nat'l Park, Austl.
62/E3 Bellerive-sur-Allier, Fr.
132/E2 Belleville, On,Can
132/B4 Belleville, Il,US.
131/H3 Belleville, Ks,US
137/F5 Belleville, NJ,US
138/C2 Bellevue, Wa,US
137/B3 Bellflower, Ca,US
51/F1 Bellingham, Eng,UK
128/C3 Bellingham, Wa,US
111/U Bellingshausen (sea), Ant.
99/K6 Bellingshausen (isl.), FrPol.
57/E2 Bellingwolde, Neth.
61/F5 Bellinzona, Swi.
137/E6 Bellmawr, NJ,US
137/G5 Bellmore, NY,US
114/C2 Bello, Col.
98/F7 Bellona (reefs), NCal.
124/G1 Bellot (str.), Nun,Can.
126/W13 Bellows A.F.B., Hi,US
137/H5 Bellport, NY,US
49/C3 Bellshill, Sc,UK
63/K3 Belluno, It.
118/E2 Bell Ville, Arg.
108/B4 Bellville, SAfr.
134/D4 Bellville, Tx,US
57/F4 Belm, Ger.
137/F5 Belmar, NJ,US
138/K11 Belmont, Ca,US
122/D4 Belmopan (cap.), Belz.
58/C2 Beloeil, Belg.
133/P6 Beloeil, Qu,Can.
83/K1 Belogorsk, Rus.
68/F4 Belogradchik, Bul.
116/D1 Belo Horizonte, Braz.
131/H3 Beloit, Ks,US
132/B3 Beloit, Wi,US
115/L5 Belo Jardim, Braz.
70/G2 Belomorsk, Rus.
110/C1 Belondo-Kundu, D.R. Congo
72/F3 Belorechensk, Rus.
71/N5 Beloretsk, Rus.
68/E4 Beloševac, Serb.
69/H4 Beloslav, Bul.
74/J4 Belovo, Rus.
70/H3 Beloye (lake), Rus.
51/G5 Belper, Eng,UK
51/G1 Belsay, Eng,UK
128/F4 Belt, Mt,US
56/D3 Belterwijde (lake), Neth.
53/H1 Belton, Eng,UK
134/D4 Belton, Tx,US
137/K7 Beltsville, Md,US
69/H2 Bel'tsy, Mol.
137/E5 Beltzville (lake), Pa,US
81/E2 Belukha, Gora (peak), Rus.
132/B3 Belvidere, Il,US
96/B3 Belyando (riv.), Austl.
74/G2 Belyy (isl.), Rus.
54/G2 Belzig, Ger.
55/M3 Bełżyce, Pol.
109/H7 Bemaraha (plat.), Madg.
109/H7 Bemarivo (riv.), Madg.
64/B1 Bembibre, Sp.
53/E5 Bembridge, Eng,UK
129/K4 Bemidji, Mn,US
56/C5 Bemmel, Neth.
51/H3 Bempton, Eng,UK
97/C3 Benalla, Austl.
64/C4 Benalmádena, Sp.
66/B4 Ben Arous (gov.), Tun.
64/C2 Benavente, Sp.
134/D5 Benavides, Tx,US
50/B1 Benbane Head (pt.), NI,UK
97/D3 Ben Boyd Nat'l Park, Austl.
50/B3 Benburb, NI,UK
128/C4 Bend, Or,US
105/G5 Bendel (state), Nga.
136/F2 Bendeleben (mtn.), Ak,US
69/J2 Bendery, Mol.
97/C3 Bendigo, Austl.
80/M8 Bene Beraq, Isr.
125/L3 Benedict (mtn.), Nf,Can.
50/D1 Beneraid (hill), Sc,UK
55/H4 Benešov, Czh.
66/D2 Benevento, It.
53/G3 Benfleet, Eng,UK
90/E4 Bengal (bay), Asia
87/D4 Bengbu, China
103/K1 Benghāzī, Libya
89/D3 Ben Giang, Viet.
92/B3 Bengkalis, Indo.
92/B3 Bengkalis (isl.), Indo.
92/C3 Bengkayang, Indo.
92/B4 Bengkulu, Indo.
129/G3 Bengough, Sk,Can.
48/E4 Bengtsfors, Swe.
110/B3 Benguela, Ang.
107/A5 Bengweulu (lake), Zam.
114/E6 Beni (riv.), Bol.
107/A2 Beni, D.R. Congo
102/E1 Beni Abbes, Alg.
65/F2 Benicarló, Sp.
138/K10 Benicia, Ca,US
65/E3 Benidorm, Sp.
65/E3 Benifayó, Sp.
102/D1 Beni Mellal, Mor.
105/F4 Benin (ctry.)
105/F5 Benin (bight), Ben., Nga.
105/G5 Benin City, Nga.
102/E1 Beni Ounif, Alg.
65/F3 Benisa, Sp.
118/B5 Benjamin (isl.), Chile
134/D3 Benjamin, Tx,US
114/D4 Benjamin Constant, Braz.
123/M7 Benjamin Hill, Mex.
131/G2 Benkelman, Ne,US
50/D5 Benllech, Wal,UK
49/C2 Ben Lomond (mtn.), Sc,UK
97/C4 Ben Lomond Nat'l Park, Austl.
49/D2 Ben Macdui (mtn.), Sc,UK
49/C2 Ben More (mtn.), Sc,UK
50/C1 Bennane Head (pt.), Sc,UK
75/R2 Bennett (isl.), Rus.
135/J3 Bennettsville, SC,US
49/C2 Ben Nevis (mtn.), Sc,UK
133/F3 Bennington, Vt,US
108/Q13 Benoni, SAfr.
109/J6 Be, Nosy (isl.), Madg.
102/H6 Bénoué Nat'l Park, Camr.
89/D2 Ben Quang, Viet.
138/Q16 Bensenville, Il,US
63/H2 Bensheim, Ger.
130/E5 Benson, Az,US
129/K4 Benson, Mn,US
51/F3 Bentham, Eng,UK
57/E4 Bentheim, Ger.
103/L6 Bentiu, Sudan
51/G4 Bentley, Eng,UK
116/B4 Bento Gonçalves, Braz.
134/E3 Benton, Ar,US
132/B4 Benton, Il,US
132/B4 Benton, Ky,US
92/B3 Bentong, Malay.
132/C3 Benton Harbor, Mi,US
134/E2 Bentonville, Ar,US

Ben T – Bongo
153

89/D4 Ben Tre, Viet.
105/G4 Benue (riv.), Nga.
105/G5 Benue (state), Nga.
68/D3 Beočin, Serb.
68/E3 Beograd (Belgrade) (cap.), Serb.
84/B4 Beppu, Japan
84/B4 Beppu (bay), Japan
102/E1 Beraber (well), Alg.
50/A2 Beragh, NI,UK
68/D4 Berane, Mont.
67/F2 Berat, Alb.
93/E4 Beratus (peak), Indo.
93/H4 Berau (bay), Indo.
93/E3 Berau (riv.), Indo.
103/Q5 Berbera, Som.
102/J7 Berberati, CAfr.
114/G2 Berbice (riv.), Guy.
58/D1 Berchem, Belg.
63/K3 Berchtesgaden, Ger.
63/K3 Berchtesgaden Nat'l Park, Ger.
58/A3 Berck, Fr.
72/D2 Berdichev, Ukr.
74/J4 Berdsk, Rus.
72/F3 Berdyansk, Ukr.
132/C4 Berea, Ky,US
72/B2 Beregovo, Ukr.
105/E5 Berekum, Gha.
106/C4 Berenice (ruins), Egypt
52/D5 Bere Regis, Eng,UK
133/H2 Beresford, NB,Can.
129/J5 Beresford, SD,US
68/E2 Berettyo (riv.), Hun.
68/E2 Berettyóújfalu, Hun.
71/N4 Berezniki, Rus.
108/B4 Berg (riv.), SAfr.
80/A2 Bergama, Turk.
63/H4 Bergamo, It.
57/G3 Bergen, Ger.
56/B3 Bergen, Neth.
48/C3 Bergen, Nor.
137/F5 Bergenfield, NJ,US
56/B6 Bergen op Zoom, Neth.
62/D4 Bergerac, Fr.
56/C6 Bergeyk, Neth.
59/F2 Bergheim, Ger.
57/E5 Bergkamen, Ger.
57/E6 Bergneustadt, Ger.
56/C2 Bergum, Neth.
56/D2 Bergumermeer (lake), Neth.
90/D4 Berhampur, India
92/C4 Berikat (cape), Indo.
75/S4 Bering (isl.), Rus.
136/E3 Bering (str.), Rus., Ak,US
59/E1 Beringen, Belg.
136/E2 Bering Land Bridge Nat'l Prsv., Ak,US
92/B4 Beritarikap (cape), Indo.
64/D4 Berja, Sp.
56/D4 Berkel (riv.), Ger.
56/B5 Berkel, Neth.
52/D3 Berkeley, Eng,UK
138/K11 Berkeley, Ca,US
137/F5 Berkeley Heights, NJ,US
53/F3 Berkhamsted, Eng,UK
138/F6 Berkley, Mi,US
111/W Berkner (isl.), Ant.
69/F4 Berkovitsa, Bul.
53/E4 Berkshire Downs (uplands), Eng,UK
58/C1 Berlare, Belg.
56/C5 Berlicum, Neth.
55/G2 Berlin (cap.), Ger.
133/G2 Berlin, NH,US
111/V Berlioz (pt.), Ant.
117/E2 Bermejo (riv.), Arg.
117/D1 Bermejo, Bol.
64/D1 Bermeo, Sp.
121/L6 Bermuda (isl.), UK
60/D3 Bern (canton), Swi.
60/D4 Bern (cap.), Swi.
114/B5 Bernal, Peru
66/E2 Bernalda, It.
130/F4 Bernalillo, NM,US
124/D1 Bernard (riv.), NW,Can.
119/J7 Bernardo O'Higgins Nat'l Park, Chile
137/G5 Bernardsville, NJ,US
62/D2 Bernay, Fr.
54/F3 Bernburg, Ger.
57/F2 Berne (riv.), Ger.
60/D5 Bernese Alps (range), Swi.
124/G1 Bernier (bay), Nun,Can.
61/G5 Bernina, Passo del (pass), Swi.
58/C3 Bernissart, Belg.
59/G4 Bernkastel-Kues, Ger.
109/H8 Beroroha, Madg.
55/H4 Beroun, Czh.
55/G4 Berounka (riv.), Czh.
68/F5 Berovo, FYROM
62/F5 Berre (lag.), Fr.
52/C1 Berriew, Wal,UK
123/F2 Berry (isls.), Bahm.
62/D3 Berry (hist. reg.), Fr.
138/K9 Berryessa (lake), Ca,US
138/K9 Berryessa (peak), Ca,US
52/C6 Berry Head (pt.), Eng,UK
134/E2 Berryville, Ar,US
102/H7 Bertoua, Camr.
119/J7 Bertrand (peak), Arg.
59/E4 Bertrix, Belg.
98/G5 Beru (atoll), Kiri.
92/D3 Beruit (isl.), Malay.
97/G5 Berwick, Austl.
133/H2 Berwick, NB,Can.
49/D3 Berwick-upon-Tweed, Eng,UK
50/E6 Berwyn (mts.), Wal,UK
138/Q16 Berwyn, Il,US
137/E5 Berwyn-Devon, Pa,US
62/E4 Bès (riv.), Fr.
109/H7 Besalampy, Madg.
60/B3 Besançon, Fr.
93/E4 Besar (peak), Indo.
62/E3 Besbre (riv.), Fr.
74/F6 Beshahr, Iran
68/E3 Beška, Serb.
55/K4 Beskids (mts.), Pol.
73/H4 Beslan, Rus.
68/F4 Besna Kobila (peak), Serb.
129/G2 Besnard (lake), Sk,Can.
51/G4 Bessacarr, Eng,UK
69/J2 Bessarabia (reg.), Mol.
50/B3 Bessbrook, NI,UK
135/G3 Bessemer, Al,US
132/B2 Bessemer, Mi,US
138/D2 Bessemer (mtn.), Wa,US
56/C6 Best, Neth.
57/F6 Bestwig, Ger.
64/A1 Betanzos, Sp.
80/N7 Beth Alpha Synagogue Nat'l Park, Isr.
131/J2 Bethany, Mo,US
50/D5 Bethesda, Wal,UK
137/J8 Bethesda, Md,US
108/E3 Bethlehem, SAfr.
137/E5 Bethlehem, Pa,US
80/K6 Bethlehem (Bayt Laḩm), WBnk.
137/G5 Bethpage, NY,US
129/G3 Bethune, Sk,Can.
58/B2 Béthune, Fr.
58/A4 Béthune (riv.), Fr.
116/C1 Betim, Braz.
109/H8 Betioky, Madg.
81/A2 Betpaqdala (des.), Kaz.
59/G6 Betschdorf, Fr.
80/K5 Bet She'an, Isr.
80/M9 Bet Shemesh, Isr.
133/G1 Betsiamites (riv.), Qu,Can.
109/H7 Betsiboka (riv.), Madg.
103/J3 Bette (peak), Libya
59/F4 Bettembourg, Lux.
90/D2 Bettiah, India
90/C3 Betūl, India
56/C5 Betuwe (reg.), Neth.
50/E5 Betws-y-Coed, Wal,UK
59/G2 Betzdorf, Ger.
129/H4 Beulah, ND,US
56/D3 Beulakerwijde (lake), Neth.
53/G4 Beult (riv.), Eng,UK
56/C5 Beuningen, Neth.
62/D3 Beuvron (riv.), Fr.
58/B2 Beuvry, Fr.
57/E4 Bever (riv.), Ger.
58/D1 Beveren, Belg.
51/H4 Beverley, Eng,UK
137/B2 Beverly Hills, Ca,US
138/F6 Beverly Hills, Mi,US
57/G5 Beverungen, Ger.
56/B4 Beverwijk, Neth.
51/F1 Bewcastle, Eng,UK
52/D2 Bewdley, Eng,UK
53/G4 Bewl Bridge (res.), Eng,UK
59/G5 Bexbach, Ger.
53/G5 Bexhill, Eng,UK
69/J5 Beykoz, Turk.
59/E2 Beyne-Heusay, Belg.
69/K5 Beypazarı, Turk.
80/B3 Beyşehir, Turk.
80/B3 Beyşehir (lake), Turk.
68/D3 Bezdan, Serb.
70/H4 Bezhetsk, Rus.
62/E5 Béziers, Fr.
90/D2 Bhabua, India
90/E3 Bhadrak, India
90/C5 Bhadrāvati, India
90/A3 Bhadreswar, India
90/E2 Bhāgalpur, India
79/K2 Bhakkar, Pak.
90/E2 Bhaktapur, Nepal
91/G3 Bhamo, Myan.
90/C2 Bharātpur, India
90/B3 Bharuch, India
90/D3 Bhātāpāra, India
79/K2 Bhatinda, India
90/B5 Bhatkal, India
90/E3 Bhātpāra, India
90/C5 Bhavāni, India
90/B3 Bhavnagar, India
90/C3 Bhawāni Mandi, India
90/D4 Bhawānipatna, India
90/D3 Bhilai, India
90/B2 Bhīlwāra, India
90/C4 Bhīma (riv.), India
90/D4 Bhīmavaram, India
90/D4 Bhimunipatnam, India
90/C2 Bhind, India
90/B3 Bhīnmāl, India
90/B4 Bhiwandi, India
90/E2 Bhojpur, Nepal
90/C3 Bhopāl, India
90/B4 Bhor, India
90/E3 Bhuban, India
90/E3 Bhubaneswar, India
90/A3 Bhūj, India
89/B2 Bhumibol (dam), Thai.
90/C3 Bhusawal, India
90/E2 Bhutan (ctry.)
81/F5 Bi (riv.), China
114/E4 Biá (riv.), Braz.
104/E5 Bia (riv.), C.d'Iv., Gui.
58/B3 Biache-Saint-Vaast, Fr.
102/G7 Biafra (bight), Afr.
93/J4 Biak (isl.), Indo.
55/M2 Biała Podlaska, Pol.
55/L3 Białobrzegi, Pol.
55/J2 Białogard, Pol.
55/K4 Białowieski Nat'l Park, Pol.
55/M2 Białystok, Pol.
61/G4 Bianca (peak), It.
66/D4 Biancavilla, It.
103/L7 Biaro, D.R. Congo
62/C5 Biarritz, Fr.
106/B2 Bibā, Egypt
116/K6 Bicas, Braz.
69/H2 Bicaz, Rom.
53/E3 Bicester, Eng,UK
68/D2 Bicske, Hun.
104/D5 Bidaga (rapids), C.d'Iv.
90/C4 Bīdar, India
133/G3 Biddeford, Me,US
51/F5 Biddulph, Eng,UK
52/B4 Bideford, Eng,UK
52/B4 Bideford (Barnstaple) (bay), Eng,UK
53/E2 Bidford on Avon, Eng,UK
89/E3 Bi Doup (peak), Viet.
65/E1 Bidouze (riv.), Fr.
110/B4 Bie (plat.), Ang.
55/M2 Biebrza (riv.), Pol.
60/D3 Biel, Swi.
55/J3 Bielawa, Pol.
57/F4 Bielefeld, Ger.
125/J1 Bieler (lake), Nun,Can.
55/K4 Bielsko-Biała, Pol.
55/M2 Bielsk Podlaski, Pol.
89/D4 Bien Hoa, Viet.
89/D1 Bien Son, Viet.
125/J3 Bienville (lake), Qu,Can.
56/B5 Biesbosch (reg.), Neth.
56/D5 Biesme (riv.), Fr.
60/D5 Bietschhorn (peak), Swi.
66/D2 Biferno (riv.), It.
97/B2 Big (des.), Austl.
125/J2 Big (isl.), Nun,Can.
124/D1 Big (riv.), NW,Can.
69/H5 Biga, Turk.
80/B2 Bigadiç, Turk.
128/F4 Big Belt (mts.), Mt,US
134/C4 Big Bend Nat'l Park, Tx,US
131/K4 Big Black (riv.), Ms,US
131/H2 Big Blue (riv.), Ks, Ne,US
52/C6 Bigbury (bay), Eng,UK
136/D2 Big Diomede (isl.), Rus.
129/K4 Big Fork (riv.), Mn,US
128/G2 Biggar, Sk,Can.
56/G1 Biggasee (lake), Ger.
57/E6 Bigge (riv.), Ger.
57/E6 Biggesee (res.), Ger.
53/F2 Biggleswade, Eng,UK
108/D3 Big Hole, SAfr.
128/E4 Big Hole (riv.), Mt,US
128/F4 Bighorn (lake), Mt, Wy,US
128/G4 Bighorn (mts.), Mt, Wy,US
128/G4 Bighorn (riv.), Mt, Wy,US
130/E1 Bighorn (basin), Wy,US
124/F4 Bighorn Canyon Nat'l Rec. Area, Mt,US
134/C4 Big Lake, Tx,US
130/D2 Big Lost (riv.), Id,US
138/P14 Big Muskego (lake), Wi,US
104/A3 Bignona, Sen.
132/C3 Big Rapids, Mi,US
128/G2 Big River, Sk,Can.
138/N16 Big Rock (cr.), Il,US
135/H4 Big Saltilla (cr.), Ga,US
131/G3 Big Sandy (cr.), Co,US
135/F2 Big Sandy (riv.), Tn,US
130/E2 Big Sandy (riv.), Wy,US
129/J5 Big Sioux (riv.), Ia, SD,US
134/C3 Big Spring, Tx,US
129/J4 Big Stone (lake), Mn, SD,US
132/D4 Big Stone Gap, Va,US
128/F4 Big Timber, Mt,US
124/H3 Big Trout (lake), On,Can.
137/B2 Big Tujunga (canyon), Ca,US
116/B3 Biguaçu, Braz.
130/D2 Big Wood (riv.), Id,US
68/B3 Bihać, Bosn.
90/E2 Bihār, India
90/D3 Bihār (state), India
68/F2 Bihor (co.), Rom.
58/F4 Bihorel, Fr.
104/A4 Bijagós (isls.), GBis.
90/C4 Bījāpur, India
78/E1 Bījār, Iran
68/D3 Bijeljina, Bosn.
68/D4 Bijelo Polje, Mont.
90/C2 Bijnor, India
90/B2 Bīkaner, India
98/G3 Bikar (atoll), Mrsh.
83/L2 Bikin, Rus.
83/M2 Bikin (riv.), Rus.
98/F3 Bikini (atoll), Mrsh.
110/C4 Bikuar Nat'l Park, Moz.
89/B3 Bilauktaung (range), Myan., Thai.
64/D1 Bilbao, Sp.
106/B2 Bilbays, Egypt
68/D4 Bileća, Bosn.
80/B2 Bilecik, Turk.
69/K5 Bilecik (prov.), Turk.
55/M3 Biłgoraj, Pol.
75/S3 Bilibino, Rus.
89/B2 Bilin (riv.), Myan.
97/C2 Billabong (cr.), Austl.
57/H1 Bille (riv.), Ger.
57/E5 Billerbeck, Ger.
62/C5 Billère, Fr.
53/G3 Billericay, Eng,UK
97/B2 Billiat Consv. Park, Austl.
51/F5 Billinge, Eng,UK
51/G2 Billingham, Eng,UK
128/F4 Billings, Mt,US
53/F4 Billingshurst, Eng,UK
77/K10 Billiton (isl.), Indo.
130/D4 Bill Williams (riv.), Az,US
96/C4 Biloela, Austl.
135/F4 Biloxi, Ms,US
90/C2 Bilsi, India
59/E2 Bilzen, Belg.
93/E5 Bima, Indo.
97/D2 Bimberi (peak), Austl.
123/F2 Bimini (isls.), Bahm.
90/C3 Bina-Etāwa, India
133/Q9 Binbrook, On,Can.
51/H5 Binbrook, Eng,UK
58/D3 Binche, Belg.
82/G2 Binder, Mong.
90/D2 Bindki, India
110/C2 Bindu, D.R. Congo
110/F4 Bindura, Zim.
65/F2 Binéfar, Sp.
53/F4 Binfield, Eng,UK
110/F4 Binga (mtn.), Moz.
63/G2 Bingen, Ger.
104/E5 Bingerville, C.d'Iv.
51/H6 Bingham, Eng,UK
132/F3 Binghamton, NY,US
51/G4 Bingley, Eng,UK
80/E2 Bingöl, Turk.
87/D4 Binhai, China
89/D4 Binh Chanh, Viet.
89/D4 Binh Chau, Viet.
91/G4 Binhon (peak), Myan.
89/E3 Binh Son, Viet.
92/A3 Binjai, Indo.
93/F5 Binongko (isl.), Indo.
92/B2 Bintang (peak), Malay.
91/J3 Binyang, China
87/D3 Binzhou, China
118/B3 Bío-Bío (riv.), Chile
118/B3 Bío-Bío (reg.), Chile
68/B4 Biograd, Cro.
68/D4 Biogradska Nat'l Park, Mont.
102/G7 Bioko (isl.), EqG.
90/C4 Bīr, India
102/H2 Birāk, Libya
102/H2 Bi'r al Ghuzayyil (well), Libya
103/K2 Bi'r al Ḩarash (well), Libya
90/E2 Birātnagar, Nepal
124/E3 Birch (mts.), Ab,Can.
129/G2 Birch Hills, Sk,Can.
129/H2 Birch River, Mb,Can.
111/X Bird (isl.), Ant.
97/D2 Birds Rock (peak), Austl.
80/D3 Birecik, Turk.
116/B2 Birigui, Braz.
116/G8 Biritiba-Mirim, Braz.
79/G2 Bīrjand, Iran
98/G4 Birkenebeu, Kiri.
51/E5 Birkenhead, Eng,UK
61/H3 Birkkarspitze (peak), Aus.
69/H2 Bîrlad, Rom.
69/H2 Bîrlad (riv.), Rom.
53/E2 Birmingham, Eng,UK
53/E2 Birmingham (co.), Eng,UK
135/G3 Birmingham, Al,US
138/F6 Birmingham, Mi,US
63/K3 Birnhorn (peak), Aus.
99/H5 Birnie (isl.), Kiri.
105/G3 Birni Nkonni, Niger
83/L2 Birobidzhan, Rus.
102/E3 Bîr Ounâne (well), Mali
60/D3 Birs (riv.), Swi.
71/M5 Birsk, Rus.
70/E4 Biržai, Lith.
69/F4 Bis (lake), Rom.
85/M9 Bisai, Japan
130/E5 Bisbee, Az,US
62/C4 Biscarrosse, Fr.
62/C4 Biscarrosse (lag.), Fr.
62/B4 Biscay (bay), Eur.
135/H5 Biscayne Nat'l Park, Fl,US
66/E2 Bisceglie, It.
60/D1 Bischheim, Fr.
63/K3 Bischofshofen, Aus.
59/G6 Bischwiller, Fr.
111/V Biscoe (isls.), Ant.
123/H6 Biscucuy, Ven.
78/D4 Bīshah (dry riv.), SAr.
81/B3 Bishkek (cap.), Kyr.
130/C3 Bishop, Ca,US
51/G2 Bishop Auckland, Eng,UK
52/D2 Bishops Castle, Eng,UK
52/D3 Bishops Cleeve, Eng,UK
133/L1 Bishop's Falls, Nf,Can.
53/G3 Bishop's Stortford, Eng,UK
53/E5 Bishops Waltham, Eng,UK
51/H4 Bishop Wilton, Eng,UK
102/G1 Biskra, Alg.
55/L2 Biskupiec, Pol.
88/E6 Bislig, Phil.
133/Q9 Bismarck, On,Can.
98/D5 Bismarck (arch.), PNG
98/D5 Bismarck (sea), PNG
129/H4 Bismarck (cap.), ND,US
80/E3 Bismil, Turk.
104/B4 Bissau (cap.), GBis.
57/F4 Bissendorf, Ger.
129/K3 Bissett, Mb,Can.
69/G2 Bistrița, Rom.
69/G2 Bistrița-Năsăud (co.), Rom.
114/E2 Bita (riv.), Col.
102/H7 Bitam, Gabon
59/F4 Bitburg, Ger.
59/G5 Bitche, Fr.
103/J5 Bitkin, Chad
80/E2 Bitlis, Turk.
68/E5 Bitola, FYROM
68/C5 Bitonto, It.
69/G2 Bitrița (riv.), Rom.
134/C2 Bitter (lakes), Egypt
128/E4 Bitterroot (range), Id, Mt,US
93/G3 Bitung, Indo.
102/H5 Biu, Nga.
85/M9 Biwa, Japan
84/E3 Biwa (lake), Japan
131/J4 Bixby, Ok,US
80/H6 Biyalā, Egypt
81/E1 Biysk, Rus.
133/N7 Bizard (isl.), Qu,Can.
66/A4 Bizerte, Tun.
66/A4 Bizerte (gov.), Tun.
66/A4 Bizerte (lake), Tun.
48/M6 Bjargtangar (pt.), Ice.
54/G1 Bjärred, Swe.
68/C3 Bjelovar, Cro.
125/S7 Bjorne (pen.), Nun,Can.
53/E1 Blaby, Eng,UK
55/K3 Blachownia, Pol.
72/D4 Black (sea), Asia, Eur.
132/B1 Black (bay), On,Can.
129/L2 Black (riv.), On,Can.
136/M3 Black (mtn.), Yk,Can.
89/C1 Black (riv.), China
72/D4 Black (sea), Eur.
60/D2 Black (for.), Ger.
108/A2 Black (pt.), Namb.
52/A6 Black (pt.), Eng,UK
52/C3 Black (mts.), Wal,UK
52/C3 Black (mts.), Wal,UK
131/K3 Black (riv.), Ar, Mo,US
130/D4 Black (mts.), Az,US
130/E4 Black (riv.), Az,US
138/L11 Black (hills), Ca,US
138/G5 Black (riv.), Mi,US
130/F4 Black (range), NM,US
132/F3 Black (riv.), NY,US
129/H5 Black (hills), SD, Wy,US
129/L4 Black (riv.), Wi,US
53/E3 Black Bourton, Eng,UK
51/F4 Blackburn, Eng,UK
51/F4 Blackburn with Darwen (co.), Eng,UK
50/D1 Blackcraig (hill), Sc,UK
89/C1 Black (Da) (riv.), Viet.
144/F3 Black Canyon of the Gunnison NP, Co,US
128/E3 Black Diamond, Ab,Can.
53/F4 Blackdown (hill), Eng,UK
52/C5 Blackdown (hills), Eng,UK
96/C3 Blackdown Tableland Nat'l Park, Austl.
128/F4 Black Eagle, Mt,US
128/E5 Blackfoot, Id,US
128/F5 Blackfoot (res.), Id,US
51/G2 Blackhall Rocks, Eng,UK
50/C2 Black Head (pt.), NI,UK
130/E3 Black Mesa (upland), Az,US
52/B6 Blackmoor (upland), Eng,UK
96/B1 Black Mountain Nat'l Park, Austl.
51/E4 Blackpool, Eng,UK
51/E4 Blackpool (co.), Eng,UK
108/A2 Black Reef (pt.), Namb.
132/B2 Black River Falls, Wi,US
130/C2 Black Rock (des.), Nv,US
51/F4 Blackrod, Eng,UK
132/D4 Blacksburg, Va,US
135/H3 Blackshear (lake), Ga,US
132/E4 Blackstone, Va,US
97/D1 Black Sugarloaf (peak), Austl.
96/G8 Blacktown, Austl.
133/H2 Blackville, NB,Can.
104/E4 Black Volta (riv.), Afr.
135/G3 Black Warrior (riv.), Al,US
96/C3 Blackwater, Austl.
50/B4 Blackwater (riv.), Ire.
49/A4 Blackwater (riv.), Ire.
53/G3 Blackwater (riv.), Eng,UK
50/B3 Blackwater (riv.), NI,UK
131/J3 Blackwater (riv.), Mo,US
131/H3 Blackwell, Ok,US
52/C3 Blackwood, Wal,UK
137/K8 Bladensburg, Md,US
96/A3 Bladensburg Nat'l Park, Austl.
50/D2 Bladnoch (riv.), Sc,UK
50/E6 Blaenau-Ffestiniog, Wal,UK
52/C3 Blaenau Gwent (co.), Wal,UK
52/C3 Blaenavon, Wal,UK
62/C5 Blagnac, Fr.
69/F4 Blagoevgrad, Bul.
83/K1 Blagoveshchensk, Rus.
128/G2 Blaine Lake, Sk,Can.
133/N6 Blainville, Qu,Can.
131/H2 Blair, Ne,US
128/E3 Blairmore, Ab,Can.
137/F5 Blairstown, NJ,US
60/A1 Blaise (riv.), Fr.
69/F2 Blaj, Rom.
135/G4 Blakely, Ga,US
102/B3 Blanc (cape), Mrta.
118/E3 Blanca (bay), Arg.
114/C5 Blanca (range), Peru
64/E3 Blanca, Sp.
65/E4 Blanca (coast), Sp.
131/F4 Blanca (peak), NM,US
63/G4 Blanc, Mont (mtn.), Fr., It.
58/A2 Blanc Nez (cape), Fr.
119/K6 Blanco (riv.), Arg.
119/K8 Blanco (lake), Chile
118/C1 Blanco (riv.), Chile
122/D6 Blanco (cape), CR
114/B4 Blanco (cape), Peru
128/B5 Blanco (cape), Or,US
131/H5 Blanco (riv.), Tx,US
52/D5 Blandford Forum, Eng,UK
130/E3 Blanding, Ut,US
65/G2 Blanes, Sp.
55/G4 Blanice (riv.), Czh.
58/C1 Blankenberge, Belg.
59/F3 Blankenheim, Ger.
123/J5 Blanquilla (isl.), Ven.
55/J4 Blansko, Czh.
110/G4 Blantyre, Malw.
62/F3 Blanzy, Fr.
56/C4 Blaricum, Neth.
54/E1 Blåvands Huk (pt.), Den.
62/B2 Blavet (riv.), Fr.
57/H2 Bleckede, Ger.
59/E2 Blégny, Belg.
58/C2 Bléharies, Belg.
68/B2 Bleiburg, Aus.
57/H6 Bleicherode, Ger.
56/B4 Bleiswijk, Neth.
48/E4 Blekinge (co.), Swe.
95/H7 Blenheim, NZ
53/E3 Blenheim Palace, Eng,UK
63/G4 Bléone (riv.), Fr.
58/C4 Blérancourt, Fr.
108/C4 Blesberg (peak), SAfr.
53/F2 Bletchley, Eng,UK
107/A2 Bleus (mts.), D.R. Congo
53/E3 Blewbury, Eng,UK
102/F1 Blida, Alg.
51/G5 Blidworth, Eng,UK
59/G5 Blies (riv.), Fr., Ger.
59/G5 Bliesbruck, Fr.
59/G5 Blieskastel, Ger.
99/Y18 Bligh Water (sound), Fiji
93/F2 Blik (mt.), Phil.
51/G6 Blithfield (res.), Eng,UK
111/L Blizzard (peak), Ant.
56/B4 Bloemendaal, Neth.
108/D3 Bloemfontein (cap.), SAfr.
108/D2 Bloemhofdam (res.), SAfr.
62/D3 Blois, Fr.
56/C3 Blokker, Neth.
129/J3 Bloodvein (riv.), Mb, On,Can.
49/A3 Bloody Foreland (pt.), Ire.
132/B2 Bloomer, Wi,US
137/F5 Bloomfield, NJ,US
130/F3 Bloomfield, NM,US
138/F6 Bloomfield Hills, Mi,US
138/P16 Bloomingdale, Il,US
137/C2 Bloomington, Ca,US
132/B3 Bloomington, Il,US
132/C4 Bloomington, In,US
129/K4 Bloomington, Mn,US
92/D5 Blora, Indo.
135/G4 Blountstown, Fl,US
111/L Blowaway (peak), Ant.
53/E3 Bloxham, Eng,UK
52/D1 Bloxwich, Eng,UK
63/K1 Blšanka (riv.), Czh.
61/F3 Bludenz, Aus.
91/F3 Blue (mtn.), India
134/D3 Blue (riv.), Ok,US
128/D4 Blue (mts.), Or, Wa,US
129/K5 Blue Earth, Mn,US
132/D4 Bluefield, Va,US
132/D4 Bluefield, WV,US
122/E5 Bluefields, Nic.
138/Q16 Blue Island, Il,US
130/C2 Bluejoint (lake), Or,US
96/D4 Blue Lake Nat'l Park, Austl.
130/F3 Blue Mesa (res.), Co,US
123/F4 Blue Mountain (pk.), Jam.
95/D4 Blue Mountains, Austl.
97/D2 Blue Mountains Nat'l Park, Austl.
103/M5 Blue Nile (riv.), Eth., Sudan
124/E2 Bluenose (lake), Nun,Can.
135/G3 Blue Ridge, Ga,US
135/H2 Blue Ridge (mts.), NC, Va,US
132/C3 Bluffton, In,US
116/B3 Blumenau, Braz.
51/G1 Blyth, Eng,UK
51/G5 Blyth, Eng,UK
53/H2 Blyth (riv.), Eng,UK
51/F6 Blythe (riv.), Eng,UK
130/D4 Blythe, Ca,US
51/F6 Blythe Bridge, Eng,UK
135/F3 Blytheville, Ar,US
89/D4 B'nom M'hai (peak), Viet.
104/C5 Bo, SLeo.
88/D5 Boac, Phil.
122/D5 Boaco, Nic.
116/C2 Boa Esperança, Braz.
115/J5 Boa Esperança (res.), Braz.
93/G4 Boano (isl.), Indo.
125/H2 Boas (riv.), Nun,Can.
115/K4 Boa Viagem, Braz.
114/F3 Boa Vista, Braz.
135/G3 Boaz, Al,US
91/J3 Bobai, China
109/J5 Bobaomby (cape), Madg.
90/D4 Bobbili, India
58/B6 Bobigny, Fr.
63/H2 Böblingen, Ger.
104/D4 Bobo Dioulasso, Burk.
68/D4 Bobotov Kuk (peak), Mont.
68/F4 Bobovdol, Bul.
55/H3 Bóbr (riv.), Pol.
72/G2 Bobrov, Rus.
109/H8 Boby (peak), Madg.
114/E5 Boca do Acre, Braz.
116/J7 Bocaina (mts.), Braz.
115/K7 Bocaiúva, Braz.
135/H5 Boca Raton, Fl,US
122/D5 Bocay, Nic.
55/L4 Bochnia, Pol.
59/E1 Bocholt, Belg.
56/D5 Bocholt, Ger.
57/E6 Bochum, Ger.
57/H4 Bockenem, Ger.
53/G3 Bocking, Eng,UK
123/G6 Boconó, Ven.
59/D3 Bocq (riv.), Belg.
103/J7 Boda, CAfr.
75/M4 Bodaybo, Rus.
54/F3 Bode (riv.), Ger.
130/B3 Bodega (bay), Ca,US
56/B4 Bodegraven, Neth.
102/J4 Bodélé (depr.), Chad
48/G2 Boden, Swe.
61/F2 Bodensee (Constance) (lake), Ger., Swi.
90/C4 Bodhan, India
90/C5 Bodināyakkanūr, India
52/B6 Bodmin, Eng,UK
52/B5 Bodmin Moor (upland), Eng,UK
48/E2 Bodø, Nor.
82/C2 Bodonchiyn (riv.), Mong.
68/E1 Bodrog (riv.), Hun.
80/A3 Bodrum, Turk.
89/D4 Bo Duc, Viet.
108/A2 Boegoeberg (peak), Namb.
56/C5 Boekel, Neth.
110/D1 Boende, D.R. Congo
131/K4 Boeuf (riv.), Ar, La,US
135/F4 Bogalusa, La,US
97/C1 Bogan (riv.), Austl.
105/E3 Bogandé, Burk.
68/D3 Bogatić, Serb.
55/H3 Bogatynia, Pol.
80/C2 Boğazlıyan, Turk.
81/E5 Bogcang (riv.), China
82/E2 Bogd, Mong.
82/B3 Bogda (mts.), China
81/E3 Bogda Feng (peak), China
53/F5 Bognor Regis, Eng,UK
59/D4 Bogny-sur-Meuse, Fr.
88/D5 Bogo, Phil.
97/C3 Bogong (peak), Austl.
97/C3 Bogong Nat'l Park, Austl.
92/C5 Bogor, Indo.
114/D3 Bogotá (cap.), Col.
68/E5 Bogovinje, FYROM
90/E3 Bogra, Bang.
50/E1 Bogrie (hill), Sc,UK
104/B2 Bogué, Mrta.
87/D3 Bohai (bay), China
87/E3 Bohai (str.), China
87/D3 Bo Hai (Chihli) (gulf), China
58/C4 Bohain-en-Vermandois, Fr.
55/G4 Bohemia (reg.), Czh.
57/G3 Böhme (riv.), Ger.
57/F4 Bohmte, Ger.
88/D6 Bohol (isl.), Phil.
91/J4 Bo Ho Su, Viet.
66/D2 Boiano, It.
64/A1 Boiro, Sp.
116/B1 Bois (riv.), Braz.
128/D5 Boise (cap.), Id,US
128/E5 Boise (riv.), Id,US
131/G3 Boise City, Ok,US
58/A5 Bois-Guillaume, Fr.
129/H3 Boissevain, Mb,Can.
57/H2 Boizenburg, Ger.
102/C2 Bojador (cape), WSah.
55/J4 Bojkovice, Czh.
79/G1 Bojnūrd, Iran
104/B4 Boké (comm.), Gui.
110/D1 Bokele, D.R. Congo
48/C4 Boknafjorden (fjord), Nor.
107/C2 Bokol (peak), Kenya
102/J5 Bokoro, Chad
108/E2 Boksburg, SAfr.
104/B4 Bolama, GBis.
79/J3 Bolān (pass), Pak.
64/D3 Bolaños de Calatrava, Sp.
62/D2 Bolbec, Fr.
69/H3 Boldești-Scăeni, Rom.
51/G2 Boldon, Eng,UK
105/E4 Bole, Gha.
55/H3 Bolesławiec, Pol.
105/E4 Bolgatanga, Gha.
138/P16 Bolingbrook, Il,US
118/E3 Bolivar, Arg.
131/J3 Bolivar, Mo,US
132/B5 Bolivar, Tn,US
123/G6 Bolívar (pk.), Ven.
114/F7 Bolivia (ctry.)
62/F4 Bollène, Fr.
60/D4 Bolligen, Swi.
51/F5 Bollin (riv.), Eng,UK
51/F5 Bollington, Eng,UK
48/F3 Bollnäs, Swe.
64/B4 Bollullos Par del Condado, Sp.
53/F5 Bolney, Eng,UK
110/C1 Bolobo, D.R. Congo
63/J4 Bologna, It.
70/G4 Bologoye, Rus.
103/J7 Bolomba, D.R. Congo
83/M2 Bolon' (lake), Rus.
110/C2 Bolongongo, Ang.
89/D3 Bolovens (plat.), Laos
66/B1 Bolsena (lake), It.
73/K1 Bol'shaya Kinel' (riv.), Rus.
71/P2 Bol'shaya Rogovaya (riv.), Rus.
71/N2 Bol'shaya Synya (riv.), Rus.
83/L2 Bol'shaya Ussurka (riv.), Rus.
75/L2 Bol'shevik (isl.), Rus.
71/M2 Bol'shezemel'skaya (tundra), Rus.
74/F2 Bol'shoy Bolvanskiy Nos (pt.), Rus.
73/H2 Bol'shoy Irgiz (riv.), Rus.
75/Q2 Bol'shoy Lyakhovskiy (isl.), Rus.
73/J2 Bol'shoy Uzen' (riv.), Rus.
82/D1 Bol'shoy Yenisey (riv.), Rus.
51/G5 Bolsover, Eng,UK
56/C2 Bolsward, Neth.
52/C6 Bolt Head (pt.), Wal,UK
133/Q8 Bolton, On,Can.
51/F4 Bolton, Eng,UK
51/F4 Bolton (co.), Eng,UK
51/G4 Bolton Abbey, Eng,UK
69/K5 Bolu, Turk.
69/K5 Bolu (prov.), Turk.
80/B2 Bolvadin, Turk.
61/H5 Bolzano (Bozen), It.
61/H4 Bolzano-Bozen (prov.), It.
110/B2 Boma, D.R. Congo
97/D2 Bomaderry, Austl.
90/B4 Bombay (Mumbai), India
93/H4 Bomberai (pen.), Indo.
116/C1 Bom Despacho, Braz.
91/G2 Bomi, China
116/J6 Bom Jardim de Minas, Braz.
116/B4 Bom Jesus, Braz.
115/K5 Bom Jesus da Gurguéia (mts.), Braz.
115/K6 Bom Jesus da Lapa, Braz.
116/B1 Bom Jesus de Goiás, Braz.
116/D2 Bom Jesus do Itabapoana, Braz.
116/G8 Bom Jesus dos Perdões, Braz.
57/G3 Bomlitz, Ger.
116/B3 Bom Retiro, Braz.
103/L6 Bomu (riv.), D.R. Congo
66/B4 Bon (cape), Tun.
136/K3 Bona (mtn.), Ak,US
123/H5 Bonaire (isl.), NAnt.
122/C4 Bonampak (ruins), Mex.
123/G4 Bonao, DRep.
95/B2 Bonaparte (arch.), Austl.
136/F3 Bonasila (mtn.), Ak,US
133/H1 Bonaventure, Qu,Can.
133/H1 Bonaventure (riv.), Qu,Can.
133/L1 Bonavista (bay), Nf,Can.
133/L1 Bonavista (cape), Nf,Can.
63/J4 Bondeno, It.
96/H8 Bondi, Austl.
103/K7 Bondo, D.R. Congo
104/E4 Bondoukou, C.d'Iv.
92/D5 Bondowoso, Indo.
93/F4 Bone (gulf), Indo.
57/E5 Bönen, Ger.
93/F5 Bonerate (isls.), Indo.
81/F5 Bong (lake), China
104/C5 Bong (co.), Libr.
104/C5 Bong (range), Libr.
93/F1 Bongabong, Phil.
103/K7 Bongandanga, D.R. Congo
93/E2 Bongao, Phil.
93/E2 Bonggi (isl.), Malay.
93/F4 Bongka (riv.), Indo.
109/H7 Bongolava (uplands), Madg.

154
Bongo – Burne

102/J5 **Bongor**, Chad
103/K6 **Bongos** (mts.), CAfr.
89/E3 **Bong Son**, Viet.
134/D3 **Bonham**, Tx,US
58/D1 **Bonheiden**, Belg.
66/A2 **Bonifacio** (str.), Fr., It.
135/G4 **Bonifay**, Fl,US
98/D2 **Bonin** (isls.), Japan
135/H5 **Bonita Springs**, Fl,US
122/D4 **Bonito** (pk.), Hon.
59/G2 **Bonn**, Ger.
128/D3 **Bonners Ferry**, Id,US
128/E4 **Bonner-West Riverside**, Mt,US
129/K3 **Bonnet** (lake), Mb,Can.
60/C5 **Bonneville**, Fr.
128/C4 **Bonneville** (dam), Or, Wa,US
138/C3 **Bonney Lake**, Wa,US
128/F2 **Bonnyville**, Ab,Can.
108/C4 **Bontberg** (peak), SAfr.
108/C4 **Bontebok Nat'l Park**, SAfr.
93/E5 **Bonthain**, Indo.
104/B5 **Bonthe**, SLeo.
88/D4 **Bontoc**, Phil.
68/D2 **Bonyhád**, Hun.
111/J **Bonzare** (coast), Ant.
58/D1 **Boom**, Belg.
129/K5 **Boone**, Ia,US
135/H2 **Boone**, NC,US
135/F3 **Booneville**, Ms,US
137/F5 **Boonton**, NJ,US
82/D2 **Bööntsagaan** (lake), Mong.
132/C4 **Boonville**, In,US
97/C1 **Booroondara** (peak), Austl.
58/A5 **Boos**, Fr.
133/G3 **Boothbay Harbor**, Me,US
111/D **Boothby** (cape), Ant.
124/G1 **Boothia** (gulf), Nun,Can.
124/G1 **Boothia** (pen.), Nun,Can.
51/E5 **Bootle**, Eng,UK
102/H8 **Booué**, Gabon
59/G3 **Boppard**, Ger.
97/C1 **Boppy** (peak), Austl.
118/C4 **Boquete** (peak), Arg.
107/C2 **Bor** (dry riv.), Kenya
71/K4 **Bor**, Rus.
103/M6 **Bor**, Sudan
80/C3 **Bor**, Turk.
68/F3 **Bor**, Serb.
99/K6 **Bora Bora** (isl.), FrPol.
128/E4 **Borah** (peak), Id,US
48/E4 **Borås**, Swe.
78/F3 **Borāzjān**, Iran
114/G4 **Borba**, Braz.
62/D3 **Borbonnais** (hist. reg.), Fr.
115/L5 **Borborema** (plat.), Braz.
68/E3 **Borča**, Serb.
57/F5 **Borchen**, Ger.
111/M **Borchgrevink** (coast), Ant.
80/E2 **Borçka**, Turk.
56/D4 **Borculo**, Neth.
116/G7 **Borda da Mata**, Braz.
62/C4 **Bordeaux**, Fr.
125/R7 **Borden** (isl.), NW,Can.
125/H2 **Borden** (pen.), Nun,Can.
137/F5 **Bordentown**, NJ,US
65/G4 **Bordj el Bahri** (cape), Alg.
102/G2 **Bordj Omar Driss**, Alg.
53/F4 **Bordon**, Eng,UK
53/F3 **Borehamwood**, Eng,UK
48/E2 **Børgefjell Nat'l Park**, Nor.
57/G5 **Borgentreich**, Ger.
56/D3 **Borger**, Neth.
134/C3 **Borger**, Tx,US
58/D1 **Borgerhout**, Belg.
48/F4 **Borgholm**, Swe.
57/F4 **Borgholzhausen**, Ger.
57/E4 **Borghorst**, Ger.
63/G4 **Borgo San Dalmazzo**, It.
105/F4 **Borgou** (prov.), Ben.
105/F4 **Borgu Game Rsv.**, Nga.
72/B2 **Borislav**, Ukr.
73/G2 **Borisoglebsk**, Rus.
109/H6 **Boriziny**, Madg.
56/D5 **Borken**, Ger.
56/D1 **Borkum** (isl.), Ger.
48/E3 **Borlänge**, Swe.
63/H4 **Bormida** (riv.), It.
56/C6 **Born**, Neth.
54/G3 **Borna**, Ger.
56/C2 **Borndiep** (chan.), Neth.
56/D4 **Borne**, Neth.
58/D1 **Bornem**, Belg.
92/E3 **Borneo** (isl.), Asia
59/F2 **Bornheim**, Ger.
55/H1 **Bornholm** (co.), Den.
55/H1 **Bornholm** (isl.), Den.
55/H1 **Bornholmsgat** (chan.), Swe.
105/H3 **Borno** (state), Nga.
64/C4 **Bornos**, Sp.
102/H5 **Bornu** (plains), Nga.
103/L6 **Boro** (riv.), Sudan
81/D3 **Borohoro** (mts.), China, Kaz.
88/E5 **Borongan**, Phil.
51/G3 **Boroughbridge**, Eng,UK
70/G4 **Borovichi**, Rus.
68/D3 **Borovo**, Cro.
72/B3 **Borşa**, Rom.
83/H1 **Borshchovochnyy** (mts.), Rus.
68/E1 **Borsod-Abaúj-Zemplén** (co.), Hun.
56/A6 **Borssele**, Neth.
81/D3 **Bortala** (riv.), China
52/B2 **Borth**, Wal,UK
78/F2 **Borūjen**, Iran
78/E2 **Borūjerd**, Iran
82/D3 **Bor Ul** (mts.), China
82/H1 **Borzya**, Rus.
66/A2 **Bosa**, It.
68/C3 **Bosanska Dubica**, Bosn.
68/C3 **Bosanska Gradiška**, Bosn.
68/C3 **Bosanska Kostajnica**, Bosn.
68/C3 **Bosanska Krupa**, Bosn.
68/D3 **Bosanski Brod**, Bosn.
68/C3 **Bosanski Petrovac**, Bosn.
68/D3 **Bosanski Šamac**, Bosn.
103/Q5 **Bosaso** (Bender Cassim), Som.
52/B5 **Boscastle**, Eng,UK
91/J3 **Bose**, China
53/F5 **Bosham**, Eng,UK
56/B4 **Boskoop**, Neth.
55/J4 **Boskovice**, Czh.
68/D3 **Bosna** (riv.), Bosn.
68/C3 **Bosnia and Herzegovina** (ctry.)
85/G3 **Bōsō** (pen.), Japan
103/J7 **Bosobolo**, D.R. Congo
69/J5 **Bosporus** (str.), Turk.
130/F4 **Bosque Farms**, NM,US
119/K6 **Bosques Petrificados Natural Mon.**, Arg.
102/J6 **Bossangoa**, CAfr.
134/E3 **Bossier City**, La,US
81/E3 **Bosten** (lake), China
51/H6 **Boston**, Eng,UK
134/E3 **Boston** (mts.), Ar,US
133/G3 **Boston** (cap.), Ma,US
134/E3 **Boston**, Tx,US
68/D3 **Bosut** (riv.), Cro.
90/B3 **Botād**, India
96/H8 **Botany** (bay), Austl.
135/H3 **Boteler** (peak), NC,US
109/F2 **Botelerpunt** (pt.), SAfr.
116/G6 **Botelhos**, Braz.
67/J1 **Botev** (peak), Bul.
69/F4 **Botevgrad**, Bul.
109/E2 **Bothaspas** (pass), SAfr.
51/E2 **Bothel**, Eng,UK
138/C2 **Bothell**, Wa,US
52/D5 **Bothenhampton**, Eng,UK
48/G2 **Bothnia** (gulf), Fin., Swe.
72/C3 **Botoşani**, Rom.
69/H2 **Botoşani** (co.), Rom.
87/D3 **Botou**, China
89/D2 **Bo Trach**, Viet.
59/F3 **Botrange** (mtn.), Belg.
110/D5 **Botswana** (ctry.)
66/E3 **Botte Donato** (peak), It.
51/H4 **Bottesford**, Eng,UK
51/H6 **Bottesford**, Eng,UK
129/H3 **Bottineau**, ND,US
56/D5 **Bottrop**, Ger.
116/B2 **Botucatu**, Braz.
133/L1 **Botwood**, Nf,Can.
104/D4 **Bou** (riv.), C.d'Iv.
104/D5 **Bouaflé**, C.d'Iv.
104/D5 **Bouaké**, C.d'Iv.
102/J6 **Bouar**, CAfr.
55/G4 **Boubín** (peak), Czh.
103/J6 **Bouca**, CAfr.
133/P6 **Boucherville**, Qu,Can.
104/C3 **Boucle du Baoulé Nat'l Park**, Mali
102/E1 **Boudenib**, Mor.
105/E2 **Boû Djébéha** (well), Mali
58/B5 **Bouffémont**, Fr.
96/B1 **Bougainville** (reef), Austl.
119/N7 **Bougainville** (cape), Falk.
98/E5 **Bougainville** (isl.), PNG
104/D4 **Bougouni**, Mali
104/E4 **Bougouriba** (prov.), Burk.
62/C3 **Bouguenais**, Fr.
102/F1 **Bouira**, Alg.
131/F2 **Boulder**, Co,US
128/E4 **Boulder**, Mt,US
130/D4 **Boulder City**, Nv,US
138/P16 **Boulder Hill**, Il,US
105/E4 **Boulgo** (prov.), Burk.
105/E3 **Boulkiemde** (prov.), Burk.
62/C3 **Boulogne** (riv.), Fr.
58/B6 **Boulogne-Billancourt**, Fr.
58/A2 **Boulogne-sur-Mer**, Fr.
51/F4 **Boulsworth** (hill), Eng,UK
136/K3 **Boundary**, Yk,Can.
130/C3 **Boundary** (peak), Nv,US
137/F5 **Bound Brook**, NJ,US
104/D4 **Boundiali**, C.d'Iv.
130/E2 **Bountiful**, Ut,US
45/T8 **Bounty** (isls.), NZ
137/B2 **Bouquet** (canyon), Ca,US
132/C3 **Bourbonnais**, Il,US
58/B2 **Bourbourg**, Fr.
105/F2 **Bouressa** (wadi), Mali
60/B5 **Bourg-en-Bresse**, Fr.
62/E3 **Bourges**, Fr.
62/F4 **Bourg-lès-Valence**, Fr.
62/B3 **Bourgneuf** (bay), Fr.
58/D5 **Bourgogne**, Fr.
62/E3 **Bourgogne** (reg.), Fr.
62/F4 **Bourgoin-Jallieu**, Fr.
53/F1 **Bourne**, Eng,UK
53/F3 **Bourne End**, Eng,UK
53/E5 **Bournemouth**, Eng,UK
53/E5 **Bournemouth** (co.), Eng,UK
53/E2 **Bournville**, Eng,UK
49/A4 **Bourn-Vincent Mem. Nat'l Park**, Ire.
57/E3 **Bourtanger Moor** (reg.), Ger.
53/E3 **Bourton on the Water**, Eng,UK
104/B2 **Boutilimit**, Mrta.
45/K8 **Bouvet** (isl.), Nor.
58/C5 **Bouzy**, Fr.
57/G5 **Bovenden**, Ger.
56/D3 **Bovenwijde** (lake), Neth.
52/C5 **Bovey Tracey**, Eng,UK
63/J4 **Bovolone**, It.
128/E3 **Bow** (riv.), Ab,Can.
129/J4 **Bowdle**, SD,US
51/F5 **Bowdon**, Eng,UK
96/C3 **Bowen**, Austl.
56/C5 **Bowen Merwede** (can.), Neth.
51/G3 **Bowes**, Eng,UK
130/E4 **Bowie**, Az,US
137/K8 **Bowie**, Md,US
128/F3 **Bow Island**, Ab,Can.
96/B2 **Bowling Green** (cape), Austl.
132/C4 **Bowling Green**, Ky,US
131/K3 **Bowling Green**, Mo,US
132/D3 **Bowling Green**, Oh,US
96/B2 **Bowling Green Bay Nat'l Park**, Austl.
111/G **Bowman** (isl.), Ant.
125/J2 **Bowman** (bay), Nun,Can.
129/H4 **Bowman**, ND,US
133/S8 **Bowmanville**, Nf,Can.
51/E2 **Bowness-on-Solway**, Eng,UK
93/F4 **Bowokan** (isls.), Indo.
97/D2 **Bowral**, Austl.
128/C2 **Bowron** (riv.), BC,Can.
129/H4 **Box Elder**, SD,US
97/C3 **Box Hill**, Austl.
97/G5 **Box Hill**, Austl.
56/C5 **Boxmeer**, Neth.
56/C5 **Boxtel**, Neth.
80/C2 **Boyabat**, Turk.
97/D2 **Boyd-Konangra Nat'l Park**, Austl.
129/K5 **Boyer** (riv.), Ia,US
128/E2 **Boyle**, Ab,Can.
50/B4 **Boyne** (riv.), Ire.
132/C2 **Boyne City**, Mi,US
135/H5 **Boynton Beach**, Fl,US
128/F5 **Boysen** (res.), Wy,US
73/J3 **Bozashchy** (pen.), Kaz.
67/J3 **Bozcaada** (isl.), Turk.
128/F4 **Bozeman**, Mt,US
80/C3 **Bozkir**, Turk.
102/J6 **Bozoum**, CAfr.
80/B2 **Bozüyük**, Turk.
63/G4 **Bra**, It.
58/D2 **Brabant** (prov.), Belg.
53/G4 **Brabourne Lees**, Eng,UK
68/C4 **Brač** (isl.), Cro.
66/B1 **Bracciano** (lake), It.
132/E2 **Bracebridge**, On,Can.
70/B3 **Bräcke**, Swe.
134/C4 **Brackettville**, Tx,US
53/E2 **Brackley**, Eng,UK
53/F4 **Bracknell**, Eng,UK
53/F4 **Bracknell Forest** (co.), Eng,UK
116/B4 **Braço do Norte**, Braz.
68/F2 **Brad**, Rom.
66/D2 **Bradano** (riv.), It.
50/D3 **Bradda Head** (pt.), IM,UK
135/H5 **Bradenton**, Fl,US
51/G4 **Bradford**, Eng,UK
51/G4 **Bradford** (co.), Eng,UK
132/E3 **Bradford**, Pa,US
52/D4 **Bradford on Avon**, Eng,UK
53/E5 **Brading**, Eng,UK
137/F5 **Bradley Beach**, NJ,US
52/C5 **Bradninch**, Eng,UK
134/D4 **Brady**, Tx,US
136/L3 **Braeburn**, Yk,Can.
49/D2 **Braemar**, Sc,UK
64/A2 **Braga**, Port.
64/A2 **Braga** (dist.), Port.
118/E2 **Bragado**, Arg.
115/J4 **Bragança**, Braz.
64/B2 **Bragança**, Port.
64/B2 **Bragança** (dist.), Port.
116/G7 **Bragança Paulista**, Braz.
77/J7 **Brahmaputra** (riv.), Asia
50/D6 **Braich-y-Pwll** (pt.), Wal,UK
50/B2 **Braid** (riv.), NI,UK
69/H3 **Brăila**, Rom.
69/H3 **Brăila** (co.), Rom.
58/D2 **Braine-l'Alleud**, Belg.
58/D2 **Braine-le-Comte**, Belg.
129/K4 **Brainerd**, Mn,US
53/G3 **Braintree**, Eng,UK
108/C3 **Brak** (riv.), SAfr.
57/F2 **Brake**, Ger.
58/C2 **Brakel**, Belg.
57/G5 **Brakel**, Ger.
104/B2 **Brakna** (reg.), Mrta.
133/Q8 **Bramalea**, On,Can.
51/G4 **Bramhope**, Eng,UK
133/Q8 **Brampton**, On,Can.
51/F2 **Brampton**, Eng,UK
57/E4 **Bramsche**, Ger.
114/F4 **Branco** (riv.), Braz.
110/B5 **Brandberg** (peak), Namb.
54/G2 **Brandenburg**, Ger.
54/G2 **Brandenburg** (state), Ger.
51/H4 **Brandesburton**, Eng,UK
129/J3 **Brandon**, Mb,Can.
53/G2 **Brandon**, Eng,UK
135/H5 **Brandon**, Fl,US
135/F3 **Brandon**, Ms,US
118/F2 **Brandsen**, Arg.
55/K1 **Braniewo**, Pol.
53/E5 **Bransgore**, Eng,UK
133/J2 **Bras d'Or** (lake), NS,Can.
115/J7 **Brasília** (cap.), Braz.
115/J7 **Brasília Nat'l Park**, Braz.
116/D1 **Brasil, Planalto do** (plat.), Braz.
69/G3 **Braşov**, Rom.
69/G3 **Braşov** (co.), Rom.
56/B6 **Brasschaat**, Belg.
135/H3 **Brasstown Bald** (peak), Ga,US
55/J4 **Bratislava** (cap.), Slvk.
55/J4 **Bratislavský** (reg.), Slvk.
75/L4 **Bratsk**, Rus.
133/F3 **Brattleboro**, Vt,US
63/K2 **Braunau am Inn**, Aus.
57/H5 **Braunlage**, Ger.
57/H4 **Braunschweig**, Ger.
52/B4 **Braunton**, Eng,UK
65/G2 **Brava** (coast), Sp.
119/T12 **Brava** (pt.), Uru.
114/F7 **Bravo** (peak), Bol.
130/D4 **Brawley**, Ca,US
125/J2 **Bray** (isl.), Nun.,Can.
50/B5 **Bray**, Ire.
62/D3 **Braye** (riv.), Fr.
50/B5 **Bray Head** (pt.), Ire.
58/B4 **Bray-sur-Somme**, Fr.
113/D3 **Brazil** (ctry.)
132/C4 **Brazil**, In,US
113/E4 **Brazilian** (plat.), Braz.
116/H7 **Brazópolis**, Braz.
134/D4 **Brazos** (riv.), Tx,US
119/K7 **Brazo Sur** (riv.), Arg.
110/C1 **Brazzaville** (cap.), Congo
68/D3 **Brčko**, Bosn.
54/J2 **Brda** (riv.), Pol.
55/G4 **Brdy** (mts.), Czh.
137/C3 **Brea**, Ca,US
52/D3 **Bream**, Eng,UK
69/G3 **Breaza**, Rom.
49/D2 **Brechin**, Sc,UK
56/B6 **Brecht**, Belg.
129/J4 **Breckenridge**, Mn,US
57/E6 **Breckerfeld**, Ger.
53/G2 **Breckland** (reg.), Eng,UK
119/K8 **Brecknock** (pen.), Chile
55/J4 **Břeclav**, Czh.
52/C3 **Brecon**, Wal,UK
52/C3 **Brecon Beacons** (mts.), Wal,UK
52/C3 **Brecon Beacons Nat'l Park**, Wal,UK
56/B5 **Breda**, Neth.
58/B1 **Bredene**, Belg.
59/E1 **Bree**, Belg.
108/L10 **Breë** (riv.), SAfr.
68/F5 **Bregalnica** (riv.), FYROM
61/F2 **Bregenz**, Aus.
48/M6 **Breiðafjördhur** (bay), Ice.
57/F2 **Bremen**, Ger.
57/F2 **Bremen** (state), Ger.
96/E7 **Bremer** (riv.), Austl.
57/F1 **Bremerhaven**, Ger.
138/B2 **Bremerton**, Wa,US
57/G2 **Bremervörde**, Ger.
52/C4 **Brendon** (hills), Eng,UK
134/D **Brenham**, Tx,US
50/E5 **Brenig, Llyn** (lake), Wal,UK
60/B4 **Brenne** (riv.), Fr.
61/H4 **Brenner** (Brennerpass) (pass), Aus.
63/J4 **Brenta** (riv.), It.
53/G3 **Brentwood**, Eng,UK
138/L11 **Brentwood**, Ca,US
137/G5 **Brentwood**, NY,US
63/J4 **Brescia**, It.
61/G5 **Brescia** (prov.), It.
58/A4 **Bresle** (riv.), Fr.
63/J3 **Bressanone**, It.
62/C3 **Bressuire**, Fr.
55/M2 **Brest**, Bela.
62/A2 **Brest**, Fr.
55/M2 **Brestskaya Voblasts**, Bela.
62/B2 **Bretagne** (mts.), Fr.
62/B2 **Bretagne** (reg.), Fr.
109/R15 **Bretagne** (pt.), Reun., Fr.
128/E2 **Breton**, Ab,Can.
133/K2 **Breton** (cape), NS,Can.
56/B4 **Breukelen**, Neth.
115/H4 **Breves**, Braz.
125/K2 **Brevoort** (isl.), Nun,Can.
133/G2 **Brewer**, Me,US
52/D1 **Brewood**, Eng,UK
131/H2 **Brewster**, Ne,US
128/D3 **Brewster**, Wa,US
135/G4 **Brewton**, Al,US
68/B3 **Brežice**, Slov.
69/G3 **Brezoi**, Rom.
103/K6 **Bria**, CAfr.
63/G4 **Briançon**, Fr.
52/C2 **Brianne, Lyn** (res.), Wal,UK
137/F5 **Brick**, NJ,US
49/A4 **Bride** (riv.), Ire.
50/D3 **Bride**, IM,UK
134/E4 **Bridge City**, Tx,US
52/C4 **Bridgend**, Wal,UK
52/C4 **Bridgend** (co.), Wal,UK
130/C3 **Bridgeport**, Ca,US
133/F3 **Bridgeport**, Ct,US
131/G2 **Bridgeport**, Ne,US
132/D4 **Bridgeport**, WV,US
128/F4 **Bridger**, Mt,US
123/K5 **Bridgetown** (cap.), Bar.
97/C4 **Bridgewater**, Austl.
133/H2 **Bridgewater**, NS,Can.
132/E4 **Bridgewater**, Va,US
52/D1 **Bridgnorth**, Eng,UK
133/G2 **Bridgton**, Me,US
52/D4 **Bridgwater**, Eng,UK
52/C4 **Bridgwater** (bay), Eng,UK
51/H3 **Bridlington**, Eng,UK
51/H3 **Bridlington** (bay), Eng,UK
52/D5 **Bridport**, Eng,UK
58/C6 **Brie** (reg.), Fr.
58/B6 **Brie-Comte-Robert**, Fr.
55/J3 **Brieg Brzeg**, Pol.
56/B5 **Brielle**, Neth.
137/F5 **Brielle**, NJ,US
51/F4 **Brierfield**, Eng,UK
52/C3 **Brigend** (co.), Wal,UK
51/H4 **Brigg**, Eng,UK
60/D5 **Brig-Glis**, Swi.
130/D2 **Brigham City**, Ut,US
51/G4 **Brighouse**, Eng,UK
53/E5 **Brighstone**, Eng,UK
53/H3 **Brightlingsea**, Eng,UK
96/F6 **Brighton**, Austl.
97/F5 **Brighton**, Austl.
53/F5 **Brighton**, Eng,UK
131/F3 **Brighton**, Co,US
53/F5 **Brighton and Hove** (co.), Eng,UK
62/F4 **Brignais**, Fr.
62/G5 **Brignoles**, Fr.
104/A3 **Brikama**, Gam.
53/E3 **Brill**, Eng,UK
115/H8 **Brillante** (riv.), Braz.
57/F6 **Brilon**, Ger.
51/G5 **Brimington**, Eng,UK
67/E2 **Brindisi**, It.
52/E3 **Brinkworth**, Eng,UK
64/A1 **Brion**, Sp.
138/K11 **Briones** (res.), Ca,US
96/F6 **Brisbane** (riv.), Austl.
96/E6 **Brisbane For. Park**, Austl.
96/E6 **Brisbane**, Austl.
97/C3 **Brisbane Ranges Nat'l Park**, Austl.
97/D2 **Brisbane Waters Nat'l Park**, Austl.
52/B4 **Bristol** (chan.), UK
52/D4 **Bristol**, Eng,UK
52/D4 **Bristol** (co.), Eng,UK
136/F4 **Bristol** (bay), Ak,US
137/F5 **Bristol**, Pa,US
135/H2 **Bristol**, Tn,US
131/H4 **Bristow**, Ok,US
136/K2 **British** (mts.), Yk,Can., Ak,US
124/D3 **British Columbia** (prov.), Can.
125/S6 **British Empire** (range), Nun.,Can.
77/G10 **British Indian Ocean Terr.**
108/P12 **Brits**, SAfr.
62/B2 **Brittany** (reg.), Fr.
129/J4 **Britton**, SD,US
62/D4 **Brive-la-Gaillarde**, Fr.
52/C6 **Brixham**, Eng,UK
53/F2 **Brixworth**, Eng,UK
81/B3 **Brlik**, Kaz.
55/J4 **Brněnský** (reg.), Czh.
55/J4 **Brno**, Czh.
96/C3 **Broad** (sound), Austl.
136/J3 **Broad** (pass), Ak,US
135/H3 **Broad** (riv.), NC, SC,US
132/E1 **Broadback** (riv.), Qu,Can.
49/D3 **Broad Lawn** (mtn.), Sc,UK
97/F5 **Broadmeadows**, Austl.
96/C3 **Broad Sound** (chan.), Austl.
53/H4 **Broadstairs**, Eng,UK
53/E5 **Broadstone**, Eng,UK
129/G4 **Broadus**, Mt,US
97/E1 **Broadwater Nat'l Park**, Austl.
53/E2 **Broadway**, Eng,UK
53/E2 **Broadway** (hill), Eng,UK
52/D5 **Broadwindsor**, Eng,UK
125/R7 **Brock** (isl.), NW,Can.
57/H5 **Brocken** (peak), Ger.
53/E5 **Brockenhurst**, Eng,UK
133/G3 **Brockton**, Ma,US
132/F2 **Brockville**, On,Can.
124/G1 **Brodeur** (pen.), Nun,Can.
137/E4 **Brodhead** (cr.), Pa,US
55/K2 **Brodnica**, Pol.
56/B3 **Broek Op Langedijk**, Neth.
97/D2 **Broken** (bay), Austl.
131/J3 **Broken Arrow**, Ok,US
131/H2 **Broken Bow**, Ne,US
131/J4 **Broken Bow**, Ok,US
131/J4 **Broken Bow** (lake), Ok,US
97/B1 **Broken Hill**, Austl.
134/B3 **Brokeoff** (mts.), NM,US
52/D2 **Bromsgrove**, Eng,UK
52/D2 **Bromyard**, Eng,UK
62/F4 **Bron**, Fr.
48/D4 **Brønderslev**, Den.
105/E5 **Brong-Ahafo** (reg.), Gha.
63/H4 **Broni**, It.
52/C3 **Bronllys**, Wal,UK
48/E2 **Brønnøysund**, Nor.
133/Q9 **Bronte**, On,Can.
66/D4 **Bronte**, It.
137/G5 **Bronx** (co.), NY,US
88/C6 **Brooke's Point**, Phil.
138/Q16 **Brookfield**, Il,US
131/J3 **Brookfield**, Mo,US
138/P13 **Brookfield**, Wi,US
135/F4 **Brookhaven**, Ms,US
137/H5 **Brookhaven**, NY,US
129/J4 **Brookings**, SD,US
137/G5 **Brooklyn** (Kings) (co.), NY,US
137/K7 **Brooklyn Park**, Md,US
53/F3 **Brookmans Park**, Eng,UK
128/F3 **Brooks**, Ab,Can.
136/E2 **Brooks** (mts.), Ak,US
136/F2 **Brooks** (range), Ak,US
135/H4 **Brooksville**, Fl,US
137/E6 **Broomall**, Pa,US
133/P7 **Brossard**, Qu,Can.
51/H2 **Brotton**, Eng,UK
51/F2 **Brough**, Eng,UK
133/R8 **Brougham**, On,Can.
50/B2 **Broughshane**, NI,UK
53/F2 **Broughton**, Eng,UK
51/E3 **Broughton in Furness**, Eng,UK
53/G4 **Broughton Street**, Eng,UK
56/A5 **Brouwersdam** (dam), Neth.
52/D2 **Brown Clee** (hill), Eng,UK
134/C3 **Brownfield**, Tx,US
53/E1 **Brownhills**, Eng,UK
128/E3 **Browning**, Mt,US
53/E5 **Brownsea** (isl.), Eng,UK
137/F6 **Browns Mills**, NJ,US
135/F3 **Brownsville**, Tn,US
134/D5 **Brownsville**, Tx,US
52/B5 **Brown Willy** (hill), Eng,UK
134/D4 **Brownwood**, Tx,US
58/B3 **Bruay-en-Artois**, Fr.
58/C3 **Bruay-sur-l'Escaut**, Fr.
95/A3 **Bruce** (peak), Austl.
132/D2 **Bruce** (pen.), On,Can.
60/D1 **Bruche** (riv.), Fr.
59/G5 **Bruchmühlbach-Miesau**, Ger.
63/H2 **Bruchsal**, Ger.
57/G5 **Brucht** (riv.), Ger.
63/K3 **Bruck an der Grossglockner-strasse**, Aus.
68/C1 **Bruck an der Leitha**, Aus.
63/L3 **Bruck an der Mur**, Aus.
54/F5 **Bruckmühl**, Ger.
52/D4 **Brue** (riv.), Eng,UK
58/C1 **Bruges** (Brugge), Belg.
56/D6 **Brüggen**, Ger.
59/F2 **Brühl**, Ger.
108/B2 **Brukkaros** (peak), Namb.
115/K6 **Brumado**, Braz.
59/G6 **Brumath**, Fr.
56/D4 **Brummen**, Neth.
48/D3 **Brumunddal**, Nor.
66/A2 **Bruncu Spina** (peak), It.
53/H1 **Brundall**, Eng,UK
58/D4 **Brune** (riv.), Fr.
130/D2 **Bruneau** (riv.), Id, Nv,US
92/D2 **Brunei** (ctry.)
63/J3 **Brunico**, It.
57/G1 **Brunsbüttel**, Ger.
59/E2 **Brunssum**, Neth.
97/F5 **Brunswick**, Austl.
119/J8 **Brunswick** (pen.), Chile
135/H4 **Brunswick**, Ga,US
133/G3 **Brunswick**, Me,US
132/D3 **Brunswick**, Oh,US
116/B3 **Brusque**, Braz.
58/D2 **Brussels** (Bruxelles) (cap.), Belg.
52/D4 **Bruton**, Eng,UK
62/C2 **Bruz**, Fr.
111/U **Bryan** (coast), Ant.
132/C3 **Bryan**, Oh,US
134/D4 **Bryan**, Tx,US
72/E1 **Bryansk**, Rus.
72/E1 **Bryanskaya Obl.**, Rus.
130/D3 **Bryce Canyon Nat'l Park**, Ut,US
51/E5 **Brymbo**, Wal,UK
52/C2 **Bryn Brawd** (mtn.), Wal,UK
52/C3 **Brynithel**, Wal,UK
52/C3 **Brynmawr**, Wal,UK
53/J3 **Brzeg Dolny**, Pol.
55/L4 **Brzesko**, Pol.
55/M4 **Brzozów**, Pol.
89/C3 **Bua Yai**, Thai.
104/B4 **Buba**, GBis.
104/B4 **Bubaque**, GBis.
78/E3 **Būbiyan** (isl.), Kuw.
80/B3 **Bucak**, Turk.
114/D2 **Bucaramanga**, Col.
65/P10 **Bucelas**, Port.
125/J1 **Buchan** (gulf), Nun,Can.
104/C5 **Buchanan**, Libr.
131/H5 **Buchanan** (lake), Tx,US
133/K1 **Buchans**, Nf,Can.
69/H3 **Bucharest** (București) (cap.), Rom.
57/G2 **Buchholz in der Nordheide**, Ger.
130/B4 **Buchon** (pt.), Ca,US
51/F3 **Buckden Pike** (mtn.), Eng,UK
57/G4 **Bückeburg**, Ger.
52/C6 **Buckfastleigh**, Eng,UK
132/D4 **Buckhannon**, WV,US
49/D2 **Buckie**, Sc,UK
132/F2 **Buckingham**, Qu,Can.
53/F3 **Buckingham**, Eng,UK
53/F3 **Buckinghamshire** (co.), Eng,UK
51/E5 **Buckley**, Wal,UK
52/D2 **Bucknell**, Eng,UK
49/D2 **Bucksburn**, Sc,UK
133/H2 **Buctouche**, NB,Can.
69/H3 **București** (Bucharest) (cap.), Rom.
132/D3 **Bucyrus**, Oh,US
68/D2 **Budaörs**, Hun.
68/D2 **Budapest** (cap.), Hun.
90/C2 **Budaun**, India
111/H **Budd** (coast), Ant.
138/B3 **Budd** (inlet), Wa,US
137/F5 **Budd Lake**, NJ,US
52/B5 **Bude**, Eng,UK
52/B5 **Bude** (bay), Eng,UK
55/H4 **Budějovický** (reg.), Czh.
56/C6 **Budel**, Neth.
54/E1 **Büdelsdorf**, Ger.
63/H1 **Büdingen**, Ger.
103/J7 **Budjala**, D.R. Congo
52/C5 **Budleigh Salterton**, Eng,UK
68/D4 **Budva**, Mont.
69/J2 **Budzhak** (reg.), Mol., Ukr.
102/G7 **Buea**, Camr.
137/C3 **Buena Park**, Ca,US
114/C3 **Buenaventura**, Col.
131/F3 **Buena Vista**, Co,US
132/E4 **Buena Vista**, Va,US
118/B4 **Bueno** (riv.), Chile
119/S12 **Buenos Aires** (cap.), Arg.
118/C5 **Buenos Aires** (lake), Arg.
118/E3 **Buenos Aires** (prov.), Arg.
64/A1 **Bueu**, Sp.
97/C3 **Buffalo** (peak), Austl.
128/E2 **Buffalo** (lake), Ab,Can.
109/E2 **Buffalo** (riv.), SAfr.
134/E2 **Buffalo** (riv.), Ar,US
129/K4 **Buffalo**, Mn,US
131/J3 **Buffalo**, Mo,US
133/S10 **Buffalo**, NY,US
131/H3 **Buffalo**, Ok,US
129/H4 **Buffalo**, SD,US
135/G3 **Buffalo** (riv.), Tn,US
128/G4 **Buffalo**, Wy,US
138/Q15 **Buffalo Grove**, Il,US
128/F2 **Buffalo Narrows**, Sk,Can.
97/B1 **Buffalo Riv. Overflow** (swamp), Austl.
108/B3 **Buffelsrivier** (dry riv.), SAfr.
135/G3 **Buford**, Ga,US
69/G3 **Buftea**, Rom.
72/B1 **Bug** (riv.), Eur.
69/K2 **Bug** (estuary), Ukr.
114/C3 **Buga**, Col.
122/E6 **Bugaba**, Pan.
65/G1 **Bugarach, Pic de** (peak), Fr.
53/E2 **Bugbrooke**, Eng,UK
92/D5 **Bugel** (pt.), Indo.
58/D1 **Buggenhout**, Belg.
68/C3 **Bugojno**, Bosn.
93/E2 **Bugsuk** (isl.), Phil.
71/M5 **Bugul'ma**, Rus.
73/K1 **Buguruslan**, Rus.
82/D4 **Buh** (riv.), China
80/D3 **Buhayrat al Asad** (lake), Turk.
78/D2 **Buḩayrat ath Tharthār** (lake), Iraq
128/E5 **Buhl**, Id,US
69/H2 **Buhuşi**, Rom.
105/E4 **Bui** (dam), Gha.
105/E4 **Bui Gorge** (res.), Gha.
52/C2 **Builth Wells**, Wal,UK
118/Q9 **Buin**, Chile
64/C4 **Bujalance**, Sp.
68/E4 **Bujanovac**, Serb.
69/H3 **Bujor**, Rom.
107/A3 **Bujumbura** (cap.), Buru.
55/J2 **Buk**, Pol.
98/E5 **Buka** (isl.), PNG
82/H1 **Bukachacha**, Rus.
81/F4 **Bukadaban Feng** (peak), China
78/E1 **Būkān**, Iran
107/A3 **Bukavu**, D.R. Congo
89/C5 **Buket Bubat** (peak), Malay.
74/G6 **Bukhara**, Uzb.
92/B4 **Bukittinggi**, Indo.
68/E1 **Bükki Nat'l Park**, Hun.
107/A3 **Bukoba**, Tanz.
92/B4 **Buku** (cape), Indo.
88/D5 **Bulan**, Phil.
90/C2 **Bulandshahr**, India
80/E2 **Bulanık**, Turk.
93/F3 **Bulawa** (peak), Indo.
110/E5 **Bulawayo**, Zim.
136/B5 **Buldir** (isl.), Ak,US
82/C2 **Bulgan** (riv.), Mong.
69/G4 **Bulgaria** (ctry.)
66/D2 **Bulgheria** (peak), It.
88/C6 **Buliluyan** (cape), Phil.
96/F7 **Bulimba** (cr.), Austl.
53/E2 **Bulkington**, Eng,UK
128/B2 **Bulkley** (riv.), BC,Can.
50/B1 **Bull** (pt.), NI,UK
64/E3 **Bullas**, Sp.
97/C3 **Buller** (peak), Austl.
130/D4 **Bullhead City**, Az,US
59/F3 **Büllingen**, Belg.
96/A5 **Bulloo** (riv.), Austl.
131/J3 **Bull Shoals** (lake), Ar, Mo,US
58/B3 **Bully-les-Mines**, Fr.
82/D2 **Bulnayn** (mts.), Mong.
118/B3 **Bulnes**, Chile
98/D5 **Bulolo**, PNG
93/F5 **Bulukumba**, Indo.
110/D2 **Bulungu**, D.R. Congo
103/K7 **Bumba**, D.R. Congo
107/C2 **Buna**, Kenya
85/L9 **Bunaga-take** (peak), Japan
107/A3 **Bunazi**, Tanz.
95/A4 **Bunbury**, Austl.
96/D4 **Bundaberg**, Austl.
57/F4 **Bünde**, Ger.
90/C2 **Būndi**, India
53/H2 **Bungay**, Eng,UK
92/C3 **Bunguran** (isls.), Indo.
107/A2 **Bunia**, D.R. Congo
135/H4 **Bunnell**, Fl,US
56/C4 **Bunnik**, Neth.
65/E3 **Buñol**, Sp.
56/C4 **Bunschoten**, Neth.
53/F3 **Buntingford**, Eng,UK
96/C4 **Bunya Mountains Nat'l Park**, Austl.
80/C2 **Bünyan**, Turk.
96/E6 **Bunya Park**, Austl.
93/E3 **Bunyu** (isl.), Indo.
89/E3 **Buon Me Thuot**, Viet.
89/E3 **Buon Mrong**, Viet.
82/B2 **Buqtyrma** (riv.), Kaz.
107/C3 **Bura**, Kenya
103/L5 **Buram**, Sudan
103/M7 **Buranga** (pass), Ugan.
103/Q6 **Burao** (Burco), Som.
135/F4 **Buras-Triumph**, La,US
88/D5 **Burauen**, Phil.
78/D3 **Buraydah**, SAr.
59/H2 **Burbach**, Ger.
137/B2 **Burbank**, Ca,US
138/Q16 **Burbank**, Il,US
103/Q6 **Burco** (Burao), Som.
96/B3 **Burdekin** (riv.), Austl.
138/J10 **Burdell** (mtn.), Ca,US
80/B3 **Burdur**, Turk.
90/E3 **Burdwān**, India
53/H1 **Bure** (riv.), Eng,UK
57/F5 **Büren**, Ger.
56/C5 **Buren**, Neth.
82/E2 **Bürengiyn** (mts.), Mong.
79/K2 **Būrewāla**, Pak.
83/L1 **Bureya** (mts.), Rus.
83/L1 **Bureya** (riv.), Rus.
53/E3 **Burford**, Eng,UK
69/H4 **Burgas**, Bul.
69/H4 **Burgas** (bay), Bul.
69/H4 **Burgas** (reg.), Bul.
57/H4 **Burgdorf**, Ger.
63/M3 **Burgenland** (prov.), Aus.
133/K2 **Burgeo**, Nf,Can.
108/D3 **Burgersdorp**, SAfr.
136/L2 **Burgess** (mtn.), Yk,Can.
53/F5 **Burgess Hill**, Eng,UK
48/E2 **Burgfjället** (peak), Swe.
51/J5 **Burgh le Marsh**, Eng,UK
63/K2 **Burglengenfeld**, Ger.
64/D1 **Burgos**, Sp.
60/A3 **Burgundy** (hist. reg.), Fr.
57/G3 **Burgwedel**, Ger.
82/D4 **Burhan Budai** (mts.), China
80/A2 **Burhaniye**, Turk.
90/C3 **Burhānpur**, India
122/E6 **Burica** (pen.), CR, Pan.
122/E6 **Burica** (pt.), Pan.
138/C3 **Burien**, Wa,US
133/L2 **Burin**, Nf,Can.
133/K2 **Burin** (pen.), Nf,Can.
89/C3 **Buriram**, Thai.
116/B2 **Buritama**, Braz.
116/B1 **Buriti Alegre**, Braz.
116/C1 **Buritizeiro**, Braz.
65/E3 **Burjasot**, Sp.
134/D3 **Burkburnett**, Tx,US
111/S **Burke** (isl.), Ant.
137/J8 **Burke**, Va,US
128/B2 **Burke Channel** (inlet), BC,Can.
105/E3 **Burkina Faso** (ctry.)
128/E5 **Burley**, Id,US
138/K11 **Burlingame**, Ca,US
133/Q9 **Burlington**, On,Can.
131/G3 **Burlington**, Co,US
129/L5 **Burlington**, Ia,US
131/J3 **Burlington**, Ks,US
135/J2 **Burlington**, NC,US
137/F5 **Burlington**, NJ,US
133/F2 **Burlington**, Vt,US
138/P14 **Burlington**, Wi,US
91/G3 **Burma** (Myanmar) (ctry.)
69/K3 **Burnas** (lake), Ukr.
134/D4 **Burnet**, Tx,US
119/J8 **Burney** (peak), Chile
130/B2 **Burney**, Ca,US

Burnh – Caspe
155

53/G3 **Burnham on Crouch**, Eng,UK
52/D4 **Burnham on Sea**, Eng,UK
97/C4 **Burnie-Somerset**, Austl.
51/F4 **Burnley**, Eng,UK
128/D5 **Burns**, Or,US
124/E2 **Burnside** (riv.), Nun.,Can.
128/B2 **Burns Lake**, BC,Can.
129/J2 **Burntwood** (riv.), Mb,Can.
53/E1 **Burntwood**, Eng,UK
97/B2 **Buronga**, Austl.
82/B2 **Burqin** (riv.), China
67/G2 **Burrel**, Alb.
97/D2 **Burrendong** (res.), Austl.
97/D2 **Burrewarra** (pt.), Austl.
65/E3 **Burriana**, Sp.
97/D2 **Burrinjuck** (res.), Austl.
96/A2 **Burrowes** (pt.), Austl.
50/D2 **Burrow Head** (pt.), Sc,UK
138/Q16 **Burr Ridge**, Il,US
96/D4 **Burrum River Nat'l Park**, Austl.
52/B3 **Burry** (inlet), Wal,UK
52/B3 **Burry Port**, Wal,UK
69/J5 **Bursa**, Turk.
69/J5 **Bursa** (prov.), Turk.
106/C3 **Būr Safājah**, Egypt
80/J6 **Būr Sa'īd** (gov.), Egypt
80/J6 **Būr Sa'īd** (Port Said), Egypt
57/E6 **Burscheid**, Ger.
51/F4 **Burscough Bridge**, Eng,UK
106/D5 **Būr Sūdān** (Port Sudan), Sudan
133/S9 **Burt**, NY,US
106/C2 **Būr Tawfīq**, Egypt
53/E5 **Burton**, Eng,UK
138/E6 **Burton**, Mi,US
53/F2 **Burton Latimer**, Eng,UK
53/E1 **Burton upon Trent**, Eng,UK
93/G4 **Buru** (isl.), Indo.
80/H6 **Burullus, Buḩayrat al** (lag.), Egypt
107/A3 **Burundi** (ctry.)
82/F2 **Burun Shibertuy** (peak), Rus.
136/L3 **Burwash Landing**, Yk,Can.
53/G2 **Burwell**, Eng,UK
131/H2 **Burwell**, Ne,US
51/F4 **Bury**, Eng,UK
51/F4 **Bury** (co.), Eng,UK
75/M4 **Buryatiya, Resp.**, Rus.
73/J3 **Burynshyk** (pt.), Kaz.
53/G2 **Bury Saint Edmunds**, Eng,UK
63/H4 **Busalla**, It.
50/B1 **Bush** (riv.), NI,UK
82/C2 **Büs Hayrhan** (peak), Mong.
53/F3 **Bushey**, Eng,UK
137/E4 **Bushkill** (falls), Pa,US
108/B3 **Bushmanland** (reg.), SAfr.
50/B1 **Bushmills**, NI,UK
103/K7 **Businga**, D.R. Congo
48/D3 **Buskerud** (co.), Nor.
55/L3 **Busko-Zdrój**, Pol.
95/A4 **Busselton**, Austl.
103/L6 **Busseri** (riv.), Sudan
56/C4 **Bussum**, Neth.
119/K7 **Bustamente** (pt.), Arg.
96/C4 **Bustard** (pt.), Austl.
69/G3 **Buşteni**, Rom.
63/H4 **Busto Arsizio**, It.
88/C5 **Busuanga** (isl.), Phil.
103/K7 **Buta**, D.R. Congo
107/A3 **Butare**, Rwa.
98/G4 **Butaritari** (atoll), Kiri.
128/B3 **Bute** (inlet), BC,Can.
49/C3 **Bute** (isl.), Sc,UK
82/E2 **Büteeliyn** (mts.), Mong.
107/A2 **Butembo**, D.R. Congo
116/B4 **Butiá**, Braz.
132/E3 **Butler**, Pa,US
93/F5 **Buton** (isl.), Indo.
128/E4 **Butte**, Mt,US
92/B2 **Butterworth**, Malay.
93/F5 **Butung** (isl.), Indo.
73/G2 **Buturlinovka**, Rus.
63/H1 **Butzbach**, Ger.
54/F2 **Bützow**, Ger.
103/Q7 **Buulo Berde**, Som.
103/P7 **Buur Hakaba**, Som.
57/G2 **Buxtehude**, Ger.
51/G5 **Buxton**, Eng,UK
70/J4 **Buy**, Rus.
73/H4 **Buynaksk**, Rus.
104/D5 **Buyo, Barrage de** (dam), C.d'Iv.
83/H2 **Buyr** (lake), Mong.
69/J5 **Büyükçekmece**, Turk.
69/J5 **Büyük Menderes** (riv.), Turk.
87/E2 **Buyun Shan** (peak), China
69/H3 **Buzău**, Rom.
69/H3 **Buzău** (co.), Rom.
69/H3 **Buzău** (riv.), Rom.
68/E3 **Buziaş**, Rom.
116/H8 **Búzios** (isl.), Braz.
73/K1 **Buzuluk**, Rus.
69/F4 **Byala Slatina**, Bul.
125/R7 **Byam Martin** (chan.), Nun,Can.
125/R7 **Byam Martin** (isl.), Nun,Can.
72/D1 **Byarezina** (riv.), Bela.
55/J2 **Bydgoszcz**, Pol.
53/E2 **Byfield**, Eng,UK
72/D1 **Bykhov**, Bela.
50/E5 **Bylchau**, Wal,UK
125/J1 **Bylot** (isl.), Nun,Can.
137/G5 **Byram** (pt.), NY,US
111/U **Byrd** (cape), Ant.
111/L **Byrd** (glac.), Ant.
119/J6 **Byron** (isl.), Chile
74/K2 **Byrranga** (mts.), Rus.
55/K4 **Bystrá** (peak), Slvk.
75/N3 **Bytantay** (riv.), Rus.
55/K3 **Bytom**, Pol.
55/J1 **Bytów**, Pol.

C

89/D2 **Ca** (riv.), Viet.
110/C3 **Caála**, Ang.
115/K5 **Caatingas** (reg.), Braz.
88/E6 **Cabadbaran**, Phil.
123/F3 **Cabaiguán**, Cuba
130/F4 **Caballo** (res.), NM,US
64/C1 **Cabañaquinta**, Sp.
88/D4 **Cabanatuan**, Phil.
52/C2 **Caban Coch** (res.), Wal,UK
133/G2 **Cabano**, Qu,Can.
62/E5 **Cabestany**, Fr.
64/C3 **Cabeza del Buey**, Sp.
64/C1 **Cabezón de la Sal**, Sp.
123/G5 **Cabimas**, Ven.
110/B2 **Cabinda**, Ang.
102/C2 **Cabo Bojador**, WSah.
107/C5 **Cabo Delgado** (prov.), Moz.
116/D2 **Cabo Frio**, Braz.
132/E2 **Cabonga** (res.), Qu,Can.
96/D4 **Caboolture**, Austl.
115/H3 **Cabo Orange Nat'l Park**, Braz.
110/F4 **Cabora Bassa** (lake), Moz.
133/J2 **Cabot** (str.), Nf, NS,Can.
116/G6 **Cabo Verde**, Braz.
64/C4 **Cabra**, Sp.
96/G8 **Cabramatta**, Austl.
66/A3 **Cabras**, It.
65/G3 **Cabrera** (isl.), Sp.
128/F3 **Cabri**, Sk,Can.
64/E3 **Cabriel** (riv.), Sp.
88/D4 **Cabugao**, Phil.
123/H5 **Cabure**, Ven.
116/B3 **Caçador**, Braz.
68/E4 **Čačak**, Serb.
116/H8 **Caçapava**, Braz.
66/A2 **Caccia** (cape), It.
114/G7 **Cáceres**, Braz.
64/B3 **Cáceres**, Sp.
118/Q10 **Cachapoal** (riv.), Chile
130/B3 **Cache** (cr.), Ca,US
128/E5 **Cache** (peak), Id,US
128/C3 **Cache Creek**, BC,Can.
104/A3 **Cacheu**, GBis.
115/G5 **Cachimbo** (mts.), Braz.
116/A4 **Cachoeira do Sul**, Braz.
116/J7 **Cachoeira Paulista**, Braz.
116/L7 **Cachoeiras de Macacu**, Braz.
116/B4 **Cachoeirinha**, Braz.
116/D2 **Cachoeiro de Itapemirim**, Braz.
116/G6 **Caconde**, Braz.
116/B1 **Caçu**, Braz.
110/B3 **Cacula**, Ang.
115/K6 **Caculé**, Braz.
65/G1 **Cadaques**, Sp.
55/K4 **Čadca**, Slvk.
134/E3 **Caddo** (mts.), Ar,US
52/C1 **Cader Idris** (mtn.), Wal,UK
132/C2 **Cadillac**, Mi,US
88/D5 **Cadiz**, Phil.
64/B4 **Cádiz**, Sp.
64/B4 **Cádiz** (gulf), Sp.
132/C4 **Cadiz**, Ky,US
53/E5 **Cadnam**, Eng,UK
62/C2 **Caen**, Fr.
52/D3 **Caerleon**, Wal,UK
50/D5 **Caernarfon**, Wal,UK
50/D5 **Caernarfon** (bay), Wal,UK
52/C3 **Caerphilly**, Wal,UK
52/C3 **Caerphilly** (co.), Wal,UK
52/C1 **Caersws**, Wal,UK
80/M7 **Caesarea Nat'l Park**, Isr.
58/B2 **Caëstre**, Fr.
117/C2 **Cafayate**, Arg.
88/D6 **Cagayan de Oro**, Phil.
88/C6 **Cagayan Sulu** (isl.), Phil.
66/A3 **Cagliari**, It.
66/A3 **Cagliari** (gulf), It.
63/G5 **Cagnes-sur-Mer**, Fr.
114/D3 **Caguán** (riv.), Col.
123/H4 **Caguas**, PR
110/B4 **Cahama**, Ang.
49/B4 **Cahore** (pt.), Ire.
62/D4 **Cahors**, Fr.
116/B4 **Cai** (riv.), Braz.
115/H7 **Caiapó** (mts.), Braz.
115/H7 **Caiapó** (riv.), Braz.
123/F3 **Caibarién**, Cuba
115/L5 **Caicó**, Braz.
123/G3 **Caicos** (isls.), Trks.
116/G8 **Caieiras**, Braz.
58/A4 **Cailly** (riv.), Fr.
89/D4 **Cai Nuoc**, Viet.
111/Y **Caird** (coast), Ant.
136/G3 **Cairn** (mtn.), Ak,US
97/B3 **Cairn Curran** (dam), Austl.
49/D2 **Cairngorm** (mts.), Sc,UK
50/C2 **Cairn Pat** (hill), Sc,UK
50/C2 **Cairnryan**, Sc,UK
96/B2 **Cairns**, Austl.
50/D1 **Cairnsmore of Carsphairn** (mtn.), Sc,UK
135/G4 **Cairo**, Ga,US
132/B4 **Cairo**, Il,US
106/B2 **Cairo** (Al Qāhirah) (cap.), Egypt
53/H1 **Caister on Sea**, Eng,UK
51/H5 **Caistor**, Eng,UK
133/Q9 **Caistor Centre**, On,Can.
133/Q9 **Caistorville**, On,Can.
110/B3 **Caitou**, Ang.
110/C4 **Caiundo**, Ang.
87/C5 **Caizi** (lake), China
114/C5 **Cajabamba**, Peru
114/C5 **Cajamarca**, Peru
105/H5 **Calabar**, Nga.
123/H6 **Calabozo**, Ven.
66/E3 **Calabria** (reg.), It.
66/E3 **Calabria Nat'l Park**, It.
64/C4 **Calaburras, Punta de** (pt.), Sp.
68/F4 **Calafat**, Rom.
64/E1 **Calahorra**, Sp.
58/A2 **Calais**, Fr.
133/H2 **Calais**, Me,US
58/A2 **Calais, Canal de** (can.), Fr.
117/C2 **Calalaste** (mts.), Arg.
117/C1 **Calama**, Chile
88/C5 **Calamian Group** (isls.), Phil.
68/F3 **Călan**, Rom.
88/D5 **Calapan**, Phil.
69/H3 **Călăraşi**, Rom.
69/H3 **Călăraşi** (co.), Rom.
64/E3 **Calasparra**, Sp.
64/E2 **Calatayud**, Sp.
138/L12 **Calaveras** (res.), Ca,US
88/D4 **Calayan**, Phil.
88/D4 **Calayan** (isl.), Phil.
88/D5 **Calbayog**, Phil.
118/B4 **Calbuco**, Chile
114/D6 **Calca**, Peru
134/E4 **Calcasieu** (riv.), La,US
132/F2 **Calcium**, NY,US
90/E3 **Calcutta** (Kolkata), India
64/A3 **Caldas da Rainha**, Port.
116/B1 **Caldas Novas**, Braz.
51/E2 **Caldbeck**, Eng,UK
57/G6 **Calden**, Ger.
51/G4 **Calder** (riv.), Eng,UK
136/M4 **Calder** (mtn.), Ak,US
51/F4 **Calderdale** (co.), Eng,UK
65/L6 **Caldes de Montbui**, Sp.
51/F2 **Caldew** (riv.), Eng,UK
52/D3 **Caldicot**, Wal,UK
128/D5 **Caldwell**, Id,US
134/D4 **Caldwell**, Tx,US
52/B3 **Caldy** (isl.), Wal,UK
108/D3 **Caledon** (riv.), Les., SAfr.
133/Q8 **Caledon East**, On,Can.
133/H2 **Caledonia** (hills), NB,Can.
65/G2 **Calella**, Sp.
118/Q9 **Calera de Tango**, Chile
123/P9 **Calera Víctor Rosales**, Mex.
123/P10 **Caleta de Campos Chutla**, Mex.
118/D5 **Caleta Olivia**, Arg.
130/D4 **Calexico**, Ca,US
51/F3 **Calf, The** (mtn.), Eng,UK
128/E3 **Calgary**, Ab,Can.
65/S12 **Calheta**, Azor.,Port.
65/U15 **Calheta**, Madr.,Port.
135/G3 **Calhoun**, Ga,US
132/C4 **Calhoun**, Ky,US
114/C3 **Cali**, Col.
90/C5 **Calicut** (Kozhikode), India
64/E4 **Calida, Costa** (coast), Sp.
130/D3 **Caliente**, Nv,US
123/M8 **California** (gulf), Mex.
130/B3 **California** (state), US
132/E4 **California**, Md,US
131/J3 **California**, Mo,US
117/D1 **Calilegua Nat'l Park**, Arg.
69/G3 **Călimăneşti**, Rom.
90/C5 **Calimere** (pt.), India
137/C2 **Calimesa**, Ca,US
122/C3 **Calkiní**, Mex.
97/A1 **Callabonna** (lake), Austl.
49/C2 **Callander**, Sc,UK
114/C6 **Callao**, Peru
135/G4 **Callaway**, Fl,US
118/Q9 **Calle Larga**, Chile
52/B6 **Callington**, Eng,UK
65/E3 **Callosa de Ensarriá**, Sp.
65/E3 **Callosa de Segura**, Sp.
52/D4 **Calne**, Eng,UK
58/B3 **Calonne-Ricouart**, Fr.
66/D2 **Calore** (riv.), It.
96/D4 **Caloundra**, Austl.
65/F3 **Calpe**, Sp.
52/B6 **Calstock**, Eng,UK
66/D4 **Caltagirone**, It.
66/D4 **Caltanissetta**, It.
62/F4 **Caluire-et-Cuire**, Fr.
138/Q16 **Calumet** (riv.), Il,US
138/Q16 **Calumet City**, Il,US
110/B3 **Caluquembe**, Ang.
128/A3 **Calvert** (isl.), BC,Can.
51/G5 **Calverton**, Eng,UK
137/K7 **Calverton**, Md,US
137/H5 **Calverton**, NY,US
65/G3 **Calviá**, Sp.
108/B3 **Calvinia**, SAfr.
64/C2 **Calvitero** (mtn.), Sp.
53/G2 **Cam** (riv.), Eng,UK
115/L6 **Camaçari**, Braz.
110/C3 **Camacupa**, Ang.
123/F3 **Camagüey**, Cuba
123/F3 **Camagüey** (arch.), Cuba
63/J5 **Camaiore**, It.
114/D7 **Camaná**, Peru
116/B4 **Camaquã**, Braz.
116/A4 **Camaquã** (riv.), Braz.
65/V15 **Câmara de Lobos**, Madr.,Port.
63/G5 **Camarat** (cape), Fr.
64/D1 **Camargo**, Sp.
137/A2 **Camarillo**, Ca,US
64/A1 **Camariñas**, Sp.
122/D4 **Camarón** (cape), Hon.
118/D5 **Camarones** (bay), Arg.
64/B4 **Camas**, Sp.
89/D4 **Ca Mau**, Viet.
89/D4 **Ca Mau** (cape), Viet.
64/A1 **Cambados**, Sp.
116/B2 **Cambará**, Braz.
90/B3 **Cambay**, India
90/B3 **Cambay** (gulf), India
116/B2 **Cambé**, Braz.
53/F4 **Camberley Frimley**, Eng,UK
89/D3 **Cambodia** (ctry.)
116/C3 **Camboriú, Ponta do** (pt.), Braz.
52/A6 **Camborne**, Eng,UK
58/C3 **Cambrai**, Fr.
52/C2 **Cambrian** (mts.), Wal,UK
132/D3 **Cambridge**, On,Can.
53/G2 **Cambridge**, Eng,UK
133/G3 **Cambridge**, Ma,US
132/E4 **Cambridge**, Md,US
129/K4 **Cambridge**, Mn,US
132/D3 **Cambridge**, Oh,US
53/G2 **Cambridgeshire** (co.), Eng,UK
65/F2 **Cambrils**, Sp.
116/G7 **Cambuí**, Braz.
116/H6 **Cambuquira**, Braz.
123/E6 **Cambutal** (mt.), Pan.
97/D2 **Camden**, Austl.
135/G4 **Camden**, Al,US
134/E3 **Camden**, Ar,US
133/G2 **Camden**, Me,US
137/E6 **Camden**, NJ,US
135/H3 **Camden**, SC,US
131/J3 **Camdenton**, Mo,US
110/D3 **Cameia Nat'l Park**, Ang.
52/B6 **Camel** (riv.), Eng,UK
137/E4 **Camelback** (mtn.), Pa,US
52/B5 **Camelford**, Eng,UK
125/R7 **Cameron** (isl.), Nun,Can.
130/E4 **Cameron**, Az,US
134/E4 **Cameron**, La,US
131/J3 **Cameron**, Mo,US
134/D4 **Cameron**, Tx,US
102/H7 **Cameroon** (ctry.)
115/J4 **Cametá**, Braz.
58/A2 **Camiers**, Fr.
88/D4 **Camiguin** (isl.), Phil.
135/G4 **Camilla**, Ga,US
114/F8 **Camiri**, Bol.
110/F5 **Camo-Camo**, Moz.
115/K4 **Camocim**, Braz.
91/F6 **Camorta** (isl.), India
58/A3 **Campagne**, Fr.
118/F2 **Campana**, Arg.
119/J7 **Campana** (isl.), Chile
118/C2 **Campanario** (peak), Arg.
66/D2 **Campanella** (cape), It.
116/H6 **Campanha**, Braz.
66/D2 **Campania** (reg.), It.
45/T8 **Campbell** (isl.), NZ
138/L12 **Campbell**, Ca,US
128/A2 **Campbell Island**, BC,Can.
128/B3 **Campbell River**, BC,Can.
132/C4 **Campbellsville**, Ky,US
133/H2 **Campbellton**, NB,Can
96/G9 **Campbelltown**, Austl.
133/Q9 **Campbellville**, On,Can.
133/R9 **Campden**, On,Can.
122/C4 **Campeche**, Mex.
122/C4 **Campeche** (bay), Mex.
122/C4 **Campeche** (state), Mex.
129/H3 **Camperville**, Mb,Can.
116/G6 **Campestre**, Braz.
89/D1 **Cam Pha**, Viet.
66/A3 **Campidano** (range), It.
64/C4 **Campillos**, Sp.
115/L5 **Campina Grande**, Braz.
116/F7 **Campinas**, Braz.
116/B1 **Campina Verde**, Braz.
114/C3 **Campoalegre**, Col.
66/D2 **Campobasso**, It.
116/C2 **Campo Belo**, Braz.
64/D3 **Campo de Criptana**, Sp.
123/G5 **Campo de la Cruz**, Col.
115/K6 **Campo Formoso**, Braz.
115/H8 **Campo Grande**, Braz.
117/G2 **Campo Largo**, Braz.
116/G8 **Campo Limpo Paulista**, Braz.
115/K4 **Campo Maior**, Braz.
64/B3 **Campo Maior**, Port.
63/H4 **Campomorone**, It.
116/A3 **Campo Mourão**, Braz.
64/C1 **Camporredondo** (res.), Sp.
116/D2 **Campos**, Braz.
115/J7 **Campos** (reg.), Braz.
116/C1 **Campos Altos**, Braz.
65/G3 **Campos del Puerto**, Sp.
116/H7 **Campos do Jordão**, Braz.
116/C2 **Campos Gerais**, Braz.
116/B3 **Campos Novos**, Braz.
137/K8 **Camp Springs**, Md,US
134/E4 **Campti**, La,US
89/E4 **Cam Ranh**, Viet.
128/E2 **Camrose**, Ab,Can.
89/D1 **Cam Thuy**, Viet.
124/* **Canada** (ctry.)
118/E2 **Cañada de Gómez**, Arg.
131/H4 **Canadian** (riv.), US
134/C3 **Canadian**, Tx,US
118/C5 **Cañadon Grande** (mts.), Arg.
123/G6 **Canagua**, Ven.
114/F2 **Canaima Nat'l Park**, Ven.
69/H5 **Çanakkale**, Turk.
69/H5 **Çanakkale** (prov.), Turk.
99/U12 **Canala**, NCal.
118/E2 **Canals**, Arg.
65/E3 **Canals**, Sp.
132/E3 **Canandaigua**, NY,US
123/M7 **Cananea**, Mex.
116/C3 **Cananéia**, Braz.
65/X16 **Canary Islands** (aut. comm.), Sp.
122/D5 **Cañas**, CR
123/P9 **Canatlán**, Mex.
135/H4 **Canaveral** (cape), Fl,US
115/L7 **Canavieiras**, Braz.
97/D2 **Canberra** (cap.), Austl.
58/A3 **Canche** (riv.), Fr.
122/D3 **Cancún**, Mex.
64/C1 **Candás**, Sp.
133/N7 **Candiac**, Qu,Can.
116/B2 **Cândido Mota**, Braz.
92/D5 **Canding** (cape), Indo.
129/G2 **Candle** (lake), Sk,Can.
129/J3 **Cando**, ND,US
88/D4 **Candon**, Phil.
116/B4 **Canela**, Braz.
63/H4 **Canelli**, It.
119/F2 **Canelones**, Uru.
119/F2 **Canelones** (dept.), Uru.
64/A1 **Cangas**, Sp.
64/B1 **Cangas de Narcea**, Sp.
64/C1 **Cangas de Onís**, Sp.
92/C5 **Cangkuang** (cape), Indo.
108/C4 **Cango Caves**, SAfr.
110/D3 **Cangombe**, Ang.
119/J7 **Cangrejo** (peak), Arg.
116/A4 **Canguçu**, Braz.
87/D3 **Cangzhou**, China
89/D1 **Canh Cuoc** (isl.), Viet.
110/B3 **Canhoca**, Ang.
96/C4 **Cania Gorge Nat'l Park**, Austl.
125/K3 **Caniapiscau** (lake), Qu,Can.
125/K3 **Caniapiscau** (riv.), Qu,Can.
66/C4 **Canicatti**, It.
62/E5 **Canigou, Pic de** (peak), Fr.
80/D2 **Canik** (mts.), Turk.
64/D4 **Caniles**, Sp.
115/L4 **Canindé**, Braz.
115/K5 **Canindé** (riv.), Braz.
80/C2 **Çankırı**, Turk.
93/F1 **Canlaon** (vol.), Phil.
128/E3 **Canmore**, Ab,Can
90/C5 **Cannanore**, India
66/E2 **Canne** (ruins), It.
59/F5 **Canner** (riv.), Fr.
63/G5 **Cannes**, Fr.
49/C2 **Cannich**, Sc,UK
52/D1 **Cannock**, Eng,UK
129/H4 **Cannonball** (riv.), ND,US
129/K4 **Cannon Falls**, Mn,US
116/B4 **Canoas**, Braz.
116/B3 **Canoas** (riv.), Braz.
97/D2 **Canobolas** (peak), Austl.
128/F2 **Canoe** (lake), Sk,Can.
116/B3 **Canoinhas**, Braz.
51/F1 **Canonbie**, Sc,UK
131/F3 **Canon City**, Co,US
129/H3 **Canora**, Sk,Can.
133/J2 **Canso** (cape), Can.
64/C1 **Cantabria** (aut. comm.), Sp.
62/E4 **Cantal** (plat.), Fr.
64/A2 **Cantanhede**, Port.
123/J6 **Cantaura**, Ven.
96/H8 **Canterbury**, Austl.
53/H4 **Canterbury**, Eng,UK
89/D4 **Can Tho**, Viet.
64/C4 **Cantillana**, Sp.
132/B3 **Canton**, Il,US
138/E7 **Canton**, Mi,US
135/F3 **Canton**, Ms,US
132/F2 **Canton**, NY,US
132/D3 **Canton**, Oh,US
131/H3 **Canton**, Ok,US
129/J5 **Canton**, SD,US
134/E3 **Canton**, Tx,US
99/H5 **Canton (Abariringa)** (atoll), Kiri.
88/B3 **Canton (Guangzhou)**, China
63/H4 **Cantù**, It.
118/F2 **Cañuelas**, Arg.
97/B3 **Canunda Nat'l Park**, Austl.
53/G3 **Canvey Island**, Eng,UK
128/G2 **Canwood**, Sk,Can.
134/C3 **Canyon**, Tx,US
130/E3 **Canyon de Chelly Nat'l Mon.**, Az,US
130/E3 **Canyonlands Nat'l Park**, Ut,US
130/E3 **Canyon of the Ancients Nat'l Mon.**, Co,US
89/D1 **Cao Bang**, Viet.
88/A2 **Caodu** (riv.), China
89/D4 **Cao Lanh**, Viet.
114/E2 **Capanaparo** (riv.), Ven.
115/J4 **Capanema**, Braz.
66/B1 **Capanne** (peak), It.
63/J5 **Capannori**, It.
116/B3 **Capão Bonito**, Braz.
116/D2 **Caparaó Nat'l Park**, Braz.
64/A3 **Caparica**, Port.
133/H1 **Cap-Chat**, Qu,Can.
133/F2 **Cap-de-la-Madeleine**, Qu,Can.
96/B3 **Cape** (riv.), Austl.
97/D4 **Cape Barren** (isl.), Austl.
133/J2 **Cape Breton** (highlands), NS,Can.
133/J2 **Cape Breton** (isl.), NS,Can.
133/J2 **Cape Breton Highlands Nat'l Park**, NS,Can.
96/B2 **Cape Cleveland Nat'l Park**, Austl.
105/E5 **Cape Coast**, Gha.
133/G3 **Cape Cod Nat'l Seashore**, Ma,US
135/H5 **Cape Coral**, Fl,US
135/J3 **Cape Fear** (riv.), NC,US
131/K3 **Cape Girardeau**, Mo,US
135/K3 **Cape Hatteras Nat'l Seashore**, NC,US
136/E2 **Cape Krusenstern Nat'l Mon.**, Ak,US
50/E5 **Capel-Curig**, Wal,UK
116/D1 **Capelinha**, Braz.
65/K6 **Capellades**, Sp.
53/H4 **Capel le Ferne**, Eng,UK
135/J3 **Cape Lookout Nat'l Seashore**, NC,US
53/H2 **Capel Saint Mary**, Eng,UK
96/B1 **Cape Melville Nat'l Park**, Austl.
96/C3 **Cape Palmerston Nat'l Park**, Austl.
137/K7 **Cape Saint Claire**, Md,US
108/B4 **Cape Town** (cap.), SAfr.
96/B2 **Cape Tribulation Nat'l Park**, Austl.
96/B2 **Cape Upstart Nat'l Park**, Austl.
44/H5 **Cape Verde** (ctry.)
96/A1 **Cape York** (pen.), Austl.
123/G4 **Cap-Haïtien**, Haiti
66/A2 **Capicciola** (pt.), Fr.
115/J4 **Capim** (riv.), Braz.
116/B1 **Capinópolis**, Braz.
116/B2 **Capirara** (res.), Braz.
134/B3 **Capitan** (mts.), NM,US
115/J4 **Capitão Poço**, Braz.
98/D3 **Capitol Hill** (cap.), NMar.
130/E3 **Capitol Reef Nat'l Park**, Ut,US
115/H8 **Capivara** (res.), Braz.
116/J6 **Capivari** (riv.), Braz.
68/C4 **Čapljina**, Bosn.
66/D3 **Capo d'Orlando**, It.
66/A3 **Capoterra**, It.
66/A1 **Capraia** (isl.), It.
132/D2 **Capreol**, On,Can.
66/D2 **Capri**, It.
96/C3 **Capricorn** (cape), Austl.
96/C3 **Capricorn** (chan.), Austl.
110/D4 **Caprivi Strip** (reg.), Namb.
134/C3 **Cap Rock Escarpment** (cliffs), Tx,US
134/C3 **Caprock, The** (cliffs), NM,US
133/G2 **Cap-Rouge**, Qu,Can.
63/G5 **Cap Roux, Pointe du** (pt.), Fr.
131/G3 **Capulin Volcano Nat'l Mon.**, NM,US
114/D4 **Caquetá** (riv.), Col.
65/N9 **Carabanchel** (nrbhd.), Sp.
69/G3 **Caracal**, Rom.
123/H5 **Caracas** (cap.), Ven.
53/E5 **Caradon** (hill), Eng,UK
116/H8 **Caraguatatuba**, Braz.
116/H8 **Caraguatatuba** (bay), Braz.
118/B3 **Carahue**, Chile
115/H5 **Carajás** (mts.), Braz.
116/D2 **Carandaí**, Braz.
116/D2 **Carangola**, Braz.
68/F3 **Caransebeş**, Rom.
66/D2 **Carapelle** (riv.), It.
116/G8 **Carapicuiba**, Braz.
133/H2 **Caraquet**, NB,Can.
68/E3 **Caraş-Severin** (co.), Rom.
122/E4 **Caratasca** (lag.), Hon.
116/D1 **Caratinga**, Braz.
114/E4 **Carauarí**, Braz.
64/E3 **Caravaca de la Cruz**, Sp.
104/A4 **Caravela** (isl.), GBis.
117/F2 **Carazinho**, Braz.
64/A1 **Carballino**, Sp.
64/A1 **Carballo**, Sp.
129/J3 **Carberry**, Mb,Can.
138/C3 **Carbon** (riv.), Wa,US
66/A3 **Carbonara** (cape), It.
66/D4 **Carbonara, Pizzo** (peak), It.
132/B4 **Carbondale**, Il,US
132/F3 **Carbondale**, Pa,US
66/A3 **Carbonia**, It.
65/E3 **Carcagente**, Sp.
118/E2 **Carcaraña**, Arg.
62/E5 **Carcassonne**, Fr.
65/P10 **Carcavelos**, Port.
64/E3 **Carche** (mtn.), Sp.
124/C2 **Carcross**, Yk,Can.
65/L6 **Cardedeu**, Sp.
119/K7 **Cardiel** (lake), Arg.
52/C4 **Cardiff** (cap.), Wal,UK
52/C3 **Cardiff** (co.), Wal,UK
52/B2 **Cardigan**, Wal,UK
65/F2 **Cardona**, Sp.
116/B2 **Cardoso**, Braz.
128/E3 **Cardston**, Ab,Can.
68/F2 **Carei**, Rom.
62/C2 **Carentan**, Fr.
68/F4 **Carev vrh** (peak), FYROM
62/B2 **Carhaix-Plouguer**, Fr.
118/E3 **Carhué**, Arg.
116/D2 **Cariacica**, Braz.
123/J5 **Cariaco**, Ven.
114/C4 **Cariamanga**, Ecu.
66/E3 **Cariati**, It.
123/G5 **Caribbean** (sea)
128/C2 **Cariboo** (mts.), BC,Can.
124/E3 **Caribou** (mts.), Ab,Can.
132/B1 **Caribou** (lake), On,Can.
136/L3 **Caribou**, Yk,Can.
128/F5 **Caribou** (range), Id,US
133/G2 **Caribou**, Me,US
88/D5 **Carigara**, Phil.
115/K6 **Carinhanha**, Braz.
66/C3 **Carini**, It.
63/K3 **Carinthia** (prov.), Aus.
123/J5 **Caripito**, Ven.
131/G3 **Carizzo** (cr.), NM, Tx,US
65/E3 **Carlet**, Sp.
133/H2 **Carleton** (peak), NB,Can.
133/H2 **Carleton** (riv.), NS,Can.
133/H1 **Carleton**, Qu,Can.
108/D2 **Carletonville**, SAfr.
130/C2 **Carlin**, Nv,US
96/H8 **Carlingford**, Austl.
50/B3 **Carlingford** (mtn.), Ire.
50/B3 **Carlingford Lough** (inlet), Ire.
132/B4 **Carlinville**, Il,US
133/Q9 **Carlisle**, On,Can.
51/F2 **Carlisle**, Eng,UK
62/D5 **Carlit** (peak), Fr.
118/E2 **Carlos Casares**, Arg.
116/D1 **Carlos Chagas**, Braz.
123/F3 **Carlos M. De Cespedes**, Cuba
50/B6 **Carlow**, Ire.
50/B6 **Carlow** (co.), Ire.
131/F4 **Carlsbad**, NM,US
131/F4 **Carlsbad Caverns Nat'l Park**, NM,US
51/G6 **Carlton**, Eng,UK
129/K4 **Carlton**, Mn,US
133/Q9 **Carluke**, On,Can.
129/G3 **Carlyle**, Sk,Can.
131/K3 **Carlyle** (lake), Il,US
124/C2 **Carmacks**, Yk,Can.
63/G4 **Carmagnola**, It.
129/J3 **Carman**, Mb,Can.
52/B3 **Carmarthen**, Wal,UK
52/B3 **Carmarthen** (bay), Wal,UK
52/B3 **Carmarthenshire** (co.), Wal,UK
62/E4 **Carmaux**, Fr.
132/C4 **Carmel**, In,US
50/D5 **Carmel Head** (pt.), Wal,UK
80/K5 **Carmel, Mount** (Har Karmel) (mtn.), Isr.
118/F2 **Carmelo**, Uru.
123/M8 **Carmen** (isl.), Mex.
123/N7 **Carmen** (riv.), Mex.
132/B4 **Carmi**, Il,US
138/M9 **Carmichael**, Ca,US
116/L6 **Carmo**, Braz.
116/C1 **Carmo do Paranaíba**, Braz.
116/C2 **Carmo do Rio Claro**, Braz.
64/C4 **Carmona**, Sp.
50/B1 **Carnanmore** (mtn.), NI,UK
95/A3 **Carnarvon**, Austl.
108/C3 **Carnarvonleegte** (dry riv.), SAfr.
96/B4 **Carnarvon Nat'l Park**, Austl.
65/P10 **Carnaxide**, Port.
50/C2 **Carncastle**, NI,UK
129/H3 **Carnduff**, Sk,Can.
50/D5 **Carnedd Dafydd** (mtn.), Wal,UK
50/E5 **Carnedd Llewelyn** (mtn.), Wal,UK
111/S **Carney** (isl.), Ant.
51/F3 **Carnforth**, Eng,UK
58/C3 **Carnières**, Fr.
50/B2 **Carnlough**, NI,UK
102/J7 **Carnot**, CAfr.
64/A1 **Carnota**, Sp.
49/D2 **Carnoustie**, Sc,UK
49/B4 **Carnsore** (pt.), Ire.
124/D2 **Carnwath** (riv.), NW,Can.
132/D3 **Caro**, Mi,US
123/H4 **Carolina**, PR
99/K5 **Caroline** (isl.), Kiri.
98/D4 **Caroline** (isls.), Micr.
138/P16 **Carol Stream**, Il,US
47/G4 **Carpathian** (mts.), Eur.
63/J4 **Carpenedolo**, It.
95/C2 **Carpentaria** (gulf), Austl.
138/P15 **Carpentersville**, Il,US
62/F4 **Carpentras**, Fr.
63/J4 **Carpi**, It.
137/A2 **Carpinteria**, Ca,US
138/B3 **Carr** (inlet), Wa,US
135/G4 **Carrabelle**, Fl,US
63/J4 **Carrara**, It.
50/D6 **Carreg Ddu** (pt.), Wal,UK
123/J5 **Carriacou** (isl.), Gren.
50/C2 **Carrickfergus**, NI,UK
50/C2 **Carrickfergus** (dist.), NI,UK
50/A2 **Carrickmore**, NI,UK
58/B6 **Carrières-sous-Poissy**, Fr.
50/B3 **Carrigatuke** (mtn.), NI,UK
129/J4 **Carrington**, ND,US
64/C1 **Carrión** (riv.), Sp.
123/G5 **Carrizal**, Col.
126/E4 **Carrizo** (mts.), Az,US
134/C2 **Carrizo** (cr.), NM,US
130/C4 **Carrizo Plain Nat'l Mon.**, Ca,US
134/D4 **Carrizo Springs**, Tx,US
131/F4 **Carrizozo**, NM,US
135/G3 **Carrollton**, Ga,US
132/C4 **Carrollton**, Ky,US
131/J3 **Carrollton**, Mo,US
129/H2 **Carrot** (riv.), Sk,Can.
129/H2 **Carrot River**, Sk,Can.
50/C2 **Carrowdore**, NI,UK
50/C2 **Carryduff**, NI,UK
80/D2 **Çarşamba**, Turk.
137/B3 **Carson**, Ca,US
130/C3 **Carson** (riv.), Nv,US
130/C3 **Carson** (sink), Nv,US
130/C3 **Carson City** (cap.), Nv,US
50/D1 **Carsphairn**, Sc,UK
128/E3 **Carstairs**, Ab,Can.
118/Q9 **Cartagena**, Chile
123/F5 **Cartagena**, Col.
65/E4 **Cartagena**, Sp.
114/C3 **Cartago**, Col.
122/E6 **Cartago**, CR
64/C4 **Cártama**, Sp.
64/A3 **Cartaxo**, Port.
64/B4 **Cartaya**, Sp.
137/F5 **Carteret**, NJ,US
135/G3 **Cartersville**, Ga,US
53/E3 **Carterton**, Eng,UK
66/B4 **Carthage** (ruins), Tun.
131/J3 **Carthage**, Mo,US
135/F3 **Carthage**, Ms,US
135/G2 **Carthage**, Tn,US
134/E3 **Carthage**, Tx,US
125/L3 **Cartwright**, Nf,Can.
115/L5 **Caruaru**, Braz.
114/F1 **Carúpano**, Ven.
131/K3 **Caruthersville**, Mo,US
58/B2 **Carvin**, Fr.
64/A3 **Carvoeiro** (cape), Port.
138/P15 **Cary**, Il,US
135/J3 **Cary**, NC,US
102/D1 **Casablanca**, Mor.
116/F6 **Casa Branca**, Braz.
123/N7 **Casa de Janos**, Mex.
130/E4 **Casa Grande**, Az,US
130/E4 **Casa Grande Nat'l Mon.**, Az,US
66/D2 **Casal di Principe**, It.
63/J4 **Casalecchio di Reno**, It.
63/H4 **Casale Monferrato**, It.
104/A3 **Casamance** (riv.), Sen.
115/J4 **Casa Nova**, Braz.
67/F3 **Casarano**, It.
123/N7 **Casas Grandes** (ruins), Mex.
123/N8 **Cascada de Bassaseachic Nat'l Park**, Mex.
128/C5 **Cascade** (range), Can., US
128/D4 **Cascade** (res.), Id,US
138/C3 **Cascade-Fairwood**, Wa,US
109/R15 **Cascades** (pt.), Reun., Fr.
128/C5 **Cascade-Siskiyou Nat'l Mon.**, Or,US
65/P10 **Cascais**, Port.
133/H1 **Cascapédia** (riv.), Qu,Can.
63/J5 **Cascina-Navacchio**, It.
138/B3 **Case** (inlet), Wa,US
66/D2 **Caserta**, It.
111/H **Casey**, Ant.
111/D **Casey** (bay), Ant.
103/R5 **Caseyr** (cape), Som.
128/C4 **Cashmere**, Wa,US
118/E2 **Casilda**, Arg.
123/P10 **Casimiro Castillo**, Mex.
97/E1 **Casino**, Austl.
137/A2 **Casitas** (lake), Ca,US
114/C5 **Casma**, Peru
65/E2 **Caspe**, Sp.
129/G5 **Casper**, Wy,US

156
Caspi – Choco

74/F6 **Caspian** (sea), Eur., Asia
65/G2 **Cassà de la Selva**, Sp.
110/D3 **Cassai** (riv.), Ang.
110/D3 **Cassamba**, Ang.
66/E3 **Cassano allo Ionio**, It.
132/D3 **Cass City**, Mi,US
116/C2 **Cássia**, Braz.
124/C3 **Cassiar** (mts.), BC,Can.
116/B1 **Cassilândia**, Braz.
66/C2 **Cassino**, It.
131/J3 **Cassville**, Mo,US
137/B2 **Castaic**, Ca,US
137/B1 **Castaic** (lake), Ca,US
65/E3 **Castalla**, Sp.
115/J4 **Castanhal**, Braz.
66/D4 **Castelbuono**, It.
63/K5 **Castelfidardo**, It.
66/C3 **Castellammare** (gulf), It.
66/D2 **Castellammare di Stabia**, It.
63/G4 **Castellamonte**, It.
65/G2 **Castellar del Vallès**, Sp.
65/K7 **Castelldefels**, Sp.
65/L7 **Castell de Montjuic**, Sp.
66/D4 **Castello Eurialo** (ruins), It.
65/E3 **Castellón de la Plana**, Sp.
80/N9 **Castel Nat'l Park**, Isr.
62/D5 **Castelnaudary**, Fr.
62/E5 **Castelnau-le-Lez**, Fr.
64/B3 **Castelo Branco**, Port.
64/B2 **Castelo Branco** (dist.), Port.
62/D4 **Castelsarrasin**, Fr.
66/C4 **Castelvetrano**, It
116/B2 **Castilho**, Braz.
114/B5 **Castilla**, Peru
64/C2 **Castille and León** (aut. comm.), Sp.
64/D3 **Castille-La Mancha** (aut. comm.), Sp.
123/G5 **Castilletes**, Col.
118/C4 **Castillo** (peak), Arg.
135/H4 **Castillo de San Marcos Nat'l Mon.**, Fl,US
119/G2 **Castillos**, Uru.
53/G1 **Castle Acre**, Eng,UK
49/A4 **Castlebar**, Ire.
52/D4 **Castle Cary**, Eng,UK
50/B3 **Castlecaulfield**, NI,UK
52/D4 **Castle Combe**, Eng,UK
130/E3 **Castle Dale**, Ut,US
50/B2 **Castledawson**, NI,UK
51/G6 **Castle Donnington**, Eng,UK
50/E2 **Castle Douglas**, Sc,UK
51/G4 **Castleford**, Eng,UK
128/D3 **Castlegar**, BC,Can.
96/H8 **Castle Hill**, Austl.
50/D2 **Castle Kennedy**, Sc,UK
97/C3 **Castlemaine**, Austl.
96/G8 **Castlereagh**, Austl.
50/B1 **Castlerock**, NI,UK
131/F3 **Castle Rock**, Co,US
129/L5 **Castle Rock** (lake), Wi,US
96/C4 **Castle Tower Nat'l Park**, Austl.
50/D3 **Castletown**, IM,UK
50/C3 **Castlewellan**, NI,UK
128/F2 **Castor**, Ab,Can.
102/D6 **Castos** (riv.), Libr.
62/E5 **Castres**, Fr.
56/B3 **Castricum**, Neth.
123/J5 **Castries** (cap.), StL.
116/B3 **Castro**, Braz.
118/B4 **Castro**, Chile
64/C4 **Castro del Río**, Sp.
64/B1 **Castro de Rey**, Sp.
57/E5 **Castrop-Rauxel**, Ger.
64/D1 **Castro-Urdiales**, Sp.
138/K11 **Castro Valley**, Ca,US
66/E3 **Castrovillari**, It.
64/C3 **Castuera**, Sp.
123/F3 **Cat** (isl.), Bahm.
129/K3 **Cat** (lake), On,Can.
88/D5 **Cataduanes** (isl.), Phil
116/L6 **Cataguases**, Braz.
88/D5 **Cataiñgan**, Phil.
93/F1 **Cataiñgan**, Phil.
69/K5 **Çatalağzı**, Turk.
116/C1 **Catalão**, Braz.
69/J5 **Çatalca**, Turk.
130/E4 **Catalina**, Az,US
65/F2 **Catalonia** (aut. comm.), Sp.
117/C2 **Catamarca**, Arg.
88/D5 **Catanduanes** (isl.), Phil.
116/B2 **Catanduva**, Braz.
66/D4 **Catania**, It.
66/D4 **Catania** (gulf), It.
66/E3 **Catanzaro**, It.
93/F1 **Catarman**, Indo.
88/D5 **Catarman**, Phil.
65/E3 **Catarroja**, Sp.
123/G6 **Catatumbo** (riv.), Col., Ven.
93/F2 **Catatungan** (mtn.), Phil.
135/H3 **Catawba** (riv.), NC, SC,US
88/D5 **Catbalogan**, Phil.
119/G2 **Catedral** (peak), Uru.
53/F4 **Caterham and Warlingham**, Eng,UK
106/C2 **Catherine, Mount** (Jabal Katrīnah) (mtn.), Egypt
123/F6 **Cativá**, Pan.
132/D4 **Catlettsburg**, Ky,US
122/D3 **Catoche** (cape), Mex.
63/K5 **Catria** (peak), It.
114/F3 **Catrimani** (riv.), Braz.
52/D2 **Catshill**, Eng,UK
132/F3 **Catskill** (mts.), NY,US
59/F5 **Cattenom**, Fr.
51/G3 **Catterick**, Eng,UK
88/D4 **Cauayan**, Phil.
88/D6 **Cauayan**, Phil.
114/C2 **Cauca** (riv.), Col.
115/L4 **Caucaia**, Braz.
114/C2 **Caucasia**, Col.
72/G4 **Caucasus** (mts.), Eur.
65/E3 **Caudete**, Sp.
58/C3 **Caudry**, Fr.
51/F1 **Cauldcleuch** (mtn.), Sc,UK
118/B2 **Cauquenes**, Chile
62/D4 **Caussade**, Fr.
66/D4 **Cava d'Ispica** (ruins), It.
64/B2 **Cávado** (riv.), Port.
62/F5 **Cavaillon**, Fr.
129/J3 **Cavalier**, ND,US
102/D6 **Cavalla** (riv.), Libr.
66/A1 **Cavallo, Capo al** (cape), Fr.
104/D5 **Cavally** (riv.), C.d'Iv.
50/A4 **Cavan** (co.), Ire.
130/E4 **Cave Creek**, Az,US
115/J3 **Caviana**, Braz.
69/F2 **Cavnic**, Rom.
88/D5 **Cawayan**, Phil.
97/B2 **Cawndilla** (lake), Austl.
51/G4 **Cawood**, Eng,UK
53/H1 **Cawston**, Eng,UK
116/J6 **Caxambu**, Braz.
115/K4 **Caxias**, Braz.
116/B4 **Caxias do Sul**, Braz.
122/D4 **Caxinas** (pt.), Hon.
110/B2 **Caxito**, Ang.
80/B2 **Çay**, Turk.
114/C3 **Cayambe** (vol.), Ecu.
135/H3 **Cayce**, SC,US
69/L5 **Çaycuma**, Turk.
80/E2 **Çayeli**, Turk.
115/H3 **Cayenne** (cap.), FrG.
123/F4 **Cayman Brac** (isl.), Cay.
122/E4 **Cayman Islands**, UK
122/E4 **Cayos Cajones** (isls.), Hon.
122/E5 **Cayos Miskitos** (isls.), Nic.
68/B3 **Cazin**, Bosn.
64/D4 **Cazorla**, Sp.
64/C1 **Cea** (riv.), Sp.
115/L5 **Ceará-Mirim**, Braz.
119/G2 **Cebollatí** (riv.), Uru.
88/D5 **Cebu**, Phil.
88/D6 **Cebu** (isl.), Phil.
66/C2 **Ceccano**, It.
109/E2 **Cecil Macks** (pass), Swaz.
63/J5 **Cecina**, It.
66/E3 **Cecita** (lake), It.
129/H2 **Cedar** (lake), Mb,Can.
132/E2 **Cedar** (lake), On,Can.
138/L11 **Cedar** (mtn.), Ca,US
129/L5 **Cedar** (riv.), Ia,US
137/F6 **Cedar** (cr.), NJ,US
138/C3 **Cedar** (riv.), Wa,US
96/B1 **Cedar Bay Nat'l Park**, Austl.
131/G3 **Cedar Bluff** (res.), Ks,US
130/D3 **Cedar Breaks Nat'l Mon.**, Ut,US
130/D3 **Cedar City**, Ut,US
134/D3 **Cedar Creek** (res.), Tx,US
129/K5 **Cedar Falls**, Ia,US
137/F5 **Cedar Grove**, NJ,US
135/H4 **Cedar Key**, Fl,US
129/L5 **Cedar Rapids**, Ia,US
135/G3 **Cedartown**, Ga,US
130/B2 **Cedarville**, Ca,US
64/A1 **Cedeira**, Sp.
115/L5 **Cedro**, Braz.
123/L8 **Cedros** (isl.), Mex.
64/A1 **Cee**, Sp.
103/Q7 **Ceel Dheere**, Som.
103/Q5 **Ceerigaabo** (Erigabo), Som.
66/D3 **Cefalù**, It.
50/D5 **Cefni** (riv.), Wal,UK
51/E6 **Cefn-mawr**, Wal,UK
64/C2 **Cega** (riv.), Sp.
68/D2 **Cegléd**, Hun.
64/E3 **Cehegín**, Sp.
69/F2 **Cehu Silvaniei**, Rom.
51/E6 **Ceiriog** (riv.), Wal,UK
72/F4 **Çekerek** (riv.), Turk.
64/B1 **Celanova**, Sp.
122/D3 **Celarain** (pt.), Mex.
122/A3 **Celaya**, Mex.
50/B5 **Celbridge**, Ire.
93/F3 **Celebes** (sea), Asia
93/E4 **Celebes** (Sulawesi) (isl.), Indo.
132/C3 **Celina**, Oh,US
68/B2 **Celje**, Slov.
68/C2 **Celldömölk**, Hun.
62/E2 **Celle** (riv.), Fr.
57/H3 **Celle**, Ger.
52/A4 **Celtic** (sea), Eur.
52/B2 **Cemaes Head** (pt.), Wal,UK
92/D3 **Cemaru** (peak), Indo.
64/E3 **Cenajo** (res.), Sp.
93/H4 **Cenderawasih** (bay), Indo.
117/C4 **Centenario**, Arg.
116/B2 **Centenario do Sul**, Braz.
130/D4 **Centennial** (wash), Az,US
128/E4 **Centennial** (mts.), Id,US
129/H4 **Center**, ND,US
134/E4 **Center**, Tx,US
137/G5 **Centereach**, NY,US
138/F7 **Center Line**, Mi,US
137/H5 **Center Moriches**, NY,US
135/G3 **Center Point**, Al,US
135/G3 **Centerville**, Tn,US
134/E4 **Centerville**, Tx,US
63/J4 **Cento**, It.
118/C4 **Central** (peak), Arg.
105/E5 **Central** (reg.), Gha.
80/K5 **Central** (dist.), Isr.
107/C3 **Central** (prov.), Kenya
103/J6 **Central African Republic** (ctry.)
128/G3 **Central Butte**, Sk,Can.
131/H2 **Central City**, Ne,US
114/C5 **Central, Cordillera** (range), SAm.
132/B4 **Centralia**, Il,US
128/C4 **Centralia**, Wa,US
137/G5 **Central Islip**, NY,US
79/H3 **Central Makrān** (range), Pak.
62/E4 **Central, Massif** (plat.), Fr.
115/J7 **Central, Planalto** (plat.), Braz.
128/C5 **Central Point**, Or,US
75/L3 **Central Siberian** (plat.), Rus.
71/N4 **Central Ural** (mts.), Rus.
62/D3 **Centre** (reg.), Fr.
135/G3 **Centreville**, Al,US
62/D4 **Céou** (riv.), Fr.
68/D3 **Čepin**, Cro.
93/G4 **Ceram** (isl.), Indo.
93/G4 **Ceram** (sea), Indo.
66/A2 **Ceraso** (cape), It.
65/L7 **Cerdanyola del Vallès**, Sp.
62/D4 **Cère** (riv.), Fr.
63/J4 **Cerea**, It.
52/B2 **Ceredigion** (co.), Wal.,UK
117/D2 **Ceres**, Arg.
115/J7 **Ceres**, Braz.
108/B4 **Ceres**, SAfr.
123/F6 **Ceretè**, Col.
58/B5 **Cergy**, Fr.
66/D2 **Cerignola**, It.
69/J5 **Çerkezköy**, Turk.
69/J3 **Cernavodă**, Rom.
52/D5 **Cerne Abbas**, Eng,UK
123/N9 **Cerralvo** (isl.), Mex.
50/E5 **Cerrig-y-Druidion**, Wal,UK
67/F2 **Cërrik**, Alb.
122/A3 **Cerritos**, Mex.
122/B3 **Cerro Azul**, Mex.
118/C3 **Cerro Colorados** (res.), Arg.
119/G2 **Cerro Largo** (dept.), Uru.
66/D2 **Cervaro** (riv.), It.
66/D2 **Cervati** (peak), It.
65/F2 **Cervera**, Sp.
63/K4 **Cervia**, It.
66/D2 **Cervialto** (peak), It.
63/K4 **Cervignano del Friuli**, It.
116/H7 **Cervo** (hills), Braz.
64/B1 **Cervo**, Sp.
123/G5 **César** (riv.), Col.
63/K4 **Cesena**, It.
63/K4 **Cesenatico**, It.
70/E4 **Cēsis**, Lat.
55/H4 **České Budějovice**, Czh.
55/H4 **Českomoravská Vysočina** (upland), Czh.
55/H4 **Český Krumlov**, Czh.
68/C3 **Česma** (riv.), Cro.
67/K3 **Çeşme**, Turk.
80/A2 **Çeşme**, Turk.
62/C2 **Cesson-Sévigné**, Fr.
104/C5 **Cestos** (riv.), Libr.
68/C4 **Cetina** (riv), Cro.
68/D4 **Cetinje**, Mont.
64/D2 **Ceurda del Pozo** (res.), Sp.
64/C5 **Ceuta**, Sp.
62/E5 **Cévennes** (mts.), Fr.
62/E4 **Cévennes Nat'l Park**, Fr.
80/C3 **Ceyhan**, Turk.
80/E3 **Ceylânpınar**, Turk.
90/D6 **Ceylon** (isl.), SrL.
62/F4 **Cèze** (riv.), Fr.
118/E2 **Chacabuco**, Arg.
114/C5 **Chachapoyas**, Peru
89/C3 **Chachoengsao**, Thai.
130/F3 **Chaco** (dry riv.), NM,US
134/B3 **Chaco** (mesa), NM,US
117/D2 **Chaco Austral** (plain), Arg.
114/G8 **Chaco Boreal** (plain), Par.
117/D1 **Chaco Central** (plain), Arg.
117/E2 **Chaco Nat'l Park**, Arg.
122/D4 **Chacujal** (ruins), Guat.
103/J4 **Chad** (ctry.)
102/H5 **Chad** (lake), Afr.
89/E4 **Cha Da** (cape), Viet.
53/E3 **Chadlington**, Eng,UK
131/G2 **Chadron**, Ne,US
69/J2 **Chadyr-Lunga**, Mol.
86/D2 **Chagang-Do** (prov.), NKor.
81/D5 **Chagdo Kangri** (peak), China
77/G10 **Chagos** (arch.), BrIn.
79/H3 **Chāh Behār** (Bandar Beheshtī), Iran
122/C4 **Chahuites**, Mex.
89/C3 **Chainat**, Thai.
89/C3 **Chaiyaphum**, Thai.
90/C5 **Chālakudi**, India
122/D5 **Chalatenango**, ESal.
107/C2 **Chalbi** (des.), Kenya
83/H2 **Chalchyn** (riv.), Mong.
133/H2 **Chaleur** (bay), NB, Qu,Can.
53/F3 **Chalfont Saint Peter**, Eng,UK
53/E3 **Chalgrove**, Eng,UK
134/C4 **Chalk** (mts.), Tx,US
62/C3 **Challans**, Fr.
125/T6 **Challenger** (mts.), Nun,Can.
59/D5 **Challerange**, Fr.
128/E4 **Challis**, Id,US
53/G4 **Challock**, Eng,UK
58/D6 **Châlons-sur-Marne**, Fr.
60/A4 **Chalon-sur-Saône**, Fr.
78/F1 **Chālūs**, Iran
63/K2 **Cham**, Ger.
130/F3 **Chama** (riv.), Co, NM,US
92/B2 **Chamah** (peak), Malay.
79/J2 **Chaman**, Pak.
79/L2 **Chamba**, India
90/C2 **Chambal** (riv.), India
62/F4 **Chambaran** (plat.), Fr.
133/G2 **Chamberlain** (lake), Me,US
129/J5 **Chamberlain**, SD,US
136/K2 **Chamberlin** (mtn.), Ak,US
132/E4 **Chambersburg**, Pa,US
62/F4 **Chambéry**, Fr.
107/A5 **Chambeshi** (riv.), Zam.
133/P7 **Chambly**, Qu,Can.
58/B5 **Chambly**, Fr.
80/F3 **Chamchamāl**, Iraq
62/F4 **Chamechaude** (mtn.), Fr.
117/C3 **Chamical**, Arg.
63/G4 **Chamonix-Mont-Blanc**, Fr.
136/L3 **Champagne**, Yk,Can.
58/C6 **Champagne** (reg.), Fr.
62/F2 **Champagne-Ardennes** (reg.), Fr.
58/B5 **Champagne-sur-Oise**, Fr.
132/B3 **Champaign**, Il,US
118/D1 **Champaqui** (peak), Arg.
59/F6 **Champigneulles**, Fr.
132/F2 **Champlain** (lake), Can., US
122/C4 **Champotón**, Mex.
58/B6 **Champs-sur-Marne**, Fr.
117/B2 **Chañaral**, Chile
64/B4 **Chança** (riv.), Port.
114/C5 **Chan Chan** (ruins), Peru
118/B2 **Chanco**, Chile
136/J2 **Chandalar** (riv.), Ak,US
90/C2 **Chandausi**, India
90/C3 **Chanderi**, India
79/L2 **Chandigarh**, India
133/H1 **Chandler**, Qu,Can.
136/H2 **Chandler** (riv.), Ak,US
134/D3 **Chandler**, Ok,US
90/C4 **Chandrapur**, India
87/C5 **Chang** (lake), China
87/L8 **Chang** (riv.), China
89/C3 **Chang** (isl.), Thai.
83/K3 **Changbai** (peak), China
86/D2 **Changbai** (mts.), China, NKor.
87/F2 **Changchun**, China
87/D5 **Changdang** (lake), China
88/B2 **Changde**, China
83/K4 **Changgi-ap** (cape), SKor.
88/D3 **Changhua**, Tai.
86/D5 **Changhŭng**, SKor.
87/D3 **Changji**, China
87/D2 **Changping**, China
86/C3 **Changsan-got** (cape), NKor.
88/B2 **Changsha**, China
87/E5 **Changshu**, China
91/J2 **Changshun**, China
86/D5 **Changsŏng**, SKor.
122/E6 **Changuinola**, Pan.
86/E5 **Ch'angwŏn**, SKor.
87/E3 **Changxing** (isl.), China
87/D5 **Chang (Yangtze)** (riv.), China
87/C3 **Changzhi**, China
87/D5 **Changzhou**, China
89/E2 **Chan May Dong** (cape), Viet.
53/H4 **Channel** (tunnel), Fr., UK
130/C4 **Channel** (isls.), Ca,US
96/A4 **Channel Country** (plain), Austl.
62/B2 **Channel Islands**, UK
130/B4 **Channel Islands Nat'l Park**, Ca,US
133/K2 **Channel-Port aux Basques**, Nf,Can.
64/B1 **Chantada**, Sp.
89/C3 **Chanthaburi**, Thai.
58/B5 **Chantilly**, Fr.
124/G2 **Chantrey** (inlet), Nun,Can.
131/J3 **Chanute**, Ks,US
87/D5 **Chao** (lake), China
83/H4 **Chaobai** (riv.), China
89/C3 **Chao Phraya** (riv.), Thai.
83/J2 **Chaor** (riv.), China
88/C3 **Chaoyang**, China
88/C3 **Chaozhou**, China
115/K6 **Chapada Diamantina Nat'l Park**, Braz.
115/J6 **Chapada dos Veadeiros Nat'l Park**, Braz.
132/F1 **Chapais**, Qu,Can.
123/P9 **Chapala** (lake), Mex.
73/J1 **Chapayevsk**, Rus.
116/A3 **Chapecó**, Braz.
51/G5 **Chapel en le Frith**, Eng,UK
51/F2 **Chapelfell Top** (mtn.), Eng,UK
135/J3 **Chapel Hill**, NC,US
58/D3 **Chapelle-Lez-Herlaimont**, Belg.
51/J5 **Chapel Saint Leonards**, Eng,UK
51/G5 **Chapeltown**, Eng,UK
138/D2 **Chaplain** (lake), Wa,US
89/D2 **Chap Le**, Viet.
132/D2 **Chapleau**, On,Can.
128/G3 **Chaplin**, Sk,Can.
131/G2 **Chappell**, Ne,US
75/M4 **Chara** (riv.), Rus.
114/C3 **Charambirá** (pt.), Col.
67/L6 **Charandra** (riv.), Gre.
117/D2 **Charata**, Arg.
122/A3 **Charcas**, Mex.
111/U **Charcot** (isl.), Ant.
52/D5 **Chard**, Eng,UK
74/G6 **Chardzhou**, Trkm.
62/C4 **Charente** (riv.), Fr.
102/J5 **Chari** (riv.), Chad
79/J1 **Chārīkār**, Afg.
53/G4 **Charing**, Eng,UK
131/J2 **Chariton** (riv.), Ia, Mo,US
53/E3 **Charlbury**, Eng,UK
50/B3 **Charlemont**, NI,UK
58/D3 **Charleroi**, Belg.
58/D2 **Charleroi à Bruxelles, Canal de** (can.), Belg.
125/J2 **Charles** (isl.), Nun,Can.
132/F4 **Charles** (cape), Va,US
129/K5 **Charles City**, Ia,US
132/B4 **Charleston**, Il,US
131/K3 **Charleston**, Mo,US
135/F3 **Charleston**, Ms,US
130/D2 **Charleston**, Nv,US
135/J3 **Charleston**, SC,US
132/D4 **Charleston** (cap.), WV,US
59/D4 **Charleville-Mézières**, Fr.
132/C2 **Charlevoix**, Mi,US
128/B2 **Charlotte** (lake), BC,Can.
132/C3 **Charlotte**, Mi,US
135/H3 **Charlotte**, NC,US
123/J4 **Charlotte Amalie** (cap.), USVI
132/E4 **Charlottesville**, Va,US
133/J2 **Charlottetown** (cap.), PE,Can.
123/J5 **Charlotteville**, Trin.
125/H3 **Charlton** (isl.), Nun,Can.
52/D3 **Charlton Kings**, Eng,UK
62/F3 **Charolais** (mts.), Fr.
81/D2 **Charsk**, Kaz.
96/B3 **Charters Towers**, Austl.
62/D2 **Chartres**, Fr.
81/D1 **Charysh** (riv.), Rus.
118/F2 **Chascomús**, Arg.
128/D3 **Chase**, BC,Can.
62/F4 **Chassezac** (riv.), Fr.
62/C3 **Chassiron, Pointe de** (pt.), Fr.
62/C3 **Châteaubriant**, Fr.
62/C3 **Château-d'Olonne**, Fr.
62/D2 **Châteaudun**, Fr.
133/N7 **Châteauguay**, Qu,Can.
62/F5 **Châteaurenard-Provence**, Fr.
62/D3 **Château-Renault**, Fr.
62/D3 **Châteauroux**, Fr.
58/C5 **Château-Thierry**, Fr.
58/D3 **Châtelet**, Belg.
62/D3 **Châtellerault**, Fr.
131/J2 **Chatfield**, Mn,US
132/D3 **Chatham**, On,Can.
119/J7 **Chatham** (isl.), Chile
53/G4 **Chatham**, Eng,UK
137/F5 **Chatham**, NJ,US
62/F3 **Châtillon-sur-Seine**, Fr.
90/D4 **Chatrapur**, India
96/H8 **Chatswood**, Austl.
137/B2 **Chatsworth** (res.), Ca,US
135/G3 **Chatsworth**, Ga,US
135/G4 **Chattahoochee**, Fl,US
135/G4 **Chattahoochee** (riv.), Fl, Ga,US
135/G3 **Chattanooga**, Tn,US
53/G2 **Chatteris**, Eng,UK
62/C2 **Chaucey** (isls.), Fr.
59/E2 **Chaudfontaine**, Belg.
133/G2 **Chaudière** (riv.), Qu,Can.
89/D4 **Chau Doc**, Viet.
91/F3 **Chauk**, Myan.
91/G2 **Chaukan** (pass), India
58/B4 **Chaulnes**, Fr.
60/B1 **Chaumont**, Fr.
58/A5 **Chaumont-en-Vexin**, Fr.
58/D4 **Chaumont-Porcien**, Fr.
75/T3 **Chaunskaya** (bay), Rus.
58/C4 **Chauny**, Fr.
132/E3 **Chautauqua** (lake), NY,US
62/D3 **Chauvigny**, Fr.
64/B2 **Chaves**, Port.
89/D1 **Chay** (riv.), Viet.
114/E7 **Chayana** (riv.), Bol.
71/M4 **Chaykovskiy**, Rus.
51/G6 **Cheadle**, Eng,UK
135/G3 **Cheaha** (peak), Al,US
54/G3 **Cheb**, Czh.
71/K4 **Cheboksary**, Rus.
71/K4 **Cheboksary** (res.), Rus.
132/C2 **Cheboygan**, Mi,US
73/H4 **Chechen'** (isl.), Rus.
73/H4 **Chechnya, Resp.**, Rus.
102/D3 **Chech, 'Erg** (des.), Afr.
86/E4 **Chech'ŏn**, SKor.
131/J4 **Checotah**, Ok,US
133/J2 **Chedabucto** (bay), NS,Can.
52/D4 **Cheddar**, Eng,UK
91/F4 **Cheduba** (isl.), Myan.
133/S10 **Cheektowaga**, NY,US
132/D1 **Cheepash** (riv.), On,Can.
132/D1 **Cheepay** (riv.), On,Can.
83/L1 **Chegdomyn**, Rus.
110/F4 **Chegutu**, Zim.
128/C4 **Chehalis**, Wa,US
63/G5 **Cheiron, Cime du** (peak), Fr.
83/K5 **Cheju**, SKor.
83/K5 **Cheju** (isl.), SKor.
83/K5 **Cheju** (str.), SKor.
128/C4 **Chelan**, Wa,US
128/C4 **Chelan** (lake), Wa,US
51/F5 **Chelford**, Eng,UK
55/M3 **Chełm**, Pol.
53/G3 **Chelmer** (riv.), Eng,UK
55/K2 **Chełmno**, Pol.
53/G3 **Chelmsford**, Eng,UK
55/K2 **Chełmża**, Pol.
97/G6 **Chelsea**, Austl.
133/Q8 **Cheltenham**, On,Can.
52/D3 **Cheltenham**, Eng,UK
71/P5 **Chelyabinsk**, Rus.
71/P5 **Chelyabinskaya Obl.**, Rus.
75/L2 **Chelyuskina** (cape), Rus.
107/A5 **Chembe**, Zam.
54/G3 **Chemnitz**, Ger.
88/A2 **Chen** (riv.), China
79/K2 **Chenāb** (riv.), India, Pak.
102/E2 **Chenachane** (well), Alg.
128/D4 **Cheney**, Wa,US
87/C3 **Cheng'anpu**, China
87/D2 **Chengde**, China
82/E5 **Chengdu**, China
87/E3 **Chengshan Jiao** (cape), China
90/D5 **Chennai** (Madras), India
60/A3 **Chenôve**, Fr.
88/B2 **Chenzhou**, China
69/G5 **Chepelare**, Bul.
99/V12 **Chépénéhé**, NCal.
118/C2 **Chépica**, Chile
123/F6 **Chepigana**, Pan.
52/D3 **Chepstow**, Wal,UK
71/M4 **Cheptsa** (riv.), Rus.
62/D3 **Cher** (riv.), Fr.
135/J3 **Cheraw**, SC,US
62/C2 **Cherbourg**, Fr.
102/F1 **Cherchell**, Alg.
82/E1 **Cheremkhovo**, Rus.
70/H4 **Cherepovets**, Rus.
72/D2 **Cherkas'ka Obl.**, Ukr.
72/E2 **Cherkasy**, Ukr.
73/G3 **Cherkessk**, Rus.
96/E6 **Chermside**, Austl.
71/M2 **Chernaya** (riv.), Rus.
72/D2 **Chernihiv**, Ukr.
72/D2 **Chernihivs'ka Obl.**, Ukr.
69/H4 **Cherni Lom** (riv.), Bul.
69/F4 **Cherni Vrŭkh** (peak), Bul.
72/C2 **Chernivtsi**, Ukr.
72/C2 **Chernivets'ka Obl.**, Ukr.
71/N4 **Chernushka**, Rus.
82/H1 **Chernyshevsk**, Rus.
131/H3 **Cherokee**, Ok,US
134/E2 **Cherokees** (lake), Ok,US
130/D3 **Cherry Creek**, Nv,US
137/E6 **Cherry Hill**, NJ,US
137/D3 **Cherry Valley**, Ca,US
75/P3 **Cherskiy** (range), Rus.
53/F4 **Chertsey**, Eng,UK
69/G4 **Cherven Bryag**, Bul.
72/C2 **Chervonograd**, Ukr.
53/E3 **Cherwell** (riv.), Eng,UK
132/C3 **Chesaning**, Mi,US
132/E4 **Chesapeake** (bay), Md, Va,US
53/F3 **Chesham**, Eng,UK
51/F5 **Cheshire** (co.), Eng,UK
51/F5 **Cheshire** (plain), Eng,UK
71/K2 **Cheshskaya** (bay), Rus.
53/F3 **Cheshunt**, Eng,UK
51/F5 **Chester**, Eng,UK
130/B2 **Chester**, Ca,US
128/F3 **Chester**, Mt,US
137/F5 **Chester**, NJ,US
137/E6 **Chester**, Pa,US
135/H3 **Chester**, SC,US
124/G2 **Chesterfield** (inlet), Nun,Can.
98/E7 **Chesterfield** (isls.), NCal.
51/G5 **Chesterfield**, Eng,UK
109/H7 **Chesterfield, Nosy** (isl.), Madg.
51/G2 **Chester-le-Street**, Eng,UK
96/B3 **Chesterton** (range), Austl.
133/G2 **Chesuncook** (lake), Me,US
122/D4 **Chetumal** (bay), Belz., Mex.
122/D4 **Chetumal**, Mex.
128/C2 **Chetwynd**, BC,Can.
52/D4 **Chew** (riv.), Eng,UK
128/D3 **Chewelah**, Wa,US
52/D4 **Chew Valley** (lake), Eng,UK
131/H4 **Cheyenne**, Ok,US
129/H4 **Cheyenne** (riv.), SD, Wy,US
129/G5 **Cheyenne** (cap.), Wy,US
131/G3 **Cheyenne Wells**, Co,US
90/C3 **Chhatarpur**, India
90/D3 **Chhattisgarh** (state), India
90/C3 **Chhindwāra**, India
89/D3 **Chhlong**, Camb.
87/D4 **Chi** (riv.), China
89/C2 **Chi** (riv.), Thai.
89/B2 **Chiang Dao** (caves), Thai.
89/B2 **Chiang Mai**, Thai.
89/B2 **Chiang Rai**, Thai.
66/C1 **Chiani** (riv.), It.
122/C4 **Chiapas** (state), Mex.
73/G4 **Chiatura**, Geo.
63/H4 **Chiavari**, It.
61/F5 **Chiavenna**, It.
88/D3 **Chiayi**, Tai.
85/G3 **Chiba**, Japan
85/G3 **Chiba** (pref.), Japan
132/F1 **Chibougamau**, Qu,Can.
132/F1 **Chibougamau** (lake), Qu,Can.
132/F1 **Chibougamau** (riv.), Qu,Can.
136/D3 **Chibukak** (pt.), Ak,US
109/F2 **Chibuto**, Moz.
138/Q16 **Chicago**, Il,US
138/Q16 **Chicago Heights**, Il,US
138/Q16 **Chicago Ridge**, Il,US
136/L4 **Chichagof** (isl.), Ak,US
79/K2 **Chīchāwatni**, Pak.
122/D3 **Chichén Itzá** (ruins), Mex.
53/F5 **Chichester**, Eng,UK
85/F3 **Chichibu**, Japan
85/F3 **Chichibu-Tama Nat'l Park**, Japan
122/D5 **Chichigalpa**, Nic.
98/D2 **Chichishima** (isls.), Japan
135/G3 **Chickamauga** (lake), Tn,US
131/H4 **Chickasha**, Ok,US
52/D5 **Chickerell**, Eng,UK
64/B4 **Chiclana de la Frontera**, Sp.
114/C5 **Chiclayo**, Peru
118/C4 **Chico** (riv.), Arg.
118/D5 **Chico** (riv.), Arg.
130/B3 **Chico**, Ca,US
133/F3 **Chicopee**, Ma,US
110/D4 **Chicote**, Ang.
133/G1 **Chicoutimi**, Qu,Can.
125/K2 **Chidley** (cape), Nf,Can.
135/H4 **Chiefland**, Fl,US
89/D1 **Chiem Hoa**, Viet.
63/K3 **Chiemsee** (lake), Ger.
66/C1 **Chienti** (riv.), It.
89/B4 **Chieo Lan** (res.), Thai.
59/E5 **Chiers** (riv.), Fr.
61/G6 **Chiese** (riv.), It.
66/D1 **Chieti**, It.
53/E4 **Chieveley**, Eng,UK
83/H3 **Chifeng**, China
117/K7 **Chifre** (mts.), Braz.
85/F3 **Chigasaki**, Japan
136/G4 **Chiginagak** (mtn.), Ak,US
133/H2 **Chignecto** (bay), NB,Can.
53/G3 **Chigwell**, Eng,UK
85/L10 **Chihayaakasaka**, Japan
87/D3 **Chihli** (Bo Hai) (gulf), China
123/N8 **Chihuahua**, Mex.
123/N8 **Chihuahua** (state), Mex.
131/H3 **Chikaskia** (riv.), Ks,US
90/C5 **Chikballāpur**, India
90/C3 **Chikhli**, India
90/C5 **Chikmagalūr**, India
82/G1 **Chikoy** (riv.), Rus.
84/B4 **Chikugo** (riv.), Japan
85/F2 **Chikuma** (riv.), Japan
85/H8 **Chikura**, Japan
90/D4 **Chilakalūrupet**, India
122/B4 **Chilapa**, Mex.
90/C6 **Chilaw**, SrL.
128/C3 **Chilcotin** (riv.), BC,Can.
135/G3 **Childersburg**, Al,US
134/C3 **Childress**, Tx,US
113/B6 **Chile** (ctry.)
122/D5 **Chile** (mt.), Hon.
117/C2 **Chilecito**, Arg.
110/E3 **Chililabombwe**, Zam.
90/E4 **Chilka** (lake), India
128/C3 **Chilko** (lake), BC,Can.
136/L4 **Chilkoot** (pass), BC,Can., Ak,US
118/B3 **Chillán**, Chile
132/B3 **Chillicothe**, Il,US
131/J3 **Chillicothe**, Mo,US
132/D4 **Chillicothe**, Oh,US
128/C3 **Chilliwack**, BC,Can.
118/B4 **Chiloé** (isl.), Chile
118/B4 **Chiloé Nat'l Park**, Chile
128/C5 **Chiloquin**, Or,US
122/B4 **Chilpancingo**, Mex.
53/F3 **Chiltern** (hills), Eng,UK
110/G4 **Chilwa** (lake), Malw.
123/F6 **Chimán**, Pan.
58/D3 **Chimay**, Belg.
74/F5 **Chimbay**, Uzb.
114/C4 **Chimborazo** (vol.), Ecu.
114/C5 **Chimbote**, Peru
123/N7 **Chimney** (peak), NM,US
91/F3 **Chin** (state), Myan.
86/D5 **Chin** (isl.), SKor.
77/J6 **China** (ctry.)
122/D5 **Chinandega**, Nic.
134/B4 **Chinati** (mts.), Tx,US
123/P8 **Chinati** (peak), Tx.,US
114/C6 **Chincha Alta**, Peru
124/E3 **Chinchaga** (riv.), Ab,Can.
132/F4 **Chincoteague**, Va,US
91/F3 **Chindwin** (riv.), Myan.
114/D3 **Chingaza Nat'l Park**, Col.
90/C5 **Chingleput**, India
110/E3 **Chingola**, Zam.
104/B1 **Chinguetti, Dhar de** (hills), Mrta.
86/E5 **Chinhae**, SKor.
110/F4 **Chinhoyi**, Zim.
136/H4 **Chiniak** (cape), Ak,US
79/K2 **Chiniot**, Pak.
89/D3 **Chinit** (riv.), Camb.
103/K6 **Chinko** (riv.), CAfr.
130/E3 **Chinle** (dry riv.), Az, Ut,US
53/F3 **Chinnor**, Eng,UK
85/F3 **Chino**, Japan
137/C2 **Chino**, Ca,US
128/F3 **Chinook**, Mt,US
123/F6 **Chinú**, Col.
110/F3 **Chipata**, Zam.
87/D3 **Chiping**, China
64/B4 **Chipiona**, Sp.
135/G4 **Chipley**, Fl,US
90/B4 **Chiplūn**, India
135/G4 **Chipola** (riv.), Fl,US
52/D4 **Chippenham**, Eng,UK
129/K4 **Chippewa** (riv.), Mn,US
132/B2 **Chippewa** (riv.), Wi,US
132/B2 **Chippewa Falls**, Wi,US
53/E2 **Chipping Campden**, Eng,UK
53/E3 **Chipping Norton**, Eng,UK
53/G3 **Chipping Ongar**, Eng,UK
52/D3 **Chipping Sodbury**, Eng,UK
133/H2 **Chiputneticook** (lakes), NB,Can., Me,US
122/D5 **Chiquimula**, Guat.
114/D2 **Chiquinquirá**, Col.
117/D3 **Chiquita, Mar** (lake), Arg.
90/D4 **Chīrāla**, India
81/A3 **Chirchik**, Uzb.
102/H3 **Chirfa**, Niger
123/N7 **Chiricahua** (peak), Az.,US
130/E4 **Chiricahua Nat'l Mon.**, Az,US
136/G4 **Chirikof** (isl.), Ak,US
122/E6 **Chiriquí** (gulf), Pan.
51/E6 **Chirk**, Eng,UK
49/D3 **Chirnside**, Sc,UK
69/G4 **Chirpan**, Bul.
122/E6 **Chirripó Grande** (mt.), CR
122/E6 **Chirripó Nat'l Park**, CR
85/N10 **Chiryu**, Japan
125/J3 **Chisasibi** (Fort-George), Qu,Can.
122/C4 **Chisec**, Guat.
53/E3 **Chiseldon**, Eng,UK
132/A2 **Chisholm**, Mn,US
79/K3 **Chishtiān Mandi**, Pak.
103/P8 **Chisimayu**, Som.
69/J2 **Chişinău** (cap.), Mol.
68/E2 **Chişineu Criş**, Rom.
71/L5 **Chistopol'**, Rus.
53/F3 **Chiswell Green**, Eng,UK
85/M10 **Chita**, Japan
85/M10 **Chita** (bay), Japan
85/M10 **Chita** (pen.), Japan
82/G1 **Chita**, Rus.
110/B4 **Chitado**, Ang.
75/M4 **Chitinskaya Obl.**, Rus.
107/B5 **Chitipa**, Malw.
90/B3 **Chitorgarh**, India
83/N3 **Chitose**, Japan
90/C5 **Chitradurga**, India
90/D2 **Chitrakut**, India
123/E6 **Chitré**, Pan.
91/F3 **Chittagong**, Bang.
90/C5 **Chittoor**, India
110/D4 **Chiume**, Ang.
63/G4 **Chivasso**, It.
123/M8 **Chivato** (pt.), Mex.
118/E2 **Chivilcoy**, Arg.
89/D3 **Choam Khsant**, Camb.
118/C1 **Choapa** (riv.), Chile
110/D4 **Chobe Nat'l Park**, Bots.
55/J4 **Choceń**, Czh.
55/H3 **Chocianów**, Pol.
130/D4 **Chocolate** (mts.), Ca,US

Chodo – Cosla
157

63/K1 Chodov, Czh.
55/J2 Chodzież, Pol.
85/F3 Chōfu, Japan
85/H7 Chōfū, Japan
98/E5 Choiseul (isl.), Sol.
58/B6 Choisy-le-Roi, Fr.
55/H2 Chojna, Pol.
55/J2 Chojnice, Pol.
55/H3 Chojnów, Pol.
83/N4 Chokai-san (mtn.), Japan
134/D4 Choke Canyon (res.), Tx,US
82/D5 Chola (mts.), China
62/C3 Cholet, Fr.
86/D5 Chŏlla-Bukto (prov.), SKor.
86/D5 Chŏlla-Namdo (prov.), SKor.
53/E3 Cholsey, Eng,UK
122/D5 Choluteca (riv.)
122/D5 Choluteca, Hon.
110/E4 Choma, Zam.
86/E4 Chŏmch'on, SKor.
90/E2 Chomo Lhāri (mtn.), Bhu.
55/G3 Chomutov, Czh.
85/J7 Chōnan, Japan
86/D4 Ch'ŏnan, SKor.
89/C3 Chon Buri, Thai.
118/B4 Chonchi, Chile
114/B4 Chone, Ecu.
86/E2 Ch'ŏngjin, NKor.
86/E2 Ch'ŏngjin-Si (prov.), NKor.
86/D4 Ch'ŏngju, SKor.
89/C3 Chong Kal, Camb.
87/L8 Chongming (isl.), China
88/A2 Chongqing, China
86/E4 Ch'ŏngsong, SKor.
86/D5 Chŏnju, SKor.
118/A5 Chonos (arch.), Chile
89/D4 Chon Thanh, Viet.
51/F4 Chorley, Eng,UK
53/F3 Chorleywood, Eng,UK
72/C2 Chortkov, Ukr.
55/K3 Chorzów, Pol.
85/G3 Chōshi, Japan
55/H2 Choszczno, Pol.
114/C5 Chota, Peru
128/E4 Choteau, Mt,US
108/A2 Chowagasberg (peak), Namb.
135/J2 Chowan (riv.), NC,US
82/G2 Choybalsan, Mong.
95/H7 Christchurch, NZ
53/E5 Christchurch, Eng,UK
53/E5 Christchurch (bay), Eng,UK
136/L4 Christian (sound), Ak,US
108/D2 Christiana, SAfr.
132/D4 Christiansburg, Va,US
128/F2 Christine (riv.), Ab,Can.
77/K11 Christmas (isl.), Austl.
99/K4 Christmas (Kiritimati) (atoll), Kiri.
55/H4 Chrudim, Czh.
55/K3 Chrzanów, Pol.
89/D2 Chu (riv.), Viet.
87/E4 Chuanchang (riv.), China
128/E5 Chubbuck, Id,US
85/F2 Chūbu (prov.), Japan
118/C4 Chubut (prov.), Arg.
118/D4 Chubut (riv.), Arg.
123/F6 Chucanti (mt.), Pan.
84/C4 Chūgoku (mts.), Japan
84/C3 Chūgoku (prov.), Japan
92/B3 Chukai, Malay.
83/M1 Chukchagirskoye (lake), Rus.
75/U3 Chukchi (pen.), Rus.
75/S3 Chukotskiy Aut. Okr., Rus.
136/D3 Chukotskiy, Mys (pt.), Rus.
130/C4 Chula Vista, Ca,US
114/B5 Chulucanas, Peru
74/J4 Chulym (riv.), Rus.
81/E1 Chulyshman (riv.), Rus.
69/G4 Chumerna (peak), Bul.
89/B4 Chumphon, Thai.
74/K4 Chuna (riv.), Rus.
86/D4 Ch'unch'ŏn, SKor.
86/D4 Ch'ungch'ŏng-Bukto (prov.), SKor.
86/D4 Ch'ungch'ŏng-Namdo (prov.), SKor.
86/D4 Ch'ungju, SKor.
86/E5 Ch'ungmu, SKor.
75/L3 Chunya (riv.), Rus.
117/C1 Chuquicamata, Chile
61/F4 Chur, Swi.
91/F3 Churachandpur, India
51/F4 Church, Eng,UK
124/D3 Churchill (peak), BC,Can.
124/G3 Churchill, Mb,Can.
124/G3 Churchill (cape), Mb,Can.
124/G3 Churchill (riv.), Mb, Sk,Can.
125/K3 Churchill (riv.), Nf,Can.
128/F1 Churchill (lake), Sk,Can.
124/G3 Churchill (riv.), Mb, Sk,Can
97/G5 Churchill Nat'l Park, Austl.
52/D1 Church Stretton, Eng,UK
51/G6 Churnet (riv.), Eng,UK
90/B2 Churu, India
123/H5 Churuguara, Ven.
130/E3 Chuska (mts.), Az, NM,US
71/N4 Chusovaya (riv.), Rus.
71/N4 Chusovoy, Rus.
71/K5 Chuvashiya, Resp., Rus.
86/E4 Chuwang-san Nat'l Park, SKor.
91/H2 Chuxiong, China
82/B1 Chuya (riv.), Rus.
89/E3 Chu Yang Sin (peak), Viet.
85/M9 Chūzu, Japan
92/C5 Ciamis, Indo.
66/C2 Ciampino, It.
92/C5 Cianjur, Indo.
138/Q16 Cicero, Il,US
115/L6 Cícero Dantas, Braz.
66/C2 Cicero Nat'l Park, It.
80/C2 Cide, Turk.
55/L2 Ciechanów, Pol.
55/K2 Ciechocinek, Pol.
123/F3 Ciego de Avilla, Cuba
123/G5 Ciénaga, Col.
123/E3 Cienfuegos, Cuba
55/H3 Cieplice Śląskie Zdrój, Pol.
55/K4 Cieszyn, Pol.
64/E3 Cieza, Sp.
80/B2 Çifteler, Turk.
64/D3 Cigüela (riv.), Sp.
80/C2 Cihanbeyli, Turk.
123/P10 Cihuatlán, Mex.
64/C3 Cijara (res.), Sp.
92/C5 Cijulang, Indo.
92/C5 Cilacap, Indo.
52/C2 Cilfaesty (hill), Wal,UK
131/G3 Cimarron, Ks,US
131/H3 Cimarron (riv.), Ks, Ok,US
134/B2 Cimarron (range), NM,US
68/F2 Cîmpeni, Rom.
69/F2 Cîmpia Turzii, Rom.
69/G3 Cîmpina, Rom.
69/G3 Cîmpulung, Rom.
69/G2 Cîmpulung Moldovenesc, Rom.
65/F1 Cinca (riv.), Sp.
68/C4 Cincar (peak), Bosn.
132/C4 Cincinnati, Oh,US
118/C3 Cinco Saltos, Arg.
52/D3 Cinderford, Eng,UK
69/G3 Cîndrelu (peak), Rom.
80/B3 Çine, Turk.
59/E3 Ciney, Belg.
137/F6 Cinnaminson, NJ,US
122/C4 Cintalapa, Mex.
66/A1 Cinto (mtn.), Fr.
68/C4 Čiovo (isl.), Cro.
118/D3 Cipolletti, Arg.
129/G4 Circle, Mt,US
132/D4 Circleville, Oh,US
92/C5 Cirebon, Indo.
52/E3 Cirencester, Eng,UK
66/E3 Cirò Marina, It.
62/C4 Ciron (riv.), Fr.
69/G3 Cisnădie, Rom.
118/B5 Cisnes (riv.), Chile
62/D3 Cisse (riv.), Fr.
66/C2 Cisterna di Latina, It.
122/B4 Citlaltépetl (mt.), Mex.
138/M9 Citrus Heights, Ca,US
63/K5 Città di Castello, It.
66/E3 Cittanova, It.
122/A2 Ciudad Acuna, Mex.
123/J6 Ciudad Bolívar, Ven.
123/N8 Ciudad Camargo, Mex.
122/C4 Ciudad del Carmen, Mex.
123/N8 Ciudad Delicias, Mex.
123/P9 Ciudad de Río Grande, Mex.
65/G3 Ciudadela, Sp.
123/J6 Ciudad Guayana, Ven.
123/N8 Ciudad Guerrero, Mex.
123/P10 Ciudad Guzmán, Mex.
123/N7 Ciudad Juárez, Mex.
123/P8 Ciudad Lerdo, Mex.
122/B3 Ciudad Madero, Mex.
122/B3 Ciudad Mante, Mex.
122/B2 Ciudad Miguel Alemán, Mex.
123/N8 Ciudad Obregón, Mex.
123/G5 Ciudad Ojeda, Ven.
64/D3 Ciudad Real, Sp.
122/B2 Ciudad Río Bravo, Mex.
64/B2 Ciudad-Rodrigo, Sp.
122/B3 Ciudad Valles, Mex.
122/B3 Ciudad Victoria, Mex.
72/F4 Civa Burnu (pt.), Turk.
63/K3 Cividale del Friuli, It.
66/C1 Civita Castellana, It.
66/B1 Civitavecchia, It.
80/B2 Çivril, Turk.
87/C3 Ci Xian, China
80/E3 Cizre, Turk.
64/E1 Cizur, Sp.
53/H3 Clacton on Sea, Eng,UK
52/C2 Claerwen (res.), Wal,UK
62/D3 Clain (riv.), Fr.
124/E3 Claire (lake), Ab,Can.
130/B2 Clair Engle (lake), Ca,US
62/D3 Claise (riv.), Fr.
53/F5 Clanfield, Eng,UK
135/G3 Clanton, Al,US
133/Q9 Clappison's Corners, On,Can.
118/D4 Clara (pt.), Arg.
49/A4 Clare (riv.), Ire.
132/C3 Clare, Mi,US
137/C2 Claremont, Ca,US
133/F3 Claremont, NH,US
131/J3 Claremore, Ok,US
97/E1 Clarence (riv.), Austl.
125/T7 Clarence (pt.), Nun,Can.
133/S9 Clarence, NY,US
123/G3 Clarence Town, Bahm.
134/C3 Clarendon, Tx,US
128/E3 Claresholm, BC,Can.
111/J Clarie (coast), Ant.
129/J4 Clark, SD,US
97/D4 Clarke (isl.), Austl.
96/B3 Clarke (range), Austl.
128/E3 Clark Fork (riv.), Id, Mt,US
135/H3 Clark Hill (lake), Ga, SC,US
132/D4 Clarksburg, WV,US
135/F3 Clarksdale, Ms,US
133/Q8 Clarkson, On,Can.
138/F6 Clarkston, Mi,US
128/D4 Clarkston, Wa,US
134/E3 Clarksville, Ar,US
135/G2 Clarksville, Tn,US
134/E3 Clarksville, Tx,US
116/B1 Claro (riv.), Braz.
58/C3 Clary, Fr.
50/D1 Clatteringshaws Loch (lake), Sc,UK
50/A2 Claudy, NI,UK
57/H5 Clausthal-Zellerfeld, Ger.
88/D4 Claveria, Phil.
138/F6 Clawson, Mi,US
131/H3 Clay Center, Ks,US
51/G5 Clay Cross, Eng,UK
53/H2 Claydon, Eng,UK
50/D3 Clay Head (pt.), IM,UK
137/E6 Claymont, De,US
138/L11 Clayton, Ca,US
135/H3 Clayton, Ga,US
131/G3 Clayton, NM,US
131/J4 Clayton, Ok,US
51/F4 Clayton-le-Moors, Eng,UK
119/S11 Clé (stream), Arg.
124/E3 Clear (hills), Ab,Can.
49/H8 Clear (cape), Ire.
130/B3 Clear (lake), Ca,US
136/J4 Cleare (cape), Ak,US
129/J4 Clear Lake, SD,US
128/C3 Clearwater, BC,Can.
135/H5 Clearwater, Fl,US
128/D4 Clearwater (mts.), Id,US
129/K4 Clearwater (riv.), Mn,US
50/E2 Cleator Moor, Eng,UK
134/D3 Cleburne, Tx,US
51/H4 Cleethorpes, Eng,UK
52/D3 Cleeve (hill), Eng,UK
135/H3 Clemson, SC,US
52/D2 Cleobury Mortimer, Eng,UK
93/E1 Cleopatra Needle (mtn.), Phil.
58/A4 Clères, Fr.
59/E3 Clerf (riv.), Belg., Lux.
58/B5 Clermont, Fr.
52/D4 Clevedon, Eng,UK
96/B2 Cleveland (cape), Austl.
51/G3 Cleveland (hills), Eng,UK
135/F3 Cleveland, Ms,US
128/E3 Cleveland (peak), Mt,US
132/D3 Cleveland, Oh,US
135/G3 Cleveland, Tn,US
134/E4 Cleveland, Tx,US
116/A3 Clevelândia, Braz.
49/A4 Clew (bay), Ire.
135/H5 Clewiston, Fl,US
58/B6 Clichy, Fr.
52/D4 Clifton, Eng,UK
130/E4 Clifton, Az,US
137/F5 Clifton, NJ,US
134/D4 Clifton, Tx,US
135/J2 Clifton Forge, Va,US
52/D2 Clifton upon Teme, Eng,UK
58/C5 Clignon (riv.), Fr.
135/H3 Clingmans (mtn.), Tn,US
128/C3 Clinton, BC,Can.
129/L5 Clinton, Ia,US
132/B3 Clinton, Il,US
135/F4 Clinton, La,US
138/G6 Clinton, Mi,US
138/F6 Clinton (riv.), Mi,US
131/J3 Clinton, Mo,US
135/F3 Clinton, Ms,US
135/J3 Clinton, NC,US
137/F5 Clinton, NJ,US
137/F4 Clinton (res.), NJ,US
131/H4 Clinton, Ok,US
135/H3 Clinton, SC,US
124/F2 Clinton-Colden (lake), NW,Can.
124/B2 Clinton Creek, Yk,Can.
137/K8 Clinton (Surrattsville), Md,US
132/D3 Clio, Mi,US
44/D5 Clipperton (isl.), Fr.
53/F2 Clipston, Eng,UK
51/F4 Clitheroe, Eng,UK
50/B4 Clogherhead, Ire.
50/B4 Clogher Head (pt.), Ire.
50/C3 Cloghy, NI,UK
49/B4 Clonmel, Ire.
57/F3 Cloppenburg, Ger.
129/K4 Cloquet, Mn,US
117/E2 Clorinda, Arg.
50/E1 Closeburn, Sc,UK
128/G4 Cloud (peak), Wy,US
134/B3 Cloudcroft, NM,US
136/G3 Cloudy (mtn.), Ak,US
50/B2 Cloughmills, NI,UK
51/H3 Cloughton, Eng,UK
52/B4 Clovelly, Eng,UK
130/B3 Cloverdale, Ca,US
130/C3 Clovis, Ca,US
131/G4 Clovis, NM,US
49/C2 Clovullin, Sc,UK
51/G5 Clowne, Eng,UK
69/F2 Cluj (co.), Rom.
69/F2 Cluj-Napoca, Rom.
52/C2 Clun, Eng,UK
52/B3 Clunderwen, Wal,UK
60/C5 Cluses, Fr.
63/H4 Clusone, It.
51/E5 Clwyd (riv.), Wal,UK
51/E5 Clwydian (range), Wal,UK
52/C3 Clydach, Wal,UK
133/H2 Clyde (riv.), NS,Can.
128/E2 Clyde, Ab,Can.
49/C3 Clyde (riv.), Sc,UK
49/C3 Clyde, Firth of (inlet), Sc,UK
52/C2 Clywedog (riv.), Wal,UK
133/R8 CN Tower, On,Can.
64/B2 Côa (riv.), Port.
130/C4 Coachella, Ca,US
50/B2 Coagh, NI,UK
122/A2 Coahuila (state), Mex.
128/E3 Coaldale, Ab,Can.
131/H4 Coalgate, Ok,US
128/E3 Coalhurst, Ab,Can.
50/B2 Coalisland, NI,UK
53/E1 Coalville, Eng,UK
130/E2 Coalville, Ut,US
114/F4 Coari, Braz.
114/F5 Coari (riv.), Braz.
124/C2 Coast (mts.), BC, Yk,Can.
107/C3 Coast (prov.), Kenya
130/B3 Coast (ranges), Ca,US
135/H4 Coastal (plain), US
122/B4 Coatepec, Mex.
133/G2 Coaticook, Qu,Can.
125/H2 Coats (isl.), Nun,Can.
111/Y Coats Land (reg.), Ant.
122/C4 Coatzacoalcos, Mex.
122/D3 Coba (ruins), Mex.
122/C4 Cobán, Guat.
97/D3 Cobberas (peak), Austl.
137/B1 Cobblestone (mtn.), Ca,US
129/K2 Cobham (riv.), Mb, On,Can.
53/F4 Cobham, Eng,UK
95/C2 Cobourg (pen.), Austl.
132/E3 Cobourg, On,Can.
118/B3 Cobquecura, Chile
97/F5 Coburg, Austl.
125/T7 Coburg (isl.), Nun,Can.
63/J1 Coburg, Ger.
65/E3 Cocentaina, Sp.
114/E7 Cochabamba, Bol.
90/C6 Cochin, India
135/H3 Cochran, Ga,US
128/E3 Cochrane, Ab,Can.
132/D1 Cochrane, On,Can.
119/J8 Cockburn (chan.), Chile
49/D3 Cockburnspath, Sc,UK
51/E2 Cockermouth, Eng,UK
108/D4 Cockscomb (peak), SAfr.
114/A2 Coco (isl.), CR
122/E5 Coco (riv.), Hon.
135/H4 Cocoa, Fl,US
130/D4 Coconino (plat.), Az,US
97/C2 Cocoparra Nat'l Park, Austl.
77/J11 Cocos (Keeling) (isls.), Austl.
125/K3 Cod (isl.), Nf,Can.
51/G3 Cod Beck (riv.), Eng,UK
118/C2 Codegua, Chile
69/G3 Codlea, Rom.
115/K4 Codó, Braz.
63/H4 Codogno, It.
123/J4 Codrington, Anti.
63/K4 Codroipo, It.
52/D1 Codsall, Eng,UK
128/F4 Cody, Wy,US
115/K4 Coelho Neto, Braz.
57/E5 Coesfeld, Ger.
45/M6 Coetivy (isl.), Sey.
128/D4 Coeur d'Alene, Id,US
128/D4 Coeur d'Alene (lake), Id,US
56/D3 Coevorden, Neth.
131/J3 Coffeyville, Ks,US
97/E1 Coffs Harbour, Austl.
53/G3 Coggeshall, Eng,UK
66/A2 Coghinas (lake), It.
62/C4 Cognac, Fr.
122/E6 Coiba (isl.), Pan.
119/K7 Coig (riv.), Arg.
118/B5 Coihaique, Chile
118/C3 Coihueco, Chile
90/C5 Coimbatore, India
64/A2 Coimbra, Port.
64/A2 Coimbra (dist.), Port.
64/C4 Coín, Sp.
65/P10 Coina (riv.), Port.
62/F4 Coise (riv.), Fr.
114/E2 Cojedes (riv.), Ven.
123/G5 Cojoro, Ven.
118/C5 Cojudo Blanco (peak), Arg.
122/D5 Cojutepeque, ESal.
128/F5 Cokeville, Wy,US
97/B3 Colac, Austl.
131/H2 Colamus (riv.), Ne,US
65/P10 Colares, Port.
116/D1 Colatina, Braz.
111/P Colbeck (cape), Ant.
118/C2 Colbún, Chile
131/G3 Colby, Ks,US
53/G3 Colchester, Eng,UK
128/F2 Cold (lake), Ab, Sk,Can.
51/F2 Cold Fell (mtn.), Eng,UK
128/F2 Cold Lake, Ab,Can.
129/K4 Cold Spring, Mn,US
134/E4 Coldspring, Tx,US
131/H3 Coldwater, Ks,US
132/C3 Coldwater, Mi,US
53/E3 Cole (riv.), Eng,UK
52/D3 Coleford, Eng,UK
134/D4 Coleman, Tx,US
80/E3 Çölemerik, Turk.
50/B1 Coleraine, NI,UK
50/B1 Coleraine (dist.), NI,UK
108/D3 Colesberg, SAfr.
53/E2 Coleshill, Eng,UK
137/J7 Colesville, Md,US
128/D4 Colfax, Wa,US
125/S6 Colgate (cape), Nun,Can.
118/C5 Colhué Huapí (lake), Arg.
89/D2 Co Lieu, Viet.
123/P10 Colima, Mex.
123/P10 Colima (state), Mex.
118/C2 Colina, Chile
115/K5 Colinas, Braz.
64/D2 Collado-Villalba, Sp.
136/J3 College, Ak,US
137/K8 College Park, Md,US
134/D4 College Station, Tx,US
63/G4 Collegno, It.
97/D1 Collie, Austl.
51/G2 Collier Law (hill), Eng,UK
135/F3 Collierville, Tn,US
52/B6 Colliford (res.), Eng,UK
51/G4 Collingham, Eng,UK
132/D2 Collingwood, On,Can.
95/H7 Collingwood, NZ
135/F4 Collins, Ms,US
131/J3 Collinsville, Ok,US
132/E4 Collinsville, Va,US
60/D1 Colmar, Fr.
64/D2 Colmenar Viejo, Sp.
119/J7 Colmillo (cape), Chile
50/D1 Colmonell, Sc,UK
53/E3 Coln (riv.), Eng UK
51/F4 Colne, Eng,UK
53/G3 Colne (riv.), Eng,UK
59/F2 Cologne (Köln), Ger.
114/D3 Colombia (ctry.)
116/B3 Colombo, Braz.
90/C6 Colombo (cap.), SrL.
62/D5 Colomiers, Fr.
118/E2 Colón, Arg.
118/F2 Colón, Arg.
123/F6 Colón, Pan.
98/C4 Colonia, Micro.
119/F2 Colonia (dept.), Uru.
119/F2 Colonia Del Sacramento, Uru.
119/K7 Colorado (peak), Arg.
118/D3 Colorado (riv.), Arg.
116/B2 Colorado, Braz.
130/D4 Colorado (riv.), Mex., US
130/E3 Colorado (plat.), US
130/F3 Colorado (state), US
134/D4 Colorado (riv.), Tx,US
131/F3 Colorado City, Co,US
134/C3 Colorado City, Tx,US
130/E3 Colorado Nat'l Mon., Co,US
117/C2 Colorados, Desagües de los (marsh), Arg.
131/F3 Colorado Springs, Co,US
114/E7 Colquiri, Bol.
128/G4 Colstrip, Mt,US
50/D1 Colt (hill), Sc,UK
118/C2 Coltauco, Chile
53/H1 Coltishall, Eng,UK
137/C2 Colton, Ca,US
137/F5 Colts Neck, NJ,US
113/D4 Coluene (riv.), Braz.
124/E3 Columbia (mtn.), Ab,Can.
128/C2 Columbia (mts.), BC,Can.
125/T6 Columbia (cape), Nun,Can.
128/C4 Columbia (riv.), Can., US
128/D4 Columbia (plat.), US
132/C4 Columbia, Ky,US
134/E3 Columbia, La,US
137/K7 Columbia, Md,US
131/J3 Columbia, Mo,US
135/F4 Columbia, Ms,US
135/H3 Columbia (cap.), SC,US
135/G3 Columbia, Tn,US
128/E3 Columbia Falls, Mt,US
108/B4 Columbine (cape), SAfr.
135/G3 Columbus, Ga,US
132/C4 Columbus, In,US
135/F3 Columbus, Ms,US
128/F4 Columbus, Mt,US
131/H2 Columbus, Ne,US
137/F5 Columbus, NJ,US
130/F5 Columbus, NM,US
132/D4 Columbus (cap.), Oh,US
134/D4 Columbus, Tx,US
130/B3 Colusa, Ca,US
124/D2 Colville (lake), NW,Can.
136/H2 Colville (riv.), Ak,US
128/D3 Colville, Wa,US
138/B3 Colvos (passg.), Wa,US
52/D2 Colwall, Eng,UK
52/C4 Colwinston, Wal,UK
50/E5 Colwyn Bay, Wal,UK
63/K4 Comacchio, It.
63/K4 Comacchio, Valli di (lag.), It.
134/D4 Comanche, Tx,US
118/F3 Comandante Nicanor Otamendi, Arg.
69/H2 Comănești, Rom.
69/G3 Comarnic, Rom.
122/E5 Comayagua, Hon.
117/E3 Combarbalá, Chile
52/B4 Combe Martin, Eng,UK
50/C2 Comber, NI,UK
58/B6 Combs-la-Ville, Fr.
96/C4 Comet (riv.), Austl.
91/F3 Comilla, Bang.
58/B2 Comines, Belg.
58/C2 Comines, Fr.
137/G5 Commack, NY,US
62/E3 Commentry, Fr.
137/B2 Commerce, Ca,US
59/E6 Commercy, Fr.
125/H2 Committee (bay), Nun,Can.
63/H4 Como, It.
61/F5 Como (lake), It.
61/F5 Como (prov.), It.
138/P14 Como (lake), Wi,US
118/D5 Comodoro Rivadavia, Arg.
104/D4 Comoé (prov.), Burk.
90/C6 Comorin (cape), India
109/G5 Comoros (ctry.)
128/B3 Comox, BC,Can.
58/B5 Compiègne, Fr.
123/P9 Compostela, Mex.
137/B3 Compton, Ca,US
134/C4 Comstock, Tx,US
104/B4 Conakry (cap.), Gui.
104/B4 Conakry (comm.), Gui.
62/B3 Concarneau, Fr.
115/E1 Conceição da Barra, Braz.
115/B1 Conceição das Alagoas, Braz.
115/J5 Conceição do Araguaia, Braz.
116/D1 Conceição do Mato Dentro, Braz.
116/H6 Conceição do Rio Verde, Braz.
114/F7 Concepción (lake), Bol.
118/B3 Concepción, Chile
117/E1 Concepción, Par.
114/C6 Concepción, Peru
122/A3 Concepción del Oro, Mex.
118/F2 Concepción del Uruguay, Arg.
130/B4 Conception (pt.), Ca,US
116/F7 Conchal, Braz.
131/F4 Conchas (lake), NM,US
131/G5 Concho (riv.), Tx,US
123/N8 Conchos (riv.), Mex.
138/K11 Concord, Ca,US
135/H3 Concord, NC,US
133/G3 Concord (cap.), NH,US
117/E3 Concordia, Arg.
116/A3 Concórdia, Braz.
131/H3 Concordia, Ks,US
128/C3 Concrete, Wa,US
89/D2 Con Cuong, Viet.
123/F3 Condado, Cuba
58/C3 Condé-sur-L'Escaut, Fr.
62/C2 Condé-sur-Noireau, Fr.
96/C4 Condamine (riv.), Austl.
128/C4 Condon, Or,US
59/D3 Condroz (plat.), Belg.
135/G4 Conecuh (riv.), Al,US
63/K4 Conegliano, It.
134/B2 Conejos, Co,US
58/B6 Conflans-Sainte-Honorine, Fr.
137/G4 Congers, NY,US
88/B3 Conghua, China
51/F5 Congleton, Eng,UK
101/E5 Congo, Dem. Rep. of the (ctry.)
101/D4 Congo, Rep. of the (ctry.)
103/K7 Congo (basin), Afr.
110/C1 Congo (riv.), Afr.
116/D2 Congonhas, Braz.
118/C3 Conguillío Nat'l Park, Chile
118/C4 Cónico, Cerro (Nevado) (peak), Arg., Chile
64/B4 Conil de la Frontera, Sp.
51/H5 Coningsby, Eng,UK
51/G5 Conisbrough, Eng,UK
51/E3 Coniston, Eng,UK
51/E3 Coniston Water (lake), Eng,UK
50/C2 Conlig, NI,UK
125/J1 Conn (lake), Nun,Can.
49/A4 Connacht (prov.), Ire.
51/E5 Connah's Quay, Wal,UK
132/D3 Conneaut, Oh,US
133/G2 Connecticut (riv.), US
133/F3 Connecticut (state), US
49/C2 Connel, Sc,UK
132/E3 Connellsville, Pa,US
49/H7 Connemara Nat'l Park, Ire.
132/C4 Connersville, In,US
49/A3 Conn, Lough (lake), Ire.
119/K7 Cono Grande (peak), Arg.
96/D4 Conondale Nat'l Park, Austl.
62/E4 Conques, Fr.
128/F3 Conrad, Mt,US
134/E4 Conroe, Tx,US
116/D2 Conselheiro Lafaiete, Braz.
116/D1 Conselheiro Pena, Braz.
51/G2 Consett, Eng,UK
137/E5 Conshohocken, Pa,US
122/E3 Consolación del Sur, Cuba
89/D4 Con Son (isl.), Viet.
61/F2 Constance (Bodensee) (lake), Ger., Swi.
69/J3 Constanța, Rom.
69/J3 Constanța (co.), Rom.
65/F2 Constantí, Sp.
64/C4 Constantina, Sp.
102/G1 Constantine, Alg.
136/G4 Constantine (cape), Ak,US
118/B2 Constitución, Chile
119/T11 Constitución (res.), Uru.
123/L7 Constitución de 1997 Nat'l Park, Mex.
64/D3 Consuegra, Sp.
90/E3 Contai, India
63/K4 Contarina, It.
115/K6 Contas (riv.), Braz.
116/C1 Contegem, Braz.
58/B4 Contigny, Fr.
128/C2 Continental (ranges), Ab, BC,Can.
138/L11 Contra Costa (can.), Ca,US
123/F3 Contramaestre, Cuba
64/E3 Contreras (res.), Sp.
136/J3 Controller (bay), Ak,US
118/B3 Contulmo, Chile
124/E2 Contwoyto (lake), Nun,Can.
58/B4 Conty, Fr.
123/G6 Convención, Col.
66/E2 Conversano, It.
96/C3 Conway (cape), Austl.
134/E3 Conway, Ar,US
133/G3 Conway, NH,US
135/J3 Conway, SC,US
96/C3 Conway Range Nat'l Park, Austl.
50/E5 Conwy, Wal,UK
50/D5 Conwy (bay), Wal,UK
50/E5 Conwy (co.), Wal,UK
50/E5 Conwy (riv.), Wal,UK
50/E5 Conwy, Vale of (val.), Wal,UK
90/E2 Cooch Behār, India
96/F7 Coochiemudlo (isl.), Austl.
119/K8 Cook (bay), Chile
95/H7 Cook (str.), NZ
136/H3 Cook (inlet), Ak,US
135/G2 Cookeville, Tn,US
111/L Cook Ice Shelf, Ant.
99/J6 Cook Islands (terr.), NZ
50/B2 Cookstown, NI,UK
50/B2 Cookstown (dist.), NI,UK
97/B3 Coola Coola (swamp), Austl.
50/B4 Cooley (pt.), Ire.
96/D4 Cooloola Nat'l Park, Austl.
97/D3 Cooma, Austl.
90/B5 Coondapoor, India
90/C5 Coonoor, India
134/E3 Cooper, Tx,US
129/J4 Cooperstown, ND,US
97/A3 Coorong Nat'l Park, Austl.
135/G3 Coosa (riv.), Al,US
128/B5 Coos Bay, Or,US
97/D2 Cootamundra, Austl.
137/G5 Copague, NY,US
118/C3 Copahué (vol.), Chile
122/D5 Copán (ruins), Hon.
64/E4 Cope (cape), Sp.
50/C2 Copeland (isl.), NI,UK
54/G1 Copenhagen (København) (cap.), Den.
67/F2 Copertino, It.
97/D1 Copeton (dam), Austl.
117/B2 Copiapó, Chile
63/J4 Copparo, It.
57/G4 Coppenbrügge, Ger.
134/D4 Copperas Cove, Tx,US
124/E2 Coppermine (riv.), NW,Nun,Can.
51/F4 Coppull, Eng,UK
69/G2 Copșa Mică, Rom.
51/F1 Coquet (riv.), Eng,UK
51/G1 Coquet Dale (val.), Eng,UK
117/B2 Coquimbo, Chile
118/C1 Coquimbo (reg.), Chile
69/G4 Corabia, Rom.
96/C1 Coral (sea)
135/H5 Coral Gables, Fl,US
95/E2 Coral Sea Is. (terr.), Austl.
135/H5 Coral Springs, Fl,US
137/H5 Coram, NY,US
62/E2 Corbeil-Essonnes, Fr.
58/B4 Corbie, Fr.
62/E5 Corbieres (mts.), Fr.
132/C4 Corbin, Ky,US
51/F2 Corbridge, Eng,UK
53/F2 Corby, Eng,UK
116/K7 Corcovado (mon.), Braz.
118/B4 Corcovado (gulf), Chile
118/B4 Corcovado (vol.), Chile
122/E6 Corcovado Nat'l Park, CR
116/D2 Cordeiro, Braz.
135/H4 Cordele, Ga,US
131/H4 Cordell (New Cordell), Ok,US
63/K4 Cordenons, It.
114/D3 Cordillera de los Picachos Nat'l Park, Col.
117/D3 Córdoba, Arg.
117/D3 Córdoba (mts.), Arg.
118/E2 Córdoba (prov.), Arg.
122/B4 Córdoba, Mex.
64/C4 Córdoba, Sp.
136/J3 Cordova (peak), Ak,US
64/E1 Corella, Sp.
114/G3 Corentyne (riv.), Guy.
67/F3 Corfu (Kérkira) (isl.), Gre.
64/B3 Coria, Sp.
64/B4 Coria del Río, Sp.
97/D2 Coricudgy (peak), Austl.
66/E3 Corigliano Calabro, It.
67/H4 Corinth (ruins), Gre.
135/F3 Corinth, Ms,US
67/H4 Corinth (Kórinthos), Gre.
116/C1 Corinto, Braz.
122/D5 Corinto, Nic.
64/A1 Coristanco, Sp.
66/C4 Corleone, It.
69/H5 Çorlu, Turk.
58/D5 Cormontreuil, Fr.
129/H2 Cormorant, Mb,Can.
129/H2 Cormorant (lake), Mb,Can.
52/C1 Corndon (hill), Wal,UK
116/B2 Cornélio Procópio, Braz.
125/K2 Cornelius Grinnell (bay), Nun,Can.
65/L7 Cornella, Sp.
97/C3 Corner (inlet), Austl.
133/K1 Corner Brook, Nf,Can.
132/E3 Corning, NY,US
96/B3 Cornish (cr.), Austl.
63/J4 Corno alle Scale (peak), It.
119/L8 Cornú (peak), Arg.
125/S7 Cornwall (isl.), Nun,Can.
132/F2 Cornwall, On,Can.
133/J2 Cornwall, PE,Can.
52/B6 Cornwall (co.), Eng,UK
125/S7 Cornwallis (isl.), Nun,Can.
123/H5 Coro, Ven.
115/K4 Coroatá, Braz.
114/E7 Corocoro, Bol.
116/C1 Coromandel, Braz.
90/D5 Coromandel (coast), India
95/H6 Coromandel, NZ
88/D5 Coron, Phil.
137/C3 Corona, Ca,US
131/F4 Corona, NM,US
122/E6 Coronado (bay), CR
128/F2 Coronation, Ab,Can.
124/E2 Coronation (gulf), Nun,Can.
118/E1 Coronda, Arg.
118/B3 Coronel, Chile
118/E3 Coronel Dorrego, Arg.
116/D1 Coronel Fabriciano, Braz.
118/D2 Coronel Moldes, Arg.
117/E2 Coronel Oviedo, Par.
118/E3 Coronel Pringles, Arg.
118/E3 Coronel Suárez, Arg.
116/A3 Coronel Vivida, Braz.
114/D7 Coropuna (peak), Peru
123/F6 Corozal, Col.
122/D4 Corozal Town, Belz.
134/D5 Corpus Christi, Tx,US
64/D3 Corral de Almaguer, Sp.
118/E2 Corral de Bustos, Arg.
65/Y16 Corralejo, Canl.
97/B3 Corrangamite (lake), Austl.
122/E6 Corredor, CR
115/J6 Corrente, Braz.
116/B1 Corrente (riv.), Braz.
49/A4 Corrib, Lough (lake), Ire.
117/E2 Corrientes, Arg.
122/E3 Corrientes (cape), Cuba
114/C4 Corrientes (riv.), Ecu., Peru
52/C1 Corris, Wal,UK
66/A1 Corse (cape), Fr.
66/A1 Corse (reg.), Fr.
50/D1 Corserine (mtn.), Sc,UK
50/C1 Corsewall (pt.), Sc,UK
52/D4 Corsham, Eng,UK
66/A1 Corsica (Corse) (isl.), Fr.
134/D3 Corsicana, Tx,US
66/A1 Corte, Fr.
130/E3 Cortez, Co,US
63/K3 Cortina d'Ampezzo, It.
132/E3 Cortland, NY,US
104/B4 Corubal (riv.), GBis.
64/A3 Coruche, Port.
80/E2 Çoruh (riv.), Turk.
114/G7 Corumbá, Braz.
116/B1 Corumbá (riv.), Braz.
128/C4 Corvallis, Or,US
52/D2 Corve (riv.), Eng,UK
65/R12 Corvo (isl.), Azor.
66/C1 Corvo (peak), It.
51/E6 Corwen, Wal,UK
66/E3 Cosenza, It.
132/D3 Coshocton, Oh,US
122/D5 Cosigüina (pt.), Nic.
64/D2 Coslada, Sp.

158
Cosmo – Denpa

116/F7 Cosmópolis, Braz.
62/E3 Cosne-Cours-sur-Loire, Fr.
64/B1 Cospeito, Sp.
117/D3 Cosquín, Arg.
62/D3 Cosson (riv.), Fr.
137/C3 Costa Mesa, Ca,US
122/E5 Costa Rica (ctry.)
123/N9 Costa Rica, Mex.
53/H1 Costessey, Eng,UK
69/G3 Costeşti, Rom.
138/M10 Cosumnes (riv.), Ca,US
88/D6 Cotabato, Phil.
104/D5 Côte d'Ivoire (Ivory Coast) (ctry.)
60/A3 Côte d'Or (dept.), Fr.
62/C2 Cotentin (pen.), Fr.
133/N7 Côte-Saint-Luc, Qu,Can.
52/B3 Cothi (riv.), Wal,UK
116/G8 Cotia, Braz.
105/F5 Cotonou, Ben.
52/D4 Cotswolds (hills), Eng,UK
128/C5 Cottage Grove, Or,US
55/H3 Cottbus, Ger.
53/G2 Cottenham, Eng,UK
130/D4 Cottonwood, Az,US
134/D2 Cottonwood (riv.), Ks,US
131/F5 Cottonwood (dry riv.), Tx,US
134/D4 Cotulla, Tx,US
62/C4 Coubre, Pointe de la (pt.), Fr.
58/C5 Coucy-le-Château-Auffrique, Fr.
58/B1 Coudekerque-Branche, Fr.
62/D2 Coulaines, Fr.
128/D4 Coulee City, Wa,US
111/M Coulman (isl.), Ant.
58/C6 Coulommiers, Fr.
132/E2 Coulonge (riv.), Qu,Can.
62/D4 Coulounieix-Chamiers, Fr.
128/D4 Council, Id,US
129/K5 Council Bluffs, Ia,US
131/H3 Council Grove, Ks,US
49/D2 Coupar Angus, Sc,UK
58/D3 Courcelles, Belg.
59/F5 Courcelles-Chaussy, Fr.
62/E4 Cournon-d'Auvergne, Fr.
124/D4 Courtenay, BC,Can.
133/S8 Courtice, On,Can
58/C2 Courtrai (Kortrijk), Belg.
62/C2 Coutances, Fr.
128/F3 Coutts, Ab,Can.
58/D3 Couvin, Belg.
65/P10 Cova da Piedade, Port.
64/B1 Cova (mt.), Sp.
64/C1 Covadonga Nat'l Park, Sp.
69/H3 Covasna, Rom.
68/G3 Covasna (co.), Rom.
53/E2 Coventry, Eng,UK
53/E1 Coventry (can.), Eng,UK
53/E2 Coventry (co.), Eng,UK
64/B2 Covilhã, Port.
137/C2 Covina, Ca,US
135/H3 Covington, Ga,US
132/C4 Covington, Ky,US
135/F3 Covington, Tn,US
132/E4 Covington, Va,US
96/H8 Cowan, Austl.
52/C4 Cowbridge, Wal,UK
53/E5 Cowes, Eng,UK
51/F2 Cow Green (res.), Eng,UK
128/C4 Cowlitz (riv.), Wa,US
135/H3 Cowpens Nat'l Bfld., SC,US
97/D2 Cowra, Austl.
51/G2 Coxhoe, Eng,UK
115/H7 Coxim, Braz.
58/B5 Coye-la-Forêt, Fr.
131/H2 Cozad, Ne,US
122/D3 Cozumel, Mex.
122/D3 Cozumel (isl.), Mex.
97/C4 Cradle (peak), Austl
97/C4 Cradle Mountain-Lake Saint Clair Nat'l Park, Austl.
108/D4 Cradock, SAfr.
136/K3 Crag (mtn.), Yk,Can.
51/F3 Crag (hill), Eng,UK
130/F2 Craig, Co,US
50/C2 Craigavad, NI,UK
50/B3 Craigavon, NI,UK
50/B3 Craigavon (dist.), NI,UK
97/F5 Craigieburn, Austl.
129/G3 Craik, Sk,Can.
63/J2 Crailsheim, Ger.
69/F3 Craiova, Rom.
51/G1 Cramlington, Eng,UK
50/A1 Crana (riv.), Ire.
129/H2 Cranberry Portage, Mb,Can.
52/D5 Cranborne Chase (for.), Eng,UK
97/C3 Cranbourne, Austl.
128/E3 Cranbrook, BC,Can.
53/G4 Cranbrook, Eng,UK
137/F5 Cranbury, NJ,US
134/C4 Crane, Tx,US
129/J3 Crane River, Mb,Can.
137/F5 Cranford, NJ,US
53/F4 Cranleigh, Eng,UK
58/C5 Craonne, Fr.
69/F2 Crasna (riv.), Rom.
128/C5 Crater (lake), Or,US
128/C5 Crater Lake Nat'l Park, Or,US
128/E5 Craters of the Moon Nat'l Mon., Id,US
115/K5 Crateús, Braz.
66/E3 Crati (riv.), It.
115/L5 Crato, Braz.
116/C2 Cravinhos, Braz.
132/C3 Crawfordsville, In,US
135/G4 Crawfordville, Fl,US
53/F4 Crawley, Eng,UK
128/F4 Crazy (mts.), Mt,US
58/A3 Crécy-en-Ponthieu, Fr.
52/D2 Credenhill, Eng,UK
133/Q8 Credit (riv.), On,Can.
52/C5 Crediton, Eng,UK
124/F3 Cree (lake), Sk,Can.
124/F3 Cree (riv.), Sk,Can.
50/D2 Cree (riv.), Sc,UK
50/D2 Creetown, Sc,UK
129/H2 Creighton, Sk,Can.
58/B5 Creil, Fr.
63/H4 Crema, It.
57/H4 Cremlingen, Ger.
63/J4 Cremona, It.
58/B5 Crépy-en-Valois, Fr.
68/B3 Cres (isl.), Cro.
130/A2 Crescent City, Ca,US
118/E2 Crespo, Arg.
62/F4 Crest, Fr.
138/P16 Crest Hill, Il,US
137/C2 Crestline, Ca,US
128/D3 Creston, BC,Can.
129/K5 Creston, Ia,US
135/G4 Crestview, Fl,US
51/G5 Creswell, Eng,UK
67/J5 Crete (isl.), Gre.
67/J5 Crete (sea), Gre.
131/H2 Crete, Ne,US
58/B6 Créteil, Fr.
65/G1 Creus (cape), Sp.
62/D3 Creuse (riv.), Fr.
59/F5 Creutzwald-la-Croix, Fr.
63/J4 Crevalcore, It.
65/E3 Crevillente, Sp.
51/F5 Crewe, Eng,UK
52/D5 Crewkerne, Eng,UK
49/C2 Crianlarich, Sc,UK
50/D6 Criccieth, Wal,UK
116/B4 Criciúma, Braz.
52/C3 Crickhowell, Wal,UK
53/E3 Cricklade, Eng,UK
49/D2 Crieff, Sc,UK
58/A3 Criel-sur-Mer, Fr.
50/E2 Criffell (hill), Eng,UK
72/E3 Crimean (pen.), Ukr.
102/H7 Cristal (mts.), Gabon
115/J7 Cristalina, Braz.
123/G5 Cristóbal (pk.), Col.
68/F2 Crişul Alb (riv.), Rom.
69/G2 Cristuru Secuiesc, Rom.
68/E2 Crişul Negru (riv.), Rom.
115/H6 Crixás-Açu (riv.), Braz.
67/G2 Crna Reka (riv.), FYROM
97/D3 Croajingolong Nat'l Park, Austl.
68/B3 Croatia (ctry.)
133/F2 Croche (riv.), Qu,Can.
93/E3 Crocker (range), Malay.
50/E1 Crocketford, Sc,UK
134/E4 Crockett, Tx,US
97/D2 Crocodile (pt.), Austl.
137/K7 Crofton, Md,US
52/B3 Crofty, Wal,UK
50/B6 Croghan (mtn.), Ire.
62/F5 Croisette (cape), Fr.
129/L3 Croix (lake), Can., US
53/H1 Cromer, Eng,UK
95/G7 Cromwell, NZ
89/E3 Crong A Na (riv.), Viet.
96/H9 Cronulla, Austl.
51/G2 Crook, Eng,UK
123/G3 Crooked (isl.), Bahm.
129/J4 Crookston, Mn,US
51/E5 Crosby, Eng,UK
129/H3 Crosby, ND,US
134/C3 Crosbyton, Tx,US
105/H5 Cross (riv.), Camr., Nga.
129/J2 Cross (lake), Mb,Can.
135/H4 Cross City, Fl,US
134/F3 Crossett, Ar,US
51/F2 Cross Fell (mtn.), Eng,UK
128/E3 Crossfield, Ab,Can.
50/C3 Crossgar, NI,UK
52/C2 Crossgates, Wal,UK
50/D1 Crosshill, Sc,UK
52/C3 Crosskeys, Wal,UK
50/B3 Crossmaglen, NI,UK
50/E2 Crossmichael, Sc,UK
105/H5 Cross River (state), Nga.
135/G3 Crossville, Tn,US
51/F4 Croston, Eng,UK
66/E3 Crotone, It.
53/G3 Crouch (riv.), Eng,UK
58/C5 Crouy-sur-Ourq, Fr.
128/G4 Crow Agency, Mt,US
53/G4 Crowborough, Eng,UK
97/E1 Crowdy Bay Nat'l Park, Austl.
132/E2 Crowe (riv.), On,Can.
128/F5 Crowheart, Wy,US
53/F1 Crowland, Eng,UK
51/H4 Crowle, Eng,UK
134/E4 Crowley, La,US
135/F3 Crowley's (ridge), Ar,US
129/K4 Crow, North Fork (riv.), Mn,US
132/C3 Crown Point, In,US
130/E4 Crownpoint, NM,US
125/H1 Crown Prince Frederik (isl.), Nun,Can.
96/D4 Crows Nest Falls Nat'l Park, Austl.
53/F4 Crowthorne, Eng,UK
53/F3 Croxley Green, Eng,UK
97/G5 Croydon, Austl.
45/M8 Crozet (isls.), FrAnt.
111/M Crozier (cape), Ant.
62/A2 Crozon, Fr.
49/E2 Cruden Bay, Sc,UK
50/B2 Crumlin, NI,UK
51/E2 Crummock Water (lake), Eng,UK
59/E5 Crusnes (riv.), Fr.
123/F4 Cruz (cape), Cuba
118/E2 Cruz Alta, Arg.
117/F2 Cruz Alta, Braz.
115/L6 Cruz das Almas, Braz.
117/D3 Cruz del Eje, Arg.
116/J7 Cruzeiro, Braz.
114/D5 Cruzeiro do Sul, Braz.
116/J6 Cruzília, Braz.
68/D3 Crvenka, Serb.
51/E5 Cryn-y-Brain (mtn.), Wal,UK
130/C3 Crystal Bay, Nv,US
134/D4 Crystal City, Tx,US
132/B2 Crystal Falls, Mi,US
138/P15 Crystal Lake, Il,US
68/E2 Csongrád, Hun.
68/E2 Csongrád (co.), Hun.
68/C2 Csorna, Hun.
68/E2 Csorvás, Hun.
68/D2 Csóványos (peak), Hun.
78/D2 Ctesiphon (ruins), Iraq
110/D4 Cuando (riv.), Ang.
110/C4 Cuangar, Ang.
110/C2 Cuango (riv.), Ang.
110/B2 Cuanza (riv.), Ang.
65/E3 Cuart de Poblet, Sp.
118/D2 Cuarto (riv.), Arg.
122/A2 Cuatrociénagas, Mex.
123/F3 Cuba (ctry.)
131/K3 Cuba, Mo,US
110/C4 Cubango (riv.), Ang.
116/G8 Cubatão, Braz.
80/C2 Çubuk, Turk.
137/C2 Cucamonga (Rancho Cucamonga), Ca,US
114/E2 Cuchivero (riv.), Ven.
53/F4 Cuckfield, Eng,UK
53/G5 Cuckmere (riv.), Eng,UK
89/D1 Cuc Phuong Nat'l Park, Viet.
114/D2 Cúcuta, Col.
138/Q14 Cudahy, Wi,US
90/C5 Cuddalore, India
90/C5 Cuddapah, India
51/F5 Cuddington, Eng,UK
64/B1 Cudillero, Sp.
51/G4 Cudworth, Eng,UK
64/C2 Cuéllar, Sp.
114/C4 Cuenca, Ecu.
64/D2 Cuenca, Sp.
64/E2 Cuenca (range), Sp.
122/B4 Cuernavaca, Mex.
134/D4 Cuero, Tx,US
62/G5 Cuers, Fr.
114/C3 Cueva de los Guarcharos Nat'l Park, Col.
64/E4 Cuevas del Almanzora, Sp.
69/F3 Cugir, Rom.
62/D5 Cugnaux-Vingtcasses, Fr.
115/G7 Cuiabá, Braz.
115/G7 Cuiabá (riv.), Braz.
56/C5 Cuijk, Neth.
110/C2 Cuilo (riv.), Ang.
110/C3 Cuima, Ang.
110/C4 Cuito (riv.), Ang.
110/C4 Cuito-Cuanavale, Ang.
114/F4 Cuiuni (riv.), Braz.
80/E3 Çukurca, Turk.
89/E4 Cu Lao (isl.), Viet.
50/A1 Culdaff (riv.), Ire.
56/C5 Culemborg, Neth.
115/H6 Culene (riv.), Braz.
97/C1 Culgoa (riv.), Austl.
123/N9 Culiacán, Mex.
88/D5 Culion (isl.), Phil.
64/D4 Cúllar Baza, Sp.
49/D2 Cullen, Sc,UK
65/E3 Cullera, Sp.
64/A1 Culleredo, Sp.
135/G3 Cullman, Al,US
52/C5 Cullompton, Eng,UK
50/B2 Cullybackey, NI,UK
50/A1 Culmore, NI,UK
96/B5 Culoga (riv.), Austl.
132/E4 Culpeper, Va,US
137/B2 Culver City, Ca,US
123/J5 Cumaná, Ven.
125/K2 Cumberland (pen.), Nun,Can.
125/K2 Cumberland (sound), Nun,Can.
129/H2 Cumberland (lake), Sk,Can.
135/G3 Cumberland (plat.), US
135/H4 Cumberland (isl.), Ga,US
135/G2 Cumberland (falls), Ky,US
132/C4 Cumberland (lake), Ky,US
135/G2 Cumberland (riv.), Ky, Tn,US
132/E4 Cumberland, Md,US
132/D4 Cumberland Gap Nat'l Hist. Park, Tn,US
129/H2 Cumberland House, Sk,Can.
123/N8 Cumbres de Majalca Nat'l Park, Mex.
122/A2 Cumbres de Monterrey Nat'l Park, Mex.
51/F2 Cumbria (co.), Eng,UK
51/E3 Cumbrian (mts.), Eng,UK
90/C4 Cumbum, India
80/C3 Çumra, Turk.
136/M5 Cumshewa (pt.), BC,Can.
118/B3 Cunco, Chile
110/B4 Cunene (riv.), Ang.
63/G4 Cuneo, It.
89/E3 Cung Son, Viet.
116/J8 Cunha, Braz.
48/H1 Čuokkarašša (peak), Nor.
63/G4 Cuorgnè, It.
49/D2 Cupar, Sc,UK
138/K12 Cupertino, Ca,US
68/E4 Ćuprija, Serb.
123/H5 Curaçao (isl.), NAnt.
118/C3 Curacautín, Chile
118/B3 Curanilahue, Chile
114/C4 Curaray (riv.), Ecu., Peru
118/Q9 Curaumilla (pt.), Chile
68/F2 Curcubăta (peak), Rom.
62/E3 Cure (riv.), Fr.
109/S15 Curepipe, Mrts.
118/B2 Curepto, Chile
118/C2 Curicó, Chile
116/B3 Curitiba, Braz.
116/B3 Curitibanos, Braz.
50/B5 Curragh, The, Ire.
115/L5 Currais Novos, Braz.
131/K3 Current (riv.), Ar, Mo,US
130/D2 Currie, Nv,US
69/G3 Curtea de Argeş, Rom.
68/E2 Curtici, Rom.
96/C3 Curtis (isl.), Austl.
98/H8 Curtis (isl.), NZ
115/G4 Curuá (riv.), Braz.
115/H5 Curuá (riv.), Braz.
114/D5 Curuçu (riv.), Braz.
92/B4 Curup, Indo.
115/K4 Cururupu, Braz.
117/E2 Curuzú Cuatiá, Arg.
116/C1 Curvelo, Braz.
132/B2 Curwood (mtn.), Mi,US
114/D6 Cusco, Peru
50/B1 Cushendall, NI,UK
50/B3 Cusher (riv.), NI,UK
131/H4 Cushing, Ok,US
62/E3 Cusset, Fr.
135/G3 Cusseta, Ga,US
128/G4 Custer, Mt,US
129/H5 Custer, SD,US
52/C5 Cut (hill), Eng,UK
128/E3 Cut Bank, Mt,US
114/C5 Cutervo, Peru
135/G4 Cuthbert, Ga,US
128/F2 Cut Knife, Sk,Can.
118/C3 Cutral-Có, Arg.
90/E3 Cuttack, India
57/F1 Cuxhaven, Ger.
130/C4 Cuyama (riv.), Ca,US
93/F1 Cuyo, Phil.
93/F1 Cuyo (isls.), Phil.
114/F2 Cuyuni (riv.), Guy., Ven.
52/C3 Cwm, Wal,UK
52/C3 Cwmafan, Wal,UK
52/C3 Cwmbran, Wal,UK
129/H5 C.W. McConaughy (lake), Ne,US
67/J4 Cyclades (isls.), Gre.
132/C4 Cynthiana, Ky,US
52/B3 Cynwyl Elfed, Wal,UK
128/F3 Cypress (hills), Ab, Sk,Can.
137/B3 Cypress, Ca,US
80/J4 Cyprus (ctry.)
103/K1 Cyrenaica (reg.), Libya
52/B3 Cywyn (riv.), Wal,UK
55/J2 Czaplinek, Pol.
55/M2 Czarna Białostocka, Pol.
55/J2 Czarnków, Pol.
55/H4 Czech Republic (ctry.)
55/K3 Częstochowa, Pol.
55/J2 Człuchów, Pol.

D

88/D2 Da (riv.), China
87/B4 Daba (mts.), China
68/D2 Dabas, Hun.
78/C3 Dabbāgh, Jabal (mtn.), SAr.
114/C2 Dabeiba, Col.
90/B3 Dabhoi, India
89/D1 Da (Black) (riv.), Viet.
138/B2 Dabob (bay), Wa,US
103/Q6 Daborow, Som.
104/D5 Dabou, C.d'Iv.
90/C2 Dabra, India
55/M2 Dąbrowa Białostocka, Pol.
55/K3 Dąbrowa Górnicza, Pol.
90/F3 Dacca (Dhaka) (cap.), Bang.
61/H1 Dachau, Ger.
89/D3 Dac Sut, Viet.
89/D3 Dac To, Viet.
135/H4 Dade City, Fl,US
93/H4 Dadi (cape), Indo.
90/B4 Dadra & Nagar Haveli (terr.), India
79/J3 Dādu, Pak.
90/D6 Daduru (riv.), SrL.
89/B4 Daen Noi (peak), Thai.
88/D5 Daet, Phil.
91/J2 Dafang, China
104/B2 Dagana, Sen.
73/H3 Dagestan, Resp., Rus.
108/D4 Daggaboersnek (pass), SAfr.
96/B2 Dagmar Range Nat'l Park, Austl.
87/D3 Dagu, China
91/H2 Daguan, China
96/E6 D'Aguilar (mtn.), Austl.
96/E6 D'Aguilar (range), Austl.
83/K2 Daguokui (peak), China
88/D4 Dagupan, Phil.
81/E5 Dagzê (lake), China
90/B4 Dāhānu, India
90/A2 Daharki, Pak.
87/B2 Dahei (riv.), China
83/K2 Daheiding (peak), China
83/J2 Da Hinggan (mts.), China
103/N4 Dahlak (arch.), Erit.
135/H3 Dahlonega, Ga,US
55/G3 Dahme (riv.), Ger.
77/D7 Dahnā' (des.), SAr.
89/D4 Da Hoa, Viet.
80/E3 Dahūk, Iraq
87/C2 Dai (lake), China
85/M9 Daian, Japan
85/G2 Daigo, Japan
90/D2 Dailekh, Nepal
50/D1 Dailly, Sc,UK
89/E3 Dai Loc, Viet.
64/D3 Daimiel, Sp.
134/E3 Daingerfield, Tx,US
96/B2 Daintree Nat'l Park, Austl.
85/E3 Daiō-zaki (pt.), Japan
118/E3 Daireaux, Arg.
84/C3 Dai-sen (mtn.), Japan
84/C3 Daisen-Oki Nat'l Park, Japan
85/L10 Daitō, Japan
98/C2 Daito (isls.), Japan
104/A3 Dakar (cap.), Sen.
104/A3 Dakar (reg.), Sen.
106/B3 Dākhilah, Wāḩāt ad (oasis), Egypt
102/B3 Dakhla, WSah.
104/A1 Dakhlet Nouadhibou (reg.), Mrta.
89/D3 Dak Nhe, Viet.
105/G3 Dakoro, Niger
131/H2 Dakota City, Ne,US
68/E4 Dakovica, Serb.
68/D3 Dakovo, Serb.
82/H3 Dalai (salt lake), China
80/B3 Dalaman, Turk.
82/F2 Dalanjargalan, Mong.
48/E3 Dalarna (reg.), Swe.
89/E4 Da Lat, Viet.
48/Q6 Dalatangi (pt.), Ice.
50/E2 Dalbeattie, Sc,UK
96/C4 Dalby, Austl.
106/B4 Dal Cataract (falls), Sudan
56/D4 Dalfsen, Neth.
134/C2 Dalhart, Tx,US
133/H1 Dalhousie, NB,Can.
136/N1 Dalhousie (cape), NW,Can.
91/H2 Dali, China
87/B3 Dali (riv.), China
64/D4 Dalías, Sp.
83/H3 Daling (riv.), China
68/D3 Dalj, Cro.
136/M4 Dall (isl.), Ak,US
136/F3 Dall (lake), Ak,US
134/D3 Dallas, Tx,US
128/C4 Dalles, The, Or,US
105/F3 Dallol Bosso (wadi), Mali, Niger
49/C2 Dalmally, Sc,UK
68/C4 Dalmatia (reg.), Cro.
50/D1 Dalmellington, Sc,UK
83/M3 Dal'negorsk, Rus.
83/L2 Dal'nerechensk, Rus.
104/D5 Daloa, C.d'Iv.
106/B4 Dalqū, Sudan
96/B3 Dalrymple (lake), Austl.
49/C3 Dalrymple, Sc,UK
135/G3 Dalton, Ga,US
90/D3 Daltonganj, India
51/E3 Dalton-in-Furness, Eng,UK
49/C2 Dalwhinnie, Sc,UK
124/H2 Daly (bay), Nun,Can.
138/K11 Daly City, Ca,US
81/F5 Dam (riv.), China
90/B3 Damān, India
90/B3 Damān & Diu (terr.), India
80/H6 Damanhūr, Egypt
93/G5 Damar (isl.), Indo.
137/J7 Damascus, Md,US
80/L5 Damascus (Dimashq) (cap.), Syria
102/H5 Damaturu, Nga.
78/F1 Damavānd (mtn.), Iran
89/D4 Dam Doi, Viet.
53/E5 Damerham, Eng,UK
79/F1 Dāmghān, Iran
80/H6 Damietta (Dumyāţ), Egypt
87/C3 Daming, China
59/D4 Damion (mtn.), Fr.
58/B5 Dammartin-en-Goële, Fr.
58/C1 Damme, Belg.
57/F3 Damme, Ger.
90/C3 Damoh, India
105/E4 Damongo, Gha.
93/H4 Dampier (str.), Indo.
89/C4 Damrei (mts.), Camb.
56/D2 Damsterdiep (riv.), Neth.
59/E5 Damvillers, Fr.
87/B4 Dan (riv.), China
135/H2 Dan (riv.), NC,US
103/P5 Danakil (reg.), Djib.
104/C5 Danané, C.d'Iv.
89/E2 Da Nang, Viet.
88/D5 Danao, Phil.
53/G3 Danbury, Eng,UK
97/G5 Dandenong, Austl.
97/G5 Dandenong (cr.), Austl.
97/G5 Dandenong (mtn.), Austl.
51/F5 Dane (riv.), Eng,UK
82/D4 Dang (riv.), China
108/B4 Danger (pt.), SAfr.
97/B2 Danggali Consv. Park, Austl.
103/N5 Dangila, Eth.
122/D4 Dangriga, Belz.
70/J4 Danilov, Rus.
87/B4 Danjiangkou, China
87/B4 Danjiangkou (res.), China
72/F1 Dankov, Rus.
81/C3 Dankova, Pik (peak), Kyr.
135/G3 Dannelly (res.), Al,US
54/F2 Dannenberg, Ger.
47/G4 Danube (riv.), Eur.
69/J3 Danube (delta), Rom.
69/H3 Danube, Borcea Branch (riv.), Rom.
69/J3 Danube, Mouths of the, Rom.
69/J3 Danube, Sfîntu Gheorghe Branch (riv.), Rom.
69/J3 Danube, Sulina Branch (riv.), Rom.
138/L11 Danville, Ca,US
132/C3 Danville, Il,US
132/C4 Danville, Ky,US
132/E4 Danville, Va,US
105/F4 Dapaong, Togo
135/G4 Daphne, Al,US
88/D6 Dapitan, Phil.
83/K2 Daqing, China
87/H7 Daqing (riv.), China
79/H2 Daqq-e Patargān (lake), Afg., Iran
80/L5 Dar'ā, Syria
79/F3 Dārāb, Iran
69/H1 Darabani, Rom.
88/D5 Daraga, Phil.
88/D5 Daram, Phil.
68/E4 Đaravica (peak), Serb.
80/L5 Dārayyā, Syria
90/E2 Darbhanga, India
136/F3 Darby (cape), Ak,US
137/E6 Darby, Pa,US
68/D3 Darda, Cro.
131/J4 Dardanelle (lake), Ar,US
69/H5 Dardanelles (str.), Turk.
97/G5 Darebin (cr.), Austl.
80/D2 Darende, Turk.
107/C4 Dar es Salaam (cap.), Tanz.
107/C4 Dar es Salaam (prov.), Tanz.
63/J4 Darfo, It.
95/H6 Dargaville, NZ
50/B5 Dargle (riv.), Ire.
82/F2 Darhan (peak), Mong.
103/Q6 Darie (hills), Som.
137/G4 Darien, Ct,US
135/H4 Darien, Ga,US
138/Q16 Darien, Il,US
123/F6 Darien Nat'l Park, Pan.
82/G2 Dariganga, Mong.
90/E2 Darjiling, India
97/B2 Darling (riv.), Austl.
96/C4 Darling Downs (upland), Austl.
51/G2 Darlington, Eng,UK
51/G2 Darlington, (co.), Eng,UK
135/J3 Darlington, SC,US
55/J1 Darłowo, Pol.
63/H2 Darmstadt, Ger.
103/K1 Darnah, Libya
58/A5 Darnétal, Fr.
111/E Darnley (cape), Ant.
124/D2 Darnley (bay), NW,Can.
51/G1 Darras Hall, Eng,UK
79/G1 Darreh Gaz, Iran
103/K6 Dar Rounga (reg.), CAfr.
111/R Dart (cape), Ant.
52/C6 Dart (riv.), Eng,UK
53/G4 Dartford, Eng,UK
52/C6 Dartington, Eng,UK
52/B5 Dartmoor (upland), Eng,UK
52/C5 Dartmoor Nat'l Park, Eng,UK
97/C3 Dartmouth (res.), Austl.
133/J2 Dartmouth, NS,Can.
52/C6 Dartmouth, Eng,UK
51/G4 Darton, Eng,UK
65/G3 Dartuch (cape), Sp.
98/D5 Daru, PNG
68/C3 Daruvar, Cro.
93/E3 Darvel (bay), Malay.
51/F4 Darwen, Eng,UK
95/C2 Darwin, Austl.
118/B5 Darwin (bay), Chile
119/K8 Darwin (mts.), Chile
79/H2 Daryācheh-ye Sīstān (lake), Iran
83/H3 Dashengtang (peak), China
87/B5 Dashennongjia (peak), China
103/N5 Dashen, Ras (peak), Eth.
79/F2 Dasht-e Kavīr (des.), Iran
79/G2 Dasht-e Lūt (des.), Iran
79/H2 Dasht-e Mārgow (des.), Afg.
79/H3 Dasht Kaur (riv.), Pak.
57/G5 Dassel, Ger.
108/B4 Dasseneiland (isl.), SAfr.
89/D4 Dat Do, Viet.
90/C2 Datia, India
130/F4 Datil, NM,US
87/C2 Datong, China
82/D4 Datong (mts.), China
82/D4 Datong (riv.), China
57/E5 Datteln, Ger.
92/C3 Datu (cape), Malay.
92/B3 Datuk (cape), Indo.
48/H4 Daugava (riv.), Lat.
70/E4 Daugava (riv.), Lat.
70/E5 Daugavpils, Lat.
59/F3 Daun, Ger.
89/B3 Daung (isl.), Myan.
129/H3 Dauphin, Mb,Can.
129/J3 Dauphin (lake), Mb,Can.
90/C5 Dāvangere, India
88/E6 Davao, Phil.
129/L5 Davenport, Ia,US
128/D4 Davenport, Wa,US
53/E2 Daventry, Eng,UK
125/T6 Davgaard-Jensen (reg.), Grld.
122/E6 David, Pan.
131/H2 David City, Ne,US
129/G3 Davidson, Sk,Can.
138/K11 Davidson (mtn.), Ca,US
111/F Davis (sea), Ant.
111/F Davis (sta.), Ant.
121/M3 Davis (str.), Can., Grld.
138/L9 Davis, Ca,US
132/E4 Davis (peak), Pa,US
134/B4 Davis (mts.), Tx,US
71/M5 Davlekanovo, Rus.
104/D5 Davo (riv.), C.d'Iv.
61/F4 Davos, Swi.
82/C1 Davst, Mong.
103/N7 Dawa Wenz (riv.), Eth.
87/D4 Dawen (riv.), China
52/C5 Dawlish, Eng,UK
96/C4 Dawson (riv.), Austl.
136/L3 Dawson, Yk,Can.
119/K8 Dawson (isl.), Chile
135/G4 Dawson, Ga,US
128/C2 Dawson Creek, BC,Can.
87/C5 Dawu Shan (mtn.), China
78/G4 Dawwah, Oman
62/C5 Dax, Fr.
87/D3 Daxing, China
91/G3 Daying (riv.), China
119/F1 Dayman (riv.), Uru.
88/B2 Dayong, China
80/K6 Dayr al Balaḩ, Gaza
78/D1 Dayr az Zawr, Syria
106/B3 Dayrūt, Egypt
128/E2 Daysland, Ab,Can.
132/C4 Dayton, Oh,US
135/G3 Dayton, Tn,US
128/D4 Dayton, Wa,US
135/H4 Daytona Beach, Fl,US
108/D3 De Aar, SAfr.
80/K6 Dead (sea), Isr., Jor.
129/H4 Deadwood, SD,US
97/C3 Deal (isl.), Austl.
53/H4 Deal, Eng,UK
137/G5 Deal, NJ,US
128/B2 Dean (riv.), BC,Can.
52/D3 Dean, Forest of (for.), Eng,UK
117/D3 Deán Funes, Arg.
138/F7 Dearborn, Mi,US
138/F7 Dearborn Heights, Mi,US
51/G4 Dearne, Eng,UK
51/G4 Dearne (riv.), Eng,UK
136/N4 Dease (riv.), BC,Can.
124/F2 Dease (str.), Nun,Can.
130/C3 Death Valley Nat'l Park, Ca, Nv,US
68/E5 Debar, FYROM
136/G3 Debauch (mtn.), Ak,US
53/H2 Deben (riv.), Eng,UK
53/H2 Debenham, Eng,UK
55/L3 Dębica, Pol.
56/C4 De Bilt, Neth.
55/L3 Dęblin, Pol.
55/H2 Dębno, Pol.
136/J3 Deborah (mtn.), Ak,US
103/N6 Debre Birhan, Eth.
68/E2 Debrecen, Hun.
103/N5 Debre Mark'os, Eth.
103/N5 Debre Tabor, Eth.
103/N6 Debre Zeyit, Eth.
135/G3 Decatur, Al,US
135/G3 Decatur, Ga,US
132/B4 Decatur, Il,US
132/C3 Decatur, In,US
134/D3 Decatur, Tx,US
62/E4 Decazeville, Fr.
90/C5 Deccan (plat.), India
55/H3 Děčín, Czh.
62/E3 Decize, Fr.
53/E3 Deddington, Eng,UK
56/D3 Dedemsvaart, Neth.
118/C5 Dedo (peak), Arg.
104/E3 Dédougou, Burk.
110/F3 Dedza, Malw.
50/B4 Dee (riv.), Ire.
50/D1 Dee (riv.), Sc,UK
49/D2 Dee (riv.), Sc,UK
51/E5 Dee (riv.), Wal,UK
50/A4 Deel (riv.), Ire.
53/F1 Deeping Saint James, Eng,UK
132/E2 Deep River, On,Can.
136/F5 Deer (isl.), Ak,US
138/Q15 Deerfield, Il,US
133/K1 Deer Lake, Nf,Can.
58/C2 Deerlijk, Belg.
128/E4 Deer Lodge, Mt,US
137/G5 Deer Park, NY,US
128/D4 Deer Park, Wa,US
90/B3 Deesa, India
96/H8 Dee Why, Austl.
103/Q6 Deex Nugaaleed (dry river), Som.
114/F8 Defensores del Chaco Nat'l Park, Par.
132/C3 Defiance, Oh,US
135/G4 De Funiak Springs, Fl,US
50/E5 Deganwy, Wal,UK
103/P6 Degeh Bur, Eth.
133/G2 Dégelis, Qu,Can.
63/K2 Deggendorf, Ger.
58/C1 De Haan, Belg.
103/P4 Dehalak (isl.), Erit.
103/P4 Dehalak Marine Nat'l Park, Erit.
79/L2 Dehra Dūn, India
90/D3 Dehri, India
58/C2 Deinze, Belg.
57/G4 Deister (mts.), Ger.
69/F2 Dej, Rom.
132/B3 De Kalb, Il,US
103/N4 Dek'emhāre, Erit.
135/H4 De Land, Fl,US
130/C4 Delano, Ca,US
79/H2 Delārām, Afg.
128/G2 Delarode (lake), Sk,Can.
138/N14 Delavan, Wi,US
132/F3 Delaware (riv.), US
132/F4 Delaware (state), US
132/D3 Delaware, Oh,US
137/F4 Delaware Water Gap Nat'l Rec. Area, NJ, Pa,US
57/F5 Delbrück, Ger.
118/D2 Del Campillo, Arg.
68/F5 Delčevo, FYROM
56/D4 Delden, Neth.
56/D2 De Leijen (lake), Neth.
60/D3 Delémont, Swi.
56/B5 Delft, Neth.
56/D2 Delfzijl, Neth.
118/E4 Delgada (pt.), Arg.
107/D5 Delgado (cape), Moz.
82/D2 Delger (riv.), Mong.
82/F2 Delgerhaan, Mong.
82/E2 Delgerhangay, Mong.
90/C2 Delhi, India
72/E5 Delice (riv.), Turk.
56/B5 De Lier, Neth.
66/D5 Delimara, Ponta Ta' (pt.), Malta
128/G3 Delisle, Sk,Can.
57/G5 Delligsen, Ger.
129/J5 Dell Rapids, SD,US
108/Q13 Delmas, SAfr.
59/F6 Delme, Fr.
57/F2 Delme (riv.), Ger.
57/F2 Delmenhorst, Ger.
131/F3 Del Norte, Co,US
129/H3 Deloraine, Mb,Can.
67/J4 Delos (ruins), Gre.
67/H3 Delphi (ruins), Gre.
132/C3 Delphos, Oh,US
137/F5 Delran, NJ,US
135/H5 Delray Beach, Fl,US
134/C4 Del Rio, Tx,US
130/E3 Delta, Co,US
130/D3 Delta, Ut,US
119/T12 Delta del Tigre, Uru.
138/M11 Delta-Mendota (can.), Ca,US
135/H4 Deltona, Fl,US
82/C2 Delüün, Mong.
138/L11 Del Valle (lake), Ca,US
71/M5 Dëma (riv.), Rus.
64/D1 Demanda (range), Sp.
136/K2 Demarcation (pt.), Ak,US
110/D2 Demba, D.R. Congo
103/M6 Dembī Dolo, Eth.
56/B7 Demer (riv.), Belg.
130/F4 Deming, NM,US
114/F3 Demini (riv.), Braz.
54/G2 Demmin, Ger.
135/G3 Demopolis, Al,US
92/B4 Dempo (peak), Indo.
58/C3 Denain, Fr.
103/P5 Denakil (reg.), Erit., Eth.
136/H3 Denali Nat'l Park & Prsv., Ak,US
129/H2 Denare Beach, Sk,Can.
51/E5 Denbigh, Wal,UK
51/E5 Denbighshire (co.), Wal,UK
56/B2 Den Burg, Neth.
51/G4 Denby Dale, Eng,UK
58/D2 Dender (riv.), Belg.
58/D2 Denderleeuw, Belg.
58/D1 Dendermonde, Belg.
56/D4 Denekamp, Neth.
56/D4 Den Ham, Neth.
56/B3 Den Helder, Neth.
51/G4 Denholme, Eng,UK
65/F3 Denia, Sp.
97/C2 Deniliquin, Austl.
130/C2 Denio, Nv,US
136/H4 Denison (mtn.), Ak,US
129/K5 Denison, Ia,US
134/D3 Denison, Tx,US
80/B3 Denizli, Turk.
111/G Denman (glac.), Ant.
48/C5 Denmark (ctry.)
121/Q3 Denmark (str.), NAm.
92/E5 Denpasar, Indo.

Dente – Easte
159

58/C2 **Dentergem**, Belg.
53/G5 **Denton**, Eng,UK
134/D3 **Denton**, Tx,US
98/D5 **D'Entrecasteaux** (isls.), PNG
131/F3 **Denver** (cap.), Co,US
137/F5 **Denville**, NJ,US
90/C2 **Deoband**, India
90/D3 **Deogarh**, India
90/E3 **Deoghar**, India
90/B4 **Deolāli**, India
90/C2 **Deoli**, India
62/D3 **Déols**, Fr.
90/D2 **Deoria**, India
58/B1 **De Panne**, Belg.
56/C6 **De Peel** (reg.), Neth.
133/S10 **Depew**, NY,US
58/C2 **De Pinte**, Belg.
103/P7 **Dera** (dry riv.), Som.
79/K2 **Dera Ghāzi Khān**, Pak.
79/K2 **Dera Ismāīl Khān**, Pak.
73/J4 **Derbent**, Rus.
51/G6 **Derby**, Eng,UK
51/G6 **Derby** (co.), Eng,UK
131/H3 **Derby**, Ks,US
51/G6 **Derbyshire** (co.), Eng,UK
68/F3 **Derdap Nat'l Park**, Serb.
68/E2 **Derecske**, Hun.
82/F2 **Deren**, Mong.
49/A4 **Derg, Lough** (lake), Ire.
134/E4 **De Ridder**, La,US
80/E3 **Derik**, Turk.
62/B2 **Déroute** (passg.), Fr., Chl,UK
50/A4 **Derravaragh, Lough** (lake), Ire.
50/B6 **Derry** (riv.), Ire.
133/G3 **Derry**, NH,US
50/C3 **Derryboy**, NI,UK
49/B3 **Derrylin**, NI,UK
53/G1 **Dersingham**, Eng,UK
68/C3 **Derventa**, Bosn.
50/B1 **Dervock**, NI,UK
97/C4 **Derwent** (riv.), Austl.
51/F2 **Derwent** (res.), Eng,UK
51/E2 **Derwent** (riv.), Eng,UK
51/G5 **Derwent** (riv.), Eng,UK
51/H4 **Derwent** (riv.), Eng,UK
51/E2 **Derwent Water** (lake), Eng,UK
118/D2 **Desaguadero** (riv.), Arg.
114/E7 **Desaguadero** (riv.), Bol.
53/F2 **Desborough**, Eng,UK
118/C2 **Descabezado Grande** (vol.), Chile
116/C2 **Descalvado**, Braz.
129/H2 **Deschambault Lake**, Sk,Can.
130/B2 **Deschutes** (riv.), Or,US
103/N5 **Desē**, Eth.
117/C6 **Deseado** (riv.), Arg.
119/J8 **Deseado** (cape), Chile
119/L7 **Desengaño** (pt.), Arg.
65/V15 **Desertas** (isls.), Madr.,Port.
87/B4 **Deshengpu**, China
129/J4 **De Smet**, SD,US
129/K5 **Des Moines** (cap.), Ia,US
129/K5 **Des Moines** (riv.), Ia, Mo,US
138/C3 **Des Moines**, Wa,US
72/D2 **Desna** (riv.), Rus., Ukr.
119/J8 **Desolación** (isl.), Chile
108/D4 **Desolation, Valley of** (val.), SAfr.
131/K3 **De Soto**, Mo,US
108/D4 **Despatch**, SAfr.
138/Q15 **Des Plaines**, Il,US
138/P16 **Des Plaines** (riv.), Il,US
54/G3 **Dessau**, Ger.
59/E1 **Dessel**, Belg.
58/C1 **Destelbergen**, Belg.
136/L3 **Destruction Bay**, Yk,Can.
68/E3 **Deta**, Rom.
57/F5 **Detmold**, Ger.
138/F7 **Detroit**, Mi,US
138/F7 **Detroit** (riv.), On,Can., Mi,US
129/K4 **Detroit Lakes**, Mn,US
48/P6 **Dettifoss** (falls), Ice.
97/D2 **Deua Nat'l Park**, Austl.
58/B2 **Deûle** (riv.), Fr.
56/B6 **Deurne**, Belg.
56/C6 **Deurne**, Neth.
63/L3 **Deutschlandsberg**, Aus.
133/N6 **Deux-Montagnes**, Qu,Can.
133/M7 **Deux-Montagnes** (lake), Qu,Can.
68/F3 **Deva**, Rom.
68/E2 **Dévaványa**, Hun.
80/C2 **Develi**, Turk.
56/D4 **Deventer**, Neth.
49/D2 **Deveron** (riv.), Sc,UK
115/H2 **Devil's** (isl.), FrG.
131/G5 **Devils** (riv.), Tx,US
129/J3 **Devils Lake**, ND,US
136/M4 **Devils Paw** (mtn.), BC,Can., Ak,US
130/C3 **Devils Postpile Nat'l Mon.**, Ca,US
129/G4 **Devils Tower Nat'l Mon.**, Wy,US
69/G5 **Devin**, Bul.
134/D4 **Devine**, Tx,US
53/E4 **Devizes**, Eng,UK
69/H4 **Devnya**, Bul.
67/G2 **Devoll** (riv.), Alb.
128/E2 **Devon**, Ab,Can.
125/S7 **Devon** (isl.), Nun,Can.
52/C5 **Devon** (co.), Eng,UK
97/C4 **Devonport**, Austl.
69/K5 **Devrek**, Turk.
72/D4 **Devrek** (riv.), Turk.
72/E4 **Devrez** (riv.), Turk.
92/A3 **Dewa** (pt.), Indo.
90/C3 **Dewās**, India
134/E2 **Dewey**, Ok,US
131/H2 **De Witt**, Ne,US
51/G4 **Dewsbury**, Eng,UK
133/G2 **Dexter**, Me,US
78/E2 **Dez** (riv.), Iran
78/E2 **Dezfūl**, Iran
136/E2 **Dezhneva, Mys** (pt.), Rus.
87/D3 **Dezhou**, China
106/C2 **Dhahab**, Egypt
90/F3 **Dhaka** (Dacca) (cap.), Bang.
90/D3 **Dhamtari**, India
90/E3 **Dhānbād**, India
90/E2 **Dhankuta**, Nepal
90/C3 **Dhār**, India
90/B3 **Dharampur**, India
90/B3 **Dhāri**, India
90/C5 **Dharmapuri**, India
90/C5 **Dharmavaram**, India
67/H3 **Dhelfoí** (Delphi) (ruins), Gre.
90/E3 **Dhenkānāl**, India
67/K2 **Dhidhimótikhon**, Gre.
67/H3 **Dhírfis** (peak), Gre.
78/F5 **Dhofar** (reg.), Oman
90/B3 **Dholka**, India
90/C2 **Dholpur**, India
90/B4 **Dhond**, India
67/J4 **Dhonoúsa** (isl.), Gre.
90/B3 **Dhorāji**, India
67/J2 **Dhráma**, Gre.
90/E2 **Dhubri**, India
90/B3 **Dhūlia**, India
90/E3 **Dhuliān**, India
90/E2 **Dhupgāri**, India
67/J5 **Día** (isl.), Gre.
63/G4 **Diable, Cime du** (peak), Fr.
136/H4 **Diablo** (mtn.), Ak,US
138/L11 **Diablo** (mt.), Ca,US
130/B3 **Diablo** (range), Ca,US
134/B4 **Diablo** (plat.), Tx,US
119/G2 **Diablo, Punta del** (pt.), Uru.
116/G8 **Diadema**, Braz.
118/E2 **Diamante**, Arg.
118/D2 **Diamante** (riv.), Arg.
116/D1 **Diamantina**, Braz.
115/K6 **Diamantina** (mts.), Braz.
115/G6 **Diamantino**, Braz.
97/G5 **Diamond** (cr.), Austl.
128/E4 **Diamond** (peak), Id,US
137/C3 **Diamond Bar**, Ca,US
126/W13 **Diamond Head** (crater), Hi,US
87/L8 **Dianshan** (lake), China
105/F3 **Diapaga**, Burk.
111/J **Dibble Iceberg Tongue**, Ant.
110/E5 **Dibete**, Bots.
106/B4 **Dibis, Bīr** (well), Egypt
134/E4 **Diboll**, Tx,US
91/F2 **Dibrugarh**, India
80/F3 **Dibs**, Iraq
134/C3 **Dickens**, Tx,US
129/H4 **Dickinson**, ND,US
135/G2 **Dickson**, Tn,US
80/E3 **Dicle** (riv.), Turk.
56/D5 **Didam**, Neth.
53/E3 **Didcot**, Eng,UK
128/E3 **Didsbury**, Ab,Can.
79/K3 **Didwāna**, India
109/E2 **Die Berg** (peak), SAfr.
104/E4 **Diébougou**, Burk.
124/F3 **Diefenbaker** (lake), Sk,Can.
119/J7 **Diego de Almagro** (isl.), Chile
77/G10 **Diego Garcia** (isl.), BrIn.
59/E4 **Diekirch** (dist.), Lux.
57/F5 **Diemel** (riv.), Ger.
56/B4 **Diemen**, Neth.
89/C1 **Dien Bien Phu**, Viet.
89/D2 **Dien Chau**, Viet.
89/E3 **Dien Khanh**, Viet.
59/E2 **Diepenbeek**, Belg.
56/D4 **Diepenveen**, Neth.
57/F3 **Diepholz**, Ger.
58/A4 **Dieppe**, Fr.
59/E2 **Diest**, Belg.
107/D2 **Dif**, Kenya
105/H3 **Diffa** (dept.), Niger
59/E4 **Differdange**, Lux.
97/B3 **Difficult** (peak), Austl.
91/G2 **Digboi**, India
133/H2 **Digby**, NS,Can.
63/G4 **Digne**, Fr.
62/E3 **Digoin**, Fr.
88/E6 **Digos**, Phil.
90/C3 **Digras**, India
58/D2 **Dijle** (Dyle) (riv.), Belg.
60/B3 **Dijon**, Fr.
105/P3 **Dikhil**, Djib.
80/H6 **Dikirnis**, Egypt
73/H4 **Diklosmt'a, Gora** (peak), Geo.
58/B1 **Diksmuide**, Belg.
102/H5 **Dikwa**, Nga.
103/N6 **Dīla**, Eth.
58/D2 **Dilbeek**, Belg.
93/G5 **Dili** (cap.), ETim.
59/H2 **Dillenburg**, Ger.
103/L5 **Dilling**, Sudan
59/F5 **Dillingen**, Ger.
135/J3 **Dillon**, SC,US
110/D3 **Dilolo**, D.R. Congo
59/E1 **Dilsen**, Belg.
91/F2 **Dimāpur**, India
80/L5 **Dimashq** (Damascus) (cap.), Syria
104/D5 **Dimbokro**, C.d'Iv.
69/G3 **Dîmbovița** (co.), Rom.
75/P2 **Dimitriya Lapteva** (str.), Rus.
69/G4 **Dimitrovgrad**, Bul.
73/J1 **Dimitrovgrad**, Rus.
68/F4 **Dimitrovgrad**, Serb.
102/H6 **Dimlang** (peak), Nga.
80/K6 **Dimona**, Isr.
80/K6 **Dimona, Hare** (mtn.), Isr.
88/E6 **Dinagat**, Phil.
88/E5 **Dinagat** (isl.), Phil.
90/E2 **Dinājpur**, Bang.
62/B2 **Dinan**, Fr.
59/D3 **Dinant**, Belg.
80/B2 **Dinar**, Turk.
62/B2 **Dinard**, Fr.
68/C3 **Dinaric Alps** (range), Bosn., Cro.
52/B2 **Dinas** (pt.), Wal,UK
52/C4 **Dinas Powys**, Wal,UK
103/N5 **Dinder Nat'l Park**, Eth.
90/C5 **Dindigul**, India
63/K2 **Dingolfing**, Ger.
88/D4 **Dingras**, Phil.
49/C2 **Dingwall**, Sc,UK
87/C3 **Dingxing**, China
87/D4 **Dingyuan**, China
89/D1 **Dinh Lap**, Viet.
57/E4 **Dinkel** (riv.), Ger.
57/F3 **Dinklage**, Ger.
51/G1 **Dinnington**, Eng,UK
130/E2 **Dinosaur**, Co,US
130/E2 **Dinosaur Nat'l Mon.**, Co, Ut,US
56/D5 **Dinslaken**, Ger.
128/G3 **Dinsmore**, Sk,Can.
56/B5 **Dintel Mark** (riv.), Neth.
130/C3 **Dinuba**, Ca,US
56/D5 **Dinxperlo**, Neth.
104/C4 **Dion** (riv.), Gui.
104/A3 **Diourbel**, Sen.
104/A3 **Diourbel** (reg.), Sen.
91/F2 **Diphu**, India
79/J4 **Diplo**, Pak.
88/D6 **Dipolog**, Phil.
96/C3 **Dipperu Nat'l Park**, Austl.
104/E2 **Diré**, Mali
103/P6 **Dire Dawa**, Eth.
122/D5 **Diriamba**, Nic.
102/H4 **Dirkou**, Niger
56/B5 **Dirksland**, Neth.
130/E3 **Dirty Devil** (riv.), Ut,US
99/L6 **Disappointment** (isls.), FrPol.
97/B3 **Discovery** (bay), Austl.
106/C3 **Dishnā**, Egypt
125/L2 **Disko** (isl.), Grld.
51/F5 **Disley**, Eng,UK
137/C3 **Disneyland**, Ca,US
59/E2 **Dison**, Belg.
91/F2 **Dispur**, India
133/G2 **Disraëli**, Qu,Can.
53/H2 **Diss**, Eng,UK
57/F4 **Dissen am Teutoburger Wald**, Ger.
50/E2 **Distington**, Eng,UK
137/J8 **District of Columbia** (cap.), US
119/S12 **Distrito Federal** (fed. dist.), Arg.
122/B4 **Distrito Federal** (state), Mex.
80/H6 **Disūq**, Egypt
53/F5 **Ditchling Beacon** (hill), Eng,UK
66/D4 **Dittaino** (riv.), It.
79/K4 **Diu** (isl.), India
90/B3 **Diu, Damān and** (terr.), India
62/D3 **Dive** (riv.), Fr.
116/C2 **Divinópolis**, Braz.
50/B2 **Divis** (mtn.), NI,UK
114/D5 **Divisor** (mts.), Braz.
104/D5 **Divo**, C.d'Iv.
80/D2 **Divriği**, Turk.
136/M4 **Dixon** (chan.), Ak,US
138/L10 **Dixon**, Ca,US
132/B3 **Dixon**, Il,US
124/C3 **Dixon Entrance** (chan.), BC,Can.
80/E2 **Diyadin**, Turk.
80/E3 **Diyarbakır**, Turk.
80/H6 **Diyarb Najm**, Egypt
105/F4 **Djado**, Niger
102/H3 **Djado** (plat.), Niger
102/G1 **Djamaa**, Alg.
110/B1 **Djambala**, Congo
102/G3 **Djanet**, Alg.
102/F1 **Djelfa**, Alg.
102/G1 **Djemila** (ruins), Alg.
104/D3 **Djénné**, Mali
105/E3 **Djibo**, Burk.
103/P5 **Djibouti** (ctry.)
103/P5 **Djibouti** (cap.), Djib.
50/B5 **Djouce** (mtn.), Ire.
105/F4 **Djougou**, Ben.
107/A2 **Djugu**, D.R. Congo
47/H3 **Dnipro** (riv.), Eur.
72/E2 **Dniprodzerzhyns'k**, Ukr.
72/E2 **Dnipropetrovs'k**, Ukr.
72/E2 **Dnipropetrovs'ka Obl.**, Ukr.
72/D3 **Dnister** (riv.), Eur.
82/E5 **Do** (riv.), China
105/E3 **Do** (lake), Mali
102/J6 **Doba**, Chad
137/G4 **Dobbs Ferry**, NY,US
70/D4 **Dobele**, Lat.
54/G3 **Döbeln**, Ger.
93/H4 **Doberai** (pen.), Indo.
68/D3 **Doboj**, Bosn.
55/L2 **Dobre Miasto**, Pol.
69/H4 **Dobruja** (reg.), Bul., Rom.
72/D1 **Dobrush**, Bela.
71/N4 **Dobryanka**, Rus.
116/D1 **Doce** (riv.), Braz.
53/G1 **Docking**, Eng,UK
135/H4 **Dock Junction**, Ga,US
117/D1 **Doctor Pedro P. Peña**, Par.
68/F2 **Doctor Petru Groza**, Rom.
132/F1 **Doda** (lake), Qu,Can.
50/B5 **Dodder** (riv.), Ire.
80/A3 **Dodecanese** (isls.), Turk.
131/G3 **Dodge City**, Ks,US
132/B3 **Dodgeville**, Wi,US
52/B6 **Dodman** (pt.), Wal,UK
107/B4 **Dodoma**, Tanz.
107/B4 **Dodoma** (prov.), Tanz.
67/G3 **Dodoni** (ruins), Gre.
128/F3 **Dodsland**, Sk,Can.
51/G4 **Dodworth**, Eng,UK
56/D4 **Doesburg**, Neth.
56/D5 **Doetinchem**, Neth.
81/E5 **Dogai Coring** (lake), China
80/D2 **Doğankent** (riv.), Turk.
84/C2 **Dōgo** (isl.), Japan
105/G3 **Dogondoutchi**, Niger
80/F2 **Doğubayazıt**, Turk.
80/E2 **Doğukaradeniz** (mts.), Turk.
78/F3 **Doha** (Ad Dawḩah) (cap.), Qatar
90/B3 **Dohad**, India
89/B2 **Doi Inthanon Nat'l Park**, Thai.
89/B2 **Doi Khun Tan Nat'l Park**, Thai.
64/B1 **Doiras** (res.)
115/K5 **Dois Irmãos** (mts.), Braz.
89/B2 **Doi Suthep-Pui Nat'l Park**, Thai.
56/D2 **Dokkum**, Neth.
56/C2 **Dokkumer Ee** (riv.), Neth.
133/F1 **Dolbeau**, Qu,Can.
60/B3 **Dôle**, Fr.
52/C1 **Dolgellau**, Wal,UK
71/W9 **Dolgoprudnyy**, Rus.
66/A3 **Dolianova**, It.
83/N2 **Dolinsk**, Rus.
69/F3 **Dolj** (co.), Rom.
57/E2 **Dollard** (Dollart) (bay), Ger., Neth.
54/D5 **Doller** (riv.), Fr.
68/C5 **Dolmen** (ruins), It.
55/J3 **Dolnośląskie** (prov.), Pol.
63/J3 **Dolomite Alps** (Alpi Dolomitiche) (range), It.
119/F3 **Dolores**, Arg.
122/D4 **Dolores**, Guat.
65/E3 **Dolores**, Sp.
118/F2 **Dolores**, Uru.
130/E3 **Dolores**, Co,US
130/E3 **Dolores** (riv.), Co, Ut,US
122/A3 **Dolores Hidalgo**, Mex.
119/N7 **Dolphin** (cape), Falk.
136/A2 **Dolphin** (pt.), Namb.
124/E1 **Dolphin and Union** (str.), Nun,Can.
51/F4 **Dolphinholme**, Eng,UK
52/B5 **Dolton**, Eng,UK
138/Q16 **Dolton**, Il,US
89/D2 **Do Luong**, Viet.
93/J4 **Dom** (peak), Indo.
61/F4 **Domat-Ems**, Swi.
54/G4 **Domažlice**, Czh.
63/G2 **Dombasle-sur-Meurthe**, Fr.
73/G4 **Dombay-Ul'gen, Gora** (peak), Geo.
68/D2 **Dombóvár**, Hun.
62/E3 **Domérat**, Fr.
117/C1 **Domeyko** (mts.), Chile
123/J4 **Dominica** (ctry.)
123/H4 **Dominican Republic** (ctry.)
56/C6 **Dommel** (riv.), Belg., Neth.
89/D3 **Dom Noi** (res.), Thai.
71/W9 **Domodedovo**, Rus.
61/E5 **Domodossola**, It.
117/F3 **Dom Pedrito**, Braz.
93/E5 **Dompu**, Indo.
68/D2 **Dömsöd**, Hun.
66/A3 **Domusnovas**, It.
118/C3 **Domuyo** (vol.), Arg.
96/C5 **Domville** (peak), Austl.
68/B2 **Domžale**, Slov.
62/C3 **Don** (riv.), Fr.
123/N8 **Don**, Mex.
73/G2 **Don** (ridge), Rus.
73/G3 **Don** (riv.), Rus.
51/G5 **Don** (riv.), Eng,UK
49/D2 **Don** (riv.), Sc,UK
50/C2 **Donaghadee**, NI,UK
50/B2 **Donaghmore**, NI,UK
135/F4 **Donaldsonville**, La,US
64/B4 **Doñana Nat'l Park**, Sp.
55/H4 **Donau** (Danube) (riv.), Aus., Ger.
64/C3 **Don Benito**, Sp.
97/G5 **Doncaster**, Austl.
51/G4 **Doncaster**, Eng,UK
51/G4 **Doncaster** (co.), Eng,UK
110/B2 **Dondo**, Ang.
90/D6 **Dondra Head** (pt.), SrL.
49/A3 **Donegal** (bay), Ire.
50/A1 **Donegal** (co.), Ire.
72/F3 **Donets'k**, Ukr.
72/F3 **Donets'ka Obl.**, Ukr.
88/B3 **Dong** (riv.), China
91/J5 **Dong** (riv.), Viet.
105/H5 **Donga** (riv.), Camr., Nga.
91/H2 **Dongchuan**, China
91/J3 **Dong Dang**, Viet.
56/B5 **Dongen**, Neth.
88/B3 **Dongguan**, China
89/D2 **Dong Ha**, Viet.
89/D2 **Donghen**, Laos
89/D2 **Dong Hoi**, Viet.
87/E2 **Dongliao** (riv.), China
89/D4 **Dong Noi** (riv.), Viet.
87/D3 **Dongping** (lake), China
88/C3 **Dongsha** (isl.), China
87/E4 **Dongtai**, China
87/L9 **Dongtaio** (riv.), China
89/D2 **Dong Tau**, Viet.
88/B2 **Dongting** (lake), China
87/D3 **Dongying**, China
118/Q10 **Donihue**, Chile
51/H6 **Donington**, Eng,UK
124/C2 **Donjek** (riv.), Yk,Can.
68/C3 **Donji Vakuf**, Bosn.
50/D1 **Doon** (riv.), Sc,UK
136/H2 **Doonerak** (mtn.), Ak,US
50/D1 **Doon, Loch** (lake), Sc,UK
132/C2 **Door** (pen.), Wi,US
56/C4 **Doorn**, Neth.
108/B3 **Doorn** (riv.), SAfr.
65/F2 **Dorada** (coast), Sp.
79/K1 **Do Rāh** (pass), Afg.
81/B4 **Dorāh Ān** (pass), Pak.
63/G4 **Dora Riparia** (riv.), It.
133/H2 **Dorchester**, NB,Can.
125/J2 **Dorchester** (cape), Nun,Can.
52/D5 **Dorchester**, Eng,UK
62/D4 **Dordogne** (riv.), Fr.
56/B5 **Dordrecht**, Neth
128/G2 **Dore** (lake), Sk,Can.
62/E4 **Dore** (mts.), Fr.
62/E4 **Dore** (riv.), Fr.
116/C1 **Dores do Indaiá**, Braz.
66/A2 **Dorgali**, It.
82/C2 **Dörgön** (lake), Mong.
105/E3 **Dori**, Burk.
133/M7 **Dorion**, Qu,Can.
53/F4 **Dorking**, Eng,UK
56/D6 **Dormagen**, Ger.
61/F3 **Dornbirn**, Aus.
68/D2 **Dorog**, Hun.
69/H2 **Dorohoi**, Rom.
53/E2 **Dorridge**, Eng,UK
97/E1 **Dorrigo Nat'l Park**, Austl.
52/D1 **Dorrington**, Eng,UK
130/B2 **Dorris**, Ca,US
66/A5 **Dorsale** (mts.), Tun.
52/D5 **Dorset** (co.), Eng,UK
56/D5 **Dorsten**, Ger.
57/E5 **Dortmund**, Ger.
57/E4 **Dortmund-Ems** (can.), Ger.
80/D3 **Dörtyol**, Turk.
57/G3 **Dörverden**, Ger.
118/D5 **Dos Bahias** (cape), Arg.
138/A2 **Dosewallips** (riv.), Wa,US
64/C4 **Dos Hermanas**, Sp.
85/H7 **Dōshi** (riv.), Japan
89/D1 **Do Son**, Viet.
123/M8 **Dos Picachos, Cerro** (mt.), Mex.
54/G2 **Dosse** (riv.), Ger.
105/F3 **Dosso**, Niger
105/F3 **Dosso** (dept.), Niger
73/K3 **Dossor**, Kaz.
135/G4 **Dothan**, Al,US
58/C3 **Douai**, Fr.
102/G7 **Douala**, Camr.
62/A2 **Douarnenez**, Fr.
62/A2 **Douarnenez** (bay), Fr.
96/D4 **Double I.** (pt.), Austl.
60/C3 **Doubs** (dept.), Fr.
60/B4 **Doubs** (riv.), Fr.
58/C3 **Douchy-les-Mines**, Fr.
62/C3 **Doué-la-Fontaine**, Fr.
104/E3 **Douentza**, Mali
66/A4 **Dougga** (ruins), Tun.
50/D3 **Douglas**, IM,UK
136/H4 **Douglas** (mtn.), Ak,US
130/E5 **Douglas**, Az,US
135/H4 **Douglas**, Ga,US
129/G5 **Douglas**, Wy,US
58/B3 **Doullens**, Fr.
63/K1 **Doupovské Hory** (mts.), Czh.
58/C3 **Dour**, Belg.
115/H8 **Dourados**, Braz.
62/E4 **Dourdou** (riv.), Fr.
64/B2 **Douro** (riv.), Port.
62/F4 **Doux** (riv.), Fr.
62/C4 **Douze** (riv.), Fr
51/G6 **Dove** (riv.), Eng,UK
51/H3 **Dove** (riv.), Eng,UK
53/H2 **Dove** (riv.), Eng,UK
130/E3 **Dove Creek**, Co,US
58/A2 **Dover** (str.), Fr., UK
53/H4 **Dover**, Eng,UK
132/F4 **Dover** (cap.), De,US
133/G3 **Dover**, NH,US
137/F5 **Dover**, NJ,US
133/G2 **Dover-Foxcroft**, Me,US
51/G6 **Doveridge**, Eng,UK
50/C3 **Down** (dist.), NI,UK
138/P16 **Downers Grove**, Il,US
137/B3 **Downey**, Ca,US
53/G1 **Downham Market**, Eng,UK
130/B3 **Downieville**, Ca,US
50/C3 **Downpatrick**, NI,UK
53/H4 **Downs, The** (har.), Eng,UK
53/E4 **Downton**, Eng,UK
137/E5 **Doylestown**, Pa,US
84/C3 **Dōzen** (isl.), Japan
132/E2 **Dozois** (res.), Qu,Can.
102/D2 **Drâa** (plat.), Alg., Mor.
102/D2 **Drâa** (wadi), Alg., Mor.
62/F4 **Drac** (riv.), Fr.
116/B2 **Dracena**, Braz.
56/D2 **Drachten**, Neth.
69/G3 **Drăgănești-Olt**, Rom.
69/G3 **Drăgășani**, Rom.
63/G5 **Draguignan**, Fr.
119/L8 **Drake** (passage), Arg., Chile
110/E6 **Drakensberg** (range), Afr.
48/D4 **Drammen**, Nor.
50/B2 **Draperstown**, NI,UK
63/L3 **Drau** (riv.), Aus.
68/C3 **Drava** (riv.), Eur.
58/B6 **Draveil**, Fr.
55/H2 **Drawa** (riv.), Pol.
55/H2 **Drawsko Pomorskie**, Pol.
129/J3 **Drayton**, ND,US
128/E2 **Drayton Valley**, Ab,Can.
93/K4 **Drei Zinnen** (peak), PNG
57/E5 **Drensteinfurt**, Ger.
56/D3 **Drenthe** (prov.), Neth.
56/D3 **Drentse Hoofdvaart** (can.), Neth.
55/G3 **Dresden**, Ger.
58/A6 **Dreux**, Fr.
55/H2 **Drezdenko**, Pol.
56/C4 **Driebergen**, Neth.
128/F5 **Driggs**, Id,US
79/J4 **Drigh Road**, Pak.
67/F2 **Drin** (gulf), Alb.
67/F1 **Drin** (riv.), Alb.
68/D3 **Drina** (riv.), Bosn., Serb.
68/E5 **Drinizi** (riv.), Alb.
68/F3 **Drobeta-Turnu Severin**, Rom.
57/G1 **Drochtersen**, Ger.
50/B4 **Drogheda**, Ire.
72/B2 **Drogobych**, Ukr.
52/D2 **Droitwich**, Eng,UK
59/G6 **Drolingen**, Fr.
57/E6 **Drolshagen**, Ger.
62/F4 **Drôme** (riv.), Fr.
50/A3 **Dromore** (riv.), Ire.
50/B3 **Dromore**, NI,UK
51/G5 **Dronfield**, Eng,UK
62/D4 **Dronne** (riv.), Fr.
56/C3 **Dronten**, Neth.
62/D4 **Dropt** (riv.), Fr.
58/A6 **Drouette** (riv.), Fr.
132/C1 **Drowning** (riv.), On,Can.
50/C3 **Drumaness**, NI,UK
50/C2 **Drumbeg**, NI,UK
128/E3 **Drumheller**, Ab,Can.
50/B5 **Drumleck** (pt.), Ire.
96/B4 **Drummond** (peak), Austl.
96/B4 **Drummond** (range), Austl.
133/F2 **Drummondville**, Qu,Can.
50/D2 **Drummore**, Sc,UK
50/A2 **Drumnakilly**, NI,UK
56/C5 **Drunen**, Neth.
51/G1 **Druridge** (bay), Eng,UK
55/M1 **Druskininkai**, Lith.
56/C5 **Druten**, Neth.
68/C3 **Drvar**, Bosn.
55/K2 **Drwęca** (riv.), Pol.
69/G4 **Dryanovo**, Bul.
136/K3 **Dry Creek**, Yk,Can.
132/A1 **Dryden**, On,Can.
134/C4 **Dryden**, Tx,US
52/C2 **Drygarn Fawr** (mtn.), Wal,UK
49/C2 **Drymen**, Sc,UK
105/H5 **Dschang**, Camr.
87/B4 **Du** (riv.), China
52/B3 **Duad** (riv.), Wal,UK
123/H4 **Duarte** (pk.), DRep.
124/F2 **Dubawnt** (lake), Nun,Can.
124/F2 **Dubawnt** (riv.), NW,Nun,Can.
79/G3 **Dubayy**, UAE
97/D2 **Dubbo**, Austl.
50/B5 **Dublin** (bay), Ire.
50/B5 **Dublin** (cap.), Ire.
50/B5 **Dublin** (co.), Ire.
138/L11 **Dublin**, Ca,US
135/H3 **Dublin**, Ga,US
70/H4 **Dubna**, Rus.
55/K4 **Dubnica nad Váhom**, Slvk.
72/C2 **Dubno**, Ukr.
132/E3 **Du Bois**, Pa,US
128/F5 **Dubois**, Wy,US
69/J2 **Dubossary** (res.), Mol.
68/D4 **Dubrovnik**, Cro.
129/L5 **Dubuque**, Ia,US
130/E2 **Duchesne**, Ut,US
130/E2 **Duchesne** (riv.), Ut,US
99/N7 **Ducie** (atoll), Pitc.
135/G3 **Duck** (riv.), Tn,US
138/A2 **Duckabush** (riv.), Wa,US
129/G2 **Duck Lake**, Sk,Can.
130/D3 **Duckwater**, Nv,US
89/D3 **Duc Lap**, Viet.
89/E3 **Duc Pho**, Viet.
89/D4 **Duc Phong**, Viet.
51/E3 **Dudden** (riv.), Eng,UK
59/F5 **Dudelange**, Lux.
57/H5 **Duderstadt**, Ger.
74/J3 **Dudinka**, Rus.
52/D2 **Dudley**, Eng,UK
52/D2 **Dudley** (co.), Eng,UK
64/C2 **Duero** (Douro) (riv.), Sp.
111/W **Dufek Massive** (mtn.), Ant.
98/F5 **Duff** (isl.), Sol.
58/D1 **Duffel**, Belg.
51/G6 **Duffield**, Eng,UK
49/D2 **Dufftown**, Sc,UK
63/G4 **Dufourspitze** (Punta Dufour) (peak), It., Swi.
68/B3 **Dugi Otok** (isl.), Cro.
130/D2 **Dugway**, Ut,US
114/E3 **Duida Marahuaca Nat'l Park**, Ven.
56/D6 **Duisburg**, Ger.
114/D2 **Duitama**, Col.
56/D5 **Duiven**, Neth.
99/L7 **Duke of Gloucester** (isls.), FrPol.
55/L4 **Dukla** (Przełęcz Dukielska) (pass), Pol.
82/D4 **Dulan**, China
117/D2 **Dulce** (riv.), Arg.
130/F3 **Dulce**, NM,US
91/J2 **Duliu** (riv.), China
57/E5 **Dülmen**, Ger.
69/H4 **Dulovo**, Bul.
129/K4 **Duluth**, Mn,US
52/C4 **Dulverton**, Eng,UK
80/L5 **Dūmā**, Syria
137/B2 **Duma** (pt.), Ca,US
88/D6 **Dumaguete**, Phil.
88/D6 **Dumalinao**, Phil.
88/C5 **Dumaran** (isl.), Phil.
97/D1 **Dumaresq** (riv.), Austl.
134/F3 **Dumas**, Ar,US
134/C3 **Dumas**, Tx,US
55/K4 **Ďumbier** (peak), Slvk.
110/C3 **Dumbo**, Ang.
69/G2 **Dumbrăveni**, Rom.
50/E1 **Dumfries**, Sc,UK
50/D1 **Dumfries & Galloway** (reg.), Sc,UK
57/F3 **Dümmer** (lake), Ger.
132/E2 **Dumoine** (lake), Qu,Can.
132/E2 **Dumoine** (riv.), Qu,Can.
137/F5 **Dumont**, NJ,US
111/K **Dumont d'Urville**, Ant.
80/H6 **Dumyāṭ** (gov.), Egypt
80/H6 **Dumyāṭ** (Damietta), Egypt
55/K5 **Duna** (Danube) (riv.), Hun.
68/D2 **Dunaföldvár**, Hun.
68/D2 **Dunaharaszti**, Hun.
55/K5 **Dunaj** (Danube) (riv.), Slvk.
55/L4 **Dunajec** (riv.), Pol.
55/K5 **Dunakeszi**, Hun.
50/B4 **Dunany** (pt.), Ire.
68/D2 **Dunaújváros**, Hun.
49/D3 **Dunbar**, Sc,UK
49/D2 **Dunblane**, Sc,UK
130/E4 **Duncan**, Az,US
131/H4 **Duncan**, Ok,US
134/D3 **Duncanville**, Tx,US
50/B3 **Dundalk**, Ire.
50/B4 **Dundalk** (bay), Ire.
137/K7 **Dundalk**, Md,US
125/R7 **Dundas** (pen.), NW,Can.
109/E3 **Dundee**, SAfr.
49/D2 **Dundee**, Sc,UK
50/C3 **Dundrum**, NI,UK
50/C3 **Dundrum** (bay), NI,UK
128/G3 **Dundurn**, Sk,Can.
95/H7 **Dunedin**, NZ
135/H4 **Dunedin**, Fl,US
49/D2 **Dunfermline**, Sc,UK
50/B2 **Dungannon**, NI,UK
50/B3 **Dungannon** (dist.), NI,UK
90/B3 **Dungarpur**, India
49/B4 **Dungarvan**, Ire.
119/K8 **Dungeness** (pt.), Arg.
53/G5 **Dungeness** (pt.), Eng,UK
50/B2 **Dungiven**, NI,UK
107/A2 **Dungu**, D.R. Congo
83/K3 **Dunhua**, China
82/C3 **Dunhuang**, China
52/C4 **Dunkery** (hill), Eng,UK
58/B1 **Dunkirk** (Dunkerque), Fr.
105/E5 **Dunkwa**, Gha.
50/B5 **Dún Laoghaire**, Ire.
50/B2 **Dunloy**, NI,UK
50/B2 **Dunmurry**, NI,UK
135/J3 **Dunn**, NC,US
50/A2 **Dunnamanagh**, NI,UK
50/B2 **Dunnamore**, NI,UK
51/H4 **Dunnington**, Eng,UK
133/Q10 **Dunnville**, On,Can.
134/B5 **Dunqulah**, Sudan
50/D2 **Dunragit**, Sc,UK
49/D3 **Duns**, Sc,UK
50/E1 **Dunscore**, Sc,UK
129/H3 **Dunseith**, ND,US
50/B1 **Dunseverick**, NI,UK
130/B2 **Dunsmuir**, Ca,US
53/F3 **Dunstable**, Eng,UK
59/E5 **Dun-sur-Meuse**, Fr.
83/J1 **Duobukur** (riv.), China
138/P16 **Du Page** (riv.), Il,US
129/H4 **Dupree**, SD,US
116/K7 **Duque de Caxias**, Braz.
119/J7 **Duque de York** (isl.), Chile
132/B4 **Du Quoin**, Il,US
62/F5 **Durance** (riv.), Fr.
123/N9 **Durango** (state), Mex.
64/D1 **Durango**, Sp.
130/F3 **Durango**, Co,US
123/P9 **Durango de Victoria**, Mex.
131/H4 **Durant**, Ok,US
119/F2 **Durazno**, Uru.
119/F2 **Durazno** (dept.), Uru.
109/E3 **Durban**, SAfr.
108/L10 **Durbanville**, SAfr.
59/E3 **Durbuy**, Belg.
68/C4 **Đurđevac**, Cro.
59/F2 **Düren**, Ger.
90/D3 **Durg**, India
90/E3 **Durgāpur**, India
51/G2 **Durham**, Eng,UK
51/F2 **Durham** (co.), Eng,UK
135/J3 **Durham**, NC,US
133/G3 **Durham**, NH,US
53/E5 **Durlston Head** (pt.), Eng,UK
58/D1 **Durme** (riv.), Belg.
68/D4 **Durmitor Nat'l Park**, Mont.
67/F2 **Durrës**, Alb.
53/E4 **Durrington**, Eng,UK
52/D3 **Dursley**, Eng,UK
80/B2 **Dursunbey**, Turk.
93/J4 **D'Urville** (cape), Indo.
132/C1 **Dusey** (riv.), On,Can.
87/D2 **Du Shan** (peak), China
74/G6 **Dushanbe** (cap.), Taj.
56/D6 **Düsseldorf**, Ger.
51/H4 **Dutch** (riv.), Eng,UK
108/L10 **Dutoitspiek** (peak), SAfr.
91/J2 **Duyun**, China
69/K5 **Düzce**, Turk.
80/D3 **Düzici**, Turk.
70/H2 **Dvina** (bay), Rus.
71/J3 **Dvina, Northern** (riv.), Rus.
70/F5 **Dvina, Western** (riv.), Bel., Rus.
90/A3 **Dwārka**, India
128/D4 **Dworshak** (res.), Id,US
50/D6 **Dwyfor** (riv.), Wal,UK
108/C4 **Dwyka** (riv.), SAfr.
72/E1 **Dyat'kovo**, Rus.
125/K2 **Dyer** (cape), Nun,Can.
119/J7 **Dyer** (cape), Chile
132/C3 **Dyer**, In,US
135/F2 **Dyersburg**, Tn,US
50/D6 **Dyffryn**, Wal,UK
52/C1 **Dyfi** (riv.), Wal,UK
55/J4 **Dyje** (riv.), Czh.
73/G4 **Dykh-tau, Gora** (peak), Rus.
58/D2 **Dyle** (Dijle) (riv.), Belg.
55/K2 **Dylewska Gora** (peak), Pol.
53/G4 **Dymchurch**, Eng,UK
73/H4 **Dyul'tydag, Gora** (peak), Rus.
82/C2 **Dzavhan** (riv.), Mong.
72/F3 **Dzenzik, Mys** (pt.), Ukr.
82/C2 **Dzereg**, Mong.
70/J4 **Dzerzhinsk**, Rus.
81/B3 **Dzhalal-Abad**, Kyr.
72/E3 **Dzhankoy**, Ukr.
74/G5 **Dzhizak**, Uzb.
75/P4 **Dzhugdzhur** (range), Rus.
55/L2 **Działdowo**, Pol.
122/D3 **Dzibilchaltún** (ruins), Mex.
122/D3 **Dzidzantún**, Mex.
55/J3 **Dzierżoniów**, Pol.
82/B3 **Dzungarian** (basin), China
81/D3 **Dzungarian Gate** (pass), China
82/E2 **Dzüünbayan-Ulaan**, Mong.
81/F2 **Dzüüngovĭ**, Mong.
82/D2 **Dzüünhangay**, Mong.
82/F2 **Dzüünharaa**, Mong.

E

131/G3 **Eads**, Co,US
125/L3 **Eagle** (riv.), Nf,Can.
132/A1 **Eagle** (lake), On,Can.
128/F3 **Eagle** (riv.), Sk,Can.
130/B2 **Eagle** (lake), Ca,US
130/F3 **Eagle**, Co,US
129/L4 **Eagle** (peak), Mn,US
138/P14 **Eagle** (lake), Wi,US
129/H4 **Eagle Butte**, SD,US
134/C4 **Eagle Pass**, Tx,US
51/E1 **Eaglesfield**, Sc,UK
51/F4 **Earby**, Eng,UK
132/A1 **Ear Falls**, On,Can.
53/G2 **Earith**, Eng,UK
130/C4 **Earlimart**, Ca,US
53/F2 **Earls Barton**, Eng,UK
53/G3 **Earls Colne**, Eng,UK
53/H2 **Earl Stonham**, Eng,UK
134/D4 **Early**, Tx,US
49/D2 **Earn** (riv.), Sc,UK
51/G2 **Easington**, Eng,UK
51/G3 **Easingwold**, Eng,UK
135/H3 **Easley**, SC,US
136/B6 **East** (cape), Ak,US
53/G2 **East Anglia** (reg.), Eng,UK
133/G2 **East Angus**, Qu,Can.
53/H3 **East Bergholt**, Eng,UK
129/K4 **East Bethel**, Mn,US
53/G5 **Eastbourne**, Eng,UK
137/F5 **East Brunswick**, NJ,US
51/G1 **East Chevington**, Eng,UK
138/R16 **East Chicago**, In,US
88/D2 **East China** (sea), Asia
52/B3 **East Cleddau** (riv.), Wal,UK
52/C5 **East Dart** (riv.), Eng,UK
53/G1 **East Dereham**, Eng,UK
138/G7 **East Detroit** (East Pointe), Mi,US
99/Q7 **Easter** (isl.), Chile
108/A2 **Easter** (pt.), Namb.

160
Easte – Faenz

105/E5 Eastern (reg.), Gha.
107/C2 Eastern (prov.), Kenya
104/C4 Eastern (prov.), SLeo.
106/C5 Eastern (reg.), Sudan
51/H4 Eastern (plain), Eng,UK
107/B5 Eastern (prov.), Zam.
108/D3 Eastern Cape (prov.), SAfr.
84/A4 Eastern Channel (str.), Japan
90/C5 Eastern Ghats (uplands), India
74/K4 Eastern Sayans (mts.), Rus.
129/J2 Easterville, Mb,Can.
119/N8 East Falkland (isl.), Falk.
58/C2 East Flanders (prov.), Belg.
57/E1 East Frisian (isls.), Ger.
53/F1 East Glen (riv.), Eng,UK
53/F4 East Grinstead, Eng,UK
128/F4 East Helena, Mt,US
138/C2 East Hill-Meridian, Wa,US
132/C2 East Jordan, Mi,US
134/D3 Eastland, Tx,US
132/C3 East Lansing, Mi,US
51/G6 East Leake, Eng,UK
53/E5 Eastleigh, Eng,UK
132/D3 East Liverpool, Oh,US
108/D4 East London, SAfr.
137/B2 East Los Angeles, Ca,US
132/F1 Eastmain (riv.), Qu,Can.
135/H3 Eastman, Ga,US
137/G5 East Meadow, NY,US
133/G2 East Millinocket, Me,US
129/K5 East Nishnabotna (riv.), Ia,US
52/D5 Easton, Eng,UK
137/E5 Easton, Pa,US
137/F5 East Orange, NJ,US
137/H5 East Patchogue, NY,US
135/G3 East Point, Ga,US
138/G7 East Pointe (East Detroit), Mi,US
133/H2 Eastport, Me,US
51/H5 East Retford, Eng,UK
51/H4 East Riding of Yorkshire, (co.), Eng,UK
51/E2 Eastriggs, Sc,UK
53/H4 Eastry, Eng,UK
132/B4 East Saint Louis, Il,US
75/S2 East Siberian (sea), Rus.
137/E5 East Stroudsburg, Pa,US
53/G5 East Sussex (co.), Eng,UK
132/D2 East Tawas, Mi,US
52/B4 East the Water, Eng,UK
93/G5 East Timor (ctry.)
128/C4 East Wenatchee, Wa,US
137/F5 East Windsor, NJ,US
53/F5 East Wittering, Eng,UK
51/G6 Eastwood, Eng,UK
133/R8 East York, On,Can.
53/E2 Eatington, Eng,UK
131/F2 Eaton, Co,US
128/F3 Eatonia, Sk,Can.
53/F2 Eaton Socon, Eng,UK
137/F5 Eatontown, NJ,US
51/H5 Eau (riv.), Eng,UK
125/J3 Eau Claire (lake), Qu,Can.
132/B2 Eau Claire, Wi,US
58/A4 Eaulne (riv.), Fr.
98/D4 Eauripik (atoll), Micr.
53/E4 Ebble (riv.), Eng,UK
52/C3 Ebbw Vale, Wal,UK
102/G3 Ebeggi (well), Alg.
63/K3 Ebensee, Aus.
55/G2 Eberswalde-Finow, Ger.
83/N3 Ebetsu, Japan
85/H7 Ebina, Japan
81/D3 Ebinur (lake), China
104/D3 Ebo (lake), Mali
66/D2 Eboli, It.
102/H7 Ebolowa, Camr.
98/F4 Ebon (atoll), Mrsh.
65/F2 Ebro (riv.), Sp.
122/B4 Ecatepec, Mex.
51/E1 Ecclefechan, Sc,UK
51/F5 Eccles, Eng,UK
51/F6 Eccleshall, Eng,UK
105/H3 Éché Fadadinga (wadi), Niger
88/B1 Echeng, China
85/M9 Echigawa, Japan
62/F4 Echirolles, Fr.
124/E2 Echo Bay, NW,Can.
129/L2 Echoing (riv.), Mb, On,Can.
56/C6 Echt, Neth.
97/C3 Echuca, Austl.
64/C4 Écija, Sp.
54/E1 Eckernförde, Ger.
52/D2 Eckington, Eng,UK
125/H1 Eclipse (sound), Nun,Can.
116/D1 Ecoporanga, Braz.
138/F7 Ecorse, Mi,US
58/A5 Écos, Fr.
62/D2 Ecouves, Signal d' (peak), Fr.
114/C4 Ecuador (ctry.)
103/P5 Ed, Erit.
49/C2 Edderton, Sc,UK
97/D4 Eddystone (pt.), Austl.
52/B6 Eddystone (rocks), Eng,UK
56/C4 Ede, Neth.
105/G5 Ede, Nga.
102/H7 Edéa, Camr.
58/D1 Edegem, Belg.
116/B1 Edéia, Braz.
68/E1 Edelény, Hun.
57/H4 Edemissen, Ger.
51/F2 Eden (riv.), Eng,UK
135/J2 Eden, NC,US
53/G4 Edenbridge, Eng,UK
109/E3 Edendale, SAfr.
51/F2 Edenside (val.), Eng,UK
57/G6 Eder (riv.), Ger.
57/F6 Edersee (res.), Ger.
57/E2 Edewecht, Ger.
53/E2 Edgbaston, Eng,UK
74/C2 Edge (isl.), Sval.
136/L4 Edgecumbe (cape), Ak,US
125/K2 Edgell (isl.), Nun,Can.
129/G5 Edgerton, Wy,US
138/C3 Edgewood-North Hill, Wa,US
52/D1 Edgmond, Eng,UK
67/H2 Édhessa, Gre.
132/D3 Edinboro, Pa,US
134/D5 Edinburg, Tx,US
49/D3 Edinburgh (cap.), Sc,UK
69/H5 Edirne, Turk.
69/H5 Edirne (prov.), Turk.
137/F5 Edison, NJ,US
135/H3 Edisto (riv.), SC,US
135/H3 Edisto Island, SC,US
105/F2 Édjérir (wadi), Mali
138/C2 Edmonds, Wa,US
128/E2 Edmonton (cap.), Ab,Can.
129/K2 Edmund (lake), Mb,Can.
96/B2 Edmund Kennedy Nat'l Park, Austl.
133/G2 Edmundston, NB,Can.
134/D4 Edna, Tx,US
85/H7 Edo (riv.), Japan
80/A2 Edremit, Turk.
72/C5 Edremit (gulf), Turk.
128/D2 Edson, Ab,Can.
115/M5 Eduardo Gomes, Braz.
107/A3 Edward (lake), Ugan., D.R. Congo
131/K2 Edwards (riv.), Il,US
134/C4 Edwards (plat.), Tx,US
132/B4 Edwardsville, Il,US
111/P Edward VII (pen.), Ant.
111/D Edward VIII (bay), Ant.
49/D2 Edzell, Sc,UK
122/C4 Edzná (ruins), Mex.
58/C1 Eeklo, Belg.
130/B3 Eel (riv.), Ca,US
56/D2 Eelde-Paterswolde, Neth.
56/C4 Eem (riv.), Neth.
56/D2 Eems (Ems) (riv.), Neth.
56/D2 Eemshaven (har.), Neth.
56/D2 Eemskanaal (can.), Neth.
56/C6 Eersel, Neth.
98/F6 Efate (isl.), Van.
129/L5 Effigy Mounds Nat'l Mon., Ia,US
133/R9 Effingham, On,Can.
132/B4 Effingham, Il,US
69/J3 Eforie, Rom.
50/E6 Efyrnwy, Llyn (lake), Wal,UK
66/C3 Egadi (isls.), It.
130/D3 Egan (range), Nv,US
63/K1 Eger (riv.), Ger.
68/E2 Eger, Hun.
48/C4 Egersund, Nor.
57/F5 Eggegebirge (ridge), Ger.
51/G3 Egglescliffe, Eng,UK
51/G2 Eggleston, Eng,UK
53/F4 Egham, Eng,UK
59/D2 Éghezée, Belg.
82/E1 Egiyn (riv.), Mong.
125/R7 Eglinton (isl.), NW,Can.
50/A1 Eglinton, NI,UK
52/C4 Eglwys Brewis, Wal,UK
56/B3 Egmond aan Zee, Neth.
50/E3 Egremont, Eng,UK
80/B3 Eğridir, Turk.
106/B3 Egypt (ctry.)
84/C4 Ehime (pref.), Japan
63/H1 Ehringshausen, Ger.
99/L5 Eiao (isl.), FrPol.
64/D1 Eibar, Sp.
56/D4 Eibergen, Neth.
59/G6 Eichel (riv.), Fr.
63/J2 Eichstätt, Ger.
48/D3 Eidsvoll, Nor.
59/F3 Eifel (plat.), Ger.
85/M9 Eigenji, Japan
90/B6 Eight Degree (chan.), India, Mald.
111/T Eights (coast), Ant.
56/B2 Eijerlandsee Gat (chan.), Neth.
59/E2 Eijsden, Neth.
97/C3 Eildon (lake), Austl.
96/A2 Einasleigh (riv.), Austl.
57/G5 Einbeck, Ger.
56/C6 Eindhoven, Neth.
114/E5 Eirunepé, Braz.
59/E4 Eisch (riv.), Lux.
57/H7 Eisenach, Ger.
63/L3 Eisenerz, Aus.
55/H2 Eisenhüttenstadt, Ger.
63/M3 Eisenstadt, Aus.
59/G2 Eiserfeld, Ger.
57/F3 Eiter (riv.), Ger.
59/G2 Eitorf, Ger.
65/E1 Ejea de los Caballeros, Sp.
123/G6 Ejido, Ven.
56/B6 Ekeren, Belg.
81/C1 Ekibastuz, Kaz.
48/E4 Eksjö, Swe.
125/H3 Ekwan (riv.), On,Can.
104/C2 El 'Acâba (reg.), Mrta.
106/B2 El Alamein (Al 'Alamayn), Egypt
78/B3 El Amra (Abydos) (ruins), Egypt
52/C2 Elan (riv.), Wal,UK
58/A6 Élancourt, Fr.
108/P12 Elands (riv.), SAfr.
108/Q12 Elandsrivier (riv.), SAfr.
64/C4 El Arahal, Sp.
96/B2 El Arish, Austl.
102/F1 El Asnam, Alg.
67/H3 Elassón, Gre.
64/D1 El Astillero, Sp.
106/C2 Elat, Isr.
98/D4 Elato (atoll), Micr.
80/D2 Elazığ, Turk.
66/B1 Elba (isl.), It.
135/G4 Elba, Al,US
123/G6 El Banco, Col.
64/B1 El Barco, Sp.
67/G2 Elbasan, Alb.
102/F1 El Bayadh, Alg.
54/E2 Elbe (riv.), Ger.
130/F3 Elbert (mtn.), Co,US
135/H3 Elberton, Ga,US
57/H2 Elbe-Seitenkanal (can.), Ger.
62/D2 Elbeuf, Fr.
80/D2 Elbistan, Turk.
55/K1 Elblag, Pol.
128/G3 Elbow, Sk,Can.
73/G4 El'brus, Gora (peak), Rus.
56/C4 Elburg, Neth.
78/E1 Elburz (mts.), Iran
130/C4 El Cajon, Ca,US
134/D4 El Campo, Tx,US
128/E4 El Capitan (peak), Mt,US
118/B3 El Carmen, Chile
123/F6 El Carmen, Col.
65/N8 El Casar de Talamanca, Sp.
130/D4 El Centro, Ca,US
138/K11 El Cerrito, Ca,US
65/E3 Elche, Sp.
118/C3 El Chocón (res.), Arg.
114/D2 El Cocuy Nat'l Park, Col.
117/E2 El Colorado, Arg.
65/E3 Elda, Sp.
54/G2 Elde (riv.), Ger.
137/K7 Eldersburg, Md,US
104/C1 El Djouf (des.), Mali, Mrta.
117/F2 Eldorado, Arg.
123/N9 Eldorado, Mex.
134/E3 El Dorado, Ar,US
134/D2 El Dorado, Ks,US
134/C4 Eldorado, Tx,US
107/B2 Eldoret, Kenya
126/W13 Eleao (peak), Hi,US
102/D2 El Eglab (plat.), Alg.
68/E2 Elek, Hun.
73/L2 Elek (riv.), Kaz.
71/X9 Elektrostal', Rus.
69/G4 Elena, Bul.
111/W Elephant (isl.), Ant.
65/M8 El Escorial, Sp.
123/F2 Eleuthera (isl.), Bahm.
131/K3 Eleven Point (riv.), Ar, Mo,US
67/L6 Elevsís, Gre.
64/A1 El Ferrol, Sp.
133/Q9 Elfrida, On,Can.
123/N8 El Fuerte, Mex.
49/D2 Elgin, Sc,UK
138/P15 Elgin, Il,US
129/H4 Elgin, ND,US
134/D4 Elgin, Tx,US
133/R8 Elgin Mills, On,Can.
122/A3 Elgogorrón Nat'l Park, Mex.
64/D1 Elgóibar, Sp.
102/F1 El Golea, Alg.
107/B2 Elgon (mtn.), Kenya, Ugan.
122/B3 El Higo, Mex.
110/D2 Elias Garcia, Ang.
131/G4 Elida, NM,US
134/C4 El Indio, Tx,US
53/E5 Eling, Eng,UK
73/H3 Elista, Rus.
108/A2 Elizabeth (bay), Namb.
137/F5 Elizabeth, NJ,US
135/J2 Elizabeth City, NC,US
135/H2 Elizabethton, Tn,US
132/C4 Elizabethtown, Ky,US
102/D1 El Jadida, Mor.
55/M2 Ełk, Pol.
134/B2 Elk (mts.), Co,US
135/H2 Elk (riv.), WV,US
131/H4 Elk City, Ok,US
138/M10 Elk Grove, Ca,US
138/Q15 Elk Grove Village, Il,US
132/C3 Elkhart, In,US
131/G3 Elkhart, Ks,US
102/D3 El Khatt (escarp.), Mrta.
129/H3 Elkhorn, Mb,Can.
131/H2 Elkhorn (riv.), Ne,US
69/H4 Elkhovo, Bul.
135/H2 Elkin, NC,US
132/E4 Elkins, WV,US
128/E2 Elk Island Nat'l Park, Ab,Can.
130/D2 Elko, Nv,US
128/F2 Elk Point, Ab,Can.
132/C2 Elk Rapids, Mi,US
137/K7 Elk Ridge, Md,US
129/K4 Elk River, Mn,US
51/G4 Elland, Eng,UK
59/F2 Elle (riv.), Ger.
125/R7 Ellef Ringnes (isl.), Nun,Can.
51/E2 Ellen (riv.), Eng,UK
129/J4 Ellendale, ND,US
128/C4 Ellensburg, Wa,US
57/H5 Eller (riv.), Ger.
59/G4 Ellerbach (riv.), Ger.
97/D3 Ellery (peak), Austl.
125/T6 Ellesmere (isl.), Nun,Can.
51/F5 Ellesmere Port, Eng,UK
118/C2 El Libertador General Bernardo O'Higgins (reg.), Chile
124/F2 Ellice (riv.), Nun,Can.
137/K7 Ellicott City, Md,US
132/D2 Elliot Lake, On,Can.
135/J2 Elliott (peak), Va,US
110/E5 Ellisras, SAfr.
123/F6 El Llano, Pan.
49/D2 Ellon, Sc,UK
51/H4 Elloughton, Eng,UK
111/T Ellsworth (mts.), Ant.
131/H3 Ellsworth, Ks,US
133/G2 Ellsworth, Me,US
132/A2 Ellsworth, Wi,US
111/U Ellsworth Land (reg.), Ant.
63/J2 Ellwangen, Ger.
133/S10 Elma, NY,US
80/C2 Elmadağ, Turk.
80/B3 Elmalı, Turk.
130/F4 El Malpais Nat'l Mon., NM,US
123/M8 El Marmol, Mex.
65/L7 El Masnou, Sp.
138/P13 Elm Grove, Wi,US
138/Q16 Elmhurst, Il,US
105/E5 Elmina, Gha.
132/E3 Elmira, NY,US
114/D7 El Misti (vol.), Peru
65/N8 El Molar, Sp.
137/G5 Elmont, NY,US
65/L6 El Montcau (peak), Sp.
137/B2 El Monte, Ca,US
118/B2 El Morrito (pt.), Chile
130/E4 El Morro Nat'l Mon., NM,US
104/C2 El Mreyyé (reg.), Mrta.
57/G1 Elmshorn, Ger.
53/G2 Elmswell, Eng,UK
138/Q16 Elmwood Park, Il,US
137/F5 Elmwood Park, NJ,US
102/D3 El Mzereb (well), Mali
118/C2 El Nevado (peak), Arg.
93/E1 El Nido, Phil.
116/H6 Elói Mendes, Braz.
62/A2 Elorn (riv.), Fr.
102/G1 El Oued, Alg.
130/E4 Eloy, Az,US
123/J6 El Palmar, Ven.
118/F1 El Palmar Nat'l Park, Arg.
65/N8 El Pardo, Sp.
134/B4 El Paso, Tx,US
123/J5 El Pilar, Ven.
90/D6 Elpitiya, SrL.
122/D4 El Placer, Mex.
123/F6 El Porvenir, Pan.
122/B2 El Potosí Nat'l Park, Mex.
65/G2 El Prat de Llobregat, Sp.
122/D4 El Progreso, Hon.
64/B4 El Puerto de Santa María, Sp.
123/N9 El Quelite, Mex.
131/H4 El Reno, Ok,US
137/A2 El Rio, Ca,US
123/H5 El Roque, Ven.
128/F3 Elrose, Sk,Can.
136/L3 Elsa, Yk,Can.
63/J5 Elsa (riv.), It.
64/B2 Elsa (res.), Sp.
64/C1 Elsa (riv.), Sp.
123/N9 El Salado, Mex.
122/D5 El Salvador (ctry.)
123/F3 El Salvador, Cuba
123/A2 El Salvador, Mex.
123/H6 El Samán de Apure, Ven.
57/F4 Else (riv.), Ger.
137/B3 El Segundo, Ca,US
123/H4 El Seibo, DRep.
81/F4 Elsen (lake), China
57/F2 Elsfleth, Ger.
106/B4 El Shab (well), Egypt
137/C3 Elsinore (lake), Ca,US
123/L7 El Socorro, Mex.
56/C5 Elst, Neth.
53/F4 Elstead, Eng,UK
122/B3 El Tajín (ruins), Mex.
114/D2 El Tama Nat'l Park, Ven.
64/B1 El Teleno (mtn.), Sp.
123/J6 El Tigre, Ven.
73/H2 El'ton (lake), Rus.
137/C3 El Toro, Ca,US
114/E3 El Tuparro Nat'l Park, Col.
63/H1 Eltville am Rhein, Ger.
90/D4 Elūru, India
64/B3 Elvas, Port.
48/D3 Elverum, Nor.
114/D2 El Viejo (peak), Col.
123/G6 El Vigía, Ven.
123/P8 El Volcán, Mex.
107/D2 El Wak, Kenya
128/F3 Elwell (lake), Mt,US
132/C3 Elwood, In,US
50/E5 Elwy (riv.), Wal,UK
53/G2 Ely, Eng,UK
129/L4 Ely, Mn,US
130/D3 Ely, Nv,US
53/G2 Ely, Isle of (reg.), Eng,UK
132/D3 Elyria, Oh,US
57/G3 Elzbach (riv.), Ger.
57/G4 Elze, Ger.
79/F1 Emāmshahr, Iran
115/H7 Emas Nat'l Park, Braz.
117/D1 Embarcación, Arg.
135/E2 Embarras (riv.), Il,US
73/L2 Embi, Kaz.
73/K3 Embi (riv.), Kaz.
114/D5 Embira (riv.), Braz.
116/C1 Emborcaçao (res.), Braz.
116/G8 Embu-Guaçu, Braz.
56/E2 Emden, Ger.
91/H2 Emei, China
97/G5 Emerald, Austl.
129/J3 Emerson, Mb,Can.
138/K11 Emeryville, Ca,US
80/B2 Emet, Turk.
63/J4 Emilia-Romagna (reg.), It.
81/D2 Emin (riv.), China
131/K3 Eminence, Mo,US
69/H4 Emine, Nos (cape), Bul.
80/B2 Emirdağ, Turk.
80/C3 Emirgazi, Turk.
109/E2 Emlembe (peak), Swaz.
56/D3 Emlichheim, Ger.
48/E4 Emmaboda, Swe.
137/E5 Emmaus, Pa,US
57/C3 Emmeloord, Neth.
56/D3 Emmen, Neth.
60/D1 Emmendingen, Ger.
57/G4 Emmer (riv.), Ger.
57/E5 Emmerbach (riv.), Ger.
56/D5 Emmerich, Ger.
128/D5 Emmett, Id,US
53/G1 Emneth, Eng,UK
134/E3 Emory, Tx,US
134/B2 Emory (peak), Tx.,US
123/M8 Empalme, Mex.
109/E3 Empangeni, SAfr.
117/E2 Empedrado, Arg.
118/B2 Empedrado, Chile
131/H3 Emporia, Ks,US
132/E4 Emporia, Va,US
57/E4 Emsbüren, Ger.
57/E4 Emsdetten, Ger.
56/D2 Ems (Eems) (riv.), Ger., Neth.
57/E2 Ems-Jade (can.), Ger.
57/E3 Emsland (reg.), Ger.
57/F3 Emstek, Ger.
48/H4 Emumägi (hill), Est.
83/J1 Emur (riv.), China
85/E3 Ena, Japan
128/G5 Encampment, Wy,US
123/L7 Encantada, Cerro de la (mt.), Mex.
123/M8 Encantada, Cerro (mt.), Mex.
117/E2 Encarnación, Par.
123/P9 Encarnación de Díaz, Mex.
104/E5 Enchi, Gha.
130/C4 Encinitas, Ca,US
97/A2 Encounter (bay), Austl.
116/A4 Encruzilhada do Sul, Braz.
93/F5 Ende, Indo.
96/B1 Endeavour River Nat'l Park, Austl.
99/H5 Enderbury (atoll), Kiri.
128/D3 Enderby, BC,Can.
111/D Enderby Land (reg.), Ant.
129/J4 Enderlin, ND,US
132/E3 Endicott, NY,US
114/D6 Ene (riv.), Peru
98/F3 Enewetak (atoll), Mrsh.
88/D4 Engaño (cape), Phil.
73/H2 Engel's, Rus.
59/G2 Engelskirchen, Ger.
56/D2 Engelsmanplaat (isl.), Neth.
116/K7 Engenheiro Paulo de Frontin, Braz.
57/F4 Enger, Ger.
92/B5 Enggano (isl.), Indo.
103/N4 Enghershatu (peak), Erit.
58/D2 Enghien, Belg.
49/D4 England, UK
62/C2 Englehart, On,Can.
137/F5 Englewood, NJ,US
137/G5 Englewood, NJ,US
111/V English (coast), Ant.
129/K3 English (riv.), On,Can.
62/B2 English (chan.), Eur.
90/E3 English Bāzār, India
57/F5 Englishtown, NJ,US
131/H3 Enid, Ok,US
56/C3 Enkhuizen, Neth.
48/F4 Enköping, Swe.
66/D4 Enna, It.
104/K4 Ennedi (plat.), Chad
57/E6 Ennepe (riv.), Ger.
57/E6 Ennepetal, Ger.
57/F5 Enningerloh, Ger.
128/F4 Ennis, Mt,US
134/D3 Ennis, Tx,US
63/L3 Enns (riv.), Aus.
69/E6 Enoggera (res.), Austl.
135/H3 Enoree (riv.), SC,US
56/D4 Enschede, Neth.
57/E6 Ense, Ger.
123/L7 Ensenada, Mex.
87/B5 Enshi, China
107/B2 Entebbe, Ugan.
63/K2 Entenbühl (peak), Ger.
135/G4 Enterprise, Al,US
118/F2 Entre Rios (prov.), Arg.
64/A3 Entroncamento, Port.
105/G5 Enugu, Nga.
105/G5 Enugu (state), Nga.
138/D3 Enumclaw, Wa,US
85/N10 Enushū (sea), Japan
58/A4 Envermeu, Fr.
63/H2 Enz (riv.), Ger.
85/F3 Enzan, Japan
59/F4 Enzbach (riv.), Ger.
56/C4 Epe, Neth.
58/C5 Épernay, Fr.
98/F6 Epi (isl.), Van.
67/H4 Epidaurus (ruins), Gre.
60/C1 Épinal, Fr.
67/G3 Epirus (reg.), Gre.
59/F5 Eppelborn, Ger.
96/H8 Epping, Austl.
53/G3 Epping, Eng,UK
96/B3 Epping Forest Nat'l Park, Austl.
53/F4 Epsom and Ewell, Eng,UK
51/H4 Epworth, Eng,UK
102/G7 Equatorial Guinea (ctry.)
91/H2 Er (lake), China
66/E2 Eraclea (ruins), It.
66/C4 Eraclea Minoa (ruins), It.
90/D6 Eravur, SrL.
89/B3 Erawan Nat'l Park, Thai.
63/H4 Erba, It.
80/D2 Erbaa, Turk.
59/G4 Erbeskopf (peak), Ger.
118/B3 Ercilla, Chile
80/E2 Erciş, Turk.
58/C3 Erclin (riv.), Fr.
68/D2 Érd, Hun.
83/K3 Erdao (riv.), China
69/H5 Erdek, Turk.
69/H5 Erdek (gulf), Turk.
80/C3 Erdemli, Turk.
82/G3 Erdene, Mong.
82/E2 Erdenedalay, Mong.
103/K4 Erdi-Ma (plat.), Chad
63/J2 Erding, Ger.
62/C3 Erdre (riv.), Fr.
111/M Erebus (vol.), Ant.
116/A3 Erechim, Braz.
82/G2 Ereen Davaanï (mts.), Mong.
69/K5 Ereğli, Turk.
80/C3 Ereğli, Turk.
81/D3 Eren Habirga (mts.), China
82/G3 Erenhot, China
69/K5 Erenler, Turk.
115/G4 Erepecu (lake), Braz.
64/C2 Eresma (riv.), Sp.
74/H4 Ereymentaū, Kaz.
102/E1 Erfoud, Mor.
59/F1 Erft (riv.), Ger.
59/F2 Erftstadt, Ger.
54/F3 Erfurt, Ger.
80/D2 Ergani, Turk.
102/D3 'Erg Chech (des.), Afr.
102/H4 'Erg du Ténéré (des.), Niger
69/H5 Ergene Nehri (riv.), Turk.
102/D2 'Erg Iguidi (des.), Afr.
102/J5 Erguig (riv.), Chad
83/H1 Ergun (riv.), China, Rus.
128/D3 Erickson, BC,Can.
129/J3 Erickson, Mb,Can.
128/J3 Erie (lake), Can., US
133/S9 Erie (can.), NY,US
132/D3 Erie, Pa,US
103/Q5 Erigabo, Som.
129/J3 Eriksdale, Mb,Can.
98/F4 Erikub (atoll), Mrsh.
67/G4 Erímanthos (peak), Gre.
83/N3 Erimo-misaki (cape), Japan
103/N4 Eritrea (ctry.)
56/D6 Erkelenz, Ger.
55/G2 Erkner, Ger.
56/D6 Erkrath, Ger.
63/J2 Erlangen, Ger.
87/F2 Erlongshan (res.), China
52/C6 Erme (riv.), Eng,UK
56/C4 Ermelo, Neth.
109/E2 Ermelo, SAfr.
80/C3 Ermenek, Turk.
67/J4 Ermoúpolis, Gre.
59/H2 Erndtebrück, Ger.
62/C2 Ernée (riv.), Fr.
90/C5 Erode, India
58/D3 Erquelinnes, Belg.
102/E1 Er Rachidia, Mor.
102/D1 Er Rif (mts.), Mor.
49/A3 Errigal (mtn.), Ire.
98/F6 Erromango (isl.), Van.
57/H4 Erse (riv.), Ger.
74/H4 Ertis (riv.), Kaz.
82/B2 Ertix (riv.), China
116/B3 Erval d'Oeste, Braz.
132/D4 Erwin, Tn,US
57/F5 Erwitte, Ger.
67/F2 Erzen (riv.), Alb.
63/K1 Erzgebirge (Krušné Hory) (mts.), Czh., Ger.
80/D2 Erzincan, Turk.
80/E2 Erzurum, Turk.
98/D5 Esa'ala, PNG
110/D1 Esambo, D.R. Congo
83/N3 Esashi, Japan
48/D5 Esbjerg, Den.
58/B6 Esbly, Fr.
48/H3 Esbo (Espoo), Fin.
130/E3 Escalante (riv.), Ut,US
135/G4 Escambia (riv.), Fl,US
132/C2 Escanaba, Mi,US
58/C3 Escaudain, Fr.
58/C3 Escaut (riv.), Belg., Fr.
59/E6 Esch (riv.), Fr.
58/B5 Esches (riv.), Fr.
59/E5 Esch-sur-Alzette, Lux.
57/H6 Eschwege, Ger.
59/F2 Eschweiler, Ger.
130/C4 Escondido, Ca,US
123/N9 Escuinapa de Hidalgo, Mex.
122/C5 Escuintla, Guat.
80/N7 Esdraelon, Plain of (plain), Isr.
102/H7 Eséka, Camr.
57/E1 Esens, Ger.
65/F1 Esera (riv.), Sp.
78/F2 Eşfahān, Iran
52/C1 Esgair Ddu (mtn.), Wal,UK
51/G2 Esh, Eng,UK
53/F4 Esher, Eng,UK
110/D2 Eshimba, D.R. Congo
51/G2 Esh Winning, Eng,UK
81/A1 Esil, Kaz.
51/E2 Esk (riv.), Eng,UK
51/H3 Esk (riv.), Eng,UK
51/E1 Eskdale (val.), Sc,UK
80/C2 Eskil, Turk.
48/F4 Eskilstuna, Swe.
80/D2 Eskimalatya, Turk.
136/M2 Eskimo (lakes), NW,Can.
80/B2 Eskişehir, Turk.
64/C1 Esla (riv.), Sp.
78/E2 Eslāmābād, Iran
57/F6 Eslohe, Ger.
80/B2 Eşme, Turk.
114/C3 Esmeraldas, Ecu.
59/E2 Esneux, Belg.
132/D2 Espanola, On,Can.
131/F4 Española, NM,US
65/K6 Esparreguera, Sp.
57/F4 Espelkamp, Ger.
95/B4 Esperance, Austl.
128/B3 Esperanza (inlet), BC,Can.
64/A3 Espichel (cape), Port.
114/D3 Espinal, Col.
101/D1 Espinhaço (mts.), Braz.
64/A2 Espinho, Port.
119/F2 Espinillo (pt.), Uru.
115/K6 Espinosa, Braz.
116/D1 Espírito Santo (state), Braz.
116/G7 Espírito Santo do Pinhal, Braz.
98/F6 Espiritu Santo (isl.), Van.
115/L6 Esplanada, Braz.
65/L7 Espluges, Sp.
48/H3 Espoo (Esbo), Fin.
118/C4 Esquel, Arg.
117/E3 Esquina, Arg.
102/D1 Essaouira, Mor.
57/G5 Esse (riv.), Ger.
56/B6 Essen, Belg.
56/E6 Essen, Ger.
97/F5 Essendon, Austl.
114/G2 Essequibo (riv.), Guy.
138/G7 Essex, On,Can.
53/G3 Essex (co.), Eng,UK
137/K7 Essex, Md,US
63/H2 Esslingen, Ger.
58/B6 Essonne (dept.), Fr.
119/L8 Estados (isl.), Arg.
78/F3 Eşţahbān, Iran
115/L6 Estância, Braz.
119/L8 Estancia La Carmen, Arg.
119/L8 Estancia La Sera, Arg.
65/F1 Estats, Pico de (peak), Sp.
109/E3 Estcourt, SAfr.
122/E3 Este (pt.), Cuba
57/G2 Este (riv.), Ger.
63/J4 Este, It.
116/B4 Esteio, Braz.
122/D5 Estelí, Nic.
64/D1 Estella, Sp.
137/C3 Estelle (mtn.), Ca,US
64/C4 Estepa, Sp.
64/C4 Estepona, Sp.
129/H3 Esterhazy, Sk,Can.
102/G7 Esterias (cape), Gabon
63/G5 Estéron (riv.), Fr.
129/H3 Estevan, Sk,Can.
58/D3 Estinnes-Au-Mont, Belg.
51/G2 Eston, Eng,UK
70/E4 Estonia (ctry.)
64/A3 Estoril, Port.
64/B2 Estrela, Serra da (mtn.), Port.
64/A3 Estrela, Serra da (range), Port.
64/B3 Estremadura (aut. comm.), Sp.
64/B3 Estremoz, Port.
115/J5 Estrondo (mts.), Braz.
68/D2 Esztergom, Hun.
98/E4 Etal (atoll), Micr.
48/H3 Etelä-Suomen (prov.) Fin.
58/A2 Étaples, Fr.
90/C2 Etāwah, India
129/H3 Ethelbert, Mb,Can.
103/N5 Ethiopia (ctry.)
103/N6 Ethiopian (plat.), Eth.
85/M9 Eti (riv.), Japan
66/D4 Etna, Monte (Mount Etna) (vol.), It.
133/Q8 Etobicoke, On,Can.
136/E3 Etolin (str.), Ak,US
83/P2 Etorofu (isl.), Rus.
110/C4 Etosha Nat'l Park, Namb.
110/C4 Etosha Pan (salt pan), Namb.
69/G4 Etropole, Bul.
85/F2 Etsu-Joshin Kogen Nat'l Park, Japan
80/M8 Et Taiyiba, Isr.
59/F4 Ettelbruck, Lux.
56/B5 Etten-Leur, Neth.
58/D2 Etterbeek, Belg.
80/M8 Et Tīra, Isr.
63/H2 Ettlingen, Ger.
51/E1 Ettrick Pen (mtn.), Sc,UK
58/A3 Eu, Fr.
99/H7 Eua (isl.), Tonga
96/B2 Eubenangee Swamp Nat'l Park, Austl.
132/D3 Euclid, Oh,US
135/F3 Eudora, Ar,US
135/G4 Eufaula, Al,US
131/J4 Eufaula, Ok,US
131/H4 Eufaula (lake), Ok,US
128/C4 Eugene, Or,US
123/L8 Eugenia (pt.), Mex.
64/B1 Eume (lake), Sp.
96/C3 Eungella Nat'l Park, Austl.
134/E4 Eunice, La,US
131/G4 Eunice, NM,US
59/F2 Eupen, Belg.
77/D6 Euphrates (riv.), Asia
62/D2 Eure (riv.), Fr.
125/S6 Eureka, Nun,Can.
125/S7 Eureka (sound), Nun,Can.
130/A2 Eureka, Ca,US
128/E3 Eureka, Mt,US
130/D3 Eureka, Nv,US
129/J4 Eureka, SD,US
58/B6 Eurodisney, Fr.
47/* Europe (cont.)
56/B5 Europoort, Neth.
59/F2 Euskirchen, Ger.
135/H4 Eustis, Fl,US
54/F1 Eutin, Ger.
107/B5 Eutini, Malw.
128/B2 Eutsuk (lake), BC,Can.
51/F4 Euxton, Eng,UK
132/E1 Évain, Qu,Can.
125/H2 Evans (str.), Nun,Can.
132/E1 Evans (lake), Qu,Can.
131/F2 Evans, Co,US
131/F3 Evans (mtn.), Co,US
138/Q15 Evanston, Il,US
128/F5 Evanston, Wy,US
132/C4 Evansville, In,US
131/F2 Evansville, Wy,US
132/C3 Evart, Mi,US
108/D2 Evaton, SAfr.
78/F3 Evaz, Iran
129/K4 Eveleth, Mn,US
75/L3 Evenkiyskiy, Aut. Okr., Rus.
53/E3 Evenlode (riv.), Eng,UK
97/D3 Everard (cape), Austl.
52/D4 Evercreech, Eng,UK
138/C2 Everett, Wa,US
58/C1 Evergem, Belg.
135/H5 Everglades Nat'l Park, Fl,US
135/G4 Evergreen, Al,US
138/Q16 Evergreen Park, Il,US
53/F3 Eversholt, Eng,UK
57/E5 Everswinkel, Ger.
53/E2 Evesham, Eng,UK
67/G3 Évinos (riv.), Gre.
64/B3 Évora, Port.
64/A3 Évora (dist.), Port.
58/A5 Évreux, Fr.
62/C2 Évron, Fr.
67/H4 Evrótas (riv.), Gre.
58/B6 Évry, Fr.
67/H3 Évvoia (gulf), Gre.
67/H3 Évvoia (isl.), Gre.
126/V13 Ewa, Hi,US
126/V13 Ewa Beach, Hi,US
137/F5 Ewing, NJ,US
131/J3 Excelsior Springs, Mo,US
52/C5 Exe (riv.), Eng,UK
52/C5 Exeter, Eng,UK
133/G3 Exeter, NH,US
52/C5 Exminster, Eng,UK
52/C4 Exmoor Nat'l Park, Eng,UK
132/F4 Exmore, Va,US
119/J7 Exmouth (pen.), Chile
52/C5 Exmouth, Eng,UK
125/L4 Exploits (riv.), Nf,Can.
116/G7 Extrema, Braz.
123/F3 Exuma (sound), Bahm.
51/G5 Eyam, Eng,UK
107/B3 Eyasi (lake), Tanz.
53/H2 Eye, Eng,UK
53/F1 Eye (brook), Eng,UK
49/D3 Eyemouth, Sc,UK
80/N9 Eyn Hemed Nat'l Park, Isr.
53/G4 Eynsford, Eng,UK
95/C4 Eyre (pen.), Austl.
95/C3 Eyre North (lake), Austl.
67/K3 Ezine, Turk.
102/H3 Ezzane (well), Alg.

F

99/L6 Faaa, FrPol.
134/B4 Fabens, Tx,US
64/B1 Fabero, Sp.
54/F1 Fåborg, Den.
63/K5 Fabriano, It.
114/D3 Facatativá, Col.
58/C2 Faches-Thumesnil, Fr.
103/K4 Fada, Chad
105/F3 Fada-N'Gourma, Burk.
63/J4 Faenza, It.

103/J6 Fafa (riv.), CAfr.
64/A2 Fafe, Port.
103/P6 Fafen Shet' (riv.), Eth.
69/G3 Făgăraş, Rom.
48/E4 Fagersta, Swe.
119/L8 Fagnano (lake), Arg.
104/D2 Faguibine (lake), Mali
65/S12 Faial (isl.), Azor.,Port.
51/F4 Failsworth, Eng,UK
136/J3 Fairbanks, Ak,US
138/J11 Fairfax, Ca,US
137/J8 Fairfax, Va,US
96/G8 Fairfield, Austl.
138/K10 Fairfield, Ca,US
137/G4 Fairfield, Ct,US
128/F4 Fairfield, Mt,US
132/C4 Fairfield, Oh,US
134/D4 Fairfield, Tx,US
53/E3 Fairford, Eng,UK
133/F3 Fair Haven, Vt,US
50/B1 Fair Head (pt.), NI,UK
137/K7 Fairland, Md,US
137/F5 Fair Lawn, NJ,US
137/F5 Fairless Hills, Pa,US
53/G5 Fairlight, Eng,UK
129/K5 Fairmont, Mn,US
132/D4 Fairmont, WV,US
138/M9 Fair Oaks, Ca,US
134/B2 Fairplay, Co,US
128/D1 Fairview, Ab,Can.
131/H3 Fairview, Ok,US
136/L4 Fairweather (cape), Ak,US
136/L4 Fairweather (mtn.), BC,Can., Ak,US
138/C3 Fairwood-Cascade, Wa,US
79/K2 Faisalabad, Pak.
67/J5 Faistós (ruins), Gre.
90/D2 Faizābād, India
99/M6 Fakahina (isl.), FrPol.
99/H5 Fakaofo (atoll), Tok.
99/L6 Fakarava (atoll), FrPol.
53/G1 Fakenham, Eng,UK
102/G7 Fako (peak), Camr.
54/G1 Fakse Bugt (bay), Den.
52/B6 Fal (riv.), Eng,UK
134/D5 Falcon (res.), Mex., US
63/K5 Falconara Marittima, It.
104/C3 Falémé (riv.), Mali, Sen.
99/S9 Faleolo, Samoa
134/D5 Falfurrias, Tx,US
128/D2 Falher, Ab,Can.
48/E4 Falkenberg, Swe.
53/H2 Falkenham, Eng,UK
119/M8 Falkland Islands (Islas Malvinas) (dpcy.), UK
48/E4 Falköping, Swe.
57/G3 Fallingbostel, Ger.
130/C3 Fallon, Nv,US
133/G3 Fall River, Ma,US
137/J8 Falls Church, Va,US
131/J2 Falls City, Ne,US
52/A6 Falmouth, Eng,UK
52/A6 Falmouth (bay), Eng,UK
123/G4 Falso (cape), DRep.
119/K8 Falso Cabo de Hornos (cape), Chile
54/G1 Falster (isl.), Den.
69/H2 Fălticeni, Rom.
48/E3 Falun, Swe.
80/J4 Famagusta, Cyp.
59/F5 Fameck, Fr.
59/E3 Famenne (reg.), Belg.
87/D5 Fanchang, China
109/H8 Fandriana, Madg.
50/B4 Fane (riv.), Ire.
99/L6 Fangatau (isl.), FrPol.
99/L7 Fangataufa (isl.), FrPol.
88/C2 Fangcun, China
88/C2 Fangdao, China
88/D3 Fangliao, Tai.
88/A2 Fanjing (peak), China
99/K4 Fanning (Tabuaeran) (atoll), Kiri.
54/E1 Fanø (isl.), Den.
63/K5 Fano, It.
89/C1 Fan Si Pan (peak), Viet.
80/H6 Fāqūs, Egypt
107/A2 Faradje, D.R. Congo
109/H8 Farafangana, Madg.
106/A3 Farāfirah, Wāḩāt al (oasis), Egypt
79/H2 Farāh, Afg.
79/H2 Farāh (riv.), Afg.
130/B3 Farallon (isls.), Ca,US
98/D3 Farallon de Medinilla (isl.), NMar.
98/D2 Farallon de Pajaros (isl.), NMar.
114/C3 Farallones de Cali Nat'l Park, Col.
104/C4 Faranah (comm.), Gui.
109/H8 Faraony (riv.), Madg.
98/D4 Faraulep (atoll), Micr.
58/D3 Farciennes, Belg.
53/E5 Fareham, Eng,UK
129/J4 Fargo, ND,US
129/K4 Faribault, Mn,US
90/C2 Farīdābād, India
90/E3 Farīdpur, Bang.
53/E3 Faringdon, Eng,UK
80/H6 Fāriskūr, Egypt
133/G2 Farmington, Me,US
138/F7 Farmington, Mi,US
131/K3 Farmington, Mo,US
130/E3 Farmington, NM,US
138/F7 Farmington Hills, Mi,US
132/E4 Farmville, Va,US
53/F4 Farnborough, Eng,UK
53/F4 Farnham, Eng,UK
51/F4 Farnworth, Eng,UK
124/C2 Faro, Yk,Can.
64/B4 Faro, Port.
64/A4 Faro (dist.), Port.
47/D2 Faroe (isls.), Den.
48/F4 Fårön (isl.), Swe.
102/H6 Faro Nat'l Park, Camr.
45/M6 Farquhar (isls.), Sey.
116/B4 Farroupilha, Braz.
90/C2 Farrukhābād, India
67/H3 Fársala, Gre.
128/F5 Farson, Wy,US
48/C4 Farsund, Nor.
78/F5 Fartak, Ra's (pt.), Yem.
121/N4 Farvel (cape), Grld.
111/T Farwell (isl.), Ant.
78/F3 Fasā, Iran
66/E2 Fasano, It.
57/H3 Fassberg, Ger.
72/D2 Fastov, Ukr.
93/H4 Fatagar Tuting (cape), Indo.
45/T6 Fataka (isl.), Sol.
90/B2 Fatehpur, India
90/D2 Fatehpur, India
104/A3 Fatick (reg.), Sen.
64/A3 Fátima, Port.
78/C4 Fāţimah (dry riv.), SAr.
80/D2 Fatsa, Turk.
99/M6 Fatu Hiva (isl.), FrPol.
60/B1 Faucilles (mts.), Fr.
50/A2 Faughan (riv.), NI,UK
129/J4 Faulkton, SD,US
48/E2 Fauske, Nor.
66/C4 Favara, It.
53/G4 Faversham, Eng,UK
53/E5 Fawley, Eng,UK
124/H3 Fawn (riv.), On,Can.
48/M7 Faxaflói (bay), Ice.
116/B2 Faxinal, Braz.
103/J4 Faya-Largeau, Chad
135/G3 Fayette, Al,US
131/J3 Fayette, Mo,US
135/F4 Fayette, Ms,US
134/E2 Fayetteville, Ar,US
135/G3 Fayetteville, Ga,US
135/J3 Fayetteville, NC,US
135/G3 Fayetteville, Tn,US
105/F4 Fazao (mts.), Gha., Togo
105/F4 Fazao Nat'l Park, Togo
49/A4 Feale (riv.), Ire.
135/J3 Fear (cape), NC,US
130/B3 Feather (riv.), Ca,US
51/G4 Featherstone, Eng,UK
62/D2 Fécamp, Fr.
138/C3 Federal Way, Wa,US
50/A2 Feeny, NI,UK
68/F2 Fehérgyarmat, Hun.
54/F1 Fehmarn (isl.), Ger.
54/F1 Fehmarn Belt (str.), Ger., Den.
87/D4 Fei (riv.), China
116/D2 Feia (lake), Braz.
58/C3 Feignies, Fr.
87/D4 Fei Huang (riv.), China
115/L6 Feira de Santana, Braz.
63/L3 Feistritz (riv.), Aus.
68/D2 Fejér (co.), Hun.
65/G3 Felanitx, Sp.
60/E2 Feldberg (peak), Ger.
61/F3 Feldkirch, Aus.
63/L3 Feldkirchen in Kärnten, Aus.
53/H3 Felixstowe, Eng,UK
123/N7 Félix U. Gómez, Mex.
51/G2 Felling, Eng,UK
57/G6 Felsberg, Ger.
53/G2 Feltwell, Eng,UK
87/C4 Fen (riv.), China
64/A1 Fene, Sp.
80/C3 Fener (pt.), Turk.
59/G6 Fénétrange, Fr.
67/J2 Fengári (peak), Gre.
83/J3 Fengcheng, China
87/D5 Fengle (riv.), China
87/D3 Fengnan, China
87/D3 Fengrun, China
83/J1 Fengshui (peak), China
87/C2 Fengzhen, China
136/C5 Fenimore (passg.), Ak,US
53/G2 Fens, The (reg.), Eng,UK
138/E6 Fenton, Mi,US
72/E3 Feodosiya, Ukr.
79/G2 Ferdows, Iran
66/C2 Ferentino, It.
66/C1 Ferento (ruins), It.
81/B3 Fergana, Uzb.
129/J4 Fergus Falls, Mn,US
124/F2 Ferguson (lake), Nun,Can.
104/D4 Ferkéssédougou, C.d'Iv.
63/L3 Ferlach, Aus.
102/C4 Ferlo (reg.), Sen.
104/B3 Ferlo, Vallée du (wadi), Sen.
50/A3 Fermanagh (dist.), NI,UK
137/B3 Fermin (pt.), Ca,US
66/C1 Fermo, It.
135/H4 Fernandina Beach, Fl,US
115/M4 Fernando de Noronha (isl.), Braz.
116/B2 Fernandópolis, Braz.
64/C4 Fernán-Núñez, Sp.
137/K7 Ferndale, Md,US
138/F7 Ferndale, Mi,US
53/E5 Ferndown, Eng,UK
128/E3 Fernie, BC,Can.
97/G5 Ferntree Gully Nat'l Park, Austl.
66/E2 Ferrandina, It.
63/J4 Ferrara, It.
64/A3 Ferreira do Alentejo, Port.
62/C4 Ferret (cape), Fr.
134/F4 Ferriday, La,US
135/F4 Ferriday, La,US
51/G2 Ferryhill, Eng,UK
52/B3 Ferryside, Wal,UK
63/M3 Fertő (Neusiedler See) (lake), Aus., Hun.
56/C2 Ferwerd, Neth.
102/E1 Fès, Mor.
110/C2 Feshi, D.R. Congo
135/F2 Festus, Mo,US
53/F4 Fetcham, Eng,UK
69/H3 Feteşti, Rom.
63/J2 Feucht, Ger.
125/J3 Feuilles (lake), Qu,Can.
125/J3 Feuilles (riv.), Qu,Can.
62/F4 Feurs, Fr.
79/K1 Feyzābād, Afg.
102/H2 Fezzan (reg.), Libya
50/E6 Ffestiniog, Wal,UK
109/H8 Fianarantsoa, Madg.
109/H8 Fianarantsoa (prov.), Madg.
102/J6 Fianga, Chad
108/D3 Ficksburg, SAfr.
63/J4 Fidenza, It.
104/C4 Fié (riv.), Gui., Mali
69/G3 Fieni, Rom.
67/F2 Fier, Alb.
67/G1 Fierzë (lake), Alb.
49/D2 Fife Ness (pt.), Sc,UK
62/E4 Figeac, Fr.
64/A2 Figueira da Foz, Port.
65/G1 Figueres, Sp.
102/E1 Figuig, Mor.
109/G8 Fiherenana (riv.), Madg.
98/G6 Fiji (ctry.)
111/X Filchner Ice Shelf, Ant.
51/H3 Filey, Eng,UK
51/H3 Filey (bay), Eng,UK
69/F3 Filiaşi, Rom.
66/D3 Filicudi (isl.), It.
105/F3 Filingué, Niger
67/J2 Filippoi (ruins), Gre.
48/E4 Filipstad, Swe.
137/B2 Fillmore, Ca,US
130/D3 Fillmore, Ut,US
52/D3 Filton, Eng,UK
111/Z Fimbul Ice Shelf, Ant.
103/J8 Fimi (riv.), D.R. Congo
63/H4 Finale Ligure, It.
104/C3 Fina Rsv., Mali
49/D2 Findhorn (riv.), Sc,UK
132/D3 Findlay, Oh,US
97/D4 Fingal, Austl.
125/H2 Finger (lake), On,Can.
132/E3 Finger (lakes), NY,US
62/E4 Finiels, Sommet de (peak), Fr.
80/B3 Finike, Turk.
64/A1 Finisterre (cape), Sp.
63/K3 Finkenstein, Aus.
48/H2 Finland (ctry.)
70/E4 Finland (gulf), Eur.
124/D3 Finlay (riv.), BC,Can.
134/B4 Finlay (mts.), Tx,US
57/E6 Finnentrop, Ger.
138/C2 Finn Hill-Inglewood, Wa,US
96/B1 Finnigan (peak), Austl.
48/G1 Finnmark (co.), Nor.
48/E4 Finspång, Swe.
50/A3 Fintona, NI,UK
66/B1 Fiora (riv.), It.
63/H4 Fiorenzuola d'Arda, It.
138/C2 Fircrest-Silver Lake, Wa,US
63/J5 Firenze (Florence), It.
118/E2 Firmat, Arg.
62/F4 Firminy, Fr.
90/C2 Firozābād, India
79/K2 Firozpur, India
78/F3 Fīrūzābād, Iran
63/L3 Fischbacher (mts.), Aus.
108/B2 Fish (riv.), Namb.
108/C3 Fish (riv.), SAfr.
51/G2 Fishburn, Eng,UK
111/E Fisher (glac.), Ant.
129/J3 Fisher (bay), Mb,Can.
125/H2 Fisher (str.), Nun,Can.
129/J3 Fisher Branch, Mb,Can.
96/F6 Fisherman (isl.), Austl.
52/B3 Fishguard, Wal,UK
72/F4 Fisht, Gora (peak), Rus.
51/J6 Fishtoft, Eng,UK
99/S9 Fito (peak), Samoa
136/L2 Fitton (mtn.), Yk,Can.
135/H4 Fitzgerald, Ga,US
128/B3 Fitz Hugo (sound), BC,Can.
119/J7 Fitzroy (peak), Arg.
96/C3 Fitzroy (riv.), Austl.
125/R7 Fitzwilliam (str.), NW,Can.
66/C2 Fiumicino, It.
50/A3 Fivemiletown, NI,UK
48/C3 Fjell, Nor.
53/F3 Flackwell Heath, Eng,UK
131/G3 Flagler, Co,US
135/H4 Flagler Beach, Fl,US
130/E4 Flagstaff, Az,US
132/B2 Flambeau (riv.), Wi,US
51/H3 Flamborough, Eng,UK
51/H3 Flamborough Head (pt.), Eng,UK
54/G2 Fläming (hills), Ger.
128/F5 Flaming Gorge Nat'l Rec. Area, Ut, Wy,US
129/K2 Flanagan (riv.), On,Can.
58/B2 Flanders (reg.), Belg., Fr.
129/J4 Flandreau, SD,US
136/L3 Flat Creek, Yk,Can.
128/E4 Flathead (lake), Mt,US
128/E4 Flathead (riv.), Mt,US
52/C4 Flat Holm (isl.), Eng,UK
131/K3 Flat River, Mo,US
138/F7 Flat Rock, Mi,US
96/B1 Flattery (cape), Austl.
128/B3 Flattery (cape), Wa,US
53/F4 Fleet, Eng,UK
51/E4 Fleetwood, Eng,UK
48/C4 Flekkefjord, Nor.
137/F5 Flemington, NJ,US
54/E1 Flensburg, Ger.
59/E2 Fleron, Belg.
62/C2 Flers, Fr.
58/D3 Fleurus, Belg.
62/D3 Fleury-les-Aubrais, Fr.
56/C4 Flevoland (prov.), Neth.
50/E2 Flimby, Eng,UK
97/D3 Flinders (isl.), Austl.
96/C2 Flinders (reefs), Austl.
96/A2 Flinders (riv.), Austl.
129/L3 Flindt (riv.), On,Can.
129/H2 Flin Flon, Mb,Can.
125/J2 Flint (lake), Nun,Can.
99/K6 Flint (isl.), Kiri.
51/E5 Flint, Wal,UK
135/G4 Flint (riv.), Ga,US
131/H3 Flint (hills), Ks,US
138/E5 Flint, Mi,US
51/E5 Flintshire (co.), Wal.,UK
53/F3 Flitwick, Eng,UK
57/F1 Flögelner See (lake), Ger.
55/G3 Flöha (riv.), Ger.
132/B4 Flora, Il,US
137/G5 Floral Park, NY,US
59/F5 Florange, Fr.
59/D3 Floreffe, Belg.
135/G3 Florence, Al,US
130/E4 Florence, Az,US
131/F3 Florence, Co,US
135/J3 Florence, SC,US
63/J5 Florence (Firenze), It.
114/C3 Florencia, Col.
58/D3 Florennes, Belg.
118/E3 Flores (riv.), Arg.
122/D4 Flores, Guat.
128/B3 Flores (isl.), BC,Can.
93/F5 Flores (isl.), Indo.
93/E5 Flores (sea), Indo.
65/R12 Flores (isl.), Azor.,Port.
119/F2 Flores (dept.), Uru.
115/L5 Floresta, Braz.
134/D4 Floresville, Tx,US
137/F5 Florham Park, NJ,US
115/K5 Floriano, Braz.
116/B3 Florianópolis, Braz.
123/F3 Florida, Cuba
123/E3 Florida (str.), NAm.
119/F2 Florida, Uru.
119/F2 Florida (dept.), Uru.
135/H4 Florida (state), US
135/H5 Florida (bay), Fl,US
135/H5 Florida Keys (isls.), Fl,US
66/D4 Floridia, It.
138/M10 Florin, Ca,US
67/G2 Flórina, Gre.
131/K3 Florissant, Mo,US
48/C3 Florø, Nor.
134/C3 Floydada, Tx,US
56/C3 Fluessen (lake), Neth.
66/A3 Flumendosa (riv.), It.
132/D3 Flushing, Mi,US
56/A6 Flushing (Vlissingen), Neth.
98/D5 Fly (riv.), PNG
111/T Flying Fish (cape), Ant.
48/P6 Fnjóská (riv.), Ice.
129/H3 Foam Lake, Sk,Can.
68/D4 Foča, Bosn.
69/H3 Focşani, Rom.
66/D2 Foggia, It.
63/L3 Fohnsdorf, Aus.
54/E1 Föhr (isl.), Ger.
62/D5 Foix, Fr.
48/C3 Folarskardnuten (peak), Nor.
48/D2 Folda (fjord), Nor.
67/J4 Folégandros (isl.), Gre.
125/J2 Foley (isl.), Nun,Can.
66/C1 Foligno, It.
53/H4 Folkestone, Eng,UK
135/H4 Folkston, Ga,US
66/B1 Follonica (gulf), It.
124/F3 Fond du Lac (riv.), Sk,Can.
132/B3 Fond du Lac, Wi,US
66/C2 Fondi, It.
48/D3 Fongen (peak), Nor.
64/B1 Fonsagrada, Sp.
122/D5 Fonseca (gulf), NAm.
62/F4 Fontaine, Fr.
62/E2 Fontainebleau, Fr.
58/D3 Fontaine-L'Evêque, Belg.
137/C2 Fontana, Ca,US
62/C3 Fontenay-le-Comte, Fr.
58/B6 Fontenay-Trésigny, Fr.
128/F5 Fontenelle (res.), Wy,US
63/G4 Font Sancte, Pic de la (peak), Fr.
48/P6 Fontur (pt.), Ice.
97/F5 Footscray, Austl.
136/H3 Foraker (mtn.), Ak,US
59/F5 Forbach, Fr.
97/D2 Forbes, Austl.
64/A1 Forcarey, Sp.
63/J2 Forchheim, Ger.
138/E7 Ford (lake), Mi,US
53/E5 Fordingbridge, Eng,UK
134/E3 Fordyce, Ar,US
52/C4 Foreland (pt.), Eng,UK
53/E5 Foreland, The (pt.), Eng,UK
128/F3 Foremost, Ab,Can.
53/H4 Foreness (pt.), Eng,UK
135/F3 Forest, Ms,US
97/D4 Forestier (cape), Austl.
133/G1 Forestville, Qu,Can.
137/K8 Forestville, Md,US
62/E4 Forez (mts.), Fr.
49/D2 Forfar, Sc,UK
133/H1 Forillon Nat'l Park, Qu,Can.
50/B3 Forkill, NI,UK
63/K4 Forlì, It.
51/E4 Formby, Eng,UK
51/E4 Formby (pt.), Eng,UK
65/F3 Formentera (isl.), Sp.
65/G3 Formentor, Cabo de (cape), Sp.
66/C2 Formia, It.
116/C2 Formiga, Braz.
117/E2 Formosa, Arg.
115/J7 Formosa, Braz.
115/G6 Formosa (mts.), Braz.
104/A4 Formosa (isl.), GBis.
108/C4 Formosa (peak), SAfr.
115/J6 Formoso (riv.), Braz.
63/J5 Fornacelle, It.
49/D2 Forres, Sc,UK
135/F3 Forrest City, Ar,US
48/G3 Forssa, Fin.
96/A3 Forsyth (range), Austl.
135/H3 Forsyth, Ga,US
128/G4 Forsyth, Mt,US
79/K3 Fort Abbās, Pak.
115/L4 Fortaleza, Braz.
119/G2 Fortaleza Santa Teresa, Uru.
108/D4 Fort Beaufort, SAfr.
128/F4 Fort Benton, Mt,US
130/B3 Fort Bragg, Ca,US
131/H4 Fort Cobb (res.), Ok,US
131/F2 Fort Collins, Co,US
134/C4 Fort Davis, Tx,US
59/E5 Fort de Douaumont, Fr.
123/J5 Fort-de-France (cap.), Mart.
59/E5 Fort de Vaux, Fr.
129/K5 Fort Dodge, Ia,US
110/D3 Forte Cameia, Ang.
133/S10 Fort Erie, On,Can.
95/A3 Fortescue (riv.), Austl.
132/A1 Fort Frances, On,Can.
135/F4 Fort Gaines, Al,US
133/R9 Fort George, On,Can.
125/J3 Fort-George (Chisasibi), Qu,Can.
131/J4 Fort Gibson, Ok,US
134/E2 Fort Gibson (lake), Ok,US
102/C3 Fort-Gouraud, Mrta.
49/C2 Forth (riv.), Sc,UK
49/D2 Forth, Firth of (inlet), Sc,UK
133/G2 Fort Kent, Me,US
135/H5 Fort Lauderdale, Fl,US
137/F5 Fort Lee, NJ,US
131/F2 Fort Lupton, Co,US
128/E3 Fort Macleod, Ab,Can.
129/L5 Fort Madison, Ia,US
135/H4 Fort Matanzas Nat'l Mon., Fl,US
124/E3 Fort McMurray, Ab,Can.
132/C2 Fort Michilimackinac, Mi,US
131/G2 Fort Morgan, Co,US
135/J3 Fort Moultrie, SC,US
135/H5 Fort Myers, Fl,US
124/D3 Fort Nelson (riv.), BC,Can.
51/F4 Forton, Eng,UK
66/D2 Fortore (riv.), It.
135/G3 Fort Payne, Al,US
128/G4 Fort Peck (lake), Mt,US
135/H5 Fort Pierce, Fl,US
129/H4 Fort Pierre, SD,US
107/A2 Fort Portal, Ugan.
129/H3 Fort Qu'Appelle, Sk,Can.
129/J5 Fort Randall (dam), SD,US
128/B2 Fort Saint James, BC,Can.
124/D3 Fort Saint John, BC,Can.
128/E2 Fort Saskatchewan, Ab,Can.
131/J3 Fort Scott, Ks,US
73/J3 Fort-Shevchenko, Kaz.
134/E3 Fort Smith, Ar,US
134/C4 Fort Stockton, Tx,US
131/F4 Fort Sumner, NM,US
129/J4 Fort Totten, ND,US
133/L2 Fortune, Nf,Can.
133/L2 Fortune (bay), Nf,Can.
52/D5 Fortuneswell, Eng,UK
131/F4 Fort Union Nat'l Mon., NM,US
135/G4 Fort Walton Beach, Fl,US
137/J8 Fort Washington Park, Md,US
132/C3 Fort Wayne, In,US
49/C2 Fort William, Sc,UK
134/D3 Fort Worth, Tx,US
129/H4 Fort Yates, ND,US
96/B2 Forty Mile Scrub Nat'l Park, Austl.
88/C3 Foshan, China
125/S7 Fosheim (pen.), Nun,Can.
51/G3 Foss (riv.), Eng,UK
63/G4 Fossano, It.
58/B5 Fosses, Fr.
59/D3 Fosses-la-Ville, Belg.
128/C4 Fossil, Or,US
128/F5 Fossil Butte Nat'l Mon., Wy,US
132/D3 Fostoria, Oh,US
62/C2 Fougères, Fr.
103/N3 Foul (bay), Egypt, Sudan
53/G3 Foulness (isl.), Eng,UK
53/G3 Foulness (pt.), Eng,UK
51/H4 Foulness (riv.), Eng,UK
53/H1 Foulsham, Eng,UK
105/H5 Foumban, Camr.
131/F3 Fountain, Co,US
137/C3 Fountain Valley, Ca,US
134/E3 Fourche La Fave (riv.), Ar,US
53/E4 Four Marks, Eng,UK
58/D4 Fourmies, Fr.
136/D5 Four Mountains (isls.), Ak,US
109/R15 Fournaise, Piton de la (peak), Reun., Fr.
104/B4 Fouta Djallon (reg.), Gha.
52/B6 Fowey, Eng,UK
52/B6 Fowey (riv.), Eng,UK
97/B1 Fowlers Gap, Austl.
78/E1 Fowman, Iran
136/M3 Fox (mtn.), Yk,Can.
136/E5 Fox (isls.), Ak,US
132/B3 Fox (riv.), Il, Wi,US
128/D2 Fox Creek, Ab,Can.
125/J2 Foxe (chan.), Nun,Can.
125/J2 Foxe (pen.), Nun,Can.
125/J2 Foxe Basin (sound), Nun,Can.
138/P15 Fox Lake, Il,US
53/G2 Foxton, Eng,UK
128/F3 Fox Valley, Sk,Can.
50/A2 Foyle (riv.), NI,UK
50/A1 Foyle, Lough (inlet), Ire., NI,UK
64/B1 Foz, Sp.
110/B4 Foz do Cunene, Ang.
117/F2 Foz do Iguaçu, Braz.
65/F2 Fraga, Sp.
116/B3 Fraiburgo, Braz.
114/E7 Frailes (range), Bol.
58/C3 Frameries, Belg.
53/H2 Framlingham, Eng,UK
116/C2 Franca, Braz.
67/E2 Francavilla Fontana, It.
62/D3 France (ctry.)
65/G1 France, Roc de (mtn.), Fr.
124/C2 Frances (lake), Yk,Can.
122/E3 Frances (cape), Cuba
123/H4 Francés Viejo (cape), DRep.
102/H8 Franceville, Gabon
60/C3 Franche-Comté (reg.), Fr.
129/J5 Francis Case (lake), SD,US
122/C4 Francisco Escárcega, Mex.
123/P8 Francisco I. Madero, Mex.
110/E5 Francistown, Bots.
116/G8 Francisco da Rocha, Braz.
128/B2 Francois (lake), BC,Can.
58/B6 Franconville, Fr.
56/C2 Franeker, Neth.
57/F6 Frankenberg (Eder), Ger.
132/D3 Frankenmuth, Mi,US
132/C3 Frankfort, In,US
132/C4 Frankfort (cap.), Ky,US
55/H2 Frankfurt, Ger.
63/H1 Frankfurt am Main, Ger.
63/J2 Frankische Alb (mts.), Ger.
63/H1 Fränkische Saale (riv.), Ger.
63/J2 Fränkische Schweiz (reg.), Ger.
97/C3 Frankland (cape), Austl.
111/M Franklin (isl.), Ant.
136/N1 Franklin (bay), NW,Can.
124/D2 Franklin (mts.), NW,Can.
136/G1 Franklin (pt.), Ak,US
132/C4 Franklin, In,US
132/C4 Franklin, Ky,US
135/H3 Franklin, NC,US
135/G3 Franklin, Tn,US
134/D4 Franklin, Tx,US
132/E4 Franklin, Va,US
138/P14 Franklin, Wi,US
132/E4 Franklin, WV,US
128/D3 Franklin D. Roosevelt (lake), Wa,US
137/F4 Franklin Lakes, NJ,US
97/C4 Franklin-Lower Gordon Wild Rivers Nat'l Park, Austl.
138/Q16 Franklin Park, Il,US
137/G5 Franklin Square, NY,US
117/F2 Fransisco Beltrão, Braz.
116/G8 Fransisco Morato, Braz.
74/F2 Franz Josef Land (arch.), Rus.
96/D4 Fraser (isl.), Austl.
128/B2 Fraser (lake), BC,Can.
128/C3 Fraser (riv.), BC,Can.
138/G6 Fraser, Mi,US
49/D2 Fraserburgh, Sc,UK
128/B2 Fraser Lake, BC,Can.
97/C3 Fraser Nat'l Park, Austl.
61/E2 Frauenfeld, Swi.
118/F2 Fray Bentos, Uru.
130/C4 Frazier Park, Ca,US
59/F2 Frechen, Ger.
108/E3 Fred (mtn.), SAfr.
54/E1 Fredericia, Den.
132/E4 Frederick, Md,US
131/H4 Frederick, Ok,US
134/D4 Fredericksburg, Tx,US
132/E4 Fredericksburg, Va,US
133/H2 Fredericton (cap.), NB,Can.
48/D4 Frederikshavn, Den.
130/D3 Fredonia, Az,US
131/J3 Fredonia, Ks,US
132/E3 Fredonia, NY,US
48/D4 Fredrikstad, Nor.
131/H3 Freedom, Ok,US
137/F5 Freehold, NJ,US
97/A1 Freeling Heights (peak), Austl.
123/F2 Freeport, Bahm.
132/B3 Freeport, Il,US
137/G5 Freeport, NY,US
134/E4 Freeport, Tx,US
134/D5 Freer, Tx,US
108/D3 Free State (prov.), SAfr.
104/B4 Freetown (cap.), SLeo.
62/B2 Fréhel (cape), Fr.
54/G3 Freib (riv.), Ger.
55/G3 Freiberg, Ger.
60/D2 Freiburg, Ger.
54/G3 Freiberger Mulde (riv.), Ger.
116/D1 Frei Inocêncio, Braz.
118/B3 Freire, Chile
59/G4 Freisen, Ger.
63/J2 Freising, Ger.
63/L2 Freistadt, Aus.
55/G3 Freital, Ger.
63/G5 Fréjus, Fr.
52/B4 Fremington, Eng,UK
138/L11 Fremont, Ca,US
132/C3 Fremont, Mi,US
131/H2 Fremont, Ne,US
132/D3 Fremont, Oh,US
130/E3 Fremont (riv.), Ut,US
128/F5 Fremont (peak), Wy,US
132/D2 French (riv.), On,Can.
99/J2 French Frigate (shoals), Hi,US
115/H3 French Guiana (dpcy.), Fr.
128/G3 Frenchman (riv.), Can., US
131/G2 Frenchman (cr.), Ne,US
133/R8 Frenchman's (bay), On,Can.
97/C4 Frenchmans Cap (peak), Austl.
99/M6 French Polynesia (terr.), Fr.
115/H5 Fresco (riv.), Braz.
53/E5 Freshwater, Eng,UK
118/B4 Fresia, Chile
123/P9 Fresnillo de González Echeverría, Mex.
130/C3 Fresno, Ca,US
97/D4 Freycinet Nat'l Park, Austl.
59/F5 Freyming-Merlebach, Fr.
63/K2 Freyung, Ger.
110/B4 Fria (cape), Namb.
117/C2 Frías, Arg.
60/D4 Fribourg, Swi.
60/D4 Fribourg (canton), Swi.
63/H1 Friedberg, Ger.
57/E2 Friedeburg, Ger.
63/H1 Friedrichsdorf, Ger.
61/F2 Friedrichshafen, Ger.
59/G5 Friedrichsthal, Ger.
57/G7 Frielendorf, Ger.
60/D1 Friesenheim, Ger.
56/C2 Friesland (prov.), Neth.
57/E2 Friesoythe, Ger.
53/F4 Frimley, Eng,UK
53/H3 Frinton, Eng,UK
44/G7 Frio (cape), Braz.
131/H5 Frio (riv.), Tx,US
57/G6 Fritzlar, Ger.
63/K3 Friuli-Venezia Giulia (reg.), It.
50/E2 Frizington, Eng,UK
125/K2 Frobisher (bay), Nun,Can.
128/F1 Frobisher (lake), Sk,Can.
51/F5 Frodsham, Eng,UK
48/D3 Frohavet (bay), Nor.
58/D3 Froidchapelle, Belg.
73/G2 Frolovo, Rus.
97/B1 Frome (lake), Austl.
52/D4 Frome, Eng,UK
52/D2 Frome (riv.), Eng,UK
52/D5 Frome (riv.), Eng,UK
131/F2 Front (range), Co,US
62/E5 Frontignan, Fr.
132/E4 Front Royal, Va,US
66/C2 Frosinone, It.
48/E3 Frösö, Swe.
111/J Frost (glac.), Ant.
59/F6 Frouard, Fr.
48/D3 Frøya (isl.), Nor.
125/H2 Frozen (str.), Nun,Can.
133/Q9 Fruitland, On,Can.
68/D3 Fruška Gora Nat'l Park, Serb.
116/C2 Frutal, Braz.
118/B4 Frutillar, Chile
71/W9 Fryazino, Rus.
55/K4 Frýdek-Místek, Czh.
87/C5 Fu (riv.), China
87/D3 Fucheng, China
59/H2 Fuchskaute (peak), Ger.
84/C3 Fuchū, Japan
87/D5 Fuchun (riv.), China
88/D2 Fuding, China
65/Y16 Fuenaventura (isl.), Canl.
64/C4 Fuengirola, Sp.
64/D2 Fuenlabrada, Sp.
65/N8 Fuente, Sp.
65/E4 Fuente-Álamo, Sp.
64/B3 Fuente del Maestre, Sp.
64/C3 Fuente Obejuna, Sp.
64/E1 Fuenterrabiá, Sp.
64/C4 Fuentes de Andalucía, Sp.
123/N8 Fuerte (riv.), Mex.
88/D4 Fuga (isl.), Phil.
54/F3 Fuhne (riv.), Ger.
57/H4 Fuhse (riv.), Ger.
85/F3 Fuji, Japan
85/F3 Fuji (riv.), Japan
85/F3 Fujieda, Japan
85/F3 Fuji-Hakone-Izu Nat'l Park, Japan
85/L10 Fujiidera, Japan
85/H7 Fujimi, Japan
85/H7 Fujino, Japan
85/F3 Fujinomiya, Japan
85/F2 Fujioka, Japan
85/F3 Fujisawa, Japan
85/J7 Fujishiro, Japan
85/M9 Fujiwara, Japan
85/F3 Fujiyama (mtn.), Japan
85/F3 Fujiyoshida, Japan
84/D3 Fukuchiyama, Japan
84/A4 Fukue, Japan
84/A4 Fukue (isl.), Japan
84/E2 Fukui, Japan
84/E3 Fukui (pref.), Japan
84/B4 Fukuoka, Japan
84/B4 Fukuoka (pref.), Japan
85/E3 Fukuroi, Japan
111/C Fukushima (peak), Ant.
85/G2 Fukushima, Japan
85/F2 Fukushima (pref.), Japan
84/C3 Fukuyama, Japan
79/J2 Fūlādī (mtn.), Afg.
53/G2 Fulbourn, Eng,UK
63/H1 Fulda, Ger.
51/G4 Fulford, Eng,UK
88/A2 Fuling, China
137/C3 Fullerton, Ca,US
137/E5 Fullerton (Whitehall), Pa,US
133/Q9 Fulton, On,Can.
132/B4 Fulton, Ky,US
131/K3 Fulton, Mo,US
132/E3 Fulton, NY,US
48/E3 Fulufjället (peak), Swe.
51/F4 Fulwood, Eng,UK
62/D4 Fumel, Fr.
85/H7 Funabashi, Japan
98/G5 Funafuti (atoll), Tuv.
98/G5 Funafuti (cap.), Tuv.
123/G5 Fundación, Col.
133/H2 Fundy (bay), NB, NS,Can.
133/H2 Fundy Nat'l Park, NB,Can.
110/F5 Funhalouro, Moz.
70/J4 Furmanov, Rus.
49/C2 Furnace, Sc,UK
116/H6 Furnas (res.), Braz.
97/C4 Furneaux Group (isls.), Austl.
57/E3 Fürstenau, Ger.
68/C2 Fürstenfeld, Aus.
61/H1 Fürstenfeldbruck, Ger.
55/H2 Fürstenwalde, Ger.
63/K2 Furth im Wald, Ger.
83/N4 Furukawa, Japan
125/H2 Fury and Hecla (str.), Nun,Can.
87/B4 Fushan, China
87/E3 Fushan, China
83/J3 Fushun, China
85/M9 Fuso, Japan
85/H7 Fussa, Japan
61/G2 Füssen, Ger.
85/M10 Futami, Japan
68/D3 Futog, Serb.
118/B4 Futrono, Chile
85/F3 Futtsu, Japan
98/H6 Futuna (isl.), Wall.
80/H6 Fuwah, Egypt
91/H3 Fuxian (lake), China
83/J3 Fuxin, China
87/C4 Fuyang, China
88/B2 Fuyi (riv.), China
83/J2 Fuyu, China
55/L5 Füzesabony, Hun.
88/C2 Fuzhou, China
54/F1 Fyn (co.), Den.
48/D5 Fyn (isl.), Den.

G

103/Q6 Gaalkacyo (Galcaio), Som.
56/D5 Gaanderen, Neth.
56/C2 Gaast, Neth.
62/C5 Gabas (riv.), Fr.
130/C3 Gabbs, Nv,US
110/B3 Gabela, Ang.
102/H1 Gabes (gulf), Tun.
102/H7 Gabon (ctry.)
108/D2 Gaborone (cap.), Bots.
69/G4 Gabrovo, Bul.
68/D4 Gacko, Bosn.
90/C4 Gadag-Betgeri, India
135/G3 Gadsden, Al,US
69/G3 Găeşti, Rom.
66/C2 Gaeta, It.
66/C2 Gaeta (gulf), It.
135/H3 Gaffney, SC,US
70/G5 Gagarin, Rus.

162
Gagno – Grand

104/D5 Gagnoa, C.d'Iv.
133/G1 Gagnon, Qu,Can.
58/B6 Gagny, Fr.
72/G4 Gagra, Geo.
68/A2 Gail (riv.), Aus.
62/D5 Gaillac, Fr.
63/K3 Gailtaler Alpen (mts.), Aus.
118/D4 Gaiman, Arg.
135/H4 Gainesville, Fl,US
135/H3 Gainesville, Ga,US
131/J3 Gainesville, Mo,US
134/D3 Gainesville, Tx,US
51/G2 Gainford, Eng,UK
51/H5 Gainsborough, Eng,UK
137/J7 Gaithersburg, Md,US
70/E4 Gaizinkalns (peak), Lat.
108/C2 Gakarosa (peak), SAfr.
64/D2 Galapagar, Sp.
44/E6 Galápagos (isls.), Ecu.
49/D3 Galashiels, Sc,UK
69/J3 Galaţi, Rom.
69/H3 Galaţi (co.), Rom.
67/F2 Galatina, It.
67/F2 Galatone, It.
132/D4 Galax, Va,US
67/H3 Galaxídhiou, Gre.
93/G3 Galela, Indo.
132/B3 Galena, Il,US
118/B3 Galera (pt.), Chile
114/B3 Galera (pt.), Ecu.
123/J5 Galera (pt.), Trin.
132/B3 Galesburg, Il,US
49/A4 Galey (riv.), Ire.
50/B2 Galgorm, NI,UK
70/J4 Galich, Rus.
55/L3 Galicia (reg.), Pol., Ukr.
64/A1 Galicia (aut. comm.), Sp.
68/E5 Galičica Nat'l Park, FYROM
80/K5 Galilee, Sea of (Tiberias) (lake), Isr.
132/D3 Galion, Oh,US
135/G2 Gallatin, Tn,US
90/D6 Galle, SrL.
119/K7 Gallegos (riv.), Arg.
123/G5 Gallinas (pt.), Col.
134/B3 Gallinas (mts.), NM,US
67/E2 Gallipoli, It.
69/H5 Gallipoli (pen.), Turk.
69/H5 Gallipoli (Gelibolu), Turk.
132/D4 Gallipolis, Oh,US
48/G2 Gällivare, Swe.
66/C3 Gallo (cape), It.
50/D2 Galloway, Mull of (pt.), Sc,UK
130/E4 Gallup, NM,US
82/D2 Galt, Mong.
138/M10 Galt, Ca,US
49/A4 Galtymore (mtn.), Ire.
82/E2 Galuut, Mong.
118/B3 Galvarino, Chile
134/E4 Galveston, Tx,US
134/E4 Galveston (bay), Tx,US
134/E4 Galveston (isl.), Tx,US
118/E2 Gálvez, Arg.
49/A4 Galway, Ire.
49/A4 Galway (bay), Ire.
89/D1 Gam (riv.), Viet.
108/C2 Gamagara (dry riv.), SAfr.
85/E3 Gamagōri, Japan
90/E2 Gamba, China
105/E4 Gambaga Scarp (escarp.), Gha., Togo
90/A2 Gambat, Pak.
103/M6 Gambēla, Eth.
103/M6 Gambela Nat'l Park, Eth.
104/B3 Gambia (ctry.)
104/A3 Gambia (Gambie) (riv.), Afr.
99/M7 Gambier (isls.), FrPol.
133/L1 Gambo, Nf,Can.
110/C1 Gamboma, Congo
108/C4 Gamka (riv.), SAfr.
108/B3 Gamkab (dry riv.), Namb.
53/F2 Gamlingay, Eng,UK
70/D2 Gammelstad, Swe.
85/M9 Gamo, Japan
107/C1 Gamud (peak), Eth.
88/C2 Gan (riv.), China
132/E2 Gananoque, On,Can.
73/H4 Gäncä, Arm.
110/D2 Gandajika, D.R. Congo
133/L1 Gander, Nf,Can.
133/L1 Gander (lake), Nf,Can.
57/F2 Ganderkesee, Ger.
90/B3 Gāndhīdhām, India
90/B3 Gandhinagar, India
90/B3 Gāndhi Sāgar (res.), India
65/E3 Gandía, Sp.
102/C4 Ganeb (well), Mrta.
90/C2 Gangāpur, India
90/E2 Gangārāmpur, India
81/D5 Gangdisê (mts.), China
59/F2 Gangelt, Ger.
90/E3 Ganges (riv.), India
66/D4 Gangi, It.
90/E2 Gangtok, India
80/N8 Gan Hashlosha Nat'l Park, Isr.
128/F5 Gannett (peak), Wy,US
81/F4 Gansu (prov.), China
102/H6 Ganye, Nga.
88/B2 Ganzhou, China
105/E3 Ganzourgou (prov.), Burk.
105/E2 Gao, Mali
105/E2 Gao (reg.), Mali
87/C3 Gaocheng, China
88/D2 Gaojian, China
104/E4 Gaoua, Burk.
87/C3 Gaoyang, China
87/D4 Gaoyou (lake), China
63/G4 Gap, Fr.
82/D5 Gar (riv.), China
73/K4 Garabogazköl (gulf), Trkm.
90/E3 Garai (riv.), Bang.
107/A2 Garamba Nat'l Park, D.R. Congo
115/L5 Garanhuns, Braz.
107/C2 Garba Tula, Kenya
57/G4 Garbsen, Ger.
116/B2 Garça, Braz.
64/C3 Garcia de Sota (res.), Sp.
62/F5 Gard (riv.), Fr.
63/J4 Garda (lake), It.
54/F2 Gardelegen, Ger.
137/B3 Gardena, Ca,US
135/H3 Garden City, Ga,US
131/G3 Garden City, Ks,US
138/F7 Garden City, Mi,US
137/G5 Garden City, NY,US
128/A2 Gardener Canal (inlet), BC,Can.
137/C3 Garden Grove, Ca,US
79/J2 Gardēz, Afg.
133/G2 Gardiner, Me,US
128/F4 Gardiner, Mt,US
99/H5 Gardner (Nikumaroro) (atoll), Kiri.
49/C2 Garelochhead, Sc,UK
102/G2 Garet el Djenoun (peak), Alg.
128/E4 Garfield (peak), Mt,US
137/F5 Garfield, NJ,US
51/G4 Garforth, Eng,UK
62/D4 Gargan (mtn.), Fr.
51/F4 Gargrave, Eng,UK
90/C3 Garhākotā, India
116/B4 Garibaldi, Braz.
107/C3 Garissa, Kenya
134/D3 Garland, Tx,US
50/D2 Garlieston, Sc,UK
61/H3 Garmisch-Partenkirchen, Ger.
131/J3 Garnett, Ks,US
97/B2 Garnpung (lake), Austl.
62/D4 Garonne (riv.), Fr.
105/E2 Garou (lake), Mali
102/H6 Garoua, Camr.
102/H6 Garoua Boulaï, Camr.
65/K7 Garraf (range), Sp.
50/D6 Garreg, Wal,UK
57/F3 Garrel, Ger.
129/H4 Garrison, ND,US
129/H4 Garrison (dam), ND,US
50/C1 Garron (pt.), NI,UK
125/H2 Garry (bay), Nun,Can.
124/F2 Garry (lake), Nun,Can.
51/F4 Garstang, Eng,UK
63/L2 Garsten, Aus.
57/H6 Garte (riv.), Ger.
62/D3 Gartempe (riv.), Fr.
52/C2 Garth, Wal,UK
92/C5 Garut, Indo.
50/B2 Garvagh, NI,UK
55/L3 Garwolin, Pol.
138/R16 Gary, In,US
114/C3 Garzón, Col.
81/F4 Gas (lake), China
48/P6 Gæsafjöll (peak), Ice.
132/C3 Gas City, In,US
131/J3 Gasconade (riv.), Mo,US
62/C5 Gascony (reg.), Fr.
116/B3 Gaspar, Braz.
92/C4 Gaspar (riv.), Indo.
133/H1 Gaspé, Qu,Can.
133/H1 Gaspé (pen.), Qu,Can.
133/H1 Gaspé, Cap de (cape), Qu,Can.
133/S9 Gasport, NY,US
135/J2 Gaston (lake), NC, Va,US
135/H3 Gastonia, NC,US
80/J4 Gata (cape), Cyp.
64/B2 Gata (range), Sp.
64/D4 Gata, Cabo de (cape), Sp.
70/F4 Gatchina, Rus.
50/D2 Gatehouse-of-Fleet, Sc,UK
124/F1 Gateshead (isl.), Nun,Can.
51/G2 Gateshead, Eng,UK
51/G2 Gateshead (co.), Eng,UK
136/H2 Gates of the Arctic Nat'l Pk. & Prsv., Ak,US
134/D4 Gatesville, Tx,US
137/G5 Gateway Nat'l Rec. Area, NJ, NY,US
62/C3 Gâtine (hills), Fr.
132/F2 Gatineau, Qu,Can.
132/F2 Gatineau (riv.), Qu,Can.
59/H4 Gau-Bickelheim, Ger.
91/F2 Gauhāti, India
51/G2 Gaunless (riv.), Eng,UK
90/E2 Gauripur, India
90/E2 Gauri Sankar (mtn.), Nepal
48/D4 Gausta (peak), Nor.
108/E2 Gauteng (prov.), SAfr.
70/E4 Gauya Nat'l Park, Lat.
65/G2 Gavà, Sp.
67/J5 Gávdhos (isl.), Gre.
64/E1 Gave de Pau (riv.), Fr.
58/C2 Gavere, Belg.
48/F3 Gävle, Swe.
48/E3 Gävleborg (co.), Swe.
97/A2 Gawler, Austl.
82/D3 Gaxun (lake), China
73/L2 Gay, Rus.
132/D4 Gay (peak), WV,US
83/K3 Gaya (riv.), China
90/E3 Gayā, India
105/F4 Gaya, Niger
132/C2 Gaylord, Mi,US
72/D2 Gaysin, Ukr.
80/K6 Gaza (Ghazzah), Gaza
80/J6 Gaza Strip
80/D3 Gaziantep, Turk.
83/H1 Gazimur (riv.), Rus.
60/C1 Gazon de Faing (peak), Fr.
103/K7 Gbadolite, D.R. Congo
104/C5 Gbarnga, Libr.
55/K1 Gdańsk, Pol.
55/K1 Gdańsk (gulf), Pol., Rus.
55/K1 Gdynia, Pol.
87/D5 Ge (lake), China
63/J1 Gebaberg (peak), Ger.
93/G3 Gebe (isl.), Indo.
106/D4 Gebeit Mine, Sudan
69/J5 Gebze, Turk.
92/C5 Gede (peak), Indo.
80/M9 Gedera, Isr.
80/B2 Gediz, Turk.
80/A2 Gediz (riv.), Turk.
59/E1 Geel, Belg.
97/C3 Geelong, Austl.
57/E3 Geeste, Ger.
57/F2 Geeste (riv.), Ger.
57/H2 Geesthacht, Ger.
81/D5 Gê'gyai, China
57/G4 Gehrden, Ger.
52/C2 Geifas (mtn.), Wal,UK
124/F3 Geikie (riv.), Sk,Can.
59/F2 Geilenkirchen, Ger.
85/M10 Geinō, Japan
63/H2 Geislingen an der Steige, Ger.
91/H3 Gejiu, China
103/L6 Gel (riv.), Sudan
66/D4 Gela, It.
66/D4 Gela (gulf), It.
103/Q6 Geladī, Eth.
56/C4 Gelderland (prov.), Neth.
56/C5 Geldermalsen, Neth.
56/D5 Geldern, Ger.
56/C6 Geldrop, Neth.
59/E2 Geleen, Neth.
72/F3 Gelendzhik, Rus.
69/H5 Gelibolu (Gallipoli), Turk.
52/C3 Gelligaer, Wal,UK
56/E5 Gelsenkirchen, Ger.
59/D2 Gembloux, Belg.
103/J7 Gemena, D.R. Congo
56/C5 Gemert, Neth.
69/J5 Gemlik, Turk.
69/J5 Gemlik (gulf), Turk.
63/K3 Gemona del Friuli, It.
108/C2 Gemsbok-Kalahari Nat'l Park, SAfr.
108/C2 Gemsbok Nat'l Park, Bots.
136/G3 Gemuk (mtn.), Ak,US
83/J1 Gen (riv.), China
103/N6 Genalē Wenz (riv.), Eth.
58/D2 Genappe, Belg.
66/A3 Genargentu (mts.), It.
80/E2 Genç, Turk.
56/D5 Gendringen, Neth.
56/C5 Gendt, Neth.
56/D3 Genemuiden, Neth.
118/D3 General Acha, Arg.
118/D3 General Alvear, Arg.
118/F2 General Belgrano, Arg.
118/E2 General Cabrera, Arg.
118/B5 General Carrera (lake), Chile
119/F3 General Juan Madariaga, Arg.
119/S12 General Las Heras, Arg.
117/C1 General Martín Miguel de Güemes, Arg.
118/E2 General Pico, Arg.
117/D2 General Pinedo, Arg.
88/E6 General Santos, Phil.
69/J4 General-Toshevo, Bul.
118/E2 General Viamonte, Arg.
118/E2 General Villegas, Arg.
132/E3 Genesee (riv.), NY,US
129/L5 Geneseo, Il,US
132/E3 Geneseo, NY,US
135/G4 Geneva, Al,US
138/P16 Geneva, Il,US
131/H2 Geneva, Ne,US
132/E3 Geneva, NY,US
138/P14 Geneva (lake), Wi,US
60/C5 Geneva (Genève), Swi.
60/C5 Geneva (Léman) (lake), Fr., Swi.
60/C5 Genève (canton), Swi.
60/E1 Gengenbach, Ger.
72/E3 Genichesk, Ukr.
64/C4 Genil (riv.), Sp.
59/E2 Genk, Belg.
59/E1 Gennep, Neth.
63/H4 Genoa (Genova), It.
63/H4 Genova (gulf), It.
58/C1 Gent-Brugge (can.), Belg.
92/C5 Genteng (cape), Indo.
58/C1 Gent (Ghent), Belg.
97/D2 George (lake), Austl.
96/C3 George (pt.), Austl.
125/K3 George (riv.), Qu,Can.
108/C4 George, SAfr.
135/H4 George (lake), Fl,US
74/E1 George Land (isl.), Rus.
96/G9 Georges (riv.), Austl.
133/Q8 Georgetown, On,Can.
122/E4 George Town (cap.), Cay.
114/G2 Georgetown (cap.), Guy.
135/H4 Georgetown, Ga,US
132/C4 Georgetown, Ky,US
135/J3 Georgetown, SC,US
134/D4 Georgetown, Tx,US
111/L George V (coast), Ant.
111/V George VI (sound), Ant.
134/D4 George West, Tx,US
73/G4 Georgia (ctry.)
128/B3 Georgia (str.), Can., US
135/G3 Georgia (state), US
132/D2 Georgian Bay Islands Nat'l Park, On,Can.
69/H4 Georgi Traykov, Bul.
57/F4 Georgsmarienhütte, Ger.
54/G3 Gera, Ger.
58/C2 Geraardsbergen, Belg.
115/J6 Geral de Goiás (Espigão Mestre) (range), Braz.
95/A3 Geraldton, Austl.
132/C1 Geraldton, On,Can.
62/F4 Gerbier de Jonc (mtn.), Fr.
57/H3 Gerdau (riv.), Ger.
136/H3 Gerdine (mtn.), Ak,US
69/L5 Gerede, Turk.
79/H2 Gereshk, Afg.
61/H2 Geretsried, Ger.
130/C2 Gerlach, Nv,US
55/L4 Gerlachovský Štít (peak), Slvk.
137/J7 Germantown, Md,US
135/F3 Germantown, Tn,US
54/E3 Germany (ctry.)
61/H1 Germering, Ger.
108/E2 Germiston, SAfr.
59/F3 Gerolstein, Ger.
65/G2 Gerona (Girona), Sp.
58/D3 Gerpinnes, Belg.
62/D5 Gers (riv.), Fr.
59/G5 Gersheim, Ger.
56/E5 Gescher, Ger.
57/F5 Geseke, Ger.
103/P6 Gestro Wenz (riv.), Eth.
64/D2 Getafe, Sp.
59/E2 Gete (riv.), Belg.
129/J4 Gettysburg, SD,US
111/S Getz Ice Shelf, Ant.
59/E2 Geul (riv.), Belg., Neth.
92/A3 Geureudong (peak), Indo.
80/E2 Gevaş, Turk.
57/E6 Gevelsberg, Ger.
68/F5 Gevgelija, FYROM
103/P5 Gewanē, Eth.
109/H6 Geyser (reef), Madg.
69/K5 Geyve, Turk.
81/B4 Gez (riv.), China
102/G1 Ghadāmis, Libya
106/C3 Ghadir, Bi'r (well), Egypt
105/E4 Ghana (ctry.)
110/D5 Ghanzi, Bots.
106/B5 Gharb Binna, Sudan
102/F1 Ghardaïa, Alg.
102/H1 Gharyān, Libya
102/H3 Ghāt, Libya
102/J5 Ghazal (riv.), Chad
90/C2 Ghaziābād, India
79/J2 Ghaznī, Afg.
80/K6 Ghazzah (Gaza), Gaza
82/G2 Ghengis Khan Wall (ruins), Mong.
58/C1 Ghent (Gent), Belg.
69/H2 Gheorghe Gheorghiu-Dej, Rom.
69/G2 Gheorgheni, Rom.
69/F2 Gherla, Rom.
118/C5 Ghio (lake), Arg.
90/A2 Ghotki, Pak.
79/H2 Ghūrīān, Afg.
89/D4 Gia Nghia, Viet.
108/E3 Giant's Castle (peak), SAfr.
130/C4 Giant Sequoia Nat'l Mon., Ca,US
66/D4 Giarre, It.
89/E3 Gia Vuc, Viet.
128/E2 Gibbons, Ab,Can.
64/B4 Gibraleón, Sp.
64/B4 Gibraltar (str.), Afr., Eur.
133/R8 Gibraltar (pt.), On,Can.
64/C4 Gibraltar (dpcy.), UK
138/F7 Gibraltar, Mi,US
97/E1 Gibraltar Range Nat'l Park, Austl.
95/B3 Gibson (des.), Austl.
134/D4 Giddings, Tx,US
106/C2 Gidi (pass), Egypt
103/N6 Gīdolē, Eth.
62/E3 Gien, Fr.
63/J2 Giengen an der Brenz, Ger.
62/F4 Gier (riv.), Fr.
63/H1 Giessen, Ger.
56/B5 Giessendam, Neth.
58/B6 Gif, Fr.
125/H1 Gifford (riv.), Nun,Can.
135/H5 Gifford, Fl,US
57/H4 Gifhorn, Ger.
85/E3 Gifu, Japan
85/E3 Gifu (pref.), Japan
51/F3 Giggleswick, Eng,UK
66/B1 Giglio (isl.), It.
64/C1 Gijón, Sp.
130/D4 Gila (riv.), Az, NM,US
130/D4 Gila Bend, Az,US
130/E4 Gila Cliff Dwellings Nat'l Mon., NM,US
51/H4 Gilberdyke Newport, Eng,UK
96/A2 Gilbert (riv.), Austl.
98/G5 Gilbert (isls.), Kiri.
132/A2 Gilbert, Mn,US
118/C2 Gil de Vilches Nat'l Park, Chile
52/C3 Gilfach Goch, Wal,UK
50/B3 Gilford, NI,UK
137/F6 Gilford Park, NJ,US
79/K1 Gilgit (riv.), Pak.
129/G4 Gillette, Wy,US
128/B3 Gillies Bay, BC,Can.
52/D4 Gillingham, Eng,UK
53/G4 Gillingham, Eng,UK
134/E3 Gilmer, Tx,US
79/K1 Gilqit (riv.), Pak.
83/K1 Gilyuy (riv.), Rus.
56/B5 Gilze, Neth.
103/N6 Gīmbī, Eth.
129/J3 Gimli, Mb,Can.
65/F1 Gimone (riv.), Fr.
85/M9 Ginan, Japan
59/E2 Gingelom, Belg.
88/E6 Gingoog, Phil.
66/E2 Ginosa, It.
64/B1 Ginzo de Limia, Sp.
103/Q7 Giohar, Som.
66/D3 Gioia (gulf), It.
66/E2 Gioia del Colle, It.
66/D3 Gioia Tauro, It.
67/J3 Gioúra (isl.), Gre.
53/G2 Gipping (riv.), Eng,UK
114/D3 Girardot, Col.
110/B4 Giraul, Ang.
80/D2 Giresun, Turk.
90/E3 Girīdīh, India
66/E3 Girifalco, It.
65/G2 Girona (Gerona), Sp.
62/C4 Gironde (riv.), Fr.
97/D1 Girraween Nat'l Park, Austl.
53/G2 Girton, Eng,UK
50/D1 Girvan, Sc,UK
50/D1 Girvan, Water of (riv.), Sc,UK
95/H6 Gisborne, NZ
58/A5 Gisors, Fr.
58/B1 Gistel, Belg.
107/A3 Gitega, Buru.
70/B2 Gittsfjället (peak), Swe.
61/F5 Giubiasco, Swi.
66/C1 Giulianova, It.
69/G4 Giurgiu, Rom.
69/G3 Giurgiu (co.), Rom.
80/M8 Giv'atayim, Isr.
59/D3 Givet, Fr.
62/F4 Givors, Fr.
59/D6 Givry-en-Argonne, Fr.
110/F5 Giyani, SAfr.
103/N6 Giyon, Eth.
106/B2 Giza, Pyramids of (Jīzah) (ruins), Egypt
75/R3 Gizhiga (bay), Rus.
55/L1 Giżycko, Pol.
67/G2 Gjirokastër, Alb.
48/D3 Gjøvik, Nor.
67/F2 Gjuhëzës, Kep i (cape), Alb.
133/K2 Glace Bay, NS,Can.
128/D3 Glacier, BC,Can.
128/C3 Glacier (peak), Wa,US
136/L4 Glacier Bay Nat'l Park & Prsv., Ak,US
128/D3 Glacier Nat'l Park, Can., US
56/D5 Gladbeck, Ger.
96/C3 Gladstone, Austl.
132/C3 Gladwin, Mi,US
51/H3 Glaisdale, Eng,UK
59/G4 Glan (riv.), Ger.
88/E6 Glan, Phil.
52/C3 Glanamman, Wal,UK
58/D4 Gland (riv.), Fr.
61/F4 Glarus (canton), Swi.
61/E4 Glarus Alps (range), Swi.
52/C2 Glasbury, Wal,UK
49/C3 Glasgow, Sc,UK
132/C4 Glasgow, Ky,US
128/G3 Glasgow, Mt,US
50/D6 Glaslyn (riv.), Wal,UK
50/D3 Glass (riv.), IM,UK
134/D2 Glass (mts.), Ok,US
134/C4 Glass (mts.), Tx,US
137/K8 Glassmanor-Oxon Hill, Md,US
52/D4 Glastonbury, Eng,UK
71/M4 Glazov, Rus.
53/G2 Glemsford, Eng,UK
51/H6 Glen (riv.), Eng,UK
97/C3 Glenaladale Nat'l Park, Austl.
132/E4 Glen Allen, Va,US
50/C2 Glenarm, NI,UK
50/C2 Glenarm (riv.), NI,UK
50/B2 Glenavy, NI,UK
97/D2 Glenbawn (dam), Austl.
129/J3 Glenboro, Mb,Can.
96/G8 Glenbrook, Austl.
137/K7 Glen Burnie, Md,US
130/E3 Glen Canyon Nat'l Rec. Area, Az, Ut,US
50/E1 Glencaple, Sc,UK
109/E3 Glencoe, SAfr.
138/Q15 Glencoe, Il,US
137/G5 Glen Cove, NY,US
130/D4 Glendale, Az,US
137/B2 Glendale, Ca,US
128/C5 Glendale, Ca,US
138/P16 Glendale Heights, Il,US
129/G4 Glendive, Mt,US
131/F2 Glendo (res.), Wy,US
137/C2 Glendora, Ca,US
50/B1 Glendun (riv.), NI,UK
97/B3 Glenelg (riv.), Austl.
50/A2 Glenelly (riv.), NI,UK
50/D2 Glenluce, Sc,UK
49/C2 Glen Mòr (val.), Sc,UK
137/E6 Glenolden, Pa,US
136/M4 Glenora, BC,Can.
96/H8 Glenorie, Austl.
131/H4 Glenpool, Ok,US
134/D3 Glen Rose, Tx,US
132/F3 Glens Falls, NY,US
50/B2 Glenshane (pass), NI,UK
137/E5 Glenside, Pa,US
50/D1 Glentrool, Sc,UK
129/H4 Glen Ullin, ND,US
138/Q15 Glenview, Il,US
133/Q8 Glen Williams, On,Can.
130/F3 Glenwood Springs, Co,US
67/L7 Glifádha, Gre.
57/H1 Glinde, Ger.
48/D3 Glittertinden (peak), Nor.
55/K3 Gliwice, Pol.
130/E4 Globe, Az,US
55/H5 Gloggnitz, Aus.
55/J3 Głogów, Pol.
55/J3 Głogówek, Pol.
48/D3 Glomma (riv.), Nor.
109/H5 Glorieuses, Iles (isls.), Reun., Fr.
96/E6 Glorious (mtn.), Austl.
136/D3 Glory of Russia (cape), Ak,US
51/G5 Glossop, Eng,UK
132/F2 Gloucester, On,Can.
52/D3 Gloucester, Eng,UK
137/E6 Gloucester City, NJ,US
52/D3 Gloucestershire (co.), Eng,UK
52/D3 Gloucester, Vale of (val.), Eng,UK
133/L1 Glovertown, Nf,Can.
55/K3 Głowno, Pol.
55/J3 Głubczyce, Pol.
55/J3 Głuchołazy, Pol.
54/E1 Glücksburg, Ger.
57/G1 Glückstadt, Ger.
72/E2 Glukhov, Ukr.
50/B4 Glyde (riv.), Ire.
52/C3 Glyncorrwg, Wal,UK
50/C2 Glynn, NI,UK
52/C3 Glyn Neath, Wal,UK
51/H4 Gmünd, Aus.
105/E3 Gnagna (prov.), Burk.
57/F2 Gnarrenburg, Ger.
55/J2 Gniezno, Pol.
68/E4 Gnjilane, Serb.
52/D1 Gnosall, Eng,UK
84/C3 Gō (riv.), Japan
90/B4 Goa (state), India
90/F2 Goālpāra, India
49/C3 Goat Fell (mtn.), Sc,UK
51/H3 Goathland, Eng,UK
103/N6 Goba, Eth.
110/C5 Gobabeb, Namb.
82/E3 Gobi (des.), China, Mong.
84/D4 Gobō, Japan
51/E6 Gobowen, Eng,UK
56/D5 Goch, Ger.
89/D4 Go Cong, Viet.
53/F4 Godalming, Eng,UK
89/D4 Go Dau Ha, Viet.
90/D4 Godāvari (riv.), India
103/P6 Godē, Eth.
68/F3 Godeanu (peak), Rom.
132/D3 Goderich, On,Can.
90/B3 Godhra, India
53/F2 Godmanchester, Eng,UK
85/M9 Gōdo, Japan
68/D2 Gödöllő, Hun.
52/A6 Godolphin Cross, Eng,UK
118/C2 Godoy Cruz, Arg.
129/K2 Gods (lake), Mb,Can.
129/K2 Gods (riv.), Mb,Can.
125/H2 Gods Mercy (bay), Nun,Can.
121/M3 Godthåb (Nuuk), Grld.
81/C4 Godwin Austen (K2) (peak), China, Pak.
132/E1 Goéland (lake), Qu,Can.
56/A5 Goerce, Neth.
56/A6 Goes, Neth.
132/B2 Gogebic (range), Mi,US
90/D2 Gogra (riv.), India
57/G3 Gohbach (riv.), Ger.
115/M5 Goiana, Braz.
115/J7 Goiânia, Braz.
115/H7 Goiás, Braz.
116/B1 Goiás (state), Braz.
116/B1 Goiatuba, Braz.
56/C5 Goirle, Neth.
84/D3 Gojō, Japan
72/E4 Gok (riv.), Turk.
84/B4 Gokase (riv.), Japan
85/M9 Gokashō, Japan
69/G5 Gökçeada (isl.), Turk.
80/D2 Göksun, Turk.
80/K5 Golan Heights (reg.), Syria
80/C2 Gölbaşı, Turk.
80/D3 Gölbaşı, Turk.
51/F5 Golborne, Eng,UK
138/B2 Gold (mtn.), Wa,US
55/M1 Gołdap, Pol.
128/B5 Gold Beach, Or,US
96/D4 Gold Coast, Austl.
105/E5 Gold Coast (reg.), Gha.
128/D3 Golden, BC,Can.
131/F3 Golden, Co,US
128/C4 Goldendale, Wa,US
54/F3 Goldene Aue (reg.), Ger.
138/J11 Golden Gate (chan.), Ca,US
108/E3 Golden Gate Highlands Nat'l Park, SAfr.
128/B3 Golden Hinde (peak), BC,Can.
57/F3 Goldenstedt, Ger.
130/C3 Goldfield, Nv,US
128/B3 Gold River, BC,Can.
135/J3 Goldsboro, NC,US
134/D4 Goldthwaite, Tx,US
80/E2 Göle, Turk.
57/H2 Goleniów, Pol.
80/B3 Gölhisar, Turk.
134/D4 Goliad, Tx,US
80/D2 Gölköy, Turk.
82/C4 Golmud, China
78/F2 Golpāyegān, Iran
69/K5 Gölpazarı, Turk.
55/K2 Golub-Dobrzyń, Pol.
69/H4 Golyama Kamchiya (riv.), Bul.
69/G5 Golyama Syutkya (peak), Bul.
69/G5 Golyam Perelik (peak), Bul.
107/A3 Goma, D.R. Congo
105/H4 Gombe (state), Nga
65/X16 Gomera (isl.), Canl.
58/B6 Gometz-le-Châtel, Fr.
123/P8 Gómez Palacio, Mex.
54/F2 Gommern, Ger.
53/F4 Gomshall, Eng,UK
79/G2 Gonābād, Iran
110/F5 Gonarezhou Nat'l Park, Zim.
123/G4 Gonâve (gulf), Haiti
79/G1 Gonbad-e Qābūs, Iran
90/D2 Gondā, India
90/B3 Gondal, India
103/N5 Gonder, Eth.
90/D3 Gondia, India
64/A2 Gondomar, Port.
64/A1 Gondomar, Sp.
69/H5 Gönen, Turk.
91/F2 Gongbo'gyamda, China
91/H2 Gongga (peak), China
82/E4 Gonghe, China
105/H4 Gongola (riv.), Nga.
105/H4 Gongola (state), Nga.
97/C1 Gongolgon, Austl.
87/F2 Gongzhuling, China
134/D4 Gonzales, Tx,US
122/B3 González, Mex.
111/J Goodenough (cape), Ant.
108/B4 Good Hope, Cape of (cape), SAfr.
128/E5 Gooding, Id,US
131/G3 Goodland, Ks,US
96/E7 Goodna, Austl.
52/B3 Goodwick, Wal,UK
108/B4 Goodwood, SAfr.
56/C4 Gooimeer (lake), Neth.
51/H4 Goole, Eng,UK
56/D4 Goor, Neth.
129/H2 Goose (lake), Mb,Can.
130/B2 Goose (lake), Ca, Or,US
125/K3 Goose Bay-Happy Valley, Nf,Can.
51/F5 Goostrey, Eng,UK
63/H2 Göppingen, Ger.
89/D4 Go Quao, Viet.
55/J3 Góra, Pol.
55/L3 Góra Kalwaria, Pol.
90/D2 Gorakhpur, India
68/D4 Goražde, Bosn.
122/E5 Gorda (pt.), Nic.
130/A2 Gorda (pt.), Ca,US
97/C4 Gordon (lake), Austl.
102/J6 Goré, Chad
103/N6 Gorē, Eth.
53/G1 Gore (pt.), Eng,UK
136/H4 Gore (pt.), Ak,US
80/D2 Görele, Turk.
62/B2 Gorey, Chl,UK
79/F1 Gorgān, Iran
59/F4 Gorge du Loup, Lux.
104/B3 Gorgol (reg.), Mrta.
104/B2 Gorgol (riv.), Mrta.
73/H4 Gori, Geo.
56/B5 Gorinchem, Neth.
53/E3 Goring, Eng,UK
53/F5 Goring by Sea, Eng,UK
63/K4 Gorizia, It.
69/F3 Gorj (co.), Rom.
72/D1 Gorki, Bela.
70/J4 Gor'kiy (res.), Rus.
71/K4 Gor'kiy (Nizhniy Novgorod), Rus.
55/L4 Gorlice, Pol.
55/H3 Görlitz, Ger.
52/C2 Gorllwyn (mtn.), Wal,UK
50/B4 Gormanston, Ire.
133/R8 Gormley, On,Can.
69/G4 Gorna Oryakhovitsa, Bul.
68/E3 Gornji Milanovac, Serb.
68/C4 Gornji Vakuf, Bosn.
74/J4 Gorno-Altay Aut. Obl., Rus.
81/E1 Gorno-Altaysk, Rus.
74/H6 Gorno-Badakhstan Aut. Obl., Taj.
71/J4 Gorodets, Rus.
98/D5 Goroka, PNG
93/H4 Gorong (isl.), Indo.
93/F3 Gorontalo, Indo.
52/B3 Gorseinon, Wal,UK
56/D4 Gorssel, Neth.
50/A2 Gortin, NI,UK
72/C2 Goryn' (riv.), Bela., Ukr.
55/H2 Gorzów Wielkopolski, Pol.
84/D3 Gōse, Japan
85/F2 Gosen, Japan
51/G2 Gosforth, Eng,UK
83/N3 Goshogawara, Japan
57/H5 Goslar, Ger.
68/B3 Gospić, Cro.
53/E5 Gosport, Eng,UK
68/E5 Gostivar, FYROM
55/J3 Gostyń, Pol.
55/K2 Gostynin, Pol.
48/D4 Göteborg, Swe.
48/D4 Göteborg och Bohus (co.), Swe.
102/H6 Gotel (mts.), Camr., Nga.
85/F3 Gotemba, Japan
57/H7 Gotha, Ger.
131/G2 Gothenburg, Ne,US
48/F4 Gotland (isl.), Swe.
84/A4 Gotō (isls.), Japan
69/F5 Gotse Delchev, Bul.
48/F4 Gotska Sandön Nat'l Park, Swe.
84/C3 Gōtsu, Japan
57/G5 Göttingen, Ger.
56/B4 Gouda, Neth.
44/J8 Gough (isl.), StH.
132/F1 Gouin (res.), Qu,Can.
132/C2 Goulais (riv.), On,Can.
97/D2 Goulburn, Austl.
97/D2 Goulburn (riv.), Austl.
111/P Gould (coast), Ant.
134/F3 Gould, Ar,US
104/E2 Goundam, Mali
105/H3 Gouré, Niger
108/C4 Gourits (riv.), SAfr.
105/F3 Gourma (prov.), Burk.
105/F3 Gourma (reg.), Burk.
105/E2 Gourma-Rharous, Mali
58/A5 Gournay-en-Bray, Fr.
103/J4 Gouro, Chad
80/D2 Gouşu (riv.), Turk.
116/D1 Gouvêa, Braz.
58/B5 Gouvieux, Fr.
116/D1 Governador Valadares, Braz.
82/D3 Govĭ Altayn (mts.), Mong.
79/H3 Gowd-e-Zereh (lake), Afg.
52/B3 Gower (pen.), Wal,UK
51/H4 Goxhill, Eng,UK
117/E2 Goya, Arg.
51/F5 Goyt (riv.), Eng,UK
85/M9 Gozaisho-yama (peak), Japan
81/D4 Gozha (lake), China
66/D4 Gozo (isl.), Malta
108/D4 Graaff-Reinet, SAfr.
56/D4 Graafschap (reg.), Neth.
108/B2 Graberberg (peak), Namb.
54/F2 Grabow, Ger.
68/B3 Gračac, Cro.
68/D3 Gračanica, Bosn.
135/G4 Graceville, Fl,US
122/E4 Gracias a Dios (cape), Nic.
65/S12 Graciosa (isl.), Azor.,Port.
68/D3 Gradačac, Bosn.
115/H5 Gradaús, Braz.
64/B1 Grado, Sp.
53/F2 Grafham Water (lake), Eng,UK
97/E1 Grafton, Austl.
96/B2 Grafton (passg.), Austl.
129/J3 Grafton, ND,US
132/D4 Grafton, WV,US
124/C3 Graham (isl.), BC,Can.
125/S7 Graham (isl.), Nun,Can.
123/N7 Graham (peak), Az,US
134/D3 Graham, Tx,US
138/C3 Graham, Wa,US
74/G1 Graham Bell (isl.), Rus.
111/V Graham Land (reg.), Ant.
108/D4 Grahamstown, SAfr.
53/G4 Grain, Eng,UK
104/C5 Grain Coast (reg.), Libr.
115/J5 Grajaú, Braz.
115/J4 Grajaú (riv.), Braz.
55/M2 Grajewo, Pol.
62/D4 Gramat (plat.), Fr.
49/C2 Grampian (mts.), Sc,UK
97/B3 Grampians Nat'l Park, Austl.
56/D3 Gramsbergen, Neth.
48/D3 Gran, Nor.
114/D3 Granada, Col.
122/D5 Granada, Nic.
64/D4 Granada, Sp.
119/K7 Gran Altiplanicie Central (plat.), Arg.
119/K7 Gran Bajo de San Julián (val.), Arg.
118/C5 Gran Bajo Oriental (val.), Arg.
134/D3 Granbury, Tx,US
131/F2 Granby, Co,US
65/X17 Gran Canaria (isl.), Canl.
117/D2 Gran Chaco (plain), SAm.
133/H2 Grand (lake), NB,Can.
133/K1 Grand (lake), Nf,Can.
125/J3 Grand (riv.), Qu,Can.
87/D4 Grand (can.), China
50/B5 Grand (can.), Ire.
130/D3 Grand (canyon), Az,US
131/J3 Grand (riv.), Ia, Mo,US
131/J5 Grand (lake), La,US
132/C2 Grand (riv.), Mi,US
134/E2 Grand (riv.), Mo,US

Grand – Hamfo
163

133/S9 Grand (isl.), NY,US
129/H4 Grand (riv.), SD,US
123/F2 Grand Bahama (isl.), Bahm.
133/L2 Grand Bank, Nf,Can.
104/C5 Grand Bassa (co.), Libr.
104/E5 Grand-Bassam, C.d'Iv.
133/H2 Grand Bay, NB,Can.
138/E6 Grand Blanc, Mi,US
130/D3 Grand Canyon Nat'l Park, Az,US
130/D3 Grand Canyon-Parashant Nat'l Mon., Az,US
104/C5 Grand Cape Mount (co.), Libr.
122/E4 Grand Cayman (isl.), Cay.
128/F2 Grand Centre, Ab,Can.
128/D4 Grand Coulee (dam), Wa,US
119/K7 Grande (bay), Arg.
119/K8 Grande (riv.), Arg.
114/F7 Grande (riv.), Bol.
116/K8 Grande (isl.), Braz.
116/J7 Grande (riv.), Braz.
123/F6 Grande (pt.), Pan.
119/T11 Grande (stream), Uru.
128/D2 Grande Cache, Ab,Can.
109/G5 Grande Comore (isl.), Com.
66/C1 Grande, Corno (peak), It.
115/H4 Grande de Gurupá, Braz.
66/C4 Grande, Monte (peak), It.
128/D2 Grande Prairie, Ab,Can.
102/H4 Grand 'Erg de Bilma (des.), Niger
102/E1 Grand Erg Occidental (des.), Alg.
102/G1 Grand Erg Oriental (des.), Alg.
134/C4 Grande, Rio (riv.), Mex., US
58/B1 Grande-Synthe, Fr.
123/J4 Grande-Terre (isl.), Guad.
133/H2 Grand Falls, NB,Can.
133/L1 Grand Falls, Nf,Can.
128/D3 Grand Forks, BC,Can.
129/J4 Grand Forks, ND,US
58/B2 Grand-Fort-Philippe, Fr.
132/C3 Grand Haven, Mi,US
131/H2 Grand Island, Ne,US
135/F4 Grand Isle, La,US
104/D5 Grand Jide (co.), Libr.
130/E3 Grand Junction, Co,US
131/J3 Grand Lake O'The Cherokees (lake), Ok,US
133/H2 Grand Manan (isl.), NB,Can.
129/L4 Grand Marais, Mn,US
58/C6 Grand Marin (riv.), Fr.
133/F2 Grand-Mère, Qu,Can.
133/K2 Grand Miquelon (isl.), StP.
60/C5 Grand Mont Ruan (mtn.), Fr.
64/A3 Grândola, Port.
129/L4 Grand Portage Nat'l Mon., Mn,US
59/D5 Grandpré, Fr.
129/J2 Grand Rapids, Mb,Can.
132/C3 Grand Rapids, Mi,US
129/K4 Grand Rapids, Mn,US
62/F5 Grand Rhône (riv.), Fr.
130/E3 Grand Staircase-Escalante Nat'l Mon., Ut,US
128/F5 Grand Teton Nat'l Park, Wy,US
123/G3 Grand Turk, Trks.
53/F3 Grand Union (can.), Eng,UK
129/H3 Grandview, Mb,Can.
128/D4 Grandview, Wa,US
118/C2 Graneros, Chile
48/E3 Granfjället (peak), Swe.
51/F3 Grange, Eng,UK
136/L3 Granger (mtn.), Yk,Can.
128/D4 Grangeville, Id,US
128/B2 Granisle, BC,Can.
128/F4 Granite (peak), Mt,US
132/B4 Granite City, Il,US
115/K4 Granja, Braz.
118/D5 Gran Laguna Salada (lake), Arg.
65/G2 Granollers, Sp.
63/G4 Gran Paradiso Nat'l Park, It.
63/J3 Gran Pilastro (peak), It.
65/Y16 Gran Tarajal, CanI.,Sp.
51/H6 Grantham, Eng,UK
49/D2 Grantown-on-Spey, Sc,UK
130/F4 Grants, NM,US
132/A2 Grantsburg, Wi,US
128/C5 Grants Pass, Or,US
114/C5 Gran Vilaya (ruins), Peru
129/H1 Granville (lake), Mb,Can.
62/C2 Granville, Fr.
138/B3 Grapeview-Allyn, Wa,US
57/F2 Grasberg, Ger.
51/E3 Grasmere, Eng,UK
63/G5 Grasse, Fr.
133/Q9 Grassie, On,Can.
51/G3 Grassington, Eng,UK
128/G3 Grasslands Nat'l Park, Sk,Can.
68/B2 Gratkorn, Aus.
61/F4 Graubünden (canton), Swi.
62/F5 Graulhet, Fr.
56/C5 Grave, Neth.
128/G3 Gravelbourg, Sk,Can.
58/B2 Gravelines, Fr.
132/E2 Gravenhurst, On,Can.
53/G4 Gravesend, Eng,UK
58/A5 Gravigny, Fr.
66/E2 Gravina di Puglia, It.
123/G4 Gravois (pt.), Haiti
62/B3 Gray, Fr.
132/C2 Grayling, Mi,US
53/G4 Grays, Eng,UK
128/F5 Grays (lake), Id,US
128/B4 Grays (har.), Wa,US
138/P15 Grayslake, Il,US
129/H3 Grayson, Sk,Can.
63/L3 Graz, Aus.
97/C4 Great (lake), Austl.
129/G3 Great (plains), Can., US
44/E3 Great (lakes), NAm.
130/C2 Great (basin), US
123/F2 Great Abaco (isl.), Bahm.
55/L5 Great Alföld (plain), Hun.
95/B4 Great Australian (bight), Austl.
123/F3 Great Bahama (bank), Bahm.
53/F2 Great Barford, Eng,UK
96/B2 Great Barrier Reef Marine Park, Austl.
53/G2 Great Barton, Eng,UK
130/D3 Great Basin Nat'l Park, Nv,US
124/D2 Great Bear (lake), NW,Can.
131/H3 Great Bend, Ks,US
108/C3 Great Brak (riv.), SAfr.
49/E3 Great Britain (isl.), UK
45/P5 Great Coco (isl.), Myan.
53/G2 Great Cornard, Eng,UK
128/F5 Great Divide (basin), Wy,US
97/B3 Great Dividing (range), Austl.
51/H4 Great Driffield, Eng,UK
53/G3 Great Dunmow, Eng,UK
105/F5 Greater Accra (reg.), Gha.
123/G4 Greater Antilles (arch.), NAm.
53/F3 Greater London (co.), Eng,UK
51/F5 Greater Manchester (co.), Eng,UK
92/C4 Greater Sunda (isls.), Indo.
123/F3 Great Exuma (isl.), Bahm.
128/F4 Great Falls, Mt,US
108/D4 Great Fish (pt.), SAfr.
108/D4 Great Fish (riv.), SAfr.
53/F2 Great Gransden, Eng,UK
123/F3 Great Guana Cay (isl.), Bahm.
51/G2 Greatham, Eng,UK
51/F4 Great Harwood, Eng,UK
90/D2 Great Himalaya (range), Asia
123/G3 Great Inagua (isl.), Bahm.
90/A2 Great Indian (des.), India, Pak.
108/C3 Great Karoo (reg.), SAfr.
108/D4 Great Kei (riv.), SAfr.
52/D2 Great Malvern, Eng,UK
53/E3 Great Milton, Eng,UK
52/B5 Great Mis Tor (hill), Eng,UK
137/G5 Great Neck, NY,US
91/F6 Great Nicobar (isl.), India
53/G1 Great Ouse (riv.), Eng,UK
97/C4 Great Oyster (bay), Austl.
135/J3 Great Pee Dee (riv.), SC,US
107/A4 Great Rift (val.), Afr.
107/B4 Great Ruaha (riv.), Tanz.
130/D2 Great Salt (lake), Ut,US
130/D2 Great Salt Lake (des.), Ut,US
131/F3 Great Sand Dunes Nat'l Park, Co,US
106/A3 Great Sand Sea (des.), Egypt, Libya
95/B2 Great Sandy (des.), Austl.
130/B2 Great Sandy (des.), Or,US
96/D4 Great Sandy Nat'l Park, Austl.
104/B4 Great Scarcies (riv.), Gui., SLeo.
53/G2 Great Shelford, Eng,UK
51/F3 Great Shunner Fell (mtn.), Eng,UK
124/E2 Great Slave (lake), NW,Can.
135/H3 Great Smoky Mts. Nat'l Park, NC, Tn,US
137/G5 Great South (bay), NY,US
53/G4 Great Stour (riv.), Eng,UK
89/B3 Great Tenasserim (riv.), Myan.
52/B5 Great Torrington, Eng,UK
95/B3 Great Victoria (des.), Austl.
87/B3 Great Wall (ruins), China
97/C4 Great Western Tiers (mts.), Austl.
108/B4 Great Winterhoek (peak), SAfr.
52/D2 Great Witley, Eng,UK
53/H1 Great Yarmouth, Eng,UK
80/F3 Great Zab (riv.), Iraq, Turk.
110/F5 Great Zimbabwe (ruins), Zim.
105/H2 Gréboun (peak), Niger
80/K4 Greco (cape), Cyp.
66/D2 Greco (peak), It.
64/C2 Gredos (range), Sp.
67/G3 Greece (ctry.)
131/F2 Greeley, Co,US
125/S6 Greely (fjord), Nun,Can.
97/D3 Green (cape), Austl.
132/C4 Green (riv.), Ky,US
129/M4 Green (bay), Mi, Wi,US
130/E3 Green (riv.), Ut, Wy,US
133/G3 Green (mts.), Vt,US
132/B2 Green Bay, Wi,US
137/K7 Greenbelt, Md,US
132/C4 Greencastle, In,US
135/H4 Green Cove Springs, Fl,US
138/Q14 Greendale, Wi,US
135/H2 Greeneville, Tn,US
132/C4 Greenfield, In,US
133/F3 Greenfield, Ma,US
138/P14 Greenfield, Wi,US
133/P7 Greenfield Park, Qu,Can.
137/K7 Green Haven, Md,US
50/C2 Greenisland, NI,UK
121/R2 Greenland (sea)
121/N2 Greenland (Kalaallit Nunaat) (dpcy.), Den.
49/D3 Greenlaw, Sc,UK
49/C3 Greenock, Sc,UK
136/K2 Greenough (mtn.), Ak,US
133/R8 Green River, On,Can.
130/E3 Green River, Ut,US
128/F5 Green River, Wy,US
135/G3 Greensboro, Al,US
135/J2 Greensboro, NC,US
132/C4 Greensburg, In,US
132/E3 Greensburg, Pa,US
133/Q9 Greens Ville, On,Can.
130/E5 Green Valley, Az,US
137/J7 Green Valley, Md,US
104/C5 Greenville, Libr.
135/G4 Greenville, Al,US
130/B2 Greenville, Ca,US
132/C4 Greenville, Ky,US
132/C3 Greenville, Mi,US
135/F3 Greenville, Ms,US
135/J3 Greenville, NC,US
132/C3 Greenville, Oh,US
135/H3 Greenville, SC,US
134/D3 Greenville, Tx,US
138/D3 Greenwater (riv.), Wa,US
137/G4 Greenwich, Ct,US
133/R8 Greenwood, On,Can.
135/F3 Greenwood, Ms,US
137/F4 Greenwood (lake), NJ, NY,US
135/H3 Greenwood, SC,US
135/H3 Greenwood (lake), SC,US
131/J4 Greers Ferry (lake), Ar,US
50/B6 Greese (riv.), Ire.
56/D6 Grefrath, Ger.
114/D5 Gregório (riv.), Braz.
96/A2 Gregory (range), Austl.
129/J5 Gregory, SD,US
55/G1 Greifswald, Ger.
55/G1 Greifswalder Bodden (bay), Ger.
68/B2 Greimberg (peak), Aus.
54/G3 Greiz, Ger.
71/N4 Gremyachinsk, Rus.
48/D4 Grenå, Den.
123/J5 Grenada (ctry.)
135/F3 Grenada, Ms,US
60/D3 Grenchen, Swi.
129/H3 Grenfell, Sk,Can.
62/F4 Grenoble, Fr.
48/E2 Gressåmoen Nat'l Park, Nor.
51/E2 Greta (riv.), Eng,UK
51/F3 Greta (riv.), Eng,UK
129/J3 Gretna, Mb,Can.
51/E2 Gretna, Sc,UK
135/F4 Gretna, La,US
53/F1 Gretton, Eng,UK
58/B6 Gretz-Armainvilliers, Fr.
56/B5 Grevelingendam (dam), Neth.
57/E4 Greven, Ger.
67/G2 Grevená, Gre.
56/D6 Grevenbroich, Ger.
59/F4 Grevenmacher (dist.), Lux.
54/F2 Grevesmühlen, Ger.
56/A5 Grevlingen (chan.), Neth.
96/A5 Grey (range), Austl.
133/K2 Grey (riv.), Nf,Can.
50/C2 Grey (pt.), NI,UK
50/C2 Grey Abbey, NI,UK
128/F4 Greybull, Wy,US
136/L3 Grey Hunter (peak), Yk,Can.
95/H7 Greymouth, NZ
96/B2 Grey Peaks Nat'l Park, Austl.
51/F2 Greystoke, Eng,UK
50/B5 Greystones, Ire.
109/E3 Greytown, SAfr.
59/D2 Grez-Doiceau, Belg.
52/B6 Gribbin (pt.), Eng,UK
56/C2 Griend (isl.), Neth.
135/G3 Griffin, Ga,US
97/C2 Griffith, Austl.
138/R16 Griffith, In,US
58/B6 Grigny, Fr.
97/C4 Grim (cape), Austl.
58/D2 Grimbergen, Belg.
52/D2 Grimley, Eng,UK
54/G1 Grimmen, Ger.
133/Q9 Grimsby, On,Can.
51/H4 Grimsby, Eng,UK
48/N6 Grimsey (isl.), Ice.
48/D4 Grimstad, Nor.
125/S7 Grinnel (pen.), Nun,Can.
68/B2 Grintavec (peak), Slov.
108/E3 Griqualand East (reg.), SAfr.
108/C2 Griqualand West (reg.), SAfr.
58/A2 Gris Nez (cape), Fr.
138/K10 Grizzly (bay), Ca,US
68/C3 Grmeč (mtn.), Bosn.
59/D1 Grobbendonk, Belg.
55/J3 Grodków, Pol.
55/J2 Grodzisk Wielkopolski, Pol.
56/D4 Groenlo, Neth.
134/D4 Groesbeck, Tx,US
56/C5 Groesbeek, Neth.
62/B3 Groix (isl.), Fr.
55/L3 Grójec, Pol.
54/F1 Grömitz, Ger.
56/E4 Gronau, Ger.
56/D2 Groningen, Neth.
56/D2 Groningen (prov.), Neth.
61/H5 Gronlait (peak), It.
108/C4 Groot (riv.), SAfr.
56/D2 Grootegast, Neth.
110/C4 Grootfontein, Namb.
108/D2 Groot-Marico (riv.), SAfr.
108/C3 Grootvloer (salt pan), SAfr.
123/J5 Gros Islet, StL.
133/K1 Gros Morne (peak), Nf,Can.
133/K1 Gros Morne Nat'l Park, Nf,Can.
62/F3 Grosne (riv.), Fr.
57/G6 Grossalmerode, Ger.
57/G3 Grosse Aue (riv.), Ger.
138/F7 Grosse Ile, Mi,US
108/A2 Grosse Münzenberg (peak), Namb.
59/G2 Grosse Nister (riv.), Ger.
57/F3 Grossenkneten, Ger.
138/G7 Grosse Pointe, Mi,US
138/G7 Grosse Pointe Farms, Mi,US
138/G7 Grosse Pointe Park, Mi,US
138/G7 Grosse Pointe Shores, Mi,US
138/G7 Grosse Pointe Woods, Mi,US
63/K2 Grosser Arber (peak), Ger.
63/L3 Grosser Bösenstein (peak), Aus.
57/F1 Grosser Knechtsand (isl.), Ger.
55/H4 Grosser Peilstein (peak), Aus.
63/L3 Grosser Priel (peak), Aus.
55/H5 Grosser Pyhrgas (peak), Aus.
63/K2 Grosser Rachel (peak), Ger.
57/E2 Grosses Meer (lake), Ger.
68/A2 Grosses Wiesbachhorn (peak), Aus.
66/B1 Grosseto, It.
63/H2 Grossgerau, Ger.
63/K3 Grossglockner (peak), Aus.
57/H1 Grosshansdorf, Ger.
63/H5 Grosso (cape), Fr.
59/F5 Grossrosseln, Ger.
59/E2 Grote Gete (riv.), Belg.
59/D1 Grote Nete (riv.), Belg.
129/J4 Groton, SD,US
66/E2 Grottaglie, It.
59/E3 Grotte de Han, Belg.
65/E1 Grottes de Bétharram, Fr.
128/D2 Grouard Mission, Ab,Can.
132/D1 Groundhog (riv.), On,Can.
56/C2 Grouw, Neth.
53/E3 Grove, Eng,UK
131/J3 Grove, Ok,US
130/B4 Grover City, Ca,US
134/E4 Groves, Tx,US
137/J8 Groveton, Va,US
73/H4 Groznyy, Rus.
69/H4 Grudovo, Bul.
55/K2 Grudziądz, Pol.
51/E2 Grune (pt.), Eng,UK
72/F1 Gryazi, Rus.
55/H2 Gryfice, Pol.
55/H2 Gryfino, Pol.
118/B4 Guabun (pt.), Chile
123/F3 Guacanayabo (gulf), Cuba
116/D2 Guaçuí, Braz.
123/P9 Guadalajara, Mex.
64/D2 Guadalajara, Sp.
98/E6 Guadalcanal (isl.), Sol.
64/E4 Guadalentín (riv.), Sp.
64/D3 Guadalimlar (riv.), Sp.
65/N8 Guadalix (riv.), Sp.
65/E2 Guadalope (riv.), Sp.
64/D4 Guadalquivir (riv.), Sp.
123/F6 Guadalupe, Pan.
64/C3 Guadalupe (range), Sp.
134/B4 Guadalupe (peak), Tx,US
134/D4 Guadalupe (riv.), Tx,US
134/B4 Guadalupe Mts. Nat'l Park, Tx,US
65/M8 Guadarrama (pass), Sp.
64/C2 Guadarrama (range), Sp.
64/C3 Guadarrama (riv.), Sp.
123/J4 Guadeloupe (dpcy.), Fr.
123/J4 Guadeloupe (passage), NAm.
64/B4 Guadiana (riv.), Sp., Port.
64/D4 Guadiana Menor (riv.), Sp.
64/D4 Guadix, Sp.
118/B4 Guafo (chan.), Chile
118/B4 Guafo (isl.), Chile
116/B4 Guaíba, Braz.
116/B4 Guaíba (riv.), Braz.
114/F2 Guaiquinima (peak), Ven.
116/B2 Guaíra, Braz.
118/B4 Guaiteca (isl.), Chile
114/E6 Guajará-Mirim, Braz.
123/G5 Guajira (pen.), Col., Ven.
130/B3 Gualala, Ca,US
66/C1 Gualdo Tadino, It.
118/F2 Gualeguay, Arg.
118/F2 Gualeguay (riv.), Arg.
118/F2 Gualeguaychú, Arg.
118/D4 Gualicho (val.), Arg.
98/D3 Guam (isl.), PacUS
118/B5 Guamblin (isl.), Chile
116/K7 Guanabara (bay), Braz.
122/A3 Guanajuato, Mex.
122/A3 Guanajuato (state), Mex.
115/K6 Guanambi, Braz.
123/H6 Guanare, Ven.
123/H6 Guanare (riv.), Ven.
87/B3 Guandi Shan (mtn.), China
91/K3 Guangdong (prov.), China
87/D5 Guangming Ding (peak), China
91/J3 Guangxi Zhuangzu Zizhiqu (aut. reg.), China
88/C2 Guangze, China
88/B3 Guangzhou (Canton), China
116/D1 Guanhães, Braz.
123/J6 Guanipa (riv.), Ven.
123/F3 Guantánamo, Cuba
87/G6 Guanting (res.), China
87/D4 Guanyun, China
116/B4 Guaporé, Braz.
114/F6 Guaporé (riv.), Braz.
115/L5 Guarabira, Braz.
115/J5 Guaraí, Braz.
116/B3 Guaramirim, Braz.
114/C4 Guaranda, Ecu.
116/D2 Guarapari, Braz.
116/B3 Guarapuava, Braz.
116/E2 Guararapes, Braz.
116/G8 Guararema, Braz.
116/H7 Guaratinguetá, Braz.
116/B3 Guaratuba, Braz.
64/B2 Guarda, Port.
64/B2 Guarda (dist.), Port.
64/B3 Guareña, Sp.
114/E2 Guárico (res.), Ven.
123/H6 Guárico (riv.), Ven.
116/G9 Guarujá, Braz.
116/G8 Guarulhos, Braz.
123/N8 Guasave, Mex.
122/C4 Guatemala (ctry.)
122/C5 Guatemala (cap.), Guat.
116/G6 Guaxupé, Braz.
123/H4 Guayama, PR
114/C4 Guayaquil, Ecu.
114/B4 Guayaquil (gulf), Ecu.
114/E6 Guayaramerín, Bol.
123/M8 Guaymas, Mex.
71/N4 Gubakha, Rus.
55/H3 Guben, Ger.
55/H3 Gubin, Pol.
72/F2 Gubkin, Rus.
82/E2 Guchin-Us, Mong.
65/E2 Gúdar (range), Sp.
57/G6 Gudensberg, Ger.
73/H4 Gudermes, Rus.
90/D4 Gudivāda, India
90/C5 Gūdūr, India
64/D1 Guecho, Sp.
104/B1 Guelb Azefal (mts.), Mrta.
132/D3 Guelph, On,Can.
102/C2 Guelta Zemmur, WSah.
59/F5 Guénange, Fr.
62/B3 Guérande, Fr.
62/D3 Guéret, Fr.
64/D1 Guernica y Luno, Sp.
62/B2 Guernsey (isl.), ChI,UK
122/B4 Guerrero (state), Mex.
62/F3 Gueugnon, Fr.
105/H3 Guézaoua, Niger
103/N6 Gugē (peak), Eth.
98/D3 Guguan (isl.), NMar.
108/L11 Guguletu, SAfr.
88/B3 Gui (riv.), China
65/X16 Guía de Isora, Sp.
114/F2 Guiana Highlands (mts.), SAm.
122/B4 Guichicovi, Mex.
102/H6 Guidder, Camr.
104/B3 Guidimaka (reg.), Mrta.
66/C2 Guidonia, It.
104/D5 Guiglo, C.d'Iv.
58/B6 Guignes, Fr.
58/C5 Guignicourt, Fr.
88/D5 Guihulngan, Phil.
53/F4 Guildford, Eng,UK
62/F4 Guilherand, Fr.
91/K2 Guilin, China
125/J3 Guillaume-Delisle (lake), Qu,Can.
64/B4 Guillena, Sp.
52/C1 Guilsfield, Wal,UK
64/A2 Guimarães, Port.
87/D4 Guimeng Ding (mtn.), China
104/C4 Guinea (ctry.)
102/F7 Guinea (gulf), Afr.
104/B3 Guinea-Bissau (ctry.)
62/B2 Guingamp, Fr.
62/A2 Guipavas, Fr.
115/H7 Guiratinga, Braz.
123/J5 Güiria, Ven.
51/G2 Guisborough, Eng,UK
58/C4 Guise, Fr.
51/G4 Guiseley, Eng,UK
64/B1 Guitiriz, Sp.
88/B2 Guiyang, China
91/J2 Guiyang, China
91/J2 Guizhou (prov.), China
62/C4 Gujan-Mestras, Fr.
90/B3 Gujarāt (state), India
79/K2 Gūjar Khān, Pak.
79/K2 Gujrānwāla, Pak.
79/K2 Gujrāt, Pak.
72/F2 Gukovo, Rus.
82/E4 Gulang, China
90/C4 Gulbarga, India
59/G3 Guldenbach (riv.), Ger.
88/C3 Guleitou, China
135/F4 Gulfport, Ms,US
135/G4 Gulf Shores, Al,US
74/G5 Gulistan, Uzb.
83/J2 Guliya (peak), China
50/B2 Gulladuff, NI,UK
128/F3 Gull Lake, Sk,Can.
80/C3 Gülnar, Turk.
52/B2 Gulpen, Neth.
107/B2 Gulu, Ugan.
69/G4 Gülübovo, Bul.
110/D4 Gumare, Bots.
85/F2 Gumma (pref.), Japan
57/E6 Gummersbach, Ger.
72/E4 Gümüşhacıköy, Turk.
80/D2 Gümüşhane, Turk.
103/N5 Guna (peak), Eth.
90/C3 Guna, India
80/E2 Güneydogu Toroslar (mts.), Turk.
129/J2 Gunisao (lake), Mb,Can.
129/J2 Gunisao (riv.), Mb,Can.
97/D1 Gunnedah, Austl.
130/F3 Gunnison, Co,US
130/F3 Gunnison (riv.), Co,US
130/E3 Gunnison, Ut,US
81/B4 Gunt (riv.), Taj.
135/G3 Guntersville, Al,US
135/G3 Guntersville (lake), Al,US
90/D4 Guntūr, India
61/G1 Günz (riv.), Ger.
63/J2 Gunzenhausen, Ger.
87/C4 Guo (riv.), China
103/N6 Gurage (peak), Eth.
69/G2 Gura Humorului, Rom.
117/F2 Gural (mts.), Braz.
81/E2 Gurbantünggut (des.), China
79/L2 Gurdāspur, India
115/K6 Gurguéia (riv.), Braz.
123/J6 Guri, Embalse de (res.), Ven.
63/L3 Gurk (riv.), Aus.
63/K3 Gurkthaler Alpen (mts.), Aus.
138/Q15 Gurnee, Il,US
69/J5 Gürsu, Turk.
115/J6 Gurupi, Braz.
115/J4 Gurupi (mts.), Braz.
115/J4 Gurupi (riv.), Braz.
90/B3 Guru Sikhar (mtn.), India
82/G2 Gurvandzagal, Mong.
70/J5 Gus'-Khrustal'nyy, Rus.
66/A3 Guspini, It.
54/G2 Güstrow, Ger.
57/F5 Gütersloh, Ger.
131/H4 Guthrie, Ok,US
131/G4 Guthrie, Tx,US
48/E3 Gutulia Nat'l Park, Nor.
114/G3 Guyana (ctry.)
58/B6 Guyancourt, Fr.
135/H2 Guyandotte (riv.), WV,US
87/B2 Guyang, China
62/C4 Guyenne (reg.), Fr.
97/E1 Guy Fawkes Riv. Nat'l Park, Austl.
53/G1 Guyhirn, Eng,UK
131/G3 Guymon, Ok,US
82/F4 Guyuan, China
82/H3 Guyuan, China
123/N7 Guzmán (lake), Mex.
79/H3 Gwādar, Pak.
90/C2 Gwalior, India
110/E5 Gwanda, Zim.
53/F1 Gwash (riv.), Eng,UK
52/C2 Gwaunceste (mtn.), Wal,UK
55/J2 Gwda (riv.), Pol.
52/A6 Gweek, Eng,UK
51/E5 Gwersyllt, Wal,UK
110/E4 Gweru, Zim.
97/D1 Gwydir (riv.), Austl.
50/D5 Gwynedd (co.), Wal,UK
83/D5 Gyaring (lake), China
105/F5 Gyasikan, Gha.
74/H2 Gyda (pen.), Rus.
96/D4 Gympie, Austl.
91/G4 Gyobingauk, Myan.
68/E2 Gyoma, Hun.
68/D2 Gyöngyös, Hun.
68/C2 Győr, Hun.
68/C2 Győr-Sopron (co.), Hun.
68/E2 Gyula, Hun.
73/G4 Gyumri, Arm.

H

58/D2 Haacht, Belg.
56/D4 Haaksbergen, Neth.
58/D2 Haaltert, Belg.
56/E6 Haan, Ger.
99/H6 Ha'apai Group (isls.), Tonga
48/H2 Haapavesi, Fin.
70/D4 Haapsalu, Est.
63/J2 Haar, Ger.
56/B4 Haarlem, Neth.
95/G7 Haast, NZ
79/J3 Hab (riv.), Pak.
59/E4 Habay, Belg.
78/D2 Habbānīyah, Iraq
91/F3 Habiganj, Bang.
85/L10 Habikino, Japan
83/N3 Haboro, Japan
57/F3 Hache (riv.), Ger.
83/N5 Hachijō (isl.), Japan
85/F3 Hachiōji, Japan
137/C3 Hacienda Heights, Ca,US
80/C2 Hacılar, Turk.
137/F5 Hackensack, NJ,US
137/F5 Hackettstown, NJ,US
89/D1 Ha Coi, Viet.
63/H1 Hadamar, Ger.
85/F3 Hadano, Japan
106/D4 Hadarba, Ras (cape), Sudan
103/J4 Haddad (wadi), Chad
53/F3 Haddenham, Eng,UK
49/D3 Haddington, Sc,UK
137/E6 Haddonfield, NJ,US
137/E6 Haddon (Westmont), NJ,US
79/G4 Ḩadd, Ra's al (pt.), Oman
105/H3 Hadejia (riv.), Nga.
57/F1 Hadelner (can.), Ger.
80/K5 Hadera, Isr.
54/E1 Haderslev, Den.
80/C3 Hadım, Turk.
68/E2 Hadjú-Bihar (co.), Hun.
124/F1 Hadley (bay), Nun,Can.
51/F1 Hadrian's Wall (ruins), Eng,UK
48/E1 Hadselfjorden (fjord), Nor.
86/C3 Haeju, NKor.
126/S9 Haena (pt.), Hi,US
80/D2 Hafik, Turk.
79/K2 Hāfizābād, Pak.
48/N7 Hafnarfjördhur, Ice.
78/E3 Ḩafr al Bāṭin, SAr.
78/E2 Haft Gel, Iran
103/R5 Hafun, Ras (pt.), Som.
98/D3 Hagåtña (cap.), Guam
136/F4 Hagemeister (isl.), Ak,US
57/E6 Hagen, Ger.
57/E4 Hagen am Teutoburger Wald, Ger.
54/F2 Hagenow, Ger.
131/F4 Hagerman, NM,US
132/E4 Hagerstown, Md,US
84/B3 Hagi, Japan
89/D1 Ha Giang, Viet.
52/D2 Hagley, Eng,UK
59/F5 Hagondange, Fr.
49/A4 Hags Head (pt.), Ire.
129/G2 Hague, Sk,Can.
62/C2 Hague, Cap de la (cape), Fr.
59/G6 Haguenau, Fr.
56/B4 Hague, The ('s-Gravenhage) (cap.), Neth.
98/D2 Hahashima (isl.), Japan
57/H6 Hahle (riv.), Ger.
59/G3 Hahnenbach (riv.), Ger.
87/D3 Hai (riv.), China
85/L10 Haibara, Japan
83/J3 Haicheng, China
89/D1 Hai Duong, Viet.
80/K5 Haifa (dist.), Isr.
80/K5 Haifa (Ḩefa), Isr.
59/H2 Haiger, Ger.
89/D1 Hai Hau, Viet.
88/B3 Haikou, China
83/H2 Hailar, China
83/J2 Hailar (riv.), China
132/E2 Haileybury, On,Can.
53/G5 Hailsham, Eng,UK
91/K4 Hainan (isl.), China
91/J4 Hainan (prov.), China
91/K3 Hainan (str.), China
58/B2 Hainaut (prov.), Belg.
63/H1 Hainburg, Ger.
135/H4 Haines City, Fl,US
136/L3 Haines Junction, Yk,Can.
57/H6 Hainich (mts.), Ger.
87/L9 Haining, China
89/D1 Haiphong (Hai Phong), Viet.
123/G4 Haiti (ctry.)
89/E2 Hai Van (pass), Viet.
87/D4 Haizhou (bay), China
55/L5 Hajdú-Bihar (co.), Hun.
68/E2 Hajdúböszormény, Hun.
68/E2 Hajdúhadház, Hun.
68/E2 Hajdúnánás, Hun.
68/E2 Hajdúszoboszló, Hun.
85/F1 Hajiki-zaki (pt.), Japan
55/M2 Hajnówka, Pol.
91/F2 Hājo, India
99/L5 Hakahau, Fr.Pol.
84/D3 Hakken-san (mtn.), Japan
83/N3 Hakodate, Japan
85/H7 Hakone, Japan
85/H8 Hakone-Fuji-Izu Nat'l Park, Japan
85/E2 Hakui, Japan
85/M10 Hakusan, Japan
85/E2 Haku-san (mtn.), Japan
85/E2 Hakusan Nat'l Park, Japan
79/J3 Hāla, Pak.
80/D3 Ḩalab (Aleppo), Syria
78/E1 Ḩalabjah, Iraq
106/D4 Ḩalā'ib, Sudan
48/D4 Halden, Nor.
54/F2 Haldensleben, Ger.
133/Q10 Haldimand, On,Can.
82/G2 Haldzan, Mong.
107/C4 Hale, Tanz.
51/F5 Hale, Eng,UK
126/T10 Haleakala Nat'l Park, Hi,US
59/E2 Halen, Belg.
138/P14 Hales Corners, Wi,US
52/D2 Halesowen, Eng,UK
53/H2 Halesworth, Eng,UK
135/G3 Haleyville, Al,US
104/E5 Half Assini, Gha.
138/K12 Half Moon Bay, Ca,US
80/K6 Ḩalḩūl, WBnk.
132/E2 Haliburton (hills), On,Can.
96/B2 Halifax (bay), Austl.
133/J2 Halifax (cap.), NS,Can.
51/G4 Halifax, Eng,UK
79/G3 Halīl (riv.), Iran
136/H1 Halkett (cape), Ak,US
125/K2 Hall (pen.), Nun,Can.
98/E4 Hall (isls.), Micr.
136/D3 Hall (isl.), Ak,US
48/E4 Halland (co.), Swe.
83/K5 Halla-san (mtn.), SKor.
58/D2 Halle, Belg.
57/F4 Halle, Ger.
48/E4 Hällefors, Swe.
63/K3 Hallein, Aus.
58/A4 Hallencourt, Fr.
54/F3 Halle-Neustadt, Ger.
111/M Hallett (cape), Ant.
134/D4 Hallettsville, Tx,US
129/J3 Hallock, Mn,US
54/B4 Hallu (riv.), Fr.
58/B3 Hallue (riv.), Fr.
58/C2 Halluin, Fr.
86/E5 Hallyŏ Haesang Nat'l Park, SKor.
93/G3 Halmahera (isl.), Indo.
93/G4 Halmahera (sea), Indo.
48/E4 Halmstad, Swe.
48/E4 Hälsingborg, Swe.
53/G3 Halstead, Eng,UK
56/B5 Halsteren, Neth.
82/C4 Haltang (riv.), China
51/H4 Haltemprice, Eng,UK
57/E5 Haltern, Ger.
51/F5 Halton (co.), Eng,UK
133/Q8 Halton Hills, On,Can.
51/F2 Haltwhistle, Eng,UK
57/E6 Halver, Ger.
57/E3 Halverder Aa (riv.), Ger.
58/C4 Ham, Fr.
84/C3 Hamada, Japan
78/E2 Hamadān, Iran
80/L4 Ḩamāh, Syria
85/M10 Hamajima, Japan
85/E3 Hamakita, Japan
85/E3 Hamamatsu, Japan
48/D3 Hamar, Nor.
106/C3 Ḩamāṭah, Jabal (mtn.), Egypt
90/D6 Hambantota, SrL.
53/E5 Hamble, Eng,UK
51/G3 Hambleton (hills), Eng,UK
57/G3 Hambühren, Ger.
57/G1 Hamburg, Ger.
57/G1 Hamburg (state), Ger.
134/F3 Hamburg, Ar,US
132/E3 Hamburg, NY,US
48/H3 Hämeenkyrö, Fin.
48/H3 Hämeenlinna, Fin.
57/G4 Hameln, Ger.
53/H3 Hamford Water (inlet), Eng,UK

164
Hamgy – Hooge

86/E2 Hamgyŏng (mts.), NKor.
86/E2 Hamgyŏng-Bukto (prov.), NKor.
86/D2 Hamgyŏng-Namdo (prov.), NKor.
86/D3 Hamhŭng, NKor.
86/D3 Hamhŭng-Si (prov.), NKor.
82/C3 Hami, China
125/L3 Hamilton (inlet), Nf,Can.
133/Q9 Hamilton, On,Can.
95/H6 Hamilton, NZ
49/C3 Hamilton, Sc,UK
135/G3 Hamilton, Al,US
138/L12 Hamilton (mt.), Ca,US
128/E4 Hamilton, Mt,US
132/C4 Hamilton, Oh,US
134/D4 Hamilton, Tx,US
90/D2 Hamīrpur, India
66/B4 Hammamet (gulf), Tun.
58/D1 Hamme, Belg.
57/F2 Hamme (riv.), Ger.
48/G1 Hammerfest, Nor.
56/D5 Hamminkeln, Ger.
138/R16 Hammond, In,US
135/F4 Hammond, La,US
59/E1 Hamont-Achel, Belg.
53/E4 Hampshire (co.), Eng,UK
53/E4 Hampshire Downs (hills), Eng,UK
132/E4 Hampton, Va,US
97/G6 Hampton Park, Austl.
102/H1 Ḩamrā (upland), Libya
138/F7 Hamtramck, Mi,US
85/H7 Hamura, Japan
87/C5 Han (riv.), China
88/C3 Han (riv.), China
86/D4 Han (riv.), SKor.
83/N4 Hanamaki, Japan
126/U11 Hanamalo (pt.), Hi,US
83/M5 Hanamatsu, Japan
107/B4 Hanang (peak), Tanz.
132/B2 Hancock, Mi,US
85/M10 Handa, Japan
87/C3 Handan, China
53/E1 Handsworth, Eng,UK
130/C3 Hanford, Ca,US
128/D4 Hanford Reach Nat'l Mon., Wa,US
82/D2 Hangayn (mts.), Mong.
52/C5 Hangingstone (hill), Eng,UK
108/L11 Hangklip (cape), SAfr.
81/B5 Hangu, Pak.
87/L9 Hangzhou, China
82/C2 Hanhöhiy (mts.), Mong.
80/E2 Hani, Turk.
129/J4 Hankinson, ND,US
129/G3 Hanley, Sk,Can.
128/F3 Hanna, Ab,Can.
128/G5 Hanna, Wy,US
85/L10 Hannan, Japan
131/K3 Hannibal, Mo,US
85/H7 Hannō, Japan
57/G4 Hannover, Ger.
59/E2 Hannut, Belg.
48/E5 Hanöbukten (bay), Swe.
89/D1 Hanoi (Ha Noi) (cap.), Viet.
132/D2 Hanover, On,Can.
119/J7 Hanover (isl.), Chile
133/F3 Hanover, NH,US
138/P16 Hanover Park, Il,US
90/C2 Hānsi, India
81/D3 Hantengri Feng (peak), China
125/J2 Hantzsch (riv.), Nun,Can.
90/B2 Hanumāngarh, India
82/E2 Hanuy (riv.), Mong.
82/F5 Hanzhong, China
99/L6 Hao (atoll), FrPol.
48/H2 Haparanda, Swe.
125/K3 Happy Valley-Goose Bay, Nf,Can.
82/D4 Har (lake), China
82/C2 Har (lake), Mong.
82/F2 Haraa (riv.), Mong.
85/G2 Haramachi, Japan
79/K2 Harappa (ruins), Pak.
110/F4 Harare (cap.), Zim.
82/F2 Har-Ayrag, Mong.
104/C5 Harbel, Libr.
83/K2 Harbin, China
133/L2 Harbour Breton, Nf,Can.
53/E2 Harbury, Eng,UK
90/C3 Hardā, India
48/C3 Hardangervidda Nat'l Park, Nor.
108/B2 Hardap (dam), Namb.
57/H3 Hardau (riv.), Ger.
57/G5 Hardegsen, Ger.
56/D3 Hardenberg, Neth.
56/C4 Harderwijk, Neth.
128/G4 Hardin, Mt,US
79/L3 Hardwār, India
119/K8 Hardy (pen.), Chile
133/L1 Hare (bay), Nf,Can.
58/C2 Harelbeke, Belg.
57/E3 Haren, Ger.
56/D2 Haren, Neth.
103/P6 Hārer, Eth.
80/N8 Har Eval (Jabal 'Aybāl) (mtn.), WBnk.
103/P6 Hargeysa, Som.
69/G2 Harghita (co.), Rom.
69/G2 Harghita (peak), Rom.
92/B4 Hari (riv.), Indo.
90/C5 Harihar, India
84/D3 Harima (sound), Japan
56/B5 Haringvliet (chan.), Neth.
79/H2 Harīrūd (riv.), Afg.
132/D4 Harlan, Ky,US
50/D6 Harlech, Wal,UK
53/H2 Harleston, Eng,UK
56/C2 Harlingen, Neth.
134/D5 Harlingen, Tx,US
53/F3 Harlington, Eng,UK
128/F4 Harlowton, Mt,US
56/B4 Harmelen, Neth.
58/B3 Harnes, Fr.
128/D5 Harney (lake), Or,US
128/D5 Harney (val.), Or,US
129/H5 Harney (peak), SD,US
48/F3 Härnösand, Swe.
123/M8 Haro (cape), Mex.
64/D1 Haro, Sp.
53/F3 Harpenden, Eng,UK
136/L3 Harper (mtn.), Yk,Can.
104/D5 Harper, Libr.
136/K3 Harper (mtn.), Ak,US
134/D2 Harper, Ks,US
138/G7 Harper Woods, Mi,US
132/E1 Harricana (riv.), Qu,Can.
135/G3 Harriman, Tn,US
132/B4 Harrisburg, Il,US
131/G2 Harrisburg, Ne,US
132/E3 Harrisburg (cap.), Pa,US
54/E1 Harrislee, Ger.
108/E3 Harrismith, SAfr.
128/C3 Harrison (lake), BC,Can.
125/L3 Harrison (cape), Nf,Can.
136/H1 Harrison (bay), Ak,US
134/E2 Harrison, Ar,US
131/G2 Harrison, Ne,US
137/G5 Harrison, NY,US
132/E4 Harrisonburg, Va,US
132/C4 Harrodsburg, Ky,US
51/G4 Harrogate, Eng,UK
131/J3 Harry S Truman (res.), Mo,US
57/G2 Harsefeld, Ger.
57/F5 Harsewinkel, Ger.
48/F1 Harstad, Nor.
124/C2 Hart (riv.), Yk,Can.
130/C2 Hart (lake), Or,US
108/C3 Hartbeesrivier (dry riv.), SAfr.
48/C3 Hårteigen (peak), Nor.
56/B5 Hartelkanaal (can.), Neth.
133/F3 Hartford (cap.), Ct,US
132/C3 Hartford City, In,US
131/H2 Hartington, Ne,US
52/B5 Hartland, Eng,UK
52/B4 Hartland (pt.), Eng,UK
52/D2 Hartlebury, Eng,UK
51/G2 Hartlepool, Eng,UK
51/G2 Hartlepool (co.), Eng,UK
53/G4 Hartley, Eng,UK
129/H3 Hartney, Mb,Can.
108/D3 Harts (riv.), SAfr.
137/G4 Hartsdale, NY,US
135/G3 Hartselle, Al,US
53/E1 Hartshill, Eng,UK
138/B3 Hartstene (isl.), Wa,US
135/H3 Hartwell, Ga,US
135/H3 Hartwell (lake), Ga, SC,US
97/C4 Hartz Mountain Nat'l Park, Austl.
59/G6 Hartzviller, Fr.
79/K3 Harūnābād, Pak.
93/E3 Harun, Bukit (peak), Indo.
81/F2 Har Us (lake), Mong.
82/D2 Har-Us (riv.), Mong.
79/H2 Hārūt (riv.), Afg.
138/Q16 Harvey, Il,US
129/J4 Harvey, ND,US
53/H3 Harwich, Eng,UK
51/G5 Harworth, Eng,UK
90/C2 Haryana (state), India
57/H5 Harz (mts.), Ger.
57/E3 Hase (riv.), Ger.
57/E3 Haselünne, Ger.
85/M9 Hashima, Japan
84/D3 Hashimoto, Japan
102/D2 Hasi el Farsia (well), WSah.
79/K3 Hāsilpur, Pak.
134/D3 Haskell, Tx,US
53/F4 Haslemere, Eng,UK
51/F4 Haslingden, Eng,UK
51/F5 Haslington, Eng,UK
90/C5 Hassan, India
125/S7 Hassel (sound), Nun,Can.
59/E2 Hasselt, Belg.
56/D3 Hasselt, Neth.
63/J1 Hassfurt, Ger.
102/G1 Hassi Messaoud, Alg.
48/E4 Hässleholm, Swe.
95/H6 Hastings, NZ
53/G5 Hastings, Eng,UK
132/C3 Hastings, Mi,US
129/K4 Hastings, Mn,US
131/H2 Hastings, Ne,US
137/G4 Hastings-on-Hudson, NY,US
85/H7 Hasuda, Japan
85/M9 Hatashō, Japan
137/E5 Hatboro, Pa,US
130/F4 Hatch, NM,US
89/B5 Hat Chao Mai Nat'l Park, Thai.
119/J7 Hatcher (peak), Arg.
68/F3 Haţeg, Rom.
53/F3 Hatfield, Eng,UK
97/E1 Hat Head Nat'l Park, Austl.
51/G5 Hathersage, Eng,UK
90/C2 Hāthras, India
78/C4 Ḩāţibah, Ra's (pt.), SAr.
89/D4 Ha Tien, Viet.
89/D2 Ha Tinh, Viet.
89/B5 Hat Nai Yang Nat'l Park, Thai.
85/H7 Hatogaya, Japan
123/H4 Hato Mayor, DRep.
85/H7 Hatoyama, Japan
90/C3 Hatta, India
97/B2 Hattah-Kulkyne Nat'l Park, Austl.
56/D4 Hattem, Neth.
57/F2 Hatten, Ger.
135/K3 Hatteras (cape), NC,US
135/F4 Hattiesburg, Ms,US
57/E6 Hattingen, Ger.
51/G6 Hatton, Eng,UK
68/D2 Hatvan, Hun.
89/C5 Hat Yai, Thai.
89/E3 Hau Bon, Viet.
58/D2 Haubourdin, Fr.
103/Q6 Haud (reg.), Eth., Som.
48/C4 Haugesund, Nor.
89/D4 Hau Giang (riv.), Viet.
48/H2 Haukipudas, Fin.
137/G5 Hauppauge, NY,US
102/D1 Haut Atlas (mts.), Mor.
60/B1 Haute-Marne (dept.), Fr.
62/D2 Haute-Normandie (reg.), Fr.
133/G1 Hauterive, Qu,Can.
60/B2 Haute-Saône (dept.), Fr.
60/C5 Haute-Savoie (dept.), Fr.
59/E3 Hautes Fagnes (uplands), Belg.
58/C3 Hautmont, Fr.
60/D2 Haut-Rhin (dept.), Fr.
58/B6 Hauts-de-Seine (dept.), Fr.
122/E3 Havana (La Habana) (cap.), Cuba
99/V13 Havannah (chan.), NCal.
53/F5 Havant, Eng,UK
130/D4 Havasu (lake), Az, Ca,US
55/G2 Havel (riv.), Ger.
54/G2 Havelland (reg.), Ger.
135/J3 Havelock, NC,US
53/G3 Havengore (isl.), Eng,UK
52/B3 Haverfordwest, Wal,UK
53/G2 Haverhill, Eng,UK
133/G3 Haverhill, Ma,US
55/K4 Havířov, Czh.
57/E5 Havixbeck, Ger.
55/H4 Havlíčkuv Brod, Czh.
128/F3 Havre, Mt,US
133/J1 Havre-Saint-Pierre, Qu,Can.
69/H5 Havsa, Turk.
126/S10 Hawaii (state), US
126/U11 Hawaii (isl.), Hi,US
99/H2 Hawaiian (isls.), Hi,US
126/U11 Hawaii Volcanoes Nat'l Park, Hi,US
78/E3 Ḩawallī, Kuw.
51/E5 Hawarden, Wal,UK
129/J5 Hawarden, Ia,US
95/H6 Hawera, NZ
51/F3 Hawes, Eng,UK
51/F2 Haweswater (res.), Eng,UK
49/D3 Hawick, Sc,UK
97/E2 Hawke (cape), Austl.
96/G8 Hawkesbury (riv.), Austl.
128/A2 Hawkesbury (isl.), BC,Can.
132/F2 Hawkesbury, On,Can.
78/E2 Hawr al Ḩammār (lake), Iraq
80/H6 Ḩawsh 'Īsá, Egypt
137/B3 Hawthorne, Ca,US
134/C1 Hawthorne, Nv,US
51/G3 Haxby, Eng,UK
96/C3 Hay (pt.), Austl.
124/E3 Hay (riv.), Ab, NW,Can.
85/H7 Hayama, Japan
59/F3 Hayange, Fr.
51/F5 Haydock, Eng,UK
51/F2 Haydon Bridge, Eng,UK
124/G3 Hayes (riv.), Mb,Can.
124/G2 Hayes (riv.), Nun,Can.
125/T7 Hayes (pen.), Grld.
136/J3 Hayes (mtn.), Ak,US
52/A6 Hayle, Eng,UK
52/A6 Hayle (riv.), Eng,UK
53/F5 Hayling (isl.), Eng,UK
134/E3 Haynesville, La,US
52/C2 Hay on Wye, Wal,UK
69/H5 Hayrabolu, Turk.
131/H3 Hays, Ks,US
131/H3 Haysville, Ks,US
138/K11 Hayward, Ca,US
132/B2 Hayward, Wi,US
53/F5 Haywards Heath, Eng,UK
79/G3 Hazār (mtn.), Iran
132/D4 Hazard, Ky,US
90/E3 Hazāribag, India
58/B2 Hazebrouck, Fr.
51/F5 Hazel Grove, Eng,UK
138/F7 Hazel Park, Mi,US
125/R7 Hazen (str.), NW,Nun,Can.
136/E3 Hazen (bay), Ak,US
56/B4 Hazerswoude-Dorp, Neth.
135/F4 Hazlehurst, Ms,US
53/F3 Hazlemere, Eng,UK
137/F5 Hazlet, NJ,US
128/B2 Hazleton (mts.), BC,Can.
132/F3 Hazleton, Pa,US
85/N10 Hazu, Japan
53/G1 Heacham, Eng,UK
53/G4 Headcorn, Eng,UK
53/G4 Headingley, Eng,UK
130/B3 Healdsburg, Ca,US
97/G5 Healesville, Austl.
51/G6 Heanor, Eng,UK
45/P8 Heard (isl.), Austl.
134/D4 Hearne, Tx,US
111/V Hearst (isl.), Ant.
132/D1 Hearst, On,Can.
129/H4 Heart (riv.), ND,US
133/J1 Heath (pt.), Qu,Can.
96/G9 Heathcote Nat'l Park, Austl.
53/G5 Heathfield, Eng,UK
134/D5 Hebbronville, Tx,US
51/F4 Hebden Bridge, Eng,UK
87/G6 Hebei (prov.), China
134/E3 Heber Springs, Ar,US
87/C4 Hebi, China
49/B2 Hebrides (isls.), Sc,UK
49/A2 Hebrides, Outer (isls.), Sc,UK
131/H2 Hebron, Ne,US
80/K6 Hebron (Al Khalīl), WBnk.
136/M5 Hecate (str.), BC,Can.
91/J3 Hechi, China
59/E1 Hechtel, Belg.
51/H6 Heckington, Eng,UK
129/J4 Hecla, SD,US
125/R7 Hecla and Griper (bay), NW,Can.
128/D3 Hector (peak), Ab,Can.
48/E3 Hedemora, Swe.
48/D3 Hedmark (co.), Nor.
51/H4 Hedon, Eng,UK
57/E4 Heek, Ger.
56/B3 Heemskerk, Neth.
56/B4 Heemstede, Neth.
56/D4 Heerde, Neth.
56/C3 Heerenveen, Neth.
56/B3 Heerhugowaard, Neth.
59/E2 Heerlen, Neth.
59/E2 Heers, Belg.
56/C5 Heesch, Neth.
56/C6 Heeze, Neth.
80/K5 Ḩefa (Haifa), Isr.
87/D5 Hefei, China
83/L2 Hegang, China
61/E2 Hegau (reg.), Ger.
85/L10 Heguri, Japan
82/D4 Hei (riv.), China
54/E1 Heide, Ger.
97/G5 Heidelberg, Austl.
63/H2 Heidelberg, Ger.
109/E2 Heidelberg, SAfr.
135/F4 Heidelberg, Ms,US
56/D5 Heiden, Ger.
83/K1 Heihe, China
54/F1 Heikendorf, Ger.
108/D2 Heilbron, SAfr.
63/H2 Heilbronn, Ger.
54/F1 Heiligenhafen, Ger.
56/D6 Heiligenhaus, Ger.
57/H6 Heiligenstadt, Ger.
83/L2 Heilong (Amur) (riv.), China
56/B3 Heiloo, Neth.
48/N7 Heimaey (isl.), Ice.
56/D4 Heino, Neth.
48/H3 Heinola, Fin.
56/D6 Heinsberg, Ger.
85/M9 Heiwa, Japan
87/D3 Hejian, China
80/D2 Hekimhan, Turk.
85/M10 Hekinan, Japan
48/N7 Hekla (vol.), Ice.
82/F4 Helan (mts.), China
56/D6 Helden, Neth.
135/F3 Helena, Ar,US
128/E4 Helena (cap.), Mt,US
54/D1 Helgoland (isl.), Ger.
54/D1 Helgoländer Bucht (bay), Ger.
78/F3 Ḩelleh (riv.), Iran
56/D4 Hellendoorn, Neth.
59/F3 Hellenthal, Ger.
56/B5 Hellevoetsluis, Neth.
64/E3 Hellín, Sp.
128/D4 Hells Canyon Nat'l Rec. Area, Id, Or,US
79/H2 Helmand (riv.), Afg.
54/F3 Helme (riv.), Ger.
136/K2 Helmet (mtn.), Ak,US
56/C6 Helmond, Neth.
51/G3 Helmsley, Eng,UK
54/F2 Helmstedt, Ger.
130/E3 Helper, Ut,US
51/F5 Helsby, Eng,UK
48/E4 Helsingør, Den.
48/H3 Helsinki (Helsingfors) (cap.), Fin.
52/A6 Helston, Eng,UK
48/G3 Helvetinjärven Nat'l Park, Fin.
58/C2 Hem, Fr.
58/B2 Hem (riv.), Fr.
53/F3 Hemel Hempstead, Eng,UK
57/E6 Hemer, Ger.
137/D3 Hemet, Ca,US
57/G4 Hemmingen, Ger.
57/G1 Hemmoor, Ger.
134/E4 Hemphill, Tx,US
137/G5 Hempstead, NY,US
53/H1 Hemsby, Eng,UK
51/G4 Hemsworth, Eng,UK
87/B4 Henan (prov.), China
64/D2 Henares (riv.), Sp.
62/C5 Hendaye, Fr.
69/K5 Hendek, Turk.
118/E3 Henderson, Arg.
99/N7 Henderson (isl.), Pitc.
132/C4 Henderson, Ky,US
135/J2 Henderson, NC,US
130/D3 Henderson, Nv,US
135/F3 Henderson, Tn,US
134/E3 Henderson, Tx,US
135/H3 Hendersonville, NC,US
135/G2 Hendersonville, Tn,US
56/B5 Hendrik-Ido-Ambacht, Neth.
108/D3 Hendrik Verwoerdam (res.), SAfr.
53/F5 Henfield, Eng,UK
87/L8 Heng (isl.), China
91/G2 Hengduan (mts.), China
56/D4 Hengelo, Neth.
87/C3 Heng Shan (mtn.), China
87/C3 Hengshui, China
88/B2 Hengyang, China
58/B3 Hénin-Beaumont, Fr.
53/E2 Henley-in-Arden, Eng,UK
53/F3 Henley-on-Thames, Eng,UK
62/B3 Hennebont, Fr.
59/G2 Hennef, Ger.
59/E2 Henri-Chapelle, Belg.
134/D3 Henrietta, Tx,US
125/H3 Henrietta Maria (cape), On,Can.
136/M5 Henry (cape), BC,Can.
130/E3 Henry (mts.), Ut,US
131/J4 Henryetta, Ok,US
58/C3 Hensies, Belg.
82/F2 Hentiyn (mts.), Mong.
91/G4 Henzada, Myan.
48/N6 Heradhsvötn (riv.), Ice.
79/H2 Herāt, Afg.
65/G1 Hérault (riv.), Fr.
96/B2 Herbert (riv.), Austl.
128/G3 Herbert, Sk,Can.
96/B2 Herbert Riv. Falls Nat'l Park, Austl.
58/B5 Herblay, Fr.
68/D4 Hercegnovi, Mont.
138/K10 Hercules, Ca,US
57/E6 Herdecke, Ger.
59/G2 Herdorf, Ger.
122/E6 Heredia, CR
52/D2 Hereford, Eng,UK
134/C3 Hereford, Tx,US
52/D2 Herefordshire (co.), Eng,UK
99/L6 Hereheretue (isl.), FrPol.
69/J5 Hereke, Turk.
64/C3 Herencia, Sp.
59/D1 Herentals, Belg.
57/F4 Herford, Ger.
131/H3 Herington, Ks,US
61/F3 Herisau, Swi.
59/E2 Herk (riv.), Belg.
59/E2 Herk-de-Stad, Belg.
82/G2 Herlen (riv.), Mong.
135/F2 Hermann, Mo,US
57/H3 Hermannsburg, Ger.
58/B5 Hermes, Fr.
128/D4 Hermiston, Or,US
80/K5 Hermon (mtn.), Leb., Syria
137/B3 Hermosa Beach, Ca,US
123/M8 Hermosillo, Mex.
118/E2 Hernando, Arg.
135/F3 Hernando, Ms,US
64/E1 Hernani, Sp.
58/D2 Herne, Belg.
57/E5 Herne, Ger.
53/H4 Herne Bay, Eng,UK
48/D4 Herning, Den.
80/N9 Herodian (ruins), WBnk.
80/N9 Herodion Nat'l Park, WBnk.
123/M7 Heroica Caborca, Mex.
123/M7 Heroica Nogales, Mex.
122/D4 Herrero (pt.), Mex.
62/D5 Hers (riv.), Fr.
57/E6 Herscheid, Ger.
136/L2 Herschel, Yk,Can.
59/D1 Herselt, Belg.
59/E2 Herstal, Belg.
53/G5 Herstmonceux, Eng,UK
57/E5 Herten, Ger.
53/F3 Hertford, Eng,UK
53/F3 Hertfordshire (co.), Eng,UK
59/E2 Herve, Belg.
96/D4 Hervey Bay, Austl.
57/H5 Herzberg am Harz, Ger.
57/F5 Herzebrock-Clarholz, Ger.
58/C2 Herzele, Belg.
80/M8 Herzliyya, Isr.
63/J2 Herzogenaurach, Ger.
68/B1 Herzogenburg, Aus.
59/F2 Herzogenrath, Ger.
59/D3 Hesbaye (plat.), Belg.
91/J3 Heshan, China
59/F4 Hesperange, Lux.
137/C2 Hesperia, Ca,US
136/M3 Hess (riv.), Yk,Can.
57/F5 Hessel (riv.), Ger.
54/E3 Hessen (state), Ger.
57/G6 Hessisch Lichtenau, Ger.
57/G4 Hessisch Oldendorf, Ger.
51/H4 Hessle, Eng,UK
51/E5 Heswall, Eng,UK
129/H4 Hettinger, ND,US
51/G2 Hetton-le-Hole, Eng,UK
57/E5 Heubach (riv.), Ger.
55/H5 Heukuppe (peak), Aus.
59/E1 Heusden-Zolder, Belg.
59/F5 Heusweiler, Ger.
62/D2 Hève, Cap de la (cape), Fr.
68/E2 Heves, Hun.
55/L5 Heves (co.), Hun.
137/G5 Hewlett (pt.), NY,US
51/F2 Hexham, Eng,UK
83/H3 Hexigten Qi, China
108/L10 Hex River (mts.), SAfr.
108/L10 Hex River (pass), SAfr.
51/F3 Heysham, Eng,UK
56/C6 Heythuysen, Neth.
51/F4 Heywood, Eng,UK
87/C4 Heze, China
135/H5 Hialeah, Fl,US
131/J3 Hiawatha, Ks,US
129/K4 Hibbing, Mn,US
97/C4 Hibbs (pt.), Austl.
136/M4 Hickman (mtn.), BC,Can.
132/B4 Hickman, Ky,US
135/H3 Hickory, NC,US
137/G5 Hicksville, NY,US
85/E3 Hida (riv.), Japan
85/H7 Hidaka, Japan
84/D4 Hidaka (riv.), Japan
122/B3 Hidalgo (state), Mex.
123/N8 Hidalgo del Parral, Mex.
57/F4 Hiddenhausen, Ger.
65/W17 Hierro (isl.), Canl.
57/E2 Hieve (lake), Ger.
85/H7 Higashikurume, Japan
85/H7 Higashimurayama, Japan
85/G1 Higashine, Japan
85/L10 Higashi-Ōsaka, Japan
85/K10 Higashiura, Japan
85/H7 Higashiyamato, Japan
128/C5 High (des.), Or,US
53/F2 Higham Ferrers, Eng,UK
52/D4 Highbridge, Eng,UK
137/F5 High Bridge, NJ,US
134/E4 High Island, Tx,US
137/C2 Highland, Ca,US
138/R16 Highland, In,US
138/Q15 Highland Park, Il,US
138/F7 Highland Park, Mi,US
137/F5 Highland Park, NJ,US
52/D2 Highley, Eng,UK
129/J4 Highmore, SD,US
135/H3 High Point, NC,US
128/D2 High Prairie, Ab,Can.
129/H2 Highrock (lake), Mb,Can.
51/F3 High Street (mtn.), Eng,UK
51/E4 Hightown, Eng,UK
137/F5 Hightstown, NJ,US
52/B5 High Willhays (hill), Eng,UK
53/E3 Highworth, Eng,UK
53/F3 High Wycombe, Eng,UK
123/H4 Higüey, DRep.
80/H6 Hihyā, Egypt
48/J3 Hiidenportin Nat'l Park, Fin.
70/D4 Hiiumaa (isl.), Est.
78/C3 Hijāz, Jabal al (mts.), SAr.
84/B4 Hiji, Japan
118/Q9 Hijuelas de Conchali, Chile
85/L9 Hikami, Japan
84/E3 Hikone, Japan
99/L6 Hikueru (atoll), FrPol.
59/H2 Hilchenbach, Ger.
63/J1 Hildburghausen, Ger.
56/D6 Hilden, Ger.
57/G4 Hildesheim, Ger.
111/L Hillary (coast), Ant.
131/H3 Hill City, Ks,US
137/F4 Hillcrest, NY,US
57/F4 Hille, Ger.
56/B4 Hillegom, Neth.
48/E5 Hillerød, Den.
50/B2 Hillhall, NI,UK
49/D2 Hill of Fearn, Sc,UK
129/J4 Hillsboro, ND,US
130/F4 Hillsboro, NM,US
132/D4 Hillsboro, Oh,US
128/C4 Hillsboro, Or,US
134/D3 Hillsboro, Tx,US
96/C3 Hillsborough (chan.), Austl.
50/B3 Hillsborough, NI,UK
138/K11 Hillsborough, Ca,US
137/F5 Hillsborough, NJ,US
132/C3 Hillsdale, Mi,US
137/F5 Hillside, NJ,US
50/B3 Hilltown, NI,UK
126/U11 Hilo, Hi,US
88/D5 Hilongos, Phil.
51/E3 Hilpsford (pt.), Eng,UK
135/H3 Hilton Head Island, SC,US
56/C6 Hilvarenbeek, Neth.
56/C4 Hilversum, Neth.
81/C5 Himachal Pradesh (state), India
90/D2 Himalaya, Great (range), Asia
88/D5 Himamaylan, Phil.
84/D3 Himeji, Japan
85/E2 Himi, Japan
103/N5 Himora, Eth.
80/L4 Ḩimş, Syria
136/J3 Hinchinbrook (chan.), Ak,US
96/B2 Hinchinbrook I. Nat'l Park, Austl.
53/E1 Hinckley, Eng,UK
51/H2 Hinderwell, Eng,UK
51/F4 Hindley, Eng,UK
97/B2 Hindmarsh (lake), Austl.
79/J1 Hindu Kush (mts.), Afg., Pak.
90/C5 Hindupur, India
135/H4 Hinesville, Ga,US
90/C3 Hinganghāt, India
79/J3 Hingol (riv.), Pak.
90/C4 Hingoli, India
79/J3 Hingorja, Pak.
80/E2 Hınıs, Turk.
85/H7 Hino, Japan
85/M9 Hino (riv.), Japan
85/H7 Hinode, Japan
64/C3 Hinojosa del Duque, Sp.
84/C3 Hino-misaki (cape), Japan
138/Q16 Hinsdale, Il,US
51/F6 Hinstock, Eng,UK
57/E2 Hinte, Ger.
128/D2 Hinton, Ab,Can.
132/D4 Hinton, WV,US
56/B3 Hippolytushoef, Neth.
51/G3 Hipswell, Eng,UK
85/L9 Hira (mts.), Japan
84/A4 Hirado, Japan
84/D3 Hirakata, Japan
90/D3 Hirakud (res.), India
84/C3 Hirata, Japan
85/H7 Hiratsuka, Japan
69/H2 Hîrlău, Rom.
83/N3 Hirosaki, Japan
84/C3 Hiroshima, Japan
84/C3 Hiroshima (pref.), Japan
63/J2 Hirschau, Ger.
58/D4 Hirson, Fr.
69/H3 Hirşova, Rom.
48/D4 Hirtshals, Den.
52/C3 Hirwaun, Wal,UK
84/E3 Hisai, Japan
90/C2 Hisār, India
82/E2 Hishig-Öndör, Mong.
123/G4 Hispaniola (isl.), DRep., Haiti
85/G2 Hitachi, Japan
85/G2 Hitachi-ōta, Japan
53/F3 Hitchin, Eng,UK
84/B4 Hitoyoshi, Japan
48/C3 Hitra (isl.), Nor.
99/M5 Hiva Oa (isl.), FrPol.
70/B2 Hjartfjellet (peak), Nor.
89/B1 Hka (riv.), Myan.
91/G2 Hkakabo (peak), Myan.
55/J4 Hlohovec, Slvk.
96/G8 Hmas-Nirimba, Austl.
91/G4 Hmawbi, Myan.
105/F5 Ho, Gha.
89/D1 Hoa Bin, Viet.
89/E4 Hoa Da, Viet.
89/C1 Hoang Lien (mts.), Viet.
125/K2 Hoare (bay), Nun,Can.
85/G2 Hobara, Japan
97/C4 Hobart, Austl.
131/H4 Hobart, Ok,US
111/Q Hobbs (coast), Ant.
131/G4 Hobbs, NM,US
58/D1 Hoboken, Belg.
137/F5 Hoboken, NJ,US
103/Q6 Hobyo, Som.
68/A2 Hochalmspitze (peak), Aus.
89/D4 Ho Chi Minh City (Saigon), Viet.
63/K3 Hochkönig (peak), Aus.
63/L3 Hochschwab (peak), Aus.
59/G3 Hochsimmer (peak), Ger.
53/G3 Hockley, Eng,UK
51/F4 Hodder (riv.), Eng,UK
53/F3 Hoddesdon, Eng,UK
128/G3 Hodgeville, Sk,Can.
104/C2 Hodh (reg.), Mrta.
80/M8 Hod HaSharon, Isr.
104/D2 Hodh ech Chargui (reg.), Mrta.
104/C2 Hodh el Gharbi (reg.), Mrta.
68/E2 Hódmezövásárhely, Hun.
51/F6 Hodnet, Eng,UK
55/J4 Hodonín, Czh.
59/E2 Hoegnel (riv.), Belg.
56/B5 Hoekse Waard (polder), Neth.
59/G6 Hoenheim, Fr.
59/E2 Hoensbroek, Neth.
59/E2 Hoeselt, Belg.
56/C4 Hoevelaken, Neth.
56/B5 Hoeven, Neth.
63/J1 Hof, Ger.
138/P15 Hoffman Estates, Il,US
57/G6 Hofgeismar, Ger.
87/B3 Hofong Qagan (salt lake), China
48/P6 Hofsá (riv.), Ice.
48/N7 Hofsjökull (glac.), Ice.
84/B3 Hōfu, Japan
56/C4 Hoge Veluwe Nat'l Park, Neth.
61/F3 Hohenems, Aus.
57/H4 Hohenhameln, Ger.
63/H2 Hohenloher Ebene (plain), Ger.
63/K3 Hoher Dachstein (peak), Aus.
57/G6 Hohes Gras (peak), Ger.
63/K3 Hohe Tauern (mts.), Aus.
63/K3 Hohe Tauern Nat'l Park, Aus.
87/B2 Hohhot, China
60/C1 Hohneck (mtn.), Fr.
59/G3 Höhr-Grenzhausen, Ger.
81/F4 Hoh Sai (lake), China
81/F4 Hoh Xil (lake), China
81/E4 Hoh Xil (mts.), China
89/E3 Hoi An, Viet.
134/D2 Hoisington, Ks,US
89/D1 Hoi Xuan, Viet.
84/C4 Hōjō, Japan
95/H7 Hokitika, NZ
83/N3 Hokkaidō (isl.), Japan
85/G2 Hokota, Japan
85/K10 Hokudan, Japan
85/M9 Hokusei, Japan
51/J6 Holbeach, Eng,UK
53/H3 Holbrook, Eng,UK
130/E4 Holbrook, Az,US
131/H4 Holdenville, Ok,US
51/H4 Holderness (pen.), Eng,UK
131/H2 Holdrege, Ne,US
123/F3 Holguín, Cuba
136/G3 Holitna (riv.), Ak,US
132/C3 Holland, Mi,US
135/F3 Hollandale, Ms,US
56/B4 Hollandse IJssel (riv.), Neth.
53/H2 Hollesley, Eng,UK
131/H4 Hollis, Ok,US
130/B3 Hollister, Ca,US
59/E2 Hollogne-aux-Pierres, Belg.
48/H3 Hollola, Fin.
135/F3 Holly Springs, Ms,US
135/H5 Hollywood, Fl,US
48/F3 Holm, Swe.
124/E1 Holman, NW,Can.
137/F5 Holmdel, NJ,US
96/C2 Holmes (reefs), Austl.
128/F4 Holmes (peak), Wy,US
51/F5 Holmes Chapel, Eng,UK
51/H4 Holme upon Spalding Moor, Eng,UK
51/G4 Holmfirth, Eng,UK
111/C Holm-Lützow (bay), Ant.
48/F3 Holmsjön (lake), Swe.
80/K5 Ḩolon, Isr.
48/D4 Holstebro, Den.
135/H2 Holston (riv.), Tn,US
52/B5 Holsworthy, Eng,UK
53/H1 Holt, Eng,UK
56/D4 Holten, Neth.
131/J3 Holton, Ks,US
137/G5 Holtsville, NY,US
50/D5 Holy (isl.), Wal,UK
50/D5 Holyhead, Wal,UK
50/D5 Holyhead (mtn.), Wal,UK
49/E3 Holy (Lindisfarne) (isl.), Eng,UK
131/G2 Holyoke, Co,US
133/F3 Holyoke, Ma,US
51/E5 Holywell, Wal,UK
50/C2 Holywood, NI,UK
54/F5 Holzkirchen, Ger.
57/G5 Holzminden, Ger.
57/E6 Holzwickede, Ger.
108/B3 Hom (dry riv.), Namb.
56/D6 Homberg, Ger.
57/G6 Homberg, Ger.
105/E3 Hombori Tondo (peak), Mali
59/F5 Hombourg-Haut, Fr.
59/G5 Homburg, Ger.
125/K2 Home (bay), Nun,Can.
59/E5 Homécourt, Fr.
134/E3 Homer, La,US
135/H5 Homestead, Fl,US
135/G3 Homewood, Al,US
138/Q16 Homewood, Il,US
135/F4 Homochitto (riv.), Ms,US
72/D1 Homyel', Bela.
72/C2 Homyel'skaya Voblasts, Bela.
90/B5 Honāvar, India
89/D4 Hon Chong, Viet.
52/C3 Honddu (riv.), Wal,UK
84/B4 Hondo, Japan
131/F4 Hondo (dry riv.), NM,US
134/D4 Hondo, Tx,US
56/D3 Hondsrug (reg.), Neth.
122/D4 Honduras (ctry.)
122/D4 Honduras (gulf), NAm.
130/B2 Honey (lake), Ca,US
53/E2 Honeybourne, Eng,UK
87/C5 Hong (lake), China
87/C4 Hong (riv.), China
91/J2 Hongdu (riv.), China
89/D1 Hon Gai, Viet.
87/C5 Honghu, China
91/J2 Hongjiang, China
88/B3 Hong Kong, China
87/B3 Hongliu (riv.), China
89/C1 Hong (Red) (riv.), Viet.
91/J3 Hongshui (riv.), China
133/H1 Honguedo (passg.), Qu,Can.
87/D4 Hongze (lake), China
98/E5 Honiara (cap.), Sol.
52/C5 Honiton, Eng,UK
126/T10 Honolulu (cap.), Hi,US
89/D4 Hon Quan, Viet.
83/M5 Honshu (isl.), Japan
138/J10 Hood (mt.), Ca,US
128/C4 Hood (mt.), Or,US
128/C4 Hood Canal (inlet), Wa,US
56/B4 Hoofddorp, Neth.
56/C6 Hoogeloon, Neth.
56/B6 Hoogerheide, Neth.
56/D3 Hoogeveen, Neth.

Hooge – İstan
165

56/D3 Hoogeveense Vaart (can.), Neth.
56/D2 Hoogezand, Neth.
90/E3 Hooghly-Chinsura, India
58/C2 Hooglede, Belg.
56/B6 Hoogstraten, Belg.
96/C3 Hook (isl.), Austl.
53/F4 Hook, Eng,UK
49/B4 Hook Head (pt.), Ire.
132/C3 Hoopeston, Il,US
56/C3 Hoorn, Neth.
56/C3 Hoornse Hop (bay), Neth.
130/D3 Hoover (dam), Az,US
80/E2 Hopa, Turk.
137/F5 Hopatcong, NJ,US
137/F5 Hopatcong (lake), NJ,US
128/C3 Hope, BC,Can.
51/E5 Hope, Wal,UK
134/E3 Hope, Ar,US
125/K2 Hopes Advance (cape), Qu,Can.
52/C6 Hope's Nose (pt.), Eng,UK
52/D2 Hope under Dinmore, Eng,UK
137/F5 Hopewell, NJ,US
132/E4 Hopewell, Va,US
97/B3 Hopkins (riv.), Austl.
132/C4 Hopkinsville, Ky,US
57/F6 Hoppecke (riv.), Ger.
57/E4 Hopsten, Ger.
128/C4 Hoquiam, Wa,US
136/J2 Horace (mtn.), Ak,US
85/L9 Hōrai-san (peak), Japan
80/E2 Horasan, Turk.
80/K5 Horbat Qesari (ruins), Isr.
51/G4 Horbury, Eng,UK
48/C3 Hordaland (co.), Nor.
51/G2 Horden, Eng,UK
69/G3 Horezu, Rom.
82/F3 Hörh (peak), Mong.
53/F4 Horley, Eng,UK
72/F2 Horlivka, Ukr.
63/L2 Horn, Aus.
48/M6 Horn (pt.), Ice.
55/L4 Hornád (riv.), Slvk.
48/E2 Hornavan (lake), Swe.
57/F5 Horn-Bad Meinberg, Ger.
133/Q8 Hornby, On,Can.
51/H5 Horncastle, Eng,UK
132/E3 Hornell, NY,US
132/C1 Hornepayne, On,Can.
119/L8 Horn (Hornos) (cape), Chile
119/L8 Hornos Nat'l Park, Cabo de, Chile
58/A4 Hornoy-le-Bourg, Fr.
96/H8 Hornsby, Austl.
51/H4 Hornsea, Eng,UK
54/E1 Hornum Odde (cape), Ger.
83/N3 Horoshiri-dake (mtn.), Japan
52/B6 Horrabridge, Eng,UK
131/F2 Horse (cr.), Ne, Wy,US
132/C4 Horse Cave, Ky,US
128/C2 Horsefly (lake), BC,Can.
48/D5 Horsens, Den.
53/H3 Horsey (isl.), Eng,UK
51/G4 Horsforth, Eng,UK
97/B3 Horsham, Austl.
53/F4 Horsham, Eng,UK
137/E5 Horsham, Pa,US
56/D6 Horst, Neth.
57/E4 Hörstel, Ger.
57/E4 Horstmar, Ger.
65/S12 Horta, Azor.,Port.
65/N9 Hortaleza, Sp.
68/E2 Hortobágyi Nat'l Park, Hun.
136/N2 Horton (riv.), NW,Can.
80/K6 Horvot 'Avedat (ruins), Isr.
80/K6 Horvot Mezada (Masada) (ruins), Isr.
51/F4 Horwich, Eng,UK
132/D2 Horwood (lake), On,Can.
90/C3 Hoshangābād, India
90/C4 Hospet, India
119/K8 Hoste (isl.), Chile
85/E2 Hotaka, Japan
85/E2 Hotaka-dake (mtn.), Japan
81/D4 Hotan (riv.), China
71/W8 Hot'kovo, Rus.
129/H5 Hot Springs, SD,US
134/E3 Hot Springs Nat'l Park, Ar,US
124/E2 Hottah (lake), NW,Can.
108/A2 Hottentot (bay), Namb.
108/A2 Hottentots (pt.), Namb.
58/B3 Houdain, Fr.
104/D4 Houet (prov.), Burk.
132/B2 Houghton, Mi,US
132/C2 Houghton Lake, Mi,US
51/G2 Houghton-le-Spring, Eng,UK
133/H2 Houlton, Me,US
87/B4 Houma, China
135/F4 Houma, La,US
58/B2 Houplines, Fr.
58/A3 Hourdel, Pointe du (pt.), Fr.
130/D3 House (range), Ut,US
128/B2 Houston, BC,Can.
131/K3 Houston, Mo,US
135/F3 Houston, Ms,US
134/E4 Houston, Tx,US
56/C4 Houten, Neth.
58/B2 Houthulst, Belg.
56/C3 Houtribdijk (dam), Neth.
53/F5 Hove, Eng,UK
57/F5 Hövelhof, Ger.
130/E3 Hovenweep Nat'l Mon., Co,US
53/H1 Hoveton, Eng,UK
48/E3 Hovfjället (peak), Swe.
51/H3 Hovingham, Eng,UK
82/E1 Hövsgöl (lake), Mong.
136/H2 Howard (hill), Ak,US
136/G2 Howard (pass), Ak,US
51/H4 Howden, Eng,UK
97/D3 Howe (cape), Austl.
132/D3 Howell, Mi,US
137/F5 Howell, NJ,US
109/E3 Howick, SAfr.
99/H4 Howland (isl.), PacUS
90/E3 Howrah, India
57/G5 Höxter, Ger.
55/H3 Hoyerswerda, Ger.
51/E5 Hoylake, Eng,UK
51/G5 Hoyland Nether, Eng,UK
65/N8 Hoyo-de-Manzanares, Sp.
59/E3 Hoyoux (riv.), Belg.
82/E2 Hoyt Tamir (riv.), Mong.
85/M9 Hozumi, Japan
55/H3 Hradec Králové, Czh.
68/D4 Hrasnica, Bosn.
68/B2 Hrastnik, Slov.
55/M2 Hrodna, Bela.
70/E5 Hrodzyenskaya Voblasts, Bela.
48/M6 Hrolleifsborg (peak), Ice.
55/K4 Hron (riv.), Slvk.
55/J3 Hronov, Czh.
55/M3 Hrubieszów, Pol.
55/J3 Hrubý Jeseník (mts.), Czh.
48/P6 Hrútafjöll (peak), Ice.
82/G5 Hua (peak), China
114/C6 Huacho, Peru
89/B3 Hua Hin, Thai.
99/K6 Huahine (isl.), FrPol.
87/C4 Huai (riv.), China
87/D4 Huai'an, China
82/H5 Huaibei, China
88/A2 Huaihua, China
87/C2 Huailai, China
87/D4 Huainan, China
87/C3 Huairen, China
87/D4 Huaiyin, China
122/B4 Huajuapan de León, Mex.
118/C2 Hualañé, Chile
88/D3 Hualien, Tai.
114/C5 Huallaga (riv.), Peru
114/C5 Huamachuco, Peru
110/C3 Huambo, Ang.
87/C5 Huan (riv.), China
114/C6 Huancavelica, Peru
114/C6 Huancayo, Peru
114/E8 Huanchaca (peak), Bol.
89/C2 Huang (riv.), Laos, Thai.
87/C4 Huangchuan, China
88/C2 Huanggang (peak), China
87/C2 Huangqi (lake), China
87/D5 Huangshan, China
87/C5 Huangshi, China
87/C5 Huangtang (lake), China
87/B4 Huangtu (plat.), China
83/H4 Huang (Yellow) (riv.), China
114/C5 Huánuco, Peru
114/E7 Huanuni, Bol.
114/C6 Huaral, Peru
114/C5 Huaráz, Peru
114/C6 Huarmey, Peru
114/C5 Huascarán (peak), Peru
114/C5 Huascarán Nat'l Park, Peru
87/B4 Hua Shan (peak), China
123/N8 Huatabampo, Mex.
114/E6 Huatunas (lake), Bol.
88/A1 Huaying, China
136/L3 Hubbard (mtn.), Ak,US, Yk,Can.
131/H4 Hubbard Creek (res.), Tx,US
87/C5 Hubei (prov.), China
87/B4 Hubei Kou (pass), China
90/C4 Hubli-Dhārwār, India
56/D6 Hückelhoven, Ger.
57/E6 Hückeswagen, Ger.
51/G5 Hucknall Torkard, Eng,UK
58/A2 Hucqueliers, Fr.
51/G4 Huddersfield, Eng,UK
70/C4 Huddinge, Swe.
57/F2 Hude, Ger.
48/F3 Hudiksvall, Swe.
111/L Hudson (cape), Ant.
125/H2 Hudson (bay), Can.
125/J2 Hudson (str.), Nun, Qu,Can.
133/M7 Hudson, Qu,Can.
132/F3 Hudson (riv.), NJ, NY,US
132/F3 Hudson, NY,US
129/H2 Hudson Bay, Sk,Can.
124/D3 Hudson's Hope, BC,Can.
89/D2 Hue, Viet.
68/F2 Huedin, Rom.
122/C4 Huehuetenango, Guat.
122/B3 Huejutla, Mex.
64/B4 Huelva, Sp.
64/B3 Huelva (riv.), Sp.
118/B4 Huequi (vol.), Chile
64/E4 Huercal-Overa, Sp.
131/F3 Huerfano (riv.), Co,US
65/E1 Huesca, Sp.
64/D4 Huéscar, Sp.
118/F3 Huesos (riv.), Arg.
122/A4 Huetamo de Nuñez, Mex.
90/E3 Hugli (riv.), India
131/G3 Hugo, Co,US
131/J4 Hugo, Ok,US
131/G3 Hugoton, Ks,US
83/H2 Hui (riv.), China
108/B2 Huib-Hock (plat.), Namb.
110/B4 Huíla (plat.), Ang.
118/D2 Huinca Renancó, Arg.
62/D2 Huisne (riv.), Fr.
56/C5 Huissen, Neth.
70/D3 Huittinen, Fin.
122/C4 Huixtla, Mex.
56/C4 Huizen, Neth.
88/B3 Huizhou, China
86/C5 Hŭksan (arch.), SKor.
82/K2 Hulan (riv.), China
82/F2 Huld, Mong.
129/G4 Hulett, Wy,US
51/H4 Hull, Eng,UK
51/H4 Hull (riv.), Eng,UK
57/F4 Hüllhorst, Ger.
99/H5 Hull (Orona) (atoll), Kiri.
56/B6 Hulst, Neth.
87/B3 Hulu (riv.), China
82/H2 Hulun (lake), China
83/K1 Huma (riv.), China
114/F5 Humaitá, Braz.
123/N8 Humaya (riv.), Mex.
110/B4 Humbe, Ang.
133/K2 Humber (riv.), Nf,Can.
133/R8 Humber (bay), On,Can.
133/Q8 Humber (riv.), On,Can.
51/H4 Humber (riv.), Eng,UK
51/H4 Humberston, Eng,UK
134/E4 Humble, Tx,US
129/G2 Humboldt, Sk,Can.
99/V12 Humboldt (peak), NCal.
130/C2 Humboldt (range), Nv,US
130/D2 Humboldt (riv.), Nv,US
135/F3 Humboldt, Tn,US
97/C2 Hume (lake), Austl.
55/L4 Humenné, Slvk.
136/K2 Humphrey (pt.), Ak,US
130/E4 Humphreys (peak), Az,US
51/F1 Humshaugh, Eng,UK
83/J3 Hun (riv.), China
83/K3 Hun (riv.), China
48/N6 Húnaflói (bay), Ice.
91/K2 Hunan (prov.), China
83/L3 Hunchun, China
68/F3 Hunedoara, Rom.
68/F2 Hunedoara (co.), Rom.
54/E3 Hünfeld, Ger.
68/D2 Hungary (ctry.)
63/H1 Hungen, Ger.
53/E4 Hungerford, Eng,UK
82/C2 Hüngüy (riv.), Mong.
89/D1 Hung Yen, Viet.
83/K3 Hunjiang, China
51/H3 Hunmanby, Eng,UK
59/G1 Hunspatch, Fr.
59/G4 Hunsrück (mts.), Ger.
53/G1 Hunstanton, Eng,UK
57/F2 Hunte (riv.), Ger.
97/C4 Hunter (isl.), Austl.
97/D2 Hunter (riv.), Austl.
128/A3 Hunter (isl.), BC,Can.
136/H3 Hunter (mtn.), Ak,US
132/C4 Huntingburg, In,US
53/F2 Huntingdon, Eng,UK
51/G4 Huntington, Eng,UK
132/C3 Huntington, In,US
137/G5 Huntington, NY,US
132/D4 Huntington, WV,US
137/C3 Huntington Beach, Ca,US
137/B3 Huntington Park, Ca,US
138/F7 Huntington Woods, Mi,US
49/D2 Huntly, Sc,UK
136/M4 Hunts Inlet, BC,Can.
132/E2 Huntsville, On,Can.
135/G3 Huntsville, Al,US
134/E4 Huntsville, Tx,US
56/D5 Hünxe, Ger.
83/H2 Huolin Gol, China
89/D2 Huong Hoa, Viet.
89/D2 Huong Khe, Viet.
89/D2 Huong Son, Viet.
91/J4 Huong Thuy, Viet.
87/B3 Huo Shan (mtn.), China
103/R5 Hurdiyo, Som.
130/E4 Hurley, NM,US
132/D2 Huron (lake), Can., US
138/F7 Huron (riv.), Mi,US
129/J4 Huron, SD,US
132/D4 Hurricane, WV,US
53/F5 Hurstpierpoint, Eng,UK
58/D4 Hurtaut (riv.), Fr.
59/F2 Hürth, Ger.
51/G3 Hurworth, Eng,UK
90/D3 Husainābād, India
53/E2 Husbands Bosworth, Eng,UK
69/J2 Huşi, Rom.
54/E1 Husum, Ger.
131/H3 Hutchinson, Ks,US
129/K4 Hutchinson, Mn,US
51/J5 Huttoft, Eng,UK
96/C4 Hutton (peak), Austl.
51/H4 Hutton Cranswick, Eng,UK
51/G3 Hutton Rudby, Eng,UK
133/Q8 Huttonville, On,Can.
87/C3 Hutuo (riv.), China
59/E2 Huy, Belg.
51/F5 Huyton-with-Roby, Eng,UK
87/E5 Huzhou, China
48/P7 Hvannadalshnúkur (peak), Ice.
68/C4 Hvar (isl.), Cro.
48/N7 Hvítá (riv.), Ice.
110/E4 Hwange, Zim.
110/E4 Hwange (Wankie) Nat'l Park, Zim.
86/D3 Hwanghae-Bukto (prov.), NKor.
86/C3 Hwanghae-Namdo (prov.), NKor.
118/B5 Hyades (peak), Chile
82/C2 Hyargas, Mong.
82/C2 Hyargas (lake), Mong.
137/K8 Hyattsville, Md,US
51/F5 Hyde, Eng,UK
90/C4 Hyderābād, India
79/J3 Hyderābād, Pak.
63/G5 Hyères, Fr.
63/G5 Hyères (isls.), Fr.
124/D2 Hyland (riv.), Yk,Can.
84/D3 Hyōgo (pref.), Japan
84/D3 Hyō-no-sen (mtn.), Japan
130/E2 Hyrum, Ut,US
53/E5 Hythe, Eng,UK
53/H4 Hythe, Eng,UK
84/B4 Hyūga, Japan
48/H3 Hyvinkää, Fin.

I

68/A2 Iâf di Montasio (peak), It.
69/H3 Ialomiţa (riv.), Rom.
116/D1 Iapu, Braz.
69/H2 Iaşi, Rom.
69/H2 Iaşi (co.), Rom.
88/C4 Iba, Phil.
105/F5 Ibadan, Nga.
114/C3 Ibagué, Col.
116/B2 Ibaiti, Braz.
88/D5 Ibajay, Phil.
130/D2 Ibapah, Ut,US
68/E4 Ibar (riv.), Serb.
84/C3 Ibara, Japan
85/L10 Ibaraki, Japan
85/F2 Ibaraki (pref.), Japan
114/C3 Ibarra, Ecu.
117/E2 Ibarreta, Arg.
103/L6 Ibba (riv.), Sudan
57/E4 Ibbenbüren, Ger.
105/F2 Ibdekhene (wadi), Mali
117/E2 Ibera, Esteros de (marshes), Arg.
64/D2 Ibérico, Sistema (range), Sp.
133/P7 Iberville, Qu,Can.
84/E3 Ibi (riv.), Japan
65/E3 Ibi, Sp.
116/C1 Ibiá, Braz.
115/L6 Ibicaraí, Braz.
116/B2 Ibitinga, Braz.
116/F8 Ibiúna, Braz.
65/F3 Ibiza, Sp.
65/F3 Ibiza (isl.), Sp.
84/D3 Ibo (riv.), Japan
115/K6 Ibotirama, Braz.
102/H8 Iboundji (peak), Gabon
55/L4 Ibrány, Hun.
106/B2 Ibshawāy, Egypt
53/E1 Ibstock, Eng,UK
93/G3 Ibu, Indo.
85/M9 Ibuki, Japan
85/M9 Ibuki-yama (peak), Japan
114/C6 Ica, Peru
48/N7 Iceland (ctry.)
90/B4 Ichalkaranji, India
90/D4 Ichchāpuram, India
85/J7 Ichihara, Japan
85/L9 Ichijima, Japan
85/H7 Ichikawa, Japan
84/E3 Ichinomiya, Japan
83/N4 Ichinoseki, Japan
85/M10 Ichishi, Japan
58/C1 Ichtegem, Belg.
115/L5 Icó, Braz.
136/K4 Icy (bay), Ak,US
136/F1 Icy (cape), Ak,US
136/L4 Icy (str.), Ak,US
131/J4 Idabel, Ok,US
128/E5 Idaho (state), US
128/E5 Idaho Falls, Id,US
90/B3 Idar, India
59/G4 Idarkopf (peak), Ger.
59/G4 Idar-Oberstein, Ger.
85/L10 Ide, Japan
82/D2 Ider (riv.), Mong.
106/C3 Idfū, Egypt
67/J5 Ídhi (peak), Gre.
80/H6 Idkū, Egypt
51/H5 Idle (riv.), Eng,UK
80/D3 Idlib, Syria
68/B3 Idrija, Slov.
58/B2 Ieper, Belg.
67/J5 Ierápetra, Gre.
107/C5 Ifakara, Tanz.
98/D4 Ifalik (isl.), Micr.
109/H8 Ifanadiana, Madg.
105/G5 Ife, Nga.
85/M10 Iga, Japan
85/M10 Iga (riv.), Japan
116/C2 Igarapava, Braz.
115/J4 Igarapé-Miri, Braz.
74/J3 Igarka, Rus.
90/B4 Igatpuri, India
80/F2 Iğdır, Turk.
136/H2 Igikpak (mtn.), Ak,US
66/A3 Iglesias, It.
132/B1 Ignace, On,Can.
69/J5 İğneada (cape), Turk.
71/M4 Igra, Rus.
116/B3 Iguaçu (riv.), Braz.
117/F2 Iguaçu Nat'l Park, Braz.
122/B4 Iguala, Mex.
65/F2 Igualada, Sp.
117/E2 Iguapa (riv.), Braz.
116/C3 Iguape, Braz.
116/C3 Iguape (riv.), Braz.
115/L5 Iguatu, Braz.
117/F2 Iguazu Nat'l Park, Arg.
102/D2 Iguidi, 'Erg (des.), Afr.
109/H8 Ihosy, Madg.
109/G8 Ihotry (lake), Madg.
74/C3 Ii (riv.), Fin.
85/E3 Iida, Japan
85/F2 Iide-san (mtn.), Japan
70/E2 Iijoki (riv.), Fin.
85/M10 Iinan, Japan
48/H3 Iisalmi, Fin.
85/M10 Iitaka, Japan
70/E3 Iitti, Fin
85/F2 Iiyama, Japan
84/B4 Iizuka, Japan
102/C3 Ijill (peak), Mrta.
56/C4 IJmeer (bay), Neth.
56/B4 IJmuiden, Neth.
104/B2 Ijnaoun (well), Mrta.
48/H2 Ijoki (riv.), Fin.
56/C4 IJssel (riv.), Neth.
56/C3 IJsselmeer (lake), Neth.
56/C3 IJsselmuiden, Neth.
56/C4 IJsselstein, Neth.
117/F2 Ijuí, Braz.
84/B5 Ijūin, Japan
58/B2 Ijzer (riv.), Belg.
71/M5 Ik (riv.), Rus.
109/H7 Ikahavo (plat.), Madg.
67/J4 Ikaría (isl.), Gre.
110/D1 Ikela, D.R. Congo
85/M10 Ikenokoya-yama (peak), Japan
69/F4 Ikhtiman, Bul.
84/A4 Iki (chan.), Japan
84/A4 Iki (isl.), Japan
85/L10 Ikoma, Japan
109/H7 Ikopa (riv.), Madg.
88/D4 Ilagan, Phil.
78/E2 Īlām, Iran
90/E2 Ilam, Nepal
88/D3 Ilan, Tai.
55/K2 Iława, Pol.
103/M4 'Ilay, Sudan
52/D4 Ilchester, Eng,UK
81/C3 Ile (riv.), Kaz.
128/G2 Ile-à-la-Crosse, Sk,Can.
129/G2 Ile-a-la-Crosse (lake), Sk,Can.
110/D1 Ilebo, D.R. Congo
62/E2 Ile-de-France (reg.), Fr.
73/K2 Ilek (riv.), Rus.
133/N7 Ile-Perrot, Qu,Can.
104/E5 Iles Ehotilés Nat'l Park, C.d'Iv.
105/G5 Ilesha, Nga.
96/B3 Ilfracombe, Austl.
52/B4 Ilfracombe, Eng,UK
72/E4 Ilgaz, Turk.
80/B2 Ilgın, Turk.
116/H8 Ilhabela, Braz.
116/J8 Ilha Grande (bay), Braz.
116/B1 Ilha Solteira (res.), Braz.
64/A2 Ílhavo, Port.
115/L6 Ilhéus, Braz.
81/D3 Ili (riv.), China
136/G4 Iliamna (lake), Ak,US
136/H3 Iliamna (vol.), Ak,US
88/D6 Iligan, Phil.
80/E3 Ilisu (res.), Turk.
69/H6 Ilium (Troy) (ruins), Turk.
51/G6 Ilkeston, Eng,UK
51/G4 Ilkley, Eng,UK
61/F3 Ill (riv.), Aus.
60/D1 Ill (riv.), Fr.
118/C1 Illapel, Chile
105/G3 Illéla, Niger
61/G1 Iller (riv.), Ger.
64/D2 Illescas, Sp.
114/E7 Illimani (peak), Bol.
59/G5 Illingen, Ger.
132/B4 Illinois (state), US
132/B3 Illinois (riv.), Il,US
52/A6 Illogan, Eng,UK
64/D4 Illora, Sp.
60/D2 Illzach, Fr.
63/J2 Ilm (riv.), Ger.
48/G3 Ilmajoki, Fin.
57/G5 Ilme (riv.), Ger.
70/F4 Il'men' (lake), Rus.
54/F3 Ilmenau, Ger.
57/H2 Ilmenau (riv.), Ger.
52/D5 Ilminster, Eng,UK
114/D7 Ilo, Peru
88/D5 Iloilo, Phil.
105/G4 Ilorin, Nga.
73/H2 Ilovlya (riv.), Rus.
57/H5 Ilse (riv.), Ger.
57/H4 Ilsede, Ger.
57/H5 Ilsenburg, Ger.
69/H5 Ilyas (pt.), Turk.
71/N3 Ilych (riv.), Rus.
63/K2 Ilz (riv.), Ger.
84/C3 Imabari, Japan
85/F2 Imaichi, Japan
109/H8 Imaloto (riv.), Madg.
80/C3 İmamoğlu, Turk.
70/F2 Imandra (lake), Rus.
84/A4 Imari, Japan
43/J3 Imatra, Fin.
84/E3 Imazu, Japan
85/J7 Imba, Japan
116/B4 Imbituba, Braz.
103/P6 Īmī, Eth.
73/J5 Imishli, Azer.
67/L7 Imittós (mtn.), Gre.
130/C2 Imlay, Nv,US
57/G6 Immenhausen, Ger.
61/G2 Immenstadt im Allgäu, Ger.
51/H4 Immingham, Eng,UK
135/H5 Immokalee, Fl,US
136/J2 Imnavait (mtn.), Ak,US
105/G5 Imo (state), Nga.
63/J4 Imola, It.
115/J5 Imperatriz, Braz.
63/H5 Imperia, It.
129/G3 Imperial, Sk,Can.
131/G2 Imperial, Ne,US
103/J7 Impfondo, Congo
91/F3 Imphāl, India
69/J5 İmrali (isl.), Turk.
80/D2 İmranlı, Turk.
61/G3 Imst, Aus.
85/E3 Ina, Japan
85/L10 Ina (riv.), Japan
55/H2 Ina (riv.), Pol.
85/M9 Inabe, Japan
85/L10 Inagawa, Japan
85/H7 Inagi, Japan
102/G2 I-n-Amenas, Alg.
85/K10 Inami, Japan
48/H1 Inari (lake), Fin.
69/G2 Inău (peak), Rom.
85/G2 Inawashiro (lake), Japan
85/M9 Inazawa, Japan
65/G3 Inca, Sp.
105/F2 I-n-Chaouâg (wadi), Mali
49/C3 Inchinnan, Sc,UK
104/B2 Inchiri (reg.), Mrta.
86/D4 Inch'ŏn, SKor.
86/D4 Inch'on-Jikhalsi (prov.), SKor.
102/E3 I-n-Dagouber (well), Mali
116/C1 Indaiá (riv.), Braz.
116/C2 Indaiatuba, Braz.
88/D6 Indanan, Phil.
59/F2 Inde (riv.), Ger.
59/F2 Inden, Ger.
122/D4 Independence, Belz.
130/C3 Independence, Ca,US
131/J3 Independence, Ks,US
131/J3 Independence, Mo,US
130/C2 Independence (mts.), Nv,US
137/E6 Independence Nat'l Hist. Park, Pa,US
77/G7 India (ctry.)
45/N6 Indian (ocean)
132/C3 Indiana (state), US
132/E3 Indiana, Pa,US
138/R16 Indiana Dunes Nat'l Lakesh., In,US
132/C4 Indianapolis (cap.), In,US
129/H3 Indian Head, Sk,Can.
135/F3 Indianola, Ms,US
135/H5 Indiantown, Fl,US
116/B1 Indiaporã, Braz.
75/Q3 Indigirka (riv.), Rus.
68/E3 Indija, Serb.
130/C4 Indio, Ca,US
89/C1 Indochina (reg.), Asia
93/E4 Indonesia (ctry.)
96/E6 Indooroopilly, Austl.
90/C3 Indore, India
92/B4 Indragiri (riv.), Indo.
92/C5 Indramayu (cape), Indo.
90/D4 Indrāvati (riv.), India
62/D3 Indre (riv.), Fr.
62/D3 Indrois (riv.), Fr.
77/F7 Indus (riv.), Asia
79/J4 Indus, Mouths of the, Pak.
80/C2 İnebolu, Turk.
105/E1 I-n-Echaï (well), Mali
80/B2 İnegöl, Turk.
68/E2 Ineu, Rom.
102/D1 Inezgane, Mor.
108/C4 Infanta (cape), SAfr.
122/A4 Infiernillo (res.), Mex.
64/C1 Infiesto, Sp.
114/C4 Ingapirca, Ecu.
58/C2 Ingelmunster, Belg.
96/G8 Ingleburn, Austl.
51/G2 Ingleton, Eng,UK
133/Q8 Inglewood, On,Can.
137/B3 Inglewood, Ca,US
138/C2 Inglewood-Finn Hill, Wa,US
135/H4 Inglis, Fl,US
82/G1 Ingoda (riv.), Rus.
51/J5 Ingoldmells, Eng,UK
63/J2 Ingolstadt, Ger.
111/E Ingrid Christianson (coast), Ant.
105/G2 I-n-Guezzâm, Alg.
72/E3 Ingulets (riv.), Ukr.
73/G4 Inguri (riv.), Geo.
73/H4 Ingushetiya, Resp., Rus.
115/J7 Inhumas, Braz.
50/A1 Inishowen (pen.), Ire.
50/B1 Inishowen Head (pt.), Ire.
138/F7 Inkster, Mi,US
84/C3 Inland (sea), Japan
91/G3 Inle (lake), Myan.
105/E2 I-n-Milach (well), Mali
63/K2 Inn (riv.), Eur.
82/G3 Inner Mongolia (reg.), China
57/H5 Innerste (riv.), Ger.
63/K3 Innichen (San Candido), It.
96/B2 Innisfail, Austl.
128/E2 Innisfail, Ab,Can.
136/G3 Innoko (riv.), Ak,US
61/H3 Innsbruck, Aus.
52/B5 Inny (riv.), Eng,UK
84/C4 Ino, Japan
110/C1 Inongo, D.R. Congo
55/K2 Inowrocław, Pol.
105/E1 I-n-Sâkâne, Erg (des.), Mali
102/F2 I-n-Salah, Alg.
49/D2 Insch, Sc,UK
91/G4 Insein, Myan.
128/A2 Inside (passg.), BC,Can.
71/P2 Inta, Rus.
105/F2 I-n-Tassik (well), Mali
128/B2 Interior (plat.), BC,Can.
129/K3 International Falls, Mn,US
89/B2 Inthanon (peak), Thai.
69/H3 Întorsura Buzăului, Rom.
85/G3 Inubō-zaki (pt.), Japan
125/J3 Inukjuak, Qu,Can.
119/K8 Inútil (bay), Chile
85/E3 Inuyama, Japan
49/C2 Inveraray, Sc,UK
95/G7 Invercargill, NZ
97/D1 Inverell, Austl.
49/C2 Invergarry, Sc,UK
49/D2 Inverkeilor, Sc,UK
129/H3 Invermay, Sk,Can.
133/J2 Inverness, NS,Can.
49/C2 Inverness, Sc,UK
135/G3 Inverness, Al,US
135/H4 Inverness, Fl,US
49/D2 Inverurie, Sc,UK
110/F4 Inyangani (peak), Zim.
136/D2 Inymney, Gora (mtn.), Rus.
130/C3 Inyo (mts.), Ca,US
73/H1 Inza, Rus.
85/J7 Inzai, Japan
67/G3 Ioánnina, Gre.
131/J3 Iola, Ks,US
79/H1 Iolotan', Trkm.
110/B4 Iona Nat'l Park, Ang.
132/C3 Ionia, Mi,US
67/F3 Ionian (sea), Eur.
67/F3 Ionian (isls.), Gre.
67/J4 Íos (isl.), Gre.
104/A2 Iouîk (cape), Mrta.
129/K5 Iowa (state), US
129/L5 Iowa (riv.), Ia,US
129/L5 Iowa City, Ia,US
129/K5 Iowa Falls, Ia,US
116/B1 Ipameri, Braz.
118/B5 Ipan (isl.), Chile
116/D1 Ipanema, Braz.
116/D1 Ipatinga, Braz.
55/K4 Ipel' (Ipoly) (riv.), Hun., Slvk.
114/C3 Ipiales, Col.
115/L6 Ipiaú, Braz.
92/B3 Ipoh, Malay.
55/K4 Ipoly (Ipel') (riv.), Hun., Slvk.
115/H7 Iporá, Braz.
67/K2 İpsala, Turk.
96/E7 Ipswich, Austl.
53/H2 Ipswich, Eng,UK
129/J4 Ipswich, SD,US
115/K4 Ipu, Braz.
116/B2 Ipuã, Braz.
125/K2 Iqaluit (cap.), Nun
114/D8 Iquique, Chile
114/D4 Iquitos, Peru
85/M10 Irago (chan.), Japan
85/E3 Irago-misaki (cape), Japan
67/J4 Iráklia (isl.), Gre.
67/J5 Iráklion, Gre.
78/F2 Iran (ctry.)
92/D3 Iran (mts.), Indo., Malay.
79/H3 Irānshahr, Iran
122/A3 Irapuato, Mex.
78/D2 Iraq (ctry.)
116/B3 Irati, Braz.
80/K5 Irbid, Jor.
80/L5 Irbid (gov.), Jor.
80/F3 Irbīl, Iraq
115/K6 Irecê, Braz.
49/A4 Ireland (ctry.)
49/B3 Ireland, Northern, UK
50/B5 Ireland's Eye (isl.), Ire.
71/N5 Iremel', Gora (peak), Rus.
52/C2 Irfon (riv.), Wal,UK
105/G2 Irhazer Oua-n-Agadez (wadi), Niger
86/D5 Iri, SKor.
93/H4 Irian Jaya (reg.), Indo.
104/D2 Irîgui (reg.), Mali, Mrta.
73/L2 Iriklinskiy (res.), Rus.
107/B4 Iringa, Tanz.
107/B5 Iringa (prov.), Tanz.
88/D3 Iriomote (isl.), Japan
115/H4 Iriri (riv.), Braz.
50/C4 Irish (sea), Ire., UK
82/E1 Irkut (riv.), Rus.
82/E1 Irkutsk, Rus.
75/L4 Irkutskaya Obl., Rus.
51/F5 Irlam, Eng,UK
52/D1 Iron Bridge, Eng,UK
68/F3 Iron Gate (gorge), Eur.
132/B2 Iron Mountain, Mi,US
132/B2 Iron River, Mi,US
132/D4 Ironton, Oh,US
132/B2 Ironwood, Mi,US
130/E4 Ironwood Forest Nat'l Mon., Az,US
132/D1 Iroquois Falls, On,Can.
85/F3 Irō-zaki (pt.), Japan
72/E1 Irput' (riv.), Bela., Rus.
59/F3 Irsen (riv.), Ger.
51/E3 Irt (riv.), Eng,UK
51/F1 Irthing (riv.), Eng,UK
53/F2 Irthlingborough, Eng,UK
74/G4 Irtysh (riv.), Rus.
85/H7 Iruma, Japan
107/A2 Irumu, D.R. Congo
64/E1 Irún, Sp.
49/C3 Irvine, Sc,UK
137/C3 Irvine, Ca,US
134/D3 Irving, Tx,US
137/F5 Irvington, NJ,US
96/C3 Isaac (riv.), Austl.
88/D6 Isabela, Phil.
125/K2 Isabella (bay), Nun,Can.
125/R7 Isachsen (cape), Nun,Can.
48/M6 Ísafjardhardjúp (fjord), Ice.
84/B4 Isahaya, Japan
109/H8 Isalo Nat'l Park, Madg.
109/H8 Isalo Ruiniform, Massif (plat.), Madg.
54/G4 Isar (riv.), Aus., Ger.
61/H4 Isarco (Eisack) (riv.), It.
66/C2 Ischia, It.
57/H3 Ise (riv.), Ger.
85/E3 Ise, Japan
85/M10 Ise (bay), Japan
53/F2 Ise (riv.), Eng,UK
85/F3 Isehara, Japan
137/F5 Iselin, NJ,US
63/K2 Isen (riv.), Ger.
63/J4 Iseo (lake), It.
62/F4 Isère (riv.), Fr.
57/E6 Iserlohn, Ger.
66/D2 Isernia, It.
85/F2 Isesaki, Japan
85/E3 Ise-Shima Nat'l Park, Japan
71/Q4 Iset' (riv.), Rus.
105/F5 Iseyin, Nga.
85/L10 Ishi (riv.), Japan
85/F2 Ishibashi, Japan
85/M9 Ishibe, Japan
98/B2 Ishigaki, Japan
88/D3 Ishigaki (isl.), Japan
85/F2 Ishige, Japan
85/G2 Ishikawa, Japan
85/E2 Ishikawa (pref.), Japan
85/N10 Ishiki, Japan
74/H4 Ishim (riv.), Kaz., Rus.
71/R4 Ishim, Rus.
73/L1 Ishimbay, Rus.
85/G1 Ishinomaki, Japan
85/G2 Ishioka, Japan
84/C4 Ishizuchi-san (mtn.), Japan
81/B4 Ismail Samani (peak), Taj.
132/C2 Ishpeming, Mi,US
114/E7 Isiboro Securé Nat'l Park, Bol.
119/G1 Isidoro, Uru.
74/H4 Isil'kul', Rus.
103/L7 Isiro, D.R. Congo
106/C4 Is, Jabal (peak), Sudan
80/D3 İskenderun, Turk.
80/C2 İskilip, Turk.
69/F4 Iskŭr (res.), Bul.
69/G4 Iskŭr (riv.), Bul.
49/D2 Isla (riv.), Sc,UK
64/B4 Isla Cristina, Sp.
118/Q9 Isla de Maipo, Chile
96/C4 Isla Gorge Nat'l Park, Austl.
123/N9 Isla Isabella Nat'l Park, Mex.
79/K2 Islāmābād (cap.), Pak.
118/B5 Isla Magdalena Nat'l Park, Chile
90/E2 Islāmpur, India
122/D3 Isla Mujeres, Mex.
129/K2 Island Lake, Mb,Can.
133/K1 Islands (bay), Nf,Can.
62/D4 Isle (riv.), Fr.
53/G2 Isleham, Eng,UK
50/D5 Isle of Anglesey (co.), Wal,UK
50/D3 Isle of Man, UK
50/D2 Isle of Whithorn, Sc,UK
53/E5 Isle of Wight, (co.), Eng,UK
132/B2 Isle Royale Nat'l Park, Mi,US
137/G5 Islip, NY,US
71/X9 Ismailovo Park, Rus.
106/C2 Ismalia (Al Ismā'īlīyah), Egypt
106/C3 Isnā, Egypt
61/G2 Isny, Ger.
85/M10 Isobe, Japan
48/H3 Isojärven Nat'l Park, Fin.
107/B5 Isoka, Zam.
66/C2 Isola del Liri, It.
66/E3 Isola di Capo Rizzuto, It.
80/B3 Isparta, Turk.
62/C5 Ispéguy, Col d' (pass), Fr.
69/H4 Isperikh, Bul.
80/E2 İspir, Turk.
80/J5 Israel (ctry.)
138/C2 Issaquah, Wa,US
56/D5 Issel (riv.), Ger.
56/D5 Isselburg, Ger.
104/D5 Issia, C.d'Iv.
62/E4 Issoire, Fr.
62/E3 Issoudun, Fr.
56/D5 Issum, Ger.
81/C3 Issyk-Kul' (lake), Kyr.
58/B6 Issy-les-Moulineaux, Fr.
68/E1 Istállós-kő (peak), Hun.
69/J5 İstanbul, Turk.
69/J5 İstanbul (prov.), Turk.

166
Istra – Kampo

69/H5 Istranca (mts.), Turk.
62/F5 Istres, Fr.
68/A3 Istria (pen.), Cro.
93/F2 Isulan, Phil.
115/L6 Itabaiana, Braz.
116/D2 Itabapoana (riv.), Braz.
115/K6 Itaberaba, Braz.
116/D1 Itabira, Braz.
116/D2 Itabirito, Braz.
116/L7 Itaboraí, Braz.
115/L7 Itabuna, Braz.
115/H5 Itacaiunas (riv.), Braz.
114/G4 Itacoatiara, Braz.
114/D5 Itacuaí (riv.), Braz.
116/K7 Itaguaí, Braz.
114/C2 Itagüí, Col.
116/B2 Itaí, Braz.
116/B3 Itaiópolis, Braz.
117/F1 Itaipu (res.), Braz., Par.
115/G4 Itaituba, Braz
116/B3 Itajaí, Braz.
116/B3 Itajaí (riv.), Braz.
116/H7 Itajubá, Braz.
85/G3 Itako, Japan
47/F4 Italy (ctry.)
115/L7 Itamaraju, Braz.
116/D1 Itamarandiba, Braz.
116/D1 Itambacuri, Braz.
116/D1 Itambé (peak), Braz.
85/L10 Itami, Japan
91/F2 Itanagar, India
116/G9 Itanhaém, Braz.
116/C2 Itanhandu, Braz.
116/D1 Itanhém (riv.), Braz.
116/D1 Itanhomi, Braz.
115/K7 Itaobim, Braz.
116/D2 Itaocara, Braz.
115/L4 Itapagé, Braz.
116/C2 Itapecerica, Braz.
115/K4 Itapecuru-Mirim, Braz.
116/D2 Itapemirim, Braz.
116/D2 Itaperuna, Braz.
115/K7 Itapetinga, Braz.
116/B2 Itapetininga, Braz.
116/B2 Itapeva, Braz.
116/G8 Itapevi, Braz.
115/K6 Itapicuru (riv.), Braz.
115/L4 Itapipoca, Braz.
116/G7 Itapira, Braz.
116/B2 Itaporanga, Braz.
116/G8 Itaquaquecetuba, Braz.
116/B3 Itararé, Braz.
90/C3 Itārsi, India
116/C2 Itatinga (res.), Braz.
48/J3 Itä-Suomen (prov.), Fin.
116/C2 Itatiaia Nat'l Park, Braz.
116/G8 Itatiba, Braz.
116/C2 Itatinga (res.), Braz.
115/K5 Itaueira (riv.), Braz.
116/C2 Itaúna, Braz.
83/N3 Itayanagi, Japan
88/D3 Itbayat (isl.), Phil.
53/E4 Itchen (riv.), Eng,UK
103/K7 Itembiri (riv.), D.R. Congo
114/F6 Iténez (riv.), Bol.
110/E4 Itezhi-Tezhi (dam), Zam.
132/E3 Ithaca, NY,US
67/G3 Ithaca (Itháki) (isl.), Gre.
57/G5 Ith (ridge), Ger.
52/C2 Ithon (riv.), Wal,UK
107/B4 Itigi, Tanz.
85/F3 Itō, Japan
85/E2 Itoigawa, Japan
62/D2 Iton (riv.), Fr.
85/H7 Itsukaichi, Japan
57/F6 Itter (riv.), Ger.
66/A2 Ittiri, It.
116/C2 Itu, Braz.
114/D5 Ituí (riv.), Braz.
116/B1 Ituiutaba, Braz.
116/B1 Itumbiara, Braz.
116/B1 Itumbiara (res.), Braz.
129/H3 Ituna, Sk,Can.
116/B3 Ituporanga, Braz.
116/B1 Iturama, Braz.
116/J6 Itutinga (res.), Braz.
116/C2 Ituverava, Braz.
114/E5 Ituxi (riv.), Braz.
80/H6 Ityāy al Bārūd, Egypt
54/E2 Itzehoe, Ger.
136/C2 Iul'tin, Gora (mtn.), Rus.
116/D2 Iuna, Braz.
116/B3 Ivaí (riv.), Braz.
116/B3 Ivaiporã, Braz.
48/H1 Ivalojoki (riv.), Fin.
63/M2 Ivančice, Czh.
132/D1 Ivanhoe (riv.), On,Can
68/E4 Ivanjica, Serb.
72/C2 Ivano-Frankivs'k, Ukr
72/C2 Ivano-Frankivs'ka Obl., Ukr.
70/J4 Ivanovo, Rus.
71/J4 Ivanovskaya Obl., Rus.
67/J2 Ivaylovgrad (res.), Bul
71/P3 Ivdel, Rus.
102/H7 Ivindo (riv.), Gabon
109/H8 Ivohibe, Madg.
109/J7 Ivondro (riv.), Madg.
63/G4 Ivrea, It.
58/B6 Ivry-sur-Seine, Fr.
136/K2 Ivvavik Nat'l Park, Yk,Can.
52/C6 Ivybridge, Eng,UK
85/F2 Iwai, Japan
85/G2 Iwaki, Japan
84/C3 Iwakuni, Japan
85/M9 Iwakura, Japan
84/D3 Iwami, Japan
83/N3 Iwamizawa, Japan
85/G1 Iwanuma, Japan
85/E3 Iwata, Japan
83/N4 Iwate-san (mtn.), Japan
85/H7 Iwatsuki, Japan
105/G5 Iwo, Nga.
98/D2 Iwo Jima (isl.), Japan
54/C3 Ixelles, Belg.
122/B4 Ixtlatepec, Mex.
123/P9 Ixtlán del Río, Mex.
53/G2 Ixworth, Eng,UK
82/D1 Iya (riv.), Rus.
84/C4 Iyo, Japan
84/C4 Iyo (sea), Japan
122/D4 Izabal (lake), Guat.
73/H4 Izberbash, Rus.
58/C2 Izegem, Belg.
136/F4 Izembek Nat'l Wild. Ref., Ak,US
71/M4 Izhevsk, Rus.
71/M2 Izhma (riv.), Rus.
136/E5 Izigan (cape), Ak,US
79/G4 Izkī, Oman
69/J3 Izmail, Ukr.
80/A2 İzmir, Turk.
69/J5 İzmit, Turk.
69/J5 İzmit (gulf), Turk.
64/C4 Iznájar, Sp.
69/J5 İznik, Turk.
69/H5 İznik (lake), Turk.
80/L5 Izra', Syria
68/D2 Izsák, Hun.
83/M5 Izu (isls.), Japan
85/F3 Izu (pen.), Japan
122/B4 Izúcar de Matamoros, Mex.
85/H8 Izu-Fuji-Hakone Nat'l Park, Japan
84/A3 Izuhara, Japan
84/D3 Izumi, Japan
85/L10 Izumi-ōtsu, Japan
84/D3 Izumi-Sano, Japan
84/C3 Izumo, Japan
72/F2 Izyum, Ukr.

J

106/B5 Jabal Abyad (plat.), Sudan
80/K4 Jabal Lubnān (gov.), Leb.
64/D3 Jabalón (riv.), Sp.
90/C3 Jabalpur, India
80/K6 Jabālyah, Gaza
58/C1 Jabbeke, Belg.
106/C4 Jabjabah, Wādī (dry riv.), Egypt, Sudan
80/K4 Jablah, Syria
67/G2 Jablanica (mts.), Alb.
55/H3 Jablonec nad Nisou, Czh.
115/L5 Jaboatão, Braz.
116/B2 Jaboticabal, Braz.
68/E3 Jabuka, Serb.
92/B4 Jabung (cape), Indo.
65/E1 Jaca, Sp.
116/C2 Jacareí, Braz.
103/Q5 Jaceel (riv.), Som.
133/G2 Jackman, Me,US
130/D2 Jackpot, Nv,US
134/D3 Jacksboro, Tx,US
135/G4 Jackson, Al,US
130/B3 Jackson, Ca,US
132/C3 Jackson, Mi,US
129/K5 Jackson, Mn,US
131/K3 Jackson, Mo,US
135/F3 Jackson (cap.), Ms,US
128/D5 Jackson (mts.), Nv,US
132/D4 Jackson, Oh,US
135/F3 Jackson, Tn,US
128/F5 Jackson, Wy,US
128/F4 Jackson (lake), Wy,US
135/G3 Jacksonville, Al,US
134/E3 Jacksonville, Ar,US
135/H4 Jacksonville, Fl,US
132/B4 Jacksonville, Il,US
135/J3 Jacksonville, NC,US
134/E4 Jacksonville, Tx,US
135/H4 Jacksonville Beach, Fl,US
123/G4 Jacmel, Haiti
79/J3 Jacobābād, Pak.
115/K6 Jacobina, Braz.
133/H1 Jacques-Cartier (mtn.), Qu,Can.
133/G2 Jacques-Cartier (riv.), Qu,Can.
117/F2 Jacuí (riv.), Braz.
115/L6 Jacuipe (riv.), Braz.
116/C3 Jacupiranga, Braz.
79/H3 Jaddi (pt.), Pak.
57/F1 Jade (bay), Ger.
57/F2 Jade (riv.), Ger.
57/F2 Jadebusen (bay), Ger.
64/D4 Jaén, Sp.
97/A3 Jaffa (cape), Austl.
90/D6 Jaffna, SrL.
90/D4 Jagdalpur, India
90/D2 Jagdīspur, India
88/D6 Jagna, Phil.
81/C5 Jagraon, India
63/J2 Jagst (riv.), Ger.
90/C4 Jagtiāl, India
115/K6 Jaguaquara, Braz.
119/G2 Jaguarão, Braz.
119/G2 Jaguarão (riv.), Braz.
116/G7 Jaguari (riv.), Braz.
116/B3 Jaguariaíva, Braz.
115/L5 Jaguaribe (riv.), Braz.
116/G7 Jaguariúna, Braz.
97/D3 Jagungal (peak), Austl.
78/F3 Jahrom, Iran
93/G3 Jailolo, Indo.
90/C2 Jaipur, India
90/B2 Jaisalmer, India
68/C3 Jajce, Bosn.
90/E3 Jājpur, India
92/C5 Jakarta (cap.), Indo.
48/G3 Jakobstad, Fin.
131/G4 Jal, NM,US
79/K2 Jalālābād, Afg.
48/G3 Jalasjärvi, Fin.
116/B2 Jales, Braz.
90/C3 Jālgaon, India
102/H6 Jalingo, Nga.
123/P9 Jalisco (state), Mex.
90/C4 Jālna, India
64/E2 Jalon (riv.), Sp.
90/B2 Jālor, India
90/E2 Jalpaiguri, India
103/K2 Jālū, Libya
98/F4 Jaluit (atoll), Mrsh.
78/E2 Jalūlā', Iraq
103/P7 Jamaame, Som.
105/H4 Jamaare (riv.), Nga.
123/F4 Jamaica (ctry.)
123/F4 Jamaica (chan.), NAm.
90/E3 Jamālpur, Bang.
90/E2 Jamālpur, India
115/G5 Jamanxim (riv.), Braz.
114/F5 Jamari (riv.), Braz.
92/B4 Jambi, Indo.
92/A2 Jambuair (cape), Indo.
125/H3 James (bay), On, Qu,Can.
118/B5 James (pt.), Chile
129/J4 James (riv.), ND, SD,US
132/E4 James (riv.), Va,US
137/F5 Jamesburg, NJ,US
124/G1 James Ross (str.), Nun,Can.
129/J4 Jamestown, ND,US
132/E3 Jamestown, NY,US
135/G2 Jamestown, Tn,US
122/B4 Jamiltepec, Mex.
81/B5 Jammu, India
81/C5 Jammu and Kashmīr (state), India
90/B3 Jāmnagar, India
79/K3 Jāmpur, Pak.
48/H3 Jämsä, Fin.
90/E3 Jamshedpur, India
48/E3 Jämtland (co.), Swe.
90/E3 Jamūi, India
129/H2 Jan (lake), Sk,Can.
70/E3 Janakkala, Fin.
115/K7 Janaúba, Braz.
115/J3 Janaucu (isl.), Braz.
116/B2 Jandaia do Sul, Braz.
64/C4 Jándula (riv.), Sp.
132/B3 Janesville, Wi,US
90/C4 Jangaon, India
90/E3 Jangipur, India
55/K2 Janikowo, Pol.
80/K5 Janīn, WBnk.
68/D3 Janja, Bosn.
47/D1 Jan Mayen (isl.), Nor.
68/D2 Jánoshalma, Hun.
55/M3 Janów Lubelski, Pol.
115/K7 Januária, Braz.
106/C2 Janūb Sīnā' (gov.), Egypt
90/C3 Jaora, India
83/M4 Japan (ctry.)
83/L4 Japan (sea), Asia
85/E3 Japanese Alps (range), Japan
85/E2 Japanese Alps Nat'l Park, Japan
114/E4 Japurá (riv.), Braz.
80/D3 Jarābulus, Syria
64/C2 Jaraíz de la Vera, Sp.
80/K5 Jarash, Jor.
102/H1 Jarbah (isl.), Tun.
117/E2 Jardín América, Arg.
116/C2 Jardinópolis, Braz.
115/H3 Jari (riv.), Braz.
90/E3 Jaridih, India
102/H1 Jarjīs, Tun.
59/E5 Jarny, Fr.
55/J3 Jarocin, Pol.
55/H3 Jaroměř, Czh.
55/M3 Jarosław, Pol.
51/G2 Jarrow, Eng,UK
89/C2 Jars (plain), Laos
59/F6 Jarville-la-Malgrange, Fr.
99/J5 Jarvis (isl.), PacUS
55/L4 Jasło, Pol.
128/D2 Jasper, Ab,Can.
135/G3 Jasper, Al,US
135/F3 Jasper, Ar,US
135/H4 Jasper, Fl,US
135/G3 Jasper, Ga,US
132/C4 Jasper, In,US
134/E4 Jasper, Tx,US
128/D2 Jasper Nat'l Park, Ab, BC,Can.
90/C2 Jaspur, India
55/J2 Jastrowie, Pol.
55/K4 Jastrzębie Zdrój, Pol.
68/E2 Jászapáti, Hun.
68/D2 Jászárokszállás, Hun.
68/D2 Jászberény, Hun.
68/E2 Jászladány, Hun.
68/E2 Jász-Nagykun-Szolnok (co.), Hun.
116/B1 Jataí, Braz.
114/G4 Jatapu (riv.), Braz.
65/E3 Játiva, Sp.
116/B2 Jaú, Braz.
114/F4 Jaú (riv.), Braz.
114/F3 Jauaperi (riv.), Braz.
115/H4 Jauaru (mts.), Braz.
114/F3 Jaua Sarisarinama Nat'l Park, Ven.
114/C6 Jauja, Peru
60/D4 Jaunpass (pass), Swi.
92/C5 Java (isl.), Indo.
92/D5 Java (sea), Indo.
114/D5 Javari (riv.), Braz.
65/F3 Jávea, Sp.
119/J6 Javier (isl.), Chile
68/D1 Javorie (peak), Slvk.
103/Q7 Jawhar (Giohar), Som.
55/J3 Jawor, Pol.
93/J4 Jaya (peak), Indo.
93/K4 Jayapura, Indo.
134/C3 Jayton, Tx,US
53/H3 Jaywick, Eng,UK
78/D5 Jazā'ir Farasān (isls.), SAr.
55/L3 Jędrzejów, Pol.
54/F2 Jeetze (riv.), Ger.
128/C4 Jefferson (peak), Or,US
134/E3 Jefferson, Tx,US
131/J3 Jefferson City (cap.), Mo,US
132/C4 Jeffersonville, In,US
128/G5 Jeffrey City, Wy,US
118/B5 Jeinemeni (peak), Chile
70/E4 Jēkabpils, Lat.
55/J3 Jelcz-Laskowice, Pol.
55/H3 Jelenia Góra, Pol.
90/E2 Jelep (pass), China
70/D4 Jelgava, Lat.
58/C3 Jemappes, Belg.
92/D5 Jember, Indo.
130/F4 Jemez Pueblo, NM,US
93/E4 Jempang (riv.), Indo.
106/C3 Jemsa, Egypt
54/F3 Jena, Ger.
134/E4 Jena, La,US
93/E5 Jeneponto, Indo.
134/E4 Jennings, La,US
124/F2 Jenny Lind (isl.), Nun,Can.
125/H2 Jens Muck (isl.), Nun,Can.
115/L6 Jequié, Braz.
115/K7 Jequitinhonha, Braz.
115/K7 Jequitinhonha (riv.), Braz.
123/G4 Jérémie, Haiti
123/P9 Jerez de García Salinas, Mex.
64/B4 Jerez de la Frontera, Sp.
64/B3 Jerez de los Caballeros, Sp.
137/G5 Jericho, NY,US
80/K6 Jericho (Arīḥā), WBnk.
128/E5 Jerome, Id,US
137/F5 Jersey City, NJ,US
132/B4 Jerseyville, Il,US
80/M9 Jerusalem (dist.), Isr.
80/N9 Jerusalem Walls Nat'l Park, Isr.
80/K6 Jerusalem (Yerushalayim) (cap.), Isr.
128/C3 Jervis (inlet), BC,Can.
68/B2 Jesenice, Slov.
63/K5 Jesi, It.
90/E3 Jessore, Bang.
135/H4 Jesup, Ga,US
133/N6 Jésus (isl.), Qu,Can.
117/D3 Jesús María, Arg.
123/F3 Jesús Menéndez, Cuba
104/A4 Jeta (isl.), GBis.
131/H3 Jetmore, Ks,US
90/B3 Jetpur, India
58/D3 Jeumont, Fr.
57/E1 Jever, Ger.
129/G5 Jewel Cave Nat'l Mon., SD,US
90/D4 Jeypore, India
67/F1 Jezerce (peak), Alb.
55/K2 Jeziorák (lake), Pol.
90/E3 Jhā Jhā, India
90/C3 Jhālawār, India
79/K2 Jhang Sadar, Pak.
90/C2 Jhānsi, India
90/D3 Jharkhand (state), India
90/D3 Jhārsuguda, India
79/K2 Jhelum (riv.), India, Pak.
79/K2 Jhelum, Pak.
90/E3 Jiāganj, India
82/F5 Jialing (riv.), China
87/C4 Jialu (riv.), China
83/L2 Jiamusi, China
88/B2 Ji'an, China
88/B3 Jian (riv.), China
89/E1 Jiang (riv.), China
88/B3 Jiangmen, China
87/D4 Jiangsu (prov.), China
87/D5 Jiangxi (prov.), China
87/E5 Jiangyin, China
88/C2 Jianyang, China
88/D2 Jiaojiang, China
83/J3 Jiaolai (riv.), China
87/C4 Jiaozuo, China
81/C4 Jiashi, China
87/E5 Jiaxing, China
82/D4 Jiayuguan, China
69/F2 Jibou, Rom.
79/G4 Jibsh, Ra's (pt.), Oman
55/H3 Jičín, Czh.
78/C4 Jiddah, SAr.
55/H4 Jihlava, Czh.
55/H4 Jihlavský (reg.), Czh.
102/G1 Jijel, Alg.
69/H2 Jijia (riv.), Rom.
103/P6 Jijiga, Eth.
65/E3 Jijona, Sp.
106/A4 Jilf al Kabīr, Ḥadabat al (upland), Egypt
116/B2 Jilhá (res.), Braz.
55/J4 Jilhava (riv.), Czh.
81/E2 Jili (lake), China
83/K3 Jilin, China
83/J1 Jiliu (riv.), China
65/E2 Jiloca (riv.), Sp.
103/N6 Jīma, Eth.
68/E3 Jimbolia, Rom.
64/C4 Jimena de la Frontera, Sp.
82/B3 Jimsar, China
88/C2 Jin (riv.), China
87/D3 Jinan, China
90/C2 Jīnd, India
55/H4 Jindřichuv Hradec, Czh.
87/B4 Jing (riv.), China
88/C2 Jingdezhen, China
88/B2 Jinggangshan, China
88/D3 Jinghai, China
87/C5 Jingmen, China
88/C2 Jinhua, China
87/C2 Jining, China
87/D4 Jining, China
107/B2 Jinja, Ugan.
122/D5 Jinotega, Nic.
122/D5 Jinotepe, Nic.
87/B4 Jinqian (riv.), China
87/E5 Jinshan, China
91/K2 Jinshi, China
88/D5 Jintotolo (chan.), Phil.
90/C4 Jintūr, India
87/E2 Jinxi, China
88/C2 Jinxi, China
87/E2 Jinzhou, China
114/F6 Ji-Paraná, Braz.
114/F5 Jiparaná (riv.), Braz.
114/B4 Jipijapa, Ecu.
106/B3 Jirgā, Egypt
88/A2 Jishou, China
80/D3 Jisr ash Shughūr, Syria
69/F4 Jiu (riv.), Rom.
88/C2 Jiujiang, China
88/A2 Jiuwan (mts.), China
87/D5 Jixi, China
87/C4 Ji Xian, China
87/D2 Ji Xian, China
106/B2 Jīzah, Pyramids of (Giza) (ruins), Egypt
87/C3 Jize, China
55/H3 Jizera (riv.), Czh.
84/C3 Jizō-zaki (pt.), Japan
78/F5 Jiz', Wādī al (dry riv.), Yem.
116/B3 Joaçaba, Braz.
116/D1 João Monlevade, Braz.
115/M5 João Pessoa, Braz.
116/C1 João Pinheiro, Braz.
117/D2 Joaquín V. González, Arg.
123/F3 Jobabo, Cuba
64/D4 Jódar, Sp.
90/B2 Jodhpur, India
58/D2 Jodoigne, Belg.
48/J3 Joensuu, Fin.
85/F2 Jōetsu, Japan
59/F5 Joeuf, Fr.
108/E2 Johannesburg, SAfr.
130/C4 Johannesburg, Ca,US
128/D4 John Day, Or,US
128/C4 John Day (riv.), Or,US
128/C4 John Day Fossil Beds Nat'l Mon., Or,US
134/C2 John Martin (res.), Co,US
135/H2 Johnson City, Tn,US
134/D4 Johnson City, Tx,US
131/G3 Johnson (Johnson City), Ks,US
136/M3 Johnsons Crossing, Yk,Can.
99/J3 Johnston (atoll), PacUS
52/B3 Johnston, Wal,UK
132/E3 Johnstown, Pa,US
92/B3 Johor Baharu, Malay.
62/B3 Joigny, Fr.
116/B3 Joinville, Braz.
111/W Joinville (isl.), Ant.
103/M6 Jokau, Sudan
48/F2 Jokkmokk, Swe.
48/P6 Jökulsargljufur Nat'l Park, Ice.
138/P16 Joliet, Il,US
132/F2 Joliette, Qu,Can.
134/D4 Jollyville, Tx,US
88/D6 Jolo, Phil.
88/D6 Jolo (isl.), Phil.
92/D5 Jombang, Indo.
61/E3 Jona, Swi.
55/N1 Jonava, Lith.
125/S7 Jones (sound), Nun,Can.
135/F3 Jonesboro, Ar,US
134/E3 Jonesboro, La,US
50/B3 Jonesborough, NI,UK
48/E4 Jönköping, Swe.
48/E4 Jönköping (co.), Swe.
133/G1 Jonquière, Qu,Can.
131/J3 Joplin, Mo,US
78/C2 Jordan (ctry.)
133/R9 Jordan, On,Can.
80/K6 Jordan (riv.), Jor., WBnk.
128/G4 Jordan, Mt,US
130/E2 Jordan (riv.), Ut,US
133/R9 Jordan Station, On,Can.
128/D5 Jordan Valley, Or,US
119/J7 Jorge (cape), Chile
57/G1 Jork, Ger.
134/B3 Jornada del Muerto (val.), NM,US
105/H4 Jos (plat.), Nga.
88/E6 Jose Abad Santos, Phil.
116/B2 José Bonifacio, Braz.
85/F2 Joshin-Etsu Kogen Nat'l Park, Japan
130/D4 Joshua Tree Nat'l Park, Ca,US
48/C3 Jotunheimen Nat'l Park, Nor.
62/C2 Jouanne (riv.), Fr.
58/C6 Jouarre, Fr.
62/D3 Joué-lès-Tours, Fr.
96/B2 Jourama Falls Nat'l Park, Austl.
134/D4 Jourdanton, Tx,US
56/C3 Joure, Neth.
48/J3 Joutseno, Fin.
78/G1 Joveyn (riv.), Iran
91/F2 Jowai, India
136/M3 Joy (mtn.), Yk,Can.
85/L10 Jōyō, Japan
104/A2 Jreïda, Mrta.
87/B5 Ju (riv.), China
123/P9 Juan Aldama, Mex.
128/B3 Juan de Fuca (str.), Can., US
109/G7 Juan de Nova (isl.), Reun., Fr.
113/A6 Juan Fernández (isls.), Chile
123/J5 Juangriego, Ven.
114/C5 Juanjuí, Peru
119/T12 Juan L. Lacaze, Uru.
118/F3 Juárez, Arg.
116/J8 Juatinga (pt.), Braz.
115/K5 Juazeiro, Braz.
115/L5 Juazeiro do Norte, Braz.
103/M7 Juba, Sudan
103/P7 Jubba (riv.), Eth., Som.
65/Y17 Juby (cape), Mor.
64/D3 Júcar (riv.), Sp.
56/D6 Jüchen, Ger.
80/N9 Judaea (reg.), WBnk.
63/L3 Judenburg, Aus.
128/F4 Judith (riv.), Mt,US
106/B3 Juhaynah, Egypt
122/D5 Juigalpa, Nic.
62/E2 Juine (riv.), Fr.
88/D3 Juishui, Tai.
56/D1 Juist (isl.), Ger.
116/K6 Juiz de Fora, Braz.
131/G2 Julesburg, Co,US
114/D7 Juliaca, Peru
63/K3 Julian Alps (mts.), It., Slov.
59/F2 Jülich, Ger.
123/F3 Julio A. Mella, Cuba
79/L2 Jullundur, India
87/C3 Juma (riv.), China
64/E3 Jumilla, Sp.
90/D2 Jumla, Nepal
57/E2 Jümme (riv.), Ger.
90/B3 Junāgadh, India
118/C2 Juncal (peak), Arg., Chile
134/D4 Junction, Tx,US
130/D3 Junction, Ut,US
131/H3 Junction City, Ks,US
128/C4 Junction City, Or,US
116/G8 Jundiaí, Braz.
87/H6 Jundu (mts.), China
136/M4 Juneau (cap.), Ak,US
60/D4 Jungfrau (peak), Swi.
114/C6 Junín, Peru
58/D5 Juniville, Fr.
87/C3 Junji Guan (pass), China
135/F5 Juno Beach, Fl,US
116/B2 Junqueirópolis, Braz.
116/E1 Juparanã (lake), Braz.
133/J1 Jupiter (riv.), Qu,Can.
135/H5 Jupiter, Fl,US
138/A2 Jupiter (mtn.), Wa,US
116/C3 Juquiá, Braz.
116/F8 Juquitiba, Braz.
103/L6 Jur (riv.), Sudan
60/B4 Jura (dept.), Fr.
60/B4 Jura (mts.), Fr.
60/D3 Jura (canton), Swi.
62/C5 Jurançon, Fr.
58/C2 Jurbise, Belg.
50/D3 Jurby Head (pt.), IM,UK
70/D4 Jūrmala, Lat.
114/E4 Juruá (riv.), Braz.
114/G6 Juruena (riv.), Braz.
115/G4 Juruti, Braz.
85/M9 Jushiyama, Japan
118/D2 Justo Daract, Arg.
114/E4 Jutaí (riv.), Braz.
122/D5 Jutiapa, Guat.
122/D5 Juticalpa, Hon.
48/D4 Jutland (pen.), Den.
48/H3 Juva, Fin.
122/E3 Juventud (Pinos) (isl.), Cuba
87/D4 Juye, China
87/C5 Juzhang (riv.), China
68/E4 Južna Morava (riv.), Serb.
48/H3 Jyväskylä, Fin.

K

81/C4 K2 (Godwin Austen) (mtn.), China, Pak.
102/F5 Ka (riv.), Nga.
108/C3 Kaap (plat.), SAfr.
70/D3 Kaarina, Fin.
56/D6 Kaarst, Ger.
68/E2 Kaba, Hun.
93/F5 Kabaena (isl.), Indo.
122/D3 Kabah (ruins), Mex.
107/A3 Kabale, Ugan.
107/A2 Kabalega Nat'l Park, Ugan.
110/E2 Kabalo, D.R. Congo
110/E2 Kabamba (lake), D.R. Congo
93/F2 Kabankalan, Phil.
73/G4 Kabardino-Balkariya, Resp., Rus.
132/C1 Kabinakagami (lake), On,Can.
110/D2 Kabinda, D.R. Congo
66/A5 Kabīyah (lag.), Tun.
110/D3 Kabompo (riv.), Zam.
110/E2 Kabongo, D.R. Congo
79/J2 Kabul (riv.), Afg.
79/J2 Kabul (Kābol) (cap.), Afg.
93/G3 Kaburuang (isl.), Indo.
110/E3 Kabwe, Zam.
68/E4 Kačanik, Serb.
136/H4 Kachemak (bay), Ak,US
91/G2 Kachin (state), Myan.
90/C6 Kadaianallur, India
89/B3 Kadan (isl.), Myan.
55/G3 Kadaň, Czh.
98/G6 Kadavu (isl.), Fiji
102/J7 Kadéï (riv.), CAfr., Congo
69/H5 Kadıköy, Turk.
80/C2 Kadınhanı, Turk.
105/E3 Kadiogo (prov.), Burk.
90/C5 Kadiri, India
80/D3 Kadirli, Turk.
129/H5 Kadoka, SD,US
85/L10 Kadoma, Japan
110/E4 Kadoma, Zim.
105/G4 Kaduna, Nga.
105/G4 Kaduna (riv.), Nga.
105/G4 Kaduna (state), Nga.
103/L5 Kāduqli, Sudan
104/B2 Kaédi, Mrta.
102/H5 Kaélé, Camr.
89/C2 Kaeng Khlo, Thai.
89/B3 Kaeng Krachan Nat'l Park, Thai.
86/D3 Kaesŏng, NKor.
86/D4 Kaesŏng-Si (prov.), NKor.
73/H5 Kafan, Arm.
79/J2 Kafar Jar Ghar (mts.), Afg.
108/D4 Kaffraria (reg.), SAfr.
104/B3 Kaffrine, Sen.
103/K6 Kafia Kingi, Sudan
67/J3 Kafirévs, Akra (cape), Gre.
80/H6 Kafr ad Dawwār, Egypt
80/H6 Kafr ash Shaykh, Egypt
80/H6 Kafr ash Shaykh (gov.), Egypt
80/H6 Kafr az Zayyāt, Egypt
80/N8 Kafr Qari', Isr.
80/M8 Kafr Qāsim, Isr.
110/E4 Kafue, Zam.
110/E4 Kafue (riv.), Zam.
110/E4 Kafue Nat'l Park, Zam.
84/E2 Kaga, Japan
102/J6 Kaga Bandoro, CAfr.
74/G6 Kagan, Uzb.
84/D3 Kagawa (pref.), Japan
69/J5 Kağıthane, Turk.
80/E2 Kağızman, Turk.
84/B5 Kagoshima, Japan
84/B5 Kagoshima (bay), Japan
84/B5 Kagoshima (pref.), Japan
69/J3 Kagul, Mol.
126/W12 Kahana, Hi,US
92/D4 Kahayan (riv.), Indo.
110/C2 Kahemba, D.R. Congo
82/D1 Kahmsara (riv.), Rus.
131/K2 Kahoka, Mo,US
126/T10 Kahoolawe (isl.), Hi,US
48/G1 Kahperusvaara (peak), Fin.
80/D3 Kahramanmaraş, Turk.
79/K3 Kahror Pakka, Pak.
80/D3 Kâhta, Turk.
126/T10 Kahuku (pt.), Hi,US
126/T10 Kahului, Hi,US
110/E1 Kahuzi-Biega Nat'l Park, D.R. Congo
93/H5 Kai (isls.), Indo.
130/D3 Kaibab (plat.), Az,US
85/L9 Kaibara, Japan
93/H5 Kai Besar (isl.), Indo.
81/E3 Kaidu (riv.), China
82/G5 Kaifeng, China
84/D4 Kaifu, Japan
93/H5 Kai Kecil (isl.), Indo.
95/H7 Kaikoura, NZ
91/J2 Kaili, China
126/U11 Kailua, Hi,US
108/B2 Kainab (dry riv.), Namb.
68/B2 Kainach (riv.), Aus.
84/D3 Kainan, Japan
105/G4 Kainji (lake), Nga.
66/A5 Kairouan, Tun.
66/A5 Kairouan (gov.), Tun.
85/H7 Kaisei, Japan
59/G5 Kaiserslautern, Ger.
95/H6 Kaitaia, NZ
81/C6 Kaithal, India
126/T10 Kaiwi (chan.), Hi,US
87/F2 Kaiyuan, China
91/H3 Kaiyuan, China
85/M9 Kaizu, Japan
85/L10 Kaizuka, Japan
48/H2 Kajaani, Fin.
86/E5 Kaji-san (mtn.), SKor.
103/M5 Kākā, Sudan
48/G3 Kakaanpää, Fin.
107/B2 Kakamega, Kenya
85/E3 Kakamigahara, Japan
68/D3 Kakanj, Bosn.
136/M4 Kaketsa (mtn.), BC,Can.
72/E3 Kakhovka, Ukr.
72/E3 Kakhovs'ke (res.), Ukr.
90/D4 Kākināda, India
85/L9 Kako (riv.), Japan
104/B4 Kakrima (riv.), Gui.
85/G2 Kakuda, Japan
107/B2 Kakuma, Kenya
107/A3 Kakuto, Ugan.
121/N2 Kalaallit Nunaat (Greenland) (dpcy.), Den.
110/D3 Kalabo, Zam.
73/G2 Kalach, Rus.
74/H4 Kalachinsk, Rus.
73/G2 Kalach-na-Donu, Rus.
91/G3 Kaladan (riv.), Myan.
126/U11 Ka Lae (cape), Hi,US
110/D5 Kalahari (des.), Afr.
108/C2 Kalahari-Gemsbok Nat'l Park, SAfr.
67/L7 Kalamáki, Gre.
102/H5 Kalamaloué Nat'l Park, Camr.
67/H2 Kalamariá, Gre.
67/H4 Kalamáta, Gre.
132/C3 Kalamazoo, Mi,US
89/C2 Kalasin, Thai.
79/J3 Kalāt, Pak.
66/B5 Kalbīyah (lake), Tun.
48/N7 Kaldakvísl (riv.), Ice.
57/H5 Kalefeld, Ger.
107/A4 Kalemie, D.R. Congo
55/K3 Kalety, Pol.
95/B4 Kalgoorlie-Boulder, Austl.
69/J4 Kaliakra, Nos (pt.), Bul.
92/C5 Kalianda, Indo.
88/D5 Kalibo, Phil.
110/E1 Kalima, D.R. Congo
92/D4 Kalimantan (reg.), Indo.
80/A3 Kálimnos, Gre.
55/L1 Kaliningrad, Rus.
71/W9 Kaliningrad, Rus.
55/K1 Kaliningrad (lag.), Rus.
70/D5 Kaliningradskaya Obl., Rus.
73/H2 Kalininsk, Rus.
72/D1 Kalinkovichi, Bela.
107/A3 Kalisizo, Ugan.
128/E3 Kalispell, Mt,US
55/K3 Kalisz, Pol.
48/G2 Kalix, Swe.
48/G2 Kalixälv (riv.), Swe.
90/E2 Kāliyāganj, India
132/C2 Kalkaska, Mi,US
67/L7 Kallithea, Gre.
48/E3 Kallsjön (lake), Swe.
48/F4 Kalmar, Swe.
48/E4 Kalmar (co.), Swe.
56/B6 Kalmthout, Belg.
73/H3 Kalmykia, Rus.
73/H3 Kalmykia, Resp., Rus.
68/D2 Kalocsa, Hun.
126/T10 Kalohi (chan.), Hi,US
90/B3 Kālol, India
110/E4 Kalomo, Zam.
90/C2 Kālpi, India
54/E2 Kaltenkirchen, Ger.
63/F4 Kaltern (Caldaro), It.
90/D6 Kalu (riv.), SrL.
70/H5 Kaluga, Rus.
70/G5 Kaluzhskaya Obl., Rus.
54/F1 Kalundborg, Den.
72/C2 Kalush, Ukr.
90/C6 Kalutara, SrL.
90/B4 Kalyān, India
71/M4 Kama (res.), Rus.
71/M3 Kama (riv.), Rus.
110/E1 Kama, D.R. Congo
85/J7 Kamagaya, Japan
83/N4 Kamaishi, Japan
126/T10 Kamakou (peak), Hi,US
85/H7 Kamakura, Japan
81/B5 Kamālia, Pak.
80/C2 Kaman, Turk.
104/E2 Kamango (lake), Mali
90/C4 Kāmāreddi, India
90/E3 Kāmārhāti, India
90/A2 Kambar, Pak.
110/E3 Kambove, D.R. Congo
93/F4 Kambuno (peak), Indo.
75/R4 Kamchatka (pen.), Rus.
75/R4 Kamchatskaya Obl., Rus.
69/H4 Kamchiya (riv.), Bul.
57/E5 Kamen, Ger.
72/C2 Kam'yanets'-Podil's'kyy, Ukr.
68/A3 Kamenjak, Rt (cape), Cro.
73/H1 Kamenka, Rus.
81/D1 Kamen'-na-Obi, Rus.
72/G2 Kamensk-Shakhtinskiy, Rus.
71/P4 Kamensk-Ural'skiy, Rus.
84/D3 Kameoka, Japan
85/M10 Kameyama, Japan
128/D4 Kamiah, Id,US
55/H2 Kamień Pomorski, Pol.
85/H7 Kamifukuoka, Japan
83/N3 Kamiisco, Japan
85/M9 Kamiishizu, Japan
126/U11 Kamilo (pt.), Hi,US
110/E2 Kamina, D.R. Congo
85/G1 Kaminoyama, Japan
136/H4 Kamishak (bay), Ak,US
84/B5 Kamiyaku, Japan
128/C3 Kamloops, BC,Can.
89/C4 Kamlot, Camb.
85/L10 Kammaki, Japan
68/B2 Kamnik, Slov.
85/J7 Kamo (riv.), Japan
85/G3 Kamogawa, Japan
84/D3 Kamojima, Japan
63/L2 Kamp (riv.), Aus.
107/B2 Kampala (cap.), Ugan.
92/B3 Kampar (riv.), Indo.
92/B3 Kampar, Malay.
56/C3 Kampen, Neth.
89/B2 Kamphaeng Phet, Thai.
55/L2 Kampinoski Nat'l Park, Pol.
56/D6 Kamp-Lintfort, Ger.
89/D4 Kampong Cham, Camb.

Kampo – Kırık
167

89/D3 **Kampong Chhnang,** Camb.
89/D3 **Kampong Khleang,** Camb.
89/C4 **Kampong Saom,** Camb.
89/C4 **Kampong Saom** (bay), Camb.
89/D4 **Kampong Spoe,** Camb.
89/D3 **Kampong Thum,** Camb.
89/D4 **Kampong Trabek,** Camb.
89/D4 **Kampot,** Camb.
93/H4 **Kamrau** (bay), Indo.
129/H3 **Kamsack,** Sk,Can.
129/H1 **Kamuchawie** (lake), Sk,Can.
122/E6 **Kámuk** (mt.), CR
73/H2 **Kamyshin,** Rus.
125/J3 **Kanaaupscow** (riv.), Qu,Can.
130/D3 **Kanab** (riv.), Az, Ut,US
130/D3 **Kanab,** Ut,US
136/C6 **Kanaga** (isl.), Ak,US
136/C6 **Kanaga** (vol.), Ak,US
85/F3 **Kanagawa** (pref.), Japan
125/K3 **Kanairiktok** (riv.), Nf,Can.
85/L10 **Kanan,** Japan
110/D2 **Kananga,** D.R. Congo
71/K5 **Kanash,** Rus.
132/D4 **Kanawha** (riv.), WV,US
85/E2 **Kanazawa,** Japan
89/B3 **Kanchanaburi,** Thai.
90/C5 **Kānchīpuram,** India
79/J2 **Kandahār,** Afg.
70/G2 **Kandalaksha,** Rus.
70/G2 **Kandalaksha** (gulf), Rus.
99/Y18 **Kandavu** (passg.), Fiji
79/J3 **Kandhkot,** Pak.
90/E3 **Kāndi,** India
93/F3 **Kandi** (cape), Indo.
69/K5 **Kandıra,** Turk.
90/C4 **Kandukūr,** India
90/D6 **Kandy,** SrL.
125/T7 **Kane Basin** (sound), Nun,Can.
102/H5 **Kanem** (reg.), Chad
126/W13 **Kaneohe,** Hi,US
126/W13 **Kaneohe** (bay), Hi,US
110/D5 **Kang,** Bots.
80/D2 **Kangal,** Turk.
92/B2 **Kangar,** Malay.
78/E2 **Kangāvar,** Iran
93/E5 **Kangean** (isls.), Indo.
125/K3 **Kangiqsualujjuaq,** Qu,Can.
125/J2 **Kangiqsujuaq,** Qu,Can.
125/J2 **Kangirsuk,** Qu,Can.
86/E4 **Kangnŭng,** SKor.
81/D5 **Kangrinboqê Feng** (peak), China
91/F2 **Kangto** (peak), China
86/D3 **Kangwŏn-Do** (prov.), NKor.
86/D4 **Kangwŏn-Do** (prov.), SKor.
90/C3 **Kanhān** (riv.), India
85/N9 **Kani,** Japan
85/M9 **Kanie,** Japan
71/K2 **Kanin** (pen.), Rus.
70/J1 **Kanin Nos** (pt.), Rus.
68/E2 **Kanjiža,** Serb.
132/C3 **Kankakee,** Il,US
132/C3 **Kankakee** (riv.), Il, In,Us
104/C4 **Kankan,** Gui.
104/C4 **Kankan** (comm.), Gui.
90/D3 **Kānker,** India
84/C3 **Kanmuri-yama** (mtn.), Japan
135/H3 **Kannapolis,** NC,US
90/C2 **Kannauj,** India
85/H7 **Kannon-zaki** (pt.), Japan
105/H4 **Kano,** Nga.
105/H3 **Kano** (state), Nga.
84/C3 **Kan'onji,** Japan
84/B5 **Kanoya,** Japan
90/D2 **Kānpur,** India
131/H3 **Kansas** (state), US
131/H3 **Kansas** (riv.), Ks,US
131/J3 **Kansas City,** Ks, Mo,US
74/K4 **Kansk,** Rus.
90/D3 **Kantābānji,** India
85/F2 **Kantō** (prov.), Japan
114/G3 **Kanuku** (mts.), Guy.
85/F2 **Kanuma,** Japan
136/H2 **Kanuti Nat'l Wild. Ref.,** Ak,US
108/D2 **Kanye,** Bots.
89/D3 **Kaoh Nhek,** Camb.
88/D3 **Kaohsiung,** Tai.
110/B4 **Kaokoveld** (reg.), Namb.
104/A3 **Kaolack,** Sen.
104/B3 **Kaolack** (reg.), Sen.
110/D3 **Kaoma,** Zam.
126/S9 **Kapaa,** Hi,US
88/E6 **Kapalong,** Phil.
110/D2 **Kapanga,** D.R. Congo
68/E4 **Kapaonik** (upland), Serb.
56/B6 **Kapellen,** Belg.
63/L3 **Kapfenberg,** Aus.
69/H5 **Kapidaği** (pen.), Turk.
98/E4 **Kapingamarangi** (isl.), Micr.
110/E3 **Kapiri Mposhi,** Zam.
125/H3 **Kapiskau** (riv.), On,Can.
103/M7 **Kapoeta,** Sudan
68/C2 **Kapos** (riv.), Hun.
68/C2 **Kaposvár,** Hun.
55/M1 **Kapsukas,** Lith.
92/C4 **Kapuas** (riv.), Indo.
92/D3 **Kapuas Hulu** (mts.), Indo., Malay.
132/D1 **Kapuskasing,** On,Can.
132/D1 **Kapuskasing** (riv.), On,Can.
68/C2 **Kapuvár,** Hun.
71/Q1 **Kara** (riv.), Rus.
74/G2 **Kara** (sea), Rus.
93/H4 **Karabra** (riv.), Indo.
80/C2 **Karabük,** Turk.
80/D3 **Karaca** (peak), Turk.
80/B2 **Karacabey,** Turk.
73/G4 **Karachayevo-Cherkesiya, Resp.,** Rus.
72/E1 **Karachev,** Rus.
79/J4 **Karāchi,** Pak.
90/B4 **Karād,** India
77/R4 **Karaginskiy** (isl.), Rus.
81/E1 **Karagoš** (peak), Rus.
90/C5 **Kāraikkudi,** India
78/F1 **Karaj,** Iran
73/L3 **Karakalpak Aut. Rep.,** Uzb.
81/C4 **Karakax** (riv.), China
80/D2 **Karakaya** (res.), Turk.
93/G3 **Karakelong** (isl.), Indo.
82/E3 **Karakhoto** (ruins), China
80/E2 **Karakoçan,** Turk.
81/C4 **Karakoram** (range), Asia
81/C4 **Karakoram** (pass), China, India
104/C3 **Karakoro** (riv.), Mali, Mrta.
82/E2 **Karakorum** (ruins), Mong.
80/E2 **Karaköse,** Turk.
81/B4 **Karakul'** (lake), Taj.
73/L5 **Karakumy** (des.), Trkm.
79/H1 **Karakyr** (peak), Trkm.
93/E4 **Karam** (riv.), Indo.
80/C3 **Karaman,** Turk.
81/D2 **Karamay,** China
81/D4 **Karamiran** (riv.), China
81/E4 **Karamiran Shankou** (pass), China
69/J5 **Karamürsel,** Turk.
91/G4 **Karan** (state), Myan.
93/E5 **Karangasem,** Indo.
75/S4 **Karanginskiy** (bay), Rus.
75/S4 **Karanginskiy** (isl.), Rus.
90/C3 **Kāranja,** India
89/B2 **Karan (Kayin)** (state), Myan.
80/C3 **Karapınar,** Turk.
84/A3 **Kara-saki** (pt.), Japan
85/M10 **Karasu,** Japan
69/K5 **Karasu,** Turk.
81/C1 **Karasuk,** Rus.
84/A4 **Karatsu,** Japan
67/G3 **Karáva** (peak), Gre.
81/B2 **Karazhal,** Kaz.
106/C5 **Karbaka,** Sudan
78/D2 **Karbalā',** Iraq
68/E2 **Karcag,** Hun.
67/G3 **Kardhítsa,** Gre.
74/D3 **Kareliya, Resp.,** Rus.
107/A4 **Karema,** Tanz.
82/H1 **Karenga** (riv.), Rus.
110/E4 **Kariba** (lake), Zam., Zim.
110/E4 **Kariba,** Zim.
92/C4 **Karimata** (isl.), Indo.
92/C4 **Karimata** (str.), Indo.
90/C4 **Karīmnagar,** India
107/A3 **Karisimbi** (vol.), Rwa.
85/M10 **Kariya,** Japan
103/Q6 **Karkaar** (mts.), Som.
90/B5 **Kārkāl,** India
98/D5 **Karkar** (isl.), PNG
72/E3 **Karkinitsk** (gulf), Ukr.
81/B4 **Karla Marksa, Pik** (peak), Taj.
68/B3 **Karlovac,** Slov.
54/G3 **Karlovarský** (reg.), Czh.
69/G4 **Karlovo,** Bul.
54/G3 **Karlovy Vary** (Karlsbad), Czh.
48/E4 **Karlshamn,** Swe.
48/E4 **Karlskoga,** Swe.
48/E4 **Karlskrona,** Swe.
63/H2 **Karlsruhe,** Ger.
48/E4 **Karlstad,** Swe.
106/B5 **Karmah,** Sudan
90/C4 **Karmāla,** India
80/K5 **Karmel, Har** (Mount Carmel) (mtn.), Isr.
90/C2 **Karnāl,** India
90/C4 **Karnataka** (state), India
134/D4 **Karnes City,** Tx,US
69/H4 **Karnobat,** Bul.
68/A2 **Kärnten** (prov.), Aus.
107/B5 **Karonga,** Malw.
108/C4 **Karoo Nat'l Park,** SAfr.
79/K2 **Karor,** Pak.
93/E5 **Karoso** (cape), Indo.
80/A3 **Kárpathos** (isl.), Gre.
108/M11 **Kars** (riv.), SAfr.
80/E2 **Kars,** Turk.
74/G6 **Karshi,** Uzb.
73/M1 **Kartaly,** Rus.
69/L3 **Kartinitsk** (gulf), Ukr.
55/K1 **Kartuzy,** Pol.
78/E2 **Kārūn** (riv.), Iran
55/K4 **Karviná,** Czh.
90/B5 **Karwar,** India
129/L2 **Kasabonika** (lake), On,Can.
90/E3 **Kāsai** (riv.), India
84/D3 **Kasai,** Japan
110/C1 **Kasai** (riv.), D.R. Congo
85/G2 **Kasama,** Japan
107/A5 **Kasama,** Zam.
85/M9 **Kasamatsu,** Japan
110/E4 **Kasane,** Bots.
84/C3 **Kasaoka,** Japan
90/C5 **Kāsaragod,** India
106/D5 **Kasar, Ras** (cape), Sudan
85/M10 **Kasartori-yama** (peak), Japan
124/F2 **Kasba** (lake), NW,Nun,Can.
84/B5 **Kaseda,** Japan
90/C2 **Kāsganj,** India
79/H1 **Kashaf** (riv.), Iran
78/F2 **Kāshān,** Iran
81/C4 **Kashi,** China
85/L10 **Kashiba,** Japan
84/D3 **Kashihara,** Japan
84/B4 **Kashima,** Japan
85/G3 **Kashima,** Japan
70/H4 **Kashin,** Rus.
85/H7 **Kashiwa,** Japan
85/L10 **Kashiwara,** Japan
85/F2 **Kashiwazaki,** Japan
79/G1 **Kāshmar,** Iran
90/A2 **Kashmor,** Pak.
70/J5 **Kasimov,** Rus.
93/G4 **Kasiruta** (isl.), Indo.
93/H4 **Kasiui** (isl.), Indo.
132/B4 **Kaskaskia** (riv.), Il,US
128/D3 **Kaslo,** BC,Can.
110/E1 **Kasongo,** D.R. Congo
110/C2 **Kasongo-Lunda,** D.R. Congo
73/H4 **Kaspiysk,** Rus.
103/N4 **Kassala,** Sudan
67/H3 **Kassándra** (pen.), Gre.
57/G6 **Kassel,** Ger.
129/K4 **Kasson,** Mn,US
80/C2 **Kastamonu,** Turk.
59/D1 **Kasterlee,** Belg.
67/G2 **Kastoría,** Gre.
67/J4 **Kastrakíou** (lake), Gre.
85/E3 **Kasugai,** Japan
85/F3 **Kasukabe,** Japan
107/A4 **Kasulu,** Tanz.
85/G2 **Kasumiga** (lake), Japan
110/F3 **Kasungu,** Malw.
79/K2 **Kasūr,** Pak.
110/E4 **Kataba,** Zam.
133/G2 **Katahdin** (mtn.), Me,US
107/A4 **Katanga** (prov.), D.R. Congo
110/E2 **Katanga** (reg.), D.R. Congo
85/L10 **Katano,** Japan
107/A4 **Katavi Nat'l Park,** Tanz.
91/F6 **Katchall** (isl.), India
110/D2 **Katea,** D.R. Congo
110/E2 **Katea,** D.R. Congo
67/H2 **Kateríni,** Gre.
136/M4 **Kates Needle** (mtn.), Ak,US
110/F3 **Katete,** Zam.
91/G3 **Katha,** Myan.
90/C2 **Kāthgodām,** India
79/K4 **Kathiawar** (pen.), India
90/E2 **Kāthmāndu** (cap.), Nepal
79/L2 **Kathua,** India
104/C3 **Kati,** Mali
104/D4 **Katiola,** C.d'Iv.
57/H5 **Katlenburg-Lindau,** Ger.
136/H4 **Katmai** (vol.), Ak,US
136/G4 **Katmai Nat'l Park & Prsv.,** Ak,US
55/K3 **Katowice,** Pol.
106/C2 **Kātrīnā, Jabal** (Mt. Catherine) (peak), Egypt
49/C2 **Katrine, Loch** (lake), Sc,UK
105/G3 **Katsina,** Nga.
105/G3 **Katsina** (state), Nga.
105/H5 **Katsina Ala** (riv.), Camr., Nga.
85/H5 **Katsura** (riv.), Japan
84/D3 **Katsuragi,** Japan
85/L10 **Katsuragi-san** (peak), Japan
85/G2 **Katsuta,** Japan
85/G3 **Katsuura,** Japan
132/E1 **Kattawagami** (riv.), On,Can.
107/B5 **Katumbi,** Malw.
81/E1 **Katun'** (riv.), Rus.
81/E1 **Katun'chuya** (riv.), Rus.
56/B4 **Katwijk aan Zee,** Neth.
63/H2 **Katzenbuckel** (peak), Ger.
126/S10 **Kauai** (chan.), Hi,US
126/S9 **Kauai** (isl.), Hi,US
61/G2 **Kaufbeuren,** Ger.
134/D3 **Kaufman,** Tx,US
57/G6 **Kaufungen,** Ger.
48/G3 **Kauhajoki,** Fin.
48/G3 **Kauhanevan-Pohjankankaan Nat'l Park,** Fin.
48/G3 **Kauhava,** Fin.
126/U10 **Kauhola** (pt.), Hi,US
126/U10 **Kauiki Head** (pt.), Hi,US
110/C5 **Kaukaveld** (mts.), Namb.
99/L6 **Kaukura** (atoll), FrPol.
126/R9 **Kaulakahi** (chan.), Hi,US
55/M1 **Kaunas,** Lith.
55/N1 **Kaunas** (res.), Lith.
89/B4 **Kau-ye** (isl.), Myan.
68/F5 **Kavadarci,** FYROM
67/F2 **Kavajë,** Alb.
67/J2 **Kavála,** Gre.
83/M3 **Kavalerovo,** Rus.
90/C5 **Kāvali,** India
98/C4 **Kavangel** (isls.), Palau
90/B5 **Kavaratti,** India
69/J4 **Kavarna,** Bul.
98/E5 **Kavieng,** PNG
134/D2 **Kaw** (lake), Ok,US
106/B5 **Kawa** (ruins), Sudan
85/L10 **Kawachi-Nagano,** Japan
85/M10 **Kawage,** Japan
85/F3 **Kawagoe,** Japan
85/M9 **Kawagoe,** Japan
85/F3 **Kawaguchi,** Japan
126/R10 **Kawaihoa** (pt.), Hi,US
126/S9 **Kawaikini** (peak), Hi,US
85/H7 **Kawajima,** Japan
85/G2 **Kawamata,** Japan
107/A5 **Kawambwa,** Zam.
85/L10 **Kawanishi,** Japan
90/D3 **Kawardha,** India
132/E2 **Kawartha** (lakes), On,Can.
85/F3 **Kawasaki,** Japan
85/M9 **Kawashima,** Japan
126/V12 **Kawela Bay** (Kawela), Hi,US
106/C3 **Kawm Umbū,** Egypt
81/D3 **Kax** (riv.), China
81/C3 **Kaxgar** (riv.), China
136/L2 **Kay** (pt.), Yk,Can.
105/E4 **Kaya,** Burk.
102/J6 **Kayagangiri** (peak), CAfr.
89/B2 **Kayah** (state), Myan.
93/E3 **Kayan** (riv.), Indo.
104/B3 **Kayanga** (riv.), Sen.
128/G5 **Kaycee,** Wy,US
130/E3 **Kayenta,** Az,US
104/C3 **Kayes,** Mali
104/C3 **Kayes** (reg.), Mali
89/B2 **Kayin (Karan)** (state), Myan.
59/F5 **Kayl,** Lux.
93/G3 **Kayoa** (isl.), Indo.
80/C2 **Kayseri,** Turk.
92/B4 **Kayuagung,** Indo.
74/G5 **Kazakhstan** (ctry.)
124/F2 **Kazan** (riv.), Nun,Can.
71/L5 **Kazan',** Rus.
69/G4 **Kazanlŭk,** Bul.
72/D2 **Kazatin,** Ukr.
73/H4 **Kazbek** (peak), Geo.
78/F3 **Kāzerūn,** Iran
55/L3 **Kazimierza Wielka,** Pol.
68/E1 **Kazincbarcika,** Hun.
83/N3 **Kazuno,** Japan
67/J4 **Kéa** (isl.), Gre.
50/B3 **Keady,** NI,UK
137/F5 **Keansburg,** NJ,US
131/H2 **Kearney,** Ne,US
50/C3 **Kearny** (pt.), NI,UK
137/F5 **Kearny,** NJ,US
126/U11 **Keawekaheka** (pt.), Hi,US
80/D2 **Keban** (res.), Turk.
48/F2 **Kebnekaise** (peak), Swe.
103/P6 **K'ebri Dehar,** Eth.
92/C5 **Kebumen,** Indo.
68/D2 **Kecel,** Hun.
68/D2 **Kecskemét,** Hun.
55/M1 **Kėdainiai,** Lith.
59/F5 **Kédange-sur Canner,** Fr.
92/D5 **Kediri,** Indo.
104/B3 **Kédougou,** Sen.
55/K3 **Kędzierzyn-Koźle,** Pol.
138/F6 **Keego Harbor,** Mi,US
124/D2 **Keele** (riv.), NW,Can.
124/C2 **Keele** (peak), Yk,Can.
88/D2 **Keelung,** Tai.
133/F3 **Keene,** NH,US
96/A1 **Keer-weer** (cape), Austl.
108/B2 **Keetmanshoop,** Namb.
67/G3 **Kefallinía** (isl.), Gre.
80/M8 **Kefar Sava,** Isr.
48/M7 **Keflavík,** Ice.
91/J5 **Ke Ga** (cape), Viet.
90/D6 **Kegalla,** SrL.
51/G6 **Kegworth,** Eng,UK
59/G6 **Kehl,** Ger.
51/G4 **Keighley,** Eng,UK
85/L9 **Keihoku,** Japan
97/F5 **Keilor,** Austl.
103/J6 **Kéita** (riv.), Chad
49/D2 **Keith,** Sc,UK
133/H2 **Kejimkujik Nat'l Park,** NS,Can.
68/D2 **Kékes** (peak), Hun.
66/B5 **Kelaa Kbira,** Tun.
93/G4 **Kelang** (isl.), Indo.
92/B3 **Kelang,** Malay.
105/H3 **Kélé-Kélé,** Niger
63/J2 **Kelheim,** Ger.
80/D2 **Kelkit,** Turk.
80/D2 **Kelkit** (riv.), Turk.
124/D2 **Keller** (lake), NW,Can.
137/C2 **Keller** (peak), Ca,US
124/D1 **Kellett** (cape), NW,Can.
128/D4 **Kellogg,** Id,US
50/B2 **Kells,** NI,UK
134/D4 **Kelly A.F.B.,** Tx,US
102/J6 **Kélo,** Chad
128/D3 **Kelowna,** BC,Can.
51/F5 **Kelsall,** Eng,UK
52/A6 **Kelsey Head** (pt.), UK
49/D3 **Kelso,** Sc,UK
128/C4 **Kelso,** Wa,US
92/B3 **Keluang,** Malay.
53/G3 **Kelvedon,** Eng,UK
129/H2 **Kelvington,** Sk,Can.
70/G2 **Kem',** Rus.
70/G2 **Kem'** (riv.), Rus.
52/D3 **Kemble,** Eng,UK
92/D3 **Kemena** (riv.), Malay.
74/J4 **Kemerovo,** Rus.
48/H2 **Kemi,** Fin.
48/H2 **Kemijärvi,** Fin.
48/H2 **Kemijoki** (riv.), Fin.
58/B2 **Kemmel,** Belg.
128/F5 **Kemmerer,** Wy,US
111/W **Kemp** (pen.), Ant.
131/H4 **Kemp** (lake), Tx,US
48/H2 **Kempele,** Fin.
56/D6 **Kempen,** Ger.
56/C6 **Kempenland** (reg.), Belg.
56/B6 **Kempisch** (can.), Belg.
97/E1 **Kempsey,** Austl.
53/F2 **Kempston,** Eng,UK
132/F2 **Kempt** (lake), Qu,Can.
61/G2 **Kempten,** Ger.
108/E2 **Kempton Park,** SAfr.
93/E3 **Kemul** (peak), Indo.
136/H3 **Kenai,** Ak,US
136/J3 **Kenai Fjords Nat'l Park,** Ak,US
51/F3 **Kendal,** Eng,UK
135/H5 **Kendall,** Fl,US
132/C3 **Kendallville,** In,US
93/F4 **Kendari,** Indo.
56/D5 **Kendel** (riv.), Neth., Ger.
90/E3 **Kendrāpāra,** India
104/D4 **Kénédougou** (prov.), Burk.
104/C5 **Kenema,** SLeo.
91/J4 **Keng Deng,** Laos
110/C1 **Kenge,** D.R. Congo
89/B1 **Kēng Tung,** Myan.
104/C3 **Kenié-Baoulé Rsv.,** Mali
53/E2 **Kenilworth,** Eng,UK
102/D1 **Kenitra,** Mor.
50/D1 **Ken, Loch** (lake), Sc,UK
129/H3 **Kenmare,** ND,US
133/S10 **Kenmore,** NY,US
138/C2 **Kenmore,** Wa,US
133/G2 **Kennebec** (riv.), Me,US
133/G3 **Kennebunk,** Me,US
125/T6 **Kennedy** (chan.), Nun,Can.
136/H4 **Kennedy** (str.), Ak,US
56/B4 **Kennemerduinen Nat'l Park,** Neth.
135/F4 **Kenner,** La,US
52/D4 **Kennet** (can.), Eng,UK
53/E4 **Kennet** (riv.), Eng,UK
132/B4 **Kennett,** Mo,US
128/D4 **Kennewick,** Wa,US
132/C1 **Kenogami** (riv.), On,Can.
136/L3 **Keno Hill,** Yk,Can.
132/A1 **Kenora,** On,Can.
138/Q14 **Kenosha,** Wi,US
124/F2 **Kent** (pen.), Nun,Can.
53/G4 **Kent** (co.), Eng,UK
51/F3 **Kent** (riv.), Eng,UK
132/D3 **Kent,** Oh,US
138/C3 **Kent,** Wa,US
81/A3 **Kentau,** Kaz.
97/C3 **Kent Group** (isls.), Austl.
132/D3 **Kenton,** Oh,US
132/C4 **Kentucky** (state), US
132/C4 **Kentucky** (riv.), Ky,US
135/F2 **Kentucky** (lake), Ky, Tn,US
53/G4 **Kent, Vale of** (val.), Eng,UK
133/H2 **Kentville,** NS,Can.
50/D1 **Ken, Water of** (riv.), Sc,UK
107/C2 **Kenya** (ctry.)
107/C3 **Kenya** (mtn.), Kenya
85/H7 **Ken-zaki** (pt.), Japan
129/L5 **Keokuk,** Ia,US
90/E3 **Keonjhar,** India
55/J3 **Kępno,** Pol.
90/C5 **Kerala** (state), India
105/F4 **Kéran Nat'l Park,** Togo
67/H4 **Keratéa,** Gre.
72/F3 **Kerch'** (str.), Rus., Ukr.
72/F3 **Kerch',** Ukr.
128/D3 **Keremeos,** BC,Can.
103/N4 **Keren,** Erit.
70/G2 **Keret'** (lake), Rus.
45/N8 **Kerguélen** (isl.), FrAnt.
92/B4 **Kerinci** (peak), Indo.
81/D4 **Keriya** (riv.), China
81/D4 **Keriya Shankou** (pass), China
56/C5 **Kerkdriel,** Neth.
56/D6 **Kerken,** Ger.
74/G6 **Kerki,** Trkm.
67/H2 **Kerkínis** (lake), Gre.
67/F3 **Kérkira** (Corfu), Gre.
59/F2 **Kerkrade,** Neth.
56/C5 **Kerkwijk,** Neth.
98/G7 **Kermadec** (isls.), NZ
79/G2 **Kermān,** Iran
134/C4 **Kermit,** Tx,US
130/C4 **Kern** (riv.), Ca,US
67/J4 **Kéros** (isl.), Gre.
135/J2 **Kerr** (res.), NC, Va,US
131/J4 **Kerr** (lake), Ok,US
128/F3 **Kerrobert,** Sk,Can.
134/D4 **Kerrville,** Tx,US
52/C2 **Kerry,** Wal,UK
82/G2 **Kerulen** (riv.), China, Mong.
132/D1 **Kesagami** (riv.), On,Can.
69/H5 **Keşan,** Turk.
83/N4 **Kesen'numa,** Japan
53/H2 **Kesgrave,** Eng,UK
90/B3 **Keshod,** India
80/C2 **Keskin,** Turk.
48/H3 **Khersons'ka** (obl.), Fin.
53/H2 **Kessingland,** Eng,UK
56/C5 **Kesteren,** Neth.
51/E2 **Keswick,** Eng,UK
68/C2 **Keszthely,** Hun.
74/J4 **Ket'** (riv.), Rus.
105/F5 **Keta,** Gha.
74/K2 **Keta** (riv.), Rus.
136/M4 **Ketchikan,** Ak,US
128/E5 **Ketchum,** Id,US
105/E5 **Kete Krachi,** Gha.
56/C3 **Ketelmeer** (lake), Neth.
55/L1 **Kętrzyn,** Pol.
53/F2 **Kettering,** Eng,UK
132/C4 **Kettering,** Oh,US
128/C3 **Kettle** (riv.), Can., US
51/F3 **Kettlewell,** Eng,UK
56/B4 **Keukenhof,** Neth.
48/H3 **Keuruu,** Fin.
56/D5 **Kevelaer,** Ger.
123/G3 **Kew,** Trks.
132/B2 **Keweenaw** (bay), Mi,US
132/B2 **Keweenaw** (pen.), Mi,US
135/H5 **Key Largo,** Fl,US
52/D4 **Keynsham,** Eng,UK
137/F5 **Keyport,** NJ,US
132/E4 **Keyser,** WV,US
134/D2 **Keystone** (lake), Ok,US
135/H5 **Key West,** Fl,US
51/G6 **Keyworth,** Eng,UK
55/L4 **Kežmarok,** Slvk.
103/Q5 **Khaanziir** (cape), Som.
83/M2 **Khabarovsk,** Rus.
75/P4 **Khabarovskiy Kray,** Rus.
73/J4 **Khachmas,** Azer.
78/E3 **Khafjī, Ra's al,** SAr.
90/D2 **Khairābād,** India
79/J3 **Khairpur,** Pak.
74/J4 **Khakasiya, Resp.,** Rus.
67/H3 **Khalándrion,** Gre.
67/H2 **Khalkhidhikhi** (pen.), Gre.
67/H3 **Khalkís,** Gre.
82/E1 **Khamar-Daban** (mts.), Rus.
90/D3 **Khamaria,** India
79/J4 **Khambaliya,** India
90/C3 **Khāmgaon,** India
78/D5 **Khamīs Mushayţ,** SAr.
90/D4 **Khammam,** India
79/J1 **Khānābād,** Afg.
78/E2 **Khānaqīn,** Iraq
90/C3 **Khandwa,** India
102/F1 **Khanem** (well), Alg.
79/K2 **Khānewāl,** Pak.
67/J5 **Khaniá,** Gre.
83/L3 **Khanka** (lake), Rus.
82/E1 **Khankh,** Mong.
81/C5 **Khanna,** India
79/K3 **Khānpur,** Pak.
74/G3 **Khanty-Mansiysk,** Rus.
74/G3 **Khanty-Mansiyskiy Aut. Okr.,** Rus.
80/K6 **Khān Yūnus,** Gaza
89/C3 **Khao Chamao-Khao Wong Nat'l Park,** Thai
89/C3 **Khao Khitchakut Nat'l Park,** Thai.
89/B3 **Khao Laem** (res.), Thai.
89/B3 **Khao Sam Roi Yot Nat'l Park,** Thai.
89/C3 **Khao Yai Nat'l Park,** Thai.
90/E3 **Kharagpur,** India
81/B5 **Kharak,** Pak.
79/J3 **Khārān,** Pak.
90/C3 **Khargon,** India
106/B3 **Khārijah, Al Wāḩāt al** (oasis), Egypt
106/C3 **Kharīt, Wādī al** (dry riv.), Egypt
72/F2 **Kharkiv,** Ukr.
72/F2 **Kharkivs'ka Obl.,** Ukr.
69/G5 **Kharmanli,** Bul.
70/J4 **Kharovsk,** Rus.
103/M4 **Khartoum** (Kharţūm) (cap.), Sudan
103/M4 **Khartoum North,** Sudan
73/H4 **Khasavyurt,** Rus.
79/H2 **Khāsh** (riv.), Afg.
79/H3 **Khāsh,** Iran
73/G4 **Khashuri,** Geo.
69/G5 **Khaskovo,** Bul.
69/G5 **Khaskovo** (reg.), Bul.
75/L2 **Khatanga** (gulf), Rus.
75/L2 **Khatanga** (riv.), Rus.
106/C2 **Khatmia** (pass), Egypt
79/G3 **Khaymah, Ra's al,** UAE
103/M4 **Khazzān Jabal Al Awliyā** (dam), Sudan
102/F1 **Khemis Miliana,** Alg.
102/D1 **Khenifra,** Mor.
78/F2 **Khersān** (riv.), Iran
72/E3 **Kherson,** Ukr.
72/E3 **Khersons'ka Obl.,** Ukr.
82/G1 **Khilok,** Rus.
82/F1 **Khilok** (riv.), Rus.
71/W9 **Khimki,** Rus.
67/K3 **Khíos,** Gre.
67/J3 **Khíos** (isl.), Gre.
69/G4 **Khisarya,** Bul.
74/G5 **Khiva,** Uzb.
72/C2 **Khmel'nyts'kyy,** Ukr.
72/C2 **Khmel'nyts'kyy Obl.,** Ukr.
79/J2 **Khojak** (pass), Pak.
89/C3 **Khok Samrong,** Thai.
79/J1 **Kholm,** Afg.
83/N2 **Kholmsk,** Rus.
78/F2 **Khomeynīshahr,** Iran
89/C2 **Khon Kaen,** Thai.
73/G2 **Khopër** (riv.), Rus.
83/M2 **Khor** (riv.), Rus.
81/B4 **Khorog,** Taj.
78/E2 **Khorramābād,** Iran
78/E2 **Khorramshahr,** Iran
89/C2 **Kho Sawai** (plat.), Thai.
136/G3 **Khotol** (mtn.), Ak,US
102/D1 **Khouribga,** Mor.
91/F3 **Khowai,** India
79/J2 **Khowst,** Afg.
67/J2 **Khrisoúpolis,** Gre.
73/L2 **Khromtaū,** Kaz.
67/J5 **Khrysi** (isl.), Gre.
89/C2 **Khuan Ubon Ratana** (res.), Thai.
81/A3 **Khudzhand,** Taj.
90/E3 **Khulna,** Bang.
79/L1 **Khūnjerāb** (pass), Pak.
90/C3 **Khurai,** India
90/E3 **Khurda,** India
90/C2 **Khurja,** India
72/B2 **Khust,** Ukr.
79/J3 **Khuzdār,** Pak.
83/L3 **Khvalynka,** Rus.
78/F2 **Khvonsār,** Iran
80/F2 **Khvoy,** Iran
81/B5 **Khyber** (pass), Afg., Pak.
97/D2 **Kiama,** Austl.
134/E3 **Kiamichi** (mts.), Ok,US
51/G2 **Kibblesworth,** Eng,UK
48/J1 **Kibergneset** (pt.), Nor.
107/A3 **Kibondo,** Tanz.
68/E5 **Kičevo,** FYROM
93/F2 **Kidapawan,** Phil.
52/D2 **Kidderminster,** Eng,UK
107/B2 **Kidepo Valley Nat'l Park,** Ugan.
51/F5 **Kidsgrove,** Eng,UK
52/B3 **Kidwelly,** Wal,UK
54/F1 **Kiel** (bay), Den., Ger.
54/F1 **Kiel,** Ger.
55/L3 **Kielce,** Pol.
51/F1 **Kielder,** Eng,UK
51/F1 **Kielder** (res.), Eng,UK
89/D1 **Kien An,** Viet.
89/D4 **Kien Duc,** Viet.
89/D4 **Kien Thanh,** Viet.
57/E6 **Kierspe,** Ger.
72/D2 **Kiev** (Kyyiv) (cap.), Ukr.
104/C2 **Kiffa,** Mrta.
67/L6 **Kifisiá,** Gre.
78/D2 **Kifrī,** Iraq
107/A3 **Kigali** (cap.), Rwa.
107/A4 **Kigoma,** Tanz.
107/A4 **Kigoma** (prov.), Tanz.
126/T10 **Kihei,** Hi,US
84/D4 **Kii** (chan.), Japan
84/D4 **Kii** (mts.), Japan
81/D3 **Kiines** (riv.), China
126/R9 **Kikepa** (pt.), Hi,US
136/H2 **Kikiktat** (mtn.), Ak,US
68/E3 **Kikinda,** Serb.
110/C2 **Kikwit,** D.R. Congo
49/C3 **Kilbirnie,** Sc,UK
133/Q9 **Kilbride,** On,Can.
50/B5 **Kildare** (co.), Ire.
70/G1 **Kil'den** (isl.), Rus.
134/E3 **Kilgore,** Tx,US
51/H3 **Kilham,** Eng,UK
125/R7 **Kilian** (isl.), Nun,Can.
107/C3 **Kilimanjaro** (prov.), Tanz.
69/K5 **Kilimli,** Turk.
107/C4 **Kilindoni,** Tanz.
80/D3 **Kilis,** Turk.
72/D3 **Kiliya,** Ukr.
50/B3 **Kilkeel,** NI,UK
49/B4 **Kilkenny,** Ire.
50/A6 **Kilkenny** (co.), Ire.
67/H2 **Kilkís,** Gre.
128/F2 **Killam,** Ab,Can.
51/G5 **Killamarsh,** Eng,UK
96/H8 **Killara,** Austl.
129/J3 **Killarney,** Mb,Can.
49/A4 **Killarney,** Ire.
129/H4 **Killdeer,** ND,US
49/C2 **Killearn,** Sc,UK
134/D4 **Killeen,** Tx,US
49/C2 **Killin,** Sc,UK
50/C3 **Killinchy,** NI,UK
125/K2 **Killinek** (isl.), Nun,Can.
67/H4 **Killíni** (peak), Gre.
50/C3 **Killough,** NI,UK
50/A2 **Killyclogher,** NI,UK
50/C3 **Killyleagh,** NI,UK
50/B5 **Kilmacanoge,** Ire.
49/C3 **Kilmarnock,** Sc,UK
52/B5 **Kilmar Tor** (hill), Eng,UK
50/B6 **Kilmichael** (pt.), Ire.
50/B1 **Kilraghts,** NI,UK
50/B2 **Kilrea,** NI,UK
107/C5 **Kilwa Masoko,** Tanz.
50/C2 **Kilwaughter,** NI,UK
49/C3 **Kilwinning,** Sc,UK
129/H5 **Kimball,** Ne,US
129/J5 **Kimball,** SD,US
98/E5 **Kimbe,** PNG
96/B2 **Kimberley** (cape), Austl.
95/B2 **Kimberley** (plat.), Austl.
128/E3 **Kimberley,** BC,Can.
108/D3 **Kimberley,** SAfr.
86/E2 **Kimch'aek,** NKor.
86/D4 **Kimch'ŏn,** SKor.
86/E5 **Kimhae,** SKor.
85/F3 **Kimitsu,** Japan
86/D5 **Kimje,** SKor.
67/J4 **Kímolos** (isl.), Gre.
72/F1 **Kimovsk,** Rus.
110/D2 **Kimpanga,** D.R. Congo
70/H4 **Kimry,** Rus.
93/E2 **Kinabalu, Gunung** (peak), Malay.
93/E2 **Kinabatangan** (riv.), Malay.
128/D2 **Kinbasket** (lake), BC,Can.
128/G3 **Kincaid,** Sk,Can.
132/D2 **Kincardine,** On,Can.
97/B2 **Kinchega Nat'l Park,** Austl.
110/D2 **Kindambi,** D.R. Congo
63/L3 **Kindberg,** Aus.
51/G5 **Kinder Scout** (mtn.), Eng,UK
104/B4 **Kindia,** Gui.
104/B4 **Kindia** (comm.), Gui.
110/E1 **Kindu,** D.R. Congo
73/J1 **Kinel',** Rus.
70/J4 **Kineshma,** Rus.
53/E2 **Kineton,** Eng,UK
97/C3 **King** (isl.), Austl.
96/B4 **King** (peak), Austl.
128/B2 **King** (isl.), BC,Can.
136/N4 **King** (mtn.), BC,Can.
136/K3 **King** (peak), Yk,Can.
96/C4 **Kingaroy,** Austl.
125/R7 **King Christian** (isl.), Nun,Can.
121/P3 **King Christian IX Land** (reg.), Grld.
121/Q2 **King Christian X Land** (reg.), Grld.
133/Q8 **King City,** On,Can.
130/B3 **King City,** Ca,US
131/H4 **Kingfisher,** Ok,US
121/N3 **King Frederik VI Coast** (reg.), Grld.
121/Q2 **King Frederik VIII Land** (reg.), Grld.
99/L6 **King George** (isl.), FrPol.
132/E4 **King George,** Va,US
97/C3 **Kinglake Nat'l Park,** Austl.
99/J4 **Kingman** (reef), PacUS
130/D4 **Kingman,** Az,US
131/H3 **Kingman,** Ks,US
137/E5 **King of Prussia,** Pa,US
130/C3 **Kings** (riv.), Ca,US
130/E2 **Kings** (peak), Ut,US
52/C6 **Kingsbridge,** Eng,UK
130/C3 **Kings Canyon Nat'l Park,** Ca,US
53/E4 **Kingsclere,** Eng,UK
53/F1 **King's Cliffe,** Eng,UK
52/D2 **Kingsland,** Eng,UK
53/F3 **Kings Langley,** Eng,UK
53/G1 **King's Lynn,** Eng,UK
135/H2 **Kingsport,** Tn,US
53/E2 **Kings Sutton,** Eng,UK
52/C5 **Kingsteignton,** Eng,UK
97/C4 **Kingston,** Austl.
132/E2 **Kingston,** On,Can.
123/F4 **Kingston** (cap.), Jam.
98/F7 **Kingston,** Austl.
132/F3 **Kingston,** NY,US
97/A3 **Kingston South East,** Austl.
51/H4 **Kingston upon Hull** (co.), Eng,UK
53/F4 **Kingston upon Thames,** Eng,UK
123/J5 **Kingstown** (cap.), StV.
135/J3 **Kingstree,** SC,US
106/C3 **Kings, Valley of the,** Egypt
134/D5 **Kingsville,** Tx,US
52/D2 **Kingswinford,** Eng,UK
52/D4 **Kingswood,** Eng,UK
52/C2 **Kington,** Eng,UK
124/G2 **King William** (isl.), Nun,Can.
108/D4 **King William's Town,** SAfr.
136/L4 **Kinkaid** (mtn.), Ak,US
110/B1 **Kinkala,** Congo
84/D3 **Kinki** (prov.), Japan
104/B4 **Kinkon, Chutes de** (falls), Gui.
50/E5 **Kinmel,** Wal,UK
48/E4 **Kinna,** Swe.
49/E2 **Kinnairds Head** (pt.), Sc,UK
84/D3 **Kino** (riv.), Japan
59/E1 **Kinrooi,** Belg.
49/D2 **Kinross,** Sc,UK
133/R8 **Kinsale,** On,Can.
110/C1 **Kinshasa** (cap.), D.R. Congo
131/H3 **Kinsley,** Ks,US
135/J3 **Kinston,** NC,US
105/E4 **Kintampo,** Gha.
49/D2 **Kintore,** Sc,UK
50/C1 **Kintyre, Mull of** (pt.), Sc,UK
85/F2 **Kinu** (riv.), Japan
103/M7 **Kinyeti** (peak), Sudan
67/G4 **Kiparissía** (gulf), Gre.
132/E2 **Kipawa** (lake), Qu,Can.
107/A4 **Kipili,** Tanz.
129/H3 **Kipling,** Sk,Can.
50/B5 **Kippure** (mtn.), Ire.
110/E3 **Kipushi,** D.R. Congo
85/N10 **Kira,** Japan
67/H3 **Kira Panayía** (isl.), Gre.
57/F6 **Kirchhundem,** Ger.
57/F4 **Kirchlengern,** Ger.
57/G3 **Kirchlinteln,** Ger.
50/C3 **Kircubbin,** NI,UK
50/D2 **Kircudbright** (bay), Sc,UK
75/L4 **Kirensk,** Rus.
81/B3 **Kirgizskiy** (mts.), Kyr.
98/H5 **Kiribati** (ctry.)
80/D3 **Kırıkhan,** Turk.
80/C2 **Kırıkkale,** Turk.

168
Kirik – Kyust

82/C3 **Kirikkuduk,** China
70/G4 **Kirishi,** Rus.
84/B5 **Kirishima-Yaku Nat'l Park,** Japan
84/B5 **Kirishima-yama** (mtn.), Japan
99/K4 **Kiritimati** (Christmas) (atoll), Kiri.
51/G4 **Kirkburton,** Eng,UK
51/F5 **Kirkby,** Eng,UK
51/G5 **Kirkby in Ashfield,** Eng,UK
51/F3 **Kirkby Lonsdale,** Eng,UK
51/H3 **Kirkbymoorside,** Eng,UK
51/F3 **Kirkby Stephen,** Eng,UK
49/D2 **Kirkcaldy,** Sc,UK
50/C2 **Kirkcolm,** Sc,UK
50/D2 **Kirkcowan,** Sc,UK
50/D2 **Kirkcudbright,** Sc,UK
90/B4 **Kirkee,** India
48/J1 **Kirkenes,** Nor.
51/F4 **Kirkham,** Eng,UK
50/D2 **Kirkinner,** Sc,UK
138/C2 **Kirkland,** Wa,US
132/D1 **Kirkland Lake,** On,Can.
69/H5 **Kırklareli,** Turk.
69/H5 **Kırklareli** (prov.), Turk.
51/G4 **Kirklees** (co.), Eng,UK
50/D3 **Kirkmichael,** IM,UK
111/M **Kirkpatrick** (mtn.), Ant.
131/J2 **Kirksville,** Mo,US
49/D2 **Kirkton of Glenisla,** Sc,UK
80/F3 **Kirkūk,** Iraq
59/G4 **Kirn,** Ger.
72/E1 **Kirov,** Rus.
71/L4 **Kirov,** Rus.
71/L4 **Kirovskaya Obl.,** Rus.
71/L4 **Kirovo-Chepetsk,** Rus.
72/E2 **Kirovohrad,** Ukr.
72/D2 **Kirovohrads'ka Obl.,** Ukr.
49/D2 **Kirriemuir,** Sc,UK
73/G1 **Kirsanov,** Rus.
80/C2 **Kırşehir,** Turk.
51/H6 **Kirton,** Eng,UK
51/H5 **Kirton in Lindsey,** Eng,UK
48/G2 **Kiruna,** Swe.
85/F2 **Kiryū,** Japan
103/L7 **Kisangani,** D.R. Congo
85/F3 **Kisarazu,** Japan
55/K5 **Kisbér,** Hun.
74/J4 **Kiselevsk,** Rus.
90/E2 **Kishanganj,** India
90/B2 **Kishangarh,** India
84/D3 **Kishiwada,** Japan
90/F3 **Kishorganj,** Bang.
79/L2 **Kishtwar,** India
138/N15 **Kishwaukee** (riv.), Il,US
107/B3 **Kisii,** Kenya
136/B6 **Kiska** (isl.), Ak,US
136/B5 **Kiska** (vol.), Ak,US
128/C2 **Kiskatinaw** (riv.), BC,Can.
129/J2 **Kiskitto** (lake), Mb,Can.
68/D2 **Kiskőrös,** Hun.
68/D2 **Kiskunfélegyháza,** Hun.
68/D2 **Kiskunhalas,** Hun.
68/D2 **Kiskunmajsa,** Hun.
68/D2 **Kiskunsági Nat'l Park,** Hun.
73/G4 **Kislovodsk,** Rus.
85/E3 **Kiso** (riv.), Japan
85/M9 **Kisogawa,** Japan
135/H4 **Kissimmee,** Fl,US
135/H4 **Kissimmee** (lake), Fl,US
129/H2 **Kississing** (lake), Mb,Can.
68/E2 **Kisújszállás,** Hun.
107/B3 **Kisumu,** Kenya
68/F1 **Kisvárda,** Hun.
85/G2 **Kita** (inlet), Japan
104/C3 **Kita,** Mali
85/M9 **Kitagata,** Japan
85/G2 **Kita-Ibaraki,** Japan
85/F2 **Kitakata,** Japan
84/B4 **Kitakyūshū,** Japan
107/B2 **Kitale,** Kenya
83/N3 **Kitami,** Japan
83/N2 **Kitami** (mts.), Japan
85/H6 **Kitamoto,** Japan
132/D3 **Kitchener,** On,Can.
48/J3 **Kitee,** Fin.
67/H4 **Kíthira** (isl.), Gre.
67/J4 **Kíthnos** (isl.), Gre.
128/A2 **Kitimat,** BC,Can.
128/A2 **Kitimat Arm** (inlet), BC,Can.
138/B2 **Kitsap Lake-Erlands Point,** Wa,US
137/E4 **Kittatinny** (mts.), NJ, Pa,US
133/G3 **Kittery,** Me,US
110/E3 **Kitwe,** Zam.
63/K3 **Kitzbühel,** Aus.
63/J2 **Kitzingen,** Ger.
48/H3 **Kiuruvesi,** Fin.
48/H2 **Kivalo** (mts.), Fin.
70/E4 **Kiviõli,** Est.
107/A3 **Kivu** (lake), Rwa., D.R. Congo
85/H7 **Kiyose,** Japan
85/M9 **Kiyosu,** Japan
110/C2 **Kizamba,** D.R. Congo
71/N4 **Kizel,** Rus.
81/B4 **Kizil** (riv.), China
80/C2 **Kızılcahamam,** Turk.
80/C2 **Kızılırmak** (riv.), Turk.
80/E3 **Kızıltepe,** Turk.
73/H4 **Kizlyar,** Rus.
85/L10 **Kizu,** Japan
84/E3 **Kizu** (riv.), Japan
73/L5 **Kizyl-Arvat,** Trkm.
70/C1 **Kjerkestinden** (peak), Nor.
48/E2 **Kjølen** (Kölen) (mts.), Nor., Swe.
68/D3 **Kladanj,** Bosn.
55/H3 **Kladno,** Czh.
68/F3 **Kladovo,** Serb.
63/L3 **Klagenfurt,** Aus.
70/D5 **Klaipėda,** Lith.
128/C5 **Klamath** (mts.), Ca, Or,US
128/C5 **Klamath** (riv.), Ca, Or,US
128/C5 **Klamath Falls,** Or,US
74/B3 **Klar** (riv.), Swe.
48/E3 **Klarälven** (riv.), Swe.
56/E3 **Klazienaveen,** Neth.
59/G5 **Kleinblittersdorf,** Ger.
133/Q8 **Kleinburg,** On,Can.
57/F3 **Kleine Aue** (riv.), Ger.
55/G3 **Kleine Elster** (riv.), Ger.
59/E2 **Kleine Gete** (riv.), Belg.
56/B6 **Kleine Nete** (riv.), Belg.
108/Q12 **Kleinolifants** (riv.), SAfr.
48/C3 **Kleppestø,** Nor.
108/D2 **Klerksdorp,** SAfr.
56/D5 **Kleve,** Ger.
72/E1 **Klintsy,** Rus.
108/E2 **Klip** (riv.), SAfr.
68/C3 **Ključ,** Bosn.
55/K2 **Kłodawa,** Pol.
55/J3 **Kłodzko,** Pol.
57/F3 **Klosterbach** (riv.), Ger.
63/M2 **Klosterneuburg,** Aus.
63/L3 **Klosterwappen** (peak), Aus.
54/F2 **Klötze,** Ger.
136/L3 **Kluane,** Yk,Can.
136/K3 **Kluane Nat'l Park,** Yk,Can.
55/K3 **Kluczbork,** Pol.
136/L3 **Klukshu,** Yk,Can.
56/B5 **Klundert,** Neth.
57/E3 **Klüstenkanal** (can.), Ger.
70/J4 **Klyaz'ma** (riv.), Rus.
75/S4 **Klyuchevskaya** (peak), Rus.
51/G3 **Knaresborough,** Eng,UK
48/C3 **Knarrevik,** Nor.
53/F3 **Knebworth,** Eng,UK
129/K2 **Knee** (lake), Mb,Can.
69/G4 **Knezha,** Bul.
128/B3 **Knight** (inlet), BC,Can.
52/C2 **Knighton,** Wa,UK
68/C3 **Knin,** Cro.
63/L3 **Knittelfeld,** Aus.
68/F4 **Knjaževac,** Serb.
93/F1 **Knob** (peak), Phil.
50/B2 **Knockcloghrim,** NI,UK
50/B1 **Knocklayd** (mtn.), NI,UK
58/C1 **Knokke-Heist,** Belg.
108/A2 **Knoll** (pt.), Namb.
67/J5 **Knosós** (Knossos) (ruins), Gre.
51/F4 **Knott End,** Eng,UK
51/G4 **Knottingley,** Eng,UK
51/F5 **Knowsley** (co.), Eng,UK
111/G **Knox** (coast), Ant.
97/G5 **Knox,** Austl.
136/M4 **Knox** (cape), BC,Can.
135/H3 **Knoxville,** Tn,US
51/F5 **Knutsford,** Eng,UK
108/C4 **Knysna,** SAfr.
83/M2 **Ko** (peak), Rus.
84/B5 **Kobayashi,** Japan
84/D3 **Kōbe,** Japan
54/G1 **København** (Copenhagen) (cap.), Den.
93/G4 **Kobipato** (peak), Indo.
59/G3 **Koblenz,** Ger.
55/N2 **Kobrin,** Bela.
136/G2 **Kobuk** (riv.), Ak,US
136/G2 **Kobuk Valley Nat'l Park,** Ak,US
85/F3 **Kobushi-ga-take** (mtn.), Japan
69/J5 **Kocaeli** (prov.), Turk.
68/F5 **Kočani,** FYROM
68/B3 **Kočevje,** Slov.
125/J2 **Koch** (isl.), Nun,Can.
63/H2 **Kocher** (riv.), Ger.
84/C4 **Kōchi,** Japan
84/C4 **Kōchi** (pref.), Japan
136/H4 **Kodiak,** Ak,US
136/H4 **Kodiak** (isl.), Ak,US
136/H4 **Kodiak Nat'l Wild. Ref.,** Ak,US
90/B3 **Kodinār,** India
103/M6 **Kodok,** Sudan
69/H2 **Kodry** (hills), Mol.
58/B1 **Koekelare,** Belg.
90/D3 **Koel** (riv.), India
59/F5 **Koenigsmacker,** Fr.
130/D4 **Kofa** (mts.), Az,US
93/G4 **Kofiau** (isl.), Indo.
105/E5 **Koforidua,** Gha.
85/F3 **Kōfu,** Japan
85/F2 **Koga,** Japan
85/H7 **Koganei,** Japan
54/G1 **Køge,** Den.
54/G1 **Køge Bugt** (bay), Den.
104/B4 **Kogon** (riv.), Gui.
79/K2 **Kohāt,** Pak.
91/F2 **Kohīma,** India
70/E4 **Kohtla-Järve,** Est.
86/D5 **Kohŭng,** SKor.
122/D4 **Kohunlich** (ruins), Mex.
108/A2 **Koichab** (dry riv.), Namb.
136/K3 **Koidern,** Yk,Can.
86/E5 **Kŏje** (isl.), SKor.
55/L4 **Kojšovská Hol'a** (peak), Slvk.
89/B1 **Kok** (riv.), Myan.
85/M10 **Kōka,** Japan
85/J7 **Kokai** (riv.), Japan
81/B3 **Kokand,** Uzb.
48/G3 **Kokkola,** Fin.
104/C3 **Kokofata,** Mali
126/W13 **Koko Head** (crater), Hi,US
107/A2 **Kokola,** D.R. Congo
132/C3 **Kokomo,** In,US
90/F2 **Kokrajhar,** India
81/C3 **Kokshaal-Tau** (mts.), Kyr.
58/B1 **Koksijde,** Belg.
125/K3 **Koksoak** (riv.), Qu,Can.
81/A1 **Kökshetaū,** Kaz.
108/E3 **Kokstad,** SAfr.
84/B5 **Kokubu,** Japan
70/H1 **Kola** (pen.), Rus.
70/G1 **Kola** (riv.), Rus.
93/F4 **Kolaka,** Indo.
90/C5 **Kolār,** India
68/D4 **Kolašin,** Mont.
54/G5 **Kolbermoor,** Ger.
55/L3 **Kolbuszowa,** Pol.
104/B3 **Kolda,** Sen.
104/B3 **Kolda** (reg.), Sen.
54/E1 **Kolding,** Den.
48/E2 **Kölen** (Kjølen) (mts.), Nor., Swe.
70/F4 **Kolgompya** (cape), Rus.
71/K1 **Kolguyev** (isl.), Rus.
90/B4 **Kolhāpur,** India
104/B3 **Koliba** (riv.), Gui.
55/H3 **Kolín,** Czh.
70/D4 **Kolkasrags** (pt.), Lat.
90/E3 **Kolkata** (Calcutta), India
56/D2 **Kollum,** Neth.
56/D7 **Köln** (Cologne), Ger.
55/L2 **Kolno,** Pol.
72/A1 **Koło,** Pol.
107/B4 **Kolo,** Tanz.
55/H1 **Kołobrzeg,** Pol.
104/C3 **Kolokani,** Mali
72/F1 **Kolomna,** Rus.
72/C2 **Kolomyya,** Ukr.
90/C6 **Kolonnawa,** SrL.
104/D3 **Kolossa** (riv.), Mali
74/J4 **Kolpashevo,** Rus.
71/T7 **Kolpino,** Rus.
68/E3 **Kolubara** (riv.), Serb
55/K3 **Koluszki,** Pol.
71/N2 **Kolva** (riv.), Rus.
110/E3 **Kolwezi,** D.R. Congo
75/R2 **Kolyma** (lowland), Rus.
75/R3 **Kolyma** (range), Rus.
75/R3 **Kolyma** (riv.), Rus.
68/F4 **Kom** (peak), Bul.
85/H7 **Koma** (riv.), Japan
68/E2 **Komádi,** Hun.
105/H4 **Komadugu Gana** (riv.), Nga.
105/H3 **Komadugu Yobé** (riv.), Nga.
85/H7 **Komae,** Japan
85/E3 **Komagane,** Japan
85/M9 **Komaki,** Japan
75/S4 **Komandorskiye** (isls.), Rus.
55/K5 **Komárno,** Slvk.
68/D2 **Komárom,** Hun.
68/D2 **Komárom-Esztergom** (co.), Hun.
84/E2 **Komatsu,** Japan
84/D4 **Komatsushima,** Japan
71/M2 **Komi, Resp.,** Rus.
71/M3 **Komi-Permyatskiy Aut. Okr.,** Rus.
68/D2 **Komló,** Hun.
72/F2 **Kommunarsk,** Ukr.
93/E5 **Komodo Isl. Nat'l Park,** Indo.
104/E5 **Komoé** (riv.), C.d'Iv.
104/E4 **Komoé Nat'l Park,** C.d'Iv.
84/E3 **Komono,** Japan
67/J2 **Komotiní,** Gre.
108/D3 **Kompasberg** (peak), SAfr.
69/J2 **Komrat,** Mol.
75/L1 **Komsomolets** (isl.), Rus.
71/P2 **Komsomol'skiy,** Rus.
83/M1 **Komsomol'sk-na-Amure,** Rus.
67/K3 **Kömür** (pt.), Turk.
70/H4 **Konakovo,** Rus.
85/M10 **Kōnan,** Japan
85/M9 **Kōnan,** Japan
97/D2 **Konangra-Boyd Nat'l Park,** Austl.
93/F4 **Konaweha** (riv.), Indo.
82/G1 **Konda** (riv.), Rus.
70/G3 **Kondopoga,** Rus.
79/J1 **Kondūz,** Afg.
89/C4 **Kong** (isl.), Camb.
81/A2 **Köng** (riv.), Kaz.
89/D3 **Kong** (riv.), Laos
86/D4 **Kongju,** SKor.
110/E2 **Kongolo,** D.R. Congo
85/L10 **Kongō-zan** (peak), Japan
48/D4 **Kongsberg,** Nor.
48/E3 **Kongsvinger,** Nor.
81/C4 **Kongur Shan** (peak), China
107/C4 **Kongwa,** Tanz.
55/K3 **Koniecpol,** Pol.
57/H4 **Königslutter am Elm,** Ger.
59/G2 **Königswinter,** Ger.
55/G2 **Königs Wusterhausen,** Ger.
55/K2 **Konin,** Pol.
60/D4 **Köniz,** Swi.
68/C4 **Konjic,** Bosn.
108/B2 **Konkiep** (dry riv.), Namb.
104/B4 **Konkouré** (riv.), Gui.
72/E2 **Konotop,** Ukr.
81/E3 **Konqi** (riv.), China
55/L3 **Końskie,** Pol.
55/L2 **Konstancin-Jeziorna,** Pol.
72/F2 **Konstantinovka,** Ukr.
55/K3 **Konstantynów Łódzki,** Pol.
61/F2 **Konstanz,** Ger.
58/D1 **Kontich,** Belg.
48/J3 **Kontiolahti,** Fin.
89/E3 **Kon Tum,** Viet.
80/C3 **Konya,** Turk.
59/F4 **Konz,** Ger.
128/E3 **Koocanusa** (lake), Can., US
128/D3 **Kootenai** (riv.), Id, Mt,US
128/D3 **Kootenay** (lake), BC,Can.
128/D3 **Kootenay Nat'l Park,** BC,Can.
90/B4 **Kopargaon,** India
48/N7 **Kópavogur,** Ice.
104/D5 **Kope** (peak), C.d'Iv.
55/G2 **Köpenick,** Ger.
71/P5 **Kopeysk,** Rus.
72/G4 **Kop Gecidi** (pass), Turk.
103/K7 **Kopia,** D.R. Congo
70/C4 **Köping,** Swe.
93/F5 **Kopondei** (cape), Indo.
48/E3 **Kopparberg** (co.), Swe.
83/M2 **Koppi** (riv.), Rus.
68/C2 **Koprivnica,** Cro.
78/F2 **Kor** (riv.), Iran
85/M9 **Kōra,** Japan
67/G2 **Korab** (peak), Alb.
63/L4 **Korana** (riv.), Bosn., Cro.
90/D4 **Koraput,** India
90/D3 **Korba,** India
57/F6 **Korbach,** Ger.
67/G2 **Korçë,** Alb.
68/C4 **Korčula** (isl.), Cro.
68/C4 **Korčulanski** (chan.), Cro.
78/F1 **Kord Kūy,** Iran
86/B3 **Korea** (bay), China, NKor.
84/A4 **Korea** (str.), Japan, SKor.
86/D3 **Korea, North** (ctry.)
86/D4 **Korea, South** (ctry.)
72/F3 **Korenovsk,** Rus.
104/D4 **Korhogo,** C.d'Iv.
67/H4 **Kórinthos** (Corinth), Gre.
68/C2 **Kőris-hegy** (peak), Hun.
85/G2 **Kōriyama,** Japan
102/J3 **Korizo, Passe de** (pass), Chad
75/R3 **Korkodon** (riv.), Rus.
80/B3 **Korkuteli,** Turk.
81/E3 **Korla,** China
80/J4 **Kormakiti** (cape), Cyp.
68/B4 **Kornat** (isl.), Cro.
99/Z18 **Koro** (isl.), Fiji
98/G6 **Koro** (sea), Fiji
69/K5 **Köroğlu** (peak), Turk.
107/C4 **Korogwe,** Tanz.
88/E6 **Koronadal,** Phil.
67/H2 **Korónia** (lake), Gre.
55/J2 **Koronowo,** Pol.
67/L7 **Koropí,** Gre.
98/C4 **Koror** (cap.), Palau
68/E2 **Körös** (riv.), Hun.
72/D2 **Korosten',** Ukr.
72/D2 **Korostyshev,** Ukr.
71/P1 **Korotaikha** (riv.), Rus.
102/J4 **Koro Toro,** Chad
136/D5 **Korovin** (vol.), Ak,US
83/N2 **Korsakov,** Rus.
56/D6 **Korschenbroich,** Ger.
54/F1 **Korsør,** Den.
58/C1 **Kortemark,** Belg.
59/E2 **Kortenaken,** Belg.
58/D2 **Kortenberg,** Belg.
59/E2 **Kortessem,** Belg.
58/C2 **Kortrijk,** Belg.
105/H5 **Korup Nat'l Park,** Camr.
77/R3 **Koryak** (range), Rus.
75/S3 **Koryakskiy Aut. Okr.,** Rus.
71/K3 **Koryazhma,** Rus.
85/L10 **Kōryō,** Japan
80/A3 **Kós** (isl.), Gre.
85/E3 **Kosai,** Japan
84/A3 **Ko-saki** (pt.), Japan
89/C3 **Ko Samut Nat'l Park,** Thai.
55/J2 **Kościan,** Pol.
55/J1 **Kościerzyna,** Pol.
97/D3 **Kosciusko** (mt.), Austl.
135/F3 **Kosciusko,** Ms,US
97/D3 **Kosciusko Nat'l Park,** Austl.
85/M10 **Kosei,** Japan
106/B4 **Kosha,** Sudan
85/F3 **Koshigaya,** Japan
73/J2 **Köshim** (riv.), Kaz.
79/H2 **Koshk,** Afg.
90/E2 **Kosi** (riv.), India
55/L4 **Košice,** Slvk.
55/L4 **Košický** (reg.), Slvk.
81/C2 **Kosoba, Gora** (peak), Kaz.
68/E4 **Kosovo** (aut. reg.), Serb.
68/E4 **Kosovo Polje,** Serb.
68/E4 **Kosovska Mitrovica,** Serb.
98/F4 **Kosrae** (isl.), Micr.
104/D3 **Kossi** (prov.), Burk.
104/D5 **Kossou** (lake), C.d'Iv.
69/F4 **Kostinbrod,** Bul.
72/C2 **Kostopol',** Ukr.
70/J4 **Kostroma,** Rus.
70/J4 **Kostroma** (riv.), Rus.
70/J4 **Kostromskaya Obl.,** Rus.
55/H2 **Kostrzyn,** Pol.
55/J2 **Kostrzyn,** Pol.
71/N4 **Kos'va** (riv.), Rus.
71/N2 **Kos'yu** (riv.), Rus.
55/J1 **Koszalin,** Pol.
90/C2 **Kota,** India
85/N10 **Kōta,** Japan
92/B5 **Kotaagung,** Indo.
92/B2 **Kota Baharu,** Malay.
93/E4 **Kotabaru,** Indo.
92/C4 **Kotabumi,** Indo.
79/K2 **Kot Addu,** Pak.
69/H4 **Kotel,** Bul.
71/L4 **Kotel'nich,** Rus.
73/G3 **Kotel'nikovo,** Rus.
75/P2 **Kotel'nyy** (isl.), Rus.
54/F3 **Köthen,** Ger.
48/H3 **Kotka,** Fin.
70/E3 **Kotka,** Fin.
79/K2 **Kot Kapūra,** India
71/K3 **Kotlas,** Rus.
85/M9 **Kotō,** Japan
68/D4 **Kotor,** Mont.
73/H2 **Kotovo,** Rus.
73/G1 **Kotovsk,** Rus.
79/J3 **Kotri,** Pak.
90/D4 **Kottagūdem,** India
90/C6 **Kottayam,** India
90/C6 **Kotte,** SrL.
103/K6 **Kotto** (riv.), CAfr.
75/L3 **Kotuy** (riv.), Rus.
136/E2 **Kotzebue** (sound), Ak,US
133/H2 **Kouchibouguac Nat'l Park,** NB,Can.
105/E3 **Koudougou,** Burk.
67/J5 **Koufonísion** (isl.), Gre.
136/E2 **Kougarok** (mtn.), Ak,US
88/D3 **Kouhu,** Tai.
125/J2 **Koukdjuak** (riv.), Nun,Can.
102/H8 **Koula-Moutou,** Gabon
104/D3 **Koulikoro,** Mali
104/B3 **Koulountou** (riv.), Gui., Sen.
104/D3 **Koumbi Saleh** (ruins), Mrta.
102/J6 **Koumra,** Chad
81/C2 **Kounradskiy,** Kaz.
134/E4 **Kountze,** Tx,US
105/H5 **Koupé** (peak), Camr.
105/E3 **Koupela,** Burk.
105/E3 **Kouritenga** (prov.), Burk.
115/H2 **Kourou,** FrG.
103/J4 **Koussi** (peak), Chad
104/D3 **Koutiala,** Mali
48/H3 **Kouvola,** Fin.
68/E3 **Kovačica,** Serb.
70/F2 **Kovdozero** (lake), Rus.
72/C2 **Kovel',** Ukr.
90/C6 **Kovilpatti,** India
70/J4 **Kovrov,** Rus.
90/C5 **Kovūr,** India
73/G1 **Kovylkino,** Rus.
79/J1 **Kowkcheh** (riv.), Afg.
79/H2 **Kowl-e Namaksār** (lake), Afg., Iran
88/B3 **Kowloon,** China
84/B5 **Kōyama,** Japan
69/G4 **Koynare,** Bul.
136/H2 **Koyukuk** (riv.), Ak,US
85/N10 **Kozakai,** Japan
80/C3 **Kozan,** Turk.
67/G2 **Kozáni,** Gre.
68/C3 **Kozara Nat'l Park,** Bosn.
90/C5 **Kozhikode** (Calicut), India
70/H3 **Kozhozero** (lake), Rus.
71/M2 **Kozhva** (riv.), Rus.
55/L3 **Kozienice,** Pol.
69/F4 **Kozloduy,** Bul.
80/E2 **Kozluk,** Turk.
55/J3 **Koźmin,** Pol.
69/F4 **Koznitsa** (peak), Bul.
55/H3 **Kożuchów,** Pol.
105/F5 **Kpalimé,** Togo
105/F5 **Kpandu,** Gha.
89/B4 **Kra** (isth.), Myan., Thai.
108/D3 **Kraai** (riv.), SAfr.
108/L10 **Kraaifontein,** SAfr.
89/B4 **Krabi,** Thai.
89/D3 **Kracheh,** Camb.
48/D4 **Kragerø,** Nor.
68/E3 **Kragujevac,** Serb.
63/H2 **Kraichgau** (reg.), Ger.
92/C5 **Krakatoa** (vol.), Indo.
89/D3 **Krakor,** Camb.
55/K3 **Kraków,** Pol.
89/C3 **Kralanh,** Camb.
123/H5 **Kralendijk,** NAnt.
68/E4 **Kraljevo,** Serb.
55/H3 **Královéhradecký** (reg.), Czh.
55/H3 **Kralupy nad Vltavou,** Czh.
72/F2 **Kramators'k,** Ukr.
48/F3 **Kramfors,** Swe.
56/B5 **Krammer** (chan.), Neth.
56/D5 **Kranenburg,** Ger.
68/B2 **Kranj,** Slov.
55/J3 **Krapkowice,** Pol.
55/M3 **Kraśnik,** Pol.
55/M3 **Kraśnik Fabryczny,** Pol.
71/X8 **Krasnoarmeysk,** Rus.
73/H2 **Krasnoarmeysk,** Rus.
72/F3 **Krasnodar,** Rus.
72/F3 **Krasnodarskiy Kray,** Rus.
71/W9 **Krasnogorsk,** Rus.
72/E2 **Krasnograd,** Ukr.
83/H1 **Krasnokamensk,** Rus.
71/M4 **Krasnokamsk,** Rus.
73/H2 **Krasnoslobodsk,** Rus.
74/G4 **Krasnotur'insk,** Rus.
71/P4 **Krasnoural'sk,** Rus.
74/K4 **Krasnoyarsk,** Rus.
55/M3 **Krasnystaw,** Pol.
73/H2 **Krasnyy Kut,** Rus.
72/F2 **Krasnyy Luch,** Ukr.
72/G3 **Krasnyy Sulin,** Rus.
89/C4 **Kravanh** (mts.), Camb.
92/C5 **Krawang,** Indo.
56/D6 **Krefeld,** Ger.
57/G5 **Kreiensen,** Ger.
67/G3 **Kremastón** (lake), Gre.
72/E2 **Kremenchuk,** Ukr.
72/E2 **Kremenchuts'ke** (res.), Ukr.
130/F2 **Kremmling,** Co,US
63/L2 **Krems an der Donau,** Aus.
75/T3 **Kresta** (gulf), Rus.
48/G5 **Kretinga,** Lith.
59/F2 **Kreuzau,** Ger.
59/G2 **Kreuztal,** Ger.
102/G7 **Kribi,** Camr.
72/D1 **Krichev,** Bela.
83/N2 **Kril'on, Mys** (cape), Rus.
56/B5 **Krimpen aan de IJssel,** Neth.
90/D4 **Krishna** (riv.), India
90/C5 **Krishnagiri,** India
48/C4 **Kristiansand,** Nor.
48/E4 **Kristianstad,** Swe.
55/H1 **Kristianstad** (co.), Swe.
48/C3 **Kristiansund,** Nor.
48/E4 **Kristinehamn,** Swe.
68/F4 **Kriva Palanka,** FYROM
68/B3 **Krk,** Cro.
68/C3 **Krka** (riv.), Cro.
55/J3 **Krnov,** Czh.
109/E2 **Krokodil** (riv.), SAfr.
108/D2 **Krokodilrivier** (riv.), SAfr.
72/E2 **Krolovets,** Ukr.
55/J4 **Kroměříž,** Czh.
63/J1 **Kronach,** Ger.
89/C4 **Krong Kaoh Kong,** Camb.
89/D4 **Krong Keb,** Camb.
48/E4 **Kronoberg** (co.), Swe.
71/S6 **Kronshtadt,** Rus.
96/C4 **Kroombit Tops Nat'l Park,** Austl.
108/D2 **Kroonstad,** SAfr.
73/G3 **Kropotkin,** Rus.
55/L4 **Krosno,** Pol.
55/H2 **Krosno Odrzańskie,** Pol.
55/J3 **Krotoszyn,** Pol.
68/B3 **Krško,** Slov.
57/G1 **Kruckau** (riv.), Ger.
110/F5 **Kruger Nat'l Park,** SAfr.
108/P13 **Krugersdorp,** SAfr.
71/N5 **Kruglitsa, Gora** (peak), Rus.
136/A5 **Krugloi** (pt.), Ak,US
56/B6 **Kruibeke,** Belg.
68/D5 **Krujë,** Alb.
69/G5 **Krumovgrad,** Bul.
89/C3 **Krung Thep** (Bangkok) (cap.), Thai.
55/K4 **Krupina,** Slvk.
136/F2 **Krusenstern** (cape), Ak,US
68/E4 **Kruševac,** Serb.
63/K1 **Krušné Hory** (Erzgebirge) (mts.), Czh., Ger.
55/K2 **Kruszwica,** Pol.
136/L4 **Kruzof** (isl.), Ak,US
72/E3 **Krym Aut. Rep.,** Ukr.
72/F3 **Krymsk,** Rus.
55/L4 **Krynica,** Pol.
72/E3 **Kryvyy Rih,** Ukr.
55/M3 **Krzna** (riv.), Pol.
55/J2 **Krzyż,** Pol.
87/D4 **Kuai** (riv.), China
92/D3 **Kuala Belait,** Bru.
92/B3 **Kuala Dungun,** Malay.
92/B3 **Kuala Lipis,** Malay.
92/B3 **Kuala Lumpur** (cap.), Malay.
92/B3 **Kuala Pilah,** Malay.
92/B2 **Kuala Terengganu,** Malay.
92/B3 **Kuantan,** Malay.
73/J4 **Kuba,** Azer.
72/F3 **Kuban'** (riv.), Rus.
70/H4 **Kubenskoye** (lake), Rus.
84/C4 **Kubokawa,** Japan
69/H4 **Kubrat,** Bul.
92/D3 **Kuching,** Malay.
67/F2 **Kuçovë,** Alb.
84/B4 **Kudamatsu,** Japan
92/D5 **Kudus,** Indo.
71/M4 **Kudymkar,** Rus.
103/K3 **Kufrah** (oasis), Libya
80/K5 **Kufrinjah,** Jor.
63/K3 **Kufstein,** Aus.
124/H2 **Kugaaruk,** Nun,Can.
48/J2 **Kuhmo,** Fin.
56/D3 **Kuinder of Tjonger** (riv.), Neth.
110/C3 **Kuito,** Ang.
136/M4 **Kuiu** (isl.), Ak,US
105/E5 **Kujani Game Rsv.,** Gha.
55/K2 **Kujawsko-Pomorskie** (prov.), Pol.
55/K2 **Kujawy** (reg.), Pol.
83/N3 **Kuji,** Japan
84/B4 **Kujū-san** (mtn.), Japan
67/G1 **Kukës,** Alb.
85/F2 **Kuki,** Japan
85/J7 **Kukizaki,** Japan
79/G3 **Kūl** (riv.), Iran
68/D3 **Kula,** Serb.
92/B3 **Kulai,** Malay.
73/J3 **Kulaly** (isl.), Kaz.
73/K4 **Kulandag** (mts.), Trkm.
73/G4 **Kulashi,** Geo.
70/D4 **Kuldīga,** Lat.
70/J5 **Kulebaki,** Rus.
89/D3 **Kulen,** Camb.
97/B2 **Kulkyne-Hattah Nat'l Park,** Austl.
79/L2 **Kullu,** India
63/J1 **Kulmbach,** Ger.
71/J2 **Kuloy** (riv.), Rus.
80/C2 **Kulu,** Turk.
74/H4 **Kulunda,** Rus.
81/C1 **Kulunda** (lake), Rus.
81/D1 **Kulunda** (riv.), Rus.
81/C1 **Kulunda Steppe** (grsld.), Kaz., Rus.
79/J1 **Kulyab,** Taj.
73/H3 **Kuma** (riv.), Rus.
85/F2 **Kumagaya,** Japan
84/B4 **Kumamoto,** Japan
84/B4 **Kumamoto** (pref.), Japan
84/E4 **Kumano,** Japan
84/D4 **Kumano** (riv.), Japan
68/E4 **Kumanovo,** FYROM
105/E5 **Kumasi,** Gha.
85/L10 **Kumatori,** Japan
105/H5 **Kumba,** Camr.
105/H5 **Kumbo,** Camr.
73/K5 **Kum-Dag,** Trkm.
88/E2 **Kumé** (isl.), Japan
73/K1 **Kumertau,** Rus.
86/E4 **Kumi,** SKor.
85/L10 **Kumiyama,** Japan
48/E4 **Kumla,** Swe.
80/B3 **Kumluca,** Turk.
91/G2 **Kumon** (range), Myan.
90/B5 **Kumta,** India
126/U11 **Kumukahi** (cape), Hi,US
83/P3 **Kunashiri** (isl.), Rus.
90/C2 **Kūnch,** India
110/E3 **Kundelungu Nat'l Park,** D.R. Congo
79/K2 **Kundiān,** Pak.
90/B3 **Kundla,** India
48/E4 **Kungsbacka,** Swe.
103/J7 **Kungu,** D.R. Congo
71/N4 **Kungur,** Rus.
68/E2 **Kunhegyes,** Hun.
84/B4 **Kunimi-dake** (mtn.), Japan
92/C5 **Kuningan,** Indo.
85/H7 **Kunitachi,** Japan
81/C4 **Kunjirap Daban** (pass), China
81/C4 **Kunlun** (mts.), China
68/E2 **Kunmadaras,** Hun.
91/H2 **Kunming,** China
86/D5 **Kunsan,** SKor.
87/E5 **Kunshan,** China
68/E2 **Kunszentmárton,** Hun.
87/E3 **Kunyu Shan** (mtn.), China
48/H3 **Kuopio,** Fin.
68/B3 **Kupa** (riv.), Cro., Slov.
93/F6 **Kupang,** Indo.
74/H4 **Kupino,** Rus.
136/M4 **Kupreanof** (isl.), Ak,US
72/F2 **Kupyansk,** Ukr.
83/L1 **Kur** (riv.), Rus.
73/J5 **Kura** (riv.), Azer., Geo.
85/L9 **Kurama-yama** (peak), Japan
84/C3 **Kurashiki,** Japan
106/B5 **Kuraymah,** Sudan
84/C3 **Kurayoshi,** Japan
78/D1 **Kurdistan** (reg.), Asia
69/G5 **Kŭrdzhali,** Bul.
67/J2 **Kŭrdzhali** (res.), Bul.
84/C3 **Kure,** Japan
80/C2 **Küre** (mts.), Turk.
98/H2 **Kure** (isl.), Hi,US
70/D4 **Kuressaare,** Est.
74/K3 **Kureyka** (riv.), Rus.
71/Q5 **Kurgan,** Rus.
71/Q5 **Kurganskaya Obl.,** Rus.
79/J1 **Kurgan-Tyube,** Taj.
98/G4 **Kuria** (isl.), Kiri.
78/G5 **Kuria Muria** (isls.), Oman
75/Q5 **Kuril** (isls.), Rus.
96/H8 **Ku-Ring-Gai Nat'l Park,** Austl.
103/M5 **Kurmuk,** Sudan
90/C4 **Kurnool,** India
85/K9 **Kurodashō,** Japan
85/G2 **Kuroiso,** Japan
85/M10 **Kuroso-yama** (peak), Japan
79/K2 **Kurram** (riv.), Pak.
70/D5 **Kuršėnai,** Lith.
90/E2 **Kurseong,** India
72/F2 **Kursk,** Rus.
55/L1 **Kurskaya** (spit), Lith., Rus.
55/L1 **Kurskiy** (lag.), Rus.
72/E2 **Kurskaya Obl.,** Rus.
68/E4 **Kuršumlija,** Serb.
80/E3 **Kurtalan,** Turk.
57/E6 **Kürten,** Ger.
106/B5 **Kūrtī,** Sudan
103/L6 **Kuru** (riv.), Sudan
73/G4 **Kuruçay** (riv.), Turk.
81/E3 **Kuruktag** (mts.), China
84/B4 **Kurume,** Japan
90/D6 **Kurunegala,** SrL.
106/B4 **Kurur, Jabal** (peak), Sudan
96/E6 **Kurwongbah** (lake), Austl.
80/A3 **Kuşadası,** Turk.
89/C2 **Ku Sathan** (peak), Thai.
85/L9 **Kusatsu,** Japan
85/M9 **Kusatsu,** Japan
85/M10 **Kushida** (riv.), Japan
84/B5 **Kushikino,** Japan
84/B5 **Kushima,** Japan
84/D4 **Kushimoto,** Japan
83/N3 **Kushiro,** Japan
82/F4 **Kushui** (riv.), China
136/F4 **Kuskokwim** (bay), Ak,US
136/G3 **Kuskokwim** (mts.), Ak,US
136/F3 **Kuskokwim** (riv.), Ak,US
103/M5 **Kūstī,** Sudan
85/M10 **Kusu,** Japan
89/C4 **Kut** (isl.), Thai.
80/B2 **Kütahya,** Turk.
73/G4 **K'ut'aisi,** Geo.
90/A3 **Kutch** (gulf), India
90/A3 **Kutch** (reg.), India
79/J4 **Kutch, Rann of** (swamp), India, Pak.
55/H4 **Kutná Hora,** Czh.
55/K2 **Kutno,** Pol.
110/C1 **Kutu,** D.R. Congo
103/K5 **Kutum,** Sudan
124/E1 **Kuujjua** (riv.), NW,Can.
125/K3 **Kuujjuaq** (Fort-Chimo), Qu,Can.
125/J3 **Kuujjuarapik,** Qu,Can.
48/J2 **Kuusamo,** Fin.
48/H3 **Kuusankoski,** Fin.
48/H4 **Kuutse Mägi** (mt.), Est.
73/L2 **Kuvandyk,** Rus.
78/E3 **Kuwait** (ctry.)
78/E3 **Kuwait** (cap.), Kuw.
90/D2 **Kuwānā** (riv.), India
84/E3 **Kuwana,** Japan
71/L5 **Kuybyshev** (res.), Rus.
87/B3 **Kuye** (riv.), China
80/F3 **Kūysanjaq,** Iraq
70/F2 **Kuyto** (lake), Rus.
81/E3 **Kuytun,** China
81/D2 **Kuytun** (riv.), China
122/E5 **Kuyu Tingni,** Nic.
136/E2 **Kuzitrin** (riv.), Ak,US
73/H1 **Kuznetsk,** Rus.
48/F1 **Kvaløy** (isl.), Nor.
68/B3 **Kvarner** (chan.), Cro.
68/B3 **Kvarnerić** (chan.), Cro.
48/E2 **Kvigtinden** (peak), Nor.
48/C4 **Kvinnherad,** Nor.
110/C1 **Kwa** (riv.), D.R. Congo
89/B3 **Kwai, River** (bridge), Thai.
98/F4 **Kwajelein** (atoll), Mrsh.
86/D5 **Kwangju,** SKor.
86/D5 **Kwangju-Jikhalsi** (prov.), SKor.
110/C1 **Kwango** (riv.), D.R.Congo
107/B2 **Kwania** (lake), Ugan.
105/G4 **Kwara** (state), Nga.
132/D1 **Kwataboahegan** (riv.), On,Can.
109/E7 **KwaZulu Natal** (prov.), SAfr.
110/E4 **Kwekwe,** Zim.
55/K2 **Kwidzyn,** Pol.
103/N5 **Kwīha,** Eth.
102/J6 **Kyabé,** Chad
89/B2 **Kyaikkami,** Myan.
89/B2 **Kyaikto,** Myan.
82/F1 **Kyakhta,** Rus.
91/G4 **Kyangin,** Myan.
89/D2 **Ky Anh,** Viet.
89/B1 **Kyaukme,** Myan.
91/F4 **Kyaukpyu,** Myan.
89/B1 **Kyaukse,** Myan.
55/J4 **Kyjov,** Czh.
128/F3 **Kyle,** Sk,Can.
59/F3 **Kyll** (riv.), Ger.
59/F3 **Kyllburg,** Ger.
53/F2 **Kym** (riv.), Eng,UK
90/C3 **Kymore,** India
107/B2 **Kyoga** (lake), Ugan.
84/D3 **Kyōga-misaki** (cape), Japan
85/F3 **Kyonan,** Japan
86/C4 **Kyŏnggi** (bay), SKor.
86/D4 **Kyŏnggi-Do** (prov.), SKor.
86/E5 **Kyŏngju,** SKor.
86/E5 **Kyŏngju Nat'l Park,** SKor.
86/E4 **Kyŏngsang-bukto** (prov.), SKor.
86/E5 **Kyŏngsang-namdo** (prov.), SKor.
84/D3 **Kyōto,** Japan
84/D3 **Kyōto** (pref.), Japan
80/J4 **Kyrenia** (dist.), Cyp.
81/B3 **Kyrgyzstan** (ctry.)
54/G2 **Kyritz,** Ger.
91/H4 **Ky Son,** Viet.
84/B5 **Kyūshū** (isl.), Japan
84/B4 **Kyūshū** (mts.), Japan
84/B4 **Kyūshū** (prov.), Japan
68/F4 **Kyustendil,** Bul.

59/E5 L'Est, Canal de (can.), Fr.
60/C4 Le Suchet (peak), Swi.
58/B6 Les Ulis, Fr.
92/D3 Lesung (peak), Indo.
67/J3 Lésvos (isl.), Gre.
50/C2 Leswalt, Sc,UK
55/J3 Leszno, Pol.
109/R15 Le Tampon, Reun., Fr.
53/F3 Letchworth, Eng,UK
128/E3 Lethbridge, Ab,Can.
57/F2 Lethe (riv.), Ger.
93/G5 Leti (isls.), Indo.
114/E4 Leticia, Col.
110/E5 Letlhakane, Bots.
110/D5 Letlhakeng, Bots.
91/G4 Letpadan, Myan.
58/A3 Le Tréport, Fr.
89/B4 Letsôk-Aw (isl.), Myan.
56/C4 Leusden-Zuid, Neth.
92/A3 Leuser (peak), Indo.
61/F2 Leutkirch im Allgäu, Ger.
59/D2 Leuven (Louvain), Belg.
58/C2 Leuze-en-Hainaut, Belg.
67/H3 Levádhia, Gre.
48/D3 Levanger, Nor.
118/B5 Level (isl.), Chile
134/C3 Levelland, Tx,US
109/F2 Leven (pt.), SAfr.
51/H4 Leven, Eng,UK
51/F3 Leven (riv.), Eng,UK
51/G3 Leven (riv.), Eng,UK
49/D2 Leven, Sc,UK
56/D6 Leverkusen, Ger.
55/K4 Levice, Slvk.
95/H7 Levin, NZ
133/G2 Lévis, Qu,Can.
137/G5 Levittown, NY,US
137/F5 Levittown, Pa,US
67/G3 Levkás, Gre.
67/G3 Levkás (isl.), Gre.
55/L4 Levoča, Slvk.
69/G4 Levski, Bul.
53/G5 Lewes, Eng,UK
133/K1 Lewis (hills), Nf,Can.
128/E3 Lewis (range), Mt,US
128/C4 Lewis (riv.), Wa,US
129/J5 Lewis & Clark (lake), Ne, SD,US
135/G3 Lewisburg, Tn,US
132/D4 Lewisburg, WV,US
133/L1 Lewisporte, Nf,Can.
135/G3 Lewis Smith (lake), Al,US
128/D4 Lewiston, Id,US
133/G2 Lewiston, Me,US
133/R9 Lewiston, NY,US
128/F4 Lewistown, Mt,US
132/E3 Lewistown, Pa,US
93/F5 Lewotobi (peak), Indo.
132/C4 Lexington, Ky,US
135/H3 Lexington, NC,US
131/H2 Lexington, Ne,US
135/H3 Lexington, SC,US
135/F3 Lexington, Tn,US
132/E4 Lexington, Va,US
132/E4 Lexington Park, Md,US
51/G3 Leyburn, Eng,UK
51/F4 Leyland, Eng,UK
88/D5 Leyte (isl.), Phil.
62/F4 Lez (riv.), Fr.
55/M3 Leżajsk, Pol.
67/F2 Lezhë, Alb.
62/E5 Lézignan-Corbières, Fr.
72/E2 L'gov, Rus.
90/F2 Lhasa, China
90/E2 Lhazê, China
65/G2 L'Hospitalet, Sp.
91/G2 Lhünzê, China
87/B5 Li (riv.), China
87/C4 Li (riv.), China
91/K2 Li (riv.), China
88/B3 Lian (riv.), China
58/B5 Liancourt, Fr.
84/B2 Liancourt (rocks), Japan, SKor.
87/C2 Liangcheng, China
92/D3 Liangpran (peak), Indo.
87/C5 Liangzi (lake), China
87/D4 Lianyungang, China
83/J3 Liao (riv.), China
87/C3 Liaocheng, China
87/E2 Liaodong (bay), China
83/J3 Liaoyang, China
87/F2 Liaoyuan, China
79/K3 Liāquatpur, Pak.
124/D2 Liard (riv.), Can.
128/E3 Libby, Mt,US
103/J7 Libenge, D.R. Congo
131/G3 Liberal, Ks,US
58/C3 Libercourt, Fr.
115/H6 Liberdade (riv.), Braz.
55/H3 Liberec, Czh.
55/H3 Liberecký (reg.), Czh.
104/C5 Liberia (ctry.)
122/D5 Liberia, CR
122/D4 Libertad, Belz.
119/F2 Libertad, Uru.
117/D1 Libertador General San Martín, Arg.
135/G2 Liberty, Ky,US
137/K7 Liberty (res.), Md,US
134/E2 Liberty, Mo,US
135/F4 Liberty, Ms,US
134/E4 Liberty, Tx,US
138/Q15 Libertyville, Il,US
93/G4 Libobo (cape), Indo.
55/G3 Liboc (riv.), Czh.
88/D5 Libon, Phil.
102/G7 Libreville (cap.), Gabon
103/J2 Libya (ctry.)
103/K2 Libyan (des.), Afr.
103/K1 Libyan (plat.), Libya
118/C2 Licantén, Chile
66/C4 Licata, It.
80/E2 Lice, Turk.
63/H1 Lich, Ger.
53/E1 Lichfield, Eng,UK
63/J1 Lichtenfels, Ger.
56/D5 Lichtenvoorde, Neth.
58/C1 Lichtervelde, Belg.
87/B5 Lichuan, China
132/C4 Licking (riv.), Ky,US
66/D2 Licosa (cape), It.
70/E5 Lida, Bela.
51/F1 Liddell Water (riv.), Sc,UK
125/R7 Liddon (gulf), NW,Can.
53/F2 Lidlington, Eng,UK
63/K4 Lido, It.
66/C2 Lido di Ostia, It.
55/K2 Lidzbark, Pol.
55/L1 Lidzbark Warmiński, Pol.
108/E2 Liebenbergsvlei (riv.), SAfr.
61/F3 Liechtenstein (ctry.)
58/D2 Liedekerke, Belg.
59/E2 Liège, Belg.
59/E3 Liège (prov.), Belg.
48/J3 Lieksa, Fin.
56/C5 Lienden, Neth.
57/E4 Lienen, Ger.
63/K3 Lienz, Aus.
70/D4 Liepāja, Lat.
58/D1 Lier, Belg.
62/E1 Lies (riv.), Belg.
59/F3 Lieser (riv.), Ger.
48/G3 Liesjärven Nat'l Park, Fin.
60/D2 Liestal, Swi.
48/G3 Lieto, Fin.
58/B3 Liévin, Fr.
132/F2 Lièvre (riv.), Qu,Can.
63/L3 Liezen, Aus.
50/B5 Liffey (riv.), Ire.
99/V12 Lifou (isl.), NCal.
52/B5 Lifton, Eng,UK
93/F1 Ligao, Phil.
63/H4 Ligure, Appenino (mts.), It.
63/H4 Liguria (reg.), It.
63/H5 Ligurian (sea), Eur.
91/H2 Lijiang (Lijiang Naxizu Zizhixian), China
110/E3 Likasi, D.R. Congo
128/C2 Likely, BC,Can.
110/F3 Likoma (isl.), Malw.
102/H7 Likouala (riv.), Congo
66/A1 L'Ile-Rousse, Fr.
57/F2 Lilienthal, Ger.
91/K2 Liling, China
59/D1 Lille, Belg.
58/C2 Lille, Fr.
48/D3 Lillehammer, Nor.
58/B2 Lillers, Fr.
48/D4 Lillestrøm, Nor.
128/C3 Lillooet, BC,Can.
128/C3 Lillooet (riv.), BC,Can.
110/F3 Lilongwe (cap.), Malw.
97/G5 Lilydale, Austl.
68/D4 Lim (riv.), Mont., Serb.
114/C6 Lima (cap.), Peru
64/A2 Lima (riv.), Port.
129/L4 Lima (peak), Mn,US
132/C3 Lima, Oh,US
118/Q9 Limache, Chile
116/K6 Lima Duarte, Braz.
55/L4 Limanowa, Pol.
80/J4 Limassol, Cyp.
50/B1 Limavady, NI,UK
50/A2 Limavady (dist.), NI,UK
118/C4 Limay (riv.), Arg.
58/A6 Limay, Fr.
66/A2 Limbara (peak), It.
90/B3 Limbdi, India
59/E2 Limburg (prov.), Belg.
59/E1 Limburg (prov.), Neth.
63/H1 Limburg an der Lahn, Ger.
133/Q8 Limehouse, On,Can.
116/C2 Limeira, Braz.
49/A4 Limerick, Ire.
64/B2 Limia (riv.), Sp.
67/J3 Límnos (isl.), Gre.
62/D4 Limoges, Fr.
62/D4 Limogne (plat.), Fr.
122/E5 Limón, CR
131/G3 Limon, Co,US
62/D4 Limousin (mts.), Fr.
62/D4 Limousin (reg.), Fr.
62/E5 Limoux, Fr.
110/F5 Limpopo (riv.), Afr.
53/G4 Limpsfield, Eng,UK
88/C5 Linapacan (isl.), Phil.
118/C2 Linares, Chile
122/B3 Linares, Mex.
64/D3 Linares, Sp.
88/C2 Linchuan, China
118/E2 Lincoln, Arg.
133/R9 Lincoln, On,Can.
121/L1 Lincoln (sea), Can.,
51/H5 Lincoln, Eng,UK
132/B3 Lincoln, Il,US
133/G2 Lincoln, Me,US
131/H2 Lincoln (cap.), Ne,US
128/B4 Lincoln Beach, Or,US
128/B4 Lincoln City, Or,US
51/H5 Lincoln Heath (woodl.), Eng,UK
138/F7 Lincoln Park, Mi,US
137/F5 Lincoln Park, NJ,US
51/H5 Lincolnshire (co.), Eng,UK
51/H5 Lincolnshire Wolds (hills), Eng,UK
135/H3 Lincolnton, NC,US
137/F5 Lincroft, NJ,US
66/A2 L'Incudine, Mont (mtn.), Fr.
56/D3 Linde (riv.), Neth.
96/C3 Lindeman (isl.), Austl.
114/G2 Linden, Guy.
135/G3 Linden, Al,US
137/F5 Linden, NJ,US
61/F2 Lindenberg im Allgäu, Ger.
138/P15 Lindenhurst, Il,US
137/G5 Lindenhurst, NY,US
137/F6 Lindenwold, NJ,US
70/B4 Lindesberg, Swe.
107/C5 Lindi, Tanz.
107/C5 Lindi (prov.), Tanz.
49/E3 Lindisfarne (Holy) (isl.), Eng,UK
57/E6 Lindlar, Ger.
97/D3 Lind Nat'l Park, Austl.
132/E2 Lindsay, On,Can.
130/C3 Lindsay, Ca,US
134/D2 Lindsborg, Ks,US
99/K4 Line (isls.), Kiri.
87/B3 Linfen, China
87/C4 Lingchuan, China
88/B2 Lingchuan, China
56/C5 Linge (riv.), Neth.
57/E3 Lingen, Ger.
53/F4 Lingfield, Eng,UK
92/B3 Lingga (isls.), Indo.
59/G6 Lingolsheim, Fr.
104/B3 Linguère, Sen.
87/D3 Ling Xian, China
88/B2 Ling Xian, China
87/E5 Lingyin Si, China
88/D2 Linhai, China
116/D1 Linhares, Braz.
48/E4 Linköping, Swe.
87/C3 Linliu Shan (mtn.), China
48/J3 Linnansaaren Nat'l Park, Fin.
52/A3 Linney Head (pt.), Wal,UK
49/C2 Linnhe, Loch (inlet), Sc,UK
59/F2 Linnich, Ger.
66/C5 Linosa (isl.), It.
87/C3 Linqing, China
116/B2 Lins, Braz.
109/H9 Linta (riv.), Madg.
53/G2 Linton, Eng,UK
132/C4 Linton, In,US
129/H4 Linton, ND,US
51/H5 Linwood, Eng,UK
87/B4 Linyi, China
87/D3 Linyi, China
87/D4 Linyi, China
63/L2 Linz, Aus.
62/E5 Lion (gulf), Fr.
66/D3 Lipari (isls.), It.
48/J3 Liperi, Fin.
72/F1 Lipetsk, Rus.
72/F1 Lipetskaya Obl., Rus.
114/E8 Lípez (range), Bol.
114/E8 Lípez (riv.), Bol.
53/F4 Liphook, Eng,UK
68/E4 Lipljan, Serb.
55/K2 Lipno, Pol.
68/E2 Lipova, Rom.
56/E5 Lippe (riv.), Ger.
57/F5 Lippstadt, Ger.
55/K4 Liptovský Mikuláš, Slvk.
97/C3 Liptrap (cape), Austl.
81/D5 Lipu La (pass), India
81/D5 Lipu Lehk Shankou (pass), China
107/B2 Lira, Ugan.
110/C1 Liranga, Congo
66/C2 Liri (riv.), It.
65/E3 Liria, Sp.
103/K7 Lisala, D.R. Congo
65/P10 Lisboa (dist.), Port.
133/G2 Lisbon, Me,US
129/J4 Lisbon, ND,US
65/P10 Lisbon (Lisboa) (cap.), Port.
50/B2 Lisburn, NI,UK
50/B3 Lisburn (dist.), NI,UK
136/E2 Lisburne (cape), Ak,US
91/H2 Lisha (riv.), China
87/B4 Li Shan (mtn.), China
88/C2 Lishui, China
99/H2 Lisianski (isl.), Hi,US
62/D2 Lisieux, Fr.
52/B6 Liskeard, Eng,UK
138/P16 Lisle, Il,US
58/B5 L'Isle-Adam, Fr.
62/F5 L'Isle-sur-la-Sorgue, Fr.
97/E1 Lismore, Austl.
50/B3 Lisnacree, NI,UK
53/F4 Liss, Eng,UK
56/B4 Lisse, Neth.
57/E6 Lister (riv.), Ger.
132/D3 Listowel, On,Can.
91/H2 Litang (riv.), China
80/K5 Līṭānī (riv.), Leb.
132/B4 Litchfield, Il,US
129/K4 Litchfield, Mn,US
56/C5 Lith, Neth.
51/F5 Litherland, Eng,UK
97/D2 Lithgow, Austl.
70/D5 Lithuania (ctry.)
70/E5 Litovskiy Nat'l Park, Lith.
96/D4 Littabella Nat'l Park, Austl.
135/H4 Little (riv.), Ga,US
131/J4 Little (riv.), La,US
135/J3 Little (riv.), NC,US
131/J4 Little (riv.), Ok,US
134/D4 Little (riv.), Tx,US
132/D1 Little Abitibi (riv.), On,Can.
55/J5 Little Alföld (plain), Hun.
91/F5 Little Andaman (isl.), India
128/F4 Little Belt (mts.), Mt,US
128/G4 Little Bighorn Nat'l Mon., Mt,US
131/H2 Little Blue (riv.), Ks, Ne,US
51/F4 Littleborough, Eng,UK
123/E4 Little Cayman (isl.), Cay.
130/E4 Little Colorado (riv.), Az,US
132/D2 Little Current, On,Can.
132/C1 Little Current (riv.), On,Can.
52/C5 Little Dart (riv.), Eng,UK
97/B3 Little Desert Nat'l Park, Austl.
136/E2 Little Diomede (isl.), Ak,US
129/K4 Little Falls, Mn,US
134/C3 Littlefield, Tx,US
129/K4 Little Fork (riv.), Mn,US
53/F5 Littlehampton, Eng,UK
123/G3 Little Inagua (isl.), Bahm.
108/C4 Little Karoo (reg.), SAfr.
133/K2 Little Miquelon (isl.), StP.
131/J4 Little Missouri (riv.), Ar,US
129/H4 Little Missouri (riv.), ND, SD,US
91/F6 Little Nicobar (isl.), India
53/G2 Little Ouse (riv.), Eng,UK
53/G2 Littleport, Eng,UK
131/J4 Little Red (riv.), Ar,US
134/E3 Little Rock (cap.), Ar,US
136/L3 Little Salmon, Yk,Can.
104/B4 Little Scarcies (riv.), Gui., SLeo.
129/K5 Little Sioux (riv.), Ia,US
136/B5 Little Sitkin (isl.), Ak,US
128/D2 Little Smoky (riv.), Ab,Can.
130/E2 Little Snake (riv.), Co, Wy,US
53/G4 Little Stour (riv.), Eng,UK
53/F2 Little Stukeley, Eng,UK
133/G2 Littleton, NH,US
132/B4 Little Wabash (riv.), Il,US
131/G2 Little White (riv.), SD,US
128/E5 Little Wood (riv.), Id,US
80/F3 Little Zab (riv.), Iraq
83/J3 Liu (riv.), China
83/K3 Liu (riv.), China
88/A3 Liu (riv.), China
110/D3 Liuwa Pan Nat'l Park, Zam.
91/J3 Liuzhou, China
135/H4 Live Oak, Fl,US
59/F6 Liverdun, Fr.
138/L11 Livermore, Ca,US
134/B4 Livermore (peak), Tx,US
96/G8 Liverpool, Austl.
133/H2 Liverpool, NS,Can.
136/M2 Liverpool (bay), NW,Can.
125/J1 Liverpool (cape), Nun,Can.
51/F5 Liverpool, Eng,UK
51/E5 Liverpool (bay), Eng,UK
51/F5 Liverpool (co.), Eng,UK
51/H2 Liverton, Eng,UK
128/F4 Livingston, Mt,US
137/F5 Livingston, NJ,US
134/E4 Livingston, Tx,US
131/J5 Livingston (lake), Tx,US
128/E3 Livingstone (range), Ab,Can.
110/E4 Livingstone, Zam.
110/B1 Livingstone, Chutes de (Livingstone) (falls), Congo
68/C4 Livno, Bosn.
72/F1 Livny, Rus.
48/H2 Livojoki (riv.), Fin.
138/F7 Livonia, Mi,US
63/J5 Livorno, It.
62/F4 Livron-sur-Drôme, Fr.
58/B6 Livry-Gargan, Fr.
107/C5 Liwale, Tanz.
52/A7 Lizard, Eng,UK
52/A7 Lizard (pt.), Eng,UK
52/A6 Lizard, The (pen.), Eng,UK
68/B2 Ljubljana (cap.), Slov.
68/C4 Ljubuški, Cro.
48/F3 Ljungan (riv.), Swe.
48/E4 Ljungby, Swe.
70/C3 Ljusdal, Swe.
48/E3 Ljusnan (riv.), Swe.
118/C2 Llaillay, Chile
118/C3 Llaima (vol.), Chile
114/E7 Llallagua, Bol.
52/B2 Llanarth, Wal,UK
50/D5 Llanberis, Wal,UK
50/D5 Llanberis, Pass of (pass), Wal,UK
118/C2 Llancañelo (lake), Arg.
52/C3 Llandeilo, Wal,UK
52/D3 Llandogo, Wal,UK
52/C3 Llandovery, Wal,UK
50/E6 Llandrillo, Wal,UK
52/C2 Llandrindod Wells, Wal,UK
50/E5 Llandudno, Wal,UK
52/C3 Llandybie, Wal,UK
52/B2 Llandyssul, Wal,UK
52/B3 Llanelli, Wal,UK
52/C1 Llanelltyd, Wal,UK
50/D6 Llanenddwyn, Wal,UK
50/D5 Llanerchymedd, Wal,UK
64/C1 Llanes, Sp.
52/C1 Llanfair Caereinion, Wal,UK
50/E5 Llanfairfechan, Wal,UK
50/D5 Llanfair-Pwllgwyngyll, Wal,UK
52/C1 Llanfyllin, Wal,UK
52/C2 Llangammarch Wells, Wal,UK
52/C3 Llangattock, Wal,UK
51/E6 Llangollen, Wal,UK
52/C2 Llangurig, Wal,UK
52/C2 Llanidloes, Wal,UK
50/D5 Llanllyfni, Wal,UK
52/B3 Llannon, Wal,UK
134/D4 Llano, Tx,US
131/H5 Llano (riv.), Tx,US
130/G4 Llano Estacado (plain), NM, Tx,US
52/B2 Llanon, Wal,UK
114/D3 Llanos (plain), Col., Ven.
118/B4 Llanquihue (lake), Chile
51/E5 Llanrhaeadr, Wal,UK
52/B2 Llanrhystyd, Wal,UK
52/A3 Llanrian, Wal,UK
50/E5 Llanrwst, Wal,UK
52/C3 Llanthony, Wal,UK
52/C3 Llantrisant, Wal,UK
52/C4 Llantwit Major, Wal,UK
50/E6 Llanuwchllyn, Wal,UK
52/C1 Llanwnog, Wal,UK
52/C2 Llanwrtyd Wells, Wal,UK
51/E5 Llay, Wal,UK
52/C2 Lledrod, Wal,UK
65/F2 Lleida (Lérida), Sp.
122/B3 Llera, Mex.
50/D6 Lleyn (pen.), Wal,UK
65/F1 Llobregat (riv.), Sp.
64/D1 Llodio, Sp.
65/G2 Lloret de Mar, Sp.
122/E6 Llorona (pt.), CR
137/G5 Lloyd (pt.), NY,US
128/F2 Lloydminster, Ab, Sk,Can.
133/K1 Lloyds (riv.), Nf,Can.
65/G3 Lluchmayor, Sp.
117/C1 Llullaillaco (vol.), Chile
52/C3 Llynfi (riv.), Wal,UK
89/D1 Lo (riv.), Viet.
117/C1 Loa (riv.), Chile
130/E3 Loa, Ut,US
63/H4 Loano, It.
65/N8 Loaoya (can.), Sp.
108/D2 Lobatse, Bots.
118/F3 Lobería, Arg.
110/B3 Lobito, Ang.
71/W8 Lobnya, Rus.
104/D5 Lobo (riv.), C.d'Iv.
118/F2 Lobos, Arg.
114/B5 Lobos de Tierra (isl.), Peru
118/B2 Lobos, Punta de (pt.), Chile
61/E5 Locarno, Swi.
50/D2 Lochans, Sc,UK
50/E1 Locharbriggs, Sc,UK
56/D4 Lochem, Neth.
49/C2 Lochgilphead, Sc,UK
50/E1 Lochmaben, Sc,UK
58/C1 Lochristi, Belg.
49/C2 Lochy, Loch (lake), Sc,UK
51/E1 Lockerbie, Sc,UK
134/D4 Lockhart, Tx,US
132/E3 Lock Haven, Pa,US
97/C3 Lockington, Austl.
138/P16 Lockport, Il,US
133/S9 Lockport, NY,US
89/D4 Loc Ninh, Viet.
66/E3 Locri, It.
131/J3 Locust (cr.), Ia, Mo,US
80/M9 Lod, Isr.
53/H1 Loddon, Eng,UK
53/E4 Loddon (riv.), Eng,UK
62/E5 Lodève, Fr.
70/G3 Lodeynoye Pole, Rus.
128/F3 Lodge (cr.), Mt,US
131/G2 Lodgepole (cr.), Ne, Wy,US
63/H4 Lodi, It.
138/M10 Lodi, Ca,US
137/F5 Lodi, NJ,US
110/D1 Lodja, D.R. Congo
107/B2 Lodwar, Kenya
55/K3 Łódź, Pol.
55/K3 Łodzkie (prov.), Pol.
65/N9 Loeches, Sp.
89/C2 Loei, Thai.
56/C4 Loenen, Neth.
104/C5 Lofa (co.), Libr.
104/C5 Lofa (riv.), Libr.
48/D2 Lofoten (isls.), Nor.
51/H2 Loftus, Eng,UK
97/C4 Lofty (range), Austl.
96/F7 Logan, Austl.
136/K3 Logan (mtn.), Yk,Can.
131/G4 Logan, NM,US
132/D4 Logan, Oh,US
130/E2 Logan, Ut,US
132/D4 Logan, WV,US
50/D2 Logan, Mull of (pt.), Sc,UK
132/C3 Logansport, In,US
102/J6 Logone (riv.), Camr., Chad
64/D1 Logroño, Sp.
57/G6 Lohfelden, Ger.
70/E3 Lohja, Fin.
59/G2 Lohmar, Ger.
57/F3 Lohne, Ger.
91/G3 Loi Lun (range), Myan., China
62/E2 Loing (riv.), Fr.
62/C3 Loir (riv.), Fr.
62/C3 Loire (riv.), Fr.
59/E5 Loisin (riv.), Fr.
107/B3 Loita (hills), Kenya
114/C4 Loja, Ecu.
64/C4 Loja, Sp.
58/C1 Lokeren, Belg.
110/D1 Lokolia, D.R. Congo
103/K8 Lokolo (riv.), D.R. Congo
103/J8 Lokoro (riv.), D.R. Congo
125/K2 Loks (isl.), Nun,Can.
103/L6 Lol (riv.), Sudan
54/F1 Lolland (isl.), Den.
128/E4 Lolo (peak), Mt,US
110/E1 Lolo, D.R. Congo
98/G5 Lolua, Tuv.
69/F4 Lom, Bul.
104/C4 Loma (mts.), Gui., SLeo.
122/B4 Loma Bonita, Mex.
137/C2 Loma Linda, Ca,US
104/C4 Loma Mansa (peak), SLeo.
103/K8 Lomami (riv.), D.R. Congo
119/S12 Lomas de Zamora, Arg.
138/P16 Lombard, Il,US
115/H3 Lombarda (mts.), Braz.
63/J4 Lombardy (reg.), It.
93/F5 Lomblen (isl.), Indo.
93/E5 Lombok (isl.), Indo.
105/F5 Lomé (cap.), Togo
110/D1 Lomela, D.R. Congo
103/K8 Lomela (riv.), D.R. Congo
137/B3 Lomita, Ca,US
62/E1 Lomme, Fr.
59/E1 Lommel, Belg.
49/C2 Lomond, Loch (lake), Sc,UK
71/S7 Lomonosov, Rus.
93/E5 Lompobatang (peak), Indo.
130/B4 Lompoc, Ca,US
89/C2 Lom Sak, Thai.
55/M2 Łomża, Pol.
90/B4 Lonāvale, India
118/B3 Loncoche, Chile
58/D2 Londerzeel, Belg.
58/A4 Londinières, Fr.
132/D3 London, On,Can.
53/F3 London (cap.), Eng,UK
132/C4 London, Ky,US
53/F3 London Colney, Eng,UK
119/J8 Londonderry (isl.), Chile
50/A2 Londonderry, NI,UK
50/A2 Londonderry (dist.), NI,UK
116/B2 Londrina, Braz.
131/H4 Lone Grove, Ok,US
96/E7 Lone Pine Sanct., Austl.
96/C4 Lonesome Nat'l Park, Austl.
123/F3 Long (isl.), Bahm.
129/J2 Long (pt.), Mb,Can.
132/C1 Long (lake), On,Can.
88/A3 Long (riv.), China
75/T2 Long (str.), Rus.
52/C1 Long (mtn.), Wal,UK
133/F3 Long (isl.), NS,Can.
118/C2 Longaví, Chile
133/R10 Long Beach, On,Can.
137/B3 Long Beach, Ca,US
137/F6 Long Beach (isl.), NJ,US
137/G5 Long Beach, NY,US
51/G1 Longbenton, Eng,UK
135/H5 Longboat Key, Fl,US
137/G5 Long Branch, NJ,US
53/E2 Long Buckby, Eng,UK
89/D1 Long Chau, Viet.
88/C3 Longchuan, China
91/G3 Longchuan, China
53/F3 Long Crendon, Eng,UK
51/G6 Long Eaton, Eng,UK
59/E5 Longeau (riv.), Fr.
133/G2 Longfellow (mts.), Me,US
49/B4 Longford, Ire.
88/B2 Longhui, China
137/G5 Long Island (sound), Ct,NY,US
132/C1 Longlac, On,Can.
52/D4 Longleat House, Eng,UK
87/C4 Longmen Shiyao (caves), China
131/F2 Longmont, Co,US
52/D1 Long Mynd, The (hill), Eng,UK
51/G5 Longnor, Eng,UK
89/D4 Long Phu, Viet.
133/K2 Long Range (mts.), Nf,Can.
51/F4 Longridge, Eng,UK
82/E4 Longshou (mts.), China
51/J6 Long Sutton, Eng,UK
51/F2 Longtown, Eng,UK
58/B2 Longuenesse, Fr.
133/N6 Longueuil, Qu,Can.
59/E5 Longuyon, Fr.
60/B3 Longvic, Fr.
134/E3 Longview, Tx,US
128/C4 Longview, Wa,US
59/E4 Longwy, Fr.
89/D4 Long Xuyen, Viet.
88/C2 Longyan, China
57/E3 Löningen, Ger.
62/C5 Lons, Fr.
60/B4 Lons-le-Saunier, Fr.
52/B6 Looe, Eng,UK
52/B6 Looe (isl.), Eng,UK
96/B1 Lookout (pt.), Austl.
135/J3 Lookout (cape), NC,US
107/B3 Loolmalasin (peak), Tanz.
128/F2 Loon Lake, Sk,Can.
56/C5 Loon op Zand, Neth.
49/G7 Loop Head (pt.), Ire.
58/C2 Loos, Fr.
81/F3 Lop (lake), China
75/R4 Lopatka, Mys (cape), Rus.
89/C3 Lop Buri, Thai.
102/G8 Lopez (cape), Gabon
56/B5 Lopik, Neth.
103/K7 Lopori (riv.), D.R. Congo
48/G1 Lopphavet (bay), Nor.
79/J3 Lora (riv.), Pak.
64/C4 Lora del Río, Sp.
79/J3 Lora, Hāmūn-i- (lake), Pak.
132/D3 Lorain, Oh,US
79/J2 Loralai, Pak.
65/E4 Lorca, Sp.
98/E8 Lord Howe (isl.), Austl.
130/E4 Lordsburg, NM,US
59/G3 Lorelei (cliff), Ger.
116/H7 Lorena, Braz.
93/J5 Lorentz (riv.), Indo.
56/C2 Lorentzsluizen (dam), Neth.
129/J3 Lorette, Mb,Can.
103/N7 Lorian (swamp), Kenya
123/F6 Lorica, Col.
62/B3 Lorient, Fr.
124/G2 Lorillard (riv.), Nun,Can.
68/D2 Lorinci, Hun.
133/Q8 Lorne Park, On,Can.
60/D2 Lörrach, Ger.
59/F6 Lorrain (plat.), Fr.
133/N6 Lorraine, Qu,Can.
60/C1 Lorraine (reg.), Fr.
51/E2 Lorton, Eng,UK
137/J8 Lorton, Va,US
137/B3 Los Alamitos, Ca,US
130/B4 Los Alamos, Ca,US
131/F4 Los Alamos, NM,US
118/C4 Los Alerces Nat'l Park, Arg.
138/K12 Los Altos, Ca,US
118/C2 Los Andes, Chile
118/B3 Los Ángeles, Chile
137/B2 Los Angeles, Ca,US
137/B2 Los Angeles (riv.), Ca,US
130/B3 Los Banos, Ca,US
64/C4 Los Barrios, Sp.
117/A6 Los Chonos (arch.), Chile
64/C1 Los Corrales de Buelna, Sp.
119/J7 Los Glaciares Nat'l Park, Arg.
59/F4 Losheim, Ger.
123/N8 Los Herreras, Mex.
55/M2 Łosice, Pol.
68/B3 Lošinj (isl.), Cro.
118/B3 Los Lagos, Chile
118/B4 Los Lagos (reg.), Chile
130/F4 Los Lunas, NM,US
123/N8 Los Mochis, Mex.
118/B4 Los Muermos, Chile
114/C2 Los Orquídeas Nat'l Park, Col.
64/C4 Los Palacios y Villafranca, Sp.
119/J8 Los Pingüinos Nat'l Park, Chile
122/A4 Los Reyes, Mex.
123/H5 Los Roques (isls.), Ven.
64/B3 Los Santos de Maimona, Sp.
118/B3 Los Sauces, Chile
56/E4 Losser, Neth.
123/H5 Los Teques, Ven.
130/D1 Lost River (range), Id,US
52/B6 Lostwithiel, Eng,UK
118/C1 Los Vilos, Chile
64/D3 Los Yébenes, Sp.
62/D4 Lot (riv.), Fr.
118/B3 Lota, Chile
79/G1 Lotfābād, Trkm.
57/E4 Lotte, Ger.
87/B5 Lou (riv.), China
89/C2 Louangphrabang, Laos
110/B1 Loubomo, Congo
62/B2 Loudéac, Fr.
88/B2 Loudi, China
62/D3 Loudun, Fr.
60/B3 Loue (riv.), Fr.
104/A3 Louga, Sen.
104/B3 Louga (reg.), Sen.
51/G6 Loughborough, Eng,UK
50/B3 Loughbrickland, NI,UK
125/R7 Lougheed (isl.), Nun,Can.
50/B3 Loughgall, NI,UK
132/E4 Louisa, Va,US
98/E6 Louisiade (arch.), PNG
134/E4 Louisiana (state), US
132/C4 Louisville, Ky,US
135/F3 Louisville, Ms,US
125/J3 Louis XIV (pt.), Qu,Can.
64/A4 Loulé, Port.
55/G3 Louny, Czh.
131/H2 Loup (riv.), Ne,US
50/B2 Loup, The, NI,UK
62/C5 Lourdes, Fr.
65/P10 Loures, Port.
64/A3 Louriçal, Port.
64/A3 Lourinhã, Port.
64/A2 Lousã, Port.
65/P10 Lousa, Port.
50/B4 Louth (co.), Ire.
51/H5 Louth, Eng,UK
67/H4 Loutrákion, Gre.
59/D2 Louvain (Leuven), Belg.
116/G8 Louveira, Braz.
58/A5 Louviers, Fr.
58/B5 Louvres, Fr.
58/C3 Louvroil, Fr.
58/B2 Lovaart (can.), Belg.
70/F4 Lovat' (riv.), Bela., Rus.
68/D4 Lovćen Nat'l Park, Mont.
69/G4 Lovech, Bul.
69/G4 Lovech (reg.), Bul.
131/F2 Loveland, Co,US
128/F4 Lovell, Wy,US
130/C2 Lovelock, Nv,US
63/J4 Lovere, It.
131/F4 Loving, NM,US
131/G4 Lovington, NM,US
70/G2 Lovozero (lake), Rus.
125/H2 Low (cape), Nun,Can.
103/L8 Lowa (riv.), D.R. Congo
51/H6 Lowdham, Eng,UK
133/G3 Lowell, Ma,US
108/B2 Löwen (dry riv.), Namb.
128/D3 Lower Arrow (lake), BC,Can.
63/L2 Lower Austria (prov.), Aus.
53/E2 Lower Brailes, Eng,UK
97/B3 Lower Glenelg Nat'l Park, Austl.
97/C4 Lower Gordon-Franklin Wild Rivers Nat'l Park, Austl.
53/E3 Lower Heyford, Eng,UK
129/K4 Lower Red (lake), Mn,US
74/K3 Lower Tunguska (riv.), Rus.
110/E4 Lower Zambezi Nat'l Park, Zam.
53/H2 Lowestoft, Eng,UK
110/E1 Lowi (riv.), D.R. Congo
55/K2 Łowicz, Pol.
50/E1 Lowther (hills), Sc,UK
133/Q9 Lowville, On,Can.
57/F2 Loxstedt, Ger.
99/V12 Loyalty (isls.), NCal.
68/D3 Loznica, Serb.
72/F2 Lozovaya, Ukr.
68/E3 Lozovik, Serb.
87/C5 Lu (riv.), China
110/D2 Luachimo, Ang.
110/E1 Lualaba (riv.), D.R. Congo
87/J6 Luam (riv.), China
126/T10 Lua Makika (crater), Hi,US
87/D5 Lu'an, China
87/D2 Luan (riv.), China
64/C1 Luanco, Sp.
110/B2 Luanda (cap.), Ang.
89/C5 Luang (lag.), Thai.
89/B4 Luang (peak), Thai.
89/C2 Luang Prabang (range), Laos
107/B5 Luangwa (riv.), Moz., Zam.
110/E3 Luanshya, Zam.
87/D3 Luan Xian, China
110/D3 Luao, Ang.
107/A5 Luapula (prov.), Zam.
64/B1 Luarca, Sp.
110/D3 Luashi, D.R. Congo
102/G7 Luba, EqG.
122/D4 Lubaantun (ruins), Belz.
55/M3 Lubaczów, Pol.
55/H3 Lubań, Pol.
110/B3 Lubango, Ang.
55/M3 Lubartów, Pol.
55/K2 Lubawa, Pol.
57/F4 Lübbecke, Ger.
59/D2 Lubbeek, Belg.
134/C3 Lubbock, Tx,US
54/F2 Lübeck, Ger.
110/D1 Lubefu, D.R. Congo
55/M3 Lubelska (upland), Pol.
55/M3 Lubelskie (prov.), Pol.
107/A3 Lubero, D.R. Congo
55/J3 Lubin, Pol.
55/M3 Lublin, Pol.
55/K3 Lubliniec, Pol.
72/E2 Lubny, Ukr.
55/J2 Luboń, Pol.
55/H3 Lubsko, Pol.
110/E2 Lubudi, D.R. Congo
92/B4 Lubuklinggau, Indo.
92/B3 Lubuksikaping, Indo.
110/E3 Lubumbashi, D.R. Congo
110/E2 Lubunda, D.R. Congo
55/H2 Lubuskie (prov.), Pol.
110/C2 Lucala, Ang.
50/B5 Lucan, Ire.
89/D1 Luc An Chau, Viet.
136/K3 Lucania (mtn.), Yk,Can.
110/D2 Lucapa, Ang.
63/J5 Lucca, It.

50/D2 Luce (bay), Sc,UK
135/F4 Lucedale, Ms,US
116/B2 Lucélia, Braz.
88/D5 Lucena, Phil.
64/C4 Lucena, Sp.
55/K4 Lučenec, Slvk.
61/E3 Lucerne (Vierwaldstättersee) (lake), Swi.
54/F2 Lüchow, Ger.
55/G2 Luckenwalde, Ger.
90/D2 Lucknow, India
128/G3 Lucky Lake, Sk,Can.
123/F3 Lucrecia (cape), Cuba
110/D3 Lucusse, Ang.
69/H4 Luda Kamchiya (riv.), Bul.
57/E6 Lüdenscheid, Ger.
108/A2 Lüderitz, Namb.
53/E4 Ludgershall, Eng,UK
79/L2 Ludhiāna, India
57/E5 Ludinghausen, Ger.
132/C3 Ludington, Mi,US
52/D2 Ludlow, Eng,UK
69/H4 Ludogorie (reg.), Bul.
69/G2 Luduş, Rom.
48/E3 Ludvika, Swe.
63/H2 Ludwigsburg, Ger.
55/G2 Ludwigsfelde, Ger.
54/F2 Ludwigslust, Ger.
110/D2 Luebo, D.R. Congo
134/E4 Lufkin, Tx,US
70/F4 Luga, Rus.
61/E6 Lugano, Swi.
57/F5 Lügde, Ger.
110/G3 Lugenda (riv.), Moz.
52/D2 Lugg (riv.), Eng,UK
50/B6 Lugnaquillia (mtn.), Ire.
64/B1 Lugo, Sp.
68/E3 Lugoj, Rom.
72/F2 Luhans'k, Ukr.
72/F2 Luhans'ka Obl., Ukr.
57/H2 Luhe (riv.), Ger.
110/D4 Luiana, Ang.
63/H4 Luino, It.
111/X Luitpold (coast), Ant.
68/D3 Lukavac, Bosn.
110/C1 Lukenie (riv.), D.R. Congo
69/G4 Lukovit, Bul.
55/M3 Łuków, Pol.
98/E4 Lukunor (atoll), Micr.
48/G2 Luleå, Swe.
48/G2 Luleälv (riv.), Swe.
69/H5 Lüleburgaz, Turk.
87/B4 Luling Guan (pass), China
98/G5 Lulua, Tuv.
110/D2 Lulua (riv.), D.R. Congo
110/D3 Lumai, Ang.
81/D5 Lumajamgdong (lake), China
135/J3 Lumberton, NC,US
134/E4 Lumberton, Tx,US
110/H4 Lumbo, Moz.
128/D3 Lumby, BC,Can.
91/F2 Lumding, India
59/E2 Lummen, Belg.
89/D3 Lumphat, Camb.
129/G3 Lumsden, Sk,Can.
95/G7 Lumsden, NZ
110/D3 Lunache, Ang.
55/G1 Lund, Swe.
130/D3 Lund, Nv,US
110/F5 Lundi (riv.), Zim.
52/B4 Lundy (isl.), Eng,UK
57/F2 Lune (riv.), Ger.
51/F3 Lune (riv.), Eng,UK
57/H2 Lüneburg, Ger.
57/G2 Lüneburger Heide (reg.), Ger.
62/F5 Lunel, Fr.
57/E5 Lünen, Ger.
133/H2 Lunenburg, NS,Can.
110/E3 Lunga (riv.), Zam.
91/F3 Lunglei, India
110/D3 Lungue-Bungo (riv.), Ang.
90/B3 Luni (riv.), India
87/B3 Luo (riv.), China
87/B4 Luo (riv.), China
87/C4 Luohe, China
87/D4 Luoma (lake), China
89/C1 Luong (mts.), Viet.
87/C4 Luoyang, China
110/B1 Luozi, D.R. Congo
110/E4 Lupane, Zim.
91/H2 Lupanshui, China
69/F3 Lupeni, Rom.
91/H2 Luquan, China
79/J2 Lūrah (riv.), Afg.
132/E4 Luray, Va,US
50/B3 Lurgan, NI,UK
110/H3 Lúrio, Moz.
110/G3 Lúrio (riv.), Moz.
110/E4 Lusaka (cap.), Zam.
110/E1 Lusambo, D.R. Congo
110/D1 Lusambo, D.R. Congo
87/D3 Lu Shan (mtn.), China
87/C5 Lu Shan (peak), China
67/F2 Lushnje, Alb.
129/G5 Lusk, Wy,US
103/J7 Lutanga (riv.), D.R. Congo
137/K7 Lutherville, Md,US
56/D1 Lütjehorn (isl.), Ger.
53/F3 Luton, Eng,UK
53/F3 Luton (co.), Eng,UK
72/C2 Lutsk, Ukr.
57/F5 Lutter (riv.), Ger.
111/C Lützow-Holm (bay), Ant.
103/P7 Luuq, Som.
129/J5 Luverne, Mn,US
59/E4 Luxembourg (ctry.)
59/E4 Luxembourg (prov.), Belg.
59/F4 Luxembourg (cap.), Lux.
59/F4 Luxembourg (dist.), Lux.
91/J2 Lu Xian, China
106/C3 Luxor (Al Uqşur), Egypt
62/C5 Luy (riv.), Fr.
116/C1 Luz, Braz.
71/L3 Luza (riv.), Rus.
60/E3 Luzern (canton), Swi.
61/E3 Luzern (Lucerne), Swi.
91/J2 Luzhou, China
115/J7 Luziânia, Braz.
88/D4 Luzon (isl.), Phil.
72/C2 L'viv, Ukr.
72/B2 L'vivs'ka Obl., Ukr.
89/C1 Lwi (riv.), Myan.
71/P3 Lyapin (riv.), Rus.
69/G4 Lyaskovets, Bul.
48/F2 Lycksele, Swe.
53/G5 Lydd, Eng,UK
111/Y Lyddan (isl.), Ant.
109/E2 Lydenburg, SAfr.
52/D3 Lydney, Eng,UK
128/F5 Lyman, Wy,US
52/C5 Lyme (bay), Eng,UK
52/D5 Lyme Regis, Eng,UK
53/E5 Lymington, Eng,UK
51/F5 Lymm, Eng,UK
55/L1 Lyna (riv.), Pol.
50/D5 Lynas (pt.), Wal,UK
137/G5 Lynbrook, NY,US
132/E4 Lynchburg, Va,US
135/H3 Lynches (riv.), SC,US
96/A2 Lynd (riv.), Austl.
53/E5 Lyndhurst, Eng,UK
137/F5 Lyndhurst, NJ,US
51/F1 Lyne (riv.), Eng,UK
48/G1 Lyngen (fjord), Nor.
133/G3 Lynn, Ma,US
135/G4 Lynn Haven, Fl,US
138/C2 Lynnwood, Wa,US
52/C4 Lynton, Eng,UK
137/B3 Lynwood, Ca,US
124/F2 Lynx (lake), NW,Can.
62/F4 Lyon, Fr.
131/H3 Lyons, Ks,US
52/C4 Lype (hill), Eng,UK
98/E5 Lyra (reef), PNG
58/B2 Lys (riv.), Fr.
55/K4 Lysá (peak), Czh.
70/E5 Lysaya, Gora (hill), Bela.
55/L3 Lysica (peak), Pol.
58/C2 Lys-lez-Lannoy, Fr.
71/N4 Lys'va, Rus.
72/F2 Lysychans'k, Ukr.
52/D5 Lytchett Matravers, Eng,UK
51/E4 Lytham Saint Anne's, Eng,UK
71/W9 Lytkarino, Rus.
128/C3 Lytton, BC,Can.
71/W9 Lyubertsy, Rus.
69/H5 Lyubimets, Bul.
72/E2 Lyubotin, Ukr.
72/E1 Lyudinovo, Rus.
52/C3 Lywd (riv.), Wal,UK

M

89/C1 Ma (riv.), Laos, Viet.
80/K5 Ma'alot, Isr.
106/C2 Ma'ān, Jor.
70/F2 Maanselkä (mts.), Fin.
87/D5 Ma'anshan, China
56/C6 Maarheeze, Neth.
56/C4 Maarssen, Neth.
54/D3 Maas (riv.), Eur.
56/C6 Maasbracht, Neth.
56/D6 Maasbree, Neth.
59/E1 Maaseik, Belg.
88/D5 Maasin, Phil.
59/E2 Maasmechelen, Belg.
56/B5 Maassluis, Neth.
59/E2 Maastricht, Neth.
80/N7 Ma'ayan Harod Nat'l Park, Isr.
88/D4 Mabalacat, Phil.
110/F5 Mabalane, Moz.
51/J5 Mablethorpe, Eng,UK
110/F5 Mabote, Moz.
118/B5 Macá (peak), Chile
116/D2 Macaé, Braz.
115/L5 Macaíba, Braz.
115/H3 Macapá, Braz.
114/C4 Macará, Ecu.
115/L5 Macau, Braz.
88/B3 Macau, China
98/H7 Macauley (isl.), NZ
114/D3 Macaya (riv.), Col.
123/G4 Macaya (pk.), Haiti
135/H4 Macclenny, Fl,US
51/F5 Macclesfield, Eng,UK
51/F5 Macclesfield (can.), Eng,UK
108/D3 Macdhui (peak), SAfr.
49/D2 Macduff, Sc,UK
67/G2 Macedonia, Former Yugoslav Rep. of (ctry.)
67/G2 Macedonia (reg.), FYROM, Gre.
115/L5 Maceió, Braz.
66/C1 Macerata, It.
111/E Macey (peak), Ant.
108/D3 Machache (peak), Les.
116/H6 Machado, Braz.
107/C3 Machakos, Kenya
114/C4 Machala, Ecu.
114/B4 Machalilla Nat'l Park, Ecu.
110/F5 Machanga, Moz.
50/D2 Machars, The (pen.), Sc,UK
110/F5 Machaze, Moz.
110/E5 Machemma (ruins), SAfr.
52/C3 Machen, Wal,UK
87/C5 Macheng, China
133/H2 Machias, Me,US
64/D1 Machichaco (cape), Sp.
65/V15 Machico, Madr.,Port.
85/H7 Machida, Japan
90/D4 Machilipatnam, India
123/G5 Machiques, Ven.
114/D6 Machu Picchu (ruins), Peru
114/F6 Machupo (riv.), Bol.
52/C1 Machynlleth, Wal,UK
69/J3 Măcin, Rom.
104/D3 Macina (reg.), Mali
97/D1 Macintyre (riv.), Austl.
130/E3 Mack, Co,US
96/C3 Mackay, Austl.
111/E MacKenzie (bay), Ant.
96/C3 Mackenzie (riv.), Austl.
128/C2 Mackenzie, BC,Can.
136/N2 Mackenzie (riv.), NW,Can.
124/C2 Mackenzie (bay), NW, Yk,Can.
124/C2 Mackenzie (mts.), NW, Yk,Can.
125/R7 Mackenzie King (is.), NW,Can.
132/C2 Mackinac Island, Mi,US
135/F1 Mackinaw (riv.), Il,US
132/C2 Mackinaw City, Mi,US
128/F2 Macklin, Sk,Can.
96/F7 Macleay (riv.), Austl.
136/L3 Macmillan (riv.), Yk,Can.
66/A2 Macomer, It.
60/A5 Mâcon, Fr.
131/K4 Macon (bayou), Ar, La,US
135/H3 Macon, Ga,US
131/J3 Macon, Mo,US
50/B1 Macosquin, NI,UK
97/C4 Macquarie (har.), Austl.
45/S8 Macquarie (isl.), Austl.
97/C1 Macquarie (riv.), Austl.
111/D Mac-Robertson Land (reg.), Ant.
114/F5 Macuim (riv.), Braz.
128/C5 Mad (riv.), Ca,US
80/K6 Ma'dabā, Jor.
109/H8 Madagascar (ctry.)
102/H3 Madama, Niger
69/G5 Madan, Bul.
90/C5 Madanapalle, India
98/D5 Madang, PNG
102/H1 Madanīyīn, Tun.
105/G3 Madaoua, Niger
90/F3 Mādārīpur, Bang.
132/E2 Madawaska (riv.), On,Can.
133/G2 Madawaska, Me,US
114/F5 Madeira (riv.), Braz.
65/V15 Madeira (isl.), Madr., Port.
65/U14 Madeira (aut. reg.), Port.
129/L4 Madelin (isl.), Wi,US
123/N8 Madera, Mex.
122/D5 Madera (vol.), Nic.
90/E2 Madhipura, India
90/C3 Madhya Pradesh (state), India
114/E6 Madidi (riv.), Bol.
131/H4 Madill, Ok,US
110/B1 Madingo-Kayes, Congo
135/G3 Madison, Al,US
135/H4 Madison, Fl,US
132/C4 Madison, In,US
135/F3 Madison, Ms,US
128/F4 Madison (riv.), Mt,US
131/H2 Madison, Ne,US
137/F5 Madison, NJ,US
129/J4 Madison, SD US
132/B3 Madison (cap.), Wi,US
132/D4 Madison, WV,US
138/F6 Madison Heights, Mi,US
132/C4 Madisonville, Ky,US
134/E4 Madisonville, Tx,US
92/D5 Madiun, Indo.
82/D5 Madoi, China
60/C1 Madon (riv.), Fr.
79/G5 Madrakah, Ra's al (pt.), Oman
90/D5 Madras (Chennai), India
128/C4 Madras, Or,US
122/B2 Madre (lag.), Mex.
134/D5 Madre (lag.), Tx,US
114/E6 Madre de Dios (riv.), Bol., Peru
119/J7 Madre de Dios (isl.), Chile
62/E5 Madrès (mtn.), Fr.
64/C2 Madrid (aut. comm.), Sp.
65/N9 Madrid (cap.), Sp.
64/D3 Madridejos, Sp.
92/D4 Madugula, India
90/C6 Madurai, India
85/F2 Maebashi, Japan
89/C2 Mae Charim, Thai.
89/B2 Mae Ping Nat'l Park, Thai.
52/C3 Maesteg, Wal,UK
89/B2 Mae Tho (peak), Thai.
98/F6 Maewo (isl.), Van.
89/B2 Mae Ya (mtn.), Thai.
107/C4 Mafia (isl.), Tanz.
108/D2 Mafikeng, SAfr.
104/C4 Mafou (riv.), Gui.
116/B3 Mafra, Braz.
64/A3 Mafra, Port.
75/R4 Magadan, Rus.
75/R3 Magadanskaya Obl., Rus.
107/C3 Magadi, Kenya
108/P12 Magalies Berg (range), SAfr.
119/K8 Magallanes (Magellan) (str.), Arg., Chile
119/K8 Magallanes y Antártica Chilena (reg.), Chile
123/G6 Magangué, Col.
88/D6 Maganoy, Phil.
105/H3 Magaria, Niger
88/D4 Magat (riv.), Phil.
131/J4 Magazine (peak), Ar,US
83/K1 Magdagachi, Rus.
133/J2 Magdalen (isls.), Qu,Can.
119/T12 Magdalena, Arg.
114/D3 Magdalena (riv.), Col.
123/M7 Magdalena de Kino, Mex.
93/E3 Magdalena, Gunung (peak), Malay.
54/F2 Magdeburg, Ger.
54/F2 Magdeburger Börde (plain), Ger.
116/K7 Magé, Braz.
135/F4 Magee, Ms,US
50/C2 Magee, Island (pen.), NI,UK
92/C5 Magelang, Indo.
119/K8 Magellan (Magallanes) (str.), Arg., Chile
48/H1 Magerøya (isl.), Nor.
63/H4 Maggiore (lake), It., Swi.
106/B2 Maghāghah, Egypt
50/B2 Maghera, NI,UK
50/B2 Magherafelt, NI,UK
50/B2 Magherafelt (dist.), NI,UK
66/A5 Maghīla (peak), Tun.
51/F4 Maghull, Eng,UK
50/B1 Magilligan, NI,UK
50/B1 Magilligan (pt.), NI,UK
68/D3 Maglaj, Bosn.
68/D4 Maglić (peak), Mont.
67/F2 Maglie, It.
132/D2 Magnetawan (riv.), On,Can.
96/B2 Magnetic (passg.), Austl.
96/B2 Magnetic I. Nat'l Park, Austl.
71/N5 Magnitogorsk, Rus.
134/E3 Magnolia, Ar,US
133/F2 Magog, Qu,Can.
103/N6 Mago Nat'l Park, Eth.
52/D3 Magor, Wal,UK
133/H1 Magpie (riv.), Qu,Can.
91/F3 Magway (Magwe), Myan.
91/F4 Magway (div.), Myan.
78/E1 Mahābād, Iran
90/B4 Mahād, India
99/X15 Mahaena, FrPol.
114/G2 Mahaica, Guy.
109/H6 Mahajamba (bay), Madg.
109/H7 Mahajamba (riv.), Madg.
109/H6 Mahajanga (prov.), Madg.
109/H7 Mahajilo (riv.), Madg.
93/E3 Mahakam (riv.), Indo.
110/E5 Mahalapye, Bots.
78/F2 Mahallāt, Iran
79/G2 Māhān, Iran
90/D3 Mahānadī (riv.), India
104/D4 Mahandiabani (riv.), C.d'Iv.
90/C2 Mahārajpur, India
90/B4 Mahārāshtra (state), India
90/D3 Mahāsamund, India
89/C2 Maha Sarakham, Thai.
109/H7 Mahavavy (riv.), Madg.
90/C4 Mahbubnagar, India
66/B5 Mahdia, Tun.
66/B5 Mahdia (gov.), Tun.
79/L2 Mahe, India
45/M6 Mahé (isl.), Sey.
109/S15 Mahébourg, Mrts.
72/D1 Mahilyow, Bela.
72/D1 Mahilyowskaya Voblasts, Bela.
91/G3 Mahlaing, Myan.
90/C2 Mahoba, India
65/H3 Mahón, Sp.
90/B3 Mahuva, India
137/F4 Mahwah, NJ,US
96/E6 Maiala Nat'l Park, Austl.
98/G4 Maiana (atoll), Kiri.
99/W15 Maiao (isl.), FrPol.
114/D1 Maicao, Col.
115/H3 Maicuru (riv.), Braz.
53/F3 Maidenhead, Eng,UK
52/D5 Maiden Newton, Eng,UK
50/D1 Maidens, Sc,UK
138/G7 Maidstone, On,Can.
128/F2 Maidstone, Sk,Can.
53/G4 Maidstone, Eng,UK
102/H5 Maiduguri, Nga.
58/B4 Maignelay-Montigny, Fr.
49/A4 Maigue (riv.), Ire.
90/D3 Maihar, India
84/E3 Maihara, Japan
103/L8 Maiko Nat'l Park, D.R. Congo
126/V13 Maili, Hi,US
79/K3 Mailsi, Pak.
63/H2 Main (riv.), Ger.
50/B2 Main (riv.), NI,UK
110/C1 Mai-Ndombe (lake), D.R. Congo
133/G3 Maine (gulf), Can., US
62/C2 Maine (hills), Fr.
49/A4 Maine (riv.), Ire.
133/G2 Maine (state), US
96/C5 Main Range Nat'l Park, Austl.
63/H2 Mainz, Ger.
118/C2 Maipo (vol.), Arg., Chile
118/Q9 Maipo (riv.), Chile
118/F3 Maipú, Arg.
118/C2 Maipú, Chile
63/G4 Maira (riv.), It.
116/G8 Mairiporã, Braz.
123/G3 Maisí (cape), Cuba
132/D3 Maitland (riv.), On,Can.
111/A Maitri, Ant.
59/F5 Maizières-lès-Metz, Fr.
84/D3 Maizuru, Japan
65/N9 Majadahonda, Sp.
67/G2 Maja e Zezë (peak), Alb.
66/A4 Majardah (riv.), Tun.
68/E3 Majdanpek, Serb.
102/J2 Majdūl, Libya
93/E4 Majene, Indo.
103/N6 Majī, Eth.
87/D3 Majia (riv.), China
65/G3 Majorca (Mallorca) (isl.), Sp.
98/G4 Majuro (atoll), Mrsh.
98/G4 Majuro (cap.), Mrsh.
110/B1 Makabana, Congo
126/V13 Makaha, Hi,US
126/V13 Makakilo City, Hi,US
83/N2 Makarov, Rus.
68/C4 Makarska, Cro.
93/E4 Makassar (str.), Indo.
99/L6 Makatea (isl.), FrPol.
109/H8 Makay (massif), Madg.
99/L6 Makemo (atoll), FrPol.
104/B4 Makeni, SLeo.
110/D5 Makgadikgadi (salt pans), Bots.
73/H4 Makhachkala, Rus.
93/G3 Makian (isl.), Indo.
98/G4 Makin (atoll), Kiri.
81/B1 Makinsk, Kaz.
72/F2 Makiyivka, Ukr.
78/C4 Makkah (Mecca), SAr.
68/E2 Makó, Hun.
102/H7 Makokou, Gabon
55/L2 Maków Mazowiecki, Pol.
79/H3 Makran (reg.), Iran, Pak.
79/K3 Makrāna, India
80/F2 Mākū, Iran
107/B5 Makumbako, Tanz.
84/B5 Makurazaki, Japan
136/E5 Makushin (vol.), Ak,US
114/C6 Mala, Peru
90/B5 Malabar (coast), India
102/G7 Malabo (cap.), EqG.
116/D1 Malacacheta, Braz.
89/B5 Malacca (str.), Malay., Thai.
55/J4 Malacky, Slvk.
128/E5 Malad City, Id,US
64/C4 Málaga, Sp.
64/D3 Malagón, Sp.
50/B5 Malahide, Ire.
98/F5 Malaita (isl.), Sol.
103/M6 Malakāl, Sudan
90/D4 Malakangiri, India
123/G5 Malambo, Col.
92/C5 Malang, Indo.
110/C2 Malange, Ang.
118/C2 Malargüe, Arg.
132/E1 Malartic, Qu,Can.
93/E5 Malasoro (pt.), Indo.
80/D2 Malatya, Turk.
110/F3 Malawi (ctry.)
89/B5 Malay (pen.), Malay.
70/G4 Malaya Vishera, Rus.
88/E6 Malaybalay, Phil.
78/E2 Malāyer, Iran
92/C2 Malaysia (ctry.)
71/L2 Malazemel'skaya (tundra), Rus.
80/E2 Malazgirt, Turk.
133/G2 Malbaie (riv.), Qu,Can.
105/G3 Malbaza-Usine, Niger
55/K1 Malbork, Pol.
54/G2 Malchin, Ger.
82/C2 Malchin, Mong.
58/C1 Maldegem, Belg.
99/K5 Malden (isl.), Kiri.
132/B4 Malden, Mo,US
77/G9 Maldives (ctry.)
53/G3 Maldon, Eng,UK
119/G2 Maldonado, Uru.
119/G2 Maldonado (dept.), Uru.
77/G9 Male (cap.), Mald.
67/H4 Maléa, Ákra (cape), Gre.
90/B3 Mālegaon, India
98/F6 Malekula (isl.), Van.
62/D4 Malemort-sur-Corrèze, Fr.
54/F1 Malente, Ger.
79/L2 Māler Kotla, India
73/H4 Malgobek, Rus.
55/G2 Malgrat de Mar, Sp.
103/L4 Malha Wells, Sudan
128/D5 Malheur (lake), Or,US
128/D5 Malheur (riv.), Or,US
109/S14 Malheureux (cape), Mrts.
102/E4 Mali (ctry.)
89/B3 Mali (isl.), Myan.
82/F4 Malian (riv.), China
137/B2 Malibu, Ca,US
103/L4 Malik (wadi), Sudan
72/D2 Malin, Ukr.
93/E3 Malinau, Indo.
107/D3 Malindi, Kenya
87/C3 Maling Guan (pass), China
109/H8 Malio (riv.), Madg.
89/D1 Malipo, China
79/J4 Malīr Cantonment, Pak.
88/E6 Malita, Phil.
103/P7 Malka Mari Nat'l Park, Kenya
69/H5 Malkara, Turk.
105/H3 Mallammaduri, Nga.
106/B3 Mallawī, Egypt
97/B2 Mallee Cliffs Nat'l Park, Austl.
118/Q10 Malloa, Chile
65/G3 Mallorca (Majorca) (isl.), Sp.
49/A4 Mallow, Ire.
48/G2 Malmberget, Swe.
59/F3 Malmédy, Belg.
108/B4 Malmesbury, SAfr.
52/D3 Malmesbury, Eng,UK
54/G1 Malmö, Swe.
55/G1 Malmöhus (co.), Swe.
71/L4 Malmyzh, Rus.
115/H5 Maloca, Braz.
98/G4 Maloelap (atoll), Mrsh.
132/F2 Malone, NY,US
55/L3 Małopolska (upland), Pol.
55/K4 Małopolskie (prov.), Pol.
48/C3 Måløy, Nor.
51/F5 Malpas, Eng,UK
114/B3 Malpelo (isl.), Col.
64/A1 Malpica, Sp.
66/D5 Malta (ctry.)
66/D5 Malta (isl.), Malta
128/G3 Malta, Mt,US
51/G2 Maltby, Eng,UK
51/G5 Maltby, Eng,UK
133/Q8 Malton, On,Can.
51/H3 Malton, Eng,UK
110/C1 Maluku, D.R. Congo
48/E3 Malung, Swe.
90/B4 Malvan, India
65/P10 Malveira, Port.
97/G5 Malvern, Austl.
134/E3 Malvern, Ar,US
52/D2 Malvern (Great Malvern), Eng,UK
119/M8 Malvinas, Islas (Falkland Islands) (dpcy.), UK
73/J2 Malyy Uzen' (riv.), Rus.
82/D1 Malyy Yenisey (riv.), Rus.
59/F6 Malzéville, Fr.
115/M5 Mamanguape, Braz.
137/G5 Mamaroneck, NY,US
110/E4 Mamba, Zam.
88/D6 Mambajao, Phil.
103/A2 Mambasa, D.R. Congo
93/J4 Mamberamo (riv.), Indo.
102/J6 Mambéré (riv.), CAfr.
80/D3 Mambij, Syria
88/D5 Mamburao, Phil.
59/F4 Mamer, Lux.
62/D2 Mamers, Fr.
58/B2 Mametz, Fr.
105/H5 Mamfé, Camr.
132/C4 Mammoth Cave Nat'l Park, Ky,US
135/F2 Mammoth Spring, Ar,US
114/E6 Mamoré (riv.), Bol.
109/H6 Mamoutzou (cap.), May.
105/E5 Mampong, Gha.
55/L1 Mamry (lake), Pol.
93/E4 Mamuju, Indo.
110/D5 Mamuno, Bots.
115/G4 Mamurí (riv.), Braz.
87/C5 Man (riv.), China
104/D5 Man, C.d'Iv.
114/F4 Manacapuru, Braz.
52/A6 Manacle (pt.), UK
65/G3 Manacor, Sp.
93/F3 Manado, Indo.
122/D5 Managua (cap.), Nic.
122/D5 Managua (lake), Nic.
109/J8 Manakara, Madg.
137/F5 Manalapan, NJ,US
78/F3 Manama (Al Manāmah) (cap.), Bahr.
109/H7 Manambaho (riv.), Madg.
109/H7 Manambolo (riv.), Madg.
109/J7 Mananara, Madg.
109/H8 Mananara (riv.), Madg.
109/J8 Mananjary, Madg.
109/H8 Mananjary (riv.), Madg.
81/D2 Manas (lake), China
81/E3 Manas (riv.), China
90/D2 Manāslu (mtn.), Nepal
137/F5 Manasquan, NJ,US
137/F5 Manasquan (riv.), NJ,US
131/F3 Manassa, Co,US
132/E4 Manassas, Va,US
67/G1 Manastir Dečani, Serb.
67/G1 Manastir Gračanica, Serb.
67/G1 Manastir Sopoćani, Serb.
85/H7 Manatsuru, Japan
114/F4 Manaus, Braz.
80/B3 Manavgat, Turk.
129/H2 Manawan (lake), Sk,Can.
85/H7 Manazuru-misaki (cape), Japan
50/D3 Man, Calf of (isl.), IM,UK
64/D4 Mancha Real, Sp.
90/C4 Mancherāl, India
95/E6 Manchester (lake), Austl.
51/F5 Manchester, Eng,UK
51/F5 Manchester (co.), Eng,UK
132/D4 Manchester, Ky,US
133/G3 Manchester, NH,US
135/G3 Manchester, Tn,US
83/J3 Manchuria (reg.), China
78/F3 Mand (riv.), Iran
107/B5 Manda, Tanz.
116/B2 Mandaguari, Braz.
48/C4 Mandal, Nor.
93/K4 Mandala (peak), Indo.
89/B1 Mandalay, Myan.
89/A1 Mandalay (div.), Myan.
75/L5 Mandalgovĭ, Mong.
78/E2 Mandalī, Iraq
129/H4 Mandan, ND,US
103/J6 Manda Nat'l Park, Chad
93/F5 Mandasavu (peak), Indo.
88/D5 Mandaue, Phil.
63/H4 Mandello del Lario, It.
59/F3 Manderscheid, Ger.
123/F4 Mandeville, Jam.
79/L2 Māndi, India
110/F4 Mandié, Moz.
93/G4 Mandioli (isl.), Indo.
90/D3 Mandla, India
54/E1 Mandø (isl.), Den.
67/L6 Mándra, Gre.
109/H9 Mandrare (riv.), Madg.
109/J6 Mandritsara, Madg.
90/C3 Mandsaur, India
95/A4 Mandurah, Austl.
67/E2 Manduria, It.
90/A3 Māndvi, India
90/C5 Mandya, India
90/D2 Mane (pass), Nepal
53/G2 Manea, Eng,UK
90/D3 Manendragarh, India
105/H5 Manengouba, Massif du (peak), Camr.
63/J4 Manerbio, It.
78/B3 Manfalūt, Egypt
66/D2 Manfredonia, It.
66/E2 Manfredonia (gulf), It.
87/B4 Mang (riv.), China
115/J6 Mangabeiras (hills), Braz.
110/C1 Mangai, D.R. Congo
99/K7 Mangaia (isl.), Cookls.
91/F2 Mangaldai, India
88/D4 Mangaldan, Phil.
69/J4 Mangalia, Rom.
90/B5 Mangalore, India
99/M7 Mangareva (isl.), FrPol.
73/K3 Mangghystaū Obl., Kaz.
73/J3 Mangghystaū (pen.), Kaz.
73/K4 Mangghystaū (plat.), Kaz.
93/E3 Mangkalihat (cape), Indo.
79/K2 Mangla, Pak.
114/C3 Manglares (pt.), Col.
105/F4 Mango, Togo
110/G3 Mangoche, Malw.
109/H8 Mangoky (riv.), Madg.
93/G4 Mangole (isl.), Indo.
109/J7 Mangoro (riv.), Madg.
52/D4 Mangotsfield, Eng,UK
90/B3 Māngrol, India
119/G2 Mangueira (lake), Braz.
131/H4 Mangum, Ok,US
131/H3 Manhattan, Ks,US
128/F4 Manhattan, Mt,US
137/B3 Manhattan Beach, Ca,US
116/D2 Manhuaçu, Braz.
116/D2 Manhumirim, Braz.
67/H4 Máni (pen.), Gre.
109/H7 Mania (riv.), Madg.
110/F4 Manica, Moz.
114/F5 Manicoré, Braz.
114/F5 Manicoré (riv.), Braz.
129/J3 Manicouagan, Mb,Can.
133/G1 Manicouagan (res.), Qu,Can.
133/G1 Manicouagan (riv.), Qu,Can.
133/H1 Manicouagan, Petit Lac (lake), Qu,Can.
96/C3 Manifold (cape), Austl.
99/L6 Manihi (isl.), FrPol.
99/J6 Manihiki (atoll), Cookls.
88/D5 Manila (cap.), Phil.
130/E2 Manila, Ut,US
109/J7 Maningory (riv.), Madg.
93/G4 Manipa (str.), Indo.
91/F3 Manipur (state), India
80/A2 Manisa, Turk.
50/D3 Man, Isle of (isl.), UK
132/C2 Manistee, Mi,US
132/C2 Manistee (riv.), Mi,US
124/G3 Manitoba (prov.), Can.
129/J3 Manitoba (lake), Mb,Can.
133/H1 Manitou (riv.), Qu,Can.
132/D2 Manitoulin (isl.), On,Can.
134/B2 Manitou Springs, Co,US
132/C1 Manitouwadge, On,Can.
132/C2 Manitowoc, Wi,US
132/F2 Maniwaki, Qu,Can.
114/C2 Manizales, Col.
90/C4 Manjlegaon, India
79/L5 Mānjra (riv.), India
129/K4 Mankato, Mn,US
104/D4 Mankono, C.d'Iv.
82/F3 Manlay, Mong.
64/D2 Manlleu, Sp.
96/H8 Manly, Austl.
90/B3 Manmād, India
89/B4 Man Mia (peak), Thai.
90/C6 Mannar (gulf), India, SrL.
90/C6 Mannar, SrL.
90/C5 Mannārgudi, India
108/C4 Mannetjiesberg (peak), SAfr.
63/H2 Mannheim, Ger.
125/Q7 Manning (cape), NW,Can.
135/H3 Manning, SC,US
53/H3 Manningtree, Eng,UK
104/C5 Mano (riv.), Libr., SLeo.
110/E2 Manono, D.R. Congo
137/H5 Manorville, NY,US
62/F5 Manosque, Fr.
133/G1 Manouane (lake), Qu,Can.
133/G1 Manouane (riv.), Qu,Can.
99/H5 Manra (Sydney) (atoll), Kiri.
65/F2 Manresa, Sp.
107/A5 Mansa, Zam.
104/B3 Mansa Konko, Gam.
93/F1 Mansalay, Phil.
125/H2 Mansel (isl.), Nun,Can.
51/G5 Mansfield, Eng,UK
134/E3 Mansfield, La,US
132/D3 Mansfield, Oh,US
51/G5 Mansfield Woodhouse, Eng,UK
114/B4 Manta, Ecu.
93/E2 Mantalingaian (mt.), Phil.
114/C6 Mantaro (riv.), Peru
130/B3 Manteca, Ca,US
116/D1 Mantena, Braz.
58/A6 Mantes-la-Jolie, Fr.
58/A6 Mantes-la-Ville, Fr.
90/C4 Manthani, India
130/E3 Manti, Ut,US
137/G5 Manticock (pt.), NY,US
116/C2 Mantiqueira (range), Braz.
63/J4 Mantova, It.
122/E3 Mantua, Cuba
71/K4 Manturovo, Rus.
48/H3 Mäntyharju, Fin.
114/E6 Manú (riv.), Peru
99/J6 Manua (isls.), ASam.
99/K6 Manuae (atoll), Cookls.
126/W13 Manuawili, Hi,US
115/J6 Manuel Alves (riv.), Braz.
92/C5 Manuk (riv.), Indo.
95/H6 Manukau, NZ
114/D6 Manú Nat'l Park, Peru
114/E6 Manuripe (riv.), Bol.
98/D5 Manus (isl.), PNG
137/F5 Manville, NJ,US
134/E4 Many, La,US
73/G3 Manych (riv.), Rus.
73/G3 Manych-Gudilo (lake), Rus.
130/E3 Many Farms, Az,US
107/B4 Manyoni, Tanz.
64/D3 Manzanares, Sp.
65/N8 Manzanares (riv.), Sp.
123/P10 Manzanillo, Mex.
134/B3 Manzano (mts.), NM,US
83/H2 Manzhouli, China
106/C2 Manzilah, Buhayrat al (lake), Egypt
109/E2 Manzini, Swaz.
123/G4 Mao, DRep.
93/J4 Maoke (mts.), Indo.
88/B3 Maoming, China
81/D5 Mapam (lake), China
122/C4 Mapastepec, Mex.
123/P8 Mapimí, Bolsón de (val.), Mex.
133/Q8 Maple, On,Can.
129/K5 Maple (riv.), Ia,US
129/J4 Maple (riv.), ND,US
128/F3 Maple Creek, Sk,Can.
137/F6 Maple Shade, NJ,US
137/F5 Maplewood, NJ,US
114/G4 Mapuera (riv.), Braz.
90/B4 Mapusa, India
109/F2 Maputo (cap.), Moz.
106/D5 Maqdam, Ras (cape), Sudan
79/J2 Maqor, Afg.
81/D5 Maquan (riv.), China
110/C2 Maquela do Zombo, Ang.
131/K2 Maquoketa (riv.), Ia,US
116/H2 Mar (range), Braz.
107/B3 Mara (prov.), Tanz.
115/J5 Marabá, Braz.
115/J3 Maracá (isl.), Braz.
123/G5 Maracaibo, Ven.
123/G6 Maracaibo (lake), Ven.
115/H7 Maracaju (mts.), Braz.

172
Marac – Mezdr

123/H5 **Maracay**, Ven.
64/D4 **Maracena**, Sp.
105/G3 **Maradi**, Niger
105/G3 **Maradi** (dept.), Niger
78/E1 **Marägheh**, Iran
114/E3 **Marahuaca** (peak), Ven.
131/J3 **Marais des Cygnes** (riv.), Ks, Mo US
115/J4 **Marajó**, Braz.
115/J4 **Marajó** (bay), Braz.
115/J4 **Marajó** (isl.), Braz.
88/E6 **Maramag**, Phil.
116/K8 **Marambaia** (isl.), Braz.
135/F2 **Maramec** (riv.), Mo,US
69/F2 **Maramureş** (co.), Rom.
130/E4 **Marana**, Az,US
115/L4 **Maranguape**, Braz.
115/J6 **Maranhão** (riv.), Braz.
96/C4 **Maranoa** (riv.), Austl.
114/C4 **Marañón** (riv.), Peru
104/D5 **Marahoue Nat'l Park**, C.d'Iv.
92/B4 **Marapi** (peak), Indo.
92/C4 **Maras** (peak), Indo.
69/H3 **Mărăşeşti**, Rom.
132/C1 **Marathon**, On,Can.
135/H5 **Marathon**, Fl,US
134/C4 **Marathon**, Tx,US
116/A4 **Marau**, Braz.
88/D6 **Marawi**, Phil.
106/B5 **Marawī**, Sudan
52/A6 **Marazion**, Eng,UK
64/C4 **Marbella**, Sp.
128/F5 **Marbleton**, Wy,US
54/E3 **Marburg**, Ger.
68/C2 **Marcali**, Hun.
110/B4 **Marca, Ponta da** (pt.), Ang.
53/G1 **March**, Eng,UK
62/D3 **Marche** (mts.), Fr.
63/K5 **Marche** (reg.), It.
59/E3 **Marche-en-Famenne**, Belg.
64/C4 **Marchena**, Sp.
117/D3 **Mar Chiquita** (lake), Arg.
58/A2 **Marck**, Fr.
135/H5 **Marco**, Fl,US
114/C7 **Marcona**, Peru
128/E3 **Marconi** (peak), BC,Can.
118/E2 **Marcos Juárez**, Arg.
58/C2 **Marcq-en-Baroeul**, Fr.
136/J3 **Marcus Baker** (mtn.), Ak,US
132/F2 **Marcy** (peak), NY,US
79/K2 **Mardān**, Pak.
119/F3 **Mar del Plata**, Arg.
53/G4 **Marden**, Eng,UK
80/E3 **Mardin**, Turk.
99/W12 **Maré** (isl.), NCal.
96/B2 **Mareeba**, Austl.
49/C2 **Maree, Loch** (lake), Sc,UK
51/H5 **Mareham le Fen**, Eng,UK
53/G5 **Maresfield**, Eng,UK
134/B4 **Marfa**, Tx,US
52/C3 **Margam**, Wal,UK
72/E3 **Marganets**, Ukr.
90/B4 **Margao**, India
123/J5 **Margarita** (isl.), Ven.
53/H4 **Margate**, Eng,UK
62/E4 **Margeride** (mts.), Fr.
107/A2 **Margherita** (peak), Ugan.
68/F2 **Marghita**, Rom.
81/B3 **Margilan**, Uzb.
81/E5 **Margog Caka** (lake), China
88/D6 **Margosatubig**, Phil.
59/E2 **Margraten**, Neth.
111/V **Marguerite** (bay), Ant.
97/D4 **Maria** (peak), Austl.
99/K7 **Maria** (isl.), FrPol.
97/D4 **Maria Island Nat'l Park**, Austl.
135/F3 **Marianna**, Ar,US
135/G4 **Marianna**, Fl,US
122/E3 **Mariano**, Cuba
54/G4 **Mariánské Lázně** (Marienbad), Czh.
128/F3 **Marias** (riv.), Mt,US
68/B2 **Maribor**, Slov.
116/L7 **Maricá**, Braz.
114/E4 **Marié** (riv.), Braz.
111/S **Marie Byrd Land** (reg.), Ant.
123/J4 **Marie-Galante** (isl.), Guad.
48/F3 **Mariehamn**, Fin.
54/G4 **Marienbad** (Mariánské Lázně), Czh.
57/E6 **Marienheide**, Ger.
48/E4 **Mariestad**, Swe.
135/G3 **Marietta**, Ga,US
132/D4 **Marietta**, Oh,US
62/F5 **Marignane**, Fr.
116/B2 **Marilia**, Braz.
64/A1 **Marín**, Sp.
137/B3 **Marina del Rey**, Ca,US
58/A5 **Marines**, Fr.
132/C2 **Marinette**, Wi,US
116/B2 **Maringá**, Braz.
64/A3 **Marinha Grande**, Port.
135/G3 **Marion**, Al,US
132/B4 **Marion**, Il,US
132/C3 **Marion**, In,US
132/B4 **Marion**, Ky,US
132/C2 **Marion**, Mi,US
132/D3 **Marion**, Oh,US
135/H3 **Marion** (lake), SC,US
132/E4 **Marion**, Va,US
130/C3 **Mariposa**, Ca,US
69/H5 **Maritsa** (riv.), Bul., Turk.
72/F3 **Mariupol'**, Ukr.
71/K4 **Mariy-El, Resp.**, Rus.
80/K5 **Marj 'Uyūn**, Leb.
56/B6 **Mark** (riv.), Belg.
48/E4 **Markaryd**, Swe.
56/C4 **Marken** (isl.), Neth.
56/C4 **Markerwaard** (polder), Neth.
53/E1 **Market Bosworth**, Eng,UK
53/F1 **Market Deeping**, Eng,UK
51/F6 **Market Drayton**, Eng,UK
53/F2 **Market Harborough**, Eng,UK
50/B3 **Markethill**, NI,UK
51/H5 **Market Rasen**, Eng,UK
51/H4 **Market Weighton**, Eng,UK
125/J2 **Markham** (bay), Nun,Can.
133/R8 **Markham**, On,Can.
55/L2 **Marki**, Pol
130/C3 **Markleeville**, Ca,US
67/L7 **Markópoulon**, Gre.
73/H2 **Marks**, Rus.
134/E4 **Marksville**, La,US
63/K2 **Marktredwitz**, Ger.
131/J3 **Mark Twain** (lake), Mo,US
57/E5 **Marl**, Ger.
137/F5 **Marlboro**, NJ,US
53/E4 **Marlborough**, Eng,UK
58/B3 **Marles-les-Mines**, Fr.
53/F3 **Marlow**, Eng,UK
137/F6 **Marlton**, NJ,US
58/C3 **Marly**, Fr.
58/B5 **Marly-la-Ville**, Fr.
58/B5 **Marly-le-Roi**, Fr.
59/F5 **Marly-sur-Seille**, Fr.
62/D4 **Marmande**, Fr.
69/H5 **Marmara** (isl.), Turk.
69/J5 **Marmara** (sea), Turk.
80/B3 **Marmaris**, Turk.
114/F5 **Marmelos** (riv.), Braz.
132/A1 **Marmion** (lake), On,Can.
63/J3 **Marmolada** (peak), It.
64/C3 **Marmolejo**, Sp.
58/C6 **Marne** (dept.), Fr.
62/E2 **Marne** (riv.), Fr.
59/D6 **Marne au Rhin, Canal de la** (can.), Fr.
52/D5 **Marnhull**, Eng,UK
103/J6 **Maro**, Chad
99/H2 **Maro** (reef), Hi,US
109/J6 **Maroantsetra**, Madg.
99/L6 **Marokau** (atoll), FrPol.
109/J8 **Marolambo**, Madg.
109/J6 **Maromokotro** (peak), Madg.
110/F4 **Marondera**, Zim.
115/H3 **Maroni** (riv.), FrG., Sur.
96/D4 **Maroochydore-Mooloolaba**, Austl.
102/H5 **Maroua**, Camr.
109/H7 **Marovoay**, Madg.
59/G5 **Marpingen**, Ger.
51/F5 **Marple**, Eng,UK
82/B2 **Marqakōl** (lake), Kaz.
82/D5 **Marqēn Gangri** (peak), China
97/C1 **Marquarie** (riv.), Austl.
99/M5 **Marquesas** (isls.), FrPol.
132/C2 **Marquette**, Mi,US
103/K5 **Marrah** (mts.), Sudan
102/D1 **Marrakech**, Mor.
107/C2 **Marsabit**, Kenya
67/C4 **Marsala**, It.
103/L1 **Marsá Matrūh**, Egypt
57/F6 **Marsberg**, Ger.
66/C1 **Marsciano**, It.
51/G4 **Marsden**, Eng,UK
56/B3 **Marsdiep** (chan.), Neth.
62/F5 **Marseille**, Fr.
134/E4 **Marsh** (isl.), La,US
128/F2 **Marshall**, Sk,Can.
129/K4 **Marshall**, Mn,US
131/J3 **Marshall**, Mo,US
134/E3 **Marshall**, Tx,US
98/G3 **Marshall Islands** (ctry.)
129/K5 **Marshalltown**, Ia,US
131/J3 **Marshfield**, Mo,US
132/B2 **Marshfield**, Wi,US
53/E3 **Marsh Gibbon**, Eng,UK
51/G2 **Marske-by-the-Sea**, Eng,UK
89/B2 **Martaban** (gulf), Myan.
128/G2 **Martensville**, Sk,Can.
133/G3 **Martha's Vineyard** (isl.), Ma,US
60/D5 **Martigny**, Swi.
62/F5 **Martigues**, Fr.
111/S **Martin** (pen.), Ant.
55/K4 **Martin**, Slvk.
135/G3 **Martin** (lake), Al,US
129/H5 **Martin**, SD,US
135/F2 **Martin**, Tn,US
66/E2 **Martina Franca**, It.
138/K10 **Martinez**, Ca,US
135/H3 **Martinez**, Ga,US
122/B3 **Martínez de la Torre**, Mex.
123/J4 **Martinique** (passage), Dom., Mart.
123/J5 **Martinique** (isl.), Fr.
116/B2 **Martinópolis**, Braz.
132/E4 **Martinsburg**, WV,US
132/C4 **Martinsville**, In,US
132/E4 **Martinsville**, Va,US
44/H7 **Martin Vaz** (isls.), Braz.
52/D2 **Martley**, Eng,UK
52/D5 **Martock**, Eng,UK
65/F2 **Martorell**, Sp.
64/D4 **Martos**, Sp.
132/F1 **Martre** (riv.), Qu,Can.
129/J5 **Marty**, SD,US
84/C3 **Marugame**, Japan
85/F2 **Maruko**, Japan
56/D2 **Marum**, Neth.
84/E2 **Maruoka**, Japan
99/M7 **Marutea** (atoll), FrPol.
85/H7 **Maruyama**, Japan
78/F3 **Marv Dasht**, Iran
96/D4 **Mary** (riv.), Austl.
79/H1 **Mary**, Trkm.
96/D4 **Maryborough**, Austl.
97/B3 **Maryborough**, Austl.
135/G4 **Mary Esther**, Fl,US
129/H3 **Maryfield**, Sk,Can.
104/C5 **Maryland** (co.), Libr.
132/E4 **Maryland** (state), US
137/K7 **Maryland City**, Md,US
50/E2 **Maryport**, Eng,UK
133/L2 **Marystown**, Nf,Can.
131/H3 **Marysville**, Ks,US
138/H6 **Marysville**, Mi,US
138/C1 **Marysville**, Wa,US
131/J2 **Maryville**, Mo,US
135/H3 **Maryville**, Tn,US
66/D2 **Marzano** (peak), It.
102/H2 **Marzūq**, Libya
102/H3 **Marzūq, Şhrā** (des.), Libya
80/K6 **Masada** (Horvot Mezada) (ruins), Isr.
107/C4 **Masai Steppe** (grsld.), Tanz.
107/A3 **Masaka**, Ugan.
65/E3 **Masamagrell**, Sp.
93/F4 **Masamba**, Indo.
86/E5 **Masan**, SKor.
107/C5 **Masasi**, Tanz.
122/D5 **Masaya**, Nic.
88/D5 **Masbate**, Phil.
88/D5 **Masbate** (isl.), Phil.
62/F1 **Mascara**, Alg.
109/S15 **Mascarene** (isls.), Mrts., Reun., Fr.
123/P9 **Mascota**, Mex.
133/N6 **Mascouche**, Qu,Can.
108/D3 **Maseru** (cap.), Les.
77/E6 **Mashad**, Iran
51/G3 **Masham**, Eng,UK
79/G1 **Mashhad**, Iran
79/H3 **Māshkel, Hāmūn-i-** (lake), Pak.
79/H3 **Māshkīd** (riv.), Iran
73/L1 **Masim** (peak), Rus.
79/G5 **Masira** (gulf), Oman
79/G4 **Maşīrah** (isl.), Oman
78/E2 **Masjed-e Soleymān**, Iran
49/A4 **Mask, Lough** (lake), Ire.
109/J6 **Masoala** (cape), Madg.
109/J6 **Masoala** (pen.), Madg.
132/C3 **Mason**, Mi,US
134/D4 **Mason**, Tx,US
138/A3 **Mason** (lake), Wa,US
129/K5 **Mason City**, Ia,US
65/X17 **Maspalomas**, Canl.,Sp.
65/K6 **Masquefa**, Sp.
63/J4 **Massa**, It.
133/F3 **Massachusetts** (state) US
133/G3 **Massachusetts** (bay), Ma,US
66/E2 **Massafra**, It.
137/G5 **Massapequa**, NY,US
132/F2 **Massena**, NY,US
125/S7 **Massey** (sound), Nun,Can.
110/D3 **Massibi**, Ang.
62/E4 **Massif Central** (plat.), Fr.
132/D3 **Massillon**, Oh,US
111/G **Masson** (isl.), Ant.
58/B6 **Massy**, Fr.
56/B5 **Mastgat** (chan.), Neth.
137/H5 **Mastic**, NY,US
79/J3 **Mastung**, Pak.
84/B3 **Masuda**, Japan
92/B4 **Masurai** (peak), Indo.
110/F5 **Masvingo**, Zim.
80/L4 **Maşyāf**, Syria
67/F2 **Mat** (riv.), Alb.
110/B2 **Matadi**, D.R. Congo
134/G3 **Matador**, Tx,US
122/D5 **Matagalpa**, Nic.
132/E1 **Matagami** (lake), Qu,Can.
134/D4 **Matagorda** (bay), Tx,US
134/D4 **Matagorda** (isl.), Tx,US
90/D6 **Matale**, SrL.
104/B3 **Matam**, Sen.
122/A2 **Matamoros**, Mex.
122/B2 **Matamoros**, Mex.
103/K3 **Ma'ţan as Sarra** (well), Libya
133/H1 **Matane**, Qu,Can.
133/H1 **Matane** (riv.), Qu,Can.
122/E3 **Matanzas**, Cuba
116/B2 **Matão**, Braz.
133/H1 **Matapedia** (riv.), Qu,Can.
118/C2 **Mataquito** (riv.), Chile
78/C6 **Matara** (ruins), Egypt
90/D6 **Matara**, SrL.
93/E5 **Mataram**, Indo.
65/G2 **Mataró**, Sp.
99/L7 **Mataura**, FrPol.
99/H6 **Mata Utu** (cap.), Wall.
137/F5 **Matawan**, NJ,US
122/A3 **Matehuala**, Mex.
66/E2 **Matera**, It.
123/F3 **Maternillos** (pt.), Cuba
68/F2 **Mátészalka**, Hun.
137/C3 **Mathews** (lake), Ca,US
134/D4 **Mathis**, Tx,US
90/C2 **Mathurā**, India
88/E6 **Mati**, Phil.
116/K6 **Matias Barbosa**, Braz.
122/B4 **Matías Romero**, Mex.
66/A4 **Mātir**, Tun.
51/G5 **Matlock**, Eng,UK
114/G7 **Mato Grosso**, Braz.
115/G6 **Mato Grosso** (plat.), Braz.
116/A1 **Mato Grosso do Sul** (state), Braz.
110/E5 **Matopos**, Zim.
64/A2 **Matosinhos**, Port.
79/G4 **Maţraḩ**, Oman
108/B4 **Matroosberg** (peak), SAfr.
106/A2 **Maţrūḩ**, Egypt
106/B2 **Maţrūḩ** (gov.), Egypt
109/H8 **Matsiatra** (riv.), Madg.
85/L10 **Matsubara**, Japan
85/H7 **Matsubushi**, Japan
85/H7 **Matsuda**, Japan
85/H7 **Matsudo**, Japan
84/C3 **Matsue**, Japan
83/N3 **Matsumae**, Japan
85/E2 **Matsumoto**, Japan
84/E3 **Matsusaka**, Japan
85/G1 **Matsushima**, Japan
84/E2 **Matsutō**, Japan
84/C4 **Matsuyama**, Japan
132/D1 **Mattagami** (riv.), On,Can.
132/E2 **Mattawa**, On,Can.
63/G4 **Matterhorn** (pk.), It., Swi.
138/Q16 **Matteson**, Il,US
136/H2 **Matthews** (mtn.), Ak,US
123/G3 **Matthew Town**, Bahm.
84/E2 **Mattō**, Japan
50/B4 **Mattock** (riv.), Ire.
132/B4 **Mattoon**, Il,US
123/J6 **Maturín**, Ven.
110/E4 **Matusadona Nat'l Park**, Zim.
93/F2 **Matutum** (mt.), Phil.
114/G3 **Maú** (riv.), Braz., Guy.
116/C2 **Mauá**, Braz.
58/C3 **Maubeuge**, Fr.
91/G4 **Ma-ubin**, Myan.
49/D2 **Maud**, Sc,UK
90/D2 **Maudaha**, India
114/G4 **Maués**, Braz.
114/G4 **Maués Açu** (riv.), Braz.
98/D3 **Maug** (isls.), NMar.
50/D3 **Maughold**, IM,UK
50/D3 **Maughold Head** (pt.), IM,UK
62/F5 **Mauguio**, Fr.
126/T10 **Maui** (isl.), Hi,US
99/K7 **Mauke** (isl.), Cookls.
58/A6 **Maule** (riv.), Fr.
118/B2 **Maule** (reg.), Chile
118/C1 **Maule** (riv.), Chile
62/C3 **Mauléon**, Fr.
118/B4 **Maullín**, Chile
132/C3 **Maumee** (riv.), In, Oh,US
110/D4 **Maun**, Bots.
126/U11 **Mauna Kea** (vol.), Hi,US
126/U11 **Mauna Loa** (vol.), Hi,US
99/K6 **Maupiti** (isl.), FrPol.
90/C2 **Mau Rānīpur**, India
56/A6 **Maurepas**, Fr.
133/F2 **Mauricie Nat'l Park**, Qu,Can.
104/B2 **Mauritania** (ctry.)
109/S15 **Mauritius** (ctry.)
132/B3 **Mauston**, Wi,US
68/E5 **Mavrovo Nat'l Park**, FYROM
89/B4 **Maw Daung** (pass), Thai.
111/D **Mawson** (coast), Ant.
111/E **Mawson** (sta.), Ant.
122/D3 **Maxcanú**, Mex.
59/F6 **Maxéville**, Fr.
132/F4 **May** (cape), NJ,US
92/C4 **Maya** (isl.), Indo.
75/P4 **Maya** (riv.), Rus.
123/G3 **Mayaguana** (isl.), Bahm.
123/H4 **Mayagüez**, PR
79/K1 **Mayakovskogo** (peak), Taj.
123/F3 **Mayarí**, Cuba
85/L10 **Maya-san** (peak), Japan
50/D1 **Maybole**, Sc,UK
103/N5 **Maych'ew**, Eth.
59/G3 **Mayen**, Ger.
62/C2 **Mayenne**, Fr.
62/C3 **Mayenne** (riv.), Fr.
128/E2 **Mayerthorpe**, Ab,Can.
132/B4 **Mayfield**, Ky,US
72/G3 **Maykop**, Rus.
53/G3 **Mayland**, Eng,UK
91/G3 **Maymyo**, Myan.
118/C5 **Mayo** (riv.), Arg.
136/L3 **Mayo**, Yk,Can.
123/N8 **Mayo** (riv.), Mex.
64/D1 **Mayor** (cape), Sp.
109/H6 **Mayotte** (terr.), Fr.
123/F4 **May Pen**, Jam.
132/D4 **Maysville**, Ky,US
129/J4 **Mayville**, ND,US
138/Q16 **Maywood**, Il,US
110/E4 **Mazabuka**, Zam.
62/E5 **Mazamet**, Fr.
66/C4 **Mazara** (val.), It.
66/C4 **Mazara del Vallo**, It.
79/J1 **Mazār-e Sharīf**, Afg.
64/A1 **Mazaricos**, Sp.
64/E4 **Mazarrón**, Sp.
114/G2 **Mazaruni** (riv.), Guy.
122/C5 **Mazatenango**, Guat.
123/N9 **Mazatlán**, Mex.
70/D4 **Mažeikiai**, Lith.
96/B3 **Mazeppa Nat'l Park**, Austl.
50/B3 **Mazetown**, NI,UK
58/B3 **Mazingarbe**, Fr.
110/C2 **Mazingu**, D.R. Congo
82/D3 **Mazong** (peak), China
55/L2 **Mazowieckie** (prov.), Pol.
55/L2 **Mazury** (reg.), Pol.
72/D1 **Mazyr**, Bela.
109/E2 **Mbabane** (cap.), Swaz.
102/H6 **Mbabo** (peak), Camr.
102/J7 **Mbaïki**, CAfr.
103/H6 **Mbakaou** (lake), Camr.
107/A5 **Mbala**, Zam.
102/H7 **Mbalam**, Camr.
107/B2 **Mbale**, Ugan.
102/H7 **Mbalmayo**, Camr.
105/H5 **Mbam** (riv.), Camr.
105/H5 **Mbam, Massif du** (peak), Camr.
103/J7 **Mbandaka**, D.R. Congo
107/A3 **Mbarara**, Ugan.
103/J7 **Mbata**, CAfr.
99/Y18 **Mbengga** (isl.), Fiji
107/B5 **Mbeya**, Tanz.
107/B5 **Mbeya** (prov.), Tanz.
107/B5 **Mbeya** (range), Tanz.
102/H8 **M'Bigou**, Gabon
102/G7 **Mbini**, EqG.
102/H7 **Mbini** (riv.), EqG.
103/L6 **Mbomou** (riv.), CAfr.
104/B3 **Mboune, Vallée du** (wadi), Sen.
104/A3 **M'Bour**, Sen.
110/D2 **Mbuji-Mayi**, D.R. Congo
131/J4 **McAlester**, Ok,US
134/D5 **McAllen**, Tx,US
128/C2 **McBride**, BC,Can.
128/D4 **McCall**, Id,US
134/C4 **McCamey**, Tx,US
138/C3 **McChord A.F.B.**, Wa,US
138/M9 **McClellan A.F.B.**, Ca,US
129/H4 **McClusky**, ND,US
135/F4 **McComb**, Ms,US
131/G2 **McConaughy** (lake), Ne,US
131/G2 **McCook**, Ne,US
135/H3 **McCormick**, SC,US
129/J3 **McCreary**, Mb,Can.
130/C2 **McDermitt**, Nv,US
45/N8 **McDonald** (isls.), Austl.
136/F3 **McDonald** (mtn.), Ak,US
136/L2 **McDougall** (pass), NW, Yk,Can.
134/F3 **McGehee**, Ar,US
135/F3 **McGehee**, Ar,US
128/C2 **McGregor** (riv.), BC,Can.
138/G7 **McGregor**, On,Can.
138/P15 **McHenry**, Il,US
99/H5 **McKean** (atoll), Kiri.
125/K2 **McKeand** (riv.), Nun,Can.
132/E3 **McKeesport**, Pa,US
135/F2 **McKenzie**, Tn,US
136/H3 **McKinley** (mtn.), Ak,US
136/J3 **McKinley Park**, Ak,US
128/B5 **McKinleyville**, Ca,US
134/D3 **McKinney**, Tx,US
129/H4 **McLaughlin**, SD,US
137/J8 **McLean**, Va,US
128/D2 **McLennan**, Ab,Can.
128/D2 **McLeod** (riv.), Ab,Can.
124/E2 **McLeod** (bay), NW,Can.
128/C2 **McLeod Lake**, BC,Can.
124/F1 **M'Clintock** (chan.), Nun,Can.
125/Q7 **M'Clure** (str.), NW,Can.
128/C4 **McMinnville**, Or,US
135/G3 **McMinnville**, Tn,US
111/M **McMurdo**, Ant.
138/B3 **McNeil** (isl.), Wa,US
110/F3 **Mcocha**, Malw.
131/H3 **McPherson**, Ks,US
82/E5 **Mē** (riv.), China
130/D3 **Mead** (lake), Az, Nv,US
136/G2 **Meade** (riv.), Ak,US
128/F2 **Meadow Lake**, Sk,Can.
133/Q8 **Meadowvale**, On,Can.
130/D3 **Meadow Valley** (riv.), Nv,US
135/F4 **Meadville**, Ms,US
132/D3 **Meadville**, Pa,US
115/J5 **Mearim** (riv.), Braz.
53/E1 **Measham**, Eng,UK
136/F2 **Meat** (mtn.), Ak,US
50/B4 **Meath** (co.), Ire.
129/G2 **Meath Park**, Sk,Can.
58/B6 **Meaux**, Fr.
78/C4 **Mecca** (Makkah), SAr.
58/D1 **Mechelen**, Belg.
54/F1 **Mecklenburger Bucht** (bay), Ger.
54/F2 **Mecklenburg-Vorpommern** (state), Ger.
110/G3 **Mecuia** (peak), Moz.
90/C4 **Medak**, India
92/A3 **Medan**, Indo.
119/L7 **Medanosa** (pt.), Arg.
53/F1 **Medbourne**, Eng,UK
57/F6 **Medebach**, Ger.
114/C2 **Medellín**, Col.
56/C3 **Medemblik**, Neth.
51/G5 **Meden** (riv.), Eng,UK
137/H5 **Medford**, NY,US
128/C5 **Medford**, Or,US
132/B2 **Medford**, Wi,US
69/J3 **Medgidia**, Rom.
69/G2 **Mediaş**, Rom.
128/D4 **Medical Lake**, Wa,US
130/F2 **Medicine Bow** (range), Co, Wy,US
129/G5 **Medicine Bow**, Wy,US
128/F3 **Medicine Hat**, Ab,Can.
53/E5 **Medina** (riv.), Eng,UK
129/J4 **Medina**, ND,US
132/D3 **Medina**, Oh,US
131/H5 **Medina**, Tx,US
78/C4 **Medina** (Al Madīnah), SAr.
64/C2 **Medina del Campo**, Sp.
64/C4 **Medina-Sidonia**, Sp.
45/K4 **Mediterranean** (sea)
128/F2 **Medley**, Ab,Can.
73/J2 **Mednogorsk**, Rus.
73/H2 **Medveditsa, Gora** (riv.), Rus.
75/S2 **Medvezh'i** (isls.), Rus.
70/G3 **Medvezh'yegorsk**, Rus.
53/G4 **Medway** (co.), Eng,UK
130/F2 **Meeker**, Co,US
57/G3 **Meerbach** (riv.), Ger.
56/D6 **Meerbusch**, Ger.
59/E1 **Meerhout**, Belg.
59/E2 **Meerssen**, Neth.
90/C2 **Meerut**, India
53/E1 **Meese** (riv.), Eng,UK
128/F4 **Meeteetse**, Wy,US
103/N7 **Mēga**, Eth.
103/P6 **Megalo**, Eth.
133/G2 **Megantic** (peak), Qu,Can.
67/H3 **Mégara**, Gre.
91/F2 **Meghalaya** (state), India
80/N7 **Megiddo** (ruins), Isr.
132/E1 **Mégiscane** (lake), Qu,Can.
132/E1 **Mégiscane** (riv.), Qu,Can.
80/B3 **Megista** (isl.), Gre.
59/E2 **Mehaigne** (riv.), Belg.
57/G1 **Mehe** (riv.), Ger.
90/C3 **Mehkar**, India
79/F3 **Mehrān** (riv.), Iran
78/F2 **Mehriz**, Iran
90/B3 **Mehsāna**, India
88/C2 **Mei** (riv.), China
88/C3 **Mei** (riv.), China
116/B1 **Meia Ponte** (riv.), Braz.
102/H6 **Meiganga**, Camr.
125/R6 **Meighen** (isl.), Nun,Can.
83/K3 **Meihekou**, China
89/A1 **Meiktila**, Myan.
57/H4 **Meine**, Ger.
57/E6 **Meinerzhagen**, Ger.
63/J1 **Meiningen**, Ger.
87/C5 **Meishan** (res.), China
55/G3 **Meissen**, Ger.
57/G6 **Meissner** (peak), Ger.
85/M10 **Meiwa**, Japan
88/C3 **Meizhou**, China
102/H7 **Mekambo**, Gabon
103/N5 **Mek'elē**, Eth.
102/D1 **Meknès**, Mor.
77/K8 **Mekong** (riv.), Asia
93/F4 **Mekongga** (peak), Indo.
89/D4 **Mekong, Mouths of the**, Viet.
92/B3 **Melaka**, Malay.
98/E5 **Melanesia** (reg.)
90/C6 **Melappālaiyam**, India
92/D4 **Melawi** (riv.), Indo.
53/G2 **Melbourn**, Eng,UK
97/F5 **Melbourne**, Austl.
124/F2 **Melbourne** (isl.), Nun,Can.
51/G6 **Melbourne**, Eng,UK
135/H4 **Melbourne**, Fl,US
118/B5 **Melchor** (isl.), Chile
122/D4 **Melchor de Mencos**, Mex.
122/A2 **Melchor Múzquiz**, Mex.
52/D5 **Melcombe Regis**, Eng,UK
54/E1 **Meldorf**, Ger.
68/E3 **Melenci**, Serb.
70/J5 **Melenki**, Rus.
73/K1 **Meleuz**, Rus.
125/J3 **Mélèzes** (riv.), Qu,Can.
103/J5 **Melfi**, Chad
66/D2 **Melfi**, It.
129/G2 **Melfort**, Sk,Can.
48/D3 **Melhus**, Nor.
102/E1 **Melilla**, Sp.
118/B5 **Melimoyu** (peak), Chile
118/Q9 **Melipilla**, Chile
67/F3 **Melissano**, It.
129/H3 **Melita**, Mb,Can.
66/D4 **Melito di Porto Salvo**, It.
72/E3 **Melitopol'**, Ukr.
63/L2 **Melk**, Aus.
103/P7 **Melka Meri**, Eth.
52/D4 **Melksham**, Eng,UK
58/C2 **Melle**, Belg.
57/F4 **Melle**, Ger.
48/E4 **Mellerud**, Swe.
64/B1 **Mellid**, Sp.
51/F3 **Melling**, Eng,UK
119/J7 **Mellizo Sur** (peak), Chile
63/J1 **Mellrichstadt**, Ger.
57/F1 **Mellum** (isl.), Ger.
55/H3 **Mělník**, Czh.
119/G2 **Melo**, Uru.
138/Q16 **Melrose Park**, Il,US
57/G6 **Melsungen**, Ger.
51/G4 **Meltham**, Eng,UK
97/C3 **Melton**, Austl.
51/H6 **Melton Mowbray**, Eng,UK
62/E2 **Melun**, Fr.
96/B1 **Melville** (cape), Austl.
95/C2 **Melville** (isl.), Austl.
125/L3 **Melville** (lake), Nf,Can.
125/R7 **Melville** (isl.), NW,Nun,Can.
125/H2 **Melville** (pen.), Nun,Can.
129/H3 **Melville**, Sk,Can.
93/E2 **Melville** (cape), Phil.
137/G5 **Melville**, NY,US
138/F7 **Melvindale**, Mi,US
68/D2 **Mélykút**, Hun.
81/D5 **Mēmar** (lake), China
56/D1 **Memmert** (isl.), Ger.
61/G2 **Memmingen**, Ger.
89/D4 **Memot**, Camb.
86/B2 **Memphis** (ruins), Egypt
138/G6 **Memphis**, Mi,US
131/J2 **Memphis**, Mo,US
135/F3 **Memphis**, Tn,US
134/C3 **Memphis**, Tx,US
134/E3 **Mena**, Ar,US
50/D5 **Menai** (str.), Wal,UK
50/D5 **Menai Bridge**, Wal,UK
56/C2 **Menaldum**, Neth.
109/H9 **Menarandra** (riv.), Madg.
134/D4 **Menard**, Tx,US
132/B2 **Menasha**, Wi,US
109/H7 **Menavava** (riv.), Madg.
92/D4 **Mendawai** (riv.), Indo.
62/E4 **Mende**, Fr.
57/E6 **Menden**, Ger.
136/E4 **Mendenhall** (cape), Ak,US
80/B3 **Menderes, Büyük** (riv.), Turk.
116/K7 **Mendes**, Braz.
103/N6 **Mendī**, Eth.
59/G3 **Mendig**, Ger.
52/D4 **Mendip** (hills), Eng,UK
130/B3 **Mendocino**, Ca,US
126/B3 **Mendocino** (cape), Ca,US
118/C2 **Mendoza**, Arg.
118/C2 **Mendoza** (prov.), Arg.
109/H9 **Mendrare** (riv.), Madg.
68/F3 **Menedinţi** (co.), Rom.
123/G6 **Mene Grande**, Ven.
80/A2 **Menemen**, Turk.
58/C2 **Menen**, Belg.
107/C3 **Menengai Crater**, Kenya
82/H2 **Menengiyn** (plain), Mong.
66/C4 **Menfi**, It.
92/C4 **Menggala**, Indo.
64/D4 **Mengibar**, Sp.
97/B2 **Menindee** (lake), Austl.
118/B5 **Menlolat** (peak), Chile
138/K12 **Menlo Park**, Ca,US
132/C2 **Menominee**, Mi,US
132/B3 **Menomonee Falls**, Wi,US
132/B2 **Menomonie**, Wi,US
65/H3 **Menorca** (Minorca) (isl.), Sp.
92/A4 **Mentawai** (isls.), Indo.
92/A4 **Mentawai** (str.), Indo.
137/C2 **Mentone**, Ca,US
134/C4 **Mentone**, Tx,US
132/D3 **Mentor**, Oh,US
93/E3 **Menyapa** (peak), Indo.
66/A4 **Menzel Bourguiba**, Tun.
66/B4 **Menzel Temime**, Tun.
136/M3 **Menzie** (mtn.), Yk,Can.
53/E5 **Meon** (riv.), Eng,UK
123/N8 **Meoquí**, Mex.
93/H4 **Meos Waar** (isl.), Indo.
110/B2 **Mepala**, Ang.
73/G4 **Mepistskaro** (peak), Geo.
56/D3 **Meppel**, Neth.
57/E3 **Meppen**, Ger.
65/E2 **Mequinenzo** (res.), Sp.
131/K3 **Meramec** (riv.), Mo,US
61/H4 **Merano**, It.
92/D4 **Meratus** (mts.), Indo.
93/K5 **Merauke**, Indo.
103/P7 **Merca**, Som.
63/G4 **Mercantour Nat'l Park**, Fr.
130/B3 **Merced**, Ca,US
130/C3 **Merced** (riv.), Ca,US
118/C1 **Mercedario** (peak), Arg.
118/D2 **Mercedes**, Arg.
118/F2 **Mercedes**, Arg.
119/F2 **Mercedes**, Uru.
138/C2 **Mercer Island**, Wa,US
137/F5 **Mercerville-Hamilton Square**, NJ,US
58/D2 **Merchtem**, Belg.
133/N7 **Mercier**, Qu,Can.
128/D2 **Mercoal**, Ab,Can.
130/D3 **Mercury**, Nv,US
125/K2 **Mercy** (cape), Yk,Can.
52/D4 **Mere**, Eng,UK
119/M8 **Meredith** (cape), Falk.
134/C3 **Meredith** (lake), Tx,US
72/F2 **Merefa**, Ukr.
58/C2 **Merelbeke**, Belg.
89/D3 **Mereuch**, Camb.
83/J2 **Mergel** (riv.), China
89/B3 **Mergui**, Myan.
89/B4 **Mergui** (arch.), Myan.
58/B3 **Méricourt**, Fr.
122/D3 **Mérida**, Mex.
64/B3 **Mérida**, Sp.
123/G6 **Mérida**, Ven.
114/D2 **Mérida**, Ven.
135/F3 **Meridian**, Ms,US
134/D4 **Meridian**, Tx,US
138/C2 **Meridian-East Hill**, Wa,US
62/C4 **Mérignac**, Fr.
58/D1 **Merksem**, Belg.
56/B6 **Merksplas**, Belg.
103/M4 **Meroe** (ruins), Sudan
80/K5 **Meron, Har** (mtn.), Isr.
97/F5 **Merri** (cr.), Austl.
137/G5 **Merrick**, NY,US
132/B2 **Merrill**, Wi,US
133/G3 **Merrimack**, NH,US
52/D5 **Merriott**, Eng,UK
128/C3 **Merritt**, BC,Can.
135/H4 **Merritt Island**, Fl,US
51/F5 **Mersey** (riv.), Eng,UK
51/F5 **Merseyside** (co.), Eng,UK
80/C3 **Mersin**, Turk.
92/B3 **Mersing**, Malay.
59/F5 **Merten**, Fr.
52/C3 **Merthyr Tydfil**, Wal,UK
52/C3 **Merthyr Tydfil** (co.), Wal,UK
111/K **Mertz** (glac.), Ant.
134/C4 **Mertzon**, Tx,US
58/B5 **Méru**, Fr.
107/C2 **Meru**, Kenya
58/B2 **Merville**, Fr.
56/C5 **Merwedekanaal** (can.), Neth.
59/F2 **Merzenich**, Ger.
80/C2 **Merzifon**, Turk.
59/F5 **Merzig**, Ger.
119/K7 **Mesa** (peak), Arg.
136/G3 **Mesa** (mtn.), Ak,US
130/E4 **Mesa**, Az,US
129/K4 **Mesabi** (range), Mn,US
123/M8 **Mesa del Seri**, Mex.
67/E2 **Mesagne**, It.
67/J5 **Mesarás** (gulf), Gre.
130/E3 **Mesa Verde Nat'l Park**, Co,US
134/C3 **Mescalero** (ridge), NM,US
57/F6 **Meschede**, Ger.
63/H4 **Mesco, Punta di** (pt.), It.
132/F1 **Mesgouez** (lake), Qu,Can.
67/G3 **Mesolóngion**, Gre.
118/F2 **Mesopotamia** (reg.), Arg.
78/D2 **Mesopotamia** (reg.), Iraq
66/E3 **Mesoraca**, It.
134/D3 **Mesquite**, Tx,US
102/E1 **Mesrouh** (peak), Mor.
102/F1 **Messaad**, Alg.
119/J7 **Messier** (chan.), Chile
66/D3 **Messina**, It.
66/D4 **Messina** (str.), It.
110/F5 **Messina**, SAfr.
67/H4 **Messini**, Gre.
67/H4 **Messini** (gulf), Gre.
69/F5 **Mesta** (riv.), Bul.
63/K4 **Mestre**, It.
104/C5 **Mesurado** (cape), Libr.
133/G1 **Métabetchouan**, Qu,Can.
133/G1 **Métabetchouane** (riv.), Qu,Can.
125/K2 **Meta Incognita** (pen.), Nun,Can.
135/F4 **Metairie**, La,US
117/D2 **Metán**, Arg.
66/E2 **Metapontum** (ruins), It.
67/G3 **Metéora**, Gre.
51/H5 **Metheringham**, Eng,UK
67/G4 **Methóni**, Gre.
68/C4 **Metković**, Cro.
132/B4 **Metropolis**, Il,US
59/D3 **Mettet**, Belg.
57/E4 **Mettingen**, Ger.
59/F5 **Mettlach**, Ger.
56/D6 **Mettmann**, Ger.
103/N6 **Metu**, Eth.
137/F5 **Metuchen**, NJ,US
59/F5 **Metz**, Fr.
58/C2 **Meulebeke**, Belg.
59/E6 **Meurthe-et-Moselle** (dept.), Fr.
59/E3 **Meuse** (riv.), Belg., Fr.
58/E6 **Meuse** (dept.), Fr.
59/E5 **Meuse, Cotes de** (uplands), Fr.
80/N9 **Mevasseret Ziyyon**, Isr.
51/G5 **Mexborough**, Eng,UK
134/D4 **Mexia**, Tx,US
115/J3 **Mexiana**, Braz.
123/L7 **Mexicali**, Mex.
122/A3 **Mexico** (ctry.)
122/B4 **México** (state), Mex.
131/J5 **Mexico** (gulf), NAm.
131/K3 **Mexico**, Mo,US
122/B4 **Mexico** (cap.), Mex.
78/F2 **Meybod**, Iran
108/Q13 **Meyerton**, SAfr.
79/H1 **Meymaneh**, Afg.
80/K6 **Mezada, Horvot** (Masada) (ruins), Isr.
69/F4 **Mezdra**, Bul.

Mezen' – Morog
173

70/J2 **Mezen'** (bay), Rus.
71/K2 **Mezen'** (riv.), Rus.
74/J4 **Mezhdurechensk,** Rus.
74/E2 **Mezhdusharskiy** (isl.), Rus.
68/E2 **Mezőberény,** Hun.
68/E2 **Mezőkovácsháza,** Hun.
68/E2 **Mezőkövesd,** Hun.
68/E2 **Mezőtúr,** Hun.
66/B4 **Mhamdia Fouchana,** Tun.
90/C3 **Mhow,** India
87/D3 **Mi** (riv.), China
122/B4 **Miahuatlán,** Mex.
64/C3 **Miajadas,** Sp.
130/E4 **Miami,** Az,US
135/H5 **Miami,** Fl,US
131/J3 **Miami,** Ok,US
135/H5 **Miami Beach,** Fl,US
87/B4 **Mianchi,** China
78/E1 **Miāndoāb,** Iran
78/E1 **Miāneh,** Iran
137/G4 **Mianus** (riv.), Ct,US
79/K2 **Miānwāli,** Pak.
82/E5 **Mianyang,** China
88/B2 **Miao'er** (peak), China
87/E3 **Miaodao** (isls.), China
71/P5 **Miass,** Rus.
71/Q5 **Miass** (riv.), Rus.
55/J2 **Miastko,** Pol.
106/C5 **Miberika,** Sudan
128/D2 **Mica Creek,** BC,Can.
55/L4 **Michalovce,** Slvk.
136/K2 **Michelson** (mtn.), Ak,US
132/C3 **Michigan** (lake), Can., US
132/C2 **Michigan** (state), US
132/C3 **Michigan City,** In,US
132/C2 **Michipicoten** (isl.), On,Can.
122/A4 **Michoacán** (state), Mex.
73/G1 **Michurinsk,** Rus.
51/F2 **Mickle Fell** (mtn.), Eng,UK
51/F2 **Mickleton,** Eng,UK
122/E5 **Mico** (riv.), Nic.
123/J5 **Micoud,** StL.
98/E3 **Micronesia** (reg.)
98/D4 **Micronesia, Fed. States of** (ctry.)
105/G2 **Midal** (well), Niger
129/H3 **Midale,** Sk,Can.
56/A6 **Middelburg,** Neth.
108/D3 **Middelburg,** SAfr.
109/E2 **Middelburg,** SAfr.
54/E1 **Middelfart,** Den.
56/B5 **Middelharnis,** Neth.
58/B1 **Middelkerke,** Belg.
130/C2 **Middle Alkali** (lake), Ca,US
91/F5 **Middle Andaman** (isl.), India
133/F2 **Middlebury,** Vt,US
134/C4 **Middle Concho** (riv.), Tx,US
51/G3 **Middleham,** Eng,UK
131/G2 **Middle Loup** (riv.), Ne,US
131/J2 **Middle Raccoon** (riv.), Ia,US
137/K7 **Middle River,** Md,US
132/D4 **Middlesboro,** Ky,US
51/G2 **Middlesbrough,** Eng,UK
51/G2 **Middlesbrough** (co.), Eng,UK
53/F4 **Middlesex** (reg.), Eng,UK
137/F5 **Middlesex,** NJ,US
128/C4 **Middle Sister** (peak), Or,US
51/F4 **Middleton,** Eng,UK
53/E2 **Middleton Cheney,** Eng,UK
51/F2 **Middleton-in-Teesdale,** Eng,UK
50/B3 **Middletown,** NI,UK
137/F5 **Middletown,** NJ,US
51/F5 **Middlewich,** Eng,UK
53/F5 **Midhurst,** Eng,UK
62/D5 **Midi** (can.), Fr.
62/D4 **Midi-Pyrénées** (reg.), Fr.
132/E2 **Midland,** On,Can.
132/C3 **Midland,** Mi,US
134/C4 **Midland,** Tx,US
138/Q16 **Midlothian,** Il,US
62/C5 **Midou** (riv.), Fr.
88/D6 **Midsayap,** Phil.
52/D4 **Midsomer Norton,** Eng,UK
98/H2 **Midway** (isls.), PacUS
97/C4 **Midway Point-Sorell,** Austl.
131/H4 **Midwest City,** Ok,US
78/C3 **Midyan** (reg.), SAr.
80/E3 **Midyat,** Turk.
72/B4 **Midzhur** (peak), Bul.
68/F4 **Midžor** (peak), Serb.
84/B4 **Mie,** Japan
84/E3 **Mie** (pref.), Japan
55/H2 **Międzychód,** Pol.
55/M3 **Międzyrzec Podlaski,** Pol.
55/H2 **Międzyrzecz,** Pol.
55/L3 **Mielec,** Pol.
102/J7 **Miéle I,** Congo
69/G2 **Miercurea Ciuc,** Rom.
64/C1 **Mieres,** Sp.
63/J3 **Miesbach,** Ger.
103/P6 **Mī'ēso,** Eth.
62/E3 **Migennes,** Fr.
122/A3 **Miguel Auza,** Mex.
116/B2 **Miguelópolis,** Braz.
116/K7 **Miguel Pereira,** Braz.
64/D3 **Miguelturra,** Sp.
84/D3 **Mihama,** Japan
84/C3 **Mihara,** Japan
85/G2 **Miharu,** Japan
79/J3 **Mihrābpur,** Pak.
65/E2 **Mijares** (riv.), Sp.
64/C4 **Mijas,** Sp.
56/B4 **Mijdrecht,** Neth.
85/N10 **Mikawa** (bay), Japan
85/N9 **Mikawa-Mino** (mts.), Japan
73/G4 **Mikha Tskhakaya,** Geo.
69/F4 **Mikhaylovgrad,** Bul.
68/F4 **Mikhaylovgrad** (reg.), Bul.
73/G2 **Mikhaylovka,** Rus.
85/K10 **Miki,** Japan
48/H3 **Mikkeli,** Fin.
67/J4 **Míkonos** (isl.), Gre.
67/G2 **Mikri Prespa** (lake), Gre.
85/M10 **Mikuma,** Japan
107/C4 **Mikumi,** Tanz.
107/C4 **Mikumi Nat'l Park,** Tanz.
84/E2 **Mikuni,** Japan
85/F2 **Mikuni-tōge** (pass), Japan
114/C4 **Milagro,** Ecu.
63/H4 **Milan** (Milano), It.
80/A3 **Milas,** Turk.
66/D3 **Milazzo,** It.
52/D5 **Milborne Port,** Eng,UK
53/G2 **Mildenhall,** Eng,UK
97/B2 **Mildura,** Austl.
134/C4 **Miles,** Tx,US
129/G4 **Miles City,** Mt,US
129/G3 **Milestone,** Sk,Can.
66/D2 **Miletto** (peak), It.
53/F4 **Milford,** Eng,UK
50/B3 **Milford,** NI,UK
134/D2 **Milford** (lake), Ks,US
130/D3 **Milford,** Ut,US
52/A3 **Milford Haven,** Wal,UK
53/E5 **Milford on Sea,** Eng,UK
98/G4 **Mili** (atoll), Mrsh.
55/J3 **Milicz,** Pol.
126/V13 **Mililani Town,** Hi,US
128/F3 **Milk** (riv.), Can., US
53/E4 **Milk** (hill), Eng,UK
128/E3 **Milk River,** Ab,Can.
111/G **Mill** (isl.), Ant.
125/J2 **Mill** (isl.), Nun,Can.
62/E4 **Millau,** Fr.
138/K11 **Millbrae,** Ca,US
52/B6 **Millbrook,** Eng,UK
135/H3 **Milledgeville,** Ga,US
133/N6 **Mille Iles** (riv.), Qu,Can.
132/B1 **Mille Lacs** (lake), On,Can.
129/K4 **Mille Lacs** (lake), Mn,US
129/J4 **Miller,** SD,US
73/G2 **Millerovo,** Rus.
50/C1 **Milleur** (pt.), Sc,UK
62/D4 **Millevaches** (plat.), Fr.
133/Q9 **Millgrove,** On,Can.
133/R8 **Milliken,** On,Can.
133/G2 **Millinocket,** Me,US
50/C2 **Millisle,** NI,UK
51/E3 **Millom,** Eng,UK
129/G5 **Mills,** Wy,US
137/F5 **Millstone** (riv.), NJ,US
51/F3 **Millthrop,** Eng,UK
138/J11 **Mill Valley,** Ca,US
134/E3 **Millwood** (lake), Ar,US
98/E5 **Milne** (bay), PNG
51/F4 **Milnrow,** Eng,UK
104/C4 **Milo** (riv.), Gui.
133/G2 **Milo,** Me,US
67/J4 **Mílos** (isl.), Gre.
138/L12 **Milpitas,** Ca,US
63/H1 **Milseburg** (peak), Ger.
133/Q8 **Milton,** On,Can.
51/F2 **Milton,** Eng,UK
53/G4 **Milton,** Eng,UK
135/G4 **Milton,** Fl,US
133/G3 **Milton,** NH,US
128/D4 **Milton-Freewater,** Or,US
133/Q8 **Milton Heights,** On,Can.
53/F2 **Milton Keynes,** Eng,UK
53/F2 **Milton Keynes** (co.), Eng,UK
49/H7 **Miltown Malbay,** Ire.
88/B2 **Miluo,** China
52/C4 **Milverton,** Eng,UK
138/Q13 **Milwaukee,** Wi,US
84/B4 **Mimi** (riv.), Japan
62/C4 **Mimizan,** Fr.
88/C2 **Min** (riv.), China
91/H2 **Min** (riv.), China
130/C3 **Mina,** Nv,US
93/F3 **Minahasa** (pen.), Indo.
85/M10 **Minakuchi,** Japan
84/B4 **Minamata,** Japan
85/F3 **Minami-Alps Nat'l Park,** Japan
85/M10 **Minamichita,** Japan
98/D2 **Minamiiō** (isl.), Japan
98/E2 **Minami-Tori-Shima** (isl.), Japan
119/G2 **Minas,** Uru.
122/E3 **Minas de Matahambre,** Cuba
64/B4 **Minas de Ríotinto,** Sp.
116/H6 **Minas Gerais** (state), Braz.
91/F3 **Minbu,** Myan.
118/C1 **Mincha,** Chile
52/D3 **Minchinhampton,** Eng,UK
118/B4 **Minchinmávida** (vol.), Chile
88/D6 **Mindanao** (isl.), Phil.
88/D6 **Mindanao** (sea), Phil.
61/G1 **Mindel** (riv.), Ger.
57/F4 **Minden,** Ger.
134/E3 **Minden,** La,US
131/H2 **Minden,** Ne,US
88/D5 **Mindoro** (isl.), Phil.
88/D5 **Mindoro** (str.), Phil.
52/C4 **Minehead,** Eng,UK
115/H7 **Mineiros,** Braz.
137/G5 **Mineola,** NY,US
73/G3 **Mineral'nye Vody,** Rus.
134/D3 **Mineral Wells,** Tx,US
63/H5 **Minerbio** (pt.), Fr.
87/C3 **Ming** (riv.), China
73/H4 **Mingäçevir,** Azer.
73/H4 **Mingäçevir** (res.), Azer.
133/J1 **Mingan** (riv.), Qu,Can.
79/K2 **Mingāora,** Pak.
89/A1 **Mingun** (ruins), Myan.
64/B1 **Minho** (riv.), Sp.
128/E5 **Minidoka Internment Nat'l Mon.,** Id,US
129/L3 **Miniss** (lake), On,Can.
129/H2 **Minitonas,** Mb,Can.
129/K4 **Minneapolis,** Mn,US
129/J3 **Minnedosa,** Mb,Can.
129/K4 **Minnesota** (state), US
129/K4 **Minnesota** (riv.), Mn,US
50/D2 **Minnigaff,** Sc,UK
132/B1 **Minnis** (lake), On,Can.
132/A1 **Minnitaki** (lake), On,Can.
85/E3 **Mino,** Japan
85/F3 **Minobu,** Japan
85/N9 **Mino-Mikawa** (mts.), Japan
85/L10 **Mino'o,** Japan
85/L10 **Mino'o** (riv.), Japan
65/G3 **Minorca** (Menorca) (isl.), Sp.
129/H3 **Minot,** ND,US
88/C2 **Minqing,** China
57/F1 **Minsener Oog** (isl.), Ger.
72/C1 **Minsk** (cap.), Bela.
55/L2 **Mińsk Mazowiecki,** Pol.
72/C1 **Minskaya Voblasts,** Bela.
53/G4 **Minster,** Eng,UK
81/B4 **Mintaka** (pass), China
133/H2 **Minto,** NB,Can.
124/E1 **Minto** (inlet), NW,Can.
136/L3 **Minto,** Yk,Can.
66/C2 **Minturno,** It.
106/B2 **Minūf,** Egypt
74/K4 **Minusinsk,** Rus.
133/K2 **Miquelon,** StP.
114/C3 **Mira** (riv.), Col., Ecu.
64/A2 **Mira,** Port.
64/A4 **Mira** (riv.), Port.
133/M6 **Mirabel,** Qu,Can.
116/D2 **Miracema,** Braz.
115/J5 **Miracema do Norte,** Braz.
118/C4 **Mirador** (pass), Chile
90/B4 **Miraj,** India
137/C2 **Mira-Loma,** Ca,US
67/J5 **Mirambéllou** (gulf), Gre.
133/H2 **Miramichi,** NB, Can.
137/A2 **Mira Monte,** Ca,US
115/G8 **Miranda** (riv.), Braz.
64/D1 **Miranda de Ebro,** Sp.
63/J4 **Mirandola,** It.
116/B2 **Mirandópolis,** Braz.
116/B2 **Mirante do Paranapanema,** Braz.
116/B2 **Mirassol,** Braz.
122/D5 **Miravalles** (vol.), CR
64/B1 **Miravalles** (mtn.), Sp.
60/C1 **Mirecourt,** Fr.
51/G4 **Mirfield,** Eng,UK
72/E2 **Mirgorod,** Ukr.
119/G2 **Mirim** (lake), Braz., Uru.
79/H3 **Mirjāveh,** Iran
111/G **Mirnyy,** Ant.
75/M3 **Mirnyy,** Rus.
129/H2 **Mirond** (lake), Sk,Can.
67/H4 **Mirtóön** (sea), Gre.
86/E5 **Miryang,** SKor.
90/D2 **Mirzāpur,** India
103/M7 **Misa,** D.R. Congo
106/A4 **Misāha, Bīr** (well), Egypt
84/D3 **Misaki,** Japan
132/C3 **Mishawaka,** In,US
136/F2 **Misheguk** (mtn.), Ak,US
85/F3 **Mishima,** Japan
66/C3 **Misilmeri,** It.
123/L7 **Misión del Rosario,** Mex.
117/F2 **Misiones** (mts.), Arg.
123/L8 **Misión San Fernando,** Mex
68/E1 **Miskolc,** Hun.
85/M10 **Misono,** Japan
93/H4 **Misool** (isl.), Indo.
129/L4 **Misquah** (hills), Mn,US
102/J1 **Mişrātah,** Libya
103/L1 **Mişrātah** (pt.), Libya
132/D1 **Missinaibi** (lake), On,Can.
132/D1 **Missinaibi** (riv.), On,Can.
134/D5 **Mission,** Tx,US
130/C4 **Mission Viejo,** Ca,US
129/M2 **Missisa** (lake), On,Can.
132/E1 **Missisicabi** (riv.), On,Can.
133/Q8 **Mississauga,** On,Can.
135/F4 **Mississippi** (delta), US
127/H5 **Mississippi** (riv.), US
135/F3 **Mississippi** (state), US
93/H4 **Missol** (isl.), Indo.
128/E4 **Missoula,** Mt,US
127/G3 **Missouri** (riv.), US
131/J3 **Missouri** (state), US
134/E4 **Missouri City,** Tx,US
129/H3 **Missouri, Coteau du** (upland), Can., US
96/B3 **Mistake** (cr.), Austl.
133/L2 **Mistaken** (pt.), Can.
133/F1 **Mistassibi** (riv.), Qu,Can.
132/F1 **Mistassini,** Qu,Can.
132/F1 **Mistassini** (lake), Qu,Can.
133/F1 **Mistassini** (riv.), Qu,Can.
55/J4 **Mistelbach an der Zaya,** Aus.
53/H3 **Mistley,** Eng,UK
67/H4 **Mistrás** (ruins), Gre.
66/D4 **Mistretta,** It.
136/M4 **Misty Fjords Nat'l Mon.,** Ak,US
85/M10 **Misugi,** Japan
123/N9 **Mita** (pt.), Mex.
85/H7 **Mitaka,** Japan
52/D3 **Mitcheldean,** Eng,UK
96/A1 **Mitchell** (riv.), Austl.
135/H3 **Mitchell** (mtn.), NC,US
131/G2 **Mitchell,** Ne,US
129/J5 **Mitchell,** SD,US
96/A1 **Mitchell & Alice Rivers Nat'l Park,** Austl.
80/H6 **Mīt Ghamr,** Egypt
90/B2 **Mithankot,** Pak.
79/J4 **Mithi,** Pak.
99/K6 **Mitiaro** (isl.), CookIs.
67/K3 **Mitilini,** Gre.
106/C2 **Mitla** (pass), Egypt
122/B4 **Mitla** (ruins), Mex.
85/G2 **Mito,** Japan
102/G7 **Mitra** (peak), EqG.
119/L8 **Mitre** (pen.), Arg.
58/B6 **Mitry-Mory,** Fr.
109/H7 **Mitsinjo,** Madg.
109/J6 **Mitsio, Nosy** (isl.), Madg.
103/N4 **Mits'iwa,** Erit.
85/F2 **Mitsukaidō,** Japan
85/F2 **Mitsuke,** Japan
57/F4 **Mittelland** (can.), Ger.
57/E3 **Mittelradde** (riv.), Ger.
54/G3 **Mittweida,** Ger.
107/A4 **Mitumba** (mts.), D.R. Congo
110/E2 **Mitwaba,** D.R. Congo
85/H7 **Miura,** Japan
85/H7 **Miura** (pen.), Japan
122/C5 **Mixco Viejo** (ruins), Guat.
85/M10 **Miya** (riv.), Japan
85/G1 **Miyagi** (pref.), Japan
83/N4 **Miyako,** Japan
88/E3 **Miyako** (isl.), Japan
84/B5 **Miyakonojō,** Japan
84/B5 **Miyanojō,** Japan
85/H6 **Miyashiro,** Japan
84/B4 **Miyazaki** (pref.), Japan
84/D3 **Miyazu,** Japan
87/D2 **Miyun,** China
87/D2 **Miyun** (res.), China
50/B6 **Mizen Head** (pt.), Ire.
69/H3 **Mizil,** Rom.
91/F3 **Mizoram** (state), India
85/E3 **Mizunami,** Japan
48/E4 **Mjölby,** Swe.
48/D3 **Mjøsa** (lake), Nor.
102/D1 **Mkorn** (peak), Mor.
109/F2 **Mkuze** (riv.), SAfr.
55/H3 **Mladá Boleslav,** Czh.
68/E3 **Mladenovac,** Serb.
107/B4 **Mlala** (hills), Tanz.
55/L2 **Mława,** Pol.
68/C4 **Mljet** (isl.), Cro.
68/C4 **Mljet Nat'l Park,** Cro.
48/E2 **Mo,** Nor.
93/G5 **Moa** (isl.), Indo.
104/C5 **Moa** (riv.), Libr., SLeo.
130/E3 **Moab,** Ut,US
98/H6 **Moala Group** (isls.), Fiji
64/A1 **Moaña,** Sp.
102/H8 **Moanda,** Gabon
78/F2 **Mobārakeh,** Iran
131/J3 **Moberly,** Mo,US
128/C2 **Moberly Lake,** BC,Can.
135/F4 **Mobile,** Al,US
129/H4 **Mobridge,** SD,US
115/J4 **Mocajuba,** Braz.
110/B4 **Moçâmedes,** Ang.
89/D4 **Moc Hoa,** Viet.
108/D2 **Mochudi,** Bots.
114/C3 **Mocoa,** Col.
116/G6 **Mococa,** Braz.
90/B3 **Modāsa,** India
52/C6 **Modbury,** Eng,UK
108/D3 **Modderrivier** (riv.), SAfr.
63/J4 **Modena,** It.
63/G2 **Moder** (riv.), Fr., Ger.
130/B3 **Modesto,** Ca,US
66/D4 **Modica,** It.
102/H4 **Modjigo** (reg.), Niger
55/J4 **Mödling,** Aus.
68/D3 **Modriča,** Bosn.
89/E3 **Mo Duc,** Viet.
66/E2 **Modugno,** It.
97/C3 **Moe,** Austl.
108/A2 **Moeb** (bay), Namb.
62/B3 **Moëlan-sur-Mer,** Fr.
51/E5 **Moel Fammau** (mtn.), Wal,UK
51/E6 **Moel Fferna** (mtn.), Wal,UK
52/C1 **Moelfre** (mtn.), UK
52/C2 **Moel Hywel** (mtn.), Wal,UK
51/E6 **Moel Sych** (mtn.), Wal,UK
52/C2 **Moel y Llyn** (mtn.), UK
98/E4 **Moen,** Micr.
130/E3 **Moenkopi** (dry riv.), Az,US
99/K7 **Moerai,** FrPol.
56/D6 **Moers,** Ger.
58/C1 **Moervaart** (can.), Belg.
50/E1 **Moffat,** Sc,UK
79/L2 **Moga,** India
103/Q7 **Mogadishu** (cap.) Som.
85/G2 **Mogami** (riv.), Japan
65/L6 **Mogent** (riv.), Sp.
116/G8 **Mogi das Cruzes,** Braz.
116/G7 **Mogi-Guaçu,** Braz.
72/C2 **Mogilev-Podol'skiy,** Ukr.
55/J2 **Mogilno,** Pol.
116/F7 **Mogi-Mirim,** Braz.
83/H1 **Mogocha,** Rus.
91/G3 **Mogok,** Myan.
119/F3 **Mogotes** (pt.), Arg.
64/B4 **Moguer,** Sp.
68/D3 **Mohács,** Hun.
129/H3 **Mohall,** ND,US
132/F3 **Mohawk** (riv.), NY,US
109/G6 **Mohéli** (isl.), Com.
110/D4 **Mohembo,** Bots
136/E3 **Mohican** (cape), Ak,US
57/F6 **Möhne** (riv.), Ger.
57/F6 **Möhnestausee** (res.), Ger.
69/H2 **Moineşti,** Rom.
81/A3 **Moinkum** (des.), Kaz.
105/E5 **Moinsi** (hills), Gha.
132/E2 **Moira** (riv.), On Can.
48/E2 **Mo i Rana,** Nor.
62/F4 **Moirans,** Fr.
125/K3 **Moisie** (riv.), Qu,Can.
62/D4 **Moissac,** Fr.
65/Q10 **Moita,** Port.
130/C4 **Mojave** (des.), Ca,US
116/G7 **Moji-Guaçu** (riv.), Braz.
129/L3 **Mojikit** (lake), On,Can.
114/E6 **Mojos** (plain), Bol.
115/J4 **Moju** (riv.), Braz.
85/F2 **Mōka,** Japan
126/W13 **Mokapu** (pt.), Hi,US
130/B3 **Mokelumne** (riv.), Ca,US
138/Q16 **Mokena,** Il,US
98/F4 **Mokil** (atoll), Micr.
66/B5 **Moknine,** Tun.
89/B3 **Mokochu** (peak), Thai.
91/F2 **Mokokchūng,** India
102/H5 **Mokolo,** Camr.
86/D5 **Mokp'o,** SKor.
68/E3 **Mokrin,** Serb.
73/G1 **Moksha** (riv.), Rus.
59/E1 **Mol,** Belg.
68/E3 **Mol,** Serb.
66/E2 **Mola di Bari,** It.
68/B3 **Molat** (isl.), Cro.
64/E3 **Molatón** (mtn.), Sp.
51/E5 **Mold,** Wal,UK
69/H2 **Moldavia** (reg.), Rom.
69/G2 **Moldavian Carpathians** (range), Rom.
48/C3 **Molde,** Nor.
72/C3 **Moldova** (ctry.)
69/H2 **Moldova** (riv.), Rom.
68/E3 **Moldova Nouă,** Rom.
69/G3 **Moldoveanu** (peak), Rom.
53/F4 **Mole** (riv.), Eng,UK
108/D2 **Molepolole,** Bots.
66/E2 **Molfetta,** It.
87/F2 **Molihong Shan** (peak), China
118/C2 **Molina,** Chile
64/E3 **Molina de Segura,** Sp.
132/B3 **Moline,** Il,US
66/D2 **Molise** (reg.), It.
63/K3 **Möll** (riv.), Aus.
48/D5 **Mollebjerg** (peak), Den.
114/D7 **Mollendo,** Peru
65/F2 **Mollerussa,** Sp.
118/C2 **Molles** (pt.), Chile
65/L6 **Mollet del Vallès,** Sp.
65/L7 **Mollins de Rei,** Sp.
54/F2 **Mölln,** Ger.
70/E5 **Molodechno,** Bela.
111/D **Molodezhnaya,** Ant.
70/H4 **Mologa** (riv.), Rus.
126/T10 **Molokai** (isl.), Hi,US
71/L4 **Moloma** (riv.), Rus.
108/C2 **Molopo** (Moloporivier) (dry riv.), Bots., SAfr.
102/J7 **Moloundou,** Camr.
129/J2 **Molson** (lake), Mb,Can.
93/H5 **Molu** (isl.), Indo.
93/G4 **Molucca** (sea), Indo.
93/G3 **Moluccas** (isls.), Indo.
115/K5 **Mombaça,** Braz.
107/C4 **Mombasa,** Kenya
83/N3 **Mombetsu,** Japan
69/G5 **Momchilgrad,** Bul.
93/H4 **Momfafa** (cape), Indo.
123/G6 **Mompós,** Col.
91/F3 **Mon** (riv.), Myan.
89/B3 **Mon** (state), Myan.
54/G1 **Møn** (isl.), Den.
123/H4 **Mona** (passage), DRep., PR
63/G5 **Monaco** (ctry.)
63/G5 **Monaco** (cap.), Mona.
50/B3 **Monaghan,** Ire.
50/A3 **Monaghan** (co.), Ire.
123/E6 **Monagrillo** (ruins), Pan.
134/C4 **Monahans,** Tx,US
128/D3 **Monashee** (mts.), BC,Can.
66/B5 **Monastir,** Tun.
66/B5 **Monastir** (gov.), Tun.
96/H8 **Mona Vale,** Austl.
65/E3 **Moncada,** Sp.
63/G4 **Moncalieri,** It.
88/E6 **Moncayo,** Phil.
64/D2 **Moncayo** (range), Sp.
70/G2 **Monchegorsk,** Rus.
56/D6 **Mönchengladbach,** Ger.
64/A4 **Monchique,** Port.
64/A4 **Monchique** (range), Port.
135/H3 **Moncks Corner,** SC,US
122/A2 **Monclova,** Mex.
133/H2 **Moncton,** NB,Can.
64/A2 **Mondego** (cape), Port.
64/A2 **Mondego** (riv.), Port.
64/B1 **Mondoñedo,** Sp.
59/F5 **Mondorf-les-Bains,** Lux.
63/G4 **Mondovì,** It.
64/D1 **Mondragón,** Sp.
66/C2 **Mondragone,** It.
64/B3 **Monesterio,** Sp.
131/J3 **Monett,** Mo,US
50/C2 **Money Head** (pt.), Sc,UK
50/B2 **Moneymore,** NI,UK
50/C2 **Moneyreagh,** NI,UK
63/K4 **Monfalcone,** It.
63/H4 **Monferrato** (reg.), It.
64/B1 **Monforte,** Sp.
116/G9 **Mongaguá,** Braz.
89/D1 **Mong Cai,** Viet.
90/E2 **Monghyr,** India
103/J5 **Mongo,** Chad
104/C4 **Mongo** (riv.), Gui., SLeo.
82/D2 **Mongolia** (ctry.)
103/K5 **Mongororo,** Chad
102/H8 **Mongoungou,** Gabon
110/D4 **Mongu,** Zam.
81/F2 **Mönh Hayrhan Uul** (peak), Mong.
82/E1 **Mönh Sarĭdag** (peak), Mong.
50/E1 **Moniaive,** Sc,UK
65/K6 **Monistrol de Montserrat,** Sp.
130/C3 **Monitor** (range), Nv,US
55/M2 **Mońki,** Pol.
110/D1 **Monkoto,** D.R. Congo
52/D3 **Monmouth,** Eng,UK
132/B3 **Monmouth,** Il,US
128/C4 **Monmouth,** Or,US
137/G5 **Monmouth Beach,** NJ,US
52/D3 **Monmouthshire** (co.), Wal,UK
52/D2 **Monnow** (riv.), UK
56/C4 **Monnickendam,** Neth.
105/F5 **Mono** (prov.), Ben.
105/F5 **Mono** (riv.), Ben., Togo
130/C3 **Mono** (lake), Ca,US
66/E2 **Monopoli,** It.
68/D2 **Monor,** Hun.
133/Q8 **Mono Road,** On,Can.
65/E3 **Monóvar,** Sp.
66/C3 **Monreale,** It.
135/H3 **Monroe,** Ga,US
134/E3 **Monroe,** La,US
132/D3 **Monroe,** Mi,US
135/H3 **Monroe,** NC,US
130/D3 **Monroe,** Ut,US
132/B3 **Monroe,** Wi,US
135/G4 **Monroeville,** Al,US
104/C5 **Monrovia** (cap.), Libr.
137/C2 **Monrovia,** Ca,US
58/C3 **Mons,** Belg.
59/F2 **Monschau,** Ger.
63/J4 **Monselice,** It.
137/F4 **Monsey,** NY,US
56/B4 **Monster,** Neth.
48/F4 **Mönsteras,** Swe.
109/J6 **Montagne d'Ambre Nat'l Park,** Madg.
133/J2 **Montague,** PE,Can.
136/L3 **Montague,** Yk,Can.
136/J4 **Montague** (isl.), Ak,US
136/J4 **Montague** (str.), Ak,US
134/D3 **Montague,** Tx,US
66/E2 **Montalbano Jonico,** It.
128/F4 **Montana** (state), US
116/D1 **Montanha,** Braz.
62/E3 **Montargis,** Fr.
58/B5 **Montataire,** Fr.
62/D4 **Montauban,** Fr.
110/E6 **Mont aux Sources** (peak), Les.
62/F3 **Montbard,** Fr.
60/C2 **Montbéliard,** Fr.
65/L7 **Montcada i Reixac,** Sp.
62/F3 **Montceau-les-Mines,** Fr.
137/C2 **Montclair,** Ca,US
62/C5 **Mont-de-Marsan,** Fr.
58/B4 **Montdidier,** Fr.
122/B4 **Monte Albán** (ruins), Mex.
115/H4 **Monte Alegre,** Braz.
116/B1 **Monte Alegre de Minas,** Braz.
116/B2 **Monte Alto,** Braz.
115/K7 **Monte Azul,** Braz.
137/B2 **Montebello,** Ca,US
117/F2 **Montecarlo,** Arg.
116/C1 **Monte Carmelo,** Braz.
123/G6 **Monte Carmelo,** Ven.
117/E3 **Monte Caseros,** Arg.
123/G4 **Monte Cristo,** DRep.
66/B1 **Montecristo** (isl.), It.
64/C4 **Montefrío,** Sp.
123/F4 **Montego Bay,** Jam.
65/P10 **Montelavar,** Port.
62/F4 **Montélimar,** Fr.
64/C4 **Montellano,** Sp.
130/D2 **Montello,** Nv,US
118/D5 **Montemayor** (plat.), Arg.
122/B2 **Montemorelos,** Mex.
64/A3 **Montemor-o-Novo,** Port.
64/A2 **Montemuro** (mtn.), Port.
116/B4 **Montenegro,** Braz.
68/D4 **Montenegro** (ctry.)
66/D2 **Montenero di Bisaccia,** It.
54/B5 **Montenoison, Butte de** (mtn.), Fr.
115/L7 **Monte Pascoal Nat'l Park,** Braz.
62/E2 **Montereau-faut-Yonne,** Fr.
130/B3 **Monterey,** Ca,US
130/B3 **Monterey** (bay), Ca,US
137/B2 **Monterey Park,** Ca,US
123/F6 **Montería,** Col.
114/F7 **Montero,** Bol.
117/C2 **Monteros,** Arg.
66/C1 **Monterotondo,** It.
122/A2 **Monterrey,** Mex.
119/K7 **Montes** (pt.), Arg.
66/D2 **Monte Sant'Angelo,** It.
66/E2 **Montescaglioso,** It.
115/K7 **Montes Claros,** Braz.
66/D1 **Montesilvano Marina,** It.
62/F4 **Monteux,** Fr.
119/F2 **Montevideo** (cap.), Uru.
119/T12 **Montevideo** (dept.), Uru.
129/K4 **Montevideo,** Mn,US
59/E5 **Montfaucon,** Fr.
56/B4 **Montfoort,** Neth.
58/B6 **Montgeron,** Fr.
52/C1 **Montgomery,** Wal,UK
135/G3 **Montgomery** (cap.), Al,US
132/D4 **Montgomery,** WV,US
137/J7 **Montgomery Village,** Md,US
137/E5 **Montgomeryville,** Pa,US
62/E5 **Montgrand** (mtn.), Fr.
60/C5 **Monthey,** Swi.
134/F3 **Monticello,** Ar,US
138/K9 **Monticello** (dam), Ca,US
135/H4 **Monticello,** Fl,US
132/C3 **Monticello,** In,US
132/C4 **Monticello,** Ky,US
131/K2 **Monticello,** Mo,US
130/E3 **Monticello,** Ut,US
132/E4 **Monticello,** Va,US
58/B3 **Montigny-en-Gohelle,** Fr.
58/B6 **Montigny-le-Bretonneux,** Fr.
59/F5 **Montigny-lès-Metz,** Fr.
58/D3 **Montigny-le-Tilleul,** Belg.
64/A3 **Montijo,** Port.
64/B3 **Montijo,** Sp.
64/C4 **Montilla,** Sp.
62/D2 **Montivilliers,** Fr.
133/G1 **Mont-Joli,** Qu,Can.
132/F2 **Mont-Laurier,** Qu,Can.
62/E3 **Montluçon,** Fr.
133/G2 **Montmagny,** Qu,Can.
62/D3 **Montmorillon,** Fr.
64/C3 **Montoro,** Sp.
104/D5 **Mont Peko Nat'l Park,** C.d'Iv.
128/F5 **Montpelier,** Id,US
133/F2 **Montpelier** (cap.), Vt,US
62/E5 **Montpellier,** Fr.
132/C2 **Montreal** (riv.), On,Can.
133/N7 **Montréal,** Qu,Can.
129/G2 **Montreal** (lake), Sk,Can.
58/A3 **Montreuil,** Fr.
60/C5 **Montreux,** Swi.
49/D2 **Montrose,** Sc,UK
130/F3 **Montrose,** Co,US
58/B6 **Montry,** Fr.
133/P6 **Mont-Saint-Hilaire,** Qu,Can.
59/E4 **Mont-Saint-Martin,** Fr.
132/F2 **Mont-Saint-Michel,** Qu,Can.
62/C2 **Mont-Saint-Michel,** Fr.
62/C2 **Mont-Saint-Michel** (bay), Fr.
104/D4 **Mont Sangbé Nat'l Park,** C.d'Iv.
65/L6 **Montseny Nat'l Park,** Sp.
104/C5 **Montserrado** (co.), Libr.
65/F2 **Montserrat** (mtn.), Sp.
123/J4 **Montserrat** (isl.), UK
137/F5 **Montville,** NJ,US
131/G4 **Monument Draw** (cr.), NM, Tx,US
91/G3 **Monywa,** Myan.
63/H4 **Monza,** It.
110/E4 **Monze,** Zam.
65/F2 **Monzón,** Sp.
108/P13 **Mool** (riv.), SAfr.
96/D4 **Mooloolaba-Maroochydore,** Austl.
97/G5 **Moorabbin,** Austl.
129/G4 **Moorcroft,** Wy,US
133/R8 **Moore** (pt.), On,Can.
131/H4 **Moore,** Ok,US
99/X15 **Moorea** (isl.), FrPol.
135/F6 **Moore Haven,** Fl,US
137/F6 **Moorestown,** NJ,US
135/H3 **Mooresville,** NC,US
129/J4 **Moorhead,** Mn,US
58/C2 **Moorslede,** Belg.
63/J2 **Moosburg,** Ger.
132/D1 **Moose** (riv.), On,Can.
129/H3 **Moose** (mtn.), Sk,Can.
132/D1 **Moose Factory,** On,Can.
133/G2 **Moosehead** (lake), Me,US
136/H3 **Mooseheart** (mtn.), Ak,US
129/G3 **Moose Jaw,** Sk,Can.
129/H3 **Moosomin,** Sk,Can.
132/D1 **Moosonee,** On,Can.
104/E3 **Mopti,** Mali
104/E3 **Mopti** (reg.), Mali
114/D7 **Moquegua,** Peru
68/D2 **Mór,** Hun.
102/H5 **Mora,** Camr.
64/D3 **Mora,** Sp.
48/E3 **Mora,** Swe.
131/F4 **Mora,** NM,US
131/F4 **Mora** (riv.), NM,US
68/D4 **Morača** (riv.), Mont.
90/C2 **Morādābād,** India
115/L5 **Morada Nova,** Braz.
116/C1 **Morada Nova de Mina,** Braz.
118/C2 **Morado Nat'l Park,** Chile
109/H7 **Morafenobe,** Madg.
55/K2 **Morąg,** Pol.
138/K11 **Moraga,** Ca,US
118/B5 **Moraleda** (chan.), Chile
64/B2 **Moraleja,** Sp.
122/D4 **Morales,** Guat.
130/E2 **Moran,** Wy,US
96/C3 **Moranbah,** Austl.
99/M7 **Morane** (isl.), FrPol.
64/E3 **Moratalla,** Sp.
55/J4 **Morava** (riv.), Czh.
67/G1 **Morava** (riv.), Serb.
55/J4 **Moravia** (reg.), Czh.
55/J4 **Moravská Třebová,** Czh.
55/H4 **Moravské Budějovice,** Czh.
59/G4 **Morbach,** Ger.
58/B2 **Morbecque,** Fr.
61/F5 **Morbegno,** It.
48/F4 **Mörbylanga,** Swe.
129/J3 **Morden,** Mb,Can.
97/G6 **Mordialloc,** Austl.
73/G1 **Mordovia,** Rus.
73/G1 **Mordoviya, Resp.,** Rus.
129/H4 **Moreau** (riv.), SD,US
49/D3 **Morebattle,** Sc,UK
51/F3 **Morecambe,** Eng,UK
51/E3 **Morecambe** (bay), Eng,UK
97/D1 **Moree,** Austl.
132/D4 **Morehead,** Ky,US
135/J3 **Morehead City,** NC,US
122/A4 **Morelia,** Mex.
122/B4 **Morelos** (state), Mex.
90/C2 **Morena,** India
64/C3 **Morena** (range), Sp.
69/G3 **Moreni,** Rom.
137/C3 **Moreno Valley,** Ca,US
48/C3 **Møre og Romsdal** (co.), Nor.
137/B2 **Morepack,** Ca,US
124/C3 **Moresby** (isl.), BC,Can.
96/F6 **Moreton** (bay), Austl.
96/D4 **Moreton** (cape), Austl.
52/C5 **Moretonhampstead,** Eng,UK
96/D4 **Moreton I. Nat'l Park,** Austl.
53/E3 **Moreton in Marsh,** Eng,UK
71/N2 **Moreyu** (riv.), Rus.
60/C4 **Morez,** Fr.
135/F4 **Morgan City,** La,US
132/C4 **Morganfield,** Ky,US
66/D4 **Morgantina** (ruins), It.
135/H3 **Morganton,** NC,US
132/C4 **Morgantown,** Ky,US
132/E4 **Morgantown,** WV,US
62/E3 **Morge** (riv.), Fr.
60/C4 **Morges,** Swi.
79/H1 **Morghāb** (riv.), Afg.
118/B3 **Morguilla** (pt.), Chile
82/C3 **Mori,** China
63/J4 **Mori,** It.
131/F4 **Moriarty,** NM,US
128/B2 **Morice** (lake), BC,Can.
85/L10 **Moriguchi,** Japan
57/G5 **Moringen,** Ger.
128/E2 **Morinville,** Ab,Can.
83/N4 **Morioka,** Japan
85/H7 **Moriya,** Japan
84/D3 **Moriyama,** Japan
62/B2 **Morlaix,** Fr.
58/D3 **Morlanwelz,** Belg.
51/G4 **Morley,** Eng,UK
90/B4 **Mormugao,** India
96/F6 **Morningside,** Austl.
119/J7 **Mornington** (isl.), Chile
79/J3 **Moro,** Pak.
88/D6 **Moro** (gulf), Phil.
102/C1 **Morocco** (ctry.)
107/C4 **Morogoro,** Tanz.
107/C4 **Morogoro** (prov.), Tanz.

174
Morok – Né

97/C3 Moroka-Wonnangatta Nat'l Park, Austl.
109/G8 Morombe, Madg.
118/F2 Morón, Arg.
123/F3 Morón, Cuba
114/C4 Morona (riv.), Ecu., Peru
109/H8 Morondara (riv.), Madg.
109/H8 Morondava, Madg.
64/C4 Morón de la Frontera, Sp.
109/G5 Moroni (cap.), Com.
93/G3 Morotai (isl.), Indo.
93/G3 Morotai (str.) Indo.
107/B2 Moroto, Ugan.
85/H7 Moroyama, Japan
73/G2 Morozovsk, Rus.
51/G1 Morpeth, Eng,UK
80/J4 Morphou, Cyp.
80/J4 Morphou (bay), Cyp.
56/C3 Morra (lake), Neth.
131/G2 Morrill, Ne,US
116/B1 Morrinhos, Braz.
129/J3 Morris, Mb,Can.
132/B3 Morris, Il,US
129/K4 Morris, Mn,US
121/P1 Morris Jesup (cape), Grld.
137/F5 Morris Plains, NJ,US
52/C3 Morriston, Wal,UK
137/F5 Morristown, NJ,US
135/H2 Morristown, Tn,US
137/F5 Morrisville, Pa,US
130/B4 Morro Bay, Ca,US
110/C3 Morro de Môco (peak), Ang.
116/B3 Morro do Capão Doce (hill), Braz.
115/K6 Morro do Chapeu, Braz.
59/G2 Morsbach, Ger.
73/G1 Morshansk, Rus.
73/J3 Morskoy (isl.), Kaz.
52/B4 Morte (pt.), UK
115/H6 Mortes (riv.), Braz.
53/E4 Mortimer, Eng,UK
52/D2 Mortimers Cross, Eng,UK
132/B3 Morton, Il,US
138/Q15 Morton Grove, Il,US
97/D2 Morton Nat'l Park, Austl.
58/D1 Mortsel, Belg.
62/E3 Morvan (plat.), Fr.
90/B3 Morvi, India
97/C3 Morwell, Austl.
64/A1 Mos, Sp.
63/H2 Mosbach, Ger.
65/P10 Moscavide, Port.
70/G5 Moscow (upland), Rus.
128/D4 Moscow, Id,US
71/X9 Moscow (Moskva) (cap.), Rus.
111/H Moscow Univ. Ice Shelf, Ant.
59/F4 Mosel (riv.), Ger.
58/F5 Moselle (dept.), Fr.
59/F5 Moselle (riv.), Fr.
128/D4 Moses Lake, Wa,US
108/C2 Moshaweng (dry riv.), SAfr.
107/C3 Moshi, Tanz.
55/J2 Mosina, Pol.
48/E2 Mosjøen, Nor.
70/H5 Moskovskaya Obl., Rus.
70/G5 Moskva (riv.), Rus.
71/X9 Moskva (Moscow) (cap.), Rus.
68/C2 Mosonmagyaróvár, Hun.
131/G4 Mosquero, NM,US
122/E6 Mosquitos (gulf), Pan.
122/E5 Mosquitos, Costa de (coast), Nic.
48/D4 Moss, Nor.
104/E4 Mossi Highlands (upland), Burk.
63/H2 Mössingen, Ger.
51/F4 Mossley, Eng,UK
50/C2 Mossley, NI,UK
115/L5 Mossoró, Braz.
135/F4 Moss Point, Ms,US
50/B1 Moss-side, NI,UK
55/G3 Most, Czh.
102/E1 Mostaganem, Alg.
68/C4 Mostar, Bosn.
64/D2 Móstoles, Sp.
51/E5 Mostyn, Wal,UK
80/E3 Mosul (Al Mawşil), Iraq
122/D4 Motagua (riv.), Guat.
48/E4 Motala, Swe.
87/E2 Motian Ling (mtn.), China
90/D2 Motīhāri, India
85/G2 Motomiya, Japan
48/K1 Motovskiy (gulf), Rus.
64/D4 Motril, Sp.
129/H4 Mott, ND,US
122/D3 Motul, Mex.
74/K4 Motygino, Rus.
104/B2 Mougris (well), Mrta.
104/E3 Mouhoun (prov.), Burk.
102/H8 Mouila, Gabon
102/H4 Moul (well), Niger
97/C2 Moulamein (riv.), Austl.
51/F5 Mouldsworth, Eng,UK
62/E3 Moulins, Fr.
89/B2 Moulmein, Myan.
102/E1 Moulouya (riv.), Mor.
53/G2 Moulton, Eng,UK
135/H4 Moultrie, Ga,US
135/H3 Moultrie (lake), SC,US
131/J3 Mound City, Ks,US
102/J6 Moundou, Chad
132/D4 Moundsville, WV,US
89/C3 Moung Roessei, Camb.
89/D3 Mounlapamok, Laos
96/B3 Mount Aberdeen Nat'l Park, Austl.
90/B3 Mount Abu, India
124/D2 Mountain (riv.), NW,Can.
52/C3 Mountain Ash, Wal,UK
135/G3 Mountain Brook, Al,US
131/J3 Mountain Grove, Mo,US
134/E2 Mountain Home, Ar,US
128/E5 Mountain Home, Id,US
134/E3 Mountain View, Ar,US
138/K12 Mountain View, Ca,US
108/D4 Mountain Zebra Nat'l Park, SAfr.
135/H2 Mount Airy, NC,US
95/A4 Mount Barker, Austl.
97/A2 Mount Barker, Austl.
96/C5 Mount Barney Nat'l Park, Austl.
97/C3 Mount Buffalo Nat'l Park, Austl.
132/C4 Mount Carmel, Il,US
103/M2 Mount Catherine (peak), Egypt
138/G6 Mount Clemens, Mi,US
96/E6 Mount Coot'tha, Austl.
110/F4 Mount Darwin, Zim.
97/B3 Mount Eccles Nat'l Park, Austl.
96/B2 Mount Elliot Nat'l Park, Austl.
97/B3 Mount Emu (cr.), Austl.
97/C4 Mount Field Nat'l Park, Austl.
97/B3 Mount Gambier, Austl.
98/D5 Mount Hagen, PNG
137/F6 Mount Holly, NJ,US
133/Q9 Mount Hope, On,Can.
97/D3 Mount Imlay Nat'l Park, Austl.
95/C3 Mount Isa, Austl.
97/D1 Mount Kaputar Nat'l Park, Austl.
137/G4 Mount Kisco, NY,US
138/C2 Mountlake Terrace, Wa,US
137/F6 Mount Laurel, NJ,US
96/D4 Mount Mistake Nat'l Park, Austl.
132/D3 Mount Morris, Mi,US
96/E6 Mount Nebo, Austl.
135/J3 Mount Olive, NC,US
67/H3 Mount Parnes Nat'l Park, Gre.
133/L2 Mount Pearl, Nf,Can.
129/L5 Mount Pleasant, Ia,US
132/C3 Mount Pleasant, Mi,US
134/E3 Mount Pleasant, Tx,US
130/E3 Mount Pleasant, Ut,US
138/Q15 Mount Prospect, Il,US
137/K8 Mount Rainier, Md,US
128/C4 Mount Rainier Nat'l Park, Wa,US
128/D3 Mount Revelstoke Nat'l Park, BC,Can.
97/B3 Mount Richmond Nat'l Park, Austl.
131/G2 Mount Rushmore Nat'l Mem., SD,US
52/A6 Mount's (bay), Eng,UK
96/B2 Mount Spec Nat'l Park, Austl.
132/D4 Mount Sterling, Ky,US
132/B4 Mount Vernon, Il,US
132/C4 Mount Vernon, In,US
137/G5 Mount Vernon, NY,US
132/D3 Mount Vernon, Oh,US
137/J8 Mount Vernon, Va,US
128/C3 Mount Vernon, Wa,US
96/C4 Mount Walsh Nat'l Park, Austl.
97/E1 Mount Warning Nat'l Park, Austl.
97/D4 Mount William Nat'l Park, Austl.
64/B3 Moura, Port.
62/C5 Mourenx, Fr.
50/B3 Mourne (dist.), NI,UK
50/B3 Mourne (mts.), NI,UK
58/C2 Mouscron, Belg.
102/J5 Moussoro, Chad
58/B5 Moussy-le-Neuf, Fr.
58/C2 Mouvaux, Fr.
50/B3 Moy, NI,UK
107/C2 Moyale, Eth.
102/D1 Moyen Atlas (mts.), Mor.
59/F5 Moyeuvre-Grande, Fr.
50/B2 Moygashel, NI,UK
50/B1 Moyle (dist.), NI,UK
93/E5 Moyo (isl.), Indo.
81/C4 Moyu, China
110/G4 Mozambique (ctry.)
110/G5 Mozambique (chan.), Afr.
70/H5 Mozhaysk, Rus.
71/M4 Mozhga, Rus.
107/A4 Mpanda, Tanz.
110/C4 Mpangu, Namb.
107/A5 Mpika, Zam.
107/A5 Mporokoso, Zam.
105/E5 Mpraeso, Gha.
109/E5 Mpumalanga (prov.), SAfr.
55/L2 Mrągowo, Pol.
68/C3 Mrkonjić Grad, Bosn.
66/B5 Msaken, Tun.
70/G4 Msta (riv.), Rus.
55/L4 Mszana Dolna, Pol.
72/F1 Mtsensk, Rus.
107/D5 Mtwara, Tanz.
107/C5 Mtwara (prov.), Tanz.
110/G4 Mualama, Moz.
89/D2 Muang Gnommarat, Laos
89/C2 Muang Kenthao, Laos
89/D3 Muang Khong, Laos
89/D3 Muang Khongxedon, Laos
89/D3 Muang Lakhonpheng, Laos
89/D1 Muang Soy, Laos
89/C2 Muang Thathom, Laos
89/D2 Muang Xamteu, Laos
89/D2 Muang Xepon, Laos
92/B3 Muar, Malay.
92/B4 Muarabungo, Indo.
79/J4 Muāri (pt.), Pak.
102/H5 Mubi, Nga.
114/F3 Mucajaí (riv.), Braz.
59/G2 Much, Ger.
107/A5 Muchinga (mts.), Zam.
52/D1 Much Wenlock, Eng,UK
50/B2 Muckamore Abbey, NI,UK
110/H3 Mucojo, Moz.
80/C2 Mucur, Turk.
116/D1 Mucuri (riv.), Braz.
110/D3 Mucussueje, Ang.
83/K3 Mudanjiang, China
69/J5 Mudanya, Turk.
83/K2 Muddan (riv.), China
48/F2 Muddus Nat'l Park, Swe.
130/E3 Muddy (riv.), Ut,US
131/H4 Muddy Boggy (cr.), Ok,US
59/G2 Mudersbach, Ger.
97/D2 Mudgee, Austl.
128/G1 Mudjatik (riv.), Sk,Can.
138/D3 Mud Mountain (lake), Wa,US
89/B2 Mudon, Myan.
119/J8 Muela (peak), Chile
80/N8 Mufjir, Nahr (dry riv.), WBnk.
110/E3 Mufulira, Zam.
64/A1 Mugardos, Sp.
63/K4 Muggia, It.
73/L2 Mughalzhar Taūy (mts.), Kaz.
64/A1 Mugia, Sp.
80/B3 Muğla, Turk.
107/A4 Mugombazi, Tanz.
106/D4 Muḩammad Qawl, Sudan
106/C3 Muḩammad, Ra's (pt.), Egypt
110/E2 Muhila (mts.), D.R. Congo
63/K2 Mühlviertel (reg.), Aus.
48/H2 Muhos, Fin.
78/C2 Mūḩ, Sabkhat al (lake), Syria
70/D4 Muhu (isl.), Est.
56/C4 Muiden, Neth.
49/C3 Muirkirk, Sc,UK
49/C2 Muir of Ord, Sc,UK
138/J11 Muir Woods Nat'l Mon., Ca,US
86/D5 Muju, SKor.
72/B2 Mukachevo, Ukr.
106/D4 Mukawwar (isl.), Sudan
129/M2 Muketei (riv.), On,Can.
80/L5 Mukhayyam al Yarmūk, Syria
138/C2 Mukilteo, Wa,US
85/L10 Mukō, Japan
98/D2 Mukoshima (isls.), Japan
89/B4 Mu Ko Similan Nat'l Park, Thai.
89/B4 Mu Ko Surin Nat'l Park, Thai.
79/K2 Muktsar, India
64/E3 Mula, Sp.
110/G4 Mulanje, Malw.
136/G4 Mulchatna (riv.), Ak,US
118/B3 Mulchén, Chile
54/G3 Mulde (riv.), Ger.
111/D Mule (pt.), Ant.
64/D4 Mulhacén, Cerro de (mtn.), Sp.
54/F3 Mülhausen, Ger.
56/D6 Mülheim an der Ruhr, Ger.
60/D2 Mulhouse, Fr.
87/D3 Muling (pass), China
83/L2 Muling (riv.), China
99/R9 Mulinu'u (cape), Samoa
79/L2 Mulkila (mtn.), India
50/B5 Mullaghcleevaun (mtn.), Ire.
50/B2 Mullaghmore (mtn.), NI,UK
131/G2 Mullen, Ne,US
92/D4 Muller (mts.), Indo.
60/D2 Müllheim, Ger.
49/B4 Mullingar, Ire.
135/J3 Mullins, SC,US
52/A6 Mullion, Eng,UK
110/C4 Mulondo, Ang.
79/K2 Multān, Pak.
128/C3 Multnomah (falls), Or,US
92/D3 Mulu, Gunung (peak), Malay.
106/B5 Mulwad, Sudan
90/B4 Mumbai (Bombay), India
110/C3 Mumbué, Ang.
110/E3 Mumbwa, Zam.
89/B5 Mum Nauk (pt.), Thai.
89/C3 Mun (riv.), Thai.
93/F4 Muna (isl.), Indo.
48/H4 Munamägi (hill), Est.
132/C3 Muncie, In,US
138/P15 Mundelein, Il,US
105/H5 Mundemba, Camr.
57/G6 Münden, Ger.
53/H1 Mundesley, Eng,UK
53/G2 Mundford, Eng,UK
90/C3 Mungaolī, India
97/B2 Mungo Nat'l Park, Austl.
81/F1 Mungun-Tayga, Gora (peak), Rus.
61/H1 Munich (München), Ger.
132/C2 Munising, Mi,US
75/L4 Munku-Sardyk (peak), Rus.
82/D1 Munku-Sasan (peak), Rus.
119/J8 Muñoz Gamero (pen.), Chile
57/E5 Münster, Ger.
57/H3 Munster, Ger.
49/A4 Munster (prov.), Ire.
138/Q16 Munster, In,US
57/E4 Münsterland (reg.), Ger.
69/F2 Muntele Mare (peak), Rom.
92/C4 Muntok, Indo.
89/D1 Muong Khuong, Viet.
48/G1 Muonioälv (riv.), Swe.
48/G1 Muoniojoki (riv.), Fin.
110/C4 Mupa Nat'l Park, Moz.
103/Q7 Muqdisho (Mogadishu) (cap.), Som.
63/L3 Mur (riv.), Aus.
68/C2 Mura (riv.), Slvk.
80/E2 Muradiye, Turk.
85/F1 Murakami, Japan
119/J7 Murallón (peak), Chile
107/C3 Murang'a, Kenya
80/E2 Murat (riv.), Turk.
72/D5 Murat Dağı (peak), Turk.
65/E4 Murcia, Sp.
64/E4 Murcia (aut. comm.), Sp.
133/H1 Murdochville, Qu,Can.
96/B1 Murdock (pt.), Austl.
69/G2 Mureş (co.), Rom.
69/G2 Mureş (riv.), Rom.
62/D5 Muret, Fr.
134/E3 Murfreesboro, Ar,US
135/G3 Murfreesboro, Tn,US
79/H1 Murgab (riv.), Trkm.
92/D5 Muria (peak), Indo.
116/D2 Muriaé, Braz.
79/G3 Mūrīān, Hāmūn-e Jaz (lake), Iran
54/G2 Müritz See (lake), Ger.
103/N6 Murle, Eth.
70/G1 Murmansk, Rus.
70/G2 Murmanskaya Obl., Rus.
85/M10 Muro, Japan
65/G3 Muro, Sp.
70/J5 Murom, Rus.
83/N3 Muroran, Japan
64/A1 Muros, Sp.
84/D4 Muroto, Japan
84/D4 Muroto-zaki (pt.), Japan
55/J2 Murowana Goślina, Pol.
135/G3 Murphy, NC,US
132/B4 Murphysboro, Il,US
97/D2 Murramarang Nat'l Park, Austl.
97/A2 Murray (riv.), Austl.
98/D5 Murray (lake), PNG
132/B4 Murray, Ky,US
135/H3 Murray (lake), SC,US
97/A2 Murray Bridge, Austl.
97/C2 Murrumbidgee (riv.), Austl.
68/C2 Murska Sobota, Slov.
51/G2 Murton, Eng,UK
99/M7 Mururoa (isl.), FrPol.
90/D3 Murwāra, India
97/E1 Murwillumbah, Austl.
55/H5 Mürz (riv.), Aus.
63/L3 Mürzzuschlag, Aus.
80/E2 Muş, Turk.
69/F4 Musala (peak), Bul.
79/G3 Musandam (pen.), Oman
85/H7 Musashino, Japan
79/G4 Muscat (Musqaţ) (cap.), Oman
137/E5 Musconetcong (riv.), NJ,US
137/C2 Muscoy, Ca,US
110/E5 Musekwapoort (pass), SAfr.
95/C3 Musgrave (ranges), Austl.
133/L1 Musgrave Harbour, Nf,Can.
90/E3 Mushābani, India
80/N9 Mushāsh, Wādī (dry riv.), WBnk.
110/C1 Mushie, D.R. Congo
92/B4 Musi (riv.), Indo.
138/P14 Muskego, Wi,US
132/C3 Muskegon, Mi,US
132/C3 Muskegon (riv.), Mi,US
132/D4 Muskingum (riv.), Oh,US
131/J4 Muskogee, Ok,US
132/E2 Muskoka (lake), On,Can.
107/B3 Musoma, Tanz.
79/G4 Musqaţ (Muscat) (cap.), Oman
133/J1 Musquaro (riv.), Qu,Can.
98/D5 Mussau (isl.), PNG
128/F4 Musselshell (riv.), Mt,US
66/C4 Mussomeli, It.
80/B2 Mustafakemalpaşa, Turk.
90/D2 Mustāng, Nepal
131/H4 Mustang, Ok,US
63/K2 Můstek (peak), Czh.
118/C5 Musters (lake), Arg.
86/E2 Musu-dan (pt.), NKor.
122/D5 Musún (mt.), Nic.
97/B3 Muswellbrook, Austl.
106/B3 Mūt, Egypt
80/C3 Mut, Turk.
110/F4 Mutare, Zim.
93/F5 Mutis (peak), Indo.
109/H6 Mutsamudu, Com.
83/N3 Mutsu, Japan
116/D1 Mutum, Braz.
73/L4 Muynak, Uzb.
79/K2 Muzaffargarh, Pak.
90/C2 Muzaffarnagar, India
90/E2 Muzaffarpur, India
116/G6 Muzambinho, Braz.
81/D3 Muzat (riv.), China
81/D4 Muztag (peak), China
81/E4 Muztag (peak), China
81/C4 Muztagata (peak), China
110/C2 Mwadi-Kalumbu, D.R. Congo
107/B3 Mwanza, Tanz.
107/B3 Mwanza (prov.), Tanz.
49/H7 Mweelrea (mtn.), Ire.
110/D1 Mweka, D.R. Congo
110/D2 Mwene-Ditu, D.R. Congo
107/A5 Mweru (lake), D.R. Congo, Zam.
97/E2 Myall Lakes Nat'l Park, Austl.
91/G4 Myanaung, Myan.
82/C2 Myangad, Mong.
91/G2 Myanmar (Burma)
91/G3 Myingyan, Myan.
91/G2 Myitkyina, Myan.
55/J4 Myjava, Slvk.
72/E3 Mykolayiv, Ukr.
72/D3 Mykolayivs'ka Obl., Ukr.
52/C2 Mynydd Eppynt (mts.), Wal,UK
52/B2 Mynydd Pencarreg (mtn.), Wal,UK
91/F3 Myohaung, Myan.
85/F2 Myōkō-san (mtn.), Japan
135/J3 Myrtle Beach, SC,US
128/C5 Myrtle Creek, Or,US
48/D4 Mysen, Nor.
55/K4 Myślenice, Pol.
55/H2 Myślibórz, Pol.
89/E3 My Son (ruins), Viet.
90/C5 Mysore, India
55/K3 Myszków, Pol.
89/D4 My Tho, Viet.
71/W9 Mytishchi, Rus.
54/G4 Mže (riv.), Czh.
107/B5 Mzuzu, Malw.

N

89/C1 Na (riv.), Viet.
63/J2 Naab (riv.), Ger.
56/B5 Naaldwijk, Neth.
56/C4 Naarden, Neth.
50/B5 Naas, Ire.
108/B3 Nababeep, SAfr.
90/E3 Nabadwīp, India
84/E3 Nabari, Japan
85/M10 Nabari (riv.), Japan
71/M5 Naberezhnye Chelny, Rus.
66/B4 Nabeul, Tun.
66/B4 Nabeul (gov.), Tun.
78/D5 Nabī Shu'ayb, Jabal an (mtn.), Yem.
133/J1 Nabisipi (riv.), Qu,Can.
88/D5 Nabua, Phil.
80/K5 Nābulus, WBnk.
84/D4 Nachi-Katsuura, Japan
55/J3 Náchod, Czh.
57/E6 Nachrodt-Wiblingwerde, Ger.
118/B3 Nacimiento, Chile
134/E4 Nacogdoches, Tx,US
52/D4 Nadder (riv.), Eng,UK
98/G6 Nadi, Fiji
90/B3 Nadiād, India
68/E2 Nădlac, Rom.
51/H3 Nafferton, Eng,UK
79/J3 Nag, Pak.
88/D5 Naga, Phil.
84/C4 Nagahama, Japan
84/E3 Nagahama, Japan
85/G1 Nagai, Japan
91/F2 Nāgāland (state), India
85/F2 Nagano, Japan
85/E3 Nagano (pref.), Japan
85/F2 Nagaoka, Japan
84/D3 Nagaokakyō, Japan
85/J7 Nagara, Japan
85/E3 Nagara (riv.), Japan
85/H7 Nagareyama, Japan
90/B4 Nagar Haveli, Dadrak (terr.), India
90/C4 Nāgārjuna Sāgar (res.), India
122/D5 Nagarote, Nic.
136/M5 Nagas (pt.), BC,Can.
84/A4 Nagasaki, Japan
84/A4 Nagasaki (pref.), Japan
85/M9 Nagashima, Japan
84/B3 Nagato, Japan
90/B2 Nāgaur, India
90/C3 Nāgda, India
90/C6 Nāgercoil, India
81/F2 Nagoonnuur, Mong.
73/H5 Nagorno-Karabakh Aut. Obl., Azer.
85/E3 Nagoya, Japan
90/C3 Nāgpur, India
82/C5 Nagqu (riv.), China
68/C2 Nagyatád, Hun.
68/E1 Nagyhalász, Hun.
68/E1 Nagykálló, Hun.
68/C2 Nagykanizsa, Hun.
68/D2 Nagykáta, Hun.
68/D2 Nagykőrös, Hun.
68/E1 Nagy-Milic (peak), Hun.
88/E2 Naha, Japan
124/D2 Nahanni Nat'l Park, NW,Can.
80/K5 Nahariyya, Isr.
98/D2 Nahashima (isls.), Japan
78/E2 Nahāvand, Iran
59/G4 Nahe (riv.), Ger.
105/E4 Nahouri (prov.), Burk.
118/B3 Nahuelbuta Nat'l Park, Chile
118/C4 Nahuel Huapí Nat'l Park, Arg.
123/N8 Naica, Mex.
82/C4 Naij Gol (riv.), China
84/C3 Naikai-Seto Nat'l Park, Japan
52/D4 Nailsea, Eng,UK
52/D3 Nailsworth, Eng,UK
90/D3 Nainpur, India
49/D2 Nairn, Sc,UK
49/D2 Nairn (riv.), Sc,UK
107/C3 Nairobi (cap.), Kenya
107/C3 Nairobi Nat'l Park, Kenya
78/F2 Najafābād, Iran
78/D3 Najd (des.), SAr.
64/D1 Nájera, Sp.
90/C2 Najībābād, India
85/K9 Naka, Japan
84/D4 Naka (riv.), Japan
85/G2 Naka (riv.), Japan
85/H7 Nakai, Japan
85/F1 Nakajō, Japan
126/T10 Nakalele (pt.), Hi,US
85/G2 Nakaminato, Japan
84/C4 Nakamura, Japan
85/F2 Nakano, Japan
84/C3 Nakano (lake), Japan
84/B5 Nakatane, Japan
85/E3 Nakatsugawa, Japan
103/N4 Nak'fa, Erit.
83/L3 Nakhodka, Rus.
89/C3 Nakhon Nayok, Thai.
89/C3 Nakhon Pathom, Thai.
89/D2 Nakhon Phanom, Thai.
89/C3 Nakhon Ratchasima, Thai.
89/C3 Nakhon Sawan, Thai.
89/B4 Nakhon Si Thammarat, Thai.
48/G3 Nakkila, Fin.
55/J2 Nakło nad Notecią, Pol.
54/F1 Nakskov, Den.
86/E5 Naktong (riv.), SKor.
107/C3 Nakuru, Kenya
128/D3 Nakusp, BC,Can.
79/J3 Nāl (riv.), Pak.
82/F2 Nalayh, Mong.
59/F5 Nalbach, Ger.
91/F2 Nalbāri, India
97/D3 Nalbaugh Nat'l Park, Austl.
73/G4 Nal'chik, Rus.
89/C2 Nale, Laos
90/C4 Nalgonda, India
69/K5 Nallıhan, Turk.
64/B1 Nalón (riv.), Sp.
102/H1 Nālūt, Libya
78/F2 Namak (lake), Iran
79/G2 Namakzār-e Shadād (salt dep.), Iran
81/B3 Namangan, Uzb.
108/B3 Namaqualand (reg.), SAfr.
93/J4 Namaripi (cape), Indo.
59/G4 Namborn, Ger.
96/D4 Nambour, Austl.
89/D4 Nam Can, Viet.
89/C1 Nam Cum, Viet.
89/D1 Nam Dinh, Viet.
132/B2 Namekagon (riv.), Wi,US
105/E3 Namentenga (prov.), Burk.
85/E2 Namerikawa, Japan
110/B5 Namib (des.), Namb.
110/C5 Namibia (ctry.)
108/A2 Namib-Naukluft Park, Namb.
85/G2 Namie, Japan
90/D2 Namja (pass), Nepal
91/G2 Namjagbarwa (peak), China
89/C2 Nam Nao Nat'l Park, Thai.
89/B4 Namnoi (peak), Myan.
97/D1 Namoi (riv.), Austl.
98/E4 Namonuito (atoll), Micr.
98/F4 Namorik (atoll), Mrsh.
128/D5 Nampa, Id,US
86/C3 Namp'o, NKor.
110/G4 Nampula, Moz.
81/D6 Namsê Shankou (pass), China
48/D2 Namsos, Nor.
89/B2 Nam Tok Mae Surin Nat'l Park, Thai.
98/F4 Namu (atoll), Mrsh.
89/C2 Nam Un (res.), Thai.
59/D3 Namur, Belg.
59/D3 Namur (prov.), Belg.
55/J3 Namysłów, Pol.
87/B4 Nan (riv.), China
89/C2 Nan, Thai.
89/C2 Nan (riv.), Thai.
128/C3 Nanaimo, BC,Can.
126/V13 Nanakuli, Hi,US
85/E2 Nanao, Japan
114/D4 Nanay (riv.), Peru
118/C2 Nancagua, Chile
88/C2 Nanchang, China
88/C2 Nancheng, China
59/F6 Nancy, Fr.
90/C4 Nānded, India
91/G3 Nanding (riv.), China
88/A4 Nandu (riv.), China
90/B3 Nandurbār, India
90/C4 Nandyāl, India
79/K1 Nanga Parbat (mtn.), Pak.
92/D4 Nangapinoh, Indo.
87/C3 Nangong, China
93/F1 Nangtud (mt.), Phil.
87/D4 Nanjing, China
84/C4 Nankoku, Japan
91/J3 Nanliu (riv.), China
83/K3 Nanlou (peak), China
91/J3 Nanning, China
85/M9 Nannō, Japan
50/B4 Nanny (riv.), Ire.
90/D2 Nānpāra, India
88/C2 Nanping, China
85/M10 Nansei, Japan
125/S6 Nansen (sound), Nun,Can.
107/B3 Nansio, Tanz.
85/F2 Nantai-san (mtn.), Japan
58/B6 Nanterre, Fr.
62/C3 Nantes, Fr.
58/B5 Nanteuil-le-Haudouin, Fr.
132/D3 Nanticoke, On,Can.
128/E3 Nanton, Ab,Can.
87/E4 Nantong, China
133/G3 Nantucket (isl.), MA,US
51/F5 Nantwich, Eng,UK
52/C3 Nantyglo, Wal,UK
137/F4 Nanuet, NY,US
99/Z18 Nanuku (chan.), Fiji
98/G5 Nanumanga (atoll), Tuv.
98/G5 Nanumea (isl.), Tuv.
116/D1 Nanuque, Braz.
87/C4 Nanwon (res.), China
87/D4 Nanyang, China
87/D4 Nanyang (lake), China
107/C2 Nanyuki, Kenya
125/J3 Naococane (lake), Qu,Can.
90/A3 Naokot, Pak.
83/L2 Naoli (riv.), China
104/D5 Naoua (falls), C.d'Iv.
138/K10 Napa, Ca,US
138/K10 Napa (riv.), Ca,US
132/E2 Napanee, On,Can.
106/B5 Napata (ruins), Sudan
138/P16 Naperville, Il,US
95/H6 Napier, NZ
108/L11 Napier, SAfr.
135/H5 Naples, Fl,US
66/D2 Naples (Napoli), It.
66/D2 Napoli (gulf), It.
96/A4 Nappa Merrie, Austl.
53/E2 Napton on the Hill, Eng,UK
99/L6 Napuka (isl.), FrPol.
84/D3 Nara, Japan
84/D3 Nara (pref.), Japan
104/D3 Nara, Mali
79/J4 Nāra (riv.), Pak.
81/D5 Nara Logna (pass), Nepal
90/D4 Narasannapeta, India
85/J7 Narashino, Japan
89/C5 Narathiwat, Thai.
90/F3 Nārāyanganj, Bang.
90/C4 Nārāyanpet, India
52/B3 Narberth, Wal,UK
62/E5 Narbonne, Fr.
64/B1 Narcea (riv.), Sp.
67/F2 Nardò, It.
52/B6 Nare (pt.), UK
125/T7 Nares (str.), Nun,Can.
55/L2 Narew (riv.), Pol.
123/F6 Narganá, Pan.
109/H6 Narinda (bay), Madg.
119/K8 Nariz (peak), Chile
90/D2 Narkatiāganj, India
90/C3 Narmada (riv.), India
80/E2 Narman, Turk.
66/C1 Narni, It.
71/P2 Narodnaya (peak), Rus.
64/A1 Narón, Sp.
79/K2 Nārowāl, Pak.
48/G3 Närpes, Fin.
88/C6 Narra, Phil.
97/D1 Narrabri, Austl.
90/C3 Narsimhapur, India
90/C3 Narsingarh, India
84/D3 Naruto, Japan
70/F4 Narva, Est.
70/E4 Narva (riv.), Est., Rus.
88/D4 Narvacan, Phil.
48/F1 Narvik, Nor.
71/M2 Nar'yan-Mar, Rus.
81/C3 Naryn, Kyr.
81/B3 Naryn (riv.), Kyr.
73/J2 Naryn Qum (des.), Kaz.
69/G2 Năsăud, Rom.
53/F3 Nash, Eng,UK
52/C4 Nash (pt.), Wal,UK
133/G3 Nashua, NH,US
134/E3 Nashville, Ar,US
135/G2 Nashville (cap.), Tn,US
68/D3 Našice, Cro.
55/L2 Nasielsk, Pol.
90/B4 Nāsik, India
103/M6 Nāşir, Sudan
90/B2 Nasīrābād, India
79/J3 Nasīrābād, Pak.
93/F1 Naso (pt.), Phil.
99/Z17 Nasorolevu (peak), Fiji
136/N4 Nass (riv.), BC,Can.
105/G4 Nassarawa (state), Nga.
123/F2 Nassau (cap.), Bahm.
119/L8 Nassau (bay), Chile
99/J6 Nassau (isl.), Cookls.
106/C4 Nasser (res.), Egypt
48/E4 Nässjö, Swe.
125/J3 Nastapoka (isls.), Nun,Can.
54/F1 Næstved, Den.
85/F2 Nasu-dake (mtn.), Japan
89/B2 Nat (peak), Myan.
110/E5 Nata, Bots.
132/C1 Natagani (riv.), On,Can.
115/L5 Natal, Braz.
133/J1 Natashquan (riv.), Qu,Can.
135/F4 Natchez, Ms,US
134/E4 Natchitoches, La,US
60/D5 Naters, Swi.
99/Z17 Natewa (bay), Fiji
90/B3 Nāthdwāra, India
128/B2 Nation (riv.), BC,Can.
130/C4 National City, Ca,US
91/G4 Nattaung (peak), Myan.
92/C3 Natuna (isls.), Indo.
130/E3 Natural Bridges Nat'l Mon., Ut,US
97/D4 Naturaliste (cape), Austl.
122/B4 Naucalpan, Mex.
108/E3 Naudesnek (pass), SAfr.
88/D5 Naujan, Phil.
70/D4 Naujoji-Akmenė, Lith.
108/A2 Naukluft-Namib Game Rsv., Namb.
98/F5 Nauru (ctry.)
65/N8 Navacarrada (pass), Sp.
130/E3 Navajo Nat'l Mon., Az,US
65/M9 Navalcarnero, Sp.
64/C3 Navalmoral de la Mata, Sp.
50/B4 Navan, Ire.
75/T3 Navarin (cape), Rus.
119/L8 Navarino (isl.), Chile
64/D1 Navarre (aut. comm.), Sp.
118/F2 Navarro, Arg.
52/A6 Navax (pt.), UK
64/B1 Navia, Sp.
64/B1 Navia (riv.), Sp.
118/C2 Navidad, Chile
115/H8 Naviraí, Braz.
69/J3 Năvodari, Rom.
74/G5 Navoi, Uzb.
123/N8 Navojoa, Mex.
123/N9 Navolato, Mex.
67/G3 Návpaktos, Gre.
67/H4 Návplion, Gre.
90/B3 Navsāri, India
125/H1 Navy Board (inlet), Nun,Can.
90/E3 Nawābganj, Bang.
90/D2 Nawābganj, India
79/J3 Nawābshāh, Pak.
79/G5 Nawş, Ra's (pt.), Oman
73/H5 Naxçıvan, Azer.
73/H5 Naxçıvan Aut. Rep., Azer.
67/J4 Náxos (isl.), Gre.
123/P9 Nayarit (state), Mex.
53/G3 Nayland, Eng,UK
91/G4 Nay Pyi Taw (cap.), Myan.
82/B2 Nayramadlīn (peak), Mong.
81/B4 Nayzatash, Pereval (pass), Taj.
64/A3 Nazaré, Port.
58/C2 Nazareth, Belg.
80/K5 Nazareth (Nazerat), Isr.
123/P8 Nazas (riv.), Mex.
114/D6 Nazca, Peru
114/C6 Nazca Lines (ruins), Peru
98/B2 Naze, Japan
53/H3 Naze, The (pt.), Eng,UK
80/B3 Nazilli, Turk.
103/N6 Nazrēt, Eth.
74/H4 Nazyvayevsk, Rus.
107/A5 Nchelenge, Zam.
110/F3 Ncheu, Malw.
110/B2 Ndalatando, Ang.
103/K6 Ndele, CAfr.
98/F6 Ndende (isl.), Sol.
102/J5 N'Djamena (cap.), Chad
102/H8 N'Djolé, Gabon
110/E3 Ndola, Zam.
105/H5 Ndop, Camr.
104/B2 Ndrhamcha, Sebkha de (dry lake), Mrta.
62/C4 Né (riv.), Fr.

175
Néa A – North

67/J5 **Néa Alikarnassós,** Gre.
50/B2 **Neagh, Lough** (lake), NI,UK
67/H3 **Néa Ionía,** Gre.
69/H2 **Neamţ** (co.), Rom.
136/A6 **Near** (isls.), Ak,US
52/C3 **Neath,** Wal,UK
52/C3 **Neath** (riv.), Wal,UK
52/C3 **Neath Port Talbot** (co.), Wal,UK
50/D3 **Neb** (riv.), IM,UK
73/K5 **Nebitdag,** Trkm.
96/E6 **Nebo** (mtn.), Austl.
131/G2 **Nebraska** (state), US
131/J2 **Nebraska City,** Ne,US
66/D4 **Nebrodi** (mts.), It.
128/B2 **Nechako** (riv.), BC,Can.
134/E4 **Neches** (riv.), Tx,US
103/N6 **Nechisar Nat'l Park,** Eth.
61/E1 **Neckar** (riv.), Ger.
99/J2 **Necker** (isl.), Hi,US
118/F3 **Necochea,** Arg.
66/C1 **Necropoli** (ruins), It.
64/A1 **Neda,** Sp.
56/C6 **Nederweert,** Neth.
56/D4 **Neede,** Neth.
53/H2 **Needham Market,** Eng,UK
53/F2 **Needingworth,** Eng,UK
130/D4 **Needles,** Ca,US
53/E5 **Needles, The** (seastacks), UK
132/B2 **Neenah,** Wi,US
129/J3 **Neepawa,** Mb,Can.
59/E1 **Neerpelt,** Belg.
57/H2 **Neetze** (riv.), Ger.
59/F2 **Neffelbach** (riv.), Ger.
71/M4 **Neftekamsk,** Rus.
77/C7 **Nefud** (des.), SAr.
50/D6 **Nefyn,** Wal,UK
132/C2 **Negaunee,** Mi,US
103/N6 **Negēlē,** Eth.
106/D2 **Negev** (phys. reg.), Isr.
69/G3 **Negoiu** (peak), Rom.
90/C6 **Negombo,** SrL.
68/F3 **Negotin,** Serb.
68/F5 **Negotino,** FYROM
114/B5 **Negra** (pt.), Peru
91/F4 **Negrais** (cape), Myan.
64/A1 **Negreira,** Sp.
69/H2 **Negreşti,** Rom.
118/C3 **Negro** (peak), Arg.
118/D3 **Negro** (riv.), Arg.
114/F7 **Negro** (riv.), Bol.
115/G7 **Negro** (riv.), Braz.
114/F4 **Negro** (riv.), Braz., Ven.
119/F2 **Negro** (riv.), Uru., Braz.
88/D6 **Negros** (isl.), Phil.
123/G4 **Neiba,** DRep.
109/R15 **Neiges, Piton des** (peak), Reun., Fr.
87/C4 **Neihuang,** China
87/B2 **Nei Monggol** (aut. reg.), China
82/G3 **Nei Monggol** (plat.), China
114/C3 **Neiva,** Col.
124/G3 **Nejanilini** (lake), Mb,Can.
103/N6 **Nejo,** Eth.
103/N6 **Nek'emtē,** Eth.
70/G4 **Nelidovo,** Rus.
131/H2 **Neligh,** Ne,US
90/C5 **Nellore,** India
97/B3 **Nelson** (cape), Austl.
128/D3 **Nelson,** BC,Can.
124/G3 **Nelson** (riv.), Mb,Can.
119/J7 **Nelson** (str.), Chile
95/H7 **Nelson,** NZ
51/F4 **Nelson,** Eng,UK
52/C3 **Nelson,** Wal,UK
136/F3 **Nelson** (isl.), Ak,US
97/E2 **Nelson Bay,** Austl.
109/E2 **Nelspruit,** SAfr.
104/D2 **Néma,** Mrta.
104/D2 **Néma, Dhar** (hills), Mrta.
63/H4 **Nembro,** It.
69/H2 **Nemira** (peak), Rom.
83/J2 **Nemor** (riv.), China
62/E2 **Nemours,** Fr.
83/P3 **Nemuro,** Japan
83/J2 **Nen** (riv.), China
53/G1 **Nene** (riv.), Eng,UK
71/M2 **Nenetskiy Aut. Okr.,** Rus.
131/J3 **Neosho** (riv.), Ks, Mo,US
131/J3 **Neosho,** Mo,US
77/H7 **Nepal** (ctry.)
90/D2 **Nepālganj,** Nepal
90/C3 **Nepanagar,** India
96/G8 **Nepean** (riv.), Austl.
132/F2 **Nepean,** Can.
130/E3 **Nephi,** Ut,US
49/A3 **Nephin** (mtn.), Ire.
133/H2 **Nepisiguit** (riv.), NB,Can.
82/H1 **Nercha** (riv.), Rus.
70/J4 **Nerekhta,** Rus.
68/D4 **Neretva** (riv.), Bosn., Cro.
70/E5 **Neris** (riv.), Lith.
64/D4 **Nerja,** Sp.
64/B4 **Nerva,** Sp.
72/C4 **Nesebŭr,** Bul.
131/H3 **Ness City,** Ks,US
57/H6 **Nesse** (riv.), Ger.
136/M4 **Nesselrode** (mtn.), Ak,US
49/C2 **Ness, Loch** (lake), Sc,UK
51/E5 **Neston,** Eng,UK
67/J2 **Néstos** (riv.), Gre.
80/M9 **Nes Ziyyona,** Isr.
80/K5 **Netanya,** Isr.
137/F5 **Netcong,** NJ,US
57/G5 **Nethe** (riv.), Ger.
52/D3 **Netherend,** Eng,UK
56/B5 **Netherlands** (ctry.)
123/H5 **Netherlands Antilles** (isls.), Neth.
53/E5 **Netley,** Eng,UK
66/E3 **Neto** (riv.), It.
59/H2 **Netphen,** Ger.
56/D6 **Nette** (riv.), Ger.
57/H5 **Nette** (riv.), Ger.
59/G3 **Nettebach** (riv.), Ger.
59/F3 **Nettersheim,** Ger.
56/D6 **Nettetal,** Ger.
125/J2 **Nettilling** (lake), Nun,Can.
51/H5 **Nettleham,** Eng,UK
66/C2 **Nettuno,** It.
55/G2 **Neubrandenburg,** Ger.
60/C4 **Neuchâtel,** Swi.
60/C4 **Neuchâtel** (canton), Swi.
60/C4 **Neuchâtel** (lake), Swi.
55/G2 **Neuenhagen,** Ger.
56/D4 **Neuenhaus,** Ger.
57/E4 **Neuenkirchen,** Ger.
57/F3 **Neuenkirchen,** Ger.
57/E6 **Neuenrade,** Ger.
59/E4 **Neufchâteau,** Belg.
60/B1 **Neufchâteau,** Fr.
58/B5 **Neuilly-en-Thelle,** Fr.
58/C5 **Neuilly-Saint-Front,** Fr.
58/B6 **Neuilly-sur-Seine,** Fr.
63/J2 **Neumarkt in der Oberpfalz,** Ger.
54/E1 **Neumünster,** Ger.
68/C2 **Neunkirchen,** Aus.
59/G5 **Neunkirchen,** Ger.
59/H2 **Neunkirchen,** Ger.
59/G2 **Neunkirchen-Seelscheid,** Ger.
118/C3 **Neuquén,** Arg.
118/C3 **Neuquén** (prov.), Arg.
118/C3 **Neuquén** (riv.), Arg.
54/G2 **Neuruppin,** Ger.
135/J3 **Neuse** (riv.), NC,US
56/D6 **Neuss,** Ger.
57/G4 **Neustadt am Rübenberge,** Ger.
63/J2 **Neustadt an der Donau,** Ger.
63/H2 **Neustadt an der Weinstrasse,** Ger.
63/J1 **Neustadt bei Coburg,** Ger.
54/F1 **Neustadt in Holstein,** Ger.
54/G2 **Neustrelitz,** Ger.
61/G1 **Neu-Ulm,** Ger.
62/G2 **Neuves-Maisons,** Fr.
57/F1 **Neuwerk** (isl.), Ger.
59/G3 **Neuwied,** Ger.
73/V7 **Neva** (riv.), Rus.
64/D4 **Nevada** (mts.), Sp.
130/C3 **Nevada** (state), US
131/J3 **Nevada,** Mo,US
118/C4 **Nevado Cónico** (peak), Chile
117/C1 **Nevado de Chañi** (peak), Arg.
123/P10 **Nevado de Colima Nat'l Park,** Mex.
117/C2 **Nevado del Candado** (peak), Arg.
114/C3 **Nevado del Huila** (peak), Col.
111/C3 **Nevado del Huila Nat'l Park,** Col.
118/C2 **Nevado, Sierra del** (mts.), Arg.
70/F4 **Nevel',** Rus.
58/C1 **Nevele,** Belg.
83/N2 **Nevel'sk,** Rus.
62/E3 **Nevers,** Fr.
68/D4 **Nevesinje,** Bosn.
73/G3 **Nevinnomyssk,** Rus.
123/J4 **Nevis** (isl.), StK.
80/C2 **Nevşehir,** Turk.
114/G3 **New** (riv.), Guy.
53/E5 **New** (for.), Eng,UK
132/D4 **New** (riv.), WV,US
50/E2 **New Abbey,** Sc,UK
132/C4 **New Albany,** In,US
135/F3 **New Albany,** Ms,US
53/E4 **New Alfresford,** Eng,UK
115/G2 **New Amsterdam,** Guy.
51/H5 **New Ancholme** (riv.), Eng,UK
138/K11 **Newark,** Ca,US
137/F5 **Newark,** NJ,US
132/D3 **Newark,** Oh,US
51/H5 **Newark-on-Trent,** Eng,UK
138/G6 **New Baltimore,** Mi,US
133/G3 **New Bedford,** Ma,US
138/P14 **New Berlin,** Wi,US
135/J3 **New Bern,** NC,US
132/C2 **Newberry,** Mi,US
135/H3 **Newberry,** SC,US
51/G1 **Newbiggin-by-the-Sea,** Eng,UK
134/D4 **New Braunfels,** Tx,US
52/C2 **Newbridge on Wye,** Wal,UK
98/D5 **New Britain** (isl.), PNG
133/F3 **New Britain,** Ct,US
133/H2 **New Brunswick** (prov.), Can.
137/F5 **New Brunswick,** NJ,US
50/A2 **New Buildings,** NI,UK
51/G2 **Newburn,** Eng,UK
53/E4 **Newbury,** Eng,UK
51/F3 **Newby Bridge,** Eng,UK
98/F6 **New Caledonia** (terr.), Fr.
99/U12 **New Caledonia** (isl.), NCal.
137/G4 **New Canaan,** Ct,US
97/D2 **Newcastle,** Austl.
133/S8 **Newcastle,** On,Can.
109/E2 **Newcastle,** SAfr.
50/C3 **Newcastle,** NI,UK
132/C4 **New Castle,** In,US
132/D3 **New Castle,** Pa,US
129/G5 **Newcastle,** Wy,US
52/B2 **Newcastle Emlyn,** Wal,UK
51/F1 **Newcastleton,** Sc,UK
51/F5 **Newcastle-under-Lyme,** Eng,UK
51/G2 **Newcastle upon Tyne,** Eng,UK
51/G1 **Newcastle upon Tyne** (co.), Eng,UK
137/G4 **New City,** NY,US
49/C3 **New Cumnock,** Sc,UK
90/C2 **New Delhi** (cap.), India
128/D3 **New Denver,** BC,Can.
137/F5 **New Egypt,** NJ,US
97/E1 **New England Nat'l Park,** Austl.
136/F4 **Newenham** (cape), Ak,US
52/D3 **Newent,** Eng,UK
133/S9 **Newfane,** NY,US
125/K3 **Newfoundland and Labrador** (prov.), Can.
133/L1 **Newfoundland** (isl.), Nf,Can.
50/D1 **New Galloway,** Sc,UK
98/E5 **New Georgia** (isls.), Sol.
98/E5 **New Georgia** (sound), Sol.
133/J2 **New Glasgow,** NS,Can.
133/N6 **New Glasgow,** Qu,Can.
98/C5 **New Guinea** (isl.) Indo., PNG
133/G3 **New Hampshire** (state), US
98/D5 **New Hanover** (isl.), PNG
53/F5 **Newhaven,** Eng,UK
132/F3 **New Haven,** Ct,US
138/G6 **New Haven,** Mi,US
98/F6 **New Hebrides** (isls.), Van.
137/F5 **New Hope,** Pa,US
134/F4 **New Iberia,** La,US
53/G5 **Newick,** Eng,UK
98/E5 **New Ireland** (isl.), PNG
132/F3 **New Jersey** (state), US
132/E3 **New Kensington,** Pa,US
134/D2 **Newkirk,** Ok,US
138/Q16 **New Lenox,** Il,US
132/E2 **New Liskeard,** On,Can.
133/F3 **New London,** Ct,US
132/B2 **New London,** Wi,US
52/A6 **Newlyn,** Eng,UK
131/K3 **New Madrid,** Mo,US
96/F6 **Newmarket,** Austl.
132/E2 **Newmarket,** On,Can.
53/G2 **Newmarket,** Eng,UK
132/D4 **New Martinsville,** WV,US
128/D4 **New Meadows,** Id,US
130/F4 **New Mexico** (state), US
51/F5 **New Mills,** Eng,UK
135/G3 **Newnan,** Ga,US
52/D3 **Newnham,** Eng,UK
97/C4 **New Norfolk,** Austl.
135/F4 **New Orleans,** La,US
132/D3 **New Philadelphia,** Oh,US
95/H6 **New Plymouth,** NZ
51/F6 **Newport,** Eng,UK
53/E5 **Newport,** Eng,UK
52/B2 **Newport,** Wal,UK
52/D3 **Newport,** Wal,UK
52/D3 **Newport** (co.), Wal,UK
135/F3 **Newport,** Ar,US
132/C4 **Newport,** Ky,US
128/B4 **Newport,** Or,US
133/G3 **Newport,** RI,US
132/D5 **Newport,** Tn,US
133/F2 **Newport,** Vt,US
128/D3 **Newport,** Wa,US
137/C3 **Newport Beach,** Ca,US
132/E4 **Newport News,** Va,US
53/F2 **Newport Pagnell,** Eng,UK
135/H4 **New Port Richey,** Fl,US
123/F3 **New Providence** (isl.), Bahm.
52/A6 **Newquay,** Eng,UK
52/B2 **New Quay,** Wal,UK
52/C2 **New Radnor,** Wal,UK
133/H1 **New Richmond,** Qu,Can.
137/G5 **New Rochelle,** NY,US
129/J4 **New Rockford,** ND,US
53/G5 **New Romney,** Eng,UK
51/G5 **New Rossington,** Eng,UK
50/B3 **Newry,** NI,UK
50/B3 **Newry** (can.), NI,UK
111/Z **New Schwabenland** (reg.), Ant.
75/P2 **New Siberian** (isls.), Rus.
135/H4 **New Smyrna Beach,** Fl,US
97/C2 **New South Wales** (state), Austl.
52/D2 **Newton,** Eng,UK
51/E1 **Newton,** Sc,UK
131/H3 **Newton,** Ks,US
133/G3 **Newton,** Ma,US
137/F4 **Newton,** NJ,US
134/E4 **Newton,** Tx,US
52/C5 **Newton Abbot,** Eng,UK
51/G2 **Newton Aycliffe,** Eng,UK
52/B6 **Newton Ferrers,** Eng,UK
51/F5 **Newton-le-Willows,** Eng,UK
49/C2 **Newtonmore,** Sc,UK
51/G1 **Newton on the Moor,** Eng,UK
50/D2 **Newton Stewart,** Sc,UK
97/B3 **Newtown,** Austl.
52/C1 **Newtown,** Wal,UK
129/H4 **New Town,** ND,US
137/F5 **Newtown,** Pa,US
50/C2 **Newtownabbey,** NI,UK
50/C2 **Newtownards,** NI,UK
49/B3 **Newtownbutler,** NI,UK
50/B3 **Newtownhamilton,** NI,UK
49/D3 **Newtown Saint Boswells,** Sc,UK
50/A2 **Newtownstewart,** NI,UK
52/C3 **New Tredegar,** Wal,UK
129/K4 **New Ulm,** Mn,US
133/J2 **New Waterford,** NS,Can.
128/C3 **New Westminster,** BC,Can.
132/F3 **New York** (state), US
137/G5 **New York,** NY,US
95/H6 **New Zealand** (ctry.)
111/L **New Zealand** (peak), Ant.
85/L10 **Neyagawa,** Japan
52/B3 **Neyland,** Wal,UK
79/F3 **Neyrīz,** Iran
79/G1 **Neyshābūr,** Iran
71/P4 **Neyva** (riv.), Rus.
90/C5 **Neyveli,** India
90/C6 **Neyyāttinkara,** India
72/D2 **Nezhin,** Ukr.
128/D4 **Nezperce,** Id,US
92/C3 **Ngabang,** Indo.
93/H5 **Ngabordamlu** (cape), Indo.
110/F4 **Ngabu,** Malw.
102/H5 **Ngala,** Nga.
81/D5 **Ngangla Ringco** (lake), China
81/E5 **Ngangzê** (lake), China
102/H6 **Ngaoundéré,** Camr.
97/B2 **Ngarkat Consv. Park,** Austl.
98/E4 **Ngatik** (isl.), Micr.
99/Z18 **Ngau** (isl.), Fiji
89/D2 **Nghia Dan,** Viet.
89/D1 **Nghia Lo,** Viet.
110/C4 **Ngiva,** Ang.
110/C1 **Ngo,** Congo
89/E4 **Ngoan Muc** (pass), Viet.
91/J4 **Ngoc Linh** (peak), Viet.
110/D4 **Ngonye** (falls), Zam.
83/D5 **Ngoring** (lake), China
102/H8 **Ngounié** (riv.), Gabon
102/H5 **Nguigmi,** Niger
98/C4 **Ngulu** (atoll), Micr.
89/C2 **Ngum** (riv.), Laos
89/D1 **Nguyen Binh,** Viet.
109/E2 **Ngwenya** (peak), Swaz.
114/G4 **Nhamundá** (riv.), Braz.
89/E3 **Nha Trang,** Viet.
104/E3 **Niafounké,** Mali
133/R9 **Niagara** (riv.), Can., US
133/R9 **Niagara Falls,** On,Can.
133/R9 **Niagara Falls,** NY,US
105/F3 **Niamey** (cap.), Niger
105/F3 **Niamey** (dept.), Niger
104/C4 **Niandan** (riv.), Gui.
103/L7 **Niangara,** D.R. Congo
104/E3 **Niangay** (lake), Mali
87/C3 **Niangzi Guan** (pass), China
92/A3 **Nias** (isl.), Indo.
107/B5 **Niassa** (prov.), Moz.
122/D5 **Nicaragua** (ctry.)
122/E5 **Nicaragua** (lake), Nic.
66/E3 **Nicastro-Sambiase,** It.
63/G5 **Nice,** Fr.
135/G4 **Niceville,** Fl,US
84/B5 **Nichinan,** Japan
91/F6 **Nicobar** (isls.), India
133/F2 **Nicolet,** Qu,Can.
80/J4 **Nicosia** (cap.), Cyp.
66/D4 **Nicosia,** It.
122/D5 **Nicoya,** CR
122/D6 **Nicoya** (gulf), CR
122/D6 **Nicoya** (pen.), CR
51/G4 **Nidd** (riv.), Eng,UK
63/H1 **Nidda,** Ger.
59/F2 **Nideggen,** Ger.
59/G6 **Niderviller,** Fr.
61/E4 **Nidwalden** (canton), Swi.
55/L2 **Nidzica,** Pol.
54/E1 **Niebüll,** Ger.
63/G2 **Nied** (riv.), Fr.
59/F5 **Nied** (riv.), Ger.
63/K3 **Niedere Tauern** (mts.), Aus.
55/G3 **Niederlausitz** (reg.), Ger.
59/H4 **Nieder-Olm,** Ger.
57/F3 **Niedersachsen** (state), Ger.
57/E1 **Niedersächsisches Wattenmeer Nat'l Park,** Ger.
68/B1 **Niederüsterreich** (prov.), Aus.
59/F2 **Niederzier,** Ger.
55/L2 **Niegocin** (lake), Pol.
57/G5 **Nieheim,** Ger.
55/J3 **Niemodlin,** Pol.
57/G3 **Nienburg,** Ger.
104/D5 **Niénokoué** (peak), C.d'Iv.
58/B2 **Nieppe,** Fr.
104/B3 **Niéri Ko** (riv.), Sen.
56/D5 **Niers** (riv.), Ger.
89/D4 **Niet Ban Tinh Xa,** Viet.
56/D5 **Nieuw-Bergen,** Neth.
56/C4 **Nieuwegein,** Neth.
56/B5 **Nieuwerkerk aan de IJssel,** Neth.
56/B4 **Nieuwkoop,** Neth.
56/D3 **Nieuwleusen,** Neth.
56/C4 **Nieuw-Loosdrecht,** Neth.
115/G2 **Nieuw-Nickerie,** Sur.
58/B1 **Nieuwpoort,** Belg.
56/D3 **Nieuw-Schoonebeek,** Neth.
80/C3 **Niğde,** Turk.
108/E2 **Nigel,** SAfr.
105/G2 **Niger** (ctry.)
105/G5 **Niger** (riv.), Afr.
105/G4 **Niger** (state), Nga.
105/G4 **Nigeria** (ctry.)
105/G5 **Niger, Mouths of the** (delta), Nga.
132/D1 **Nighthawk** (lake), On,Can.
64/A1 **Nigrán,** Sp.
67/H2 **Nigríta,** Gre.
99/J2 **Nihoa** (isl.), Hi,US
85/G2 **Nihonmatsu,** Japan
85/F3 **Nii** (isl.), Japan
85/F2 **Niigata,** Japan
85/F2 **Niigata** (pref.), Japan
84/C4 **Niihama,** Japan
126/R10 **Niihau** (isl.), Hi,US
84/C3 **Niimi,** Japan
85/F2 **Niitsu,** Japan
85/H7 **Niiza,** Japan
64/D4 **Níjar,** Sp.
56/C4 **Nijkerk,** Neth
58/D1 **Nijlen,** Belg.
56/C5 **Nijmegen,** Neth.
70/F1 **Nikel',** Rus.
85/F2 **Nikkō,** Japan
85/F2 **Nikkō Nat'l Park,** Japan
75/Q4 **Nikolayevsk-na-Amure,** Rus.
73/H1 **Nikol'sk,** Rus.
72/E3 **Nikopol',** Ukr.
80/D2 **Niksar,** Turk
68/D4 **Nikšíc,** Mont.
99/H5 **Nikumaroro** (Gardner) (atoll), Kiri.
98/G5 **Nikunau** (isl.), Kiri.
103/M2 **Nile** (riv.), Afr.
80/H6 **Nile** (delta), Egypt
138/Q15 **Niles,** Il,US
132/C3 **Niles,** Mi,US
132/D3 **Niles,** Oh,US
116/K7 **Nilópolis,** Braz.
48/J3 **Nilsiä,** Fin.
90/B3 **Nīmach,** India
83/L1 **Niman** (riv.), Rus.
104/C5 **Nimba** (peak), C.d'Iv.
104/C5 **Nimba** (co.), Libr.
62/F5 **Nîmes,** Fr.
111/L **Nimrod** (glac.), Ant.
59/F4 **Nimsbach** (riv.), Ger.
107/A2 **Nimule Nat'l Park,** Sudan
78/D1 **Nineveh** (ruins), Iraq
118/D4 **Ninfas** (pt.), Arg.
88/D2 **Ningbo,** China
87/C4 **Ningling,** China
87/B3 **Ningxia Huizu Zizhiqu** (aut. reg.), China
89/D1 **Ninh Binh,** Viet.
89/E3 **Ninh Hoa,** Viet.
98/D5 **Niningo** (isl.), PNG
111/K **Ninnis** (glac.), Ant.
85/H7 **Ninomiya,** Japan
58/D2 **Ninove,** Belg.
131/G2 **Niobrara** (riv.), Ne,US
104/B3 **Niokolo-Koba Nat'l Park,** Sen.
104/D3 **Niono,** Mali
104/B3 **Nioro-du-Rip,** Sen.
104/C3 **Nioro du Sahel,** Mali
62/C3 **Niort,** Fr.
129/H2 **Nipawin,** Sk,Can.
132/B1 **Nipigon,** On,Can.
132/B1 **Nipigon** (lake), On,Can.
132/E2 **Nipissing** (lake), On,Can.
118/C3 **Ñiquén,** Chile
85/F3 **Nirasaki,** Japan
96/H8 **Nirimba-Hmas,** Austl.
90/C4 **Nirmal,** India
68/E4 **Niš,** Serb.
64/B3 **Nisa,** Port.
67/H1 **Nišava** (riv.), Serb.
66/D4 **Niscemi,** It.
85/M9 **Nishiharu,** Japan
84/C3 **Nishiki** (riv.), Japan
85/L10 **Nishinomiya,** Japan
84/B5 **Nishino'omote,** Japan
85/E3 **Nishio,** Japan
84/D3 **Nishiwaki,** Japan
55/M3 **Nisko,** Pol.
138/B3 **Nisqually Reach** (str.), Wa,US
98/E5 **Nissan** (isl.), PNG
85/N9 **Nisshin,** Japan
129/K4 **Nisswa,** Mn,US
116/K7 **Niterói,** Braz.
50/E1 **Nith** (riv.), Sc,UK
50/E1 **Nithsdale** (val.), Sc,UK
81/C5 **Niti** (pass), India
55/K4 **Nitra,** Slvk.
55/K4 **Nitra** (riv.), Slvk.
55/K4 **Nitrianský** (reg.), Slvk.
71/P4 **Nitsa** (riv.), Rus.
99/H6 **Niuafo'ou** (isl.), Tonga
99/H6 **Niuatoputapu Group** (isls.), Tonga
99/J7 **Niue** (terr.), NZ
98/G6 **Niulakita** (isl.), Tuv.
91/H2 **Niulan** (riv.), China
92/C3 **Niut** (peak), Indo.
98/G5 **Niutau** (isl.), Tuv.
58/D2 **Nivelles,** Belg.
62/E3 **Nivernais** (hills), Fr.
129/J3 **Niverville,** Mb,Can.
130/C3 **Nixon,** Nv,US
81/D4 **Niya** (riv.), China
84/C4 **Niyodo** (riv.), Japan
90/C4 **Nizāmābād,** India
71/M4 **Nizhnekama** (res.), Rus.
71/L5 **Nizhnekamsk,** Rus.
75/K4 **Nizhneudinsk,** Rus.
74/H3 **Nizhnevartovsk,** Rus.
73/G1 **Nizhniy Lomov,** Rus.
71/K4 **Nizhniy Novgorod** (Gor'kiy), Rus.
71/K4 **Nizhegorodskaya Obl.,** Rus.
71/N4 **Nizhniy Tagil,** Rus.
80/D3 **Nizip,** Turk.
55/K4 **Nízke Tatry Nat'l Park,** Slvk.
107/B5 **Njombe,** Tanz.
105/H5 **Nkambe,** Camr.
110/B1 **Nkayi,** Congo
107/B5 **Nkhata Bay,** Malw.
105/H5 **Nkogam, Massif du** (peak), Camr.
105/H5 **N'Kongsamba,** Camr.
91/G2 **Nmai** (riv.), Myan.
58/B5 **Noailles,** Fr.
90/F3 **Noākhāli,** Bang.
90/E3 **Noāmundi,** India
136/F2 **Noatak** (riv.), Ak,US
136/F2 **Noatak Nat'l Prsv.,** Ak,US
84/B4 **Nobeoka,** Japan
131/H4 **Noble,** Ok,US
132/C3 **Noblesville,** In,US
133/Q8 **Nobleton,** On,Can.
83/N3 **Noboribetsu,** Japan
68/C5 **Noci,** It.
85/H7 **Noda,** Japan
58/B3 **Noeux-les-Mines,** Fr.
130/E5 **Nogales,** Az,US
84/B4 **Nogata,** Japan
62/D2 **Nogent-le-Rotrou,** Fr.
58/B5 **Nogent-sur-Oise,** Fr.
71/X9 **Noginsk,** Rus.
96/B4 **Nogoa** (riv.), Austl.
82/C2 **Nogoonuur,** Mong.
118/F2 **Nogoyá,** Arg.
55/K5 **Nógrád** (co.), Hun.
65/F1 **Noguera Pallarosa** (riv.), Sp.
86/E4 **Nogwak-san** (mtn.), SKor.
90/B2 **Nohar,** India
59/G4 **Nohfelden,** Ger.
132/E2 **Noire** (riv.), Qu,Can.
62/B2 **Noires** (mts.), Fr.
62/B3 **Noirmoutier** (isl.), Fr.
58/B6 **Noisiel,** Fr.
58/B6 **Noisy-le-Sec,** Fr.
85/F3 **Nojima-zaki** (pt.), Japan
48/G3 **Nokia,** Fin.
93/F4 **Nokilalaki** (peak), Indo.
79/H3 **Nok Kundi,** Pak.
102/J7 **Nola,** CAfr.
97/D2 **Nomadgi Nat'l Park,** Austl.
136/F3 **Nome** (cape), Ak,US
84/B5 **Nomo-misaki** (cape), Japan
84/A4 **Nomo-zaki** (pt.), Japan
82/D2 **Nömrög,** Mong.
124/F2 **Nonacho** (lake), NW,Can.
63/G4 **None,** It.
58/B5 **Nonette** (riv.), Fr.
87/F1 **Nong'an,** China
89/D2 **Nong Han** (res.), Thai.
89/C2 **Nong Het,** Laos
89/C2 **Nong Khai,** Thai.
89/C2 **Nong Pet,** Laos
59/F4 **Nonnweiler,** Ger.
98/G5 **Nonouti** (atoll), Kiri.
87/E5 **Nonri** (isl.), China
86/D4 **Nonsan,** SKor.
56/A5 **Noordbeveland** (isl.), Neth.
56/B3 **Noorderhaaks** (isl.), Neth.
56/B3 **Noordhollandsch** (can.), Neth.
56/C3 **Noordostpolder** (polder), Neth.
56/B4 **Noordwijk aan Zee,** Neth.
56/B4 **Noordwijkerhout,** Neth.
56/B4 **Noordzeekanaal** (can.), Neth.
96/D4 **Noosa-Tewantin,** Austl.
128/B3 **Nootka** (isl.), BC,Can.
128/B3 **Nootka** (sound), BC,Can.
122/B4 **Nopala,** Mex.
83/L1 **Nora** (riv.), Rus.
70/B4 **Nora,** Swe.
93/F2 **Norala,** Phil.
137/C3 **Norco,** Ca,US
133/M6 **Nord** (riv.), Qu,Can.
58/C3 **Nord** (dept.), Fr.
58/B3 **Nord, Canal du** (can.), Fr.
57/E1 **Norden,** Ger.
57/F2 **Nordenham,** Ger.
74/K2 **Nordenskjöld** (arch.), Rus.
57/E1 **Norderney,** Ger.
57/E1 **Norderney** (isl.), Ger.
57/G1 **Norderstedt,** Ger.
54/F3 **Nordhausen,** Ger.
57/F1 **Nordholz,** Ger.
57/E4 **Nordhorn,** Ger.
48/H1 **Nordkapp** (North) (cape), Nor.
48/H1 **Nordkinn** (pt.), Nor.
57/E5 **Nordkirchen,** Ger.
107/A3 **Nord-Kivu** (prov.), D.R. Congo.
48/E2 **Nordland** (co.), Nor.
48/F3 **Nordmaling,** Swe.
54/E1 **Nord-Ostsee** (can.), Ger.
105/H5 **Nord-Ouest** (prov.), Camr.
62/D1 **Nord-Pas-de-Calais** (reg.), Fr.
57/E3 **Nord-Radde** (riv.), Ger.
54/E3 **Nordrhein-Westfalen** (state), Ger.
57/E3 **Nord-Sud** (can.), Ger.
48/E2 **Nord-Trøndelag** (co.), Nor.
57/E4 **Nordwalde,** Ger.
49/B4 **Nore** (riv.), Ire.
62/E5 **Nore, Pic de** (peak), Fr.
98/F7 **Norfolk** (isl.), Austl.
97/C4 **Norfolk** (peak), Austl.
53/G1 **Norfolk** (co.), Eng,UK
131/H2 **Norfolk,** Ne,US
132/E4 **Norfolk,** Va,US
53/H1 **Norfolk Broads** (swamp), Eng,UK
131/J3 **Norfork** (lake), Ar, Mo,US
56/D2 **Norg,** Neth.
85/E2 **Norikura-dake** (mtn.), Japan
74/J3 **Noril'sk,** Rus.
132/B3 **Normal,** Il,US
96/A2 **Norman** (riv.), Austl.
131/H4 **Norman,** Ok,US
98/E6 **Normanby** (isl.), PNG
138/C3 **Normandy Park,** Wa,US
51/G4 **Normanton,** Eng,UK
108/B3 **Norotshama** (peak), Namb.
129/H3 **Norquay,** Sk,Can.
48/F2 **Norrbotten** (co.), Swe.
64/B1 **Norrea** (riv.), Sp.
58/B2 **Norrent-Fontes,** Fr.
138/Q16 **Norridge,** Il,US
135/H2 **Norris** (lake), Tn,US
137/E5 **Norristown,** Pa,US
48/F4 **Norrköping,** Swe.
48/F2 **Norrland** (reg.), Swe.
48/F4 **Norrtälje,** Swe.
118/E4 **Norte** (pt.), Arg.
119/F3 **Norte** (pt.), Arg.
114/G6 **Norte** (mts.), Braz.
115/J3 **Norte, Cabo do** (cape), Braz.
119/J6 **Norte, Campo de Hielo** (glacier), Chile
115/G6 **Nortelândia,** Braz.
57/G5 **Nörten-Hardenberg,** Ger.
97/C3 **North** (pt.), Austl.
97/C4 **North** (pt.), Austl.
132/D2 **North** (chan.), On,Can.
133/J2 **North** (cape), PE,Can.
47/E3 **North** (sea), Eur.
95/H6 **North** (cape), NZ
95/H6 **North** (isl.), NZ
50/C1 **North** (chan.), UK
136/D5 **North** (cape), Ak,US
136/F3 **North** (peak), Ak,US
68/D4 **North Albanian Alps** (mts.), Eur.
51/G3 **Northallerton,** Eng,UK
95/A4 **Northam,** Austl.
52/B4 **Northam,** Eng,UK
121/* **North America** (cont.)
53/F2 **Northampton,** Eng,UK
53/E2 **Northampton** (uplands), Eng,UK
132/F3 **Northampton,** Ma,US
137/E5 **Northampton,** Pa,US
53/F2 **Northamptonshire** (co.), Eng,UK
91/F5 **North Andaman** (isl.), India
125/K3 **North Aulatsivik** (isl.), Nf,Can.
49/C2 **North Ballachulish,** Sc,UK
50/D3 **North Barrule** (mtn.), IM,UK
128/F2 **North Battleford,** Sk,Can.
132/E2 **North Bay,** On,Can.
128/B5 **North Bend,** Or,US
137/F5 **North Bergen,** NJ,US
49/D2 **North Berwick,** Sc,UK
56/C5 **North Brabant** (prov.), Neth.
138/Q15 **Northbrook,** Il,US
137/F5 **North Brunswick,** NJ,US
131/H3 **North Canadian** (riv.), Ok,US
129/L2 **North Caribou** (lake), On,Can.
135/H3 **North Carolina** (state), US
128/C3 **North Cascades Nat'l Park,** Wa,US
135/J3 **North Charleston,** SC,US
138/Q15 **North Chicago,** Il,US
51/H5 **North Collingham,** Eng,UK
128/C3 **North Cowichan,** BC,Can.
129/H4 **North Dakota** (state), US
52/D5 **North Dorset Downs** (uplands), Eng,UK
50/C2 **North Down** (dist.), NI,UK
53/F4 **North Downs** (hills), Eng,UK
96/C3 **North East** (pt.), Austl.
123/G3 **Northeast** (pt.), Bahm.
136/E3 **Northeast** (cape), Ak,US
107/D2 **North Eastern** (prov.), Kenya
74/C2 **Northeast Land** (isl.), Sval.
51/H4 **Northeast Lincolnshire** (co.), Eng,UK
57/G5 **Northeim,** Ger.
53/G1 **North Elmham,** Eng,UK
95/C2 **Northern** (terr.), Austl.
105/E4 **Northern** (reg.), Gha.
80/K5 **Northern** (dist.), Isr.
107/B5 **Northern** (reg.), Malw.
104/B4 **Northern** (prov.), SLeo.
106/B4 **Northern** (reg.), Sudan
107/A5 **Northern** (prov.), Zam.
81/B4 **Northern Areas** (terr.), Pak.
108/C3 **Northern Cape** (prov.), SAfr.
99/J6 **Northern Cook** (isls.), CookIs.
47/J2 **Northern Dvina** (riv.), Rus.
49/B3 **Northern Ireland,** UK
132/B1 **Northern Light** (lake), On,Can, Mn,US
98/D3 **Northern Marianas,** US
109/E6 **Northern Province** (prov.), SAfr.
74/G3 **Northern Sos'va** (riv.), Rus.
67/J3 **Northern Sporades** (isls.), Gre.
71/N3 **Northern Ural** (mts.), Rus.
71/K4 **Northern Uval** (hills), Rus.
74/E4 **Northern Wals** (upland), Rus.
129/K4 **Northfield,** Mn,US
53/G4 **Northfleet,** Eng,UK
53/H4 **North Foreland** (pt.), Eng,UK
135/H5 **North Fort Myers,** Fl,US
132/D1 **North French** (riv.), On,Can.
54/E1 **North Frisian** (isls.), Den., Ger.
133/F2 **North Hero,** Vt,US
138/M9 **North Highlands,** Ca,US
138/C3 **North Hill-Edgewood,** Wa,US
56/B3 **North Holland** (prov.), Neth.
51/H5 **North Hykeham,** Eng,UK
71/Q5 **North Kazakhstan Obl.,** Rus.
86/D3 **North Korea**
91/F2 **North Lakhimpur,** India
130/D3 **North Las Vegas,** Nv,US
51/H4 **North Lincolnshire** (co.), Eng,UK
134/E3 **North Little Rock,** Ar,US
107/B5 **North Luangwa Nat'l Park,** Zam.
125/R7 **North Magnetic Pole,** NAm.
129/J2 **North Moose** (lake), Mb,Can.
135/J3 **North Myrtle Beach,** SC,US
48/H1 **North** (Nordkapp) (cape), Nor.
73/G4 **North Ossetian Aut. Rep.,** Rus.
133/R9 **North Pelham,** On,Can.
52/C4 **North Petherton,** Eng,UK
96/E6 **North Pine** (riv.), Austl.
137/F5 **North Plainfield,** NJ,US
131/G2 **North Platte** (riv.), US
131/G2 **North Platte,** Ne,US
135/G3 **Northport,** Al,US
137/G5 **Northport** (Old Northport), NY,US
137/J7 **North Potomac,** Md,US
130/D3 **North Rim,** Az,US
128/F2 **North Saskatchewan** (riv.), Ab, Sk,Can.
51/G2 **North Shields,** Eng,UK
74/K2 **North Siberian** (plain), Rus.

176
North – Orton

51/J5 **North Somercotes**, Eng,UK
52/D4 **North Somerset** (co.), Eng,UK
96/D4 **North Stradbroke** (isl.), Austl.
137/G4 **North Tarrytown**, NY,US
51/H5 **North Thoresby**, Eng,UK
53/E4 **North Tidworth**, Eng,UK
133/S9 **North Tonawanda**, NY,US
51/F1 **North Tyne** (riv.), Eng,UK
51/G1 **North Tyneside** (co.), Eng,UK
133/J2 **Northumberland** (str.), Can.
51/F1 **Northumberland** (co.), Eng,UK
51/F1 **Northumberland Nat'l Park**, Eng,UK
130/B2 **North Umpqua** (riv.), Or,US
124/D4 **North Vancouver**, BC,Can.
138/F7 **Northville**, Mi,US
53/H1 **North Walsham**, Eng,UK
95/A3 **North West** (cape), Austl.
108/D2 **North-West** (prov.), SAfr.
81/B4 **Northwest Frontier** (prov.), Pak.
133/L1 **North West Gander** (riv.), Nf,Can.
49/C2 **North West Highlands** (mts.), Sc,UK
124/E2 **Northwest Territories** (terr.), Can.
51/H5 **North Wheatley**, Eng,UK
51/F5 **Northwich**, Eng,UK
51/G5 **North Wingfield**, Eng,UK
129/J4 **Northwood**, ND,US
133/R8 **North York**, On,Can.
51/H3 **North York Moors Nat'l Park**, Eng,UK
51/G3 **North Yorkshire** (co.), Eng,UK
136/F3 **Norton** (bay), Ak,US
136/E3 **Norton** (sound), Ak,US
131/H3 **Norton**, Ks,US
132/D4 **Norton**, Va,US
51/F6 **Norton Bridge**, Eng,UK
132/C3 **Norton Shores**, Mi,US
54/E1 **Nortorf**, Ger.
133/Q8 **Norval**, On,Can.
111/Z **Norvegia** (cape), Ant.
59/F2 **Nörvenich**, Ger.
137/B3 **Norwalk**, Ca,US
137/G4 **Norwalk**, Ct,US
132/D3 **Norwalk**, Oh,US
48/B3 **Norway** (ctry.)
129/J2 **Norway House**, Mb,Can.
125/S7 **Norwegian** (bay), Nun,Can.
47/D2 **Norwegian** (sea), Eur.
53/H1 **Norwich**, Eng,UK
132/F3 **Norwich**, NY,US
85/L10 **Nose**, Japan
79/K1 **Noshaq** (mtn.), Pak.
83/N3 **Noshiro**, Japan
69/H4 **Nos Maslen Nos** (pt.), Bul.
92/E2 **Nosong** (cape), Malay.
108/C2 **Nosop** (dry riv.), Bots.
72/D2 **Nosovka**, Ukr.
79/G3 **Noșratābād**, Iran
119/J7 **Notch** (cape), Chile
55/J2 **Noteć** (riv.), Pol.
66/D4 **Noto**, It.
66/D4 **Noto** (gulf), It.
85/E2 **Noto** (pen.), Japan
66/D4 **Noto Antica** (ruins), It.
85/M9 **Notogawa**, Japan
133/L1 **Notre Dame** (bay), Nf,Can.
133/G1 **Notre Dame** (mts.), Qu,Can.
133/N7 **Notre-Dame-de-l'Ile-Perrot**, Qu,Can.
132/E1 **Nottaway** (riv.), Qu,Can.
125/H2 **Nottingham** (isl.), Nun,Can.
51/G6 **Nottingham**, Eng,UK
51/G6 **Nottingham** (co.), Eng,UK
51/H5 **Nottinghamshire** (co.) Eng,UK
57/E5 **Nottuln**, Ger.
102/B3 **Nouadhibou**, Mrta.
104/B2 **Nouakchott** (cap.), Mrta.
99/V13 **Nouméa** (cap.), NCal.
108/D3 **Noupoort**, SAfr.
58/A3 **Nouvion**, Fr.
59/D4 **Nouzonville**, Fr.
115/H8 **Nova Andradina**, Braz.
69/F3 **Novaci**, Rom.
115/L5 **Nova Cruz**, Braz.
55/K4 **Nová Dubnica**, Slvk.
116/L7 **Nova Friburgo**, Braz.
68/C3 **Nova Gradiška**, Cro.
116/K7 **Nova Iguaçu**, Braz.
114/G4 **Nova Olinda do Norte**, Braz.
68/E3 **Nova Pazova**, Serb.
116/B4 **Nova Prata**, Braz.
63/H4 **Novara**, It.
61/E5 **Novara** (prov.), It.
133/J2 **Nova Scotia** (prov.), Can.
138/J10 **Novato**, Ca,US
68/D4 **Nova Varoš**, Serb.
116/D1 **Nova Venécia**, Braz.
115/H6 **Nova Xavantina**, Braz.
72/E3 **Novaya Kakhovka**, Ukr.
75/R2 **Novaya Sibir'** (isl.), Rus.
74/E2 **Novaya Zemlya** (isl.), Rus.
69/H4 **Nova Zagora**, Bul.
65/E3 **Novelda**, Sp.
55/J4 **Nové Mesto nad Váhom**, Slvk.
55/K5 **Nové Zámky**, Slvk.
70/F4 **Novgorod**, Rus.
70/G4 **Novgorodskaya Obl.**, Rus.
138/F7 **Novi**, Mi,US
68/E3 **Novi Bečej**, Serb.
69/F4 **Novi Iskŭr**, Bul.
63/H4 **Novi Ligure**, It.
69/H4 **Novi Pazar**, Bul.
68/E4 **Novi Pazar**, Serb.
68/D3 **Novi Sad**, Serb.
116/K6 **Novo** (riv.), Braz.
73/G2 **Novoanninskiy**, Rus.
114/F5 **Novo Aripuanã**, Braz.
71/K4 **Novocheboksarsk**, Rus.
72/G3 **Novocherkassk**, Rus.
72/C2 **Novograd-Volynskiy**, Ukr.
70/E5 **Novogrudok**, Bela.
116/B4 **Novo Hamburgo**, Braz.
116/B2 **Novo Horizonte**, Braz.
73/J1 **Novokuybyshevsk**, Rus.
74/J4 **Novokuznetsk**, Rus.
111/A **Novolazarevskaya**, Ant.
68/B3 **Novo Mesto**, Slov.
68/E3 **Novo Miloševo**, Serb.
72/F1 **Novomoskovsk**, Rus.
72/E3 **Novomoskovsk**, Ukr.
70/F5 **Novopolotsk**, Bela.
72/F3 **Novorossiysk**, Rus.
72/F3 **Novoshakhtinsk**, Rus.
74/J4 **Novosibirsk**, Rus.
73/L2 **Novotroitsk**, Rus.
72/D2 **Novoukrainka**, Ukr.
72/C2 **Novovolynsk**, Ukr.
71/L4 **Novovyatsk**, Rus.
72/D1 **Novozybkov**, Rus.
68/C3 **Novska**, Cro.
55/K4 **Nový Jičín**, Czh.
73/K4 **Novyy Uzen'**, Kaz.
55/L3 **Nowa Dęba**, Pol.
55/K3 **Nowa Ruda**, Pol.
55/M3 **Nowa Sarzyna**, Pol.
55/H3 **Nowa Sól**, Pol.
131/J3 **Nowata**, Ok,US
55/K2 **Nowe**, Pol.
55/K2 **Nowe Miasto Lubawskie**, Pol.
90/F2 **Nowgong**, India
91/F2 **Nowgong**, India
136/H3 **Nowitna** (riv.), Ak,US
136/H3 **Nowitna Nat'l Wild. Ref.**, Ak,US
55/H2 **Nowogard**, Pol.
130/F1 **Nowood** (riv.), Wy,US
79/K2 **Nowshera**, Pak.
55/K1 **Nowy Dwór Gdański**, Pol.
55/L4 **Nowy Sącz**, Pol.
55/L4 **Nowy Targ**, Pol.
55/J2 **Nowy Tomyśl**, Pol.
64/A1 **Noya**, Sp.
58/B5 **Noye** (riv.), Fr.
58/C4 **Noyon**, Fr.
110/G4 **Nsanje**, Malw.
105/E5 **Nsawam**, Gha.
82/D5 **Nu** (riv.), China
103/M5 **Nūbah** (mts.), Sudan
106/C4 **Nubian** (des.), Sudan
130/E3 **Nucla**, Co,US
134/D4 **Nueces** (riv.), Tx,US
124/G2 **Nueltin** (lake), Nun,Can.
56/C6 **Nuenen**, Neth.
122/C5 **Nueva Concepción**, Guat.
122/E3 **Nueva Gerona**, Cuba
119/F2 **Nueva Helvecia**, Uru.
118/B3 **Nueva Imperial**, Chile
114/C3 **Nueva Loja**, Ecu.
119/S11 **Nueva Palmira**, Uru.
122/A2 **Nueva Rosita**, Mex.
123/F3 **Nuevitas**, Cuba
118/D4 **Nuevo** (gulf), Arg.
123/N7 **Nuevo Casas Grandes**, Mex.
123/N9 **Nuevo Ideal**, Mex.
122/B2 **Nuevo Laredo**, Mex.
122/A2 **Nuevo León** (state), Mex.
119/S11 **Nuevo Palmira**, Uru.
98/E5 **Nuguria** (isls.), PNG
99/J2 **Nuhau** (isl.), Hi,US
57/F6 **Nuhne** (riv.), Ger.
98/G5 **Nui** (atoll), Tuv.
85/N10 **Nukata**, Japan
136/F4 **Nuklunek** (mtn.), Ak,US
99/H7 **Nuku'alofa** (cap.), Tonga
98/G5 **Nukufetau** (atoll), Tuv.
99/L5 **Nuku Hiva** (isl.), FrPol.
98/H5 **Nukulaelae** (isl.), Tuv.
98/F5 **Nukumanu** (atoll), PNG
99/H5 **Nukunonu** (atoll), Tok.
98/E4 **Nukuoro** (isl.), Micr.
74/F5 **Nukus**, Uzb.
99/M6 **Nukutavake** (isl.), FrPol.
65/E3 **Nules**, Sp.
95/B4 **Nullarbor** (plain), Austl.
102/H6 **Numan**, Nga.
56/B5 **Numansdorp**, Neth.
85/F2 **Numata**, Japan
85/J7 **Numazu**, Japan
59/G2 **Nümbrecht**, Ger.
93/H4 **Numfoor** (isl.), Indo.
124/G2 **Nunavut** (terr.), Can.
97/G5 **Nunawading**, Austl.
53/E1 **Nuneaton**, Eng,UK
97/D3 **Nungatta Nat'l Park**, Austl.
136/E4 **Nunivak** (isl.), Ak,US
56/C4 **Nunspeet**, Neth.
51/G2 **Nunthorpe**, Eng,UK
83/J1 **Nuomin** (riv.), China
104/C5 **Nuon** (riv.), C.d'Iv., Libr.
66/A2 **Nuoro**, It.
81/B2 **Nura** (riv.), Kaz.
59/F3 **Nürburgring**, Ger.
80/D3 **Nurhak**, Turk.
106/B5 **Nuri** (ruins), Sudan
63/J2 **Nürnberg**, Ger.
97/C1 **Nurri** (peak), Austl.
63/H2 **Nürtingen**, Ger.
80/L4 **Nuşayrīyah, Jabal an** (mts.), Syria
80/E3 **Nusaybin**, Turk.
136/G4 **Nushagak** (riv.), Ak,US
79/J3 **Nushki**, Pak.
59/E2 **Nuth**, Neth.
137/F5 **Nutley**, NJ,US
121/M3 **Nuuk** (Godthåb), Grld.
99/X15 **Nuupere** (pt.), FrPol.
106/C2 **Nuwaybi'**, Egypt
108/L10 **Nuy** (riv.), SAfr.
110/E4 **Nxai Pan Nat'l Park**, Bots.
137/G4 **Nyack**, NY,US
107/B4 **Nyahua**, Tanz.
81/F5 **Nyainqêntanglha Feng** (peak), China
103/K5 **Nyala**, Sudan
103/L6 **Nyamlell**, Sudan
70/J3 **Nyandoma**, Rus.
107/B3 **Nyanza** (prov.), Kenya
107/A4 **Nyanza-Lac**, Buru.
107/B5 **Nyasa** (Malawi) (lake), Afr.
54/F1 **Nyborg**, Den.
48/E4 **Nybro**, Swe.
55/L5 **Nyíradony**, Hun.
68/F2 **Nyírbátor**, Hun.
68/E2 **Nyíregyháza**, Hun.
107/C2 **Nyiru** (peak), Kenya
54/F1 **Nykøbing**, Den.
48/F4 **Nyköping**, Swe.
108/E2 **Nylstroom**, SAfr.
48/F4 **Nynäshamn**, Swe.
60/C5 **Nyon**, Swi.
55/G4 **Nýřany**, Czh.
55/J3 **Nysa**, Pol.
128/D5 **Nyssa**, Or,US
83/M4 **Nyūdo-zaki** (pt.), Japan
70/F2 **Nyuk** (lake), Rus.
110/E2 **Nyunzu**, D.R. Congo
85/E2 **Nyūzen**, Japan
104/C5 **Nzérékoré**, Gui.
104/C4 **Nzérékoré** (comm.), Gui.
104/D5 **Nzi** (riv.), C.d'Iv.

O

53/E1 **Oadby**, Eng,UK
129/H4 **Oahe** (lake), ND, SD,US
126/V13 **Oahu** (isl.), Hi,US
129/J3 **Oakbank**, Mb,Can.
138/Q14 **Oak Creek**, Wi,US
129/J4 **Oakes**, ND,US
138/Q16 **Oak Forest**, Il,US
53/F1 **Oakham**, Eng,UK
132/D4 **Oak Hill**, WV,US
130/C3 **Oakhurst**, Ca,US
138/K11 **Oakland**, Ca,US
137/F4 **Oakland**, NJ,US
138/A3 **Oakland** (bay), Wa,US
138/Q16 **Oak Lawn**, Il,US
53/E3 **Oakley**, Eng,UK
53/F2 **Oakley**, Eng,UK
138/L11 **Oakley**, Ca,US
131/G3 **Oakley**, Ks,US
138/Q16 **Oak Park**, Il,US
138/F7 **Oak Park**, Mi,US
128/C5 **Oakridge**, Or,US
132/C4 **Oak Ridge**, Tn,US
133/R8 **Oak Ridges**, On,Can.
52/D3 **Oaksey**, Eng,UK
137/A2 **Oak View**, Ca,US
133/Q9 **Oakville**, On,Can.
95/H7 **Oamaru**, NZ
122/B4 **Oaxaca**, Mex.
122/B4 **Oaxaca** (state), Mex.
74/H3 **Ob'** (gulf), Rus.
74/G3 **Ob'** (riv.), Rus.
98/F6 **Oba** (isl.), Van.
71/Q5 **Obaghan** (riv.), Kaz.
132/D2 **Obabika** (lake), On,Can.
84/D3 **Obama**, Japan
105/H5 **Oban** (hills), Camr., Nga.
95/G7 **Oban**, NZ
132/D1 **Obasatika** (riv.), On,Can.
85/M10 **Obata**, Japan
117/E2 **Oberá**, Arg.
56/D6 **Oberhausen**, Ger.
55/H3 **Oberlausitz** (reg.), Ger.
131/G3 **Oberlin**, Ks,US
61/E1 **Oberndorf am Neckar**, Ger.
57/G4 **Obernkirchen**, Ger.
59/G4 **Oberthal**, Ger.
63/L3 **Oberwölz**, Aus.
93/G4 **Obi** (isls.), Indo.
93/G4 **Obi** (str.), Indo.
115/G4 **Óbidos**, Braz.
83/N3 **Obihiro**, Japan
68/E4 **Obilić**, Serb.
85/J7 **Obitsu** (riv.), Japan
89/B2 **Ob Luang Gorge**, Thai.
83/L2 **Obluch'ye**, Rus.
70/H5 **Obninsk**, Rus.
103/P5 **Obock**, Djib.
55/J2 **Oborniki**, Pol.
55/J3 **Oborniki Śląskie**, Pol.
55/J2 **Obra** (riv.), Pol.
68/E3 **Obrenovac**, Serb.
85/M10 **Ōbu**, Japan
105/E5 **Obuasi**, Gha.
61/E4 **Obwalden** (canton), Swi.
135/H4 **Ocala**, Fl,US
62/C5 **Occabe, Sommet d'** (peak), Fr.
114/E7 **Occidental, Cordillera** (range), SAm.
136/L4 **Ocean** (cape), Ak,US
137/G5 **Ocean Beach**, NY,US
132/F4 **Ocean City**, Md,US
128/B2 **Ocean Falls**, BC,Can.
137/F5 **Ocean Grove**, NJ,US
98/* **Oceania**
130/C4 **Oceanside**, Ca,US
137/G5 **Oceanside**, NY,US
89/D4 **Oc-Eo** (ruins), Viet.
73/G4 **Ochamchira**, Geo.
83/P3 **Ochiishi-misaki** (cape), Japan
123/F4 **Ocho Rios**, Jam.
57/E4 **Ochtrup**, Ger.
57/F2 **Ochtum** (riv.), Ger.
53/E3 **Ock** (riv.), Eng,UK
70/C3 **Ockelbo**, Swe.
135/H4 **Ocmulgee** (riv.), Ga,US
69/F2 **Ocna Mureș**, Rom.
135/H3 **Oconee** (lake), Ga,US
135/H3 **Oconee** (riv.), Ga,US
122/D5 **Ocotal**, Nic.
122/A3 **Ocotlán**, Mex.
122/B4 **Ocotlán**, Mex.
62/C2 **Octeville**, Fr.
75/L1 **October Revolution** (isl.), Rus.
105/E5 **Oda**, Gha.
84/C3 **Oda**, Japan
85/M10 **Ōdai**, Japan
84/E3 **Ōdaigahara-san** (mtn.), Japan
106/D4 **Oda, Jabal** (peak), Sudan
83/N3 **Ōdate**, Japan
85/F3 **Odawara**, Japan
48/C3 **Odda**, Nor.
103/P7 **Oddur**, Som.
57/F6 **Odeborn** (riv.), Ger.
54/A2 **Odemira**, Port.
80/A2 **Ödemiş**, Turk.
108/D2 **Odendaalsrus**, SAfr.
54/F1 **Odense**, Den.
57/E6 **Odenthal**, Ger.
137/K7 **Odenton**, Md,US
55/H2 **Oderhaff** (lag.), Ger., Pol.
55/H2 **Oder** (Odra) (riv.), Ger., Pol.
63/K4 **Oderzo**, It.
72/D3 **Odesa**, Ukr.
69/J2 **Odes'ka Obl.**, Ukr.
134/C4 **Odessa**, Tx,US
128/D4 **Odessa**, Wa,US
62/B2 **Odet** (riv.), Fr.
104/D4 **Odienné**, C.d'Iv.
71/W9 **Odintsovo**, Rus.
88/D5 **Odiongan**, Phil.
65/P10 **Odivelas**, Port.
69/H3 **Odobești**, Rom.
62/C2 **Odon** (riv.), Fr.
89/D4 **Odongk**, Camb.
56/D3 **Odoorn**, Neth.
69/G2 **Odorheiu Secuiesc**, Rom.
55/H2 **Odra** (Oder) (riv.), Ger., Pol.
68/D3 **Odžaci**, Serb.
102/J7 **Odzala Nat'l Park**, Congo
85/L9 **Ōe**, Japan
56/B4 **Oegstgeest**, Neth.
115/K5 **Oeiras**, Braz.
57/F5 **Oelde**, Ger.
63/K1 **Oelsnitz**, Ger.
99/M7 **Oeno** (atoll), Pitc.,UK
57/E5 **Oer-Erkenschwick**, Ger.
59/E4 **Oesling** (mts.), Lux.
56/B6 **Oesterdam** (dam), Neth.
63/H2 **Oestrich-Winkel**, Ger.
67/H3 **Oeta Nat'l Park**, Gre.
80/E2 **Of**, Turk.
66/D2 **Ofanto** (riv.), It.
80/K6 **Ofaqim**, Isr.
50/A5 **Offaly** (co.), Ire.
63/H1 **Offenbach**, Ger.
60/D1 **Offenburg**, Ger.
63/G3 **Oftringen**, Swi.
83/M4 **Oga**, Japan
103/P6 **Ogadēn** (reg.), Eth.
84/E3 **Ōgaki**, Japan
131/G2 **Ogallala**, Ne,US
98/D2 **Ogasawara**, Japan
105/G4 **Ogbomosho**, Nga.
130/E2 **Ogden**, Ut,US
132/F2 **Ogdensburg**, NY,US
135/H3 **Ogeechee** (riv.), Ga,US
132/D2 **Ogidaki** (mtn.), On,Can.
136/L3 **Ogilvie** (mts.), Yk,Can.
124/C2 **Ogilvie** (riv.), Yk,Can.
63/J4 **Oglio** (riv.), It.
52/C4 **Ogmore by Sea**, Wal,UK
60/B3 **Ognon** (riv.), Fr.
93/F3 **Ogoamas** (peak), Indo.
129/M3 **Ogoki** (lake), On,Can.
129/L3 **Ogoki** (res.), On,Can.
129/M3 **Ogoki** (riv.), On,Can.
102/G8 **Ogooué** (riv.), Gabon
85/H7 **Ogose**, Japan
69/F4 **Ogosta** (riv.), Bul.
70/E4 **Ogre**, Lat.
85/M9 **Oguchi**, Japan
105/F5 **Ogun** (riv.), Nga.
105/F5 **Ogun** (state), Nga.
73/K5 **Ogurchinskiy** (isl.), Trkm.
102/G2 **Ohanet**, Alg.
96/G8 **O'Hares** (cr.), Austl.
57/E2 **Ohe** (riv.), Ger.
119/J7 **O'Higgins** (lake), Chile
132/B4 **Ohio** (riv.), US
132/D3 **Ohio** (state), US
51/F1 **Oh Me Edge** (hill), Eng,UK
135/H3 **Ohoopee** (riv.), Ga,US
63/K1 **Ohře** (riv.), Czh.
54/F2 **Ohre** (riv.), Ger.
68/E5 **Ohrid** (lake), Alb., FYROM
68/E5 **Ohrid**, FYROM
91/G2 **Oi** (riv.), China
85/H7 **Ōi**, Japan
85/F3 **Ōi** (riv.), Japan
115/H3 **Oiapoque** (riv.), Braz.
65/P10 **Oieras**, Port.
58/B3 **Oignies**, Fr.
132/E3 **Oil City**, Pa,US
56/C5 **Oirschot**, Neth.
58/B5 **Oise** (dept.), Fr.
58/B5 **Oise** (riv.), Fr.
58/C5 **Oise à l'Aisne, Canal de** (can.), Fr.
58/A4 **Oisemont**, Fr.
85/H7 **Ōiso**, Japan
56/C5 **Oisterwijk**, Neth.
58/C3 **Oisy-le-Verger**, Fr.
84/B4 **Ōita**, Japan
84/B4 **Ōita** (pref.), Japan
84/B4 **Ōita** (riv.), Japan
137/A2 **Ojai**, Ca,US
55/K3 **Ojcowski Nat'l Park**, Pol.
85/L10 **Ōji**, Japan
123/P8 **Ojinaga**, Mex.
85/F2 **Ojiya**, Japan
122/A3 **Ojocaliente**, Mex.
117/C2 **Ojos del Salado** (peak), Arg., Chile
123/L7 **Ojos Negros**, Mex.
71/J4 **Oka** (riv.), Rus.
125/K3 **Okak** (isl.), Nf,Can.
128/C3 **Okanagan** (lake), BC,Can.
128/D3 **Okanagan Falls**, BC,Can.
110/B1 **Okanda Nat'l Park**, Gabon
128/D3 **Okanogan**, Wa,US
128/D3 **Okanogan** (riv.), Wa,US
79/K2 **Okāra**, Pak.
110/C4 **Okaukuejo**, Namb.
110/D4 **Okavango Delta** (reg.), Bots.
84/B4 **Ōkawa**, Japan
85/F2 **Okaya**, Japan
84/C3 **Okayama**, Japan
84/C3 **Okayama** (pref.), Japan
85/E3 **Okazaki**, Japan
135/H5 **Okeechobee**, Fl,US
135/H5 **Okeechobee** (lake), Fl,US
85/H7 **Okegawa**, Japan
52/C5 **Okehampton**, Eng,UK
52/B5 **Okement** (riv.), Eng,UK
57/H4 **Oker** (riv.), Ger.
75/Q4 **Okha**, Rus.
67/J3 **Okhi** (peak), Gre.
75/Q4 **Okhotsk** (sea), Japan, Rus.
84/C2 **Oki** (isls.), Japan
84/C2 **Oki-Daisen Nat'l Park**, Japan
88/E2 **Okinawa** (isls.), Japan
98/C2 **Okino-Tori-Shima** (Parece Vela) (isl.), Japan
91/G4 **Okkan**, Myan.
131/H4 **Oklahoma** (state), US
131/H4 **Oklahoma City** (cap.), Ok,US
135/H4 **Oklawaha** (riv.), Fl,US
131/J4 **Okmulgee**, Ok,US
129/K5 **Okoboji** (lakes), Ia,US
135/F3 **Okolona**, Ms,US
128/E3 **Okotoks**, Ab,Can.
106/C4 **Oko, Wādī** (dry riv.), Sudan
48/E2 **Oksskolten** (peak), Nor.
73/J1 **Oktyabr'sk**, Rus.
71/M5 **Oktyabr'skiy**, Rus.
70/G4 **Okulovka**, Rus.
83/M3 **Okushiri** (isl.), Japan
85/H7 **Okutama**, Japan
110/D5 **Okwa** (riv.), Bots.
130/C3 **Olancha**, Ca,US
122/D4 **Olanchito**, Hon.
48/F4 **Öland** (isl.), Swe.
48/F4 **Ölands södra udde** (pt.), Swe.
63/G4 **Olan, Pic d'** (peak), Fr.
66/D2 **Olanto** (riv.), It.
130/F3 **Olathe**, Co,US
131/J3 **Olathe**, Ks,US
118/E3 **Olavarría**, Arg.
55/J3 **Oława**, Pol.
57/F5 **Ölbach** (riv.), Ger.
66/A2 **Olbia**, It.
61/H1 **Olching**, Ger.
133/S9 **Olcott**, NY,US
138/D3 **Old Baldy** (mtn.), Wa,US
137/F5 **Old Bridge**, NJ,US
136/L2 **Old Crow**, Yk,Can.
56/C4 **Oldebroek**, Neth.
57/F2 **Oldenburg**, Ger.
56/D4 **Oldenzaal**, Neth.
51/F4 **Oldham**, Eng,UK
51/F4 **Oldham** (co.), Eng,UK
128/E3 **Oldman** (riv.), Ab,Can.
53/F2 **Old Nene** (riv.), Eng,UK
137/G5 **Old Northport** (Northport), NY,US
57/F1 **Oldoog** (isl.), Ger.
133/G2 **Old Town**, Me,US
53/F4 **Old Windsor**, Eng,UK
129/G3 **Old Wives** (lake), Sk,Can.
132/E3 **Olean**, NY,US
55/M1 **Olecko**, Pol.
64/A1 **Oleiros**, Sp.
75/N4 **Olekma** (riv.), Rus.
138/B2 **Olele** (pt.), Wa,US
70/G1 **Olenegorsk**, Rus.
75/N2 **Olenek** (bay), Rus.
75/N2 **Olenëk** (riv.), Rus.
81/B1 **Ölengti** (riv.), Kaz.
62/C4 **Oléron** (isl.), Fr.
65/K6 **Olesa de Montserrat**, Sp.
55/J3 **Oleśnica**, Pol.
55/K3 **Olesno**, Pol.
57/E5 **Olfen**, Ger.
82/B2 **Ölgiy**, Mong.
64/B4 **Olhão**, Port.
63/L4 **Olib** (isl.), Cro.
66/A2 **Oliena**, It.
108/B2 **Olifants** (dry riv.), Namb.
108/B3 **Olifants** (riv.), SAfr.
108/E2 **Olifantsrivier** (riv.), SAfr.
98/D4 **Olimarao** (atoll), Micr.
67/H2 **Ólimbos** (Mount Olympus) (peak), Gre.
116/B2 **Olímpia**, Braz.
115/M5 **Olinda**, Braz.
73/K3 **Oli Qoltyq Sory** (salt marsh), Kaz.
118/E2 **Oliva**, Arg.
65/E3 **Oliva**, Sp.
64/B3 **Oliva de la Frontera**, Sp.
64/A3 **Olivais**, Port.
116/C2 **Oliveira**, Braz.
64/B3 **Olivenza**, Sp.
128/D3 **Oliver**, BC,Can.
62/D3 **Olivet**, Fr.
114/E8 **Ollagüe** (vol.), Bol.
65/E3 **Ollería**, Sp.
90/C5 **Ollūr**, India
118/Q9 **Olmué**, Chile
53/F2 **Olney**, Eng,UK
132/B4 **Olney**, Il,US
137/J7 **Olney**, Md,US
133/J1 **Olomane** (riv.), Qu,Can.
55/J4 **Olomouc**, Czh.
55/J4 **Olomoucký** (reg.), Czh.
88/D5 **Olongapo**, Phil.
62/C3 **Olonne-sur-Mer**, Fr.
62/C5 **Oloron-Sainte-Marie**, Fr.
65/G1 **Olot**, Sp.
75/S3 **Oloy** (range), Rus.
57/E6 **Olpe**, Ger.
57/F6 **Olsberg**, Ger.
56/D4 **Olst**, Neth.
55/L2 **Olsztyn**, Pol.
55/L2 **Olsztynek**, Pol.
69/G3 **Olt** (co.), Rom.
69/G4 **Olt** (riv.), Rom.
118/C4 **Olte** (mts.), Arg.
60/D3 **Olten**, Swi.
69/H3 **Oltenița**, Rom.
69/F3 **Olteț** (riv.), Rom.
80/E2 **Oltu**, Turk.
80/E2 **Oltu** (riv.), Turk.
88/D3 **Oluanpi**, Tai.
64/C4 **Olvera**, Sp.
138/B3 **Olympia** (cap.), Wa,US
67/G4 **Olympia** (Olímbia) (ruins), Gre.
128/B4 **Olympic** (mts.), Wa,US
128/B4 **Olympic Nat'l Park**, Wa,US
80/J4 **Olympus** (mtn.), Cyp.
128/C4 **Olympus** (peak), Wa,US
67/H2 **Olympus, Mount** (Ólimbos) (peak), Gre.
67/H2 **Olympus Nat'l Park**, Gre.
75/S3 **Olyutorskiy** (bay), Rus.
71/K2 **Oma** (riv.), Rus.
85/E2 **Ōmachi**, Japan
85/F3 **Omae-zaki** (pt.), Japan
50/A2 **Omagh**, NI,UK
50/A2 **Omagh** (dist.), NI,UK
131/J2 **Omaha**, Ne,US
128/D3 **Omak**, Wa,US
79/G4 **Oman** (ctry.)
79/G4 **Oman** (gulf), Asia
110/C4 **Omatako** (riv.), Namb.
93/F5 **Ombai** (str.), ETim., Indo.
52/D2 **Ombersley**, Eng,UK
110/B4 **Ombombo**, Namb.
102/G8 **Omboué**, Gabon
80/B1 **Ombrone** (riv.), It.
103/M4 **Omdurman** (Umm Durmān), Sudan
85/H7 **Ōme**, Japan
63/H4 **Omegna**, It.
122/B4 **Ometepec**, Mex.
85/M9 **Ōmihachiman**, Japan
66/E1 **Omiš**, Cro.
85/G2 **Ōmiya**, Japan
136/M4 **Ommaney** (cape), Ak,US
56/D3 **Ommen**, Neth.
82/F2 **Ömnödelger**, Mong.
82/C2 **Ömnögovĭ**, Mong.
66/A2 **Omodeo** (lake), It.
77/Q3 **Omolon** (riv.), Rus.
103/N6 **Omo Nat'l Park**, Eth.
103/N6 **Omo Wenz** (riv.), Eth.
74/H4 **Omskaya Obl.**, Rus.
69/G3 **Omul** (peak), Rom.
69/H4 **Omurtag**, Bul.
84/B4 **Ōmuta**, Japan
71/M4 **Omutninsk**, Rus.
85/G1 **Onagawa**, Japan
131/J5 **Onalaska**, Tx,US
64/D1 **Oñate**, Sp.
132/C2 **Onaway**, Mi,US
118/E1 **Oncativo**, Arg.
50/D3 **Onchan**, IM,UK
110/B4 **Oncocúa**, Ang.
65/E3 **Onda**, Sp.
110/C4 **Ondangua**, Namb.
55/L4 **Ondava** (riv.), Slvk.
110/C4 **Ondjiva**, Ang.
105/G5 **Ondo** (state), Nga.
82/G2 **Öndörhaan**, Mong.
82/C2 **Öndörhangay**, Mong.
70/H3 **Onega**, Rus.
70/H2 **Onega** (bay), Rus.
70/G3 **Onega** (lake), Rus.
70/H2 **Onega** (pen.), Rus.
70/H3 **Onega** (riv.), Rus.
128/C3 **One Hundred Mile House**, BC,Can.
132/F3 **Oneida**, NY,US
131/H2 **O'Neill**, Ne,US
132/F3 **Oneonta**, NY,US
82/E2 **Ongiyn** (riv.), Mong.
90/D4 **Ongole**, India
129/H4 **Onida**, SD,US
65/E3 **Onil**, Sp.
109/G8 **Onilahy** (riv.), Madg.
105/G5 **Onitsha**, Nga.
109/H7 **Onive** (riv.), Madg.
58/C3 **Onnaing**, Fr.
52/D2 **Onny** (riv.), Eng,UK
84/D3 **Ono**, Japan
84/E3 **Ōno**, Japan
84/B4 **Onoda**, Japan
84/C3 **Onomichi**, Japan
82/G1 **Onon** (riv.), Mong., Rus.
98/G5 **Onotoa** (atoll), Kiri.
85/E3 **Ontake-san** (mtn.), Japan
124/H3 **Ontario** (prov.), Can.
132/E3 **Ontario** (lake), Can., US
137/C2 **Ontario**, Ca,US
128/D4 **Ontario**, Or,US
65/E3 **Onteniente**, Sp.
132/B2 **Ontonagon**, Mi,US
98/F5 **Ontong Java** (isl.), Sol.
134/E2 **Oologah** (lake), Ok,US
56/A6 **Oostburg**, Neth.
56/C4 **Oostelijk Flevoland** (polder), Neth.
58/B1 **Oostende**, Belg.
56/B5 **Oosterhout**, Neth.
56/A5 **Oosterschelde** (chan.), Neth.
58/C2 **Oosterzele**, Belg.
58/C1 **Oostkamp**, Belg.
56/C4 **Oostvaarderplassen** (lake), Neth.
56/B4 **Oostzaan**, Neth.
90/C5 **Ootacamund**, India
129/B2 **Ootsa** (lake), BC,Can.
110/D1 **Opala**, D.R. Congo
55/J2 **Opalenica**, Pol.
68/B3 **Opatija**, Cro.
55/L3 **Opatów**, Pol.
55/J4 **Opava**, Czh.
135/G3 **Opelika**, Al,US
134/E4 **Opelousas**, La,US
132/E2 **Opeongo** (lake), On,Can.
59/E1 **Opglabbeek**, Belg.
56/C5 **Oploo**, Neth.
56/B3 **Opmeer**, Neth.
55/L3 **Opoczno**, Pol.
55/J3 **Opole**, Pol.
55/L3 **Opole Lubelskie**, Pol.
55/J3 **Opolskie** (prov.), Pol.
135/G4 **Opp**, Al,US
48/D3 **Oppdal**, Nor.
48/D3 **Oppland** (co.), Nor.
128/D4 **Opportunity**, Wa,US
58/D2 **Opwijk**, Belg.
68/E2 **Oradea**, Rom.
68/E4 **Orahovac**, Serb.
90/C2 **Orai**, India
73/J2 **Oral**, Kaz.
102/E1 **Oran**, Alg.
108/B3 **Orange** (riv.), Afr.
97/D2 **Orange**, Austl.
62/F4 **Orange**, Fr.
115/H3 **Orange** (mts.), Sur.
137/C3 **Orange**, Ca,US
137/F5 **Orange**, NJ,US
134/E4 **Orange**, Tx,US
132/E4 **Orange**, Va,US
135/H3 **Orangeburg**, SC,US
135/H4 **Orange Park**, Fl,US
132/D3 **Orangeville**, On,Can.
122/D4 **Orange Walk**, Belz.
104/A4 **Orango** (isl.), GBis.
55/G2 **Oranienburg**, Ger.
56/D3 **Oranjekanaal** (can.), Neth.
123/G5 **Oranjestad** (cap.), Aru.
110/E5 **Orapa**, Bots.
80/M8 **Or 'Aqiva**, Isr.
88/E5 **Oras**, Phil.
69/F3 **Orăștie**, Rom.
68/E3 **Oravița**, Rom.
62/E5 **Orb** (riv.), Fr.
64/C1 **Órbigo** (riv.), Sp.
134/B2 **Orchard City**, Co,US
128/E4 **Orchard Homes**, Mt,US
138/F6 **Orchard Lake Village**, Mi,US
88/D3 **Orchid** (isl.), Tai.
63/G4 **Orco** (riv.), It.
62/F3 **Or, Côte d'** (uplands), Fr.
131/H2 **Ord**, Ne,US
64/A1 **Órdenes**, Sp.
65/F1 **Ordesa y Monte Perdido Nat'l Park**, Sp.
87/B3 **Ordos** (des.), China
80/D2 **Ordu**, Turk.
131/G3 **Ordway**, Co,US
48/E4 **Örebro**, Swe.
48/E4 **Örebro** (co.), Swe.
128/C4 **Oregon** (state), US
130/B2 **Oregon Caves Nat'l Mon.**, Or,US
128/C4 **Oregon City**, Or,US
72/F1 **Orël**, Rus.
72/E2 **Orel'** (riv.), Ukr.
72/E1 **Orel Obl.**, Rus.
130/E2 **Orem**, Ut,US
73/K2 **Orenburg**, Rus.
73/K1 **Orenburgskaya Obl.**, Rus.
64/B1 **Orense**, Sp.
67/K2 **Orestiás**, Gre.
53/H2 **Orford**, Eng,UK
53/H2 **Orford Ness** (pt.), UK
130/D4 **Organ Pipe Cactus Nat'l Mon.**, Az,US
116/L7 **Órgãos** (mts.), Braz.
69/J2 **Orgeyev**, Mol.
72/D5 **Orhaneli**, Turk.
69/J5 **Orhangazi**, Turk.
82/F2 **Orhon** (riv.), Mong.
62/C5 **Orhy, Pic d'** (peak), Fr.
117/C6 **Oriental** (val.), Arg.
114/D6 **Oriental, Cordillera** (range), SAm.
107/A2 **Orientale** (prov.), D.R. Congo
65/E3 **Orihuela**, Sp.
132/E2 **Orillia**, On,Can.
138/K11 **Orinda**, Ca,US
114/F2 **Orinoco** (riv.), Col., Ven.
123/J6 **Orinoco** (delta), Ven.
138/F6 **Orion** (lake), Mi,US
90/D3 **Orissa** (state), India
66/A3 **Oristano**, It.
66/A3 **Oristano** (gulf), It.
48/H3 **Orivesi**, Fin.
115/G4 **Oriximiná**, Braz.
122/B4 **Orizaba**, Mex.
68/D4 **Orjen** (peak), Mont.
57/F6 **Orke** (riv.), Ger.
47/D3 **Orkney** (isls.), Sc,UK
134/C4 **Orla**, Tx,US
116/C2 **Orlândia**, Braz.
135/H4 **Orlando**, Fl,US
66/D3 **Orlando, Capo d'** (cape), It.
138/Q16 **Orland Park**, Il,US
62/D2 **Orléanais** (hist. reg.), Fr.
62/D3 **Orléans**, Fr.
130/B2 **Orleans**, Ca,US
55/K4 **Orlová**, Czh.
72/E1 **Orlovskaya Obl.**, Rus.
88/D5 **Ormoc**, Phil.
135/H4 **Ormond Beach**, Fl,US
51/F4 **Ormskirk**, Eng,UK
62/F2 **Ornain** (riv.), Fr.
59/F5 **Orne** (riv.), Fr.
48/E2 **Ørnes**, Nor.
55/L1 **Orneta**, Pol.
48/F3 **Örnsköldsvik**, Swe.
123/N8 **Oro** (riv.), Mex.
61/F6 **Orobie, Alpi** (range), It.
104/D2 **Orodara**, Burk.
65/E1 **Oroel** (peak), Sp.
128/D4 **Orofino**, Id,US
99/L6 **Orohena** (peak), FrPol.
98/E4 **Oroluk** (atoll), Micr.
133/H2 **Oromocto**, NB,Can.
66/A1 **Oro, Monte d'** (mtn.), Fr.
99/H5 **Orona** (Hull) (atoll), Kiri.
133/G2 **Orono**, Me,US
80/L4 **Orontes** (riv.), Asia
83/J1 **Oroqen Zizhiqi**, China
88/D6 **Oroquieta**, Phil.
66/A2 **Orosei** (gulf), It.
68/E2 **Orosháza**, Hun.
68/D2 **Oroszlány**, Hun.
130/C2 **Orovada**, Nv,US
130/E4 **Oro Valley**, Az,US
130/B3 **Oroville**, Ca,US
128/D3 **Oroville**, Wa,US
51/F4 **Orrell**, Eng,UK
58/B5 **Orry-la-Ville**, Fr.
48/E3 **Orsa**, Swe.
58/B6 **Orsay**, Fr.
70/F5 **Orsha**, Bela.
73/L2 **Orsk**, Rus.
68/F3 **Orșova**, Rom.
48/C3 **Ørsta**, Nor.
63/H4 **Orta** (lake), It.
80/C2 **Orta**, Turk.
80/B3 **Ortaca**, Turk.
66/D2 **Orta Nova**, It.
64/B1 **Ortegal** (cape), Sp.
62/C5 **Orthez**, Fr.
64/B1 **Ortigueira**, Sp.
61/G5 **Ortles** (mts.), It., Swi.
114/E6 **Ortón** (riv.), Bol.
83/H2 **Orton** (riv.), China
66/D1 **Ortona**, It.
138/F6 **Ortonville**, Mi,US

129/J4 Ortonville, Mn,US
57/H3 Örtze (riv.), Ger.
80/F3 Orūmīyeh, Iran
114/E7 Oruro, Bol.
66/C1 Orvieto, It.
111/V Orville (coast), Ant.
53/H2 Orwell (riv.), Eng,UK
82/H3 Orxon (riv.), China
69/F4 Oryakhovo, Bul.
80/M8 Or Yehuda, Isr.
71/M4 Osa, Rus.
131/J3 Osage (riv.), Mo,US
131/J3 Osage Beach, Mo,US
84/L10 Ōsaka, Japan
85/L10 Ōsaka (bay), Japan
84/D3 Ōsaka (pref.), Japan
86/D4 Osan, SKor.
116/G8 Osasco, Braz.
136/E3 Osborn (mtn.), Ak,US
131/H3 Osborne, Ks,US
135/F3 Osceola, Ar,US
54/F2 Oschersleben, Ger.
134/B3 Oscura (mts.), NM,US
81/B3 Osh, Kyr.
110/C4 Oshakati, Namb.
133/S8 Oshawa, On,Can.
83/M3 Oshima (pen.), Japan
110/C4 Oshivelo, Namb.
129/H5 Oshkosh, Ne,US
132/B2 Oshkosh, Wi,US
80/F3 Oshnovīyeh, Iran
105/G5 Oshogbo, Nga.
110/C1 Oshwe, D.R. Congo
68/D3 Osijek, Cro.
63/K5 Osimo, It.
72/D1 Osipovichi, Bela.
129/K5 Oskaloosa, Ia,US
48/F4 Oskarshamn, Swe.
81/D2 Öskemen, Kaz.
72/F2 Oskol (riv.), Rus., Ukr.
48/D4 Oslo (cap.), Nor.
90/C4 Osmānābād, India
80/C2 Osmancık, Turk.
69/K5 Osmaneli, Turk.
80/D3 Osmaniye, Turk.
57/F4 Osnabrück, Ger.
58/B5 Osny, Fr.
116/B4 Osório, Braz.
118/B4 Osorno, Chile
128/D3 Osoyoos, BC,Can.
96/B1 Osprey (reef), Austl.
56/C5 Oss, Neth.
97/C4 Ossa (peak), Austl.
54/B3 Ossa (range), Port.
105/G5 Osse (riv.), Nga.
58/C1 Ossett, Eng,UK
137/G4 Ossining, NY,US
70/G4 Ostashkov, Rus.
57/E4 Ostbevern, Ger.
57/G1 Oste (riv.), Ger.
58/B1 Ostend (Oostende), Belg.
54/F2 Osterburg, Ger.
57/F4 Ostercappeln, Ger.
56/D1 Osterems (chan.), Neth.
48/E4 Östergötland (co.), Swe.
63/K2 Osterhofen, Ger.
57/F2 Osterholz-Scharmbeck, Ger.
57/H5 Osterode am Harz, Ger.
48/E3 Östersund, Swe.
48/D4 Østfold (co.), Nor.
57/E2 Ostfriesland (reg.), Ger.
48/F3 Östhammar, Swe.
66/C2 Ostia Antica (ruins), It.
63/J4 Ostiglia, It.
55/K4 Ostrava, Czh.
55/J4 Ostravský (reg.), Czh.
57/E2 Ostrhauderfehn, Ger.
58/C3 Ostricourt, Fr.
68/D4 Oštri Rt (cape), Mont.
55/K2 Ostróda, Pol.
72/F2 Ostrogozhsk, Rus.
55/L2 Ostrołęka, Pol.
54/G3 Ostrov, Czh.
70/F4 Ostrov, Rus.
55/L3 Ostrowiec Świętokrzyski, Pol.
55/L2 Ostrów Mazowiecka, Pol.
55/J3 Ostrów Wielkopolski, Pol.
55/J3 Ostrzeszów, Pol.
57/H1 Oststeinbek, Ger.
66/E2 Ostuni, It.
67/G2 Osum (riv.), Alb.
69/G4 Osŭm (riv.), Bul.
84/B5 Ōsumi (isls.), Japan
84/B5 Ōsumi (pen.), Japan
84/B5 Ōsumi (str.), Japan
64/C4 Osuna, Sp.
116/B2 Osvaldo Cruz, Braz.
51/G3 Oswaldkirk, Eng,UK
51/F4 Oswaldtwistle, Eng,UK
132/E3 Oswego, NY,US
51/E6 Oswestry, Eng,UK
55/K3 Oświęcim (Auschwitz), Pol.
84/F2 Ota, Japan
84/C3 Ōta (riv.), Japan
84/C3 Ōtake, Japan
85/G2 Ōtakine-yama (mtn.), Japan
55/G4 Otava (riv.), Czh.
85/G2 Ōtawara, Japan
68/F3 Oţelu Roşu, Rom.
99/L6 Otepa, FrPol.
123/N8 Oteros (riv.), Mex.
82/D2 Otgon, Mong.
82/D2 Otgon Tenger (peak), Mong.
128/D4 Othello, Wa,US
58/B5 Othis, Fr.
67/F3 Othonoí (isl.), Gre.
105/F4 Oti (riv.), Gui.
110/C5 Otjikango, Namb.
110/C5 Otjinene, Namb.
110/C5 Otjiwarongo, Namb.
110/B4 Otjokavare, Namb.
51/G4 Otley, Eng,UK
87/A3 Otog Qi, China
129/L3 Otoskwin (riv.), On,Can.
85/N10 Otowa, Japan
48/C4 Otra (riv.), Nor.
73/J1 Otradnyy, Rus.
67/F2 Otranto (str.), Alb., It.
55/J4 Otrokovice, Czh.
84/D3 Ōtsu, Japan
48/D3 Otta, Nor.
132/F2 Ottawa (cap.), Can.
125/H3 Ottawa (isls.), Nun,Can.
132/E2 Ottawa (riv.), On, Qu,Can.
132/B3 Ottawa, Il,US
131/J3 Ottawa, Ks,US
132/C3 Ottawa, Oh,US
52/C5 Otter (riv.), Eng,UK
51/F1 Otterburn, Eng,UK
57/F1 Otterndorf, Ger.
57/G2 Ottersberg, Ger.
52/C5 Ottery Saint Mary, Eng,UK
58/D2 Ottignies-Louvain-La-Neuve, Belg.
63/J2 Ottobrunn, Ger.
129/K5 Ottumwa, Ia,US
59/G5 Ottweiler, Ger.
97/B3 Otway (cape), Austl.
119/J8 Otway (bay), Chile
119/K8 Otway (sound), Chile
97/B3 Otway Nat'l Park, Austl.
55/L2 Otwock, Pol.
61/G4 Ötztal Alps (mts.), Aus., It.
89/C1 Ou (riv.), Laos
134/E3 Ouachita (riv.), Ar, La,US
131/J4 Ouachita (mts.), Ar, Ok,US
102/C3 Ouadane, Mrta.
103/J5 Ouaddaï (reg.), Chad
105/E3 Ouagadougou (cap.), Burk.
103/K6 Ouaka (riv.), CAfr.
104/D2 Oualâta, Dhar (hills), Mrta.
62/E3 Ouanne (riv.), Fr.
102/C3 Ouarane (reg.), Mrta.
102/G1 Ouargla, Alg.
102/D1 Ouarzazate, Mor.
133/F1 Ouasiemsca (riv.), Qu,Can.
103/J6 Oubangui (riv.), CAfr.
105/E3 Oubritenga (prov.), Burk.
85/L10 Ōuda, Japan
105/E3 Oudalan (prov.), Burk.
56/B5 Oud-Beijerland, Neth.
56/A5 Ouddorp, Neth.
56/D5 Oude IJssel (riv.), Neth.
58/C2 Oudenaarde, Belg.
56/B5 Oudenbosch, Neth.
58/B1 Oudenburg, Belg.
56/E2 Oude Pekela, Neth.
62/C3 Oudon (riv.), Fr.
108/C4 Oudtshoorn, SAfr.
56/B6 Oud-Turnhout, Belg.
104/E2 Oued el Hadjar (well), Mali
102/D1 Oued Zem, Mor.
105/F5 Ouémé (prov.), Ben.
105/F5 Ouémé (riv.), Ben.
99/V13 Ouen (isl.), NCal.
62/A2 Ouessant (isl.), Fr.
102/J7 Ouesso, Congo
105/H5 Ouest (prov.), Camr.
123/G4 Ouest (pt.), Haiti
102/D1 Ouezzane, Mor.
103/J6 Ouham (riv.), CAfr., Chad
58/C5 Ouichy-le-Château, Fr.
102/E1 Oujda, Mor.
48/J2 Oulangan Nat'l Park, Fin.
97/A2 Oulnina (peak), Austl.
48/H2 Oulu, Fin.
48/H2 Oulun (prov.), Fin.
48/H2 Oulujärvi (lake), Fin.
102/D1 Oum er Rhia (riv.), Mor.
103/J5 Oum Hadjer, Chad
70/E2 Ounasjoki (riv.), Fin.
53/F2 Oundle, Eng,UK
103/K4 OuniangaKebir, Chad
59/E2 Oupeye, Belg.
59/F4 Our (riv.), Eur.
60/A2 Ource (riv.), Fr.
58/C5 Ourcq (riv.), Fr.
48/H1 Øure Anarjokka Nat'l Park, Nor.
48/F1 Øure Dividal Nat'l Park, Nor.
103/J3 Ouri, Chad
115/K5 Ouricuri, Braz.
116/B2 Ourinhos, Braz.
105/H3 Ourofané, Niger
116/G7 Ouro Fino, Braz.
116/D2 Ouro Preto, Braz.
59/E3 Ourthe (riv.), Belg.
51/H4 Ouse (riv.), Eng,UK
53/G5 Ouse (riv.), Eng,UK
62/B3 Oust (riv.), Fr.
65/Q11 Outão, Port.
132/E2 Outaouais (riv.), Qu,Can.
133/G1 Outardes (riv.), Qu,Can.
133/G1 Outardes Quatre (res.), Qu,Can.
104/D2 Outeid Arkas (well), Mali
49/A2 Outer Hebrides (isls.), Sc,UK
64/A1 Outes, Sp.
128/G3 Outlook, Sk,Can.
58/A2 Outreau, Fr.
99/V12 Ouvéa (atoll), NCal.
63/H4 Ovada, It.
99/Y18 Ovalau (isl.), Fiji
117/B3 Ovalle, Chile
64/A2 Ovar, Port.
59/G2 Overath, Ger.
56/B5 Overflakkee (isl.), Neth.
58/D2 Overijse, Belg.
56/D3 Overijssel (prov.), Neth.
56/D4 Overijssels (can.), Neth.
131/J3 Overland Park, Ks,US
137/K7 Overlea, Md,US
118/C5 Overo (peak), Arg.
59/E1 Overpelt, Belg.
53/E1 Overseal, Eng,UK
53/H1 Overstrand, Eng,UK
53/E4 Overton, Eng,UK
51/F6 Overton, Wal,UK
130/D3 Overton, Nv,US
48/G2 Övertorneå, Swe.
64/C1 Oviedo, Sp.
48/J1 Øvre Pasvik Nat'l Park, Nor.
110/C1 Owando, Congo
85/N9 Owariasahi, Japan
84/E3 Owase, Japan
131/J3 Owasso, Ok,US
129/K4 Owatonna, Mn,US
132/E3 Owego, NY,US
50/A2 Owenkillew (riv.), NI,UK
130/C3 Owens (riv.), Ca,US
132/C4 Owensboro, Ky,US
132/D2 Owen Sound, On,Can.
130/C2 Owhyee (mts.), Id,US
137/K7 Owings Mills, Md,US
128/F4 Owl Creek (mts.), Wy,US
132/C3 Owosso, Mi,US
128/D5 Owyhee (riv.), Id, Or,US
130/C2 Owyhee, Nv,US
130/C2 Owyhee (lake), Or,US
78/E1 Owzan (riv.), Iran
129/H3 Oxbow, Sk,Can.
129/K2 Oxford (lake), Mb,Can.
53/E3 Oxford, Eng,UK
53/E3 Oxford (can.), Eng,UK
138/F6 Oxford, Mi,US
135/F3 Oxford, Ms,US
132/C4 Oxford, Oh,US
53/E3 Oxfordshire (co.), Eng,UK
96/E7 Oxley (cr.), Austl.
137/A2 Oxnard, Ca,US
137/K8 Oxon Hill-Glassmanor, Md,US
53/F4 Oxted, Eng,UK
85/E2 Oyabe, Japan
85/F2 Oyama, Japan
85/M10 Ōyamada, Japan
85/L10 Ōyamazaki, Japan
115/H3 Oyapock (riv.), FrG.
102/H7 Oyem, Gabon
128/F3 Oyen, Ab,Can.
105/F5 Oyo, Nga.
105/F4 Oyo (state), Nga.
85/L10 Ōyodo, Japan
84/B5 Ōyodo (riv.), Japan
137/G5 Oyster Bay, NY,US
57/G2 Oyten, Ger.
73/K2 Oyyl (riv.), Kaz.
88/D6 Ozamiz, Phil.
62/D2 Ozanne (riv.), Fr.
131/J3 Ozark (plat.), US
135/G4 Ozark, Al,US
134/E3 Ozark, Ar,US
134/E3 Ozark (mts.), Ar, Mo,US
131/J3 Ozarks, Lake of the (lake), Mo,US
68/E1 Ózd, Hun.
75/S4 Ozernoy (cape), Rus.
128/B3 Ozette (lake), Wa,US
129/L3 Ozhiski (lake), On,Can.
66/A2 Ozieri, It.
55/K3 Ozimek, Pol.
58/B6 Ozoir-la-Ferrière, Fr.
134/C4 Ozona, Tx,US
55/K3 Ozorków, Pol.
84/C4 Ōzu, Japan

P

61/H1 Paar (riv.), Ger.
108/B4 Paarl, SAfr.
55/K3 Pabianice, Pol.
90/E3 Pābna, Bang.
114/F6 Pacaás Novos (mts.), Braz.
114/F6 Pacaás Novos Nat'l Park, Braz.
115/H4 Pacajá (riv.), Braz.
114/C5 Pacasmayo, Peru
66/C4 Paceco, It.
114/C6 Pachacamac (ruins), Peru
66/D4 Pachino, It.
90/C3 Pachmarhī, India
44/B4 Pacific (ocean)
128/B3 Pacific (ranges), BC,Can.
138/K11 Pacifica, Ca,US
137/B2 Pacifico (mtn.), Ca,US
124/D4 Pacific Rim Nat'l Park, BC,Can.
92/D5 Pacinan (cape), Indo.
92/D5 Pacitan, Indo.
65/P10 Paço de Arcos, Port.
92/B4 Padang, Indo.
92/B4 Padangpanjang, Indo.
92/A3 Padangsidempuan, Indo.
53/G4 Paddock Wood, Eng,UK
57/F5 Paderborn, Ger.
79/J3 Pad Īdan, Pak.
51/F4 Padiham, Eng,UK
68/E3 Padina, Serb.
48/E2 Padjelanta Nat'l Park, Swe.
63/J4 Padova (Padua), It.
110/B2 Padrão, Ponta do (pt.), Ang.
134/D5 Padre Island Nat'l Seashore, Tx,US
64/A1 Padrón, Sp.
108/D4 Padrone (cape), SAfr.
52/B5 Padstow, Eng,UK
63/J4 Padua (Padova), It.
132/B4 Paducah, Ky,US
134/C3 Paducah, Tx,US
86/E4 Paektŏk-san (mtn.), SKor.
86/D2 Paektu-San (mtn.), NKor.
86/C4 Paengnyŏng (isl.), SKor.
68/B3 Pag (isl.), Cro.
88/D6 Pagadian, Phil.
92/B4 Pagai Selatan (isl.), Indo.
92/A4 Pagai Utara (isl.), Indo.
98/D3 Pagan (isl.), NMar.
130/E3 Page, Az,US
99/T10 Pago Pago (cap.), ASam.
130/F3 Pagosa Springs, Co,US
132/C1 Pagwachuan (riv.), On,Can.
92/B3 Pahang (riv.), Malay.
130/D3 Pahrump, Nv,US
130/C3 Pahute Mesa (upland), Nv,US
87/C5 Pai (lake), China
67/L7 Paiania, Gre.
52/C6 Paignton, Eng,UK
48/H3 Päijänne (lake), Fin.
89/C3 Pailin, Camb.
126/T10 Pailolo (chan.), Hi,US
70/D3 Paimio, Fin.
118/C2 Paine, Chile
119/J7 Paine (peak), Chile
132/D3 Painesville, Oh,US
52/C2 Painscastle, Wal,UK
129/J2 Paint (lake), Mb,Can.
130/E4 Painted (des.), Az,US
134/D4 Paint Rock, Tx,US
132/D4 Paintsville, Ky,US
49/C3 Paisley, Sc,UK
90/C4 Paithan, India
48/G2 Pajala, Swe.
55/K3 Pajęczno, Pol.
123/E6 Pajonal Abajo, Pan.
92/B3 Pakanbaru, Indo.
97/G6 Pakenham, Austl.
119/J7 Pakenham (cape), Chile
67/J5 Pákhnes (peak), Gre.
71/X9 Pakhra (riv.), Rus.
79/H3 Pakistan (ctry.)
68/B3 Paklenica Nat'l Park, Cro.
91/G3 Pakokku, Myan.
128/F3 Pakowki (lake), Ab,Can.
79/K2 Pākpattan, Pak.
91/H6 Pak Phanang, Thai.
68/C3 Pakrac, Cro.
68/D2 Paks, Hun.
89/D3 Pakxe, Laos
102/H6 Pala, Chad
65/N9 Palacio Real, Sp.
65/G2 Palafrugell, Sp.
66/D4 Palagonia, It.
66/E1 Palagruža (isls.), Cro.
67/F3 Palaiokastritsa, Gre.
90/D4 Pālakolla, India
65/G2 Palamós, Sp.
92/D4 Palangkaraya, Indo.
90/B3 Pālanpur, India
126/T10 Palaoa (pt.), Hi,US
110/E5 Palapye, Bots.
90/C5 Palar (riv.), India
64/B1 Palas de Rey, Sp.
138/P15 Palatine, Il,US
135/H4 Palatka, Fl,US
98/C4 Palau (ctry.)
88/C6 Palawan (isl.), Phil.
88/C5 Palawan (passage), Phil.
90/C6 Pālayankottai, India
66/D4 Palazzolo Acreide, It.
102/G8 Palé, EqG.
93/F3 Paleleh, Indo.
92/B4 Palembang, Indo.
118/B4 Palena (riv.), Chile
64/C1 Palencia, Sp.
133/Q9 Palermo, On,Can.
66/C3 Palermo, It.
134/E4 Palestine, Tx,US
134/E3 Palestine (lake), Tx,US
79/K5 Pālghar, India
86/E4 P'algong-san (mtn.), SKor.
116/B3 Palhoça, Braz.
90/B2 Pāli, India
119/K8 Pali Aike Nat'l Park, Chile
68/D2 Palić, Serb.
126/V13 Palikea (peak), Hi,US
98/E4 Palikir (cap.), Micr.
67/H3 Paliouríon, Ákra (cape), Gre.
137/F5 Palisades Park, NJ,US
90/B3 Pālitāna, India
68/C3 Paljenik (peak), Bosn.
90/C6 Palk (str.), India, SrL.
48/H1 Pallas-Ounastunturin Nat'l Park, Fin.
48/H1 Pallastunturi (peak), Fin.
115/J6 Palma (riv.), Braz.
65/G3 Palma, Sp.
64/C4 Palma del Río, Sp.
66/C4 Palma di Montechiaro, It.
115/L5 Palmares, Braz.
116/B3 Palmas, Braz.
104/D5 Palmas (cape), Libr.
123/F3 Palma Soriano, Cuba
135/H4 Palm Bay, Fl,US
96/H8 Palm Beach, Austl.
137/B1 Palmdale, Ca,US
116/B3 Palmeira, Braz.
115/L5 Palmeira dos Índios, Braz.
110/B2 Palmeirinhas, Ponta das (pt.), Ang.
65/Q10 Palmela, Port.
111/V Palmer (arch.), Ant.
111/V Palmer Land (reg.), Ant.
96/C3 Palmerston (cape), Austl.
99/J6 Palmerston (atoll), CookIs.
95/H7 Palmerston, NZ
96/B2 Palmerston Nat'l Park, Austl.
95/H7 Palmerston North, NZ
135/H5 Palmetto, Fl,US
135/H4 Palm Harbor, Fl,US
66/D3 Palmi, It.
118/C2 Palmilla, Chile
114/C3 Palmira, Col.
130/C4 Palm Springs, Ca,US
99/J4 Palmyra (isl.), PacUS
78/C2 Palmyra (ruins), Syria
90/E3 Palmyras (pt.), India
50/E2 Palnackie, Sc,UK
90/C5 Palni, India
88/D5 Palo, Phil.
138/K12 Palo Alto, Ca,US
123/M8 Palo Bola, Mex.
131/G3 Palo Duro (cr.), Ok, Tx,US
63/J4 Palon (peak), It.
134/D3 Palo Pinto, Tx,US
65/E4 Palos, Cabo de (cape), Sp.
138/Q16 Palos Hills, Il,US
137/B3 Palos Verdes Estates, Ca,US
122/D5 Palo Verde Nat'l Park, Mex.
90/D2 Pālpa, Nepal
117/C1 Palpalá, Arg.
93/G4 Palpetu (cape), Indo.
80/D2 Palu, Turk.
88/D5 Paluan, Phil.
92/C3 Pamangkat, Indo.
62/D5 Pamiers, Fr.
81/B4 Pamir (riv.), Afg., Taj.
81/B4 Pamir (reg.), China, Taj.
135/J3 Pamlico (riv.), NC,US
135/J3 Pamlico (sound), NC,US
134/C3 Pampa, Tx,US
118/E2 Pampa Humida (plain), Arg.
118/E3 Pampas (plain), Arg.
118/D3 Pampa Seca (plain), Arg.
114/D2 Pamplona, Col.
64/E1 Pamplona, Sp.
69/K5 Pamukova, Turk.
88/E6 Panabo, Phil.
130/D3 Panaca, Nv,US
90/C6 Panadura, SrL.
69/G4 Panagyurishte, Bul.
92/B5 Panaitan (isl.), Indo.
90/B4 Pānāji, India
123/E6 Panama (ctry.)
123/E6 Panama (can.), Pan.
123/F6 Panamá (cap.), Pan.
123/F6 Panama (gulf), Pan.
123/F6 Panama (isth.), Pan.
135/G4 Panama City, Fl,US
130/C3 Panamint (range), Ca,US
63/J4 Panaro (riv.), It.
88/D5 Panay (isl.), Phil.
130/C3 Pancake (range), Nv,US
68/E3 Pančevo, Serb.
68/E4 Pančičev vrh (peak), Serb.
69/H3 Panciu, Rom.
110/E4 Pandamatenga, Bots.
117/B2 Pan de Azúcar Nat'l Park, Chile
90/C4 Pandharpur, India
119/G2 Pando, Uru.
70/E5 Panevėžys, Lith.
81/D3 Panfilov, Kaz.
89/B1 Pang (riv.), Myan.
99/H7 Pangai, Tonga
67/J2 Pangaion (peak), Gre.
107/C3 Pangani (riv.), Tanz.
53/E4 Pangbourne, Eng,UK
92/A3 Pangkalanberandan, Indo.
93/F4 Pangkalaseang (cape), Indo.
92/C4 Pangkalpinang, Indo.
130/D3 Panguitch, Ut,US
93/F2 Pangutaran, Phil.
88/D6 Pangutaran (isl.), Phil.
134/C3 Panhandle, Tx,US
93/J4 Paniai (lake), Indo.
126/R10 Paniau (peak), Hi,US
98/F7 Panié (peak), NCal.
90/C2 Pānīpat, India
79/K1 Panj (Pyandzh) (riv.), Afg., Taj.
90/D3 Panna, India
96/F7 Pannikin (isl.), Austl.
116/B2 Panorama, Braz.
51/E6 Pant, Eng,UK
53/G3 Pant (riv.), Eng,UK
115/G7 Pantanal Matogrossense Nat'l Park, Braz.
66/B4 Pantelleria (isl.), It.
58/B5 Pantin, Fr.
64/B1 Pantón, Sp.
122/B3 Pánuco, Mex.
122/B3 Pánuco (riv.), Mex.
91/H2 Panzhihua, China
66/E3 Paola, It.
131/J3 Paola, Ks,US
130/F3 Paonia, Co,US
102/J6 Paoua, CAfr.
89/C3 Paoy Pet, Camb.
68/C2 Pápa, Hun.
122/D5 Papagayo (gulf), CR
122/B3 Papantla de Olarte, Mex.
99/X15 Papara, FrPol.
99/X15 Papeete (cap.), FrPol.
57/E2 Papenburg, Ger.
56/B5 Papendrecht, Neth.
99/X15 Papenoo, FrPol.
99/X15 Papetoai, FrPol.
80/J4 Paphos, Cyp.
131/H2 Papillion, Ne,US
67/G2 Papingut, Maj'e (peak), Alb.
93/H4 Papisoi (cape), Indo.
98/D5 Papua (gulf), PNG
98/D5 Papua New Guinea (ctry.)
116/C1 Pará (riv.), Braz.
116/K7 Paracambi, Braz.
115/J7 Paracatu, Braz.
88/B4 Paracel (isls.)
77/N7 Parace Vela (Okino-Tori-Shima) (isl.), Japan
68/E4 Paraćin, Serb.
65/N8 Paracuellos, Sp.
116/C1 Pará de Minas, Braz.
90/E3 Paradip, India
128/F2 Paradise Hill, Sk,Can.
115/J4 Paragominas, Braz.
135/F2 Paragould, Ar,US
114/F6 Paraguá (riv.), Bol.
114/F2 Paragua (riv.), Ven.
115/H6 Paraguaçu, Braz.
115/L6 Paraguaçu (riv.), Braz.
115/B2 Paraguaçu Paulista, Braz.
115/G6 Paraguai (riv.), Braz.
123/G5 Paraguaná (pen.), Ven.
117/E2 Paraguarí, Par.
117/D3 Paraguay (ctry.)
116/D2 Paraíba do Sul (riv.), Braz.
116/H8 Paraibuna (riv.), Braz.
115/J6 Paraíso do Norte de Goiás, Braz.
116/G7 Paraisópolis, Braz.
105/F4 Parakou, Ben.
115/G2 Paramaribo (cap.), Sur.
114/C2 Paramillo Nat'l Park, Col.
115/K6 Paramirim (riv.), Braz.
137/B3 Paramount, Ca,US
137/F5 Paramus, NJ,US
75/R4 Paramushir (isl.), Rus.
116/B3 Paraná (state), Braz.
117/E3 Paraná (riv.), SAm.
116/B3 Paranaguá, Braz.
116/B1 Paranaíba, Braz.
116/B1 Paranaíba (riv.), Braz.
116/B2 Paranapanema (riv.), Braz.
116/B3 Paranapiacaba (range), Braz.
113/D4 Paranatinga (riv.), Braz.
115/H8 Paranavaí, Braz.
93/F2 Parang, Phil.
116/C1 Paraopeba, Braz.
115/J8 Parapanema (riv.), Braz.
114/F7 Parapetí (riv.), Bol.
116/J8 Parati, Braz.
116/H8 Paratinga (riv.), Braz.
90/C4 Parbhani, India
54/F2 Parchim, Ger.
55/M3 Parczew, Pol.
80/M8 Pardes Hanna-Karkur, Isr.
90/B3 Pārdi, India
116/G6 Pardo (riv.), Braz.
55/H3 Pardubice, Czh.
55/J4 Pardubický (reg.), Czh.
92/D5 Pare, Indo.
114/F6 Parecis (mts.), Braz.
65/P10 Parede, Port.
118/C2 Paredones, Chile
132/E1 Parent (lake), Qu,Can.
93/E4 Parepare, Indo.
65/L6 Parets del Vallès, Sp.
67/G3 Párga, Gre.
123/J5 Paria (gulf), Trin., Ven.
130/E3 Paria (riv.), Az, Ut,US
123/J5 Paria (pen.), Ven.
123/J6 Pariaguán, Ven.
92/B4 Pariaman, Indo.
114/E7 Parinacota (peak), Bol.
115/G4 Parintins, Braz.
58/B6 Paris (cap.), Fr.
134/E3 Paris, Ar,US
132/B4 Paris, Tn,US
134/E3 Paris, Tx,US
130/F2 Park (range), Co,US
130/D4 Parker, Az,US
131/F3 Parker, Co,US
132/D4 Parkersburg, WV,US
97/D2 Parkes, Austl.
53/H3 Parkeston, Eng,UK
132/B2 Park Falls, Wi,US
50/B2 Parkgate, NI,UK
52/A5 Park Head (pt.), UK
53/E5 Parkhurst, Eng,UK
138/C3 Parkland, Wa,US
129/K4 Park Rapids, Mn,US
138/Q15 Park Ridge, Il,US
137/F4 Park Ridge, NJ,US
129/J3 Park River, ND,US
137/K7 Parkville, Md,US
138/L9 Parkway-Sacramento, Ca,US
64/D2 Parla, Sp.
90/D4 Parlakhemundi, India
90/C4 Parli, India
63/J4 Parma, It.
132/D3 Parma, Oh,US
115/K4 Parnaíba, Braz.
115/K4 Parnaíba (riv.), Braz.
67/H3 Parnassos Nat'l Park, Gre.
67/H3 Párnis (peak), Gre.
67/H4 Párnon (mts.), Gre.
70/E4 Pärnu, Est.
97/C1 Paroo (riv.), Austl.
67/J4 Páros (isl.), Gre.
108/B4 Parow, SAfr.
130/D3 Parowan, Ut,US
118/C3 Parral, Chile
96/H8 Parramatta, Austl.
122/A2 Parras de la Fuente, Mex.
52/D4 Parrett (riv.), Eng,UK
122/E6 Parrita, CR
125/H2 Parry (bay), Nun,Can.
124/F1 Parry (chan.), Nun,Can.
125/R7 Parry (isls.), NW,Nun,Can.
132/D2 Parry Sound, On,Can.
61/G3 Parseierspitze (peak), Aus.
129/H4 Parshall, ND,US
137/F5 Parsippany, NJ,US
128/C2 Parsnip (riv.), BC,Can.
131/J3 Parsons, Ks,US
70/C2 Pårtefjället (peak), Swe.
62/C3 Parthenay, Fr.
66/C3 Partinico, It.
83/L3 Partizansk, Rus.
132/D1 Partridge (riv.), On,Can.
90/C4 Partūr, India
115/H4 Paru (riv.), Braz.
90/D4 Pārvathīpuram, India
51/G5 Parwich, Eng,UK
108/D2 Parys, SAfr.
133/K1 Pasadena, Nf,Can.
137/B2 Pasadena, Ca,US
137/K7 Pasadena, Md,US
134/E4 Pasadena, Tx,US
114/C4 Pasaje, Ecu.
89/C3 Pa Sak (riv.), Thai.
92/B3 Pasaman (peak), Indo.
135/F4 Pascagoula, Ms,US
69/H2 Paşcani, Rom.
128/D4 Pasco, Wa,US
119/J7 Pascua (riv.), Chile
58/A3 Pas-de-Calais (dept.), Fr.
58/B3 Pas-en-Artois, Fr.
88/D5 Pasig, Phil.
91/G2 Pāsighāt, India
80/E2 Pasinler, Turk.
55/K1 Pasłęk, Pol.
55/L2 Pasłęka (riv.), Pol.
68/B4 Pašman (isl.), Cro.
79/H3 Pasni, Pak.
117/E2 Paso de Los Libres, Arg.
118/C2 Paso del Planchón (peak), Chile
130/B4 Paso Robles (El Paso de Robles), Ca,US
136/M3 Pass (peak), Yk,Can.
137/F5 Passaic, NJ,US
137/F5 Passaic (riv.), NJ,US
116/J7 Passa Quatro, Braz.
63/K2 Passau, Ger.
58/C2 Passendale, Belg.
66/D4 Passero (pt.), It.
117/F2 Passo Fundo, Braz.
116/A3 Passo Fundo (res.), Braz.
105/E3 Passoré (prov.), Burk.
116/C2 Passos, Braz.
63/G4 Passy, Fr.
114/C4 Pastaza (riv.), Ecu., Peru
114/C3 Pasto, Col.
136/F3 Pastol (bay), Ak,US
92/D5 Pasuruan, Indo.
68/D2 Pásztó, Hun.
118/D4 Patagonia (reg.), Arg.
92/B4 Patah (peak), Indo.
90/B3 Pātan, India
137/K7 Patapsco (riv.), Md,US
137/G5 Patchogue, NY,US
52/D3 Patchway, Eng,UK
51/G3 Pateley Bridge, Eng,UK
65/E3 Paterna, Sp.
137/F5 Paterson, NJ,US
79/L2 Pathānkot, India
128/G5 Pathfinder (res.), Wy,US
92/D5 Pati, Indo.
114/C3 Patía (riv.), Col.
79/L2 Patiāla, India
93/F2 Patikul, Phil.
90/E2 Patna, India
50/D1 Patna, Sc,UK
93/F1 Patnongon, Phil.
80/E2 Patnos, Turk.
116/A3 Pato Branco, Braz.
135/G2 Patoka (riv.), In,US
67/F2 Patos, Alb.
115/L5 Patos, Braz.
116/B4 Patos (lake), Braz.
116/C1 Patos de Minas, Braz.
67/G3 Pátrai, Gre.
67/G3 Patrai (gulf), Gre.
119/J7 Patricio Lynch (isl.), Chile
51/H4 Patrington, Eng,UK
116/C1 Patrocínio, Braz.
89/C5 Pattani, Thai.
89/C3 Pattaya, Thai.
57/G4 Pattensen, Ger.
66/D3 Patti, It.
52/D1 Pattingham, Eng,UK
90/C5 Pattukkottai, India
136/N4 Pattullo (mtn.), BC,Can.
122/E4 Patuca (pt.), Hon.
122/D5 Patuca (riv.), Hon.
137/K8 Patuxent (riv.), Md,US
62/C5 Pau, Fr.
115/L7 Pau Brasil, Braz.
114/E5 Pauini (riv.), Braz.
116/F7 Paulínia, Braz.
115/L5 Paulo Afonso, Braz.
115/L5 Paulo Afonso Nat'l Park, Braz.
137/E6 Paulsboro, NJ,US
131/H4 Pauls Valley, Ok,US
52/D4 Paulton, Eng,UK
91/G4 Paungde, Myan.
81/C5 Pauri, India
63/H4 Pavia, It.
69/G4 Pavlikeni, Bul.
81/C1 Pavlodar, Kaz.
136/F4 Pavlof (vol.), Ak,US
72/E2 Pavlograd, Ukr.
70/J5 Pavlovo, Rus.
63/J4 Pavullo nel Frignano, It.
92/D4 Pawan (riv.), Indo.
131/H3 Pawhuska, Ok,US
89/B2 Pawn (riv.), Myan.
131/H3 Pawnee (riv.), Ks,US
132/C3 Paw Paw, Mi,US
133/G3 Pawtucket, RI,US
67/F3 Paxoí (isl.), Gre.
67/G3 Paxoí (Yáios), Gre.
92/B4 Payakumbuh, Indo.
118/C3 Payén, Altiplanicie del (plat.), Arg.
128/D4 Payette, Id,US
128/D5 Payette (riv.), Id,US
71/P1 Pay-Khoy (mts.), Rus.
125/J3 Payne (lake), Qu,Can.
119/F2 Paysandú, Uru.
119/F1 Paysandú (dept.), Uru.
62/C3 Pays de la Loire (reg.), Fr.
130/E4 Payson, Az,US
130/E2 Payson, Ut,US
117/C3 Payún (peak), Arg.
80/D3 Pazarcık, Turk.
69/G4 Pazardzhik, Bul.
72/D5 Pazaryeri, Turk.
116/A2 Peabiru, Braz.
124/E3 Peace (riv.), Ab, BC,Can.
135/H5 Peace (riv.), Fl,US
128/D1 Peace River, Ab,Can.
128/D3 Peachland, BC,Can.
135/G3 Peachtree City, Ga,US
51/G5 Peak District Nat'l Park, Eng,UK
126/W13 Pearl (har.), Hi,US
135/F4 Pearl (riv.), La, Ms,US
135/F3 Pearl, Ms,US
137/B1 Pearland, Ca,US
99/H2 Pearl and Hermes (reef), Hi,US
126/W13 Pearl City, Hi,US
88/B3 Pearl River (inlet), China
137/F4 Pearl River, NY,US
134/D4 Pearsall, Tx,US
125/R7 Peary (chan.), Nun,Can.
131/H4 Pease (riv.), Tx,US
53/E2 Pebworth, Eng,UK
68/E4 Peć, Serb.
71/N2 Pechora, Rus.
71/M1 Pechora (bay), Rus.
71/M2 Pechora (riv.), Rus.
131/G5 Pecos (riv.), NM, Tx,US
134/C4 Pecos, Tx,US
131/F4 Pecos Nat'l Mon., NM,US
58/C3 Pecquencourt, Fr.
68/D2 Pécs, Hun.
123/E6 Pedasí, Pan.
97/C4 Pedder (lake), Austl.
123/G4 Pedernales, DRep.
116/B2 Pederneiras, Braz.
137/C3 Pedley, Ca,US
115/K7 Pedra Azul, Braz.
116/G7 Pedreira, Braz.
115/K5 Pedreiras, Braz.
90/D6 Pedro (pt.), SrL.
123/F4 Pedro Cays (isls.), Jam.
114/E3 Pedro II, Braz.
117/E1 Pedro Juan Caballero, Par.
116/C1 Pedro Leopoldo, Braz.
116/A4 Pedro Osório, Braz.
49/D3 Peebles, Sc,UK
96/F6 Peel (isl.), Austl.
124/G1 Peel (sound), Nun,Can.
136/L2 Peel (riv.), Yk,Can.
50/D3 Peel, IM,UK
51/F1 Peel Fell (mtn.), Eng,UK
59/E1 Peer, Belg.

Porcu – Radcl
179

136/K2 **Porcupine** (riv.), Yk,Can, Ak,US
96/B3 **Porcupine Gorge Nat'l Park**, Austl.
129/H2 **Porcupine Plain**, Sk,Can.
63/K4 **Pordenone**, It.
48/G3 **Pori**, Fin.
95/H7 **Porirua**, NZ
70/E4 **Porkhov**, Rus.
123/J5 **Porlamar**, Ven.
52/C4 **Porlock**, Eng,UK
83/N2 **Poronaysk**, Rus.
111/J **Porpoise** (bay), Ant.
64/A1 **Porriño**, Sp.
48/H1 **Porsangen** (fjord), Nor.
48/D4 **Porsgrunn**, Nor.
80/B2 **Porsuk** (riv.), Turk.
114/F7 **Portachuelo**, Bol.
50/B3 **Portadown**, NI,UK
50/C3 **Portaferry**, NI,UK
132/C3 **Portage**, Mi,US
132/B3 **Portage**, Wi,US
129/J3 **Portage la Prairie**, Mb,Can.
128/B3 **Port Alberni**, BC,Can.
64/B3 **Portalegre**, Port.
64/B3 **Portalegre** (dist.), Port.
131/G4 **Portales**, NM,US
108/D4 **Port Alfred**, SAfr.
128/B3 **Port Alice**, BC,Can.
128/C3 **Port Angeles**, Wa,US
123/F4 **Port Antonio**, Jam.
49/C2 **Port Appin**, Sc,UK
134/E4 **Port Arthur**, Tx,US
133/K1 **Port au Choix**, Nf,Can.
95/C4 **Port Augusta**, Austl.
123/G4 **Port-au-Prince** (cap.), Haiti
50/C3 **Portavogie**, NI,UK
57/F4 **Porta Westfalica**, Ger.
91/F5 **Port Blair**, India
134/E4 **Port Bolivar**, Tx,US
104/E5 **Port-Bouët**, C.d'Iv.
125/K2 **Port Burwell**, Qu,Can.
133/H1 **Port-Cartier**, Qu,Can.
135/H5 **Port Charlotte**, Fl,US
137/G5 **Port Chester**, NY,US
132/D3 **Port Clinton**, Oh,US
133/R10 **Port Colborne**, On,Can.
133/Q8 **Port Credit**, On,Can.
133/S8 **Port Darlington**, On,Can.
97/C4 **Port Davey** (har.), Austl.
123/G4 **Port-de-Paix**, Haiti
92/B3 **Port Dickson**, Malay.
136/M4 **Port Edward**, BC,Can.
115/H4 **Portel**, Braz.
132/D2 **Port Elgin**, Can.
108/D4 **Port Elizabeth**, SAfr.
50/D3 **Port Erin**, IM,UK
108/L10 **Porterville**, SAfr.
130/C3 **Porterville**, Ca,US
62/F4 **Portes-lès-Valence**, Fr.
102/B3 **Port-Étienne**, Mrta.
62/D5 **Portet-sur-Garonne**, Fr.
52/B3 **Port Eynon**, Wal,UK
52/B3 **Port Eynon** (pt.), Wal,UK
102/G8 **Port-Gentil**, Gabon
49/C3 **Port Glasgow**, Sc,UK
50/B2 **Portglenone**, NI,UK
52/C3 **Porth**, Wal,UK
105/G5 **Port Harcourt**, Nga.
128/B3 **Port Hardy**, BC,Can.
133/J2 **Port Hawkesbury**, NS,Can.
52/C4 **Porthcawl**, Wal,UK
95/A3 **Port Hedland**, Austl.
52/A6 **Porthleven**, Eng,UK
50/D6 **Porthmadog**, Wal,UK
137/A2 **Port Hueneme**, Ca,US
132/D3 **Port Huron**, Mi,US
64/A4 **Portimão**, Port.
52/B5 **Port Isaac**, Eng,UK
52/D4 **Portishead**, Eng,UK
137/G5 **Port Jefferson**, NY,US
97/C4 **Portland** (cape), Austl.
123/F4 **Portland** (pt.), Jam.
52/D6 **Portland** (pt.), Eng,UK
136/N4 **Portland** (inlet), BC,Can, Ak,US
132/C3 **Portland**, In,US
133/G3 **Portland**, Me,US
128/C4 **Portland**, Or,US
135/G2 **Portland**, Tn,US
52/D5 **Portland, Isle of** (pen.), Eng,UK
134/D4 **Port Lavaca**, Tx,US
95/C4 **Port Lincoln**, Austl.
109/S15 **Port Louis** (cap.), Mrts.
97/E1 **Port Macquarie**, Austl.
50/B5 **Portmarnock**, Ire.
128/B3 **Port McNeill**, BC,Can.
133/H1 **Port-Menier**, Qu,Can.
98/D5 **Port Moresby** (cap.), PNG
133/G1 **Portneuf** (riv.), Qu,Can.
66/A1 **Porto** (gulf), Fr.
64/A2 **Porto**, Port.
64/A2 **Porto** (dist.), Port.
116/B4 **Pôrto Alegre**, Braz.
110/B3 **Porto Amboim**, Ang.
63/K5 **Portocivitanova**, It.
66/C4 **Porto Empedocle**, It.
66/B1 **Portoferraio**, It.
116/C2 **Pôrto Ferreira**, Braz.
123/J5 **Port-of-Spain** (cap.), Trin.
63/K4 **Portogruaro**, It.
63/J4 **Portomaggiore**, It.
115/J6 **Porto Nacional**, Braz.
105/F5 **Porto-Novo** (cap.), Ben.
135/H4 **Port Orange**, Fl,US
66/C1 **Porto San Giorgio**, It.
66/B1 **Porto Santo Stefano**, It.
66/A2 **Porto Torres**, It.
116/B3 **Porto União**, Braz.
114/F5 **Porto Velho**, Braz.
114/B4 **Portoviejo**, Ecu.
50/C2 **Portpatrick**, Sc,UK
97/C3 **Port Phillip** (bay), Austl.
95/C4 **Port Pirie**, Austl.
50/B1 **Portrush**, NI,UK
106/C2 **Port Said** (Būr Sa'īd), Egypt
135/G4 **Port Saint Joe**, Fl,US
62/F5 **Port-Saint-Louis-du-Rhône**, Fr.
135/H5 **Port Saint Lucie**, Fl,US
50/D3 **Port Saint Mary**, IM,UK
53/E5 **Portsea** (isl.), Eng,UK
136/M4 **Port Simpson**, BC,Can.
53/F5 **Portslade by Sea**, Eng,UK
53/E5 **Portsmouth**, Eng,UK
53/E5 **Portsmouth** (co.), Eng,UK
133/G3 **Portsmouth**, NH,US
132/D4 **Portsmouth**, Oh,US
132/E4 **Portsmouth**, Va,US
97/E2 **Port Stephens** (bay), Austl.
50/B1 **Portstewart**, NI,UK
106/D5 **Port Sudan** (Būr Sūdān), Sudan
52/C3 **Port Talbot**, Wal,UK
128/C3 **Port Townsend**, Wa,US
64/A3 **Portugal** (ctry.)
64/D1 **Portugalete**, Sp.
123/H6 **Portuguesa** (riv.), Ven.
98/F6 **Port-Vila** (cap.), Van.
137/G5 **Port Washington**, NY,US
132/C3 **Port Washington**, Wi,US
50/D2 **Port William**, Sc,UK
117/E2 **Posadas**, Arg.
64/C4 **Posadas**, Sp.
68/C3 **Posavina** (val.), Bosn., Cro.
93/F4 **Poso** (lake), Indo.
86/D5 **Posŏng**, SKor.
138/C2 **Possession** (sound), Wa,US
134/C3 **Post**, Tx,US
70/E5 **Postavy**, Bela.
102/F3 **Poste Maurice Cortier** (ruins), Alg.
102/F3 **Poste Weygand** (ruins), Alg.
128/D4 **Post Falls**, Id,US
108/C3 **Postmasburg**, SAfr.
68/B3 **Postojna**, Slov.
108/D2 **Potchefstroom**, SAfr.
131/J4 **Poteau**, Ok,US
66/D2 **Potenza**, It.
66/C1 **Potenza** (riv.), It.
128/D4 **Potholes** (res.), Wa,US
115/K5 **Poti** (riv.), Braz.
73/G4 **P'ot'i**, Geo.
137/J7 **Potomac**, Md,US
132/E4 **Potomac** (riv.), Md, Va,US
114/E7 **Potosí**, Bol.
131/K3 **Potosi**, Mo,US
117/C2 **Potrerillos**, Chile
54/G2 **Potsdam**, Ger.
132/F2 **Potsdam**, NY,US
53/F3 **Potters Bar**, Eng,UK
53/F2 **Potterspury**, Eng,UK
53/F2 **Potton**, Eng,UK
90/D6 **Pottuvil**, SrL.
132/F3 **Poughkeepsie**, NY,US
50/B5 **Poulaphouca** (res.), Ire.
51/G5 **Poulter** (riv.), Eng,UK
51/F4 **Poulton-le-Fylde**, Eng,UK
63/G4 **Pourri** (mtn.), Fr.
116/H7 **Pouso Alegre**, Braz.
89/C3 **Pouthisat**, Camb.
89/C3 **Pouthisat** (riv.), Camb.
55/K4 **Považská Bystrica**, Slvk.
64/A2 **Póvoa de Varzim**, Port.
73/G2 **Povorino**, Rus.
83/L3 **Povorotnyy, Mys** (cape), Rus.
125/J2 **Povungnituk** (riv.), Qu,Can.
129/G4 **Powder** (riv.), Mt, Wy,US
130/E3 **Powell** (lake), Az, Ut,US
128/F4 **Powell**, Wy,US
128/B3 **Powell River**, BC,Can.
133/R9 **Power** (res.), NY,US
52/C2 **Powys** (co.), Wal,UK
52/C1 **Powys, Vale** (val.), Wal,UK
115/H7 **Poxoréo**, Braz.
88/C2 **Poyang** (lake), China
51/F5 **Poynton**, Eng,UK
64/A1 **Poyo**, Sp.
68/E3 **Požarevac**, Serb.
122/B3 **Poza Rica**, Mex.
68/E4 **Požega**, Serb.
53/J2 **Poznań**, Pol.
64/D4 **Pozo Alcón**, Sp.
64/C3 **Pozoblanco**, Sp.
65/N9 **Pozuelo de Alarcón**, Sp.
66/D4 **Pozzallo**, It.
55/K2 **Prabuty**, Pol.
89/B4 **Pracham Hiang** (pt.), Thai.
55/H4 **Prachatice**, Czh.
89/C3 **Prachin Buri**, Thai.
89/C3 **Prachin Buri** (riv.), Thai.
89/B4 **Prachuap Khiri Khan**, Thai.
55/J3 **Praděd** (peak), Czh.
115/L7 **Prado**, Braz.
137/C3 **Prado** (dam), Ca,US
55/H3 **Prague** (Praha) (cap.), Czh.
55/H3 **Praha** (reg.), Czh.
69/G3 **Prahova** (co.), Rom.
65/S12 **Praia de Victória**, Azor.,Port.
116/G9 **Praia Grande**, Braz.
132/B3 **Prairie du Chien**, Wi,US
133/N6 **Prairies** (riv.), Qu,Can.
129/J4 **Prairies, Coteau des** (upland), US
134/E4 **Prairie View**, Tx,US
89/B3 **Pran Buri** (res.), Thai.
90/D4 **Prānhita** (riv.), India
92/A3 **Prapat**, Indo.
89/D3 **Prasat Preah Vihear**, Camb.
55/K3 **Praszka**, Pol.
116/B1 **Prata**, Braz.
63/J5 **Prato**, It.
66/C1 **Pratola Peligna**, It.
119/J7 **Pratt** (isl.), Chile
131/H3 **Pratt**, Ks,US
135/G3 **Prattville**, Al,US
64/B1 **Pravia**, Sp.
52/C6 **Prawle** (pt.), Eng,UK
93/E5 **Praya**, Indo.
69/G3 **Predeal**, Rom.
129/H3 **Preeceville**, Sk,Can
51/F6 **Prees**, Eng,UK
51/F4 **Preesall**, Eng,UK
54/F1 **Preetz**, Ger.
55/L1 **Pregolya** (riv.), Rus.
132/E1 **Preissac** (lake), On,Can.
89/D4 **Prek Pouthi**, Camb.
65/L7 **Premiá de Mar**, Sp
55/G2 **Prenzlau**, Ger.
55/J4 **Přerov**, Czh.
61/G5 **Presanella** (peak), It.
51/F5 **Prescot**, Eng,UK
132/F2 **Prescott**, On,Can.
130/D4 **Prescott**, Az,US
68/E4 **Preševo**, Serb.
117/D2 **Presidencia Roque Sáenz Peña**, Arg.
115/K5 **Presidente Dutra**, Braz.
116/A2 **Presidente Epitácio**, Braz.
116/B2 **Presidente Prudente**, Braz.
118/B5 **Presidente Ríos** (lake), Chile
116/B2 **Presidente Venceslau**, Braz.
134/B4 **Presidio**, Tx,US
69/H4 **Preslav**, Bul.
58/B6 **Presles-en-Brie**, Fr.
55/L4 **Prešov**, Slvk.
55/L4 **Prešovský** (reg.), Slvk.
55/G2 **Prespa** (lake), Eur.
133/G2 **Presque Isle**, Me,US
51/E5 **Prestatyn**, Wal,UK
105/E5 **Prestea**, Gha.
52/D2 **Presteigne**, Wal,UK
55/G4 **Přeštice**, Czh.
97/G5 **Preston**, Austl.
51/F4 **Preston**, Eng,UK
52/D5 **Preston**, Eng,UK
128/F5 **Preston**, Id,US
132/D4 **Prestonsburg**, Ky,US
51/F4 **Prestwich**, Eng,UK
49/C3 **Prestwick**, Sc,UK
53/F3 **Prestwood**, Eng,UK
115/J6 **Prêto** (riv.), Braz.
108/E2 **Pretoria** (cap.), SAfr.
57/F4 **Preussisch Oldendorf**, Ger.
55/G3 **Préveza**, Gre.
136/D4 **Pribilof** (isls.), Ak,US
68/D4 **Priboj**, Serb.
55/G4 **Příbram**, Czh.
130/E3 **Price**, Ut,US
130/E3 **Price** (riv.), Ut,US
135/F4 **Prichard**, Al,US
64/C4 **Priego de Córdoba**, Sp.
108/C3 **Prieska**, SAfr.
128/D3 **Priest** (lake), Id,US
128/D3 **Priest River**, Id,US
62/C1 **Prieta** (mtn.), Sp.
55/K4 **Prievidza**, Slvk.
54/F2 **Prignitz** (reg.), Ger.
68/C3 **Prijedor**, Bosn.
68/D4 **Prijepolje**, Serb.
73/H3 **Prikaspian** (plain), Kaz., Rus.
73/H3 **Prikumsk**, Rus.
68/E5 **Prilep**, FYROM
72/E2 **Priluki**, Ukr.
66/C2 **Prima Porta**, It.
119/J7 **Primero** (cape), Chile
53/E1 **Primethorpe**, Eng,UK
75/P5 **Primorskiy Kray**, Rus.
72/F3 **Primorsko-Akhtarsk**, Rus
128/F2 **Primrose** (lake), Ab, Sk,Can.
59/F5 **Prims** (riv.), Ger.
124/E1 **Prince Albert** (pen.), NW,Can.
124/E1 **Prince Albert** (sound), NW,Can.
129/G2 **Prince Albert**, Sk,Can.
129/G2 **Prince Albert Nat'l Park**, Sk,Can.
124/D1 **Prince Alfred** (cape), NW,Can.
125/J2 **Prince Charles** (isl.), Nun,Can.
45/L8 **Prince Edward** (isls.), SAfr.
133/J2 **Prince Edward Island** (prov.), Can.
133/J2 **Prince Edward Island Nat'l Park**, PE,Can.
128/C2 **Prince George**, BC,Can.
125/R7 **Prince Gustav Adolf** (sea), Nun,Can.
111/C **Prince Harold** (coast), Ant.
124/G1 **Prince Leopold** (isl.), Nun,Can.
56/C2 **Princenhof** (lake), Neth.
124/G1 **Prince of Wales** (isl.), Nun,Can.
124/E1 **Prince of Wales** (str.), NW,Can.
136/M4 **Prince of Wales** (isl.), Ak,US
111/C **Prince Olav** (coast), Ant.
125/R7 **Prince Patrick** (isl.), NW,Can.
124/G1 **Prince Regent** (inlet), Nun,Can.
136/M4 **Prince Rupert**, BC,Can.
53/F3 **Princes Risborough**, Eng,UK
111/A **Princess Astrid** (coast), Ant.
96/A1 **Princess Charlotte** (bay), Austl.
125/S6 **Princess Margaret** (range), Nun,Can.
111/Z **Princess Martha** (coast), Ant.
111/B **Princess Ragnhild** (coast), Ant.
128/A2 **Princess Royal** (isl.), BC,Can.
123/J5 **Princes Town**, Trin.
128/C3 **Princeton**, BC,Can.
132/B3 **Princeton**, Il,US
132/C4 **Princeton**, In,US
132/C4 **Princeton**, Ky,US
129/K4 **Princeton**, Mn,US
137/F5 **Princeton**, NJ,US
132/D4 **Princeton**, WV,US
136/J3 **Prince William** (sound), Ak,US
102/G7 **Príncipe** (isl.), SaoT.
136/K3 **Prindle** (vol.), Ak,US
128/C4 **Prineville**, Or,US
56/B5 **Prinsenbeek**, Neth.
56/C2 **Prinses Margriet** (can.), Neth.
122/E5 **Prinzapolka**, Nic.
66/D4 **Priolo di Gargallo**, It.
64/A1 **Prior** (cape), Sp.
70/F3 **Priozersk**, Rus.
72/C2 **Pripet** (marshes), Bela., Ukr.
68/E4 **Priština**, Serb.
54/G2 **Pritzwalk**, Ger.
62/F4 **Privas**, Fr.
73/H2 **Privolzhskiy**, Rus.
73/K1 **Priyutovo**, Rus.
68/E4 **Prizren**, Serb.
68/C3 **Prnjavor**, Bosn.
92/D5 **Probolinggo**, Indo.
134/D3 **Proctor** (lake), Tx,US
90/C5 **Proddatūr**, India
59/D3 **Profondeville**, Belg.
122/E6 **Progreso**, Pan.
119/T12 **Progreso**, Uru.
83/K2 **Progress**, Rus.
73/H4 **Prokhladnyy**, Rus.
81/E1 **Prokop'yevsk**, Rus.
68/E4 **Prokuplje**, Serb.
91/G4 **Prome**, Myan.
116/B2 **Promissão**, Braz.
116/B2 **Promissão** (res.), Braz.
115/L6 **Propriá**, Braz.
55/J2 **Prosna** (riv.), Pol.
136/L3 **Prospector** (mtn.), Yk,Can.
88/E6 **Prosperidad**, Phil.
55/J4 **Prostějov**, Czh.
55/L3 **Prószowice**, Pol.
69/H4 **Provadiya**, Bul.
63/G5 **Provence** (mts.), Fr.
62/F5 **Provence** (reg.), Fr.
63/G4 **Provence-Alpes-Côte d'Azur** (reg.), Fr.
114/F6 **Providência** (mts.), Braz.
133/G3 **Providence** (cap.), RI,US.
122/E5 **Providencia** (isl.), Col.
62/E2 **Provins**, Fr.
130/E2 **Provo**, Ut,US
65/T13 **Provoação**, Azor.,Port.
128/F2 **Provost**, Ab,Can.
68/C4 **Prozor**, Bosn.
116/B3 **Prudentópolis**, Braz.
51/G2 **Prudhoe**, Eng,UK
136/J1 **Prudhoe** (bay), Ak,US
55/J3 **Prudnik**, Pol.
59/F3 **Prüm** (riv.), Ger.
55/K1 **Pruszcz Gdański**, Pol.
55/L2 **Pruszków**, Pol.
69/J2 **Prut** (riv.), Eur.
111/F **Prydz** (bay), Ant.
134/E2 **Pryor** (cr.), Ok,US
55/L2 **Przasnysz**, Pol.
55/H3 **Przemków**, Pol.
55/M4 **Przemyśl**, Pol.
55/M3 **Przeworsk**, Pol.
81/C3 **Przheval'sk**, Kyr.
70/C5 **Przylądek Rozewie** (cape), Pol.
55/L3 **Przysucha**, Pol.
67/J3 **Psará** (isl.), Gre.
70/F4 **Pskov** (lake), Est., Rus.
70/F4 **Pskov**, Rus.
70/F4 **Pskovskaya Obl.**, Rus.
55/K4 **Pszczyna**, Pol.
67/G2 **Ptolemaís**, Gre.
68/B2 **Ptuj**, Slov.
89/C2 **Pua**, Thai.
114/D5 **Pucallpa**, Peru
138/G7 **Puce**, On,Can.
87/B4 **Pucheng**, China
118/Q9 **Puchuncaví**, Chile
69/G3 **Pucioasa**, Rom.
55/K1 **Puck**, Pol.
53/G3 **Puckeridge**, Eng,UK
118/C3 **Pucón**, Chile
48/H2 **Pudasjärvi**, Fin.
52/D5 **Puddletown**, Eng,UK
51/G4 **Pudsey**, Eng,UK
91/H2 **Pudu** (riv.), China
90/C5 **Pudukkottai**, India
122/B4 **Puebla**, Mex.
122/B4 **Puebla** (state), Mex.
64/A1 **Puebla del Caramiñal**, Sp.
131/F3 **Pueblo**, Co,US
122/C5 **Pueblo Nuevo Tiquisate**, Guat.
118/C2 **Puente Alto**, Chile
64/A1 **Puenteareas**, Sp.
64/A1 **Puente Caldelas**, Sp.
64/A1 **Puente-Ceso**, Sp.
118/C2 **Puente del Inca**, Arg.
64/A1 **Puentedeume**, Sp.
64/C4 **Puente-Genil**, Sp
64/B1 **Puentes de García Rodríguez**, Sp.
126/R10 **Pueo** (pt.), Hi,US
130/E4 **Puerco** (riv.), Az, NM,US
130/F4 **Puerco** (riv.), NM,US
118/B5 **Puerto Aisén**, Chile
114/C3 **Puerto Asís**, Col.
114/E2 **Puerto Ayacucho**, Ven.
122/D4 **Puerto Barrios**, Guat.
123/H5 **Puerto Cabello**, Ven.
122/E5 **Puerto Cabezas**, Nic.
123/H5 **Puerto Cumarebo**, Ven.
65/X16 **Puerto de la Cruz**, Canl.
64/A1 **Puerto del Son**, Sp.
122/B4 **Puerto Escondido**, Mex.
117/F2 **Puerto Iguazú**, Arg.
123/J5 **Puerto La Cruz**, Ven.
122/E4 **Puerto Lempira**, Hon.
64/C3 **Puertollano**, Sp.
64/E4 **Puerto Lumbreras**, Sp.
118/D4 **Puerto Madryn**, Arg.
114/E6 **Puerto Maldonado**, Peru
118/B4 **Puerto Montt**, Chile
122/D3 **Puerto Morelos**, Mex.
119/J7 **Puerto Natales**, Chile
123/F6 **Puerto Obaldía**, Pan.
123/G4 **Puerto Plata**, DRep.
88/C6 **Puerto Princesa**, Phil.
118/B4 **Puerto Quellón**, Chile
64/B4 **Puerto Real**, Sp.
123/H4 **Puerto Rico** (commonwealth), US
122/C5 **Puerto San José**, Guat.
114/G7 **Puerto Suárez**, Bol.
123/N9 **Puerto Vallarta**, Mex.
118/B4 **Puerto Varas**, Chile
118/C5 **Pueyrredón** (lake), Arg.
50/D5 **Puffin** (isl.), Wal,UK
73/J1 **Pugachev**, Rus.
138/C2 **Puget** (sound), Wa,US
66/E2 **Puglia** (reg.), It.
65/G1 **Puigsacalm** (mtn.), Sp.
92/C5 **Pujut** (cape), Indo.
99/J6 **Pukapuka** (isl.), Cookls.
99/M6 **Puka Puka** (atoll), FrPol.
99/M6 **Pukarua** (isl.), FrPol.
132/C1 **Pukaskwa Nat'l Park**, On,Can.
93/F1 **Pulanduta** (pt.), Phil.
98/D4 **Pulap** (atoll), Micr.
135/G3 **Pulaski**, Tn,US
132/D4 **Pulaski**, Va,US
55/L3 **Puławy**, Pol.
53/F5 **Pulborough**, Eng,UK
56/D7 **Pulheim**, Ger.
93/G3 **Pulisan** (cape), Indo.
128/D4 **Pullman**, Wa,US
60/C5 **Pully**, Swi.
55/G3 **Pulsnitz** (riv.), Ger.
55/L2 **Pułtusk**, Pol.
98/D4 **Puluwat** (atoll), Micr.
52/C2 **Pumpsaint**, Wal,UK
91/F2 **Pumu** (pass), China
99/X15 **Punaauia**, FrPol.
114/E7 **Punata**, Bol.
79/K2 **Pūnch**, India
90/B4 **Pune** (Poona), India
92/B3 **Punggai** (cape), Malay.
110/E1 **Punia**, D.R. Congo
81/C5 **Punjab** (state), India
79/K2 **Punjab** (plains), Pak.
114/D7 **Puno**, Peru
122/D4 **Punta Allen**, Mex.
119/K8 **Punta Arenas**, Chile
123/G5 **Punta Cardón**, Ven.
123/J5 **Punta de Mata**, Ven.
122/D4 **Punta Gorda**, Belz.
122/E5 **Punta Gorda** (bay), Nic.
135/H5 **Punta Gorda**, Fl,US
123/M7 **Punta Peñasco**, Mex.
122/E6 **Puntarenas**, CR
64/B4 **Punta Umbría**, Sp.
126/S10 **Puolo** (pt.), Hi,US
114/D6 **Puquio**, Peru
74/H3 **Pur** (riv.), Rus.
114/C3 **Puracé Nat'l Park**, Col.
52/D5 **Purbeck, Isle of** (pen.), Eng,UK
131/H4 **Purcell**, Ok,US
118/B3 **Purén**, Chile
131/G3 **Purgatoire** (riv.), Co,US
90/D3 **Purī**, India
70/E4 **Purikari** (pt.), Est.
56/B3 **Purmerend**, Neth.
90/C4 **Pūrna**, India
90/C3 **Pūrna** (riv.), India
117/B5 **Purranque**, Chile
53/E3 **Purton**, Eng,UK
114/F4 **Purús** (riv.), Braz.
69/G4 **Pŭrvomay**, Bul.
92/C5 **Purwokerto**, Indo.
90/C4 **Pusad**, India
86/E5 **Pusan**, SKor.
86/D5 **Pusan-Jikhalsi** (prov.), SKor.
92/A2 **Pusat Gayo** (mts.), Indo.
71/T7 **Pushkin**, Rus.
71/W8 **Pushkino**, Rus.
68/E2 **Püspökladány**, Hun.
118/C2 **Putaendo**, Chile
92/C4 **Puting** (cape), Indo.
122/E4 **Putla**, Mex.
118/B4 **Putomayo** (riv.), Col.
74/K3 **Putorana** (mts.), Rus.
118/C4 **Putrachoique** (peak), Arg.
90/C6 **Puttalam**, SrL.
58/D1 **Putte**, Belg.
56/C4 **Putten**, Neth.
56/B5 **Putten** (isl.), Neth.
59/F5 **Püttlingen**, Ger.
104/C5 **Putu** (range), Libr.
114/D4 **Putumayo** (riv.), SAm.
92/D3 **Putussibau**, Indo.
126/T10 **Puu Kukui** (peak), Hi,US
59/D1 **Puurs**, Belg.
87/B3 **Pu Xian**, China
128/C3 **Puyallup**, Wa,US
138/C3 **Puyallup** (riv.), Wa,US
87/C4 **Puyang**, China
62/E4 **Puy de Sancy** (peak), Fr.
118/B4 **Puyehue** (vol.), Chile
118/B4 **Puyehué Nat'l Park**, Chile
62/D5 **Puymorens, Col de** (pass), Fr.
65/E3 **Puzal**, Sp.
107/C4 **Pwani** (prov.), Tanz.
107/A5 **Pweto**, D.R. Congo
50/D6 **Pwllheli**, Wal,UK
79/K1 **Pyandzh** (Panj) (riv.), Afg., Taj.
70/F2 **Pyaozero** (lake), Rus.
91/G4 **Pyapon**, Myan.
74/J2 **Pyasina** (riv.), Rus.
73/G3 **Pyatigorsk**, Rus.
62/F4 **Pyfara** (mtn.), Fr.
48/H3 **Pyhä-Häkin Nat'l Park**, Fin.
48/H3 **Pyhäjärvi**, Fin.
48/H2 **Pyhäntunturi** (peak), Fin.
89/B2 **Pyinmana**, Myan.
52/C3 **Pyle**, Wal,UK
86/C2 **P'yŏngan-Bukto** (prov.), NKor.
86/C3 **P'yŏngan-Namdo** (prov.), NKor.
86/D4 **Pyŏngt'aek**, SKor.
86/C3 **P'yŏngyang** (cap.), NKor.
86/C3 **P'yŏngyang-Si** (prov.), NKor.
136/M4 **Pyramid** (mtn.), BC,Can.
137/B1 **Pyramid** (lake), Ca,US
130/C3 **Pyramid** (lake), Nv,US
65/E1 **Pyrenees** (range), Eur.
62/C5 **Pyrénées Occidentales Nat'l Park**, Fr.
55/H2 **Pyrzyce**, Pol.
71/Q4 **Pyshma** (riv.), Rus.
89/B2 **Pyu**, Myan.

Q

80/L6 **Qā'al Jafr** (salt pan), Jor.
80/K5 **Qabātiyah**, WBnk.
102/H1 **Qābis**, Tun.
78/F1 **Qā'emshahr**, Iran
67/G1 **Qafa e Malit** (pass), Alb.
102/G1 **Qafşah**, Tun.
83/J2 **Qagan** (lake), China
87/C2 **Qahar Youyi Qianqi**, China
82/C4 **Qaidam** (basin), China
80/M8 **Qalansuwa**, Isr.
80/F3 **Qal'at Dizah**, Iraq
80/H6 **Qallīn**, Egypt
80/K5 **Qalqīlyah**, WBnk.
81/A1 **Qalqotan** (riv.), Kaz.
78/F5 **Qamar, Ghubbat al** (bay), Yem.
80/N8 **Qanah, Wādī** (dry riv.), WBnk.
73/H5 **Qapıcıq Daği** (peak), Azer.
81/C3 **Qapshaghay**, Kaz.
81/C3 **Qapshaghay** (res.), Kaz.
81/B2 **Qaraghandy**, Kaz.
80/E3 **Qarah Qōsh**, Iraq
81/C2 **Qaratal** (riv.), Kaz.
81/B3 **Qarataū**, Kaz.
81/A3 **Qarataū** (mts.), Kaz.
81/A3 **Qaratau Zhotasy** (uplands), Kaz.
103/Q6 **Qardho**, Som.
78/E2 **Qareh Chāy** (riv.), Iran
81/F4 **Qarqan** (riv.), China
67/G2 **Qarrit, Qaf'e** (pass), Alb.
66/B4 **Qarţājannah** (ruins), Tun.
106/B2 **Qārūn, Birkat** (lake), Egypt
78/E2 **Qaşr-e-Shīrīn**, Iran
106/A3 **Qaşr Farāfirah**, Egypt
80/L5 **Qaţanā**, Syria
78/F3 **Qatar** (ctry.)
106/A2 **Qattara** (depr.), Egypt
80/L4 **Qaţţīnah** (lake), Syria
73/K3 **Qaydaq Sory** (salt marsh), Kaz.
81/B2 **Qazaqtyng Usaqshoqylyghy** (uplands), Kaz.
90/A2 **Qāzi Ahmad**, Pak.
78/F1 **Qazvīn**, Iran
67/F2 **Qendrevica** (peak), Alb.
79/G3 **Qeshm** (isl.), Iran
78/E1 **Qezel** (riv.), Iran
91/J2 **Qi** (riv.), China
87/D4 **Qian** (can.), China
87/D5 **Qian** (riv.), China
87/D5 **Qianqiu Guan** (pass), China
87/B5 **Qifeng Guan** (pass), China
82/D4 **Qilian** (mts.), China
82/D4 **Qilian** (peak), China
80/N9 **Qilt, Wādī** (dry riv.), WBnk.
81/F4 **Qimantag** (mts.), China
87/B4 **Qin** (mts.), China
87/C4 **Qin** (riv.), China
106/C3 **Qinā**, Egypt
106/C3 **Qinā** (gov.), Egypt
88/B1 **Qing** (riv.), China
87/E3 **Qingdao**, China
82/D4 **Qinghai** (lake), China
82/D4 **Qinghai** (mts.), China
88/C2 **Qingjiang**, China
88/A2 **Qingshui** (riv.), China
83/H4 **Qingzhou**, China
87/D3 **Qinhuangdao**, China
87/C3 **Qinyuan**, China
88/B4 **Qiongshan**, China
83/J2 **Qiqihar**, China
80/K5 **Qiryat Ata**, Isr.
80/K5 **Qiryat Bialik**, Isr.
80/K6 **Qiryat Gat**, Isr.
80/M9 **Qiryat Mal'akhi**, Isr.
80/K5 **Qiryat Shemona**, Isr.
80/K5 **Qiryat Yam**, Isr.
83/L2 **Qitaihe**, China
87/C4 **Qi Xian**, China
83/L2 **Qixing** (riv.), China
74/G5 **Qizilqum** (des.), Kaz.,Uzb.
78/F2 **Qom**, Iran
78/F2 **Qom** (riv.), Iran
90/E2 **Qomolangma** (Everest) (peak), China
79/J1 **Qondūz** (riv.), Afg.
73/M1 **Qostanay**, Kaz.
73/M2 **Qostanay Obl.**, Kaz.
88/C2 **Qu** (riv.), China
133/F3 **Quabbin** (res.), Ma,US
53/F3 **Quainton**, Eng,UK
57/E3 **Quakenbrück**, Ger.
137/E5 **Quakertown**, Pa,US
82/H5 **Quan** (riv.), China
134/D3 **Quanah**, Tx,US
87/B4 **Quanbao Shan** (mtn.), China
89/E3 **Quang Ngai**, Viet.
89/D2 **Quang Trach**, Viet.
89/D2 **Quang Tri**, Viet.
52/C4 **Quantock** (hills), Eng,UK
88/B2 **Quanzhou**, China
129/G3 **Qu'Appelle** (riv.), Mb, Sk,Can.
129/H3 **Qu'Appelle**, Sk,Can.
129/G3 **Qu'Appelle** (dam), Sk,Can.
125/K2 **Quaqtaq**, Qu,Can.
58/C3 **Quaregnon**, Belg.
93/E4 **Quarles** (mts.), Indo.
63/J5 **Quarrata**, It.
66/A3 **Quartu Sant'Elena**, It.
137/B1 **Quartz Hill**, Ca,US
66/A4 **Quballāt**, Tun.
79/G1 **Qūchān**, Iran
97/D2 **Queanbeyan**, Austl.
125/J3 **Québec** (prov.), Can.
133/G2 **Québec** (cap.), Qu,Can.
116/J7 **Quebra-Cangalha** (mts.), Braz.
118/B4 **Quedal** (pt.), Chile
52/D3 **Quedgeley**, Eng,UK
124/C3 **Queen Charlotte** (isls.), BC,Can.
124/C3 **Queen Charlotte** (sound), BC,Can.
128/B3 **Queen Charlotte** (str.), BC,Can.
134/E3 **Queen City**, Tx,US
125/R7 **Queen Elizabeth** (isls.), NW,Nun,Can.
111/G **Queen Mary** (coast), Ant.
111/P **Queen Maud** (mts.), Ant.
124/F2 **Queen Maud** (gulf), Nun,Can.
111/Z **Queen Maud Land** (reg.), Ant.
125/S7 **Queens** (chan.), Nun,Can.
50/E1 **Queensberry** (mtn.), Sc,UK
51/G4 **Queensbury**, Eng,UK
51/E5 **Queensferry**, Wal,UK
96/B3 **Queensland** (state), Austl.
133/R9 **Queenston**, On,Can.
108/D3 **Queenstown**, SAfr.
118/B4 **Queilén**, Chile
115/H4 **Queimada**, Braz.
110/G4 **Quelimane**, Moz.
64/A3 **Queluz**, Port.
53/E3 **Quenington**, Eng,UK
118/F3 **Quequén**, Arg.
118/F3 **Quequén Grande** (riv.), Arg.
122/A3 **Querétaro**, Mex.
122/A3 **Querétaro** (state), Mex.
122/E5 **Quesada**, CR
64/D4 **Quesada**, Sp.
87/C4 **Queshan**, China
128/C2 **Quesnel**, BC,Can.
128/C2 **Quesnel** (lake), BC,Can.
89/E3 **Que Son**, Viet.
131/F3 **Questa**, NM,US
79/J2 **Quetta**, Pak.
118/B5 **Queulat Nat'l Park**, Chile
114/C4 **Quevedo**, Ecu.
122/C5 **Quezaltenango**, Guat.
88/E6 **Quezon**, Phil.
88/D5 **Quezon City**, Phil.
87/D4 **Qufu**, China
110/B3 **Quibala**, Ang.
114/C2 **Quibdó**, Col.
62/B3 **Quiberon** (bay), Fr.
110/B2 **Quiçama Nat'l Park**, Ang.
57/G1 **Quickborn**, Ger.
59/G5 **Quierschied**, Ger.
130/D4 **Quijotoa**, Az,US
118/B4 **Quilán** (cape), Chile
118/Q9 **Quilicura**, Chile
129/G2 **Quill** (lakes), Sk,Can.
114/D6 **Quillabamba**, Peru
114/E7 **Quillacollo**, Bol.
118/B4 **Quillagua** (pt.), Chile
118/C3 **Quilleco**, Chile
118/C2 **Quillota**, Chile
90/C6 **Quilon**, India
118/C2 **Quilpué**, Chile
62/A3 **Quimper**, Fr.
135/G4 **Quincy**, Fl,US
132/B4 **Quincy**, Il,US
133/G3 **Quincy**, Ma,US
128/D4 **Quincy**, Wa,US
89/E3 **Qui Nhon**, Viet.
130/C2 **Quinn** (riv.), Nv,US
64/D3 **Quintanar de la Orden**, Sp.
122/D4 **Quintana Roo** (state), Mex.
118/Q9 **Quintero**, Chile
118/D2 **Quinto** (riv.), Arg.
123/N8 **Quiriego**, Mex.
118/B3 **Quirihue**, Chile
107/D5 **Quirimba** (arch.), Moz.
116/B1 **Quirinópolis**, Braz.
123/J6 **Quiriquire**, Ven.
133/H2 **Quispamsis**, NB,Can.
117/D2 **Quitilipi**, Arg.
135/H4 **Quitman**, Ga,US
135/F3 **Quitman**, Ms,US
134/E3 **Quitman**, Tx,US
114/C4 **Quito** (cap.), Ecu.
115/L4 **Quixadá**, Braz.
115/L5 **Quixeramobim**, Braz.
91/H2 **Qujing**, China
73/K3 **Qulsary**, Kaz.
82/C4 **Qumar** (riv.), China
124/G2 **Quoich** (riv.), Nun,Can.
50/C3 **Quoile** (riv.), NI,UK
108/B4 **Quoin** (pt.), SAfr.
80/L4 **Qurnat as Sawdā'** (mtn.), Leb.
106/C3 **Qūş**, Egypt
71/Q5 **Qusmuryn** (lake), Kaz.
125/T6 **Quttinirpaaq Nat'l Park**, Nun,Can.
82/F4 **Quwu** (mts.), China
89/C1 **Quynh Nhai**, Viet.
87/C3 **Quzhou**, China
88/C2 **Quzhou**, China
68/D5 **Qyteti Stalin**, Alb.
74/G5 **Qyzylorda**, Kaz.

R

63/L3 **Raab** (riv.), Aus.
48/H2 **Raahe**, Fin.
56/D4 **Raalte**, Neth.
56/B5 **Raamsdonk**, Neth.
80/M8 **Ra'anana**, Isr.
125/S7 **Raanes** (pen.), Nun,Can.
107/D3 **Raas Jumbo**, Som.
68/B3 **Rab** (isl.), Cro.
68/C2 **Rába** (riv.), Hun.
66/D5 **Rabat**, Malta
102/D1 **Rabat** (cap.), Mor.
98/E5 **Rabaul**, PNG
63/K4 **Rabbi** (riv.), It.
55/K4 **Rabka**, Pol.
90/C4 **Rabkavi**, India
133/S8 **Raby** (pt.), On,Can.
63/G4 **Racconigi**, It.
135/F4 **Raccoon** (pt.), La,US
125/L4 **Race** (cape), Nf,Can.
89/D4 **Rach Gia**, Viet.
89/D4 **Rach Gia** (bay), Viet.
55/K3 **Racibórz**, Pol.
138/Q14 **Racine**, Wi,US
68/D2 **Ráckeve**, Hun.
69/G2 **Rădăuţi**, Rom.
54/G4 **Radbuza** (riv.), Czh.
51/F4 **Radcliffe**, Eng,UK

180

Radcl – Rose B

51/G6 Radcliffe on Trent, Eng,UK
68/A2 Radenthein, Aus.
57/E6 Radevormwald, Ger.
132/D4 Radford, Va,US
90/B3 Rādhanpur, India
128/G2 Radisson, Sk,Can.
53/F3 Radlett, Eng,UK
69/G4 Radnevo, Bul.
55/L3 Radom, Pol.
68/F4 Radomir, Bul.
55/K3 Radomsko, Pol.
68/F5 Radoviš, FYROM
52/D4 Radstock, Eng,UK
70/D5 Radviliškis, Lith.
52/C3 Radyr, Wal,UK
55/K2 Radziejów, Pol.
55/L2 Radzymin, Pol.
55/M3 Radzyń Podlaski, Pol.
125/H3 Rae (isth.), Nun,Can.
124/E2 Rae (riv.), Nun,Can.
90/D2 Rae Bareli, India
135/J3 Raeford, NC,US
59/F2 Raeren, Belg.
56/D5 Raesfeld, Ger.
117/D3 Rafaela, Arg.
80/K6 Rafah, Gaza
79/G2 Rafsanjān, Iran
128/E5 Raft (riv.), Id, Ut,US
103/L6 Raga, Sudan
119/J8 Ragged (pt.), Chile
50/A1 Raghtin More (mtn.), Ire.
52/D3 Raglan, Wal,UK
48/E2 Rago Nat'l Park, Nor.
66/D4 Ragusa, It.
57/F4 Rahden, Ger.
79/K3 Rahīmyār Khān, Pak.
137/F5 Rahway, NJ,US
99/K6 Raiatea (isl.), FrPol.
90/C4 Raichūr, India
90/D3 Raigarh, India
130/E3 Rainbow Bridge Nat'l Mon., Ut,US
51/F4 Rainford, Eng,UK
128/C4 Rainier (mt.), Wa,US
135/G3 Rainsville, Al,US
51/G5 Rainworth, Eng,UK
129/K3 Rainy (lake), Can., US
129/K3 Rainy (riv.), Can., US
132/A1 Rainy River, On,Can.
90/D3 Raipur, India
54/F1 Raisdorf, Ger.
138/E8 Raisin (riv.), Mi,US
48/G3 Raisio, Fin.
58/C3 Raismes, Fr.
99/L7 Raivavae (isl.), FrPol.
92/A3 Raja (pt.), Indo.
90/D4 Rājahmundry, India
90/C5 Rājampet, India
92/D3 Rajang (riv.), Malay.
79/K3 Rājanpur, Pak.
90/C6 Rājapālaiyam, India
90/B4 Rājāpur, India
90/B2 Rājasthān (state), India
79/L3 Rajgarh, India
90/C3 Rājgarh, India
90/B3 Rājkot, India
90/D3 Rāj-Nāndagaon, India
79/L2 Rājpura, India
90/E3 Rājshāhi, Bang.
90/B3 Rājula, India
99/J5 Rakahanga (atoll), Cookls.
79/K1 Rakaposhi (mtn.), Pak.
91/F4 Rakhine (state), Myan.
79/H3 Rakhshān (riv.), Pak.
110/D5 Rakops, Bots.
69/G4 Rakovski, Bul.
70/E4 Rakvere, Est.
135/J3 Raleigh (cap.), NC,US
98/F4 Ralik Chain (arch.), Mrsh.
128/F3 Ralston, Ab,Can.
115/K6 Ramalho (mts.), Braz.
80/K6 Rām Allāh, WBnk.
90/B4 Ramas (cape), India
80/K5 Ramat Gan, Isr.
80/M8 Ramat HaSharon, Isr.
99/Z17 Rambi (isl.), Fiji
58/A6 Rambouillet, Fr.
52/B6 Rame (pt.), UK
90/E2 Rāmechhāp, Nepal
71/X9 Ramenskoye, Rus.
90/C6 Rāmeshwaram, India
78/E2 Rāmhormoz, Iran
80/K6 Ramla, Isr.
106/C2 Ramm, Jabal (mt.), Jor.
50/A4 Ramor, Lough (lake), Ire.
91/F4 Ramree (isl.), Myan.
78/F1 Ramsar (Sakht Sar), Iran
51/F4 Ramsbottom, Eng,UK
53/E4 Ramsbury, Eng,UK
132/D2 Ramsey (lake), On,Can.
53/F2 Ramsey, Eng,UK
50/D3 Ramsey, IM,UK
52/A3 Ramsey (isl.), Wal,UK
53/H4 Ramsgate, Eng,UK
59/G5 Ramstein-Miesenbach, Ger.
98/D5 Ramu (riv.), PNG
90/E3 Rānāghāt, India
118/C2 Rancagua, Chile
62/B2 Rance (riv.), Fr.
116/B2 Rancharia, Braz.
128/G4 Ranchester, Wy,US
90/E3 Rānchī, India
138/M9 Rancho Cordova, Ca,US
137/C2 Rancho Cucamonga (Cucamonga), Ca,US
137/B3 Rancho Palos Verdes, Ca,US
118/B4 Ranco (lake), Chile
103/P5 Randa, Djib.
137/K7 Randallstown, Md,US
50/B2 Randalstown, NI,UK
66/D4 Randazzo, It.
108/P13 Randburg, SAfr.
48/D4 Randers, Den.
137/F5 Randolph, NJ,US
55/H2 Randow (riv.), Ger.
96/H8 Randwick, Austl.
89/C2 Rang (peak), Thai.
91/F3 Rāngāmāti, Bang.
93/E4 Rangasa (cape), Indo.
130/E2 Rangely, Co,US
134/D3 Ranger, Tx,US
99/L6 Rangiroa (atoll), FrPol.
89/B2 Rangoon (Yangon) (cap.), Myan.
90/E2 Rangpur, Bang.
90/C5 Rānībennur, India
134/C4 Rankin, Tx,US
89/B4 Ranong, Thai.
59/G3 Ransbach-Baumbach, Ger.
133/S9 Ransomville, NY,US
58/D1 Ranst, Belg.
93/F4 Rantekombola (peak), Indo.
132/B3 Rantoul, Il,US
89/D2 Rao Co (peak), Laos
60/C1 Raon-L'Étape, Fr.
98/H7 Raoul (isl.), NZ
87/C3 Raoyang, China
99/L7 Rapa (isl.), FrPol.
118/Q10 Rapel (lake), Chile
118/B5 Raper (cape), Chile
129/H4 Rapid City, SD,US
132/E4 Rappahannock (riv.), Va,US
90/D2 Rapti (riv.), India
137/F5 Raritan (bay), NJ,US
137/F5 Raritan (riv.), NJ,US
99/L6 Raroia (atoll), FrPol.
99/J7 Rarotonga (isl.), Cookls.
118/E4 Rasa (pt.), Arg.
80/E3 Ra's al 'Ayn, Syria
103/J7 Ra's al Unūf, Libya
106/C2 Ras Gharib, Egypt
50/B2 Rasharkin, NI,UK
80/K5 Rāshayyā, Leb.
80/H6 Rashīd (Rosetta), Egypt
78/E1 Rasht, Iran
68/E4 Raška, Serb.
124/G2 Rasmussen (basin), Nun,Can.
65/P10 Raso (cape), Port.
73/G1 Rasskazovo, Rus.
63/H2 Rastatt, Ger.
57/F2 Rastede, Ger.
136/B6 Rat (isls.), Ak,US
92/B5 Rata (cape), Indo.
90/B2 Ratangarh, India
89/B3 Rat Buri, Thai.
90/C2 Rāth, India
129/K5 Rathbun (lake), Ia,US
54/G2 Rathenow, Ger.
50/B3 Rathfriland, NI,UK
50/B1 Rathlin (isl.), NI,UK
50/B1 Rathlin (sound), NI,UK
98/F4 Ratik Chain (arch.), Mrsh.
56/D6 Ratingen, Ger.
90/C3 Ratlām, India
90/B4 Ratnāgiri, India
90/D6 Ratnapura, SrL.
131/F3 Raton, NM,US
48/E3 Rättvik, Swe.
54/F2 Ratzeburg, Ger.
92/B3 Raub, Malay.
118/F3 Rauch, Arg.
48/D3 Raufoss, Nor.
116/D2 Raul Soares, Braz.
53/F2 Raunds, Eng,UK
90/D3 Raurkela, India
66/C4 Ravanusa, It.
56/C6 Ravels, Belg.
51/E3 Ravenglass, Eng,UK
63/K4 Ravenna, It.
61/F2 Ravensburg, Ger.
51/G5 Ravenshead, Eng,UK
132/D4 Ravenswood, WV,US
79/K2 Rāvi (riv.), India, Pak.
68/B2 Ravne na Koroškem, Slov.
99/H5 Rawaki (Phoenix) (atoll), Kiri.
79/K2 Rāwalpindi, Pak.
55/L3 Rawa Mazowiecka, Pol.
55/J3 Rawicz, Pol.
128/G5 Rawlins, Wy,US
51/G5 Rawmarsh, Eng,UK
118/D4 Rawson, Arg.
51/F4 Rawtenstall, Eng,UK
133/K2 Ray (cape), Nf,Can.
92/D4 Raya (peak), Indo.
90/C5 Rāyadrug, India
90/D4 Rāyagada, India
83/K2 Raychikhinsk, Rus.
53/G3 Rayleigh, Eng,UK
128/E3 Raymond, Ab,Can.
134/D5 Raymondville, Tx,US
129/G3 Raymore, Sk,Can.
89/C3 Rayong, Thai.
73/H4 Razdan, Arm.
69/J3 Razelm (lake), Rom.
69/H4 Razgrad, Bul.
67/K1 Razgrad (reg.), Bul.
69/F5 Razlog, Bul.
62/A2 Raz, Pointe du (pt.), Fr.
62/C3 Ré (isl.), Fr.
52/D2 Rea (riv.), Eng,UK
53/F4 Reading, Eng,UK
53/E4 Reading (co.), Eng,UK
89/C3 Reang Kesei, Camb.
99/M6 Reao (atoll), FrPol.
83/N2 Rebun (isl.), Japan
63/K5 Recanati, It.
59/F6 Réchicourt-le-Château, Fr.
72/D1 Rechitsa, Bela.
115/M5 Recife, Braz.
108/D4 Recife (cape), SAfr.
57/E4 Recke, Ger.
57/E5 Recklinghausen, Ger.
54/G2 Recknitz (riv.), Ger.
89/B2 Reclining Buddha (Shwethalyaung) (ruins), Myan.
117/E2 Reconquista, Arg.
78/C4 Red (sea), Afr., Asia
91/H3 Red (riv.), China, Viet.
50/B1 Red (bay), NI,UK
131/J5 Red (riv.), US
134/D2 Red (hills), Ks,US
55/K1 Reda, Pol.
137/F5 Red Bank, NJ,US
130/B2 Red Bluff, Ca,US
131/G4 Red Bluff (lake), NM, Tx,US
53/F3 Redbourn, Eng,UK
51/G2 Redcar, Eng,UK
51/G2 Redcar & Cleveland (co.), Eng,UK
128/F3 Redcliff, Ab,Can.
96/F6 Redcliffe, Austl.
131/H2 Red Cloud, Ne,US
128/E2 Red Deer, Ab,Can.
128/F3 Red Deer (riv.), Ab,Can.
129/H2 Red Deer (lake), Mb,Can.
129/H2 Red Deer (riv.), Mb, Sk,Can.
130/B2 Redding, Ca,US
53/E2 Redditch, Eng,UK
51/F1 Rede (riv.), Eng,UK
129/J4 Redfield, SD,US
138/F7 Redford, Mi,US
53/F4 Redhill, Eng,UK
126/T10 Red Hill (peak), Hi,US
133/K1 Red Indian (lake), Nf,Can.
59/G6 Réding, Fr.
129/K3 Red Lake, On,Can.
129/K3 Red Lake (riv.), Mn,US
137/J7 Redland, Md,US
96/F7 Redland Bay, Austl.
137/C2 Redlands, Ca,US
128/F4 Red Lodge, Mt,US
128/C4 Redmond, Or,US
138/C2 Redmond, Wa,US
62/B3 Redon, Fr.
64/A1 Redondela, Sp.
64/B3 Redondo, Port.
137/B3 Redondo Beach, Ca,US
136/H3 Redoubt (vol.), Ak,US
129/J3 Red River of the North (riv.), Can., US
129/K5 Red Rock (lake), Ia,US
52/A6 Redruth, Eng,UK
106/D4 Red Sea (hills), Sudan
124/D2 Redstone (riv.), NW,Can.
129/K2 Red Sucker (lake), Mb,Can.
129/H3 Redvers, Sk,Can.
105/E4 Red Volta (riv.), Burk., Gui.
128/E2 Redwater, Ab,Can.
130/B2 Redway, Ca,US
131/G2 Red Willow (cr.), Ne,US
132/A2 Red Wing, Mn,US
138/K12 Redwood City, Ca,US
129/K4 Redwood Falls, Mn,US
130/A2 Redwood Nat'l Park, Ca,US
132/C3 Reed City, Mi,US
53/H1 Reedham, Eng,UK
130/C3 Reedley, Ca,US
132/B3 Reedsburg, Wi,US
128/B5 Reedsport, Or,US
97/B3 Reedy (cr.), Austl.
98/F6 Reef (isls.), Sol.
95/H7 Reefton, NZ
49/A4 Ree, Lough (lake), Ire.
53/H1 Reepham, Eng,UK
56/D5 Rees, Ger.
130/C3 Reese (riv.), Nv,US
56/D3 Reest (riv.), Neth.
51/G3 Reeth, Eng,UK
56/B4 Reeuwijk, Neth.
134/D4 Refugio, Tx,US
51/H2 Rega (riv.), Pol.
116/E1 Regência, Pontal de (pt.), Braz.
115/K5 Regeneração, Braz.
63/K2 Regensburg, Ger.
63/K2 Regenstauf, Ger.
96/H8 Regents Park, Austl.
102/F2 Reggane, Alg.
56/D4 Regge (riv.), Neth.
66/D3 Reggio di Calabria, It.
63/J4 Reggio nell'Emilia, It.
69/G2 Reghin, Rom.
129/G3 Regina (cap.), Sk,Can.
130/F3 Regina, NM,US
129/G3 Regina Beach, Sk,Can.
116/C3 Registro, Braz.
63/J2 Regnitz (riv.), Ger.
64/B3 Reguengosde Monsaraz, Port.
57/G4 Rehburg-Loccum, Ger.
59/F5 Rehlingen-Siersburg, Ger.
110/C5 Rehoboth, Namb.
80/M9 Rehovot, Isr.
59/G2 Reichshof, Ger.
128/F3 Reid (lake), Sk,Can.
135/J2 Reidsville, NC,US
53/F4 Reigate, Eng,UK
58/D5 Reims, Fr.
119/J7 Reina Adelaida (arch.), Chile
57/H1 Reinbek, Ger.
129/J2 Reindeer (isl.), Mb,Can.
129/H1 Reindeer (lake), Mb, Sk,Can.
129/H1 Reindeer (riv.), Sk,Can.
64/C1 Reinosa, Sp.
48/G1 Reisduoddarhal'di (peak), Nor.
56/D2 Reitdiep (riv.), Neth.
128/F5 Reliance, Wy,US
102/F1 Relizane, Alg.
57/G1 Rellingen, Ger.
59/G2 Remagen, Ger.
115/K5 Remanso, Braz.
92/D5 Rembang, Indo.
115/H3 Rémire, FrG.
63/H2 Rems (riv.), Ger.
57/E6 Remscheid, Ger.
87/B5 Ren (riv.), China
118/C2 Renca, Chile
135/F2 Rend (lake), Il,US
54/E1 Rendsburg, Ger.
60/C4 Renens, Swi.
132/E2 Renfrew, On,Can.
92/B4 Rengat, Indo.
118/C2 Rengo, Chile
72/D3 Reni, Ukr.
56/C5 Renkum, Neth.
98/F6 Rennell (isl.), Sol.
62/C2 Rennes, Fr.
63/J4 Reno (riv.), It.
130/C3 Reno, Nv,US
108/C3 Renoster (riv.), SAfr.
108/D2 Renoster (riv.), SAfr.
87/D3 Renqiu, China
132/C3 Rensselaer, In,US
64/E1 Rentería, Sp.
138/C3 Renton, Wa,US
133/P6 Repentigny, Qu,Can.
51/G6 Repton, Eng,UK
128/D3 Republic, Wa,US
131/H2 Republican (riv.), Ks, Ne,US
96/C3 Repulse (bay), Austl.
114/D4 Requena, Peru
65/E3 Requena, Sp.
118/C2 Requiñoa, Chile
118/B5 Rescue (pt.), Chile
68/E5 Resen, FYROM
116/J7 Resende, Braz.
130/E4 Reserve, NM,US
117/E2 Resistencia, Arg.
68/E3 Reşiţa, Rom.
124/G1 Resolute, Nun,Can.
125/K2 Resolution (isl.), Nun,Can.
52/C3 Resolven, Wal,UK
116/D1 Resplendor, Braz.
58/B4 Ressons-sur-Matz, Fr.
133/H2 Restigouche (riv.), NB,Can.
129/H3 Reston, Mb,Can.
137/J8 Reston, Va,US
138/C2 Restoration (pt.), Wa,US
122/C5 Retalhuleu, Guat.
58/D4 Rethel, Fr.
67/J5 Réthimnon, Gre.
59/E1 Retie, Belg.
68/F3 Retrezap Nat'l Park, Rom.
109/R15 Réunion (dpcy.), Fr.
65/F2 Reus, Sp.
56/C6 Reusel, Neth.
54/G2 Reuterstadt Stavenhagen, Ger.
61/F1 Reutlingen, Ger.
71/W9 Reutov, Rus.
62/D5 Revel, Fr.
128/D3 Revelstoke, BC,Can.
96/H8 Revesby, Austl.
58/D4 Revin, Fr.
81/B4 Revolyutsii, Pik (peak), Taj.
48/G1 Revsbotn (fjord), Nor.
90/D3 Rewa, India
90/C2 Rewāri, India
136/J3 Rex (mtn.), Ak,US
128/F5 Rexburg, Id,US
58/B2 Rexpoëde, Fr.
123/F6 Rey (isl.), Pan.
53/H2 Reydon, Eng,UK
130/B3 Reyes (pt.), Ca,US
80/D3 Reyhanlı, Turk.
48/N7 Reykjavík (cap.), Ice.
122/B2 Reynosa, Mex.
62/C3 Rezé, Fr.
70/E4 Rēzekne, Lat.
61/F4 Rhaetian Alps (mts.), It., Swi.
61/F3 Rhätikon (mts.), Aus., Swi.
52/C2 Rhayader, Wal,UK
57/F5 Rheda-Wiedenbrück, Ger.
56/D5 Rheden, Neth.
53/F2 Rhee (Cam) (riv.), Eng,UK
59/F2 Rheinbach, Ger.
56/D5 Rheinberg, Ger.
57/E4 Rheine, Ger.
59/F3 Rheinland-Pfalz (state), Ger.
102/E2 Rhemiles (well), Alg.
56/C5 Rhenen, Neth.
54/D3 Rhine (riv.), Eur.
57/E5 Rhine-Herne (can.), Ger.
132/B2 Rhinelander, Wi,US
59/D3 Rhisnes, Belg.
52/C1 Rhiw (riv.), Wal,UK
133/G3 Rhode Island (state), US
80/B3 Rhodes (isl.), Gre.
80/B3 Rhodes (Ródhos), Gre.
69/F4 Rhodope (mts.), Bul.
52/C3 Rhondda, Wal,UK
52/C3 Rhondda Cynon Taff (co.), Wal,UK
62/F4 Rhône (riv.), Fr., Swi.
62/F4 Rhône-Alpes (reg.), Fr.
58/C3 Rhonelle (riv.), Fr.
51/E6 Rhosllanerchrugog, Wal,UK
52/B3 Rhossili, Wal,UK
50/E5 Rhuddlan, Wal,UK
57/H5 Rhume (riv.), Ger.
52/C2 Rhyddhywel (mtn.), Wal,UK
52/B2 Rhydowen, Wal,UK
50/E5 Rhyl, Wal,UK
52/C3 Rhymney, Wal,UK
115/K6 Riacho de Santana, Braz.
137/C2 Rialto, Ca,US
64/A1 Rianjo, Sp.
92/B3 Riau (isls.), Indo.
64/A1 Ribadavia, Sp.
64/B1 Ribadeo, Sp.
64/C1 Ribadesella, Sp.
109/H8 Riban'i Manamby (mts.), Madg.
51/F4 Ribble (riv.), Eng,UK
54/E1 Ribe, Den.
54/E1 Ribe (co.), Den.
116/B3 Ribeira (riv.), Braz.
115/L6 Ribeira do Pombal, Braz.
65/T13 Ribeira Grande, Azor.
116/B2 Ribeirão do Pinha, Braz.
116/C2 Ribeirão Preto, Braz.
58/C4 Ribemont, Fr.
66/C4 Ribera, It.
114/E6 Riberalta, Bol.
54/G1 Ribnitz-Damgarten, Ger.
132/E2 Rice (lake), On,Can.
132/B2 Rice Lake, Wi,US
124/C2 Richards (isl.), NW,Can.
133/G2 Richardson (lakes), Me,US
56/C2 Richel (isl.), Neth.
130/D3 Richfield, Ut,US
50/B1 Richhill, NI,UK
128/D4 Richland, Wa,US
135/H3 Richland Balsam (peak), NC,US
132/B3 Richland Center, Wi,US
134/D4 Richland Creek (res.), Tx,US
97/D2 Richmond, Austl.
133/F2 Richmond, Qu,Can.
51/G3 Richmond, Eng,UK
138/K11 Richmond, Ca,US
132/C4 Richmond, In,US
132/C4 Richmond, Ky,US
134/E4 Richmond, Tx,US
132/E4 Richmond (cap.), Va,US
138/C2 Richmond Beach-Innis Arden, Wa,US
133/R8 Richmond Hill, On,Can.
96/G8 Richmond-Raaf, Austl.
53/F3 Rickmansworth, Eng,UK
56/B5 Ridderkerk, Neth.
132/E2 Rideau (lake), On,Can.
130/C4 Ridgecrest, Ca,US
137/F5 Ridgewood, NJ,US
51/G2 Riding Mill, Eng,UK
129/H3 Riding Mountain Nat'l Park, Mb,Can.
63/K2 Ried im Innkreis, Aus.
59/F5 Riegelsberg, Ger.
59/E2 Riemst, Belg.
55/G3 Riesa, Ger.
119/J8 Riesco (isl.), Chile
108/D3 Riet (riv.), SAfr.
57/F5 Rietberg, Ger.
66/C1 Rieti, It.
51/G3 Rievaulx, Eng,UK
128/C4 Riffe (lake), Wa,US
130/F3 Rifle, Co,US
48/N6 Rifsnes (pt.), Ice.
107/B2 Rift Valley (prov.), Kenya
70/E4 Riga (Rīga) (cap.), Lat.
128/F5 Rigby, Id,US
79/H2 Rīgestan (reg.), Afg.
128/D4 Riggins, Id,US
90/D3 Rihand Sāgar (res.), India
48/H3 Riihimäki, Fin.
111/C Riiser-Larsen (pen.), Ant.
48/J2 Riisitunturin Nat'l Park, Fin.
68/B3 Rijeka, Cro.
56/B4 Rijnsburg, Neth.
56/D4 Rijssen, Neth.
56/B4 Rijswijk, Neth.
99/M7 Rikitea, FrPol.
69/F4 Rila (mts.), Bul.
67/H1 Rilski Manastir, Bul.
99/K7 Rimatara (isl.), FrPol.
55/L4 Rimavská Sobota, Slvk.
78/D3 Rīma, Wādī (dry riv.), SAr.
128/E2 Rimbey, Ab,Can.
103/J5 Rimé (wadi), Chad
63/K4 Rimini, It.
69/H3 Rîmnicu Sărat, Rom.
69/G3 Rîmnicu Vîlcea, Rom.
133/G1 Rimouski, Qu,Can.
82/D1 Rinchinlhümbe, Mong.
64/C4 Rincón de la Victoria, Sp.
122/D5 Rincon de la Vieja Nat'l Park, CR
123/P9 Rincón de Romos, Mex.
50/C3 Ringboy (pt.), NI,UK
48/D4 Ringkøbing, Den.
53/G5 Ringmer, Eng,UK
137/F5 Ringoes, NJ,US
50/B1 Ringsend, NI,UK
54/F1 Ringsted, Den.
56/B4 Ringvaart (can.), Neth.
48/F1 Ringvassøy (isl.), Nor.
97/G5 Ringwood, Austl.
53/E5 Ringwood, Eng,UK
137/F4 Ringwood, NJ,US
67/J4 Rínia (isl.), Gre.
50/C2 Rinns, The (pen.), Sc,UK
57/G4 Rinteln, Ger.
114/C5 Río Abiseo Nat'l Park, Peru
114/C4 Riobamba, Ecu.
116/L7 Rio Bonito, Braz.
114/E5 Rio Branco, Braz.
119/G2 Río Branco, Uru.
116/B3 Rio Branco do Sul, Braz.
132/C4 Río Bravo del Norte (Río Grande) (riv.), Mex., US
118/B4 Río Bueno, Chile
116/D2 Rio Casca, Braz.
119/T12 Riochuelo, Uru.
118/C2 Río Clarillo Nat'l Park, Chile
116/J7 Rio Claro, Braz.
118/D3 Río Colorado, Arg.
118/D2 Río Cuarto, Arg.
116/K7 Rio de Janeiro, Braz.
116/K7 Rio de Janeiro (state), Braz.
128/B5 Rio Dell, Ca,US
116/B3 Rio do Sul, Braz.
65/Q10 Rio Frio, Port.
119/K7 Río Gallegos, Arg.
119/L8 Río Grande, Arg.
116/A5 Rio Grande, Braz.
134/C4 Rio Grande (riv.), Mex., US
134/D5 Rio Grande City, Tx,US
116/G8 Rio Grande da Serra, Braz.
122/E5 Río Grande de Matagalpa (riv.), Nic.
116/A4 Rio Grande do Sul (state), Braz.
123/G5 Riohacha, Col.
123/E6 Río Hato, Pan.
114/C5 Rioja, Peru
114/F4 Rio Jaú Nat'l Park, Braz.
115/L5 Rio Largo, Braz.
62/E4 Riom, Fr.
64/A3 Rio Maior, Port.
128/D3 Riondel, BC,Can.
118/C4 Río Negro (prov.), Arg.
119/F2 Río Negro (dept.), Uru.
119/F2 Río Negro (res.), Uru.
66/D2 Rionero in Vulture, It.
116/C1 Rio Paranaíba, Braz.
116/A4 Rio Pardo, Braz.
117/E2 Río Pilcomayo Nat'l Park, Arg.
130/F4 Rio Rancho, NM,US
62/F3 Riorges, Fr.
118/E1 Río Segundo, Arg.
118/B5 Río Simpson Nat'l Park, Chile
118/D2 Río Tercero, Arg.
116/B1 Rio Verde, Braz.
122/B3 Rioverde, Mex.
115/H7 Rio Verde de Mato Grosso, Braz.
68/E3 Ripanj, Serb.
135/F3 Ripley, Ms,US
135/F3 Ripley, Tn,US
65/G1 Ripoll, Sp.
65/L6 Ripoll (riv.), Sp.
65/L6 Ripollet, Sp.
51/G3 Ripon, Eng,UK
129/L5 Ripon, Wi,US
66/D4 Riposto, It.
51/G4 Ripponden, Eng,UK
52/C3 Risca, Wal,UK
83/N2 Rishiri (isl.), Japan
80/K6 Rishon LeZiyyon, Isr.
62/D2 Risle (riv.), Fr.
68/B3 Risnjak (peak), Cro.
68/B3 Risnjak Nat'l Park, Cro.
69/G3 Rîşnov, Rom.
134/E3 Rison, Ar,US
48/D4 Risør, Nor.
114/D2 Ritacuba (peak), Col.
98/C2 Ritaiō (isl.), Japan
57/F2 Ritterhude, Ger.
85/L9 Rittō, Japan
128/D4 Ritzville, Wa,US
63/J4 Riva, It.
118/E2 Rivadavia, Arg.
63/G4 Rivarolo Canavese, It.
122/D5 Rivas, Nic.
62/F4 Rive-de-Gier, Fr.
118/B5 Rivera (isl.), Chile
117/E3 Rivera, Uru.
119/G1 Rivera (dept.), Uru.
138/F7 River Rouge, Mi,US
128/B3 Rivers (inlet), BC,Can.
129/H3 Rivers, Mb,Can.
105/G5 Rivers (state), Nga.
108/C4 Riversdale, SAfr.
137/C3 Riverside, Ca,US
96/G8 Riverstone, Austl.
129/J3 Riverton, Mb,Can.
128/F5 Riverton, Wy,US
133/H2 Riverview, NB,Can.
138/F7 Riverview, Mi,US
135/H5 Riviera Beach, Fl,US
137/K7 Riviera Beach, Md,US
133/G2 Rivière-du-Loup, Qu,Can.
108/L11 Riviersonde-rendreeks (mts.), SAfr.
72/C2 Rivne, Ukr.
72/C2 Rivnens'ka Obl., Ukr.
63/G4 Rivoli, It.
58/D2 Rixensart, Belg.
78/E4 Riyadh (Ar Riyāḑ) (cap.), SAr.
80/E2 Rize, Turk.
87/D4 Rizhao, China
66/E3 Rizzuto (cape), It.
48/D4 Rjukan, Nor.
104/B2 Rkîz (lake), Mrta.
48/D3 Roa, Nor.
53/F2 Roade, Eng,UK
49/D2 Roadside, Sc,UK
123/J4 Road Town (cap.), BVI
130/E3 Roan (plat.), Co,US
51/F1 Roan Fell (hill), Sc,UK
135/H2 Roan High (peak), NC,US
62/F3 Roanne, Fr.
135/G3 Roanoke, Al,US
135/J2 Roanoke (riv.), NC, Va,US
132/E4 Roanoke, Va,US
135/J2 Roanoke Rapids, NC,US
122/D4 Roatán (isl.), Hon.
97/C4 Robbins (isl.), Austl.
97/B1 Robe (peak), Austl.
49/A4 Robe (riv.), Ire.
59/E6 Robert-Espagne, Fr.
134/C4 Robert Lee, Tx,US
136/E4 Roberts (mtn.), Ak,US
53/G5 Robertsbridge, Eng,UK
48/G2 Robertsfors, Swe.
90/D3 Robertsganj, India
108/B4 Robertson, SAfr.
133/F1 Roberval, Qu,Can.
51/H3 Robin Hood's Bay, Eng,UK
132/C4 Robinson, Il,US
138/C3 Robinson (pt.), Wa,US
113/B6 Robinson Crusoe (isl.), Chile
96/C4 Robinson Gorge Nat'l Park, Austl.
129/H3 Roblin, Mb,Can.
114/G7 Roboré, Bol.
128/D2 Robson (peak), BC,Can.
134/D5 Robstown, Tx,US
134/C3 Roby, Tx,US
64/A3 Roca, Cabo da (cape), Port.
122/B4 Roca Partida (pt.), Mex.
115/M4 Rocas, Braz.
63/G4 Rocciamelone (peak), It.
65/G1 Roc de France (mtn.), Fr.
119/G2 Rocha, Uru.
119/G2 Rocha (dept.), Uru.
51/F4 Rochdale, Eng,UK
51/F4 Rochdale (co.), Eng,UK
52/B6 Roche, Eng,UK
62/C4 Rochefort, Fr.
53/G4 Rochester, Eng,UK
132/C3 Rochester, In,US
138/F6 Rochester, Mi,US
129/K4 Rochester, Mn,US
133/G3 Rochester, NH,US
132/E3 Rochester, NY,US
138/F6 Rochester Hills, Mi,US
53/G3 Rochford, Eng,UK
132/B3 Rock (riv.), Il, Wi,US
128/C4 Rock (cr.), Or,US
47/C3 Rockall (isl.), UK
136/L3 Rock Creek, Yk,Can.
96/H8 Rockdale, Austl.
111/R Rockefeller (plat.), Ant.
132/B3 Rockford, Il,US
133/G2 Rock Forest, Qu,Can.
129/G3 Rockglen, Sk,Can.
96/C3 Rockhampton, Austl.
135/H3 Rock Hill, SC,US
95/A4 Rockingham, Austl.
135/J3 Rockingham, NC,US
132/B3 Rock Island, Il,US
132/F2 Rockland, On,Can.
133/G2 Rockland, Me,US
97/B3 Rocklands (res.), Austl.
135/H4 Rockledge, Fl,US
134/D4 Rockport, Tx,US
134/C4 Rocksprings, Tx,US
128/F5 Rock Springs, Wy,US
137/J7 Rockville, Md,US
137/G5 Rockville Center, NY,US
134/D3 Rockwall, Tx,US
135/G3 Rockwood, Tn,US
121/E4 Rocky (mts.), NAm.
132/D4 Rocky (peak), Ky,US
97/C4 Rocky Cape Nat'l Park, Austl.
133/K1 Rocky Harbour, Nf,Can.
132/D2 Rocky Island (lake), On,Can.
135/J3 Rocky Mount, NC,US
132/E4 Rocky Mount, Va,US
128/E2 Rocky Mountain House, Ab,Can.
131/F2 Rocky Mountain Nat'l Park, Co,US
137/H5 Rocky Point, NY,US
59/G5 Rodalben, Ger.
133/K1 Roddickton, Nf,Can.
52/D1 Roden (riv.), Eng,UK
138/K10 Rodeo, Ca,US
62/E4 Rodez, Fr.
80/B3 Ródhos (Rhodes), Gre.
63/K2 Roding, Ger.
57/F4 Rödinghausen, Ger.
67/F2 Rodonit, Kep i (cape), Alb.
45/N6 Rodrigues (isl.), Mrts.
50/B2 Roe (riv.), NI,UK
56/D6 Roer (riv.), Neth.
56/C6 Roermond, Neth.
58/C2 Roeselare, Belg.
138/D2 Roesiger (lake), Wa,US
125/H2 Roes Welcome (sound), Nun,Can.
72/D1 Rogachev, Bela.
48/C4 Rogaland (co.), Nor.
68/D4 Rogatica, Bosn.
134/E2 Rogers, Ar,US
132/D4 Rogers (peak), Va,US
132/D2 Rogers City, Mi,US
135/H2 Rogersville, Tn,US
60/B1 Rognon (riv.), Fr.
55/J2 Rogoźno, Pol.
130/B2 Rogue (riv.), Or,US
103/L6 Rohl (riv.), Sudan
79/J3 Rohri, Pak.
89/C2 Roi Et, Thai.
58/C4 Roisel, Fr.
118/E2 Rojas, Arg.
122/B3 Rojo (cape), Mex.
123/H4 Rojo (cape), PR
92/B3 Rokan (riv.), Indo.
96/A1 Rokeby-Croll Creek Nat'l Park, Austl.
104/C4 Rokel (riv.), SLeo.
85/L10 Rokkō-san (peak), Japan
116/B2 Rolândia, Braz.
56/D3 Rolde, Neth.
128/C2 Rolla, BC,Can.
131/K3 Rolla, Mo,US
129/J3 Rolla, ND,US
138/P15 Rolling Meadows, Il,US
96/C4 Roma, Austl.
62/E4 Romagnat, Fr.
59/E5 Romagne-sous-Montfaucon, Fr.
135/J3 Romain (cape), SC,US
125/K3 Romaine (riv.), Qu,Can.
69/H2 Roman, Rom.
93/G5 Romang (isl.), Indo.
93/G5 Romang (str.), Indo.
69/F3 Romania (ctry.)
62/F4 Romans-sur-Isère, Fr.
136/E3 Romanzof (cape), Ak,US
66/C2 Roma (Rome) (cap.), It.
59/F5 Rombas, Fr.
88/D5 Romblon, Phil.
135/G3 Rome, Ga,US
132/F3 Rome, NY,US
138/P16 Romeoville, Il,US
66/C2 Rome (Roma) (cap.), It.
62/E2 Romilly-sur-Seine, Fr.
56/D6 Rommerskirchen, Ger.
53/G4 Romney Marsh (reg.), Eng,UK
72/E2 Romny, Ukr.
54/E1 Rømø (isl.), Den.
62/D3 Romorantin-Lanthenay, Fr.
53/E5 Romsey, Eng,UK
138/F7 Romulus, Mi,US
89/D2 Ron, Viet.
128/E4 Ronan, Mt,US
115/H6 Roncador (mts.), Braz.
123/F5 Roncador Cay (isl.), Col.
66/C1 Ronciglione, It.
58/C2 Roncq, Fr.
64/C4 Ronda, Sp.
48/D3 Rondane Nat'l Park, Nor.
115/H7 Rondonópolis, Braz.
91/J2 Rong (riv.), China
129/G2 Ronge (lake), Sk,Can.
98/F3 Rongelap (atoll), Mrsh.
98/F3 Rongerik (atoll), Mrsh.
99/X15 Roniu (peak), FrPol.
137/G5 Ronkonkoma, NY,US
55/H1 Rønne, Den.
48/E4 Ronneby, Swe.
111/U Ronne Entrance (inlet), Ant.
57/G4 Ronnenberg, Ger.
58/C2 Ronse, Belg.
115/H6 Ronuro (riv.), Braz.
108/P13 Roodepoort-Maraisburg, SAfr.
108/B2 Rooiberg (peak), Namb.
90/C2 Roorkee, India
56/B5 Roosendaal, Neth.
111/N Roosevelt (isl.), Ant.
114/F6 Roosevelt (riv.), Braz.
124/D3 Roosevelt (mtn.), BC,Can.
130/E2 Roosevelt, Ut,US
136/L4 Root (mtn.), Ak,US
138/Q14 Root (riv.), Wi,US
64/D4 Roquetas de Mar, Sp.
114/F2 Roraima (peak), Guy.
129/J3 Rorketon, Mb,Can.
118/E2 Rosario, Arg.
115/K4 Rosário, Braz.
123/N9 Rosario, Mex.
119/F2 Rosario, Uru.
117/D2 Rosario de la Frontera, Arg.
119/S11 Rosario del Tala, Arg.
117/F3 Rosário do Sul, Braz.
123/M8 Rosarito, Mex.
65/G1 Rosas (gulf), Sp.
114/C3 Rosa Zárate, Ecu.
57/G6 Rosdorf, Ger.
99/J6 Rose (isl.), ASam.
136/M4 Rose (pt.), BC,Can.
129/J3 Roseau (riv.), Can., US
123/J4 Roseau (cap.), Dom.
129/K3 Roseau, Mn,US
109/S15 Rose Belle, Mrts.

181
Roseb – Salin

128/C5 Roseburg, Or,US
137/K7 Rosedale, Md,US
135/F3 Rosedale, Ms,US
49/D2 Rosehearty, Sc,UK
138/P16 Roselle, Il,US
137/F5 Roselle, NJ,US
133/N6 Rosemère, Qu,Can.
134/E4 Rosenberg, Tx,US
54/G5 Rosenheim, Ger.
65/G1 Roses, Sp.
66/D1 Roseto degli Abruzzi, It.
128/G3 Rosetown, Sk,Can.
80/H6 Rosetta (Rashīd), Egypt
138/M9 Roseville, Ca,US
138/G6 Roseville, Mi,US
80/M8 Rosh Ha'Ayin, Isr.
80/K5 Rosh HaNiqra (pt.), Isr.
69/G3 Roşiori de Vede, Rom.
54/G1 Roskilde, Den.
54/F1 Roskilde (co.), Den.
72/E1 Roslavl', Rus.
56/C5 Rosmalen, Neth.
66/D4 Rosolini, It.
62/B3 Rosporden, Fr.
59/G2 Rösrath, Ger.
111/M Ross (isl.), Ant.
111/P Ross (sea), Ant.
129/J2 Ross (isl.), Mb,Can.
63/K3 Rossa (peak), It.
51/E4 Rossall (pt.), Eng,UK
66/E3 Rossano, It.
98/E6 Rossel (isl.), PNG
111/N Ross Ice Shelf, Ant.
133/H2 Rossignol (lake), NS,Can.
49/H6 Rosskeeragh (pt.), Ire.
128/D3 Rossland, BC,Can.
50/A3 Rosslea, NI,UK
104/B2 Rosso, Mrta.
52/D3 Ross on Wye, Eng,UK
72/F2 Rossosh', Rus.
136/M3 Ross River, Yk,Can.
129/G2 Rosthern, Sk,Can.
54/G1 Rostock, Ger.
72/F1 Rostov, Rus.
73/G2 Rostovskaya Obl., Rus.
50/B3 Rostrevor, NI,UK
135/G3 Roswell, Ga,US
131/F4 Roswell, NM,US
61/F1 Rot (riv.), Ger.
98/D3 Rota (isl.), NMar.
64/B4 Rota, Sp.
57/G2 Rotenburg, Ger.
57/G7 Rotenburg an der Fulda, Ger.
59/F2 Rötgen, Ger.
54/E3 Rothaargebirge (mts.), Ger.
51/G1 Rothbury, Eng,UK
51/G5 Rother (riv.), Eng,UK
53/F5 Rother (riv.), Eng,UK
51/G5 Rotherham, Eng,UK
51/G5 Rotherham (co.), Eng,UK
49/D2 Rothes, Sc,UK
59/E2 Rotheux-Rimière, Belg.
53/F2 Rothwell, Eng,UK
93/F6 Roti (isl.), Indo.
95/H6 Rotorua, NZ
59/D2 Rotselaar, Belg.
63/K2 Rott (riv.), Ger.
59/F6 Rotte (riv.), Fr.
56/B5 Rotterdam, Neth.
56/D2 Rottumeroog (isl.), Neth.
56/D2 Rottumerplaat (isl.), Neth.
61/E1 Rottweil, Ger.
98/G6 Rotuma (isl.), Fiji
58/C2 Roubaix, Fr.
62/F4 Roubion (riv.), Fr.
62/D2 Rouen, Fr.
132/F2 Rouge (riv.), Qu,Can.
138/F6 Rouge (riv.), Mi,US
135/G2 Rough (riv.), Ky,US
96/C4 Round Hill (pt.), Austl.
50/B1 Round Knowe (mtn.), NI,UK
138/P15 Round Lake, Il,US
138/P15 Round Lake Beach, Il,US
130/C3 Round Mountain, Nv,US
134/D4 Round Rock, Tx,US
128/F4 Roundup, Mt,US
52/E4 Roundway (hill), Eng,UK
96/G8 Rouse Hill, Austl.
59/E5 Rouvres-en-Woëvre, Fr.
132/E1 Rouyn-Noranda, Qu,Can.
48/H2 Rovaniemi, Fin.
89/D3 Rovieng Tbong, Camb.
63/J4 Rovigo, It.
125/J2 Rowley (isl.), Nun,Can.
104/B4 Roxa (isl.), GBis.
88/C5 Roxas, Phil.
88/D4 Roxas, Phil.
93/F1 Roxas City, Indo.
135/J2 Roxboro, NC,US
123/J5 Roxborough, Trin.
104/A3 Roxo (cape), Sen.
131/F4 Roy, NM,US
130/D2 Roy, Ut,US
63/G4 Roya (riv.), Fr.
49/B4 Royal (can.), Ire.
124/H4 Royale (isl.), Mi,US
53/E2 Royal Leamington Spa, Eng,UK
53/G4 Royal Military (can.), Eng,UK
108/E3 Royal Natal Nat'l Park, SAfr.
96/H9 Royal Nat'l Park, Austl.
138/F6 Royal Oak, Mi,US
53/G4 Royal Tunbridge Wells, Eng,UK
62/C4 Royan, Fr.
53/F2 Royston, Eng,UK
51/F4 Royton, Eng,UK
68/E4 Rožaje, Serb.
55/L4 Rožňava, Slvk.
58/D4 Rozoy-sur-Serre, Fr.
55/M3 Roztoczański Nat'l Park, Pol.
134/E3 R.S. Kerr (lake), Ok,US
73/G1 Rtishchevo, Rus.
51/E6 Ruabon, Wal,UK
110/B4 Ruacana (falls), Ang.
110/B4 Ruacana, Namb.
107/B2 Ruaha Nat'l Park, Tanz.
78/E5 Rub' al Khali (des.), SAr.
72/F2 Rubezhnoye, Ukr.
65/G2 Rubí, Sp.
137/C3 Rubidoux, Ca,US
81/D1 Rubtsovsk, Rus.
130/D2 Ruby (mts.), Nv,US
130/D2 Ruby Valley, Nv,US
56/B5 Rucphen, Neth.
55/K2 Ruda Woda (lake), Pol.
51/G6 Ruddington, Eng,UK
55/G2 Rüdersdorf, Ger.
55/M3 Rudnik, Pol.
73/M1 Rudnyy, Kaz.
74/F1 Rudolf (isl.), Rus.
54/F3 Rudolstadt, Ger.
78/F1 Rūdsar, Iran
51/H3 Rudston, Eng,UK
50/B1 Rue (pt.), NI,UK
62/D4 Ruelle-sur-Touvre, Fr.
68/F4 Ruen (Rujen) (peak), Bul., FYROM
103/M5 Rufā'ah, Sudan
67/F3 Ruffano, It.
107/C4 Rufiji (riv.), Tanz.
118/E2 Rufino, Arg.
53/E2 Rugby, Eng,UK
129/J3 Rugby, ND,US
53/E1 Rugeley, Eng,UK
55/G1 Rügen (isl.), Ger.
56/D6 Ruhr (riv.), Ger.
57/D6 Ruhrgebiet (reg.), Ger.
131/F4 Ruidoso, NM,US
56/D3 Ruinen, Neth.
123/N9 Ruiz, Mex.
68/F4 Rujen (Ruen) (peak), Bul., FYROM
103/J8 Ruki (riv.), D.R. Congo
107/B4 Rukwa (lake), Tanz.
107/A4 Rukwa (prov.), Tanz.
68/D3 Ruma, Serb.
103/L6 Rumbek, Sudan
123/G3 Rum Cay (isl.), Bahm.
133/G2 Rumford, Me,US
55/K1 Rumia, Pol.
52/C4 Rumney, Wal,UK
83/N3 Rumoi, Japan
107/B5 Rumphi, Malw.
137/F5 Rumson, NJ,US
58/D1 Rumst, Belg.
50/B1 Runabay Head (pt.), NI,UK
51/F5 Runcorn, Eng,UK
103/L7 Rungu, D.R. Congo
107/B4 Rungwa, Tanz.
107/B5 Rungwe (peak), Tanz.
137/E6 Runnemede, NJ,US
137/C2 Running Springs, Ca,US
82/D3 Ruo (riv.), China
81/E4 Ruoqiang, China
92/B3 Rupat (isl.), Indo.
69/G2 Rupea, Rom.
58/D1 Rupel (riv.), Belg.
132/E1 Rupert (riv.), Qu,Can.
128/E5 Rupert, Id,US
125/J3 Rupert House (Waskaganish), Qu,Can.
59/G2 Ruppichteroth, Ger.
59/F1 Rur (riv.), Ger.
99/K7 Rurutu (isl.), FrPol.
110/F4 Rusape, Zim.
53/E4 Rushall, Eng,UK
129/K4 Rush City, Mn,US
53/F2 Rushden, Eng,UK
132/C4 Rushville, In,US
131/G2 Rushville, Ne,US
134/E4 Rusk, Tx,US
51/H5 Ruskington, Eng,UK
115/L4 Russas, Braz.
96/F7 Russell (isl.), Austl.
129/H3 Russell, Mb,Can.
129/H1 Russell (lake), Mb,Can.
124/F1 Russell (isl.), Nun,Can.
135/H3 Russell (lake), Ga, SC,US
131/H3 Russell, Ks,US
135/G3 Russellville, Al,US
134/E3 Russellville, Ar,US
132/C4 Russellville, Ky,US
74/* Russia (ctry.)
130/B3 Russian (riv.), Ca,US
73/H4 Rust'avi, Geo.
108/D2 Rustenburg, SAfr.
134/E3 Ruston, La,US
64/C4 Rute, Sp.
93/F5 Ruteng, Indo.
110/F5 Rutenga, Zim.
130/D3 Ruth, Nv,US
57/F6 Rüthen, Ger.
51/E5 Ruthin, Wal,UK
133/F3 Rutland, Vt,US
53/F1 Rutland (co.), Eng,UK
53/F1 Rutland Water (res.), Eng,UK
81/C5 Rutog, China
107/A3 Rutshuru, D.R. Congo
56/D4 Ruurlo, Neth.
66/E2 Ruvo di Puglia, It.
107/C5 Ruvuma (prov.), Tanz.
107/B5 Ruvuma (riv.), Tanz.
80/F3 Ruwāndūz, Iraq
107/A2 Ruwenzori (range), Ugan.
73/H1 Ruzayevka, Rus.
55/K4 Ružomberok, Slvk.
107/A3 Rwanda (ctry.)
97/D2 Ryan (mt.), Austl.
50/C2 Ryan, Loch (inlet), Sc,UK
72/F1 Ryazan', Rus.
70/J5 Ryazanskaya Obl., Rus.
72/G1 Ryazhsk, Rus.
70/G1 Rybachiy (pen.), Rus.
81/C3 Rybach'ye, Kyr.
70/H4 Rybinsk, Rus.
70/H4 Rybinsk (res.), Rus.
55/K3 Rybnik, Pol.
69/J2 Rybnitsa, Mol.
128/D2 Rycroft, Ab,Can.
96/H8 Ryde, Austl.
53/E5 Ryde, Eng,UK
53/G5 Rye, Eng,UK
53/G5 Rye (bay), Eng,UK
51/H3 Rye (riv.), Eng,UK
130/C2 Rye Patch (res.), Nv,US
55/L3 Ryki, Pol.
85/F1 Ryōtsu, Japan
85/M9 Ryōzen-yama (peak), Japan
55/K2 Rypin, Pol.
55/L4 Rysy (peak), Slvk.
51/G2 Ryton, Eng,UK
53/E2 Ryton on Dunsmore, Eng,UK
55/H1 Rytterknægten (peak), Den.
85/G3 Ryūgasaki, Japan
85/M9 Ryūō, Japan
55/M3 Rzeszów, Pol.
70/G4 Rzhev, Rus.

S

56/C4 's-Graveland, Neth.
56/B5 's-Gravendeel, Neth.
56/B4 's-Gravenhage (The Hague) (cap.), Neth.
56/D5 's-Heerenberg, Neth.
56/C5 's-Hertogenbosch, Neth.
57/G4 Saale (riv.), Ger.
54/F3 Saalfeld, Ger.
63/K3 Saalfelden am Steinernen Meer, Aus.
128/C3 Saanich, BC,Can.
59/F5 Saar (riv.), Ger.
59/F5 Saarbrücken, Ger.
70/D4 Saaremaa (isl.), Est.
59/F5 Saarland (state), Ger.
59/F5 Saarlouis, Ger.
89/D3 Sab (riv.), Camb.
123/J4 Saba (isl.), NAnt.
68/D3 Šabac, Serb.
65/G2 Sabadell, Sp.
84/E3 Sabae, Japan
93/E2 Sabah (state), Malay.
92/A2 Sabang, Indo.
123/F6 Sabanita, Pan.
103/M6 Sabat (riv.), Eth., Sudan
79/H2 Şāberi, Hāmūn-e (lake), Afg.
102/H2 Sabhā, Libya
106/B3 Sabie, Egypt
109/F2 Sabie (Sabierivier) (riv.), Moz., SAfr.
65/E1 Sabiñánigo, Sp.
122/A2 Sabinas, Mex.
122/A2 Sabinas (riv.), Mex.
122/A2 Sabinas Hidalgo, Mex.
134/E4 Sabine (lake), La, Tx,US
134/E4 Sabine (riv.), La, Tx,US
131/J5 Sabine Pass (waterway), La, Tx,US
66/C1 Sabini (mts.), It.
116/D1 Sabinópolis, Braz.
78/F4 Sabkhat Maţţī (salt marsh), UAE
88/D5 Sablayan, Phil.
133/J3 Sable (isl.), Can.
133/H3 Sable (cape), NS,Can.
135/H5 Sable (cape), Fl,US
62/C3 Sablé-sur-Sarthe, Fr.
64/B2 Sabor (riv.), Port.
93/H4 Sabra (cape), Indo.
111/J Sabrina (coast), Ant.
79/G1 Sabzevār, Iran
128/D4 Sacajawea (peak), Or,US
130/E4 Sacaton, Az,US
64/A3 Sacavém, Port.
66/C2 Sacco (riv.), It.
69/G3 Săcele, Rom.
129/L2 Sachigo (lake), On,Can.
129/L2 Sachigo (riv.), On,Can.
55/G3 Sachsen (state), Ger.
54/F3 Sachsen-Anhalt (state), Ger.
133/H2 Sackville, NB,Can.
133/G3 Saco, Me,US
116/C1 Sacramento, Braz.
138/M9 Sacramento (cap.), Ca,US
130/B2 Sacramento (riv.), Ca,US
131/F4 Sacramento (mts.), NM,US
64/D4 Sacratif (cape), Sp.
126/W12 Sacred (falls), Hi,US
51/G2 Sacriston, Eng,UK
66/E2 Sacro (peak), It.
64/A1 Sada, Sp.
128/C2 Saddle (hills), Ab, BC,Can.
51/G4 Saddleworth, Eng,UK
89/D4 Sa Dec, Viet.
79/K3 Sādiqābād, Pak.
91/G2 Sadiya, India
85/F2 Sado (isl.), Japan
64/A3 Sado (riv.), Port.
84/B4 Sadowara, Japan
90/B2 Sādri, India
102/H1 Şafāqis, Tun.
78/E3 Saffānīyah, Ra's as (pt.), SAr.
48/E4 Säffle, Swe.
130/E4 Safford, Az,US
53/G2 Saffron Walden, Eng,UK
102/D1 Safi, Mor.
79/H2 Safīd (mts.), Afg.
79/J1 Safīd (riv.), Afg.
79/K1 Safīd Khers (mts.), Afg., Taj.
80/L4 Şāfītā, Syria
70/G5 Safonovo, Rus.
80/C2 Safranbolu, Turk.
90/E2 Saga, China
84/B4 Saga, Japan
84/A4 Saga (pref.), Japan
85/G1 Sagae, Japan
91/G3 Sagaing, Myan.
91/F3 Sagaing (div.), Myan.
85/H7 Sagami (bay), Japan
85/H7 Sagami (riv.), Japan
85/F3 Sagami (sea), Japan
85/F3 Sagamihara, Japan
85/H7 Sagamiko, Japan
90/C3 Sāgar, India
136/J2 Sagavanirktok (riv.), Ak,US
93/F1 Sagay, Phil.
73/K2 Saghyz (riv.), Kaz.
132/D3 Saginaw, Mi,US
132/D3 Saginaw (bay), Mi,US
125/K3 Saglek (bay), Nf,Can.
66/A1 Sagone (gulf), Fr.
64/A4 Sagres, Port.
81/E2 Sagsay (riv.), Mong.
123/F3 Sagua de Tánamo, Cuba
130/E4 Saguaro Nat'l Park, Az,US
133/G1 Saguenay (riv.), Qu,Can.
102/C2 Saguia el Hamra (wadi), Mor., WSah.
65/E3 Sagunto, Sp.
90/E2 Sa'gya, China
80/L6 Saḩāb, Jor.
106/B5 Sahaba, Sudan
123/F6 Sahagún, Col.
78/E1 Sahand (mtn.), Iran
102/G3 Sahara (des.), Afr.
79/L3 Sahāranpur, India
90/E2 Saharsa, India
90/E2 Sāhibganj, India
79/K2 Sāhīwāl, Pak.
102/H2 Şaḩrā' Awbārī (des.), Libya
102/H3 Şaḩrā' Marzūq (des.), Libya
103/K2 Sahra' Rabyānah (des.), Libya
122/A3 Sahuayo, Mex.
90/D2 Sai (riv.), India
85/E2 Sai (riv.), Japan
102/F1 Saïda, Alg.
90/D2 Saidpur, India
84/C2 Saigō, Japan
89/D4 Saigon (Ho Chi Minh City), Viet.
84/C4 Saijō, Japan
84/A4 Saikai Nat'l Park, Japan
84/B4 Saiki, Japan
90/C4 Sailu, India
48/J3 Saimaa (lake), Fin.
58/C4 Sains-Richaumont, Fr.
49/D3 Saint Abb's Head (pt.), Sc,UK
62/E5 Saint-Affrique, Fr.
52/A6 Saint Agnes, Eng,UK
133/L2 Saint Alban's, Nf,Can.
133/F2 Saint Albans, Vt,US
132/D4 Saint Albans, WV,US
128/E2 Saint Albert, Ab,Can.
52/D5 Saint Aldhelm's Head (pt.), Eng,UK
58/C3 Saint-Amand-les-Eaux, Fr.
62/E3 Saint-Amand-Montrond, Fr.
133/G1 Saint-Ambroise, Qu,Can.
109/R15 Saint-André, Reun., Fr.
62/F2 Saint-André-les-Vergers, Fr.
49/D2 Saint Andrews, Sc,UK
104/B5 Saint Ann (cape), SLeo.
123/F4 Saint Ann's Bay, Jam.
62/B2 Saint Anne, Chl,UK
133/Q9 Saint Anns, On,Can.
52/A3 Saint Ann's (pt.), UK
133/L1 Saint Anthony, Nf,Can.
128/F5 Saint Anthony, Id,US
133/N6 Saint-Antoine, Qu,Can.
58/D6 Saint-Armand-sur-Fion, Fr.
50/E5 Saint Asaph, Wal,UK
52/C4 Saint Athan, Wal,UK
62/B2 Saint Aubin, Chl,UK
133/N6 Saint-Augustin, Qu,Can.
135/H4 Saint Augustine, Fl,US
52/B6 Saint Austell, Eng,UK
62/B3 Saint-Avé, Fr.
59/F5 Saint-Avold, Fr.
62/D5 Saint-Barthélemy, Pic de (peak), Fr.
50/E3 Saint Bees, Eng,UK
50/E3 Saint Bees Head (pt.), Eng,UK
133/M6 Saint-Benoît, Qu,Can.
109/R15 Saint-Benoît, Reun., Fr.
133/P7 Saint-Blaise, Qu,Can.
108/C4 Saint Blaize (cape), SAfr.
52/D3 Saint Briavels, Eng,UK
52/A3 Saint Brides (bay), Wal,UK
62/B2 Saint-Brieuc, Fr.
62/B2 Saint-Brieuc (bay), Fr.
133/P6 Saint-Bruno-de-Montarville, Qu,Can.
133/M6 Saint-Canut, Qu,Can.
133/R9 Saint Catharines, On,Can.
123/J5 Saint Catherine (mt.), Gren.
53/E5 Saint Catherine's (pt.), Eng,UK
62/F4 Saint-Chamond, Fr.
138/P16 Saint Charles, Il,US
132/E4 Saint Charles, Md,US
131/K3 Saint Charles, Mo,US
138/G7 Saint Clair (lake), On,Can, Mi,US
138/H6 Saint Clair (riv.), On,Can, Mi,US
138/G6 Saint Clair Shores, Mi,US
60/B5 Saint-Claude, Fr.
52/B3 Saint Clears, Wal UK
58/B6 Saint-Cloud, Fr.
129/K4 Saint Cloud, Mn,US
52/B6 Saint Columb Major, Eng,UK
133/N7 Saint-Constant, Qu,Can.
129/K4 Saint Croix (riv.), Mn, Wi,US
123/H4 Saint Croix (isl.), USVI
136/M3 Saint Cyr (mtn.), Yk,Can.
58/B6 Saint-Cyr-l'École, Fr.
52/A3 Saint David's, Wal,UK
52/A3 Saint David's Head (pt.), Wal,UK
58/B6 Saint-Denis, Fr.
109/R15 Saint-Denis (cap.), Reun., Fr.
60/C1 Saint-Dié, Fr.
62/F2 Saint-Dizier, Fr.
62/E3 Saint-Doulchard, Fr.
132/F2 Sainte-Agathe-des-Monts, Qu,Can.
133/H1 Sainte-Anne-des-Monts, Qu,Can.
133/N6 Sainte-Anne-des-Plaines, Qu,Can.
131/K3 Sainte Genevieve, Mo,US
58/B6 Sainte-Geneviève-des-Bois, Fr.
133/P6 Sainte-Julie-de-Verchères, Qu,Can.
133/J2 Saint Eleanors, PE,Can.
136/K3 Saint Elias (mts.), Can., US
136/K4 Saint Elias (cape), Ak,US
136/K3 Saint Elias (mt.), Ak,US
136/K3 Saint Elias-Wrangell Nat'l Park and Prsv., Ak,US
133/H1 Sainte-Marguerite (riv.), Qu,Can.
133/G2 Sainte-Marie, Qu,Can.
109/J7 Sainte Marie, Nosy (isl.), Madg.
63/G5 Sainte-Maxime, Fr.
58/C5 Saint-Erme-Outre-et-Ramecourt, Fr.
129/J3 Sainte Rose du Lac, Mb,Can.
62/C4 Saintes, Fr.
133/M6 Sainte-Scholastique, Qu,Can.
62/E5 Saint-Estève, Fr.
133/N6 Sainte-Thérèse, Qu,Can.
62/F4 Saint-Étienne, Fr.
62/D2 Saint-Étienne-du-Rouvray, Fr.
133/N6 Saint-Eustache, Qu,Can.
133/F1 Saint-Félicien, Qu,Can.
50/C3 Saintfield, NI,UK
62/E2 Saint-Florentin, Fr.
62/E3 Saint-Florent-sur-Cher, Fr.
103/K6 Saint-Floris Nat'l Park, CAfr.
62/E4 Saint-Flour, Fr.
108/D4 Saint Francis (cape), SAfr.
131/K4 Saint Francis (riv.), Ar, Mo,US
131/G3 Saint Francis, Ks,US
138/Q14 Saint Francis, Wi,US
135/F4 Saint Francisville, La,US
135/F2 Saint Francois (mts.), Mo,US
62/D5 Saint-Gaudens, Fr.
133/H2 Saint George, NB,Can.
133/K1 Saint George (cape), Nf,Can.
136/E4 Saint George (isl.), Ak,US
130/A2 Saint George (pt.), Ca,US
135/H3 Saint George, SC,US
130/D3 Saint George, Ut,US
133/K1 Saint George's, Nf,Can.
133/J2 Saint Georges (bay), NS,Can.
133/G2 Saint-Georges, Qu,Can.
123/J5 Saint George's (cap.), Gren.
50/C6 Saint George's (chan.), Ire., UK
58/B6 Saint-Germain-en-Laye, Fr.
58/B6 Saint-Germain-sur-Morin, Fr.
58/A5 Saint-Germer-de-Fly, Fr.
58/C3 Saint-Ghislain, Belg.
62/F5 Saint-Gilles, Fr.
62/C3 Saint-Gilles-Croix-de-Vie, Fr.
62/D5 Saint-Girons, Fr.
52/B3 Saint Govan's Head (pt.), Wal,UK
96/F6 Saint Helena (isl.), Austl.
108/B4 Saint Helena (bay), SAfr.
101/B6 Saint Helena (isl.), UK
138/J9 Saint Helena (mtn.), Ca,US
97/C4 Saint Helens (pt.), Austl.
51/F5 Saint Helens, Eng,UK
51/F5 Saint Helens (co.), Eng,UK
128/C4 Saint Helens, Or,US
128/C4 Saint Helens, Mount (vol.), Wa,US
62/B2 Saint Helier, Chl,UK
62/C3 Saint-Herblain, Fr.
133/M6 Saint-Hermas, Qu,Can.
90/E3 Sainthia, India
133/G1 Saint-Honoré, Qu,Can.
133/P7 Saint-Hubert, Qu,Can.
133/F2 Saint-Hyacinthe, Qu,Can.
132/C1 Saint Ignace (isl.), On,Can.
132/C2 Saint Ignace, Mi,US
96/H8 Saint Ives, Austl.
52/A6 Saint Ives, Eng,UK
53/F2 Saint Ives, Eng,UK
133/P7 Saint-Jacques-le-Mineur, Qu,Can.
124/C3 Saint James (cape), BC,Can.
129/K5 Saint James, Mn,US
137/G5 Saint James, NY,US
133/G1 Saint-Jean (lake), Qu,Can.
133/H1 Saint-Jean (riv.), Qu,Can.
62/C4 Saint-Jean-d'Angély, Fr.
62/D3 Saint-Jean-de-la-Ruelle, Fr.
62/C5 Saint-Jean-de-Luz, Fr.
133/G2 Saint-Jean-Port-Joli, Qu,Can.
133/F2 Saint-Jean-sur-Richelieu, Qu,Can.
133/N6 Saint-Jérôme, Qu,Can.
128/D4 Saint Joe (riv.), Id,US
133/H2 Saint John, NB,Can.
133/H2 Saint John (riv.), Can., US
62/B2 Saint John, Chl,UK
123/J4 Saint John's (cap.), Anti.
133/L2 Saint John's (cap.), Nf,Can.
50/C3 Saint John's (pt.), IM,UK
130/E4 Saint Johns, Az,US
135/H4 Saint Johns (riv.), Fl,US
133/F2 Saint Johnsbury, Vt,US
132/B1 Saint Joseph (lake), On,Can.
109/R15 Saint-Joseph, Reun., Fr.
132/C2 Saint Joseph (isl.), Mi,US
132/C3 Saint Joseph (riv.), Mi,US
131/J3 Saint Joseph, Mo,US
62/E5 Saint-Juéry, Fr.
62/D4 Saint-Junien, Fr.
52/A6 Saint Just, Eng,UK
52/A6 Saint Just in Roseland, Eng,UK
97/F5 Saint Kilda, Austl.
49/A2 Saint Kilda (isl.), Sc,UK
123/J4 Saint Kitts and Nevis (ctry.)
133/P6 Saint-Lambert, Qu,Can.
129/J3 Saint Laurent, Mb,Can.
58/B3 Saint-Laurent-Blangy, Fr.
115/H2 Saint-Laurent du Maroni, FrG.
133/J1 Saint Lawrence (gulf), Can.
133/L2 Saint Lawrence, Nf,Can.
133/G1 Saint Lawrence (riv.), Can, US
136/D3 Saint Lawrence (isl.), Ak,US
132/E2 Saint Lawrence Islands Nat'l Park, Can.
133/M7 Saint-Lazare, Qu,Can.
97/G5 Saint Leonard (mtn.), Austl.
109/R15 Saint-Leu, Reun., Fr.
62/C2 Saint-Lô, Fr.
133/N7 Saint Louis (lake), Qu,Can.
129/G2 Saint Louis, Sk,Can.
109/R15 Saint-Louis, Reun., Fr.
104/A2 Saint-Louis, Sen.
104/B3 Saint-Louis (reg.), Sen.
128/A2 Saint Louis (riv.), Mn,US
131/K3 Saint Louis, Mo,US
133/H2 Saint-Louis-de-Kent, NB,Can.
123/G4 Saint-Louis du Nord, Haiti
133/P7 Saint-Luc, Qu,Can.
123/J5 Saint Lucia (ctry.)
109/F3 Saint Lucia, Lake (lag.), SAfr.
62/C3 Saint-Maixent-L'École, Fr.
129/J3 Saint Malo, Mb,Can.
62/B2 Saint-Malo, Fr.
62/B2 Saint-Malo (gulf), Fr.
62/F5 Saint-Mandrier-sur-Mer, Fr.
58/B5 Saint-Mard, Fr.
53/H4 Saint Margaret's at Cliffe, Eng,UK
128/D4 Saint Maries, Id,US
129/J3 Saint Martin (lake), Mb,Can.
123/J4 Saint-Martin (isl.), Fr.
58/A2 Saint-Martin-Boulogne, Fr.
58/C6 Saint-Martin-d'Ablois, Fr.
62/F4 Saint-Martin-d'Hères, Fr.
104/A3 Saint Mary (cape), Gam.
96/G8 Saint Marys, Austl.
132/D3 Saint Mary's, Nf,Can.
133/J2 Saint Marys (riv.), NS,Can.
136/F3 Saint Marys, Ak,US
135/H4 Saint Marys, Ga,US
132/E3 Saint Marys, Pa,US
133/N7 Saint-Mathieu, Qu,Can.
136/D3 Saint Matthew (isl.), Ak,US
135/H3 Saint Matthews, SC,US
98/E5 Saint Matthias (isls.), PNG
58/B6 Saint-Maur-des-Fossés, Fr.
132/F1 Saint-Maurice (riv.), Qu,Can.
52/A6 Saint Mawes, Eng,UK
59/F6 Saint-Max, Fr.
52/C3 Saint Mellons, Wal,UK
58/D6 Saint-Memmie, Fr.
58/B6 Saint-Michel-sur-Orge, Fr.
62/B3 Saint-Nazaire, Fr.
53/F2 Saint Neots, Eng,UK
59/E2 Saint-Nicolas, Belg.
58/B2 Saint-Omer, Fr.
58/A4 Saint-Omer-en-Chaussée, Fr.
133/G2 Saint-Pamphile, Qu,Can.
133/G2 Saint-Pascal, Qu,Can.
16/H5 Saint Paul (isls.), Braz.
128/F2 Saint Paul, Ab,Can.
45/N7 Saint Paul (isl.), FrAnt.
105/F5 Saint Paul (cape), Gha.
104/C5 Saint Paul (riv.), Gui., Libr.
109/R15 Saint-Paul, Reun., Fr.
136/E4 Saint Paul (isl.), Ak,US
131/J3 Saint Paul, Ks,US
129/K4 Saint Paul (cap.), Mn,US
62/C5 Saint-Paul-lès-Dax, Fr.
62/F4 Saint-Paul-Trois-Châteaux, Fr.
129/K4 Saint Peter, Mn,US
115/M3 Saint Peter and Saint Paul (rocks), Braz.
62/B2 Saint Peter Port, Chl,UK
53/H4 Saint Peter's, Eng,UK
71/V7 Saint Petersburg (Leningrad), Rus.
135/H5 Saint Petersburg, Fl,US
133/P7 Saint-Philippe-de-La Prairie, Qu,Can.
123/J5 Saint-Pierre, Mart.
109/R15 Saint-Pierre, Reun., Fr.
133/K2 Saint Pierre & Miquelon (dpcy.), Fr.
62/D3 Saint-Pierre-des-Corps, Fr.
62/C5 Saint-Pierre-du-Mont, Fr.
129/J3 Saint Pierre-Jolys, Mb,Can.
62/B2 Saint-Pol-de-Léon, Fr.
58/B1 Saint-Pol-sur-Mer, Fr.
58/B5 Saint-Prix, Fr.
58/C4 Saint-Quentin, Fr.
63/G5 Saint-Raphaël, Fr.
62/F5 Saint-Rémy-de-Provence, Fr.
58/A3 Saint-Riquier, Fr.
62/B2 Saint Sampson's, Chl,UK
58/C3 Saint-Saulve, Fr.
135/H4 Saint Simons Island, Ga,US
133/H2 Saint Stephen, NB,Can.
52/B6 Saint Stephen in Brannel, Eng,UK
132/D3 Saint Thomas, On,Can.
123/H4 Saint Thomas (isl.), USVI
133/N7 Saint-Urbain-Premier, Qu,Can.
62/F3 Saint-Vallier, Fr.
58/B2 Saint-Venant, Fr.
97/C4 Saint Vincent (pt.), Austl.
123/J5 Saint Vincent & the Grenadines (ctry.)
59/F3 Saint Vith, Belg.
128/F2 Saint Walburg, Sk,Can.
90/E2 Saipal (mtn.), Nepal
98/D3 Saipan (isl.), NMar.
85/F2 Saitama (pref.), Japan
84/B4 Saito, Japan
89/B3 Sai Yok Nat'l Park, Thai.
114/E7 Sajama Nat'l Park, Bol.
68/E1 Sajószentpéter, Hun.
108/C3 Sak (riv.), SAfr.
85/H7 Sakado, Japan
85/J7 Sakae, Japan
85/M9 Sakahogi, Japan
85/F2 Sakai, Japan
84/C3 Sakaide, Japan
84/C3 Sakaiminato, Japan
129/H3 Sakakawea (lake), ND,US
125/J3 Sakami (lake), Qu,Can.
69/K5 Sakarya (prov.), Turk.
80/B2 Sakarya (riv.), Turk.
83/M4 Sakata, Japan
84/C4 Sakawa, Japan
75/M3 Sakha (Yakutiya), Resp., Rus.
75/Q4 Sakhalin (gulf), Rus.
75/Q4 Sakhalin (isl.), Rus.
75/Q4 Sakhalinskaya Obl., Rus.
78/F1 Sakht Sar (Ramsar), Iran
73/H4 Şaki, Azer.
72/E3 Saki, Ukr.
88/D3 Sakishima (isls.), Japan
73/L1 Sakmara (riv.), Rus.
89/D2 Sakon Nakhon, Thai.
79/J3 Sakrand, Pak.
85/F2 Saku, Japan
85/J7 Sakura, Japan
85/L10 Sakurai, Japan
73/G3 Sal (riv.), Rus.
55/J4 Šal'a, Slvk.
48/F4 Sala, Swe.
66/D2 Sala Consilina, It.
117/E2 Saladas, Arg.
118/F2 Saladillo, Arg.
118/D3 Salado (riv.), Arg.
118/F2 Salado (riv.), Arg.
122/B2 Salado (riv.), Mex.
113/C5 Salado del Norte (riv.), Arg.
105/E4 Salaga, Gha.
93/G4 Salahatu (mtn.), Indo.
68/F2 Sălaj (co.), Rom.
102/J5 Salal, Chad
106/D4 Şalālah, Sudan
118/D5 Salamanca (plain), Arg.
118/C1 Salamanca, Chile
122/A3 Salamanca, Mex.
64/C2 Salamanca, Sp.
132/E3 Salamanca, NY,US
103/J6 Salamat (riv.), Chad
67/H3 Salamís, Gre.
67/L7 Salamís (isl.), Gre.
80/L4 Salamīyah, Syria
89/C1 Sala Mok, Laos
64/B1 Salas, Sp.
73/K1 Salavat, Rus.
93/F5 Salayar (isl.), Indo.
16/D7 Sala y Gomez (isls.), Chile
62/E3 Salbris, Fr.
52/C6 Salcombe, Eng,UK
97/C3 Sale, Austl.
102/D1 Salé, Mor.
51/F5 Sale, Eng,UK
93/G3 Salebabu (isl.), Indo.
74/G3 Salekhard, Rus.
90/C5 Salem, India
132/C4 Salem, In,US
131/K3 Salem, Mo,US
133/G3 Salem, NH,US
128/C4 Salem (cap.), Or,US
132/D4 Salem, Va,US
66/C4 Salemi, It.
66/F2 Salentina (pen.), It.
66/D2 Salerno, It.
66/D2 Salerno (gulf), It.
53/G3 Sales (pt.), UK
51/F5 Salford, Eng,UK
51/F5 Salford (co.), Eng,UK
68/D1 Salgótarján, Hun.
115/L5 Salgueiro, Braz.
131/F3 Salida, Co,US
80/B2 Salihli, Turk.
72/C1 Salihorsk, Bela.
110/F3 Salima, Malw.
106/B4 Salīmah (oasis), Sudan
64/B1 Salime (res.), Sp.
123/G3 Salina (pt.), Bahm.
66/D3 Salina (isl.), It.
131/H3 Salina, Ks,US
130/E3 Salina, Ut,US
122/B4 Salina Cruz, Mex.
115/K7 Salinas, Braz.

Salin – Sapar

Sapel – Shuan
183

135/H4 Sapelo (isl.), Ga,US
67/G4 Sapiéndza (isl.), Gre.
56/D2 Sappemeer, Neth.
83/N3 Sapporo, Japan
66/D2 Sapri, It.
116/H7 Sapucaí (riv.), Braz.
78/E1 Saqqez, Iran
68/E4 Šar (mts.), Serb.
78/E1 Sarāb, Iran
89/C3 Sara Buri, Thai.
65/E2 Saragossa (Zaragoza), Sp.
68/D4 Sarajevo (cap.), Bosn.
135/F4 Saraland, Al,US
92/D4 Saran (peak), Indo.
81/B2 Saran', Kaz.
132/F2 Saranac Lake, NY,US
67/L6 Sarandapótamos (riv.), Gre.
67/G3 Sarandë, Alb.
119/G2 Sarandí Del Yi, Uru.
90/C3 Sārangpur, India
73/H1 Saransk, Rus.
71/M4 Sarapul, Rus.
135/H5 Sarasota, Fl,US
138/K12 Saratoga, Ca,US
128/G5 Saratoga, Wy,US
132/F3 Saratoga Springs, NY,US
73/H2 Saratov, Rus.
73/J1 Saratov (res.), Rus.
73/H2 Saratovskaya Obl., Rus.
92/D3 Sarawak (state), Malay.
80/B3 Sarayköy, Turk.
80/C2 Sarayönü, Turk.
68/D2 Sárbogárd, Hun.
58/B5 Sarcelles, Fr.
90/B2 Sardārshahar, India
66/A2 Sardegna (reg.), It.
63/G5 Sardinaux, Cap de (cape), Fr.
66/A2 Sardinia (isl.), It.
131/K4 Sardis (lake), Ms,US
131/J4 Sardis (lake), Ok,US
48/F2 Sareks Nat'l Park, Swe.
48/F2 Sarektjåkko (peak), Swe.
93/E4 Sarempaka (peak), Indo.
79/K2 Sargodha, Pak.
103/J6 Sarh, Chad
78/F1 Sārī, Iran
93/J4 Saribi (cape), Indo.
98/D3 Sarigan (isl.), NMar.
80/E2 Sarıkamış, Turk.
80/C2 Sarıkaya, Turk.
60/D4 Sarine (riv.), Swi.
103/K2 Sarīr Kalanshiyū (des.), Libya
103/J3 Sarīr Tibasti (des.), Libya
134/D5 Sarita, Tx,US
68/E2 Sarkad, Hun.
73/L4 Sarkamyshskoye (lake), Trkm., Uzb.
74/H5 Sarkant, Kaz.
80/B2 Şarkikaraağaç, Turk.
80/D2 Şarkışla, Turk.
69/H5 Şarköy, Turk.
62/D4 Sarlat-La-Canéda, Fr.
119/K8 Sarmiento (peak), Chile
61/E4 Sarnen, Swi.
138/H6 Sarnia, On,Can.
72/C2 Sarny, Ukr.
67/H4 Saronic (gulf), Gre.
67/L7 Saronikós (gulf), Gre.
69/H5 Saros (gulf), Turk.
68/E1 Sárospatak, Hun.
59/F6 Sarre (riv.), Fr.
59/G6 Sarrebourg, Fr.
59/G5 Sarreguemines, Fr.
64/B1 Sarria, Sp.
57/G4 Sarstedt, Ger.
75/P3 Sartang (riv.), Rus.
62/C3 Sarthe (riv.), Fr.
58/B6 Sartrouville, Fr.
68/D2 Sárvíz (riv.), Hun.
81/C2 Saryesik Atyraū Qumy (des.), Kaz.
81/B2 Saryshaghan, Kaz.
81/A2 Sarysu (riv.), Kaz.
63/H4 Sarzana, It.
129/K3 Sasaginnigak (lake), Mb,Can.
90/D3 Sasarām, India
85/L9 Sasayama, Japan
85/L9 Sasayama (riv.), Japan
84/A4 Sasebo, Japan
124/F3 Saskatchewan (prov.), Can.
128/F3 Saskatchewan (riv.), Can.
128/G2 Saskatoon, Sk,Can.
122/D5 Saslaya (mt.), Nic.
73/G1 Sasovo, Rus.
104/D5 Sassandra, C.d'Iv.
104/D5 Sassandra (riv.), C.d'Iv.
66/A2 Sassari, It.
57/E4 Sassenberg, Ger.
56/B4 Sassenheim, Neth.
55/G1 Sassnitz, Ger.
63/J4 Sassuolo, It.
56/A6 Sas Van Gent, Neth.
81/D2 Sasykköl (lake), Kaz.
84/B5 Sata-misaki (cape), Japan
90/B4 Sātāra, India
98/E4 Satawan (atoll), Micr.
114/D6 Satipo, Peru
51/G2 Satley, Eng,UK
90/D3 Satna, India
68/E1 Sátoraljaújhely, Hun.
81/A2 Satpayev, Kaz.
90/C3 Satpura (range), India
68/F2 Satu Mare, Rom.
68/F2 Satu Mare (co.), Rom.
89/C5 Satun, Thai.
99/R9 Satupaitea, Samoa
118/E3 Sauce Grande (riv.), Arg.
78/D4 Saudi Arabia (ctry.)
59/F4 Sauer (riv.), Ger., Lux.
59/G1 Sauerland (reg.), Ger.
114/G6 Sauêruiná (riv.), Braz.
129/K4 Sauk (riv.), Mn,US
129/K4 Sauk Centre, Mn,US
129/K4 Sauk Rapids, Mn,US
62/D3 Sauldre (riv.), Fr.
132/C2 Sault Sainte Marie, On,Can.
132/C2 Sault Sainte Marie, Mi,US
59/E6 Saulx (riv.), Fr.
96/D3 Saumarez (reefs), Austl.
62/C3 Saumur, Fr.
52/B3 Saundersfoot, Wal,UK
110/D2 Saurimo, Ang.
138/K11 Sausalito, Ca,US
68/B9 Sava (riv.), Eur.
66/E2 Sava, It.
99/H6 Savai'i (isl.), Samoa
133/G1 Savane (riv.), Qu,Can.
135/H3 Savannah, Ga,US
135/H3 Savannah (riv.), Ga, SC,US
135/F3 Savannah, Tn,US
91/H4 Savannaket, Laos
89/D2 Savannakhet, Laos
123/F4 Savanna-la-Mar, Jam.
132/B1 Savant (lake), On,Can.
90/B4 Sāvantvādi, India
110/C4 Savate, Ang.
110/F5 Save (riv.), Moz., Zim.
78/F1 Sāveh, Iran
69/H2 Săveni, Rom.
59/G6 Saverne, Fr.
63/G4 Savigliano, It.
63/K4 Savignano sul Rubicone, It.
58/B6 Savigny, Fr.
63/K5 Savio (riv.), It.
128/C3 Savona, BC,Can.
63/H4 Savona, It.
48/J3 Savonlinna, Fin.
60/C6 Savoy Alps (mts.), Fr.
48/E4 Sävsjö, Swe.
93/F5 Savu (sea), Indo.
92/B4 Sawahlunto, Indo.
106/D5 Sawākin, Sudan
89/B2 Sawankhalok, Thai.
85/G3 Sawara, Japan
85/F2 Sawasaki-bana (pt.), Japan
130/F3 Sawatch (range), Co,US
53/G3 Sawbridgeworth, Eng,UK
102/J2 Sawdā (mts.), Libya
78/D5 Sawdā', Jabal (mtn.), SAr.
103/L5 Sawdirī, Sudan
93/H4 Saweba (cape), Indo.
50/A2 Sawel (mtn.), NI,UK
106/B3 Sawhāj, Egypt
106/B3 Sawhāj (gov.), Egypt
91/F6 Sāwi, India
78/G5 Sawqirah, Ghubbat (bay), Oman
53/G2 Sawston, Eng,UK
97/E1 Sawtell, Austl.
128/E4 Sawtooth (range), Id,US
93/F6 Sawu (isls.), Indo.
65/E3 Sax, Sp.
51/H5 Saxilby, Eng,UK
53/H2 Saxmundham, Eng,UK
85/F3 Sayama, Japan
122/D3 Sayil (ruins), Mex.
59/G1 Saynbach (riv.), Ger.
81/D3 Sayram (lake), China
137/F5 Sayreville, NJ,US
137/G5 Sayville, NY,US
67/F2 Sazan (isl.), Alb.
63/L2 Sázava (riv.), Czh.
51/E3 Scafell Pikes (mtn.), Eng,UK
51/H3 Scalby, Eng,UK
66/D3 Scalea, It.
63/J5 Scandicci, It.
133/R8 Scarborough, On,Can.
51/H3 Scarborough, Eng,UK
58/B3 Scarpe (riv.), Fr.
137/G4 Scarsdale, NY,US
50/E1 Scar Water (riv.), Sc,UK
58/D2 Schaerbeek, Belg.
61/E2 Schaffhausen, Swi.
61/E2 Schaffhausen (canton), Swi.
56/B3 Schagen, Neth.
56/C5 Schaijk, Neth.
57/E6 Schalksmühle, Ger.
97/C3 Schanck (cape), Austl.
57/F1 Scharhörn (isl.), Ger.
138/P15 Schaumburg, Il,US
56/B2 Scheemda, Neth.
57/G2 Scheessel, Ger.
58/C2 Schelde (Scheldt) (riv.), Belg.
130/D3 Schell Creek (range), Nv,US
57/H4 Schellerten, Ger.
132/F3 Schenectady, NY,US
57/G1 Schenefeld, Ger.
138/R16 Schererville, In,US
56/D5 Schermbeck, Ger.
56/C3 Scherpenzeel, Neth.
56/B5 Schiedam, Neth.
57/G5 Schieder-Schwalenberg, Ger.
56/D2 Schiermonnikoog (isl.), Neth.
59/G5 Schiffweiler, Ger.
56/C5 Schijndel, Neth.
58/D1 Schilde, Belg.
56/D2 Schildmeer (lake), Neth.
57/F1 Schillighörn (cape), Ger.
59/G6 Schiltigheim, Fr.
59/E2 Schinnen, Neth.
56/D4 Schipbeek (riv.), Neth.
67/G2 Schkumbin (riv.), Alb.
57/F5 Schlangen, Ger.
59/F2 Schleiden, Ger.
54/E1 Schleswig, Ger.
54/E1 Schleswig-Holstein (state), Ger.
54/E1 Schleswig-Holsteinisches Wattenmeer Nat'l Park, Ger.
57/F5 Schloss Holte-Stukenbrock, Ger.
63/H1 Schlüchtern, Ger.
54/F3 Schmalkalden, Ger.
57/F6 Schmallenberg, Ger.
59/F5 Schmelz, Ger.
59/F3 Schneifel (upland), Ger.
57/G2 Schneverdingen, Ger.
126/V12 Schofield Barracks, Hi,US
119/L7 Scholl, Cerro (mtn.), Arg.
54/F2 Schönebeck, Ger.
54/F2 Schöningen, Ger.
56/D3 Schoonebeek, Neth.
56/B5 Schoonhoven, Neth.
56/B3 Schoorl, Neth.
57/E1 Schortens, Ger.
58/D1 Schoten, Belg.
97/D4 Schouten (isl.), Austl
98/C5 Schouten (isls.), Indo.
56/A5 Schouwen (isl.), Neth.
61/E1 Schramberg, Ger.
132/C1 Schreiber, On,Can.
108/B2 Schroffenstein (peak), Namb.
134/D4 Schulenburg, Tx,US
57/H4 Schunter (riv.), Ger.
57/E4 Schüttorf, Ger.
137/E5 Schuylkill (riv.), Pa,US
63/J2 Schwabach, Ger.
61/E1 Schwäbische Alb (range), Ger.
63/H2 Schwäbisch Hall, Ger.
59/F5 Schwalbach, Ger.
57/F6 Schwalm (riv.), Ger
56/D6 Schwalmtal, Ger.
63/K2 Schwandorf im Bayern, Ger.
92/D4 Schwaner (mts.), Indo.
57/F2 Schwanewede, Ger.
55/G3 Schwartz Elster (riv.), Ger.
108/B2 Schwartzerberg (peak), Namb.
57/H2 Schwarzenbek, Ger.
59/F3 Schwarzer Mann (peak), Ger
63/J3 Schwaz, Aus.
55/J4 Schwechat, Aus.
55/H2 Schwedt, Ger.
63/J1 Schweinfurt, Ger.
57/E6 Schwelm, Ger.
54/F2 Schwerin, Ger.
54/F2 Schweriner (lake), Ger.
57/E6 Schwerte, Ger.
57/G1 Schwinge (riv.), Ger.
61/E3 Schwyz, Swi.
61/E3 Schwyz (canton), Swi.
56/C4 Sciacca, It.
66/D4 Scicli, It.
132/D4 Scioto (riv.), Oh,US
129/G3 Scobey, Mt,US
53/G1 Scolt (pt.), UK
66/D4 Scordia, It.
51/G3 Scotch Corner, Eng,UK
137/F5 Scotch Plains, NJ,US
111/W Scotia (sea), Ant.
49/C2 Scotland, UK
111/M Scott, Ant.
111/L Scott (coast), Ant.
124/D3 Scott (cape), BC,Can.
125/R7 Scott (cape), NW,Can.
124/F2 Scott (lake), NW,Can.
131/G3 Scott City, Ks,US
51/F1 Scottish Borders (reg.), Sc,UK
131/G2 Scottsbluff, Ne,US
131/F2 Scotts Bluff Nat'l Mon., Ne,US
135/G3 Scottsboro, Al,US
132/C4 Scottsburg, In,US
130/E4 Scottsdale, Az,US
97/C4 Scotts Peak (dam), Austl.
132/C4 Scottsville, Ky,US
132/C3 Scottville, Mi,US
51/H4 Scunthorpe, Eng,UK
68/D4 Scutari (lake), Alb., Mont.
127/K5 Sea (isls.), Ga,US
53/G5 Seaford, UK
50/C3 Seaforde, NI,UK
51/G2 Seaham, Eng,UK
125/H2 Seahorse (pt.), Nun,Can.
124/G3 Seal (riv.), Mb,Can.
118/B5 Seal (pt.), Chile
108/C4 Seal (cape), SAfr.
137/B3 Seal Beach, Ca,US
51/H3 Seamer, Eng,UK
130/D4 Searchlight, Nv,US
134/F3 Searcy, Ar,US
50/E3 Seascale, Eng,UK
128/C4 Seaside, Or,US
138/C3 SeaTac, Wa,US
52/C5 Seaton, Eng,UK
52/B6 Seaton (riv.), Eng,UK
51/G2 Seaton Carew, Eng,UK
51/G1 Seaton Valley, Eng,UK
138/C2 Seattle, Wa,US
135/H5 Sebastian, Fl,US
123/M8 Sebastián Vizcaíno (bay), Mex.
97/B3 Sebastopol, Austl.
92/D4 Sebayan (peak), Indo.
69/F3 Sebeș, Rom.
80/D2 Şebinkarahisar, Turk.
68/F2 Sebiș, Rom.
66/B5 Sebkhet Kelbia (dry lake), Tun.
55/H3 Sebnitz, Ger.
93/F2 Seboto (pt.), Phil.
135/H5 Sebring, Fl,US
93/E4 Sebuku (isl.), Indo.
63/J4 Secchia (riv.), It.
114/B5 Sechura, Peru
114/B5 Sechura (bay), Peru
114/B5 Sechura (des.), Peru
58/C2 Seclin, Fr.
119/L7 Seco (riv.), Arg.
90/C4 Secunderābād, India
114/E7 Securé (riv.), Bol.
131/J3 Sedalia, Mo,US
59/D4 Sedan, Fr.
89/B3 Sedaung (mtn.), Myan.
51/F3 Sedbergh, Eng,UK
106/B4 Seddenga Temple (ruins), Sudan
80/K6 Sederot, Isr.
51/G2 Sedgefield, Eng,UK
136/L2 Sedgwick (mtn.), Yk,Can.
104/B3 Sedhiou, Sen.
63/L1 Sedlo (peak), Czh.
130/E4 Sedona, Az,US
55/L3 Sędziszów, Pol.
62/C2 Sée (riv.), Fr.
108/D3 Seekooi (riv.), SAfr.
57/H5 Seesen, Ger.
57/G2 Seeve (riv.), Ger.
51/E4 Sefton (co.), Eng,UK
92/B3 Segamat, Malay.
69/F3 Segarcea, Rom.
66/C4 Segesta (ruins), It.
70/G3 Segezha, Rus.
65/E3 Segorbe, Sp.
104/D3 Ségou, Mali
104/D3 Ségou (reg.), Mali
64/C2 Segovia, Sp.
70/G3 Segozero (lake), Rus.
62/C3 Segré, Fr.
65/F2 Segre (riv.), Sp.
136/D5 Seguam (isl.), Ak,US
102/H3 Séguédine, Niger
104/D5 Séguéla, C.d'Iv.
134/D4 Seguin, Tx,US
64/D3 Segura (riv.), Sp.
110/D5 Sehithwa, Bots.
90/C3 Sehore, India
79/J3 Sehwān, Pak.
85/L10 Seika, Japan
131/H3 Seiling, Ok,US
59/F6 Seille (riv.), Fr.
48/G3 Seinäjoki, Fin.
129/L3 Seine (riv.), On,Can.
62/C2 Seine (bay), Fr.
62/D2 Seine (riv.), Fr.
58/B5 Seine-et-Marne (dept.), Fr.
58/B6 Seine-Saint-Denis (dept.), Fr.
48/G3 Seitsemisen Nat'l Park, Fin.
85/M10 Seiwa, Japan
85/E3 Seki, Japan
85/M9 Sekigahara, Japan
85/H6 Sekiyado, Japan
105/E5 Sekondi, Gha.
128/C4 Selah, Wa,US
66/A3 Selargius, It.
93/H5 Selaru (isl.), Indo.
92/D4 Selatan (cape), Indo.
136/F2 Selawik (lake), Ak,US
93/F5 Selayar (isl.), Indo.
63/K1 Selb, Ger.
51/G4 Selby, Eng,UK
129/H4 Selby, SD,US
137/G5 Selden, NY,US
66/D2 Sele (riv.), It.
110/E5 Selebi-Phikwe, Bots.
83/L1 Selemdzha (riv.), Rus.
82/F1 Selenga (riv.), Rus.
82/E2 Selenge, Mong.
82/E2 Selenge (riv.), Mong.
60/D1 Sélestat, Fr.
81/B1 Seletyteniz (lake), Kaz.
70/G4 Seliger (lake), Rus.
130/D4 Seligman, Az,US
66/C4 Selinunte (ruins), It.
128/D3 Selkirk (mts.), BC,Can.
129/J3 Selkirk, Mb,Can.
49/D3 Selkirk, Sc,UK
130/E5 Sells, Az,US
52/E2 Selly Oak, Eng,UK
57/E5 Selm, Ger.
135/G3 Selma, Al,US
135/F3 Selmer, Tn,US
136/M3 Selous (mtn.), Yk,Can.
53/F5 Selsey, Eng,UK
53/F5 Selsey Bill (pt.), Eng,UK
62/C2 Sélune (riv.), Fr.
114/E5 Selvas (for.), Braz.
63/H2 Selz (riv.), Ger.
102/C2 Semara, WSah.
92/D5 Semarang, Indo.
80/F3 Şemdinli, Turk.
71/K4 Semenov, Rus.
92/D5 Semeru (peak), Indo.
81/D1 Semey, Kaz.
136/G4 Semidi (isls.), Ak,US
72/F2 Semiluki, Rus.
128/G5 Seminoe (res.), Wy,US
135/G4 Seminole (lake), Ga,US
134/C3 Seminole, Tx,US
136/B5 Semisopochnoi (isl.), Ak,US
92/D4 Semitau, Indo.
78/F1 Semnān, Iran
62/C3 Semnon (riv.), Fr.
59/E4 Semois (riv.), Belg.
59/D4 Semoy (riv.), Fr.
70/B2 Semskefjellet (peak), Nor.
89/D3 Sen (riv.), Camb.
89/C3 Sena, Thai.
88/C6 Senaja, Malay.
110/D4 Senanga, Zam.
135/F3 Senatobia, Ms,US
53/E2 Sence (riv.), Eng,UK
84/B5 Sendai, Japan
85/G1 Sendai (bay), Japan
84/B5 Sendai (riv.), Japan
84/D3 Sendai (riv.), Japan
57/E5 Senden, Ger.
57/E5 Sendenhorst, Ger.
55/J4 Senec, Slvk.
58/D2 Seneffe, Belg.
104/B3 Senegal (ctry.)
104/B2 Sénégal (riv.), Afr.
108/D3 Senekal, SAfr.
55/H3 Senftenberg, Ger.
81/D5 Sênggê (riv.), China
118/C5 Senguerr (riv.), Arg.
115/L6 Senhor do Bonfim, Braz.
55/J4 Senica, Slvk.
63/K5 Senigallia, It.
80/B2 Senirkent, Turk.
66/E2 Senise, It.
68/B3 Senj, Cro.
48/F1 Senja (isl.), Nor.
58/B5 Senlis, Fr.
85/L10 Sennan, Japan
103/M5 Sennar (dam), Sudan
58/D2 Senne (riv.), Belg.
132/E1 Senneterre, Qu,Can.
52/C3 Sennybridge, Wal,UK
105/F3 Séno (prov.), Burk.
62/E2 Sens, Fr.
68/E3 Senta, Serb.
110/E2 Sentery, D.R. Congo
128/C2 Sentinel (peak), BC,Can.
98/E4 Senyavin (isls.), Micr.
90/C3 Seoni, India
90/C3 Seonī Mālwā, India
86/D4 Seoul-Jikhalsi (prov.), SKor.
86/D4 Seoul (Sŏul) (cap.), SKor.
116/K8 Sepetiba (bay), Braz.
98/D5 Sepik (riv.), PNG
55/J2 Sępólno Krajeńskie, Pol.
69/G4 Septemvri, Bul.
133/H1 Sept-Îles, Qu,Can.
138/A1 Sequim (bay), Wa,US
130/C3 Sequoia Nat'l Park, Ca,US
59/E2 Seraing, Belg.
92/C5 Serang, Indo.
92/C3 Serasan (str.), Indo., Malay.
68/E4 Serbia (rep.), Serb.
68/D3 Serbia (ctry.)
73/H1 Serdobsk, Rus.
136/D2 Serdtse-Kamen, Mys (pt.), Rus.
80/C2 Şereflikoçhisar, Turk.
62/F3 Serein (riv.), Fr
92/B3 Seremban, Malay.
107/B3 Serengeti (plain), Tanz.
107/B3 Serengeti Nat'l Park, Tanz.
110/F3 Serenje, Zam.
71/K5 Sergach, Rus.
74/J2 Sergeya Kirova (isls.), Rus.
70/H4 Sergiyev Posad, Rus.
92/D3 Seria, Bru.
63/H4 Seriate, It.
67/J4 Sérifos (isl.), Gre.
80/B3 Serik, Turk.
115/H5 Seringa (mts.), Braz.
80/B3 Serinhisar, Turk.
93/G5 Sermata (isl.), Indo.
74/G4 Serov, Rus.
110/E5 Serowe, Bots.
64/B4 Serpa, Port.
66/A3 Serpeddi (peak), It.
104/C3 Serpent, Vallée du (wadi), Mali
70/H5 Serpukhov, Rus.
116/D2 Serra, Braz.
116/J8 Serra da Bocaina Nat'l Park, Braz.
116/C2 Serra da Canastra Nat'l Park, Braz.
115/K5 Serra de Capivara Nat'l Park, Braz.
116/D1 Serra do Cipó Nat'l Park, Braz.
116/K7 Serra dos Órgãos Nat'l Park, Braz.
67/H2 Sérrai, Gre.
66/E3 Serralta di San Vito (peak), It.
66/A3 Serramanna, It.
123/F5 Serrana (bank), Col.
114/E3 Serranía de la Neblina Nat'l Park, Ven.
123/F4 Serranilla (bank), Col.
66/A4 Serrat (cape), Tun.
115/L5 Serra Talhada, Braz.
58/C4 Serre (riv.), Fr.
115/L6 Serrinha, Braz.
64/A3 Sertã, Port.
116/C2 Sertãozinho, Braz.
82/C4 Serteng (mts.), China
92/D4 Seruyan (riv.), Indo.
106/B4 Sesebi (ruins), Sudan
63/H4 Sesia (riv.), It.
64/A3 Sesimbra, Port.
64/D1 Sestao, Sp.
63/J5 Sesto Fiorentino, It.
63/H4 Sesto San Giovanni, It.
71/S6 Sestroretsk, Rus.
66/A3 Sestu, It.
68/C3 Sesvete, Cro.
62/E5 Sète, Fr.
115/K4 Sete Cidades Nat'l Park, Braz.
116/C1 Sete Lagoas, Braz.
79/J3 Sethārja, Pak.
102/G1 Sétif, Alg.
85/E3 Seto, Japan
84/C3 Seto-Naikai Nat'l Park, Japan
63/G4 Settimo Torinese, It.
129/J2 Setting (lake), Mb,Can.
51/F3 Settle, Eng,UK
85/L10 Settsu, Japan
64/A3 Setúbal, Port.
65/Q11 Setúbal (bay), Port.
64/A3 Setúbal (dist.), Port.
62/C4 Seudre (riv.), Fr.
62/C4 Seugne (riv.), Fr.
132/A1 Seul (lake), On,Can.
73/H4 Sevan (lake), Arm.
72/E3 Sevastopol', Ukr.
49/G7 Seven Hogs, The (isls.), Ire.
53/G4 Sevenoaks, Eng,UK
129/L2 Severn (riv.), On,Can.
52/D3 Severn (riv.), Eng,UK
137/K7 Severn, Md,US
52/C4 Severn, Mouth of the (estuary), Eng,UK
137/K7 Severna Park, Md,US
73/G4 Severnaya Osetiya-Alaniya, Resp., Rus.
71/P3 Severnaya Sos'va (riv.), Rus.
77/K2 Severnaya Zemlya (arch.), Rus.
71/Q2 Severnyy, Rus.
72/F2 Severodonetsk, Ukr.
70/H2 Severodvinsk, Rus.
75/R4 Severo-Kuril'sk, Rus.
70/G1 Severomorsk, Rus.
71/N3 Severoural'sk, Rus.
130/D3 Sevier (des.), Ut,US
130/D3 Sevier (riv.), Ut,US
135/H3 Sevierville, Tn,US
64/C4 Seville, Sp.
69/G4 Sevlievo, Bul.
104/C5 Sewa (riv.), SLeo.
136/E2 Seward (pen.), Ak,US
131/H2 Seward, Ne,US
136/M5 Sewell Inlet, BC,Can.
128/D2 Sexsmith, Ab,Can.
45/M6 Seychelles (ctry.)
80/B3 Seydişehir, Turk.
80/C2 Seyhan (riv.), Turk.
97/C3 Seymour, Austl.
134/D3 Seymour, Tx,US
58/C6 Sézanne, Fr.
64/A3 Sezimbra, Port.
66/C2 Sezze, It.
69/G3 Sfîntu Gheorghe, Rom.
49/C2 Sgurr Mór (mtn.), Sc,UK
87/C4 Sha (riv.), China
87/B4 Shaanxi (prov.), China
103/P7 Shabeelle, Webi (riv.), Som.
110/E1 Shabunda, D.R. Congo
111/M Shackleton (coast), Ant.
111/G Shackleton Ice Shelf, Ant.
71/P4 Shadrinsk, Rus.
134/B4 Shafter, Tx,US
52/D4 Shaftesbury, Eng,UK
81/C2 Shaghan (riv.), Kaz.
79/J3 Shāhdādkot, Pak.
79/J3 Shāhdādpur, Pak.
90/D3 Shahdol, India
103/K1 Shaḥḥāt, Libya
90/C2 Shāhjahānpur, India
79/K3 Shāhpura, India
90/A2 Shāhpur Chākar, Pak.
106/C3 Sha'ib al Banāt, Jabal (mtn.), Egypt
90/C3 Shājāpur, India
79/L2 Shakargarh, Pak.
110/D4 Shakawe, Bots.
74/H5 Shakhtinsk, Kaz.
72/G3 Shakhty, Rus.
70/K4 Shakhun'ya, Rus.
73/H4 Shalbuzdag, Gora (peak), Rus.
52/C5 Shaldon, Eng,UK
73/L3 Shalqar, Kaz.
107/B4 Shama (riv.), Tanz.
80/J6 Shamal Sīnā' (gov.), Egypt
129/M2 Shamattawa (riv.), On,Can.
90/C3 Shāmgarh, India
90/C2 Shāmli, India
78/D3 Shammar, Jabal (mts.), SAr.
136/L3 Shamrock (mtn.), Yk,Can.
134/C3 Shamrock, Tx,US
89/B1 Shan (plat.), Myan.
89/B1 Shan (state), Myan.
103/M4 Shandī, Sudan
87/D3 Shandong (pen.), China
87/C5 Shangcheng, China
87/L8 Shanghai, China
87/C4 Shangqiu, China
88/C2 Shangrao, China
53/E5 Shanklin, Eng,UK
49/A4 Shannon (riv.), Ire.
75/P4 Shantar (isls.), Rus.
88/C3 Shantou, China
88/B3 Shaoguan, China
88/D2 Shaoxing, China
88/E2 Shaoyang, China
51/F2 Shap, Eng,UK
111/L Shapeless (peak), Ant.
71/M2 Shapkina (riv.), Rus.
80/F3 Shaqlāwah, Iraq
79/G5 Sharbatāt, Ra's ash (pt.), Oman
106/C3 Sharm ash Shaykh, Egypt
53/F2 Sharnbrook, Eng,UK
132/D3 Sharon, Pa,US
129/K2 Sharpe (lake), Mb,Can.
129/J4 Sharpe (lake), SD,US
71/K4 Shar'ya, Rus.
81/C3 Sharyn (riv.), Kaz.
103/N6 Shashemenē, Eth.
87/C5 Shashi, China
130/B2 Shasta (dam), Ca,US
130/B2 Shasta (peak), Ca,US
72/B2 Shatskiy Nat'l Park, Ukr.
102/G1 Shaṭṭ al Jarīd (dry lake), Tun.
131/H3 Shattuck, Ok,US
128/F3 Shaunavon, Sk,Can.
53/E4 Shaw, Eng,UK
132/B2 Shawano, Wi,US
133/M6 Shawbridge, Qu,Can.
52/D1 Shawbury, Eng,UK
133/F2 Shawinigan, Qu,Can.
131/H4 Shawnee, Ok,US
83/E3 Shaykhān, Iraq
72/C1 Shchara (riv.), Bela.
72/F1 Shchekino, Rus.
71/X9 Shchelkovo, Rus.
72/F2 Shchigry, Rus.
81/B1 Shchūchīnsk, Kaz.
103/P6 Shebelē Wenz (riv.), Eth.
79/J1 Sheberghān, Afg.
132/C3 Sheboygan, Wi,US
133/H2 Shediac, NB,Can.
50/A4 Sheelin, Lough (lake), Ire.
136/F2 Sheep (mtn.), Ak,US
51/G5 Sheffield, Eng,UK
51/G5 Sheffield (co.), Eng,UK
135/G3 Sheffield, Al,US
53/F2 Shefford, Eng,UK
103/P6 Shēh Husēn, Eth.
119/K7 Shehuen (riv.), Arg.
132/C1 Shekak (riv.), On,Can.
79/K2 Shekhūpura, Pak.
75/T2 Shelagskiy (cape), Rus.
133/H3 Shelburne, NS,Can.
135/F3 Shelby, Ms,US
128/F3 Shelby, Mt,US
135/H3 Shelby, NC,US
135/F2 Shelbyville (lake), Il,US
132/C4 Shelbyville, In,US
135/G3 Shelbyville, Tn,US
75/R3 Shelekhov (gulf), Rus.
136/H4 Shelikof (str.), Ak,US
129/G2 Shellbrook, Sk,Can.
132/B2 Shell Lake, Wi,US
129/K5 Shell Rock (riv.), Ia,US
138/A3 Shelton, Wa,US
73/J4 Shemakha, Azer.
136/A5 Shemya (isl.), Ak,US
129/K5 Shenandoah, Ia,US
132/E4 Shenandoah Nat'l Park, Va,US
104/B5 Shenge (pt.), SLeo.
81/E3 Shengli Daban (pass), China
87/B5 Shennongjia, China
53/E1 Shenstone, Eng,UK
83/J3 Shenyang, China
91/K3 Shenzhen, China
90/B2 Sheoganj, India
90/C2 Sheopur, India
72/C2 Shepetovka, Ukr.
134/E4 Shepherd, Tx,US
98/F6 Shepherd (isls.), Van.
53/G4 Sheppey (isl.), Eng,UK
53/E1 Shepshed, Eng,UK
52/D4 Shepton Mallet, Eng,UK
125/H1 Sherard (cape), Nun,Can.
52/D5 Sherborne, Eng,UK
104/B5 Sherbro (isl.), SLeo.
133/G2 Sherbrooke, Qu,Can.
51/G2 Sherburn, Eng,UK
105/H4 Shere (hill), Nga.
90/D3 Sherghāti, India
134/E3 Sheridan, Ar,US
128/G4 Sheridan, Wy,US
53/H1 Sheringham, Eng,UK
134/D3 Sherman, Tx,US
128/E2 Sherwood Park, Ab,Can.
47/D2 Shetland (isls.), Sc,UK
87/D4 Sheyang (riv.), China
129/J4 Sheyenne (riv.), ND,US
87/C4 Shi (riv.), China
138/E6 Shiawassee (riv.), Mi,US
85/F2 Shibata, Japan
106/B2 Shibīn al Kaum, Egypt
129/L2 Shibogama (lake), On,Can.
84/B5 Shibushi (bay), Japan
81/B1 Shiderti (riv.), Kaz.
84/D3 Shido, Japan
52/D1 Shifnal, Eng,UK
85/L9 Shiga, Japan
84/E3 Shiga (pref.), Japan
85/M10 Shigaraki, Japan
81/E3 Shihezi, China
67/F2 Shijak, Alb.
87/C3 Shijiazhuang, China
79/J3 Shikārpur, Pak.
85/M9 Shikatsu, Japan
85/H7 Shiki, Japan
84/C4 Shikoku (isl.), Japan
84/C4 Shikoku (mts.), Japan
83/P3 Shikotan (isl.), Rus.
51/G2 Shildon, Eng,UK
82/H1 Shilka, Rus.
83/H1 Shilka (riv.), Rus.
79/L2 Shilla (mtn.), India
80/N8 Shillo, Naḥal (dry riv.), WBnk.
91/F2 Shillong, India
82/D2 Shilüüstey, Mong.
85/M10 Shima (pen.), Japan
84/B4 Shimabara, Japan
84/D3 Shimamoto, Japan
84/C3 Shimane (pref.), Japan
83/K1 Shimanovsk, Rus.
85/M9 Shimasahi, Japan
103/Q5 Shimber Berris (peak), Som.
91/H2 Shimian, China
85/F3 Shimizu, Japan
85/F3 Shimoda, Japan
85/F3 Shimodate, Japan
90/C5 Shimoga, India
85/L10 Shimoichi, Japan
84/A5 Shimo-koshiki (isl.), Japan
84/B4 Shimonoseki, Japan
85/F2 Shinano (riv.), Japan
79/H2 Shindand, Afg.
84/D4 Shingū, Japan
84/C3 Shinji (lake), Japan
83/N4 Shinjō, Japan
85/M9 Shinkawa, Japan
85/E2 Shinminato, Japan
85/M9 Shinsei, Japan
107/B3 Shinyanga, Tanz.
107/B3 Shinyanga (prov.), Tanz.
85/G1 Shiogama, Japan
84/D4 Shio-no-misaki (cape), Japan
51/G4 Shipley, Eng,UK
133/H2 Shippegan, NB,Can.
85/M9 Shippo, Japan
130/E3 Shiprock, NM,US
53/E2 Shipston on Stour, Eng,UK
81/C5 Shipuqi Shankou (pass), China
78/F2 Shīr (mtn.), Iran
85/H8 Shirahama, Japan
84/E3 Shirakawa-tōge (pass), Japan
85/F3 Shirane-san (mtn.), Japan
85/H6 Shiraoka, Japan
78/F3 Shīrāz, Iran
80/H6 Shirbīn, Egypt
51/G1 Shiremoor, Eng,UK
87/C5 Shirjiu (lake), China
85/J7 Shiroi, Japan
85/G2 Shiroishi, Japan
85/F2 Shirone, Japan
85/H7 Shiroyama, Japan
79/G1 Shīrvān, Iran
81/D2 Shi San Ling, China
136/F5 Shishaldin (vol.), Ak,US
82/D1 Shishhid (riv.), Mong.
87/C5 Shishou, China
85/J7 Shisui, Japan
90/C2 Shivpurī, India
87/B4 Shiyan, China
82/F4 Shizuishan, China
83/N3 Shizunai, Japan
85/F3 Shizuoka, Japan
85/F3 Shizuoka (pref.), Japan
67/F1 Shkodër, Alb.
67/G2 Shkumbin (riv.), Alb.
136/C2 Shmidta, Mys (pt.), Rus.
97/D2 Shoalhaven (riv.), Austl.
129/H3 Shoal Lake, Mb,Can.
96/C3 Shoalwater (bay), Austl.
84/C3 Shōbara, Japan
84/D3 Shōdo (isl.), Japan
53/G3 Shoeburyness, Eng,UK
90/C4 Sholāpur, India
80/N8 Shomron (ruins), WBnk.
85/M9 Shonai (riv.), Japan
85/J7 Shōnan, Japan
90/C4 Shorāpur, India
53/F5 Shoreham by Sea, Eng,UK
138/P16 Shorewood, Il,US
138/Q13 Shorewood, Wi,US
79/K2 Shorkot, Pak.
96/F6 Shorncliffe, Austl.
135/G3 Short (peak), Tn,US
98/E5 Shortland (isl.), Sol.
53/E5 Shorwell, Eng,UK
130/C3 Shoshone (mts.), Nv,US
128/F4 Shoshone (riv.), Wy,US
128/F5 Shoshoni, Wy,US
72/E2 Shostka, Ukr.
53/H3 Shotley, Eng,UK
51/G2 Shotton, Eng,UK
85/H7 Shōwa, Japan
130/E4 Show Low, Az,US
72/D2 Shpola, Ukr.
134/E3 Shreveport, La,US
52/D1 Shrewsbury, Eng,UK
52/D1 Shropshire (co.), Eng,UK
51/F6 Shropshire Union (can.), Eng,UK
87/D4 Shu (riv.), China
87/D5 Shu (riv.), China
81/B3 Shū (riv.), Kaz.
83/K3 Shuangyang, China

184
Shuan – South

83/L2 Shuangyashan, China
80/H6 Shubrā Khīt, Egypt
80/K6 Shu'fāt, WBnk.
87/D5 Shuiyang (riv.), China
79/K3 Shujāābād, Pak.
82/D4 Shule (riv.), China
136/G4 Shumagin (isls.), Ak,US
69/H4 Shumen, Bul.
71/K5 Shumerlya, Rus.
81/B2 Shunak, Gora (peak), Kaz.
87/C3 Shuo Xian, China
79/G2 Shūr (riv.), Iran
110/F4 Shurugwi, Zim.
81/F1 Shushenskoye, Rus.
78/E2 Shūshtar, Iran
128/D3 Shuswap (lake), BC,Can.
103/N5 Shuwak, Sudan
70/J4 Shuya, Rus.
89/A1 Shwebo, Myan.
89/B2 Shwemawdaw Pagoda (ruins), Myan.
74/J5 Shyghys Qazaqstan Obl., Kaz.
81/A3 Shymkent, Kaz.
81/C5 Shyok (riv.), India
79/H2 Siāh (mts.), Afg.
92/B3 Siak (riv.), Indo.
79/K2 Siālkot, Pak.
88/E6 Siargao (isl.), Phil.
88/D6 Siasi, Phil.
93/F2 Siaton (pt.), Phil.
93/G3 Siau (isl.), Indo.
70/D5 Šiauliai, Lith.
88/D5 Sibalom, Phil.
73/L1 Sibay, Rus.
68/B4 Šibenik, Cro.
74/K3 Siberia (reg.), Rus.
79/J3 Sibi, Pak.
107/C1 Sibiloi Nat'l Park, Kenya
110/B1 Sibiti, Congo
69/G3 Sibiu, Rom.
69/G2 Sibiu (co.), Rom.
53/G3 Sible Hedingham, Eng,UK
92/A3 Sibolga, Indo.
93/F2 Sibuco, Phil.
93/F1 Sibuyan (isl.), Phil.
88/D5 Sibuyan (sea), Phil.
128/D3 Sicamous, BC,Can.
91/H2 Sichuan (prov.), China
66/C4 Sicilia (reg.), It.
66/C3 Sicily (isl.), It.
66/B4 Sicily (str.), It., Tun.
122/D4 Sico (riv.), Hon.
114/D6 Sicuani, Peru
68/D3 Šid, Serb.
90/C4 Siddipet, India
66/E3 Siderno Marina, It.
116/B4 Sidérópolis, Braz.
137/C1 Sidewinder (mtn.), Ca,US
67/F3 Sidhári, Gre.
90/D3 Sidhi, India
67/H2 Sidhirókastron, Gre.
90/B3 Sidhpur, India
106/A2 Sīdī Barrānī, Egypt
102/E1 Sidi Bel-Abbes, Alg.
66/A5 Sidi Bou Zid (gov.), Tun.
102/C2 Sidi Ifni, Mor.
80/H6 Sīdī Sālim, Egypt
111/R Sidley (mtn.), Ant.
96/A1 Sidmouth (cape), Austl.
52/C5 Sidmouth, Eng,UK
128/C3 Sidney, BC,Can.
129/G4 Sidney, Mt,US
131/G2 Sidney, Ne,US
132/C3 Sidney, Oh,US
135/G3 Sidney Lanier (lake), Ga,US
80/K5 Sidon (Şaydā), Leb.
102/J1 Sidra (gulf), Libya
57/F3 Siede (riv.), Ger.
55/M2 Siedlce, Pol.
59/G2 Sieg (riv.), Ger.
59/G2 Siegburg, Ger.
59/H2 Siegen, Ger.
55/M2 Siemianówka (lake), Pol.
55/M2 Siemiatycze, Pol.
89/D3 Siempang, Camb.
89/C3 Siemreab, Camb.
63/J5 Siena, It.
62/C2 Sienne (riv.), Fr.
55/K3 Sieradz, Pol.
59/F5 Sierk-les-Bains, Fr.
55/K2 Sierpc, Pol.
134/B4 Sierra Blanca, Tx,US
114/D3 Sierra de la Macarena Nat'l Park, Col.
122/A2 Sierra del Carmen Nat'l Park, Mex.
123/M7 Sierra de San Pedro Mártir, Mex.
118/D4 Sierra Grande, Arg.
104/B4 Sierra Leone (ctry.)
104/B4 Sierra Leone (cape), SLeo.
137/B2 Sierra Madre, Ca,US
122/B4 Sierra Madre del Sur (mts.), Mex.
123/N8 Sierra Madre Occidental (range), Mex.
122/B3 Sierra Madre Oriental (mts.), Mex.
122/A2 Sierra Mojada, Mex.
130/B3 Sierra Nevada (range), Ca,US
123/G5 Sierra Nevada de Santa Marta, Col.
123/G6 Sierra Nevada Nat'l Park, Ven.
130/E5 Sierra Vista, Az,US
60/D5 Sierre, Swi.
65/M8 Siete (peak), Sp.
118/C2 Siete Tazas Nat'l Park, Chile
67/J4 Sífnos (isl.), Gre.
69/F2 Sighetu Marmaţiei, Rom.
69/G2 Sighişoara, Rom.
51/F1 Sighty Crag (hill), Eng,UK
92/A2 Sigli, Indo.
61/F1 Sigmaringen, Ger.
70/C4 Sigtuna, Swe.
90/D3 Sihorā, India
48/H3 Siilinjärvi, Fin.
80/E3 Siirt, Turk.
124/D3 Sikanni Chief (riv.), BC,Can.
90/C2 Sīkar, India
104/D4 Sikasso, Mali
104/D4 Sikasso (reg.), Mali
131/K3 Sikeston, Mo,US
83/M2 Sikhote-Alin' (mts.), Rus.
67/J4 Síkinos (isl.), Gre.
90/E2 Sikkim (state), India
68/D3 Siklós, Hun.
64/B1 Sil (riv.), Sp.
61/G4 Silandro (Schlanders), It.
122/A3 Silao, Mex.
88/D5 Silay, Phil.
91/F3 Silchar, India
69/J5 Şile, Turk.
53/E1 Sileby, Eng,UK
55/H3 Silesia (reg.), Pol.
102/F3 Silet, Alg.
81/B1 Sileti (riv.), Kaz.
66/A4 Siliana, Tun.
66/A4 Siliana (gov.), Tun.
80/C3 Silifke, Turk.
90/E2 Silīguri, India
81/E5 Siling (lake), China
99/R9 Silisili (peak), Samoa
69/H3 Silistra, Bul.
69/J5 Silivri, Turk.
48/D4 Silkeborg, Den.
51/G2 Silksworth, Eng,UK
65/E3 Silla, Sp.
70/E4 Sillamäe, Est.
64/A1 Silleda, Sp.
51/E2 Silloth, Eng,UK
134/E2 Siloam Springs, Ar,US
78/D1 Silopi, Turk.
134/E4 Silsbee, Tx,US
51/G4 Silsden, Eng,UK
102/J4 Siltou (well), Chad
55/L1 Šilutė, Lith.
80/E2 Silvan, Turk.
90/B3 Silvassa, India
128/D5 Silver (cr.), Or,US
130/B2 Silver (lake), Or,US
129/L4 Silver Bay, Mn,US
130/E4 Silver City, NM,US
136/L3 Silver Creek, Yk,Can.
51/F3 Silverdale, Eng,UK
138/B2 Silverdale, Wa,US
138/C2 Silver Lake-Fircrest, Wa,US
137/J8 Silver Spring, Md,US
53/E2 Silverstone, Eng,UK
52/C5 Silverton, Eng,UK
130/F3 Silverton, Co,US
128/C4 Silverton, Or,US
134/C3 Silverton, Tx,US
64/A4 Silves, Port.
66/D1 Silvi, It.
130/C2 Silvies (riv.), Or,US
61/G4 Silvretta (mts.), Aus., Swi.
92/D3 Simanggang, Malay.
132/E2 Simard (lake), Qu,Can.
80/B2 Simav, Turk.
73/H1 Simbirsk Obl., Rus.
132/D3 Simcoe, On,Can.
132/E2 Simcoe (lake), On,Can.
103/N5 Simēn (mts.), Eth.
68/F3 Simeria, Rom.
92/A3 Simeulue (isl.), Indo.
72/E3 Simferopol', Ukr.
69/F5 Simitli, Bul.
137/B2 Simi Valley, Ca,US
79/L2 Simla, India
68/F2 Şimleu Silvaniei, Rom.
61/D4 Simme (riv.), Swi.
59/F2 Simmerath, Ger.
59/G4 Simmerbach (riv.), Ger.
122/C4 Simojovel, Mex.
128/D2 Simonette (riv.), Ab,Can.
108/B4 Simonstown, SAfr.
56/D1 Simonszand (isl.), Neth.
92/A3 Simpang-kiri (riv.), Indo.
59/E2 Simpelveld, Neth.
124/H2 Simpson (pen.), Nun,Can.
124/G2 Simpson (riv.), Nun,Can.
55/H1 Simrishamn, Swe.
93/E3 Simunul, Phil.
103/Q6 Sinadhago, Som.
78/B3 Sinafir (isl.), SAr.
106/C2 Sinai (pen.), Egypt
123/N8 Sinaloa (state), Mex.
123/F6 Sincelejo, Col.
135/H3 Sinclair (lake), Ga,US
128/G5 Sinclair, Wy,US
90/C2 Sind (riv.), India
79/J3 Sind (prov.), Pak.
88/D6 Sindañgan, Phil.
92/C5 Sindangbarang, Indo.
63/H2 Sindelfingen, Ger.
64/A4 Sines, Port.
64/A4 Sines, Cabo de (cape), Port.
104/D5 Sinfra, C.d'Iv.
92/B3 Singapore (ctry.)
92/B3 Singapore (cap.), Sing.
89/C3 Sing Buri, Thai.
61/E2 Singen, Ger.
69/G2 Sîngeorz-Băi, Rom.
107/B4 Singida, Tanz.
107/B4 Singida (prov.), Tanz.
67/H2 Singitic (gulf), Gre.
93/F4 Singkang, Indo.
92/C3 Singkawang, Indo.
92/B4 Singkep (isl.), Indo.
97/D2 Singleton, Austl.
66/A2 Siniscola, It.
103/M5 Sinjah, Sudan
80/E3 Sinjār, Iraq
106/D5 Sinkāt, Sudan
58/C3 Sin-le-Noble, Fr.
90/B4 Sinnar, India
66/E2 Sinni (riv.), It.
68/E2 Sînnicolau Mare, Rom.
106/B2 Sinnūris, Egypt
104/C5 Sino (co.), Libr.
69/J3 Sinoe (lake), Rom.
115/G6 Sinop, Braz.
80/C1 Sinop, Turk.
92/D3 Sintang, Indo.
58/D2 Sint-Genesius-Rode, Belg.
58/D1 Sint-Gillis-Waas, Belg.
58/D1 Sint-Katelijne-Waver, Belg.
58/C1 Sint-Laureins, Belg.
123/J4 Sint Maarten (isl.), NAnt.
56/C5 Sint-Michielsgestel, Neth.
58/D1 Sint-Niklaas, Belg.
56/C5 Sint-Oedenrode, Neth.
134/D4 Sinton, Tx,US
58/D2 Sint-Pieters-Leeuw, Belg.
64/A3 Sintra, Port.
65/P10 Sintra (mts.), Port.
59/E2 Sint-Truiden, Belg.
123/F6 Sinú (riv.), Col.
86/C2 Sinŭiju, NKor.
59/G2 Sinzig, Ger.
68/D2 Sió (riv.), Hun.
93/F2 Siocon, Phil.
68/D2 Siófok, Hun.
110/D4 Sioma Ngwezi Nat'l Park, Zam.
60/D5 Sion, Swi.
62/E4 Sioule (riv.), Fr.
129/J5 Sioux City, Ia,US
129/J5 Sioux Falls, SD,US
132/B1 Sioux Lookout, On,Can.
66/E1 Šipan (isl.), Cro.
87/F2 Siping, China
129/J2 Sipiwesk (lake), Mb,Can.
111/Q Siple (coast), Ant.
111/R Siple (isl.), Ant.
135/G3 Sipsey (riv.), Al,US
92/A4 Sipura (isl.), Indo.
116/B2 Siqueira Campos, Braz.
122/E5 Siquia (riv.), Nic.
48/C4 Sira (riv.), Nor.
66/D4 Siracusa (Syracuse), It.
90/E3 Sirājganj, Bang.
128/C2 Sir Alexander (peak), BC,Can.
80/D2 Şiran, Turk.
69/H2 Siret, Rom.
69/H3 Siret (riv.), Rom.
92/D3 Sirik (cape), Malay.
89/C2 Sirikit (res.), Thai.
91/H4 Sirit (res.), Thai.
136/B5 Sirius (pt.), Ak,US
124/D2 Sir James MacBrien (peak), NW,Can.
79/G3 Sīrjan, Iran
97/D4 Sir John (cape), Austl.
80/E3 Şırnak, Turk.
90/B3 Sirohi, India
90/C3 Sironj, India
67/J4 Síros (isl.), Gre.
90/C2 Sirsa, India
90/B5 Sirsi, India
68/C3 Sisak, Cro.
89/D3 Sisaket, Thai.
91/H4 Si Sa Ket, Thai.
89/B2 Si Satchanalai (ruins), Thai.
129/H2 Sisipuk (lake), Mb, Sk,Can.
89/C3 Sisophon, Camb.
129/J4 Sisseton, SD,US
105/E4 Sissili (prov.), Burk.
135/H2 Sissonville, WV,US
91/F3 Sitākund, Bang.
65/F2 Sitges, Sp.
67/H2 Sithoniá (pen.), Gre.
67/K5 Sitía, Gre.
136/M2 Sitidgi (lake), NW,Can.
136/L4 Sitka, Ak,US
68/D1 Sitno (peak), Slvk.
89/B2 Sittang (riv.), Myan.
56/C7 Sittard, Neth.
53/G4 Sittingbourne, Eng,UK
91/F3 Sittwe (Akyab), Myan.
68/D3 Sivac, Serb.
90/C6 Sivakāsi, India
80/D2 Sivas, Turk.
80/D3 Siverek, Turk.
80/B2 Sivrihisar, Turk.
58/D3 Sivry-Rance, Belg.
103/L2 Sīwah, Egypt
90/D2 Siwān, India
50/A2 Sixmilecross, NI,UK
136/K3 Sixtymile, Yk,Can.
82/G3 Siziwang, China
48/D5 Sjælland (isl.), Den.
68/E4 Sjenica, Serb.
48/M6 Sjónfridh (peak), Ice.
48/P7 Skaftafell Nat'l Park, Ice.
48/D4 Skagen, Den.
48/D4 Skagens (cape), Den.
48/D4 Skagerrak (str.), Eur.
48/P6 Skálfandafljót (riv.), Ice.
55/J4 Skalica, Slvk.
63/K2 Skalice (riv.), Czh.
67/J3 Skantzoura (isl.), Gre.
48/E4 Skaraborg (co.), Swe.
55/L3 Skarżysko-Kamienna, Pol.
55/K4 Skawina, Pol.
124/D3 Skeena (range), BC,Can.
128/A2 Skeena (riv.), BC,Can.
51/J5 Skegness, Eng,UK
48/F2 Skellefteälven (riv.), Swe.
48/G2 Skellefteå, Swe.
51/G4 Skelmanthorpe, Eng,UK
51/F4 Skelmersdale, Eng,UK
51/H2 Skelton, Eng,UK
51/G2 Skerne (riv.), Eng,UK
50/B4 Skerries, Ire.
67/G4 Skhiza (isl.), Gre.
131/H3 Skiatook, Ok,US
51/E2 Skiddaw (mtn.), Eng,UK
48/D4 Skien, Nor.
55/L3 Skierniewice, Pol.
102/G1 Skikda, Alg.
67/G4 Skinári, Ákra (cape), Gre.
51/H4 Skipsea, Eng,UK
51/F4 Skipton, Eng,UK
51/F3 Skirfare (riv.), Eng,UK
67/J3 Skíros (isl.), Gre.
48/D4 Skjeberg, Nor.
70/B2 Skjelåtinden (peak), Nor.
48/D5 Skjern, Den.
52/A3 Skokholm (isl.), Wal,UK
138/Q15 Skokie, Il,US
52/A3 Skomer (isl.), Wal,UK
89/D3 Skon, Camb.
67/H3 Skópelos (isl.), Gre.
72/F1 Skopin, Rus.
68/E5 Skopje (cap.), FYROM
48/E4 Skövde, Swe.
83/J1 Skovorodino, Rus.
133/G2 Skowhegan, Me,US
136/L3 Skukum (mtn.), Yk,Can.
131/K2 Skunk (riv.), Ia,US
55/H2 Skwierzyna, Pol.
138/D2 Skykomish (riv.), Wa,US
119/J8 Skyway (sound), Chile
48/D5 Slagelse, Den.
51/F4 Slaidburn, Eng,UK
55/L4 Slaná (riv.), Slvk.
49/B4 Slaney (riv.), Ire.
70/F4 Slantsy, Rus.
55/K3 Śląskie (prov.), Pol.
69/G3 Slatina, Rom.
124/E2 Slave (riv.), Can.
105/F5 Slave Coast (reg.), Afr.
128/E2 Slave Lake, Ab,Can.
81/C1 Slavgorod, Rus.
68/C3 Slavonia (reg.), Cro.
68/C3 Slavonska Požega, Cro.
68/D3 Slavonski Brod, Cro.
72/C2 Slavuta, Ukr.
72/F3 Slavyansk-na-Kubani, Rus.
55/J1 Sławno, Pol.
129/K5 Slayton, Mn,US
51/H6 Sleaford, Eng,UK
56/D3 Sleen, Neth.
125/H3 Sleeper (isls.), Nun,Can.
129/K4 Sleepy Eye, Mn,US
50/A4 Sliabh na Caillighe (mtn.), Ire.
135/F4 Slidell, La,US
56/B5 Sliedrecht, Neth.
66/D5 Sliema, Malta
50/A3 Slieve Beagh (mtn.), NI,UK
50/C3 Slieve Binnian (mtn.), NI,UK
50/C3 Slieve Croob (mtn.), NI,UK
50/C3 Slieve Donard (mtn.), NI,UK
50/B3 Slieve Gullion (mtn.), NI,UK
50/A1 Slieve Snaght (mtn.), Ire.
49/A3 Sligo, Ire.
49/A3 Sligo (bay), Ire.
69/H4 Sliven, Bul.
68/F4 Slivnitsa, Bul.
133/S10 Sloan, NY,US
71/L4 Slobodskoy, Rus.
69/H3 Slobozia, Rom.
56/D2 Slochteren, Neth.
72/C1 Slonim, Bela.
56/C3 Slotermeer (lake), Neth.
53/F4 Slough, Eng,UK
53/F3 Slough (co.), Eng,UK
55/K4 Slovakia (ctry.)
68/B3 Slovenia (ctry.)
68/B2 Slovenska Bistrica, Slov.
55/L4 Slovenské Rudohorie (mts.), Slvk.
72/F2 Slov'yans'k, Ukr.
55/J1 Słowiński Nat'l Park, Pol.
55/H2 Słubice, Pol.
72/C2 Sluch' (riv.), Ukr.
55/J2 Słupca, Pol.
55/J1 Słupia (riv.), Pol.
55/J1 Słupsk, Pol.
72/C1 Slutsk, Bela.
82/E1 Slyudyanka, Rus.
53/F4 Smallfield, Eng,UK
125/K3 Smallwood (res.), Nf,Can.
129/G2 Smeaton, Sk,Can.
68/E3 Smederevo, Serb.
68/E3 Smederevska Palanka, Serb.
48/E3 Smedjebacken, Swe.
72/D2 Smela, Ukr.
56/D3 Smilde, Neth.
111/V Smith (pen.), Ant.
128/B3 Smith (inlet), BC,Can.
125/J2 Smith (isl.), Nun,Can.
128/F4 Smith (riv.), Mt,US
128/B2 Smithers, BC,Can.
135/J3 Smithfield, NC,US
130/E2 Smithfield, Ut,US
132/E4 Smith Mountain (lake), Va,US
132/E2 Smiths Falls, On,Can.
137/G5 Smithtown, NY,US
133/Q9 Smithville, On,Can.
131/J4 Smithville, Ok,US
97/E1 Smoky (cape), Austl.
128/D2 Smoky (riv.), Ab,Can.
131/H3 Smoky (hills), Ks,US
131/G3 Smoky Hill (riv.), Ks,US
128/E2 Smoky Lake, Ab,Can.
48/C3 Smøla (isl.), Nor.
70/G5 Smolensk, Rus.
70/F5 Smolenskaya Obl., Rus.
67/G2 Smólikas (peak), Gre.
69/G5 Smolyan, Bul.
111/U Smyley (isl.), Ant.
135/G3 Smyrna, Ga,US
50/D3 Snaefell (mtn.), IM,UK
136/M2 Snake (riv.), Yk,Can.
128/D4 Snake (riv.), US
131/G2 Snake (riv.), Ne,US
56/C2 Sneek, Neth.
56/C2 Sneekermeer (lake), Neth.
108/D3 Sneeuberg (mts.), SAfr.
108/B4 Sneeuberg (peak), SAfr.
133/Q8 Snelgrove, On,Can.
53/G1 Snettisham, Eng,UK
55/H3 Sněžka (peak), Czh.
68/B3 Snežnik (peak), Slov.
55/L2 Śniardwy (lake), Pol.
53/G4 Snodland, Eng,UK
48/D3 Snøhetta (peak), Nor.
138/C2 Snohomish, Wa,US
138/C2 Snohomish (riv.), Wa,US
138/D2 Snoqualmie (riv.), Wa,US
48/E2 Snøtind (peak), Nor.
50/D5 Snowdon (mtn.), Wal,UK
50/D5 Snowdonia Nat'l Park, Wal,UK
130/E4 Snowflake, Az,US
129/H2 Snow Lake, Mb,Can.
136/K2 Snowy (peak), Ak,US
97/D3 Snowy River Nat'l Park, Austl.
134/C3 Snyder, Tx,US
109/H7 Soalala, Madg.
109/J7 Soanierana-Ivongo, Madg.
51/G6 Soar (riv.), Eng,UK
63/L2 Soběslav, Czh.
93/K4 Sobger (riv.), Indo.
79/J3 Sobhādero, Pak.
115/K6 Sobradinho (res.), Braz.
115/K4 Sobral, Braz.
85/M9 Sobue, Japan
55/L2 Sochaczew, Pol.
72/F4 Sochi, Rus.
99/K6 Society (isls.), FrPol.
116/G7 Socorro, Braz.
130/F4 Socorro, NM,US
134/B4 Socorro, Tx,US
77/E8 Socotra (isl.), Yem.
89/D4 Soc Trang, Viet.
64/D3 Socuéllamos, Sp.
48/H2 Sodankylä, Fin.
128/F5 Soda Springs, Id,US
85/H7 Sodegaura, Japan
48/F3 Söderhamn, Swe.
48/F4 Södertälje, Swe.
103/N6 Sodo, Eth.
57/F5 Soest, Ger.
56/C4 Soest, Neth.
57/E3 Soeste (riv.), Ger.
109/J6 Sofia (riv.), Madg.
69/F4 Sofia (Sofiya) (cap.), Bul.
68/F4 Sofiya (reg.), Bul.
114/D2 Sogamoso, Col.
48/B3 Sognafjorden (fjord), Nor.
48/C3 Sogn og Fjordane (co.), Nor.
102/J4 Sogollé (well), Chad
83/K5 Sŏgwip'o, SKor.
53/G2 Soham, Eng,UK
86/C3 Sŏhan (bay), NKor.
58/D2 Soignies, Belg.
58/C5 Soissons, Fr.
84/C3 Sōja, Japan
90/B2 Sojat, India
73/J1 Sok (riv.), Rus.
89/C3 Sok (pt.), Thai.
85/H7 Sōka, Japan
86/E3 Sokch'o, SKor.
80/A3 Söke, Turk.
82/F1 Sokhor (peak), Rus.
73/G4 Sokhumi, Arm.
68/E4 Sokobanja, Geo.
105/F4 Sokodé, Togo
70/J4 Sokol, Rus.
55/M2 Sokółka, Pol.
54/G3 Sokolov, Czh.
55/M2 Sokołów Podlaski, Pol.
105/G4 Sokoto (plains), Nga.
105/G4 Sokoto (riv.), Nga.
105/G3 Sokoto (state), Nga.
48/C4 Sola, Nor.
88/D4 Solana, Phil.
114/C2 Solano (pt.), Col.
64/C4 Sol, Costa del (coast), Sp.
65/P10 Sol, Costa do (reg.), Port.
131/J2 Soldier (riv.), Ia,US
123/G5 Soledad, Col.
137/B2 Soledad (canyon), Ca,US
123/J6 Soledad, Ven.
122/A3 Soledad Diez Guiterrez, Mex.
116/A4 Soledade, Braz.
53/E5 Solent (chan.), Eng,UK
59/E4 Soleuvre (mtn.), Lux.
80/E2 Solhan, Turk.
53/E2 Solihull, Eng,UK
53/E2 Solihull (co.), Eng,UK
71/N4 Solikamsk, Rus.
73/K2 Sol'-Iletsk, Rus.
57/E6 Solingen, Ger.
48/F3 Sollefteå, Swe.
65/G3 Sóller, Sp.
57/G5 Solling (mts.), Ger.
48/D3 Søln (peak), Nor.
60/B5 Solnan (riv.), Fr.
71/V8 Solnechnogorsk, Rus.
71/W9 Solntsevo, Rus.
92/D5 Solo (riv.), Indo.
92/B4 Solok, Indo.
122/C5 Sololá, Guat.
98/E5 Solomon (sea), PNG, Sol.
134/D2 Solomon (riv.), Ks,US
98/E6 Solomon Islands (ctry.)
73/L4 Solonchak Goklenkui (salt marsh), Trkm.
60/D3 Solothurn, Swi.
60/D3 Solothurn (canton), Swi.
70/G2 Solovetskiy (isls.), Rus.
65/F2 Solsona, Sp.
68/D2 Solt, Hun.
68/B4 Šolta (isl.), Cro.
57/G3 Soltau, Ger.
68/D2 Soltvadkert, Hun.
68/E5 Solunska (peak), FYROM
52/A3 Solva (riv.), Wal,UK
130/B4 Solvang, Ca,US
48/E4 Sölvesborg, Swe.
50/E2 Solway Firth (inlet), Eng, Sc,UK
110/E3 Solwezi, Zam.
85/G2 Sōma, Japan
80/A2 Soma, Turk.
58/C3 Somain, Fr.
103/Q6 Somalia (ctry.)
133/F1 Somaqua (riv.), Qu,Can.
68/D3 Sombor, Cro.
123/P9 Sombrerete, Mex.
116/B4 Sombrio, Braz.
51/G5 Somercotes, Eng,UK
56/C6 Someren, Neth.
48/G3 Somero, Fin.
128/E3 Somers, Mt,US
124/G1 Somerset (isl.), Nun,Can.
52/D4 Somerset (co.), Eng,UK
132/C4 Somerset, Ky,US
137/F5 Somerset, NJ,US
133/S9 Somerset, NY,US
97/C4 Somerset-Burnie, Austl.
108/D4 Somerset East, SAfr.
108/B4 Somerset West, SAfr.
53/F2 Somersham, Eng,UK
133/G3 Somersworth, NH,US
52/D4 Somerton, Eng,UK
130/D4 Somerton, Az,US
137/F5 Somerville, NJ,US
131/H5 Somerville (lake), Tx,US
69/F2 Someş (riv.), Rom.
69/G2 Someşul Mare (riv.), Rom.
62/D1 Somme (bay), Fr.
58/B4 Somme (dept.), Fr.
58/A3 Somme (riv.), Fr.
58/D6 Somme (riv.), Fr.
58/D5 Somme-Soude (riv.), Fr.
68/C2 Somogy (co.), Hun.
122/D5 Somoto, Nic.
53/F5 Somptin, Eng,UK
48/D5 Sønderborg, Den.
108/L11 Sonderend (riv.), SAfr.
54/E1 Sønderjylland (co.), Den.
61/F5 Sondrio, It.
90/C2 Sonepat, India
90/D3 Sonepur, India
89/E3 Song Cau, Viet.
89/D4 Song Dinh, Viet.
61/F5 Sondrio (prov.), It.
107/B5 Songea, Tanz.
87/F1 Songhua (riv.), China
89/C5 Songkhla, Thai.
89/C2 Songkhram (riv.), Thai.
81/B3 Song-Köl (lake), Kyr.
83/J2 Songling, China
89/C1 Song Ma, Viet.
110/F4 Songo, Moz.
87/C4 Song Shan (peak), China
86/D4 Songt'an, SKor.
87/C5 Songzi Guan (pass), China
89/E3 Son Ha, Viet.
82/G3 Sonid Youqi, China
82/G3 Sonid Zuoqi, China
89/C1 Son La, Viet.
79/J3 Sonmiāni (bay), Pak.
63/J1 Sonneberg, Ger.
53/F4 Sonning, Eng,UK
54/G5 Sonntagshorn (peak), Ger.
115/J5 Sono (riv.), Braz.
84/D3 Sonobe, Japan
138/K10 Sonoma, Ca,US
138/J10 Sonoma (mts.), Ca,US
123/M8 Sonora (riv.), Mex.
123/M8 Sonora (state), Mex.
130/B3 Sonora, Ca,US
134/C4 Sonora, Tx,US
130/D4 Sonoran Desert Nat'l Mon., Az,US
123/M7 Sonoyta (riv.), Mex.
78/E2 Sonqor, Iran
56/D5 Sonsbeck, Ger.
64/D3 Sonseca, Sp.
122/D5 Sonsonate, ESal.
98/C4 Sonsorol (isls.), Palau
68/D3 Sonta, Serb.
89/D1 Son Tay, Viet.
57/G6 Sontra, Ger.
93/G3 Sopi (cape), Indo.
89/C1 Sopka, Laos
79/K2 Sopore, India
69/G4 Sopot, Bul.
55/K1 Sopot, Pol.
68/C2 Sopron, Hun.
52/D3 Sôr (riv.), Wal,UK
66/C2 Sora, It.
86/E3 Sŏrak-san (mtn.), SKor.
133/F2 Sorel, Qu,Can.
80/M9 Soreq, Nabel (dry riv.), Isr.
63/H4 Soresina, It.
62/F5 Sorgues, Fr.
80/C2 Sorgun, Turk.
64/D2 Soria, Sp.
119/F2 Soriano (dept.), Uru.
92/A3 Sorikmerapi (peak), Indo.
73/K3 Sor Karatuley (salt pan), Kaz.
58/D4 Sormonne (riv.), Fr.
54/F1 Sorø, Den.
116/C2 Sorocaba, Braz.
73/K1 Sorochinsk, Rus.
69/J1 Soroki, Mol.
98/D4 Sorol (atoll), Micr.
93/H4 Sorong, Indo.
107/B2 Soroti, Ugan.
48/G1 Sørøya (isl.), Nor.
48/G1 Sørøysundet (chan.), Nor.
57/E6 Sorpestausee (res.), Ger.
64/A3 Sorraia (riv.), Port.
66/D2 Sorrento, It.
110/B5 Sorris-Sorris, Namb.
66/A2 Sorso, It.
88/D5 Sorsogon, Phil.
70/F3 Sortavala, Rus.
70/D4 Sõrve (pt.), Est.
57/H5 Söse (riv.), Ger.
72/F1 Sosna (riv.), Rus.
118/C2 Sosneado (peak), Arg.
71/M3 Sosnogorsk, Rus.
71/L4 Sosnovka, Rus.
55/K3 Sosnowiec, Pol.
123/G4 Sosúa, DRep.
58/D6 Soude (riv.), Fr.
123/J4 Soufrière (mt.), Guad.
123/J5 Soufrière (mt.), StV.
102/G1 Souk Ahras, Alg.
59/G1 Soultz-sous-Forets, Fr.
105/E3 Soum (prov.), Burk.
59/E2 Soumagne, Belg.
108/E3 Sources, Mont aux (peak), Les.
115/J4 Soure, Braz.
64/A2 Soure, Port.
129/H3 Souris, Mb,Can.
133/J2 Souris, PE,Can.
129/H3 Souris (riv.), Can., US
104/E3 Sourou (prov.), Burk.
102/D2 Sous (wadi), Mor.
115/L5 Sousa, Braz.
64/B3 Sousel, Port.
66/B5 Sousse, Tun.
66/B5 Sousse (gov.), Tun.
108/C3 Sout (riv.), SAfr.
96/G8 South (cr.), Austl.
133/H2 South (mts.), NS,Can.
125/H2 South (bay), Nun,Can.
95/G7 South (cape), NZ
95/H7 South (isl.), NZ
110/D6 South Africa (ctry.)
53/E2 Southam, Eng,UK
135/* South America (cont.)
125/H2 Southampton (cape), Nun,Can.
125/H2 Southampton (isl.), Nun,Can.
132/D2 Southampton, On,Can.
53/E5 Southampton, Eng,UK
53/E5 Southampton (co.), Eng,UK
91/F5 South Andaman (isl.), India
135/J2 South Anna (riv.), Va,US
135/H3 South Augusta, Ga,US
125/K3 South Aulatsivik (isl.), Nf,Can.
95/C3 South Australia (state), Austl.
135/F3 Southaven, Ms,US
50/D1 South Ayrshire (reg.), Sc,UK
50/D3 South Barrule (mtn.), IM,UK
132/C3 South Bend, In,US
53/G4 Southborough, Eng,UK
132/E4 South Boston, Va,US
53/F5 Southbourne, Eng,UK
52/C6 South Brent, Eng,UK
133/F2 South Burlington, Vt,US
135/H3 South Carolina (state), US
77/L8 South China (sea), Asia
129/H4 South Dakota (state), US
52/D5 South Dorset Downs (uplands), Eng,UK
53/F5 South Downs (hills), Eng,UK
45/S8 South East (cape), Austl.
97/C3 South East (pt.), Austl.
123/G3 Southeast (pt.), Bahm.
136/E3 Southeast (cape), Ak,US
138/P16 South Elgin, Il,US
51/G4 South Elmsall, Eng,UK
50/C1 Southend, Sc,UK
53/G3 Southend-on-Sea, Eng,UK
53/G3 Southend-on-Sea (co.), Eng,UK
80/K6 Southern (dist.), Isr.
104/B5 Southern (prov.), SLeo.
99/J6 Southern Cook (isls.), Cookls.
124/G3 Southern Indian (lake), Mb,Can.
135/J3 Southern Pines, NC,US
50/D1 Southern Uplands (mts.), Sc,UK
53/G1 Southery, Eng,UK
97/C4 South Esk (riv.), Austl.
138/F7 Southfield, Mi,US
53/H4 South Foreland (pt.), Eng,UK
130/F3 South Fork, Co,US
135/F2 South Fulton, Tn,US
137/B3 South Gate, Ca,US
138/F7 Southgate, Mi,US
111/X South Georgia (isl.), UK
52/D3 South Gloucestershire (co.), Eng,UK
52/C6 South Hams (plain), Eng,UK
53/F5 South Hayling, Eng,UK
132/E4 South Hill, Va,US
56/B5 South Holland (prov.), Neth.
138/Q16 South Holland, Il,US
51/G4 South Kirkby, Eng,UK
86/D4 South Korea
130/C3 South Lake Tahoe, Ca,US
110/F3 South Luangwa Nat'l Park, Zam.
111/K South Magnetic Pole, Ant.
138/Q14 South Milwaukee, Wi,US
53/G3 Southminster, Eng,UK
52/C4 South Molton, Eng,UK
129/J2 South Moose (lake), Mb,Can.
136/M5 South Moresby Nat'l Park Rsv., BC,Can.
51/G5 South Normanton, Eng,UK
111/W South Orkney (isls.), UK
73/G4 South Ossetian Aut. Obl., Geo.
53/F3 South Oxhey, Eng,UK
52/D5 South Petherton, Eng,UK
96/E6 South Pine (riv.), Austl.
137/F5 South Plainfield, NJ,US
131/G2 South Platte (riv.), Co, Ne,US
111/A South Pole, Ant.
51/E4 Southport, Eng,UK
135/J3 Southport, NC,US
137/F5 South River, NJ,US
111/Y South Sandwich (isls.), UK
138/K11 South San Francisco, Ca,US
128/F3 South Saskatchewan (riv.), Ab, Sk,Can.
111/W South Shetland (isls.), UK
51/G2 South Shields, Eng,UK
131/H2 South Sioux City, Ne,US
90/E3 South Suburban, India
51/F2 South Tyne (riv.), Eng,UK
51/G2 South Tyneside (co.), Eng,UK
93/F2 South Ubian, Phil.
51/H5 Southwell, Eng,UK
97/C4 South West (cape), Austl.
97/C4 South West Nat'l Park, Austl.
53/H2 Southwold, Eng,UK
53/G3 South Woodham Ferrers, Eng,UK

96/C4 Southwood Nat'l Park, Austl.
69/G2 Sovata, Rom.
66/E3 Soverato Marina, It.
55/L1 Sovetsk, Rus.
70/D5 Sovetsk, Rus.
70/L4 Sovetsk, Rus.
83/N2 Sovetskaya Gavan', Rus.
51/G4 Sowerby Bridge, Eng,UK
108/D2 Soweto, SAfr.
70/J2 Soyana (riv.), Rus.
86/D4 Soyang (lake), SKor.
62/D4 Soyaux, Fr.
111/E Soyuz, Ant.
72/D1 Sozh (riv.), Eur.
59/E3 Spa, Belg.
111/U Spaatz (isl.), Ant.
64/C2 Spain (ctry.)
51/H6 Spalding, Eng,UK
138/C3 Spanaway, Wa,US
123/F4 Spanish Town, Jam.
130/C3 Sparks, Nv,US
135/H2 Sparta, NC,US
137/F4 Sparta, NJ,US
135/G3 Sparta, Tn,US
132/B3 Sparta, Wi,US
135/H3 Spartanburg, SC,US
67/H4 Sparta (Spárti), Gre.
66/A3 Spartivento (cape), It.
66/E4 Spartivento (cape), It.
128/E3 Sparwood, BC,Can.
83/L3 Spassk-Dal'niy, Rus.
67/H5 Spátha, Ákra (cape), Gre.
49/C2 Spean (riv.), Sc,UK
49/C2 Spean Bridge, Sc,UK
129/H4 Spearfish, SD,US
51/F5 Speke, Eng,UK
95/C4 Spencer (gulf), Austl.
136/E2 Spencer (pt.), Ak,US
129/K5 Spencer, Ia,US
57/F4 Spenge, Ger.
51/G2 Spennymoor, Eng,UK
67/H3 Sperkhiós (riv.), Gre.
50/A2 Sperrin (mts.), NI,UK
49/D2 Spey (riv.), Sc,UK
53/F1 Speyer, Ger.
133/Q8 Speyside, On,Can.
66/E3 Spezzano Albanese, It.
125/H2 Spicer (isl.), Nun,Can.
57/E1 Spiekeroog (isl.), Ger.
60/D4 Spiez, Swi.
56/B5 Spijkenisse, Neth.
136/K2 Spike (mtn.), Ak,US
68/A2 Spilimbergo, It.
51/J5 Spilsby, Eng,UK
66/A2 Spina, Bruncu (peak), It.
79/J2 Spin Būldak, Afg.
59/E5 Spincourt, Fr.
128/D2 Spirit River, Ab,Can.
128/G2 Spiritwood, Sk,Can.
55/L4 Spišská Nová Ves, Slvk.
53/E5 Spithead (chan.), Eng,UK
74/B2 Spitsbergen (isl.), Sval.
63/K3 Spittal an der Drau, Aus.
129/K2 Split (lake), Mb,Can.
68/C4 Split, Cro.
61/F4 Splugenpass (pass), It., Swi.
128/D4 Spokane (riv.), Id, Wa,US
128/D4 Spokane, Wa,US
66/C1 Spoleto, It.
132/B3 Spoon (riv.), Il,US
132/B2 Spooner, Wi,US
129/J3 Sprague, Mb,Can.
56/C5 Sprang-Capelle, Neth.
88/B5 Spratly (isls.)
55/H2 Spree (riv.), Ger.
63/K4 Spresiano, It.
59/E3 Sprimont, Belg.
135/G4 Spring (cr.), Ga,US
134/E4 Spring, Tx,US
133/K1 Springdale, Nf,Can.
134/E2 Springdale, Ar,US
57/G4 Springe, Ger.
131/F3 Springer, NM,US
130/E4 Springerville, Az,US
131/G3 Springfield, Co,US
132/B4 Springfield (cap.), Il,US
133/F3 Springfield, Ma,US
131/J3 Springfield, Mo,US
132/D4 Springfield, Oh,US
128/C4 Springfield, Or,US
135/G2 Springfield, Tn,US
137/J8 Springfield, Va,US
133/F3 Springfield, Vt,US
133/H2 Springhill, NS,Can.
134/E3 Springhill, La,US
108/E2 Springs, SAfr.
129/H3 Springside, Sk,Can.
97/G5 Springvale
129/K5 Spring Valley, Mn,US
137/F4 Spring Valley, NY,US
57/E6 Sprockhövel, Ger.
53/H1 Sprowston, Eng,UK
132/E4 Spruce (peak), WV,US
137/E5 Spruce Run (res.), NJ,US
56/B5 Spui (riv.), Neth.
51/J4 Spurn Head (pt.), Eng,UK
128/C3 Squamish, BC,Can.
66/E3 Squillace (gulf), It.
67/F2 Squinzano, It.
68/D3 Srbobran, Serb.
89/C4 Sre Ambel, Camb.
68/D3 Srebrenica, Bosn.
69/G4 Sredna (mts.), Bul.
69/G4 Srednogorie, Bul.
89/D3 Sre Khtum, Camb.
55/J2 Śrem, Pol.
68/E3 Sremčica, Serb.
68/D3 Sremska Mitrovica, Serb.
89/C3 Sreng (riv.), Camb.
89/D3 Sre Noy, Camb.
89/D3 Srepok (riv.), Camb.
83/H1 Sretensk, Rus.
79/K3 Sri Dungargarh, India
79/K3 Sri Gangānagar, India
90/D6 Sri Jayewardenepura Kotte (cap.), SrL.
90/D4 Srikākulam, India
90/D6 Sri Lanka (ctry.)
79/K2 Srīnagar, India
90/B4 Srīvardhan, India
55/J3 Środa Śląska, Pol.
55/J2 Środa Wielkopolska, Pol.
96/A2 Staaten River Nat'l Park, Austl.
48/H1 Stabbursdalen Nat'l Park, Nor.
56/B6 Stabroek, Belg.
57/G1 Stade, Ger.
58/C2 Staden, Belg.
56/D3 Stadskanaal, Neth.
57/G4 Stadthagen, Ger.
56/D5 Stadtlohn, Ger.
61/E3 Stäfa, Swi.
55/G1 Staffanstorp, Swe.
51/F6 Stafford, Eng,UK
52/D2 Stafford & Worcester (can.), Eng,UK
51/F5 Staffordshire (co.), Eng,UK
66/B4 Stagnone (isls.), It.
51/G2 Staindrop, Eng,UK
53/F4 Staines, Eng,UK
138/M12 Stakes (mtn.), Ca,US
72/F2 Stakhanov, Ukr.
52/D5 Stalbridge, Eng,UK
53/H1 Stalham, Eng,UK
125/S6 Stallworthy (cape), Nun,Can.
55/M3 Stalowa Wola, Pol.
51/F5 Stalybridge, Eng,UK
69/G4 Stamboliyski, Bul.
53/F1 Stamford, Eng,UK
137/G4 Stamford, Ct,US
51/H4 Stamford Bridge, Eng,UK
48/E1 Stamsund, Nor.
50/B4 Stamullin, Ire.
108/E2 Standerton, SAfr.
51/F4 Standish-with-Langtree, Eng,UK
53/G4 Stanford le Hope, Eng,UK
48/D3 Stange, Nor.
109/E3 Stanger, SAfr.
51/F2 Stanhope, Eng,UK
137/F5 Stanhope, NJ,US
130/B3 Stanislaus (riv.), Ca,US
69/F4 Stanke Dimitrov, Bul.
97/C4 Stanley (peak), Austl.
133/H2 Stanley, NB,Can.
90/C5 Stanley (res.), India
51/G2 Stanley, Eng,UK
129/H3 Stanley, ND,US
103/L8 Stanley (falls), D.R. Congo
68/E4 Stanovo, Serb.
75/N4 Stanovoy (range), Rus.
53/G3 Stansted Mountfitchet, Eng,UK
53/G2 Stanton, Eng,UK
137/C3 Stanton, Ca,US
132/D4 Stanton, Ky,US
134/C3 Stanton, Tx,US
56/D3 Staphorst, Neth.
53/E4 Stapleford, Eng,UK
53/G4 Staplehurst, Eng,UK
55/L3 Starachowice, Pol.
68/E3 Stara Pazova, Serb.
68/F3 Stara Planina (mts.), Serb.
70/F4 Staraya Russa, Rus.
69/G4 Stara Zagora, Bul.
99/K5 Starbuck (isl.), Kiri.
96/B1 Starcke Nat'l Park, Austl.
55/H2 Stargard Szczeciński, Pol.
135/H4 Starke, Fl,US
135/F3 Starkville, Ms,US
72/F3 Staroderevyan-kovskaya, Rus.
72/E1 Starodub, Rus.
55/K2 Starogard Gdański, Pol.
72/F3 Staroshcher-binovskaya, Rus.
52/C6 Start (bay), Eng,UK
52/C6 Start (pt.), Eng,UK
55/L3 Staszów, Pol.
132/E3 State College, Pa,US
137/F5 Staten (isl.), NY,US
135/H3 Statesboro, Ga,US
135/H3 Statesville, NC,US
54/E3 Staufenberg, Ger.
52/D3 Staunton, Eng,UK
132/E4 Staunton, Va,US
52/D2 Staunton on Wye, Eng,UK
48/C4 Stavanger, Nor.
51/F3 Staveley, Eng,UK
51/G5 Staveley, Eng,UK
73/G3 Stavropol', Rus.
73/G3 Stavropol'skiy Kray, Rus.
97/B3 Stawell, Austl.
128/C4 Stayton, Or,US
130/F2 Steamboat Springs, Co,US
57/H3 Stederau (riv.), Ger.
97/F5 Steele (cr.), Austl.
129/J4 Steele, ND,US
109/E2 Steelpoortrivier (riv.), SAfr.
56/B5 Steenbergen, Neth.
130/C2 Steens (mtn.), Or,US
125/J1 Steensby (inlet), Nun,Can.
56/D3 Steenwijk, Neth
129/G1 Steephill (lake), Sk,Can.
52/C4 Steep Holm (isl.), Eng,UK
51/J5 Steeping (riv.), Eng,UK
136/J2 Steese Nat'l Rec. Area, Ak,US
124/F1 Stefansson (isl.), Nun,Can.
118/C5 Steffen (peak), Chile
60/D4 Steffisburg, Swi.
68/A2 Steiermark (prov.), Aus.
63/J2 Steigerwald (for.), Ger.
54/F4 Stein, Ger.
59/E2 Stein, Neth.
129/J3 Steinbach, Mb,Can.
57/E4 Steinfurt, Ger.
57/F4 Steinhagen, Ger.
57/G5 Steinheim, Ger.
57/G4 Steinhuder Meer (lake), Ger.
48/D2 Steinkjer, Nor.
58/D1 Stekene, Belg.
133/J2 Stellarton, NS,Can.
57/H2 Stelle, Ger.
108/B4 Stellenbosch, SAfr.
63/H5 Stello (mtn.), Fr.
61/G4 Stelvio Nat'l Park, It.
54/F2 Stendal, Ger.
69/G4 Steneto Nat'l Park, Bul.
48/D4 Stenungsund, Swe.
97/B1 Stephens Creek, Austl.
133/K1 Stephenville, Nf,Can.
134/D3 Stephenville, Tx,US
131/G2 Sterling, Co,US
134/C4 Sterling City, Tx,US
138/F6 Sterling Heights, Mi,US
73/K1 Sterlitamak, Rus.
128/E2 Stettler, Ab,Can.
132/D3 Steubenville, Oh,US
53/F3 Stevenage, Eng,UK
129/J2 Stevenson (lake), Mb,Can.
136/H4 Stevenson (str.), Ak,US
132/B2 Stevens Point, Wi,US
128/E4 Stevensville, Mt,US
56/C3 Stevinsluizen (dam), Neth.
136/L3 Stewart (riv.), Yk,Can.
136/L3 Stewart Crossing, Yk,Can.
136/L3 Stewart River, Yk,Can.
50/B2 Stewartstown, NI,UK
129/K5 Stewartville, Mn,US
53/F5 Steyning, Eng,UK
63/L2 Steyr, Aus.
63/L3 Steyr (riv.), Aus.
56/C2 Stiens, Neth.
131/J4 Stigler, Ok,US
136/M4 Stikine (riv.), BC,Can.
129/K4 Stillwater, Mn,US
130/C3 Stillwater (range), Nv,US
131/H3 Stillwater, Ok,US
131/J4 Stilwell, Ok,US
50/D1 Stinchar (riv.), Sc,UK
134/C3 Stinnett, Tx US
68/F5 Štip, FYROM
59/F5 Stiring-Wendel, Fr
49/D2 Stirling, Sc,UK
133/L2 St. John's (cap.), Nf,Can.
48/D3 Stjørdal, Nor.
53/E4 Stockbridge, Eng,UK
55/J4 Stockerau, Aus.
48/F4 Stockholm (cap.), Swe.
51/F5 Stockport, Eng,UK
51/F5 Stockport (co.), Eng,UK
51/F4 Stocks (res.), Eng,UK
51/G5 Stocksbridge, Eng,UK
138/M11 Stockton, Ca,US
131/J3 Stockton (lake), Mo,US
134/C4 Stockton (plat.), Tx,US
51/G2 Stockton-on-Tees, Eng,UK
51/G2 Stockton-on-Tees (co.), Eng,UK
89/D3 Stoeng Treng, Camb.
52/B6 Stoke (pt.), Eng,UK
51/F5 Stoke-on-Trent, Eng,UK
51/F6 Stoke-on-Trent (co.), Eng,UK
97/B4 Stokes (pt.), Austl.
68/C4 Stolac, Bosn.
57/F2 Stolberg, Ger.
75/P2 Stolbovoy (isl.), Rus.
108/K10 Stompneuspunt (pt.), SAfr.
51/F6 Stone, Eng,UK
49/D2 Stonehaven, Sc,UK
53/E4 Stonehenge (ruins), Eng,UK
52/D3 Stonehouse, Eng,UK
129/J3 Stonewall, Mb,Can.
129/J2 Stony (pt.), Mb,Can.
137/G5 Stony Brook, NY,US
129/J3 Stony Mountain, Mb,Can.
137/G4 Stony Point, NY,US
74/K3 Stony Tunguska (riv.), Rus.
132/D1 Stooping (riv.), On,Can.
125/S7 Stor (isl.), Nun,Can.
57/G1 Stör (riv.), Ger.
48/F2 Stora Sjöfallets Nat'l Park, Swe.
48/F2 Storavan (lake), Swe.
54/F1 Store Bælt (chan.), Den.
48/D3 Støren, Nor.
97/C4 Storm (bay), Austl.
129/K5 Storm Lake, Ia,US
50/C2 Stormont, NI,UK
53/F5 Storrington, Eng,UK
48/F1 Storsteinsfjellet (peak), Nor.
54/F1 Storstrøm (co.), Den.
53/G3 Stort (riv.), Eng,UK
48/F2 Storuman, Swe.
128/G4 Story, Wy,US
119/J7 Stosch (isl.), Chile
53/F2 Stotfold, Eng,UK
129/H3 Stoughton, Sk,Can.
52/D5 Stour (riv.), Eng,UK
53/E2 Stour (riv.), Eng,UK
53/H3 Stour (riv.), Eng,UK
53/H4 Stour (riv.), Eng,UK
52/D2 Stourbridge, Eng,UK
53/G4 Stour, Great (riv.), Eng,UK
52/D2 Stourport on Severn, Eng,UK
53/G2 Stowmarket, Eng,UK
53/E3 Stow on the Wold, Eng,UK
50/A2 Strabane (dist.), NI,UK
49/D2 Strachan, Sc,UK
49/C2 Strachur, Sc,UK
63/H4 Stradella, It.
56/D6 Straelen, Ger.
55/G4 Strakonice, Czh.
69/H4 Straldzha, Bul.
54/G1 Stralsund, Ger.
108/B4 Strand, SAfr.
50/C3 Strangford, NI,UK
50/C3 Strangford Lough (inlet), NI,UK
70/C4 Strängnäs, Swe.
50/B1 Stranocum, NI,UK
50/C2 Stranraer, Sc,UK
129/G3 Strasbourg, Sk,Can.
60/D1 Strasbourg, Fr.
132/D3 Stratford, On,Can.
95/H6 Stratford, NZ
137/E6 Stratford, NJ,US
53/E2 Stratford upon Avon, Eng,UK
49/C3 Strathaven, Sc,UK
128/E3 Strathmore, Ab,Can.
52/B5 Stratton, Eng,UK
63/K2 Straubing, Ger.
48/M6 Straumnes (pt.), Ice.
55/G2 Strausberg, Ger.
137/B2 Strawberry (peak), Ca,US
138/P15 Streamwood, Il,US
53/E3 Streatley, Eng,UK
132/B3 Streator, Il,US
55/H4 Středočeská Žulová Vrchovina (mts.), Czh.
55/H3 Středočeský (reg.), Czh.
52/D4 Street, Eng,UK
133/Q8 Streetsville, On,Can.
69/F3 Strehaia, Rom.
70/H2 Strel'na (riv.), Rus.
51/F5 Stretford, Eng,UK
53/G2 Stretham, Eng,UK
56/B5 Strijen, Neth.
67/H2 Strimón (gulf), Gre.
67/H2 Strimónas (riv.), Gre.
119/K7 Strobel (lake), Arg.
67/G4 Strofádhes (isls.), Gre.
66/D3 Stromboli (isl.), It.
48/D4 Strømmen, Nor.
48/D4 Strömstad, Swe.
48/E3 Strömsund, Swe.
55/J3 Stronie Śląskie, Pol.
52/D3 Stroud, Eng,UK
68/E5 Struga, FYROM
108/C4 Struisbaai (bay), SAfr.
50/A2 Strule (riv.), NI,UK
67/H2 Struma (riv.), Bul., Gre.
52/A2 Strumble Head (pt.), UK
68/F5 Strumica, FYROM
48/C3 Stryn, Nor.
55/J3 Strzegom, Pol.
55/H2 Strzelce Krajeńskie, Pol.
96/A5 Strzelecki (cr.), Austl.
97/D4 Strzelecki (peak), Austl.
55/J3 Strzelin, Pol.
55/L4 Strzyżów, Pol.
128/B2 Stuart (lake), BC,Can.
128/B2 Stuart (riv.), BC,Can.
135/H5 Stuart, Fl,US
132/E4 Stuarts Draft, Va,US
55/G1 Stubbenkammer (pt.), Ger.
53/E5 Studland, Eng,UK
53/E2 Studley, Eng,UK
55/J4 Stupava, Slvk.
70/H5 Stupino, Rus.
129/J3 Sturgeon (bay), Mb,Can.
132/B1 Sturgeon (lake), On,Can.
132/C2 Sturgeon Bay, Wi,US
132/E2 Sturgeon Falls, On,Can.
132/C3 Sturgis, Mi,US
129/H4 Sturgis, SD,US
52/D5 Sturminster Newton, Eng,UK
53/H4 Sturry, Eng,UK
96/A5 Sturt (des.), Austl.
97/B1 Sturt (peak), Austl.
97/B1 Sturt Nat'l Park, Austl.
108/D4 Stutterheim, SAfr.
63/H2 Stuttgart, Ger.
135/F3 Stuttgart, Ar,US
72/C2 Styr (riv.), Ukr.
63/L3 Styria (prov.), Aus.
116/D1 Suaçuí Grande (riv.), Braz.
106/D5 Suakin (arch.), Sudan
88/D3 Suao, Tai.
92/C5 Subang, Indo.
92/C3 Subi (isl.), Indo.
68/D2 Subotica, Serb.
137/F5 Succasunna-Kenvil, NJ,US
69/H2 Suceava, Rom.
69/G2 Suceava (co.), Rom.
55/L3 Suchedniów, Pol.
49/A4 Suck (riv.), Ire.
114/E7 Sucre (cap.), Bol.
114/G5 Sucunduri (riv.), Braz.
116/B2 Sucuriú (riv.), Braz.
70/H4 Suda (riv.), Rus.
103/L5 Sudan (ctry.)
102/H5 Sudan (phys. reg.), Afr.
132/D2 Sudbury, On,Can.
53/G2 Sudbury, Eng,UK
57/H2 Sude (riv.), Ger.
55/H3 Sudeten (mts.), Czh., Pol.
107/A3 Sud-Kivu (prov.), D.R. Congo
56/D5 Südlohn, Ger.
105/H5 Sud-Ouest (prov.), Camr.
103/L6 Sue (riv.), Sudan
65/E3 Sueca, Sp.
69/G4 Süedinenie, Bul.
106/C2 Suez (can.), Egypt
106/C2 Suez (gulf), Egypt
106/C2 Suez (As Suways), Egypt
80/K5 Sūf, Jor.
137/F4 Suffern, NY,US
53/G2 Suffolk (co.), Eng,UK
132/E4 Suffolk, Va,US
131/K2 Sugar (riv.), Il, Wi,US
134/E4 Sugar Land, Tx,US
52/C3 Sugar Loaf (mtn.), Wal,UK
135/H2 Sugarloaf (peak), Ky,US
82/F1 Sühbaatar, Mong.
63/J1 Suhl, Ger.
80/B2 Şuhut, Turk.
88/B3 Sui (riv.), China
89/B4 Sui (pt.), Thai.
115/H6 Suia-Missu (riv.), Braz.
83/L2 Suibin, China
83/L3 Suifenhe, China
83/K2 Suihua, China
83/K2 Suileng, China
58/D5 Suippe (riv.), Fr.
49/B4 Suir (riv.), Ire.
138/K10 Suisun City, Ca,US
85/L10 Suita, Japan
137/K8 Suitland-Silver Hill, Md,US
88/B2 Suizhou, China
90/B2 Sūjāngarh, India
92/C5 Sukabumi, Indo.
92/C4 Sukadana, Indo.
92/C4 Sukadana (bay), Indo.
85/G2 Sukagawa, Japan
72/E1 Sukhinichi, Rus.
70/J4 Sukhona (riv.), Rus.
89/B2 Sukhothai, Thai.
79/J3 Sukkur, Pak.
84/C4 Sukumo, Japan
93/G4 Sula (isls.), Indo.
71/L2 Sula (riv.), Rus.
79/J3 Sulaimān (range), Pak.
93/E4 Sulawesi (Celebes) (isl.), Indo.
106/B4 Sulb Temple (ruins), Sudan
50/D3 Sulby (riv.), IM,UK
55/H2 Sulechów, Pol.
55/H2 Sulęcin, Pol.
55/L2 Sulejówek, Pol.
57/F3 Sulingen, Ger.
82/D4 Sulin Gol (riv.), China
48/F2 Sulitjelma (peak), Nor.
114/B4 Sullana, Peru
128/F3 Sullivan (lake), Ab,Can.
132/C4 Sullivan, In,US
132/E1 Sullivan Mines, Qu,Can.
52/C4 Sully, Wal,UK
66/C1 Sulmona, It.
131/J4 Sulphur (riv.), Ar, Tx,US
134/E4 Sulphur, La,US
131/H4 Sulphur, Ok,US
134/E3 Sulphur Springs, Tx,US
88/C6 Sulu (sea), Malay., Phil.
88/D6 Sulu (arch.), Phil.
80/C2 Suluova, Turk.
103/K1 Sulūq, Libya
59/G2 Sülz (riv.), Ger.
59/G5 Sulzbach, Ger.
63/J2 Sulzbach-Rosenberg, Ger.
111/P Sulzberger (bay), Ant.
111/Q Sulzberger Ice Shelf, Ant.
68/E3 Šumadija (reg.), Serb.
114/D3 Sumapaz Nat'l Park, Col.
92/B4 Sumatra (isl.), Indo.
93/E5 Sumba (isl.), Indo.
93/E5 Sumba (str.), Indo.
73/L5 Sumbar (riv.), Trkm.
93/E5 Sumbawa (isl.), Indo.
93/E5 Sumbawa Besar, Indo.
107/A5 Sumbawanga, Tanz.
110/B3 Sumbe, Ang.
82/F2 Sümber, Mong.
136/M4 Sumdum (mtn.), Ak,US
68/C2 Sümeg, Hun.
92/D5 Sumenep, Indo.
51/G3 Summer Bridge, Eng,UK
128/D3 Summerland, BC,Can.
133/J2 Summerside, PE,Can.
132/D4 Summersville, WV,US
135/G3 Summerville, Ga,US
135/H3 Summerville, SC,US
137/F5 Summit, NJ,US
138/C3 Sumner, Wa,US
84/D3 Sumoto, Japan
55/J4 Šumperk, Czh.
73/J4 Sumqayıt, Azer.
72/E2 Sums'ka Obl., Ukr.
135/H3 Sumter, SC,US
72/E2 Sumy, Ukr.
128/E4 Sun (riv.), Mt,US
85/M9 Sunami, Japan
97/C3 Sunbury, Austl.
53/F4 Sunbury on Thames, Eng,UK
86/D5 Sunch'ŏn, SKor.
130/D4 Sun City, Az,US
137/C3 Sun City, Ca,US
133/G3 Suncook, NH,US
92/B5 Sunda (str.), Indo.
129/G4 Sundance, Wy,US
90/E3 Sundarbans (reg.), Bang., India
90/D3 Sundargarh, India
79/L2 Sundarnagar, India
108/D4 Sundays (riv.), SAfr.
51/G2 Sunderland, Eng,UK
51/G2 Sunderland (co.), Eng,UK
57/F6 Sundern, Ger.
97/D1 Sundown Nat'l Park, Austl.
128/E3 Sundre, Ab,Can.
48/F3 Sundsvall, Swe.
92/B4 Sungaipenuh, Indo.
92/B2 Sungai Petani, Malay.
80/C2 Sungurlu, Turk.
134/E4 Sunland Park, NM,US
48/C3 Sunndalsøra, Nor.
48/E4 Sunne, Swe.
53/F4 Sunninghill, Eng,UK
138/K12 Sunnyvale, Ca,US
85/H8 Su-no-saki (cape), Japan
132/B3 Sun Prairie, Wi,US
137/B3 Sunset Beach, Ca,US
97/B2 Sunset Country (reg.), Austl.
130/E4 Sunset Crater Nat'l Mon., Az,US
97/F5 Sunshine, Austl.
75/P3 Suntar-Khayata (mts.), Rus.
57/G4 Süntel (mts.), Ger.
105/E5 Sunyani, Gha.
107/A5 Sunzu (peak), Zam.
84/B4 Suo (sea), Japan
89/D1 Suoi Rut, Viet.
48/H3 Suomenselkä (reg.), Fin.
89/D4 Suong, Camb.
114/C6 Supe, Peru
132/C2 Superior (lake), Can., US
130/E4 Superior, Az,US
126/E4 Superior, Mt,US
132/A2 Superior, Wi,US
132/B2 Superior (upland), Wi,US
89/C3 Suphan Buri, Thai.
93/J4 Supiori (isl.), Indo.
78/E2 Sūq ash Shuyūkh, Iraq
83/J4 Şuqaylabīyah, Syria
87/D4 Suqian, China
119/F3 Sur (pt.), Arg.
59/E4 Sûr (riv.), Belg.
130/B3 Sur (pt.), Ca,US
73/H1 Sura (riv.), Rus.
92/D5 Surabaya, Indo.
93/D4 Surada, India
92/D5 Surakarta, Indo.
88/D6 Surallah, Phil.
55/K4 Šurany, Slvk.
90/B3 Surat, India
90/B2 Suratgarh, India
89/B4 Surat Thani, Thai.
59/G6 Surbourg, Fr.
119/J7 Sur, Campo de Hielo (glacier), Chile
68/E3 Surčin, Serb.
68/F4 Surdulica, Serb.
59/E4 Sûre (riv.), Belg., Lux.
90/B3 Surendranagar, India
62/C3 Surgères, Fr.
74/H3 Surgut, Rus.
90/E3 Suri, India
65/F2 Súria, Sp.
88/E6 Surigao, Phil.
89/C3 Surin, Thai.
115/G3 Suriname (ctry.)
81/A4 Surkhob (riv.), Taj.
137/K8 Surrattsville (Clinton), Md,US
128/D3 Surrey, BC,Can.
53/F4 Surrey (co.), Eng,UK
102/J1 Surt, Libya
48/D3 Sur-Trøndelag (co.), Nor.
80/K5 Şūr (Tyre), Leb.
80/D3 Sürüç, Turk.
85/F3 Suruga (bay), Japan
84/C4 Susaki, Japan
78/E2 Süsangerd, Iran
130/B2 Susanville, Ca,US
80/D2 Suşehri, Turk.
87/B4 Susha (riv.), China
136/J3 Susitna (riv.), Ak,US
85/F3 Susono, Japan
132/E3 Susquehanna (riv.), US
133/H2 Sussex, NB,Can.
53/F4 Sussex, Vale of (val.), Eng,UK
56/C6 Susteren, Neth.
75/Q3 Susuman, Rus.
96/H9 Sutherland, Austl.
68/C4 Sutjeska Nat'l Park, Bosn.
79/K2 Sutlej (riv.), India, Pak.
51/H6 Sutterton, Eng,UK
51/J6 Sutton Bridge, Eng,UK
53/E1 Sutton Coldfield, Eng,UK
51/G5 Sutton in Ashfield, Eng,UK
51/J5 Sutton on Sea, Eng,UK
51/H5 Sutton on Trent, Eng,UK
108/D4 Suurberge (mts.), SAfr.
99/Y18 Suva (cap.), Fiji
85/F2 Suwa, Japan
55/M1 Suwałki, Pol.
135/H4 Suwannee (riv.), Fl,US
99/J6 Suwarrow (atoll), Cookls.
80/K5 Şuwaylih, Jor.
87/D4 Suzhou, China
87/E5 Suzhou, China
85/E2 Suzu, Japan
84/E3 Suzuka, Japan
85/M10 Suzuka (range), Japan
85/E2 Suzu-misaki (cape), Japan
63/J4 Suzzara, It.
74/C2 Svalbard (arch.), Nor.
89/D4 Svay Rieng, Camb.
48/E4 Svealand (reg.), Swe.
54/F1 Svendborg, Den.
125/S7 Svendsen (pen.), Nun,Can.
48/E4 Svenljunga, Swe.
71/P4 Sverdlovsk (Yekaterinburg), Rus.
71/P4 Sverdlovskaya Obl., Rus.
125/S7 Sverdrup (chan.), Nun,Can.
125/R7 Sverdrup (isls.), Nun,Can.
74/H2 Sverdrup (isl.), Rus.
72/D1 Svetlogorsk, Bela.
73/G3 Svetlograd, Rus.
68/E4 Svetozarevo, Serb.
48/P7 Svíahnúkar (peak), Ice.
68/E3 Svilajnac, Serb.
69/H5 Svilengrad, Bul.
69/G4 Svishtov, Bul.
55/J4 Svitavy, Czh.
83/K1 Svobodnyy, Rus.
69/F4 Svoge, Bul.
48/E1 Svolvær, Nor.
75/Q2 Svyatyy Nos (cape), Rus.
53/E1 Swadlincote, Eng,UK
53/G1 Swaffham, Eng,UK
96/D3 Swain (reefs), Austl.
135/H3 Swainsboro, Ga,US
99/H5 Swains Island (atoll), ASam.
110/C2 Swa-Kibula, D.R. Congo
110/B5 Swakopmund, Namb.
51/G3 Swale (riv.), Eng,UK
53/H4 Swalecliffe, Eng,UK
53/G4 Swale, The (chan.), Eng,UK
56/D6 Swalmen, Neth.
128/D2 Swan (hills), Ab,Can.
129/H2 Swan (riv.), Mb, Sk,Can.
122/E4 Swan (isls.), Hon.
53/E5 Swanage, Eng,UK
97/B2 Swan Hill, Austl.
53/G4 Swanley-Hextable, Eng,UK
129/H2 Swan River, Mb,Can.
52/C3 Swansea, Wal,UK
52/C3 Swansea (bay), Wal,UK
52/B3 Swansea (co.), Wal,UK
137/E6 Swarthmore, Pa,US
108/D3 Swart Kei (riv.), SAfr.
55/J2 Swarzędz, Pol.
108/B2 Swarzrand (mts.), Namb.
50/B2 Swatragh, NI,UK
53/E5 Sway, Eng,UK
109/E2 Swaziland (ctry.)
48/E3 Sweden (ctry.)
128/C4 Sweet Home, Or,US
134/C3 Sweetwater, Tx,US
128/F5 Sweetwater (riv.), Wy,US
108/C4 Swellendam, SAfr.
55/J3 Świdnica, Pol.
55/M3 Świdnik, Pol.
55/H2 Świdwin, Pol.
55/J3 Świebodzice, Pol.
55/H2 Świebodzin, Pol.
55/K2 Świecie, Pol.
55/L3 Świętokrzyskie (prov.), Pol.
128/G3 Swift Current, Sk,Can.
53/E3 Swindon, Eng,UK
53/E3 Swindon (co.), Eng,UK
51/H6 Swineshead, Eng,UK
55/H2 Świnoujście, Pol.
51/G5 Swinton, Eng,UK
60/D4 Swiss (plat.), Swi.
59/F2 Swistbach (riv.), Ger.
60/D4 Switzerland (ctry.)
50/B5 Swords, Ire.
70/G3 Syamozero (lake), Rus.
55/J3 Syców, Pol.
96/H8 Sydney, Austl.
133/J2 Sydney, NS,Can.
99/H5 Sydney (Manra) (atoll), Kiri.
133/J2 Sydney Mines, NS,Can.
57/F3 Syke, Ger.
71/L3 Syktyvkar, Rus.
135/G3 Sylacauga, Al,US
48/E3 Sylarna (peak), Swe.
91/F3 Sylhet, Bang.
54/E1 Sylt (isl.), Ger.
71/N4 Sylva (riv.), Rus.
132/D3 Sylvania, Oh,US
138/F6 Sylvan Lake, Mi,US
67/L6 Syntagma Square, Gre.
137/G5 Syosset, NY,US
111/C Syowa, Ant.
131/G3 Syracuse, Ks,US
132/E3 Syracuse, NY,US
66/D4 Syracuse (Siracusa), It.
74/G5 Syrdar'ya (riv.), Asia
78/C1 Syria (ctry.)
91/G4 Syriam, Myan.
71/L3 Sysola (riv.), Rus.
53/E1 Syston, Eng,UK
73/J1 Syzran', Rus.
68/E1 Szabolcs-Szatmár-Bereg (co.), Hun.
55/J2 Szamotuły, Pol.
68/E2 Szarvas, Hun.
68/D2 Százhalombatta, Hun.
55/H2 Szczecin, Pol.
55/J2 Szczecinek, Pol.
55/L2 Szczytno, Pol.
68/E2 Szeged, Hun.
68/E2 Szeghalom, Hun.
68/E2 Szegvár, Hun.
68/D2 Székesfehérvár, Hun.
68/D2 Szekszárd, Hun.
68/D2 Szentendre, Hun.
68/E2 Szentes, Hun.
68/E1 Szerencs, Hun.
55/M1 Szeskie (peak), Pol.
68/C2 Szigetvár, Hun.
68/E2 Szolnok, Hun.
68/C2 Szombathely, Hun.
55/H3 Szprotawa, Pol.
55/K2 Sztum, Pol.
55/J2 Szubin, Pol.
55/L3 Szydłowiec, Pol.

T

88/D5 Tabaco, Phil.
79/G2 Ţabas, Iran
122/C4 Tabasco (state), Mex.
115/K6 Tabatinga (mts.), Braz.
128/E3 Taber, Ab,Can.
65/E3 Tabernes de Valldigna, Sp.
98/G5 Tabiteuea (atoll), Kiri.
88/D5 Tablas (isl.), Phil.
108/B4 Table (bay), SAfr.
108/L10 Table (mtn.), SAfr.
131/J3 Table Rock (lake), Ar, Mo,US
64/B1 Taboada, Sp.
55/H4 Tábor, Czh.
107/B4 Tabora, Tanz.
107/B4 Tabora (prov.), Tanz.
104/D5 Tabou, C.d'Iv.
99/K4 Tabuaeran (Fanning) (atoll), Kiri.
88/D4 Tabuk, Phil.
78/C3 Tabūk, SAr.
98/F6 Tabwemasana (mtn.), Van.
123/F6 Tacarcuna (mt.), Pan.
81/D2 Tacheng, China
88/D3 Tachia (riv.), Tai.
84/A4 Tachibana (bay), Japan
85/F3 Tachikawa, Japan
88/D3 Tachoshui, Tai.
54/G4 Tachov, Czh.
88/E5 Tacloban, Phil.
114/D7 Tacna, Peru
138/C3 Tacoma, Wa,US
114/E7 Tacora (vol.), Chile
65/X16 Tacoronte, Canl.,Sp.
119/G1 Tacuarembó, Uru.
119/G2 Tacuarembó (dept.), Uru.
85/F2 Tadami (riv.), Japan
85/L10 Tadaoka, Japan
51/G4 Tadcaster, Eng,UK
102/F2 Tademaït (plat.), Alg.
90/D4 Tādepallegūdem, India
99/V12 Tadine, NCal.
53/E4 Tadley, Eng,UK
78/C2 Tadmur, Syria
85/M9 Tado, Japan
84/C3 Tadotsu, Japan
90/C5 Tādpatri, India
102/H2 Tadrart (mts.), Alg., Libya
86/D3 T'aebaek (mts.), NKor., SKor.
86/D4 Taech'ŏn, SKor.
86/D3 Taegang-got (pt.), NKor.
86/E5 Taegu, SKor.
86/E5 Taegu-Jikhalsi (prov.), SKor.
86/D4 Taejŏn, SKor.
52/B3 Taf (riv.), Wal,UK
64/E1 Tafalla, Sp.
52/C3 Taff (riv.), Wal,UK
117/C2 Tafí Viejo, Arg.
78/F2 Taft, Iran
79/H3 Taftān (mtn.), Iran
85/M9 Taga, Japan

186
Tagan – Tian S

72/F3 Taganrog, Rus.
72/F3 Taganrog (gulf), Rus., Ukr.
104/C2 Tagant (reg.), Mrta.
79/G1 Tagarav (peak), Trkm.
84/B4 Tagawa, Japan
88/D6 Tagbilaran, Phil.
63/G5 Taggia, It.
102/E1 Taghit, Alg.
136/M3 Tagish, Yk,Can.
63/K3 Tagliamento (riv.), It.
58/D5 Tagnon, Fr.
93/F2 Tagolo (pt.), Phil.
115/J7 Taguatinga, Braz.
98/E6 Tagula (isl.), PNG
88/E6 Tagum, Phil.
71/P4 Tagun (riv.), Rus.
64/B3 Tagus (riv.), Port., Sp.
92/B3 Tahan (peak), Malay.
85/N10 Tahara, Japan
102/G3 Tahat (peak), Alg.
99/L6 Tahenea (atoll), FrPol.
99/X15 Tahiti (isl.), FrPol.
134/E3 Tahlequah, Ok,US
136/J3 Tahneta (pass), Ak,US
130/C3 Tahoe (lake), Ca, Nv,US
134/C3 Tahoka, Tx,US
105/G3 Tahoua, Niger
105/G3 Tahoua (dept.), Niger
128/B3 Tahsis, BC,Can.
106/B3 Ṭahṭā, Egypt
99/L6 Tahuata (isl.), FrPol.
93/G3 Tahulandang (isl.), Indo.
87/L8 Tai (lake), China
83/H4 Tai'an, China
99/X15 Taiarapu (pen.), FrPol.
88/D3 T'aichung, Tai.
87/C3 Taihang (mts.), China
88/D3 Taihsi, Tai.
85/L10 Taima, Japan
49/C2 Tain, Sc,UK
88/D3 T'ainan, Tai.
67/H4 Taínaron, Ákra (cape), Gre.
104/D5 Taï Nat'l Park, C.d'Iv.
99/L5 Taiohae, FrPol.
88/D2 T'aipei (cap.), Tai.
83/J2 Taiping (peak), China
92/B3 Taiping, Malay.
84/C3 Taisha, Japan
85/L10 Taishi, Japan
87/E3 Taishun, China
118/B5 Taitao (pen.), Chile
88/D3 Taitung, Tai.
88/D3 Taiwan (ctry.)
88/C3 Taiwan (str.), China, Tai.
67/H4 Taïyetos (mts.), Gre.
87/C3 Taiyuan, China
87/D4 Taizhou, China
87/E2 Taizi (riv.), China
92/C4 Tajam (peak), Indo.
102/H3 Tajarhī, Libya
74/H6 Tajikistan (ctry.)
85/F2 Tajima, Japan
85/E3 Tajimi, Japan
85/L10 Tajiri, Japan
64/C3 Tajo (Tagus) (riv.), Sp.
78/F1 Tajrīsh, Iran
122/C4 Tajumulco (vol.), Guat.
64/D2 Tajuña (riv.), Sp.
89/B2 Tak, Thai.
85/G2 Takahagi, Japan
84/D3 Takahama, Japan
84/C3 Takahashi, Japan
84/C3 Takahashi (riv.), Japan
85/G2 Takahata, Japan
85/L10 Takaishi, Japan
84/D3 Takamatsu, Japan
85/M10 Takami-yama (peak), Japan
84/B4 Takanabe, Japan
85/E2 Takaoka, Japan
95/H6 Takapuna, NZ
85/L10 Takarazuka, Japan
99/L6 Takaroa (isl.), FrPol.
85/F2 Takasaki, Japan
85/M9 Takashima, Japan
85/L10 Takatori, Japan
84/D3 Takatsuki, Japan
85/E2 Takayama, Japan
84/E3 Takefu, Japan
84/C3 Takehara, Japan
78/E1 Tākestān, Iran
84/B4 Taketa, Japan
85/M10 Taketoyo, Japan
89/D4 Takev, Camb.
91/H4 Ta Khli, Thai.
103/R2 Takht-e Jamshīd (Persepolis) (ruins), Iran
85/M10 Taki, Japan
124/E2 Takijuq (lake), Nun,Can.
83/N3 Takikawa, Japan
85/K10 Takino, Japan
128/B2 Takla (lake), BC,Can.
81/D4 Takla Makan (des.), China
105/E5 Takoradi, Gha.
80/H6 Ṭalā, Egypt
51/E5 Talacre, Wal,UK
118/Q9 Talagante, Chile
90/B3 Talāja, India
105/G2 Talak (reg.), Niger
110/C2 Tala Mugongo, Ang.
92/B4 Talang (peak), Indo.
59/F5 Talange, Fr.
60/A3 Talant, Fr.
114/B4 Talara, Peru
81/B3 Talas (riv.), Kaz.
80/C2 Talas, Turk.
93/G3 Talaud (isls.), Indo
64/C3 Talavera de la Reina, Sp.
90/D6 Talawakele, SrL.
103/M5 Talawdī, Sudan
64/C3 Talayuela, Sp.
118/C2 Talca, Chile
118/B3 Talcahuano, Chile
90/E3 Tālcher, India
81/C3 Taldyqorghan, Kaz.
62/C4 Talence, Fr.
74/H5 Talgar, Kaz.
52/C3 Talgarth, Wal,UK
93/F4 Taliabu (isl.), Indo.
103/M6 Tali Post, Sudan
93/E5 Taliwang, Indo.
80/H6 Ṭalkhā, Egypt
135/G3 Talladega, Al,US
80/E3 Tall 'Afar, Iraq
135/G4 Tallahassee (cap.), Fl,US
135/F3 Tallahatchie (riv.), Ms,US
80/N9 Tall 'Āsūr (Ba'al Hazor) (mtn.), WBnk.
137/E6 Talleyville, De,US
70/E4 Tallinn (cap.), Est.
80/E3 Tall Kayf, Iraq
135/H3 Tallulah (falls), Ga,US
135/F3 Tallulah, La,US
103/N5 Talo (peak), Eth.
90/B3 Taloda, India
79/J1 Tāloqān, Afg.
124/G2 Taloyoak, Nun,Can.
117/B2 Taltal, Chile
124/E2 Taltson (riv.), NW,Can.
89/C4 Talumphuk (pt.), Thai.
79/L2 Talwāra, India
85/H7 Tama, Japan
85/H7 Tama (riv.), Japan
85/M10 Tamaki, Japan
105/E4 Tamale, Gha.
98/G5 Tamana (atoll), Kiri.
102/G3 Tamanghasset, Alg.
52/B5 Tamar (riv.), Eng,UK
68/D2 Tamási, Hun.
122/B3 Tamazunchale, Mex.
85/L9 Tamba, Japan
85/L9 Tamba (hills), Japan
104/B3 Tambacounda, Sen.
104/B3 Tambacounda (reg.), Sen.
104/C3 Tambaoura, Falaise de (escarp.), Mali
92/C3 Tambelan (isls.), Indo.
93/E5 Tambora (peak), Indo.
97/C3 Tamboritha (peak), Austl.
73/G1 Tambov, Rus.
73/G1 Tambovskaya Obl., Rus.
64/A1 Tambre (riv.), Sp.
103/L6 Tambura, Sudan
53/E1 Tame (riv.), Eng,UK
64/B2 Tâmega (riv.), Port.
51/F5 Tameside (co.), Eng,UK
105/H2 Tamgak (peak), Niger
104/B3 Tamgue, Massif du (reg.), Gui., Sen.
90/C5 Tamil Nadu (state), India
89/E3 Tam Ky, Viet.
89/D2 Tam Le, Viet.
135/H5 Tampa, Fl,US
48/G3 Tampere, Fin.
122/B3 Tampico, Mex.
92/A3 Tampulonanjing (peak), Indo.
122/B3 Tamuín, Mex.
122/B3 Tamulipas (state), Mex.
97/D1 Tamworth, Austl.
53/E1 Tamworth, Eng,UK
91/K3 Tan (riv.), China
103/N5 Tana (lake), Eth.
107/C3 Tana (riv.), Kenya
48/H1 Tana (riv.), Nor.
84/D4 Tanabe, Japan
116/B2 Tanabi, Braz.
48/J1 Tanafjorden (fjord), Nor.
136/C6 Tanaga (isl.), Ak,US
66/D2 Tanagro (riv.), It.
85/G2 Tanagura, Japan
89/C5 Tanah Merah, Malay.
89/D4 Tan An, Viet.
136/J3 Tanana (riv.), Ak,US
63/H4 Tanaro (riv.), It.
90/C2 Tānda, India
90/D2 Tānda, India
104/D3 Tanda (lake), Mali
103/M5 Tandaltī, Sudan
69/H3 Ţăndărei, Rom.
118/F3 Tandil, Arg.
79/J3 Tando Ādam, Pak.
79/J3 Tando Allāhyār, Pak.
79/J3 Tando Muhammad Khān, Pak.
97/B2 Tandou (lake), Austl.
50/B3 Tandragee, NI,UK
84/B5 Tanega (isl.), Japan
89/B2 Tanem (range), Myan., Thai.
102/E3 Tanezrouft (des.), Alg., Mali
87/C3 Tang (riv.), China
87/C4 Tang (riv.), China
107/C4 Tanga, Tanz.
107/C4 Tanga (prov.), Tanz.
109/H8 Tangainony, Madg.
107/A4 Tanganyika (lake), Afr.
115/G6 Tangará da Serra, Braz.
136/G1 Tangent (pt.), Ak,US
54/F2 Tangerhütte, Ger.
81/E5 Tanggula (mts.), China
81/F5 Tanggula Shankou (pass), China
102/D1 Tangier (Tanger), Mor.
138/B3 Tanglewilde-Thompson Place, Wa,US
81/E5 Tangra (lake), China
88/D6 Tangub, Phil.
93/H5 Tanimbar (isls.), Indo.
88/D6 Tanjay, Phil.
92/A3 Tanjungbalai, Indo.
92/C5 Tanjungkarang-Telukbetung, Indo.
92/C4 Tanjungpandan, Indo.
92/A3 Tanjungpura, Indo.
79/K2 Tānk, Pak.
98/F6 Tanna (isl.), Van.
85/L9 Tannan, Japan
81/F1 Tannu-Ola (mts.), Mong., Rus.
105/E5 Tano (riv.), C.d'Iv., Ghana
80/H6 Ṭanṭā, Egypt
103/M1 Ṭanṭā, Egypt
102/C2 Tan-Tan, Mor.
122/B3 Tantoyuca, Mex.
90/D4 Tanuku, India
107/B4 Tanzania (ctry.)
85/H7 Tanzawa-yama (peak), Japan
88/B2 Tao (riv.), China
89/B4 Tao (isl.), Thai.
83/J2 Tao'er (riv.), China
66/D4 Taormina, It.
131/F3 Taos, NM,US
102/E3 Taoudenni, Mali
88/B2 Taoyuan, China
88/D3 Taoyuan, Tai.
70/E4 Tapa, Est.
122/C5 Tapachula, Mex.
115/G4 Tapajós (riv.), Braz.
115/G3 Tapanahoni (riv.), Sur.
114/E5 Tapauá (riv.), Braz.
88/D5 Tapaz, Phil.
116/B4 Tapejara, Braz.
116/B4 Tapes, Braz.
92/B3 Tapis (peak), Malay.
105/F3 Tapoa (prov.), Burk.
68/C2 Tapolca, Hun.
132/E4 Tappahannock, Va,US
137/G4 Tappan, NY,US
137/G4 Tappan Zee (reach), NY,US
138/C3 Tapps (lake), Wa,US
90/B3 Tāpti (riv.), India
106/B5 Taqab, Sudan
106/D5 Taqātu' Hayyā, Sudan
116/B4 Taquara, Braz.
116/B4 Taquari, Braz.
115/G7 Taquari (riv.), Braz.
116/B2 Taquaritinga, Braz.
116/B2 Taquarituba, Braz.
81/B3 Tar (riv.), Kyr.
68/D4 Tara (riv.), Bosn., Mont.
74/H4 Tara, Rus.
105/H4 Taraba (riv.), Nga.
80/K4 Ţarābulus (Tripoli), Leb.
102/H1 Ţarābulus (Tripoli) (cap.), Libya
50/B4 Tara, Hill of (hill), Ire.
93/E3 Tarakan, Indo.
64/D2 Tarancón, Sp.
107/B3 Tarangire Nat'l Park, Tanz.
66/E2 Taranto, It.
66/E3 Taranto (gulf), It.
114/C5 Tarapoto, Peru
62/F4 Tarare, Fr.
62/F5 Tarascon, Fr.
114/D5 Tarauacá, Braz.
99/M7 Taravai (isl.), FrPol.
98/G4 Tarawa (atoll), Kiri.
98/G4 Tarawa (cap.), Kiri.
64/E2 Tarazona, Sp.
64/E3 Tarazona de la Mancha, Sp.
81/D2 Tarbagatay (mts.), Kaz.
79/K2 Tarbela (res.), Pak.
62/D5 Tarbes, Fr.
135/J3 Tarboro, NC,US
68/A2 Tarcento, It.
62/E3 Tardes (riv.), Fr.
62/D4 Tardoire (riv.), Fr.
83/M2 Tardoki-Jani (peak), Rus.
97/E1 Taree, Austl.
106/C2 Ţarfā', Wādī al (dry riv.), Egypt
106/B4 Tarfāwī, Bīr (well), Egypt
49/C2 Tarf Water (riv.), Sc,UK
69/G3 Târgovişte, Rom.
69/H3 Târgu Bujor, Rom.
69/F3 Târgu Cărbuneşti, Rom.
69/H2 Târgu Frumos, Rom.
69/F3 Târgu Jiu, Rom.
69/F2 Târgu Lăpuş, Rom.
69/G2 Târgu Mureş, Rom.
69/H2 Târgu Neamţ, Rom.
69/H2 Târgu Ocna, Rom.
69/H3 Târgu Secuiesc, Rom.
102/H1 Tarhūnah, Libya
64/C4 Tarifa, Sp.
114/F8 Tarija, Bol.
93/J4 Tariku (riv.), Indo.
93/J4 Tariku-taritatu (plain), Indo.
82/B4 Tarim (basin), China
81/D3 Tarim (riv.), China
79/J2 Tarin (riv.), Afg.
93/J4 Taritatu (riv.), Indo.
72/E3 Tarkhankut, Mys (cape), Ukr.
105/E5 Tarkwa, Gha.
88/D4 Tarlac, Phil.
114/C6 Tarma, Peru
62/D5 Tarn (riv.), Fr.
82/E2 Tarna (riv.), Mong.
79/J2 Tarnak (riv.), Afg.
55/L3 Tarnobrzeg, Pol.
55/L3 Tarnów, Pol.
81/D5 Taro (lake), China
63/J4 Taro (riv.), It.
102/D1 Taroudannt, Mor.
135/H4 Tarpon Springs, Fl,US
51/F5 Tarporley, Eng,UK
66/B1 Tarquinia, It.
65/F2 Tarragona, Sp.
65/F2 Tàrrega, Sp.
137/G4 Tarrytown, NY,US
80/C3 Tarsus, Turk.
70/E4 Tartu, Est.
80/K4 Ţarţūs, Syria
80/K4 Ţarţūs (dist.), Syria
85/M9 Tarui, Japan
84/B5 Tarumizu, Japan
89/B5 Tarutao Nat'l Park, Thai.
82/D2 Tarvagatay (mts.), Mong.
51/F5 Tarvin, Eng,UK
89/D3 Ta Seng, Camb.
81/E2 Tashanta, Rus.
74/F5 Tashauz, Trkm.
73/L4 Tashauz Obl., Trkm.
81/A3 Tashkent (cap.), Uzb.
81/B3 Tash-Kumyr, Kyr.
92/C5 Tasikmalaya, Indo.
80/C3 Taşkent, Turk.
80/C2 Taşköprü, Turk.
98/E8 Tasman (sea)
97/C4 Tasman (pen.), Austl.
97/C4 Tasman Head (cape), Austl.
97/C4 Tasmania (state), Austl.
68/F2 Tăşnad, Rom.
68/D2 Tata, Hun.
102/D2 Tata, Mor.
68/D2 Tatabánya, Hun.
132/D2 Tatachikapika (riv.), On,Can.
99/M6 Tatakoto (isl.), FrPol.
82/D4 Tatalin (riv.), China
83/N2 Tatar (str.), Rus.
74/H4 Tatarsk, Rus.
71/L5 Tatarstan, Resp., Rus.
102/H1 Tatāwīn, Tun.
85/F3 Tateyama, Japan
85/E2 Tate-yama (mtn.), Japan
124/E2 Tathlina (lake), NW,Can.
104/B2 Tatilt (well), Mrta.
124/G3 Tatnam (cape), Mb,Can.
105/H3 Tatokou, Niger
55/K4 Tatranský Nat'l Park, Slvk.
55/K4 Tatrzański Nat'l Park, Pol.
53/G4 Tatsfield, Eng,UK
85/E3 Tatsuno, Japan
51/H5 Tattershall, Eng,UK
80/E2 Tatvan, Turk.
115/K5 Tauá, Braz.
116/H8 Taubaté, Braz.
63/H2 Tauberbischofsheim, Ger.
63/K3 Tauern, Hohe (mts.), Aus.
63/K2 Taufkirchen, Ger.
131/K3 Taum Sauk (peak), Mo,US
91/G3 Taungdwingyi, Myan.
89/B1 Taunggyi, Myan.
79/K2 Taunsa, Pak.
133/S8 Taunton, On,Can.
52/C4 Taunton, Eng,UK
133/G3 Taunton, Ma,US
63/H1 Taunusstein, Ger.
95/H6 Taupo, NZ
55/M1 Tauragė, Lith.
95/H6 Tauranga, NZ
62/D3 Taurion (riv.), Fr.
80/C3 Taurus (mts.), Turk.
64/E2 Tauste, Sp.
62/C2 Taute (riv.), Fr.
99/X15 Tautira, FrPol.
98/E5 Tauu (isls.), PNG
130/E3 Tavaputs (plat.), Ut,US
135/H4 Tavares, Fl,US
80/B3 Tavas, Turk.
71/Q4 Tavda (riv.), Rus.
53/H1 Taverham, Eng,UK
58/B5 Taverny, Fr.
99/Z17 Taveuni (isl.), Fiji
64/B4 Tavira, Port.
52/B5 Tavistock, Eng,UK
89/B3 Tavoy, Myan.
83/L3 Tavrichanka, Rus.
80/B2 Tavşanlı, Turk.
52/B5 Tavy (riv.), Eng,UK
52/B4 Taw (riv.), Eng,UK
85/L10 Tawaramoto, Japan
132/D2 Tawas City, Mi,US
93/E3 Tawau, Malay.
52/C3 Tawe (riv.), Wal,UK
88/C6 Tawi-tawi (isl.), Phil.
106/D5 Ţawkar, Sudan
102/G1 Tawzar, Tun.
122/B4 Taxco, Mex.
79/K2 Taxila (ruins), Pak.
81/C4 Taxkorgan (Taxkorgan Tajik Zizhixian), China
49/D2 Tay (riv.), Sc,UK
49/C2 Tay, Loch (lake), Sc,UK
131/H2 Taylor, Ne,US
132/B4 Taylorville, Il,US
75/L2 Taymyr (isl.), Rus.
74/K2 Taymyr (pen.), Rus.
74/K2 Taymyr (riv.), Rus.
74/J2 Taymyrskiy Aut. Okr., Rus.
89/D4 Tay Ninh, Viet.
74/K4 Tayshet, Rus.
88/C5 Taytay, Phil.
74/J3 Taz (riv.), Rus.
102/B1 Taza, Mor.
135/H2 Tazewell, Tn,US
132/D4 Tazewell, Va,US
103/K2 Tāzirbū (oasis), Libya
122/D5 Tazumal (ruins), ESal.
73/H4 T'bilisi (cap.), Geo.
102/H8 Tchibanga, Gabon
102/H6 Tcholliré, Camr.
55/K1 Tczew, Pol.
114/E4 Tea (riv.), Braz.
51/H5 Tealby, Eng,UK
95/G7 Te Anau, NZ
137/F5 Teaneck, NJ,US
122/C4 Teapa, Mex.
92/B4 Tebak (peak), Indo.
102/G1 Tébessa, Alg.
105/F2 Tebesselamane (well), Mali
117/E2 Tebicuary (riv.), Par.
92/A3 Tebingtinggi, Indo.
73/H4 Tebulos-mta (peak), Rus.
65/E5 Tech (riv.), Fr.
69/J3 Techirghiol, Rom.
118/C4 Tecka (riv.), Arg.
123/P10 Tecomán, Mex.
123/N9 Tecuala, Mex.
69/H3 Tecuci, Rom.
138/G7 Tecumseh, On,Can.
132/D3 Tecumseh, Mi,US
131/H2 Tecumseh, Ne,US
79/H1 Tedzhen, Trkm.
74/G6 Tedzhen (riv.), Trkm.
51/G2 Tees (bay), Eng,UK
51/G2 Tees (riv.), Eng,UK
114/F4 Tefé, Braz.
114/E4 Tefé (riv.), Braz.
92/C5 Tegal, Indo.
56/D6 Tegelen, Neth.
102/H2 Tegheri (well), Libya
50/E6 Tegid, Llyn (lake), Wal,UK
105/H3 Tégouma (wadi), Niger
122/D5 Tegucigalpa (cap.), Hon.
124/G2 Tehek (lake), Nun,Can.
78/F1 Tehrān (cap.), Iran
81/C5 Tehri, India
122/B4 Tehuacán, Mex.
122/C4 Tehuantepec (gulf), Mex.
122/C4 Tehuantepec (isth.), Mex.
65/X16 Teide (peak), Canl.,Sp.
52/B2 Teifi (riv.), Wal,UK
103/L4 Teiga (plat.), Sudan
52/C5 Teignmouth, Eng,UK
64/B3 Tejo (Tagus) (riv.), Port.
131/H2 Tekamah, Ne,US
95/H6 Te Kao, NZ
122/D3 Tekax, Mex.
81/C3 Tekeli, Kaz.
81/D3 Tekes (riv.), China
78/C6 Tekezē Wenz (reg.), Eth.
103/N5 Tekezē Wenz (riv.), Eth., Sudan
81/D4 Tekiliktag (peak), China
69/H5 Tekirdağ, Turk.
90/D4 Tekkali, India
90/D3 Tel (riv.), India
122/D4 Tela, Hon.
73/H4 Telavi, Geo.
80/K5 Tel Aviv (dist.), Isr.
80/K5 Tel Aviv-Yafo, Isr.
65/X17 Telde, Canl.
104/E2 Télé (lake), Mali
81/G2 Telem (lake), Mong.
116/B3 Telemaco Borba, Braz.
48/D4 Telemark (co.), Nor.
93/E3 Telen (riv.), Indo.
69/G4 Teleorman (co.), Rom.
102/G3 Telertheba (peak), Alg.
115/G5 Teles Pires (riv.), Braz.
52/D1 Telford, Eng,UK
60/H3 Telfs, Aus.
57/G5 Telgte, Ger.
104/B4 Télimélé, Gui.
80/N9 Tel Jericho Nat'l Park, WBnk.
128/B2 Telkwa, BC,Can.
132/C4 Tell City, In,US
90/C5 Tellicherry, India
130/F3 Telluride, Co,US
80/N7 Tel Megiddo Nat'l Park, Isr.
82/D2 Telmen (lake), Mong.
92/B3 Telok Anson, Malay.
81/E1 Telotskoye (lake), Rus.
70/D5 Telšiai, Lith.
55/G2 Teltow (reg.), Ger.
105/E5 Tema, Gha.
132/D2 Temagami (lake), On,Can.
108/E2 Tembisa, SAfr.
123/J6 Temblador, Ven.
110/C2 Tembo, D.R. Congo
52/D2 Teme (riv.), Eng,UK
68/D3 Temerin, Serb.
93/B3 Temerloh, Malay.
81/B1 Temirtau, Kaz.
133/F1 Témiscamie (riv.), Qu,Can.
132/E2 Témiscaming, Qu,Can.
82/E1 Temnik (riv.), Rus.
99/M7 Temoe (isl.), FrPol.
130/E4 Tempe, Az,US
66/A2 Tempio Pausania, It.
134/D4 Temple, Tx,US
50/B2 Templepatrick, NI,UK
97/G5 Templestowe, Austl.
55/G2 Templin, Ger.
122/B3 Tempoal, Mex.
110/C3 Tempué, Ang.
72/F3 Temryuk, Rus.
58/D1 Temse, Belg.
118/B3 Temuco, Chile
102/D5 Tena Kourou (peak), Burk.
90/D4 Tenāli, India
89/B3 Tenasserim (range), Myan.
89/B4 Tenasserim (Thanintharyi) (div.), Myan.
56/D2 Ten Boer, Neth.
52/D2 Tenbury, Eng,UK
52/B3 Tenby, Wal,UK
103/P5 Tendaho, Eth.
85/G1 Tendō, Japan
102/G3 Ténéré du Tafassasset (des.), Niger
105/H2 Ténéré, 'Erg du (des.), Niger
65/X16 Tenerife (isl.), Canl.
65/L6 Tenes (riv.), Sp.
89/B1 Teng (riv.), Myan.
93/E4 Tenggarong, Indo.
82/E4 Tengger (des.), China
81/A1 Tengiz (lake), Kaz.
63/G4 Tenibres (peak), It.
117/D1 Teniente Enciso Nat'l Park, Par.
68/D3 Tenja, Cro.
105/E4 Tenkodogo, Burk.
135/F2 Tennessee (riv.), US
135/G3 Tennessee (state), US
118/C2 Teno, Chile
48/H1 Tenojoki (riv.), Fin.
122/C4 Tenosique, Mex.
85/L10 Tenri, Japan
85/E3 Tenryū (riv.), Japan
53/G4 Tenterden, Eng,UK
89/B2 Ten Thousand Buddhas, Cave of, Myan.
93/F3 Tentolomatinan (peak), Indo.
64/A1 Teo, Sp.
122/A3 Teocaltiche, Mex.
116/A2 Teodoro Sampaio, Braz.
116/D1 Teófilo Otoni, Braz.
123/P9 Tepatitlán de Morelos, Mex.
123/P9 Tepic, Mex.
55/G3 Teplice, Czh.
123/M7 Tepoca (cape), Mex.
99/L6 Tepoto (isl.), FrPol.
123/P9 Tequila, Mex.
65/G1 Ter (riv.), Sp.
105/F3 Téra, Niger
64/B1 Tera (riv.), Sp.
56/B4 Ter Aar, Neth.
99/K4 Teraina (Washington) (atoll), Kiri.
66/C1 Teramo, It.
80/E2 Tercan, Turk.
65/S12 Terceira (isl.), Azor.,Port.
118/E2 Tercero (riv.), Arg.
69/K2 Terderovsk (bay), Ukr.
73/H4 Terek (riv.), Rus.
115/K5 Teresina, Braz.
116/L7 Teresópolis, Braz.
58/C4 Tergnier, Fr.
82/D4 Tergun Daba (mts.), China
56/B5 Terheijden, Neth.
70/G1 Teriberskiy, Mys (pt.), Rus.
81/A1 Terisaqqan (riv.), Kaz.
56/C2 Terkaplesterpoelen (lake), Neth.
69/H5 Terkirdağ (prov.), Turk.
79/J1 Termez, Uzb.
66/C4 Termini Imerese, It.
122/C4 Términos (lag.), Mex.
130/B2 Termo, Ca,US
66/D1 Termoli, It.
52/D1 Tern (riv.), Eng,UK
93/G3 Ternate, Indo.
56/A6 Terneuzen, Neth.
66/C1 Terni, It.
62/F3 Ternin (riv.), Fr.
58/B3 Ternoise (riv.), Fr.
72/C2 Ternopil', Ukr.
72/C2 Ternopil's'ka Obl., Ukr.
83/N2 Terpeniya (bay), Rus.
128/A2 Terrace, BC,Can.
132/C1 Terrace Bay, On,Can.
66/C2 Terracina, It.
133/Q8 Terra Cotta, On,Can.
66/A3 Terralba, It.
133/L1 Terra Nova Nat'l Park, Nf,Can.
65/G2 Terrassa, Sp.
62/D4 Terrasson-la-Villedieu, Fr.
133/N6 Terrebonne, Qu,Can.
135/G2 Terre Haute, In,US
96/H8 Terrey Hills, Austl.
53/G1 Terrington Saint Clement, Eng,UK
129/G4 Terry, Mt,US
56/C2 Terschelling (isl.), Neth.
65/E1 Teruel, Sp.
89/B5 Terutao (isl.), Thai.
69/H4 Tervel, Bul.
63/K3 Terza Grande (peak), It.
82/C1 Tes, Mong.
82/D2 Tes, Mong.
62/D5 Tescou (riv.), Fr.
136/G1 Teshekpuk (lake), Ak,US
83/N3 Teshio-dake (mtn.), Japan
82/D2 Tesiyn (riv.), Mong.
82/C1 Tes-Khem (riv.), Rus.
68/C3 Teslić, Bosn.
124/C3 Teslin (lake), BC,Can.
136/M3 Teslin, Yk,Can.
124/C2 Teslin (riv.), Yk,Can.
105/G3 Tessaoua, Niger
59/E1 Tessenderlo, Belg.
53/E4 Test (riv.), Eng,UK
65/G1 Têt (riv.), Fr.
52/D3 Tetbury, Eng,UK
63/G4 Tête de l'Estrop (peak), Fr.
69/G4 Teteven, Bul.
51/H5 Tetford, Eng,UK
99/L6 Tetiaroa (isl.), FrPol.
59/F5 Teting-sur-Nied, Fr.
136/K3 Tetlin Nat'l Wild. Ref., Ak,US
128/F4 Teton (riv.), Mt,US
102/D1 Tétouan, Mor.
68/E4 Tetovo, FYROM
65/N9 Tetuan, Sp.
117/D1 Teuco (riv.), Arg.
66/A3 Teulada (cape), It.
129/J3 Teulon, Mb,Can.
57/F4 Teutoburger Wald (for.), Ger.
63/K5 Tevere (Tiber) (riv.), It.
80/K5 Teverya (Tiberias), Isr.
49/D3 Teviot (riv.), Sc,UK
96/D4 Tewantin-Noosa, Austl.
52/D3 Tewkesbury, Eng,UK
134/E3 Texarkana, Ar, Tx,US
134/C4 Texas (state), US
134/E4 Texas City, Tx,US
56/B2 Texel (isl.), Neth.
131/G3 Texoma, Ok,US
70/J4 Teykovo, Rus.
122/B4 Teziutlán, Mex.
89/C1 Tha (riv.), Laos
124/G2 Tha-anne (riv.), Nun,Can.
108/E3 Thabana-Ntlenyana (peak), Les.
109/E2 Thabankulu (peak), SAfr.
108/D2 Thabazimbi, SAfr.
89/B3 Tha Chin (riv.), Thai.
89/B4 Thaen (pt.), Thai.
89/D1 Thai Binh, Viet.
89/C3 Thailand (ctry.)
89/C4 Thailand (gulf), Thai.
89/D1 Thai Nguyen, Viet.
79/K2 Thal, Pak.
81/B5 Thal (des.), Pak.
89/C5 Thaleban Nat'l Park, Thai.
78/E6 Thamar, Jabal (mtn.), Yem.
53/F3 Thame, Eng,UK
53/F3 Thame (riv.), Eng,UK
132/D3 Thames (riv.), On,Can.
53/G3 Thames (riv.), Eng,UK
90/B4 Thāna, India
53/H4 Thanet, Isle of (isl.), Eng,UK
91/J5 Thang Duc, Viet.
89/D2 Thanh Hoa, Viet.
91/J4 Thanh Lang Xa, Viet.
89/D4 Thanh Phu, Viet.
89/D4 Thanh Tri, Viet.
89/B4 Thanintharyi (Tenasserim) (div.), Myan.
90/C5 Thanjavur, India
79/J3 Thar (des.), India, Pak.
90/B3 Tharād, India
91/G4 Tharrawaddy, Myan.
67/J2 Thásos (isl.), Gre.
53/E4 Thatcham, Eng,UK
91/G4 That Khe, Viet.
89/B2 Thaton, Myan.
91/H4 Tha Uthen, Thai.
53/G3 Thaxted, Eng,UK
55/H4 Thaya (riv.), Aus.
91/G4 Thayetmyo, Myan.
91/G3 Thazi, Myan.
53/E4 Theale, Eng,UK
106/C3 Thebes (ruins), Egypt
134/C3 The Caprock (cliffs), NM,US
128/C4 The Dalles, Or,US
97/B3 The Grampians (mts.), Austl.
56/B4 The Hague (s'-Gravenhage) (cap.), Neth.
97/C3 The Lakes Nat'l Park, Austl.
124/F2 Thelon (riv.), NW,Nun,Can.
50/B2 The Loup, NI,UK
129/H3 Theodore, Sk,Can.
130/E4 Theodore Roosevelt (lake), Az,US
129/G4 Theodore Roosevelt Nat'l Park, ND,US
129/H2 The Pas, Mb,Can.
58/B5 Thérain (riv.), Fr.
67/H3 Thermaic (Salonika) (gulf), Gre.
67/H3 Thermopílai (Thermopylae) (pass), Gre.
128/F5 Thermopolis, Wy,US
132/D2 Thessalon, On,Can.
67/H2 Thessaloníki (Salonika), Gre.
67/H3 Thessaly (reg.), Gre.
53/G2 Thet (riv.), Eng,UK
53/G2 Thetford, Eng,UK
133/G2 Thetford Mines, Qu,Can.
59/E2 Theux, Belg.
123/J4 The Valley (cap.), Angu.
53/G1 The Wash (bay), Eng,UK
53/G4 The Weald (reg.), Eng,UK
134/E4 The Woodlands, Tx,US
52/D1 The Wrekin (co.), Eng,UK
52/D1 The Wrekin (hill), Eng,UK
67/G3 Thíamis (riv.), Gre.
135/F4 Thibodaux, La,US
129/J3 Thief River Falls, Mn,US
128/C5 Thielsen (peak), Or,US
89/D4 Thien Ngon, Viet.
62/E4 Thiers, Fr.
104/A3 Thiès, Sen.
104/A3 Thiès (reg.), Sen.
107/C3 Thika, Kenya
90/E2 Thimphu (cap.), Bhu.
48/N7 Thingvellir Nat'l Park, Ice.
59/F5 Thionville, Fr.
67/J4 Thíra (isl.), Gre.
51/E2 Thirlmere (lake), Eng,UK
51/G3 Thirsk, Eng,UK
48/D4 Thisted, Den.
48/P6 Thistilfjördhur (bay), Ice.
136/L3 Thistle (mtn.), Yk,Can.
99/Z18 Thithia (isl.), Fiji
88/B5 Thitu (isl.)
67/H3 Thívai, Gre.
48/N7 Thjórsa (riv.), Ice.
124/G2 Thlewiaza (riv.), Nun,Can.
89/D4 Thoi Binh, Viet.
56/B5 Tholen, Neth.
56/B5 Tholen (isl.), Neth.
59/G5 Tholey, Ger.
135/G3 Thomaston, Ga,US
135/G4 Thomasville, Al,US
135/H4 Thomasville, Ga,US
135/H3 Thomasville, NC,US
128/C3 Thompson (riv.), BC,Can.
129/J2 Thompson, Mb,Can.
131/J2 Thompson (riv.), Ia, Mo,US
128/E4 Thompson Falls, Mt,US
138/B3 Thompson Place-Tanglewilde, Wa,US
124/E1 Thomsen (riv.), NW,Can.
96/A4 Thomson (riv.), Austl.
135/H3 Thomson, Ga,US
89/C3 Thon Buri, Thai.
91/J4 Thon Cam Lo, Viet.
89/B2 Thongwa, Myan.
89/E4 Thon Lac Nghiep, Viet.
60/C5 Thonon-les-Bains, Fr.
89/E4 Thon Song Pha, Viet.
130/E4 Thoreau, NM,US
128/E2 Thorhild, Ab,Can.
58/B6 Thorigny, Fr.
51/G2 Thornaby-on-Tees, Eng,UK
52/D3 Thornbury, Eng,UK
51/H4 Thorne, Eng,UK
133/R8 Thornhill, On,Can.
50/E1 Thornhill, Sc,UK
51/G2 Thornley, Eng,UK
51/G3 Thornthwaite, Eng,UK
51/E4 Thornton Cleveleys, Eng,UK
51/H3 Thornton Dale, Eng,UK
133/R9 Thorold, On,Can.
53/H3 Thorpe le Soken, Eng,UK
51/G2 Thorpe Thewles, Eng,UK
62/C3 Thouars, Fr.
62/C3 Thouet (riv.), Fr.
137/B2 Thousand Oaks, Ca,US
72/C4 Thracian (sea), Gre., Turk.
128/F4 Three Forks, Mt,US
136/L4 Three Guardsmen (mtn.), BC,Can.
128/E3 Three Hills, Ab,Can.
97/C4 Three Hummock (isl.), Austl.
98/G8 Three Kings (isls.), NZ
89/B3 Three Pagodas (pass), Myan.
105/E5 Three Points (cape), Gha.
132/C3 Three Rivers, Mi,US
134/D3 Throckmorton, Tx,US
52/B5 Thrushel (riv.), Eng,UK
52/D2 Thruxton, Eng,UK
89/D4 Thu Dau Mot, Viet.
89/D4 Thu Duc, Viet.
58/D3 Thuin, Belg.
62/E5 Thuir, Fr.
125/T7 Thule Air Base, Grld.
60/D4 Thun, Swi.
132/B1 Thunder Bay, On,Can.
89/C2 Thung Salaeng Luang Nat'l Park, Thai.
61/E2 Thur (riv.), Swi.
61/F2 Thurgau (canton), Swi.
54/F3 Thüringen (state), Ger.
63/H1 Thüringer Wald (for.), Ger.
53/E2 Thurlaston, Eng,UK
49/B4 Thurles, Ire.
53/G3 Thurrock (co.), Eng,UK
111/T Thurston (isl.), Ant.
122/B4 Tiacolula, Mex.
114/E7 Tiahuanaco (ruins), Bol.
136/M5 Tian (pt.), BC,Can.
115/K4 Tianguá, Braz.
87/D3 Tianjin, China
87/D3 Tianjin (prov.), China
87/C5 Tianmen, China
87/K9 Tianmu (mts.), China
74/H5 Tian Shan (range), Asia

Tians – Tunce
187

82/F5 Tianshui, China
102/F1 Tiaret, Alg.
99/S9 Ti'avea, Samoa
116/B2 Tibaji (riv.), Braz.
102/H6 Tibati, Camr.
51/F6 Tibberton, Eng,UK
104/C4 Tibé, Pic de (peak), Gui.
80/K5 Tiberias (Sea of Galilee) (lake), Isr., Syria
80/K5 Tiberias (Teverya), Isr.
63/K5 Tiber (Tevere) (riv.), It.
102/J3 Tibesti (mts.), Chad, Libya
81/D5 Tibet (Xizang) Aut. Reg., China
51/G5 Tibshelf, Eng,UK
123/G4 Tiburon (cape), Haiti
123/M8 Tiburón (isl.), Mex.
138/K11 Tiburon, Ca,US
53/G4 Ticehurst, Eng,UK
138/P14 Tichigan (lake), Wi,US
104/C2 Tichît, Dhar (hills), Mrta.
102/C3 Tichla, WSah.
63/H4 Ticino (riv.), It.
61/E5 Ticino (canton), Swi.
51/G5 Tickhill, Eng,UK
132/F3 Ticonderoga, NY,US
122/D3 Ticul, Mex.
48/E4 Tidaholm, Swe.
51/G5 Tideswell, Eng,UK
102/F2 Tidikelt (plain), Alg.
104/C2 Tidjikdja, Mrta.
93/G3 Tidore (isl.), Indo.
104/A2 Tidra (isl.), Mrta.
65/X16 Tiede Nat'l Park, Canl.
56/C5 Tiel, Neth.
83/J3 Tieling, China
65/N9 Tielmes, Sp.
58/C1 Tielt, Belg.
59/D2 Tielt-Winge, Belg.
104/D4 Tiemba (riv.), C.d'Iv.
81/E3 Tiemen Guan (pass), China
59/D2 Tienen, Belg.
77/H5 Tien Shan (range), China
89/D1 Tien Yen, Viet.
89/D2 Tien Yen, Viet.
103/J3 Tieroko (peak), Chad
48/F3 Tierp, Swe.
130/F3 Tierra Amarilla, NM,US
119/L8 Tierra del Fuego (isl.), Arg., Chile
119/L8 Tierra del Fuego, Antártida e Islas del Atlántico Sur (prov.), Arg.
119/K8 Tierra del Fuego Nat'l Park, Arg.
64/C2 Tiétar (riv.), Sp.
116/B2 Tietê (riv.), Braz.
102/C2 Tifariti, WSah.
132/D3 Tiffin, Oh,US
135/H4 Tifton, Ga,US
99/V12 Tiga (isl.), NCal.
102/H6 Tignère, Camr.
119/S12 Tigre, Arg.
114/C4 Tigre (riv.), Peru
123/J6 Tigre (riv.), Ven.
78/D1 Tigris (riv.), Iraq, Turk.
103/J4 Tigui (well), Chad
105/G2 Tiguidit, Falaise de (escarp.), Niger
122/B3 Tihuatlán, Mex.
48/J3 Tiilikkajärven Nat'l Park, Fin.
104/B1 Tijirît (reg.), Mrta.
123/L7 Tijuana, Mex.
116/K8 Tijuca Nat'l Park, Braz.
116/B3 Tijucas, Braz.
116/B1 Tijuco (riv.), Braz.
122/C4 Tikal Nat'l Park, Guat.
90/C3 Tīkamgarh, India
136/G3 Tikchik (lakes), Ak,US
99/L6 Tikehau (atoll), FrPol.
72/G3 Tikhoretsk, Rus.
70/G4 Tikhvin, Rus.
67/H2 Tikveš (lake), FYROM
56/C5 Tilburg, Neth.
53/G4 Tilbury, Eng,UK
134/D4 Tilden, Tx,US
51/H5 Till (riv.), Eng,UK
128/C4 Tillamook, Or,US
60/B3 Tille (riv.), Fr.
48/D4 Tilst, Den.
49/D2 Tilt (riv.), Sc,UK
118/Q9 Tiltil, Chile
71/L2 Timan (ridge), Rus.
95/H7 Timaru, NZ
72/F3 Timashevsk, Rus.
115/L5 Timbaúba, Braz.
129/H4 Timber Lake, SD,US
116/B3 Timbó, Braz.
104/E2 Timbuktu (Tombouctou), Mali
93/H4 Timbuni (riv.), Indo.
67/G3 Timfristós (peak), Gre.
102/F2 Timimoun, Alg.
104/A2 Timiris (cape), Mrta.
68/E3 Timiş (co.), Rom.
68/E3 Timiş (riv.), Rom.
68/E3 Timişoara, Rom.
105/G2 Ti-m-Mershoï (wadi), Niger
132/D1 Timmins, On,Can.
132/B2 Timms (hill), Wi,US
115/K5 Timon, Braz.
137/K7 Timonium, Md,US
95/B2 Timor (sea)
93/F5 Timor (isl.), ETim., Indo.
116/D1 Timóteo, Braz.
75/N4 Timpton (riv.), Rus.
48/F3 Timrå, Swe.
135/G3 Tims Ford (lake), Tn,US
108/E3 Tina (riv.), SAfr.
88/E6 Tinaca (pt.), Phil.
90/C5 Tindivanam, India
102/D2 Tindouf, Alg.
64/B1 Tineo, Sp.
88/C2 Ting (riv.), China
96/F7 Tingalpa (res.), Austl.
97/D3 Tingaringy Nat'l Park, Austl.
102/H2 Tinghert (upland), Libya
104/C4 Tingi (mts.), Gui., SLeo.
136/F2 Tingmerkpuk (mtn.), Ak,US
114/C5 Tingo María, Peru
118/C2 Tinguiririca (vol.), Chile
115/L6 Tinharé, Braz.
115/L6 Tinharé (isl.), Braz.
89/D2 Tinh Gia, Viet.
98/D3 Tinian (isl.), NMar.
104/C4 Tinkisso (riv.), Gui.
138/Q16 Tinley Park, Il,US
117/C2 Tinogasta, Arg.
67/J4 Tinos (isl.), Gre.
58/C5 Tinqueux, Fr.
102/G2 Tinrhert (plat.), Alg.
102/D1 Tinrhir, Mor.
91/G2 Tinsukia, India
52/B5 Tintagel, Eng,UK
64/B4 Tinto (riv.), Sp.
137/F5 Tinton Falls, NJ,US
51/G5 Tintwistle, Eng,UK
102/F4 Ti-n-Zaouâten, Alg.
129/H3 Tioga, ND,US
92/B3 Tioman (isl.), Malay.
53/G3 Tiptree, Eng,UK
90/C5 Tiptūr, India
99/L6 Tiputa, FrPol.
115/J4 Tiracambu (mts.), Braz.
106/C2 Tiran (str.), Egypt
67/F2 Tiranë (cap.), Alb.
106/C3 Tiran, Jazīrat (isl.), Egypt
61/G5 Tirano, It.
69/J2 Tiraspol', Mol.
80/A2 Tire, Turk.
72/F4 Tirebolu, Turk.
105/F1 Tirest (well), Mali
79/K1 Tirich Mīr (mtn.), Pak.
69/G2 Tîrnava Mare (riv.), Rom.
69/G2 Tîrnava Mică (riv.), Rom.
69/G2 Tîrnăveni, Rom.
67/H3 Tírnavos, Gre.
61/G3 Tirol (prov.), Aus.
52/C1 Tir Rhiwiog (mtn.), Wa,UK
63/K2 Tirschenreuth, Ger.
66/A2 Tirso (riv.), It.
90/C5 Tiruchchendūr, India
90/C5 Tiruchchirāppalli, India
90/C6 Tiruchendūr, India
90/C6 Tirunelveli, India
90/C5 Tirupati, India
90/C5 Tiruppattūr, India
90/C5 Tiruppūr, India
90/C5 Tirūr, India
90/C5 Tiruvannāmalai, India
72/B2 Tisa (riv.), Eur.
52/D4 Tisbury, Eng,UK
129/G2 Tisdale, Sk,Can.
131/H4 Tishomingo, Ok,US
68/E2 Tisza (riv.), Hun.
68/E2 Tiszaföldvár, Hun.
68/E2 Tiszafüred, Hun.
68/E2 Tiszakécske, Hun.
68/E1 Tiszalök, Hun.
68/E2 Tiszavasvári, Hun.
68/E3 Titel, Serb.
114/E7 Titicaca (lake), Bol., Peru
90/D3 Titlagarh, India
61/E4 Titlis (peak), Swi.
68/E5 Titov Veles, FYROM
68/E5 Titov vrh (peak), FYROM
69/G3 Titu, Rom.
135/H4 Titusville, Fl,US
104/A3 Tivaouane, Sen.
68/D4 Tivat, Mont.
52/C5 Tiverton, Eng,UK
122/D3 Tizimín, Mex.
79/L1 Tiznap (riv.), China
102/D2 Tiznit, Mor.
56/C3 Tjeukemeer (lake), Neth.
123/P8 Tlahualilo de Zaragoza, Mex.
122/B4 Tlalnepantla, Mex.
122/B4 Tlapa, Mex.
122/B4 Tlaxcala, Mex.
122/B4 Tlaxcala (state), Mex.
102/E1 Tlemcen, Alg.
102/J2 Tmassah, Libya
69/G2 Toaca (peak), Rom.
109/J7 Toamasina, Madg.
109/J7 Toamasina (prov.), Madg.
138/B2 Toandos (pen.), Wa,US
99/L6 Toau (atoll), FrPol.
128/B3 Toba (inlet), BC,Can.
82/D5 Toba, China
92/A3 Toba (lake), Indo.
85/E3 Toba, Japan
123/J5 Tobago (isl.), Trin.
79/J2 Toba Kākar (range), Pak.
64/E3 Tobarra, Sp.
81/B5 Toba Tek Singh, Pak.
50/B2 Tobermore, NI,UK
115/L6 Tobias Barreto, Braz.
129/H2 Tobin (lake), Sk,Can.
133/H2 Tobique (riv.), NB,Can.
74/G4 Tobol'sk, Rus.
103/K1 Tobruk, Libya
137/E4 Tobyhanna (lake), Pa,US
71/Q4 Tobyl (riv.), Kaz., Rus.
71/L2 Tobysh (riv.), Rus.
115/J5 Tocantinópolis, Braz.
115/J5 Tocantins (riv.), Braz.
135/H3 Toccoa, Ga,US
61/E5 Toce (riv.), It.
85/F2 Tochigi, Japan
85/F2 Tochigi (pref.), Japan
85/F2 Tochio, Japan
64/C4 Tocina, Sp.
117/B1 Tocopilla, Chile
123/F6 Tocumen, Pan.
123/H5 Tocuyito, Ven.
123/H5 Tocuyo (riv.), Ven.
85/H7 Toda, Japan
90/C2 Toda Bhīm, India
53/F3 Toddington, Eng,UK
66/C1 Todi, It.
51/F4 Todmorden, Eng,UK
115/G3 Toekomstig (res.), Sur.
128/E2 Tofield, Ab,Can
48/E3 Töfsingdalens Nat'l Park, Swe.
99/H6 Tofua (isl.), Tonga
104/C2 Togba (well), Mrta.
136/G4 Togiak Nat'l Wild. Ref., Ak,US
105/F4 Togo (ctry.)
85/N9 Tōgō, Japan
130/E4 Tohatchi, NM,US
99/X15 Tohivea (peak), FrPol.
85/F2 Tōhoku (prov.), Japan
85/F3 Toi, Japan
85/M9 Tōin, Japan
130/C3 Toiyabe (range), Nv,US
84/C3 Tojō, Japan
85/L10 Tōjō, Japan
85/E3 Tōkai, Japan
85/F2 Tōkamachi, Japan
106/D5 Tokar, Sudan
98/B1 Tokara (isls.), Japan
106/D5 Tokar Game Rsv., Sudan
80/D2 Tokat, Turk.
99/H5 Tokelau (terr.), NZ
85/N9 Toki, Japan
85/N9 Toki (riv.), Japan
85/H6 Tokigawa, Japan
85/M10 Tokoname, Japan
95/H6 Tokoroa, NZ
85/F3 Tokorozawa, Japan
82/B2 Toksun, China
81/B3 Toktogul (res.), Kyr.
84/D3 Tokushima, Japan
84/C4 Tokushima (pref.), Japan
85/H7 Tokyo (bay), Japan
85/H7 Tōkyō (cap.), Japan
109/H9 Tôlanaro, Madg.
69/H4 Tolbukhin, Bul.
117/F1 Toledo, Braz.
88/D5 Toledo, Phil.
64/C3 Toledo, Sp.
64/C3 Toledo (mts.), Sp.
132/D3 Toledo, Oh,US
134/E4 Toledo Bend (res.), La, Tx,US
66/C1 Tolentino, It.
118/C3 Tolhuaca Nat'l Park, Chile
81/D2 Toli, China
109/G8 Toliara, Madg.
109/H8 Toliara (prov.), Madg.
93/F3 Tolitoli, Indo.
50/B5 Tolka (riv.), Ire.
68/A2 Tolmezzo, It.
68/D2 Tolna, Hun.
68/D2 Tolna (co.), Hun.
93/F4 Tolo (gulf), Indo.
64/D1 Tolosa, Sp.
138/D2 Tolt (riv.), Wa,US
118/B3 Toltén, Chile
118/B3 Toltén (riv.), Chile
122/B4 Toluca, Mex.
73/J1 Tol'yatti, Rus.
74/J4 Tom' (riv.), Rus.
132/B3 Tomah, Wi,US
83/N3 Tomakomai, Japan
99/Y18 Tomanivi (peak), Fiji
64/A3 Tomar, Port.
67/G3 Tómaros (peak), Gre.
55/M3 Tomaszów Lubelski, Pol.
55/L3 Tomaszów Mazowiecki, Pol.
49/D2 Tomatin, Sc,UK
114/G6 Tombador (mts.), Braz.
103/M6 Tombe, Sudan
135/F4 Tombigbee (riv.), Al, Ms,US
110/B2 Tomboco, Ang.
104/E2 Tombouctou (Timbuktu), Mali
130/E5 Tombstone, Az,US
110/B4 Tombua, Ang.
118/B3 Tomé, Chile
62/B2 Tomé (isl.), Fr.
55/G1 Tomelilla, Swe.
64/D3 Tomelloso, Sp.
93/F4 Tomini (gulf), Indo.
64/A2 Tomiño, Sp.
85/H7 Tomiura, Japan
75/N4 Tommot, Rus.
114/E2 Tomo (riv.), Col.
132/C4 Tompkinsville, Ky,US
74/J4 Tomsk, Rus.
74/J4 Tomskaya Obl., Rus.
137/F6 Toms River, NJ,US
136/K3 Tom White (mtn.), Ak,US
128/D3 Tonasket, Wa,US
133/S9 Tonawanda, NY,US
53/G4 Tonbridge, Eng,UK
85/L10 Tondabayashi, Japan
93/F3 Tondano, Indo.
48/D5 Tønder, Den.
103/K6 Tondou (mts.), CAfr.
85/J7 Tone, Japan
85/G3 Tone (riv.), Japan
52/C4 Tone (riv.), Eng,UK
78/F1 Tonekābon, Iran
82/F5 Tong (riv.), China
99/H7 Tonga (ctry.)
99/K5 Tongareva (Penrhyn) (atoll), CookIs.
99/H7 Tonga-tapu (isl.), Tonga
82/F4 Tongchuan, China
59/E2 Tongeren, Belg.
88/B2 Tonggu, China
86/D3 Tonghan (bay), NKor.
83/K3 Tonghua, China
93/E5 Tongo (peak), Indo.
91/J2 Tongren, China
82/D5 Tongtian (riv.), China
128/G4 Tongue (riv.), Mt, Wy,US
56/D6 Tönisvorst, Ger.
103/L6 Tonj, Sudan
90/C2 Tonk, India
131/H3 Tonkawa, Ok,US
89/D1 Tonkin (gulf), China, Viet.
104/D5 Tonkoui (peak), C.d'Iv.
89/C3 Tonle Sap (lake), Camb.
62/D4 Tonneins, Fr.
130/D4 Tonopah, Az,US
130/C3 Tonopah, Nv,US
84/D3 Tonoshō, Japan
110/E5 Tonota, Bots.
48/D4 Tønsberg, Nor.
130/E4 Tonto Nat'l Mon., Az,US
130/D2 Tooele, Ut,US
97/G6 Toomuc (cr.), Austl.
96/C4 Toowoomba, Austl.
137/B2 Topanga, Ca,US
131/J3 Topeka (cap.), Ks,US
128/B2 Topley, BC,Can.
69/G2 Toplița, Rom.
55/K4 Topol'čany, Slvk.
69/G3 Topoloveni, Rom.
69/H4 Topolovgrad, Bul.
70/F2 Topozero (lake), Rus.
128/C4 Toppenish, Wa,US
52/C5 Topsham, Eng,UK
103/M6 Tor, Eth.
85/M9 Torahime, Japan
114/D7 Torata, Peru
93/G3 Torawitan (cape), Indo.
80/A2 Torbalı, Turk.
79/G1 Torbat-e Ḩeydarīyeh, Iran
52/C6 Torbay, Eng,UK
52/C6 Torbay (co.), Eng,UK
136/H3 Torbert (mtn.), Ak,US
54/E1 Törder, Den.
65/L6 Tordera (riv.), Sp.
64/C2 Tordesillas, Sp.
65/G1 Torelló, Sp.
52/C3 Torfaen (co.), Wal.,UK
55/G2 Torgelow, Ger.
58/C1 Torhout, Belg.
85/J7 Toride, Japan
85/E3 Torii-tōge (pass), Japan
64/A1 Toriñana (cape), Sp.
63/G4 Torino (Turin), It.
98/D1 Tori-Shima (isl.), Japan
103/M7 Torit, Sudan
79/H1 Torkestān (mts.), Afg.
64/C2 Tormes (riv.), Sp.
51/H4 Torne (riv.), Eng,UK
57/G1 Tornesch, Ger.
68/D4 Tornik (peak), Serb.
48/G2 Torniojoki (Torneälven) (riv.), Fin., Swe.
64/C2 Toro, Sp.
117/C2 Toro, Cerro del (peak), Arg.
68/E2 Törökszentmiklós, Hun.
67/H2 Toronaic (gulf), Gre.
133/R8 Toronto (cap.), On,Can.
70/F4 Toropets, Rus.
107/B2 Tororo, Ugan.
65/N8 Torote (riv.), Sp.
52/B6 Torpoint, Eng,UK
52/C6 Torquay, Eng,UK
137/B3 Torrance, Ca,US
64/D4 Torre del Campo, Sp.
64/D4 Torredonjimeno, Sp.
64/D2 Torrejón de Ardoz, Sp.
64/C1 Torrelavega, Sp.
65/N8 Torrelodones, Sp.
96/B3 Torrens (cr.), Austl.
95/C4 Torrens (lake), Austl.
65/E3 Torrente, Sp.
123/P8 Torreón, Mex.
65/E4 Torre-Pacheco, Sp.
64/D3 Torreperogil, Sp.
95/D1 Torres (str.), Austl.
116/B4 Tôrres, Braz.
98/F6 Torres (isls.), Van.
119/J7 Torres del Paine Nat'l Park, Chile
64/A3 Torres Novas, Port.
64/A3 Torres Vedras, Port.
65/E4 Torrevieja, Sp.
50/B1 Torr Head (pt.), NI,UK
52/B5 Torridge (riv.), Eng,UK
64/C3 Torrijos, Sp.
129/G5 Torrington, Wy,US
64/D4 Torrox, Sp.
47/D2 Tórshavn, Den.
62/B2 Torteval, Chl,UK
123/J4 Tortola (isl.), BVI
66/A3 Tortolì, It.
63/H4 Tortona, It.
65/F2 Tortosa, Sp.
65/F2 Tortosa (cape), Sp.
81/C3 Torugart, Pereval (pass), Kyr.
55/K2 Toruń, Pol.
49/A3 Tory (isl.), Ire.
55/L4 Torysa (riv.), Slvk.
70/G4 Torzhok, Rus.
84/C4 Tosa, Japan
84/C4 Tosa (bay), Japan
84/C4 Tosashimizu, Japan
110/B5 Toscanini, Namb.
63/J4 Tosco-Emiliano (range), It.
82/D4 Toson (lake), China
82/D2 Tosontsengel, Mong.
61/E3 Töss (riv.), Swi.
51/G1 Tosson (hill), Eng,UK
117/D2 Tostado, Arg.
57/G2 Tostedt, Ger.
84/B4 Tosu, Japan
80/C2 Tosya, Turk.
64/E4 Totana, Sp.
53/E5 Totland, Eng,UK
52/C6 Totnes, Eng,UK
122/A4 Totolapan, Mex.
118/E2 Totoras, Arg.
111/H Totten (glac.), Ant.
51/F4 Tottington, Eng,UK
53/E5 Totton, Eng,UK
84/D3 Tottori, Japan
84/C3 Tottori (pref.), Japan
102/D1 Toubkal, Jebel (peak), Mor.
88/D3 Toucheng, Tai.
129/G3 Touchwood (hills), Sk,Can.
104/E3 Tougan, Burk.
102/G1 Touggourt, Alg.
59/E6 Toul, Fr.
133/H1 Toulnustouc (riv.), Qu,Can.
62/F5 Toulon, Fr.
62/D5 Toulouse, Fr.
102/H3 Toumo (well), Niger
104/D5 Toumodi, C.d'Iv.
88/D3 Tounan, Tai.
89/B2 Toungoo, Myan.
104/D5 Toura (mts.), C.d'Iv.
58/C2 Tourcoing, Fr.
64/A1 Touriñan (cape), Sp.
62/C2 Tourlaville, Fr.
58/C2 Tournai, Belg.
60/A4 Tournus, Fr.
62/D3 Tours, Fr.
65/E3 Tous (res.), Sp.
62/B2 Toussaines, Signal de (peak), Fr.
102/J3 Toussidé (peak), Chad
103/K6 Toussoro (peak), CAfr.
108/C4 Touws (riv.), SAfr.
123/G6 Tovar, Ven.
53/E2 Tove (riv.), Eng,UK
82/E2 Tövshrüüleh, Mong.
85/G2 Towada, Japan
53/F2 Towcester, Eng,UK
51/G2 Tow Law, Eng,UK
129/H3 Towner, ND,US
128/F4 Townsend, Mt,US
138/A2 Townsend (mt.), Wa,US
96/C3 Townshend (cape), Austl.
96/B2 Townsville, Austl.
79/H1 Towraghondi, Afg.
137/K7 Towson, Md,US
93/F4 Towuti (lake), Indo.
81/C3 Toxkan (riv.), China, Kyr.
134/C4 Toyah, Tx,US
134/C4 Toyahvale, Tx,US
85/E2 Toyama, Japan
85/E2 Toyama (bay), Japan
85/E2 Toyama (pref.), Japan
85/N9 Toyoake, Japan
85/E3 Toyohashi, Japan
85/E3 Toyokawa, Japan
85/L10 Toyonaka, Japan
85/L10 Toyono, Japan
84/D3 Toyo'oka, Japan
85/M9 Toyosato, Japan
85/E2 Toyoshina, Japan
85/E3 Toyota, Japan
85/M9 Toyoyama, Japan
136/H2 Tozi (mtn.), Ak,US
89/E3 Tra Bong, Viet.
80/D2 Trabzon, Turk.
133/H2 Tracadie, NB,Can.
89/D4 Tra Cu, Viet.
137/F2 Tracy, Qu,Can.
138/M11 Tracy, Ca,US
64/B4 Trafalgar (cape), Sp.
65/P10 Trafaria, Port.
51/F5 Trafford (co.), Eng,UK
118/B3 Traiguén, Chile
128/D3 Trail, BC,Can.
63/L3 Traisen (riv.), Aus.
55/J4 Traiskirchen, Aus.
49/A4 Tralee, Ire.
89/D1 Tra Linh, Viet.
116/B4 Tramandaí, Braz.
89/E3 Tra Mi, Viet.
131/G3 Tramperos (cr.), NM, Tx,US
48/E4 Tranås, Swe.
59/D4 Tranet (mtn.), Fr.
89/B5 Trang, Thai.
93/H5 Trangan (isl.), Indo.
66/E2 Trani, It.
111/W Transantarctic (mts.), Ant.
68/F2 Transylvania (reg.), Rom.
68/F3 Transylvanian Alps (range), Rom.
89/D4 Tra On, Viet.
66/C3 Trapani, It.
89/D3 Trapeang Veng, Camb.
128/E4 Trapper (peak), Mt,US
58/B6 Trappes, Fr.
97/C3 Traralgon, Austl.
104/B2 Trarza (reg.), Mrta.
66/C1 Trasimeno (lake), It.
64/B2 Trás-os-Montes e Alto Douro (dist.), Port.
108/E2 Trasvaal (prov.), SAfr.
89/C3 Trat, Thai.
63/L2 Traun, Aus.
63/L2 Traun (riv.), Aus.
63/K3 Traunreut, Ger.
63/K3 Traunsee (lake), Aus.
63/K3 Traunstein, Ger.
54/F2 Trave (riv.), Ger.
97/B2 Travellers (lake), Austl.
136/G2 Traverse (peak), Ak,US
129/J4 Traverse (lake), SD,US
132/C2 Traverse City, Mi,US
89/D4 Tra Vinh, Viet.
134/D4 Travis (lake), Tx,US
68/C3 Travnik, Bosn.
52/C2 Trawsallt (mtn.), Wal,UK
50/E6 Trawsfynydd, Wal,UK
50/E6 Trawsfynydd, Llyn (lake), Wal,UK
68/B2 Trbovlje, Slov.
63/H4 Trebbia (riv.), It.
54/G1 Trebel (riv.), Ger.
55/H4 Třebíč, Czh.
68/D4 Trebinje, Bosn.
66/E3 Trebisacce, It.
55/H4 Třeboň, Czh.
64/B4 Trebujena, Sp.
52/C3 Tredegar, Wal,UK
52/C2 Trefeglwys, Wal,UK
50/E5 Trefnant, Wal,UK
52/C2 Tregaron, Wal,UK
119/G2 Treinta y Tres, Uru.
119/G2 Treinta y Tres (dept.), Uru.
62/C3 Trélazé, Fr.
52/B3 Trelech, Wal,UK
118/D4 Trelew, Arg.
62/D4 Trélissac, Fr.
54/G1 Trelleborg, Swe.
50/D6 Tremadoc (bay), Wal,UK
50/B4 Tremblestown (riv.), Ire.
128/B2 Trembleur (lake), BC,Can.
59/D2 Tremelo, Belg.
66/D1 Tremiti (isls.), It.
130/D2 Tremonton, Ut,US
133/F1 Trenche (riv.), Qu,Can.
55/J4 Trenčiansky (reg.), Slvk.
55/K4 Trenčín, Slvk.
118/E2 Trenque Lauquen, Arg.
51/F5 Trent (riv.), Eng,UK
51/F6 Trent and Mersey (can.), Eng,UK
63/J3 Trentino-Alto Adige (reg.), It.
61/H5 Trento, It.
61/H5 Trento (prov.), It.
132/E2 Trenton, On,Can.
135/H4 Trenton, Fl,US
135/G3 Trenton, Ga,US
138/F7 Trenton, Mi,US
131/J2 Trenton, Mo,US
137/F5 Trenton (cap.), NJ,US
135/F3 Trenton, Tn,US
52/C3 Treorchy, Wal,UK
67/F2 Trepuzzi, It.
119/T11 Tres Arboles, Uru.
118/E3 Tres Arroyos, Arg.
116/H6 Três Corações, Braz.
116/B2 Três Irmãos (res.), Braz.
117/J2 Tres Isletas, Arg.
116/B2 Três Lagoas, Braz.
116/C1 Três Marias, Braz.
116/C1 Três Marias (res.), Braz.
123/N9 Tres Marías (isls.), Mex.
118/B5 Tres Montes (cape), Chile
118/C4 Tres Picos (peak), Arg.
118/E3 Tres Picos (peak), Arg.
116/H6 Três Pontas, Braz.
118/D5 Tres Puntas (cape), Arg.
116/K7 Três Rios, Braz.
63/J2 Treuchtlingen, Ger.
54/G2 Treuenbrietzen, Ger.
63/H4 Treviglio, It.
63/K4 Treviso, It.
52/A5 Trevose Head (pt.), Eng,UK
137/J7 Triadelphia (res.), Md,US
96/B2 Tribulation (cape), Austl.
67/F3 Tricase, It.
90/C5 Trichūr, India
93/J4 Tricora (peak), Indo.
58/A5 Trie-Château, Fr.
59/F4 Trier, Ger.
66/E2 Triggiano, It.
68/A2 Triglav (peak), Slov.
68/A2 Triglav Nat'l Park, Slov.
66/D2 Trigno (riv.), It.
64/B4 Trigueros, Sp.
67/G3 Trikala, Gre.
67/G3 Trikhonís (lake), Gre.
60/D3 Trimbach, Swi.
51/G2 Trimdon, Eng,UK
90/D6 Trincomalee, SrL.
115/J7 Trindade, Braz.
55/K4 Třinec, Czh.
53/F3 Tring, Eng,UK
118/E3 Trinidad (isl.), Arg.
114/F6 Trinidad, Bol.
119/J7 Trinidad (gulf), Chile
119/F2 Trinidad, Uru.
131/F3 Trinidad, Co,US
123/J5 Trinidad and Tobago (ctry.)
115/N8 Trinidade, Braz.
133/L2 Trinity (bay), Nf,Can.
136/H4 Trinity (isls.), Ak,US
130/B2 Trinity (riv.), Ca,US
130/C2 Trinity (range), Nv,US
134/E4 Trinity (riv.), Tx,US
106/D5 Trinkitat, Sudan
109/S15 Triolet, Mrts.
80/K4 Tripoli (Ţarābulus), Leb.
102/H1 Tripoli (Ţarābulus) (cap.), Libya
67/H4 Trípolis, Gre.
102/H1 Tripolitania (reg.), Libya
90/C6 Tripunittura, India
91/F3 Tripura (state), India
16/J7 Tristan da Cunha (isls.), StH.
104/B4 Tristao (isls.), Guin.
118/D4 Triste (peak), Arg.
89/D4 Tri Ton, Viet.
57/H1 Trittau, Ger.
90/C6 Trivandrum, India
55/J4 Trnava, Slvk.
55/J4 Trnavský (reg.), Slvk.
98/E5 Trobriand (isls.), PNG
58/A5 Troesne (riv.), Fr.
63/L3 Trofaiach, Aus.
66/D2 Troia, It.
65/Q11 Tróia, Port.
59/G2 Troisdorf, Ger.
59/G6 Troisfontaines, Fr.
133/G1 Trois-Pistoles, Qu,Can.
133/F2 Trois-Rivières, Qu,Can.
71/P5 Troitsk, Rus.
48/E4 Trollhättan, Swe.
115/G4 Trombetas (riv.), Braz.
45/M6 Tromelin (isl.), Reu.
48/F1 Troms (co.), Nor.
48/F1 Tromsø, Nor.
118/C4 Tronador (peak), Arg., Chile
48/D3 Trondheim, Nor.
66/C1 Tronto (riv.), It.
80/J4 Troodos (mts.), Cyp.
50/D1 Trool, Loch (lake), Sc,UK
49/C3 Troon, Sc,UK
66/D3 Tropea, It.
130/D3 Tropic, Ut,US
50/B1 Trostan (mtn.), NI,UK
124/D2 Trout (lake), NW,Can.
129/K3 Trout (lake), On,Can.
51/F3 Troutbeck, Eng,UK
128/E1 Trout Lake, BC,Can.
52/D4 Trowbridge, Eng,UK
135/G4 Troy, Al,US
138/F6 Troy, Mi,US
132/F3 Troy, NY,US
135/G1 Troy, Oh,US
69/G4 Troyan, Bul.
69/G4 Troyanski Prokhod (pass), Bul.
62/F2 Troyes, Fr.
67/K3 Troy (Ilium) (ruins), Turk.
68/E4 Trstenik, Serb.
136/M3 Truitt (peak), Yk,Can.
122/D4 Trujillo, Hon.
114/C5 Trujillo, Peru
64/C3 Trujillo, Sp.
123/G6 Trujillo, Ven.
98/E4 Truk (isls.), Micr.
137/G4 Trumbull, Ct,US
52/D2 Trumpet, Eng,UK
39/D1 Trung Khanh, Viet.
133/J2 Truro, NS,Can.
52/A6 Truro, Eng,UK
130/F4 Truth Or Consequences, NM,US
55/H3 Trutnov, Czh.
62/E4 Truyère (riv.), Fr.
50/D6 Trwyn Cilan (pt.), Wal,UK
69/G4 Tryavna, Bul.
48/E3 Trysil, Nor.
55/J2 Trzcianka, Pol.
55/H1 Trzebiatów, Pol.
55/J3 Trzebnica, Pol.
55/J2 Trzemeszno, Pol.
68/B2 Tržič, Slov.
82/D3 Tsagaan Bogd (peak), Mong.
82/G2 Tsagaan-Ovoo, Mong.
82/E1 Tsagaan-Üür, Mong.
109/J6 Tsaratanana Massif (plat.), Madg.
108/B2 Tsarisberge (mts.), Namb.
81/F2 Tsast Uul (peak), Mong.
108/E3 Tsatsana (peak), Les.
110/D5 Tsau, Bots.
107/C3 Tsavo, Kenya
107/C3 Tsavo East Nat'l Park, Kenya
107/C3 Tsavo West Nat'l Park, Kenya
82/F2 Tsenhermandal, Mong.
82/D2 Tsetsen-Uul, Mong.
110/B1 Tshela, D.R. Congo
110/D2 Tshibwika, D.R. Congo
110/D2 Tshikapa, D.R. Congo
103/K8 Tshuapa (riv.), D.R. Congo
71/L2 Tsil'ma (riv.), Rus.
73/G2 Tsimlyansk (res.), Rus.
109/H9 Tsiombe, Madg.
109/H7 Tsiribihina (riv.), Madg.
109/H7 Tsiroanomandidy, Madg.
108/C4 Tsitsikamma Forest & Coastal Nat'l Park, SAfr.
73/G4 Ts'khinvali, Geo.
70/G4 Tsna (riv.), Rus.
82/D2 Tsogt, Mong.
82/F3 Tsogt-Ovoo, Mong.
82/F3 Tsogttsetsiy, Mong.
82/F2 Tsöh (riv.), Mong.
108/D3 Tsomo (riv.), SAfr.
84/E3 Tsu, Japan
84/A3 Tsushima (isls.), Japan
85/F2 Tsubame, Japan
84/E2 Tsubata, Japan
85/G2 Tsuchiura, Japan
85/M10 Tsuchiyama, Japan
83/M3 Tsugaru (str.), Japan
85/L10 Tsuge, Japan
85/H7 Tsukui, Japan
84/B4 Tsukumi, Japan
110/C4 Tsumeb, Namb.
85/K10 Tsuna, Japan
85/F3 Tsuru, Japan
84/E3 Tsuruga, Japan
85/H7 Tsurugashima, Japan
85/E2 Tsurugi, Japan
84/D4 Tsurugi-san (mtn.), Japan
85/M9 Tsushima, Japan
84/D3 Tsuyama, Japan
92/C5 Tua (cape), Indo.
64/B2 Tua (riv.), Port.
118/B4 Tuamapu (chan.), Chile
99/L6 Tuamotu (arch.), FrPol.
87/B4 Tuan (riv.), China
92/A3 Tuan (pt.), Indo.
89/C1 Tuan Giao, Viet.
92/A3 Tuangku (isl.), Indo.
89/D2 Tuan Thuong, Viet.
88/D4 Tuao, Phil.
72/F3 Tuapse, Rus.
130/E3 Tuba City, Az,US
92/D5 Tuban, Indo.
78/D6 Tuban (riv.), Yem.
116/B4 Tubarão, Braz.
56/D4 Tubbergen, Neth.
61/E1 Tübingen, Ger.
58/D2 Tubize, Belg.
104/C5 Tubmanburg, Libr.
98/H6 Tubou, Fiji
103/K1 Ţubruq (Tobruk), Libya
99/K7 Tubuaï (isls.), FrPol.
99/K7 Tubuaï (isl.), FrPol.
55/J2 Tuchola, Pol.
130/E4 Tucson, Az,US
131/G4 Tucumcari, NM,US
123/H6 Tucupido, Ven.
123/J6 Tucupita, Ven.
115/J4 Tucuruí, Braz.
115/H4 Tucuruí (res.), Braz.
64/E1 Tudela, Sp.
108/E3 Tugela (falls), SAfr.
109/E3 Tugela (riv.), SAfr.
135/H2 Tug Fork (riv.), WV,US
88/D4 Tuguegarao, Phil.
93/F5 Tukangbesi (isls.), Indo.
70/D4 Tukums, Lat.
92/D4 Tukung (peak), Indo.
138/B3 Tukwila, Wa,US
122/B3 Tula, Mex.
72/F1 Tula, Rus.
81/F4 Tulagt Ar (riv.), China
122/B3 Tulancingo, Mex.
130/C3 Tulare, Ca,US
131/F4 Tularosa, NM,US
131/F4 Tularosa (val.), NM,US
108/L10 Tulbagh, SAfr.
114/C3 Tulcán, Ecu.
69/J3 Tulcea, Rom.
69/J3 Tulcea (co.), Rom.
73/J3 Tüledi (isls.), Kaz.
134/C3 Tulia, Tx,US
136/E5 Tulik (vol.), Ak,US
98/E5 Tulin (isls.), PNG
80/K5 Ţūlkarm, WBnk.
135/G3 Tullahoma, Tn,US
49/B4 Tullamore, Ire.
62/D4 Tulle, Fr.
55/J4 Tulln, Aus.
70/G1 Tuloma (riv.), Rus.
131/J3 Tulsa, Ok,US
72/F1 Tul'skaya Obl., Rus.
114/C3 Tuluá, Col.
75/L4 Tulun, Rus.
122/D5 Tuma (riv.), Nic.
135/E5 Tumacacori Nat'l Mon., Az,US
115/H3 Tumac-Humac (mts.), Braz.
114/C3 Tumaco, Col.
88/D4 Tumauini, Phil.
103/J8 Tumba (lake), D.R. Congo
114/B4 Tumbes, Peru
89/C3 Tumbot (peak), Camb.
83/K3 Tumen, China
123/J6 Tumeremo, Ven.
90/C5 Tumkūr, India
49/C2 Tummel (riv.), Sc,UK
83/M1 Tumnin (riv.), Rus.
92/B2 Tumpat, Malay.
93/F4 Tumpu (peak), Indo.
97/D2 Tumut, Austl.
138/B3 Tumwater, Wa,US
80/D2 Tunceli, Turk.

Vet – Weiss
189

108/D3 Vet (riv.), SAfr.
48/E4 Vetlanda, Swe.
71/K4 Vetluga (riv.), Rus.
66/C1 Vetralla, It.
62/D3 Veude (riv.), Fr.
58/B1 Veurne, Belg.
60/C5 Vevey, Swi.
59/F2 Veybach (riv.), Ger.
62/D4 Vézère (riv.), Fr.
80/C2 Vezirköprü, Turk.
114/E7 Viacha, Bol.
115/K4 Viana, Braz.
64/B1 Viana del Bollo, Sp.
64/A2 Viana do Castelo, Port.
64/A2 Viana do Castelo (dist.), Port.
56/C5 Vianen, Neth.
89/C2 Viangchan (Vientiane) (cap.), Laos
64/C4 Viar (riv.), Sp.
63/J5 Viareggio, It.
62/E4 Viaur (riv.), Fr.
48/D4 Viborg, Den.
66/E3 Vibo Valentia, It.
65/G2 Vic, Sp.
64/D4 Vicar, Sp.
119/S12 Vicente López, Arg.
63/J4 Vicenza, It.
70/J4 Vichuga, Rus.
62/E3 Vichy, Fr.
135/F3 Vicksburg, Ms,US
66/C1 Vico (lake), It.
116/D2 Viçosa, Braz.
67/G3 Vicou Gorge Nat'l Park, Gre.
58/C5 Vic-sur-Aisne, Fr.
59/F6 Vic-sur-Seille, Fr.
107/B3 Victoria (lake), Afr.
118/E2 Victoria, Arg.
97/C3 Victoria (state), Austl.
122/D4 Victoria (peak), Belz.
128/C3 Victoria (cap.), BC,Can.
124/E1 Victoria (isl.), NW,Nun,Can.
124/F2 Victoria (str.), Nun,Can.
133/Q8 Victoria, On,Can.
118/B3 Victoria, Chile
88/B3 Victoria, China
91/F3 Victoria (peak), Myan.
93/E2 Victoria (peak), Phil.
69/G3 Victoria, Rom.
45/M6 Victoria (cap.), Sey.
134/D4 Victoria, Tx,US
123/F3 Victoria de las Tunas, Cuba
111/L Victoria Land (reg.), Ant.
107/B2 Victoria Nile (riv.), Ugan.
133/G2 Victoriaville, Qu,Can.
137/C1 Victorville, Ca,US
109/F3 Vidal (cape), SAfr.
135/H3 Vidalia, Ga,US
135/F4 Vidalia, La,US
116/B3 Videira, Braz.
69/G3 Videle, Rom.
68/F4 Vidin, Bul.
90/C3 Vidisha, India
71/W9 Vidnoye, Rus.
134/E4 Vidor, Tx,US
62/E5 Vidourle (riv.), Fr.
62/C3 Vie (riv.), Fr.
118/E4 Viedma, Arg.
119/J7 Viedma (lake), Arg.
134/B4 Vieja (mts.), Tx,US
59/E3 Vielsalm, Belg.
57/H5 Vienenburg, Ger.
137/J8 Vienna, Va,US
132/D4 Vienna, WV,US
55/J4 Vienna (Wien) (cap.), Aus.
62/F4 Vienne, Fr.
62/D3 Vienne (riv.), Fr.
89/C2 Vientiane (Viangchan) (cap.), Laos
59/D6 Viere (riv.), Fr.
56/D5 Vierlingsbeek, Neth.
59/E4 Vierre (riv.), Fr.
56/D6 Viersen, Ger.
62/E3 Vierzon, Fr.
66/E2 Vieste, It.
89/D2 Vietnam (ctry.)
89/D1 Viet Tri, Viet.
58/C3 Vieux-Condé, Fr.
123/J5 Vieux Fort, StL.
88/D5 Viga, Phil.
88/D4 Vigan, Phil.
63/H4 Vigevano, It.
115/J4 Vigia, Braz.
66/C2 Viglio (peak), It.
62/C5 Vignemale (mtn.), Fr.
58/B6 Vigneux, Fr.
63/J4 Vignola, It.
64/A1 Vigo, Sp.
59/F5 Vigy, Fr.
79/K2 Vihāri, Pak.
48/H3 Viitasaari, Fin.
90/D4 Vijayawada, India
67/F2 Vijosë (riv.), Alb.
48/D4 Vikersund, Nor.
69/F5 Vikhren (peak), Bul.
128/F2 Viking, Ab,Can.
65/G2 Viladecans, Sp.
65/V14 Vila de Porto Santo, Madr.,Port.
110/G4 Vila de Sena, Moz.
64/A2 Vila do Conde, Port.
65/T13 Vila do Porto, Azor,Port.
65/K7 Vilafranca del Penedès, Sp.
64/A3 Vila Franca de Xira, Port.
65/T13 Vila Franca do Campo, Azor.,Port.
62/B3 Vilaine (riv.), Fr.
109/H7 Vilanandro (cape), Madg.
64/A2 Vila Nova de Gaia, Port.
65/F2 Vilanova i la Geltrù, Sp.
65/K7 Vilanova i la Geltru, Sp.
64/B2 Vila Real, Port.
64/B2 Vila Real (dist.), Port.
64/B4 Vila Real de Santo António, Port.
116/D2 Vila Velha Argolas, Braz.
69/F3 Vîlcea (co.), Rom.
48/F2 Vilhelmina, Swe.
114/F6 Vilhena, Braz.
70/E5 Viliya (riv.), Bela.
70/E4 Viljandi, Est.
75/K2 Vil'kitsogo (str.), Rus.
118/Q9 Villa Alemana, Chile
117/D2 Villa Ángela, Arg.
64/E1 Villaba, Sp.
64/B1 Villablino, Sp.
123/H6 Villa Bruzual, Ven.
118/E2 Villa Cañas, Arg.
64/D3 Villacañas, Sp.
117/D3 Villa Carlos Paz, Arg.
64/D3 Villacarrillo, Sp.
63/K3 Villach, Aus.
118/E2 Villa Constitución, Arg.
64/A1 Villa de Cruces, Sp.
64/C4 Villa del Río, Sp.
117/C3 Villa Dolores, Arg.
122/C4 Villa Flores, Mex.
64/B3 Villafranca de los Barros, Sp.
122/A2 Villa Frontera, Mex.
64/A1 Villagarcía, Sp.
134/E4 Village Mills, Tx,US
119/F3 Villa Gesell, Arg.
118/F1 Villaguay, Arg.
122/C4 Villahermosa, Mex.
123/N7 Villa Hidalgo, Mex.
65/E3 Villajoyosa, Sp.
64/B1 Villalba, Sp.
64/B2 Villalcampo (res.), Sp.
118/E2 Villa María, Arg.
64/C4 Villamartín, Sp.
114/F8 Villa Montes, Bol.
122/D4 Villanueva, Hon.
64/A1 Villanueva de Arosa, Sp.
64/C3 Villanueva de Córdoba, Sp.
64/D3 Villanueva del Arzobispo, Sp.
64/C3 Villanueva de la Serena, Sp.
64/D3 Villanueva de los Infantes, Sp.
137/C3 Villa Park, Ca,US
138/Q16 Villa Park, Il,US
118/D3 Villa Regina, Arg.
65/E3 Villarreal de los Infantes, Sp.
118/B3 Villarrica, Chile
118/B3 Villarrica (lake), Chile
117/E2 Villarrica, Par.
118/C3 Villarrica Nat'l Park, Chile
64/D3 Villarrobledo, Sp.
64/D3 Villarrubia de los Ojos, Sp.
118/F2 Villa San José, Arg.
114/F7 Villa Serrano, Bol.
117/C2 Villa Unión, Arg.
123/N9 Villa Unión, Mex.
114/D3 Villavicencio, Col.
64/C1 Villaviciosa, Sp.
65/N9 Villaviciosa de Odon, Sp.
114/E8 Villazón, Bol.
62/E4 Villefranche-de-Rouergue, Fr.
62/F4 Villefranche-sur-Saône, Fr.
58/B6 Villejuif, Fr.
65/E3 Villena, Sp.
58/C2 Villeneuve-d'Ascq, Fr.
62/F5 Villeneuve-lès-Avignon, Fr.
58/B6 Villeneuve-Saint-Georges, Fr.
62/D4 Villeneuve-sur-Lot, Fr.
62/D5 Villeneuve-Tolosane, Fr.
58/B6 Villeparisis, Fr.
134/E4 Ville Platte, La,US
58/C5 Villers-Cotterêts, Fr.
59/F6 Villers-lès-Nancy, Fr.
58/C3 Villers-Outreaux, Fr.
59/E5 Villerupt, Fr.
61/E1 Villingen-Schwenningen, Ger.
90/C5 Villupuram, India
55/N1 Vilnius (cap.), Lith.
48/H3 Vilppula, Fin.
63/K2 Vils (riv.), Ger.
63/K2 Vilshofen, Ger.
58/D2 Vilvoorde, Belg.
75/L3 Vilyuy (range), Rus.
75/N3 Vilyuy (riv.), Rus.
61/H4 Vipiteno (Sterzing), It.
64/B1 Vimianzo, Sp.
48/E4 Vimmerby, Swe.
58/B3 Vimy, Fr.
102/H6 Vina (riv.), Camr.
118/C2 Viña del Mar, Chile
65/F2 Vinaroz, Sp.
111/H Vincennes (bay), Ant.
58/B6 Vincennes, Fr.
132/C4 Vincennes, In,US
137/B2 Vincent, Ca,US
48/F2 Vindeln, Swe.
133/R9 Vineland, On,Can.
137/F4 Vineland, NJ,US
89/D2 Vinh, Viet.
116/G8 Vinhedo, Braz.
89/D4 Vinh Long, Viet.
89/D4 Vinh Quoi, Viet.
89/E3 Vinh Thanh, Viet.
89/D1 Vinh Yen, Viet.
68/F5 Vinica, FYROM
131/J3 Vinita, Ok,US
68/F3 Vînju Mare, Rom.
68/D3 Vinkovci, Cro.
72/D2 Vinnytsya, Ukr.
72/D2 Vinnyts'ka Obl., Ukr.
72/B2 Vinogradov, Ukr.
111/U Vinson (peak), Ant.
58/A5 Viosne (riv.), Fr.
61/H4 Vipiteno (Sterzing), It.
88/D5 Virac, Phil.
80/D3 Viranşehir, Turk
90/B4 Virār, India
129/H3 Virden, Mb,Can.
62/C2 Vire, Fr.
110/B4 Virei, Ang.
117/C7 Virgenes (cape), Arg.
133/R9 Virgil, On,Can.
123/J4 Virgin (isls.), UK, US
130/D3 Virgin (riv.), US
132/E5 Virginia (state), US
129/K4 Virginia, Mn,US
132/F4 Virginia Beach, Va,US
130/C3 Virginia City, Nv,US
89/D3 Virochey, Camb.
58/D3 Viroin (riv.), Belg.
132/B3 Viroqua, Wi,US
68/C3 Virovitica, Cro.
59/E4 Virton, Belg.
90/C6 Virudunagar, India
58/B6 Viry-Châtillon, Fr.
66/D1 Vis (isl.), Cro.
90/D4 Visākhapatnam, India
130/C3 Visalia, Ca,US
88/D5 Visayan (sea), Phil.
57/F3 Visbek, Ger.
48/F4 Visby, Swe.
116/D2 Visconde do Rio Branco, Braz.
125/R7 Viscount Melville (sound), NW,Nun,Can.
59/E2 Visé, Belg.
68/D4 Višegrad, Bosn.
64/B2 Viseu, Port.
64/B2 Viseu (dist.), Port.
69/G2 Vişeu de Sus, Rom.
71/N3 Vishera (riv.), Rus.
108/B4 Vishoek, SAfr.
90/B3 Visnagar, India
68/D3 Višnjevac, Cro.
68/D4 Visoko, Bosn.
57/G3 Visselhövede, Ger.
130/C4 Vista, Ca,US
67/J2 Vistonís (lake), Gre.
55/K2 Vistula (Wisła) (riv.), Pol.
69/G4 Vit (riv.), Bul.
129/J3 Vita, Mb,Can.
66/C1 Viterbo, It.
89/D4 Vi Thanh, Viet.
99/Y18 Viti Levu (isl.), Fiji
82/G1 Vitim (plat.), Rus.
82/G1 Vitim (riv.), Rus.
116/D2 Vitória, Braz.
64/D1 Vitoria, Sp.
115/K6 Vitória da Conquista, Braz.
115/L5 Vitória de Santo Antão, Braz.
69/F4 Vitosha Nat'l Park, Bul.
62/C2 Vitré, Fr.
62/F5 Vitrolles, Fr.
58/D6 Vitry-le-François, Fr.
58/B6 Vitry-sur-Seine, Fr.
70/F5 Vitsyebsk, Bela.
70/E5 Vitsyebskaya Voblasts, Bela.
66/D4 Vittoria, It.
63/K4 Vittorio Veneto, It.
62/F4 Vivarais (mts.), Fr.
64/B1 Vivero, Sp.
69/H5 Vize, Turk.
71/K2 Vizhas (riv.), Rus.
90/D4 Vizianagaram, India
56/B5 Vlaardingen, Neth.
68/F2 Vlădeasa (peak), Rom.
73/H4 Vladikavkaz, Rus.
70/J4 Vladimir, Rus.
70/J5 Vladimirskaya Obl., Rus.
72/C2 Vladimir-Volynskiy, Ukr.
83/L3 Vladivostok, Rus.
57/E2 Vlagtwedde, Neth.
69/G2 Vlăhiţa, Rom.
68/E4 Vlajna (peak), Serb.
68/D3 Vlasenica, Bosn.
55/H4 Vlašim, Czh.
68/F4 Vlasotince, Serb.
56/B2 Vlieland (isl.), Neth.
56/C2 Vliestroom (chan.), Neth.
56/C5 Vlijmen, Neth.
56/A6 Vlissingen, Neth.
67/F2 Vlorë, Alb.
57/F4 Vlotho, Ger.
63/L1 Vltava (riv.), Czh.
63/K2 Vöcklabruck, Aus.
70/H3 Vodlozero (lake), Rus.
56/D5 Voerde, Ger.
63/H1 Vogelsberg (mts.), Ger.
63/H4 Voghera, It.
68/D4 Vogošća, Bosn.
63/J1 Vogtland (reg.), Ger.
99/U12 Voh, NCal.
63/K2 Vohenstrauss, Ger.
109/H9 Vohimena (cape), Madg.
109/G7 Vohipeno, Madg.
107/C3 Voi, Kenya
62/F4 Voiron, Fr.
62/D2 Voise (riv.), Fr.
125/K3 Voisey (bay), Nf,Can.
58/B5 Voisne (riv.), Fr.
68/D5 Vojosë (riv.), Alb.
68/D3 Vojvodina (aut. prov.), Serb.
59/F5 Völklingen, Ger.
98/C2 Volcano (isls.), Japan
48/C3 Volda, Nor.
56/C4 Volendam, Neth.
47/J3 Volga (riv.), Rus.
70/H3 Volga-Baltic Wtwy., Rus.
73/G3 Volgodonsk, Rus.
73/H2 Volgograd, Rus.
73/H2 Volgograd (res.), Rus.
73/G2 Volgogradskaya Obl., Rus.
56/B5 Volkerakdam (dam), Neth.
63/L3 Völkermarkt, Aus.
70/G4 Volkhov, Rus.
70/F4 Volkhov (riv.), Rus.
59/F5 Völklingen, Ger.
57/G6 Volkmarsen, Ger.
55/N2 Volkovysk, Bela.
109/E2 Volksrust, SAfr.
59/G5 Volmunster, Fr.
70/H4 Vologda, Rus.
70/J3 Vologodskaya Obl., Rus.
60/C1 Vologne (riv.), Fr.
67/H3 Vólos, Gre.
67/H3 Volos (gulf), Gre.
73/H1 Vol'sk, Rus.
105/E4 Volta (lake), Gha.
105/F5 Volta (reg.), Gha.
105/F5 Volta (riv.), Gha.
116/J7 Volta Redonda, Braz.
63/J5 Volterra, It.
66/D2 Volturno (riv.), It.
67/H2 Vólvi (lake), Gre.
72/C2 Volyns'ka Obl., Ukr.
71/L5 Volzhsk, Rus.
73/H2 Volzhskiy, Rus.
136/H3 Von Frank (mtn.), Ak,US
62/D3 Vonne (riv.), Fr.
56/B4 Voorburg, Neth.
56/B5 Voorne (isl.), Neth.
56/B4 Voorschoten, Neth.
56/D4 Voorst, Neth.
61/F3 Vorarlberg (prov.), Aus.
56/D4 Vorden, Neth.
61/E4 Vorderrhein (riv.), Swi.
62/F4 Voreppe, Fr.
71/Q2 Vorkuta, Rus.
73/G1 Vorona (riv.), Rus.
72/F2 Voronezh, Rus.
72/F1 Voronezh (riv.), Rus.
73/G2 Voronezhskaya Obl., Rus.
70/G1 Voron'ya (riv.), Rus.
59/E1 Vorst, Belg.
70/E4 Võru, Est.
60/C1 Vosges (dept.), Fr.
60/C2 Vosges (mts.), Fr.
70/H5 Voskresensk, Rus.
48/C3 Voss, Nor.
111/V Vostock (cape), Ant.
111/H Vostok, Ant.
99/K6 Vostok (isl.), Kiri.
71/M4 Votkinsk, Rus.
71/M4 Votkinsk (res.), Rus.
116/C2 Votorantim, Braz.
116/B2 Votuporanga, Braz.
64/B2 Vouga (riv.), Port.
67/H5 Voúxa, Ákra (cape), Gre.
129/K3 Voyageurs Nat'l Park, Mn,US
111/J Voyeykov Ice Shelf, Ant.
71/M3 Voy-Vozh, Rus.
70/H3 Vozhe (lake), Rus.
72/D3 Voznesensk, Ukr.
69/H3 Vrancea (co.), Rom.
77/S2 Vrangelya (isl.), Rus.
68/E4 Vranje, Serb.
55/L4 Vranov nad Teplou, Slvk.
69/F4 Vratsa, Bul.
68/C3 Vrbas (riv.), Bosn.
68/D3 Vrbas, Serb.
108/E2 Vrede, SAfr.
56/D4 Vreden, Ger.
108/B4 Vredenburg, SAfr.
63/L4 Vrhnika, Slov.
56/D2 Vries, Neth.
56/D4 Vriezenveen, Neth.
54/B5 Vrin (riv.), Fr.
90/C2 Vrindāban, India
68/E4 Vrnjačka Banja, Serb.
68/E3 Vršac, Serb.
108/D2 Vryburg, SAfr.
109/E2 Vryheid, SAfr.
55/K4 Vsetín, Czh.
136/E5 Vsevidof (mtn.), Ak,US
71/T6 Vsevolozhsk, Rus.
55/K4 Vtáčnik (peak), Slvk.
68/E4 Vučitrn, Serb.
56/C5 Vught, Neth.
68/D3 Vukovar, Cro.
128/E3 Vulcan, Ab,Can.
69/F3 Vulcan, Rom.
66/D3 Vulcano (isl.), It.
69/F4 Vŭlchedrŭm, Bul.
66/B1 Vulci (ruins), It.
89/D2 Vu Liet, Viet.
89/D4 Vung Tau, Viet.
98/G7 Vunisea, Fiji
136/K2 Vuntut Nat'l Park, Yk,Can.
70/E1 Vuotso, Fin.
69/F4 Vŭrshets, Bul.
90/B3 Vyāra, India
71/L4 Vyatka (riv.), Rus.
71/L4 Vyatskiye Polyany, Rus.
83/L2 Vyazemskiy, Rus.
70/G5 Vyaz'ma, Rus.
70/F3 Vyborg, Rus.
71/K3 Vychegda (riv.), Rus.
70/G3 Vygozero (lake), Rus.
55/M4 Vyhorlat (peak), Slvk.
70/J5 Vyksa, Rus.
71/L3 Vym' (riv.), Rus.
52/C1 Vyrnwy (riv.), Wal,UK
70/G4 Vyshniy Volochek, Rus.
55/J4 Vyškov, Czh.

W

105/E4 Wa, Gha.
56/C5 Waal (riv.), Neth.
56/C6 Waalre, Neth.
56/C5 Waalwijk, Neth.
58/C1 Waarschoot, Belg.
128/E2 Wabasca, Ab,Can.
124/E3 Wabasca (riv.), Ab,Can.
132/C4 Wabash (riv.), Il, In,US
132/C3 Wabash, In,US
57/G6 Wabern, Ger.
129/K3 Wabigoon (lake), On,Can.
129/J2 Wabowden, Mb,Can.
55/K2 Wąbrzeźno, Pol.
87/D4 Wabu (lake), China
85/L9 Wachi, Japan
58/C1 Wachtebeke, Belg.
56/D6 Wachtendonk, Ger.
134/D4 Waco, Tx,US
134/D2 Waconda (lake), Ks,US
129/K4 Waconia, Mn,US
97/D3 Wadbilliga Nat'l Park, Austl.
102/J2 Waddān, Libya
56/C2 Waddenzee (sound), Neth.
128/B3 Waddington (mtn.), BC,Can.
51/F4 Waddington, Eng,UK
51/H5 Waddington, Eng,UK
56/B4 Waddinxveen, Neth.
96/D4 Waddy (pt.), Austl.
52/B5 Wadebridge, Eng,UK
129/H3 Wadena, Sk,Can.
129/K4 Wadena, Mn,US
61/E3 Wädenswil, Swi.
59/F4 Wadern, Ger.
57/F5 Wadersloh, Ger.
59/F5 Wadgassen, Ger.
53/G4 Wadhurst, Eng,UK
80/K6 Wādī As Sīr, Jor.
106/B4 Wādī Ḩalfā', Sudan
103/M5 Wad Medanī, Sudan
55/K4 Wadowice, Pol.
83/J4 Wafangdian, China
57/F3 Wagenfeld, Ger.
57/F3 Wagenfelder (riv.), Ger.
56/C5 Wageningen, Neth
124/G2 Wager (bay), Nun,Can.
97/C2 Wagga Wagga, Austl.
55/J2 Wągrowiec, Pol.
79/K2 Wāh, Pak.
93/G4 Wahai, Indo.
106/B4 Wāḩat Salīmah (well), Sudan
126/V12 Wahiawa, Hi,US
131/H2 Wahoo, Ne,US
129/J4 Wahpeton, ND,US
130/D3 Wah Wah (range), Ut,US
90/B4 Wai, India
126/V13 Waianae, Hi,US
63/L3 Waidhofen an der Ybbs, Aus.
93/H3 Waigeo (isl.), Indo.
93/E5 Waikabubak, Indo.
95/H7 Waikari, NZ
126/T10 Wailuku, Hi,US
126/V12 Waimea (falls), Hi,US
133/R10 Wainfleet, On,Can.
51/J5 Wainfleet All Saints, Eng,UK
90/C3 Waingangā (riv.), India
93/F5 Waingapu, Indo.
128/F2 Wainwright, Ab,Can.
126/V13 Waipahu, Hi,US
126/U10 Waipio, Hi,US
95/H6 Wairoa, NZ
95/H6 Waitemata, NZ
99/Z17 Waiyevo, Fiji
85/E2 Wajima, Japan
107/D2 Wajir, Kenya
93/G4 Waka (cape), Indo.
84/D3 Wakasa, Japan
84/D3 Wakasa (bay), Japan
129/G2 Wakaw, Sk,Can.
84/D3 Wakayama, Japan
84/D4 Wakayama (pref.), Japan
98/F3 Wake (isl.), PacUS
134/D2 Wakeeney, Ks,US
51/G4 Wakefield, Eng,UK
51/G4 Wakefield (co.), Eng,UK
132/B2 Wakefield, Mi,US
91/G4 Wakema, Myan.
84/D3 Waki, Japan
83/N2 Wakkanai, Japan
85/H7 Wakō, Japan
132/D1 Wakwayowkastic (riv.), On,Can.
69/G3 Walachia (range), Rom.
69/G3 Walachia (reg.), Rom.
55/J3 Wałbrzych, Pol.
53/E4 Walbury (hill), Eng,UK
56/A5 Walcheren (isl.), Neth.
58/D3 Walcourt, Belg.
55/J2 Wałcz, Pol.
59/G2 Waldbröl, Ger.
57/G6 Waldeck, Ger.
137/F2 Walden, Co,US
128/G2 Waldheim, Sk,Can.
60/D1 Waldkirch, Ger.
63/L2 Waldviertel (reg.), Aus.
93/F4 Walea (str.), Indo.
93/F4 Waleabahi (isl.), Indo.
125/H2 Wales (isl.), Nun,Can.
49/C4 Wales, UK
111/T Walgreen (coast), Ant.
129/J3 Walhalla, ND,US
135/H3 Walhalla, SC,US
110/E1 Walikale, D.R. Congo
108/L11 Walker (bay), SAfr.
130/C3 Walker (lake), Nv,US
130/C3 Walker (riv.), Nv,US
132/D2 Walkerton, On,Can.
128/E4 Wallace, Id,US
138/H6 Wallaceburg, On,Can.
51/E5 Wallasey, Eng,UK
128/D4 Walla Walla, Wa,US
138/F6 Walled (lake), Mi,US
138/F6 Walled Lake, Mi,US
57/F4 Wallenhorst, Ger.
58/C3 Wallers, Fr.
53/E3 Wallingford, Eng,UK
99/H6 Wallis (isls.), Wall.
98/G6 Wallis & Futuna (terr.), Fr.
128/D4 Wallowa (mts.), Or,US
51/G2 Wallsend, Eng,UK
51/E3 Walney, Isle of (isl.), Eng,UK
137/C2 Walnut, Ca,US
130/E4 Walnut Canyon Nat'l Mon., Az,US
138/K11 Walnut Creek, Ca,US
135/F2 Walnut Ridge, Ar,US
136/F4 Walrus (isls.), Ak,US
52/D1 Walsall, Eng,UK
52/E1 Walsall (co.), Eng,UK
125/K2 Walsingham (cape), Nun,Can.
53/G1 Walsingham, Eng,UK
57/G3 Walsrode, Ger.
135/H3 Walterboro, SC,US
135/G4 Walter F. George (res.), Al, Ga,US
53/G3 Waltham Holy Cross, Eng,UK
51/F4 Walton-le-Dale, Eng,UK
53/F4 Walton on Thames, Eng,UK
53/H3 Walton on the Naze, Eng,UK
57/E5 Waltrop, Ger.
110/B5 Walvis Bay, Namb.
110/C3 Wama, Ang.
103/L7 Wamba, D.R. Congo
56/C5 Wamel, Neth.
51/E2 Wampool (riv.), Eng,UK
128/G5 Wamsutter, Wy,US
87/D5 Wan (riv.), China
137/F4 Wanaque, NJ,US
137/F4 Wanaque (res.), NJ,US
83/L2 Wanda (mts.), China
91/G3 Wanding, China
89/B2 Wang (riv.), Thai.
95/H7 Wanganui, NZ
97/C3 Wangaratta, Austl.
61/F2 Wangen, Ger.
57/E1 Wangerooge (isl.), Ger.
93/F6 Wanggamet (peak), Indo.
89/B4 Wang Hip (peak), Thai.
87/E5 Wangpan (bay), China
93/F4 Wani (peak), Indo.
85/M9 Wanouchi, Japan
81/D5 Wanquan (lake), China
51/G1 Wansbeck (riv.), Eng,UK
53/E3 Wantage, Eng,UK
82/F5 Wanxian, China
59/E2 Wanze, Belg.
132/C3 Wapakoneta, Oh,US
129/G2 Wapawekka (lake), Sk,Can.
128/D2 Wapiti (riv.), Ab, BC,Can.
93/J4 Wapoga (riv.), Indo.
131/K3 Wappapello (lake), Mo,US
129/K5 Wapsipinicon (riv.), Ia,US
85/H7 Warabi, Japan
90/C4 Warangal, India
53/F2 Warboys, Eng,UK
57/G6 Warburg, Ger.
59/F3 Warche (riv.), Belg.
53/G4 Warden (pt.), Eng,UK
57/F2 Wardenburg, Ger.
90/C3 Wardha, India
51/F3 Ward's Stone (mtn.), Eng,UK
53/F3 Ware, Eng,UK
58/C2 Waregem, Belg.
52/D5 Wareham, Eng,UK
59/E2 Waremme, Belg.
54/G2 Waren, Ger.
57/E5 Warendorf, Ger.
53/F3 Wargrave, Eng,UK
89/D3 Warin Chamrap, Thai.
50/B3 Waringstown, NI,UK
51/F1 Wark, Eng,UK
55/L3 Warka, Pol.
52/D2 Warley, Eng,UK
129/G2 Warman, Sk,Can.
108/E2 Warmbad, SAfr.
57/G6 Warmebach (riv.), Ger.
57/H5 Warme Bode (riv.), Ger.
55/K1 Warmia (reg.), Pol.
55/L2 Warmińsko-Mazurskie (prov.), Pol.
52/D4 Warminster, Eng,UK
137/E5 Warminster, Pa,US
130/B2 Warner (mts.), Ca,US
135/H3 Warner Robins, Ga,US
54/G2 Warnow (riv.), Ger.
56/D4 Warnsveld, Neth.
97/G5 Warrandyte, Austl.
96/B4 Warrego (range), Austl.
96/B4 Warrego (riv.), Austl.
136/M2 Warren (pt.), NW,Can.
134/E3 Warren, Ar,US
138/F6 Warren, Mi,US
129/K3 Warren, Mn,US
132/D3 Warren, Oh,US
137/F5 Warren, NJ,US
132/E3 Warren, Pa,US
50/B3 Warrenpoint, NI,UK
131/J3 Warrensburg, Mo,US
108/D3 Warrenton, SAfr.
132/E4 Warrenton, Va,US
138/P16 Warrenville, Il,US
51/F5 Warrington, Eng,UK
51/F5 Warrington (co.), Eng,UK
135/G4 Warrington, Fl,US
97/B3 Warrnambool, Austl.
129/K3 Warroad, Mn,US
97/D1 Warrumbungle Nat'l Park, Austl.
55/L2 Warsaw (Warszawa) (cap.), Pol.
132/C3 Warsaw, In,US
131/J3 Warsaw, Mo,US
55/H5 Warscheneck (peak), Aus.
51/G5 Warslow, Eng,UK
51/G5 Warsop, Eng,UK
57/F6 Warstein, Ger.
55/H2 Warta (riv.), Pol.
96/D5 Warwick, Austl.
53/E2 Warwick, Eng,UK
133/G3 Warwick, RI,US
53/E2 Warwickshire (co.), Eng,UK
130/E2 Wasatch (range), Ut,US
130/C4 Wasco, Ca,US
129/K4 Waseca, Mn,US
124/F1 Washburn (lake), Nun,Can.
51/G4 Washburn (riv.), Eng,UK
129/M3 Washi (lake), On,Can.
51/H5 Washingborough, Eng,UK
51/G2 Washington, Eng,UK
128/C4 Washington (state), US
137/J8 Washington (cap.), DC,US
132/B3 Washington, Il,US
132/C4 Washington, In,US
135/J3 Washington, NC,US
133/G2 Washington (mtn.), NH,US
137/F5 Washington, NJ,US
132/D3 Washington, Pa,US
138/C2 Washington (lake), Wa,US
132/C2 Washington (isl.), Wi,US
132/D4 Washington Court House, Oh,US
99/K4 Washington (Teraina) (atoll), Kiri.
131/H4 Washita (riv.), Ok, Tx,US
53/G1 Wash, The (bay), Eng,UK
55/M2 Wasilków, Pol.
132/E1 Waskaganish (Rupert House), Qu,Can.
136/G4 Waskey (mtn.), Ak,US
56/B4 Wassenaar, Neth.
56/D6 Wassenberg, Ger.
63/H1 Wasserkuppe (peak), Ger.
126/C4 Wassuk (range), Nv,US
51/E3 Wast Water (lake), Eng,UK
132/E1 Waswanipi (lake), Qu,Can.
93/E4 Watampone, Indo.
85/M10 Watarai, Japan
85/F2 Watarase (riv.), Japan
85/G1 Watari, Japan
52/C4 Watchet, Eng,UK
53/E3 Watchfield, Eng,UK
53/G2 Waterbeach, Eng,UK
133/F3 Waterbury, Ct,US
135/H3 Wateree (lake), SC,US
135/H3 Wateree (riv.), SC,US
49/B4 Waterford, Ire.
138/F6 Waterford, Mi,US
52/A6 Watergate (bay), Eng,UK
129/J2 Waterhen (lake), Mb,Can.
128/F2 Waterhen (riv.), Sk,Can.
58/D2 Waterloo, Belg.
132/D3 Waterloo, On,Can.
131/J2 Waterloo, Ia,US
132/B4 Waterloo, Il,US
58/D2 Waterloo Battlesite, Belg.
53/E5 Waterlooville, Eng,UK
58/D2 Watermael-Boitsfort, Belg.
128/E3 Waterton Lakes Nat'l Park, Ab,Can.
132/F3 Watertown, NY,US
129/J4 Watertown, SD,US
132/B3 Watertown, Wi,US
109/E2 Waterval-Bo, SAfr.
133/G2 Waterville, Me,US
128/C4 Waterville, Wa,US
53/F3 Watford, Eng,UK
129/H4 Watford City, ND,US
51/G5 Wath-upon-Dearne, Eng,UK
123/G3 Watling (San Salvador) (isl.), Bahm.
53/F3 Watlington, Eng,UK
89/B2 Wat Mahathat, Thai.
131/H4 Watonga, Ok,US
93/G3 Watowato (peak), Indo.
89/D3 Wat Phu, Laos
129/G3 Watrous, Sk,Can.
107/A2 Watsa, D.R. Congo
132/C3 Watseka, Il,US
124/D2 Watson Lake, Yk,Can.
130/B3 Watsonville, Ca,US
63/J3 Wattens, Aus.
58/C2 Wattignies, Fr.
53/G1 Watton, Eng,UK
58/C2 Wattrelos, Fr.
89/C2 Wat Xieng Thong, Laos
135/H5 Wauchula, Fl,US
138/P15 Wauconda, Il,US
138/Q15 Waukegan, Il,US
138/P13 Waukesha, Wi,US
52/C3 Waun Fâch (mtn.), Wal,UK
52/C1 Waun Oer (mtn.), Wal,UK
132/B3 Waupun, Wi,US
131/H4 Waurika, Ok,US
132/B2 Wausau, Wi,US
132/C3 Wauseon, Oh,US
138/P13 Wauwatosa, Wi,US
53/H2 Waveney (riv.), Eng,UK
51/E2 Waver (riv.), Eng,UK
97/G5 Waverly, Austl.
135/G2 Waverly, Tn,US
58/D2 Wavre, Belg.
58/B2 Wavrin, Fr.
103/L6 Wāw, Sudan
132/C2 Wawa, On,Can.
132/E1 Wawagosic (riv.), Qu,Can.
134/D3 Waxahachie, Tx,US
59/F3 Waxweiler, Ger.
135/H4 Waycross, Ga,US
138/F7 Wayne, Mi,US
131/H2 Wayne, Ne,US
137/F5 Wayne, NJ,US
135/H3 Waynesboro, Ga,US
135/F4 Waynesboro, Ms,US
132/E4 Waynesboro, Pa,US
132/E4 Waynesboro, Va,US
131/J3 Waynesville, Mo,US
135/H3 Waynesville, NC,US
58/C3 Waziers, Fr.
85/L10 Wazuka, Japan
54/K2 Wda (riv.), Pol.
105/F3 W du Niger Nat'l Park, Afr.
92/A2 We (isl.), Indo.
53/G4 Weald, The (reg.), Eng,UK
51/G2 Wear (riv.), Eng,UK
51/F2 Wear Head, Eng,UK
131/H4 Weatherford, Ok,US
134/D3 Weatherford, Tx,US
51/F5 Weaver (riv.), Eng,UK
130/B2 Weaverville, Ca,US
129/J4 Webster, SD,US
129/K5 Webster City, Ia,US
107/B2 Webuye, Kenya
111/W Weddell (sea), Ant.
119/M7 Weddell (isl.), Falk.
97/C2 Weddin Mountains Nat'l Park, Austl.
57/G1 Wedel, Ger.
57/G3 Wedemark, Ger.
52/D4 Wedmore, Eng,UK
52/D1 Wednesbury, Eng,UK
52/D1 Wednesfield, Eng,UK
130/B2 Weed, Ca,US
53/E2 Weedon Bec, Eng,UK
135/H4 Weeki Wachee Springs, Fl,US
52/B5 Week Saint Mary, Eng,UK
56/D4 Weerselo, Neth.
56/C6 Weert, Neth.
56/C4 Weesp, Neth.
56/D6 Wegberg, Ger.
55/L1 Węgorzewo, Pol.
55/M2 Węgrów, Pol.
57/G6 Wehre (riv.), Ger.
83/H4 Wei (riv.), China
83/H3 Weichang, China
54/G3 Weida, Ger.
63/K2 Weiden, Ger.
87/D3 Weifang, China
83/J4 Weihai, China
63/H1 Weilburg, Ger.
59/F2 Weilerswist, Ger.
61/H2 Weilheim, Ger.
54/F3 Weimar, Ger.
61/F2 Weingarten, Ger.
55/J4 Weinviertel (reg.), Aus.
132/D3 Weirton, WV,US
128/D4 Weiser, Id,US
128/D4 Weiser (riv.), Id,US
87/D4 Weishan (lake), China
59/F4 Weiskirchen, Ger.
135/G3 Weiss (lake), Al,US
63/J2 Weissenburg im Bayern, Ger.
54/F3 Weissenfels, Ger.
59/G3 Weissenthurm, Ger.
59/F3 Weisser Stein (peak), Ger.
61/G4 Weisskugel (mt.), Aus., It.

60/E5 Weissmies (peak), Swi.
55/H3 Weisswasser, Ger.
63/L3 Weiz, Aus.
91/J3 Weizhou (isl.), China
55/K1 Wejherowo, Pol.
132/D4 Welch, WV,US
103/N5 Weldiya, Eth.
53/F2 Weldon, Eng,UK
103/M6 Welel (peak), Eth.
53/E4 Welford, Eng,UK
53/E3 Welham Green, Eng,UK
90/D6 Weligama, SrL.
59/E2 Welkenraedt, Belg.
108/D3 Welkom, SAfr.
133/R10 Welland, On,Can.
133/R10 Welland (can.), On,Can.
53/F1 Welland (riv.), Eng,UK
133/R10 Wellandport, On,Can.
59/E2 Wellen, Belg.
53/F2 Wellingborough, Eng,UK
97/C3 Wellington (inlet), Austl.
125/S7 Wellington (chan.), Nun,Can.
119/J7 Wellington (isl.), Chile
95/H7 Wellington (cap.), NZ
108/B4 Wellington, SAfr.
52/C5 Wellington, Eng,UK
52/D2 Wellington, Eng,UK
134/D2 Wellington, Ks,US
134/C3 Wellington, Tx,US
128/C2 Wells, BC,Can.
52/D4 Wells, Eng UK
128/E5 Wells, Nv,US
53/G1 Wells-next-the-Sea, Eng,UK
132/D4 Wellston, Oh,US
63/J2 Wels, Aus.
52/C1 Welshpool Wal,UK
57/E5 Welver, Ger.
53/F3 Welwyn, Eng,UK
53/F3 Welwyn Garden City, Eng,UK
51/F6 Wem, Eng,UK
107/B4 Wembere (riv.), Tanz.
128/D2 Wembley, Ab,Can.
52/B6 Wembury, Eng,UK
125/J3 Wemindji, Qu,Can.
58/D2 Wemmel, Belg.
128/C4 Wenatchee, Wa,US
88/B4 Wenchang, China
105/E5 Wenchi, Gha.
57/H4 Wendeburg, Ger.
59/G2 Wenden, Ger.
53/F3 Wendover, Eng,UK
130/D2 Wendover, Nv,US
52/A6 Wendron, Eng,UK
52/D2 Wenlock Edge (ridge), Eng,UK
57/F6 Wenne (riv.), Ger.
57/G4 Wennigsen, Ger.
51/F3 Wennington, Eng,UK
51/F3 Wensleydale (val.), Eng,UK
53/H1 Wensum (riv.), Eng,UK
53/H1 Went (riv.), Eng,UK
88/D2 Wenzhou, China
54/G3 Werdau, Ger.
103/G6 Werdēr, Eth
57/E6 Werdohl, Ger.
56/B5 Werkendam, Neth.
57/E5 Werl, Ger.
57/E3 Werlte, Ger.
57/E6 Wermelskirchen, Ger.
57/E5 Werne an der Lippe, Ger.
63/J2 Werneck, Ger.
57/H5 Wernigerode, Ger.
97/D2 Werong (pt.), Austl.
57/G6 Werra (riv.), Ger.
57/F4 Werre (riv.), Ger.
97/E1 Werrikimbe Nat'l Park, Austl.
51/F5 Werrington, Eng,UK
57/E5 Werse (riv.), Ger.
63/H2 Wertheim, Ger.
57/F4 Werther, Ger.
56/C3 Wervershoof, Neth.
58/C2 Wervik, Belg.
56/D5 Wesel, Ger.
57/E5 Wesel-Datteln-Kanal (can.), Ger.
57/F2 Weser (riv.), Ger.
57/G2 Wesergebirge (ridge), Ger.
134/D5 Weslaco, Tx,US
52/D4 Wessex (reg.), Eng,UK
129/J2 Wessington Springs, SD,US
97/C3 West (pt.), Austl.
138/P13 West Allis, Wi,US
135/H3 West Augusta, Va,US
137/G5 West Babylon, NY,US
80/K5 West Bank (occ. zone)
132/B3 West Bend, Wi,US
90/E3 West Bengal (state), India
53/G3 West Bergholt, Eng,UK
53/E4 West Berkshire (co.), Eng,UK
132/C2 West Branch, Mi,US
51/G6 West Bridgford, Eng,UK
53/E1 West Bromwich, Eng,UK
52/D4 Westbury, Eng,UK
137/G5 Westbury, NY,US
138/P16 West Chicago, Il,US
52/B3 West Cleddau (riv.), Wal,UK
135/H3 West Columbia, SC,US

51/G2 West Cornforth, Eng,UK
137/C2 West Covina, Ca,US
56/A6 Westdorpe, Neth.
70/E5 West Dvina (riv.), Eur.
134/B2 West Elk (mts.), Co,US
56/D3 Westerbork, Neth.
57/E4 Westerkappeln, Ger.
54/E1 Westerland, Ger.
59/D1 Westerlo, Belg.
107/B2 Western (des.), Egypt
105/E5 Western (reg.), Gha.
107/B2 Western (prov.), Kenya
104/B4 Western (area), SLeo.
95/B3 Western Australia (state), Austl.
108/P4 Western Cape (prov.), SAfr.
84/A3 Western Channel (str.), Japan, SKor.
90/B4 Western Ghats (mts.), India
102/B3 Western Sahara
82/C1 Western Sayan (mts.), Rus.
56/A6 Westerschelde (chan.), Neth.
57/E2 Westerstede, Ger.
132/D3 Westerville, Oh,US
56/C5 Westervoort, Neth.
59/G2 Westerwald (for.), Ger.
57/F4 Westfalica, Porta (pass), Ger.
119/M8 West Falkland (isl.), Falk.
129/J4 West Fargo, ND,US
98/D4 West Fayu (isl.), Micr.
137/F5 Westfield, NJ,US
58/B2 West Flanders (prov.), Belg.
132/B4 West Frankfort, Il,US
56/C2 West Frisian (isls.), Neth.
53/F1 West Glen (riv.), Eng,UK
137/G4 West Haverstraw, NY,US
135/F3 West Helena, Ar,US
49/D2 Westhill, Sc,UK
51/F4 Westhoughton, Eng,UK
133/Q8 West Humber (riv.), On,Can.
123/F4 West Indies (isls.), NAm.
137/G5 West Islip, NY,US
130/E2 West Jordan, Ut,US
51/E5 West Kirby, Eng,UK
138/F7 Westland, Mi,US
128/E2 Westlock, Ab,Can.
110/E3 West Lunga Nat'l Park, Zam.
50/A4 Westmeath (co.), Ire.
135/F3 West Memphis, Ar,US
53/G3 West Mersea, Eng,UK
53/E2 West Midlands (co.), Eng,UK
137/F4 West Milford, NJ,US
138/Q16 Westmont, Il,US
137/E6 Westmont (Haddon), NJ,US
51/F3 Westmoreland (reg.), Eng,UK
133/N7 Westmount, Qu,Can.
131/J3 Weston, Mo,US
132/D4 Weston, WV,US
108/P13 Westonaria, SAfr.
52/D4 Weston-super-Mare, Eng,UK
52/D4 Weston Zoyland, Eng,UK
137/K7 West Orange, NJ,US
135/H5 West Palm Beach, Fl,US
131/K3 West Pensacola, Fl,US
131/K3 West Plains, Mo,US
135/G3 West Point (lake), Al, Ga,US
135/F3 West Point, Ms,US
131/H2 West Point, Ne,US
137/G4 Westport, Ct,US
128/B2 West Road (riv.), BC,Can.
138/L9 West Sacramento, Ca,US
133/S10 West Seneca, NY,US
74/H3 West Siberian (plain), Rus.
53/F4 West Sussex (co.), Eng,UK
128/F4 West Valley City, Ut,US
128/C3 West Vancouver, BC,Can.
132/D4 West Virginia (state), US
105/E4 West Volta (riv.), Burk.,Gha.
52/B4 Westward Ho!, Eng,UK
137/F5 Westwood, NJ,US
51/H4 West Yorkshire (co.), Eng,UK
134/B2 Wet (riv.), Eng,UK
93/G5 Wetar (isl.), Indo.
93/G5 Wetar (str.), Indo.
107/C4 Wete, Tanz.
132/E1 Wetetnagami (riv.), Qu,Can.
51/F2 Wetheral, Eng,UK
51/G4 Wetherby, Eng,UK
57/B2 Wetherell (lake), Austl.
134/B2 Wet, Eng,UK
57/E6 Wetter, Ger.
58/C1 Wetteren, Ger.
57/E4 Wettringen, Ger.
58/C2 Wevelgem, Belg.

98/D5 Wewak, PNG
131/H4 Wewoka, Ok,US
49/B4 Wexford (co.), Ire.
50/B6 Wexford (co.), Ire.
53/H1 Weybourne, Eng,UK
129/H3 Weyburn, Sk,Can.
52/D5 Weymouth, Eng,UK
52/D5 Weymouth (bay), Eng,UK
95/H6 Whakatane, NZ
51/G5 Whaley Bridge, Eng,UK
51/F4 Whalley, Eng,UK
95/H6 Whangarei, NZ
51/G4 Wharfe (riv.), Eng,UK
134/D4 Wharton, Tx,US
129/G5 Wheatland, Wy,US
53/E3 Wheatley, Eng,UK
138/P16 Wheaton, Il,US
52/D1 Wheaton Aston, Eng,UK
137/J7 Wheaton-Glenmont, Md,US
135/G3 Wheeler (lake), Al,US
131/F3 Wheeler (peak), NM,US
130/D3 Wheeler (peak), Nv,US
138/Q15 Wheeling, Il,US
132/D3 Wheeling, WV,US
51/F3 Whernside (mtn.), Eng,UK
51/G2 Whickham, Eng,UK
138/B1 Whidbey (isl.), Wa,US
130/B2 Whiskeytown-Shasta-Trinity Nat'l Rec. Area, Ca,US
51/G2 Whitburn, Eng,UK
133/S8 Whitby, On,Can.
51/H3 Whitby, Eng,UK
51/F6 Whitchurch, Eng,UK
53/E4 Whitchurch, Eng,UK
53/E4 Whitchurch, Eng,UK
52/C4 Whitchurch, Wal,UK
111/D White (isl.), Ant.
133/K1 White (bay), Nf,Can.
132/C1 White (lake), On,Can.
70/H2 White (sea), Rus.
136/L4 White (pass), Ak,US
135/F3 White (riv.), Ar,US
130/E2 White (riv.), Co, Ut,US
52/C4 White (riv.), In,US
131/J5 White (lake), La,US
131/K4 White (riv.), La, Mo,US
131/G2 White (riv.), Ne, SD,US
130/D3 White (riv.), Nv,US
134/C3 White (riv.), Tx,US
132/D4 White (peak), Va,US
133/K1 White Bear (riv.), Nf,Can.
129/G3 White City, Sk,Can.
128/E2 Whitecourt, Ab,Can.
51/E1 White Esk (riv.), Sc,UK
129/K4 Whiteface (riv.), Mn,US
51/F4 Whitefield, Eng,UK
132/C2 Whitefish (bay), On,Can, Mi,US
128/E3 Whitefish (lake), NW,Can.
136/L2 Whitefish Station, Yk,Can.
52/B3 Whiteford (pt.), Wal,UK
129/G2 White Fox, Sk,Can.
128/E4 Whitehall, Mt,US
137/E5 Whitehall (Fullerton), Pa,US
50/E2 Whitehaven, Eng,UK
50/C2 Whitehead, NI,UK
136/L3 Whitehorse (cap.), Yk,Can.
53/E3 Whitehorse (hill), Eng,UK
137/K7 White Marsh, Md,US
136/J2 White Mountains Nat'l Rec. Area, Ak,US
129/K3 Whitemouth (riv.), Mb,Can.
103/M5 White Nile (riv.), Sudan
137/K7 White Oak, Md,US
132/A1 White Otter (lake), On,Can.
137/G4 White Plains, NY,US
132/C1 White River, On,Can.
130/E4 Whiteriver, Az,US
134/B3 White Rock, NM,US
130/F4 White Sands, NM,US
130/F4 White Sands Nat'l Mon., NM,US
119/K8 Whiteside (chan.), Chile
128/F4 White Sulphur Springs, Mt,US
132/D4 White Sulphur Springs, WV,US
135/J3 Whiteville, NC,US
130/D4 Whitewater, Az,US
129/L3 Whitewater (lake), On,Can.
129/H3 Whitewood, Sk,Can.
50/D2 Whithorn, Sc,UK
52/B3 Whitland, Wal,UK
51/G1 Whitley Bay, Eng,UK
131/H4 Whitney (lake), Tx,US
130/C3 Whitney (mtn.), Ca,US
52/B6 Whitsand (bay), Eng,UK
53/H4 Whitstable, Eng,UK
96/C3 Whitsunday I. Nat'l Park, Austl.
137/B3 Whittier, Ca,US
53/F1 Whittlesey, Eng,UK
51/G5 Whitwell, Eng,UK
51/G2 Whitworth, Eng,UK
124/F2 Wholdaia (lake), NW,Can.
95/C4 Whyalla, Austl.

89/B2 Wiang Ko Sai Nat'l Park, Thai.
132/D2 Wiarton, On,Can.
58/C2 Wichelen, Belg.
131/H3 Wichita, Ks,US
131/H4 Wichita (mts.), Ok,US
134/D3 Wichita Falls, Tx,US
100/D4 Wickenburg, Az,US
53/G3 Wickford, Eng,UK
97/C3 Wickham (cape), Austl.
53/H2 Wickham Market, Eng,UK
50/B6 Wicklow (co.), Ire.
50/B5 Wicklow (mts.), Ire.
50/B5 Wicklow Gap (pass), Ire.
50/C6 Wicklow Head (pt.), Ire.
57/F4 Wickriede (riv.), Ger.
51/F5 Widnes, Eng,UK
59/G2 Wied (riv.), Ger.
57/G2 Wiedau (riv.), Ger.
57/F2 Wiefelstede, Ger.
57/F4 Wiehengebirge (ridge), Ger.
59/G2 Wiehl, Ger.
55/L4 Wieliczka, Pol.
55/J2 Wielkopolskie (prov.), Pol.
58/C2 Wielsbeke, Belg.
55/K3 Wieluń, Pol.
55/J4 Wien (prov.), Aus.
55/J4 Wien (Vienna) (cap.), Aus.
55/J5 Wiener Neustadt, Aus.
63/L2 Wienwald (reg.), Aus.
55/M3 Wieprz (riv.), Pol.
56/B3 Wieringermeerpolder (polder), Neth.
56/C3 Wieringerwerf, Neth.
52/C4 Wieruszów, Pol.
63/H1 Wiesbaden, Ger.
60/D2 Wiese (riv.), Ger.
74/H2 Wiese (isl.), Rus.
57/E2 Wiesmoor, Ger.
57/E3 Wietmarschen, Ger.
57/G3 Wietze, Ger.
57/G3 Wietze (riv.), Ger.
55/K1 Wieżyca (peak), Pol.
51/F4 Wigan, Eng,UK
51/F5 Wigan (co.), Eng,UK
135/F4 Wiggins, Ms,US
130/D3 Wight, Isle of (isl.), Eng,UK
52/E1 Wigston, Eng,UK
51/E2 Wigton, Eng,UK
50/D2 Wigtown, Sc,UK
50/D2 Wigtown (bay), Sc,UK
56/C5 Wijchen, Neth.
56/D4 Wijhe, Neth.
56/C5 Wijk bij Duurstede, Neth.
103/N5 Wik'ro, Eth.
131/H2 Wilber, Ne,US
51/H4 Wilberfoss, Eng,UK
131/J4 Wilburton, Ok,US
74/G1 Wilczek (isl.), Rus.
108/E4 Wild Coast (reg.), SAfr.
57/F3 Wildeshausen, Ger.
133/Q8 Wildfield, On,Can.
129/J4 Wild Rice (riv.), Mn,US
61/G4 Wildspitze (peak), Aus.
137/K8 Wild World, Md,US
108/E2 Wilge (riv.), SAfr.
111/F Wilhelm II (coast), Ant.
115/G4 Wilhelmina (mts.), Sur.
56/C5 Wilhelminakanaal (can.), Neth.
57/F1 Wilhelmshaven, Ger.
135/H2 Wilkesboro, NC,US
111/J Wilkes Land (reg.), Ant.
51/E4 Wilkie, Sk,Can.
111/V Wilkins (sound), Ant.
136/N4 Will (mtn.), BC,Can.
97/C2 Willandra Nat'l Park, Austl.
134/F3 Willapa (bay), Wa,US
51/F4 Willaston, Eng,UK
130/E4 Willcox, Az,US
57/G5 Willebadessen, Ger.
58/D1 Willebroek, Belg.
123/H5 Willemstad (cap.), NAnt.
97/B3 William (peak), Austl.
130/D4 Williams, Az,US
132/E4 Williamsburg, Ky,US
135/H2 Williamsburg, Va,US
128/C2 Williams Lake, BC,Can.
132/D4 Williamson, WV,US
97/D2 Williamstown, Austl.
133/S10 Williamsville, NY,US
52/D3 Willingboro, NJ,US
51/G2 Willington, Eng,UK
51/G2 Willington, Eng,UK
134/E4 Willis, Tx,US
133/G2 Williston (lake), BC,Can.
135/H4 Williston, Fl,US
129/H3 Williston, ND,US
52/C4 Williton, Eng,UK
131/H3 Willmar, Mn,US
50/C2 Willow (cr.), Or,US
138/Q16 Willowbrook, Il,US

129/G3 Willow Bunch, Sk,Can.
137/G5 Willow Grove, Pa,US
128/C2 Willow River, BC,Can.
130/B3 Willows, Ca,US
138/Q15 Wilmette, Il,US
137/E6 Wilmington, De,US
135/J3 Wilmington, NC,US
130/D4 Wilmington, Oh,US
135/H4 Wilmington Island, Ga,US
51/F5 Wilmslow, Eng,UK
59/H2 Wilnsdorf, Ger.
59/H4 Wilrijk, Belg.
57/G2 Wilseder Berg (peak), Ger.
125/P2 Wilson (cape), Nun,Can.
137/B2 Wilson (mt.), Ca,US
135/J3 Wilson, NC,US
133/S9 Wilson, NY,US
137/H3 Wilson, Pa,US
97/C3 Wilsons Promontory Nat'l Park, Austl.
53/E4 Wilton, Eng,UK
53/E4 Wiltshire (co.), Eng,UK
52/E5 Wimborne Minster, Eng,UK
58/A2 Wimereux, Fr.
108/D3 Winburg, SAfr.
52/D4 Wincanton, Eng,UK
53/G5 Winchcombe, Eng,UK
53/G5 Winchelsea, Eng,UK
132/C4 Winchester, Ky,US
135/G3 Winchester, Tn,US
135/G3 Winchester, Va,US
53/E4 Winchester, Eng,UK
129/G5 Wind Cave Nat'l Park, SD,US
135/H3 Winder, Ga,US
51/F3 Windermere, Eng,UK
51/F3 Windermere (lake), Eng,UK
110/C5 Windhoek (cap.), Namb.
129/K5 Windom, Mn,US
130/E4 Window Rock, Az,US
128/F5 Wind River (range), Wy,US
53/E4 Windrush (riv.), Eng,UK
96/G8 Windsor, Austl.
133/L1 Windsor, NF,Can.
133/H2 Windsor, NS,Can.
138/F7 Windsor, On,Can.
133/G2 Windsor, Qu,Can.
53/F4 Windsor, Eng,UK
53/F3 Windsor and Maidenhead (co.), Eng,UK
123/K5 Windward (isls.), NAm.
123/G4 Windward (passage), NAm.
128/D3 Winfield, BC,Can.
131/H3 Winfield, Ks,US
53/H4 Wingham, Eng,UK
129/M2 Winisk, On,Can.
129/M2 Winisk (lake), On,Can.
129/M2 Winisk (riv.), On,Can.
129/J3 Winkler, Mb,Can.
105/E5 Winneba, Gha.
132/B3 Winnebago (lake), Wi,US
130/C2 Winnemucca, Nv,US
129/J5 Winner, SD,US
138/Q15 Winnetka, Il,US
128/F4 Winnett, Mt,US
129/J3 Winnipeg (cap.), Mb,Can.
129/J3 Winnipeg (lake), Mb,Can.
129/K3 Winnipeg (riv.), Mb, On,Can.
129/J3 Winnipeg Beach, Mb,Can.
129/J3 Winnipegosis, Mb,Can.
129/J3 Winnipegosis (lake), Mb,Can.
134/F3 Winnsboro, La,US
135/J3 Winnsboro, SC,US
133/Q9 Winona, Mn,US
129/L4 Winona, Mn,US
56/E2 Winschoten, Neth.
52/D4 Winscombe, Eng,UK
51/F5 Winsford, Eng,UK
52/D4 Winsley, Eng,UK
130/E4 Winslow, Az,US
53/F3 Winslow, Eng,UK
135/H2 Winston-Salem, NC,US
56/D2 Winsum, Neth.
57/F6 Winterberg, Ger.
108/D4 Winterberge (mts.), SAfr.
52/D5 Winterbourne, Eng,UK
135/H4 Winter Haven, Fl,US
135/H4 Winter Park, Fl,US
56/D5 Winterswijk, Neth.
61/E2 Winterthur, Swi.
86/D3 Winton, Austl.
54/F3 Wipper (riv.), Ger.
57/H2 Wipperau (riv.), Ger.
57/E6 Wipperfürth, Ger.
51/G5 Wirksworth, Eng,UK
53/G1 Wirral (co.), Eng,UK
51/E5 Wirral (pen.), Eng,UK
53/G1 Wisbech, Eng,UK
132/B2 Wisconsin (state), US

132/B2 Wisconsin Rapids, Wi,US
129/J4 Wishek, ND,US
55/K4 Wisła (riv.), Pol.
55/K1 Wiślany (lag.), Pol.
55/K2 Wisła (Vistula) (riv.), Pol.
55/K1 Wisłok (riv.), Pol.
55/L4 Wisłoka (riv.), Pol.
54/F2 Wismar, Ger.
59/G5 Wissembourg, Fr.
59/G2 Wissen, Ger.
53/G1 Wissey (riv.), Eng,UK
59/H2 Witbank, SAfr.
108/A2 Witberg (peak), Namb.
53/G3 Witham, Eng,UK
51/H5 Witham (riv.), Eng,UK
51/J4 Withernsea, Eng,UK
136/J3 Witherspoon (mtn.), Ak,US
135/H4 Withlacoochee (riv.), Fl, Ga,US
51/F4 Withnell, Eng,UK
55/J2 Witkowo, Pol.
53/E3 Witney, Eng,UK
55/J2 Witnica, Pol.
59/E2 Wittem, Neth.
57/E6 Witten, Ger.
54/G2 Wittenberg, Ger.
54/F2 Wittenberge, Ger.
60/D2 Wittenheim, Fr.
53/F1 Wittering, Eng,UK
57/H3 Wittingen, Ger.
59/F4 Wittlich, Ger.
57/E1 Wittmund, Ger.
55/J1 Wittow (pen.), Ger.
54/G1 Wittstock, Ger.
108/P13 Witwatersrand (reg.), SAfr.
57/G6 Witzenhausen, Ger.
52/C4 Wiveliscombe, Eng,UK
53/G3 Wivenhoe, Eng,UK
138/E6 Wixom, Mi,US
55/J2 Wkra (riv.), Pol.
55/K1 Włocławek, Pol.
55/K2 Włocławskie (lake), Pol.
55/M3 Włodawa, Pol.
55/K3 Włoszczowa, Pol.
52/C1 Wnion (riv.), Wal,UK
53/F3 Woburn Sands, Eng,UK
97/C3 Wodonga, Austl.
56/B4 Woerden, Neth.
59/G6 Woerth, Fr.
83/K2 Woken (riv.), China
53/F4 Woking, Eng,UK
53/F4 Wokingham, Eng,UK
53/F4 Wokingham (co.), Eng,UK
93/H5 Wokam (isl.), Indo.
133/S9 Wolcottsville, NY,US
98/D4 Woleai (atoll), Micr.
136/F3 Wolf (mtn.), Ak,US
131/G3 Wolf (cr.), Ok, Tx,US
132/B2 Wolf (riv.), Wi,US
136/F3 Wolf Creek (mtn.), Ak,US
128/E4 Wolf Creek, Mt,US
54/G3 Wolfen, Ger.
57/H4 Wolfenbüttel, Ger.
57/G6 Wolfhagen, Ger.
57/H4 Wolfsburg, Ger.
54/F1 Wolgast, Ger.
55/H2 Woliński Nat'l Park, Pol.
124/E2 Wollaston (pen.), NW,Nun,Can.
124/F3 Wollaston (lake), Sk,Can.
119/L8 Wollaston (isl.), Chile
53/F2 Wollaston, Eng,UK
97/D2 Wollongong, Austl.
108/D2 Wolmaransstad, SAfr.
63/J3 Wolnzach, Ger.
102/C6 Wologizi (range), Libr.
55/J2 Wołomin, Pol.
55/J3 Wołów, Pol.
108/L10 Wolseley, SAfr.
51/G2 Wolsingham, Eng,UK
55/K1 Wolsztyn, Pol.
58/D2 Woluwé-Saint-Lambert, Belg.
56/D3 Wolvega, Neth.
52/D1 Wolverhampton, Eng,UK
52/D1 Wolverhampton (co.), Eng,UK
53/E1 Wolverton, Eng,UK
52/D3 Wombourne, Eng,UK
51/G5 Wombwell, Eng,UK
97/C3 Wonnangatta-Moroka Nat'l Park, Austl.
97/C1 Wongalarroo (lake), Austl.
81/D3 Wŏnsan, NKor.
90/C3 Woni, India
129/H2 Wood (lake), Sk,Can.
128/G3 Wood (mtn.), Sk,Can.
81/D3 Wushi, China
57/H2 Wipperau --
133/Q8 Woodbridge, On,Can.
51/H5 Wragby, Eng,UK
137/H2 Woodbridge, NJ,US
51/E5 Woodbridge, Eng,UK
124/E2 Wood Buffalo Nat'l Park, Ab, Yk,Can.
133/Q9 Woodburn, On,Can.
50/C2 Woodburn, NI,UK

128/C4 Woodburn, Or,US
137/E6 Woodbury, NJ,US
96/D4 Woodgate Nat'l Park, Austl.
51/H5 Woodhall Spa, Eng,UK
138/L9 Woodland, Ca,US
131/F3 Woodland Park, Co,US
98/E5 Woodlark (isl.), PNG
137/K7 Woodlawn, Md,US
53/F4 Woodley, Eng,UK
137/F5 Woodmere, NY,US
138/P16 Woodridge, Il,US
51/F6 Woodseaves, Eng,UK
133/H2 Woodstock, NB,Can.
53/E3 Woodstock, Eng,UK
138/P15 Woodstock, Il,US
132/E4 Woodville, Oh,US
134/E4 Woodville, Tx,US
131/H3 Woodward, Ok,US
52/D5 Wool, Eng,UK
52/D4 Woolavington, Eng,UK
51/G1 Woolsington, Eng,UK
131/H1 Woonsocket, SD,US
51/F6 Woore, Eng,UK
132/D3 Wooster, Oh,US
53/E3 Wootton Basset, Eng,UK
108/B4 Worcester, SAfr.
52/D2 Worcester, Eng,UK
133/G3 Worcester, Ma,US
53/D2 Worcester & Birmingham (can.), Eng,UK
52/D2 Worcestershire (co.), Eng,UK
63/K3 Wörgl, Aus.
50/E2 Workington, Eng,UK
51/G5 Worksop, Eng,UK
128/G4 Worland, Wy,US
44/* World
56/A4 Wormer, Neth.
63/H2 Worms, Ger.
57/F2 Worpswede, Ger.
51/G4 Worsbrough, Eng,UK
53/F5 Worthing, Eng,UK
129/K5 Worthington, Mn,US
98/F3 Wotho (atoll), Mrsh.
98/G4 Wotje (atoll), Mrsh.
52/D3 Wotton under Edge, Eng,UK
56/C4 Woudenberg, Neth.
56/C5 Woudrichem, Neth.
56/B5 Wouw, Neth.
93/F4 Wowoni (isl.), Indo.
131/K3 Wray, Co,US
51/H6 Wreake (riv.), Eng,UK
108/B3 Wreck (pt.), SAfr.
52/D1 Wrekin, The (co.), Eng,UK
52/D1 Wrekin, The (hill), Eng,UK
51/F5 Wrenbury, Eng,UK
51/F5 Wrexham, Wal,UK
51/F5 Wrexham (co.), Wal,UK
129/G5 Wright, Wy,US
137/F5 Wrightstown, NJ,US
137/C2 Wrightwood, Ca,US
53/G3 Writtle, Eng,UK
55/J3 Wrocław, Pol.
124/D1 Wrottesley (cape), NW,Can.
52/D2 Wroxeter, Eng,UK
53/H1 Wroxham, Eng,UK
55/J2 Września, Pol.
55/J3 Wschowa, Pol.
91/K2 Wu (riv.), China
87/K2 Wu'an, China
87/D5 Wuchang (lake), China
83/K2 Wudalianchi, China
87/B4 Wudang Shan (mtn.), China
87/D5 Wuding (riv.), China
87/D5 Wuhan, China
82/F3 Wujia (riv.), China
87/D5 Wuhu, China
88/B2 Wuling (mts.), China
105/H5 Wum, Camr.
57/F2 Wümme (riv.), Ger.
57/F5 Wünnenberg, Ger.
57/E6 Wupper (riv.), Ger.
57/E6 Wuppertal, Ger.
81/C4 Wuqia, China
59/F2 Würm (riv.), Ger.
57/E5 Würselen, Ger.
63/H2 Würzburg, Ger.
83/H5 Wushan (lake), China
87/C5 Wusheng Guan (pass), China
81/C3 Wushi, China
57/G6 Wüstegarten (peak), Ger.
83/L2 Wusuli (Ussuri) (riv.), China, Rus.
87/D5 Wutai Shan (peak), China
104/C4 Wuteve (peak), Libr.
87/D4 Wuwei, China
87/E5 Wuxi, China
87/D5 Wuxue, China
91/J4 Wuyi, China
83/K2 Wuyur (riv.), China
89/E2 Wuzhi (mts.), China
87/D2 Wuzhi Shan (peak), China
91/K3 Wuzhou, China
138/F7 Wyandotte, Mi,US
97/D2 Wyangale (dam), Austl.
137/F5 Wyckoff, NJ,US
52/D3 Wye, Eng,UK
52/D4 Wylye (riv.), Eng,UK
53/H1 Wymondham, Eng,UK
135/F3 Wynne, Ar,US
96/F6 Wynnum, Austl.
129/G3 Wynyard, Sk,Can.
128/F5 Wyoming (state), US
132/C3 Wyoming, Mi,US
128/F5 Wyoming (peak), Wy,US
130/E2 Wyoming (range), Wy,US
97/B2 Wyperfeld Nat'l Park, Austl.
51/F4 Wyre (riv.), Eng,UK
55/L2 Wyszków, Pol.
132/D3 Wytheville, Va,US

X

89/D4 Xa Binh Long, Viet.
122/B4 Xadani, Mex.
81/E5 Xainza, China
90/E2 Xaitongmoin, China
109/F2 Xai-Xai, Moz.
89/D1 Xam Nua, Laos
89/D3 Xan (riv.), Laos
73/H5 Xankändi, Azer.
56/D5 Xanten, Ger.
116/A3 Xanxerê, Braz.
103/Q7 Xarardheere, Som.
89/E4 Xa Song Luy, Viet.
110/C3 Xassengue, Ang.
89/D3 Xa Tho Thanh, Viet.
115/J6 Xavantes (mts.), Braz.
116/B2 Xavantes (res.), Braz.
89/D4 Xa Vo Dat, Viet.
81/D3 Xayar, China
122/D4 Xel-há (ruins), Mex.
132/D4 Xenia, Oh,US
89/D2 Xeno, Laos
87/E2 Xi (lake), China
87/E3 Xi (riv.), China
83/H5 Xi (riv.), China
88/B3 Xi (riv.), China
88/B3 Xi'an, China
87/C4 Xiang (riv.), China
87/C4 Xiangfan, China
89/C2 Xiang Khoang (plat.), Laos
88/B2 Xiangtan, China
88/B2 Xiangxiang, China
87/C5 Xianning, China
108/B3 Xiantao, China
82/F5 Xianyang, China
87/C4 Xiao (riv.), China
88/B2 Xiao (riv.), China
91/H2 Xiao (riv.), China
83/J1 Xiaobole (peak), China
83/K2 Xiaogan, China
83/K2 Xiao Hinggan (mts.), China
87/D3 Xiaoqing (riv.), China
87/C3 Xiaoshan, China
87/C3 Xiaowutai Shan (peak), China
122/B3 Xicohténcatl, Mex.
122/B2 Xicotepec, Mex.
87/C4 Xifei (riv.), China
82/F4 Xifeng, China
83/J3 Xifeng, China
88/A2 Xifeng, China
90/E2 Xigazê, China
82/E5 Xihan (riv.), China
81/F4 Xijir Ulan (lake), China
87/C5 Xiliao (riv.), China
88/C2 Xin (riv.), China
87/D5 Xin'an (riv.), China
87/D5 Xin'anjiang (res.), China
88/B3 Xinfengjiang (res.), China
87/E2 Xingcheng, China
110/C2 Xinge, Ang.
87/D4 Xinghua, China
81/D3 Xingjiang Uygur Aut. Reg., China
83/L3 Xingkai (lake), China
111/H6 Xingo Nat'l Park, Braz.
82/C3 Xingtai, China
115/H4 Xingu (riv.), Braz.
87/C4 Xingyang, China
82/E4 Xining (Xining Shi), China
87/D4 Xintai, China
87/C4 Xinxiang, China
88/B2 Xinyang, China
88/B2 Xinyu, China
81/D3 Xinyuan, China
82/E5 Xiqing (mts.), China
115/K6 Xique-Xique, Braz.
88/B2 Xiu (riv.), China
90/E2 Xixabangma (peak), China
91/J3 Xiyang (riv.), China
93/J3 Xiji (isl.), China
88/C2 Xu (riv.), China
87/C2 Xuanhua, China